Current Law

Case Citator

2017

Current Law

Case Citator

2017

SWEET & MAXWELL

SWEET & MAXWELL THOMSON REUTERS

Published in 2018 by Thomson Reuters, trading as Sweet & Maxwell. Thomson Reuters is registered in England & Wales, Company No.1679046. Registered Office and address for service: 5 Canada Square, Canary Wharf, London E14 5AQ.

For further information on our products and services, visit
http://www.sweetandmaxwell.co.uk.

Computerset by Sweet & Maxwell
Printed and bound by CPI Group (UK) Ltd, Croydon, CR0 4YY.

A CIP catalogue record for this book is available from the British Library.

Orders by email to: trluki.orders@thomsonreuters.com.

No natural forests were destroyed to make this product: only farmed timber was used and replanted.

ISBN: 978-0-414-06250-4

CONTENTS

PREFACE

The Sweet & Maxwell Current Law Service

The Current Law Service began in 1947 and provides a comprehensive guide to developments in case law, primary legislation and secondary legislation in the United Kingdom and mainland Europe. The Current Law Service presently consists of the Monthly Digests, the Year Book, Current Law Statutes Annotated, the Legislation Citator, the Case Citator, Current Law Weekly and European Current Law.

The Case Citators

The Current Law Case Citators comprise four cumulative volumes covering the years 1947-1976, 1977-1997, 1998-2001, and 2002-2004. Single volumes have been produced since 2005. Together they provide a comprehensive reference guide to case law after 1946.

How to use the Citators

When searching for a case, users should consult the most recent citator volume first, since it provides the most comprehensive and authoritative information. The current volume contains a guide to cases digested or judicially considered in 2017. For earlier case law not considered since 2017, users should consult previous citator volumes.

The material in this volume is arranged in alphabetical order in three sections:

English Citator
Scottish Citator
Ships' Names Index

The details in each entry can be used on a number of different levels, including identifying law report series in which a full report of a case can be found, the judicial history of a case and the location of an abstract of a case within a Current Law Yearbook. The following information is provided:

(a) The full name of any case reported between 1947 and 2017
Cases are listed alphabetically by the first party's name, giving the most recent Current Law Year Book paragraph reference to the appropriate digest. Most references have a year before the paragraph number, e.g. 17/**239** alludes to the 2017 Year Book, paragraph 239. If no year is given, the case is contained in the Current Law Consolidation 1947-1951. (For Scotland see the Scottish Year Books 1948-1951.)

(b) An extensive list of references to the law reports and journals reporting each case
Each entry gives details about one case, beginning with the case name and any joined cases or other names by which the case might be known, followed by the reports in descending order of authority and the court in which the case was heard. Where cases go on to an appellate court, the entry states whether the higher court affirmed or reversed the decision of the lower court.

(c) The judicial history of a case
If a case has been applied, considered, approved, distinguished, overruled, etc., since it was decided, Current Law Year Book references to digests of cases in which the judicial consideration took place are provided. These references are in normal type while the paragraph number of the actual digest of each case is given in bold.

(d) Details of Scottish cases
Part II of the Citator contains details of cases decided or judicially considered in the Scottish Courts. References to English cases judicially considered in Scotland are also included in this part, so subscribers wishing to follow the full history of an English case should consult both parts of the Citator. Scottish cases published in English Law Reports are included in both the Scottish and English sections.

(e) Ships' Names Index
This is an alphabetical listing of all ships' names and their law report citations to assist where only the ship's name is known by the user. The official party names for these cases will be located in the main body of the Citator.

Whilst every effort has been made to ensure that details of cases in this citator are correct, there may be occasions when a citation is wrong. The editor would be grateful for notification of any errors to enable them to be rectified on the database from which this volume was derived.

Case Citator Editor
Sweet & Maxwell
The Hatchery
Hall Bank Lane
Mytholmroyd, Hebden Bridge
West Yorkshire
HX7 5HQ

TABLE OF ABBREVIATIONS

Court Abbreviations

AAT = Administrative Appeals Tribunal (Australia)
AD = Anotato Dikastirio (Cyprus)
Afr Comm HPR = African Commission on Human and Peoples Rights
AG = Amtsgericht (Germany)
AGO = Advocate Generals Opinion
AIT = Asylum and Immigration Tribunal
APDPK = Arkhe Prostasias Dedomenon Prosopikou Kharaktera (Greece)
App (B) = Cour d'Appel (Belgium)
App (I) = Corte di Appello (Italy)
App Person = Trade Marks Registry (Appointed Person)
Ar Pag = Areios Pagos (Greece)
ArbG = Arbeitsgericht (Germany)
ARRS = Afdeling Rechtspraak van de Raad van State (NL)
As Huk Mah = Asliye Hukuk Mahkemesi (Turkey)
As Tic Mah = Asliye Ticaret Mahkemesi (Turkey)
AT = Augstakas Tiesas (Latvia)
ATMC = Administrative Trade Mark Committee (Greece)
Aud = Audiencia Provincial (Spain)
BAG = Bundesarbeitsgericht (Germany)
Bar Standards Bd = Bar Standards Board Review Panel
Bd of Trade = Board of Trade
BezG = Bezirksgericht (Switzerland)
BFH = Bundesfinanzhof (Germany)
BG = Bundesgericht (Switzerland)
BGH = Bundesgerichtshof (Germany)
BKA = Bundeskartellamt (Germany)
BOIP = Benelux Office for Intellectual Property
BPG = Bundespatentgericht (Germany)
BRB = Burgerlijke Rechtbank (Belgium)
BsozG = Bundessozialgericht (Germany)
BverfG = Bundesverfassungsgericht (Germany)
BverwG = Bundesverwaltungsgericht (Germany)
C Adm A = Cour Administrative d'Appel (Belgium/France)
C Concurrence = Conseil de la Concurrence (Belgium/France)
C Cost = Corte Costituzionale (Italy)
C d'A = Cour d'Appel (France/Luxembourg)
CA = Court of Appeal
CA (Civ Div) = Court of Appeal (Civil Division)
CA (Crim Div) = Court of Appeal (Criminal Division)
CA (Irl) = Court of Appeal (Ireland)
CA (Sey) = Court of Appeal (Seychelles)
CAC = Central Arbitration Committee
CAEW = Central Authority for England and Wales
Care Standards Tr = Care Standards Tribunal
Cass = Cour de Cassation (Belgium/France/Luxembourg)
CAT = Competition Appeal Tribunal
CC = County Court
CCA = Court of Criminal Appeal
CCAT = Competition Commission Appeal Tribunal
CCP = Court of Common Pleas
CE = Conseil d'Etat (Belgium/France)
CE (Col) = Consejo de Estado (Colombia)
CEC = Commission of the European Communities
Cent Crim Ct = Central Criminal Court (Ireland)
Central Crim Ct = Central Criminal Court
CFA (HK) = Court of Final Appeal (Hong Kong)
CFI = Court of First Instance
CFI (HK) = Court of First Instance of the High Court (Hong Kong Special Administrative Region)
CFI (Phl) = Court of First Instance (Philippines)
Charity Comm = Charity Commissioners
Ch D = Chancery Division
Ch D (Bankruptcy Ct) = Chancery Division (Bankruptcy Court)
Ch D (Companies Ct) = Chancery Division (Companies Court)
Ch D (Irl) = Chancery Division (Ireland)
Ch D (NI) = Chancery Division (Northern Ireland)
Ch D (Patents Ct) = Chancery Division (Patents Court)
Ch D (RPC) = Chancery Division (Restrictive Practices Court)
CICA = Criminal Injuries Compensation Authority
CICAP = Criminal Injuries Compensation Appeals Panel
CICB = Criminal Injuries Compensation Board
Circ Ct = Circuit Court (Ireland)
Civil Ct = Civil Court (M)
CJ = Court of Justice
CJ (Gen Div) (Ont) = Ontario Court of Justice (General Division)
CMAC = Courts Martial Appeal Court
CollvB = College van Beroep voor het Bedrijfsleven (NL)
Comm Cartels = Commission des Cartels (Switzerland)
Comm Conc = Commission de la Concurrence (France)
Comm Ministers = Committee of Ministers
Commr Pat = Commissioner of Patents (Australia)
Comm Sec Cons (F) = Commission de la Securite des Consommateurs
Comm Tributaria PG = Commissione Tributaria di Primo Grado (Italy)
Comm Tributaria SG = Commissione Tributaria di Secondo Grado (Italy)
Comp Auth = Competition Authority (Ireland)
Company Names Tr = Company Names Tribunal
Cons Const = Conseil Constitutionnel (France)
Cons Ct = Consistory Court
Cons Stato = Consiglio di Stato (Italy)
Const Ct = Constitutional Court
Cour d'Arb = Cour d'Arbitrage (Belgium)
Cour Const = Cour Constitutionnelle (Belgium)
CP = Court of Protection
CPD = Common Pleas Division
CRC = Commission Federale de Recours en Matiere de Contributions (Switzerland)
Crim CA = Criminal Court of Appeal (Ireland)
CRvB = Centrale Raad van Beroep (Netherlands)
CS = Court of Session
CSJ = Cour Superieure de Justice (Luxembourg)
CST = Civil Service Tribunal
Ct Sup = Corte Suprema de Justicia (Argentina)
DC = Divisional Court
DR = District Registry
EAT = Employment Appeal Tribunal
EC Council = European Council
Eccl Ct = Court of Ecclesiastical Causes Reserved
ECHR = European Court of Human Rights

TABLE OF ABBREVIATIONS

ECHR (Grand Chamber) = European Court of Human Rights (Grand Chamber)
ECJ = European Court of Justice
ECSR = European Committee of Social Rights
ED = Eparhiako Dikastrio (Cyprus)
EFTA = EFTA Court of Justice
Epit Antag = Epitropi Antagonismou (Greece)
EPO = European Patent Office
ERGI (Swi) = Eidgenossische Rekurskommission fur Geistiges Eigentum (Switzerland)
ES = Eidgenossisches Steuerrekurskommission (Switzerland)
ET = Employment Tribunal
EUIPO = European Union Intellectual Property Office
Eur Comm HR = European Commission on Human Rights
Ex Chamber = Court of Exchequer Chamber
Ex Ct = Court of Exchequer
Ex Div = Extra Division
Fam Ct = Family Court
Fam Div = Family Division
FAS Mosk Okr (RF) = Federalnyi Arbitrazhnyi Sud Moskovskogo Okruga (Russian Federation)
Fed CA = Federal Court of Appeal
Fed Circ Ct (Aus) = Federal Circuit Court (Australia)
Fed Ct = Federal Court
Fed HC = Federal High Court
FG = Finanzgericht (Germany)
FET= Fair Employment Tribunal (Northern Ireland)
FSMT = Financial Services & Markets Tribunal
FTT = First-Tier Tribunal
GC = General Court
GC = Giudice Conciliatore (Italy)
HC = High Court
HCJ = High Court of Justiciary
HD = Hogsta Domstolen (Finland/Sweden)
HerrR = Herredsrett (Norway)
HFD = Hogsta forvaltningsdomstolen (Finland)
HL = House of Lords
HO = Hovioikeus/Hovratt (Finland)
Hof = Gerechtshof (Netherlands)
HR (DK) = Hojesteret (Denmark)
HR (N) = Hoyesterett (Norway)
HR (NL) = Hoge Raad (NL)
HR (Swe) = Hovratt (Sweden)
HR Ch = Human Rights Chamber for Bosnia and Herzegovina
HvB = Hof van Beroep (Belgium)
HvC = Hof van Cassatie (Belgium)
IA Comm HR = Inter American Commission on Human Rights
IACHR = Inter American Court of Human Rights
IAT = Immigration Appeal Tribunal
ICC = International Chamber of Commerce, Arbitration Tribunal
ICJ = International Court of Justice
ICTA Tr = Tribunal constituted under the Income and Corporation Taxes Act 1988 s.706
IH = Inner House
IH = Court of Session (Inner House)
IH (1 Div) = Court of Session (Inner House, First Division)
IH (2 Div) = Court of Session (Inner House, Second Division)
IH (Ex Div) = Court of Session (Inner House, Extra Division)
IPEC = Intellectual Property Enterprise Court
IPO = Intellectual Property Office
IPT = Investigatory Powers Tribunal
IT = Industrial Tribunal
ITAT (Ind) = Income Tax Appellate Tribunal (India)
It Cass = Corte di Cassazione (Italy)
J de Paix = Justices de la Paix (Luxembourg)
JP = Juge de Paix (Belgium)
JPI = Juzgado de Primera Instancia (Spain)
KBD = King's Bench Division
KBD (Comm) = King's Bench Division (Commercial Court)
KBD (Irl) = King's Bench Division (Ireland)
KBD (NI) = King's Bench Division (Northern Ireland)
KG (Ger) = Kammergericht (Germany)
KG (Swi) = Kassationsgericht (Switzerland)
KHO = Korkein Hallinto-Oikeus (Finland)
KKO = Korkein Oikeus (Finland)
KO = Kihlakunnanoikeus/Haradsratt (Finland)
Ktg = Kantongerecht (Netherlands)
Lab Ct = Labour Court (Ireland)
Land Ct (IoM) = Land Court (Isle of Man)
LArbG = Landesarbeitsgericht (Germany)
LCD = Lord Chancellors Department
Legf Bir = Legfelsobb Birosag (Hungary)
LG (A) = Landesgericht (Austria)
LG (Ger) = Landgericht (Germany)
LGO = Local Government Ombudsman
LJ in Lunacy = Lords Justices sitting in Lunacy
LR = Lagmannsrett (Norway)
LSozG = Landessozialgericht (Germany)
LVAC = Lands Valuation Appeal Court
LVT = Leasehold Valuation Tribunal
MC = Magistrates Court
MCLC = Mayor's and City of London Court
MD = Marknadsdomstolen (Sweden)
MMC = Monopolies and Mergers Commission
MR = Markedsradet (Norway)
Nat Ct = National Court
NI Comm = National Insurance Commissioner
NIRC = National Industrial Relations Court
NO = Naringsfrihetotombudsman (Swe)
NS CR = Nejvyssi soud Ceske republiky (Czech Republic)
NSA (PL) = Naczelny Sad Administracyjny (Poland)
ObG = Obergericht (Switzerland)
ODEI = Office of the Director of Equality Investigations (Ireland)
OGH = Oberster Gerichtshof (Austria)
OH = Outer House
OHIM = Office for Harmonization in the Internal Market
Okr Sod = Okrozno Sodisce (Slovenia)
OL = Ostre Landsret (Denmark)
OLG = Oberlandesgericht (Austria/Germany)
OPM = Oberster Patent- und Markensenat (Austria)
OR = Official Referee
OVG = Oberverwaltungsgericht (Germany)
Pat App Tr = Patents Appeal Tribunal
Pat Val Apel Pad = Patentu Valdes Apelacijas Padome (Latvia)
PC = Privy Council
PCA = Parliamentary Commissioner for Administration
PCC = Patents County Court
PDAD = Probate, Divorce & Admiralty Division
PO = Patent Office
Prer Ct = Prerogative Court
Pret = Pretura (Italy)
PVO = Plant Variety Office
PVST = Plant Varieties & Seeds Tribunal
QB = Court of Queen's Bench
QBD = Queen's Bench Division
QBD (Admin) = Queen's Bench Division (Administrative Court)
QBD (Admlty) = Queen's Bench Division (Admiralty Court)

QBD (Comm) = Queen's Bench Division (Commercial Court)
QBD (Merc) = Queen's Bench Division (Mercantile Court)
QBD (NI) = Queen's Bench Division (Northern Ireland)
QBD (OR) = Queen's Bench Division (Official Referee)
QBD (TCC) = Queen's Bench Division (Technology & Construction Court)
QBD (UK-Irl) = Queen's Bench Division (UK - Ireland)
R = Riigikohus (Estonia)
RB (B) = Tribunal de Premiere Instance (Belgium)
RB (NL) = Arrondissementsrechtbank (Netherlands)
RDAT = Registered Designs Appeal Tribunal
Refugees Status Apps = Refugees Status Appeals Authority (New Zealand)
Rel = Tribunal de Relacao (Portugal)
RP Comm = Restrictive Practices Commission (Ireland)
RPC = Restrictive Practices Court
RR = Regeringsratten (Sweden)
RvK = Rechtbank van Koophandel (Belgium)
Ry & Canal Comm = Railway and Canal Commission
Ry Rates Tr = Railway Rates Tribunal
SAC = Sheriff Appeal Court
Sad Apel = Sad Apelacyjny (Poland)
Sad Rej = Sad Rejonowy (Poland)
SC = Supreme Court
SCSL (UN) = Special Court for Sierra Leone (Appeals Chamber)
Sen Cts = Senior Courts
Sen Cts Costs Office = Senior Courts Costs Office
SENT = Special Educational Needs Tribunal
SH = So- og Handelsret (Denmark)
Sh Ct = Sheriff Court
Sh Pr = Sheriff Principal
Solicitors Disc Ctte (SC) = Solicitors Discipline (Scotland) Committee
Solicitors Disc Tr = Solicitors Disciplinary Tribunal
SozG = Sozialgericht (Germany)
Sp Comm = Special Commissioners
Sp Imm App Comm = Special Immigration Appeals Commission
Spec Crim Ct = Special Criminal Court (Ireland)
SPIC = Sheriff Personal Injury Court
SS Comm = Social Security Commissioner
Star Chamber = Star Chamber
Sup Ct = Supreme Court
STJ = Superior Tribunal de Justica (Brazil)
Sup Trib = Supremo Tribunal de Justica (Portugal)
Sup Trib Admin = Supremo Tribunal Administrativo (Portugal)
Sym Ep = Symvoulio tis Epikrateias (Greece)
TAR = Tribunale Amministrativo (Italy)
TMR = Trade Marks Registry
Tr = Tribunal
TR = Tingsratt (Sweden)
Transport Arb Tr = Transport Arbitration Tribunal
Trib = Tribunale (Italy)
Trib Ad = Tribunal Administratif (France)
Trib Civil = Tribunal Civil (Belgium)
Trib Comm = Tribunal de Commerce (Belgium/France)
Trib Comp = Tribunal de Defensa de la Competencia (Spain)
Trib Const = Tribunal Constitucional (Spain)
Trib Corr = Tribunal Correctionnel (France)
Trib Correct = Tribunal Correctionnel (Belgium)
Trib d'Arr = Tribunal d'Arrondissement (Luxembourg)
Trib Fed = Tribunal Federal (Switzerland)
Trib Gde Inst = Tribunal de Grande Instance (Belgium/France)
Trib Police = Tribunal de Police (France)
Trib Prem Inst = Tribunal de Premiere Instance (Monaco)
Trib Reg Fed = Tribunal Regional Federal (Brazil)
Trib Sup = Tribunal Supremo (Spain)
Trib Travail = Tribunal du Travail (Belgium)
Tryb Konst = Trybunal Konstytucyjny (Poland)
UN CAT = UN Committee Against Torture
UN CED = United Nations Committee on Enforced Disappearances
UN CEDW = UN Committee on the Elimination of Discrimination against Women
UN CERD = UN Committee on the Elimination of Racial Discrimination
UN CRPD - UN Committee on the Rights of Persons with Disabilities
UN HRC = UN Human Rights Committee
UN ICT = UN International Criminal Tribunal
Ur Last = Urad Republike Slovenije za Intelektualno Lastnino (Slovenia)
US CR = Ustavni Soud Ceske Republiky (Czech Republic)
US Ct = US Court
UT = Upper Tribunal
V&DTr = VAT and Duties Tribunal
VAC = Valuation Appeal Court
VfGH = Verfassungsgerichtshof (Austria)
VGH = Verwaltungsgericht (Germany/Switzerland)
Visje Sod = Visje Sodisce (Slovenia)
VKS = Vurhoven Kasatsionen Sud (Bulgaria)
VL = Vestre Landsret (Denmark)
VrS = Vrchni soud (Prague)
VT = Valuation Tribunal
VwGH = Verwaltungsgerichtshof (Austria)
Yrg = Yargitay (Turkey)

Jurisdiction Abbreviations

A = Austria
Abu = Abu Dhabi (United Arab Emirates)
ACT = Australian Capital Territory
Afg = Afghanistan
AI = Ascension Island (St Helena)
AL = Albania
Ald = Alderney
Alg = Algeria
Alta = Alberta
And = Andorra
Ang = Anguilla
Ango = Angola
Ant = Antigua and Barbuda
Arg = Argentina
Arm = Armenia (CIS)
Aus = Australia
Aze = Azerbaijan (CIS)
B = Belgium
Bah = Bahamas
Bahr = Bahrain
Bang = Bangladesh
Bar = Barbados
BC = British Columbia
BEL = Belarus (CIS)
Ben = Benin
Ber = Bermuda
BF = Burkina Faso
BG = British Guiana

TABLE OF ABBREVIATIONS

BH = British Honduras
Bhu = Bhutan
BIH = Bosnia Herzegovina
Bol = Bolivia
Bots = Botswana
Bru = Brunei
Bul = Bulgaria
Bur = Burundi
BVI = British Virgin Islands
Bze = Belize
Bzl = Brazil
Camb = Cambodia
Camn = Cameroon
Can = Canada
Canary I = Canary Islands (Spain)
Cape = Cape of Good Hope
CAR = Central African Republic
Cey = Ceylon
CI = Cayman Islands
CIS = Commonwealth of Independent States
Col = Colombia
Com = Comoros
Con = Congo
Cook I = Cook Islands
CR = Costa Rica
CV = Cape Verde
Cy = Cyprus
CZ = Czech Republic
Dji = Djibouti
DK = Denmark
Dom = Dominica
DomR = Dominican Republic
Dub = Dubai
EA = Eastern Africa
EC = European Communities
ECHR = European Commission on Human Rights
Ecu = Ecuador
Egy = Egypt
ElS = El Salvador
EPO = European Patent Office
EqG = Equatorial Guinea
Eri = Eritrea
Eth = Ethiopia
EU = European Union
EW = Estonia
F = France
FI = Falkland Islands
Fin = Finland
FL = Lichtenstein/Liechtenstein
FMS = Federated Malay States
FRY = Yugoslavia
Gab = Gabon
Gam = Gambia, The
GBi = Guinea Bissau
Geo = Georgia (CIS)
Ger = Germany
Gha = Ghana
Gib = Gibraltar
Gld = Greenland (Denmark)
GR = Greece
Gren = Grenada
Gua = Guatemala
Gue = Guernsey
Gui = Guinea
Guy = Guyana
H = Hungary
HK = Hong Kong
Hon = Honduras
HR = Croatia
I = Italy
Ind = India
Indo = Indonesia
IoM = Isle of Man
Iran = Iran
Iraq = Iraq
Irl = Ireland
IS = Iceland
Isr = Israel
Ivo = Ivory Coast
Jam = Jamaica
Jer = Jersey
Jor = Jordan
Jpn = Japan
Kaz = Kazakhstan (CIS)
Ken = Kenya
Kir = Kiribati
Kuw = Kuwait
Kyr = Kyrgyzstan (CIS)
L = Luxembourg
LA = Latvia
Leb = Lebanon
Les = Lesotho
Libe = Liberia
Libya = Libya
LT = Lithuania
M = Malta
Mace = Macedonia
Mad = Madagascar
Made = Madeira (Portugal)
Mal = Malaysia
Man = Manitoba
Mar = Martinique
Marshall I = Marshall Islands (Micronesia)
Mau = Mauritius
MC = Monaco
Mex = Mexico
Mic = Micronesia
Mnegro = Montenegro
Mnia = Mauritania
Mol = Moldova (CIS)
Mong = Mongolia
Mor = Morocco
Moz = Mozambique
Mrat = Montserrat
Mves = Maldives
Mwi = Malawi
Mya = Myanmar
N = Norway
Nam = Namibia
NAnt = Netherlands Antilles
Nau = Nauru
NB = New Brunswick
Nfld = Newfoundland
NI = Northern Ireland
Nic = Nicaragua
Nig = Nigeria
NK = North Korea
NL = Netherlands
NS = Nova Scotia
NSW = New South Wales
NT = Northern Territory
NWT = North West Territories
NZ = New Zealand
OAS = Organisation of American States
OECS = Organization of Eastern Caribbean States
OAU = Organisation of African Unity
Oman = Oman
Ont = Ontario
P = Portugal
Pak = Pakistan
Pal = Palestine
Pan = Panama
Par = Paraguay
PEI = Prince Edward Island

Phl = Philippines
PI = Pitcairn Islands (New Zealand)
PL = Poland
PNG = Papua New Guinea
Poly = Polynesia
PR = Puerto Rico
PRC = People's Republic of China
Qat = Qatar
Qld = Queensland
Que = Quebec
RF = Russian Federation
Rho = Rhodesia
RI = Rhode Island
RO = Romania
Rwa = Rwanda
SA = South Africa
Sask = Saskatchewan
Saudi = Saudi Arabia
SAus = South Australia
SC = Scotland
Sen = Senegal
Serb = Serbia
Sey = Seychelles
Sing = Singapore
SK = South Korea
SL = Sierra Leone
Slo = Slovakia
Slove = Slovenia
Smld = Somaliland
Sol = Solomon Islands
Som = Somalia
Sp = Spain
SrL = Sri Lanka
StC = Saint Christopher and Nevis
StH = St Helena
StL = Saint Lucia
StV = Saint Vincent and the Grenadines
Sud = Sudan
Sur = Surinam
Swa = Swaziland
Swe = Sweden
Swi = Switzerland
Syria = Syria
Tai = Taiwan
Taj = Tajikistan (CIS)
Tan = Tanzania
Tas = Tasmania
TCI = Turks and Caicos Islands
TDC = Tristan Da Cunha (St Helena)
Thai = Thailand
Tka = Tanganyika
Ton = Tonga
TR = Turkey
Trin = Trinidad and Tobago
Tun = Tunisia
Turkn = Turkmenistan (CIS)
Tuv = Tuvalu
UAE = United Arab Emirates
Ug = Uganda
UK = United Kingdom
UK-Irl = UK - Ireland (pre 1922)
UKEW = England and Wales
UKR = Ukraine (CIS)
UN = United Nations
Uru = Uruguay
US = United States
Uzb = Uzbekistan (CIS)
Van = Vanuatu
Ven = Venezuela
VI = Virgin Islands
Vic = Victoria
Viet = Vietnam
WA = Western Australia
WI = West Indies
Wind = Windward Islands
WS = Western Samoa
WSah = Western Sahara
YT = Yukon Territory
Yug = Yugoslavia
Zai = Zaire
Zam = Zambia
Zim = Zimbabwe

Law Reports/Journal Abbreviations

A.2d = Atlantic Reporter 2nd
A.B.C. = Australian Bankruptcy Cases
A.C. = Appeal Cases
A.C.D. = Administrative Court Digest
A.C.L.C. = Australian Company Law Cases
A.C.L.R. = Australian Company Law Reports
A.C.S.R. = Australian Companies and Securities Reports
A.C.T.R. = Australian Capital Territory Reports
A.D. = Appellate Division Reports (NY)
A.D.2d = Appellate Division Reports 2nd (NY)
A.F.T.R. = American Federal Tax Reports
A.I.R. All. = All India Reporter, Allahabad Series
A.I.R. Bom. = All India Reporter, Bombay Series
A.I.R. Delhi = All India Reporter, Delhi Series
A.I.R. Mad. = All India Reporter, Madras Series
A.I.R. P.C. = All India Reporter, Privy Council Series
A.I.R. S.C. = All India Reporter, Supreme Court Series
A.L.J. = Australian Law Journal
A.L.J.R. = Australian Law Journal Reports
A.L.M.D. = Australian Legal Monthly Digest
A.L.R. = Australian Law Reports
A.L.R. = American Law Reports (1919-48)
A.L.R. (C.N.) = Argus Law Reports, Current Notes (Australia)
A.L.R. Fed. = American Law Reports Federal
A.L.R. Int'l = American Law Reports International
A.L.R.2d = American Law Reports 2nd (1948-65)
A.L.R.3d = American Law Reports 3rd (1965-80)
A.M.C. = American Maritime Cases
A.R. = Alberta Reports (Canada)
A.T.C. = Annotated Tax Cases
A.T.R. = Australian Tax Reports
Act. = Acton's Prize Causes Reports
Ad. & El. = Adolphus & Ellis' Reports
Adam = Adam's Justiciary Reports (Scotland)
Add. = Addams' Ecclesiastical Reports
Admin. L.R. = Administrative Law Reports
Al. = Aleyn's Select Cases
All E.R. = All England Law Reports
All E.R. (Comm) = All England Law Reports (Commercial Cases)
All E.R. (EC) = All England Law Reports (European Cases)
All E.R. Rep. = All England Law Reports Reprints
All N.L.R. = All Nigeria Law Reports
Am.Dec. = American Decisions
Am.Rep. = American Reports
Am.St.Rep. = American State Reports
Amb. = Ambler's Chancery Reports
And. = Anderson's Common Pleas Reports
Andr. = Andrews' King's Bench Reports
Anst. = Anstruther's Exchequer Reports
Arb. L.R.= Arbitration Law Reports and Review

TABLE OF ABBREVIATIONS

Ark. = Arkley's Justiciary Reports (Scotland)
Asp. = Aspinall's Maritime Cases (1870-1940)
Atk. = Atkyn's Chancery Reports
B. & Ad. = Barnewall and Adolphus's King's Bench Reports
B. & Ald. = Barnewall and Alderson's King's Bench Reports
B. & C. = Barnewall and Cresswell's King's Bench Reports
B. & C.R. = Reports of Bankruptcy and Companies (Winding up) Cases (1918-41)
B. & S. = Best and Smith's Queen's Bench Reports
B.C.C. = British Company Cases
BCCA = Court of Appeal of British Columbia (media neutral cite)
B.C.L.C. = Butterworths Company Law Cases
B.C.L.R. = British Columbia Law Reports (Canada)
BCSC = Supreme Court of British Columbia (media neutral cite)
B.H.R.C. = Butterworths Human Rights Cases
B.L.G.R. = Butterworths Local Government Reports
B.L.R. = Building Law Reports
B.M.L.R. = Butterworths Medico Legal Reports
B.N.C. = Brooke's New Cases
B.P.I.R. = Bankruptcy and Personal Insolvency Reports
B.R. = Bankruptcy Reporter
B.T.C. = British Tax Cases
B.T.L.C. = Butterworths Trading Law Cases Cases
B.V.C. = British VAT Cases
B.W.C.C. = Butterworths Workmen's Compensation Cases
Ball & B. = Ball and Beatty's Irish Chancery Reports
Bank. L.R. = Banking Law Reports
Bankr.Ct.Dec. = Bankruptcy Court Decisions (CRR)
Barn. Ch. = Barnardiston's Chancery Reports
Barn. K.B. = Barnardiston's King's Bench Reports
Barnes = Barnes' Notes of Cases in Common Pleas
Beat. = Beatty's Irish Chancery Reports
Beav. = Beavan's Rolls Court Reports
Bel. = Bellewe's Reports (Les Ans du Roy Richard le Second)
Bell C.C. = Bell's Crown Cases Reserved
Belt's Supp. = Belt's Supplement to Vesey Senior's Reports
Benl. = Benloe's Reports
Benl. & Dal. Benloe = Benloe & Dalison's Reports (Benloe)
Benl. & Dal. Dalison = Benloe & Dalison's Reports (Dalison)
Bing. = Bingham's Common Pleas Reports
Bing. N.C. = Bingham, New Cases, English Common Pleas
Binn. = Binney's Reports (U.S.A.)
Bli. = Bligh's House of Lords Reports
Bli. N.S. = Bligh's House of Lords Reports, New Series
Bos. & P. = Bosanquet and Puller's Common Pleas Reports
Bos. & P. N.R. = Bosanquet and Puller's New Reports, Common Pleas
Bott P.L. = Bott's Poor Law Cases
Br. & Col. Pri. Cas. = British and Colonial Prize Cases
Bro. C.C. = W. Brown's Chancery Reports
Bro. P.C. = J. Brown's Parliamentary Cases
Bro. Sup. = Brown's Supplement to the Dictionary of Decisions of the Court of Session
Brod. & Bing. = Broderip and Bingham's Common Pleas Reports
Broun = Broun's Justiciary Reports (Scotland)
Brown. & Lush. = Browning and Lushington's Admiralty Reports
Brownl. = Brownlow and Goldesborough's Common Pleas Reports
Bull. N.P. = Buller's Nisi Prius Reports
Bulst. = Bulstrode's King's Bench Reports
Bunb. = Bunbury's Exchequer Reports
Burr. = Burrow's King's Bench Reports tempore Mansfield
Burrell = Burrell's Admiralty Reports
Bus. L.R. = Business Law Reports
Bus. L.R. D = Business Law Reports Digest Pages
C. Rob. = Christopher Robinson's Admiralty Reports
C.B. = Common Bench Reports (Manning)
C.B. N.S. = Common Bench Reports (Manning), New Series
C.C.C. = Canadian Criminal Cases
C.C.C. (2d) = Canadian Criminal Cases, 2nd Series
C.C.C. (3d) = Canadian Criminal Cases, 3rd Series
C.C.L. Rep. = Community Care Law Reports
C.C.L.R. = Consumer Credit Law Reports
C.C.L.T. = Canadian Cases on the Law of Torts
C.C.P.A. = Court of Customs & Patent Appeals Reports
C.E.C. = European Community Cases
C.I.L.L. = Construction Industry Law Letter
C.I.L.R. = Cayman Islands Law Reports
C.L.C. = Commercial Law Cases
C.L.R. = Commonwealth Law Reports
C.M.L. Rev. = Common Market Law Review
C.M.L.R. = Common Market Law Reports
C.M.L.R. D = Common Market Law Reports Restrictive Practices Supplement
C.M.L.R. M = Common Market Law Reports Merger Decisions
C.O.D. = Crown Office Digest
C.O.P.L.R. = Court of Protection Law Reports
C.P. Rep. = Civil Procedure Reports
C.P.C. (2d) = Carswell's Practice Cases, Second Series
C.P.C. (3d) = Carswell's Practice Cases, Third Series
C.P.L. = Current Property Law (1952-53)
C.P.L.R. = Civil Practice Law Reports
C.P.R. = Canadian Patent Reporter
C.P.R. (2d) = Canadian Patent Reporter, 2nd Series
C.P.R. (3d) = Canadian Patent Reporter, 3rd Series
C.P.R. (4th) = Canadian Patent Reporter, 4th Series
C.R. = Criminal Reports (Canada, 1946-67)
C.R. N.S. = Criminal Reports (New Series) (Canada, 1967-78)
C.R.R. = Canadian Rights Reporter
C.S. = Rapports Judiciaires de Quebec, Cour Superieure
CAT = Competition Commission Appeal Tribunal (media neutral cite)
CJ C.A.R. = Colorado Appellate Report
CSIH = Court of Session, Inner House (media neutral cite)
CSOH = Court of Session, Outer House (media neutral cite)
Cab. & Ell. = Cababe and Ellis' Queen's Bench Reports
Cal. = California Reports
Cal. Daily Op. Serv. = California Daily Opinion Service
Cal.3d = California Reports 3rd
Cal.4th = California Reports, 4th Series
Cal.Rptr.2d = California Reporter 2d (West's)
Cald. M.C. = Caldecott's Magistrates Cases
Calth. = Calthrop's City of London Special Cases
Camp. = Campbell's Nisi Prius Reports
Can. B.R. = Canadian Bar Review
Car. & K. = Carrington and Kirwan's Nisi Prius Reports

TABLE OF ABBREVIATIONS

Car. & M. = Carrington and Marshman's Nisi Prius Reports
Car. & P. = Carrington and Payne's Nisi Prius Reports
CarswellFor = Carswell Foreign
Cart. = Carter's Common Pleas Reports
Carth. = Carthew's King's Bench Reports
Cary = Cary's Chancery Reports
Cas. t. Hard. = Lee's King's Bench Cases tempore Hardwicke
Cas. t. Talb. = Cases in Equity tempore Talbot
Ch. = Chancery Division
Ch. Cas. = Cases Argued and Decreed in Chancery (Select Cases in Chancery)
Ch. Cas. in Ch. = Choyce Cases in Chancery
Chit. = Chitty's King's Bench Practice and Pleading Reports
Cl. & F. = Clark and Finnelly's House of Lords Reports
Clark's Rep. = Clark's Reports (Jamaica)
Clay. = Clayton's Reports and Pleas of Assises at Yorke
Clunet = Journal du Droit International (France)
Co. Rep. = Coke's King's Bench Reports
Coll. = Collyer's Chancery Cases tempore Bruce
Colles = Colles' Parliament Reports
Com. = Comyns' King's Bench, Common Pleas and Exchequer Reports
Com. Cas. = Commercial Cases
Com. L.R. = Commercial Law Reports
Comb. = Comberbach's King's Bench Reports
Comp. A.R. = Competition Appeal Reports
Con. L.R. = Construction Law Reports
Const. L.J. = Construction Law Journal
C.T.L.C.= Consumer and Trading Law Cases
Cooke = Cooke's Common Pleas Reports
Coop. Pr. Cas. = Cooper's Practice Cases
Coop. t. Brough. = Cooper's Select Cases of Lord Brougham
Coop. t. Cott. = Cooper's Chancery Reports tempore Cottenham
Costs L.O. = Costs Law Reports Online
Costs L.R. = Costs Law Reports
Costs L.R. Online = Costs Law Reports Online
Costs L.R. (Core Vol.) = Costs Law Reports, Core Volume
Coup. = Couper's Justiciary Reports (Scotland)
Cowp. = Cowper's King's Bench Reports
Cox C.C. = Cox's Criminal Cases
Cox Eq. Cas. = Cox's Equity Cases
Cr. & J. = Crompton and Jervis' Exchequer Reports
Cr. & M. = Crompton and Meeson's Exchequer Reports
Cr. & Ph. = Craig and Phillip's Chancery Reports
Cr. App. R. = Criminal Appeal Reports
Cr. App. R. (S.) = Criminal Appeal Reports (Sentencing)
Cr. M. & R. = Crompton, Meeson and Roscoe's Exchequer Reports
Cr. S. & P. = Craigie, Stewart and Paton's Scottish Appeal Cases
Cranch = Cranch's United States Supreme Court Reports
Crim. L.R. = Criminal Law Review
Cro. Car. = Croke's King's Bench Reports tempore Charles
Cro. Eliz. = Croke's King's Bench Reports tempore Elizabeth
Cro. Jac. = Croke's King's Bench Reports tempore James
Cun. = Cunningham's King's Bench Reports
Curt. = Curteis' Ecclesiastical Reports
D. = Dunlop, Bell and Murray's Reports, Session Cases, 2nd series (Scotland)
D. & R. = Decisions and Reports of the European Commission of Human Rights
D. (H.L.) = Dunlop's Session Cases, 2nd Series (House of Lords cases, Scotland)
D.L.R. = Dominion Law Reports (Canada, 1912-55)
D.L.R. (2d) = Dominion Law Reports (2d) (Canada, 1956-68)
D.L.R. (3d) = Dominion Law Reports (3d) (Canada, 1969-84)
D.L.R. (4th) = Dominion Law Reports (4th) (Canada, 1985-94)
D.R.A. = De-rating Appeals
D.T.C. = Dominion Tax Cases
Daily Telegraph = Daily Telegraph
Dan. = Daniell's Exchequer Reports
Dav. = Davis' Irish Reports
De G. = De Gex's Bankruptcy Reports
De G. & J. = De Gex and Jones' Chancery Reports
De G. & Sm. = De Gex and Smale's Chancery Reports
De G.F. & J. = De Gex, Fisher and Jones' Chancery Reports
De G.J. & S. = De Gex, Jones and Smith's Chancery Reports
De G.M. & G. = De Gex, Macnaghten and Gordons' Chancery Reports
Dea. & Sw. = Deane and Swabey's Ecclesiastical Reports
Deac. & Ch. = Deacon and Chitty's Bankruptcy Reports
Dears. = Dearsley's Crown Cases Reserved
Dears. & B. = Dearsley and Bell's Crown Cases Reserved
Den. = Denison and Pearce's Crown Cases Reserved
Dick. = Dickens' Chancery Reports
Disc. L.R. = Discrimination Law Reports
Dods. = Dodson's Admiralty Reports
Donn. = Donnelly's Chancery Cases
Doug. K.B. = Douglas' King's Bench Reports
Dow = Dow's House of Lords Cases
Dow. & Cl. = Dow and Clark's House of Lords Reports
Dowl. & L. = Dowling and Lowndes' Bail Court Reports
Dowl. & Ry. K.B. = Dowling and Ryland's King's Bench Reports
Dowl. & Ry. N.P. = Dowling and Ryland's Nisi Prius Cases
Dowl. N.S. = Dowling's Bail Court Reports, New Series
Dowl. Pr. Cas. = Dowling's Bail Court Practice Cases
Dr. & War. = Drury and Warren's Irish Chancery Reports
Dr. t. Sug. = Drury's Irish Chancery Cases tempore Sugden
Drew. = Drewry's Chancery Reports tempore Kindersley
Drew. & Sm. = Drewry and Smales' Chancery Reports
Dyer = Dyer's King's Bench Reports
E.A. = East African Law Reports
E.A.C.A. = Law Reports of the Court of Appeals for Eastern Africa
E.A.T.C. = East African Tax Cases
E.B.L.R. = Electronic Business Law Reports
E.C.C. = European Commercial Cases
E.C.D.R. = European Copyright and Design Reports
E.C.D.R. CN = European Copyright and Design Reports Case Notes
E.C.R. = European Court Reports
E.C.R. IA = European Court Reports
E.G. = Estates Gazette
E.G.C.S. = Estates Gazette Case Summaries
E.G.D. = Estates Gazette Digest of Cases

E.G.L.R. = Estates Gazette Law Reports (Bound Volume)
E.H.L.R. = Environmental Health Law Reports
E.H.L.R. Dig. = Environmental Health Reports Digest Pages
E.H.R.R. = European Human Rights Reports
E.H.R.R. CD = European Human Rights Reports, Commission Decisions
E.H.R.R. SE = European Human Rights Reports, Summaries and Extracts
E.L.R. = Education Law Reports
E.M.L.R. = Entertainment and Media Law Reports
E.N.P.R. = European National Patent Reports
E.P.O.R. = European Patent Office Reports
E.P.O.R. A = European Patent Office Reports A (1979-85, J decisions)
E.P.O.R. B = European Patent Office Reports B (1979-85, T decisions)
E.P.O.R. C = European Patent Office Reports C (1979-85, T decisions)
E.R. = English Reports
E.T.M.R. = European Trade Mark Reports
E.T.M.R. CN = European Trade Mark Reports Case Notes
Elchies = Elchies' Decisions of the Court of Session
ERC = Environment Reporter Cases (BNA)
EWCA Civ = Court of Appeal (Civil)
EWCA Crim = Court of Appeal (Criminal)
EWCOP = Court of Protection
EWFC = Family Court
EWHC = High Court
EWHC Admin = High Court (Administrative Court)
EWPCC = Patents County Court
East = East's King's Bench Reports
East P.C. = East's Pleas of the Crown
Ed. C.R. = Education Case Reports
Ed. Law Rep. = Education Law Reporter
Eden = Eden's Chancery Reports
Edw. = Edward's Admiralty Reports
El. & Bl. = Ellis and Blackburn's Queen's Bench Reports
El. & El. = Ellis and Ellis' Queen's Bench Reports
El. Bl. & El. = Ellis, Blackburn and Ellis' Queen's Bench Reports
Emp. L.R. = Employment Law Reports
Employee Benefits Cas. = Employee Benefits Cases
Env. L.R. = Environmental Law Reports
Env. L.R. D = Environmental Law Reports Digest Pages
Envtl. L. Rep. = Environmental Law Reporter (ELR) (cases only)
Eq. Cas. Abr. = Abridgment of Cases in Equity
Eq. L.R. = Equality Law Reports
Eq. Rep. = Equity Reports
Esp. = Espinasse's Nisi Prius Reports
EU:C = European Case Law Identifier (European Court of Justice)
EU:F = European Case Law Identifier (Civil Service Tribunal)
EU:T = European Case Law Identifier (General Court)
Eu. L.R. = European Law Reports
Ex. = Exchequer Reports (Welsby, Hurlstone and Gordon)
Ex. C.R. = Canada Law Reports, Exchequer Court
Extradition L.R. = Extradition Law Reports
F. = Federal Reporter (U.S.A.)
F. = Fraser's Session Cases, 5th Series (Scotland)
F. & F. = Foster and Finlason's Nisi Prius Reports
F. (Ct. of Sess.) = Faculty Decisions, Court of Session (Scotland)
F. (H.L.) = Fraser's Session Cases, 5th Series (House of Lords, Scotland)
F. (J.) = Fraser's Session Cases, 5th Series (Justiciary cases, Scotland)
F.2d = Federal Reporter, 2nd Series (U.S.A.)
F.3d = Federal Reporter, 3rd Series (U.S.A.)
F.C. = Canada Law Reports, Federal Court
F.C.R. = Family Court Reporter
F.L.R. = Family Law Reports
F.R.D. = Federal Rules Decisions (U.S.A.)
F.S.R. = Fleet Street Reports
F.Supp. = Federal Supplement (U.S.A.)
F.Supp.2d = Federal Supplement, Second Series
F.T.L.R. = Financial Times Law Reports
F.T.R. = Federal Trial Reports
FCA = Federal Court of Australia (media neutral cite)
FCA = Federal Court of Appeal of Canada (media neutral cite)
FCAFC = Federal Court of Australia, Full Court (media neutral cite)
Fam. = Family Division
Fam. L.R. = Family Law Reports (Scotland)
Fam. Law = Family Law
FamCA = Family Court of Australia (media neutral cite)
Fed. L.R. = Federal Law Reports (Australia)
Fed. R. Evid. Serv. = Federal Rules of Evidence Service (Callaghan's)
Fed. Sec. L. Rep. P = Federal Securities Law Reports (CCH)
Fed.R.Serv.2d = Federal Rules Service 2nd (Callaghan's)
Fed.R.Serv.3d = Federal Rules Service 3rd (Callaghan's)
Fed.Sent.R. = Federal Sentencing Reporter (U.S.A.)
Fin. L.R. = Financial Law Reports
Financial Times = Financial Times
Fitzg. = Fitz-Gibbons' King's Bench Reports
Fla. L. Weekly Fed. S = Florida Law Weekly, United States Supreme Court
Forr. = Forrest's Exchequer Reports
Fort. = Fortescue's Courts of Westminster Hall Reports
Fost. = Foster's Crown Cases
Freem. Ch. = Freeman's Chancery Reports
Freem. K.B. = Freeman's King's Bench and Common Pleas Reports
G. Coop. = Cooper's Chancery Reports
G.W.D. = Green's Weekly Digest (Scotland)
GRUR = Gewerblicher Rechtsschutz und Urheberrecht
Ga. = Georgia Reports
Giff. = Giffard's Chancery Reports
Gilb. Ch. = Gilbert's Cases in Equity
Gilb. K.B. = Gilbert's King's Bench Cases
Gl. & J. = Glyn and Jameson's Bankruptcy Reports
Godb. = Godbolt's Courts of Record at Westminster Reports
Gould. = Gouldsborough's King's Bench Reports
Gow = Gow's Nisi Prius Reports
Guardian = Guardian
H. & Tw. = Hall and Twells' Chancery Reports
H. Bl. = H. Blackstone's Common Pleas Reports
H.B.R. = Hansell's Bankruptcy Reports (1915-17)
H.K. Cases = Hong Kong Cases
H.K.L.R. = Hong Kong Law Reports
H.K.L.R.D. = Hong Kong Law Reports and Digest
H.L. Cas. = Clark's House of Lords Cases
H.L.R. = Housing Law Reports
H.R.C.D. = Human Rights Case Digest
H.R.L.R. = Human Rights Law Reports - UK Cases
Hailes = Hailes' Decisions of the Lords of Council and Session
HCA = High Court of Australia (media neutral cite)

TABLE OF ABBREVIATIONS

HCJAC = High Court of Justiciary, Appeal (media neutral cite)
HCJT = High Court of Justiciary, Trial (media neutral cite)
Hag. Adm. = Haggard's Admiralty Reports
Hag. Con. = Haggard's Consistorial Reports
Hag. Ecc. = Haggard's Ecclesiastical Reports
Har. & Woll. = Harrison and Wollaston's King's Bench and Bail Court Reports
Hardres = Hardres' Exchequer Reports
Hare = Hare's Chancery Reports
Hay & M. = Hay and Marriott's Admiralty Reports
Hayes = Hayes' Irish Exchequer Reports
Hayes & J. = Hayes and Jones' Irish Exchequer Reports
Hem. & M. = Hemming and Miller's Chancery Reports
Het. = Hetley's Reports
Hob. = Hobart's Reports (Common Pleas and King's Bench)
Hodg. = Hodges' Common Pleas Reports
Holt Eq. = Holt's Equity Reports
Holt K.B. = Holt's King's Bench Reports
Holt N.P. = Holt's Nisi Prius Reports
Hous. L.R. = Housing Law Reports (Scottish)
Hov. Supp. = Hovenden's Supplement to Vesey Junior's Reports
How. = Howard's United States Supreme Court Reports
Hume = Hume's Session Cases (Scotland)
Hurl. & C. = Hurlstone and Coltman's Exchequer Reports
Hurl. & N. = Hurlstone and Norman's Exchequer Reports
Hut. = Hutton's Reports
I.C.L.R. = Irish Common Law Reports, Second Series (1850-66)
I.C.R. = Industrial Cases Reports
I.C.R.D. = Industrial Cases Reports Digest Pages
I.H.R.R. = International Human Rights Reports
I.L.Pr. = International Litigation Procedure
I.L.R. = International Law Reports
I.L.R.M. = Irish Law Reports Monthly
I.L.T. = Irish Law Times
I.L.T.R. = Irish Law Times Reports
I.N.L.R. = Immigration and Nationality Law Reports
I.P.D. = Intellectual Property Decisions
I.P.L.R. = Industrial Property Law Reports (India)
I.P.R. = Intellectual Property Reports (Australia)
I.P.&.T. = Intellectual Property and Technology Cases
I.R. = Irish Reports
I.R. C.L. = Irish Reports, Common Law
I.R.L.R. = Industrial Relations Law Reports
I.T.C. = Srinivasan's Reports of Income Tax Cases (India)
I.T.C.L.R. = IT & Communications Law Reports
I.T.E.L.R. = International Trust and Estate Law Reports
I.T.L. Rep. = International Tax Law Reports
I.T.R. = Industrial Tribunal Reports
IEHC = High Court of Ireland (media neutral cite)
IESC = Supreme Court of Ireland (media neutral cite)
ITRD = International Trade Reporter Decisions (BNA)
Ill.2d = Illinois Reports, 2nd Series
Ill.Dec. = Illinois Decisions
Imm. A.R. = Immigration Appeal Reports
Ind. = Indiana Reports
Ind. Cas. = Indian Cases
Ind. L.R. = Indian Law Reports
Ind. L.R. All. = Indian Law Reports, Allahabad Series
Ind. L.R. Cal. = Indian Law Reports, Calcutta Series
Ind. L.R. Mad. = Indian Law Reports, Madras Series
Ind. L.R. Pat. = Indian Law Reports, Patna Series
Independent = Independent
Info. T.L.R. = Information Technology Law Reports
Inquest L.R. = Inquest Law Reports
Ir. Ch. R. = Irish Chancery Reports (1850-66)
Ir. Eq. = Irish Reports, Equity (1866-77)
Ir. Eq. R. = Irish Equity Reports, First Series (1838-50)
Ir. Jur. Rep. = Irish Jurist Reports
Ir. L.J. = Irish Law Journal
Ir. L.R. = Irish Law Reports
Irvine = Irvine's High Court and Circuit Courts of Justiciary Reports (Scotland)
J. & Lat. = Jones and La Touche's Irish Chancery Reports (1844-46)
J. Bridg. = Sir John Bridgman's Reports
J. Shaw. = Shaw's Justiciary Reports (Scotland)
J.C. = Justiciary Cases (Scotland)
J.J. = Jersey Judgments
J.L.R. = Jamaica Law Reports
J.P. = Justice of the Peace Reports
J.P. Rep. = Local Government Review Reports
J.P.I. Law = Journal of Personal Injury Law
J.P.I.L. = Journal of Personal Injury Litigation
J.P.L. = Journal of Planning & Environment Law
J.P.N. = Justice of the Peace Notes of Cases
Jac. = Jacob's Chancery Reports
Jac. & W. = Jacob and Walker's Chancery Reports
JCA = Jersey Court of Appeal (media neutral cite)
Jebb. & Sym. = Jebb and Syme's Queen's Bench Reports (Ireland, 1838-41)
Jenk. = Jenkins' Eight Centuries of Reports
Jer. L.R. = Jersey Law Reports
John. = Johnson's Chancery Reports
John. & H. = Johnson and Hemming's Chancery Reports
JRC = Jersey Royal Court (media neutral cite)
Jur. = Jurist
Jur. N.S. = Jurist, New Series
K.B. = King's Bench
K.I.R. = Knight's Industrial Law Reports
Kay = Kay's Chancery Reports
Kay & J. = Kay and Johnson's Chancery Reports
Keb. = Keble's King's Bench Reports
Keen = Keen's Rolls Court Reports
Keil. = Keilwey's Reports
Kel. = Kelyng's Divers Cases
Kel. W. = W Kelynge's King's Bench and Chancery Reports
Keny. = Kenyon's King's Bench Reports
Kn. = Knapp's Privy Council Appeal Cases
Ky. = Kentucky Reports
L. & T.R. = Landlord and Tenant Reports
L.D.B. = Legal Decisions Affecting Bankers
L.Ed. = Lawyers' Edition, United States Supreme Court Reporter
L.Ed.2d = Lawyers' Edition 2nd Series, United States Supreme Court Reporter
L.G. Rev. = Local Government Review
L.G.L.R. = Local Government Law Reports
L.G.R. = Local Government Reports
L.G.R.A. = Local Government Reports of Australia
L.J. = Law Journal (Newspaper)
L.J. Bcy. = Law Journal Reports, Bankruptcy (1832-80)
L.J. C.P. = Law Journal Reports, Common Pleas (1831-75)
L.J. Ch. = Law Journal Reports, Chancery (1831-1946)
L.J. Ex. = Law Journal Reports, Exchequer (1831-75)
L.J. K.B. = Law Journal Reports, King's Bench (1831-1946)
L.J. M.C. = Law Journal Reports, Magistrates Cases (1831-96)

TABLE OF ABBREVIATIONS

L.J. N.C. = Law Journal, Notes of Cases
L.J. N.C.C.R. = Law Journal, County Court Reports (1934-47)
L.J. N.S. = Law Journal Reports, New Series (1832-1946)
L.J. O.S. = Law Journal Reports, Old Series (1822-31)
L.J. P. = Law Journal Reports, Probate, Divorce and Admiralty (1875-1946)
L.J. P. & M. = Law Journal Reports, Probate, Divorce and Matrimonial (1858-59, 1866-75)
L.J. P.C. = Law Journal Reports, Privy Council (1831-1946)
L.J. P.M. & A. = Law Journal Reports, Probate, Matrimonial and Admiralty (1860-65)
L.J. Q.B. = Law Journal Reports, Queen's Bench (1831-1946)
L.J.R. = Law Journal Reports (1947-49)
L.L.R. = Licensing Law Reports
L.M.C.L.Q. = Lloyd's Maritime and Commercial Law Quarterly
L.R. A. & E. = Admiralty and Ecclesiastical Cases (1865-75)
L.R. App. Cas. = Appeal Cases (1875-90)
L.R. C.C.R. = Crown Cases Reserved
L.R. C.P. = Common Pleas (1865-75)
L.R. C.P.D. = Common Pleas Division (1875-80)
L.R. Ch. App. = Chancery Appeals (1865-75)
L.R. Ch. D. = Chancery Division (1875-90)
L.R. Eq. = Equity Cases
L.R. Ex. = Exchequer (1865-75)
L.R. Ex. D. = Exchequer Division (1875-80)
L.R. H.L. = English and Irish Appeals (1866-75)
L.R. Ind. App. = Indian Appeals
L.R. Ir. = Ireland
L.R. P. & D. = Probate and Divorce (1865-75)
L.R. P.C. = Privy Council
L.R. P.D. = Probate Division (1875-90)
L.R. Q.B. = Queen's Bench (1865-75)
L.R. Q.B.D. = Queen's Bench Division (1875-90)
L.R. R.P. = Restrictive Practices (1958-72)
L.R. Sc. = Scotch and Divorce Appeals
L.R.B. = Law Reports of the Bahamas
L.R.C. = Law Reports of the Commonwealth
L.R.C. (Const) = Law Reports of the Commonwealth (Constitutional & Administrative Reports)
L.R.L.R. = Lloyd's Reinsurance Law Reports
L.R.R.M. (BNA) = Labor Relations Reference Manual (BNA)
L.S.G. = Law Society Gazette
L.T. = Law Times (1859-1965)
L.T. O.S. = Law Times (Old Series) (1843-59)
L.T.R. = Law Times Reports (1859-1947)
LS Law Medical = LS Law Medical
Lab.Cas. P = Labor Cases (CCH)
Lane = Lane's Exchequer Reports
Lat. = Latch's King's Bench Reports
Ld. Raym. = Lord Raymond's King's Bench Reports
Le. & Ca. = Leigh and Cave's Crown Cases Reserved
Leach = Leach's Cases in Crown Law
Lee = Lee's Ecclesiastical Reports
Leo. = Leonard's Reports of the Courts at Westminster
Lev. = Levinz's King's Bench and Common Pleas Reports
Lewin = Lewin's Crown Cases Reserved
Ley = Ley's Court of Wards Reports
Lil. = Lilly's Assise Cases
Litt. = Littleton's Common Bank and Exchequer Reports
Ll. & G. t Sug. = Lloyd and Goold's Reports of Chancery in Ireland tempore Sugden
Ll. L. Pr. Cas. = Lloyd's List Prize Cases (1914-24)
Ll. L. Pr. Cas. (N.S.) = Lloyd's List Prize Cases, Second Series (1939-53)
Ll. L. Rep. = Lloyd's List Law Reports (1919-50)
Lloyd's List = Lloyd's List
Lloyd's Rep. = Lloyd's Law Reports (1951-)
Lloyd's Rep. Bank. = Lloyd's Law Reports Banking
Lloyd's Rep. F.C. = Lloyd's Law Reports Financial Crime
Lloyd's Rep. I.R. = Lloyd's Law Reports, Insurance & Reinsurance
Lloyd's Rep. Med. = Lloyd's Law Reports Medical
Lloyd's Rep. P.N. = Lloyd's Law Reports Professional Negligence
Lofft = Lofft's King's Bench Reports
Lush. = Lushington's Admiralty Reports
Lut. = Lutwyche's Reports (Livre des Entries)
Lut. Reg. Cas. = Lutwyche's Entries and Reports, Common Pleas (Registration Cases)
M'Cle. = M'Cleland's Exchequer Reports
M'Cle. & Y. = M'Cleland and Younge's Exchequer Reports
M. = Macpherson's Session Cases, 3rd Series (Scotland)
M. & S. = Maule and Selwyn's King's Bench Reports
M. & W. = Meeson and Welsby's Exchequer Reports
M. (H.L.) = Macpherson's Session Cases, 3rd Series (House of Lords cases, Scotland)
M.C.C. = MacGillivray's Copyright Cases
M.H.L.R. = Mental Health Law Reports
M.L.J. = Malaysian Law Journal
M.P.L.R. = Municipal and Planning Law Reports (Canada)
M.P.R. = Maritime Provinces Reports (Canada)
M.R. = Mauritius Reports
Mac. & G. = Macnaghten and Gordon's Chancery Reports
Macl. & R. = Maclean and Robinson's House of Lords Cases
Macq. = Macqueen's Scottish Appeal Cases
Madd. = Maddock's Chancery Reports
Man. & G. = Manning and Granger's Common Pleas Reports
Man. & Ry. K.B. = Manning and Ryland's King's Bench Reports
Man. & Ry. M.C. = Manning and Ryland's Magistrates Cases Reports
Man. Law = Managerial Law
Mans. = Manson's Bankruptcy and Companies Winding up Cases (1894-1913)
Manx L.R. = Manx Law Reports
March N.C. = March's New Cases
Masons C.L.R. = Masons Computer Law Reports
Masons C.L.R. Rep. = Masons Computer Law Reports Reprints (Case Digests, 1994-97)
Mass. = Massachusetts Reports
Med. L.R. = Medical Law Reports
Media L. Rep. = Media Law Reporter (BNA)
Mer. = Merivale's Chancery Reports
Misc. = New York Miscellaneous Reports
Misc.2d = Miscellaneous Reports, 2nd Series (New York)
Mod. = Modern Reports
Mol. = Molloy's Chancery Reports (Ireland, 1927-31)
Mont. D. & De G. = Montagu, Deacon and De Gex's Bankruptcy Reports
Moo. Ind. App. = Moore's Appeals from the East Indies Reports
Moo. K.B. = Moore's King's Bench Reports
Moo. P.C. = Moore's Privy Council Cases
Moo. P.C. N.S. = Moore's Privy Council Cases, New Series
Mood. & M. = Moody and Malkin's Nisi Prius Reports

TABLE OF ABBREVIATIONS

Mood. & R. = Moody and Robinson's Nisi Prius Reports
Mood. C.C. = Moody's Crown Cases Reserved
Mor. Dic. = Morison's Dictionary of Decisions (Scotland)
Morr. = Morrell's Bankruptcy Reports
Mos. = Moseley's Chancery Reports
My. & C. = Mylne and Craig's Chancery Reports
My. & K. = Mylne and Keen's Chancery Reports
N.B. Eq. = New Brunswick Equity Reports
N.B.R. = National Bankruptcy Register Reports
N.B.R. 2d = New Brunswick Reports, 2nd Series
N.C. = Notes of Cases, Ecclesiastical and Maritime (ed. Thornton)
N.E. = North Eastern Reporter (U.S.A.)
N.E.2d = North Eastern Reporter 2nd
N.H. = New Hampshire Reports
N.I. = Northern Ireland Law Reports
N.I.J.B. = Northern Ireland Judgment Bulletin
N.I.L.Q. = Northern Ireland Legal Quarterly
N.J. = New Jersey Reports
N.L.J. = New Law Journal
N.L.J. Rep. = New Law Journal Reports
N.L.R. = New Law Reports (Sri Lanka)
N.P.C. = New Property Cases
N.R. = National Reporter (Canada)
N.S.R. 2d = Nova Scotia Reports, 2nd Series
N.S.W.L.R. = New South Wales Law Reports
N.S.W.R. = New South Wales Reports (1960-70)
N.W. = North Western Reporter (U.S.A.)
N.W.2d = North Western Reporter, 2nd Series (U.S.A.)
N.Y. = New York Reports
N.Y.2d = New York Reports, 2nd Series
N.Y.S. = New York Supplement Reporter
N.Y.S.2d = New York Supplement Reporter, 2nd Series
N.Z.L.R. = New Zealand Law Reports
NDLR P = National Disability Law Reporter
NICA = Court of Appeal (Northern Ireland) (media neutral cite)
NICh = Chancery Division (Northern Ireland) (media neutral cite)
NIFam = Family Division (Northern Ireland) (media neutral cite)
NIQB = Queen's Bench Division (Northern Ireland) (media neutral cite)
NSWCA = Court of Appeal of New South Wales (media neutral cite)
NSWSC = Supreme Court of New South Wales (media neutral cite)
NZCA = Court of Appeal of New Zealand (media neutral cite)
NZHC = High Court of New Zealand (media neutral cite)
NZSC = Supreme Court of New Zealand (media neutral cite)
Nels. = Nelson's Chancery Reports
Nev. & M. K.B. = Neville and Manning's King's Bench Reports
New Rep. = New Reports
Nfld. & P.E.I.R. = Newfoundland and Prince Edward Island Reports
Noy = Noy's Reports
O'M. & H. = O'Malley and Hardcastle's Election Cases
O. Bridg. = Sir Orlando Bridgman's Reports
O.F.L.R. = Offshore Financial Law Reports
O.J. E.P.O. = Official Journal of the European Patent Office
O.L.R. = Ontario Law Reports (1901-30)
O.P.L.R. = Occupational Pensions Law Reports
O.R. = Ontario Reports (1882-1900, 1931-)
O.R. (2d) = Ontario Reports, 2nd Series
O.R. (3d) = Ontario Reports, 3rd Series
Owen = Owen's King's Bench and Common Pleas Reports
P. = Pacific Reporter (U.S.A.)
P. = Probate
P. & C.R. = Property, Planning and Compensation Reports
P. & C.R. D = Property and Compensation Reports Digest Pages
P. & C.R. DG = Property, Planning and Compensation Reports Digest Pages
P. Wms. = Peere Williams' Chancery Reports
P.2d = Pacific Reporter, 2nd Series (U.S.A.)
P.A.D. = Planning Appeal Decisions
P.C.C. = Palmer's Company Cases
P.I.Q.R. P = Personal Injury and Quantum Reports
P.I.Q.R. Q = Personal Injury and Quantum Reports
P.L.C.R. = Planning Law Case Reports
P.L.R. = Planning Law Reports
P.N.G.L.R. = Papua New Guinea Law Reports
P.N.L.R. = Professional Negligence and Liability Reports
P.T.S.R. = Public and Third Sector Law Reports
P.T.S.R. (C.S.) = Public and Third Sector Law Reports (Case Summaries)
P.T.S.R D = Public and Third Sector Law Reports Digest Pages
Pal. L.R. = Palestine Law Reports
Palm. = Palmer's Reports
Park on Ins. = Park on Insurance, 8th ed.
Park. = Parker's Exchequer Reports
Pat. = Paton's Scottish Appeals, House of Lords
Peake = Peake's Nisi Prius Reports
Peake Add. Cas. = Peake's Additional Cases
Pens. App. R. = Pensions Appeal Reports
Pens. L.R. = Pensions Law Reports
Perry & K. = Perry and Knapp's Election Cases
Ph. = Phillips' Chancery Reports
Phil. Ecc. = Phillimore's Ecclesiastical Reports
Plow. = Plowden's Commentaries
Po. L.R. = Police Law Reports
Pollex. = Pollexfen's Special Cases
Pop. = Sir John Popham's Reports
Prec. Ch. = Precedents in Chancery
Price = Price's Exchequer Reports
Prison L.R. = Prison Law Reports
Q.B. = Queen's Bench
Q.B. = Queen's Bench Reports (1841-1856)
Q.J.P. = Queensland Justice of the Peace Reports
Q.L.J. = Queensland Law Journal Reports (1897-1901)
Q.R. = Quantum Reports (Kemp & Kemp)
Q.S.R. = Queensland State Reports (1902-57)
Q.W.N. = Queensland Law Reporter and Weekly Notes (1908-72)
QCA = Court of Appeal of Queensland (media neutral cite)
QSC = Supreme Court of Queensland (media neutral cite)
Qd. R. = Queensland State Reports (1958-)
R. = Retties Session Cases, 4th Series (Scotland)
R. & I.T. = Rating and Income Tax Reports
R. (H.L.) = Retties Session Cases, 4th Series (House of Lords cases, Scotland)
R. (J.) = Retties Session Cases, 4th Series (Justiciary cases, Scotland)
R.A. = Rating Appeals
R.C.N. = Rating Case Notes
R.F.L. = Reports of Family Law (Canada)
R.I.C.S. = Royal Institution of Chartered Surveyors, Scottish Lands Valuation Appeal Reports

R.J.Q. B.R. = Rapports Judiciares de Quebec, Cour du Banc du Roi (1875-91)
R.L.R. = Road Law Reports
R.P.C. = Reports of Patent Cases
R.P.R. = Real Property Reports (Canada)
R.R.C. = Ryde's Rating Cases
R.T.R. = Road Traffic Reports
R.V.R. = Rating and Valuation Reporter
RICO Bus.Disp.Guide = RICO Business Disputes Guide (CCH)
Ram. = Ramanathan's Reports, Sri Lanka
Re. L.R. = Reinsurance Law Reports
Recueil = Recueil de la Jurisprudence de la Cour (ECJ)
Rep. Ch. = Reports of Cases in Chancery
Rep. L.R. = Reparation Law Reports (Scottish)
Rep. L.R. (Quantum) = Reparation Law Reports, Quantum Cases (Scottish)
Rep. t. Finch = Reports in Chancery tempore Finch
Ridge. t. Hard. = Ridgeway's King's Bench and Chancery Reports tempore Hardwicke
Rob. = Robinson's Scottish Appeal Cases, House of Lords
Rob. Ecc. = Robertson's Ecclesiastical Reports
Roll. Abr. = Rolle's Abridgment des Plusieurs Cases
Rolle = Rolle's King's Bench Reports
Rose = Rose's Bankrupty Cases
Russ. = Russell's Chancery Reports
Russ. & M. = Russell and Mylne's Chancery Reports
Russ. & Ry. = Russell and Ryan's Crown Cases Reserved
Russ. Cr. = Russell on Crime
Ry. & M. = Ryan and Moody's Nisi Prius Reports
S. = Shaw's Session Cases, 1st Series (Scotland)
S. (H.L.) = Shaw's Session Cases, 1st Series (House of Lords cases, Scotland)
S.A. = South African Law Reports
S.A. (A.D.) = South African Law Reports (Appellate Division)
S.A. (T.P.D.) = South African Law Reports (Transvaal Provincial Division)
S.A.C.R. = South African Criminal Law Reports
S.A.L.J. = South African Law Journal
S.A.S.R. = South Australian State Reports
S.C. = Session Cases (Scotland)
S.C. (H.L.) = Session Cases (House of Lords cases, Scotland)
S.C. (J.) = Session Cases (Justiciary 1907-16, Scotland)
S.C. (P.C.) = Session Cases (Privy Council Cases, Scotland)
S.C. (S.A.) = Supreme Court Reports (South Africa)
S.C. (S.A.C.) = Session Cases (Sheriff Appeal Court, Scotland)
S.C. (U.K.S.C.) = Session Cases (Supreme Court cases, Scotland)
S.C.C.R. = Scottish Criminal Case Reports
S.C.C.R. (Supp.) = Scottish Criminal Case Reports Supplement
S.C.L. = Scottish Criminal Law
S.C.L.R. = Scottish Civil Law Reports
S.C.R. = Canada Law Reports, Supreme Court
S.C.R. = Supreme Court Reports (India)
S.Ct. = Supreme Court Reporter
S.E. = South Eastern Reporter (U.S.A.)
S.E.2d = South Eastern Reporter, 2nd Series (U.S.A.)
S.F.T.D. = Simon's First-tier Tax Decisions
S.J. = Solicitors Journal (Old)
S.J.L.B. = Solicitors Journal Law Brief
S.L.C.R. = Scottish Land Court Reports
S.L.C.R. App. = Scottish Land Court Reports (Appendix)
S.L.L.P. = Scottish Licensing Law and Practice
S.L.R. = Scottish Law Reporter (1865-1924)
S.L.T. = Scots Law Times
S.L.T. (Land Ct) = Scots Law Times (Land Court Reports)
S.L.T. (Land Ct.) = Scots Law Times (Land Ct)
S.L.T. (Lands Tr) = Scots Law Times (Lands Tribunal Reports)
S.L.T. (Lands Tr.) = Scots Law Times (Lands Tr)
S.L.T. (Lyon Ct) = Scots Law Times (Lyon Court Reports)
S.L.T. (Lyon Ct.) = Scots Law Times (Lyon Ct)
S.L.T. (Notes) = Scots Law Times (Notes)
S.L.T. (P.L.) = Scots Law Times (Poor Law Reports)
S.L.T. (Sh Ct) = Scots Law Times (Sheriff Court Reports)
S.L.T. (Sh Ct.) = Scots Law Times (Sheriff Court)
S.L.T. (Sh. Ct.) = Scots Law Times (Sheriff Court)
S.N. = Session Notes
S.R. (N.S.W.) = New South Wales State Reports (1901-)
S.S.L.R. = Straits Settlements Law Reports (Malaysia)
S.T.C. = Simons Tax Cases
S.T.C. (S.C.D.) = Simons Tax Cases: Special Commissioners Decisions
S.T.I. = Simon's Tax Intelligence
S.W.2d = South Western Reporter, 2nd Series (U.S.A.)
SAC (Civ) = Sheriff Appeal Court (Civil)
SAC (Crim) = Sheriff Appeal Court (Criminal)
SCC = Supreme Court of Canada (media neutral cite)
SGCA = Court of Appeal of Singapore (media neutral cite)
SGHC = High Court of Singapore (media neutral cite)
Salk. = Salkeld's King's Bench Reports
Sask. R. = Saskatchewan Reports
Saund. = Saunder's King's Bench Reports
Sav. = Savile's Common Bench Reports
Say. = Sayer's King's Bench Reports
Sc. Jur. = Scottish Jurist
Sch. & L. = Schoales and Lefroy's Irish Chancery Reports
Scotsman = Scotsman
Scott N.R. = Scott's New Common Pleas Reports
Sel. Cas. Ch. = Select Cases in Chancery tempore King
Sess. Cas. K.B. = Session Cases touching settlements (England, 1710-48)
Sh. App. = Shaw's Scottish Appeal Cases, House of Lords
Sh. Ct. Rep. = Scottish Law Review, Sheriff Court Reports (1885-1963)
Shaw = Shaw's Justiciary Cases (Scotland)
Ship. Gaz. = Shipping Gazette
Show. K.B. = Shower's King's Bench Reports
Show. Parl. Cas. = Shower's Cases in Parliament
Sid. = Siderfin's King's Bench Reports
Sim. = Simon's Vice Chancellors Reports
Sim. & St. = Simon and Stuart's Chancery Reports
Sim. N.S. = Simon's Vice Chancellors Reports, New Series
Skin. = Skinner's King's Bench Reports
Sm. & G. = Smales and Giffard's Chancery Reports
Smith & B. = Smith and Batty's King's Bench Reports (Ireland, 1824-25)
Smith L.C. = Smith's Leading Cases on Various Branches of the Law
Sneed (TN) = Sneed's Tennessee Reports
So.2d = Southern Reporter, 2nd Series (U.S.A.)
Sol. = The Solicitor
Sp. Ecc. & Ad. = Spinks' Ecclesiastical and Admiralty Reports

Sp. Pri. Cas. = Spinks' Admiralty Prize Court Reports
St. Tr. = Cobbett and Howell's State Trials
St. Tr. (N.S.) = MacDonnell's State Trials, New Series
Stark. = Starkie's Nisi Prius Reports
Str. = Strange's King's Bench Reports
Sty. = Style's Modern Reports
Sw. = Swabey's Admiralty Reports
Sw. & Tr. = Swabey and Tristram's Reports
Swans. = Swanston's Chancery Reports
Swin. = Swinton's Justiciary Reports (Scotland)
Syme = Syme's Justiciary Reports (Scotland)
T. Jones = Sir Thomas Jones' King's Bench Reports
T. Raym. = Sir Thomas Raymond's King's Bench Reports
T.C. = Tax Cases
T.C.L.R. = Technology and Construction Law Reports
T.L.R. = Times Law Reports
T.R. = Taxation Reports (1939-81)
T.S. = Transvaal Supreme Court Reports (South Africa)
TCC = Tax Court of Canada (media neutral cite)
Taml. = Tamlyn's Chancery Reports
Tang. L.R. (R.) = Tanganyika Law Reports
Tas. R. = Tasmanian Reports (1979-)
Tas. S.R. = Tasmanian State Reports (1941-98)
Taunt. = Taunton's Common Pleas Reports
Tenn. = Tennessee Reports
Term Rep. = Durnford and East's Term Reports
Times = Times
Toth. = Tothill's Chancery Transactions
Tr. Consist. J. = Tristram's Consistory Judgments
Tr. L. = Trading Law
Tr. L.R. = Trading Law Reports
Traff. Cas. = Traffic Cases
Trin. L.R. = Trinidad Law Reports
Turn. & R. = Turner and Russell's Chancery Reports
Tyr. = Tyrwhitt's Exchequer Reports
U.C.R. = Upper Canada Reports
U.K.C.L.R. = UK Competition Law Reports
U.K.H.R.R. = United Kingdom Human Rights Reports
U.K.T. = UK Transcripts
U.S. = United States Supreme Court Reports
U.S.App.D.C. = United States District Court for the District of Columbia
U.S.P.Q. = United States Patent Quarterly (BNA)
U.S.P.Q.2d = United States Patent Quarterly 2nd (BNA)
USTC P = United States Tax Cases
UCC Rep.Serv. = Uniform Commercial Code Reporting Service (Callaghan's)
UKAIT = Asylum and Immigration Tribunal (media neutral cite)
UKHL = House of Lords
UKIAT = Immigration Appeal Tribunal
UKPC = Privy Council
UKPC D = Privy Council (Devolution)
UKSC = Supreme Court
USLW = United States Law Week
V. & B. = Vesey and Beames' Chancery Reports
V. & D.R. = Value Added Tax and Duties Reports
V.A.T.T.R. = Value Added Tax Tribunal Reports
V.L.R. = Victorian Law Reports (1875-1956)
V.R. = Victorian Reports (1957 -)
VSC = Supreme Court of Victoria (media neutral cite)
VSCA = Court of Appeal of Victoria (media neutral cite)
Va. = Virginia Reports
Vaugh. = Vaughan's Common Pleas Reports
Vent. = Ventris' King's Bench Reports
Vern. = Vernon's Chancery Reports
Ves. Jr. = Vesey Junior's Chancery Reports
Ves. Sen. = Vesey Senior's Chancery Reports
W. & S. = Wilson and Shaw's Scottish Appeal Cases, House of Lords
W. Jones = Sir William Jones' Reports
W. Rob. = W. Robinson's Admiralty Reports
W.A.C.A. = West African Court of Appeal Reports
W.A.L.R. = Western Australian Law Reports (1875-1956)
W.A.R. = Western Australian Reports (1957-)
W.I.R. = West Indian Reports
W.L.R. = Weekly Law Reports
W.N. = Weekly Notes (1866-1952)
W.N. (N.S.W.) = Weekly Notes, New South Wales
W.P.A.R. = War Pensions Appeal Reports
W.P.C. = Webster's Patent Cases
W.R. = Weekly Reporter (1853-1906)
W.T.L.R. = Wills & Trusts Law Reports
W.W.R. = Western Weekly Law Reports (Canada)
Wall. = Wallace's United States Supreme Court Reports
West H.L. = West's House of Lords Cases
West t. Hard. = West's Chancery Reports tempore Hardwicke
Wheat. = Wheaton's Supreme Court Reports (U.S.A.)
White = White's Justiciary Reports (Scotland)
Wight. = Wightwick's Exchequer Reports
Will. Woll. & Dav. = Willmore, Wollaston and Davison's Queen's Bench Reports
Willes = Willes' Common Pleas Reports
Wilm. = Wilmot's Notes and Opinions, King's Bench
Wils. Ch. = Wilson's Chancery Reports
Wils. Ex. = Wilson's Exchequer in Equity Reports
Wils. K.B. = Wilson's King's Bench Reports
Winch = Winch's Reports
Wm. Bl. = W. Blackstone's King's Bench Reports
Y. = Younge's Exchequer in Equity Reports
Y. & C. Ch. = Younge and Collier's Chancery Cases
Y. & C. Ex. = Younge and Collier's Exchequer Reports
Y. & J. = Younge and Jervis' Exchequer Reports
Y.B. = Year Books
Y.B. (R.S.) = Year Books, Rolls Series
Y.B. (S.S.) = Year Books, Selden Society
Yel. = Yelverton's King's Bench Reports
Yer. = Yerger's Tennessee Reports
Z.L.R. = Zimbabwe Law Reports

CURRENT LAW
PART I

CASE CITATOR 2017 (ENGLAND)

The Current Law Case Citator comprises in a single table:
(i) Full case name of cases reported in 2017
(ii) The judicial history of any case of whatever date which has been considered, applied, overruled, etc., in 2017
Note: Figures appearing in bold type indicate the paragraph in the Current Law Year Book at which the case is digested

'Spotting the Ball' Partnership v Revenue and Customs Commissioners see Revenue and Customs Commissioners v IFX Investment Co Ltd
'Sveda' UAB v Valstybine mokesciu inspekcija prie Lietuvos Respublikos finansu ministerijos (C-126/14) EU:C:2015:712; [2016] S.T.C. 447; [2015] B.V.C. 36, ECJ (5th Chamber)
Followed 17/2241, 17/2272

1-6 Dunloe Passage, London, E2 8JS see Fluss v Queensbridge Terrace Residents Ltd
125 OBS (Nominees1) v Lend Lease Construction (Europe) Ltd [2017] EWHC 25 (TCC); [2017] T.C.L.R. 8; 174 Con. L.R. 105, QBD (TCC)
19 Entertainment Ltd, Re [2016] EWHC 1545 (Ch); [2017] B.C.C. 347, Ch D (Companies Ct)

24 Lea Bridge Road, Re see Meghnagi v Hackney LBC

3-15 Queensbridge Road, Haggeston, London, E2 8NP see Fluss v Queensbridge Terrace Residents Ltd
3D Garages Ltd v Prolatis Co Ltd 2017 S.L.T. (Sh Ct) 9; 2016 G.W.D. 34-617, Sh Ct (Lothian) (Edinburgh) .... *Digested,* 17/**2781**
3H Investments Ltd v West Devon BC [2017] P.A.D. 1, Planning Inspector

4 Eng Ltd v Harper [2008] EWHC 915 (Ch); [2009] Ch. 91; [2008] 3 W.L.R. 892; [2008] Bus. L.R. 1698; Times, June 23, 2008, Ch D .... *Digested,* 08/**893**:
Applied 10/2291: *Considered* 10/828, 11/857, 17/1298
4-6 Trinity Church Square Freehold Ltd v Corp of the Trinity House of Deptford Strond [2016] UKUT 484 (LC); [2017] L. & T.R. 25, UT (Lands) .... *Digested,* 17/**1830**

68 Applications by Entities Under the Control of Michael Gleissner to Revoke 68 Trade Marks Owned by Apple Inc for Non-Use see Sherlock Systems CV v Apple Inc

7 Strathray Gardens Ltd v Pointstar Shipping & Finance Ltd; *sub nom* Pointstar Shipping & Finance Ltd v 7 Strathray Gardens Ltd [2004] EWCA Civ 1669; [2005] H.L.R. 20; [2005] L. & T.R. 16; [2005] 1 E.G.L.R. 53; [2005] 07 E.G. 144; Times, January 10, 2005; Independent, January 19, 2005; [2005] 1 E.G. 95 (C.S.); (2005) 102(6) L.S.G. 32; (2005) 149 S.J.L.B. 58; [2005] 1 P. & C.R. DG23, CA (Civ Div) .... *Digested,* 05/**2652**:
Applied 14/2011: *Followed* 15/1576, 17/1463
7E Communications Ltd v Vertex Antennentechnik GmbH [2007] EWCA Civ 140; [2007] 1 W.L.R. 2175; [2007] 2 All E.R. (Comm) 798; [2008] Bus. L.R. 472; [2007] 2 Lloyd's Rep. 411; [2007] C.P. Rep. 23; [2007] 1 C.L.C. 417; [2007] I.L.Pr. 18; Times, March 19, 2007, CA (Civ Div) .... *Digested,* 07/**364**:
Considered 10/637, 12/618, 16/434, 17/295: *Followed* 11/472

A v A [2016] EWCA Civ 72; [2017] 1 F.L.R. 72; [2016] 2 F.C.R. 139; [2016] Fam. Law 292, CA (Civ Div) .... *Digested,* 16/**897**

A v A (Children) (Habitual Residence); *sub nom* ZA v NA (Abduction: Habitual Residence); A (Children) (Jurisdiction: Return of Child), Re [2013] UKSC 60; [2014] A.C. 1; [2013] 3 W.L.R. 761; [2014] 1 All E.R. 827; [2014] 1 F.L.R. 111; [2013] 3 F.C.R. 559; Times, October 15, 2013; [2013] Fam. Law 1528; (2013) 157(36) S.J.L.B. 37, SC .... *Digested,* 13/**1250**:
Applied 14/2806, 15/1021, 15/1106, 15/1107, 15/1124, 15/1751, 16/1486, 16/860: *Considered* 14/1381, 16/833, 16/852, 17/941: *Followed* 14/1307, 14/1378, 14/2186, 15/1022, 15/1023, 15/1024, 15/1025, 15/1027, 15/1028, 15/1037, 16/849, 16/850, 16/851, 16/853, 16/948

A v A (Maintenance Pending Suit: Provision for Legal Costs) see A v A (Maintenance Pending Suit: Provision for Legal Fees)

A v A (Maintenance Pending Suit: Provision for Legal Fees); *sub nom* A v A (Maintenance Pending Suit: Provision for Legal Costs) [2001] 1 W.L.R. 605; [2001] 1 F.L.R. 377; [2001] 1 F.C.R. 226; Times, November 14, 2000; Independent, December 11, 2000; [2001] Fam. Law 96; (2000) 97(44) L.S.G. 45; (2000) 144 S.J.L.B. 273, Fam Div .... *Digested,* 00/**2528**:
Applied 03/1586: *Considered* 14/1364, 17/1017

A v A (Setting aside Consent Order on Ground of Duress); *sub nom* SA v FA [2017] EWHC 1731 (Fam); [2017] 3 F.C.R. 150, Fam Div .... *Digested,* 17/**996**

A v Abu [2017] EWHC 1946 (QB); [2017] I.R.L.R. 1113, QBD

A v B [2016] EWHC 3003 (Comm); [2017] 1 W.L.R. 2030; [2017] 3 All E.R. 856; [2017] 2 All E.R. (Comm) 746; [2017] 1 Lloyd's Rep. 1, QBD (Comm) .... *Digested,* 17/**77**

A v B [2017] EWHC 596 (Comm); [2018] 1 All E.R. (Comm) 509; [2017] 2 Lloyd's Rep. 1, QBD (Comm) .... *Digested,* 17/**67**

A v B 2016 S.L.T. (Sh Ct) 389; 2016 G.W.D. 27-492, Sh Ct (Lothian) (Edinburgh) .... *Digested,* 17/**2618**

A v B (Investigatory Powers Tribunal: Jurisdiction); *sub nom* R. (on the application of A) v Director of Establishments of the Security Service [2009] UKSC 12; [2010] 2 A.C. 1; [2010] 2 W.L.R. 1; [2010] 1 All E.R. 1149; [2010] H.R.L.R. 11; [2010] U.K.H.FR.R. 568; Times, December 11, 2009, SC .... *Digested,* 10/**25**:
Considered 17/26

A v B see Yegiazaryan v Smagin

A v BBC see BBC, Re

A v Birmingham City Council see S v Birmingham City Council

A v C [2016] EWFC 42; [2017] 2 F.L.R. 101; [2016] Fam. Law 1225, Fam Ct .... *Digested,* 17/**1059**

A v C (No.1); *sub nom* A & B v C, D, E, F, G and H (No.1) [1981] Q.B. 956; [1981] 2 W.L.R. 629; [1980] 2 All E.R. 347; [1980] 2 Lloyd's Rep. 200, QBD (Comm) .... *Digested,* 82/**2503**:
Applied 17/300

A v City of Edinburgh Council 2017 Hous. L.R. 4; 2017 G.W.D. 5-67, Sh Ct (Lothian) (Edinburgh) .... *Digested,* 17/**2659**

A v Criminal Injuries Compensation Board [2017] CSIH 46; 2017 S.L.T. 984; 2017 G.W.D. 22-381, IH (2 Div) .... *Digested,* 17/**2386**

A v D [2017] EWHC 2222 (Ch); [2017] W.T.L.R. 799, Ch D

A v D; *sub nom* ADS v DSM [2017] EWCOP 8; [2017] C.O.P.L.R. 231; [2017] W.T.L.R. 819, CP .... *Digested,* 17/**1551**

A v DPP; *sub nom* A, Re [2016] EWCA Crim 1393; [2017] 1 W.L.R. 713; [2017] C.P. Rep. 2; [2017] 1 Cr. App. R. 6; [2016] Lloyd's Rep. F.C. 567, CA (Crim Div) .... *Digested,* 17/**600**

A v Enfield LBC see R. (on the application of A) v Enfield LBC

A v Essex CC; *joined cases* B v Suffolk CC; S v Hertfordshire CC; J v Worcestershire CC [2010] UKSC 33; [2011] 1 A.C. 280; [2010] 3 W.L.R. 509; [2010] 4 All E.R. 199; [2010] P.T.S.R. 1332; [2010] H.R.L.R. 32; [2010] U.K.H.R.R. 937; 30 B.H.R.C. 1; [2010] E.L.R. 531; (2010) 13 C.C.L. Rep. 314; Times, July 15, 2010; (2010) 154(28) S.J.L.B. 30, SC .... *Digested,* 10/**989**:
Applied 16/2236, 17/675: *Followed* 16/1032

A v H see M (Children), Re

A v Hoare; *joined cases* X v Wandsworth LBC; H v Suffolk CC; C v Middlesbrough Council; Young v Catholic Care (Diocese of Leeds) [2008] UKHL 6; [2008] 1 A.C. 844; [2008] 2 W.L.R. 311; [2008] 2 All E.R. 1; [2008] 1 F.L.R. 771; [2008] 1 F.C.R. 507; (2008) 11 C.C.L. Rep. 249; (2008) 100 B.M.L.R. 1; Times, January 31, 2008; [2008] Fam. Law 402; (2008) 105(6) L.S.G. 27; (2008) 158 N.L.J. 218; (2008) 152(6) S.J.L.B. 28, HL .... *Digested,* 08/**385**:
Applied 09/418, 09/427, 16/1606: *Considered* 09/421, 09/465, 11/856, 13/393, 17/2191: *Followed* 09/2854, 09/425, 10/379, 11/2370, 11/353, 17/320

A v Liverpool City Council [1982] A.C. 363; [1981] 2 W.L.R. 948; [1981] 2 All E.R. 385; 79 L.G.R. 621; (1981) 125 S.J. 396, HL .... *Digested,* 81/**1796**: *Applied* 81/1763, 82/2045, 83/2469, 84/2210, 84/2211, 84/2243, 84/2247, 84/2254, 85/2255, 85/36.u, 86/2150, 86/2181, 86/2214, 86/2216, 86/2218, 87/2457, 87/2485, 88/1215, 90/3122, 90/3146, 91/2587, 93/2782, 15/1741: *Considered* 82/2081, 85/2262, 86/2144, 86/2171, 86/2213, 87/2460, 87/2518, 87/2522, 87/2523, 87/3052, 89/2485, 91/2512, 93/2771, 95/3554, 17/1070: *Distinguished* 86/2212: *Followed* 85/2200, 85/2429, 86/2160, 87/2524, 88/2285, 88/2344, 89/2409, 02/315, 17/1069: *Not followed* 95/3398: *Referred to* 88/2331

A v Local Authority see LG (A Child) (Adoption: Leave to Oppose), Re

A v Minister van Buitenlandse Zaken (C-158/14) EU:C:2017:202; [2017] 4 W.L.R. 90; [2017] 3 C.M.L.R. 20; Times, April 3, 2017, ECJ (Grand Chamber)

A v Murphy [2014] HCJAC 96; 2014 S.C.L. 784; 2014 G.W.D. 28-565, HCJ .... *Digested,* 14/**3784**: *Applied* 17/2819

A v National Blood Authority (No.1); *sub nom* Hepatitis C Litigation (No.1), Re [2001] 3 All E.R. 289; [2001] Lloyd's Rep. Med. 187; (2001) 60 B.M.L.R. 1; Times, April 4, 2001; Daily Telegraph, April 3, 2001, QBD .... *Digested,* 01/**2933**: *Doubted* 17/483

A v Nautilus Trustees Ltd [2015] JRC 259; 19 I.T.E.L.R. 363, Royal Ct (Jer)

A v Norway (24130/11); *joined case* B v Norway (29758/11) (2017) 65 E.H.R.R. 4; 19 I.T.L. Rep. 868, ECHR (Grand Chamber)

A v P Council see M (Notification of Step-parent Adoption), Re

A v Revenue and Customs Commissioners [2012] UKFTT 541 (TC); [2012] S.F.T.D. 1257; [2013] S.T.I. 65, FTT (Tax) .... *Digested,* 13/**2995**: *Applied* 17/199

A v Secretary of State for the Home Department see AA (Nigeria) v Secretary of State for the Home Department

A v Secretary of State for the Home Department see BBC, Re

A v Secretary of State for the Home Department see HMA v Secretary of State for the Home Department

A v X see Z (A Child) (Surrogacy Agreements: Child Arrangements Orders), Re

A & B v C, D, E, F, G and H (No.1) see A v C (No.1)

A (A Child) (Contact: Section 91(14)), Re [2009] EWCA Civ 1548; [2010] 2 F.L.R. 151; [2010] Fam. Law 450, CA (Civ Div) .... *Digested,* 10/**1394**: *Considered* 17/978

A (A Child) (Vulnerable Witness: Fact Finding), Re; *sub nom* J (A Child) (Vulnerable Witness: Sexual Abuse: Fact Finding), Re [2014] EWCA Civ 875; [2015] 1 F.L.R. 1152; [2014] 3 F.C.R. 534; [2014] Fam. Law 1388, CA (Civ Div) .... *Digested,* 15/**1073**: *Considered* 17/993

A (A Child) (Ward of Court: Security Service Interview), Re see Ward of Court (Wardship: Interview), Re

A (A Child) (Withdrawal of Medical Treatment), Re [2016] EWCA Civ 759; [2016] Med. L.R. 427; (2016) 151 B.M.L.R. 39, CA (Civ Div) .... *Digested,* 16/**1003**: *Followed* 17/1125

A (A Minor) (Fact Finding: Unrepresented Party), Re [2017] EWHC 1195 (Fam); [2017] 3 F.C.R. 494, Fam Div

A (A Protected Party) v Persons Unknown [2016] EWHC 3295 (Ch); [2017] E.M.L.R. 11, Ch D .... *Digested,* 17/**3**

A (Abduction: Child's Objections to Return), Re; *sub nom* KP (A Child) (Abduction: Judge Meeting Child: Conduct of Interview), Re; KP (A Child) (Abduction: Child's Objections), Re; Z v Y; KP (A Child) (Abduction: Rights of Custody), Re [2014] EWCA Civ 554; [2014] 1 W.L.R. 4326; [2014] 2 F.L.R. 660; [2014] 2 F.C.R. 545; [2014] Fam. Law 945; (2014) 158(19) S.J.L.B. 37, CA (Civ Div) .... *Digested,* 14/**1310**: *Applied* 17/971

A (Application for Care Placement Orders: Local Authority Failings), Re; *sub nom* Darlington Borough Council v M [2015] EWFC 11; [2016] 1 F.L.R. 1; [2015] Fam. Law 367, Fam Ct .... *Digested,* 16/**821**: *Applied* 17/992

A (Baby Relinquished for Adoption: Case Management), Re; *sub nom* RA (Baby Relinquished for Adoption), Re [2016] EWFC 25; [2016] 4 W.L.R. 104; [2017] 1 F.L.R. 1610; [2016] Fam. Law 801, Fam Ct .... *Digested,* 16/**804**

A (Baby Relinquished for Adoption: Final Hearing), Re [2016] EWFC 47; [2017] 2 F.L.R. 1271, Fam Ct .... *Digested,* 17/**911**

A (C-453/15) EU:C:2016:933; [2016] B.V.C. 44; [2017] S.T.I. 41, ECJ (2nd Chamber)

A (Children) (Adoption: Scottish Children's Hearing), Re; *sub nom* A (Children) (Scotland), Re [2017] EWHC 1293 (Fam); [2017] 4 W.L.R. 122; [2018] 1 F.L.R. 1; [2017] 3 F.C.R. 215, Fam Div .... *Digested,* 17/**920**

A (Children) (Adoption: Scottish Permanence Orders), Re [2017] EWHC 35 (Fam); [2018] 2 W.L.R. 770; [2017] 2 F.L.R. 995; [2017] 2 F.C.R. 103, Fam Div .... *Digested,* 17/**917**
A (Children) (Contact: Ultra-Orthodox Judaism: Transgender Parent), Re; *sub nom* J v B (Ultra-Orthodox Judaism: Transgender) [2017] EWFC 4; [2017] 4 W.L.R. 201; [2018] 1 F.L.R. 59; [2017] 2 F.C.R. 230, Fam Ct .... *Digested,* 17/**979**
A (Children) (Jurisdiction: Return of Child), Re see A v A (Children) (Habitual Residence)
A (Children) (Placement Orders: Cultural Heritage), Re [2015] EWCA Civ 1254; [2017] 1 F.L.R. 1; [2016] 2 F.C.R. 35; [2016] Fam. Law 269, CA (Civ Div) .... *Digested,* 16/**815**
A (Children) (Restrictions on Parental Responsibility: Extremism and Radicalisation in Private Law), Re; *sub nom* M v F [2016] EWFC 40; [2016] 2 F.L.R. 977; [2016] Fam. Law 1081, Fam Ct .... *Digested,* 17/**949**
A (Children) (Scotland), Re see A (Children) (Adoption: Scottish Children's Hearing), Re
A (Children), Re see D v ED (Parental Order: Time Limit)
A (Human Fertilisation and Embryology Act 2008: Assisted Reproduction: Parent), Re; *sub nom* Human Fertilisation and Embryology Act 2008, Re; In re A (Legal Parenthood: Written Consents) [2015] EWHC 2602 (Fam); [2016] 1 W.L.R. 1325; [2016] 1 All E.R. 273; [2017] 1 F.L.R. 366; [2015] 3 F.C.R. 555; (2015) 146 B.M.L.R. 123; [2015] Fam. Law 1333, Fam Div .... *Digested,* 16/**928**:
Applied 16/926, 16/929, 16/931, 17/1052, 17/1053, 17/1054, 17/1141
A (Letter to a Young Person), Re see Father v Mother
A (Medical Treatment: Male Sterilisation), Re see A (Mental Patient: Sterilisation), Re
A (Mental Patient: Sterilisation), Re; *sub nom* A (Medical Treatment: Male Sterilisation), Re; R-B (A Patient) v Official Solicitor; RB (Male Patient: Sterilisation), Re [2000] 1 F.L.R. 549; [2000] 1 F.C.R. 193; [2000] Lloyd's Rep. Med. 87; (2000) 53 B.M.L.R. 66; Times, March 15, 2000; [2000] Fam. Law 242; (2000) 97(2) L.S.G. 30, CA (Civ Div) .... *Digested,* 00/**2780**:
Applied 04/3648, 05/1794, 05/1848, 08/1437, 11/2220, 12/2279, 12/2282, 14/2187, 16/999: *Considered* 04/1690, 09/3727, 13/2069, 17/1123
A (Prohibited Steps Order), Re see R (A Child) (Prohibited Steps Order), Re
A Ahlstrom Osakeyhtio v Commission of the European Communities (C-89/85) EU:C:1988:447; [1988] E.C.R. 5193; [1988] 4 C.M.L.R. 901; Times, September 29, 1988, ECJ .... *Digested,* 90/**2062**:
Applied 10/466, 17/416, 17/426
A Child (No Approved Secure Accommodation Available: Deprivation of Liberty), Re see A Local Authority v AT
A Company, Re [1983] B.C.L.C. 492
Applied 15/1436, 17/1294: *Considered* 03/2352, 03/2365: *Distinguished* 95/2863
A County Council v AB [2016] EWCOP 41; [2016] C.O.P.L.R. 576, CP .... *Digested,* 17/**1548**
A County Council v M; *sub nom* B (Children) (Foreign Adoption: Refusal of Recognition), Re [2013] EWHC 1501 (Fam); [2014] 1 F.L.R. 881; [2013] Fam. Law 933, Fam Div .... *Digested,* 14/**1242**:
Considered 17/1034, 17/914
A I Walgate & Son v Scottish Natural Heritage; *sub nom* Walgate & Son v Scottish Natural Heritage [2017] CSOH 51; [2017] L.L.R. 651; 2017 G.W.D. 12-167, OH *Digested,* 17/**2407**:
Cited 17/2408
A Local Authority v A Mother see T (A Child) (Care Proceedings: Request to Assume Jurisdiction), Re
A Local Authority v AT; *sub nom* A Child (No Approved Secure Accommodation Available: Deprivation of Liberty), Re [2017] EWHC 2458 (Fam); [2018] 1 F.L.R. 621; [2017] 3 F.C.R. 621, Fam Div
A Local Authority v D; *sub nom* C (A Child), Re [2016] EWHC 3473 (Fam); [2017] 2 F.L.R. 875; (2017) 20 C.C.L. Rep. 219, Fam Div .... *Digested,* 17/**966**
A Local Authority v D see AB (A Child) (Deprivation of Liberty: Consent), Re
A Local Authority v Father see E (A Child) (Care Proceedings: Placement Outside Jurisdiction), Re
A Local Authority v M [2016] EWCOP 42, CP
Reversed 17/218
A Local Authority v M [2016] EWHC 1599 (Fam); [2017] 1 F.L.R. 1389; [2016] Fam. Law 1218, Fam Div
A Local Authority v M see M (Children), Re
A Local Authority v MA see SA (Vulnerable Adult with Capacity: Marriage), Re
A Local Authority v Mother [2017] EWHC 1515 (Fam); [2017] 2 F.L.R. 1321, Fam Div
A Local Authority v X [2016] EWCOP 44; [2017] C.O.P.L.R. 1, CP
A Local Authority v X [2016] EWCOP 50; [2017] C.O.P.L.R. 8, CP .... *Digested,* 17/**1543**
A London Borough v M see N (Children: Welfare Decision), Re
A London Borough Council v JL see JL (Babies Relinquished for Adoption), Re

A Ltd, Petitioner 2016 S.L.T. (Sh Ct) 425; 2016 G.W.D. 35-635, Sh Ct (Lothian) (Edinburgh) .... *Digested,* 17/**2685**
A McC v Wandsworth LBC see J (Children) (Care Proceedings: Issues Resolution Hearing), Re
A Oy v Veronsaajien oikeudenvalvontayksikko (C-33/16) see Proceedings Brought by A Oy (C-33/16)
A Western Circuit Local Authority v A Mother see JL (Babies Relinquished for Adoption), Re
A's Curator Bonis v Criminal Injuries Compensation Board see P's Curator Bonis v Criminal Injuries Compensation Board
A, Re see A v DPP
A. M. Gillespie & Company v James Howden & Company (1885) 12 R. 800, IH (2 Div) *Considered* 17/472
AA v BB 2015 G.W.D. 17-288, Sh Ct (South Strathclyde) (Dumfries) *Reversed* 17/2616
AA v Sweden (14499/09) (2017) 64 E.H.R.R. 20, ECHR
AA v United Kingdom (8000/08) [2012] Imm. A.R. 107; [2012] I.N.L.R. 1; Times, September 28, 2011; (2011) 161 N.L.J. 1336, ECHR .... *Digested,* 12/**1677**: *Applied* 16/1120, 17/1200
AA (Iraq) v Secretary of State for the Home Department [2017] EWCA Civ 944; [2018] 1 W.L.R. 1083; [2017] Imm. A.R. 1440; [2018] I.N.L.R. 1, CA (Civ Div)
AA (Nigeria) v Secretary of State for the Home Department; *sub nom* A v Secretary of State for the Home Department [2016] CSIH 39; 2016 S.L.T. 1208; 2016 G.W.D. 17-317, IH (2 Div) .... *Digested,* 17/**2672**
AA (Nigeria) v Secretary of State for the Home Department [2017] CSIH 38; 2017 S.L.T. 1088; [2018] Imm. A.R. 1; 2017 G.W.D. 22-377, IH (2 Div) .... *Digested,* 17/**2673**
AA, LDA v BB—Sociedade Industrial de Refrigerantes SA (2470/08) [2017] E.C.C. 26, Sup Trib (P)
Aabar Block Sarl v Maud see Maud v Aabar Block Sarl
Aabar Blocks Sarl v Maud [2016] EWHC 1016 (Ch); [2016] B.P.I.R. 803, Ch D (Bankruptcy Ct) .... *Digested,* 16/**1198**: *Reversed* 17/1294
Aadan v Brent LBC [2000] C.P. Rep. 17; (2000) 32 H.L.R. 848; Times, December 3, 1999; Independent, December 20, 1999, CA (Civ Div) .... *Digested,* 00/**366**: *Applied* 17/323: *Cited* 02/2344
AAZ v BBZ [2016] EWHC 3234 (Fam); [2018] 1 F.L.R. 153; [2017] 2 F.C.R. 415; [2017] W.T.L.R. 765, Fam Div .... *Digested,* 17/**1004**
AAZ v BBZ [2016] EWHC 3361 (Fam); [2017] 2 F.C.R. 461, Fam Div
AAZ v BBZ see Z v Z (Legal Professional Privilege: Fraud Exemption)
AB v AT see Contempt of Court Proceedings in Respect of M and L
AB v BB [2013] EWHC 227 (Fam); [2014] 1 F.L.R. 178; [2013] Fam. Law 531, Fam Div .... *Digested,* 14/**1320**: *Applied* 17/949
AB v CD 19 I.T.E.L.R. 316, HC (IoM)
AB v CD (Financial Remedy Consent Order: Non-Disclosure) [2016] EWHC 10 (Fam); [2016] 4 W.L.R. 36; [2017] 1 F.L.R. 13; [2016] Fam. Law 443, Fam Div .... *Digested,* 16/**895**
AB v FC (Financial Provision) (Short Marriage: Needs: Stockpiling) see B v C (Short Marriage: Needs: Stockpiling)
AB v HM Advocate; *sub nom* B v HM Advocate [2017] UKSC 25; 2017 S.C. (U.K.S.C.) 101; 2017 S.L.T. 401; 2017 S.C.L. 434; 2017 S.C.C.R. 244; 2017 G.W.D. 12-178, SC .... *Digested,* 17/**537**
AB v JJB (EU Maintenance Regulation: Modification Application Procedure) [2015] EWHC 192 (Fam); [2015] 2 F.L.R. 1143; [2015] Fam. Law 373, Fam Div .... *Digested,* 15/**1116**: *Applied* 17/1042
AB v Minister of Social Development 42 B.H.R.C. 571, Const Ct (SA)
AB v Nugent Care Society see B v Nugent Care Society
AB v Secretary of State for the Home Department see AB (British Citizenship: Deprivation: Deliallisi Considered: Nigeria), Re
AB (A Child) (Deprivation of Liberty: Consent), Re; *sub nom* A Local Authority v D [2015] EWHC 3125 (Fam); [2016] 1 W.L.R. 1160; [2016] 2 F.L.R. 601; [2015] Fam. Law 1464, Fam Div *Applied* 17/966: *Considered* 16/1524
AB (British Citizenship: Deprivation: Deliallisi Considered: Nigeria), Re; *sub nom* AB v Secretary of State for the Home Department [2016] UKUT 451 (IAC); [2017] Imm. A.R. 226, UT (IAC)
AB (Care Proceedings: Service on Husband Ignorant of Child's Existence), Re see B (A Child) (Parentage: Knowledge of Proceedings), Re

AB (Surrogacy: Consent), Re; *sub nom* C v E [2016] EWHC 2643 (Fam); [2017] 2 F.L.R. 217, Fam Div .... *Digested,* 17/**1058**

AB Bank Ltd v Abu Dhabi Commercial Bank PJSC [2016] EWHC 2082 (Comm); [2017] 1 W.L.R. 810; [2016] C.P. Rep. 47; [2016] 2 C.L.C. 372, QBD (Comm) .. *Digested,* 16/**288**

AB, Petitioner see Contempt of Court Proceedings in Respect of M and L

Abacha v National Crime Agency see National Crime Agency v Abacha

ABB AB/Device and Method for Stabilising a Metallic Object (T1689/12) [2017] E.P.O.R. 11, EPO (Technical Bd App)

Abbey National Building Society v Cann [1991] 1 A.C. 56; [1990] 2 W.L.R. 832; [1990] 1 All E.R. 1085; [1990] 2 F.L.R. 122; (1990) 22 H.L.R. 360; (1990) 60 P. & C.R. 278; Times, March 30, 1990; (1990) 87(17) L.S.G. 32; (1990) 140 N.L.J. 477, HL .... *Digested,* 90/**707**: *Applied* 94/4028, 96/4953, 01/4867, 09/3168, 12/2734, 14/2505, 17/158: *Considered* 93/2538, 96/5031, 97/4258, 04/3248, 10/2724, 17/159: *Distinguished* 09/2208: *Followed* 90/706, 17/1841

Abbey National Plc v Chagger; *joined case* Chagger v Abbey National Plc [2009] EWCA Civ 1202; [2010] I.C.R. 397; [2010] I.R.L.R. 47; (2009) 153(44) S.J.L.B. 34, CA (Civ Div) .... *Digested,* 10/**1026**: *Applied* 11/1130, 13/991: *Considered* 17/848: *Followed* 13/1055

Abbey National Plc v Office of Fair Trading see Office of Fair Trading v Abbey National Plc

Abbey National Treasury Services Plc v Revenue and Customs Commissioners [2015] UKFTT 341 (TC); [2015] S.F.T.D. 929, FTT (Tax) *Not followed* 17/2106

Abbey National Treasury Services Plc, Re see Barclays Bank Plc, Re

Abboud (Mohammed) v HM Advocate [2016] HCJAC 124; 2017 S.C.L. 234; 2017 S.C.C.R. 93; 2016 G.W.D. 40-708, HCJ .... *Digested,* 17/**2553**

ABC v St George's Healthcare NHS Foundation Trust [2015] EWHC 1394 (QB); [2015] P.I.Q.R. P18; [2015] Med. L.R. 307; (2015) 145 B.M.L.R. 154, QBD .... *Digested,* 15/**1767**: *Reversed* 17/1558

ABC v St George's Healthcare NHS Foundation Trust [2017] EWCA Civ 336; [2017] P.I.Q.R. P15; [2017] Med. L.R. 368; (2018) 160 B.M.L.R. 19, CA (Civ Div) .... *Digested,* 17/**1558**

ABC Ltd v M (Inspector of Taxes) see Barclays Mercantile Business Finance Ltd v Mawson (Inspector of Taxes)

Abdi v Secretary of State for the Home Department see R. (on the application of Lumba) v Secretary of State for the Home Department

Abdi v Secretary of State for the Home Department see R. (on the application of Nadarajah) v Secretary of State for the Home Department

Abdulla v Whelan [2017] EWHC 605 (Ch); [2017] 1 W.L.R. 3318; [2018] 1 All E.R. 533; [2017] B.P.I.R. 791; [2017] 2 P. & C.R. DG13, Ch D .... *Digested,* 17/**1275**

Abdullah v Shropshire CC see R. v Barnet LBC Ex p. Shah

Abdullahi v Bundesasylamt (C-394/12) EU:C:2013:813; [2014] 1 W.L.R. 1895; [2014] Imm. A.R. 727; [2014] I.N.L.R. 411, ECJ (Grand Chamber) *Applied* 16/1066: *Considered* 17/1177

Abdulle v Commissioner of Police of the Metropolis; *sub nom* Commissioner of Police of the Metropolis v Abdulle [2015] EWCA Civ 1260; [2016] 1 W.L.R. 898; [2016] C.P. Rep. 14, CA (Civ Div) .... *Digested,* 16/**170**: *Followed* 17/1293

Abela v Baadarani [2013] UKSC 44; [2013] 1 W.L.R. 2043; [2013] 4 All E.R. 119; [2013] 2 C.L.C. 92; [2013] I.L.Pr. 40; Times, August 7, 2013, SC .... *Digested,* 13/**425**: *Applied* 14/1139, 14/478, 16/313, 16/315, 17/367: *Followed* 14/128, 16/2153, 16/316

Abercrombie & Fitch Italia Srl v Bordonaro (C-143/16) EU:C:2017:566; [2018] 1 C.M.L.R. 27; [2017] I.R.L.R. 1018, ECJ (1st Chamber)

Aberdeen Construction Group Ltd v Inland Revenue Commissioners [1978] A.C. 885; [1978] 2 W.L.R. 648; [1978] 1 All E.R. 962; [1978] S.T.C. 127; 1978 S.C. (H.L.) 72; 1978 S.L.T. 146; 52 T.C. 281; [1978] T.R. 25; (1978) 122 S.J. 249, HL .... *Digested,* 79/**371**: *Applied* 79/1450, 09/3743, 17/2097: *Cited* 97/1073: *Considered* 97/1071, 12/3233: *Distinguished* 80/1453: *Followed* 78/359, 05/4003: *Referred to* 95/527

Aberdeen Journals Ltd v Director General of Fair Trading [2002] CAT 4; [2002] Comp. A.R. 167, CCAT .... *Digested,* 03/**5306**: *Applied* 08/540: *Considered* 17/410: *Followed* 05/565

Abertawe Bro Morgannwg University Local Health Board v RY [2017] EWCOP 2; [2017] C.O.P.L.R. 143, CP .... *Digested,* 17/**1124**

Ablack v Inner London Education Authority see R. v Barnet LBC Ex p. Shah

Abouraya v Sigmund [2014] EWHC 277 (Ch); [2015] B.C.C. 503, Ch D *Approved* 17/287

Abraham v Thompson [1997] 4 All E.R. 362; [1997] C.L.C. 1370; Times, August 19, 1997; (1997) 94(37) L.S.G. 41; (1997) 141 S.J.L.B. 217, CA (Civ Div) .... *Digested,* 97/**562**: *Applied* 02/393: *Considered* 98/411, 99/546: *Distinguished* 00/436: *Followed* 99/417, 16/280, 17/1570

Absolute Lofts South West London Ltd v Artisan Home Improvements Ltd [2015] EWHC 2608 (IPEC); [2017] E.C.D.R. 6, Ch D

Abu Qatada v United Kingdom (8139/09) see Othman v United Kingdom (8139/09)

Abu-Qulbain v Secretary of State for the Home Department see Huang v Secretary of State for the Home Department

Abuja International Hotels Ltd v Meridien SAS [2012] EWHC 87 (Comm); [2012] 1 Lloyd's Rep. 461, QBD (Comm) .... *Digested,* 12/**114**: *Applied* 14/118, 17/66, 17/67

AC (Wholesale) Ltd v Revenue and Customs Commissioners [2015] UKFTT 457 (TC), FTT (Tax) *Affirmed* 17/2277

AC (Wholesale) Ltd v Revenue and Customs Commissioners [2017] UKUT 191 (TCC); [2017] B.V.C. 515, UT (Tax) .... *Digested,* 17/**2277**

ACCENTURE GLOBAL SERVICES/Cross-community invitation (T1033/16) [2017] E.P.O.R. 6, EPO (Technical Bd App)

Accenture Services Ltd v Revenue and Customs Commissioners; *joined case* Barclays Bank Plc v Revenue and Customs Commissioners [2009] EWHC 857 (Admin); [2009] S.T.C. 1503; [2009] B.T.C. 5430; [2009] B.V.C. 429; [2009] S.T.I. 1601, QBD (Admin) .... *Digested,* 09/**4110**: *Applied* 14/2971: *Considered* 17/825

ACCG v MN see N (An Adult) (Court of Protection: Jurisdiction), Re

Accident Exchange Ltd v Broom [2017] EWHC 1096 (Admin); [2017] A.C.D. 93, QBD (Admin)

Accountant in Bankruptcy v Farrell see Accountant in Bankruptcy v Walker

Accountant in Bankruptcy v Walker; *sub nom* Accountant in Bankruptcy v Farrell [2017] CSOH 78; 2017 S.L.T. 890; [2017] B.P.I.R. 803; 2017 G.W.D. 16-255, OH .... *Digested,* 17/**2684**

Accountant in Bankruptcy, Appellant [2017] SAC (Civ) 5; 2017 S.L.T. (Sh Ct) 77; 2017 G.W.D. 5-71, SAC .... *Digested,* 17/**2682**

Ace Capital Ltd v CMS Energy Corp [2008] EWHC 1843 (Comm); [2008] 2 C.L.C. 318; [2009] Lloyd's Rep. I.R. 414, QBD (Comm) .... *Digested,* 09/**607**: *Considered* 17/367

Ace Insurance SA NV v Seechurn see Seechurn v Ace Insurance SA NV

Achbita v G4S Secure Solutions NV (C-157/15) EU:C:2017:203; [2017] 3 C.M.L.R. 21; [2017] C.E.C. 1319; [2018] I.C.R. 102; [2017] I.R.L.R. 466; Times, March 27, 2017, ECJ (Grand Chamber)

Achieving Perfection Ltd v Gray A01BN108, CC (Brighton) *Doubted* 17/1829

Acornwood LLP v Revenue and Customs Commissioners [2016] UKUT 361 (TCC); [2016] S.T.C. 2317; [2016] B.T.C. 517, UT (Tax) .... *Digested,* 17/**2137**

Acornwood LLP v Revenue and Customs Commissioners [2014] UKFTT 416 (TC); [2014] S.F.T.D. 694, FTT (Tax) .... *Digested,* 14/**2975**: *Affirmed* 17/2137

Acrow (Automation) Ltd v Rex Chainbelt Inc [1971] 1 W.L.R. 1676; [1971] 3 All E.R. 1175; (1971) 115 S.J. 642, CA (Civ Div) .... *Digested,* 71/**9259**: *Applied* 73/2661, 79/350: *Considered* 86/1501: *Followed* 17/160

Actavis Group PTC EHF v Icos Corp [2016] EWHC 2690 (Pat); [2016] 6 Costs L.R. 1051, Ch D (Patents Ct) .... *Digested,* 17/**260**

Actavis Group PTC EHF v Warner-Lambert Co LLC see Generics (UK) Ltd (t/a Mylan) v Warner-Lambert Co LLC

Actavis UK Ltd v Competition and Markets Authority see Generics (UK) Ltd v Competition and Markets Authority

Actavis UK Ltd v Eli Lilly & Co; *sub nom* Eli Lilly & Co v Actavis UK Ltd [2017] UKSC 48; [2018] 1 All E.R. 171; [2017] Bus. L.R. 1731; [2017] R.P.C. 21; (2017) 157 B.M.L.R. 96; Times, August 3, 2017, SC .... *Digested,* 17/**1366**

Actavis UK Ltd v Eli Lilly & Co [2015] EWCA Civ 555; [2016] 4 All E.R. 666; [2017] 1 All E.R. (Comm) 24; [2015] Bus. L.R. 1068; [2016] R.P.C. 2, CA (Civ Div) .... *Digested,* 15/**1502**: *Reversed in part* 17/1366

Actavis UK Ltd v Eli Lilly & Co [2014] EWHC 1511 (Pat); [2014] 4 All E.R. 331; [2014] 2 All E.R. (Comm) 669; [2015] Bus. L.R. 154; [2015] R.P.C. 6, Ch D (Patents Ct) .... *Digested,* 14/**1894**: *Applied* 17/425: *Considered* 17/1377: *Reversed* 15/1502

Actavis UK Ltd v Novartis AG [2010] EWCA Civ 82; [2010] F.S.R. 18, CA (Civ Div) .... *Digested,* 10/**1973**: *Followed* 17/1376

Action Storage Systems Ltd v G-Force Europe.Com Ltd [2016] EWHC 3151 (IPEC); [2017] F.S.R. 18, IPEC .... *Digested,* 17/**1363**
AD (A Child) (Fact-finding Hearing: Application for Re-hearing), Re [2016] EWHC 326 (Fam); [2016] 2 F.L.R. 1247; [2016] Fam. Law 559, Fam Div .... *Digested,* 17/**1047**
AD (Children) (Fact-finding: Rehearing), Re [2016] EWHC 2912 (Fam); [2017] 4 W.L.R. 23, Fam Div .... *Digested,* 17/**1048**
AD (Human Fertilisation and Embryology Act 2008), Re [2017] EWHC 1026 (Fam), Fam Div
Considered 17/1054
AD (Human Fertilisation and Embryology Act 2008), Re see D (Practice: Declaration of Parentage), Re
Adamczewski v Jelenia Gora District Court, Poland see Adamczewski v Poland
Adamczewski v Poland; *sub nom* Adamczewski v Jelenia Gora District Court, Poland [2014] EWHC 2958 (Admin), QBD (Admin)
Considered 17/909
Adams v Aroca Seiquer & Asociados see Adams v Atlas International Property Services Ltd
Adams v Atlas International Property Services Ltd; *joined case* Adams v Aroca Seiquer & Asociados [2016] EWHC 2680 (QB); [2017] Bus. L.R. 287, QBD ...... *Digested,* 17/**49**
Adams v British Telecommunications Plc [2017] I.C.R. 382, EAT
Adams v Crown Prosecution Service; *sub nom* R. v Adams (Terence George) [2017] EWCA Civ 185; [2017] 1 W.L.R. 3732; [2017] Lloyd's Rep. F.C. 519, CA (Civ Div) .... *Digested,* 17/**578**
Adams, Re; *sub nom* R. v Adams (Terence George) [2014] EWHC 2639 (Admin), QBD (Admin)
Affirmed 17/578
Adcock (Edward) v Archibald 1925 J.C. 58; 1925 S.L.T. 258, HCJ
Considered 17/2512
Addis v Burrows [1948] 1 K.B. 444; [1948] 1 All E.R. 177; 64 T.L.R. 169; [1948] L.J.R. 1033; (1948) 92 S.J. 124, CA .... *Digested,* 47-51/**5533**:
Applied 68/547: *Considered* 17/1440
Adecco UK Ltd v Revenue and Customs Commissioners [2017] UKUT 113 (TCC); [2017] S.T.C. 787; [2017] B.V.C. 509, UT (Tax) .... *Digested,* 17/**2254**
Adecco UK Ltd v Revenue and Customs Commissioners [2015] UKFTT 600 (TC); [2016] S.T.I. 102, FTT (Tax)
Affirmed 17/2254
Adelson v Associated Newspapers Ltd [2007] EWCA Civ 701; [2008] 1 W.L.R. 585; [2007] 4 All E.R. 330; [2007] C.P. Rep. 40; [2008] E.M.L.R. 9; Times, July 18, 2007, CA (Civ Div) .... *Digested,* 07/**534**:
Applied 10/430, 16/1424: *Considered* 10/1887, 15/209, 17/195: *Explained* 10/428:
Followed 13/445, 15/374
Adepoju v Akinola [2016] EWHC 3160 (Ch); [2017] W.T.L.R. 187, Ch D .... *Digested,* 17/**2068**
Adesina v Nursing and Midwifery Council; *sub nom* R. (on the application of Adesina) v Nursing and Midwifery Council; *joined case* Baines v Nursing and Midwifery Council [2013] EWCA Civ 818; [2013] 1 W.L.R. 3156; (2013) 133 B.M.L.R. 196; Times, July 22, 2013, CA (Civ Div) .... *Digested,* 13/**1490**:
Considered 15/1127, 17/202: *Followed* 14/392, 15/1249, 15/2071
Adesokan v Sainsbury's Supermarkets Ltd [2017] EWCA Civ 22; [2017] I.C.R. 590; [2017] I.R.L.R. 346; Times, February 21, 2017, CA (Civ Div) .... *Digested,* 17/**803**
Adidas AG v Shoe Branding Europe BVBA (R 1515/2016-2) [2017] E.T.M.R. 22, EUIPO
Adigun v Ireland (Admissibility) (19673/16) (2017) 64 E.H.R.R. SE16, ECHR
Admiral Casinos & Entertainment v Balmatic Handelsgesellschaft mbH (C-464/15) EU:C:2016:500; [2017] 1 C.M.L.R. 14, ECJ (7th Chamber)
Adobe Systems Inc v Assistant Director of Income Tax 19 I.T.L. Rep. 44, HC (Ind)
Adoption Application (96 AO 147), Re (Unreported, January 31, 1997), CC
Approved 17/1034: *Considered* 00/2434
ADS v DSM see A v D
ADVA Optical Networking Ltd v Optron Holding Ltd; *joined case* Rotronic Instruments (UK) Ltd v A One Distribution (UK) Ltd [2017] EWHC 1813 (TCC); [2017] B.L.R. 516, QBD (TCC) .... *Digested,* 17/**350**
Advent Computer Training Ltd, Re see Gould v Advent Computer Training Ltd
Advice Centre for Mortgages Ltd v McNicoll 2006 S.L.T. 591; 2006 S.C.L.R. 602; 2006 Hous. L.R. 22; 2006 G.W.D. 19-413, OH .... *Digested,* 06/**5548**:
Applied 16/2487, 17/2470: *Followed* 14/3631
Advocate General for Scotland v Murray Group Holdings Ltd see Murray Group Holdings Ltd v Revenue and Customs Commissioners

Advocate General for Scotland v Murray Group Holdings Ltd see RFC 2012 Plc (In Liquidation) (formerly Rangers Football Club Plc) v Advocate General for Scotland
Advocate General for Scotland, Petitioner; *sub nom* Spring Salmon & Seafood Ltd, Re [2010] CSOH 82; 2010 G.W.D. 25-465, OH
Considered 17/402
AECOM Design Build Ltd v Staptina Engineering Services Ltd [2017] EWHC 723 (TCC); [2017] B.L.R. 329; 171 Con. L.R. 247, QBD (TCC) .... *Digested,* 17/**450**
Aer Lingus Plc v Gildacroft Ltd [2006] EWCA Civ 4; [2006] 1 W.L.R. 1173; [2006] 2 All E.R. 290; [2006] C.P. Rep. 21; [2006] P.I.Q.R. P16; Times, January 23, 2006; Independent, January 19, 2006; (2006) 103(6) L.S.G. 32; (2006) 156 N.L.J. 147; (2006) 150 S.J.L.B. 129; [2006] N.P.C. 4, CA (Civ Div) .... *Digested,* 06/**480**: *Applied* 17/322
Aeroflot - Russian Airlines v Berezovsky; *sub nom* Joint Stock Co Aeroflot Russian Airlines v Berezovsky [2013] EWCA Civ 784; [2013] 2 Lloyd's Rep. 242; [2013] 2 C.L.C. 206, CA (Civ Div) .... *Digested,* 13/**509**: *Applied* 16/434, 17/377: *Considered* 17/295: *Followed* 14/136
AES Barry Ltd v TXU Europe Energy Trading (In Administration) [2004] EWHC 1757 (Ch); [2005] 2 B.C.L.C. 22; [2006] B.P.I.R. 1109, Ch D .... *Digested,* 05/**2258**: *Applied* 10/1837, 10/1844: *Considered* 09/2316, 17/337, 17/453
AF v RF [2017] SAC (Civ) 18; 2017 Fam. L.R. 61; 2017 G.W.D. 16-261, SAC .... *Digested,* 17/**2615**
Affum v Prefet du Pas-de-Calais (C-47/15) EU:C:2016:408; [2017] 1 C.M.L.R. 9, ECJ (Grand Chamber)
Afonso da Trindade v Hackney LBC [2017] EWCA Civ 942; [2017] H.L.R. 37, CA (Civ Div) .... *Digested,* 17/**1159**
African Export-Import Bank v Shebah Exploration and Production Co Ltd [2016] EWHC 311 (Comm); [2016] 2 All E.R. (Comm) 307; [2016] 2 B.C.L.C. 412; [2016] 1 C.L.C. 292, QBD (Comm) .... *Digested,* 16/**441**: *Affirmed* 17/508
African Export-Import Bank v Shebah Exploration and Production Co Ltd [2017] EWCA Civ 845; [2018] 1 W.L.R. 487; [2018] 2 All E.R. 144; [2018] 1 All E.R. (Comm) 535; [2017] 2 Lloyd's Rep. 111; [2017] B.L.R. 469; 173 Con. L.R. 53; Times, September 1, 2017, CA (Civ Div) .... *Digested,* 17/**508**
Agarwal v ABN AMRO Bank NV [2017] B.P.I.R. 816, Ch D .... *Digested,* 17/**162**
Agarwal v Canara Bank [2017] B.P.I.R. 842, Ch D
Agarwal v Cardiff University [2017] I.C.R. 967; [2017] I.R.L.R. 600, EAT .... *Digested,* 17/**854**: *Not followed* 17/853
Agarwala v Agarwala [2016] EWCA Civ 1252; Times, January 20, 2017; [2017] 1 P. & C.R. DG17, CA (Civ Div) .... *Digested,* 17/**635**
Agassi v Robinson (Inspector of Taxes) (Costs); *sub nom* Agassi v Robinson (Inspector of Taxes) (No.2) [2005] EWCA Civ 1507; [2006] 1 W.L.R. 2126; [2006] 1 All E.R. 900; [2006] S.T.C. 580; [2006] 2 Costs L.R. 283; [2006] B.T.C. 3; Times, December 22, 2005; Independent, December 7, 2005; [2005] S.T.I. 1994; (2005) 155 N.L.J. 1885; (2006) 150 S.J.L.B. 28; [2005] N.P.C. 140, CA (Civ Div) .... *Digested,* 06/**392**: *Considered* 17/220: *Followed* 15/315, 16/215
Agassi v Robinson (Inspector of Taxes) (No.2) see Agassi v Robinson (Inspector of Taxes) (Costs)
AGC Glass Europe SA v European Commission (C-517/15 P) EU:C:2017:598; [2017] 5 C.M.L.R. 13, ECJ (6th Chamber)
Ageas (UK) Ltd v Kwik-Fit (GB) Ltd [2013] EWHC 3261 (QB), QBD
Considered 17/368
Agents Mutual Ltd v Gascoigne Halman Ltd; *joined case* Agents Mutual Ltd v Moginie James Ltd [2016] CAT 15; [2017] Comp. A.R. 39; [2016] 5 Costs L.R. 893, CAT .... *Digested,* 17/**422**
Agents Mutual Ltd v Gascoigne Halman Ltd (t/a Gascoigne Halman) [2016] CAT 21; [2017] Comp. A.R. 58, CAT .... *Digested,* 17/**421**
Agents Mutual Ltd v Moginie James Ltd see Agents Mutual Ltd v Gascoigne Halman Ltd
Agents' Mutual Ltd v Gascoigne Halman Ltd (t/a Gascoigne Halman) [2016] CAT 20; [2017] Comp. A.R. 47; [2017] 1 Costs L.O. 17, CAT .... *Digested,* 17/**423**
Agents' Mutual Ltd v Gascoigne Halman Ltd (t/a Gascoigne Halman) [2017] CAT 15; [2017] Comp. A.R. 392, CAT
Agents' Mutual Ltd v Gascoigne Halman Ltd (t/a Gascoigne Halman) [2016] EWHC 2315 (Ch); [2017] U.K.C.L.R. 269, Ch D .... *Digested,* 17/**360**
Agents' Mutual Ltd v Gascoigne Halman Ltd (t/a Gascoigne Halman) [2017] CAT 3; [2017] Comp. A.R. 114, CAT

Agents' Mutual Ltd v Gascoigne Halman Ltd (t/a Gascoigne Halman) [2017] CAT 5; [2017] Comp. A.R. 117, CAT

Agents' Mutual Ltd v Gascoigne Halman Ltd (t/a Gascoigne Halman) [2016] EWHC 2789 (Ch); [2017] U.K.C.L.R. 278, Ch D ..... *Digested,* 17/**364**

Agenzia delle Entrate v Federal Express Europe Inc. (C-273/16) EU:C:2017:733; [2017] B.V.C. 45; [2017] S.T.I. 2128, ECJ (1st Chamber)

Agenzia delle Entrate v Identi (C-493/15) EU:C:2017:219; [2017] S.T.C. 1916; [2017] B.V.C. 14; [2017] S.T.I. 917, ECJ (7th Chamber)

Aggeliki Charis Compania Maritima SA v Pagnan SpA (The Angelic Grace) [1995] 1 Lloyd's Rep. 87, CA (Civ Div)
Applied 98/239, 05/2357, 05/599, 12/312, 13/96, 14/301, 16/166, 16/367: *Considered* 97/880, 99/4441, 99/733, 99/745, 01/950, 05/625, 09/172, 11/468, 17/2000, 17/377: *Followed* 16/164: *Referred to* 15/1471

AGN (Adoption: Foreign Adoption), Re see N (A Child) (Adoption: Foreign Guardianship), Re

Agnew's Application for Judicial Review, Re see McCord's Application for Judicial Review, Re

Agnew's Application for Judicial Review, Re see R. (on the application of Miller) v Secretary of State for Exiting the European Union

Agria Polska sp z oo v European Commission (T-480/15) EU:T:2017:339; [2017] 5 C.M.L.R. 1, GC (1st Chamber)

Aguilar Quila v Secretary of State for the Home Department see R. (on the application of Aguilar Quila) v Secretary of State for the Home Department

Agyemang-Prempeh v Facilicom Services Group [2017] I.R.L.R. 688, CAC ..... *Digested,* 17/**801**

AH v CH see H v H

Ahmad v Secret Garden (Cheshire) Ltd [2013] EWCA Civ 1005; [2013] 3 E.G.L.R. 42; [2014] 1 P. & C.R. DG3, CA (Civ Div) ..... *Digested,* 14/**1991**:
Considered 17/196

Ahmed v Amnesty International; *sub nom* Amnesty International v Ahmed [2009] I.C.R. 1450; [2009] I.R.L.R. 884; Times, October 6, 2009; (2009) 159 N.L.J. 1400, EAT ..... *Digested,* 09/**1228**:
Applied 12/1150: *Considered* 17/820, 17/840: *Followed* 11/1063

Ahmed v Crown Prosecution Service [2017] EWHC 1272 (Admin); [2017] A.C.D. 85, QBD (Admin)

Ahmed v HM Treasury see Guardian News and Media Ltd, Re

Ahmed v Mogul Eastern Foods [2005] EWHC 3532 (Ch); [2007] B.P.I.R. 975, Ch D
Applied 10/1858, 11/1851, 12/1834, 15/1405, 15/1410, 17/1290

Ahmed v National College for Teaching and Leadership see Anwar v National College for Teaching and Leadership

Ahmed v Secretary of State for the Home Department [2017] EWCA Civ 99; [2017] 1 W.L.R. 3977; [2017] 2 C.M.L.R. 27; [2017] Imm. A.R. 1191, CA (Civ Div) ..... *Digested,* 17/**1246**

Ahmed v United Kingdom (59727/13) (2017) 65 E.H.R.R. 18; Times, April 27, 2017, ECHR ..... *Digested,* 17/**1204**

Ahmed (Tanveer) v HM Advocate [2016] HCJAC 125; 2017 J.C. 130; 2017 S.C.L. 306; 2016 G.W.D. 40-727, HCJ ..... *Digested,* 17/**2806**:
Considered 17/2807

AI v Secretary of State for the Home Department see R. (on the application of XH) v Secretary of State for the Home Department

AIB Group (UK) Plc v Mark Redler & Co Solicitors [2014] UKSC 58; [2015] A.C. 1503; [2014] 3 W.L.R. 1367; [2015] 1 All E.R. 747; [2015] 2 All E.R. (Comm) 189; [2015] P.N.L.R. 10; [2015] W.T.L.R. 187; 18 I.T.E.L.R. 216; (2014) 158(43) S.J.L.B. 49, SC ..... *Digested,* 15/**167**:
Followed 16/2160, 17/1276

AIC Ltd v ITS Testing Services (UK) Ltd (The Kriti Palm) [2006] EWCA Civ 1601; [2007] 1 All E.R. (Comm) 667; [2007] 1 Lloyd's Rep. 555; [2007] 2 C.L.C. 223; Times, December 21, 2006, CA (Civ Div) ..... *Digested,* 07/**482**:
Applied 08/232, 16/277, 17/325

Aidiniantz v Sherlock Holmes International Society Ltd see Sherlock Holmes International Society Ltd, Re

AIG Europe Ltd v OC320301 LLP; *sub nom* AIG Europe Ltd v Woodman [2017] UKSC 18; [2017] 1 W.L.R. 1168; [2018] 1 All E.R. 936; [2017] Lloyd's Rep. I.R. 209; [2017] P.N.L.R. 22; Times, March 28, 2017, SC ..... *Digested,* 17/**1351**

AIG Europe Ltd v OC320301 LLP; *sub nom* AIG Europe Ltd v Woodman [2016] EWCA Civ 367; [2017] 1 All E.R. 143; [2016] 2 All E.R. (Comm) 1058; [2016] Lloyd's Rep. I.R. 289, CA (Civ Div) ..... *Digested,* 16/**1274**:
Reversed 17/1351

AIG Europe Ltd v Woodman see AIG Europe Ltd v OC320301 LLP

Ailsa Craig Fishing Co Ltd v Malvern Fishing Co Ltd (The Strathallan); *joined case* Malvern Fishing Co Ltd v Ailsa Craig Fishing Co Ltd (The Strathallan) [1983] 1 W.L.R. 964; [1983] 1 All E.R. 101; [1983] 1 Lloyd's Rep. 183 (Note); 1982 S.C. (H.L.) 14; 1982 S.L.T. 377; (1983) 80 L.S.G. 2516; (1983) 127 S.J. 508, HL ...... *Digested,* 83/**440**: *Applied* 83/3314, 95/5569, 00/895: *Followed* 17/468

Ainsworth v Inland Revenue Commissioners see Inland Revenue Commissioners v Ainsworth

Aintree University Hospitals NHS Foundation Trust v James; *sub nom* James v Aintree University Hospitals NHS Foundation Trust [2013] UKSC 67; [2014] A.C. 591; [2013] 3 W.L.R. 1299; [2014] 1 All E.R. 573; [2014] 1 F.C.R. 153; (2013) 16 C.C.L. Rep. 554; [2014] Med. L.R. 1; (2014) 135 B.M.L.R. 1; Times, November 19, 2013; (2013) 163(7583) N.L.J. 16; (2013) 157(43) S.J.L.B. 53, SC ...... *Digested,* 14/**1526**: *Applied* 14/2182, 15/1227, 16/1000, 16/1514, 16/999: *Considered* 15/1740, 16/2032: *Followed* 15/1224, 15/1738, 16/1003, 16/1496, 17/1122, 17/1125

Air Berlin Plc & Co Luftverkehrs KG v Bundesverband der Verbraucherzentralen und Verbraucherverbande - Verbraucherzentrale Bundesverband eV (C-290/16) EU:C:2017:523; [2017] Bus. L.R. 1680; [2018] 1 C.M.L.R. 21, ECJ (4th Chamber)

Airbus Industrie GIE v Patel [1999] 1 A.C. 119; [1998] 2 W.L.R. 686; [1998] 2 All E.R. 257; [1998] 1 Lloyd's Rep. 631; [1998] C.L.C. 702; [1999] I.L.Pr. 238; Times, April 6, 1998; (1998) 95(18) L.S.G. 32; (1998) 148 N.L.J. 551; (1998) 142 S.J.L.B. 139, HL ...... *Digested,* 98/**755**: *Considered* 00/758, 02/641: *Followed* 03/606, 17/430

Airedale NHS Trust v Bland [1993] A.C. 789; [1993] 2 W.L.R. 316; [1993] 1 All E.R. 821; [1993] 1 F.L.R. 1026; [1994] 1 F.C.R. 485; [1993] 4 Med. L.R. 39; (1993) 12 B.M.L.R. 64; Times, February 5, 1993; Independent, February 5, 1993; [1993] Fam. Law 473; Guardian, February 5, 1993; (1993) 143 N.L.J. 199, HL .. *Digested,* 93/**2712**: *Applied* 94/3015, 95/4266, 01/2934, 07/1986, 09/4389: *Considered* 94/1004, 95/4104, 97/2593, 97/6070, 98/958, 00/3246, 01/2662, 01/2935, 12/1674, 13/619, 15/1221: *Distinguished* 97/5783: *Followed* 98/2650, 98/2651, 01/3571, 02/1888, 12/1517, 12/1558, 15/1738, 17/1124

Airtours Holiday Transport Ltd (formerly My Travel Group) v Revenue and Customs Commissioners; *sub nom* Airtours Holidays Transport Ltd v Revenue and Customs Commissioners; Revenue and Customs Commissioners v Airtours Holiday Transport Ltd [2016] UKSC 21; [2016] 4 W.L.R. 87; [2016] 4 All E.R. 1; [2016] S.T.C. 1509; [2016] B.V.C. 17; [2016] S.T.I. 1529, SC ...... *Digested,* 16/**2185**: *Applied* 17/2249: *Followed* 17/2254

Airtours Holidays Transport Ltd v Revenue and Customs Commissioners see Airtours Holiday Transport Ltd (formerly My Travel Group) v Revenue and Customs Commissioners

AJE v HM Advocate see E v HM Advocate

AK (A Child) (Human Fertilisation and Embryology: Declaration of Parentage), Re; *sub nom* AK (Human Fertilisation and Embryology Act 2008), Re [2017] EWHC 1154 (Fam); [2017] 4 W.L.R. 169, Fam Div ...... *Digested,* 17/**1052**

AK (Afghanistan) v Secretary of State for the Home Department [2007] EWCA Civ 535, CA (Civ Div) *Followed* 17/1208

AK (Human Fertilisation and Embryology Act 2008), Re see AK (A Child) (Human Fertilisation and Embryology: Declaration of Parentage), Re

AK (Sierra Leone) v Secretary of State for the Home Department [2016] EWCA Civ 999; [2017] Imm. A.R. 319; [2017] I.N.L.R. 681, CA (Civ Div) ...... *Digested,* 17/**1187**

AK Investment CJSC v Kyrgyz Mobil Tel Ltd; *joined cases* Altimo Holdings and Investment Ltd v Kyrgyz Mobil Tel Ltd; CP-Credit Prive SA v Kyrgyz Mobil Tel Ltd; Fellowes International Holdings Ltd v Kyrgyz Mobil Tel Ltd [2011] UKPC 7; [2012] 1 W.L.R. 1804; [2011] 4 All E.R. 1027; [2012] 1 All E.R. (Comm) 319; [2011] 1 C.L.C. 205, PC (IoM) *Applied* 15/433, 17/314, 17/369, 17/426: *Considered* 11/139, 12/120, 12/472, 12/557, 15/85, 17/371: *Followed* 14/477

AKB v Willerton see H v Craven

Akbar v Secretary of State for the Home Department see Secretary of State for the Home Department v Akbar

Akbarali v Brent LBC see R. v Barnet LBC Ex p. Shah

Akerman v Richmond upon Thames LBC [2017] EWHC 84 (Admin); [2017] P.T.S.R. 351; [2017] A.C.D. 36, DC ...... *Digested,* 17/**562**

Akerman-Livingstone v Aster Communities Ltd (formerly Flourish Homes Ltd); *sub nom* Aster Communities Ltd (formerly Flourish Homes Ltd) v Akerman-Livingstone [2015] UKSC 15; [2015] A.C. 1399; [2015] 2 W.L.R. 721; [2015] 3 All E.R. 725; [2015] H.L.R. 20; [2015] B.L.G.R. 765; [2015] 2 P. & C.R. 10; [2015] L. & T.R. 13, SC .... *Digested,* 15/**1592**: *Followed* 17/1155, 17/1459

Akers v Motor Insurers' Bureau [2003] EWCA Civ 18; [2003] Lloyd's Rep. I.R. 427, CA (Civ Div) .... *Digested,* 03/**2472**: *Applied* 17/1350

Akers v Samba Financial Group [2014] EWCA Civ 1516; [2015] Ch. 451; [2015] 2 W.L.R. 1281; [2016] 1 B.C.L.C. 657; [2015] B.P.I.R. 411; [2015] W.T.L.R. 931; 17 I.T.E.L.R. 921, CA (Civ Div) .... *Digested,* 15/**441**: *Reversed* 17/1335

Akers v Samba Financial Group [2017] UKSC 6; [2017] A.C. 424; [2017] 2 W.L.R. 713; [2017] 2 All E.R. 799; [2017] 2 All E.R. (Comm) 97; [2017] B.C.C. 511; [2017] 1 B.C.L.C. 151; [2017] B.P.I.R. 263; [2017] W.T.L.R. 373; 20 I.T.E.L.R. 554; Times, February 6, 2017, SC .... *Digested,* 17/**1335**

Akinfolarin v Secretary of State for the Home Department [2016] EWHC 2101 (Admin); [2017] Imm. A.R. 402, QBD (Admin) .... *Digested,* 17/**1180**

Akinyemi v Secretary of State for the Home Department [2017] EWCA Civ 236; [2017] 1 W.L.R. 3118; [2017] Imm. A.R. 1216; [2017] I.N.L.R. 819; Times, May 18, 2017, CA (Civ Div) .... *Digested,* 17/**1194**: *Considered* 17/1197

Akita Holdings Ltd v Attorney General of the Turks and Caicos Islands [2017] UKPC 7; [2017] A.C. 590; [2017] 2 W.L.R. 1153; [2017] W.T.L.R. 407; 20 I.T.E.L.R. 593; Times, April 4, 2017, PC (TCI)

Aksenchik v Russia (961/11) see Khamtokhu v Russia (60367/08)

Akzo Nobel NV v European Commission (C-516/15 P) EU:C:2017:314; [2017] 5 C.M.L.R. 7, ECJ (5th Chamber)

Al v Advocate General for Scotland [2015] CSOH 95; 2015 S.L.T. 507; 2015 G.W.D. 25-439, OH .... *Digested,* 15/**3148**: *Considered* 17/2663

Al Rushaid Parker Drilling Ltd v Shetty see Shetty v Al Rushaid Petroleum Investment Co

Al Shamsi v Terna Bahrain Holding Co WLL see Terna Bahrain Holding Co WLL v Al Shamsi

Al-Dulimi v Switzerland (5809/08) 42 B.H.R.C. 163, ECHR (Grand Chamber)

Al-Fayed v Commissioner of Police of the Metropolis (No.1) [2002] EWCA Civ 780; Times, June 17, 2002; (2002) 99(30) L.S.G. 39; (2002) 146 S.J.L.B. 153, CA (Civ Div) .... *Digested,* 02/**421**: *Applied* 04/872, 17/183: *Considered* 16/156: *Not followed* 14/294

Al-Ghabra v HM Treasury see Guardian News and Media Ltd, Re

Al-Jeffery v Al-Jeffery; *sub nom* Al-Jeffery (Vulnerable Adult: British Citizen), Re [2016] EWHC 2151 (Fam); [2016] Fam. Law 1319, Fam Div *Applied* 17/13

Al-Jeffery (Vulnerable Adult: British Citizen), Re see Al-Jeffery v Al-Jeffery

Al-Khawaja v United Kingdom (26766/05); *joined case* Tahery v United Kingdom (22228/06) (2009) 49 E.H.R.R. 1; 26 B.H.R.C. 249; [2009] Crim. L.R. 352, ECHR .... *Digested,* 09/**757**: *Considered* 09/761, 10/658, 17/2603

Al-Khawaja v United Kingdom (26766/05); *joined case* Tahery v United Kingdom (22228/06) [2012] 2 Costs L.O. 139; (2012) 54 E.H.R.R. 23; 32 B.H.R.C. 1; Times, December 22, 2011; [2012] Crim. L.R. 375, ECHR (Grand Chamber) .... *Digested,* 12/**657**: *Applied* 12/653: *Considered* 13/600, 14/287, 17/2474

Al-Rawas v Hassan Khan & Co; *sub nom* Hassan Khan & Co v Al-Rawas; Hassan Khan & Co v v Al-Shanfari; *joined case* Al-Shanfari v Hassan Khan & Co [2017] EWCA Civ 42; [2017] 1 W.L.R. 2301; [2017] P.N.L.R. 13, CA (Civ Div) .... *Digested,* 17/**329**

Al-Rawas v Pegasus Energy Ltd [2008] EWHC 617 (QB); [2009] 1 All E.R. 346; [2009] 1 All E.R. (Comm) 393, QBD .... *Digested,* 09/**467**: *Applied* 17/1298: *Considered* 13/783, 15/680

Al-Saadoon v Secretary of State for Defence see R. (on the application of Al-Saadoon) v Secretary of State for Defence

Al-Saadoon v Secretary of State for Defence see R. (on the application of Al-Saadoon) v Secretary of State for Defence

Al-Shabib v Bradford Hospitals NHS Trust; *sub nom* Bradford Hospitals NHS Trust v Al-Shabib [2003] I.R.L.R. 4; [2002] Emp. L.R. 1228, EAT .... *Digested,* 03/**1300**: *Applied* 17/856

Al-Shanfari v Hassan Khan & Co see Al-Rawas v Hassan Khan & Co

Al-Skeini v United Kingdom (55721/07) (2011) 53 E.H.R.R. 18; 30 B.H.R.C. 561; [2011] Inquest L.R. 73; Times, July 13, 2011, ECHR (Grand Chamber) .... *Digested,* 11/**1696**: *Applied* 13/121, 13/1551, 13/1929, 14/2044, 15/101, 17/180, 17/83: *Considered* 16/1094: *Followed* 15/1558

Al-Waheed v Ministry of Defence [2014] EWHC 2714 (QB), QBD *Affirmed* 17/1407

Al-Waheed v Ministry of Defence see Mohammed v Secretary of State for Defence

Alakor Gabonatermelo es Forgalmazo Kft v Nemzeti Ado- es Vamhivatal Eszak-alfoldi Regionalis Ado Foigazgatosaga (C-191/12) EU:C:2013:315; [2013] S.T.I. 1904, ECJ (7th Chamber) *Applied* 17/2289

Alam v Covea Insurance Plc (Unreported, March 3, 2017), CC (Coventry) [*Robert Rees, Barrister, New Walk Chambers, 27 New Walk, Leicester*] .... *Digested,* 17/**1648**

Alam v Denmark (Admissibility) (33809/15) (2017) 65 E.H.R.R. SE10, ECHR

Alame v Royal Dutch Shell Plc see His Royal Highness Okpabi v Royal Dutch Shell Plc

Albano, The v Allan Line Steamship Co Ltd; *joined case* Union Dampfschiffsrhederei AG v SS Parisian [1907] A.C. 193, PC (Can) *Considered* 47-51/9537: *Not applied* 17/2020

Alberg v Revenue and Customs Commissioners [2016] UKFTT 621 (TC); [2017] S.F.T.D. 406; [2016] S.T.I. 3171, FTT (Tax) .... *Digested,* 17/**2140**

Alcorn v MGN Ltd see Gulati v MGN Ltd

Aldcroft v International Cotton Association Ltd [2017] EWHC 642 (Comm); [2018] 2 W.L.R. 793; [2018] 1 All E.R. (Comm) 721; [2017] 1 Lloyd's Rep. 635, QBD (Comm) .... *Digested,* 17/**75**

Aldi Stores Ltd v WSP Group Plc [2007] EWCA Civ 1260; [2008] 1 W.L.R. 748; [2008] C.P. Rep. 10; [2008] B.L.R. 1; 115 Con. L.R. 49; [2008] P.N.L.R. 14; Times, December 4, 2007; (2008) 24 Const. L.J. 334; [2008] C.I.L.L. 2549; (2007) 104(48) L.S.G. 24; [2007] N.P.C. 128, CA (Civ Div) .... *Digested,* 07/**346**: *Applied* 08/271, 14/2993, 15/430, 17/1375: *Considered* 09/976, 16/1388, 17/322: *Explained* 17/206: *Followed* 16/1313, 16/159

Alexander v France; *sub nom* Alexander v Public Prosecutor's Office, Marseille District Court of First Instance, France; Di Benedetto v Court of Palermo, Italy; *joined case* Di Benedetto v Italy [2017] EWHC 1392 (Admin); [2018] Q.B. 408; [2017] 3 W.L.R. 1427; [2018] 1 All E.R. 963; [2017] 3 C.M.L.R. 42, DC

Alexander v Public Prosecutor's Office, Marseille District Court of First Instance, France see Alexander v France

Alexander v Standard Telephones & Cables Ltd (No.2); *joined case* Wall v Standard Telephones & Cables Ltd (No.2) [1991] I.R.L.R. 286; Independent, July 31, 1989, Ch D .... *Digested,* 91/**1620**: *Applied* 98/2107, 12/1528, 16/721, 17/773: *Considered* 04/1200, 07/1396, 08/1124: *Followed* 98/2110, 11/1531

Alexander v West Bromwich Mortgage Co Ltd [2016] EWCA Civ 496; [2017] 1 All E.R. 942; [2017] 1 All E.R. (Comm) 667, CA (Civ Div) .... *Digested,* 17/**175**: *Followed* 17/474

Alexander v West Bromwich Mortgage Co Ltd [2015] EWHC 135 (Comm); [2015] 2 All E.R. (Comm) 224, QBD (Comm) .... *Digested,* 15/**186**: *Reversed* 17/175

Alexander-Thedotou v Michael Kyprianou & Co LLC see Alexander-Theodotou v Michael Kyprianou & Co LLC

Alexander-Theodotou v Michael Kyprianou & Co LLC; *sub nom* Alexander-Thedotou v Michael Kyprianou & Co LLC [2016] EWHC 1493 (Ch); [2016] B.P.I.R. 1114, Ch D .... *Digested,* 17/**1326**

Alexandros T, The see Starlight Shipping Co v Allianz Marine & Aviation Versicherungs AG

Alfa Acciai SpA v European Commission (C-87/15 P) see Ferriera Valsabbia SpA v European Commission (C-86/15 P)

Alhashem v Secretary of State for Work and Pensions [2016] EWCA Civ 395; [2017] Q.B. 52; [2016] 3 W.L.R. 853; [2016] 3 C.M.L.R. 20, CA (Civ Div) .... *Digested,* 16/**1980**

Ali v Ansar-Ali [2016] EWCA Civ 781; [2017] 1 F.C.R. 1; [2016] Fam. Law 1318, CA (Civ Div) .... *Digested,* 17/**1005**

Ali v Birmingham City Council; *sub nom* Birmingham City Council v Ali; *joined cases* Tomlinson v Birmingham City Council; Ibrahim v Birmingham City Council; Moran v Manchester City Council; R. (on the application of Aweys) v Birmingham City Council [2010] UKSC 8; [2010] 2 A.C. 39; [2010] 2 W.L.R. 471; [2010] 2 All E.R. 175; [2010] P.T.S.R. 524; [2010] H.R.L.R. 18; [2010] U.K.H.R.R. 417; [2010] H.L.R. 22; [2010] B.L.G.R. 401; Times, February 19, 2010; (2010) 154(7) S.J.L.B. 37, SC .... *Digested,* 10/**1694**: *Considered* 10/3180, 12/1625, 14/2181: *Followed* 16/35, 17/1147: *Not applied* 17/180

Ali v Carr (Unreported, August 18, 2017), QBD [*Isaac Hogarth, Barrister, 12 King's Bench Walk, Temple, London*] .... *Digested,* 17/**1662**

Ali v Entry Clearance Officer see Mahad (Ethiopia) v Entry Clearance Officer

Ali v Pattni see Pattni v Ali

Ali v Petroleum Co of Trinidad and Tobago [2017] UKPC 2; [2017] I.C.R. 531; [2017] I.R.L.R. 432, PC (Trin)

Ali v Revenue and Customs Commissioners see Balti Hut (Gloucester) Ltd v Revenue and Customs Commissioners

Ali v Secretary of State for the Home Department; *sub nom* HA (Iraq) v Secretary of State for the Home Department [2016] UKSC 60; [2016] 1 W.L.R. 4799; [2017] 3 All E.R. 20; [2017] Imm. A.R. 484; [2017] I.N.L.R. 109; Times, December 5, 2016, SC .... *Digested,* 17/**1200**: *Applied* 17/1209: *Considered* 17/1197: *Followed* 17/1186, 17/1194, 17/1235, 17/1239

Ali v Secretary of State for the Home Department; *sub nom* HA (Iraq) v Secretary of State for the Home Department [2014] EWCA Civ 1304; [2015] Imm. A.R. 207, CA (Civ Div) .... *Digested,* 15/**1325**: *Affirmed* 17/1200

Ali v United Kingdom (40378/10) (2016) 63 E.H.R.R. 20; [2015] H.L.R. 46; Times, January 13, 2016, ECHR .... *Digested,* 16/**1052**: *Applied* 17/180: *Not followed* 17/1147

Aline Tramp SA v Jordan International Insurance Co; *joined case* London Steam-Ship Owners' Mutual Insurance Association Ltd v Jordan International Insurance Co [2016] EWHC 1317 (Comm); [2017] 1 Lloyd's Rep. 467, QBD (Comm) .... *Digested,* 17/**2000**

Alireza v Radwan [2017] EWCA Civ 1545; [2017] 4 W.L.R. 206; [2018] 1 F.C.R. 289; Times, October 30, 2017, CA (Civ Div)

Alker v Collingwood Housing Association [2007] EWCA Civ 343; [2007] 1 W.L.R. 2230; [2007] H.L.R. 29; [2007] L. & T.R. 23; [2007] 2 E.G.L.R. 43; [2007] 25 E.G. 184; Times, February 14, 2007, CA (Civ Div) .... *Digested,* 07/**2738**: *Applied* 16/1536, 17/1563: *Considered* 16/1366

All Leisure Holidays Ltd (In Administration), Re [2017] EWHC 870 (Ch); [2017] B.C.C. 354; [2017] B.P.I.R. 1131, Ch D (Birmingham) .... *Digested,* 17/**311**

All Saints and Saint Andrews, Honington with Sapiston, Re [2017] P.T.S.R. 664, Cons Ct

Allan v Plexus Corp (UK) Ltd 2017 S.C.L.R. 214; 2016 Rep. L.R. 119; 2018 Rep. L.R. 32; 2016 G.W.D. 28-502, Sh Ct (Lothian) (Edinburgh) .... *Digested,* 17/**2441**

Allan v Revenue and Customs Commissioners [2015] UKUT 16 (TCC); [2015] S.T.C. 890; [2015] B.T.C. 502, UT (Tax) .... *Digested,* 15/**2480**: *Applied* 17/2091, 17/2150

Allan v Tant (Michael Norman) 1986 J.C. 62; 1986 S.C.C.R. 175, HCJ .... *Digested,* 86/**3893**: *Considered* 17/2478, 17/2479

Allen v Allen [1985] Fam. 8; [1985] 2 W.L.R. 65; [1985] 1 All E.R. 93; [1985] Fam. Law 25; (1984) 81 L.S.G. 2618; (1984) 128 S.J. 721, Fam Div .... *Digested,* 85/**2115**: *Applied* 17/384: *Disapproved* 85/1689, 86/2094

Allen v Mohammed [2017] Lloyd's Rep. I.R. 73, CC (Birmingham) .... *Digested,* 17/**1349**

Allen v Unigate Dairies Ltd see Ridehalgh v Horsefield

Allen v Young see Young (A Bankrupt), Re

Allen (Joint Liquidator), Re see Longmeade Ltd (In Administration), Re

Allen (Valuation Officer) v Bassetlaw DC see Allen (Valuation Officer) v Mansfield DC

Allen (Valuation Officer) v Mansfield DC; *joined case* Allen (Valuation Officer) v Bassetlaw DC [2008] R.A. 338, Lands Tr .... *Digested,* 09/**2679**: *Applied* 17/1528: *Considered* 14/2129

Alliance Bank JSC v Aquanta Corp [2012] EWCA Civ 1588; [2013] 1 All E.R. (Comm) 819; [2013] 1 Lloyd's Rep. 175; [2012] 2 C.L.C. 1027, CA (Civ Div) .... *Digested,* 13/**428**: *Applied* 13/427: *Considered* 15/1471: *Followed* 17/369

Allied Domecq Retailing Ltd v Williams (Valuation Officer) see Williams (Valuation Officer) v Scottish & Newcastle Retail Ltd

Allied Irish Bank Plc v Maguire & Co [2016] IESC 57; [2017] P.N.L.R. 6, Sup Ct (Irl)

Allied Maples Group Ltd v Simmons & Simmons [1995] 1 W.L.R. 1602; [1995] 4 All E.R. 907; [1996] C.L.C. 153; 46 Con. L.R. 134; [1955-95] P.N.L.R. 701; (1995) 145 N.L.J. 1646; [1995] N.P.C. 83; (1995) 70 P. & C.R. D14, CA (Civ Div) .... *Digested*, 96/**4489**: *Applied* 97/3832, 98/1447, 98/3604, 00/4266, 00/4276, 03/3015, 03/946, 05/2880, 05/3419, 06/1026, 07/1316, 10/2286, 10/461, 10/827, 11/2266, 13/487, 16/1544: *Considered* 96/4482, 96/4505, 97/3839, 97/3903, 00/4264, 02/1318, 06/2900, 08/3446, 09/430, 10/832, 13/2094: *Distinguished* 03/3121, 04/913: *Followed* 05/2877, 10/2291, 14/2214, 15/1780, 15/860, 16/1545, 17/2201: *Not applied* 01/537: *Referred to* 97/3917

Allonby v Accrington and Rossendale College (C-256/01) EU:C:2004:18; [2004] E.C.R. I-873; [2004] 1 C.M.L.R. 35; [2005] All E.R. (EC) 289; [2004] I.C.R. 1328; [2004] I.R.L.R. 224; [2004] O.P.L.R. 83; [2004] Pens. L.R. 199, ECJ .... *Digested*, 04/**1258**: *Applied* 11/127, 13/959, 15/823: *Considered* 12/1181: *Followed* 17/840

Allsop v Derbyshire Dales DC [2012] EWHC 3562 (Admin), QBD (Admin) *Applied* 17/1747

Almos Agrarkulkereskedelmi Kft v Nemzeti Ado- es Vamhivatal Kozep-magyarorszagi Regionalis Ado Foigazgatosaga (C-337/13) EU:C:2014:328; [2014] B.V.C. 26; [2014] S.T.I. 1949, ECJ (7th Chamber) *Considered* 17/2230

Alokpa v Ministre du Travail, de l'Emploi et de l'Immigration (C-86/12) EU:C:2013:645; [2017] 1 C.M.L.R. 40; [2014] I.N.L.R. 145, ECJ (2nd Chamber)

Aloys F Dornbracht GmbH & Co KG v European Commission (C-604/13 P) EU:C:2017:45; [2017] 4 C.M.L.R. 22, ECJ (1st Chamber)

Alpine Taxis Ltd v Rochford DC [2017] P.A.D. 21, Planning Inspector

Alsaifi v Amunwa [2017] EWHC 1443 (QB); [2017] 4 W.L.R. 172, QBD .... *Digested*, 17/**653**

Alsaifi v Secretary of State for Education [2016] EWHC 1519 (Admin); [2016] P.T.S.R. 1497; [2017] E.L.R. 1; [2016] A.C.D. 107, QBD (Admin) .... *Digested*, 17/**720**: *Considered* 17/653

Alsop Wilkinson v Neary [1996] 1 W.L.R. 1220; [1995] 1 All E.R. 431; Times, November 4, 1994; Independent, November 3, 1994, Ch D .... *Digested*, 95/**2213**: *Applied* 05/4290, 10/321, 17/2216: *Considered* 97/3952, 97/4939, 03/4470: *Distinguished* 05/4314

Alstom Transport UK Ltd v London Underground Ltd [2017] EWHC 1521 (TCC); 174 Con. L.R. 194, QBD (TCC)

Altimo Holdings and Investment Ltd v Kyrgyz Mobil Tel Ltd see AK Investment CJSC v Kyrgyz Mobil Tel Ltd

Altomart Ltd v Salford Estates (No.2) Ltd; *sub nom* Salford Estates (No.2) Ltd v Altomart Ltd [2014] EWCA Civ 1408; [2015] 1 W.L.R. 1825; [2016] 2 All E.R. 328; [2015] C.P. Rep. 8; [2014] 6 Costs L.R. 1013; Times, December 9, 2014, CA (Civ Div) .... *Digested*, 15/**298**: *Applied* 15/295: *Followed* 15/299, 16/1194, 17/297, 17/350

Altun v Turkey (Admissibility) (4353/16) (2017) 64 E.H.R.R. SE13, ECHR

Alvis v Harrison 1991 S.L.T. 64; (1991) 62 P. & C.R. 10, HL .... *Digested*, 91/**5109**: *Applied* 99/6239, 10/4308: *Considered* 17/1840

Alway Sheet Metal Ltd v Revenue and Customs Commissioners [2017] UKFTT 198 (TC); [2017] S.F.T.D. 719; [2017] S.T.I. 1200, FTT (Tax) .... *Digested*, 17/**2105**

AM v DF (Temporary Removal) see M (Children) (Temporary Relocation), Re

AM v Hungary (21320/15) (2017) 65 E.H.R.R. SE2, ECHR

AM v Switzerland (144/1999) (2002) 9 I.H.R.R. 36, UN CAT .... *Digested*, 02/**2544**: *Considered* 17/1176

AM (Afghanistan) v Secretary of State for the Home Department [2017] EWCA Civ 1123; [2018] 2 All E.R. 350; [2017] C.P. Rep. 41; [2017] Imm. A.R. 1508; [2017] I.N.L.R. 839, CA (Civ Div) .... *Digested*, 17/**1173**

AM (Ethiopia) v Entry Clearance Officer see Mahad (Ethiopia) v Entry Clearance Officer

Amalgamated Investment & Property Co Ltd (In Liquidation) v Texas Commerce International Bank Ltd [1982] Q.B. 84; [1981] 3 W.L.R. 565; [1981] 3 All E.R. 577; [1982] 1 Lloyd's Rep. 27; [1981] Com. L.R. 236; (1981) 125 S.J. 623, CA (Civ Div) .... *Digested*, 81/**1273**: *Applied* 84/3161, 86/1883, 86/44, 89/1531, 94/4047, 96/1229, 11/219, 15/514: *Considered* 82/421, 85/407, 93/2456, 96/3694, 97/1005, 01/410, 03/2483, 09/1573, 10/3358, 11/533: *Followed* 91/1865, 97/3171, 17/406: *Not followed* 96/1230: *Referred to* 82/1145

Amalgamated Metal Corp Plc v Revenue and Customs Commissioners [2017] UKFTT 705 (TC); [2018] S.F.T.D. 410; [2017] S.T.I. 2276, FTT (Tax)

Amalgamated Metal Trading Ltd v City of London Police Financial Investigation Unit [2003] EWHC 703 (Comm); [2003] 1 W.L.R. 2711; [2003] 4 All E.R. 1225; [2003] 1 All E.R. (Comm) 900; (2003) 153 N.L.J. 564, QBD (Comm) .... *Digested,* 03/**795**: *Applied* 17/173

Amalgamated Metal Trading Ltd v International Tin Council see JH Rayner (Mincing Lane) Ltd v Department of Trade and Industry

Amantilla v Telefusion 9 Con. L.R. 139 .... *Digested,* 88/**2163**: *Approved* 13/392: *Considered* 17/2219

Amaryllis Ltd v McLeod UKEAT/0273/15/RN, EAT *Applied* 17/841

Ambisig - Ambiente e Sistemas de Informacao Geografica SA v AICP - Associacao de Industriais do Concelho de Pombal (C-46/15) EU:C:2016:530; [2017] 1 C.M.L.R. 18, ECJ (5th Chamber)

AMD Environmental Ltd v Cumberland Construction Co Ltd [2016] EWHC 285 (TCC); [2017] 1 All E.R. (Comm) 823; 165 Con. L.R. 191, QBD (TCC) .... *Digested,* 16/**389**

AMEC Capital Projects Ltd v Whitefriars City Estates Ltd [2004] EWCA Civ 1418; [2005] 1 All E.R. 723; [2005] B.L.R. 1; 96 Con. L.R. 142; Times, November 8, 2004; (2005) 21 Const. L.J. 249; (2004) 154 N.L.J. 1690; (2004) 148 S.J.L.B. 1285, CA (Civ Div) .... *Digested,* 05/**646**: *Applied* 10/845, 16/390, 17/659: *Considered* 06/671, 09/650, 17/4: *Followed* 11/493

AMEC Group Ltd v Thames Water Utilities Ltd [2010] EWHC 419 (TCC), QBD (TCC) *Applied* 17/465: *Considered* 10/845

American Energy Group Ltd v Hycarbex Asia Pte Ltd (In Liquidation) [2014] EWHC 1091 (Ch), Ch D (Companies Ct) *Considered* 17/337

AMERICAN EXPRESS/Metal-containing Transaction Card (T519/12) [2017] E.P.O.R. 29, EPO (Technical Bd App)

Ames v Spamhaus Project Ltd [2015] EWHC 127 (QB); [2015] 1 W.L.R. 3409; [2015] E.M.L.R. 13, QBD .... *Digested,* 15/**693**: *Considered* 17/646

Amey v Peter Symonds College [2013] EWHC 2788 (QB); [2014] I.R.L.R. 206, QBD .. *Digested,* 14/**1124**: *Applied* 15/863: *Doubted* 17/808

Amey LG Ltd v Cumbria CC [2016] EWHC 2946 (TCC); [2016] 6 Costs L.R. 1113, QBD (TCC) .... *Digested,* 17/**227**

Amey Wye Valley Ltd v Herefordshire DC [2016] EWHC 2368 (TCC); [2016] B.L.R. 698, QBD (TCC) .... *Digested,* 17/**467**

Amin v Amin [2017] EWCA Civ 1114; [2017] 4 W.L.R. 138; [2017] 3 F.C.R. 1, CA (Civ Div) .... *Digested,* 17/**1025**

Amin v Reigate and Banstead BC [2017] P.A.D. 29, Planning Inspector

Amirteymour v Secretary of State for the Home Department see Amirteymour (EEA Appeals: Human Rights: United States)

Amirteymour (EEA Appeals: Human Rights: United States); *sub nom* Secretary of State for the Home Department v HF (Gambia); Secretary of State for the Home Department v Izvira; Amirteymour v Secretary of State for the Home Department [2015] UKUT 466 (IAC); [2015] Imm. A.R. 1365, UT (IAC) .... *Digested,* 16/**1144**: *Affirmed* 17/1245: *Considered* 16/1149

Amirteymour (EEA Appeals: Human Rights: United States); *sub nom* Secretary of State for the Home Department v HF (Gambia); Secretary of State for the Home Department v Izvira; Amirteymour v Secretary of State for the Home Department [2017] EWCA Civ 353; [2017] Imm. A.R. 1368; [2017] I.N.L.R. 691, CA (Civ Div) .... *Digested,* 17/**1245**

Amissah v Trainpeople.co.uk Ltd [2017] I.C.R. 581; [2017] I.R.L.R. 318, EAT .... *Digested,* 17/**761**

Amlin UK Ltd v Geo-Rope Ltd [2016] CSOH 165; [2017] Lloyd's Rep. I.R. 277; 2017 Rep. L.R. 46; 2016 G.W.D. 39-689, OH .... *Digested,* 17/**2754**

Amministrazione delle Finanze dello Stato v San Giorgio SpA (199/82) EU:C:1983:318; [1983] E.C.R. 3595; [1985] 2 C.M.L.R. 658, ECJ .... *Digested,* 85/**1433**: *Applied* 95/5067, 96/2803, 00/2406, 09/3771, 10/3278, 15/2422, 17/2080, 17/2289: *Cited* 12/3430: *Considered* 10/3268, 10/3512, 15/2610, 17/2255: *Referred to* 15/2613

Amnesty International v Ahmed see Ahmed v Amnesty International

AMR (Adoption: Procedure), Re [1999] 2 F.L.R. 807; [1999] 3 F.C.R. 734; [1999] Fam. Law 684, Fam Div .... *Digested,* 00/**2436**: *Applied* 17/1034: *Considered* 00/2434

AMS Neve Ltd v Heritage Audio S.L. [2016] EWHC 2563 (IPEC); [2017] F.S.R. 16, IPEC .... *Digested,* 17/**1398**

AMT Futures Ltd v Marzillier, Dr Meier & Dr Guntner Rechtsanwaltsgesellschaft mbH; *sub nom* Marzillier, Dr Meier & Dr Guntner Rechtsanwaltsgesellschaft mbH v AMT Futures Ltd [2017] UKSC 13; [2017] 2 W.L.R. 853; [2017] 4 All E.R. 382; [2017] 2 All E.R. (Comm) 1041; [2017] 1 C.L.C. 178; [2017] I.L.Pr. 22, SC .... *Digested,* 17/**430**

AMT Futures Ltd v Marzillier, Dr Meier & Dr Guntner Rechtsanwaltsgesellschaft mbH; *sub nom* Marzillier, Dr Meier & Dr Guntner Rechtsanwaltsgesellschaft mbH v AMT Futures Ltd [2015] EWCA Civ 143; [2015] Q.B. 699; [2015] 3 W.L.R. 282; [2016] 1 All E.R. (Comm) 486; [2015] 1 C.L.C. 219; [2015] I.L.Pr. 20, CA (Civ Div) .... *Digested,* 15/**438**: *Affirmed* 17/430: *Applied* 16/2145: *Followed* 17/160

AmTrust Europe Ltd v Trust Risk Group SpA; *sub nom* Trust Risk Group SpA v AmTrust Europe Ltd [2015] EWCA Civ 437; [2016] 1 All E.R. (Comm) 325; [2015] 2 Lloyd's Rep. 154, CA (Civ Div) .... *Digested,* 15/**430**: *Followed* 17/493

AN v Lithuania (17280/08) (2017) 65 E.H.R.R. 23; [2017] M.H.L.R. 38, ECHR

AN (Sri Lanka) v Secretary of State for the Home Department [2008] UKAIT 63, AIT *Superseded* 17/1208

An NHS Trust v CS see CS (Termination of Pregnancy), Re

Anan Kasei Co Ltd v Molycorp Chemicals & Oxides (Europe) Ltd [2016] EWHC 1722 (Pat); [2016] Bus. L.R. 945; [2017] I.L.Pr. 8; [2017] F.S.R. 13, Ch D (Patents Ct) .... *Digested,* 16/**1306**: *Applied* 17/1377

Anangel Atlas Compania Naviera SA v Ishikawajima-Harima Heavy Industries Co (No.2) [1990] 2 Lloyd's Rep. 526, QBD (Comm) .... *Digested,* 91/**496**: *Applied* 17/461

Anchor Line (Henderson Bros) Ltd, Re; *sub nom* Companies Act 1929, Re [1937] Ch. 483; [1937] 2 All E.R. 823, Ch D *Considered* 47-51/1270, 17/2447

Anderson v Imrie [2016] CSOH 171; 2017 Rep. L.R. 21; 2017 G.W.D. 1-11, OH .... *Digested,* 17/**2737**

Anderson v Revenue and Customs Commissioners [2016] UKFTT 335 (TC); [2017] S.F.T.D. 100; [2016] S.T.I. 2319, FTT (Tax) .... *Digested,* 17/**2088**

Anderson (Craig) v HM Advocate [2017] HCJAC 33; 2017 J.C. 287; 2017 S.C.L. 621; 2017 G.W.D. 17-269, HCJ Appeal .... *Digested,* 17/**2499**

Anderson (James McAulay) v HM Advocate 1996 J.C. 29; 1996 S.L.T. 155, HCJ Appeal .... *Digested,* 96/**6764**: *Applied* 04/4679, 06/5173, 08/4663, 15/3114, 17/2532: *Cited* 09/4820: *Considered* 06/5192, 07/5078, 09/4815, 14/3459, 17/2438, 17/2538: *Distinguished* 00/6091, 08/4677: *Followed* 03/5379: *Referred to* 97/5804

Anderson Brown & Co v Morris 1987 S.L.T. (Sh. Ct.) 96; 1987 S.C.L.R. 187, Sh Pr ..... *Digested,* 87/**5078**: *Applied* 17/2413: *Followed* 90/5797, 96/7332

Anderson Owen Ltd (In Liquidation), Re; *sub nom* Merrygold v Bates [2009] EWHC 2837 (Ch); [2011] I.L.Pr. 11; [2010] B.P.I.R. 37, Ch D (Companies Ct) .... *Digested,* 10/**416**: *Considered* 17/1295

Anderson Strathern LLP v Scottish Legal Complaints Commission [2016] CSIH 71; 2017 S.C. 120; 2016 S.L.T. 967; 2016 G.W.D. 28-511, IH (2 Div) .... *Digested,* 16/**2715**: *Cited* 17/2711

Andrews v Bohm [2005] EWHC 3520 (Ch), Ch D *Considered* 17/1295

Aneco Reinsurance Underwriting Ltd v Johnson & Higgs Ltd see Aneco Reinsurance Underwriting Ltd (In Liquidation) v Johnson & Higgins Ltd

Aneco Reinsurance Underwriting Ltd (In Liquidation) v Johnson & Higgins Ltd; *sub nom* Aneco Reinsurance Underwriting Ltd v Johnson & Higgs Ltd [2001] UKHL 51; [2001] 2 All E.R. (Comm) 929; [2002] 1 Lloyd's Rep. 157; [2002] C.L.C. 181; [2002] Lloyd's Rep. I.R. 91; [2002] P.N.L.R. 8, HL .... *Digested,* 02/**3292**: *Applied* 06/2897, 10/238: *Considered* 08/2219, 17/641

Angel Group Ltd v British Gas Trading Ltd [2012] EWHC 2702 (Ch); [2013] B.C.C. 265, Ch D .... *Digested,* 13/**1718**: *Applied* 17/1337

Angiotech Pharmaceuticals Inc v Conor Medsystems Inc see Conor Medsystems Inc v Angiotech Pharmaceuticals Inc

Angiotech Pharmaceuticals Inc's Patent (No.706376) see Conor Medsystems Inc v Angiotech Pharmaceuticals Inc

Anglian Water Services Ltd v Laing O'Rourke Utilities Ltd [2010] EWHC 1529 (TCC); [2011] 1 All E.R. (Comm) 1143; 131 Con. L.R. 94; [2010] 3 E.G.L.R. 104; [2010] C.I.L.L. 2873, QBD (TCC) .... *Digested,* 10/**575**: *Considered* 17/162

Anglian Water Services Ltd v Revenue and Customs Commissioners [2017] UKFTT 386 (TC); [2017] S.T.I. 1179, FTT (Tax)

Anglo Financial SA v Goldberg [2014] EWHC 3192 (Ch), Ch D
Considered 17/300

Angove Pty Ltd v Bailey see D&D Wines International Ltd (In Liquidation), Re

Angus v Nisbet [2010] HCJAC 76; 2011 J.C. 69; 2011 S.L.T. 98; 2011 S.C.L. 33; 2010 S.C.C.R. 873; 2010 G.W.D. 27-532, HCJ .... *Digested,* 11/**4102**:
Considered 17/2494

Angus Growers Ltd v Scottish Ministers [2016] CSOH 26; 2016 S.L.T. 529; 2016 G.W.D. 6-125, OH .... *Digested,* 16/**2428**:
Considered 17/2773

Anheuser-Busch Inc v Budejovicky Budvar Narodni Podnik (Application for Revocation); *sub nom* BUD and BUDWEISER BUDBRAU Trade Marks; Budejovicky Budvar Narodni Podnik's Registered Trade Marks (Nos 807395 and 1070309) [2002] EWCA Civ 1534; [2003] R.P.C. 25, CA (Civ Div) .... *Digested,* 03/**2635**:
Applied 08/2395: *Considered* 17/1356

Anisminic Ltd v Foreign Compensation Commission [1969] 2 A.C. 147; [1969] 2 W.L.R. 163; [1969] 1 All E.R. 208; Times, December 18, 1968; (1968) 113 S.J. 55, HL .... *Digested,* 69/**1866**:
Applied 70/2778, 74/3742, 78/2324, 79/19, 80/163, 84/447, 93/2167, 96/4839, 00/5979, 01/81: *Considered* 70/2436, 73/3295, 82/289, 84/3483, 85/2217, 85/2791, 85/3415, 86/950, 88/2417, 90/4424, 94/1803, 96/2508, 02/658, 05/2163, 10/3926: *Distinguished* 76/19, 92/2740, 92/3464, 94/5367, 10/25: *Explained* 80/273: *Followed* 17/26: *Not applied* 93/63: *Referred to* 92/6511

Annon v Nursing and Midwifery Council [2017] EWHC 1879 (Admin); [2017] A.C.D. 107, QBD (Admin)

Anonymi Geniki Etairia Tsimenton Iraklis (AGET Iraklis) v Ypourgos Ergasias, Koinonikis Asfalisis kai Koinonikis Allilengyis (C-201/15) EU:C:2016:972; [2017] 2 C.M.L.R. 32; [2017] C.E.C. 1121; [2017] I.R.L.R. 282, ECJ (Grand Chamber)

Ansari v Aberdeen City Council [2017] CSIH 5; 2017 S.C. 274; 2017 S.L.T. 358; 2017 G.W.D. 4-57, IH (Ex Div) .... *Digested,* 17/**2746**

Ansari v Aberdeen City Council [2015] CSOH 168; 2016 S.L.T. 73; 2016 G.W.D. 1-24, OH .... *Digested,* 16/**2750**:
Affirmed 17/2746

Anson v Revenue and Customs Commissioners; *sub nom* Revenue and Customs Commissioners v Anson; Swift v Revenue and Customs Commissioners [2015] UKSC 44; [2015] 4 All E.R. 288; [2015] S.T.C. 1777; [2015] B.T.C. 21; 17 I.T.L. Rep. 1007; [2015] S.T.I. 2019, SC .... *Digested,* 15/**2462**:
Applied 16/2081: *Followed* 17/2130

Anticosti Shipping Co v Viateur St Amand [1959] 1 Lloyd's Rep. 352, Sup Ct (Can) ..... *Digested,* 59/**3031**:
Applied 79/2434, 17/2015

Antonelli v Secretary of State for Trade and Industry [1998] Q.B. 948; [1998] 2 W.L.R. 826; [1998] 1 All E.R. 997; (1998) 10 Admin. L.R. 75; [1998] 1 E.G.L.R. 9; [1998] 14 E.G. 133; Times, October 3, 1997; Independent, October 14, 1997; [1998] C.O.D. 178; (1997) 94(35) L.S.G. 35; (1997) 141 S.J.L.B. 198; [1997] N.P.C. 123, CA (Civ Div) .... *Digested,* 97/**82**:
Applied 06/2219, 07/1952, 17/719

Antonelli v Wade Gery Farr (A Firm) see Ridehalgh v Horsefield

Antonio Gramsci Shipping Corp v Lembergs see Antonio Gramsci Shipping Corp v Recoletos Ltd

Antonio Gramsci Shipping Corp v Recoletos Ltd; *sub nom* Antonio Gramsci Shipping Corp v Lembergs [2013] EWCA Civ 730; [2013] 4 All E.R. 157; [2013] 2 All E.R. (Comm) 781; [2014] Bus. L.R. 239; [2013] 2 Lloyd's Rep. 295; [2014] 1 B.C.L.C. 581; [2013] 2 C.L.C. 44; [2013] I.L.Pr. 36, CA (Civ Div) .... *Digested,* 13/**362**:
Considered 17/295

Anwar v National College for Teaching and Leadership; *joined case* Ahmed v National College for Teaching and Leadership [2016] EWHC 2507 (Admin); [2016] E.L.R. 459; [2016] A.C.D. 127, QBD (Admin) .... *Digested,* 17/**716**

Anyanwu v South Bank Student Union see Anyanwu v South Bank Students Union

Anyanwu v South Bank Students Union; *sub nom* Anyanwu v South Bank Student Union [2001] UKHL 14; [2001] 1 W.L.R. 638; [2001] 2 All E.R. 353; [2001] I.C.R. 391; [2001] I.R.L.R. 305; [2001] Emp. L.R. 420; [2001] E.L.R. 511; Times, March 27, 2001; Independent, March 28, 2001; (2001) 98(21) L.S.G. 39; (2001) 151 N.L.J. 501; (2001) 145 S.J.L.B. 110, HL .... *Digested,* 01/**2300**:
Applied 06/1363, 10/1109, 16/701: *Considered* 07/1428, 11/348: *Followed* 01/3492, 13/1053, 15/844, 17/821

Aon Trust Corp Ltd v KPMG [2005] EWCA Civ 1004; [2006] 1 W.L.R. 97; [2006] 1 All E.R. 238; [2006] I.C.R. 18; [2005] O.P.L.R. 189; [2005] Pens. L.R. 301; Times, September 7, 2005, CA (Civ Div) .... *Digested,* 05/**3042**:
Considered 08/2759, 17/1628: *Distinguished* 08/2748

AP v Duncan [2016] CSOH 111; 2017 S.C.L.R. 341; 2016 G.W.D. 26-480, OH .... *Digested,* 17/**2428**
AP v Tameside MBC [2017] EWHC 65 (QB); [2017] 1 W.L.R. 2127; (2017) 20 C.C.L. Rep. 5, QBD (Manchester) .... *Digested,* 17/**299**
AP v TD (Relocation: Retention of Jurisdiction) [2010] EWHC 2040 (Fam); [2011] 1 F.L.R. 1851; [2011] Fam. Law 16, Fam Div .... *Digested,* 11/**1448**: *Considered* 17/941
AP Racing Ltd v Alcon Components Ltd [2016] EWHC 116 (IPEC), IPEC *Considered* 17/1359
Apex Global Management Ltd v Fi Call Ltd see Prince Abdulaziz v Apex Global Management Ltd
Apex Global Management Ltd v Global Torch Ltd [2017] EWCA Civ 315; [2017] C.P. Rep. 28, CA (Civ Div) .... *Digested,* 17/**375**
Apollo Fuels Ltd v Revenue and Customs Commissioners; *sub nom* Revenue and Customs Commissioners v Apollo Fuels Ltd [2014] UKUT 95 (TCC); [2014] B.T.C. 510; [2014] S.T.I. 875, UT (Tax) .... *Digested,* 14/**2911**: *Affirmed in part* 16/2084: *Followed* 17/2133
Apollo Fuels Ltd v Revenue and Customs Commissioners; *sub nom* Revenue and Customs Commissioners v Apollo Fuels Ltd [2016] EWCA Civ 157; [2016] 4 W.L.R. 96; [2016] 4 All E.R. 464; [2016] S.T.C. 1594; [2016] R.T.R. 24; [2016] B.T.C. 12; Times, May 10, 2016; [2016] S.T.I. 1155, CA (Civ Div) .... *Digested,* 16/**2084**: *Considered* 17/2090: *Followed* 17/2133
Apostu v Romania (22765/12) (2017) 65 E.H.R.R. 8; 38 B.H.R.C. 485, ECHR
Appellant v Billing Authority [2017] R.V.R. 101, VT
Apple and Pear Development Council v Customs and Excise Commissioners; *sub nom* Customs and Excise Commissioners v Apple and Pear Development Council [1986] S.T.C. 192; [1987] 2 C.M.L.R. 634, HL .... *Digested,* 86/**3485**: *Applied* 90/4626, 90/4627, 03/4553, 07/4309, 17/2262: *Considered* 98/4922: *Preliminary ruling given* 88/1572
Apple Inc v Arcadia Trading Ltd [2017] EWHC 440 (Ch); [2017] E.C.C. 12; [2017] E.T.M.R. 28; [2017] F.S.R. 40, Ch D .... *Digested,* 17/**1405**
Apple Inc v Swatch AG [2017] EWHC 713 (Ch); [2017] E.C.C. 18; [2017] E.T.M.R. 29; [2017] F.S.R. 41, Ch D .... *Digested,* 17/**1388**
APPLE/Authenticating an accessory (T1321/11) [2017] E.P.O.R. 3, EPO (Technical Bd App)
Appleyard v Wewelwala [2012] EWHC 3302 (Ch); [2013] 1 W.L.R. 752; [2013] 1 All E.R. 1383; [2013] B.P.I.R. 15; (2012) 162 N.L.J. 1534, Ch D .... *Digested,* 13/**1714**: *Applied* 15/1410: *Considered* 16/1204, 17/1310
Approved Prescription Services Ltd v Licensing Authority (C36/03) EU:C:2004:781; [2004] E.C.R. I-11583, ECJ *Applied* 06/2466, 17/1137
AR v AS [2015] EWHC 3440 (Fam); [2016] 2 F.L.R. 1280; [2016] Fam. Law 173, Fam Div .... *Digested,* 17/**1035**
AR v RN see R, Petitioner
AR (Bail: Conditions: Variation: Article 9 ECHR); *sub nom* R. (on the application of AR) v Secretary of State for the Home Department [2016] UKUT 132 (IAC), UT (IAC) *Reversed* 17/41
AR (Pakistan) v Secretary of State for the Home Department see R. (on the application of AR (Pakistan)) v Secretary of State for the Home Department
AR (Sri Lanka) v Secretary of State for the Home Department see R. (on the application of MA (Pakistan)) v Upper Tribunal (Immigration and Asylum Chamber)
AR, Petitioner see R, Petitioner
ARA Foreclosure (Management of Packaging Waste Recycling in Austria), Re (COMP/At.39523) [2017] 4 C.M.L.R. 11, CEC
Arab Monetary Fund v Hashim (No.8) (1994) 6 Admin. L.R. 348; Times, May 4, 1993; Independent, April 30, 1993, CA (Civ Div) .... *Digested,* 95/**3938**: *Applied* 15/28: *Considered* 95/3112, 99/3796: *Followed* 17/5
Arada v Windle see Windle v Secretary of State for Justice
Aramis, The [1989] 1 Lloyd's Rep. 213; Financial Times, November 22, 1988, CA (Civ Div) .... *Digested,* 90/**4057**: *Applied* 06/1315, 07/1347, 11/1073, 17/507: *Followed* 14/1064
Aramis, The [1987] 2 Lloyd's Rep. 58, QBD (Admlty) .... *Digested,* 87/**3379**: *Applied* 17/2003: *Reversed* 90/4057
Arawak Homes Ltd v Attorney General of the Bahamas [2016] UKPC 34; [2016] 1 W.L.R. 5214; [2017] R.V.R. 193, PC (Bah)
Arbuthnot Pensions & Investments Ltd v Padden see Padden v Arbuthnot Pensions & Investments Ltd

Arcadia Group Ltd v Arcadia Group Pension Trust Ltd [2014] EWHC 2683 (Ch); [2014] B.T.C. 40; [2014] I.C.R. D35, Ch D .... *Digested,* 14/**2283**: *Considered* 17/1628

Arcadis Consulting (UK) Ltd (formerly Hyder Consulting (UK) Ltd) v AMEC (BCS) Ltd (formerly CV Buchan Ltd) [2016] EWHC 2509 (TCC); 169 Con. L.R. 41, QBD (TCC) .... *Digested,* 17/**469**

ArcelorMittal Rodange et Schifflange SA v Luxembourg (C-321/15) EU:C:2017:179; [2017] Env. L.R. 30, ECJ (5th Chamber)

Arch Initiatives v Greater Manchester West Mental Health NHS Foundation Trust [2016] I.C.R. 607; [2016] I.R.L.R. 406, EAT .... *Digested,* 16/**726**: *Applied* 17/843

Archer v Fabian Investments Ltd [2017] UKPC 9; [2017] B.C.C. 367, PC (Bah)

Ardagh Glass Ltd v Chester City Council; *sub nom* R. (on the application of Ardagh Glass Ltd) v Cheshire West and Chester Council [2009] EWHC 745 (Admin); [2009] Env. L.R. 34; [2009] N.P.C. 59, QBD (Admin)
Affirmed 10/2617: *Applied* 17/1784

Arena Corp Ltd (In Provisional Liquidation) v Schroeder; *sub nom* Arena Corp Ltd (In Provisional Liquidation) v Shroeder [2003] EWHC 1089 (Ch), Ch D
Applied 11/1298, 14/496: *Considered* 17/377

Arena Corp Ltd (In Provisional Liquidation) v Shroeder see Arena Corp Ltd (In Provisional Liquidation) v Schroeder

Argentina v NML Capital Ltd see NML Capital Ltd v Argentina

Argos Distributors Ltd v Customs and Excise Commissioners (C-288/94) EU:C:1996:398; [1997] Q.B. 499; [1997] 2 W.L.R. 477; [1996] S.T.C. 1359; [1996] E.C.R. I-5311; [1996] 3 C.M.L.R. 569; [1996] C.E.C. 963; [1997] B.V.C. 64; Times, November 18, 1996; Independent, November 25, 1996, ECJ (6th Chamber) .... *Digested,* 96/**5909**:
Applied 99/6472, 03/4580, 05/4417, 09/4044: *Cited* 16/2190: *Considered* 02/4775, 17/2258: *Distinguished* 00/5364, 01/5614: *Followed* 97/4980: *Referred to* 00/5317

Argos Ltd v Argos Systems Inc [2017] EWHC 231 (Ch); [2017] Bus. L.R. 958; [2017] E.T.M.R. 19; [2017] F.S.R. 26, Ch D .... *Digested,* 17/**1399**

Argyll and Bute Council v Gordon [2017] SAC (Civ) 6; 2017 S.L.T. (Sh Ct) 53; 2017 G.W.D. 6-87, SAC .... *Digested,* 17/**2834**

Argyll and Bute Council v Gordon 2016 S.L.T. (Sh Ct) 196; 2016 S.C.L.R. 192; 2016 G.W.D. 6-135, Sh Ct (Lothian) (Edinburgh) .... *Digested,* 16/**2825**: *Affirmed* 17/2834

Ariel v Revenue and Customs Commissioners see Revenue and Customs Commissioners v Ariel

Arjo Wiggins Ltd v Ralph [2009] EWHC 3198 (Ch); [2010] Pens. L.R. 11, Ch D .... *Digested,* 10/**2377**: *Applied* 17/1625

Arkin v Borchard Lines Ltd (Costs Order) [2005] EWCA Civ 655; [2005] 1 W.L.R. 3055; [2005] 3 All E.R. 613; [2005] 2 Lloyd's Rep. 187; [2005] C.P. Rep. 39; [2005] 4 Costs L.R. 643; Times, June 3, 2005; Independent, June 7, 2005; (2005) 155 N.L.J. 902, CA (Civ Div) .... *Digested,* 05/**385**:
Applied 07/405, 15/282, 17/253: *Considered* 07/421, 14/1835

Arlewin v Sweden (22302/10) 41 B.H.R.C. 571, ECHR

ARM Asset Backed Securities SA, Re [2013] EWHC 3351 (Ch); [2014] B.C.C. 252, Ch D (Companies Ct) .... *Digested,* 14/**1817**: *Applied* 17/1257

Armada Shipping SA, Re see Cosco Bulk Carrier Co Ltd v Armada Shipping SA

Armagas Ltd v Mundogas SA (The Ocean Frost) [1985] 3 W.L.R. 640; [1985] 3 All E.R. 795; [1985] 1 Lloyd's Rep. 1; (1984) 81 L.S.G. 2169; (1984) 129 S.J. 362, CA (Civ Div) .... *Digested,* 85/**27**:
Affirmed 86/37: *Applied* 99/456, 10/1931, 17/320: *Followed* 16/1610

Armani Da Silva v United Kingdom (5878/08) see Da Silva v United Kingdom (5878/08)

Armes v Godfrey Morgan Solicitors Ltd; *sub nom* Godfrey Morgan Solicitors v Armes [2017] EWCA Civ 323; [2018] 1 W.L.R. 936; [2017] C.P. Rep. 29; [2017] P.N.L.R. 30, CA (Civ Div) .... *Digested,* 17/**195**

Armes v Nottinghamshire CC see NA v Nottinghamshire CC

Armia Ltd v Daejan Developments Ltd 1979 S.C. (H.L.) 56; 1979 S.L.T. 147, HL .... *Digested,* 79/**3117**:
Applied 89/3854, 96/6570, 00/6467, 05/5470: *Followed* 91/5346, 93/5383, 17/2696

Armstrong v Glasgow City Council see HBJ Claimants v Glasgow City Council

Armstrong v Onyearu [2015] EWHC 1937 (Ch), Ch D
Affirmed 17/890

Armstrong v Onyearu [2017] EWCA Civ 268; [2018] Ch. 137; [2017] 3 W.L.R. 1304; [2017] B.P.I.R. 869; [2017] W.T.L.R. 415; Times, June 9, 2017; [2017] 2 P. & C.R. DG14, CA (Civ Div) .... *Digested,* 17/**890**

Armstrong Whitworth Securities Co Ltd, Re [1947] Ch. 673; [1947] 2 All E.R. 479; [1948] L.J.R. 172; (1947) 91 S.J. 544, Ch D .... *Digested,* 47-51/**1390**: *Applied* 69/2846: *Considered* 12/1788, 17/1258

Arnhold & Co Ltd v Attorney General of Hong Kong 47 B.L.R. 129; (1989) 5 Const. L.J. 263, HC (HK) .... *Digested,* 90/**648**: *Applied* 17/461: *Followed* 91/532

Arnold v Britton [2015] UKSC 36; [2015] A.C. 1619; [2015] 2 W.L.R. 1593; [2016] 1 All E.R. 1; [2015] H.L.R. 31; [2015] 2 P. & C.R. 14; [2015] L. & T.R. 25; [2015] C.I.L.L. 3689, SC .... *Digested,* 15/**1606**: *Applied* 15/1802, 16/137, 16/1764, 16/426, 17/2468, 17/498: *Cited* 17/2471: *Considered* 16/2704: *Followed* 16/413, 16/440, 17/1334, 17/1443, 17/1455, 17/1474, 17/2463, 17/474, 17/478, 17/493, 17/506

Arnold v National Westminster Bank Plc (No.1) [1991] 2 A.C. 93; [1991] 2 W.L.R. 1177; [1991] 3 All E.R. 41; (1991) 62 P. & C.R. 490; [1991] 2 E.G.L.R. 109; [1991] 30 E.G. 57; Times, April 26, 1991; [1991] E.G. 49 (C.S.); (1991) 135 S.J. 574, HL .... *Digested,* 91/**1736**: *Applied* 95/3781, 97/487, 00/3772, 03/1579, 06/2591, 07/3225, 08/2278, 09/431, 10/3536: *Considered* 96/2578, 97/3886, 97/766, 17/1856: *Distinguished* 98/2162, 17/1013: *Followed* 99/370, 12/1178, 13/266, 14/1393, 17/372: *Referred to* 94/2807

Arnold v Secretary of State for Communities and Local Government [2017] EWCA Civ 231; [2017] J.P.L. 923, CA (Civ Div) .... *Digested,* 17/**1710**

Arnold v Secretary of State for Communities and Local Government [2015] EWHC 1197 (Admin); [2015] J.P.L. 1053, QBD (Admin) .... *Digested,* 15/**1942**: *Affirmed* 17/1710

Arnold Clark Automobiles Ltd v Spoor [2017] I.R.L.R. 500, EAT .... *Digested,* 17/**844**

Arorangi Timberland Ltd v Minister of the Cook Islands National Superannuation Fund [2016] UKPC 32; [2017] 1 W.L.R. 99, PC (Cook I)

Arranz v Spain [2016] EWHC 3029 (Admin); [2017] A.C.D. 12, DC

Arrow Generics Ltd v Merck & Co Inc [2007] EWHC 1900 (Pat); [2008] Bus. L.R. 487; [2007] F.S.R. 39; (2007) 30(9) I.P.D. 30058, Ch D (Patents Ct) .... *Digested,* 08/**2334**: *Applied* 12/1265: *Approved* 17/1371

Arrow Shipping Co Ltd v Tyne Improvement Commissioners [1894] A.C. 508, HL *Followed* 17/2019

Arrowsmith v Nottingham Trent University [2011] EWCA Civ 797; [2012] I.C.R. 159, CA (Civ Div) .... *Digested,* 12/**1088**: *Applied* 13/336: *Considered* 15/827: *Followed* 17/795

Arroyo v BP Exploration Co (Colombia) Ltd; *sub nom* Ocensa Pipeline Group Litigation, Re [2010] EWHC 1643 (QB), QBD *Disapproved* 17/205

Arroyo v Equion Energia Ltd (formerly BP Exploration Co (Colombia) Ltd) [2016] EWHC 3348 (TCC); [2017] 1 Costs L.O. 31, QBD (TCC) .... *Digested,* 17/**241**

Arscott v Coal Authority [2004] EWCA Civ 892; [2005] Env. L.R. 6; (2004) 148 S.J.L.B. 880; [2004] N.P.C. 114, CA (Civ Div) .... *Digested,* 05/**2893**: *Applied* 09/2743: *Considered* 17/2297

Arshad v Secretary of State for the Home Department see Arshad (Tier 1 Applicants: Funding: Availability)

Arshad (Tier 1 Applicants: Funding: Availability); *sub nom* Arshad v Secretary of State for the Home Department [2016] UKUT 334 (IAC); [2016] Imm. A.R. 1381, UT (IAC) .... *Digested,* 17/**1236**

Arthur JS Hall & Co v Simons; *sub nom* Barratt v Ansell (t/a Woolf Seddon); Harris v Scholfield Roberts & Hall; *joined cases* Harris v Scholfield Roberts & Hill; Cockbone v Atkinson Dacre & Slack; Barratt v Woolf Seddon [2002] 1 A.C. 615; [2000] 3 W.L.R. 543; [2000] 3 All E.R. 673; [2000] B.L.R. 407; [2000] E.C.C. 487; [2000] 2 F.L.R. 545; [2000] 2 F.C.R. 673; [2001] P.N.L.R. 6; Times, July 21, 2000; Independent, July 25, 2000; [2000] Fam. Law 806; [2000] E.G. 99 (C.S.); (2000) 97(32) L.S.G. 38; (2000) 150 N.L.J. 1147; (2000) 144 S.J.L.B. 238; [2000] N.P.C. 87, HL .... *Digested,* 00/**4269**: *Applied* 03/509, 05/2869, 05/363, 09/2737: *Cited* 01/525, 07/2946: *Considered* 01/4515, 08/272, 09/3957, 10/250, 11/238, 12/538, 13/249: *Followed* 13/1020, 17/191

Arthur Williams & Co, Re; *sub nom* Official Receiver, Ex p. [1913] 2 K.B. 88, CA *Considered* 17/244

Artist Court Collective Ltd v Khan [2016] EWHC 2453 (Ch); [2017] Ch. 53; [2016] 3 W.L.R. 1619; [2017] 1 P. & C.R. 9; [2017] L. & T.R. 1, Ch D .... *Digested,* 17/**1462**

Artist Court Collective Ltd v Khan 3CL10528, CC (Central London) *Reversed* 17/1462

Arts & Antiques Ltd v Richards [2013] EWHC 3361 (Comm); [2014] Lloyd's Rep. I.R. 219; [2014] P.N.L.R. 10, QBD (Comm) .... *Digested,* 14/**1842**: *Approved* 17/191

AS v HM Advocate see S (A) v HM Advocate

AS v Switzerland (39350/13) (2017) 65 E.H.R.R. 12, ECHR

AS v TH (False Allegations of Abuse) see S v H (False Allegations of Abuse)

ASA International Ltd v Kashmiri Properties (Ireland) Ltd [2016] CSIH 70; 2017 S.C. 107; 2016 G.W.D. 27-493, IH (Ex Div) .... *Digested,* 17/**2655**

Asda Stores Ltd v Brierley [2016] EWCA Civ 566; [2017] 3 All E.R. 636; [2016] C.P. Rep. 38; [2016] I.C.R. 945; [2016] I.R.L.R. 709; Times, July 28, 2016, CA (Civ Div) .... *Digested,* 16/**685**

Asda Stores Ltd v Brierley [2018] I.C.R. 384; [2017] I.R.L.R. 1058, EAT

Asda Stores Ltd v Brierley see Farmah v Birmingham City Council

Asda Stores Ltd v Mastercard Inc [2017] EWHC 93 (Comm); [2017] U.K.C.L.R. 283; [2017] 4 C.M.L.R. 32, QBD (Comm) .... *Digested,* 17/**411**

Asghar v Bhatti [2017] EWHC 1702 (QB); [2017] 4 Costs L.O. 427, QBD .... *Digested,* 17/**274**

Ashfaq v International Insurance Co of Hannover Plc [2017] EWCA Civ 357; [2017] H.L.R. 29, CA (Civ Div) .... *Digested,* 17/**1340**

Ashif (Mohammed) v HM Advocate; *joined case* Ashraf (Aliah) v HM Advocate [2015] HCJAC 100; 2017 J.C. 7; 2016 S.L.T. 1079; 2016 S.C.L. 934; 2016 S.C.C.R. 437; 2016 G.W.D. 33-589, HCJ .... *Digested,* 17/**2496**

Ashington and Ellington Social Club and Institute Ltd v Revenue and Customs Commissioners [2017] S.T.I. 1902, FTT (Tax)

Ashley v Chief Constable of Sussex [2008] UKHL 25; [2008] 1 A.C. 962; [2008] 2 W.L.R. 975; [2008] 3 All E.R. 573; [2008] Po. L.R. 203; Times, April 24, 2008; (2008) 158 N.L.J. 632; (2008) 152(17) S.J.L.B. 29, HL .... *Digested,* 08/**3895**: *Applied* 17/21

Ashman (Setting of Minimum Term), Re see Jones (Setting of Minimum Term), Re

Ashori v Secretary of State for the Home Department see R. (on the application of Lumba) v Secretary of State for the Home Department

Ashraf (Aliah) v HM Advocate see Ashif (Mohammed) v HM Advocate

Ashton v Revenue and Customs Commissioners [2016] UKFTT 727 (TC); [2017] S.T.I. 215, FTT (Tax)

Ashurst v Pollard; *sub nom* Pollard v Ashurst [2001] Ch. 595; [2001] 2 W.L.R. 722; [2001] 2 All E.R. 75; [2001] B.P.I.R. 131; Times, November 29, 2000; (2001) 98(3) L.S.G. 42; (2000) 150 N.L.J. 1787, CA (Civ Div) .... *Digested,* 01/**3736**: *Applied* 05/619, 09/2214, 10/372: *Considered* 10/500, 12/563: *Not followed* 17/1849

Ashworth v MGN Ltd see Gulati v MGN Ltd

Ashworth v Newnote Ltd [2007] EWCA Civ 793; [2007] B.P.I.R. 1012, CA (Civ Div) ..... *Digested,* 07/**2453**: *Followed* 10/1897, 17/1326

Ashworth Hospital Authority v MGN Ltd; *sub nom* Ashworth Security Hospital v MGN Ltd [2002] UKHL 29; [2002] 1 W.L.R. 2033; [2002] 4 All E.R. 193; [2002] C.P.L.R. 712; [2002] E.M.L.R. 36; [2002] H.R.L.R. 41; [2002] U.K.H.R.R. 1263; 12 B.H.R.C. 443; [2003] F.S.R. 17; (2002) 67 B.M.L.R. 175; Times, July 1, 2002; Independent, July 3, 2002; (2002) 99(30) L.S.G. 37; (2002) 146 S.J.L.B. 168, HL .... *Digested,* 02/**3221**: *Applied* 06/990: *Considered* 05/2064, 08/408, 13/397, 14/383, 17/286: *Distinguished* 03/2922, 06/2096: *Followed* 07/486, 12/1921, 12/1922

Ashworth Security Hospital v MGN Ltd see Ashworth Hospital Authority v MGN Ltd

Ashworth Trading v Revenue and Customs Commissioners [2017] UKFTT 517 (TC); [2017] S.T.I. 1665, FTT (Tax)

Asif v Secretary of State for the Home Department 1999 S.L.T. 890; 1999 S.C.L.R. 427; 1999 G.W.D. 6-311, OH .... *Digested,* 99/**6291**: *Affirmed* 02/5878: *Approved* 00/6491: *Considered* 17/2825

Asklepios Dienstleistungsgesellschaft mbH v Graf (C□681/15) see Asklepios Kliniken Langen-Seligenstadt GmbH v Felja (C-680/15)

Asklepios Kliniken Langen-Seligenstadt GmbH v Felja (C-680/15); *joined case* Asklepios Dienstleistungsgesellschaft mbH v Graf (C□681/15) EU:C:2017:317; [2017] I.R.L.R. 653, ECJ (3rd Chamber)

Aslam v Uber BV [2017] I.R.L.R. 4, ET .... *Digested,* 17/**791**

Aspect Capital Ltd v Revenue and Customs Commissioners [2014] UKUT 81 (TCC); [2014] S.T.C. 1360; [2014] B.T.C. 508; [2014] S.T.I. 873, UT (Tax) .... *Digested,* 14/**2873**: *Applied* 17/2279

Aspect Contracts (Asbestos) Ltd v Higgins Construction Plc; *sub nom* Higgins Construction Plc v Aspect Contracts (Asbestos) Ltd [2015] UKSC 38; [2015] 1 W.L.R. 2961; [2015] 4 All E.R. 482; [2015] 2 All E.R. (Comm) 965; [2015] Bus. L.R. 830; [2015] 2 C.L.C. 203; [2015] B.L.R. 503; 160 Con. L.R. 28; Times, June 22, 2015; [2015] C.I.L.L. 3696, SC .... *Digested,* 15/**469**:
Considered 17/329: *Followed* 17/379

Aspen Insurance UK Ltd v Pectel Ltd [2008] EWHC 2804 (Comm); [2009] 2 All E.R. (Comm) 873; [2009] Lloyd's Rep. I.R. 440, QBD (Comm) .... *Digested,* 09/**2286**:
Applied 17/1338: *Distinguished* 15/524

Aspen Underwriting Ltd v Kairos Shipping Ltd [2017] EWHC 1904 (Comm); [2018] 1 All E.R. (Comm) 228; [2017] 2 Lloyd's Rep. 295; [2017] Lloyd's Rep. I.R. 635, QBD (Comm) .... *Digested,* 17/**429**

Aspinall (Deceased), Re; *sub nom* Cronin v de Hamel [2017] EWHC 454 (Ch); [2017] W.T.L.R. 447, Ch D (Manchester) .... *Digested,* 17/**2075**

Asprey & Garrard Ltd v WRA (Guns) Ltd (t/a William R Asprey Esquire) [2001] EWCA Civ 1499; [2002] E.T.M.R. 47; [2002] F.S.R. 31; (2002) 25(1) I.P.D. 25001, CA (Civ Div) .... *Digested,* 02/**2785**:
Applied 09/2452, 16/2083: *Considered* 02/2907: *Explained* 10/1996: *Followed* 17/1394

Assange v Sweden; *sub nom* Assange v Swedish Prosecution Authority [2011] EWHC 2849 (Admin); (2011) 108(44) L.S.G. 17, DC
Affirmed 12/1284: *Applied* 13/606, 14/1227, 15/963: *Considered* 13/1179, 13/667, 17/2597

Assange v Swedish Prosecution Authority see Assange v Sweden

Assens Havn v Navigators Management (UK) Ltd (C-368/16) EU:C:2017:546; [2018] Q.B. 463; [2018] 2 W.L.R. 250; [2018] C.E.C. 104; [2017] I.L.Pr. 30; [2018] Lloyd's Rep. I.R. 10, ECJ (8th Chamber)

Assessor for Glasgow v Schuh Ltd [2012] CSIH 40; 2012 S.L.T. 904; [2012] R.A. 245; 2012 G.W.D. 17-355, LVAC .... *Digested,* 12/**4244**:
Applied 17/2726: *Cited* 14/3676

Assethold Ltd v 110 Boulevard RTM Co Ltd [2017] UKUT 316 (LC); [2017] 4 W.L.R. 181; [2018] H.L.R. 14; [2018] L. & T.R. 1, UT (Lands)

Assethold Ltd v 369 Upland Road RTM Co Ltd see Elim Court RTM Co Ltd v Avon Freeholds Ltd

Associated British Ports v Tata Steel UK Ltd [2017] EWHC 694 (Ch); [2018] 1 All E.R. (Comm) 170; [2017] 2 Lloyd's Rep. 11; 172 Con. L.R. 174, Ch D .... *Digested,* 17/**74**

Associated Newspapers Ltd v Dingle; *sub nom* Dingle v Associated Newspapers Ltd [1964] A.C. 371; [1962] 3 W.L.R. 229; [1962] 2 All E.R. 737; (1962) 106 S.J. 488, HL .... *Digested,* 62/**1741**:
Applied 71/6775, 97/2033, 08/899, 08/900: *Considered* 66/7003, 13/794: *Followed* 17/645

Associated Newspapers Ltd v HRH Prince of Wales see HRH Prince of Wales v Associated Newspapers Ltd

Associated Newspapers Ltd v Murray see Murray v Associated Newspapers Ltd

Associated Newspapers Ltd v Revenue and Customs Commissioners; *sub nom* Revenue and Customs Commissioners v Associated Newspapers Ltd [2015] UKUT 641 (TCC); [2016] S.T.C. 1143; [2015] B.V.C. 538; [2016] S.T.I. 66, UT (Tax) .... *Digested,* 16/**2184**:
Affirmed 17/2272: *Applied* 17/2241

Associated Newspapers Ltd v Revenue and Customs Commissioners; *sub nom* Revenue and Customs Commissioners v Associated Newspapers Ltd [2017] EWCA Civ 54; [2017] S.T.C. 843; [2017] B.V.C. 10, CA (Civ Div) .... *Digested,* 17/**2272**

Association Francaise des Entreprises Privees (AFEP) v Ministre des Finances et des Comptes Publics (C-365/16) EU:C:2017:378; [2017] B.T.C. 13, ECJ (1st Chamber)

Assoun v Assoun [2017] EWCA Civ 370; [2017] 2 F.C.R. 538, CA (Civ Div) .... *Digested,* 17/**1062**

Assoun v Assoun [2017] EWCA Civ 21; [2017] 2 F.L.R. 1137; [2017] 2 F.C.R. 519, CA (Civ Div) .... *Digested,* 17/**1010**

Assoun v Assoun [2017] EWCA Civ 179; [2017] 2 F.L.R. 1149; [2017] 2 F.C.R. 533, CA (Civ Div) .... *Digested,* 17/**1011**

Aster Communities Ltd (formerly Flourish Homes Ltd) v Akerman-Livingstone see Akerman-Livingstone v Aster Communities Ltd (formerly Flourish Homes Ltd)

Astex Therapeutics Ltd v Astrazeneca AB [2016] EWHC 2759 (Ch), Ch D
Applied 17/186

Astlaslos v Hungary see Asztaslos v Hungary

Aston v Burgundy (Unreported, November 4, 2016), CC (Walsall) [*Irwin Mitchell LLP, Riverside West, 1 Millsands, Sheffield*] .... *Digested,* 17/**1687**

Astor Management AG v Atalaya Mining Plc [2017] EWHC 425 (Comm); [2018] 1 All E.R. (Comm) 547; [2017] Bus. L.R. 1634; [2017] 1 Lloyd's Rep. 476; [2017] 2 B.C.L.C. 119, QBD (Comm) .... *Digested,* 17/**503**

Astral Construction Ltd v Revenue and Customs Commissioners; *sub nom* Revenue and Customs Commissioners v Astral Construction Ltd [2015] UKUT 21 (TCC); [2015] S.T.C. 1033; [2015] B.V.C. 505; [2015] S.T.I. 252, UT (Tax) .... *Digested,* 15/**2629**: *Not applied* 17/2292

AstraZeneca AB v KRKA dd Novo Mesto [2015] EWCA Civ 484; (2015) 145 B.M.L.R. 188, CA (Civ Div) .... *Digested,* 15/**1510**: *Considered* 17/302

Asztaslos v Hungary; *sub nom* Astlaslos v Hungary [2010] EWHC 237 (Admin); [2011] 1 W.L.R. 252; [2011] 1 All E.R. 1027, DC .... *Digested,* 11/**1272**: *Distinguished* 17/908

Atkinson v Bank of Scotland Plc see Teasdale v HSBC Bank Plc

Atlanska Plovidba v Consignaciones Asturianas SA (The Lapad) [2004] EWHC 1273 (Admlty); [2004] 2 Lloyd's Rep. 109; [2004] 2 C.L.C. 886, QBD (Admlty) .... *Digested,* 04/**193**: *Applied* 13/104, 17/64: *Considered* 08/151, 11/133, 11/134

Atlantic Computer Systems Plc, Re [1992] Ch. 505; [1992] 2 W.L.R. 367; [1992] 1 All E.R. 476; [1990] B.C.C. 859; [1991] B.C.L.C. 606; Financial Times, August 1, 1990, CA (Civ Div) .... *Digested,* 91/**2127**: *Applied* 93/2325, 93/4812, 03/644, 05/2258, 08/2121, 09/2191, 09/2316, 11/1827, 13/287, 17/1272: *Considered* 95/566, 99/3349, 00/3432, 00/3433, 01/507, 01/733, 06/2318, 10/2051, 11/1818, 17/453: *Distinguished* 96/400: *Followed* 93/2315, 94/2591, 99/3267, 99/3358, 13/1882, 16/1369: *Referred to* 90/514

Atlantic Electronics Ltd v Revenue and Customs Commissioners; *sub nom* Revenue and Customs Commissioners v Atlantic Electronics Ltd [2012] UKUT 45 (TCC); [2012] S.T.C. 931; [2012] B.V.C. 1577; (2012) 109(33) L.S.G. 20, UT (Tax) .... *Digested,* 12/**3425**: *Applied* 13/3074, 13/3200: *Considered* 13/3198, 17/2269

Atlantisrealm Ltd v Intelligent Land Investments (Renewable Energy) Ltd [2017] EWCA Civ 1029; [2018] 4 W.L.R. 6; [2017] C.P. Rep. 39; [2017] B.L.R. 489; [2017] C.I.L.L. 4009, CA (Civ Div) .... *Digested,* 17/**183**

Atlasnavios Navegacao Lda (formerly Bnavios Navegacao Lda) v Navigators Insurance Co Ltd [2016] EWCA Civ 808; [2017] 1 W.L.R. 1303; [2017] 1 All E.R. (Comm) 401; [2016] 2 Lloyd's Rep. 351; [2016] 2 C.L.C. 349; [2016] Lloyd's Rep. I.R. 565, CA (Civ Div) .... *Digested,* 16/**1279**

Atrium Gestion (Societe) v X [2017] E.C.C. 23, Cass (F)

Attorney General v Blake [2001] 1 A.C. 268; [2000] 3 W.L.R. 625; [2000] 4 All E.R. 385; [2000] 2 All E.R. (Comm) 487; [2001] I.R.L.R. 36; [2001] Emp. L.R. 329; [2000] E.M.L.R. 949; Times, August 3, 2000; Independent, November 6, 2000; (2000) 23(12) I.P.D. 23098; (2000) 97(32) L.S.G. 37; (2000) 150 N.L.J. 1230; (2000) 144 S.J.L.B. 242, HL .... *Digested,* 00/**797**: *Applied* 06/1018, 08/2669, 12/858, 14/2991, 15/800: *Complaint upheld* 07/2224: *Considered* 03/717, 04/912, 05/956, 07/1054, 09/3956, 16/564: *Followed* 16/1315, 17/2196

Attorney General v Dallas [2012] EWHC 156 (Admin); [2012] 1 W.L.R. 991; [2012] 1 Cr. App. R. 32; Times, February 13, 2012; [2012] Crim. L.R. 694; [2012] A.C.D. 21; (2012) 109(6) L.S.G. 23, DC .... *Digested,* 12/**8**: *Applied* 14/14: *Complaint dismissed* 17/1166: *Considered* 16/19

Attorney General v Growfar see Attorney General v Times Newspapers Ltd

Attorney General v Guardian Newspapers Ltd (No.2) see Attorney General v Observer Ltd

Attorney General v Knowles [2017] UKPC 5; [2017] Lloyd's Rep. F.C. 225, PC (Bah)

Attorney General v Newspaper Publishing Plc; *sub nom* R. v Blackledge (William Stuart) [1997] 1 W.L.R. 926; [1997] 3 All E.R. 159; [1997] E.M.L.R. 429; Times, May 2, 1997; Independent, April 29, 1997; (1997) 147 N.L.J. 757, CA (Crim Div) .... *Digested,* 97/**19**: *Followed* 17/8

Attorney General v Newspaper Publishing Plc see Attorney General v Times Newspapers Ltd

Attorney General v Nissan; *sub nom* Nissan v Attorney General [1970] A.C. 179; [1969] 2 W.L.R. 926; [1969] 1 All E.R. 629; (1969) 113 S.J. 207, HL .... *Digested,* 69/**111**: *Considered* 17/1425

Attorney General v Observer and Guardian Newspapers see Attorney General v Times Newspapers Ltd

Attorney General v Observer Ltd; *joined cases* Attorney General v Guardian Newspapers Ltd (No.2); Attorney General v Times Newspapers Ltd (No.2) [1990] 1 A.C. 109; [1988] 3 W.L.R. 776; [1988] 3 All E.R. 545; [1989] 2 F.S.R. 181; Times, October 14, 1988; Independent, October 14, 1988; (1988) 85(42) L.S.G. 45; (1988) 138 N.L.J. Rep. 296; (1988) 132 S.J. 1496, HL .... *Digested,* 89/**3103**:
Applied 89/4740, 90/3099, 92/2791, 02/1610, 06/2853, 17/2195, 17/333:
Considered 92/3474, 94/3552, 96/1219, 99/5990, 01/1057, 02/3224, 08/60:
Followed 97/2040, 10/1937, 10/408, 11/2200, 11/369

Attorney General v Sunday Telegraph see Attorney General v Times Newspapers Ltd

Attorney General v Times Newspapers Ltd; *sub nom* Attorney General v Observer and Guardian Newspapers; *joined cases* Attorney General v Sunday Telegraph; Attorney General v Growfar; Attorney General v Newspaper Publishing Plc [1992] 1 A.C. 191; [1991] 2 W.L.R. 994; [1991] 2 All E.R. 398; Times, April 12, 1991; Independent, April 23, 1991; Guardian, April 12, 1991; (1991) 141 N.L.J. 528; (1991) 135 S.J.L.B. 508, HL .... *Digested,* 91/**2809**:
Applied 02/444, 03/773, 14/14: *Cited* 91/777: *Considered* 96/27, 01/18, 06/2880, 11/862, 12/469, 15/1719: *Followed* 17/8

Attorney General v Times Newspapers Ltd (No.2) see Attorney General v Observer Ltd

Attorney General ex rel Sutcliffe v Calderdale MBC (1983) 46 P. & C.R. 399; [1983] J.P.L. 310, CA (Civ Div) .... *Digested,* 84/**3451**:
Applied 85/2927, 17/1737: *Considered* 86/2814, 00/4473, 02/3694, 08/2908:
Distinguished 87/3195

Attorney General of Hong Kong v Ng Yuen Shiu [1983] 2 A.C. 629; [1983] 2 W.L.R. 735; [1983] 2 All E.R. 346; (1983) 127 S.J. 188, PC (HK) .... *Digested,* 83/**44**:
Applied 85/1702: *Considered* 83/3031, 87/3736, 91/79, 94/2466, 94/8, 95/3252, 06/2224, 13/2016, 17/1108

Attorney General of Nigeria v Abacha see Compagnie Noga d'Importation et d'Exportation SA v Abacha (No.3)

Attorney General of Trinidad and Tobago v Dumas [2017] UKPC 12; [2017] 1 W.L.R. 1978, PC (Trin)

Attorney General's Reference (No.1 of 2003); *sub nom* R. v W [2003] EWCA Crim 1286; [2003] 2 Cr. App. R. 29, CA (Crim Div) .... *Digested,* 04/**692**:
Applied 17/514: *Considered* 15/536

Attorney General's Reference (No.2 of 1999) [2000] Q.B. 796; [2000] 3 W.L.R. 195; [2000] 3 All E.R. 182; [2001] B.C.C. 210; [2000] 2 B.C.L.C. 257; [2000] 2 Cr. App. R. 207; [2000] I.R.L.R. 417; Times, February 29, 2000; [2000] Crim. L.R. 475; (2000) 97(9) L.S.G. 39, CA (Crim Div) .... *Digested,* 00/**980**:
Applied 17/553

Attorney General's Reference (No.2 of 2002) [2002] EWCA Crim 2373; [2003] 1 Cr. App. R. 21; Times, October 17, 2002; [2003] Crim. L.R. 192, CA (Crim Div) ...... *Digested,* 02/**748**:
Applied 17/2559: *Considered* 03/760

Attorney General's Reference (No.3 of 1989), Re see Attorney General's Reference (Nos 3 and 5 of 1989)

Attorney General's Reference (No.3 of 2003) [2004] EWCA Crim 868; [2005] Q.B. 73; [2004] 3 W.L.R. 451; [2005] 4 All E.R. 303; [2004] 2 Cr. App. R. 23; Times, April 22, 2004, CA (Crim Div) .... *Digested,* 04/**753**:
Considered 11/669, 11/767, 13/649: *Followed* 17/522

Attorney General's Reference (No.5 of 1989), Re see Attorney General's Reference (Nos 3 and 5 of 1989)

Attorney General's Reference (No.5 of 2011); *sub nom* R. v Troninas (Paulias) [2011] EWCA Crim 1244; [2012] 1 Cr. App. R. (S.) 20; Times, May 18, 2011; [2011] Crim. L.R. 730, CA (Crim Div) .... *Digested,* 11/**2892**:
Followed 17/1895

Attorney General's Reference (No.27 of 2013); *sub nom* R. v Burinskas (Gintas); *joined cases* R. v P (Anthony); R. v Ahmad (Goran Kamal); R. v Hanson (John); R. v Donegan (David); R. v Smith (Paul Simon); R. v Mathews (Michael Richard); R. v C [2014] EWCA Crim 334; [2014] 1 W.L.R. 4209; [2015] 1 All E.R. 93; [2014] 2 Cr. App. R. (S.) 45, CA (Crim Div) .... *Digested,* 14/**2613**:
Applied 15/2185, 17/1897: *Considered* 15/2196: *Followed* 17/1928

Attorney General's Reference (No.29 of 2014) [2014] EWCA Crim 1314, CA (Crim Div)
Applied 17/1942

Attorney General's Reference (No.34 of 2014); *sub nom* R. v Jenkin (John) [2014] EWCA Crim 1394; [2014] 2 Cr. App. R. (S.) 84; [2015] M.H.L.R. 442, CA (Crim Div) .... *Digested,* 15/**2239**:
Applied 16/1897: *Considered* 17/545

Attorney General's Reference (No.54 of 2011) [2011] EWCA Crim 2276; [2012] 1 Cr. App. R. (S.) 106; [2012] M.H.L.R. 87; [2012] Crim. L.R. 144, CA (Crim Div) .... *Digested,* 12/**2946**: *Applied* 14/2649, 15/2234: *Followed* 17/1906

Attorney General's Reference (No.58 of 2007); *sub nom* R. v S [2007] EWCA Crim 2057; [2008] 1 Cr. App. R. (S.) 71, CA (Crim Div) .... *Digested,* 08/**3416**: *Considered* 17/1886

Attorney General's Reference (No.68 of 2008); *sub nom* R. v Myrie (Owen Anthony) [2008] EWCA Crim 3188; [2009] 2 Cr. App. R. (S.) 48, CA (Crim Div) .... *Digested,* 09/**3337**: *Considered* 10/2837, 12/2836, 14/2590, 16/1849, 17/1886

Attorney General's Reference (No.68 of 2009); *sub nom* R. v Turner (Mark Simon) [2009] EWCA Crim 2219; [2010] 1 Cr. App. R. (S.) 108; Times, November 10, 2009, CA (Crim Div) .... *Digested,* 10/**2903**: *Considered* 11/2946, 12/2952, 17/1946

Attorney General's Reference (No.69 of 2013); *sub nom* R. v Newell (Lee William); R. v McLoughlin (Ian) [2014] EWCA Crim 188; [2014] 1 W.L.R. 3964; [2014] 3 All E.R. 73; [2014] 2 Cr. App. R. (S.) 40; [2014] H.R.L.R. 7; Times, February 24, 2014; [2014] Crim. L.R. 471; (2014) 158(8) S.J.L.B. 37, CA (Crim Div) .... *Digested,* 14/**2701**: *Applied* 15/1296, 17/1938

Attorney General's Reference (No.75 of 2007); *sub nom* R. v C (Peter Charles) [2007] EWCA Crim 2266, CA (Crim Div)
Considered 17/1982

Attorney General's Reference (No.103 of 2015); *sub nom* R. v S [2016] EWCA Crim 129; [2016] 2 Cr. App. R. (S.) 31; [2016] Crim. L.R. 941, CA (Crim Div) .... *Digested,* 17/**1942**

Attorney General's Reference (No.105 of 2014); *sub nom* R. v Harrak (Musa) [2014] EWCA Crim 2751; [2015] 1 Cr. App. R. (S.) 45, CA (Crim Div) .... *Digested,* 15/**2186**: *Applied* 17/1896

Attorney General's Reference (No.126 of 2006); *sub nom* R. v H [2007] EWCA Crim 53; [2007] 1 All E.R. 1254; [2007] 2 Cr. App. R. (S.) 59; [2007] M.H.L.R. 64; Times, February 13, 2007; [2007] Crim. L.R. 399; (2007) 151 S.J.L.B. 200, CA (Crim Div) .... *Digested,* 07/**3787**: *Considered* 17/1952

Attorney General's Reference (No.323 of 2016) see R. v Abdallah (Abdalraouf)

Attorney General's Reference (Nos 3 and 5 of 1989); *sub nom* Attorney General's Reference (No.5 of 1989), Re; Attorney General's Reference (No.3 of 1989), Re; R. v Hill-Trevor (Mark Charles); R. v Sumner (Peter Anthony) (1990) 90 Cr. App. R. 358; (1989) 11 Cr. App. R. (S.) 489; (1989) 11 Cr. App. R. (S.) 486; [1989] R.T.R. 337; Times, October 18, 1989; Independent, November 10, 1989; [1990] Crim. L.R. 277, CA (Crim Div) .... *Digested,* 90/**1226**: *Cited* 93/1048, 93/1127, 93/1331: *Considered* 92/1428, 93/1050, 96/2094: *Followed* 17/1899

Attorney General's Reference (Nos 3, 73 and 75 of 2010); *sub nom* R. v Anigbugu (Michael); R. v Pyo (Hyung-Woo); R. v McGee (Mark Stuart) [2011] EWCA Crim 633; [2011] 2 Cr. App. R. (S.) 100; Times, March 28, 2011; [2011] Crim. L.R. 580, CA (Crim Div) .... *Digested,* 11/**3046**: *Applied* 13/2770: *Considered* 13/2629, 13/2772, 13/2774: *Explained* 14/2622: *Followed* 17/1895

Attorney General's Reference (Nos 60, 62 and 63 of 2009); *joined cases* R. v Cowles (Tom Andew); R. v Cowles (Ben Kevin); R. v Roberts (Peter Jason); R. v Bryan (Thomas); R. v Appleby (Declan Paul) [2009] EWCA Crim 2693; [2010] 2 Cr. App. R. (S.) 46; Times, December 24, 2009; [2010] Crim. L.R. 325, CA (Crim Div) .... *Digested,* 10/**2899**: *Applied* 11/2933, 11/2937, 11/582, 12/2949, 13/2686, 15/2240, 17/1939, 17/1942, 17/1944: *Considered* 10/2901, 11/2932, 11/2940, 11/2942, 11/2944, 12/2941, 12/2945, 12/2948, 13/2681, 13/2687, 13/2688, 15/2242, 17/1943

Attorney General's Reference (Nos 128 to 141 of 2015 and 8 to 10 of 2016); *sub nom* R. v Stephenson (Nosakhere); R. v Nazran (Sundish Singh); R. v McDermott (Louis Junior); R. v Wiggan (Theodore Junior); R. v Gul (Rowan); R. v Ducram (Fitzroy); R. v Mattu (Joga Singh); R. v Miah (Mohammed Selu); R. v Ghalib (Amar); R. v Abdin (Joynal); R. v Hussain (Ifran); R. v Hussain (Usman); R. v Fedar (Mohammed); R. v Mohammed (Janed); R. v Officer (Clinton); R. v Smith (Jamal Shaka); R. v Mentore (Darren) [2016] EWCA Crim 54; [2016] 4 W.L.R. 83; [2016] 2 Cr. App. R. (S.) 12, CA (Crim Div) .... *Digested,* 16/**1886**: *Considered* 17/2802

Austen v Crown Prosecution Service [2016] EWHC 2247 (Admin); (2017) 181 J.P. 181; [2017] A.C.D. 3, DC .... *Digested,* 17/**556**

Austin v United Kingdom (39692/09); *joined cases* Black v United Kingdom (40713/09); Lowenthal v United Kingdom (41008/09) (2012) 55 E.H.R.R. 14; 32 B.H.R.C. 618; Times, March 26, 2012; [2012] Crim. L.R. 544, ECHR .... *Digested,* 12/**1667**: *Applied* 17/19: *Considered* 13/2386: *Followed* 12/2663
Austria v Germany (C-648/15) EU:C:2017:664; 20 I.T.L. Rep. 385, ECJ (Grand Chamber)
Austria Asphalt GmbH & Co OG v Bundeskartellanwalt (C-248/16) EU:C:2017:643; [2018] Bus. L.R. 462; [2017] B.C.C. 745; [2017] 5 C.M.L.R. 21, ECJ (5th Chamber)
Authentik Language Learning Resources Ltd (In Liquidation) v Revenue and Customs Commissioners [2016] UKFTT 826 (TC); [2017] S.T.I. 170, FTT (Tax)
Autobrokers Ltd v Dymond [2015] EWHC 2691 (Admin); [2017] B.C.C. 291, DR (Birmingham)
Automatic Bottle Makers Ltd, Re; *sub nom* Osborne v Automatic Bottle Makers Ltd [1926] Ch. 412, CA *Considered* 17/159
Autoridad del Canal de Panama v Sacyr SA [2017] EWHC 2228 (Comm); [2017] 2 Lloyd's Rep. 351, QBD (Comm) .... *Digested,* 17/**456**
Autortiesibu un Komunicesanas Konsultaciju Agentura/Latvijas Autoru Apvieniba v Konkurences Padome (C-177/16) EU:C:2017:689; [2018] Bus. L.R. 703; [2017] 5 C.M.L.R. 19; [2018] E.C.D.R. 11, ECJ (2nd Chamber)
Auzins v Latvia; *sub nom* Auzins v Prosecutor General's Office [2017] EWHC 48 (Admin); [2017] 1 W.L.R. 2981; [2017] A.C.D. 33, DC .... *Digested,* 17/**902**
Auzins v Latvia [2016] EWHC 802 (Admin); [2016] 4 W.L.R. 75; [2017] 3 All E.R. 481, DC .... *Digested,* 16/**793**
Auzins v Prosecutor General's Office see Auzins v Latvia
AV v AJF [2017] CSOH 103; 2017 Fam. L.R. 110; 2017 G.W.D. 24-408, OH .... *Digested,* 17/**2599**
Aviemore Highland Resort Ltd v Cairngorms National Park Authority 2009 S.L.T. (Sh Ct) 97; 2009 G.W.D. 24-388, Sh Ct (Grampian) (Inverness) .... *Digested,* 09/**4984**: *Distinguished* 17/2643
Aviva Insurance Ltd v Randive [2016] EWHC 3152 (QB); [2017] R.T.R. 16, QBD .... *Digested,* 17/**7**
Avon Freeholds Ltd v Garnier [2016] UKUT 477 (LC); [2017] L. & T.R. 2, UT (Lands) .. *Digested,* 17/**1429**
Avonwick Holdings Ltd v Shlosberg see Shlosberg v Avonwick Holdings Ltd
Avotins v Latvia (17502/07) (2017) 64 E.H.R.R. 2, ECHR
Avrahami v Biran [2013] EWHC 1776 (Ch), Ch D *Applied* 17/1298
Aw-Aden v Birmingham City Council [2005] EWCA Civ 1834, CA (Civ Div) *Considered* 17/1159
AWB (Geneva) SA v North America Steamships Ltd [2007] EWCA Civ 739; [2007] 2 Lloyd's Rep. 315; [2007] 2 C.L.C. 117; [2007] B.P.I.R. 1023; (2007) 104(31) L.S.G. 27, CA (Civ Div) .... *Digested,* 07/**530**: *Applied* 16/165, 17/432
AWG Group Ltd v HCP II Properties 101 GP Ltd [2017] CSOH 69; 2017 Hous. L.R. 30; 2017 G.W.D. 15-245, OH .... *Digested,* 17/**2696**
Awuah v Secretary of State for the Home Department; *sub nom* Awuah (Wasted Costs Order: HOPOs: Tribunal Powers), Re [2017] UKFTT 555 (IAC); [2017] 4 Costs L.R. 615; [2017] I.N.L.R. 858; [2018] P.N.L.R. 7, FTT (IAC) .... *Digested,* 17/**1219**
Awuah (Wasted Costs Order: HOPOs: Tribunal Powers), Re see Awuah v Secretary of State for the Home Department
Awuku v Secretary of State for the Home Department [2017] EWCA Civ 178; [2017] Imm. A.R. 1066; [2017] I.N.L.R. 487, CA (Civ Div) .... *Digested,* 17/**1247**
AX v Federal Tax Administration 19 I.T.L. Rep. 1, BG (Swi)
AXA Seguros SA De CV v Allianz Insurance Plc (t/a Allianz Global Risks) [2011] EWHC 268 (Comm); [2011] Lloyd's Rep. I.R. 544, QBD (Comm) .... *Digested,* 11/**1930**: *Applied* 17/530
Axa Versicherung AG v Arab Insurance Group (BSC) [2017] EWCA Civ 96; [2017] 1 All E.R. (Comm) 929; [2017] Lloyd's Rep. I.R. 216, CA (Civ Div) .... *Digested,* 17/**1354**
Axa Versicherung AG v Arab Insurance Group (BSC) [2015] EWHC 1939 (Comm); [2016] Lloyd's Rep. I.R. 1, QBD (Comm) .... *Digested,* 16/**1276**: *Affirmed* 17/1354
Axel Springer AG v Germany (39954/08) [2012] E.M.L.R. 15; (2012) 55 E.H.R.R. 6; 32 B.H.R.C. 493, ECHR (Grand Chamber) *Applied* 16/285, 17/698: *Considered* 15/695
AXN v Worboys [2012] EWHC 1730 (QB); [2013] Lloyd's Rep. I.R. 207; [2013] L.L.R. 256, QBD .... *Digested,* 13/**1744**: *Considered* 17/1877
Ayliffe v DPP see R. v Jones (Margaret)
AZ v Kirklees Council see CZ (Human Rights Claim: Costs), Re

AZ (Pakistan) v Secretary of State for the Home Department see R. (on the application of MA (Pakistan)) v Upper Tribunal (Immigration and Asylum Chamber)
AZ (Syria) v Secretary of State for the Home Department see R. (on the application of AZ) v Secretary of State for the Home Department
Azevedo v CED Portugal Unipessoal Lda (C-558/15); *sub nom* Vieira de Azevedo v CED Portugal Unipessoal Lda (C-558/15) EU:C:2016:957; [2017] Lloyd's Rep. I.R. 284, ECJ (6th Chamber)
Azhar v Dundee City Council [2017] L.L.R. 429; 2017 G.W.D. 19-311, Sh Ct (Tayside) (Dundee) .... *Digested,* 17/**2718**
Azimi v Newham LBC (2001) 33 H.L.R. 51, CA (Civ Div)
Applied 17/1221
Azizi v Aghaty [2016] EWHC 110 (Fam); [2017] 1 F.L.R. 351; [2016] Fam. Law 293, Fam Div .... *Digested,* 17/**1012**
Azumi Ltd v Zuma's Choice Pet Products Ltd; *joined case* Vanderbilt v Wallace [2017] EWHC 609 (IPEC); [2017] E.T.M.R. 24, IPEC .... *Digested,* 17/**1396**

B v B (Maintenance Enforcement: Stay); *sub nom* B v B (Maintenance Regulation: Stay) [2017] EWHC 1029 (Fam); [2018] 2 W.L.R. 987; [2018] 1 F.L.R. 658; [2017] 3 F.C.R. 240, Fam Div .... *Digested,* 17/**1042**
B v B (Maintenance Regulation: Stay) see B v B (Maintenance Enforcement: Stay)
B v B (Post Nuptial Settlements) (Pension Fund), Re see Brooks v Brooks
B v B see B (A Child) (Residence: Second Appeal), Re
B v B see MB v KB
B v C (Short Marriage: Needs: Stockpiling); *sub nom* AB v FC (Financial Provision) (Short Marriage: Needs: Stockpiling) [2016] EWHC 3285 (Fam); [2017] 4 W.L.R. 35; [2018] 1 F.L.R. 965; [2017] 1 F.C.R. 467, Fam Div .... *Digested,* 17/**1019**
B v Calderdale MBC see R. (on the application of B) v Calderdale MBC
B v Chief Constable of Northern Ireland [2015] EWHC 3691 (Admin); [2016] Crim. L.R. 428; [2016] A.C.D. 30, DC
Applied 17/1802
B v D [2015] CSOH 24; 2015 S.L.T. 217; 2015 G.W.D. 8-148, OH .... *Digested,* 15/**2886**: *Affirmed* 17/2452
B v D; *sub nom* D (Medical Treatment), Re [2017] EWCOP 15; [2017] C.O.P.L.R. 347, CP
B v G [2017] EWHC 223 (Fam); [2017] 2 F.C.R. 205, Fam Div .... *Digested,* 17/**946**
B v HM Advocate [2016] HCJAC 101; 2017 S.C.L. 64; 2016 G.W.D. 37-665, HCJ .... *Digested,* 17/**2550**
B v HM Advocate see AB v HM Advocate
B v L (Divorce: Jurisdiction and Forum Conveniens) [2016] EWFC 67; [2017] 2 F.L.R. 1020; [2017] 2 F.C.R. 212, Fam Div .... *Digested,* 17/**985**
B v Norway (29758/11) see A v Norway (24130/11)
B v Nugent Care Society; *sub nom* GR v Wirral MBC; AB v Nugent Care Society; *joined case* R v Wirral MBC [2009] EWCA Civ 827; [2010] 1 W.L.R. 516; [2010] 1 F.L.R. 707; [2010] P.I.Q.R. P3; [2009] LS Law Medical 524; [2009] Fam. Law 1045; (2009) 153(30) S.J.L.B. 28, CA (Civ Div) .... *Digested,* 10/**379**: *Applied* 11/2370, 11/353: *Followed* 11/856, 15/1113, 17/2191, 17/320
B v Secretary of State for the Home Department see MIAB v Secretary of State for the Home Department
B v Secretary of State for Work and Pensions [2005] EWCA Civ 929; [2005] 1 W.L.R. 3796; Times, September 16, 2005, CA (Civ Div) .... *Digested,* 06/**3978**: *Considered* 17/2772
B v Suffolk CC see A v Essex CC
B v Willerton see H v Craven
B v X CC see P (Children) (Placement Orders: Parental Consent), Re
B & K Lavery Property Trading Partnership v Revenue and Customs Commissioners [2015] UKFTT 470 (TC); [2016] S.T.I. 315, FTT (Tax)
Affirmed 17/2101
B & K Lavery Property Trading Partnership v Revenue and Customs Commissioners [2016] UKUT 525 (TCC); [2017] S.T.C. 829; [2016] B.T.C. 521, UT (Tax) .... *Digested,* 17/**2101**
B (A Child) (Adoption Proceedings: Joinder of Presumed Father), Re see B (A Child) (Parentage: Knowledge of Proceedings), Re
B (A Child) (Care Order: Adjournment of Fact-Finding Hearing), Re [2009] EWCA Civ 1243; [2010] 2 F.L.R. 1445; [2010] Fam. Law 246; (2009) 153(41) S.J.L.B. 28, CA (Civ Div) .... *Digested,* 11/**247**: *Applied* 17/999
B (A Child) (Care Order: Proportionality: Criterion for Review), Re see B (A Child) (Care Proceedings: Appeal), Re

B (A Child) (Care Proceedings: Appeal), Re; *sub nom* B (A Child) (Care Order: Proportionality: Criterion for Review), Re; B (A Child) (Care Proceedings: Threshold Criteria), Re [2013] UKSC 33; [2013] 1 W.L.R. 1911; [2013] 3 All E.R. 929; [2013] 2 F.L.R. 1075; [2013] 2 F.C.R. 525; [2013] H.R.L.R. 29; [2013] Fam. Law 946; (2013) 157(24) S.J.L.B. 37, SC .... *Digested,* 13/**1213**: *Applied* 14/1238, 14/1247, 14/1250, 14/1283, 14/1323, 14/1346, 14/1672, 14/2444, 15/1004, 15/1013, 15/1368, 15/300, 15/979, 15/985, 16/786, 16/810, 16/815, 16/860: *Considered* 14/1243, 14/1404, 15/1020, 15/976, 15/986, 16/808, 17/1356, 17/2200, 17/912: *Distinguished* 16/805: *Followed* 13/1221, 14/1245, 14/1579, 15/1053, 15/1135, 15/975, 15/980, 15/983, 16/797, 16/807, 16/821, 17/913, 17/934

B (A Child) (Care Proceedings: Threshold Criteria), Re see B (A Child) (Care Proceedings: Appeal), Re

B (A Child) (Disclosure), Re see Kent CC v B (A Child)

B (A Child) (Evidence: Passport Order), Re see B (A Child) (Wrongful Removal: Orders against Non-Parties), Re

B (A Child) (Habitual Residence: Inherent Jurisdiction), Re [2016] UKSC 4; [2016] A.C. 606; [2016] 2 W.L.R. 557; [2017] 1 All E.R. 899; [2016] 1 F.L.R. 561; [2016] 2 F.C.R. 307; Times, February 3, 2016; [2016] Fam. Law 298, SC .... *Digested,* 16/**851**: *Considered* 17/1066, 17/941, 17/957: *Followed* 16/833, 17/1020, 17/962

B (A Child) (Looked After Child), Re; *sub nom* Redcar and Cleveland BC v B [2013] EWCA Civ 964; [2014] 1 F.L.R. 277; [2013] Fam. Law 1382, CA (Civ Div) .... *Digested,* 14/**1434**: *Considered* 17/950

B (A Child) (Medical Treatment), Re [2008] EWHC 1996 (Fam); [2009] 1 F.L.R. 1264; [2009] LS Law Medical 214; [2009] Fam. Law 397, Fam Div .... *Digested,* 09/**1570**: *Considered* 17/958

B (A Child) (Non-Accidental Injury), Re [2002] EWCA Civ 752; [2002] 2 F.L.R. 1133; [2002] 3 F.C.R. 85; [2002] Fam. Law 879, CA (Civ Div) .... *Digested,* 03/**1533**: *Applied* 09/1529: *Considered* 03/1525, 17/1049

B (A Child) (Parentage: Knowledge of Proceedings), Re; *sub nom* B (A Child) (Adoption Proceedings: Joinder of Presumed Father), Re; AB (Care Proceedings: Service on Husband Ignorant of Child's Existence), Re [2003] EWCA Civ 1842; [2004] 1 F.L.R. 527; [2004] 1 F.C.R. 473; [2004] Fam. Law 178, CA (Civ Div) .... *Digested,* 04/**1504**: *Considered* 11/1371: *Followed* 17/930

B (A Child) (Removal from Jurisdiction: Removal of Family's Passports as Coercive Measure), Re see B (A Child) (Wrongful Removal: Orders against Non-Parties), Re

B (A Child) (Residence Order: Biological Parent), Re see B (A Child) (Residence: Second Appeal), Re

B (A Child) (Residence: Second Appeal), Re; *sub nom* B (A Child) (Residence Order: Biological Parent), Re; B v B [2009] UKSC 5; [2009] 1 W.L.R. 2496; [2010] 1 All E.R. 223; [2010] 1 F.L.R. 551; [2010] 1 F.C.R. 1; Times, November 23, 2009; [2010] Fam. Law 143; (2009) 106(46) L.S.G. 18, SC .... *Digested,* 10/**1435**: *Applied* 10/1434: *Followed* 15/1007, 17/965

B (A Child) (Welfare: Child Arrangement Order), Re; *sub nom* J v R [2017] EWHC 488 (Fam); [2017] 2 F.L.R. 1326; [2017] 2 F.C.R. 727, Fam Div .... *Digested,* 17/**963**

B (A Child) (Wrongful Removal: Orders against Non-Parties), Re; *sub nom* B (A Child) (Removal from Jurisdiction: Removal of Family's Passports as Coercive Measure), Re; B (A Child) (Evidence: Passport Order), Re [2014] EWCA Civ 843; [2015] Fam. 209; [2015] 2 W.L.R. 392; [2015] 1 All E.R. 230; [2015] 1 F.L.R. 871; [2015] 1 F.C.R. 75; [2014] Fam. Law 1250, CA (Civ Div) .... *Digested,* 15/**1144**: *Applied* 15/1032: *Considered* 17/931

B (A Child), Re [2017] EWCA Civ 264; [2017] 3 F.C.R. 9, CA (Civ Div) .... *Digested,* 17/**915**

B (A Minor), Re [1990] F.C.R. 409; Times, December 20, 1989, Fam Div .... *Digested,* 90/**3198**: *Applied* 17/1069

B (Children Act Proceedings: Issue Estoppel), Re see B (Minors) (Care Proceedings: Issue Estoppel), Re

B (Children) (Allegation of Sexual Abuse: Child's Evidence), Re; *joined case* B and O (Children), Re [2006] EWCA Civ 773; [2006] 2 F.L.R. 1071; [2006] 2 F.C.R. 386; [2006] Fam. Law 847, CA (Civ Div) .... *Digested,* 07/**1720**: *Applied* 08/1440: *Followed* 17/952

B (Children) (Foreign Adoption: Refusal of Recognition), Re see A County Council v M

B (Children) (Relocation outside Jurisdiction: Enforcement of Contact: Wardship), Re see B (Children) (Removal from Jurisdiction: Enforcement of Contact Order), Re

B (Children) (Relocation to UAE: Enforcability of Charge over Property and Issues of Wardship), Re see B (Children) (Removal from Jurisdiction: Enforcement of Contact Order), Re

B (Children) (Removal from Jurisdiction: Enforcement of Contact Order), Re; *sub nom* B (Children) (Relocation to UAE: Enforcability of Charge over Property and Issues of Wardship), Re; B (Relocation: Appeal), Re; B (Children) (Relocation outside Jurisdiction: Enforcement of Contact: Wardship), Re [2015] EWCA Civ 1302; [2016] 1 W.L.R. 2326; [2017] 1 All E.R. 1099; [2016] 2 F.L.R. 1131; [2016] 2 F.C.R. 151; [2016] Fam. Law 309, CA (Civ Div) .... *Digested,* 16/**860**

B (Children) (Sexual Abuse: Standard of Proof), Re; *sub nom* Local Authority X v B [2008] UKHL 35; [2009] 1 A.C. 11; [2008] 3 W.L.R. 1; [2008] 4 All E.R. 1; [2008] 2 F.L.R. 141; [2008] 2 F.C.R. 339; Times, June 12, 2008; [2008] Fam. Law 619; [2008] Fam. Law 837, HL .... *Digested,* 08/**1501**:
Applied 09/1553, 10/1330, 10/1355, 11/1335, 12/3259, 13/1215, 13/420, 14/1293, 15/2499: *Considered* 08/3774, 08/5003, 09/1519, 09/1611, 09/2649, 10/1305, 10/1327, 10/1416, 10/975, 15/1158, 17/953: *Followed* 09/1096, 09/1523, 10/1317, 10/1325, 10/1428, 11/1346, 11/1451, 12/1347, 12/1354, 12/437, 13/1222, 13/1227, 17/993

B (Family Proceedings) (Litigants in Person: Timely Service of Documents), Re [2016] EWHC 2365 (Fam); [2016] 4 W.L.R. 158; [2017] 1 F.C.R. 159; [2016] Fam. Law 1400, Fam Div .... *Digested,* 16/**884**

B (Incapacitated Person) (Representatives and Advocates: Duties and Powers), Re see D (Incapacitated Person) (Representatives and Advocates: Duties and Powers), Re

B (JP) v HM Advocate [2017] HCJAC 28; 2017 S.C.L. 690; 2017 G.W.D. 18-287, HCJ Appeal .... *Digested,* 17/**2520**

B (Minors) (Care Proceedings: Evidence), Re see B (Minors) (Care Proceedings: Issue Estoppel), Re

B (Minors) (Care Proceedings: Issue Estoppel), Re; *sub nom* B (Minors) (Care Proceedings: Evidence), Re; B (Minors: Issue Estoppel), Re; B (Children Act Proceedings: Issue Estoppel), Re [1997] Fam. 117; [1997] 3 W.L.R. 1; [1997] 2 All E.R. 29; [1997] 1 F.L.R. 285; [1997] 1 F.C.R. 477; Times, December 16, 1996; Independent, November 25, 1996; [1997] Fam. Law 235; (1997) 161 J.P.N. 358; (1996) 93(44) L.S.G. 30; (1996) 140 S.J.L.B. 252, Fam Div .... *Digested,* 96/**685**:
Applied 07/1685, 15/1005: *Considered* 98/1981, 17/1047

B (Minors) (Wardship: Power to Detain), Re [1994] 2 F.L.R. 479; [1994] 2 F.C.R. 1142; Times, May 24, 1994; Independent, July 25, 1994; [1994] Fam. Law 607, CA (Civ Div) .... *Digested,* 94/**3277**:
Applied 97/639, 15/1144: *Considered* 17/931

B (Minors: Issue Estoppel), Re see B (Minors) (Care Proceedings: Issue Estoppel), Re

B (R) v HM Advocate; *sub nom* RB v HM Advocate [2017] HCJAC 24; 2017 J.C. 278; 2017 S.L.T. 714; 2017 S.C.L. 545; 2017 S.C.C.R. 278; 2017 G.W.D. 14-216, HCJ .... *Digested,* 17/**2486**

B (Relocation: Appeal), Re see B (Children) (Removal from Jurisdiction: Enforcement of Contact Order), Re

B Ambition Shipping Co Ltd, Re see Northsea Base Investment Ltd, Re

B and O (Children), Re see B (Children) (Allegation of Sexual Abuse: Child's Evidence), Re

B Endeavour Shipping Co Ltd, Re see Northsea Base Investment Ltd, Re

B Faith Shipping Co Ltd, Re see Northsea Base Investment Ltd, Re

B Force Shipping Co Ltd, Re see Northsea Base Investment Ltd, Re

B Marshall Shipping Co Ltd, Re see Northsea Base Investment Ltd, Re

B Merchant Shipping Co Ltd, Re see Northsea Base Investment Ltd, Re

B&M Retail Ltd v Revenue and Customs Commissioners; *sub nom* Revenue and Customs Commissioners v B&M Retail Ltd [2016] UKUT 429 (TCC); [2016] S.T.C. 2456, UT (Tax) .... *Digested,* 17/**632**

B&M Retail Ltd v Revenue and Customs Commissioners; *sub nom* Revenue and Customs Commissioners v B&M Retail Ltd [2014] UKFTT 902 (TC); [2015] S.F.T.D. 72, FTT (Tax)
Reversed 17/632

B, Petitioner see Contempt of Court Proceedings in Respect of M and L

B, Re see R. v B

B-S (Children) (Adoption Order: Leave to Oppose), Re see B-S (Children) (Adoption: Leave to Oppose), Re

B-S (Children) (Adoption: Application of s.47(5)), Re see B-S (Children) (Adoption: Leave to Oppose), Re

B-S (Children) (Adoption: Leave to Oppose), Re; *sub nom* B-S (Children) (Adoption: Application of s.47(5)), Re; B-S (Children) (Adoption Order: Leave to Oppose), Re [2013] EWCA Civ 1146; [2014] 1 W.L.R. 563; [2014] 1 F.L.R. 1035; [2013] 3 F.C.R. 481; [2013] Fam. Law 1515; (2013) 157(36) S.J.L.B. 37, CA (Civ Div) .... *Digested,* 14/**1245**: *Applied* 14/1238, 14/1246, 14/1283, 14/1284, 15/979, 15/982, 16/805, 16/812, 16/859, 17/992: *Considered* 15/986, 17/912: *Explained* 15/975: *Followed* 14/1243, 14/1247, 14/1248, 14/1252, 14/1254, 14/1291, 15/1135, 15/981, 15/983, 15/985, 15/993, 16/797, 16/807, 16/819, 17/925, 17/932: *Not applied* 16/810

B010 v Canada 2015 SCC 58; 41 B.H.R.C. 653, Sup Ct (Can)

B2 v Secretary of State for the Home Department see Pham v Secretary of State for the Home Department

BA (Ghana) v Secretary of State for the Home Department see GS (India) v Secretary of State for the Home Department

BA (Turkey) v Secretary of State for the Home Department [2017] CSOH 27; 2017 S.L.T. 1061; 2017 G.W.D. 8-116, OH .... *Digested,* 17/**2668**

BAA Ltd v Competition Commission [2012] CAT 3; [2012] Comp. A.R. 134; Times, February 22, 2012, CAT .... *Digested,* 12/**547**: *Applied* 15/418, 17/414: *Considered* 14/547: *Followed* 14/535

Babiarz v Poland (1955/10) [2017] 2 F.L.R. 613, ECHR

Applied 17/981

Bacciottini v Gotelee & Goldsmith (A Firm) [2016] EWCA Civ 170; [2016] 4 W.L.R. 98; [2016] P.N.L.R. 22, CA (Civ Div) .... *Digested,* 16/**572**: *Not applied* 17/1838

Backwell v Royal Bank of Scotland Plc see Teasdale v HSBC Bank Plc

Badenach v Calvert [2016] HCA 18; [2017] W.T.L.R. 873; 19 I.T.E.L.R. 790, HC (Aus)

BAE Systems (Operations) Ltd v Konczak UKEAT/0097/15/DA, EAT

Affirmed 17/826

BAE Systems (Operations) Ltd v Konczak [2017] EWCA Civ 1188; [2018] I.C.R. 1; [2017] I.R.L.R. 893; Times, September 27, 2017, CA (Civ Div) .... *Digested,* 17/**826**

BAE Systems (Operations) Ltd v Konczak; *joined case* Konczak v BAE Systems (Operations) Ltd [2014] I.R.L.R. 676, EAT .... *Digested,* 14/**1039**: *Applied* 17/827

Bagarea v Caras Severin Tribunal, Romania see Grecu v Romania

Bagarea v Romania see Grecu v Romania

Bagum v Hafiz [2015] EWCA Civ 801; [2016] Ch. 241; [2015] 3 W.L.R. 1495; [2015] C.P. Rep. 44; [2016] 2 F.L.R. 337; [2015] W.T.L.R. 1303; Times, September 7, 2015; [2015] Fam. Law 1192; [2015] 2 P. & C.R. DG21, CA (Civ Div) .... *Digested,* 15/**2127**: *Followed* 17/1847

Bahamas Oil Refining Co International Ltd v Owners of the Cape Bari Tankschiffahrts GmbH & Co KG [2016] UKPC 20; [2017] 1 All E.R. (Comm) 189; [2016] 2 Lloyd's Rep. 469; [2016] 2 C.L.C. 157, PC (Bah)

Bailey v Angove's Pty Ltd see D&D Wines International Ltd (In Liquidation), Re

Bailey v Revenue and Customs Commissioners [2017] UKFTT 658 (TC); [2017] S.T.I. 2184, FTT (Tax)

Bain v Brand (1876) 1 App. Cas. 762; (1876) 3 R. (H.L.) 16, HL

Considered 07/5285, 16/2709: *Explained* 86/4106: *Followed* 81/3242, 89/4524, 17/2710

Baines v Nursing and Midwifery Council see Adesina v Nursing and Midwifery Council

Bains v Moore [2017] EWHC 242 (QB); [2017] E.M.L.R. 20, QBD .... *Digested,* 17/**286**

Baisley v South Lanarkshire Council [2017] I.C.R. 365, EAT (SC) .... *Digested,* 17/**2582**

Baka v Hungary (20261/12) (2017) 64 E.H.R.R. 6, ECHR (Grand Chamber)

Bakanova v Lithuania (11167/12) [2017] Inquest L.R. 60, ECHR

Baker v Craggs [2016] EWHC 3250 (Ch); [2017] Ch. 295; [2017] 2 W.L.R. 1483; [2017] 2 P. & C.R. 3; [2017] 1 P. & C.R. DG14, Ch D (Bristol) .... *Digested,* 17/**1841**

Baker v Dunne [2016] EWHC 2318 (Ch); [2016] W.T.L.R. 1489, Ch D .... *Digested,* 17/**2220**

Baker v Secretary of State for Communities and Local Government see R. (on the application of Baker) v Secretary of State for Communities and Local Government

Baker v Turner [1950] A.C. 401; [1950] 1 All E.R. 834; 66 T.L.R. (Pt. 1) 780; (1950) 94 S.J. 335, HL .... *Digested,* 47-51/**8525**: *Applied* 47-51/8509, 17/1441: *Considered* 54/2864, 69/1637: *Distinguished* 52/2947, 58/2891: *Doubted* 47-51/8523

Baker Refractories Ltd v Bishop see Barber v Somerset CC

Balbosa v Ali [1990] 1 W.L.R. 914; (1990) 87(20) L.S.G. 35; (1990) 134 S.J. 545, PC (Trin) .... *Digested,* 90/**689**: *Considered* 17/503

Balfour (Bruce James) v HM Advocate see Ferguson (James Douglas) v HM Advocate
Balfour Beatty Building Ltd v Chestermount Properties Ltd 62 B.L.R. 1; 32 Con. L.R. 139; (1993) 9 Const. L.J. 117, QBD .... *Digested,* 94/**335**: *Considered* 00/232, 17/478
Balfour Beatty Regional Construction Ltd v Grove Developments Ltd see Grove Developments Ltd v Balfour Beatty Regional Construction Ltd
Balfour Beatty Regional Construction Ltd v Grove Developments Ltd see Grove Developments Ltd v Balfour Beatty Regional Construction Ltd
Balhousie Holdings Ltd v Revenue and Customs Commissioners [2016] UKFTT 377 (TC); [2017] S.F.T.D. 126; [2016] S.T.I. 1779, FTT (Tax) .... *Digested,* 17/**2287**
Ball v Ball [2017] EWHC 1750 (Ch); [2017] W.T.L.R. 891, Ch D (Bristol)
Ball UK Holdings Ltd v Revenue and Customs Commissioners [2017] UKFTT 457 (TC); [2018] 1 B.C.L.C. 229; [2017] S.T.I. 1775, FTT (Tax)
Ballard v Solicitors' Regulation Authority [2017] EWHC 164 (Admin); [2017] A.C.D. 41, DC
Balogun v Boyes Sutton and Perry [2017] EWCA Civ 75; [2017] P.N.L.R. 20, CA (Civ Div) .... *Digested,* 17/**1573**
Balti Hut (Gloucester) Ltd v Revenue and Customs Commissioners; *joined case* Ali v Revenue and Customs Commissioners [2017] UKFTT 231 (TC); [2017] S.T.I. 1046, FTT (Tax)
Baltic Tankers Holding Ltd, Re see Northsea Base Investment Ltd, Re
Bamber v United Kingdom (130/10) see Vinter v United Kingdom (66069/09)
Bamford v Harvey [2012] EWHC 2858 (Ch); [2013] Bus. L.R. 589; [2013] B.C.C. 311; Times, December 7, 2012, Ch D .... *Digested,* 13/**354**: *Considered* 17/2423
Banco Nacional de Comercio Exterior SNC v Empresa de Telecomunicationes de Cuba SA [2007] EWCA Civ 662; [2008] 1 W.L.R. 1936; [2007] 2 All E.R. (Comm) 1093; [2008] Bus. L.R. 1265; [2007] 2 Lloyd's Rep. 484; [2007] C.P. Rep. 39; [2007] 2 C.L.C. 34; [2007] I.L.Pr. 51; (2007) 104(29) L.S.G. 22; (2007) 151 S.J.L.B. 923, CA (Civ Div) .... *Digested,* 07/**457**: *Applied* 17/301: *Considered* 16/261
Banco Popular Espamol SA v Irles Lopez (C-308/15) see Gutierrez Naranjo v Cajasur Banco SAU (C-154/15)
Banco Primus SA v Gutierrez Garcia (C-421/14) EU:C:2017:60; [2017] 2 C.M.L.R. 26, ECJ (2nd Chamber)
Banco Santander Totta SA v Companhia de Carris de Ferro de Lisboa SA [2016] EWHC 465 (Comm); [2016] 4 W.L.R. 49, QBD (Comm) .... *Digested,* 16/**135**: *Affirmed* 17/163
Banco Santander Totta SA v Companhia de Carris de Ferro de Lisboa SA [2016] EWCA Civ 1267; [2017] 1 W.L.R. 1323; [2017] 3 All E.R. 838; [2017] 2 All E.R. (Comm) 551; [2017] 1 Lloyd's Rep. 113; [2016] 2 C.L.C. 980; Times, January 16, 2017, CA (Civ Div) .... *Digested,* 17/**163**
Bank Mellat v HM Treasury [2016] EWCA Civ 452; [2017] Q.B. 67; [2016] 3 W.L.R. 1117; [2017] 2 All E.R. 139; [2017] 1 All E.R. (Comm) 807; [2016] 1 C.L.C. 868, CA (Civ Div) .... *Digested,* 16/**568**
Bank Mellat v HM Treasury [2015] EWCA Civ 1052; [2016] 1 W.L.R. 1187; [2016] C.P. Rep. 7, CA (Civ Div) .... *Digested,* 16/**180**: *Applied* 16/1157: *Followed* 17/1250
Bank Mellat v HM Treasury [2013] UKSC 38; [2014] A.C. 700; [2013] 4 All E.R. 495; [2013] Lloyd's Rep. F.C. 557, SC .... *Digested,* 14/**48**: *Applied* 14/2102, 14/45, 16/1157, 16/2599, 17/2693: *Considered* 15/3243, 17/1231: *Followed* 14/663, 16/1975, 16/632, 17/1155, 17/1513
Bank Mellat v HM Treasury [2013] UKSC 39; [2014] A.C. 700; [2013] 3 W.L.R. 179; [2013] 4 All E.R. 533; [2013] H.R.L.R. 30; [2013] Lloyd's Rep. F.C. 580, SC ...... *Digested,* 13/**194**: *Applied* 16/1040, 16/180, 17/1624: *Considered* 14/2744, 14/545, 15/2512, 15/763, 16/2050, 16/2748: *Followed* 15/49, 16/2115, 16/326, 17/1464
Bank of Baroda, GCC Operations v Nawany Marine Shipping FZE [2016] EWHC 3089 (Comm); [2017] 2 All E.R. (Comm) 763, QBD (Comm) .... *Digested,* 17/**366**
Bank of Credit and Commerce International SA (In Liquidation) v Ali (No.1) [2001] UKHL 8; [2002] 1 A.C. 251; [2001] 2 W.L.R. 735; [2001] 1 All E.R. 961; [2001] I.C.R. 337; [2001] I.R.L.R. 292; [2001] Emp. L.R. 359; Times, March 6, 2001; (2001) 98(15) L.S.G. 32; (2001) 151 N.L.J. 351; (2001) 145 S.J.L.B. 67; (2001) 145 S.J.L.B. 70, HL .... *Digested,* 01/**2228**: *Applied* 02/207, 02/217, 03/2723, 06/203, 06/2411, 07/2760, 08/663, 12/2023, 14/381: *Considered* 07/2500, 08/2178, 08/2195, 08/648, 09/722, 10/613, 12/2389, 13/578, 14/3354, 17/823: *Distinguished* 02/703: *Followed* 15/368

Bank of Credit and Commerce International SA (In Liquidation) (No.8), Re; *sub nom* Morris v Rayners Enterprises Inc; Morris v Agrichemicals Ltd; Bank of Credit and Commerce International SA (No.3), Re [1996] Ch. 245; [1996] 2 W.L.R. 631; [1996] 2 All E.R. 121; [1996] B.C.C. 204; [1996] 2 B.C.L.C. 254; Times, January 8, 1996; (1996) 140 S.J.L.B. 36, CA (Civ Div) ..... *Digested,* 96/**3463**: *Affirmed* 97/3047: *Disapproved* 17/1259

Bank of Credit and Commerce International SA (No.3), Re see Bank of Credit and Commerce International SA (In Liquidation) (No.8), Re

Bank of Cyprus UK Ltd v Menelaou see Menelaou v Bank of Cyprus Plc

Bank of Cyprus UK Ltd v Menelaou see Menelaou v Bank of Cyprus Plc

Bank of Ireland v Hollicourt (Contracts) Ltd see Hollicourt (Contracts) Ltd (In Liquidation) v Bank of Ireland

Bank of Ireland v Watts Group Plc [2017] EWHC 1667 (TCC); [2017] T.C.L.R. 7; 173 Con. L.R. 240, QBD (TCC) ..... *Digested,* 17/**1571**

Bank of Ireland v Watts Group Plc [2017] EWHC 2472 (TCC); [2017] B.L.R. 626; 174 Con. L.R. 84; [2017] 5 Costs L.R. 899, QBD (TCC)

Bank of Scotland v A Ltd [2001] EWCA Civ 52; [2001] 1 W.L.R. 751; [2001] 3 All E.R. 58; [2001] 1 All E.R. (Comm) 1023; [2001] Lloyd's Rep. Bank. 73; (2000-01) 3 I.T.E.L.R. 503; Times, February 6, 2001; Independent, January 23, 2001; (2001) 98(9) L.S.G. 41; (2001) 151 N.L.J. 102; (2001) 145 S.J.L.B. 21, CA (Civ Div) ..... *Digested,* 01/**370**: *Considered* 03/1598, 05/261: *Distinguished* 03/795: *Explained* 17/173

Bank of Scotland v Bennett see Royal Bank of Scotland Plc v Etridge (No.2)

Bank of Scotland Plc v King [2007] EWHC 2747 (Ch); [2008] 1 E.G.L.R. 65; [2008] 13 E.G. 150, Ch D ..... *Digested,* 08/**3082**: *Considered* 16/1817, 17/1456

Bank of Scotland Plc, Re see Barclays Bank Plc, Re

Bankovic v Belgium (Admissibility) (52207/99); *sub nom* Bankovic v United Kingdom (Admissibility) (52207/99) 11 B.H.R.C. 435; (2007) 44 E.H.R.R. SE5, ECHR ..... *Digested,* 02/**2535**: *Applied* 05/2065, 05/2129, 06/2163, 07/2212, 07/2239, 08/1882, 09/1986, 09/21, 10/1737: *Considered* 03/2162, 04/2008, 08/1975, 11/1696, 13/121, 16/1094: *Doubted* 17/83: *Not applied* 15/101

Bankovic v United Kingdom (Admissibility) (52207/99) see Bankovic v Belgium (Admissibility) (52207/99)

Banks v Goodfellow (Costs) (1870-71) L.R. 11 Eq. 472, Ct of Chancery *Applied* 11/3267, 17/2076, 17/2078

Banks v Mecca Bookmakers (Scotland) Ltd 1982 S.C. 7; 1982 S.L.T. 150, OH ..... *Digested,* 82/**3945**: *Distinguished* 93/5461, 17/2696

Banque Financiere de la Cite SA v Parc (Battersea) Ltd [1999] 1 A.C. 221; [1998] 2 W.L.R. 475; [1998] 1 All E.R. 737; [1998] C.L.C. 520; Times, March 2, 1998; [1998] E.G. 36 (C.S.); (1998) 95(15) L.S.G. 31; (1998) 148 N.L.J. 365; (1998) 142 S.J.L.B. 101, HL ..... *Digested,* 98/**2521**: *Applied* 01/3793, 03/3610, 03/3613, 04/3242, 04/3267, 06/3509, 09/991, 13/2472, 15/2131, 17/2285: *Cited* 00/3550: *Considered* 08/2170, 17/637: *Followed* 11/2716, 12/2768, 14/2529: *Referred to* 00/1460

Banque Populaire Alsace Lorraine Champagne v X [2017] E.C.C. 2, Cass (F)

Banstonian Co v United Kingdom (9265/81) see Lithgow v United Kingdom (A/102)

Bar Standards Board v Howd; *sub nom* Howd v Bar Standards Board [2017] EWHC 210 (Admin); [2017] 4 W.L.R. 54; [2017] I.R.L.R. 423; [2017] A.C.D. 45, QBD (Admin) ..... *Digested,* 17/**1487**

Barber v Somerset CC; *sub nom* Somerset CC v Barber; Bishop v Baker Refractories Ltd; Hatton v Sutherland; Jones v Sandwell MBC; *joined cases* Sandwell MBC v Jones; Sutherland v Hatton; Baker Refractories Ltd v Bishop [2002] EWCA Civ 76; [2002] 2 All E.R. 1; [2002] I.C.R. 613; [2002] I.R.L.R. 263; [2002] Emp. L.R. 288; [2002] P.I.Q.R. P21; (2002) 68 B.M.L.R. 115; Times, February 12, 2002; Independent, February 13, 2002; Daily Telegraph, February 14, 2002; (2002) 99(12) L.S.G. 34; (2002) 146 S.J.L.B. 43, CA (Civ Div) ..... *Digested,* 02/**3264**: *Applied* 03/3134, 03/3135, 04/1194, 04/2860, 05/2883, 06/2892, 06/2916, 07/1316, 07/2940, 07/2941, 15/685: *Considered* 03/5830, 07/1322, 09/2833, 11/1046: *Explained* 07/2942, 17/826: *Followed* 10/1092: *Reversed* 04/2713

Barbulescu v Romania (61496/08) [2016] I.R.L.R. 235; 41 B.H.R.C. 44, ECHR

Barbulescu v Romania (61496/08) [2017] I.R.L.R. 1032, ECHR (Grand Chamber)

Barcham, Re see French v Barcham

Barclay Pharmaceuticals Ltd v Waypharm LP [2012] EWHC 306 (Comm); (2012) 109(26) L.S.G. 19, QBD (Comm) *Considered* 17/1998

Barclays Bank Ltd v WJ Simms Son & Cooke (Southern) Ltd [1980] Q.B. 677; [1980] 2 W.L.R. 218; [1979] 3 All E.R. 522; [1980] 1 Lloyd's Rep. 225; (1979) 123 S.J. 785, QBD (Comm) .... *Digested,* 79/**157**: *Applied* 83/182, 99/2218, 99/292, 01/374, 17/466: *Considered* 83/447, 90/1993, 90/3918, 00/2331, 17/909: *Followed* 97/319

Barclays Bank Plc v Christie Owen & Davies Ltd (t/a Christie & Co) [2016] EWHC 2351 (Ch); [2017] P.N.L.R. 8, Ch D .... *Digested,* 17/**1579**

Barclays Bank Plc v Coleman see Royal Bank of Scotland Plc v Etridge (No.2)

Barclays Bank Plc v Ente Nazionale di Previdenza ed Assistenza dei Medici e Degli Odontoiatri [2016] EWCA Civ 1261; [2017] 2 All E.R. (Comm) 432; [2016] 2 C.L.C. 859, CA (Civ Div) .... *Digested,* 17/**428**

Barclays Bank Plc v Ente Nazionale di Previdenza ed Assistenza dei Medici e Degli Odontoiatri [2015] EWHC 2857 (Comm); [2015] 2 Lloyd's Rep. 527, QBD (Comm) .... *Digested,* 16/**362**: *Affirmed* 17/428

Barclays Bank Plc v Eustice [1995] 1 W.L.R. 1238; [1995] 4 All E.R. 511; [1995] B.C.C. 978; [1995] 2 B.C.L.C. 630; Times, August 3, 1995; (1995) 145 N.L.J. 1503; (1995) 70 P. & C.R. D29, CA (Civ Div) .... *Digested,* 96/**3510**: *Applied* 01/398, 11/2116, 15/201: *Considered* 98/355, 98/356, 15/200: *Followed* 12/1822, 17/1488

Barclays Bank Plc v Harris see Royal Bank of Scotland Plc v Etridge (No.2)

Barclays Bank Plc v Inland Revenue Commissioners see National Westminster Bank Plc v Inland Revenue Commissioners

Barclays Bank Plc v O'Brien [1994] 1 A.C. 180; [1993] 3 W.L.R. 786; [1993] 4 All E.R. 417; [1994] 1 F.L.R. 1; [1994] 1 F.C.R. 357; (1994) 26 H.L.R. 75; (1994) 13 Tr. L.R. 165; [1994] C.C.L.R. 94; Times, October 22, 1993; Independent, October 22, 1993; [1994] Fam. Law 78; [1993] E.G. 169 (C.S.); (1993) 143 N.L.J. 1511; (1993) 137 S.J.L.B. 240; [1993] N.P.C. 135, HL .... *Digested,* 94/**3300**: *Applied* 94/3294, 95/2443, 95/2451, 96/419, 98/4363, 99/6431, 01/4878, 01/4880, 03/2379, 12/1824, 14/2588: *Cited* 98/305, 00/4644, 00/4662, 01/2653: *Considered* 94/2246, 95/2196, 95/2444, 95/2446, 95/2449, 95/2450, 95/4659, 96/411, 96/4967, 96/4970, 96/4973, 97/4232, 97/4240, 97/4244, 99/3715, 99/4377, 00/2333, 00/6670, 01/669, 10/224, 11/2688, 17/504: *Disapproved* 97/6087: *Distinguished* 94/5914, 04/1526: *Explained* 98/4358: *Followed* 97/4238, 99/4390, 00/4273, 02/3839: *Not followed* 94/5881, 96/6577: *Referred to* 95/2447, 99/310

Barclays Bank Plc v Quincecare Ltd [1992] 4 All E.R. 363; [1988] 1 F.T.L.R. 507; [1988] Fin. L.R. 166; Times, March 2, 1988; Independent, March 3, 1988; Financial Times, March 1, 1988; Daily Telegraph, March 14, 1988, QBD (Comm) .... *Digested,* 88/**177**: *Applied* 17/174: *Followed* 09/306

Barclays Bank Plc v Revenue and Customs Commissioners see Accenture Services Ltd v Revenue and Customs Commissioners

Barclays Bank Plc, Re; *sub nom* Abbey National Treasury Services Plc, Re; Santander UK Plc, Re; HSBC Plc, Re; Bank of Scotland Plc, Re; Lloyds Bank Plc, Re; Woolwich Plan Managers Ltd, Re [2017] EWHC 1482 (Ch); [2018] 1 All E.R. 893; [2018] 1 All E.R. (Comm) 592; [2017] Bus. L.R. 2006, Ch D (Companies Ct)

Barclays Mercantile Business Finance Ltd v Mawson (Inspector of Taxes); *sub nom* ABC Ltd v M (Inspector of Taxes) [2004] UKHL 51; [2005] 1 A.C. 684; [2004] 3 W.L.R. 1383; [2005] 1 All E.R. 97; [2005] S.T.C. 1; 76 T.C. 446; [2004] B.T.C. 414; 7 I.T.L. Rep. 383; Times, November 27, 2004; [2004] S.T.I. 2435; (2004) 154 N.L.J. 1830; (2004) 148 S.J.L.B. 1403, HL .... *Digested,* 05/**3988**: *Applied* 06/4213, 07/3992, 07/4085, 08/3662, 08/3840, 09/3754, 09/3755, 09/3849, 09/3876, 11/3277, 12/3234, 16/2098: *Considered* 06/4257, 08/3765, 09/3916, 10/3390, 11/3285, 11/3347, 14/2851, 15/2476, 16/2120, 17/2180: *Distinguished* 06/4125: *Followed* 05/4022, 10/3249, 10/3329, 11/3383, 13/3095, 14/2873, 15/2433, 16/2045, 16/2119, 17/2094, 17/2131, 17/2137, 17/2144

Barclays Wealth Trustees (Jersey) Ltd v Revenue and Customs Commissioners [2017] EWCA Civ 1512; [2017] S.T.C. 2465; [2017] B.T.C. 27; [2017] W.T.L.R. 917, CA (Civ Div) .... *Digested,* 17/**2157**

Barclays Wealth Trustees (Jersey) Ltd v Revenue and Customs Commissioners [2015] EWHC 2878 (Ch); [2015] B.T.C. 28; [2015] W.T.L.R. 1675, Ch D .... *Digested,* 15/**2501**: *Reversed* 17/2157

Barings Bank Plc v Coopers & Lybrand see Barings Plc (In Liquidation) v Coopers & Lybrand (No.6) (Application to Set Aside Permission to Appeal)

Barings Plc (In Liquidation) v Coopers & Lybrand (No.6) (Application to Set Aside Permission to Appeal); *sub nom* Barings Bank Plc v Coopers & Lybrand [2002] EWCA Civ 1155; [2003] C.P. Rep. 2, CA (Civ Div) .... *Digested,* 03/**305**: *Applied* 03/306: *Followed* 17/1282

Barings Plc (In Liquidation) (No.1), Re; *sub nom* Hamilton v Law Debenture Trustees Ltd [2001] 2 B.C.L.C. 159; [2002] B.P.I.R. 85, Ch D .... *Digested,* 02/**2692**: *Not applied* 17/1319

Barker Mill Estates Trustees v Secretary of State for Communities and Local Government see Barker Mill Estates Trustees v Test Valley BC

Barker Mill Estates Trustees v Test Valley BC; *joined case* Barker Mill Estates Trustees v Secretary of State for Communities and Local Government [2016] EWHC 3028 (Admin); [2017] P.T.S.R. 408; [2017] J.P.L. 417, QBD (Admin) ..... *Digested,* 17/**1780**: *Applied* 17/1767, 17/1769: *Approved* 17/1779

Barkhuysen v Hamilton [2016] EWHC 3371 (QB); [2016] 6 Costs L.R. 1217, QBD (Truro) .... *Digested,* 17/**271**

Barking and Dagenham LBC v Jones (Unreported, July 30, 1999), CA (Civ Div) *Followed* 17/619

Barnaby v DPP [2015] EWHC 232 (Admin); [2015] 2 Cr. App. R. 4; (2015) 179 J.P. 143; [2015] Crim. L.R. 729; [2015] A.C.D. 50, DC .... *Digested,* 15/**536**: *Applied* 17/514

Barnardo's v Buckinghamshire see Buckinghamshire v Barnardo's

Barnes v Chief Constable of the Police Service of Scotland [2017] CSOH 92; 2017 S.L.T. 844; 2017 G.W.D. 21-328, OH .... *Digested,* 17/**2769**

Barnes v St Helens MBC; *sub nom* St Helens MBC v Barnes [2006] EWCA Civ 1372; [2007] 1 W.L.R. 879; [2007] 3 All E.R. 525; [2007] C.P. Rep. 7; [2007] P.I.Q.R. P10; Times, November 17, 2006; Independent, October 27, 2006, CA (Civ Div) *Digested,* 07/**477**: *Applied* 07/373, 12/449, 17/1433, 17/1625: *Considered* 16/179: *Followed* 16/274

Barnes (Inspector of Taxes) v Hilton Main Construction Ltd [2005] EWHC 1355 (Ch); [2005] S.T.C. 1532; 77 T.C. 255; [2005] B.T.C. 568; [2005] S.T.I. 834, Ch D ..... *Digested,* 05/**4036**: *Applied* 16/2050, 17/2103: *Explained* 12/3409

Barnet v Crozier [1987] 1 W.L.R. 272; [1987] 1 All E.R. 1041; (1987) 84 L.S.G. 658; (1987) 131 S.J. 298, CA (Civ Div) .... *Digested,* 87/**2301**: *Applied* 04/939, 10/842, 14/840: *Considered* 97/4857: *Followed* 15/694, 17/374

Barnet LBC v AL; *sub nom* SL (Permission to Vaccinate), Re [2017] EWHC 125 (Fam); [2017] 4 W.L.R. 53; [2017] 2 F.L.R. 1499; (2017) 155 B.M.L.R. 135, Fam Div .... *Digested,* 17/**923**: *Not applied* 17/967

Barnet LBC v T see H (A Child) (Hair Strand Testing), Re

Barnett v Creggy; *sub nom* Creggy v Barnett [2016] EWCA Civ 1004; [2017] Ch. 273; [2017] 2 W.L.R. 1054; [2017] C.P. Rep. 3; [2017] P.N.L.R. 4; [2017] 1 P. & C.R. DG8, CA (Civ Div) .... *Digested,* 17/**2219**

Barnett v Creggy; *sub nom* Creggy v Barnett [2014] EWHC 3080 (Ch); [2015] P.N.L.R. 13; [2016] W.T.L.R. 17, Ch D .... *Digested,* 15/**1657**: *Reversed* 17/2219

Barnett v Medway NHS Foundation Trust [2015] EWHC 440 (QB), QBD *Affirmed* 17/1639

Barnett v Medway NHS Foundation Trust [2017] EWCA Civ 235; [2017] Med. L.R. 217, CA (Civ Div) .... *Digested,* 17/**1639**

Barnett v South Downs NPA [2017] P.A.D. 5, Planning Inspector

Barney-Smith v Tonbridge and Malling BC [2016] EWCA Civ 1264; [2017] P.T.S.R. 583; [2017] L.L.R. 225, CA (Civ Div) .... *Digested,* 17/**1783**

Barnfield v Solihull MBC see Sim v Rotherham MBC

Barnsley v Noble [2016] EWCA Civ 799; [2017] Ch. 191; [2017] 2 W.L.R. 1231; [2016] W.T.L.R. 1501; 19 I.T.E.L.R. 532; [2017] 1 P. & C.R. DG3, CA (Civ Div) .... *Digested,* 16/**2164**

Barnsley MBC v Yerrakalva see Yerrakalva v Barnsley MBC

Barnwell Manor Wind Energy Ltd v East Northamptonshire DC see East Northamptonshire DC v Secretary of State for Communities and Local Government

Baron, Re; *joined case* Ex p. the Debtor v Official Receiver [1943] Ch. 177; [1943] 2 All E.R. 662, Ch D *Applied* 17/1310

Baroness Cumberlege of Newick v Secretary of State for Communities and Local Government [2017] EWHC 2057 (Admin); [2017] P.T.S.R. 1513; [2018] Env. L.R. 10; [2018] J.P.L. 37, QBD (Admin)

Baronetcy of Pringle of Stichill, Re [2016] UKPC 16; [2016] 1 W.L.R. 2870; [2017] 1 All E.R. 106; 2016 S.C. (P.C.) 1; 2016 S.L.T. 723; [2016] W.T.L.R. 1117; 2016 G.W.D. 20-360, PC (Sc) .... *Digested,* 16/**2744**

Barras v Aberdeen Steam Trawling & Fishing Co Ltd [1933] A.C. 402; [1933] All E.R. Rep. 52; (1933) 45 Ll. L. Rep. 199; 1933 S.C. (H.L.) 21; 1933 S.L.T. 338, HL
Applied 14/2936, 16/2102: *Considered* 47-51/9934, 83/538, 16/2697, 17/2679
Barratt v Ansell (t/a Woolf Seddon) see Arthur JS Hall & Co v Simons
Barratt v Woolf Seddon see Arthur JS Hall & Co v Simons
Barratt Homes Ltd v Dwr Cymru Cyfyngedig (Welsh Water) see Dwr Cymru Cyfyngedig (Welsh Water) v Barratt Homes Ltd
Barratt Scotland Ltd v Keith 1993 S.C. 142; 1994 S.L.T. 1343; 1993 S.C.L.R. 120, IH (2 Div) .... *Digested,* 93/**5686**:
Cited 10/4482: *Considered* 04/5093: *Followed* 17/2771
Barrett Bros (Taxis) Ltd v Davies; *sub nom* Lickiss v Milestone Motor Policies at Lloyds [1966] 1 W.L.R. 1334; [1966] 2 All E.R. 972; [1966] 2 Lloyd's Rep. 1; (1966) 110 S.J. 600, CA .... *Digested,* 66/**10684**:
Considered 70/1378, 17/503: *Distinguished* 82/1669, 08/3471: *Followed* 94/2661
Barron v Vines [2015] EWHC 1161 (QB), QBD
Considered 17/651
Barry v Midland Bank Plc [1998] 1 All E.R. 805; [1999] I.C.R. 319; [1998] I.R.L.R. 138; Times, December 29, 1997, CA (Civ Div) .... *Digested,* 98/**2189**:
Affirmed 99/2117: *Considered* 12/1036, 17/1800
Barthelemy v F&C Alternative Investments (Holdings) Ltd see F&C Alternative Investments (Holdings) Ltd v Barthelemy
Barthelemy v F&C Alternative Investments (Holdings) Ltd see F&C Alternative Investments (Holdings) Ltd v Barthelemy (Costs)
Bartles v Barclays Bank Plc see CGL Group Ltd v Royal Bank of Scotland Plc
Barton v DPP [2001] EWHC 527 (Admin); (2001) 165 J.P. 779; (2001) 165 J.P.N. 887, QBD (Admin) .... *Digested,* 02/**866**:
Applied 17/601: *Considered* 05/3742
Barton v Golden Sun Holidays Ltd (In Liquidation) [2007] EWHC 3455 (QB); [2007] I.L.Pr. 57; (2007) 151 S.J.L.B. 1128, QBD .... *Digested,* 08/**275**:
Applied 17/338
Barton v Secretary of State for Communities and Local Government [2017] EWHC 573 (Admin); [2017] P.T.S.R. 705, QBD (Admin) .... *Digested,* 17/**1702**
Barty Party Co Ltd v Revenue and Customs Commissioners [2017] UKFTT 697 (TC); [2017] S.T.I. 2072, FTT (Tax)
Barwood Strategic Land II LLP v East Staffordshire BC see East Staffordshire BC v Secretary of State for Communities and Local Government
Basnet v Secretary of State for the Home Department see Basnet (Validity of Application: Respondent: Nepal), Re
Basnet (Validity of Application: Respondent: Nepal), Re; *sub nom* Basnet v Secretary of State for the Home Department [2012] UKUT 113 (IAC); [2012] Imm. A.R. 673; [2012] I.N.L.R. 585, UT (IAC) .... *Digested,* 13/**1628**:
Applied 17/1229: *Considered* 15/1361, 17/1237
BAT Caribbean SA v PHP Tobacco Carib Sarl see PHP Tobacco Carib Sarl v BAT Caribbean SA
BAT Industries Plc v Sequana SA see BTI 2014 LLC v Sequana SA
Bates v Chief Constable of Avon and Somerset [2009] EWHC 942 (Admin); (2009) 173 J.P. 313; [2009] Po. L.R. 186, DC .... *Digested,* 09/**936**:
Considered 11/814, 17/625
Bates v Green see Pettit v Bradford Bulls (Northern) Ltd (In Administration)
Bates van Winkelhof v Clyde & Co LLP; *joined case* Clyde & Co LLP v Bates van Winkelhof [2012] EWCA Civ 1207; [2013] 1 All E.R. 844; [2013] I.C.R. 883; [2012] I.R.L.R. 992; (2012) 109(38) L.S.G. 19; (2012) 156(37) S.J.L.B. 31, CA (Civ Div) .... *Digested,* 13/**993**:
Applied 13/1075: *Followed* 17/849: *Reversed* 14/1067
Bath Society v Secretary of State for the Environment [1991] 1 W.L.R. 1303; [1992] 1 All E.R. 28; 89 L.G.R. 834; (1991) 4 Admin. L.R. 77; (1991) 62 P. & C.R. 565; [1991] 2 P.L.R. 51; Times, February 14, 1991; [1991] J.P.L. 663; [1991] C.O.D. 427; [1991] E.G. 14 (C.S.); (1991) 135 S.J. 382, CA (Civ Div) .... *Digested,* 92/**4184**:
Applied 14/2388: *Cited* 95/4751: *Considered* 91/3446, 92/4186, 94/43:
Followed 17/1751
Bathurst v Bathurst [2016] EWHC 3033 (Ch); [2017] W.T.L.R. 437; [2017] 1 P. & C.R. DG13, Ch D .... *Digested,* 17/**2218**
Batmore Capital Ltd v European Union Intellectual Property Office (EUIPO) (T-596/15) EU:T:2017:103; [2017] E.T.M.R. 21, GC (4th Chamber)
Baugniet v Capita Employee Benefits Ltd (t/a Teachers' Pensions) [2017] EWHC 501 (Ch); [2017] Pens. L.R. 13, Ch D .... *Digested,* 17/**1607**

Bavaird v Sir Robert McAlpine Ltd [2013] CSIH 98; 2014 S.C. 322; 2014 S.L.T. 39; 2013 G.W.D. 39-752, IH (Ex Div) .... *Digested,* 14/**3696**: *Applied* 17/872

BAWAG PSK Bank fur Arbeit und Wirtschaft und Osterreichische Postsparkasse AG v Verein fur Konsumenteninformation (C-375/15) EU:C:2017:38; [2017] Bus. L.R. 616; [2017] 2 C.M.L.R. 35; [2017] C.T.L.C. 129, ECJ (3rd Chamber)

Baxter v Camden LBC (No.2) see Southwark LBC v Mills

Baxter v Mannion [2011] EWCA Civ 120; [2011] 1 W.L.R. 1594; [2011] 2 All E.R. 574; [2011] 2 E.G.L.R. 29; [2011] 20 E.G. 114; (2011) 161 N.L.J. 326; (2011) 155(8) S.J.L.B. 31, CA (Civ Div) .... *Digested,* 11/**2695**: *Not followed* 17/1848

Bayer Pharma AG v Genentech Inc see Regeneron Pharmaceuticals Inc v Genentech Inc

Bayerische Motoren Werke AG v Acacia Srl (C-433/16) EU:C:2017:550; [2018] Bus. L.R. 419; [2018] C.E.C. 226; [2017] E.C.D.R. 18; [2017] I.L.Pr. 33, ECJ (2nd Chamber)

Bayerische Motoren Werke AG v Technosport London Ltd [2016] EWHC 797 (IPEC); [2017] R.T.R. 11; [2016] E.C.C. 20; [2016] E.T.M.R. 31; [2016] F.S.R. 34, IPEC *Digested,* 16/**1337**: *Reversed* 17/1390

Bayerische Motoren Werke AG v Technosport London Ltd [2017] EWCA Civ 779; [2018] R.T.R. 1; [2017] E.C.C. 29; [2017] E.T.M.R. 32; [2017] F.S.R. 35, CA (Civ Div) .... *Digested,* 17/**1390**

Baylis v Revenue and Customs Commissioners [2016] UKFTT 725 (TC); [2017] S.F.T.D. 217, FTT (Tax) .... *Digested,* 17/**2128**

Baylis (Inspector of Taxes) v Gregory see Craven (Inspector of Taxes) v White (Stephen)

Bayliss v Revenue and Customs Commissioners [2016] UKFTT 500 (TC); [2017] S.F.T.D. 370; [2016] S.T.I. 2687, FTT (Tax)

Baynham v Royal Wolverhampton Hospitals NHS Trust [2016] EWCA Civ 1249; [2017] Med. L.R. 1, CA (Civ Div) .... *Digested,* 17/**1641**

Baynham v Royal Wolverhampton Hospitals NHS Trust [2014] EWHC 3780 (QB), QBD *Affirmed* 17/1641

Bayswater Trading Co Ltd, Re [1970] 1 W.L.R. 343; [1970] 1 All E.R. 608; (1969) 114 S.J. 29, Ch D .... *Digested,* 70/**289**: *Applied* 70/305, 78/259: *Considered* 17/409: *Distinguished* 87/338

BBC, Re; *sub nom* A v Secretary of State for the Home Department; A v BBC [2014] UKSC 25; [2015] A.C. 588; [2014] 2 W.L.R. 1243; [2014] 2 All E.R. 1037; 2014 S.C. (U.K.S.C.) 151; 2014 S.L.T. 613; 2014 S.C.L.R. 593; [2014] E.M.L.R. 25; 37 B.H.R.C. 664; Times, May 15, 2014; 2014 G.W.D. 15-266, SC .... *Digested,* 14/**43**: *Considered* 14/790, 17/332: *Followed* 15/4

BC v DE (Proceedings under Children Act 1989: Legal Costs Funding) see F (A Child) (Financial Provision: Legal Costs Funding), Re

BC (A Minor) (Care Order: Appropriate Local Authority), Re [1995] 3 F.C.R. 598; (1996) 160 L.G. Rev. 13, Fam Div .... *Digested,* 96/**485**: *Applied* 17/925: *Considered* 99/2352: *Followed* 99/2312

BC&G Care Homes Ltd, Re; *sub nom* Crowley v Bessell [2016] EWHC 1303 (Ch); [2016] B.C.C. 664, Ch D .... *Digested,* 17/**407**

BD v FD (Financial Remedies: Needs) [2016] EWHC 594 (Fam); [2017] 1 F.L.R. 1420; [2016] Fam. Law 670, Fam Div *Applied* 16/904: *Considered* 17/1019

BDW Trading Ltd (t/a David Wilson Homes (Central, Mercia and West Midlands)) v Secretary of State for Communities and Local Government; *sub nom* Secretary of State for Communities and Local Government v BDW Trading Ltd (t/a David Wilson Homes (Central, Mercia and West Midlands)) [2016] EWCA Civ 493; [2017] P.T.S.R. 1337, CA (Civ Div) *Applied* 17/1779

Beaconside Country House and Cottages v Gidman (Valuation Officer) [2016] UKUT 497 (LC); [2017] R.A. 61, UT (Lands) .... *Digested,* 17/**1517**

Beaney v Beaney see Beaney (Deceased), Re

Beaney (Deceased), Re; *sub nom* Beaney v Beaney [1978] 1 W.L.R. 770; [1978] 2 All E.R. 595; (1977) 121 S.J. 832, Ch D .... *Digested,* 78/**1538**: *Applied* 02/4330, 03/3556, 03/3561, 10/2751, 12/3192, 15/2406, 17/1307: *Considered* 95/2196, 96/1529, 11/3249, 15/1725

Beatt v Croydon Health Services NHS Trust see Croydon Health Services NHS Trust v Beatt

Beattie v Public Guardian see Miles v Public Guardian

Beaumont v Ferrer [2016] EWCA Civ 768; [2016] R.T.R. 25; [2017] P.I.Q.R. P1; Times, October 4, 2016, CA (Civ Div) .... *Digested,* 16/**1542**

Bechtel v Finanzamt Offenburg (C-20/16) EU:C:2017:488; [2017] S.T.I. 1453, ECJ (10th Chamber)

Beck v Ministry of Defence [2003] EWCA Civ 1043; [2005] 1 W.L.R. 2206; [2003] C.P. Rep. 62; [2004] P.I.Q.R. P1; Times, July 21, 2003; (2003) 100(31) L.S.G. 31, CA (Civ Div) .... *Digested,* 03/**400**: *Considered* 11/327: *Explained* 05/296: *Followed* 17/298

Becker v Finanzamt Munster-Innenstadt (8/81) EU:C:1982:7; [1982] E.C.R. 53; [1982] 1 C.M.L.R. 499, ECJ .... *Digested,* 82/**1333**: *Applied* 91/3640, 98/2111, 99/4984, 00/5321, 03/4559, 03/4568, 07/1565, 07/4351, 14/3057, 17/2285: *Cited* 00/5317: *Considered* 92/4815, 06/4475: *Followed* 04/1206: *Referred to* 13/3190

Beckford v Southwark LBC [2016] I.R.L.R. 178; [2016] I.C.R. D1, EAT .... *Digested,* 16/**671**: *Applied* 17/782, 17/827

Bedat v Switzerland (56925/08) (2016) 63 E.H.R.R. 15; 42 B.H.R.C. 75, ECHR

Bedford v Bedfordshire CC [2013] EWHC 1717 (QB); [2014] P.T.S.R. 351; [2013] H.R.L.R. 33; [2014] B.L.G.R. 44; [2014] Med. L.R. 89, QBD .... *Digested,* 14/**1638**: *Applied* 17/299

Bedriftsforbundet v Norway (103/2013) (2017) 64 E.H.R.R. SE4, ECSR

Bee v Jenson [2006] EWHC 3359 (Comm); [2007] R.T.R. 32; Times, January 16, 2007; (2007) 104(4) L.S.G. 33; (2007) 157 N.L.J. 66, QBD (Comm) *Affirmed* 07/2497: *Applied* 17/644

Beesley v New Century Group Ltd [2008] EWHC 3033 (QB), QBD *Considered* 16/1607, 17/1553

Begg v HM Treasury [2016] EWCA Civ 568; [2016] 1 W.L.R. 4113; [2017] 3 All E.R. 146; [2016] C.P. Rep. 39; Times, September 15, 2016, CA (Civ Div) .... *Digested,* 16/**300**

Beggs v Scottish Information Commissioner [2016] CSIH 23; 2016 S.C. 615; 2016 G.W.D. 11-225, IH (Ex Div) .... *Digested,* 17/**2395**

Begum (Rikha) v Tower Hamlets LBC; *sub nom* Tower Hamlets LBC v Begum (Rikha) [2005] EWCA Civ 340; [2005] 1 W.L.R. 2103; [2005] H.L.R. 34; [2005] B.L.G.R. 503; Independent, April 6, 2005; (2005) 149 S.J.L.B. 393; [2005] N.P.C. 49, CA (Civ Div) .... *Digested,* 05/**1986**: *Considered* 13/1523: *Followed* 16/1036, 17/1148, 17/1157

BEH Electricity, Re (AT.39767) [2017] 5 C.M.L.R. 9, CEC

Behic v Northumberland CC [2017] UKUT 269 (LC); [2017] R.V.R. 352, UT (Lands)

Belcher v Revenue and Customs Commissioners [2017] UKFTT 427 (TC); [2017] S.T.I. 1215, FTT (Tax)

Belco Trading Co v Kondo [2008] EWCA Civ 205, CA (Civ Div) *Considered* 10/411, 15/357, 17/358

Belfast International Airport Ltd v Commissioner of Valuation [2017] R.A. 407, Lands Tr (NI)

Belgium v Oxycure Belgium SA (C-573/15) EU:C:2017:189; [2017] B.V.C. 12; [2017] S.T.I. 793, ECJ (6th Chamber)

Belgium v Recolta Recycling SPRL (C-440/04) see Kittel v Belgium (C-439/04)

Belgium v Temco Europe SA (C-284/03) EU:C:2004:730; [2005] S.T.C. 1451; [2004] E.C.R. I-11237; [2005] 1 C.M.L.R. 23; [2005] C.E.C. 20; [2007] B.T.C. 5339; [2007] B.V.C. 308; Times, November 25, 2004; [2004] S.T.I. 2399, ECJ (1st Chamber) .... *Digested,* 05/**4351**: *Applied* 06/4493, 09/4106, 17/2236: *Considered* 12/3414, 13/3194, 17/2237

Belgium v Wereldhave Belgium Comm VA (C-448/15) EU:C:2017:180; [2017] B.T.C. 6, ECJ (5th Chamber)

Belhaj v Straw; *joined case* Rahmatullah v Ministry of Defence [2014] EWCA Civ 1394; [2015] 2 W.L.R. 1105; [2016] 1 All E.R. 121, CA (Civ Div) .... *Digested,* 15/**1566**: *Affirmed* 17/1426: *Followed* 17/379

Belhaj v Straw; *joined case* Rahmatullah v Ministry of Defence [2017] UKSC 3; [2017] A.C. 964; [2017] 2 W.L.R. 456; [2017] 3 All E.R. 337; [2017] H.R.L.R. 4, SC ..... *Digested,* 17/**1426**: *Followed* 17/157

Bell v Birchall see Birchall (A Bankrupt), Re

Bell v Lever Brothers Ltd; *sub nom* Lever Bros Ltd v Bell [1932] A.C. 161, HL *Applied* 47-51/9247, 47-51/9254, 53/3290, 57/596, 80/592, 83/430, 89/430, 91/408, 91/425, 02/720, 06/2926, 06/767, 07/2715, 08/2743: *Considered* 68/3999, 69/1819, 99/2111, 07/339, 11/1068: *Distinguished* 66/1854, 68/2240, 83/1254, 03/518, 05/524: *Followed* 17/2069

Bellinger v Mercer Ltd; *sub nom* Mercer Ltd v Ballinger [2014] EWCA Civ 996; [2014] 1 W.L.R. 3597; [2014] Pens. L.R. 669; (2014) 158(31) S.J.L.B. 37, CA (Civ Div) .... *Digested,* 14/**426**: *Followed* 17/340, 17/343

Bellman v Northampton Recruitment Ltd [2016] EWHC 3104 (QB); [2017] I.C.R. 543; [2017] I.R.L.R. 124, QBD .... *Digested,* 17/**2205**

Benedictus v Jalaram (1989) 58 P. & C.R. 330; [1989] 1 E.G.L.R. 251; [1988] E.G. 173 (C.S.), CA (Civ Div) .... *Digested,* 90/**2804**: *Considered* 10/2592, 17/433

Beng Tan v Commissioner of Taxation 19 I.T.L. Rep. 719, AAT (Aus)

Benjamin Cope & Sons Ltd, Re; *sub nom* Marshall v Benjamin Cope & Sons Ltd [1914] 1 Ch. 800, Ch D *Considered* 17/159

Bent v Highways and Utilities Construction see Pattni v First Leicester Buses Ltd

Bentine v Bentine see Wilsons Solicitors LLP v Bentine

Benyon v Customs and Excise Commissioners see Beynon v Customs and Excise Commissioners

Berardi v San Marino (24705/16) (2017) 65 E.H.R.R. SE11, ECHR

Berezovsky v Abramovich [2011] EWCA Civ 153; [2011] 1 W.L.R. 2290; [2011] 1 C.L.C. 359; (2011) 108(10) L.S.G. 23, CA (Civ Div) .... *Digested,* 11/**362**: *Considered* 12/120, 17/285: *Followed* 11/139

Berg v Besselsen (C144/87); *joined case* Busschers v Besselsen (C145/87) EU:C:1988:236; [1988] E.C.R. 2559; [1989] 3 C.M.L.R. 817; [1990] I.C.R. 396; [1989] I.R.L.R. 447, ECJ (5th Chamber) *Approved* 95/5911: *Considered* 95/2063, 96/2640: *Distinguished* 94/2004: *Followed* 17/769

Berkeley Applegate (Investment Consultants) Ltd (No.1), Re; *joined case* Harris v Conway [1989] Ch. 32; [1988] 3 W.L.R. 95; [1988] 3 All E.R. 71; (1988) 4 B.C.C. 274; [1989] B.C.L.C. 28; [1989] P.C.C. 261; (1988) 132 S.J. 896, Ch D (Companies Ct) .... *Digested,* 88/**362**: *Cited* 04/2170: *Considered* 14/2493, 15/1448, 16/1166, 17/1272: *Referred to* 11/1898

Berlioz Investment Fund SA v Directeur de l'administration des contributions directes (C-682/15) see Berlioz Investment Fund SA v Director of the Direct Taxation Administration, Luxembourg (C-682/15)

Berlioz Investment Fund SA v Director of the Direct Taxation Administration, Luxembourg (C-682/15); *sub nom* Berlioz Investment Fund SA v Directeur de l'administration des contributions directes (C-682/15) EU:C:2017:373; [2018] 1 C.M.L.R. 1; [2017] B.T.C. 15, ECJ (Grand Chamber)

Bermingham v United States see R. (on the application of Bermingham) v Director of the Serious Fraud Office

Bernard v Attorney General of Jamaica [2004] UKPC 47; [2005] I.R.L.R. 398; (2004) 148 S.J.L.B. 1281, PC (Jam) .... *Digested,* 05/**4200**: *Applied* 05/4199, 06/2916, 12/2298, 17/2205: *Considered* 08/3906: *Distinguished* 07/4201

Bernard Sport Surfaces Ltd v Astrosoccer4U Ltd see Bernhards Sport Surfaces Ltd v Astrosoccer4U Ltd

Bernhards Sport Surfaces Ltd v Astrosoccer4U Ltd; *sub nom* Bernard Sport Surfaces Ltd v Astrosoccer4U Ltd [2017] EWHC 2425 (TCC); [2017] C.I.L.L. 4041, QBD (TCC)

Berriello v Felixstowe Dock & Railway Co [1989] 1 W.L.R. 695; [1989] I.C.R. 467; (1989) 133 S.J. 918, CA (Civ Div) .... *Digested,* 89/**1292**: *Applied* 17/827

Berry v Iceland Foods Ltd; *sub nom* Iceland Foods Ltd v Berry (Valuation Officer) [2016] EWCA Civ 1150; [2017] Bus. L.R. 766; [2017] R.A. 1, CA (Civ Div) .... *Digested,* 17/**1520**

Berry v Iceland Foods Ltd; *sub nom* Iceland Foods Ltd v Berry (Valuation Officer) [2015] UKUT 14 (LC); [2015] R.A. 201, UT (Lands) *Affirmed* 17/1520: *Applied* 17/1526

Bessant v South Cone Inc see REEF Trade Mark

Best Buys Supplies Ltd v Revenue and Customs Commissioners [2011] UKUT 497 (TCC); [2012] S.T.C. 885; [2012] B.V.C. 1501, UT (Tax) .... *Digested,* 12/**3392**: *Approved* 17/2229

Besterman v British Motor Cab Co Ltd [1914] 3 K.B. 181, CA *Considered* 47-51/7577, 17/223: *Distinguished* 47-51/9883

Bestfort Development LLP v Ras Al Khaimah Investment Authority [2015] EWHC 3197 (Ch), Ch D *Reversed* 17/362

Bestfort Developments LLP v Ras Al Khaimah Investment Authority [2016] EWCA Civ 1099; [2017] C.P. Rep. 9; [2016] 2 C.L.C. 714, CA (Civ Div) .... *Digested,* 17/**362**

Bethell Construction Ltd v Deloitte and Touche [2011] EWCA Civ 1321, CA (Civ Div) *Considered* 15/359, 17/367

Betriebsrat der Ruhrlandklinik gGmbH v Ruhrlandklinik gGmbH (C-216/15) EU:C:2016:883; [2017] 2 C.M.L.R. 13; [2017] I.R.L.R. 194, ECJ (5th Chamber)

Betterment Properties (Weymouth) Ltd v Dorset CC; *sub nom* Taylor v Betterment Properties (Weymouth) Ltd [2010] EWHC 3045 (Ch); [2011] 1 E.G.L.R. 129; [2010] 48 E.G. 84 (C.S.); [2010] N.P.C. 115, Ch D
Affirmed 12/2763: *Applied* 17/1860

Betterment Properties (Weymouth) Ltd v Dorset CC; *sub nom* Taylor v Betterment Properties (Weymouth) Ltd [2012] EWCA Civ 250; [2012] 2 P. & C.R. 3; [2012] 11 E.G. 93 (C.S.), CA (Civ Div) .... *Digested,* 12/**2763**:
Affirmed 14/2507: *Considered* 15/2047: *Followed* 16/1821, 17/1860

Beumer Group UK Ltd v Vinci Construction UK Ltd [2016] EWHC 2283 (TCC); [2018] 1 All E.R. (Comm) 80; [2017] Bus. L.R. 449; [2017] B.L.R. 53; 168 Con. L.R. 113; (2018) 34 Const. L.J. 68; [2016] C.I.L.L. 3897, QBD (TCC) .... *Digested,* 17/**659**

Bewley Homes Plc v CNM Estates (Surbiton) Ltd [2010] EWHC 2619 (TCC); [2011] B.L.R. 67; [2011] C.I.L.L. 2953, QBD (TCC) .... *Digested,* 11/**495**:
Applied 17/471

Beynon v Customs and Excise Commissioners; *sub nom* Benyon v Customs and Excise Commissioners [2004] UKHL 53; [2005] 1 W.L.R. 86; [2004] 4 All E.R. 1091; [2005] S.T.C. 55; [2004] B.T.C. 5794; [2005] B.V.C. 3; Times, November 26, 2004; [2004] S.T.I. 2434; (2004) 148 S.J.L.B. 1404, HL .... *Digested,* 05/**4397**:
Considered 06/4449, 14/3102, 17/2294: *Distinguished* 08/4061: *Followed* 14/3050

Beyts v Trump International Golf Club Scotland Ltd 2017 S.L.T. (Sh Ct) 93; 2017 G.W.D. 12-187, Sh Ct (Lothian) (Edinburgh) .... *Digested,* 17/**2675**

Bezeliansky v Bezelianskaya [2017] EWCA Civ 76; [2017] 2 F.C.R. 1, CA (Civ Div) .... *Digested,* 17/**1016**

BGC Brokers LP v Tullett Prebon Plc see Tullett Prebon Plc v BGC Brokers LP

BGZ Leasing sp z oo v Dyrektor Izby Skarbowej w Warszawie (C-224/11) EU:C:2013:15; [2013] S.T.C. 2162; [2013] S.T.I. 295, ECJ (6th Chamber)
Applied 13/3229: *Followed* 14/3050, 17/2265

BH v Lord Advocate see H v Lord Advocate

Bhandal, Re see R. (on the application of Bhandal) v Revenue and Customs Commissioners

Bhatia v General Medical Council [2016] EWHC 3221 (Admin); [2017] A.C.D. 26, QBD (Admin)

Bhayani v Taylor Bracewell LLP [2016] EWHC 3360 (IPEC); [2017] E.T.M.R. 14, IPEC .... *Digested,* 17/**1394**

BHL v Leumi ABL Ltd [2017] EWHC 1871 (QB); [2017] 2 Lloyd's Rep. 237, QBD (Merc) .... *Digested,* 17/**154**

BHS Group Ltd (In Administration) v Retail Acquisitions Ltd [2017] EWHC 1057 (Ch); [2017] 2 B.C.L.C. 472; [2017] B.P.I.R. 892, Ch D (Companies Ct) .... *Digested,* 17/**1333**

BHS Ltd (In Administration), Re [2016] EWHC 1965 (Ch); [2016] B.C.C. 609, Ch D (Companies Ct) .... *Digested,* 17/**1270**

Bi v Mohammed [2016] EWHC 506 (Fam), Fam Div
Considered 17/997

Biao v Denmark (38590/10) (2017) 64 E.H.R.R. 1; 41 B.H.R.C. 243; [2016] Imm. A.R. 1165, ECHR

Bibby v Coventry City Council [2016] EWHC 2554 (Admin); [2017] R.V.R. 4, DC .... *Digested,* 17/**1518**

Bibi v Secretary of State for the Home Department see R. (on the application of Aguilar Quila) v Secretary of State for the Home Department

Bieber v Teathers Ltd (In Liquidation) [2014] EWHC 4205 (Ch); [2015] C.I.L.L. 3609, Ch D
Applied 17/2066

Biffa Waste Services Ltd v Maschinenfabrik Ernst Hese GmbH [2008] EWCA Civ 1257; [2009] Q.B. 725; [2009] 3 W.L.R. 324; [2009] Bus. L.R. 696; [2009] B.L.R. 1; 122 Con. L.R. 1; [2009] P.N.L.R. 12; Times, November 21, 2008; (2008) 152(45) S.J.L.B. 25, CA (Civ Div) .... *Digested,* 09/**2732**:
Applied 11/2272: *Considered* 17/477

Biffin Ltd v Revenue and Customs Commissioners [2016] EWHC 2926 (Admin); [2016] B.T.C. 48, QBD (Admin) .... *Digested,* 17/**317**

Big Bad Wolff Ltd v Revenue and Customs Commissioners [2017] UKFTT 729 (TC); [2018] S.F.T.D. 468; [2017] S.T.I. 2257, FTT (Tax)

Biggin & Co Ltd v Permanite Ltd [1951] 2 K.B. 314; [1951] 2 All E.R. 191; [1951] 2 T.L.R. 159; (1951) 95 S.J. 414, CA .... *Digested,* 47-51/**2491**:
Applied 53/3273, 84/3104, 99/1379, 99/1400, 00/826: *Considered* 75/179, 76/58u, 82/230, 99/244, 99/789, 03/670, 07/745: *Followed* 85/3479, 09/671, 10/307, 17/350

Biggin & Co Ltd v Permanite Ltd [1951] 1 K.B. 422; [1950] 2 All E.R. 859; (1950) 66 T.L.R. (Pt. 2) 944, KBD
Considered 04/677, 17/1771: *Reversed in part* 47-51/2491

Bijl v General Medical Council [2001] UKPC 42; [2002] Lloyd's Rep. Med. 60; (2002) 65 B.M.L.R. 10; Times, October 24, 2001, PC (UK) .... *Digested,* 01/**3287**: *Applied* 05/1919: *Considered* 17/1114

Bikam OOD v Adria Cable Sarl [2012] EWHC 621 (Comm), QBD (Comm) *Considered* 17/468

Billson v Residential Apartments Ltd; *sub nom* Residential Apartments Ltd v Billson [1991] 3 W.L.R. 264; [1991] 3 All E.R. 265; (1991) 62 P. & C.R. 505; [1991] 1 E.G.L.R. 70; [1991] 19 E.G. 122; [1991] 18 E.G. 169; Times, February 26, 1991; [1991] E.G. 17 (C.S.), CA (Civ Div) .... *Digested,* 91/**2232**: *Applied* 92/2749, 92/3426, 17/1447: *Considered* 92/2682, 92/2703, 92/3579: *Reversed* 92/2678

Bilta (UK) Ltd (In Liquidation) v Nazir; *sub nom* Jetivia SA v Bilta (UK) Ltd (In Liquidation) [2015] UKSC 23; [2016] A.C. 1; [2015] 2 W.L.R. 1168; [2015] 2 All E.R. 1083; [2015] 2 All E.R. (Comm) 281; [2015] 2 Lloyd's Rep. 61; [2015] B.C.C. 343; [2015] 1 B.C.L.C. 443; [2015] B.V.C. 20, SC .... *Digested,* 15/**1421**: *Applied* 16/1224, 17/2193: *Considered* 16/1230: *Followed* 16/961, 17/2276

Bimbo SA v Office for Harmonisation in the Internal Market (Trade Marks and Designs) (OHIM) (T-569/10) EU:T:2012:535; [2013] E.T.M.R. 7, GC (7th Chamber) *Considered* 17/2690

Birch v Birch [2015] EWCA Civ 833; [2016] 2 F.L.R. 467; [2015] 3 F.C.R. 249; [2015] Fam. Law 1327, CA (Civ Div) .... *Digested,* 15/**1094**: *Reversed* 17/1008

Birch v Birch [2017] UKSC 53; [2017] 1 W.L.R. 2959; [2018] 1 All E.R. 108; [2017] 2 F.L.R. 1031; [2017] 3 F.C.R. 111; Times, August 7, 2017, SC .... *Digested,* 17/**1008**

Birchall (A Bankrupt), Re; *sub nom* Bell v Birchall [2015] EWHC 1541 (Ch); [2017] 1 W.L.R. 667; [2016] 4 All E.R. 766; [2015] B.P.I.R. 751, Ch D (Manchester) .... *Digested,* 15/**1448**

Bird v Acorn Group Ltd [2016] EWCA Civ 1096; [2017] 1 W.L.R. 1915; [2017] C.P. Rep. 8; [2016] 6 Costs L.O. 959; [2017] P.I.Q.R. P7, CA (Civ Div) .... *Digested,* 17/**235**

Bird Precision Bellows Ltd, Re; *sub nom* Company (No.003420 of 1981), Re [1984] Ch. 419; [1984] 2 W.L.R. 869; [1984] 3 All E.R. 444; (1984) 1 B.C.C. 98992; Times, November 4, 1983; (1984) 81 L.S.G. 187; (1984) 128 S.J. 348, Ch D .... *Digested,* 84/**312**: *Affirmed* 85/309: *Considered* 85/308: *Referred to* 17/1575

Birdi v Price [2017] EWHC 1859 (Ch); [2017] B.P.I.R. 1140, Ch D .... *Digested,* 17/**210**

Birdlip Ltd v Hunter [2015] EWHC 808 (Ch), Ch D *Reversed* 17/1828

Birdlip Ltd v Hunter [2016] EWCA Civ 603; [2017] 1 P. & C.R. 1, CA (Civ Div) .... *Digested,* 17/**1828**

Birkett (t/a Orchards Residential Home) v Revenue and Customs Commissioners [2017] UKUT 89 (TCC); [2017] B.T.C. 511, UT (Tax) .... *Digested,* 17/**2150**: *Applied* 17/2125

Birmingham City Council v Ali see Ali v Birmingham City Council

Birmingham City Council v Bagshaw [2017] I.C.R. 263, EAT .... *Digested,* 17/**798**

Birmingham City Council v Equal Opportunities Commission (No.1) see R. v Birmingham City Council Ex p. Equal Opportunities Commission (No.1)

Birmingham City Council v Frisby see Hounslow LBC v Powell

Birmingham City Council v H; *sub nom* Birmingham City Council v H (No.2); Birmingham City Council v H (No.3) [1993] 1 F.L.R. 883; [1993] Fam. Law 459, CA (Civ Div) *Applied* 17/958: *Reversed* 94/3180

Birmingham City Council v H (No.2) see Birmingham City Council v H

Birmingham City Council v H (No.3) see Birmingham City Council v H

Birmingham City Council v SA see S v Birmingham City Council

Birmingham City Council v SS see S v Birmingham City Council

Birmingham City Council v Stephenson [2016] EWCA Civ 1029; [2016] H.L.R. 44; [2017] L.L.R. 249, CA (Civ Div) .... *Digested,* 17/**1459**

Birmingham City Council v Wilson [2016] EWCA Civ 1137; [2017] H.L.R. 4, CA (Civ Div) .... *Digested,* 17/**1146**

Bishop v Baker Refractories Ltd see Barber v Somerset CC

Biskup v Poland see Wolkowicz v Poland

Bitumen Invest AS v Richmond Mercantile Ltd FZC [2016] EWHC 2957 (Comm); [2017] 1 Lloyd's Rep. 219; [2017] B.L.R. 74, QBD (Comm) .... *Digested,* 17/**2010**

Biuro podrozy Partner sp z oo sp k w Dabrowie Gorniczej v Prezes Urzedu Ochrony Konkurencji i Konsumentow (C-119/15) EU:C:2016:987; [2017] 2 C.M.L.R. 34, ECJ (5th Chamber)

BJ Crabtree (Insulation) Ltd v GPT Communication Systems Ltd 59 B.L.R. 43, CA (Civ Div) *Followed* 17/363

Black v Carmichael; *joined case* Carmichael v Black 1992 S.L.T. 897; 1992 S.C.C.R. 709; Times, June 25, 1992; Independent, July 27, 1992; Guardian, July 8, 1992, HCJ Appeal .... *Digested,* 92/**5545**: *Applied* 17/2597: *Distinguished* 96/5698

Black v Sumitomo Corp [2001] EWCA Civ 1819; [2002] 1 W.L.R. 1562; [2003] 3 All E.R. 643; [2002] 1 Lloyd's Rep. 693; [2002] C.P.L.R. 148; Times, January 25, 2002; Independent, December 13, 2001, CA (Civ Div) .... *Digested,* 02/**422**: *Applied* 02/426, 05/456, 06/430, 06/431, 07/500, 07/503, 08/356, 08/402, 09/397, 09/434, 16/295: *Considered* 07/502, 08/401, 08/403: *Followed* 10/398, 14/438, 15/289, 16/294, 17/188

Black v United Kingdom (40713/09) see Austin v United Kingdom (39692/09)

Black Diamond Offshore Ltd v Fomento de Construcciones y Contratas SA; *sub nom* Fomento de Construcciones y Contratas SA v Black Diamond Offshore Ltd [2016] EWCA Civ 1141; [2017] 1 B.C.L.C. 196, CA (Civ Div) .... *Digested,* 17/**168**

Black Diamond Offshore Ltd v Fomento de Construcciones y Contratas SA; *sub nom* Fomento de Construcciones y Contratas SA v Black Diamond Offshore Ltd HC-2015-000148, Ch D
Affirmed 17/168

Blackbay Ventures Ltd (t/a Chemistree) v Gahir [2014] I.C.R. 747; [2014] I.R.L.R. 416, EAT .... *Digested,* 14/**1096**: *Applied* 17/815

Blackburn v Chief Constable of the West Midlands see Chief Constable of the West Midlands v Blackburn

Blackrock Investment Management (UK) Ltd v Revenue and Customs Commissioners [2017] UKFTT 633 (TC); [2018] S.F.T.D. 232; [2017] S.T.I. 1905, FTT (Tax)

Blackshaw v MFS Portfolio Ltd [2016] EWHC 3708 (Ch); [2017] C.T.L.C. 217, Ch D

Blackwell v Revenue and Customs Commissioners; *sub nom* Revenue and Customs Commissioners v Blackwell [2015] UKUT 418 (TCC); [2016] S.T.C. 598; [2015] B.T.C. 526, UT (Tax) .... *Digested,* 15/**2432**: *Affirmed* 17/2097

Blackwell v Revenue and Customs Commissioners; *sub nom* Revenue and Customs Commissioners v Blackwell [2017] EWCA Civ 232; [2017] 4 W.L.R. 164; [2017] 4 All E.R. 188; [2017] S.T.C. 1159; [2017] B.T.C. 9; Times, June 5, 2017; [2017] S.T.I. 1099, CA (Civ Div) .... *Digested,* 17/**2097**

Blagdon Cemetery, Re [2002] Fam. 299; [2002] 3 W.L.R. 603; [2002] 4 All E.R. 482; (2002) 99(20) L.S.G. 31; (2002) 146 S.J.L.B. 108, Arches Ct
Applied 04/943, 05/993: *Considered* 06/1058, 13/810: *Followed* 13/803: *Not applied* 17/660

Bland (Millwood Designer Homes Ltd) v Maidstone BC [2017] P.A.D. 11, Planning Inspector

Blasi v Finanzamt Munchen I (C-346/95) EU:C:1998:51; [1998] S.T.C. 336; [1998] E.C.R. I-481; [1998] All E.R. (EC) 211; [1998] C.E.C. 408; [1998] B.T.C. 5188; [1998] B.V.C. 247, ECJ (5th Chamber) .... *Digested,* 98/**4897**: *Applied* 17/2264: *Considered* 04/3976, 05/4351, 10/3475: *Followed* 13/3232

Blast 106 Ltd's Application for Judicial Review, Re [2014] NIQB 95, QBD (NI)
Reversed 17/2302

Blast 106 Ltd's Application for Judicial Review, Re [2015] NICA 16; [2016] N.I. 189, CA (NI) .... *Digested,* 17/**2302**

Blavo v Law Society [2017] EWHC 561 (Ch); [2017] 1 W.L.R. 4514; [2017] B.P.I.R. 909, Ch D .... *Digested,* 17/**1323**

Blenheim Leisure (Restaurants) Ltd (No.1), Re [2000] B.C.C. 554; Times, August 13, 1999; Independent, November 8, 1999; (1999) 96(33) L.S.G. 29; [1999] N.P.C. 105, CA (Civ Div) .... *Digested,* 99/**602**: *Applied* 03/505: *Followed* 17/402

Blewitt v Derbyshire Waste Ltd see R. (on the application of Blewett) v Derbyshire CC

Blindley Heath Investments Ltd v Bass; *sub nom* Dixon v Blindley Heath Investments Ltd [2014] EWHC 1366 (Ch), Ch D
Affirmed 17/406

Blindley Heath Investments Ltd v Bass; *sub nom* Dixon v Blindley Heath Investments Ltd [2015] EWCA Civ 1023; [2017] Ch. 389; [2017] 3 W.L.R. 166; [2016] 4 All E.R. 490; [2017] 1 All E.R. (Comm) 319, CA (Civ Div) .... *Digested,* 17/**406**

Blohn v Desser [1962] 2 Q.B. 116; [1961] 3 W.L.R. 719; [1961] 3 All E.R. 1; (1961) 105 S.J. 724, QBD .... *Digested,* 61/**1319**: *Considered* 17/432: *Disapproved* 71/1548

Blomqvist v Aziz see Zavarco Plc, Re

Blomqvist v Peng see Blomqvist v Zavarco Plc

Blomqvist v Teoh see Blomqvist v Zavarco Plc

Blomqvist v Zavarco Plc; *sub nom* Blomqvist v Peng; *joined case* Blomqvist v Teoh [2016] EWHC 1143 (Ch); [2016] Bus. L.R. 907; [2016] B.C.C. 542; [2017] 1 B.C.L.C. 373, Ch D (Companies Ct) .... *Digested,* 16/**353**

Blomqvist v Zavarco Plc see Zavarco Plc, Re

Bloom v Pensions Regulator; *sub nom* Lehman Brothers International (Europe) (In Administration), Re; Nortel Networks UK Pension Trust Ltd, Re; Nortel GmbH (In Administration), Re; Nortel Companies, Re; Lehman Companies, Re; *joined case* Lomas v Pensions Regulator [2013] UKSC 52; [2014] A.C. 209; [2013] 3 W.L.R. 504; [2013] 4 All E.R. 887; [2013] Bus. L.R. 1056; [2013] B.C.C. 624; [2013] 2 B.C.L.C. 135; [2013] B.P.I.R. 866; [2013] Pens. L.R. 299, SC .... *Digested,* 13/**2138**: *Applied* 14/1773, 16/1165, 16/1258, 16/2694, 17/1259: *Cited* 17/1359: *Considered* 14/1752, 16/1180: *Followed* 15/1395, 15/1396, 15/177, 15/230, 17/1258

Bloomberg LP v Sandberg (A Firm) [2016] EWHC 488 (TCC); [2017] 1 Costs L.O. 1, QBD (TCC)

Bloomsbury Law Solicitors v MacPherson [2016] EWHC 3394 (QB); [2016] 6 Costs L.R. 1227, QBD .... *Digested,* 17/**204**

Bloomsbury Publishing Group Ltd v Newsgroup Newspapers Ltd (Continuation of Injunction) see Bloomsbury Publishing Group Plc v News Group Newspapers Ltd (Continuation of Injunction)

Bloomsbury Publishing Group Plc v News Group Newspapers Ltd (Continuation of Injunction); *sub nom* Bloomsbury Publishing Group Ltd v Newsgroup Newspapers Ltd (Continuation of Injunction) [2003] EWHC 1205 (Ch); [2003] 1 W.L.R. 1633; [2003] 3 All E.R. 736; [2003] C.P. Rep. 55; [2003] F.S.R. 45; Times, June 5, 2003; (2003) 100(29) L.S.G. 35; (2003) 153 N.L.J. 882, Ch D ... *Digested,* 03/**422**: *Applied* 17/1878

Bloor Construction (UK) Ltd v Bowmer and Kirkland (London) Ltd [2000] B.L.R. 314; (2000) 2 T.C.L.R. 914, QBD (TCC) *Applied* 09/649, 10/566: *Considered* 07/732, 08/607, 17/2461

Bloor Homes East Midlands Ltd v Secretary of State for Communities and Local Government [2014] EWHC 754 (Admin); [2017] P.T.S.R. 1283, QBD (Admin) *Applied* 16/1748, 17/1725: *Approved* 17/1779: *Considered* 16/1728

BLP Group Plc v Customs and Excise Commissioners (C-4/94) EU:C:1995:107; [1996] 1 W.L.R. 174; [1995] S.T.C. 424; [1995] E.C.R. I-983; [1995] 2 C.M.L.R. 750; [1995] All E.R. (E.C.) 401; [1995] B.V.C. 159; Times, April 17, 1995, ECJ (5th Chamber) .... *Digested,* 95/**5059**: *Applied* 00/5309, 01/5585, 03/4551, 03/4556, 04/3990, 04/3994, 06/4456, 08/3990, 08/4013, 09/4059, 12/3396, 13/3245, 15/2584, 16/2177: *Considered* 98/4932, 99/5015, 11/3553, 14/3089, 17/2272: *Distinguished* 96/5869, 99/4994: *Followed* 96/5866, 97/5003, 01/5606, 12/3426, 17/2295: *Referred to* 00/5337

Blue v Ashley [2017] EWHC 1553 (Comm); [2017] 1 W.L.R. 3630; [2018] 2 All E.R. 284; [2017] E.M.L.R. 27, QBD (Comm) .... *Digested,* 17/**189**

Blue Chip Hotels Ltd v Revenue and Customs Commissioners [2016] UKFTT 309 (TC); [2016] S.T.I. 1574, FTT (Tax) *Affirmed* 17/2236

Blue Chip Hotels Ltd v Revenue and Customs Commissioners [2017] UKUT 204 (TCC); [2017] B.V.C. 516, UT (Tax) .... *Digested,* 17/**2236**

Blue Holdings (1) Pte Ltd v National Crime Agency see National Crime Agency v Abacha

Bluhdorn v Germany (62054/12) [2017] M.H.L.R. 144, ECHR

Bluu Solutions Ltd v Revenue and Customs Commissioners [2015] UKFTT 95 (TC); [2015] S.T.I. 1582, FTT (Tax) *Applied* 17/2082

BM v HM Advocate [2017] HCJAC 55; 2017 S.C.L. 882; 2017 G.W.D. 23-388, HCJ .... *Digested,* 17/**2498**

BM (Albania) v Advocate General for Scotland [2017] CSOH 17; 2017 S.L.T. 247; [2017] Imm. A.R. 1143; 2017 G.W.D. 5-70, OH .... *Digested,* 17/**2671**

BMC Software Ltd v Shaikh [2017] I.R.L.R. 1074, EAT .... *Digested,* 17/**800**

BMG (Mansfield) Ltd v Galliford Try Construction Ltd [2013] EWHC 3183 (TCC); [2014] C.P. Rep. 3; [2017] T.C.L.R. 4; [2014] C.I.L.L. 3437, QBD (TCC) .... *Digested,* 14/**291**: *Applied* 16/154: *Followed* 16/152

BMO v BMP [2017] SGHC 127; [2017] 2 Lloyd's Rep. 57, HC (Sing)

BNP Paribas v Ahab CO X19 [2011] EWHC 1081 (Comm), QBD (Comm) *Applied* 17/371

BNP Paribas v Deloitte & Touche LLP [2003] EWHC 2874 (Comm); [2004] 1 Lloyd's Rep. 233; [2004] 1 C.L.C. 530; [2004] B.L.R. 90; (2003) 153 N.L.J. 1841, QBD (Comm) .... *Digested,* 05/**209**: *Applied* 05/211, 17/334

BNP Paribas SA v Open Joint Stock Company Russian Machines [2011] EWHC 308 (Comm); [2012] 1 Lloyd's Rep. 61; [2011] 2 C.L.C. 942; [2011] Arb. L.R. 49, QBD (Comm)
Affirmed 12/313: *Considered* 17/334

BNP Paribas SA (London Branch) v Revenue and Customs Commissioners [2017] UKFTT 487 (TC); [2017] S.T.I. 1933, FTT (Tax)

BNY Corporate Trustee Services Ltd v Eurosail-UK 2007-3BL Plc; *joined case* BNY Corporate Trustee Services Ltd v v Neuberger Berman Europe Ltd [2010] EWHC 2005 (Ch); [2011] 1 W.L.R. 1200; [2010] Bus. L.R. 1731; Times, September 23, 2010, Ch D .... *Digested,* 10/**236**:
Affirmed 11/216: *Applied* 17/1333

BNY Corporate Trustee Services Ltd v v Neuberger Berman Europe Ltd see BNY Corporate Trustee Services Ltd v Eurosail-UK 2007-3BL Plc

BNY Mellon Corporate Trustee Services Ltd v LBG Capital No.1 Plc; *sub nom* LBG Capital No.1 Plc v BNY Mellon Corporate Trustee Services Ltd [2016] UKSC 29; [2017] 1 All E.R. 497; [2016] 2 All E.R. (Comm) 851; [2016] Bus. L.R. 725; [2016] 2 Lloyd's Rep. 119; [2016] 2 B.C.L.C. 163; Times, June 20, 2016, SC .... *Digested,* 16/**140**:
Applied 17/157

Boam v Information Commissioner [2017] E.L.R. 176, FTT (GRC) .... *Digested,* 17/**696**

Board (otherwise Checkland) v Checkland [1987] 2 F.L.R. 257; [1987] Fam. Law 236, CA (Civ Div) .... *Digested,* 87/**1731**:
Applied 04/1521: *Followed* 17/1002

Bogendorff von Wolffersdorff v Standesamt der Stadt Karlsruhe (C-438/14) EU:C:2016:401; [2017] 1 C.M.L.R. 4, ECJ (2nd Chamber)

Boggis v Revenue and Customs Commissioners [2016] UKFTT 794 (TC); [2017] S.T.I. 114, FTT (Tax)

Boland v Bridgend CBC; *sub nom* Bridgend CBC v Boland [2017] EWCA Civ 1004; [2017] R.V.R. 243; [2018] J.P.L. 13, CA (Civ Div) .... *Digested,* 17/**1698**

Boland v Bridgend CBC; *sub nom* Bridgend CBC v Boland [2016] UKUT 174 (LC); [2017] R.V.R. 186, UT (Lands)
Affirmed 17/1698

Boldhurst Properties Ltd v Sevenoaks DC [2017] P.A.D. 13, Planning Inspector

Bolitho v City and Hackney Health Authority [1998] A.C. 232; [1997] 3 W.L.R. 1151; [1997] 4 All E.R. 771; [1998] P.I.Q.R. P10; [1998] Lloyd's Rep. Med. 26; (1998) 39 B.M.L.R. 1; [1998] P.N.L.R. 1; Times, November 27, 1997; (1997) 94(47) L.S.G. 30; (1997) 141 S.J.L.B. 238, HL .... *Digested,* 97/**3789**:
Applied 98/3977, 99/3994, 01/4263, 01/4542, 02/3294, 03/5826, 04/2698, 06/2869, 07/2917, 07/2926, 08/2644, 08/2763, 09/2840, 09/2842, 09/2844, 09/73, 14/2197, 17/1561: *Considered* 98/3986, 03/2989, 07/2923, 07/3068, 16/2731, 17/1568, 17/2736: *Distinguished* 98/3969, 05/2863: *Followed* 98/3963, 99/3989

Bolkiah v KPMG; *sub nom* HRH Prince Jefri Bolkiah v KPMG [1999] 2 A.C. 222; [1999] 2 W.L.R. 215; [1999] 1 All E.R. 517; [1999] 1 B.C.L.C. 1; [1999] C.L.C. 175; [1999] P.N.L.R. 220; Times, April 20, 1999; Independent, January 12, 1999; (1999) 149 N.L.J. 16; (1999) 143 S.J.L.B. 35, HL .... *Digested,* 99/**1**:
Applied 00/2504, 00/4008, 02/216, 02/3108, 04/2569, 05/2724, 12/2097, 14/2060, 17/184, 17/2712, 17/458: *Considered* 99/2, 99/3796, 00/4007, 03/2821, 06/1042, 11/287, 12/1051, 12/1140, 12/334: *Distinguished* 12/418: *Followed* 00/2469, 10/1379

Bolton v Law Society [1994] 1 W.L.R. 512; [1994] 2 All E.R. 486; Times, December 8, 1993; [1994] C.O.D. 295, CA (Civ Div) .... *Digested,* 94/**4220**:
Applied 98/3724, 03/1724, 05/1807, 05/3349, 09/1000, 09/2587, 10/1545, 17/1790: *Approved* 03/1733: *Considered* 07/2800, 10/1539: *Followed* 97/3375, 05/1805, 13/1952, 14/2056, 14/2057

Bolton v Stone; *sub nom* Stone v Bolton [1951] A.C. 850; [1951] 1 All E.R. 1078; [1951] 1 T.L.R. 977; 50 L.G.R. 32; (1951) 95 S.J. 333, HL .... *Digested,* 47-51/**6897**:
Applied 47-51/6863, 47-51/9855, 53/2524, 57/2376, 57/2416, 61/5875, 62/2033, 69/2400, 74/3364, 98/3994, 07/4196: *Considered* 62/2083, 70/1067, 75/2291, 75/2324, 77/2146, 77/2597, 87/4737, 95/3659, 09/2847: *Distinguished* 66/3445:
Referred to 17/1564

Bolton MBC v Municipal Mutual Insurance Ltd [2006] EWCA Civ 50; [2006] 1 W.L.R. 1492; [2006] 1 C.L.C. 242; [2007] Lloyd's Rep. I.R. 173; Times, February 9, 2006; Independent, February 9, 2006; (2006) 103(9) L.S.G. 31; (2006) 150 S.J.L.B. 226, CA (Civ Div) .... *Digested,* 06/**2431**:
Applied 17/493: *Distinguished* 09/2277: *Followed* 11/1905

Bolton MBC v Secretary of State for the Environment; *sub nom* R. v Secretary of State for the Environment Ex p. Bolton MDC [2017] P.T.S.R. 1063; (1991) 61 P. & C.R. 343; [1991] J.P.L. 241; [1990] E.G. 106 (C.S.), CA (Civ Div) .... *Digested,* 91/**94**:
Applied 93/3840, 96/4764, 97/4130, 01/2038, 02/3733, 07/3291, 09/3038, 13/2358, 17/1761: *Considered* 94/43, 96/4734, 96/4754, 97/4031, 97/4061, 99/4230, 06/3339, 10/2595, 17/1772: *Followed* 94/4400, 97/4125

Bolton MDC v Manchester Ship Canal Co see Bolton MDC v Secretary of State for the Environment

Bolton MDC v Secretary of State for the Environment; *joined cases* Bolton MDC v Trafford Park Development Corp; Bolton MDC v Manchester Ship Canal Co [2017] P.T.S.R. 1091; 94 L.G.R. 387; (1996) 71 P. & C.R. 309; Times, May 25, 1995; Independent, July 10, 1995; [1995] J.P.L. 1043; (1996) 160 L.G. Rev. 361; [1995] E.G. 94 (C.S.); (1995) 139 S.J.L.B. 190; [1995] N.P.C. 99; (1995) 70 P. & C.R. D25, HL .... *Digested,* 96/**4834**:
Applied 96/4674, 97/4130, 01/4684: *Considered* 96/4777, 97/4090: *Followed* 95/4886, 96/4753, 97/4122, 98/4222

Bolton MDC v Trafford Park Development Corp see Bolton MDC v Secretary of State for the Environment

Bolton School v Evans [2006] I.R.L.R. 500; [2006] E.L.R. 255, EAT .... *Digested,* 06/**1401**:
Affirmed 07/1438: *Considered* 17/815

Bolton St Catherine's Academy v O'Brien; *sub nom* O'Brien v Bolton St Catherine's Academy [2017] EWCA Civ 145; [2017] I.C.R. 737; [2017] I.R.L.R. 547; Times, May 8, 2017, CA (Civ Div) .... *Digested,* 17/**846**

Bolton St Catherine's Academy v O'Brien; *sub nom* O'Brien v Bolton St Catherine's Academy UKEAT/0051/15/LA, EAT
Reversed 17/846

Bombardier Transportation Ltd v Merseytravel [2017] EWHC 575 (TCC); 171 Con. L.R. 241, QBD (TCC) .... *Digested,* 17/**215**

Bomford v Osborne (Inspector of Taxes) [1942] A.C. 14; [1941] 2 All E.R. 426, HL
Applied 47-51/4678, 47-51/4772: *Considered* 67/3363, 15/1700, 17/2146

Bond v Dunster Properties Ltd [2011] EWCA Civ 455; (2011) 108(19) L.S.G. 21; (2011) 161 N.L.J. 634, CA (Civ Div)
Considered 15/88: *Followed* 13/2095, 17/1847

Bonifacti v Italy (C-9/90) see Francovich v Italy (C-6/90)

Bonner Properties Ltd v McGurran Construction Ltd [2009] NICA 49; [2010] N.I. 97, CA (NI) .... *Digested,* 10/**3615**:
Followed 17/2328

Bonnick v Morris [2002] UKPC 31; [2003] 1 A.C. 300; [2002] 3 W.L.R. 820; [2002] E.M.L.R. 37; 12 B.H.R.C. 558; Times, June 18, 2002; (2002) 146 S.J.L.B. 161, PC (Jam) .... *Digested,* 02/**953**:
Applied 06/1050: *Considered* 05/977, 06/1044, 08/901, 17/651

Bonomini Associates Ltd v Revenue and Customs Commissioners [2017] UKFTT 683 (TC); [2017] S.T.I. 2069, FTT (Tax)

Bonus Malus System, Re (C-346/02) see Commission of the European Communities v Luxembourg (C-346/02)

Bookit Ltd v Revenue and Customs Commissioners (C-607/14) EU:C:2016:355; [2016] B.V.C. 21; Times, June 8, 2016, ECJ (2nd Chamber)
Considered 17/2233

Booth v Parole Board see Reilly's Application for Judicial Review, Re

Boreh v Djibouti; *sub nom* Gray v Boreh [2017] EWCA Civ 56; Times, April 28, 2017, CA (Civ Div) .... *Digested,* 17/**335**

Born London Ltd v Spire Production Services Ltd [2017] I.C.R. 998; [2017] I.R.L.R. 493, EAT .... *Digested,* 17/**842**

Borrows v HM Coroner for Preston see Burrows v HM Coroner for Preston

Bosma v Larsen [1966] 1 Lloyd's Rep. 22, QBD (Comm) .... *Digested,* 66/**11212**:
Considered 17/1342

Boss Holdings Ltd v Grosvenor West End Properties Ltd; *joined case* Mallett & Sons (Antiques) Ltd v Grosvenor West End Properties Ltd [2008] UKHL 5; [2008] 1 W.L.R. 289; [2008] 2 All E.R. 759; [2008] H.L.R. 29; [2008] 2 P. & C.R. 20; [2008] L. & T.R. 10; [2008] 1 E.G.L.R. 51; [2008] 15 E.G. 174; [2008] R.V.R. 313; Times, February 4, 2008; [2008] 5 E.G. 167 (C.S.); (2008) 152(6) S.J.L.B. 31; [2008] N.P.C. 9, HL .... *Digested,* 08/**2450**:
Considered 12/3423, 13/2439: *Followed* 10/2716, 14/1770, 17/1843

Bossen v Brussels Airlines SA/NV (C-559/16) EU:C:2017:644; [2018] Bus. L.R. 486; [2017] 2 Lloyd's Rep. 571, ECJ (8th Chamber)

Botham v Ministry of Defence see Lawson v Serco Ltd

Bougnaoui v Micropole SA (C-188/15) EU:C:2017:204; [2017] 3 C.M.L.R. 22; [2018] I.C.R. 139; [2017] I.R.L.R. 447; Times, March 27, 2017, ECJ (Grand Chamber)

Boultif v Switzerland (54273/00) [2001] 2 F.L.R. 1228; (2001) 33 E.H.R.R. 50; [2001] Fam. Law 875, ECHR ... *Digested,* 02/**2516**: *Applied* 06/2178, 06/2180, 07/2252, 10/1745, 10/1773, 17/1200: *Considered* 04/2063, 05/2120, 07/2262, 09/2070, 10/1266, 11/1762, 11/4388, 15/3157: *Distinguished* 06/5522

Bourne Leisure (Hopton) Ltd v Great Yarmouth Port Authority [2016] UKUT 44 (LC); [2016] R.V.R. 371, UT (Lands) ... *Digested,* 17/**1832**

Bouygues UK Ltd v Dahl-Jensen UK Ltd [2000] B.L.R. 49; (2000) 2 T.C.L.R. 308; 70 Con. L.R. 41; Independent, February 7, 2000, QBD (TCC) *Affirmed* 00/3489: *Applied* 02/654, 10/566, 14/581, 15/459: *Considered* 17/2461: *Followed* 01/6289

Bouygues UK Ltd v Dahl-Jensen UK Ltd [2001] 1 All E.R. (Comm) 1041; [2001] C.L.C. 927; [2000] B.L.R. 522; (2001) 3 T.C.L.R. 2; 73 Con. L.R. 135; Times, August 17, 2000; (2000) 97(35) L.S.G. 36, CA (Civ Div) ... *Digested,* 00/**3489**: *Applied* 03/667, 05/644, 06/333, 10/845, 10/847, 12/600, 14/578: *Considered* 02/655, 11/486, 16/405: *Distinguished* 10/556: *Followed* 10/558, 10/846, 17/452

Bovey Cranbrook RBS, Re; *joined case* Pensions Regulator v Dalriada Trustees Ltd [2013] EWHC 4346 (Ch), Ch D *Applied* 17/1609

Bow v Harvie see Paterson v Harvie

Bowes v Highland Council [2017] CSOH 53; 2017 S.L.T. 749; 2017 Rep. L.R. 52; 2017 G.W.D. 12-193, OH ... *Digested,* 17/**2738**

Bowling and Welby's Contract, Re [1895] 1 Ch. 663, CA *Considered* 17/409

Bowman v Guthrie 1998 S.L.T. (Land Ct) 2; 1997 S.L.C.R. 40, Land Ct ... *Digested,* 98/**6030**: *Considered* 17/2402

Boyle v SCA Packaging Ltd see SCA Packaging Ltd v Boyle

BP v DP (Children) (Wrongful Retention: Anticipatory Breach) [2016] EWHC 633 (Fam); [2017] 4 W.L.R. 33, Fam Div ... *Digested,* 17/**1040**

BP Europa SE v Hauptzollamt Hamburg-Stadt (C-64/15) EU:C:2016:62, ECJ *Applied* 17/632

BP Gas Marketing Ltd v La Societe Sonatrach [2016] EWHC 2461 (Comm); 169 Con. L.R. 141, QBD (Comm) ... *Digested,* 17/**506**

BP's Application for Judicial Review, Re [2015] NICA 20; [2017] N.I. 40, CA (NI)

BPE Solicitors v Gabriel see Gabriel v Little

bpost NV van Publiek Recht (formerly De Post NV van Publiek Recht) v European Commission (T-514/09) EU:T:2011:689; [2011] E.C.R. II-420, GC *Applied* 17/1816

BPP Holdings Ltd v Revenue and Customs Commissioners [2016] EWCA Civ 121; [2016] 1 W.L.R. 1915; [2016] 3 All E.R. 245; [2016] S.T.C. 841; [2017] R.V.R. 132; [2016] B.V.C. 9; Times, April 13, 2016; [2016] S.T.I. 516, CA (Civ Div) ... *Digested,* 16/**2204**: *Affirmed* 17/2182

BPP Holdings Ltd v Revenue and Customs Commissioners [2017] UKSC 55; [2017] 1 W.L.R. 2945; [2017] 4 All E.R. 756; [2017] S.T.C. 1655; [2018] R.V.R. 8; [2017] B.V.C. 36; [2017] S.T.I. 1742, SC ... *Digested,* 17/**2182**

Brabners LLP v Revenue and Customs Commissioners [2017] UKFTT 666 (TC); [2017] S.T.I. 2011, FTT (Tax)

Bracking v Secretary of State for Work and Pensions see R. (on the application of Bracking) v Secretary of State for Work and Pensions

Bradbury v BBC [2015] EWHC 1368 (Ch); [2015] Pens. L.R. 457, Ch D ... *Digested,* 15/**834**: *Affirmed* 17/1602

Bradbury v BBC [2012] EWHC 1369 (Ch); [2012] Pens. L.R. 283, Ch D ... *Digested,* 12/**2376**: *Affirmed* 17/1602

Bradbury v BBC [2017] EWCA Civ 1144; [2018] I.C.R. 61; [2017] Pens. L.R. 20; Times, September 19, 2017, CA (Civ Div) ... *Digested,* 17/**1602**

Bradford Hospitals NHS Trust v Al-Shabib see Al-Shabib v Bradford Hospitals NHS Trust

Bradley v Bradley [2017] SAC (Civ) 29; 2017 S.L.T. (Sh Ct) 201; 2017 Fam. L.R. 123; 2017 G.W.D. 31-502, SAC ... *Digested,* 17/**2607**

Bradley v Secretary of State for Business, Innovation and Skills [2016] CSIH 80; 2017 S.C. 153; 2016 S.L.T. 1097; 2016 G.W.D. 33-587, IH (Ex Div) ... *Digested,* 17/**2459**

Bradley & Essex & Suffolk Accident Indemnity Society, Re [1912] 1 K.B. 415, CA *Considered* 17/1338

Bradley Saul v Revenue and Customs Commissioners [2017] UKFTT 520 (TC); [2017] S.T.I. 1668, FTT (Tax)

Brady v Revenue and Customs Commissioners [2017] UKFTT 94 (TC); [2017] S.T.I. 228, FTT (Tax)

Braganza v BP Shipping Ltd [2015] UKSC 17; [2015] 1 W.L.R. 1661; [2015] 4 All E.R. 639; [2015] 2 Lloyd's Rep. 240; [2015] I.C.R. 449; [2015] I.R.L.R. 487; [2015] Pens. L.R. 431; Times, April 6, 2015, SC .... *Digested,* 15/**798**: *Applied* 16/380: *Considered* 17/772: *Followed* 16/657, 16/658, 17/1470, 17/154, 17/399

Bragg v Oceanus Mutual Underwriting Association (Bermuda) Ltd; *joined case* Ulster Marine Insurance Co Ltd v Oceanus Mutual Underwriting Association (Bermuda) Ltd [1982] 2 Lloyd's Rep. 132; [1982] Com. L.R. 165, CA (Civ Div) .. *Digested,* 82/**2514**: *Applied* 92/1950, 17/191: *Doubted* 90/3542

Brain Disorders Research Ltd Partnership v Revenue and Customs Commissioners [2015] UKFTT 325 (TC); [2015] S.F.T.D. 1043; [2015] S.T.I. 2691, FTT (Tax) *Affirmed* 17/2180

Brain Disorders Research Ltd Partnership v Revenue and Customs Commissioners [2017] UKUT 176 (TCC); [2017] S.T.C. 1170; [2017] B.T.C. 516, UT (Tax) .... *Digested,* 17/**2180**

Brake (t/a Stay in Style), Re see Patley Wood Farm LLP v Brake

Bramley Ferry Supplies Ltd v Revenue and Customs Commissioners [2017] UKUT 214 (TCC); [2017] B.T.C. 523, UT (Tax) .... *Digested,* 17/**305**

Bramston v Haut [2012] EWCA Civ 1637; [2013] 1 W.L.R. 1720; [2013] B.P.I.R. 25, CA (Civ Div) .... *Digested,* 13/**1700**: *Applied* 14/1795, 14/1796: *Considered* 14/1832: *Followed* 17/1281, 17/1300

Bramwell (Deceased), Re; *sub nom* Campbell v Tobin [1988] 2 F.L.R. 263; [1988] Fam. Law 391, Fam Div .... *Digested,* 89/**3812**: *Considered* 17/2072

Branded Garden Products Ltd v Revenue and Customs Commissioners [2017] UKFTT 86 (TC); [2017] S.T.I. 225, FTT (Tax)

Brandeis Goldschmidt & Co Ltd v Western Transport Ltd [1981] Q.B. 864; [1981] 3 W.L.R. 181; [1982] 1 All E.R. 28; [1981] F.S.R. 481; (1981) 125 S.J. 395, CA (Civ Div) .... *Digested,* 81/**2654**: *Applied* 91/3408: *Considered* 94/1758, 00/5107: *Distinguished* 90/4308: *Not applied* 17/1276

Brangman v Queen, The see Myers v Queen, The

Brauer v Germany (24062/13) [2017] M.H.L.R. 165, ECHR

Bray & Slaughter Ltd v Kersfield Developments (Bridge Road) Ltd see Kersfield Developments (Bridge Road) Ltd v Bray & Slaughter Ltd

Braymist Ltd v Wise Finance Co Ltd; *sub nom* Wise Finance Ltd v Braymist Ltd Times, March 27, 2001; [2001] 11 E.G. 174 (C.S.); [2001] N.P.C. 55, Ch D .... *Digested,* 01/**704**: *Affirmed* 02/62: *Considered* 17/497

Brazil v Durant International Corp [2015] UKPC 35; [2016] A.C. 297; [2015] 3 W.L.R. 599; [2016] 1 All E.R. (Comm) 722; [2015] 2 Lloyd's Rep. 460; [2015] Lloyd's Rep. F.C. 593; [2015] W.T.L.R. 1323; 18 I.T.E.L.R. 334; Times, September 23, 2015; [2015] 2 P. & C.R. DG24, PC (Jer) *Applied* 17/1277

Breasley Pillows Ltd v Vita Cellular Foams (UK) Ltd [2016] CAT 8; [2016] Comp. A.R. 15, CAT .... *Digested,* 17/**419**

Breasley Pillows Ltd v Vita Cellular Foams (UK) Ltd [2016] CAT 9; [2016] Comp. A.R. 26, CAT .... *Digested,* 17/**420**

Breen v Slater see Goodwood Recoveries Ltd v Breen

Brennan v Good see Good (Deceased), Re

Brennan v Health Professions Council [2011] EWHC 41 (Admin); (2011) 119 B.M.L.R. 1, QBD (Admin) .... *Digested,* 11/**1617**: *Applied* 17/1116

Brent LBC v C [2016] EWHC 1335 (Fam); [2017] 2 F.L.R. 12; [2016] Fam. Law 1095, Fam Div .... *Digested,* 17/**927**

Brent LBC v Risk Management Partners Ltd; *sub nom* Risk Management Partners Ltd v Brent LBC [2011] UKSC 7; [2011] 2 A.C. 34; [2011] 2 W.L.R. 166; [2011] 2 All E.R. 209; [2011] P.T.S.R. 481; [2011] 2 C.M.L.R. 26; [2011] Eu. L.R. 615; [2011] B.L.G.R. 169; Times, February 10, 2011; (2011) 155(6) S.J.L.B. 31, SC . *Digested,* 11/**2635**: *Applied* 15/849, 17/1815: *Followed* 14/1619

Brent LBC v Shulem B Association Ltd [2011] EWHC 1663 (Ch); [2011] 1 W.L.R. 3014; [2011] 4 All E.R. 778; [2011] L. & T.R. 22; [2011] 27 E.G. 77 (C.S.); [2011] N.P.C. 69, Ch D .... *Digested,* 12/**2066**: *Applied* 17/1468: *Considered* 12/2065, 14/2013, 17/1469

Breslin v Murphy [2013] NICA 75; [2017] N.I. 1, CA (NI)

Brett v Solicitors Regulation Authority [2014] EWHC 2974 (Admin); [2015] P.N.L.R. 2, DC .... *Digested,* 15/**1661**: *Explained* 17/1492

Brevan Howard Asset Management LLP v Reuters Ltd [2017] EWCA Civ 950; [2017] E.M.L.R. 28, CA (Civ Div) .... *Digested,* 17/**333**

Brevan Howard Asset Management LLP v Reuters Ltd [2017] EWHC 644 (QB), QBD *Affirmed* 17/333

Brewster v Northern Ireland Local Government Officers' Superannuation Committee; *sub nom* Brewster's Application for Judicial Review, Re [2013] NICA 54; [2014] Pens. L.R. 103, CA (NI) .... *Digested,* 14/**3226**: *Reversed* 17/1624

Brewster v Northern Ireland Local Government Officers' Superannuation Committee; *sub nom* Brewster's Application for Judicial Review, Re [2017] UKSC 8; [2017] 1 W.L.R. 519; [2017] 2 All E.R. 1001; [2017] N.I. 326; [2017] I.C.R. 434; [2017] I.R.L.R. 366; [2017] Pens. L.R. 9; Times, February 13, 2017, SC .... *Digested,* 17/**1624**: *Considered* 17/1466

Brewster's Application for Judicial Review, Re see Brewster v Northern Ireland Local Government Officers' Superannuation Committee

Breyer v Germany (C-582/14) EU:C:2016:779; [2017] 1 W.L.R. 1569; [2017] 2 C.M.L.R. 3; [2017] C.E.C. 691; 42 B.H.R.C. 700, ECJ (2nd Chamber)

Breyer Group Plc v RBK Engineering Ltd [2017] EWHC 1206 (Ch); [2017] T.C.L.R. 6, Ch D .... *Digested,* 17/**1337**

Bridgend CBC v Boland see Boland v Bridgend CBC

Bridport and West Dorset Golf Club Ltd v Revenue and Customs Commissioners; *sub nom* Revenue and Customs Commissioners v Bridport and West Dorset Golf Club Ltd [2012] UKUT 272 (TCC); [2012] S.T.C. 2244; [2012] B.V.C. 1758; [2012] S.T.I. 2552, UT (Tax) .... *Digested,* 12/**3386**: *Applied* 15/2606, 17/2240

Briers v Briers [2017] EWCA Civ 15; [2017] 1 F.C.R. 309, CA (Civ Div) .... *Digested,* 17/**1020**

Briggs v Briggs (No.2); *sub nom* Briggs (Incapacitated Person) (MedicalTreatment: Best Interests Decision), Re [2016] EWCOP 53; [2017] 4 W.L.R. 37; [2017] C.O.P.L.R. 42; [2017] Med. L.R. 88; (2017) 154 B.M.L.R. 26, CP .... *Digested,* 17/**1122**

Briggs v Briggs (Preliminary Issue) (No.1) see Briggs (Incapacitated Person), Re

Briggs v First Choice Holidays [2017] EWHC 2012 (QB); [2017] 4 Costs L.R. 595, QBD .... *Digested,* 17/**238**

Briggs v Gleeds see Gleeds Retirement Benefits Scheme, Re

Briggs (Incapacitated Person) (MedicalTreatment: Best Interests Decision), Re see Briggs v Briggs (No.2)

Briggs (Incapacitated Person), Re; *sub nom* Briggs v Briggs (Preliminary Issue) (No.1); Director of Legal Aid Casework v Briggs; *joined case* Walton Centre NHS Foundation Group v Briggs [2016] EWCOP 48; [2017] Fam. 207; [2017] 2 W.L.R. 926; [2017] C.O.P.L.R. 16; (2017) 154 B.M.L.R. 1, CP *Reversed* 17/1534

Briggs (Incapacitated Person), Re; *sub nom* Briggs v Briggs (Preliminary Issue) (No.1); Director of Legal Aid Casework v Briggs; *joined case* Walton Centre NHS Foundation Group v Briggs [2017] EWCA Civ 1169; [2018] Fam. 63; [2018] 2 W.L.R. 152; [2017] C.P. Rep. 45; [2017] C.O.P.L.R. 370; (2017) 158 B.M.L.R. 88, CA (Civ Div) .... *Digested,* 17/**1534**

Brightlife Ltd, Re [1987] Ch. 200; [1987] 2 W.L.R. 197; [1986] 3 All E.R. 673; (1986) 2 B.C.C. 99359; [1986] P.C.C. 435; (1987) 84 L.S.G. 653; (1987) 131 S.J. 132, Ch D (Companies Ct) .... *Digested,* 88/**306**: *Applied* 00/3483, 17/159: *Followed* 92/2549, 93/2332

Brighton University v Dovehouse Interiors Ltd; *sub nom* University of Brighton v Dovehouse Interiors Ltd [2014] EWHC 940 (TCC); [2014] B.L.R. 432; 153 Con. L.R. 147, QBD (TCC) .... *Digested,* 14/**577**: *Applied* 16/584: *Considered* 15/696, 17/453

Brightside Group Ltd (formerly Brightside Group Plc) v RSM UK Audit LLP [2017] EWHC 6 (Comm); [2017] 1 W.L.R. 1943, QBD (Comm) .... *Digested,* 17/**368**

Brill & Co v Penn see Penn v Bristol & West Building Society

Brims Construction Ltd v A2M Development Ltd [2013] EWHC 3262 (TCC), QBD (TCC) *Considered* 16/393, 17/453

Brisal-Auto Estradas do Litoral SA v Fazenda Publica (C-18/15) EU:C:2016:549; [2016] S.T.C. 2078; [2017] 1 C.M.L.R. 20; [2016] B.T.C. 39; [2016] S.T.I. 2599, ECJ (5th Chamber)

Bristol & West Building Society v Fancy & Jackson [1997] 4 All E.R. 582; [1997] N.P.C. 109, Ch D .... *Digested,* 98/**4027**: *Applied* 15/683: *Considered* 01/4529, 14/2195, 15/1792: *Followed* 99/4036, 99/4379, 13/1950: *Not applied* 11/2259: *Overruled in part* 17/641

Bristol & West Plc v Revenue and Customs Commissioners; *sub nom* Revenue and Customs Commissioners v Bristol & West Plc [2016] EWCA Civ 397; [2017] 1 W.L.R. 2792; [2017] 1 All E.R. 480; [2016] S.T.C. 1491; [2016] B.T.C. 18; [2016] S.T.I. 1464, CA (Civ Div) .... *Digested,* 16/**2060**: *Applied* 17/2129, 17/2187

Bristol Alliance Ltd Partnership v EUI Ltd see Bristol Alliance Ltd Partnership v Williams

Bristol Alliance Ltd Partnership v Williams; *sub nom* EUI Ltd v Bristol Alliance Ltd Partnership; Bristol Alliance Ltd Partnership v EUI Ltd [2012] EWCA Civ 1267; [2013] Q.B. 806; [2013] 2 W.L.R. 1029; [2013] 1 All E.R. (Comm) 257; [2013] R.T.R. 9; [2013] Lloyd's Rep. I.R. 351, CA (Civ Div) .... *Digested,* 13/**1742**: *Applied* 17/1349: *Followed* 17/1348

Bristol Missing Link Ltd v Bristol City Council [2015] EWHC 876 (TCC); [2015] P.T.S.R. 1470; 160 Con. L.R. 93; [2015] B.L.G.R. 480, QBD (TCC) .... *Digested,* 15/**2077**: *Considered* 16/1790, 16/1791, 17/1810

Brit UW Ltd v Starlight Shipping Co see Starlight Shipping Co v Allianz Marine & Aviation Versicherungs AG

Britaniacrest Ltd v Bamborough [2016] UKUT 144 (LC), UT (Lands) *Applied* 17/1161

Britaniacrest Ltd, Re [2013] UKUT 521 (LC), UT (Lands) *Applied* 17/1161

British Airline Pilots Association v Jet2.com Ltd [2015] EWHC 1110 (QB); [2015] I.R.L.R. 543, QBD .... *Digested,* 15/**797**: *Reversed* 17/764

British Airline Pilots Association v Jet2.com Ltd [2017] EWCA Civ 20; [2017] I.C.R. 457; [2017] I.R.L.R. 233, CA (Civ Div) .... *Digested,* 17/**764**

British Airways Plc v Airways Pension Scheme Trustee Ltd [2017] EWHC 1191 (Ch); [2017] Pens. L.R. 16, Ch D .... *Digested,* 17/**1622**

British Airways Plc v Williams (C-155/10) see Williams v British Airways Plc (C-155/10)

British American Nickel Corp Ltd v MJ O'Brien Ltd [1927] A.C. 369, PC (Can) *Applied* 71/1238, 17/405: *Considered* 14/275

British American Tobacco Denmark A/S v Exel Europe Ltd see British American Tobacco Switzerland SA v Exel Europe Ltd

British American Tobacco Denmark A/S v Kazemier Transport BV see British American Tobacco Switzerland SA v Exel Europe Ltd

British American Tobacco Switzerland SA v Exel Europe Ltd; *sub nom* British American Tobacco Switzerland SA v H Essers Security Logistics BV; British American Tobacco Denmark A/S v Kazemier Transport BV; *joined case* British American Tobacco Denmark A/S v Exel Europe Ltd [2015] UKSC 65; [2016] A.C. 262; [2015] 3 W.L.R. 1173; [2016] 4 All E.R. 389; [2017] 1 All E.R. (Comm) 68; [2016] 1 Lloyd's Rep. 463; [2015] 2 C.L.C. 637; [2016] R.T.R. 1; Times, November 16, 2015, SC .... *Digested,* 15/**2551**

British American Tobacco Switzerland SA v H Essers Security Logistics BV see British American Tobacco Switzerland SA v Exel Europe Ltd

British Credit Trust Holdings v UK Insurance Ltd [2003] EWHC 2404 (Comm); [2004] 1 All E.R. (Comm) 444; [2004] C.P. Rep. 25, QBD (Comm) .... *Digested,* 04/**395**: *Applied* 17/197

British Fermentation Products Ltd v Compair Reavell Ltd [1999] 2 All E.R. (Comm) 389; [1999] B.L.R. 352; (2000) 2 T.C.L.R. 704; 66 Con. L.R. 1, QBD (TCC) ...... *Digested,* 99/**843**: *Applied* 17/508: *Considered* 16/441

British Film Institute v Revenue and Customs Commissioners (C-592/15) see Revenue and Customs Commissioners v British Film Institute (C-592/15)

British Gas Trading Ltd v Lock see Lock v British Gas Trading Ltd

British Gurkha Welfare Society v United Kingdom (44818/11) (2017) 64 E.H.R.R. 11; Times, November 8, 2016, ECHR

British Nursing Association v Inland Revenue (National Minimum Wage Compliance Team) [2002] EWCA Civ 494; [2003] I.C.R. 19; [2002] I.R.L.R. 480; [2002] Emp. L.R. 668, CA (Civ Div) .... *Digested,* 02/**1386**: *Applied* 02/5575, 08/1177: *Considered* 11/1100, 12/1112: *Distinguished* 03/1286: *Followed* 16/696, 17/812

British Red Cross v Werry [2017] EWHC 875 (Ch); [2017] W.T.L.R. 441, Ch D .... *Digested,* 17/**2069**

British Reinforced Concrete Engineering Co Ltd v Schelff [1921] 2 Ch. 563, Ch D *Considered* 84/405, 17/823: *Followed* 54/1205

British Sky Broadcasting Ltd v Office of Communications see British Telecommunications Plc v Office of Communications

British South Africa Co v Companhia de Mocambique; *sub nom* Companhia de Mocambique v British South Africa Co; *joined case* De Sousa v British South Africa Co [1893] A.C. 602; [1891-94] All E.R. Rep. 640, HL
Applied 90/609, 99/731, 07/510, 10/1943: *Approved* 67/128: *Considered* 77/341, 97/901, 11/1944, 17/1377: *Distinguished* 47-51/9624, 04/2255: *Followed* 78/286, 13/361

British Telecommunications Plc v Office of Communications; *joined cases* Cable and Wireless Worldwide Plc v Office of Communications; British Sky Broadcasting Ltd v Office of Communications [2014] CAT 14, CAT
Applied 17/2190

British Telecommunications Plc v One in a Million Ltd; *joined cases* Marks & Spencer Plc v One in a Million Ltd; Virgin Enterprises Ltd v One in a Million Ltd; J Sainsbury Plc v One in a Million Ltd; Ladbroke Group Plc v One in a Million Ltd [1999] 1 W.L.R. 903; [1998] 4 All E.R. 476; [1999] E.T.M.R. 61; [1997-98] Info. T.L.R. 423; [1998] I.T.C.L.R. 146; [2001] E.B.L.R. 2; [1999] F.S.R. 1; Times, July 29, 1998; Independent, July 31, 1998; [1998] Masons C.L.R. 165; (1998) 95(37) L.S.G. 37; (1998) 148 N.L.J. 1179, CA (Civ Div) .... *Digested,* 98/**3520**:
Applied 04/2272, 06/2593, 07/2545, 14/1025, 17/1396: *Considered* 00/3592, 01/5357, 02/2782, 02/2891, 03/2648, 07/2674: *Followed* 11/1943, 16/1339

British Telecommunications Plc v Revenue and Customs Commissioners see Revenue and Customs Commissioners v GMAC UK Plc

British Telecommunications Plc v Revenue and Customs Commissioners see Revenue and Customs Commissioners v GMAC UK Plc

British Westinghouse Electric & Manufacturing Co Ltd v Underground Electric Railways Co of London Ltd (No.2) [1912] A.C. 673, HL
Applied 47-51/431, 53/3775, 55/2483, 56/936, 65/993, 69/3313, 70/748, 72/826, 78/312, 78/704, 79/658, 00/2566, 16/572, 16/573, 17/412: *Approved* 66/3146: *Considered* 75/18.u, 75/248, 76/59.u, 79/849, 85/1860, 91/1503, 91/3194, 94/3438, 95/4510, 97/1808, 01/894, 11/538, 14/827: *Distinguished* 90/1565: *Followed* 95/3704, 97/3843, 14/2210

British-American Tobacco (Holdings) Ltd v Revenue and Customs Commissioners [2017] UKFTT 167 (TC); [2017] S.F.T.D. 550, FTT (Tax) .... *Digested,* 17/**633**

Britt v Buckinghamshire CC [1964] 1 Q.B. 77; [1963] 2 W.L.R. 722; [1963] 2 All E.R. 175; (1963) 127 J.P. 389; 61 L.G.R. 223; (1963) 14 P. & C.R. 318; [1963] R.V.R. 215; (1963) 107 S.J. 153, CA .... *Digested,* 63/**3360**:
Applied 91/3422: *Distinguished* 72/3341: *Followed* 17/1747

Brittain v Whyte [2016] B.P.I.R. 1314, Ch D .... *Digested,* 17/**1287**

Broadhurst v Tan; *joined case* Smith v Taylor [2016] EWCA Civ 94; [2016] 1 W.L.R. 1928; [2017] 2 All E.R. 60; [2016] C.P. Rep. 22; [2016] 2 Costs L.O. 155; [2017] R.T.R. 1; [2016] P.I.Q.R. P12, CA (Civ Div) .... *Digested,* 16/**255**:
Applied 16/236: *Considered* 17/1359

Broads Authority v Fry [2015] EWHC 4139 (Admin); [2017] P.T.S.R. 1; [2016] 2 Lloyd's Rep. 61, DC .... *Digested,* 16/**2149**

Brockenhurst College v Revenue and Customs Commissioners (C-699/15) see Revenue and Customs Commissioners v Brockenhurst College (C-699/15)

Brogden v Investec Bank Plc [2014] EWHC 2785 (Comm); [2014] I.R.L.R. 924, QBD (Comm) .... *Digested,* 15/**519**:
Affirmed 17/771: *Considered* 16/657

Brogden v Investec Bank Plc [2016] EWCA Civ 1031; [2017] I.R.L.R. 90, CA (Civ Div) *Digested,* 17/**771**

Bromley LBC v C [2006] EWHC 1110 (Admin); [2006] E.L.R. 358; Times, April 12, 2006; (2006) 103(12) L.S.G. 29, DC .... *Digested,* 06/**1135**:
Considered 16/613: *Overruled* 17/704

Bromley LBC v Special Educational Needs Tribunal (No.2) [1999] 3 All E.R. 587; (1999) 1 L.G.L.R. 970; [1999] B.L.G.R. 747; [1999] Ed. C.R. 907; [1999] E.L.R. 260; (1999) 2 C.C.L. Rep. 239; Times, June 14, 1999; Independent, June 17, 1999; [1999] C.O.D. 409, CA (Civ Div) .... *Digested,* 99/**1890**:
Applied 02/1167, 07/1266, 14/943: *Considered* 03/1123, 07/1262, 12/993: *Followed* 17/711

Brookes v Borough Care Services [1998] I.C.R. 1198; [1998] I.R.L.R. 636, EAT .... *Digested,* 98/**2212**:
Applied 17/769

Brookes v HSBC Bank Plc see Teasdale v HSBC Bank Plc

Brookes v Revenue and Customs Commissioners [2017] UKFTT 671 (TC); [2017] S.T.I. 2013, FTT (Tax)

Brooks v Armstrong [2016] EWHC 2893 (Ch); [2017] B.C.C. 99, Ch D .... *Digested,* 17/**1318**

Brooks v Brooks; *sub nom* B v B (Post Nuptial Settlements) (Pension Fund), Re [1996] A.C. 375; [1995] 3 W.L.R. 141; [1995] 3 All E.R. 257; [1995] 2 F.L.R. 13; [1995] 3 F.C.R. 214; [1995] Pens. L.R. 173; Times, July 3, 1995; Independent, July 4, 1995; [1995] Fam. Law 545; (1995) 145 N.L.J. 995; (1995) 139 S.J.L.B. 165, HL .... *Digested,* 95/**2354**:
Applied 09/1489: *Considered* 13/1303: *Distinguished* 05/1682: *Followed* 17/1026

Broomleigh Housing Association Ltd v Okonkwo [2010] EWCA Civ 1113; [2011] C.P. Rep. 4; [2011] H.L.R. 5; Times, November 18, 2010; [2010] 42 E.G. 104 (C.S.); (2010) 107(41) L.S.G. 22, CA (Civ Div) .... *Digested,* 11/**336**:
Considered 14/391, 17/380

Brophy v Simmonds (Valuation Officer) [2016] UKUT 217 (LC); [2016] R.V.R. 293, UT (Lands) .... *Digested,* 17/**1515**

Brown v Bower [2017] EWHC 1388 (QB); [2017] 1 W.L.R. 4703; [2017] E.M.L.R. 24, QBD .... *Digested,* 17/**646**

Brown v Complete Building Solutions Ltd [2016] EWCA Civ 1; [2016] B.L.R. 98; 164 Con. L.R. 21, CA (Civ Div) .... *Digested,* 16/**583**:
Considered 17/462

Brown v Haringey LBC; *sub nom* Haringey LBC v Brown [2015] EWCA Civ 483; [2017] 1 W.L.R. 542; [2016] 4 All E.R. 754; [2015] H.L.R. 30, CA (Civ Div) .... *Digested,* 15/**1647**

Brown v McPherson see Brown v Procurator Fiscal, Ayr

Brown v Natural Resources Body for Wales [2016] UKUT 514 (LC); [2017] R.V.R. 211, UT (Lands) .... *Digested,* 17/**883**

Brown v Oceancrown Ltd see Joint Administrators of Oceancrown Ltd v Stonegale Ltd

Brown v Pelosi see Joint Administrators of Oceancrown Ltd v Stonegale Ltd

Brown v Procurator Fiscal, Ayr; *sub nom* Brown v McPherson [2016] SAC (Crim) 32; 2017 S.L.T. (Sh Ct) 63; 2017 S.C.L. 315; 2016 S.C.C.R. 564; 2016 G.W.D. 36-644, SAC .... *Digested,* 17/**2510**

Brown v Stonegale Ltd see Joint Administrators of Oceancrown Ltd v Stonegale Ltd

Brown v Trumper 53 E.R. 800; (1858) 26 Beav. 11, Ct of Chancery
Applied 17/1440

Brown Bear Foods Ltd, Re; *sub nom* Shaw v Webb [2014] EWHC 1132 (Ch), Ch D (Birmingham)
Considered 17/1266

Browning v Howard (Unreported, June 19, 2017), CC (Horsham) [*Irwin Mitchell LLP, 1 Millsands, Riverside West, Sheffield*] .... *Digested,* 17/**1656**

Brownlie v Four Seasons Holdings Inc [2015] EWCA Civ 665; [2016] 1 W.L.R. 1814; [2015] C.P. Rep. 40; [2015] 2 C.L.C. 151; [2016] P.I.Q.R. P2, CA (Civ Div) .... *Digested,* 15/**365**:
Applied 17/377: *Followed* 17/369

Brownsville Holdings Ltd v Adamjee Insurance Co Ltd (The Milasan) [2000] 2 All E.R. (Comm) 803; [2000] 2 Lloyd's Rep. 458, QBD (Comm) .... *Digested,* 00/**4724**:
Applied 17/2021: *Distinguished* 09/2290

Bruart (Liquidator) v Point S France (Societe) [2017] E.C.C. 1, Cass (F)

Brucefield Estate Trustee Co Ltd v Computacenter (UK) Ltd 2017 Hous. L.R. 66; 2017 G.W.D. 21-350, Sh Ct (Lothian) (Livingston) .... *Digested,* 17/**2697**

Brunel University v Webster see Wong v Igen Ltd (formerly Leeds Careers Guidance)

Brunner v Greenslade [1971] Ch. 993; [1970] 3 W.L.R. 891; [1970] 3 All E.R. 833; (1971) 22 P. & C.R. 54; (1970) 114 S.J. 787, Ch D .... *Digested,* 70/**2427**:
Applied 17/1595: *Approved* 73/2793

Bruton v Governor of Swaleside Prison [2017] EWHC 704 (Admin); [2017] A.C.D. 69, QBD (Admin)

BRUTT Trade Marks see Target Fixings Ltd v Brutt Beteiligungsgesellschaft MBH

Bryan v Westminster Bank see Mulholland's Will Trusts, Re

Bryanston Finance Ltd v De Vries (No.2) [1976] Ch. 63; [1976] 2 W.L.R. 41; [1976] 1 All E.R. 25; (1975) 119 S.J. 709, CA (Civ Div) .... *Digested,* 76/**276**:
Applied 86/339, 06/2399, 17/1294

Bryant Homes Southern Ltd v Stein Management Ltd [2016] EWHC 2435 (Ch); [2017] 1 P. & C.R. 6, Ch D .... *Digested,* 17/**1857**

Bryen & Langley Ltd v Boston [2005] EWCA Civ 973; [2005] B.L.R. 508, CA (Civ Div) . *Digested,* 06/**677**:
Applied 07/724, 17/469: *Considered* 09/676: *Followed* 17/473

BS v Court of First Instance Brussels (Belgium) [2017] EWHC 571 (Admin); [2017] A.C.D. 59, DC

BS v Secretary of State for the Home Department DA/01997/2013, UT (IAC)
Affirmed 17/1188

BS (Congo) v Secretary of State for the Home Department [2017] EWCA Civ 53; [2017] 4 W.L.R. 45, CA (Civ Div) .... *Digested,* 17/**1188**

BTI 2014 LLC v Sequana SA; *joined case* BAT Industries Plc v Sequana SA [2016] EWHC 1686 (Ch); [2017] Bus. L.R. 82; [2017] 1 B.C.L.C. 453, Ch D .... *Digested,* 17/**393**: *Considered* 17/394

BTS Specialised Equipment Ltd v Revenue and Customs Commissioners; *joined case* NTS Specialised Equipment Ltd v Revenue and Customs Commissioners [2017] UKUT 159 (TCC); [2017] B.V.C. 512, UT (Tax) .... *Digested,* 17/**2274**

BTS Specialised Equipment Ltd v Revenue and Customs Commissioners; *joined case* NTS Specialised Equipment Ltd v Revenue and Customs Commissioners [2015] UKFTT 137 (TC), FTT (Tax) *Affirmed* 17/2274

Bucci v Carman see Casa Estates (UK) Ltd (In Liquidation), Re

Buchanan v Commissioner of Police of the Metropolis [2017] I.C.R. 184; [2016] I.R.L.R. 918, EAT .... *Digested,* 17/**779**

Buchanan v Milton [1999] 2 F.L.R. 844; (2000) 53 B.M.L.R. 176; [1999] Fam. Law 692, Fam Div .... *Digested,* 00/**4905**: *Applied* 09/6, 12/3184, 12/3186, 17/961

Buchleither v Germany (20106/13) [2017] 1 F.L.R. 1445; [2016] Fam. Law 679, ECHR

Buckinghamshire v Barnardo's; *sub nom* Barnardo's v Buckinghamshire [2016] EWCA Civ 1064; [2017] Pens. L.R. 2, CA (Civ Div) .... *Digested,* 17/**1628**: *Followed* 17/1617

Buckinghamshire v Barnardo's; *sub nom* Barnardo's v Buckinghamshire [2015] EWHC 2200 (Ch); [2015] Pens. L.R. 501, Ch D .... *Digested,* 15/**1861**: *Affirmed* 17/1628

Bucknall v Dacorum BC see Dacorum BC v Bucknall (formerly Acheampong)

BUD and BUDWEISER BUDBRAU Trade Marks see Anheuser-Busch Inc v Budejovicky Budvar Narodni Podnik (Application for Revocation)

Budejovicky Budvar Narodni Podnik's Registered Trade Marks (Nos 807395 and 1070309) see Anheuser-Busch Inc v Budejovicky Budvar Narodni Podnik (Application for Revocation)

Budniok v Adjudicator, Insolvency Service see Budniok, Re

Budniok, Re; *sub nom* Budniok v Adjudicator, Insolvency Service [2017] EWHC 368 (Ch); [2017] B.P.I.R. 521, Ch D (Bankruptcy Ct) .... *Digested,* 17/**1278**

Bugdaycay v Secretary of State for the Home Department; *sub nom* R. v Secretary of State for the Home Department Ex p. Bugdaycay; *joined cases* Musisi v Secretary of State for the Home Department; Norman v Secretary of State for the Home Department; Nelidow Santis v Secretary of State for the Home Department [1987] A.C. 514; [1987] 2 W.L.R. 606; [1987] 1 All E.R. 940; [1987] Imm. A.R. 250; (1987) 84 L.S.G. 902; (1987) 137 N.L.J. 199; (1987) 131 S.J. 297, HL .... *Digested,* 87/**1989**: *Applied* 89/1951, 89/1954, 92/2450, 94/2452, 96/3220, 97/4111, 01/3421, 03/3944, 07/2344: *Cited* 94/2498, 95/2695: *Considered* 87/1983, 87/23, 88/14, 91/1965, 92/28, 94/2455, 96/3231, 96/3236, 96/3278, 05/3882, 17/1241: *Followed* 97/2929, 98/3196, 07/2295, 16/1139: *Referred to* 89/1939, 95/2676

Bugeja v Customs and Excise Commissioners (No.2) see Lex Services Plc v Customs and Excise Commissioners

Bujdoso v Hungary (4/2011) [2017] M.H.L.R. 129, UN CRPD

Bula Ltd, Re; *sub nom* Bula Mines Ltd, Re [1990] 1 I.R. 440, Sup Ct (Irl) *Applied* 16/1198, 16/1199: *Considered* 17/1294

Bula Mines Ltd, Re see Bula Ltd, Re

Bull v Hall see Hall v Bull

Bullring Ltd Partnership v Laing O'Rourke Midlands Ltd [2016] EWHC 3092 (TCC); 170 Con. L.R. 112, QBD (TCC) .... *Digested,* 17/**460**

Bund Naturschutz in Bayern eV v Freistaat Bayern (C-645/15) EU:C:2016:898; [2017] Env. L.R. D3, ECJ (6th Chamber)

Bunter v Revenue and Customs Commissioners see Lee v Revenue and Customs Commissioners

Burberry Group Plc v Fox-Davies; *sub nom* Fox-Davies v Burberry Plc [2015] EWHC 222 (Ch); [2015] 2 B.C.L.C. 66, Ch D (Companies Ct) .... *Digested,* 15/**400**: *Affirmed* 17/400

Burberry Group Plc v Fox-Davies; *sub nom* Fox-Davies v Burberry Plc [2017] EWCA Civ 1129; [2018] Bus. L.R. 332; [2017] B.C.C. 387, CA (Civ Div) .... *Digested,* 17/**400**

Burdiashvili v Georgia (26290/12) (2017) 65 E.H.R.R. SE3, ECHR

Burdis v Livsey see Lagden v O'Connor

Burford v Secretary of State for Communities and Local Government [2017] EWHC 1493 (Admin); [2017] J.P.L. 1300, QBD (Admin) .... *Digested,* 17/**1737**

Burge v South Gloucestershire Council [2016] UKUT 300 (LC); [2017] R.V.R. 71, UT (Lands) .... *Digested,* 17/**1782**

Burge v South Gloucestershire Council [2017] EWCA Civ 1313; [2018] P.T.S.R. 485; [2017] R.V.R. 360; Times, October 16, 2017, CA (Civ Div)

Burgerausschuss fur die Burgerinitiative Minority SafePack - one million signatures for diversity in Europe v European Commission (T-646/13) EU:T:2017:59; [2017] 2 C.M.L.R. 31, GC (1st Chamber)

Burgess v Hawes; *sub nom* Hawes v Burgess; Burgess's Estate, Re [2013] EWCA Civ 94; [2013] W.T.L.R. 453, CA (Civ Div) .... *Digested,* 13/**2985**: *Applied* 14/2843: *Considered* 13/2984: *Followed* 14/2840, 17/2078

Burgess v Lejonvarn; *sub nom* Lejonvarn v Burgess [2017] EWCA Civ 254; [2017] B.L.R. 277; [2017] T.C.L.R. 5; 171 Con. L.R. 118; [2017] P.N.L.R. 25, CA (Civ Div) .... *Digested,* 17/**2204**

Burgess v Lejonvarn; *sub nom* Lejonvarn v Burgess [2016] EWHC 40 (TCC); [2016] T.C.L.R. 3; 164 Con. L.R. 165, QBD (TCC) .... *Digested,* 16/**396**: *Affirmed* 17/2204

Burgess (Churchill Retirement Living) v South Gloucestershire Council [2017] P.A.D. 31, Planning Inspector

Burgess's Estate, Re see Burgess v Hawes

Burke v Laing [2016] SAC (Crim) 31; 2017 S.C.L. 112; 2016 G.W.D. 34-622, SAC ...... *Digested,* 17/**2795**

Burke-Monerville v HM Senior Coroner for Inner North London [2016] Inquest L.R. 217, QBD (Admin) .... *Digested,* 17/**23**

Burnden Group Ltd, Re; *sub nom* Fielding v Hunt [2017] EWHC 406 (Ch); [2017] 2 Costs L.O. 191; [2017] B.P.I.R. 585, Ch D (Manchester) .... *Digested,* 17/**244**

Burnden Group Ltd, Re; *sub nom* Fielding v Hunt [2017] EWHC 247 (Ch); [2017] B.P.I.R. 554, Ch D (Manchester) .... *Digested,* 17/**1320**

Burnden Holdings (UK) Ltd v Fielding [2016] EWCA Civ 557; [2017] 1 W.L.R. 39; [2016] C.P. Rep. 41, CA (Civ Div) .... *Digested,* 16/**272**

Burnett (Andrew) v Procurator Fiscal, Hamilton [2017] SAC (Crim) 4; 2017 S.C.L. 569; 2017 G.W.D. 11-151, SAC .... *Digested,* 17/**2494**

Burnie Port Authority v General Jones Pty Ltd [1994] HCA 13, HC (Aus) *Applied* 17/470

Burnip v Birmingham City Council; *joined cases* Trengove v Walsall MBC; Gorry v Wiltshire CC [2012] EWCA Civ 629; [2013] P.T.S.R. 117; [2012] H.R.L.R. 20; [2012] Eq. L.R. 701; [2013] H.L.R. 1; [2012] B.L.G.R. 954; Times, August 21, 2012, CA (Civ Div) .... *Digested,* 12/**3111**: *Applied* 14/2757: *Distinguished* 16/1443, 17/2030: *Followed* 13/2885, 16/1982

Burnley BC v Huron Properties Ltd [2016] EWHC 3803 (Admin); [2017] R.V.R. 279, QBD (Admin)

Buron v Denman 154 E.R. 327; (1848) 2 Ex. 167; (1848) 1 Ex. 769, Ex Ct *Considered* 69/111, 17/1425

Burrell v Clifford [2016] EWHC 294 (Ch); [2017] E.M.L.R. 2, Ch D .... *Digested,* 17/**2198**

Burrell v Helical (Bramshott Place) Ltd [2015] EWHC 3727 (Ch); [2017] E.C.C. 3; [2016] H.L.R. 18; [2016] C.T.L.C. 1; [2016] 1 P. & C.R. DG21, Ch D .... *Digested,* 16/**1368**

Burridge v Stafford; *joined case* Khan v Ali [2000] 1 W.L.R. 927; [1999] 4 All E.R. 660; [1999] C.P.L.R. 645; [2001] 1 Costs L.R. 77; Times, September 14, 1999; (1999) 149 N.L.J. 1474, CA (Civ Div) .... *Digested,* 99/**3760**: *Applied* 10/2121: *Considered* 16/1406: *Followed* 17/1477

Burrow Down Support Services Ltd v Rossiter [2008] I.C.R. 1172, EAT .... *Digested,* 08/**1177**: *Applied* 10/1120, 14/1091, 14/1092, 17/812: *Considered* 11/1100, 16/696

Burrows v HM Coroner for Preston; *sub nom* Borrows v HM Coroner for Preston [2008] EWHC 1387 (Admin); [2008] 2 F.L.R. 1225; [2008] Inquest L.R. 72; [2008] Fam. Law 984, QBD .... *Digested,* 09/**6**: *Applied* 17/961: *Doubted* 12/3186

Burry & Knight Ltd v Knight see Burry & Knight Ltd, Re

Burry & Knight Ltd, Re; *sub nom* Hoburne Ltd, Re; Burry & Knight Ltd v Knight [2014] EWCA Civ 604; [2014] 1 W.L.R. 4046; [2015] 1 All E.R. 37; [2014] B.C.C. 393; [2015] 1 B.C.L.C. 61, CA (Civ Div) .... *Digested,* 14/**518**: *Applied* 15/400, 17/400

Burton v Liden; *sub nom* Liden v Burton [2016] EWCA Civ 275; [2017] 1 F.L.R. 310; [2016] Fam. Law 687, CA (Civ Div) .... *Digested,* 17/**1825**

Bury MBC v SU [2010] UKUT 406 (AAC); [2011] E.L.R. 14, UT (AAC) .... *Digested,* 11/**982**: *Applied* 17/709

Burzala (Steven) v HM Advocate [2007] HCJAC 67; 2008 S.L.T. 61; 2008 S.C.L. 305; 2008 S.C.C.R. 199; 2008 G.W.D. 1-10, HCJ .... *Digested,* 08/**4664**: *Applied* 17/2532: *Considered* 10/4116

Bush v Bank Mandiri (Europe) Ltd [2011] B.P.I.R. 19, Ch D .... *Digested,* 11/**1841**: *Doubted* 17/1295

Bush v Bush [2008] EWCA Civ 865; [2008] 2 F.L.R. 1437; [2008] 3 F.C.R. 139; [2008] Fam. Law 989; (2008) 105(31) L.S.G. 17, CA (Civ Div) .... *Digested,* 08/**1557**: *Applied* 17/941: *Followed* 13/1335, 15/1026

Busschers v Besselsen (C145/87) see Berg v Besselsen (C144/87)

Butt v Butt [1987] 1 W.L.R. 1351; [1987] 3 All E.R. 657; [1987] F.S.R. 574; (1987) 84 L.S.G. 2194; (1987) 131 S.J. 1286, CA (Civ Div) .... *Digested,* 87/**3031**: *Distinguished* 17/365: *Referred to* 95/4240

Butt v Revenue and Customs Commissioners [2017] UKUT 325 (TCC); [2017] B.V.C. 525, UT (Tax)

Butt v Secretary of State for the Home Department see R. (on the application of Butt) v Secretary of State for the Home Department

Butterworth v Supplementary Benefits Commission see Crake v Supplementary Benefits Commission

Buttes Gas & Oil Co v Hammer (No.3); *joined case* Occidental Petroleum Corp v Buttes Gas & Oil Co (No.2) [1982] A.C. 888; [1981] 3 W.L.R. 787; [1981] 3 All E.R. 616; [1981] Com. L.R. 257; Times, October 31, 1981; (1981) 125 S.J. 776, HL .... *Digested,* 81/**1473**: *Applied* 96/3659, 06/2396, 15/1566: *Cited* 93/3224: *Considered* 92/203, 96/1086, 99/723, 00/1756, 00/5107, 03/4204, 05/212, 06/501, 13/40, 16/965, 17/1426: *Distinguished* 90/3689: *Explained* 14/38: *Not followed* 89/1699

Buttes Gas & Oil Co v Hammer (No.3); *joined case* Occidental Petroleum Corp v Buttes Gas & Oil Co (No.2) [1981] Q.B. 223; [1980] 3 W.L.R. 668; [1980] 3 All E.R. 475; (1980) 124 S.J. 630, CA (Civ Div) .... *Digested,* 80/**2184**: *Applied* 87/3060, 17/216: *Considered* 84/2700, 92/3479, 93/3224, 96/681, 05/212, 08/358, 09/399: *Distinguished* 85/2651: *Reversed* 81/1473

Buyco Ltd v Revenue and Customs Commissioners [2006] V. & D.R. 57, V&DTr (London) .... *Digested,* 07/**4286**: *Applied* 17/2281: *Considered* 15/2583

Buzadji v Moldova (23755/07) 42 B.H.R.C. 398, ECHR (Grand Chamber)

Buzzoni v Revenue and Customs Commissioners; *sub nom* Kamhi (Deceased), Re [2013] EWCA Civ 1684; [2014] 1 W.L.R. 3040; [2014] 1 E.G.L.R. 181; [2014] B.T.C. 1; [2014] W.T.L.R. 421, CA (Civ Div) .... *Digested,* 14/**2938**: *Distinguished* 17/2155

BW Estates Ltd, Re; *sub nom* Randhawa v Turpin [2016] EWHC 2156 (Ch); [2016] B.C.C. 814; [2017] 1 B.C.L.C. 240, Ch D (Birmingham) *Reversed* 17/409

BW Estates Ltd, Re; *sub nom* Randhawa v Turpin [2015] EWHC 517 (Ch); [2016] B.C.C. 475; [2016] 1 B.C.L.C. 708, Ch D (Birmingham) .... *Digested,* 17/**1271**

BW Estates Ltd, Re; *sub nom* Randhawa v Turpin [2017] EWCA Civ 1201; [2018] 2 W.L.R. 1175; [2017] B.C.C. 406; Times, October 5, 2017, CA (Civ Div) .... *Digested,* 17/**409**

Bwllfa and Merthyr Dare Steam Collieries (1891) Ltd v Pontypridd Waterworks Co; *sub nom* Bwllfa and Merthyr Dare Steam Collieries (1891) Ltd and Pontypridd Waterworks Co's Arbitration, Re [1903] A.C. 426, HL *Applied* 62/2560, 68/1862, 68/4074, 75/3666, 79/297, 03/3023, 07/3816, 08/2147, 11/537, 15/508: *Considered* 69/433, 95/4829, 03/1230, 05/2671, 08/1131, 13/1900: *Distinguished* 79/2873, 83/3143, 91/3062, 17/2135: *Followed* 13/484

Bwllfa and Merthyr Dare Steam Collieries (1891) Ltd and Pontypridd Waterworks Co's Arbitration, Re see Bwllfa and Merthyr Dare Steam Collieries (1891) Ltd v Pontypridd Waterworks Co

Byford v Butler see Byford (Deceased), Re

Byford (Deceased), Re; *sub nom* Byford v Butler [2003] EWHC 1267 (Ch); [2004] 1 F.L.R. 56; [2004] 2 F.C.R. 454; [2003] B.P.I.R. 1089; [2004] 1 P. & C.R. 12; Times, June 13, 2003; [2004] Fam. Law 14; (2003) 100(31) L.S.G. 32; (2003) 100(24) L.S.G. 38; [2003] N.P.C. 77, Ch D .... *Digested,* 03/**3542**: *Applied* 08/3064, 09/2204, 10/1853: *Considered* 17/1826

Byrne (Andrew) v HM Advocate [2016] HCJAC 84; 2016 S.C.L. 998; 2016 G.W.D. 31-562, HCJ Appeal .... *Digested,* 17/**2808**

Bywater Investments Ltd v Commissioner of Taxation; *joined case* Hua Wang Bank Berhad v Commissioner of Taxation [2016] HCA 45; 19 I.T.L. Rep. 287, HC (Aus)

C v A (A Minor) [2011] EWHC 4033 (Fam), Fam Div *Applied* 14/1304, 17/923

C v C [2016] SAC (Civ) 6; 2016 S.L.T. (Sh Ct) 433; 2016 Fam. L.R. 141; 2016 G.W.D. 26-472, SAC .... *Digested,* 17/**2458**

C v Central Criminal Court see R. (on the application of A) v Central Criminal Court

C v E see AB (Surrogacy: Consent), Re

C v G [2017] CSOH 5; 2017 S.L.T. 79; 2017 G.W.D. 3-33, OH .... *Digested,* 17/**2779**

C v HM Advocate; *sub nom* RC v HM Advocate [2017] HCJAC 61; 2018 J.C. 1; 2017 S.C.L. 854; 2017 G.W.D. 27-437, HCJ .... *Digested,* 17/**2473**
C v HM Advocate [2016] HCJAC 100; 2017 S.C.L. 53; 2016 G.W.D. 37-658, HCJ .... *Digested,* 17/**2487**
C v MGN Ltd see Cairns v Modi
C v Middlesbrough Council see A v Hoare
C v P see S (Children), Re
C v Secretary of State for Justice; *sub nom* R. (on the application of C) v Secretary of State for Justice [2016] UKSC 2; [2016] 1 W.L.R. 444; [2017] 1 All E.R. 513; [2016] E.M.L.R. 13; [2016] H.R.L.R. 7; (2016) 19 C.C.L. Rep. 5; (2016) 149 B.M.L.R. 1; Times, February 9, 2016, SC .... *Digested,* 16/**172**: *Applied* 17/353: *Considered* 16/309: *Distinguished* 17/1906
C (A Child) (Application for Public Interest Immunity) (No.2), Re; *sub nom* Tower Hamlets LBC v M [2017] EWHC 692 (Fam); [2017] 2 F.L.R. 1342; [2017] 2 F.C.R. 621, Fam Div .... *Digested,* 17/**933**
C (A Child) (Care Proceedings: Disclosure of Documents), Re [2015] EWFC 79; [2017] 1 F.L.R. 82; [2016] 3 F.C.R. 581; [2015] Med. L.R. 531; (2016) 151 B.M.L.R. 122; [2015] Fam. Law 1457, Fam Ct .... *Digested,* 16/**994**
C (A Child) (Care Proceedings: Disclosure), Re; *sub nom* Tower Hamlets LBC v M [2016] EWHC 3171 (Fam); [2017] 4 W.L.R. 19; [2017] 1 F.L.R. 1665, Fam Div . *Digested,* 17/**990**
C (A Child) (Internal Relocation), Re [2015] EWCA Civ 1305; [2016] Fam. 253; [2016] 3 W.L.R. 1; [2017] 1 F.L.R. 103; [2016] 2 F.C.R. 576; [2016] Fam. Law 284, CA (Civ Div) .... *Digested,* 16/**858**: *Considered* 16/883, 17/938
C (A Child) (Private Judgment: Publicity), Re; *sub nom* C (A Child) (Publicity), Re [2016] EWCA Civ 798; [2016] 1 W.L.R. 5204; [2017] 2 F.L.R. 105; Times, November 10, 2016; [2016] Fam. Law 1223, CA (Civ Div) .... *Digested,* 16/**27**
C (A Child) (Publicity), Re see C (A Child) (Private Judgment: Publicity), Re
C (A Child), Re see A Local Authority v D
C (A Minor) (Family Assistance Order), Re [1996] 1 F.L.R. 424; [1996] 3 F.C.R. 514; [1996] Fam. Law 202; (1996) 160 J.P.N. 697, Fam Div .... *Digested,* 96/**579**: *Considered* 17/1057
C (A Minor) (Medical Treatment: Refusal of Parental Consent), Re see T (A Minor) (Wardship: Medical Treatment), Re
C (C-122/15) EU:C:2016:391; [2017] 1 C.M.L.R. 2; [2016] I.R.L.R. 643, ECJ (1st Chamber)
C (Care Proceedings: Publication of Judgment), Re; *sub nom* Sutton LBC v Gray [2016] EWHC 1608 (Fam); [2017] 2 F.L.R. 146; [2016] Fam. Law 1097, Fam Div
Reversed 16/27
C (Children) (Abduction), Re; *sub nom* P (Children) (Child Abduction: Anticipatory Breach), Re; C (Children) (Anticipatory Retention), Re [2017] EWCA Civ 980; [2018] 1 All E.R. 476; [2018] 1 F.L.R. 186; [2017] 3 F.C.R. 719, CA (Civ Div)
C (Children) (Anticipatory Retention), Re see C (Children) (Abduction), Re
C (Children) (Child in Care: Choice of Forename), Re; *sub nom* C (Children) (Power to Choose Forenames), Re [2016] EWCA Civ 374; [2017] Fam. 137; [2016] 3 W.L.R. 1557; [2017] 1 F.L.R. 487; [2016] Fam. Law 666, CA (Civ Div) .... *Digested,* 17/**958**: *Not applied* 17/967
C (Children) (Power to Choose Forenames), Re see C (Children) (Child in Care: Choice of Forename), Re
C (Deceased), Re; *sub nom* V v Associated Newspapers Ltd [2016] EWCOP 21; [2016] C.O.P.L.R. 236; [2016] Inquest L.R. 169, CP .... *Digested,* 16/**309**: *Applied* 17/1645, 17/353
C (Zimbabwe) v Secretary of State for the Home Department; *sub nom* Chikwamba v Secretary of State for the Home Department [2008] UKHL 40; [2008] 1 W.L.R. 1420; [2009] 1 All E.R. 363; [2008] H.R.L.R. 39; [2008] U.K.H.R.R. 1008; [2008] Imm. A.R. 700; [2008] I.N.L.R. 502; Times, June 26, 2008; (2008) 152(26) S.J.L.B. 31, HL .... *Digested,* 08/**2052**: *Applied* 10/1789, 12/1765, 17/1212: *Considered* 09/2163, 13/1633, 15/1336: *Followed* 14/1715, 17/1239
C Jenkin and Son Ltd v Revenue and Customs Commissioners; *sub nom* Revenue and Customs Commissioners v C Jenkin and Son Ltd [2017] UKUT 239 (TCC); [2017] B.V.C. 517; [2017] S.T.I. 1654, UT (Tax) .... *Digested,* 17/**2293**
C Jenkin and Son Ltd v Revenue and Customs Commissioners; *sub nom* Revenue and Customs Commissioners v C Jenkin and Son Ltd [2015] UKFTT 242 (TC); [2015] S.T.I. 1940, FTT (Tax)
Reversed 17/2293

C Plc v P; *sub nom* W v P [2007] EWCA Civ 493; [2008] Ch. 1; [2007] 3 W.L.R. 437; [2007] 3 All E.R. 1034; [2007] C.P. Rep. 35; Times, May 28, 2007, CA (Civ Div) *Digested,* 07/**855**: *Followed* 12/413, 17/291

C Trust, Re 19 I.T.E.L.R. 814, Sup Ct (Ber)

C&MB Holdings Ltd, Re see Hamilton v Brown

C, Re [2016] EWCOP 46; [2017] C.O.P.L.R. 84, CP .... *Digested,* 17/**13**

C-W (A Child) (Contact Overseas: Risk of Non-Return), Re; *sub nom* C-W (A Child) (Temporary Leave to Remove from Jurisdiction: Safeguards), Re [2015] EWCA Civ 1272; [2017] 4 W.L.R. 51; [2017] 1 F.L.R. 131; [2016] 1 F.C.R. 572; [2016] Fam. Law 286, CA (Civ Div) .... *Digested,* 16/**933**

C-W (A Child) (Temporary Leave to Remove from Jurisdiction: Safeguards), Re see C-W (A Child) (Contact Overseas: Risk of Non-Return), Re

CA (Natural Delivery or Caesarean Section), Re; *sub nom* University Hospital NHS Trust v CA [2016] EWCOP 51; (2017) 154 B.M.L.R. 142, CP .... *Digested,* 17/**1544**

CA Webber (Transport) Ltd v Network Rail Infrastructure Ltd (formerly Railtrack Plc) see CA Webber (Transport) Ltd v Railtrack Plc

CA Webber (Transport) Ltd v Railtrack Plc; *sub nom* CA Webber (Transport) Ltd v Network Rail Infrastructure Ltd (formerly Railtrack Plc) [2003] EWCA Civ 1167; [2004] 1 W.L.R. 320; [2004] 3 All E.R. 202; [2004] 1 P. & C.R. 20; [2004] L. & T.R. 2; [2004] 1 E.G.L.R. 49; [2004] 14 E.G. 142; Times, August 5, 2003; (2003) 100(36) L.S.G. 40; (2003) 147 S.J.L.B. 902; [2003] 2 P. & C.R. DG21, CA (Civ Div) .... *Digested,* 03/**2757**: *Applied* 17/1433: *Considered* 05/2584, 12/462: *Followed* 12/2742: *Not applied* 13/2449

Cabinet de Maitrise d'oeuvre (CMO) v Lavalin (Societes) [2017] I.L.Pr. 21, Cass (F)

Cable and Wireless Worldwide Plc v Office of Communications see British Telecommunications Plc v Office of Communications

Cadbury Schweppes Plc v Somji; *sub nom* Somji v Cadbury Schweppes Plc [2000] B.P.I.R. 950, Ch D *Affirmed* 01/3791: *Applied* 17/1302

Cadbury UK Ltd v Comptroller General of Patents Designs and Trade Marks [2016] EWHC 796 (Ch); [2016] E.T.M.R. 33; [2017] F.S.R. 2, Ch D .... *Digested,* 16/**1331**

Cadbury UK Ltd v Comptroller General of Patents Designs and Trade Marks (Costs) [2016] EWHC 1609 (Ch); [2016] Bus. L.R. 872; [2017] F.S.R. 3, Ch D .... *Digested,* 16/**1342**

Cadbury UK Ltd v Societe des Produits Nestle SA see Societe des Produits Nestle SA v Cadbury UK Ltd

Cadder (Peter) v HM Advocate [2010] UKSC 43; [2010] 1 W.L.R. 2601; 2011 S.C. (U.K.S.C.) 13; 2010 S.L.T. 1125; 2010 S.C.L. 1265; 2010 S.C.C.R. 951; [2011] H.R.L.R. 1; [2010] U.K.H.R.R. 1171; 30 B.H.R.C. 257; Times, October 28, 2010; (2010) 107(43) L.S.G. 21; (2010) 154(41) S.J.L.B. 30, SC .... *Digested,* 10/**1733**: *Cited* 11/4134, 12/3876, 12/3881, 12/3925, 13/3567, 13/3589: *Considered* 11/1674, 11/4078, 11/4079, 12/1039, 12/3875, 12/3896, 12/3907, 12/3910, 12/771, 13/760, 16/2573, 17/551: *Referred to* 11/4127, 11/4131, 17/623

Cadlock v Dunn [2015] EWHC 1318 (Ch); [2015] B.P.I.R. 739, Ch D (Leeds) .... *Digested,* 15/**2116**: *Approved* 17/890

Cadmus Management Ltd, Re; *sub nom* Hanbury v Hogan [2016] EWHC 3330 (Ch); [2017] B.P.I.R. 317, Ch D (Companies Ct) .... *Digested,* 17/**1331**

Cafferkey (Daniel) v HM Advocate; *joined case* Frew (Laura) v HM Advocate [2016] HCJAC 114; 2017 S.C.L. 149; 2017 S.C.C.R. 14; 2016 G.W.D. 38-671, HCJ .... *Digested,* 17/**2495**

Caffoor (Trustees of the Abdul Gaffoor Trust) v Income Tax Commissioner (Colombo); *sub nom* Gaffoor (Abdul) Trustees v Ceylon Commissioner of Income Tax; Trustees of Abdul Gaffoor Trust v Income Tax Commissioner, Colombo [1961] A.C. 584; [1961] 2 W.L.R. 794; [1961] 2 All E.R. 436; (1961) 40 A.T.C. 93; [1961] T.R. 97; (1961) 105 S.J. 383, PC (Cey) .... *Digested,* 61/**943**: *Applied* 01/5291: *Considered* 66/5957, 70/158, 10/3536, 14/3079, 17/2125: *Distinguished* 07/4001: *Explained* 09/4053: *Followed* 88/247

Cahill v Cahill 19 I.T.E.L.R. 883, CA (Ont)

Cahillane, Re see National Asset Loan Management Ltd v Cahillane

Cain v Francis; *joined case* McKay v Hamlani [2008] EWCA Civ 1451; [2009] Q.B. 754; [2009] 3 W.L.R. 551; [2009] 2 All E.R. 579; [2009] C.P. Rep. 19; [2009] R.T.R. 18; [2009] LS Law Medical 82; (2009) 106(2) L.S.G. 20, CA (Civ Div) .... *Digested,* 09/**420**: *Applied* 09/2854, 15/1113, 17/320: *Considered* 10/376, 11/860: *Followed* 14/421

Caine v Allianz (Unreported, March 16, 2017), CC (Bath) [*Irwin Mitchell LLP, Riverside West, 1 Millsands, Sheffield*] .... *Digested,* 17/**1689**

Cairns v Modi; *sub nom* C v MGN Ltd; *joined case* KC v MGN Ltd [2012] EWCA Civ 1382; [2013] 1 W.L.R. 1015; [2013] E.M.L.R. 8; Times, January 2, 2013, CA (Civ Div) .... *Digested,* 13/**794**: *Applied* 17/645

Caja de Ahorros y Monte de Piedad de Madrid v Asociacion de Usuarios de Servicios Bancarios (Ausbanc) (C-484/08) EU:C:2010:309; [2010] 3 C.M.L.R. 43, ECJ (1st Chamber)
Considered 17/485

Cakmakci v Turkey (Admissibility) (3952/11) (2017) 65 E.H.R.R. SE5, ECHR

Calderdale MBC v S [2004] EWHC 2529 (Fam); [2005] 1 F.L.R. 751; Times, November 18, 2004; [2005] Fam. Law 353; (2004) 101(47) L.S.G. 30, Fam Div *Digested,* 05/**1629**:
Applied 07/1725, 17/998

Calderwood v Renfrewshire Council 2004 S.C. 691; 2004 S.L.T. 219; [2004] L.L.R. 171; [2004] 29 S.L.L.P. 22; 2004 G.W.D. 6-100, IH (Ex Div) .... *Digested,* 04/**5024**:
Applied 17/2719: *Considered* 16/2721

Caledonian Modular Ltd v Mar City Developments Ltd [2015] EWHC 1855 (TCC); [2015] B.L.R. 694; [2015] T.C.L.R. 6; 160 Con. L.R. 42; [2015] C.I.L.L. 3705, QBD (TCC) .... *Digested,* 15/**481**:
Considered 17/475: *Followed* 17/452

Callaghan v Birmingham City Council see Farmah v Birmingham City Council

Calltel Telecom Ltd v Revenue and Customs Commissioners see Mobilx Ltd (In Administration) v Revenue and Customs Commissioners

Calow v Calow see Calow, Re

Calow, Re; *sub nom* Calow v Calow [1928] Ch. 710, Ch D
Applied 17/2075

Calverton Parish Council v Nottingham City Council see Nottingham City Council v Calverton Parish Council

Cambridge Associates in Management v Ofsted [2013] EWHC 1157 (Admin), QBD (Admin)
Considered 17/697

Camden LBC v Humphreys see R. (on the application of Humphreys) v Parking and Traffic Appeals Service

Camden LBC v RZ [2015] EWHC 3751 (Fam); [2017] 1 F.L.R. 873; [2016] Fam. Law 279, Fam Div

Camden LBC v Thomas McInerney & Sons Ltd 9 Con. L.R. 99; (1986) 2 Const. L.J. 293, QBD (OR) .... *Digested,* 87/**237**:
Applied 17/408

Camden Primary Care Trust v Atchoe [2007] EWCA Civ 714; (2007) 151 S.J.L.B. 672, CA (Civ Div)
Followed 17/853

Camera di Commercio, Industria, Artigianato e Agricoltura di Lecce v Manni (C-398/15) EU:C:2017:197; [2018] Bus. L.R. 25; [2017] 3 C.M.L.R. 18; [2017] C.E.C. 1282, ECJ (2nd Chamber)

Cameron v Hussain [2017] EWCA Civ 366; [2018] 1 W.L.R. 657; [2017] R.T.R. 23; [2017] Lloyd's Rep. I.R. 487; [2017] P.I.Q.R. P16, CA (Civ Div) .... *Digested,* 17/**1878**

Cameron (David) v HM Advocate [2017] HCJAC 74; 2017 S.C.L. 923; 2017 G.W.D. 31-496, HCJ .... *Digested,* 17/**2567**

Cameron (Stuart) v HM Advocate see Ferguson (James Douglas) v HM Advocate

Cameron New Homes Ltd v Customs and Excise Commissioners 17039, V&DTr
Considered 17/2288

Cammell Laird & Co Ltd v Manganese Bronze & Brass Co Ltd [1934] A.C. 402; (1934) 48 Ll. L. Rep. 209, HL
Applied 52/634, 54/2976, 68/3544, 70/2613, 17/472: *Considered* 60/2869, 65/3516, 68/3526: *Followed* 71/10517, 11/2780

Campbell v Bromley Magistrates' Court see R. (on the application of Campbell) v Independent Police Complaints Commission

Campbell v Commissioner of Police of the Metropolis see R. (on the application of Campbell) v Independent Police Complaints Commission

Campbell v Gordon see Campbell v Peter Gordon Joiners Ltd

Campbell v Narine 19 I.T.E.L.R. 750, Sup Ct (OECS)

Campbell v OCS Group UK Ltd [2017] I.C.R. D19, EAT

Campbell v Peter Gordon Joiners Ltd; *sub nom* Campbell v Gordon [2016] UKSC 38; [2016] A.C. 1513; [2016] 3 W.L.R. 294; [2017] 2 All E.R. 161; 2017 S.C. (U.K.S.C.) 13; 2016 S.L.T. 887; 2016 S.C.L.R. 434; [2016] 2 B.C.L.C. 287; [2016] I.C.R. 862; [2016] Lloyd's Rep. I.R. 591; [2016] P.I.Q.R. P15; Times, July 20, 2016; 2016 G.W.D. 21-380, SC .... *Digested,* 16/**1257**

Campbell v Revenue and Customs Commissioners [2017] UKFTT 104 (TC); [2017] S.T.I. 227, FTT (Tax)

Campbell v Tobin see Bramwell (Deceased), Re

Campbell (Sharon) v Vannet 1997 S.C.C.R. 787; 1997 G.W.D. 40-2039, HCJ Appeal . *Digested,* 98/**5603**:
Distinguished 09/5154: *Followed* 17/2472

Campsa Estaciones de Servicio SA v Administracion del Estado (C-285/10) EU:C:2011:381; [2011] S.T.C. 1603; [2012] B.V.C. 258; [2011] S.T.I. 1906, ECJ (8th Chamber)
Applied 17/2262

Canada Steamship Lines Ltd v King, The [1952] A.C. 192; [1952] 1 All E.R. 305; [1952] 1 Lloyd's Rep. 1; [1952] 1 T.L.R. 261; (1952) 96 S.J. 72, PC (Can) .... *Digested,* 52/**610**: *Applied* 55/3036, 71/9949, 74/296, 74/447, 75/273, 78/3186, 80/359, 82/2909, 88/461, 90/636, 93/499, 95/778, 96/1216, 99/836, 01/947, 02/712, 10/3040, 13/574: *Cited* 99/3311: *Considered* 68/2647, 73/407, 81/110.u, 81/304, 81/3603, 82/403, 97/937, 00/5991, 00/895, 09/715, 10/621, 14/599, 15/507, 17/463: *Followed* 96/5302: *Referred to* 95/5571

Canadian Transport, The see Owners of the Eleftherotria v Owners of the Despina R

Canal and River Trust v Jones see Jones v Canal and River Trust

Canal Digital Danmark A/S, Re (C-611/14) see Criminal Proceedings against Canal Digital Danmark A/S (C-611/14)

Cancino v Secretary of State for the Home Department; *sub nom* Cancino (Costs: First-tier Tribunal: New Powers), Re [2015] UKFTT 59 (IAC); [2015] Imm. A.R. 574; [2015] I.N.L.R. 731, FTT (IAC)
Applied 16/307, 17/1460

Cancino (Costs: First-tier Tribunal: New Powers), Re see Cancino v Secretary of State for the Home Department

Candy v Holyoake see Holyoake v Candy

Cangoz v Turkey (7469/06) (2017) 65 E.H.R.R. 3, ECHR

Canning v Irwin Mitchell LLP [2017] EWHC 718 (Ch); [2017] B.P.I.R. 934, Ch D .... *Digested,* 17/**1295**

CANON/Liquid container (T1811/13) [2017] E.P.O.R. 20, EPO (Technical Bd App)

Cantillon Ltd v Urvasco Ltd [2008] EWHC 282 (TCC); [2008] B.L.R. 250; 117 Con. L.R. 1; [2008] C.I.L.L. 2564, QBD (TCC) .... *Digested,* 08/**606**: *Applied* 09/653, 10/565, 12/579, 16/388, 17/451, 17/467, 17/658: *Considered* 10/564, 12/586, 12/871, 13/520, 16/393, 16/395, 17/450, 17/453

Caparo Industries Plc v Dickman [1990] 2 A.C. 605; [1990] 2 W.L.R. 358; [1990] 1 All E.R. 568; [1990] B.C.C. 164; [1990] B.C.L.C. 273; [1990] E.C.C. 313; [1955-95] P.N.L.R. 523; Times, February 12, 1990; Independent, February 16, 1990; Financial Times, February 13, 1990; Guardian, February 15, 1990; Daily Telegraph, February 15, 1990; (1990) 87(12) L.S.G. 42; (1990) 140 N.L.J. 248; (1990) 134 S.J. 494, HL .... *Digested,* 90/**3266**: *Applied* 91/2650, 91/2652, 92/1915, 92/2605, 93/2982, 94/3365, 95/2906, 95/3668, 95/3686, 95/3701, 95/4519, 95/4730, 96/4440, 96/4484, 97/331, 97/3778, 97/3816, 98/3997, 99/3956, 99/3963, 99/3966, 99/4025, 99/5435, 00/4201, 00/4246, 00/4249, 00/6162, 00/6586, 00/679, 01/1509, 01/1989, 01/4462, 01/4464, 01/4541, 04/2119, 04/2704, 04/658, 05/2845, 05/2848, 05/2851, 05/2861, 05/2868, 06/2885, 06/4380, 06/684, 07/1682, 08/2644, 08/4861, 09/2725, 09/2726, 09/2727, 09/2848, 10/4300, 11/2553, 11/4482, 14/2203, 15/3235: *Cited* 00/4218, 07/1755: *Considered* 91/2657, 91/35, 93/2044, 93/2958, 93/2983, 93/2994, 93/2997, 95/3452, 95/3652, 95/3667, 95/3721, 98/3921, 98/3951, 98/3999, 99/3953, 00/4205, 01/550, 03/5821, 04/386, 04/5103, 05/2891, 06/2880, 06/5590, 06/5600, 07/2937, 07/2952, 07/733, 08/2653, 08/4946, 08/4947, 08/4949, 09/4702, 10/2281, 10/81, 11/2370, 11/4485, 12/4236, 12/4257, 13/2087, 13/565, 15/3229, 16/2735, 16/2737: *Distinguished* 91/2653: *Followed* 93/5553, 97/4087, 97/424, 98/3930, 98/3987, 99/3959, 99/4015, 00/4219, 00/4224, 01/4470, 09/265, 10/2278, 11/2254, 11/2255, 11/2256, 12/2294, 12/2297, 14/2202, 14/2205, 14/2210, 15/1777, 15/1815, 15/2539, 16/1537, 16/1538, 16/1539, 17/1565, 17/169, 17/2194, 17/44: *Referred to* 92/6078, 94/6386, 95/5841, 99/4023

Cape Distribution Ltd v Cape Intermediate Holdings Plc; *sub nom* Cape Intermediate Holdings Plc v Aviva Plc [2016] EWHC 1786 (QB); [2017] Lloyd's Rep. I.R. 1, QBD .... *Digested,* 17/**1342**

Cape Intermediate Holdings Plc v Aviva Plc see Cape Distribution Ltd v Cape Intermediate Holdings Plc

Capelloni and Aquilini v Pelkmans (C-119/84) EU:C:1985:388; [1985] E.C.R. 3147; [1986] 1 C.M.L.R. 388, ECJ (4th Chamber) .... *Digested,* 86/**1379**: *Applied* 17/301: *Considered* 07/457

Capita (Banstead 2011) Ltd v RFIB Group Ltd [2017] EWCA Civ 1032; [2017] C.P. Rep. 38; [2017] 4 Costs L.R. 669, CA (Civ Div) .... *Digested,* 17/**249**

Capita Plc v Darch [2017] EWHC 1248 (Ch); [2017] I.R.L.R. 718, Ch D .... *Digested,* 17/**768**

Capita Translation and Interpreting Ltd v Siacunas (Debarred) [2017] I.C.R. 887, EAT *Digested,* 17/**788**

Capital Home Loans Ltd v Hewitt & Gilpin Solicitors Ltd [2016] NICA 45; [2017] P.N.L.R. 12, CA (NI) .... *Digested,* 17/**2327**

Capparrelli (EEA Nationals: British Nationality); *sub nom* Secretary of State for the Home Department v Capparelli [2017] UKUT 162 (IAC); [2017] Imm. A.R. 970; [2017] I.N.L.R. 629, UT (IAC)

Capsky v Czech Republic (25784/09) (2017) 64 E.H.R.R. SE15, ECHR

Car Giant Ltd v Hammersmith LBC [2017] EWHC 464 (TCC); [2017] 2 Costs L.O. 235, QBD (TCC) .... *Digested,* 17/**246**

Caradon DC v Bussell see Caradon DC v Paton

Caradon DC v Paton; *joined case* Caradon DC v Bussell (2001) 33 H.L.R. 34; [2000] 3 E.G.L.R. 57; [2000] 35 E.G. 132; Times, May 17, 2000; Independent, June 19, 2000; [2000] E.G. 59 (C.S.); (2000) 97(22) L.S.G. 44, CA (Civ Div) .... *Digested,* 00/**4625**: *Considered* 17/1443

Carapeto v Good see Good (Deceased), Re

Carbondesk Group Plc v Revenue and Customs Commissioners [2015] UKFTT 367 (TC), FTT (Tax) *Considered* 17/2261

Card Protection Plan Ltd v Customs and Excise Commissioners (C-349/96) EU:C:1999:93; [1999] 2 A.C. 601; [1999] 3 W.L.R. 203; [1999] S.T.C. 270; [1999] E.C.R. I-973; [1999] 2 C.M.L.R. 743; [1999] All E.R. (E.C.) 339; [1999] C.E.C. 133; [1999] B.T.C. 5121; [1999] B.V.C. 155; Times, March 18, 1999, ECJ (6th Chamber) .... *Digested,* 99/**4972**: *Applied* 00/5343, 00/5346, 00/5369, 02/4745, 02/4750, 02/4782, 03/4538, 03/4545, 03/4576, 03/4580, 04/3968, 04/4009, 05/4354, 05/4355, 05/4397, 06/4449, 06/4476, 06/4514, 07/4341, 07/4342, 08/4025, 08/4035, 08/4040, 08/4048, 09/4098, 11/3562, 15/2594, 15/2596: *Considered* 01/5599, 03/4537, 03/4558, 04/3977, 04/4018, 04/4020, 05/4419, 06/4438, 06/4490, 08/3999, 08/4061, 09/4041, 09/4135, 09/5224, 11/1465, 11/3550, 14/3102, 17/2284: *Distinguished* 00/5294, 01/5564, 05/4394: *Explained* 12/3431: *Followed* 99/4983, 00/5344, 04/3981, 06/4501, 10/3519, 12/3387, 13/3221, 13/3227, 14/3050, 17/2265, 17/2294

Carder v Secretary of State for Health; *sub nom* Carder v University of Exeter [2016] EWCA Civ 790; [2017] I.C.R. 392; [2016] Med. L.R. 562, CA (Civ Div) .... *Digested,* 16/**1527**

Carder v University of Exeter see Carder v Secretary of State for Health

Cardiff CC v Lee; *sub nom* Lee v Cardiff CC [2016] EWCA Civ 1034; [2017] 1 W.L.R. 1751; [2016] H.L.R. 45, CA (Civ Div) .... *Digested,* 17/**1475**

Care Matters Partnership Ltd (In Administration), Re; *sub nom* Solomons v Cheal [2011] EWHC 2543 (Ch); [2011] B.C.C. 957; [2012] 2 B.C.L.C. 311, Ch D (Companies Ct) .... *Digested,* 12/**1796**: *Considered* 12/1803, 12/1804, 17/1268

Carillion Construction Ltd v Devonport Royal Dockyard Ltd [2005] EWCA Civ 1358; [2006] B.L.R. 15; 104 Con. L.R. 1; Times, November 24, 2005; (2005) 102(47) L.S.G. 26, CA (Civ Div) .... *Digested,* 06/**670**: *Applied* 07/395, 07/728, 09/658, 10/845, 11/490, 14/581, 16/583: *Considered* 09/4839, 10/556, 10/558, 10/563, 10/580, 17/453: *Distinguished* 09/651: *Followed* 06/666, 13/1719, 17/452

Carillion Construction Ltd v Emcor Engineering Services Ltd see Carillion Construction Ltd v Woods Bagot Europe Ltd

Carillion Construction Ltd v Woods Bagot Europe Ltd; *sub nom* Carillion Construction Ltd v Emcor Engineering Services Ltd [2016] EWHC 905 (TCC); [2016] B.L.R. 382; 166 Con. L.R. 52; [2016] C.I.L.L. 3833, QBD (TCC) .... *Digested,* 16/**413**: *Affirmed* 17/478

Carillion Construction Ltd v Woods Bagot Europe Ltd; *sub nom* Carillion Construction Ltd v Emcor Engineering Services Ltd [2017] EWCA Civ 65; [2017] B.L.R. 203; 170 Con. L.R. 1; [2017] C.I.L.L. 3945, CA (Civ Div) .... *Digested,* 17/**478**

Carillion JM Ltd v PHI Group Ltd; *sub nom* PHI Group Ltd v Robert West Consulting Ltd; *joined case* Carillion JM Ltd v Robert West Consulting Ltd [2012] EWCA Civ 588; [2012] C.P. Rep. 37; [2012] B.L.R. 329; [2012] T.C.L.R. 5; 142 Con. L.R. 96; [2012] 4 Costs L.O. 523; [2012] C.I.L.L. 3180, CA (Civ Div) .... *Digested,* 12/**340**: *Applied* 15/261, 17/242

Carillion JM Ltd v Robert West Consulting Ltd see Carillion JM Ltd v PHI Group Ltd

Carlill v Carbolic Smoke Ball Co [1893] 1 Q.B. 256, CA *Applied* 57/592, 67/1745, 95/799, 14/275: *Approved* 66/3146: *Considered* 64/3479, 80/1888, 88/2020, 17/1114: *Distinguished* 52/2194

Carman v Bucci see Casa Estates (UK) Ltd (In Liquidation), Re

Carmarthenshire CC v Y [2017] EWFC 36; [2017] 4 W.L.R. 136; [2018] 1 F.L.R. 361, Fam Ct .... *Digested,* 17/**993**

Carmichael v Black see Black v Carmichael

Carmichael (Alan) v HM Advocate [2016] HCJAC 123; 2017 S.C.L. 230; 2016 G.W.D. 40-709, HCJ .... *Digested,* 17/**2571**

Caroopen v Secretary of State for the Home Department; *joined case* Myrie v Secretary of State for the Home Department [2016] EWCA Civ 1307; [2017] 1 W.L.R. 2339; [2017] Imm. A.R. 930; [2017] I.N.L.R. 283, CA (Civ Div) .... *Digested,* 17/**1231**

Carpet Decor (Guildford) v Secretary of State for the Environment (1982) 261 E.G. 56; [1981] J.P.L. 806 .... *Digested,* 81/**2679**: *Considered* 85/1928, 14/2408, 17/1749

Carr v Esure Group Plc (Unreported, June 7, 2017), CC (Chester) [*Irwin Mitchell LLP, Riverside West, 1 Millsands, Sheffield*] .... *Digested,* 17/**1651**

Carr v Larussa 19 I.T.E.L.R. 894, Sup Ct (WA) (Sgl judge)

Carr-Glynn v Frearsons (A Firm) [1999] Ch. 326; [1999] 2 W.L.R. 1046; [1998] 4 All E.R. 225; [1999] 1 F.L.R. 8; [1998] 3 F.C.R. 487; [1999] P.N.L.R. 13; [1998] Fam. Law 739; [1998] E.G. 128 (C.S.); (1998) 148 N.L.J. 1487; [1998] N.P.C. 136, CA (Civ Div) .... *Digested,* 98/**4595**: *Applied* 01/4537, 04/2733: *Considered* 00/4225, 10/2267, 17/1569

Carrasco v Revenue and Customs Commissioners [2016] UKFTT 731 (TC); [2017] W.T.L.R. 1, FTT (Tax) .... *Digested,* 17/**2093**

Carrefour Hypermarches SAS v ITM Alimentaire International SASU (C-562/15) EU:C:2017:95; [2017] 3 C.M.L.R. 1; [2017] C.E.C. 1009; [2017] E.T.M.R. 18, ECJ (2nd Chamber)

Carse (Liquidator) v Coppen 1951 S.C. 233; 1951 S.L.T. 145, IH (1 Div) .... *Digested,* 47-51/**1270**: *Considered* 17/2447: *Distinguished* 17/2781

Carson v Secretary of State for Work and Pensions see R. (on the application of Carson) v Secretary of State for Work and Pensions

Carson v United Kingdom (42184/05) (2010) 51 E.H.R.R. 13; 29 B.H.R.C. 22, ECHR (Grand Chamber) .... *Digested,* 10/**1721**: *Applied* 17/1466: *Considered* 17/1095

Carswell v Secretary of State for Transport; *sub nom* Carswell (Deceased), Re [2010] EWHC 3230 (QB); [2011] Eu. L.R. 406; [2011] Lloyd's Rep. I.R. 644, QBD .... *Digested,* 11/**1923**: *Considered* 17/1878

Carswell (Deceased), Re see Carswell v Secretary of State for Transport

Cartel Damage Claims (CDC) Hydrogen Peroxide SA v Akzo Nobel NV (C-352/13); *sub nom* Hydrogen Peroxide SA v Akzo Nobel NV (C-352/13) EU:C:2015:335; [2015] Q.B. 906; [2015] 3 W.L.R. 909; [2015] 5 C.M.L.R. 4; [2016] C.E.C. 123, ECJ (4th Chamber) *Considered* 17/377

Carter v Brine 19 I.T.E.L.R. 1, Sup Ct (SAus) (Sgl judge)

Carter v Brine 19 I.T.E.L.R. 145, Sup Ct (SAus) (Sgl judge)

Carter v Chief Constable of Cumbria [2008] EWHC 1072 (QB); [2008] Po. L.R. 66, QBD *Considered* 17/325

Carter v McIntosh (1862) 24 D. 925, IH (2 Div) *Applied* 55/3507, 17/2610: *Considered* 97/6106, 07/5335

Carter & Ellis Ex p. Savill Bros, Re [1905] 1 K.B. 735, CA *Applied* 17/1331

Carter-Brown v Crown Prosecution Service [2017] EWHC 1955 (QB); [2017] A.C.D. 113, DC

Cartier International AG v British Sky Broadcasting Ltd [2016] EWCA Civ 658; [2017] 1 All E.R. 700; [2017] 1 All E.R. (Comm) 507; [2017] Bus. L.R. 1; [2016] E.T.M.R. 43; [2016] E.M.L.R. 23; [2016] Info. T.L.R. 1; [2017] R.P.C. 3, CA (Civ Div) .... *Digested,* 16/**1325**: *Followed* 17/1358, 17/1450

Casa Estates (UK) Ltd (In Liquidation), Re; *sub nom* Carman v Bucci; Bucci v Carman [2014] EWCA Civ 383; [2014] B.C.C. 269; [2014] 2 B.C.L.C. 49; [2014] B.P.I.R. 523, CA (Civ Div) .... *Digested,* 14/**1793**: *Applied* 16/1232, 17/1333

Casehub Ltd v Wolf Cola Ltd [2017] EWHC 1169 (Ch); [2017] 5 Costs L.R. 835, Ch D *Digested,* 17/**485**

Casseldine v Diocese of Llandaff Board for Social Responsibility (A Charity) 3YU56348, CC (Cardiff) *Doubted* 17/226

Cassell v Queen, The; *sub nom* R. v Cassell (Warren) [2016] UKPC 19; [2017] 1 W.L.R. 2738; [2017] 2 All E.R. 904; Times, July 12, 2016, PC (Mrat)

Casson v Hudson [2017] EWCA Civ 125; [2017] P.I.Q.R. P12, CA (Civ Div) .... *Digested,* 17/**2203**

Castellain v Preston (1883) 11 Q.B.D. 380, CA *Applied* 57/1763, 61/8360, 71/6016, 79/1509, 89/3392, 10/2113: *Considered* 73/1046, 74/1885, 96/3605, 99/793: *Distinguished* 93/2414: *Followed* 97/3151, 17/1343

Catalano v Espley-Tyas Development Group Ltd [2017] EWCA Civ 1132; [2017] C.P. Rep. 42; [2017] 4 Costs L.R. 769; [2018] P.I.Q.R. Q1, CA (Civ Div) .... *Digested,* 17/**226**

Catana v Revenue and Customs Commissioners [2012] UKUT 172 (TCC); [2012] S.T.C. 2138; [2012] B.T.C. 1625, UT (Tax) .... *Digested,* 12/**3286**: *Considered* 17/2153

Catchpole v Revenue and Customs Commissioners [2012] UKFTT 309 (TC); [2012] S.T.I. 2100, FTT (Tax) *Considered* 17/2288

Catlow v Kemeny (Unreported, June 20, 2017), CC (Preston) [*Irwin Mitchell LLP, 1 Millsands, Sheffield*] .... *Digested,* 17/**1688**

Cattle v Stockton Waterworks Co (1874-75) L.R. 10 Q.B. 453; [1874-80] All E.R. Rep. 492, QBD *Applied* 72/2341, 17/2455: *Considered* 89/3392: *Followed* 65/2671

Caudle v Sharp; *joined case* Grove v Sharp [1995] L.R.L.R. 433; [1995] C.L.C. 642; [1995] 4 Re. L.R. 389; Lloyd's List, August 3, 1995, CA (Civ Div) .... *Digested,* 95/**2923**: *Considered* 02/2731, 17/1355

Cavanna Homes (Devon) Ltd v East Devon DC [2017] P.A.D. 15, Planning Inspector

Cavendish Green Ltd v Revenue and Customs Commissioners [2016] UKFTT 620 (TC); [2017] S.F.T.D. 197; [2016] S.T.I. 2608, FTT (Tax) .... *Digested,* 17/**2288**

Cavendish Square Holding BV v Makdessi see Makdessi v Cavendish Square Holdings BV

Cay's Trustee v Cay 1998 S.C. 780; 1999 S.L.T. 321; 1998 S.C.L.R. 456; 1998 G.W.D. 14-722, IH (2 Div) .... *Digested,* 98/**6001**: *Applied* 17/2684: *Followed* 02/5891

CB (A Child) (International Relocation: Domestic Abuse: Child Arrangements), Re [2017] EWFC 39; [2017] 3 F.C.R. 273, Fam Ct

CB (Brazil) v Secretary of State for the Home Department see CB (Validity of Marriage: Proxy Marriage: Brazil), Re

CB (Validity of Marriage: Proxy Marriage: Brazil), Re; *sub nom* CB (Brazil) v Secretary of State for the Home Department [2008] UKAIT 80, AIT *Considered* 17/1247

CCC Films (London) Ltd v Impact Quadrant Films Ltd [1985] Q.B. 16; [1984] 3 W.L.R. 245; [1984] 3 All E.R. 298; (1984) 81 L.S.G. 1046; (1984) 134 N.L.J. 657; (1984) 128 S.J. 297, QBD .... *Digested,* 84/**371**: *Applied* 17/502: *Considered* 11/538, 13/1870: *Distinguished* 09/430: *Followed* 96/1235

CCHG Ltd (t/a Vaporized) v Vapouriz Ltd [2017] CSOH 100; 2017 S.L.T. 907; [2017] E.T.M.R. 35; 2017 G.W.D. 22-378, OH .... *Digested,* 17/**2690**

CD (A Child), Re see X (A Child) (Care Proceedings: Notice to Father without Parental Responsibility), Re

CE (Female Genital Mutilation), Re; *sub nom* E v E [2016] EWHC 1052 (Fam); [2017] 1 F.L.R. 1255; [2016] Fam. Law 817, Fam Div

CEF Holdings Ltd v Mundey [2012] EWHC 1524 (QB); [2012] I.R.L.R. 912; [2012] F.S.R. 35, QBD .... *Digested,* 12/**1142**: *Considered* 17/823

Celaya Emparanza y Galdos Internacional SA (Cegasa) v Proyectos Integrales de Balizamiento SL (C-488/10) EU:C:2012:88; [2012] E.C.D.R. 17, ECJ (1st Chamber) *Considered* 17/386

Celine Sarl v Celine SA (C-17/06) EU:C:2007:497; [2007] E.C.R. I-7041; [2007] E.T.M.R. 80, ECJ (Grand Chamber) .... *Digested,* 08/**2380**: *Applied* 08/2383, 10/2005, 13/1831: *Followed* 17/1396

Celltech R&D Ltd v MedImmune Inc [2004] EWCA Civ 1331; [2005] F.S.R. 21; Independent, November 12, 2004; (2005) 28(1) I.P.D. 27109; (2004) 148 S.J.L.B. 1250, CA (Civ Div) .... *Digested,* 04/**2344**: *Followed* 17/1377

Celsa Steel (UK) Ltd v Webb (Valuation Officer) [2017] UKUT 133 (LC); [2017] R.A. 143, UT (Lands) .... *Digested,* 17/**1526**

Celtic Bioenergy Ltd v Knowles Ltd [2017] EWHC 472 (TCC); [2018] 1 All E.R. (Comm) 608; [2017] 1 Lloyd's Rep. 495; [2017] B.L.R. 312; 171 Con. L.R. 160; [2017] C.I.L.L. 3961, QBD (TCC) .... *Digested,* 17/**71**

Central A1 Ltd, Re; *sub nom* Rubin & Partners v Cohen [2017] EWHC 220 (Ch); [2017] B.C.C. 69, Ch D (Companies Ct) .... *Digested,* 17/**1316**

Central Bank of Nigeria v Williams see Williams v Central Bank of Nigeria

Centre for Advice on Individual Rights in Europe v Secretary of State for the Home Department [2017] EWHC 1878 (Admin); [2017] 4 W.L.R. 129; [2017] A.C.D. 108, QBD (Admin) .... *Digested,* 17/**1796**

Cevrioglu v Turkey (69546/12) [2017] Inquest L.R. 37, ECHR

CF v MF [2017] CSIH 44; 2017 S.L.T. 945; 2017 Fam. L.R. 83; 2017 G.W.D. 23-394, IH (Ex Div) .... *Digested,* 17/**2604**

CFC 26 Ltd v Brown Shipley & Co Ltd [2017] EWHC 1594 (Ch); [2017] 1 W.L.R. 4589, Ch D
CFL Finance Ltd v Rubin [2017] EWHC 111 (Ch); [2017] B.P.I.R. 336, Ch D .... *Digested,* 17/**1302**
CG v Facebook Ireland Ltd [2015] NIQB 28, QBD (NI)
Reversed in part 17/2367
CG v Facebook Ireland Ltd [2016] NICA 54; [2017] 2 C.M.L.R. 29; [2017] E.M.L.R. 12, CA (NI) .... *Digested,* 17/**2367**
CGI Holding LLC v Minister of National Revenue 19 I.T.L. Rep. 692, Fed Ct (Can)
CGL Group Ltd v Royal Bank of Scotland Plc; *joined cases* Bartles v Barclays Bank Plc; WW Property Investments Ltd v National Westminster Bank Plc [2017] EWCA Civ 1073; [2017] C.T.L.C. 97, CA (Civ Div)
CH v A Metropolitan Council [2017] EWCOP 12; [2017] C.O.P.L.R. 341; (2018) 160 B.M.L.R. 198, CP
CH v SM see X (Foreign Surrogacy: Child's Name), Re
CH v WH (Financial Provision: Approval of Consent Order); *sub nom* CH v WH (Power to Order Indemnity) [2017] EWHC 2379 (Fam); [2017] 4 W.L.R. 178; [2018] 1 F.L.R. 495; [2017] 3 F.C.R. 626; [2018] 1 P. & C.R. DG5, Fam Ct
CH v WH (Power to Order Indemnity) see CH v WH (Financial Provision: Approval of Consent Order)
Chachani Misti y Pichu Pichu SRL v Hostplanet Ltd [2016] EWHC 983 (Ch); [2017] I.L.Pr. 34, Ch D .... *Digested,* 17/**294**
Chadwick v Nash [2012] B.P.I.R. 70, Ch D .... *Digested,* 12/**1816**:
Considered 14/1796, 17/1300
Chadwick v National Crime Agency [2017] UKFTT 656 (TC); [2017] B.P.I.R. 1429; [2017] S.T.I. 2103, FTT (Tax)
Chagger v Abbey National Plc see Abbey National Plc v Chagger
Chagos Islanders v Attorney General [2003] EWHC 2222 (QB); Times, October 10, 2003, QBD
Affirmed 05/4197: *Considered* 17/379
Chai v Peng [2017] EWHC 792 (Fam); [2018] 1 F.L.R. 248; [2017] 3 F.C.R. 29, Fam Div .... *Digested,* 17/**1031**
Chai v Peng; *sub nom* Peng v Chai [2015] EWCA Civ 1312; [2017] 1 F.L.R. 318; [2016] Fam. Law 303, CA (Civ Div)
Challacombe's Ltd v Revenue and Customs Commissioners [2017] UKFTT 664 (TC); [2017] S.T.I. 2010, FTT (Tax)
Chalmers v Diageo Scotland Ltd [2017] CSOH 36; [2017] L.L.R. 256; 2017 G.W.D. 9-126, OH .... *Digested,* 17/**2740**
Chalmers (Robert Davidson) v HM Advocate [2014] HCJAC 24; 2014 J.C. 220; 2014 S.L.T. 688; 2014 S.C.L. 442; 2014 S.C.C.R. 291; 2014 G.W.D. 13-249, HCJ .... *Digested,* 14/**3775**:
Considered 17/2807
Chambelin Solicitors v Emokpae see Wong v Igen Ltd (formerly Leeds Careers Guidance)
Chamberlain-Davidson (Mark) v HM Advocate [2013] HCJAC 54; 2013 S.C.L. 560; 2013 S.C.C.R. 295; 2013 G.W.D. 18-365, HCJ .... *Digested,* 13/**3580**:
Considered 17/623
Chamberlin v Revenue and Customs Commissioners; *sub nom* Revenue and Customs Commissioners v Chamberlin [2011] EWCA Civ 271; [2011] S.T.C. 1237; [2011] B.P.I.R. 691; [2011] B.V.C. 162; [2011] S.T.I. 1213; [2011] N.P.C. 33, CA (Civ Div) .... *Digested,* 11/**3579**:
Applied 12/1867, 17/1327
Chambers v Chambers [2016] NZHC 583; 20 I.T.E.L.R. 1, HC (NZ)
Chambers v Starkings see Sage v Double A Hydraulics Ltd
Champion v North Norfolk DC see R. (on the application of Champion) v North Norfolk DC
Chan Wing Siu v R.; *sub nom* R. v Chan Wing Siu [1985] A.C. 168; [1984] 3 W.L.R. 677; [1984] 3 All E.R. 877; (1985) 80 Cr. App. R. 117; [1984] Crim. L.R. 549; (1984) 81 L.S.G. 216; (1984) 128 S.J. 685, PC (HK) .... *Digested,* 84/**667**:
Applied 90/1131, 91/949, 93/917: *Approved* 87/801: *Cited* 97/1221:
Considered 93/966, 08/743, 11/675, 17/551: *Distinguished* 89/840, 90/1121:
Explained 92/639: *Followed* 95/1238, 11/676: *Referred to* 84/489:
Superseded 16/482
Chancepixies Animal Welfare v North Kesteven DC [2017] EWHC 1927 (Admin); [2017] P.T.S.R. 1368; [2017] L.L.R. 685, QBD (Admin)
Chancery Client Partners Ltd v MRC 957 Ltd [2016] EWHC 2142 (Ch); [2016] Lloyd's Rep. F.C. 578, Ch D (Manchester) .... *Digested,* 17/**504**
Chand v Linden Mews Ltd see Das v Linden Mews Ltd
Chandi (Setting of Minimum Term), Re see Jones (Setting of Minimum Term), Re

Chandler v Camden LBC see R. (on the application of Chandler) v Secretary of State for Children, Schools and Families
Chandler v Cape Plc [2012] EWCA Civ 525; [2012] 1 W.L.R. 3111; [2012] 3 All E.R. 640; [2012] I.C.R. 1293; [2012] P.I.Q.R. P17, CA (Civ Div) .... *Digested,* 12/**2400**:
Applied 16/1539, 17/2194: *Followed* 14/2202
Chandra v Mayor; *joined case* Mayor v Mahendru [2016] EWHC 2636 (Ch); [2017] 1 W.L.R. 729, Ch D (Birmingham) .... *Digested,* 17/**354**
Chanel Ltd v FW Woolworth & Co Ltd [1981] 1 W.L.R. 485; [1981] 1 All E.R. 745; [1981] F.S.R. 196; Times, November 14, 1980; (1981) 125 S.J. 202, CA (Civ Div) .... *Digested,* 81/**2126**:
Applied 92/576, 93/587, 17/365: *Considered* 93/3211, 94/3675: *Distinguished* 87/3031, 97/2721, 07/437: *Followed* 97/3904: *Referred to* 95/4240, 99/435
Changtel Solutions UK Ltd (formerly Enta Technologies Ltd) v Revenue and Customs Commissioners see Enta Technologies Ltd, Re
Chaplin v United Kingdom (59842/10) see Eweida v United Kingdom (48420/10)
Chapman v Honig [1963] 2 Q.B. 502; [1963] 3 W.L.R. 19; [1963] 2 All E.R. 513; (1963) 107 S.J. 374, CA .... *Digested,* 63/**2729**:
Considered 16/2145, 17/160: *Distinguished* 91/119: *Followed* 71/2133
Chapman v United Kingdom (27238/95) (2001) 33 E.H.R.R. 18; 10 B.H.R.C. 48; Times, January 30, 2001, ECHR .... *Digested,* 01/**4744**:
Applied 02/3684, 03/3380, 03/3485, 05/3285, 06/2823, 09/3018, 13/1582, 17/1730: *Considered* 02/3686, 03/3424, 04/1376, 04/3040, 04/3095, 06/3331, 07/2137, 07/2879, 07/3293, 08/2918, 08/4302, 09/3007, 10/2608, 14/2744, 15/1972: *Distinguished* 02/3069, 04/1992, 09/1941: *Followed* 06/3381
Chappell v Revenue and Customs Commissioners [2016] EWCA Civ 809; [2017] 1 W.L.R. 2701; [2017] 1 All E.R. 550; [2016] S.T.C. 1980; [2016] B.T.C. 36; [2016] S.T.I. 2293, CA (Civ Div) .... *Digested,* 16/**2120**
Chard v Trowbridge Office Cleaning Services Ltd [2017] I.C.R. D21, EAT
Chargeable Batteries Cartel, Re (AT.39904) [2017] 5 C.M.L.R. 2, CEC
Charity Commission for Northern Ireland v Bangor Provident Trust [2015] NICA 21; [2017] N.I. 59, CA (NI)
Charles v Mugla Chief Public Prosecution Office see Charles v Turkey
Charles v Turkey; *sub nom* Charles v Mugla Chief Public Prosecution Office [2017] EWHC 952 (Admin); [2017] A.C.D. 84, DC
Charman v Charman [2005] EWCA Civ 1606; [2006] 1 W.L.R. 1053; [2006] 2 F.L.R. 422; [2006] W.T.L.R. 1; (2006-07) 9 I.T.E.L.R. 43; Independent, January 13, 2006; [2006] Fam. Law 516; (2006) 103(5) L.S.G. 28, CA (Civ Div) .... *Digested,* 06/**1625**:
Applied 09/1494, 11/1301, 11/1307, 12/1439, 14/1373, 14/1374: *Followed* 12/1440, 17/1023
Charman v Charman [2007] EWCA Civ 503; [2007] 1 F.L.R. 1246; [2007] 2 F.C.R. 217; [2007] W.T.L.R. 1151; (2006-07) 9 I.T.E.L.R. 913; [2007] Fam. Law 682; (2007) 157 N.L.J. 814; (2007) 151 S.J.L.B. 710, CA (Civ Div) .... *Digested,* 07/**1691**:
Applied 08/1426, 09/1488, 09/1495, 09/1510, 12/1308, 12/1427, 13/1310: *Considered* 07/1692, 08/1434, 10/1288, 10/26, 11/1290, 17/983: *Distinguished* 11/1302: *Followed* 11/1296, 15/1102, 17/1032
Chartbrook Ltd v Persimmon Homes Ltd [2009] UKHL 38; [2009] 1 A.C. 1101; [2009] 3 W.L.R. 267; [2009] 4 All E.R. 677; [2010] 1 All E.R. (Comm) 365; [2009] Bus. L.R. 1200; [2009] B.L.R. 551; 125 Con. L.R. 1; [2010] 1 P. & C.R. 9; [2009] 3 E.G.L.R. 119; Times, July 2, 2009; [2009] C.I.L.L. 2729; [2009] 27 E.G. 91 (C.S.); (2009) 153(26) S.J.L.B. 27; [2009] N.P.C. 87; [2009] N.P.C. 86, HL .... *Digested,* 09/**722**:
Applied 10/1038, 10/2709, 11/236, 11/505, 11/550, 12/2042, 12/2057, 13/1886, 13/3185, 13/571, 14/2707, 15/2310, 16/137, 16/140, 16/1536, 16/234, 16/438, 17/1817: *Considered* 10/1920, 10/574, 10/578, 10/622, 10/623, 11/175, 11/187, 11/2704, 12/516, 13/2454, 14/2279, 14/2503, 16/1409, 17/792: *Followed* 10/516, 12/1797, 12/2759, 12/626, 12/627, 15/1606, 16/1264, 16/1596, 16/399, 16/424
Chartridge Developments Ltd v Revenue and Customs Commissioners [2016] UKFTT 766 (TC); [2017] S.F.T.D. 419; [2017] S.T.I. 332, FTT (Tax) .... *Digested,* 17/**2082**
Chartwell Estate Agents Ltd v Fergies Properties SA [2014] EWCA Civ 506; [2014] C.P. Rep. 36; [2014] 3 Costs L.R. 588; [2014] C.I.L.L. 3513, CA (Civ Div) .... *Digested,* 14/**461**:
Applied 16/170: *Considered* 17/352: *Followed* 14/447, 15/195
Chase Manhattan Bank v HIH Casualty & General Insurance Ltd see HIH Casualty & General Insurance Ltd v Chase Manhattan Bank
Chatfield & Co Ltd v Commissioner of Inland Revenue [2016] NZHC 1234; 19 I.T.L. Rep. 63, HC (NZ)
Chatfield & Co Ltd v Commissioner of Inland Revenue [2016] NZCA 614; 19 I.T.L. Rep. 706, CA (NZ)

Chaudhary v Yavuz [2011] EWCA Civ 1314; [2013] Ch. 249; [2012] 3 W.L.R. 987; [2012] 2 All E.R. 418; [2012] H.L.R. 17; [2012] 1 P. & C.R. 9; Times, December 29, 2011; [2011] N.P.C. 120, CA (Civ Div) .... *Digested,* 12/**2730**: *Considered* 17/1841

Chaudhry v Advocate General for Scotland [2013] CSOH 36; 2013 S.L.T. 548; 2013 S.C.L.R. 635; 2013 G.W.D. 10-211, OH .... *Digested,* 13/**3541**: *Considered* 17/2447

Chaudhry (Tariq) v Procurator Fiscal, Hamilton [2017] SAC (Crim) 7; 2017 S.C.L. 646; 2017 G.W.D. 14-231, SAC .... *Digested,* 17/**2818**

Chaudhry (Tariq) v Procurator Fiscal, Hamilton [2017] SAC (Crim) 5; 2017 S.C.L. 573; 2017 G.W.D. 11-153, SAC .... *Digested,* 17/**2543**

Chavez-Vilchez v Raad van Bestuur van de Sociale Verzekeringsbank (C-133/15) EU:C:2017:354; [2018] Q.B. 103; [2017] 3 W.L.R. 1326; [2017] 3 C.M.L.R. 35; [2018] C.E.C. 53; [2017] Imm. A.R. 1387; [2017] I.N.L.R. 708, ECJ (Grand Chamber)

Chawda, Re; *sub nom* Lemon v Chawda [2014] B.P.I.R. 49, Ch D (Bankruptcy Ct) ...... *Digested,* 14/**1203**: *Considered* 15/2116, 17/890

Cheesman, Re [1891] 2 Ch. 289, CA
Considered 17/288: *Followed* 11/2127

Cheltenham & Gloucester Plc v Appleyard [2004] EWCA Civ 291; Times, March 29, 2004; [2004] 13 E.G. 127 (C.S.); (2004) 101(13) L.S.G. 37; (2004) 101(14) L.S.G. 26; (2004) 148 S.J.L.B. 356; [2004] N.P.C. 42, CA (Civ Div) .... *Digested,* 04/**3242**: *Considered* 11/2716, 17/637

Chennell, Re; *sub nom* Jones v Chennell (1878) 8 Ch. D. 492, CA
Applied 17/1221

Cherkasov v Olegovich see Dalnyaya Step LLC (In Liquidation), Re

Cherney v Neuman [2009] EWHC 1743 (Ch), Ch D
Considered 17/301

Cherry Tree Investments Ltd v Landmain Ltd [2012] EWCA Civ 736; [2013] Ch. 305; [2013] 2 W.L.R. 481; [2013] 1 B.C.L.C. 484; [2012] 2 P. & C.R. 10; [2012] 2 E.G.L.R. 141; [2012] 23 E.G. 97 (C.S.), CA (Civ Div) .... *Digested,* 13/**2454**: *Applied* 16/1596: *Considered* 17/178: *Distinguished* 14/2278: *Followed* 14/2521

Cheshire and Wirral Partnership NHS Foundation Trust v Z [2016] EWCOP 56; [2017] C.O.P.L.R. 165, Fam Div .... *Digested,* 17/**1120**

Cheshire East BC v NA see PN (A Child) (Care Proceedings: Flawed Assessments), Re

Cheshire East BC v Secretary of State for Communities and Local Government [2016] EWHC 571 (Admin); [2016] P.T.S.R. 1052; [2016] J.P.L. 909, QBD (Admin) ..... *Digested,* 16/**1751**: *Applied* 17/1767, 17/1769, 17/1780: *Approved* 17/1779

Cheshire East BC v Secretary of State for Communities and Local Government see Secretary of State for Communities and Local Government v Hopkins Homes Ltd

heshire West and Chester Council v P; *sub nom* P v Surrey CC; P v Cheshire West and Chester Council; *joined case* Surrey CC v P [2014] UKSC 19; [2014] A.C. 896; [2014] 2 W.L.R. 642; [2014] 2 All E.R. 585; [2014] P.T.S.R. 460; [2014] 2 F.C.R. 71; [2014] C.O.P.L.R. 313; [2014] H.R.L.R. 13; (2014) 17 C.C.L. Rep. 5; [2014] Med. L.R. 321; (2014) 137 B.M.L.R. 16; [2014] M.H.L.R. 394; Times, April 1, 2014; (2014) 158(13) S.J.L.B. 37, SC .... *Digested,* 14/**2189**: *Applied* 15/1745, 15/1747, 16/1517: *Cited* 15/1757, 16/1522: *Considered* 15/1748, 16/14, 16/1483, 16/1518, 17/1546: *Distinguished* 15/1758, 17/19: *Followed* 15/1734, 16/1480, 16/1499, 17/966: *Referred to* 15/1720, 15/1746, 16/4, 17/1539

Chester v Afshar [2004] UKHL 41; [2005] 1 A.C. 134; [2004] 3 W.L.R. 927; [2004] 4 All E.R. 587; [2005] P.I.Q.R. P12; [2005] Lloyd's Rep. Med. 109; (2005) 81 B.M.L.R. 1; [2005] P.N.L.R. 14; Times, October 19, 2004; (2004) 101(43) L.S.G. 34; (2004) 154 N.L.J. 1589; (2004) 148 S.J.L.B. 1215, HL .... *Digested,* 05/**2841**: *Applied* 09/2842, 15/1769: *Considered* 12/1535, 14/2198, 17/1557, 17/1640: *Distinguished* 05/2863: *Followed* 06/2866, 17/1560

Chesterton Global Ltd (t/a Chestertons) v Nurmohamed [2017] EWCA Civ 979; [2018] 1 All E.R. 947; [2017] I.R.L.R. 837, CA (Civ Div) .... *Digested,* 17/**816**

Chesterton Global Ltd (t/a Chestertons) v Nurmohamed [2015] I.C.R. 920; [2015] I.R.L.R. 614, EAT .... *Digested,* 15/**842**: *Affirmed* 17/816

Chet v Capita Translation and Interpreting Ltd UKEAT/0086/15/DM, EAT
Cited 17/788

Chetwynd v Tunmore [2016] EWHC 156 (QB); [2017] Q.B. 188; [2016] 3 W.L.R. 1159; [2016] Env. L.R. 23, QBD .... *Digested,* 16/**2137**

Chevron Australia Holdings Pty Ltd v Commissioner of Taxation [2017] FCAFC 62; 19 I.T.L. Rep. 971, Fed Ct (Aus) (Full Ct)

Chevron Australia Holdings Pty Ltd v Commissioner of Taxation [2015] FCA 1092; 19 I.T.L. Rep. 159, Fed Ct (Aus) (Sgl judge)

Chhokar v Chhokar [1984] F.L.R. 313; [1984] Fam. Law 269; (1983) 80 L.S.G. 3243, CA (Civ Div) .... *Digested,* 84/**1696**: *Applied* 17/1826

Chief Adjudication Officer v Bath [2000] 1 F.L.R. 8; [2000] 1 F.C.R. 419; [2001] W.T.L.R. 55; Times, October 28, 1999; Independent, November 9, 1999; [2000] Fam. Law 91, CA (Civ Div) .... *Digested,* 99/**4523**: *Considered* 09/1573, 12/1443, 17/1045: *Distinguished* 11/1437

Chief Adjudication Officer v Wolke see Secretary of State for Social Security v Remilien

Chief Constable of Greater Manchester v Bailey [2017] EWCA Civ 425; Times, June 28, 2017, CA (Civ Div) .... *Digested,* 17/**820**

Chief Constable of Greater Manchester v Bailey UKEAT/0166/15/DA, EAT *Reversed* 17/820

Chief Constable of Thames Valley v Police Misconduct Panel [2017] EWHC 923 (Admin); [2017] A.C.D. 83, QBD (Admin)

Chief Constable of the Police Service of Scotland v A (M) 2017 S.L.T. (Sh Ct) 192; 2017 G.W.D. 21-356, Sh Ct (Lothian) (Edinburgh) .... *Digested,* 17/**2819**

Chief Constable of the West Midlands v Blackburn; *sub nom* Blackburn v Chief Constable of the West Midlands [2008] EWCA Civ 1208; [2009] I.R.L.R. 135; [2008] Po. L.R. 346; (2008) 105(44) L.S.G. 20; (2008) 158 N.L.J. 1603, CA (Civ Div) .... *Digested,* 09/**1211**: *Considered* 17/1800

Chief Constable of West Midlands v Fowkes see Harrod v Chief Constable of West Midlands

Chief Constable of West Midlands v Harrod see Harrod v Chief Constable of West Midlands

Chief Constable of West Yorkshire v Vento (No.2) see Vento v Chief Constable of West Yorkshire

Chief Executive of Ministry of Social Development v TS see JSB (A Child), Re

Chiesa v Financial Conduct Authority [2017] UKUT 275 (TCC); [2017] Lloyd's Rep. F.C. 501, UT (Tax) .... *Digested,* 17/**1073**

Chihaia v Bacau Court of Law see Romania v Zagrean

Chihaia v Romania see Romania v Zagrean

Chikwamba v Secretary of State for the Home Department see C (Zimbabwe) v Secretary of State for the Home Department

Child and Family Agency v D (C-428/15); *sub nom* Child and Family Agency v JD (C-428/15) EU:C:2016:819; [2017] Fam. 248; [2017] 2 W.L.R. 949; [2017] I.L.Pr. 5; [2017] 1 F.L.R. 223; [2017] 1 F.C.R. 320, ECJ (3rd Chamber)

Child and Family Agency v JD (C-428/15) see Child and Family Agency v D (C-428/15)

China National Chartering Co Ltd v Daiichii Chuo Kisen Kaisha see Gard Marine & Energy Ltd v China National Chartering Co Ltd

China Shipbuilding Corp v Nippon Yusen Kabukishi Kaisha (The Seta Maru, The Saikyo and The Suma) [2000] 1 Lloyd's Rep. 367; [2000] C.L.C. 566, QBD (Comm) .... *Digested,* 00/**4738**: *Applied* 17/505

Chiswell v Chiswell [2016] CSOH 45; 2017 S.C.L.R. 49; 2016 G.W.D. 10-186, OH ...... *Digested,* 17/**2677**

Chiswell v Griffon Land and Estates Ltd [1975] 1 W.L.R. 1181; [1975] 2 All E.R. 665; (1975) 30 P. & C.R. 211; (1975) 119 S.J. 338, CA (Civ Div) .... *Digested,* 75/**1879**: *Applied* 03/2724, 03/2757, 17/1433: *Considered* 90/2782: *Followed* 12/462

Chocoladefabriken Lindt & Sprungli AG v Franz Hauswirth GmbH (C-529/07) EU:C:2009:361; [2010] Bus. L.R. 443; [2009] E.C.R. I-4893; [2009] E.T.M.R. 56, ECJ (1st Chamber) .... *Digested,* 09/**2416**: *Applied* 11/1998, 11/2002, 11/2009, 13/1832: *Considered* 13/1791, 17/1395: *Followed* 10/1996

Chodiev v Stein [2015] EWHC 1428 (Comm), QBD (Comm) *Applied* 17/194

Chodoreck v District Court of Kielce see Chodorek v Poland

Chodorek v Poland; *sub nom* Chodoreck v District Court of Kielce [2017] EWHC 995 (Admin); [2018] 1 Cr. App. R. 6; [2017] Lloyd's Rep. F.C. 395; [2017] A.C.D. 82, QBD (Admin) .... *Digested,* 17/**909**

Choudhary v Bhattar; *sub nom* Choudhury v Bhatter [2009] EWCA Civ 1176; [2010] 2 All E.R. 1031; [2010] 2 All E.R. (Comm) 419; [2010] 2 B.C.L.C. 17; [2010] I.L.Pr. 8; Times, November 20, 2009; (2009) 159 N.L.J. 1628, CA (Civ Div) ...... *Digested,* 10/**501**: *Considered* 15/220: *Not applied* 17/212

Choudhry v Luton BC [2017] EWHC 960 (Ch); [2017] B.P.I.R. 1150; [2017] R.V.R. 208, Ch D ...... *Digested,* 17/**1279**

Choudhury v Bhatter see Choudhary v Bhattar

Chouhan v Earls High School [2016] UKUT 405 (LC); [2017] L. & T.R. 3, UT (Lands) .. *Digested,* 17/**1431**

Christ Church, Alsager, Re [1999] Fam. 142; [1998] 3 W.L.R. 1394; [1999] 1 All E.R. 117; Times, October 22, 1998, Chancery Ct of York ...... *Digested,* 98/**1786**: *Applied* 01/1848, 01/3481: *Considered* 00/1770, 06/1058: *Followed* 17/660

Christ Church, Harwood, Re [2002] 1 W.L.R. 2055; Times, May 7, 2002; (2002) 99(20) L.S.G. 32; (2002) 146 S.J.L.B. 110, Cons Ct (Manchester) ...... *Digested,* 02/**966**: *Applied* 17/662

Christian Institute v Lord Advocate; *sub nom* Christian Institute, Petitioners; Christian Institute v Scottish Ministers [2016] UKSC 51; 2017 S.C. (U.K.S.C.) 29; 2016 S.L.T. 805; 2016 S.C.L.R. 448; [2016] H.R.L.R. 19; [2016] E.L.R. 474; (2016) 19 C.C.L. Rep. 422; Times, September 26, 2016; 2016 G.W.D. 22-401, SC ...... *Digested,* 16/**848**

Christian Institute v Scottish Ministers see Christian Institute v Lord Advocate

Christian Institute, Petitioners see Christian Institute v Lord Advocate

Christianuyi Ltd v Revenue and Customs Commissioners; *joined cases* Jonny Tooze Physiotherapy Services Ltd v Revenue and Customs Commissioners; Dr Jacek Trzaski Ltd v Revenue and Customs Commissioners; Haddassah Ltd v Revenue and Customs Commissioners; Fanning Social Care Ltd v Revenue and Customs Commissioners [2016] UKFTT 272 (TC); [2017] S.F.T.D. 252, FTT (Tax) ...... *Digested,* 17/**2139**

Christopher Linnett Ltd v Harding (t/a MJ Harding Contractors) [2017] EWHC 1781 (TCC); [2018] Bus. L.R. 179; [2017] B.L.R. 498; 173 Con. L.R. 66; [2017] C.I.L.L. 4012, QBD (TCC) ...... *Digested,* 17/**657**

Chugai Pharmaceutical Co Ltd v UCB Biopharma SPRL see Chugai Pharmaceutical Co Ltd v UCB Pharma SA

Chugai Pharmaceutical Co Ltd v UCB Pharma SA; *sub nom* Chugai Pharmaceutical Co Ltd v UCB Biopharma SPRL [2017] EWHC 1216 (Pat); [2017] Bus. L.R. 1455; [2017] F.S.R. 45, Ch D (Patents Ct) ...... *Digested,* 17/**1377**

Chuku v Chuku [2017] EWHC 541 (Ch); [2017] 1 W.L.R. 3137; [2017] 2 Costs L.R. 267, Ch D ...... *Digested,* 17/**363**

Chung v Towey [2017] UKUT 157 (LC); [2017] 2 P. & C.R. DG11, UT (Lands)

Church of England Children's Society v Customs and Excise Commissioners; *sub nom* Church of England Children's Society v Revenue and Customs Commissioners [2005] EWHC 1692 (Ch); [2005] S.T.C. 1644; [2005] B.T.C. 5559; [2005] B.V.C. 590; Times, September 21, 2005; [2005] S.T.I. 1340; (2005) 102(34) L.S.G. 33, Ch D ...... *Digested,* 05/**4371**: *Applied* 15/2593, 17/2241: *Cited* 10/3488

Church of England Children's Society v Revenue and Customs Commissioners see Church of England Children's Society v Customs and Excise Commissioners

Churchill Retirement Living v Christchurch BC [2017] P.A.D. 4, Planning Inspector

Churchmanor Estates Co Plc v Colchester BC [2017] P.A.D. 6, Planning Inspector

Ciccone v Ritchie [2016] EWHC 608 (Fam); [2016] 4 W.L.R. 60; [2017] 1 F.L.R. 795; [2016] 3 F.C.R. 419; [2016] Fam. Law 660, Fam Div ...... *Digested,* 16/**951**

Ciccone v Ritchie [2016] EWHC 616 (Fam); [2016] 1 W.L.R. 3545; [2016] 3 All E.R. 335; [2017] 1 F.L.R. 812; [2016] 3 F.C.R. 438; [2016] Fam. Law 435, Fam Div .. *Digested,* 16/**916**

Ciola v Land Vorarlberg (C-224/97) EU:C:1999:212; [1999] E.C.R. I-2517; [1999] 2 C.M.L.R. 1220, ECJ ...... *Digested,* 99/**2252**: *Considered* 07/1640, 17/807

Ciorap v Moldova (7481/06) (Unreported, July 20, 2010), ECHR *Applied* 17/1169

CIP Properties (AIPT) Ltd v Galliford Try Infrastructure Ltd [2014] EWHC 3546 (TCC); [2015] 1 All E.R. (Comm) 765; 156 Con. L.R. 202; [2014] 6 Costs L.R. 1026, QBD (TCC) ...... *Digested,* 15/**468**: *Applied* 17/772

CIP Properties (AIPT) Ltd v Galliford Try Infrastructure Ltd [2015] EWHC 1345 (TCC); 160 Con. L.R. 73, QBD (TCC) ...... *Digested,* 15/**329**: *Applied* 17/196

Circuit Systems Ltd (In Liquidation) v Zuken-Redac (UK) Ltd see Norglen Ltd (In Liquidation) v Reeds Rains Prudential Ltd

CIT Group Securities (Canada) Inc v R. 2016 TCC 163; 19 I.T.L. Rep. 73, Tax Ct (Can)

Citizens UK v Secretary of State for the Home Department see R. (on the application of Citizens UK) v Secretary of State for the Home Department
Citroen Commerce GmbH v Zentralvereinigung des Kraftfahrzeuggewerbes zur Aufrechterhaltung lauteren Wettbewerbs eV (ZLW) (C-476/14) EU:C:2016:527; [2016] Bus. L.R. 1024; [2017] R.T.R. 6; [2017] 1 C.M.L.R. 19, ECJ (4th Chamber)
Citta Metropolitana di Bari v Edilizia Mastrodonato srl (C-147/15) EU:C:2016:606; [2017] P.T.S.R. 94, ECJ (4th Chamber)
City Index v Leslie [1992] Q.B. 98; [1991] 3 W.L.R. 207; [1991] 3 All E.R. 180; [1991] B.C.L.C. 643; Times, March 21, 1991; Independent, April 5, 1991; Financial Times, March 19, 1991; (1991) 141 N.L.J. 419, CA (Civ Div) .... *Digested,* 92/**3730**: *Considered* 95/789, 17/171
City of Edinburgh Council v O; *sub nom* City of Edinburgh Council v RO [2016] SAC (Civ) 15; 2017 Fam. L.R. 27; 2016 G.W.D. 40-716, SAC .... *Digested,* 17/**2602**
City of Edinburgh Council v RO see City of Edinburgh Council v O
City of Edinburgh Council v X 2017 S.L.T. (Sh Ct) 225; 2017 Hous. L.R. 61; 2017 G.W.D. 28-447, Sh Ct (Lothian) (Edinburgh) .... *Digested,* 17/**2704**
City of London v Reeve & Co Ltd; *joined case* G Lawrence Wholesale Meat Co Ltd v Citigen (London) Ltd [2000] C.P. Rep. 73; [2000] B.L.R. 211, QBD (TCC) .... *Digested,* 00/**878**: *Applied* 17/1342
City of London Building Society v Flegg [1988] A.C. 54; [1987] 2 W.L.R. 1266; [1987] 3 All E.R. 435; [1988] 1 F.L.R. 98; (1987) 19 H.L.R. 484; (1987) 54 P. & C.R. 337; [1988] Fam. Law 17; (1987) 84 L.S.G. 1966; (1987) 137 N.L.J. 475; (1987) 131 S.J. 806, HL .... *Digested,* 87/**2540**: *Considered* 89/2342: *Distinguished* 00/4658: *Followed* 17/1841
City of London Corp v Devlin (1997) 29 H.L.R. 58, CA (Civ Div) .... *Digested,* 97/**2745**: *Considered* 17/1458
City of Los Angeles v Patel 41 B.H.R.C. 71, US Court
City of York Council v Sykes (Valuation Officer) [2016] R.V.R. 287, VT *Considered* 17/1529
City of York Council v Sykes (Valuation Officer) see York City Council v Sykes (Valuation Officer)
City of York Council v Trinity One (Leeds) Ltd [2017] EWHC 318 (Ch); [2017] 2 P. & C.R. 12, Ch D .... *Digested,* 17/**1771**
City West Housing Trust v Massey; *sub nom* Manchester and District Housing Association v Roberts [2016] EWCA Civ 704; [2017] 1 W.L.R. 129; [2016] H.L.R. 31; [2016] 2 P. & C.R. 14, CA (Civ Div) .... *Digested,* 16/**1045**
CJM v HM Advocate see M v HM Advocate (No.2)
CK v Slovenia (C-578/16 PPU) EU:C:2017:127; [2017] 3 C.M.L.R. 10, ECJ (5th Chamber)
CL (Vietnam) v Secretary of State for the Home Department [2008] EWCA Civ 1551; [2009] 1 W.L.R. 1873; [2009] Imm. A.R. 403; [2009] I.N.L.R. 449; Times, January 7, 2009, CA (Civ Div) .... *Digested,* 09/**2096**: *Applied* 11/1722, 17/1173
Clarise Properties Ltd v Rees [2017] EWCA Civ 1135; [2017] H.L.R. 39; [2018] 1 P. & C.R. 7; [2018] L. & T.R. 3; [2018] R.V.R. 84, CA (Civ Div) .... *Digested,* 17/**1461**
Clark v Ardington Electrical Services see Lagden v O'Connor
Clark v Greater Glasgow Health Board [2016] CSOH 126; 2016 Rep. L.R. 126; 2016 G.W.D. 28-507, OH .... *Digested,* 17/**2755**
Clark v Greater Glasgow Health Board [2017] CSIH 17; 2017 S.C. 297; 2017 G.W.D. 7-96, IH (1 Div) .... *Digested,* 17/**2435**
Clark v Syme (William) 1957 J.C. 1; 1957 S.L.T. 32, HCJ .... *Digested,* 57/**3889**: *Followed* 01/6334, 17/2514
Clark v Tull (t/a Ardington Electrical Services) see Lagden v O'Connor
Clark v University of Lincolnshire and Humberside [2000] 1 W.L.R. 1988; [2000] 3 All E.R. 752; [2000] Ed. C.R. 553; [2000] E.L.R. 345; Times, May 3, 2000; Independent, May 3, 2000; [2000] C.O.D. 293; (2000) 150 N.L.J. 616; (2000) 144 S.J.L.B. 220, CA (Civ Div) .... *Digested,* 00/**2001**: *Applied* 05/2497, 06/1227, 07/1281, 13/913: *Considered* 07/51, 09/1056, 09/341, 13/909, 17/192: *Followed* 14/916
Clark (A Bankrupt), Re; *sub nom* Trustees Ex p. v Texaco [1975] 1 W.L.R. 559; [1975] 1 All E.R. 453; Times, October 29, 1974; (1974) 118 S.J. 862, Ch D .... *Digested,* 75/**170**: *Applied* 17/1285
Clarke v General Optical Council [2017] EWHC 521 (Admin); (2017) 155 B.M.L.R. 192, QBD (Admin) .... *Digested,* 17/**1106**
Clarke v Vedel [1979] R.T.R. 26, CA (Civ Div) .... *Digested,* 79/**2346**: *Considered* 98/506, 17/1878

Clarke Homes Ltd v Secretary of State for the Environment [2017] P.T.S.R. 1081; (1993) 66 P. & C.R. 263; [1993] E.G. 29 (C.S.); [1993] N.P.C. 26, CA (Civ Div) . *Digested,* 93/**3925**: *Applied* 99/4236, 09/1866, 12/1459, 15/2046, 16/1703, 16/972
Clarke-Jervoise v Scutt [1920] 1 Ch. 382, Ch D *Considered* 17/464
Classica Shipping Co Ltd v CMA CGM SA see CMA CGM SA v Classica Shipping Co Ltd (The CMA Djakarta)
Claughton v Charalambous [1999] 1 F.L.R. 740; [1998] B.P.I.R. 558; [1999] Fam. Law 205, Ch D .... *Digested,* 99/**3244**: *Applied* 17/1288
Claughton (Liquidator of Hollicourt (Contracts) Ltd) v Bank of Ireland see Hollicourt (Contracts) Ltd (In Liquidation) v Bank of Ireland
Clayton v Clayton [2016] NZSC 30; 19 I.T.E.L.R. 448, SC (NZ)
Clayton v Clayton [2016] NZSC 29; [2016] W.T.L.R. 955; 19 I.T.E.L.R. 406, SC (NZ)
Clayton v EUI Ltd (t/a Admiral Insurance) see McBride v UK Insurance Ltd
Clear Call Ltd v Central London Investments Ltd [2016] EWCA Civ 1231; [2017] L. & T.R. 13; [2017] 1 P. & C.R. DG16, CA (Civ Div) .... *Digested,* 17/**1452**
CLECE SA v Martin Valor (C-463/09) EU:C:2011:24; [2011] 2 C.M.L.R. 30; [2011] I.C.R. 1319; [2011] I.R.L.R. 251, ECJ (3rd Chamber) *Followed* 17/769
Cleeves v University of Oxford [2017] EWHC 702 (QB); [2017] E.L.R. 303, QBD .... *Digested,* 17/**193**
Cleghorn v Duncan [2017] CSOH 114; 2017 S.L.T. 1189; 2017 G.W.D. 29-456, OH .... *Digested,* 17/**2417**
Clenshaw v Tanner [2002] EWCA Civ 1848, CA (Civ Div) *Considered* 17/827
Cleveleys Investment Trust Co v Inland Revenue Commissioners (No.2) [1975] S.T.C. 457; 1975 S.C. 283; 1975 S.L.T. 237; 51 T.C. 26; [1975] T.R. 209, IH (1 Div) .... *Digested,* 75/**465**: *Applied* 17/2092: *Distinguished* 79/1450
CLFIS (UK) Ltd v Reynolds see Reynolds v CLFIS (UK) Ltd
Clibbery v Allan; *sub nom* Cliberry v Allan [2002] EWCA Civ 45; [2002] Fam. 261; [2002] 2 W.L.R. 1511; [2002] 1 All E.R. 865; [2002] 1 F.L.R. 565; [2002] 1 F.C.R. 385; [2002] U.K.H.R.R. 697; Times, February 5, 2002; Independent, February 5, 2002; [2002] Fam. Law 260; (2002) 99(11) L.S.G. 37; (2002) 152 N.L.J. 222; (2002) 146 S.J.L.B. 38, CA (Civ Div) .... *Digested,* 02/**1695**: *Applied* 14/1353, 16/907: *Considered* 04/185, 15/1101, 17/1015, 17/1029: *Followed* 12/22
Cliberry v Allan see Clibbery v Allan
ClientEarth v Secretary of State for the Environment, Food and Rural Affairs [2016] EWHC 2740 (Admin); [2017] P.T.S.R. 203; [2017] Env. L.R. 16; [2016] A.C.D. 137, QBD (Admin) .... *Digested,* 17/**875**
Clifton v Liverpool City Council [2017] UKUT 74 (LC); [2017] L. & T.R. 14; [2017] R.V.R. 214, UT (Lands) .... *Digested,* 17/**1437**
Clifton Place Garage Ltd, Re [1970] Ch. 477; [1970] 2 W.L.R. 243; [1970] 1 All E.R. 353; Times, October 23, 1969; (1969) 113 S.J. 895, CA (Civ Div) .... *Digested,* 70/**310**: *Considered* 17/1334
Clunes v Revenue and Customs Commissioners [2017] UKFTT 204 (TC); [2017] S.T.I. 1070, FTT (Tax) .... *Digested,* 17/**199**
Clunis v Camden and Islington HA [1998] Q.B. 978; [1998] 2 W.L.R. 902; [1998] 3 All E.R. 180; (1997-98) 1 C.C.L. Rep. 215; (1998) 40 B.M.L.R. 181; [1998] P.N.L.R. 262; Times, December 10, 1997; Independent, December 9, 1997; (1998) 95(2) L.S.G. 23; (1998) 142 S.J.L.B. 38, CA (Civ Div) .... *Digested,* 98/**3937**: *Applied* 03/935, 09/2836: *Considered* 08/2648, 08/2649, 10/2251, 10/2285: *Distinguished* 08/2767, 16/1835: *Followed* 99/1413, 03/3122, 17/2202
Clyde & Co LLP v Bates van Winkelhof see Bates van Winkelhof v Clyde & Co LLP
Clyde and Co (Scotland) LLP v Richardson [2016] HCJAC 93; 2016 S.L.T. 1200; 2016 S.C.L. 961; 2016 S.C.C.R. 480; 2016 G.W.D. 32-572, HCJ .... *Digested,* 17/**2565**
CM v Aviva Insurance UK Ltd see M v Aviva Insurance UK Ltd
CM v FC (Abduction: Consent) [2017] EWHC 1104 (Fam); [2017] 2 F.C.R. 635, Fam Div
CM v State Hospitals Board for Scotland see McCann v State Hospitals Board for Scotland
CM (EM Country Guidance: Disclosure: Zimbabwe), Re; *sub nom* CM (Zimbabwe) v Secretary of State for the Home Department [2013] UKUT 59 (IAC), UT (IAC) *Affirmed* 14/1664: *Considered* 17/1201
CM (Zimbabwe) v Secretary of State for the Home Department see CM (EM Country Guidance: Disclosure: Zimbabwe), Re
CM, Petitioner see McCann v State Hospitals Board for Scotland

CMA CGM SA v Classica Shipping Co Ltd (The CMA Djakarta); *sub nom* Classica Shipping Co Ltd v CMA CGM SA [2004] EWCA Civ 114; [2004] 1 All E.R. (Comm) 865; [2004] 1 Lloyd's Rep. 460; [2004] 1 C.L.C. 468; Times, February 27, 2004; (2004) 101(11) L.S.G. 36, CA (Civ Div) .... *Digested,* 04/**3487**: *Approved* 17/2017: *Considered* 09/3580, 14/2732

CN v United Kingdom (4239/08) (2013) 56 E.H.R.R. 24; 34 B.H.R.C. 1, ECHR .... *Digested,* 13/**1543**: *Applied* 17/1222

CNH Global NV v PGN Logistics Ltd [2009] EWHC 977 (Comm); [2009] 1 C.L.C. 807, QBD (Comm) .... *Digested,* 10/**175**: *Considered* 15/92, 17/66

Co-operative Bank Plc v Phillips [2017] EWHC 1320 (Ch); [2017] B.P.I.R. 1156, Ch D *Digested,* 17/**1304**

Co-operative Group Ltd v Baddeley [2014] EWCA Civ 658, CA (Civ Div) *Applied* 17/763

Co-operative Group Ltd v Birse Developments Ltd [2013] EWCA Civ 474; [2013] B.L.R. 383; 148 Con. L.R. 264; [2013] 19 E.G. 96 (C.S.), CA (Civ Div) .... *Digested,* 13/**403**: *Applied* 17/370

Coal Staff Superannuation Scheme Trustees Ltd v Revenue and Customs Commissioners [2017] UKUT 137 (TCC); [2017] S.T.C. 1064; [2017] B.T.C. 514; [2017] S.T.I. 1120, UT (Tax) .... *Digested,* 17/**2085**

Coates v Octagon Overseas Ltd see Octagon Overseas Ltd v Coates

Coats (Colin) v HM Advocate see Wade (Philip) v HM Advocate

Cobbe v Yeoman's Row Management Ltd; *sub nom* Yeoman's Row Management Ltd v Cobbe [2008] UKHL 55; [2008] 1 W.L.R. 1752; [2008] 4 All E.R. 713; [2009] 1 All E.R. (Comm) 205; [2008] 3 E.G.L.R. 31; [2008] 35 E.G. 142; [2008] 36 E.G. 142; [2008] W.T.L.R. 1461; (2008-09) 11 I.T.E.L.R. 530; Times, September 8, 2008; [2008] 31 E.G. 88 (C.S.); (2008) 152(31) S.J.L.B. 31; [2008] N.P.C. 95, HL .... *Digested,* 08/**3081**: *Applied* 09/2204, 11/2710, 16/1282: *Considered* 09/3175, 09/3188, 09/3723, 10/3217, 16/1795, 16/1801, 17/1837: *Followed* 09/3145, 12/2024

Cockbone v Atkinson Dacre & Slack see Arthur JS Hall & Co v Simons

Cockburn v Edwards (1881) 18 Ch. D. 449, CA *Applied* 06/1027, 17/1298: *Considered* 47-51/6353, 03/260

Coco v AN Clark (Engineers) Ltd [1968] F.S.R. 415; [1969] R.P.C. 41, Ch D .... *Digested,* 68/**1458**: *Applied* 88/3403, 99/3437, 01/4415, 03/1217, 07/4190, 09/2049, 13/1776, 13/1804, 14/1864, 15/795, 17/2197: *Considered* 03/2923, 08/60, 08/71, 15/1511

Codona v Showmen's Guild of Great Britain 2002 S.L.T. 299; 2001 G.W.D. 18-689, OH .... *Digested,* 02/**5247**: *Applied* 17/2393

Cofely Ltd v Bingham [2016] EWHC 240 (Comm); [2016] 2 All E.R. (Comm) 129; [2016] B.L.R. 187; 164 Con. L.R. 39; [2016] C.I.L.L. 3801, QBD (Comm) .... *Digested,* 16/**71**: *Applied* 17/659

Coin-a-Drink Ltd v Revenue and Customs Commissioners [2015] UKFTT 495 (TC); [2016] S.F.T.D. 96, FTT (Tax) *Affirmed* 17/2255

Coin-a-Drink Ltd v Revenue and Customs Commissioners [2017] UKUT 211 (TCC); [2017] S.T.C. 1351; [2017] B.T.C. 520, UT (Tax) .... *Digested,* 17/**2255**

Coinstar Ltd v Revenue and Customs Commissioners; *sub nom* Revenue and Customs Commissioners v Coinstar Ltd [2016] UKFTT 610 (TC); [2017] S.F.T.D. 177; [2016] S.T.I. 2607, FTT (Tax) *Affirmed* 17/2235

Coinstar Ltd v Revenue and Customs Commissioners; *sub nom* Revenue and Customs Commissioners v Coinstar Ltd [2017] UKUT 256 (TCC); [2017] S.T.C. 1519; [2017] B.V.C. 520; [2017] S.T.I. 1652, UT (Tax) .... *Digested,* 17/**2235**

Colaingrove Ltd v Revenue and Customs Commissioners; *sub nom* Revenue and Customs Commissioners v Colaingrove Ltd [2015] UKUT 80 (TCC); [2015] S.T.C. 1725; [2015] B.V.C. 510; [2015] S.T.I. 1530, UT (Tax) .... *Digested,* 15/**2594**: *Affirmed* 17/2284

Colaingrove Ltd v Revenue and Customs Commissioners; *sub nom* Revenue and Customs Commissioners v Colaingrove Ltd [2017] EWCA Civ 332; [2017] 1 W.L.R. 4668; [2017] S.T.C. 1287; [2017] B.V.C. 19, CA (Civ Div) .... *Digested,* 17/**2284**

Coleman v Magnet Joinery Ltd [1975] I.C.R. 46; [1974] I.R.L.R. 343; [1975] K.I.R. 139, CA (Civ Div) .... *Digested,* 75/**1176**: *Applied* 16/737: *Followed* 17/851

Colin Dawson Windows Ltd v Howard see Colin Dawson Windows Ltd v King's Lynn and West Norfolk BC

Colin Dawson Windows Ltd v King's Lynn and West Norfolk BC; *sub nom* Colin Dawson Windows Ltd v Howard [2005] EWCA Civ 9; [2005] 2 P. & C.R. 19; [2005] N.P.C. 8, CA (Civ Div) .... *Digested,* 05/**3439**: *Applied* 06/3452: *Considered* 17/1824

Coll v Secretary of State for Justice see R. (on the application of Coll) v Secretary of State for Justice

Collector of Stamp Revenue v Arrowtown Assets Ltd 6 I.T.L. Rep. 454, CFA (HK) *Applied* 07/3992, 09/3825, 14/2878: *Considered* 05/4084, 09/3755, 15/2105, 15/2433, 16/2085, 16/2120, 17/2156

Collie v Tesco Stores Ltd [2016] CSOH 149; 2016 S.L.T. 1213; 2017 S.C.L.R. 401; 2016 G.W.D. 33-593, OH .... *Digested,* 17/**2431**

Collins v Devonport Royal Dockyard Ltd AGS/1602954, Sen Cts Costs Office *Considered* 17/276

Collins v Lawrence [2017] 1 Lloyd's Rep. 13, CC (Canterbury) .... *Digested,* 17/**2002**

Collins (Gordon) v HM Advocate see HM Advocate v Collins (Gordon)

Collis v Revenue and Customs Commissioners [2011] UKFTT 588 (TC), FTT (Tax) *Applied* 17/2088

Coloroll Pension Trustees Ltd v Russell (C-200/91) see Ten Oever v Stichting Bedrijfspensioenfonds voor het Glazenwassers- en Schoonmaakbedrijf (C-109/91)

Colzani v RUWA Polstereimaschinen GmbH (24/76) see Estasis Salotti di Colzani Aimo e Gianmario Colzani v RUWA Polstereimaschinen GmbH (24/76)

Combinatie Spijker Infrabouw-De Jonge Konstruktie v Provincie Drenthe (C-568/08) EU:C:2010:751, ECJ *Applied* 16/1792: *Followed* 17/1813

Comic Enterprises Ltd v Twentieth Century Fox Film Corp [2016] EWCA Civ 41; [2016] E.C.C. 24; [2016] E.T.M.R. 22; [2016] F.S.R. 30, CA (Civ Div) .... *Digested,* 16/**1330**: *Followed* 16/1293, 17/1390

Comlex Ltd (In Liquidation) v Allianz Insurance Plc [2016] CSOH 87; [2016] Lloyd's Rep. I.R. 631; 2016 G.W.D. 21-379, OH .... *Digested,* 17/**2686**

Commercial First Business Ltd v Pickup [2017] C.T.L.C. 1, Ch D (Manchester) .... *Digested,* 17/**482**

Commerzbank Aktiengesellschaft v Liquimar Tankers Management Inc; *joined case* Commerzbank Aktiengesellschaft v Pauline Shipping Ltd [2017] EWHC 161 (Comm); [2017] 1 W.L.R. 3497; [2017] 2 All E.R. (Comm) 829; [2017] 1 Lloyd's Rep. 273; [2017] 1 C.L.C. 136, QBD (Comm) .... *Digested,* 17/**436**

Commerzbank Aktiengesellschaft v Pauline Shipping Ltd see Commerzbank Aktiengesellschaft v Liquimar Tankers Management Inc

Commissaire General aux Refugies et aux Apatrides v Lounani (C-573/14) EU:C:2017:71; [2017] 4 W.L.R. 52; [2017] 2 C.M.L.R. 36; [2017] C.E.C. 971; [2017] Imm. A.R. 984, ECJ (Grand Chamber)

Commission of the European Communities v Anic Partecipazioni SpA (C-49/92 P) [1999] E.C.R. I-4125, AGO *Followed* 17/412

Commission of the European Communities v Finland (C-246/08) EU:C:2009:671; [2009] E.C.R. I-10605; [2010] B.V.C. 1062, ECJ (3rd Chamber) *Applied* 15/2606, 16/2216: *Considered* 15/2628, 17/2262: *Followed* 16/2187, 17/2295

Commission of the European Communities v France (C-404/99) EU:C:2001:192; [2001] E.C.R. I-2667, ECJ *Applied* 09/4040: *Considered* 04/4021, 05/4419, 17/2262

Commission of the European Communities v France (C-68/92); *sub nom* VAT on Advertising, Re; *joined cases* Commission of the European Communities v Spain (C73/92); Commission of the European Communities v Luxembourg (C-69/92) EU:C:1993:888; [1997] S.T.C. 684; [1993] E.C.R. I-5881; [1995] 2 C.M.L.R. 1; Financial Times, November 23, 1993, ECJ .... *Digested,* 97/**5015**: *Applied* 97/5019, 01/5558, 17/2260: *Considered* 98/4962: *Followed* 17/2278

Commission of the European Communities v France (C-60/96) EU:C:1997:340; [1999] S.T.C. 480; [1997] E.C.R. I-3827, ECJ (6th Chamber) .... *Digested,* 99/**4971**: *Applied* 14/3052: *Considered* 17/2238

Commission of the European Communities v Italy (C-518/06) EU:C:2009:270; [2009] E.C.R. I-3491; [2009] 3 C.M.L.R. 22, ECJ (Grand Chamber) .... *Digested,* 09/**2291**: *Applied* 17/1090

Commission of the European Communities v Italy (C59/01) EU:C:2003:102; [2003] E.C.R. I-1759, ECJ *Applied* 17/1090: *Distinguished* 05/2381, 05/2382

Commission of the European Communities v Luxembourg (C-69/92) see Commission of the European Communities v France (C-68/92)

Commission of the European Communities v Luxembourg (C-346/02); *sub nom* Bonus Malus System, Re (C346/02) EU:C:2004:485; [2004] E.C.R. I-7517; [2004] 3 C.M.L.R. 50, ECJ .... *Digested,* 05/**2382**: *Applied* 17/1090

Commission of the European Communities v Luxembourg (C69/92) EU:C:1993:889; [1997] S.T.C. 712; [1993] E.C.R. I-5907; Financial Times, November 23, 1993, ECJ .... *Digested,* 97/**5016**: *Applied* 01/5558: *Followed* 17/2278

Commission of the European Communities v Spain (C73/92) see Commission of the European Communities v France (C-68/92)

Commission of the European Communities v United Kingdom (C-484/04); *sub nom* UK Working Time Guidelines, Re (C-484/04) EU:C:2006:526; [2006] E.C.R. I-7471; [2006] 3 C.M.L.R. 48; [2007] C.E.C. 56; [2007] I.C.R. 592; [2006] I.R.L.R. 888; Times, September 21, 2006, ECJ (3rd Chamber) .... *Digested,* 07/**1442**: *Followed* 17/855

Commissioner of Police of the Metropolis v A Local Authority; *sub nom* X (Disclosure to the Security Service), Re [2016] EWHC 2400 (Fam); [2016] 4 W.L.R. 153; [2017] 2 F.L.R. 583, Fam Div .... *Digested,* 16/**834**

Commissioner of Police of the Metropolis v Abdulle see Abdulle v Commissioner of Police of the Metropolis

Commodore Royal Bahamas Defence Force v Laramore [2017] UKPC 13; [2017] 1 W.L.R. 2752; Times, June 12, 2017, PC (Bah)

Commune de Laguiole v X [2017] E.C.C. 8, Cass (F)

Comninos v Prudential Assurance Co Ltd see National Justice Compania Naviera SA v Prudential Assurance Co Ltd (The Ikarian Reefer) (No.2)

Compagnie Noga d'Importation et d'Exportation SA v Abacha (No.3); *sub nom* Compagnie Noga d'Importation et d'Exportation SA v Australia and New Zealand Banking Group Ltd; Compagnie Noga d'Importation et d'Exportation SA v Russia; *joined case* Attorney General of Nigeria v Abacha [2002] EWCA Civ 1142; [2003] 1 W.L.R. 307; [2003] C.P. Rep. 5, CA (Civ Div)
Applied 10/1990, 14/37: *Considered* 17/335, 17/999: *Followed* 15/2433, 15/369

Compagnie Noga d'Importation et d'Exportation SA v Australia and New Zealand Banking Group Ltd see Compagnie Noga d'Importation et d'Exportation SA v Abacha (No.3)

Compagnie Noga d'Importation et d'Exportation SA v Russia see Compagnie Noga d'Importation et d'Exportation SA v Abacha (No.3)

Companhia de Mocambique v British South Africa Co see British South Africa Co v Companhia de Mocambique

Companies Act 1929, Re see Anchor Line (Henderson Bros) Ltd, Re

Company (No.003420 of 1981), Re see Bird Precision Bellows Ltd, Re

Compass Contract Services Ltd v Revenue and Customs Commissioners (C-38/16) EU:C:2017:454; [2017] 4 W.L.R. 168; [2017] S.T.C. 1358; [2017] B.V.C. 30; Times, June 23, 2017; [2017] S.T.I. 1393, ECJ (4th Chamber) .... *Digested,* 17/**2244**

Compass Group UK and Ireland Ltd v Morgan [2017] I.C.R. 73; [2016] I.R.L.R. 924, EAT .... *Digested,* 17/**760**

Concurrence SARL v Samsung Electronics France SAS (C-618/15) EU:C:2016:976; [2017] Bus. L.R. 758; [2017] I.L.Pr. 11, ECJ (3rd Chamber)

Conde Nast Publications Ltd v Revenue and Customs Commissioners see Fleming (t/a Bodycraft) v Customs and Excise Commissioners

Conder Structures v Kvaerner Construction Ltd (Unreported, 2000)
Applied 00/228: *Considered* 17/79

Condon Ex p. James, Re (1873-74) L.R. 9 Ch. App. 609; [1874-80] All E.R. Rep. 388, CA in Chancery
Applied 70/310, 72/189, 74/357, 75/170, 09/399, 16/1165: *Considered* 99/3258, 00/3433, 05/2261, 11/187, 14/608: *Distinguished* 72/197, 82/195, 87/3806, 88/3612, 02/2655: *Followed* 17/1285: *Not applied* 99/3230

Confiance Ltd, Re see Twin Benefits Ltd v Barker

Conlon v Black Horse Ltd see Plevin v Paragon Personal Finance Ltd

Connect Plus (M25) Ltd v Highways England Co Ltd [2016] EWHC 2614 (TCC); [2017] B.L.R. 33; 169 Con. L.R. 107; [2017] C.I.L.L. 3913, QBD (TCC) .... *Digested,* 17/**476**

Connect Shipping Inc v Sveriges Anfgartygs Assurans Forening (The Swedish Club) [2016] EWHC 1580 (Comm); [2017] 2 All E.R. (Comm) 1122; [2016] Bus. L.R. 1184; [2016] 2 Lloyd's Rep. 364; [2016] 2 C.L.C. 58; [2016] Lloyd's Rep. I.R. 601, QBD (Comm) .... *Digested,* 16/**1966**

Connelly (Alexander) v HM Advocate [2017] HCJAC 42; 2017 S.C.L. 716, HCJ Appeal .... *Digested,* 17/**2820**

Connex South Eastern Ltd v MJ Building Services Group Plc [2005] EWCA Civ 193; [2005] 1 W.L.R. 3323; [2005] 2 All E.R. 871; [2005] B.L.R. 201; 100 Con. L.R. 16; Times, May 13, 2005; (2005) 102(18) L.S.G. 23; (2005) 149 S.J.L.B. 296, CA (Civ Div) .... *Digested,* 05/**649**: *Followed* 17/656

Connexxion Taxi Services BV v Staat der Nederlanden (C-171/15) EU:C:2016:948; [2017] P.T.S.R. 1197, ECJ (4th Chamber)

Connors v United Kingdom (66746/01) (2005) 40 E.H.R.R. 9; 16 B.H.R.C. 639; [2004] H.L.R. 52; [2004] 4 P.L.R. 16; Times, June 10, 2004; [2004] N.P.C. 86, ECHR . *Digested,* 04/**1992**: *Applied* 06/2173, 06/2708, 08/1978, 11/2066: *Considered* 06/1649, 06/2046, 08/1934, 08/2467, 12/2743, 13/1560: *Distinguished* 05/190, 07/2242: *Explained* 05/3424: *Followed* 17/562

Conor Medsystems Inc v Angiotech Pharmaceuticals Inc; *sub nom* Angiotech Pharmaceuticals Inc v Conor Medsystems Inc; Angiotech Pharmaceuticals Inc's Patent (No.706376) [2008] UKHL 49; [2008] 4 All E.R. 621; [2008] R.P.C. 28; (2008) 103 B.M.L.R. 100; (2008) 31(8) I.P.D. 31049; (2008) 105(28) L.S.G. 16; (2008) 152(29) S.J.L.B. 31, HL .... *Digested,* 08/**2325**: *Applied* 09/2394, 10/1967, 16/1322: *Considered* 14/1896: *Followed* 12/1948, 17/1374

Conrath v Germany see Puceviciene v Lithuania

Constancia v Netherlands (73560/12) [2017] M.H.L.R. 138, ECHR

Conteh v Parking Partners Ltd [2011] I.C.R. 341; [2011] Eq. L.R. 332, EAT .... *Digested,* 11/**1108**: *Considered* 11/1107, 17/840

Contempt of Court Proceedings in Respect of M and L; *sub nom* AB v AT; B, Petitioner; AB, Petitioner [2015] CSIH 25; 2015 S.C. 545; 2015 S.L.T. 269; 2015 S.C.L.R. 664; 2015 Fam. L.R. 58; 2015 G.W.D. 12-198, IH (2 Div) .... *Digested,* 15/**2888**: *Considered* 17/2438

Continental Assurance Co of London Plc (In Liquidation), Re see Singer v Beckett

Continental Tyre & Rubber Co (Great Britain) Ltd v Daimler Co Ltd see Daimler Co Ltd v Continental Tyre & Rubber Co (Great Britain) Ltd

Continental Tyre & Rubber Co (Great Britain) Ltd v Thomas Tilling Ltd see Daimler Co Ltd v Continental Tyre & Rubber Co (Great Britain) Ltd

Conville v Richmond upon Thames LBC see R. (on the application of Conville) v Richmond upon Thames LBC

Cook v Alexander [1974] Q.B. 279; [1973] 3 W.L.R. 617; [1973] 3 All E.R. 1037; (1973) 117 S.J. 618, CA (Civ Div) .... *Digested,* 73/**1959**: *Considered* 17/653

Cook v Mortgage Business Plc see North East Property Buyers Litigation, Re

Cook v Virgin Media Ltd; *joined case* McNeil v Tesco Plc [2015] EWCA Civ 1287; [2016] 1 W.L.R. 1672; [2017] 1 All E.R. 929; [2016] C.P. Rep. 16; [2016] I.L.Pr. 6; [2016] P.I.Q.R. P5, CA (Civ Div) .... *Digested,* 16/**250**

Coope v Ward see Ward v Coope

Cooper v Dean and Chapter of York Minster [2017] P.T.S.R. 225, Cons Ct (York) .... *Digested,* 17/**668**

Cooper v Monarch Financial Services Ltd see Monarch Financial Services Ltd, Re

Cooper-Hohn v Hohn [2014] EWHC 4122 (Fam); [2015] 1 F.L.R. 745; [2015] Fam. Law 124, Fam Div .... *Digested,* 15/**1102**: *Considered* 17/1020, 17/1032: *Explained* 15/1091

Copenhagen Reinsurance Co (UK) Ltd, Re; *sub nom* Marlon Insurance Co Ltd, Re [2016] EWHC 944 (Ch); [2016] Bus. L.R. 741; [2016] Lloyd's Rep. I.R. 683, Ch D .... *Digested,* 17/**1339**

Copin v Adamson; *joined case* Copin v Strachan (1875) 1 Ex. D. 17, CA *Considered* 17/432

Copin v Strachan see Copin v Adamson

Copolo (John Murray) v HM Advocate; *sub nom* Copolo (John Murray) (also known as McIntosh) v HM Advocate; Ironside (Joanne Mary) (also known as Mitchell) v HM Advocate; *joined case* Ironside (Joanne Mary) v HM Advocate [2016] HCJAC 119; 2017 J.C. 143; 2017 S.L.T. 45; 2017 S.C.L. 247; 2017 S.C.C.R. 45; 2016 G.W.D. 39-692, HCJ .... *Digested,* 17/**2557**

Copolo (John Murray) (also known as McIntosh) v HM Advocate see Copolo (John Murray) v HM Advocate

Corbitt's Application for Judicial Review, Re [2016] NIQB 23; [2017] N.I. 288, QBD (NI)

Corby BC v da Silva [2016] EWHC 2503 (Admin); [2017] R.A. 48; [2016] A.C.D. 125, DC .... *Digested,* 17/**1506**

Corich v Lobo see Lobo v Corich

Corporacion Habanos SA v Mastercigars Direct Ltd see Mastercigars Direct Ltd v Hunters & Frankau Ltd

Correia v University Hospital of North Staffordshire NHS Trust [2017] EWCA Civ 356; [2017] E.C.C. 37; [2017] Med. L.R. 292, CA (Civ Div) .... *Digested,* 17/**1557**

Cortas v Poland see Kortas v Poland

Cory Bros & Co Ltd v Owners of the Turkish Steamship Mecca [1897] A.C. 286, HL
Applied 86/38, 17/2279: *Considered* 03/260

Cosco Bulk Carrier Co Ltd v Armada Shipping SA; *sub nom* Armada Shipping SA, Re [2011] EWHC 216 (Ch); [2011] 2 All E.R. (Comm) 481; [2011] B.P.I.R. 626; [2011] Arb. L.R. 5, Ch D (Companies Ct) .... *Digested,* 11/**3111**:
Applied 16/58: *Considered* 17/337

Cosmetic Warriors Ltd v Gerrie [2017] EWCA Civ 324; [2017] 2 B.C.L.C. 456, CA (Civ Div)

Costain Ltd v Tarmac Holdings Ltd [2017] EWHC 319 (TCC); [2017] 2 All E.R. (Comm) 645; [2017] 1 Lloyd's Rep. 331; [2017] B.L.R. 239; 171 Con. L.R. 183, QBD (TCC) .... *Digested,* 17/**493**

Costello v MacDonald see MacDonald Dickens & Macklin v Costello

Cott UK Ltd v FE Barber Ltd [1997] 3 All E.R. 540, QBD .... *Digested,* 97/**271**:
Applied 07/528: *Considered* 17/476

Cotter v Revenue and Customs Commissioners see Revenue and Customs Commissioners v Cotter

Cottingham Park Lodges Ltd v Revenue and Customs Commissioners [2017] UKFTT 10 (TC); [2017] S.T.I. 222, FTT (Tax)

Coty Germany GmbH v First Note Perfumes NV (C-360/12) EU:C:2014:1318; [2014] Bus. L.R. 1294; [2015] C.E.C. 511; [2014] E.T.M.R. 49; [2015] I.L.Pr. 13, ECJ (4th Chamber)
Applied 17/1398: *Followed* 17/430

Coudert Bros v Normans Bay Ltd (formerly Illingworth Morris) see Normans Bay Ltd (formerly Illingworth Morris Ltd) v Coudert Bros

Couling v Coxe 136 E.R. 1424; (1848) 6 C.B. 703, CCP
Considered 17/160

Coulter v Chief Constable of Dorset [2005] EWCA Civ 1113; [2006] B.P.I.R. 10, CA (Civ Div) .... *Digested,* 06/**2333**:
Applied 10/1858, 16/1239, 17/1324

Council for Healthcare Regulatory Excellence v Nursing and Midwifery Council [2011] EWHC 927 (Admin); [2011] A.C.D. 72, QBD (Admin) .... *Digested,* 11/**1540**:
Applied 13/1440, 17/1116

Council for the Regulation of Health Care Professionals v General Medical Council; *sub nom* Council for the Regulation of Health Care Professionals v Solanke [2004] EWHC 944 (Admin); [2004] 1 W.L.R. 2432; [2004] Lloyd's Rep. Med. 377; Times, May 10, 2004; [2004] A.C.D. 55, QBD (Admin) .... *Digested,* 04/**1675**:
Applied 17/1115

Council for the Regulation of Health Care Professionals v General Medical Council; *sub nom* Council for the Regulation of Health Care Professionals v Truscott; Ruscillo v Council for the Regulation of Health Care Professionals; *joined case* Council for the Regulation of Health Care Professionals v Nursing and Midwifery Council [2004] EWCA Civ 1356; [2005] 1 W.L.R. 717; [2005] Lloyd's Rep. Med. 65; Times, October 27, 2004; Independent, October 28, 2004; [2005] A.C.D. 69; [2005] A.C.D. 99; (2004) 148 S.J.L.B. 1248, CA (Civ Div) ...... *Digested,* 05/**1796**:
Applied 05/1801, 05/1919, 07/1953, 10/1540, 11/1540, 14/1518, 15/1203, 17/1105, 17/1109: *Considered* 17/2635: *Followed* 14/1497, 15/1190, 17/1115

Council for the Regulation of Health Care Professionals v Nursing and Midwifery Council see Council for the Regulation of Health Care Professionals v General Medical Council

Council for the Regulation of Health Care Professionals v Solanke see Council for the Regulation of Health Care Professionals v General Medical Council

Council for the Regulation of Health Care Professionals v Truscott see Council for the Regulation of Health Care Professionals v General Medical Council

Council for the Regulation of Healthcare Professionals v General Medical Council; *sub nom* Council for the Regulation of Healthcare Professionals v Southall [2005] EWHC 579 (Admin); [2005] Lloyd's Rep. Med. 365; (2005) 84 B.M.L.R. 7; [2005] A.C.D. 87, QBD (Admin) .... *Digested,* 05/**1919**:
Considered 17/1109

Council for the Regulation of Healthcare Professionals v Southall see Council for the Regulation of Healthcare Professionals v General Medical Council

Council of the European Union v Front Polisario (C-104/16 P) EU:C:2016:973; [2017] 2 C.M.L.R. 28, ECJ (Grand Chamber)

Council of the Law Society of Scotland v Scottish Legal Complaints Commission [2017] CSIH 36; 2017 S.C. 718; 2017 S.L.T. 816; 2017 G.W.D. 20-327, IH (Ex Div) .... *Digested,* 17/**2711**

Countrywide Assured Group Plc v Marshall [2002] EWHC 2082 (Comm); [2003] 1 All E.R. (Comm) 237; [2003] Lloyd's Rep. I.R. 195; [2003] Lloyd's Rep. P.N. 1; [2002] Pens. L.R. 537; (2002) 99(44) L.S.G. 32, QBD (Comm) .... *Digested,* 03/**2453**: *Applied* 17/1345

County & District Properties Ltd v C Jenner & Son [1976] 2 Lloyd's Rep. 728; 3 B.L.R. 38; (1974) 230 E.G. 1589, QBD .... *Digested,* 77/**1796**: *Applied* 17/1342: *Followed* 81/1619, 85/2013

County Leasing Asset Management Ltd v Hawkes; *sub nom* Hawkes v County Leasing Asset Management Ltd [2015] EWCA Civ 1251; [2016] C.P. Rep. 12; [2016] B.C.C. 102; [2016] 2 B.C.L.C. 427, CA (Civ Div) .... *Digested,* 16/**346**: *Followed* 17/398

Couper v Albion Properties Ltd [2013] EWHC 2993 (Ch), Ch D *Considered* 17/562

Courage Ltd v Crehan (C-453/99); *sub nom* Crehan v Courage Ltd (C-453/99) EU:C:2001:465; [2002] Q.B. 507; [2001] 3 W.L.R. 1646; [2001] E.C.R. I-6297; [2002] U.K.C.L.R. 171; [2001] 5 C.M.L.R. 28; [2001] All E.R. (EC) 886; [2001] C.E.C. 297; [2002] I.C.R. 457; Times, October 4, 2001; Daily Telegraph, September 25, 2001, ECJ .... *Digested,* 01/**783**: *Applied* 07/626, 13/496, 16/2180, 17/285: *Considered* 06/2592: *Followed* 10/1938, 10/446

Courtney's Executors v Campbell; *sub nom* Igoe v Campbell [2016] CSOH 136; 2017 S.C.L.R. 387; 2016 G.W.D. 31-564, OH .... *Digested,* 17/**2846**

Coutts & Co v Stock [2000] 1 W.L.R. 906; [2000] 2 All E.R. 56; [2000] Lloyd's Rep. Bank. 14; [2000] B.C.C. 247; [2000] 1 B.C.L.C. 183; [2000] B.P.I.R. 400; Times, November 30, 1999; (1999) 96(48) L.S.G. 39; (2000) 144 S.J.L.B. 24, Ch D .... *Digested,* 00/**3465**: *Applied* 15/1447: *Doubted* 17/1334

Coventry v Lawrence see Coventry (t/a RDC Promotions) v Lawrence

Coventry (t/a RDC Promotions) v Lawrence; *sub nom* Coventry v Lawrence; Lawrence v Coventry (t/a RDC Promotions); Lawrence v Fen Tigers Ltd [2014] UKSC 13; [2014] A.C. 822; [2014] 2 W.L.R. 433; [2014] 2 All E.R. 622; [2014] P.T.S.R. 384; [2014] B.L.R. 271; 152 Con. L.R. 1; [2014] Env. L.R. 25; [2014] H.L.R. 21; [2014] 2 P. & C.R. 2; [2014] 1 E.G.L.R. 147; [2014] L.L.R. 423; (2014) 158(9) S.J.L.B. 37, SC .... *Digested,* 14/**2223**: *Applied* 14/2526: *Considered* 16/264, 17/2740: *Followed* 16/1554

Coventry City Council v C [2012] EWHC 2190 (Fam); [2013] 2 F.L.R. 987; [2013] 1 F.C.R. 54; [2012] Fam. Law 1316; (2012) 162 N.L.J. 1078; (2012) 156(31) S.J.L.B. 31, Fam Div .... *Digested,* 13/**1196**: *Applied* 16/824: *Considered* 17/950

Cowan v Cowan [2001] EWCA Civ 679; [2002] Fam. 97; [2001] 3 W.L.R. 684; [2001] 2 F.L.R. 192; [2001] 2 F.C.R. 331; Times, May 17, 2001; [2001] Fam. Law 498, CA (Civ Div) .... *Digested,* 01/**2633**: *Applied* 06/1621, 15/1102: *Considered* 07/1691, 07/1704, 12/1313: *Distinguished* 03/1590: *Followed* 17/1032

Cowderoy v Cranfield [2011] EWHC 1616 (Ch); [2011] W.T.L.R. 1699, Ch D .... *Digested,* 12/**3199**: *Applied* 12/3200, 13/2980, 13/2984, 17/2076

Cowthorpe Road 1-1A Freehold Ltd v Wahedally [2017] L. & T.R. 4, CC (Central London) .... *Digested,* 17/**1829**

Cox v Bankside Members Agency Ltd [1995] C.L.C. 180; Times, January 27, 1995, QBD (Comm) *Applied* 05/2366: *Considered* 16/1273, 17/1338

Cox v Bankside Members Agency Ltd [1995] 2 Lloyd's Rep. 437; [1995] C.L.C. 671; Times, May 16, 1995; Independent, June 9, 1995; Lloyd's List, August 29, 1995, CA (Civ Div) *Applied* 04/2216: *Considered* 95/2907, 96/3581, 96/3599, 17/1352

Cox v Ergo Versicherung AG (formerly Victoria); *sub nom* Cox (Deceased), Re [2014] UKSC 22; [2014] A.C. 1379; [2014] 2 W.L.R. 948; [2014] 2 All E.R. 926; [2014] 1 C.L.C. 430; [2014] R.T.R. 20; Times, April 14, 2014, SC .... *Digested,* 14/**825**: *Applied* 17/418: *Considered* 16/2459: *Followed* 15/1559

Cox v Ministry of Justice [2016] UKSC 10; [2016] A.C. 660; [2016] 2 W.L.R. 806; [2017] 1 All E.R. 1; [2016] I.C.R. 470; [2016] I.R.L.R. 370; [2016] P.I.Q.R. P8; Times, March 10, 2016, SC .... *Digested,* 16/**1553**: *Applied* 17/1033: *Referred to* 16/2146

Cox v Queen, The see Myers v Queen, The

Cox v Varey (Unreported, December 15, 2016), CC (Derby) [*IMe Law Ltd, Riverside West, 1 Millsands, Sheffield*] .... *Digested,* 17/**1683**

Cox (Deceased), Re see Cox v Ergo Versicherung AG (formerly Victoria)

Coyle (James Thomas) v HM Advocate [2007] HCJAC 52; 2008 J.C. 107; 2008 S.C.L. 131; 2007 S.C.C.R. 479; 2007 G.W.D. 29-508, HCJ .... *Digested,* 08/**5043**: *Applied* 08/5055: *Cited* 17/2814

CP-Credit Prive SA v Kyrgyz Mobil Tel Ltd see AK Investment CJSC v Kyrgyz Mobil Tel Ltd

CR Taylor (Wholesale) Ltd v Hepworths Ltd [1977] 1 W.L.R. 659; [1977] 2 All E.R. 784; (1976) 244 E.G. 631; (1977) 121 S.J. 15, QBD .... *Digested,* 77/**2020**: *Applied* 78/2061, 89/1185, 89/1199, 90/1522, 92/1537, 17/1850: *Approved* 03/943: *Considered* 80/631, 85/2313, 94/3079: *Followed* 86/982

Crabbe v Townsend; *sub nom* Townsend (Deceased), Re [2016] EWHC 2450 (Ch); [2017] W.T.L.R. 13, Ch D .... *Digested,* 17/**2066**

Craddock Bros v Transport and General Workers Union (Non-Payment of Fine: Accountability of Union) see Heatons Transport (St Helens) Ltd v Transport and General Workers Union

Craig v Mair's Trustees; *sub nom* Healy & Young's Trustee v Mair's Trustees 1914 S.C. 893; 1914 2 S.L.T. 118, IH (1 Div) *Applied* 17/2704

Crailsheimer Volksbank eG v Conrads (C-229/04) EU:C:2005:640; [2005] E.C.R. I-9273; [2006] 1 C.M.L.R. 21; [2006] C.E.C. 221, ECJ (2nd Chamber) .... *Digested,* 06/**708**: *Considered* 17/479

Crake v Supplementary Benefits Commission; *joined case* Butterworth v Supplementary Benefits Commission [1982] 1 All E.R. 498; (1981) 2 F.L.R. 264, QBD .... *Digested,* 82/**3035**: *Considered* 83/3179, 91/2313, 13/1868, 17/2825: *Followed* 00/2542

Crammer v West Bromwich Building Society [2012] EWCA Civ 517; [2012] B.P.I.R. 963, CA (Civ Div) .... *Digested,* 13/**1679**: *Followed* 15/1405, 17/1290

Cramp v Hastings BC; *joined case* Phillips v Camden LBC [2005] EWCA Civ 1005; [2005] 4 All E.R. 1014; [2005] H.L.R. 48; [2005] N.P.C. 109, CA (Civ Div) .... *Digested,* 06/**2022**: *Applied* 08/1842, 08/1849, 08/2469, 13/1531: *Followed* 17/239: *Superseded in part* 11/1648

Crane v Secretary of State for Communities and Local Government [2015] EWHC 425 (Admin), QBD (Admin) *Applied* 17/1769: *Considered* 16/1760

Crane (t/a Indigital Satellite Services) v Sky In-Home Ltd [2008] EWCA Civ 978, CA (Civ Div) *Followed* 15/2474, 17/1876

Cranwell v Cullen UKEATPAS/0046/14/SM, EAT (SC) *Applied* 17/2582

Craven (Inspector of Taxes) v White (Brian) see Craven (Inspector of Taxes) v White (Stephen)

Craven (Inspector of Taxes) v White (Stephen); *joined cases* Inland Revenue Commissioners v Bowater Property Developments Ltd; Craven (Inspector of Taxes) v White (Brian); Baylis (Inspector of Taxes) v Gregory [1989] A.C. 398; [1988] 3 W.L.R. 423; [1988] 3 All E.R. 495; [1988] S.T.C. 476; (1988) 85(34) L.S.G. 49; (1988) 138 N.L.J. Rep. 219; (1988) 132 S.J. 1120, HL .... *Digested,* 88/**257**: *Applied* 92/2518, 92/2519, 92/611, 95/876, 00/5043: *Considered* 90/2685, 93/337, 96/428, 96/5891, 17/2111: *Distinguished* 17/2098: *Referred to* 95/527

Crawley v Barnsley MBC [2017] EWCA Civ 36; [2017] 1 W.L.R. 2329; [2017] R.T.R. 12; Times, March 17, 2017, CA (Civ Div) .... *Digested,* 17/**1512**

Cream Holdings Ltd v Banerjee [2004] UKHL 44; [2005] 1 A.C. 253; [2004] 3 W.L.R. 918; [2004] 4 All E.R. 617; [2005] E.M.L.R. 1; [2004] H.R.L.R. 39; [2004] U.K.H.R.R. 1071; 17 B.H.R.C. 464; Times, October 15, 2004; (2005) 28(2) I.P.D. 28001; (2004) 101(42) L.S.G. 29; (2004) 154 N.L.J. 1589; (2004) 148 S.J.L.B. 1215, HL .... *Digested,* 05/**2041**: *Applied* 05/4191, 06/1037, 06/454, 07/2189, 07/2672, 07/2887, 07/2893, 10/1939, 11/339: *Considered* 05/970, 06/456, 08/2379, 09/4260: *Followed* 11/2200, 11/341, 14/1864, 15/1541, 15/311, 17/342

Credit Agricole Indosuez v Generale Bank (No.1) [1999] 2 All E.R. (Comm) 1009, QBD (Comm) .... *Digested,* 00/**283**: *Considered* 17/166

Credit Enterprise v Woodcocks Sussex see P&J Macrae Ltd, Re

Credit Lyonnais SA v Russell Jones & Walker [2002] EWHC 1310 (Ch); [2003] Lloyd's Rep. P.N. 7; [2003] P.N.L.R. 2; [2002] 2 E.G.L.R. 65; [2002] 33 E.G. 99; Times, October 9, 2002; [2002] 28 E.G. 128 (C.S.); (2002) 152 N.L.J. 1071; [2002] N.P.C. 91, Ch D .... *Digested,* 02/**3306**: *Applied* 13/1950, 16/1421, 17/1567: *Considered* 07/752, 15/1789

Creditsights Ltd v Dhunna see Dhunna v Creditsights Ltd

Creggy v Barnett see Barnett v Creggy
Creggy v Barnett see Barnett v Creggy
Crehan v Courage Ltd (C-453/99) see Courage Ltd v Crehan (C-453/99)
Crescent Farm (Sidcup) Sports v Sterling Offices [1972] Ch. 553; [1972] 2 W.L.R. 91; [1971] 3 All E.R. 1192; (1972) 116 S.J. 59, Ch D .... *Digested,* 72/**2732**: *Considered* 90/3666: *Not applied* 17/1286
Crest Nicholson (Wainscott) v Revenue and Customs Commissioners [2017] UKFTT 134 (TC); [2017] S.F.T.D. 451, FTT (Tax) .... *Digested,* 17/**2175**
Cretu v Local Court of Suceava see Cretu v Romania
Cretu v Romania; *sub nom* Cretu v Local Court of Suceava [2016] EWHC 353 (Admin); [2016] 1 W.L.R. 3344; [2016] A.C.D. 70, DC .... *Digested,* 16/**792**: *Considered* 17/1905
Crigglestone Coal Co Ltd, Re [1906] 2 Ch. 327, CA
Applied 72/388, 17/1294
Crime Reduction Initiatives (CRI) v Lawrence UKEAT/0319/13/DA, UKEAT/0321/13/DA, EAT
Considered 17/779
Criminal Injuries Compensation Authority v First-tier Tribunal (Social Entitlement Chamber) [2017] EWCA Civ 139; [2017] 4 W.L.R. 60; [2017] P.I.Q.R. P13, CA (Civ Div) .... *Digested,* 17/**1644**
Criminal Practice Directions 2015 see Practice Direction (CA (Crim Div): Criminal Proceedings: General Matters)
Criminal Proceedings against Aranyosi (C-404/15 PPU); *sub nom* Execution of a European Arrest Warrant against Aranyosi (C-404/15 PPU); *joined case* Criminal Proceedings against Caldararu (C-659/15 PPU) EU:C:2016:198; [2016] Q.B. 921; [2016] 3 W.L.R. 807; [2016] 3 C.M.L.R. 13; 42 B.H.R.C. 551, ECJ (Grand Chamber)
Considered 17/904
Criminal Proceedings against Baldetti (C-350/15) see Criminal Proceedings against Orsi (C-217/15)
Criminal Proceedings against Bob-Dogi (C-241/15); *sub nom* Execution of a European Arrest Warrant against Bob-Dogi (C-241/15) EU:C:2016:385; [2016] 1 W.L.R. 4583; [2017] 3 C.M.L.R. 40, ECJ (2nd Chamber)
Followed 16/789
Criminal Proceedings against Caldararu (C-659/15 PPU) see Criminal Proceedings against Aranyosi (C-404/15 PPU)
Criminal Proceedings against Canal Digital Danmark A/S (C-611/14); *sub nom* Canal Digital Danmark A/S, Re (C-611/14) EU:C:2016:800; [2017] Bus. L.R. 1099; [2017] 2 C.M.L.R. 4, ECJ (5th Chamber)
Criminal Proceedings against Grundza (C-289/15); *sub nom* Grundza v Krajska prokuratura Presov (C-289/15) EU:C:2017:4; [2017] 4 W.L.R. 66, ECJ (5th Chamber)
Criminal Proceedings against Hoffmann (C-144/00); *sub nom* Hoffmann (C-144/00) EU:C:2003:192; [2004] S.T.C. 740; [2003] E.C.R. I-2921; [2004] 1 C.M.L.R. 37; [2005] B.T.C. 5010; [2005] B.V.C. 41; Times, April 17, 2003; [2003] S.T.I. 587, ECJ (6th Chamber) .... *Digested,* 03/**4527**: *Applied* 09/4048, 13/3190: *Considered* 14/3043, 17/2266
Criminal Proceedings against Kossowski (C-486/14); *sub nom* Kossowski v Generalstaatsanwaltschaft Hamburg (C-486/14) EU:C:2016:483; [2016] 1 W.L.R. 4393; [2017] 1 C.M.L.R. 11; [2017] C.E.C. 157, ECJ (Grand Chamber)
Criminal proceedings against Kovalkovas (C-477/16) EU:C:2016:861; [2017] 4 W.L.R. 10, ECJ (4th Chamber)
Criminal Proceedings against Milev (C-439/16 PPU); *sub nom* Milev (C-439/16 PPU) EU:C:2016:818; [2017] 2 C.M.L.R. 5, ECJ (4th Chamber)
Criminal Proceedings against Noria Distribution SARL (C-672/15) EU:C:2017:310; [2017] 3 C.M.L.R. 32, ECJ (1st Chamber)
Criminal Proceedings against Ognyanov (C-554/14) EU:C:2016:835; [2017] Q.B. 732; [2017] 2 W.L.R. 1249, ECJ (Grand Chamber)
Criminal Proceedings against Orsi (C-217/15); *joined case* Criminal Proceedings against Baldetti (C-350/15) EU:C:2017:264; [2017] B.V.C. 25; [2017] S.T.I. 1068, ECJ (4th Chamber)
Criminal proceedings against Ozcelik (C-453/16 PPU) EU:C:2016:860; [2017] 4 W.L.R. 9, ECJ (4th Chamber)
Criminal Proceedings against Petruhhin (C-182/15); *sub nom* Petruhhin (C-182/15) EU:C:2016:630; [2017] Q.B. 299; [2016] 3 W.L.R. 1491; [2017] 1 C.M.L.R. 28; [2017] C.E.C. 415, ECJ (Grand Chamber)
Criminal proceedings against Poltorak (C-452/16 PPU) EU:C:2016:858; [2017] 4 W.L.R. 8, ECJ (4th Chamber)

Criminal Proceedings against Pupino (C-105/03) EU:C:2005:386; [2006] Q.B. 83; [2005] 3 W.L.R. 1102; [2005] E.C.R. I-5285; [2005] 2 C.M.L.R. 63; [2006] All E.R. (EC) 142; [2006] C.E.C. 448; Times, July 14, 2005, ECJ .... *Digested,* 06/**1581**: *Applied* 07/1657, 12/1284, 16/792, 17/1905

Criminal Proceedings against Ranks (C-166/15) EU:C:2016:762; [2017] Bus. L.R. 290; [2017] C.E.C. 617; [2017] E.C.D.R. 12, ECJ (3rd Chamber)

Criminal Proceedings against Tupikas (C-270/17 PPU) EU:C:2017:628; [2017] 4 W.L.R. 188, ECJ (5th Chamber)

Criminal Proceedings against van Vemde (C-582/15) EU:C:2017:37; [2017] 4 W.L.R. 50, ECJ (5th Chamber)

Criminal Proceedings against Vanderborght (C-339/15) EU:C:2017:335; [2017] 3 C.M.L.R. 37, ECJ (3rd Chamber)

Criminal Proceedings against Zdziaszek (C-271/17 PPU) EU:C:2017:629; [2017] 4 W.L.R. 189, ECJ (5th Chamber)

Criminal Proceedings concerning Vilkas (C-640/15) EU:C:2017:39; [2017] 4 W.L.R. 69, ECJ (3rd Chamber)

Croftbell Ltd, Re [1990] B.C.C. 781; [1990] B.C.L.C. 844, Ch D (Companies Ct) *Applied* 17/159

Crofters Commission's Reference, Re 2012 S.L.C.R. 159, Land Ct .... *Digested,* **14/3627**: *Considered* 17/2402

Crofton v NHS Litigation Authority [2007] EWCA Civ 71; [2007] 1 W.L.R. 923; [2007] B.L.G.R. 507; (2007) 10 C.C.L. Rep. 123; [2007] P.I.Q.R. Q3; [2007] LS Law Medical 254; Times, February 15, 2007; (2007) 104(8) L.S.G. 36; (2007) 151 S.J.L.B. 262, CA (Civ Div) .... *Digested,* 07/**1065**: *Applied* 11/244, 17/1540: *Considered* 09/2834, 11/1619: *Distinguished* 15/1887

Crofton v Yeboah; *sub nom* Yeboah v Crofton [2002] EWCA Civ 794; [2002] I.R.L.R. 634; Times, June 20, 2002, CA (Civ Div) .... *Digested,* 02/**1398**: *Applied* 04/1309, 07/1316, 07/1391, 11/1076, 13/1071: *Considered* 06/1369, 12/1035: *Followed* 13/970, 17/811

Crofts v Veta Ltd see Lawson v Serco Ltd

Croitoru v Crown Prosecution Service; *sub nom* Croitoru v DPP [2016] EWHC 1645 (Admin); [2017] 1 W.L.R. 1130; (2016) 180 J.P. 451; [2017] R.T.R. 17, DC .... *Digested,* 17/**1872**

Croitoru v DPP see Croitoru v Crown Prosecution Service

Croke v Secretary of State for Communities and Local Government [2016] EWHC 2484 (Admin); [2017] P.T.S.R. 116; [2016] A.C.D. 131, QBD (Admin) .... *Digested,* 17/**12**

Croke (A Minor) v Wiseman [1982] 1 W.L.R. 71; [1981] 3 All E.R. 852, CA (Civ Div) .... *Digested,* 82/**787**: *Applied* 84/1042: *Considered* 82/794: *Distinguished* 07/3071, 17/638: *Followed* 08/892, 15/1890

Croly (Theresa) v HM Advocate 2004 S.C.C.R. 389; 2004 G.W.D. 15-334, HCJ *Considered* 17/2482

Cronin v de Hamel see Aspinall (Deceased), Re

Crossley v Newsquest (Midlands South) Ltd [2008] EWHC 3054 (QB), QBD *Considered* 17/653

Crossman v St George's Healthcare NHS Trust [2016] EWHC 2878 (QB); (2017) 154 B.M.L.R. 204, QBD .... *Digested,* 17/**1640**

Crowley v Bessell see BC&G Care Homes Ltd, Re

Crown Prosecution Service v Ahmed see Ready Rentals Ltd (In Liquidation) v Ahmed

Crown Prosecution Service v C [2017] Crim. L.R. 61, MC

Crown Prosecution Service v J see Jennings v Crown Prosecution Service

Crown Prosecution Service v M; *joined case* R. v M [2009] EWCA Crim 2615; [2011] 1 W.L.R. 822; [2010] 4 All E.R. 51; [2010] 2 Cr. App. R. 33, CA (Crim Div) .... *Digested,* 10/**679**: *Distinguished* 17/540

Croydon Health Services NHS Trust v Beatt; *sub nom* Beatt v Croydon Health Services NHS Trust [2017] EWCA Civ 401; [2017] I.C.R. 1240; [2017] I.R.L.R. 748, CA (Civ Div) .... *Digested,* 17/**817**

Croydon Health Services NHS Trust v Beatt; *sub nom* Beatt v Croydon Health Services NHS Trust UKEAT/0136/15/JOJ, EAT *Reversed* 17/817

Croydon LBC v Lopes [2017] EWHC 33 (QB); [2017] H.L.R. 15, QBD .... *Digested,* 17/**239**

Croydon LBC v Persons Unknown [2016] EWHC 3018 (QB); [2017] L.L.R. 98, QBD

Croydon LBC v Y; *sub nom* R. (on the application of Y) v Croydon LBC [2016] EWCA Civ 398; [2016] 1 W.L.R. 2895; [2016] Imm. A.R. 965; (2016) 19 C.C.L. Rep. 229; (2016) 152 B.M.L.R. 77; Times, May 13, 2016, CA (Civ Div) .... *Digested,* 16/**1058**: *Explained* 17/2048

Cruden Buildings and Renewals Ltd v Scottish Water [2017] CSOH 98; [2017] B.L.R. 575; 2017 G.W.D. 22-363, OH .... *Digested,* 17/**2455**

Cruise and Maritime Services International Ltd v Navigators Underwriting Agency Ltd [2017] EWHC 843 (Comm); [2017] 1 Lloyd's Rep. 575; [2017] Lloyd's Rep. I.R. 347, QBD (Comm) .... *Digested,* 17/**2009**

Crump v Gilmore 68 L.G.R. 56; Times, November 5, 1969; (1969) 113 S.J. 998, DC ... *Digested,* 69/**1189**: *Considered* 99/1832: *Overruled* 17/704

Crumpler v Candey Ltd see Peak Hotels and Resorts Ltd, Re

Cruz City 1 Mauritius Holdings v Unitech Ltd [2014] EWHC 3704 (Comm); [2015] 1 All E.R. (Comm) 305; [2015] 1 Lloyd's Rep. 191; [2014] 2 C.L.C. 784, QBD (Comm) .... *Digested,* 15/**364**: *Applied* 15/1471, 17/334

Crystal Decisions (UK) Ltd v Vedatech [2006] EWHC 3500 (Ch), Ch D *Applied* 17/381

Crystal Properties (London) Ltd v Secretary of State for Communities and Local Government see Crystal Property (London) Ltd v Secretary of State for Communities and Local Government

Crystal Property (London) Ltd v Secretary of State for Communities and Local Government; *sub nom* Crystal Properties (London) Ltd v Secretary of State for Communities and Local Government [2016] EWCA Civ 1265; [2017] J.P.L. 594, CA (Civ Div) .... *Digested,* 17/**1734**

CS v ACS see S v S

CS (Termination of Pregnancy), Re; *sub nom* An NHS Trust v CS [2016] EWCOP 10; [2017] 1 F.L.R. 635; [2016] C.O.P.L.R. 187; (2017) 153 B.M.L.R. 141; [2016] Fam. Law 437, CP .... *Digested,* 16/**1514**

CSC Media Group Ltd (formerly Chart Show Channels Ltd) v Video Performance Ltd (Unreported, September 9, 2009), Copyright Tr *Applied* 17/1384

Csonka v Magyar Allam (C-409/11) EU:C:2013:512; [2014] 1 C.M.L.R. 14; [2014] C.E.C. 763, ECJ (1st Chamber) *Applied* 17/1349: *Considered* 14/1853: *Followed* 15/1469

CUB Pty Ltd v Union of India 19 I.T.L. Rep. 147, HC (Ind)

Cullen v Advocate General for Scotland [2016] CSOH 170; 2017 S.L.T. 1; 2016 G.W.D. 40-726, OH .... *Digested,* 17/**2772**

Cumberland Consolidated Holdings Ltd v Ireland [1946] K.B. 264; [1946] 1 All E.R. 284, CA *Applied* 57/2796, 86/3523: *Considered* 04/2496: *Followed* 17/1474

Cumbria CC v X see Cumbria CC, Petitioner

Cumbria CC, Petitioner; *sub nom* Cumbria CC v X [2016] CSIH 92; 2017 S.C. 451; 2017 S.L.T. 34; 2017 Fam. L.R. 15; 2016 G.W.D. 40-703, IH (Ex Div) .... *Digested,* 17/**2379**

Cumbria NHS Clinical Commissioning Group v S [2016] EWCOP 32; (2017) 153 B.M.L.R. 168, CP .... *Digested,* 17/**1123**

Cumming v SSE Plc 2016 Rep. L.R. 75; 2016 G.W.D. 15-286, Sh Ct (Lothian) (Edinburgh) .... *Digested,* 16/**2460**: *Affirmed* 17/2429

Cumming v SSE Plc [2017] SAC (Civ) 17; 2017 Rep. L.R. 82; 2017 G.W.D. 15-238, SAC .... *Digested,* 17/**2429**

Cummings v Crown Prosecution Service [2016] EWHC 3624 (Admin); (2017) 181 J.P. 269, DC .... *Digested,* 17/**531**

Cunningham (t/a Urban Developments) v Buckley [2017] EWCA Civ 224; [2017] B.V.C. 28, CA (Civ Div) .... *Digested,* 17/**459**

Cupi v Albania [2016] EWHC 3288 (Admin); [2017] A.C.D. 27, DC

Currey v Currey [2006] EWCA Civ 1338; [2007] 2 Costs L.R. 227; [2007] 1 F.L.R. 946; Times, November 3, 2006; Independent, October 25, 2006; [2007] Fam. Law 12; (2006) 156 N.L.J. 1651; (2006) 150 S.J.L.B. 1393, CA (Civ Div) .... *Digested,* 07/**1707**: *Considered* 11/1412, 17/1017: *Followed* 11/1295

Cursitan v Keenan [2011] NICh 23, Ch D (NI) *Applied* 17/1257

Curtis v Sheffield (Application for Leave to Appeal) (1882) 21 Ch. D. 1, CA *Applied* 17/972

Curzon v Wolstenholme [2015] UKUT 173 (LC); [2015] L. & T.R. 26; [2015] R.V.R. 347, UT (Lands) .... *Digested,* 15/**1577**: *Reversed* 17/1434

Curzon v Wolstenholme [2017] EWCA Civ 1098; [2018] 1 P. & C.R. 9; [2017] L. & T.R. 26; [2018] R.V.R. 125, CA (Civ Div) .... *Digested,* 17/**1434**

Custins v Peacock see Peacock v Custins

Customs and Excise Commissioners v Apple and Pear Development Council see Apple and Pear Development Council v Customs and Excise Commissioners

Customs and Excise Commissioners v Barclays Bank Plc [2006] UKHL 28; [2007] 1 A.C. 181; [2006] 3 W.L.R. 1; [2006] 4 All E.R. 256; [2006] 2 All E.R. (Comm) 831; [2006] 2 Lloyd's Rep. 327; [2006] 1 C.L.C. 1096; Times, June 22, 2006; (2006) 103(27) L.S.G. 33; (2006) 156 N.L.J. 1060; (2006) 150 S.J.L.B. 859, HL *Digested,* 06/**2880**: *Applied* 07/1755, 07/4144, 08/2642, 09/2727, 10/3406, 16/2145: *Considered* 11/2585, 11/4485, 12/1784, 13/1660, 16/2: *Followed* 09/265, 10/2267, 10/2281, 13/2087, 15/1761, 15/1777, 16/1537, 17/160

Customs and Excise Commissioners v British United Provident Association Ltd see Customs and Excise Commissioners v Wellington Private Hospital Ltd

Customs and Excise Commissioners v Cardholder Services see Customs and Excise Commissioners v Diners Club Ltd

Customs and Excise Commissioners v D&D Marketing (UK) Ltd; *sub nom* D&D Marketing (UK) Ltd, Re [2002] EWHC 660 (Ch); [2003] B.P.I.R. 539; [2003] B.T.C. 5015; [2003] B.V.C. 71, Ch D .... *Digested,* 03/**4523**: *Applied* 17/1327

Customs and Excise Commissioners v Diners Club Ltd; *joined case* Customs and Excise Commissioners v Cardholder Services [1989] 1 W.L.R. 1196; [1989] 2 All E.R. 385; [1989] S.T.C. 407; [1989] C.C.L.R. 107, CA (Civ Div) .... *Digested,* 89/**3739**: *Applied* 94/4583, 95/5088: *Considered* 90/4623, 17/2283: *Followed* 91/3668

Customs and Excise Commissioners v Gus Merchandise Corp Ltd (No.2) see GUS Merchandise Corp Ltd v Customs and Excise Commissioners (No.2)

Customs and Excise Commissioners v Leicester University Student Union see Customs and Excise Commissioners v Leicester University Students Union

Customs and Excise Commissioners v Leicester University Students Union; *sub nom* Customs and Excise Commissioners v University of Leicester Students Union; Customs and Excise Commissioners v Leicester University Student Union [2001] EWCA Civ 1972; [2002] S.T.C. 147; [2002] E.L.R. 347; [2002] B.T.C. 5064; [2002] B.V.C. 269; Times, January 25, 2002; [2002] S.T.I. 38; (2002) 99(10) L.S.G. 33, CA (Civ Div) .... *Digested,* 02/**4741**: *Applied* 16/2171, 17/2234: *Considered* 14/3041, 14/3045

Customs and Excise Commissioners v Lex Services Plc see Lex Services Plc v Customs and Excise Commissioners

Customs and Excise Commissioners v Lord Fisher; *sub nom* Lord Fisher DSC v Customs and Excise Commissioners [1981] 2 All E.R. 147; [1981] S.T.C. 238, QBD .... *Digested,* 81/**2849**: *Applied* 84/3038, 03/4606, 05/4383, 08/3793, 10/3531, 12/3220: *Considered* 88/3454, 06/4429, 07/4336, 10/3526: *Doubted* 17/2295

Customs and Excise Commissioners v Loyalty Management UK Ltd see Revenue and Customs Commissioners v Loyalty Management UK Ltd

Customs and Excise Commissioners v Marchday Holdings Ltd; *sub nom* Marchday Holdings Ltd v Customs and Excise Commissioners [1997] S.T.C. 272; [1997] B.T.C. 5054; [1997] B.V.C. 165; Times, December 20, 1996; [1996] E.G. 204 (C.S.); (1997) 94(4) L.S.G. 26; (1997) 141 S.J.L.B. 28, CA (Civ Div) .... *Digested,* 97/**5050**: *Applied* 15/2629: *Superseded* 17/2292

Customs and Excise Commissioners v Parkwood Landfill Ltd see Parkwood Landfill Ltd v Customs and Excise Commissioners

Customs and Excise Commissioners v Pegasus Birds Ltd see Pegasus Birds Ltd v Customs and Excise Commissioners

Customs and Excise Commissioners v Plantiflor Ltd; *sub nom* Plantiflor Ltd v Customs and Excise Commissioners [2002] UKHL 33; [2002] 1 W.L.R. 2287; [2002] S.T.C. 1132; [2002] 3 C.M.L.R. 5; [2002] B.T.C. 5413; [2002] B.V.C. 572; Times, July 31, 2002; Independent, November 11, 2002; [2002] S.T.I. 1093; (2002) 99(36) L.S.G. 39; (2002) 152 N.L.J. 1385, HL .... *Digested,* 02/**4785**: *Applied* 04/3992, 05/4346, 07/4310: *Followed* 07/4293, 17/2260

Customs and Excise Commissioners v Redrow Group Plc [1999] 1 W.L.R. 408; [1999] 2 All E.R. 1; [1999] S.T.C. 161; [1999] B.T.C. 5062; [1999] B.V.C. 96; Times, February 18, 1999; Independent, February 18, 1999; [1999] E.G. 20 (C.S.); (1999) 96(9) L.S.G. 32; (1999) 143 S.J.L.B. 58; [1999] N.P.C. 18, HL .... *Digested,* 99/**4994**: *Applied* 02/4774, 04/3992, 05/4346, 05/4375, 06/5741, 07/4310, 08/4018, 14/3061: *Considered* 03/4529, 13/3209, 17/2249: *Distinguished* 05/4379, 06/4468: *Explained* 08/4020: *Followed* 10/3515, 11/3542, 13/3204, 17/2260

Customs and Excise Commissioners v Reed Personnel Services Ltd [1995] S.T.C. 588; Times, April 13, 1995; Independent, May 1, 1995, QBD .... *Digested,* 95/**5089**: *Applied* 09/4114, 10/3504, 11/3565, 17/2254: *Considered* 10/3520, 13/3216: *Followed* 10/3515: *Referred to* 97/4979

Customs and Excise Commissioners v Rysaffe Trustee Co (CI) Ltd see Rysaffe Trustee Co (CI) Ltd v Inland Revenue Commissioners

Customs and Excise Commissioners v School of Finance and Management (London) Ltd see School of Finance and Management (London) Ltd v Customs and Excise Commissioners

Customs and Excise Commissioners v St Martin's Hospital see Customs and Excise Commissioners v Wellington Private Hospital Ltd

Customs and Excise Commissioners v Steptoe [1992] S.T.C. 757; Times, September 22, 1992; Independent, September 25, 1992, CA (Civ Div) .... *Digested,* 93/**4053**: *Applied* 93/4076, 97/5014, 03/4526, 04/3737, 10/3523, 17/2170, 17/2273

Customs and Excise Commissioners v Total Network SL; *sub nom* Revenue and Customs Commissioners v Total Network SL; Total Network SL v Revenue and Customs Commissioners [2008] UKHL 19; [2008] 1 A.C. 1174; [2008] 2 W.L.R. 711; [2008] 2 All E.R. 413; [2008] S.T.C. 644; [2008] Lloyd's Rep. F.C. 275; [2008] B.P.I.R. 699; [2008] B.T.C. 5216; [2008] B.V.C. 340; Times, March 13, 2008; [2008] S.T.I. 938; (2008) 152(12) S.J.L.B. 29, HL .... *Digested,* 08/**3907**: *Applied* 16/2145: *Considered* 11/3157: *Followed* 17/160

Customs and Excise Commissioners v University of Leicester Students Union see Customs and Excise Commissioners v Leicester University Students Union

Customs and Excise Commissioners v Wellington Private Hospital Ltd; *joined cases* Customs and Excise Commissioners v St Martin's Hospital; Customs and Excise Commissioners v British United Provident Association Ltd [1997] S.T.C. 445; [1997] B.T.C. 5140; [1997] B.V.C. 251; Times, February 11, 1997, CA (Civ Div) .... *Digested,* 97/**5057**: *Applied* 01/5604, 06/4438, 14/3102: *Considered* 17/2294: *Doubted* 14/3050: *Followed* 99/4978

Cuthbertson v Tesco Personal Finance Plc see Teasdale v HSBC Bank Plc

CW (Sri Lanka) v Secretary of State for the Home Department see R. (on the application of MA (Pakistan)) v Upper Tribunal (Immigration and Asylum Chamber)

Cyprus Popular Bank Co Ltd v Vgenopoulos [2016] EWHC 1695 (QB); [2017] Q.B. 453; [2017] 2 W.L.R. 67; [2016] 1 C.L.C. 936, QBD .... *Digested,* 17/**301**

Cyprus Popular Bank Co Ltd v Vgenopoulos [2016] EWHC 1442 (QB); [2017] Q.B. 453; [2017] 2 W.L.R. 67; [2016] 2 Lloyd's Rep. 177; [2016] 1 C.L.C. 908, QBD . *Digested,* 16/**261**

CZ (A Child) (Convention Rights Claim: Costs), Re see CZ (Human Rights Claim: Costs), Re

CZ (Human Rights Claim: Costs), Re; *sub nom* AZ v Kirklees Council; CZ (A Child) (Convention Rights Claim: Costs), Re [2017] EWFC 11; [2017] 1 W.L.R. 2467; [2017] 1 Costs L.R. 201; [2018] 1 F.L.R. 23; [2017] 2 F.C.R. 465, Fam Ct .... *Digested,* 17/**995**: *Applied* 17/975

D v D see D (A Child) (Abduction: Rights of Custody), Re

D v East Berkshire Community NHS Trust see JD v East Berkshire Community Health NHS Trust

D v ED (Parental Order: Time Limit); *sub nom* A (Children), Re [2015] EWHC 911 (Fam); [2016] 2 F.L.R. 530; [2017] 1 F.C.R. 77; [2015] Fam. Law 1052, Fam Div

D v Lothian Health Board; *sub nom* JD v Lothian Health Board [2017] CSIH 27; 2018 S.C.L.R. 1; 2017 G.W.D. 15-234, IH (Ex Div) *Considered* 17/2697

D v R [2014] EWHC 4306 (Fam); [2015] 2 F.L.R. 978; [2015] Fam. Law 261, Fam Div *Digested,* 15/**1114**: *Considered* 17/1001

D v Southwark LBC see R. (on the application of D) v Southwark LBC

D (A Child) (Abduction: Foreign Custody Right), Re see D (A Child) (Abduction: Rights of Custody), Re

D (A Child) (Abduction: Rights of Custody), Re; *sub nom* D (A Child) (Abduction: Foreign Custody Right), Re; D v D [2006] UKHL 51; [2007] 1 A.C. 619; [2006] 3 W.L.R. 989; [2007] 1 All E.R. 783; [2007] 1 F.L.R. 961; [2007] 1 F.C.R. 1; Times, November 17, 2006; Independent, November 21, 2006; [2007] Fam. Law 102; (2006) 103(46) L.S.G. 29; (2006) 156 N.L.J. 1803; (2006) 150 S.J.L.B. 1532, HL .... *Digested,* 07/**1775**: *Applied* 07/1743, 08/1460, 09/1641, 10/1341, 14/1323, 15/1104, 17/1038: *Considered* 07/1736, 09/1573, 09/1635, 11/1349, 16/951: *Followed* 09/1539, 11/1348, 14/1310, 15/1041, 15/1110, 16/846

D (A Child) (Care Proceedings: Adoption), Re [2016] EWFC 1; [2017] 4 W.L.R. 55; [2017] 1 F.L.R. 237; [2016] Fam. Law 272, Fam Ct .... *Digested,* 17/**919**

D (A Child) (Deprivation of Liberty: Parental Responsibility), Re; *sub nom* Trust A v X (A Child) [2015] EWHC 922 (Fam); [2016] 1 F.L.R. 142; [2015] 3 F.C.R. 60; [2015] C.O.P.L.R. 209; (2015) 144 B.M.L.R. 210; [2015] Fam. Law 636, Fam Div .... *Digested,* 15/**1747**: *Applied* 17/966

D (A Child) (Transfer of Proceedings), Re; *sub nom* M (Brussels II Revised: Art.15), Re; *joined case* Nottingham City Council v LM [2014] EWCA Civ 152; [2014] 2 F.L.R. 1372; [2014] 2 F.C.R. 585; [2014] Fam. Law 966, CA (Civ Div) .... *Digested,* 14/**1287**: *Considered* 15/1006: *Followed* 16/824, 17/926

D (A Child), Re; *sub nom* F v L (Child Arrangements Order: Relocation); F v L (Permission to Relocate: Appeal) [2017] EWHC 1377 (Fam); [2017] 4 W.L.R. 111; [2018] 1 F.L.R. 375; [2017] 3 F.C.R. 460, Fam Div .... *Digested,* 17/**943**

D (A Child), Re [2017] EWCA Civ 196; [2017] 2 F.C.R. 493, CA (Civ Div) .... *Digested,* 17/**1049**

D (Appeal: Failure of Case Management), Re see H v D (Appeal: Failure of Case Management: Cross-examination by Alleged Abuser)

D (Children) v Wakefield MDC; *sub nom* GD v Wakefield MDC [2016] EWHC 3312 (Fam); [2017] 2 F.L.R. 1353, Fam Div *Applied* 17/995

D (Children) (Care: Change of Forename), Re [2003] 1 F.L.R. 339; [2003] Fam. Law 77, Fam Div .... *Digested,* 03/**1527**: *Applied* 17/958

D (Children) (Child Abduction: Practice), Re [2016] EWHC 504 (Fam); [2016] 4 W.L.R. 62; [2017] 1 F.L.R. 1125; [2016] Fam. Law 553, Fam Div .... *Digested,* 16/**917**

D (Incapacitated Person) (Representatives and Advocates: Duties and Powers), Re; *sub nom* RD v Herefordshire Council; RD (Duties and Powers of Relevant Person's Representatives and Section 39 IMCAs), Re; *joined cases* B (Incapacitated Person) (Representatives and Advocates: Duties and Powers), Re; P (Incapacitated Person) (Representatives and Advocates: Duties and Powers), Re; W (Incapacitated Person) (Representatives and Advocates: Duties and Powers), Re [2016] EWCOP 49; [2017] 1 W.L.R. 1723; [2017] C.O.P.L.R. 87, CP .... *Digested,* 17/**1550**

D (Inherent Jurisdiction: Power of Arrest), Re see D (Vulnerable Adult) (Injunction: Power of Arrest), Re

D (Medical Treatment), Re see B v D

D (Minors) (Adoption Reports: Confidentiality), Re [1996] A.C. 593; [1995] 3 W.L.R. 483; [1995] 4 All E.R. 385; [1995] 2 F.L.R. 687; [1996] 1 F.C.R. 205; [1996] Fam. Law 8; (1995) 145 N.L.J. 1612, HL .... *Digested,* 96/**474**: *Applied* 96/508, 97/356, 99/2360, 99/6065, 00/2534, 02/1609, 06/1671, 10/1312, 11/1327, 13/1189, 14/2184, 17/928: *Considered* 08/922, 11/1328: *Distinguished* 99/6064: *Followed* 13/1223

D (Practice: Declaration of Parentage), Re; *sub nom* AD (Human Fertilisation and Embryology Act 2008), Re [2017] EWHC 1782 (Fam); [2017] 4 W.L.R. 128; [2017] 3 F.C.R. 298, Fam Div .... *Digested,* 17/**1054**

D (Vulnerable Adult) (Injunction: Power of Arrest), Re; *sub nom* FD (Inherent Jurisdiction: Power of Arrest), Re; D (Inherent Jurisdiction: Power of Arrest), Re [2016] EWHC 2358 (Fam); [2017] Fam. 105; [2017] 2 W.L.R. 698; [2016] Fam. Law 1398, Fam Ct .... *Digested,* 17/**1050**

D Geddes (Contractors) Ltd v Neil Johnson Health & Safety Services Ltd [2017] CSOH 42; [2017] P.N.L.R. 21; 2017 G.W.D. 10-134, OH .... *Digested,* 17/**2735**

D&D Marketing (UK) Ltd, Re see Customs and Excise Commissioners v D&D Marketing (UK) Ltd

D&D Wines International Ltd (In Liquidation), Re; *sub nom* Angove Pty Ltd v Bailey; Bailey v Angove's Pty Ltd [2016] UKSC 47; [2016] 1 W.L.R. 3179; [2017] 1 All E.R. 773; [2017] 1 All E.R. (Comm) 583; [2016] 2 Lloyd's Rep. 409; [2016] B.C.C. 594; [2017] 1 B.C.L.C. 1; [2016] 2 C.L.C. 228; [2016] E.C.C. 28; [2016] B.P.I.R. 1361; [2016] W.T.L.R. 1309; [2017] 1 P. & C.R. DG2, SC .... *Digested,* 16/**47**

D'Arcy v Revenue and Customs Commissioners see Revenue and Customs Commissioners v D'Arcy

D'Este v D'Este [1973] Fam. 55; [1973] 2 W.L.R. 183, Fam Div .... *Digested,* 73/**3074**: *Applied* 93/1905: *Approved* 17/1282: *Considered* 06/1624

D'Eye, Re; *sub nom* Thomas v Mariner Properties Ltd [2017] B.P.I.R. 598, Ch D (Bankruptcy Ct) .... *Digested,* 17/**1274**

D'Eye, Re; *sub nom* Thomas v Mariner Properties Ltd [2017] B.P.I.R. 1174, QBD .... *Digested,* 17/**1277**

D's Application for Leave to Apply for Judicial Review, Re [2015] NIQB 78; [2017] N.I. 91, QBD (NI)

D-Media Communications Ltd v Revenue and Customs Commissioners [2016] UKFTT 430 (TC); [2017] S.F.T.D. 1; [2016] S.T.I. 2656, FTT (Tax) .... *Digested,* 17/**2127**

Da Costa v Sargaco [2016] EWCA Civ 764; [2016] C.P. Rep. 40; [2017] R.T.R. 2, CA (Civ Div) .... *Digested,* 16/**1552**

Da Silva v United Kingdom (5878/08); *sub nom* Armani Da Silva v United Kingdom (5878/08) (2016) 63 E.H.R.R. 12; 40 B.H.R.C. 159; [2017] Inquest L.R. 73; Times, April 26, 2016, ECHR (Grand Chamber) .... *Digested,* 16/**1054**: *Considered* 17/21

Dacorum BC v Bucknall (formerly Acheampong); *sub nom* Bucknall v Dacorum BC [2017] EWHC 2094 (QB); [2017] H.L.R. 40, QBD .... *Digested,* 17/**1150**

Dacy Building Services Ltd v IDM Properties LLP [2016] EWHC 3007 (TCC); [2017] B.L.R. 114; 170 Con. L.R. 176, QBD (TCC) .... *Digested,* 17/**494**

Dad v General Dental Council [2000] 1 W.L.R. 1538; [2000] Lloyd's Rep. Med. 299; (2000) 56 B.M.L.R. 130; Times, April 19, 2000, PC (UK) .... *Digested,* 00/**38**: *Considered* 02/1832, 17/1807

Dahou v Serco Ltd see Serco Ltd v Dahou

Daiichi Sankyo Co Ltd v DEMO Anonimos Viomikhaniki kai Emporiki Etairia Farmakon (C-414/11) EU:C:2013:520; [2014] Bus. L.R. 1, ECJ (Grand Chamber) *Considered* 17/386

Daiichii Chuo Kisen Kaisha v Gard Marine & Energy Ltd see Gard Marine & Energy Ltd v China National Chartering Co Ltd

Daimler Co Ltd v Continental Tyre & Rubber Co (Great Britain) Ltd; *sub nom* Continental Tyre & Rubber Co (Great Britain) Ltd v Daimler Co Ltd; *joined case* Continental Tyre & Rubber Co (Great Britain) Ltd v Thomas Tilling Ltd [1916] 2 A.C. 307, HL *Applied* 55/2805: *Considered* 62/1718: *Distinguished* 17/390: *Doubted* 64/468

Dainford Navigation Inc v PDVSA Petroleo SA [2017] EWHC 2150 (Comm); [2018] Bus. L.R. 410; [2017] 2 Lloyd's Rep. 409, QBD (Comm)

Dalecroft Properties Ltd v Underwriters [2017] EWHC 1263 (Comm); [2017] Lloyd's Rep. I.R. 511, QBD (Comm) .... *Digested,* 17/**1344**

Dallas v United Kingdom (38395/12) (2016) 63 E.H.R.R. 13; 41 B.H.R.C. 420; Times, April 5, 2016, ECHR .... *Digested,* 17/**1166**

Dallaway (Deceased), Re [1982] 1 W.L.R. 756; [1982] 3 All E.R. 118; (1982) 126 S.J. 314, Ch D .... *Digested,* 82/**1346**: *Considered* 97/4939, 17/2216: *Distinguished* 85/1513

Dallow and Moscrop v Codd see Macadam, Re

Dalnyaya Step LLC (In Liquidation), Re; *sub nom* Cherkasov v Olegovich; Cherkasov v Nogotkov [2017] EWHC 756 (Ch); [2017] 1 W.L.R. 4264; [2017] 2 B.C.L.C. 233, Ch D (Companies Ct) .... *Digested,* 17/**361**

Dalriada Trustees Ltd v Bluefin Trustees Ltd [2017] EWHC 1085 (Ch); [2017] Pens. L.R. 12, Ch D .... *Digested,* 17/**1609**

Dalriada Trustees Ltd v Mcauley [2017] EWHC 202 (Ch); [2017] Pens. L.R. 8, Ch D ... *Digested,* 17/**1619**

Dalriada Trustees Ltd v Nidd Vale Trustees Ltd see PI Consulting (Trustee Services) Ltd v Pensions Regulator

Dammermann v Lanyon Bowdler LLP [2017] EWCA Civ 269; [2017] C.P. Rep. 25; [2017] 2 Costs L.R. 393, CA (Civ Div) .... *Digested,* 17/**222**

Dance with Mr D Ltd v Revenue and Customs Commissioners [2017] UKFTT 374 (TC); [2017] S.T.I. 1178, FTT (Tax)

Danfoss A/S v Skatteministeriet (C-371/07) EU:C:2008:711; [2009] S.T.C. 701; [2008] E.C.R. I-9549; [2009] 1 C.M.L.R. 46; [2009] B.V.C. 781; [2008] S.T.I. 2788, ECJ (4th Chamber) .... *Digested,* 09/**4057**: *Considered* 17/2272: *Followed* 10/3492

Danfoss A/S v Skatteministeriet (C-94/10) EU:C:2011:674; [2013] S.T.C. 1651; [2011] E.C.R. I-9963; [2013] B.T.C. 315, ECJ (1st Chamber) *Applied* 12/3430, 17/2289

Daniels v Daniels [1978] Ch. 406; [1978] 2 W.L.R. 73; [1978] 2 All E.R. 89; (1977) 121 S.J. 605, Ch D .... *Digested,* 78/**241**: *Applied* 82/330, 17/287

Danks v Qinetiq Holdings Ltd [2012] EWHC 570 (Ch); [2012] Pens. L.R. 131, Ch D .... *Digested,* 12/**2383**: *Considered* 14/2283, 17/1628

Danvers v Revenue and Customs Commissioners [2016] UKFTT 3 (TC); [2016] Pens. L.R. 49, FTT (Tax) .... *Digested,* 16/**1584**: *Affirmed* 17/2099

Danvers v Revenue and Customs Commissioners [2016] UKUT 569 (TCC); [2017] S.T.C. 555; [2017] Pens. L.R. 6; [2017] B.T.C. 502; [2017] S.T.I. 138, UT (Tax) *Digested,* 17/**2099**

Dany Lions Ltd v Bristol Cars Ltd [2014] EWHC 817 (QB); [2014] 2 All E.R. (Comm) 403; [2014] Bus. L.R. D11, QBD .... *Digested,* 14/**630**: *Considered* 17/503

Daouidi v Bootes Plus SL (C-395/15) EU:C:2016:917; [2017] 2 C.M.L.R. 21; [2017] I.C.R. 420; [2017] I.R.L.R. 151, ECJ (3rd Chamber)

Dar Al Arkan Real Estate Development Co v Al-Refai [2014] EWCA Civ 715; [2015] 1 W.L.R. 135; [2014] 1 C.L.C. 855, CA (Civ Div) .... *Digested,* 15/**220**: *Applied* 17/380: *Followed* 17/212

Dardana Ltd v Yukos Oil Co (No.1); *sub nom* Petroalliance Services Co Ltd v Yukos Oil Co; Yukos Oil Co v Dardana Ltd [2002] EWCA Civ 543; [2002] 1 All E.R. (Comm) 819; [2002] 2 Lloyd's Rep. 326; [2002] C.L.C. 1120, CA (Civ Div) .... *Digested,* 03/**196**: *Approved* 17/68: *Considered* 05/463, 09/188, 14/122, 16/67

Darlington Borough Council v M see A (Application for Care Placement Orders: Local Authority Failings), Re

Darnley v Croydon Health Services NHS Trust [2015] EWHC 2301 (QB); [2016] P.I.Q.R. P4; [2015] Med. L.R. 506; (2015) 146 B.M.L.R. 216; [2015] P.T.S.R. D54, QBD .... *Digested,* 16/**1538**: *Affirmed* 17/1565

Darnley v Croydon Health Services NHS Trust [2017] EWCA Civ 151; [2018] 2 W.L.R. 54; [2017] P.I.Q.R. P14; [2017] Med. L.R. 245; (2017) 156 B.M.L.R. 104, CA (Civ Div) .... *Digested,* 17/**1565**

Darroch v Football Association Premier League Ltd; *sub nom* Hull & Holderness Magistrates' Court v Darroch [2016] EWCA Civ 1220; [2017] 4 W.L.R. 6; [2017] Lloyd's Rep. F.C. 65; [2017] L.L.R. 290, CA (Civ Div) .... *Digested,* 17/**270**

Darroch v Football Association Premier League Ltd see Hull and Holderness Magistrates' Court v Darroch

Dartford BC v Secretary of State for Communities and Local Government [2017] EWCA Civ 141; [2017] P.T.S.R. 737; [2017] 2 P. & C.R. 9; Times, May 4, 2017, CA (Civ Div) .... *Digested,* 17/**1724**

Dartford BC v Secretary of State for Communities and Local Government [2016] EWHC 635 (Admin), QBD (Admin) *Affirmed* 17/1724

Das v Linden Mews Ltd; *sub nom* Chand v Linden Mews Ltd [2002] EWCA Civ 590; [2003] 2 P. & C.R. 4; [2002] 2 E.G.L.R. 76; [2002] 28 E.G. 130; Independent, May 9, 2002; [2002] 2 P. & C.R. DG14, CA (Civ Div) .... *Digested,* 02/**3820**: *Considered* 03/3600, 17/1840: *Not followed* 03/3558

Daventry DC v Daventry and District Housing Ltd [2011] EWCA Civ 1153; [2012] 1 W.L.R. 1333; [2012] 2 All E.R. (Comm) 142; [2012] Bus. L.R. 485; [2012] Pens. L.R. 57; [2012] 1 P. & C.R. 5; [2011] 42 E.G. 120 (C.S.), CA (Civ Div) .... *Digested,* 12/**626**: *Applied* 12/2042, 12/2371, 13/571, 14/1991, 16/137: *Followed* 17/1626, 17/1627

Daventry DC v Secretary of State for Communities and Local Government; *sub nom* Gladman Developments Ltd v Daventry District Council [2015] EWHC 3459 (Admin); [2016] J.P.L. 578, QBD (Admin) .... *Digested,* 16/**1740**: *Affirmed* 17/1776: *Considered* 16/1760

Daventry DC v Secretary of State for Communities and Local Government; *sub nom* Gladman Developments Ltd v Daventry District Council [2016] EWCA Civ 1146; [2017] J.P.L. 402, CA (Civ Div) .... *Digested,* 17/**1776**

Davey v General Dental Council [2015] EWHC 3594 (Admin); (2017) 153 B.M.L.R. 200, QBD (Admin) .... *Digested,* 17/**1111**

Davey (A Bankrupt), Re; *sub nom* Lismore v Davey [2014] NICh 2; [2017] N.I. 32; [2015] B.P.I.R. 1425, Ch D (NI)

David T Morrison & Co Ltd (t/a Gael Home Interiors) v ICL Plastics Ltd [2014] UKSC 48; 2014 S.C. (U.K.S.C.) 222; 2014 S.L.T. 791; 2014 S.C.L.R. 711; [2014] C.I.L.L. 3561; 2014 G.W.D. 25-504, SC .... *Digested,* 14/**2470**: *Considered* 17/2449: *Followed* 16/2456

Davidson (William) v HM Advocate [2016] HCJAC 110; 2017 S.C.L. 198; 2016 G.W.D. 38-686, HCJ .... *Digested,* 17/**2813**

Davies v Davies [2016] EWCA Civ 463; [2017] 1 F.L.R. 1286; [2016] 2 P. & C.R. 10; [2016] Fam. Law 815, CA (Civ Div) .... *Digested,* 16/**780**

Davies v Revenue and Customs Commissioners [2017] UKFTT 188 (TC); [2017] S.F.T.D. 707, FTT (Tax) .... *Digested,* 17/**2174**

Davies (Deceased), Re see Ellenborough Park, Re

Davis v Catto [2011] CSIH 85; 2012 Rep. L.R. 40; 2012 G.W.D. 3-54, IH (Ex Div) .... *Digested,* 12/**4208**: *Considered* 17/2442

Davis v Jackson [2017] EWHC 698 (Ch); [2017] 1 W.L.R. 4005; [2017] 2 F.L.R. 1153; [2017] B.P.I.R. 950; [2017] W.T.L.R. 465, Ch D .... *Digested,* 17/**1826**

Davy v Pickering; *sub nom* Pickering v Davy [2015] EWHC 380 (Ch); [2016] B.C.C. 50; [2015] 2 B.C.L.C. 116, Ch D (Cardiff) .... *Digested,* 15/**398**: *Applied* 16/1255: *Reversed* 17/398

Davy v Pickering; *sub nom* Pickering v Davy [2017] EWCA Civ 30; [2017] Bus. L.R. 1239; [2017] B.C.C. 171; [2017] 2 B.C.L.C. 260; Times, March 8, 2017, CA (Civ Div) .... *Digested,* 17/**398**

Davy's of London (Wine Merchants) Ltd v City of London Corp; *joined case* Davy's of London (Wine Merchants) Ltd v Saxon Land BV [2004] EWHC 2224 (Ch); [2004] 3 E.G.L.R. 39; [2004] 49 E.G. 136; [2004] 42 E.G. 161 (C.S.); [2004] N.P.C. 144; [2005] 1 P. & C.R. DG8, Ch D .... *Digested,* 05/**2671**: *Considered* 17/1452

Davy's of London (Wine Merchants) Ltd v Saxon Land BV see Davy's of London (Wine Merchants) Ltd v City of London Corp

Dawnus Construction Holdings Ltd v Marsh Life Ltd [2017] EWHC 1066 (TCC); 172 Con. L.R. 162; [2017] C.I.L.L. 3977, QBD (TCC) .... *Digested,* 17/**451**

Dawson-Damer v Taylor Wessing LLP [2015] EWHC 2366 (Ch); [2016] 1 W.L.R. 28; [2016] W.T.L.R. 253, Ch D .... *Digested,* 16/**1057**: *Reversed* 17/1171

Dawson-Damer v Taylor Wessing LLP [2017] EWCA Civ 74; [2017] 1 W.L.R. 3255, CA (Civ Div) .... *Digested,* 17/**1171**: *Considered* 17/1165

Day v Health Education England see Day v Lewisham and Greenwich NHS Trust

Day v Hosebay Ltd; *sub nom* Lexgorge Ltd v Howard de Walden Estates Ltd; Hosebay Ltd v Day; *joined case* Howard de Walden Estates Ltd v Lexgorge Ltd [2012] UKSC 41; [2012] 1 W.L.R. 2884; [2012] 4 All E.R. 1347; [2012] H.L.R. 48; [2013] 1 P. & C.R. 9; [2013] L. & T.R. 3; [2012] 3 E.G.L.R. 33; [2012] 43 E.G. 116; [2012] R.V.R. 359; Times, October 26, 2012; [2012] 42 E.G. 132 (C.S.); (2012) 156(39) S.J.L.B. 31, SC .... *Digested,* 13/**2439**: *Considered* 14/1982, 17/1843: *Followed* 16/1814

Day v Lewisham and Greenwich NHS Trust; *sub nom* Day v Health Education England [2016] I.C.R. 878; [2016] I.R.L.R. 415; [2016] Med. L.R. 269, EAT .... *Digested,* 16/**705**: *Reversed* 17/818

Day v Lewisham and Greenwich NHS Trust; *sub nom* Day v Health Education England [2017] EWCA Civ 329; [2017] I.C.R. 917; [2017] I.R.L.R. 623; (2017) 158 B.M.L.R. 76; Times, June 26, 2017, CA (Civ Div) .... *Digested,* 17/**818**

DB v Chief Constable of Police Service of Northern Ireland see DB's Application for Judicial Review, Re

DB v DLJ see J v B (Challenge to Arbitral Award)

DB v General Medical Council [2016] EWHC 2331 (QB); (2016) 152 B.M.L.R. 106, QBD (Manchester) .... *Digested,* 17/**1112**

DB v PB (Financial Provision) (Prenuptial Agreement: Prorogation Clause); *sub nom* DB v PB (Prenuptial Agreement: Jurisdiction) [2016] EWHC 3431 (Fam); [2017] 4 W.L.R. 44; [2017] 2 F.L.R. 1540, Fam Div .... *Digested,* 17/**1027**

DB v PB (Prenuptial Agreement: Jurisdiction) see DB v PB (Financial Provision) (Prenuptial Agreement: Prorogation Clause)

DB Group Services (UK) Ltd v Revenue and Customs Commissioners see UBS AG v Revenue and Customs Commissioners

DB UK Bank Ltd (t/a DB Mortgages) v Jacobs Solicitors [2016] EWHC 1614 (Ch); [2016] 4 W.L.R. 184, Ch D .... *Digested,* 17/**373**

DB UK Bank Ltd (t/a DB Mortgages) v Sinclair Solicitors Ltd HC-2015-000987, Ch D *Doubted* 17/368

DB's Application for Judicial Review, Re; *sub nom* DB v Chief Constable of Police Service of Northern Ireland [2017] UKSC 7; [2017] N.I. 301, SC

DC v Hertfordshire CC [2016] UKUT 379 (AAC); [2017] E.L.R. 27, UT (AAC) .... *Digested,* 17/**711**

DCC Holdings (UK) Ltd v Revenue and Customs Commissioners; *sub nom* Revenue and Customs Commissioners v DCC Holdings (UK) Ltd [2010] UKSC 58; [2011] 1 W.L.R. 44; [2011] 1 All E.R. 537; [2011] S.T.C. 326; 80 T.C. 301; [2011] B.T.C. 13; [2011] S.T.I. 133, SC .... *Digested,* 11/**3311**: *Applied* 12/2385, 17/2112: *Considered* 15/2447

DCC Holdings (UK) Ltd v Revenue and Customs Commissioners; *sub nom* Revenue and Customs Commissioners v DCC Holdings (UK) Ltd [2009] EWCA Civ 1165; [2010] S.T.C. 80; [2009] B.T.C. 724; [2009] S.T.I. 2933, CA (Civ Div) ...... *Digested,* 10/**220**: *Affirmed* 11/3311: *Applied* 17/2111: *Considered* 14/2972, 15/2447, 15/2451

DCM (Optical Holdings) Ltd v Revenue and Customs Commissioners [2017] UKFTT 785 (TC); [2018] S.F.T.D. 333; [2017] S.T.I. 1143, FTT (Tax)

De Keyser's Royal Hotel Ltd v King, The see De Keyser's Royal Hotel Ltd, Re

De Keyser's Royal Hotel Ltd, Re; *sub nom* De Keyser's Royal Hotel Ltd v King, The [1920] A.C. 508, HL

Applied 54/480, 64/543, 72/1101, 79/321, 87/2868, 99/5188, 17/1068: *Considered* 71/5455, 77/150, 83/359, 94/15, 08/581, 16/1723: *Followed* 67/128, 16/370

De Lange v Staatssecretaris van Financien (C-548/15) EU:C:2016:850; [2017] I.R.L.R. 278, ECJ (6th Chamber)

De Sousa v British South Africa Co see British South Africa Co v Companhia de Mocambique
De Souza v Vinci Construction UK Ltd see Pereira de Souza v Vinci Construction UK Ltd
De Tommaso v Italy (43395/09) (2017) 65 E.H.R.R. 19, ECHR
De Wilde v Belgium (No.1) (A/12) (1979-80) 1 E.H.R.R. 373, ECHR
Applied 02/3869, 03/3067, 08/2690, 14/2233, 17/1538: *Considered* 09/1960, 09/2761, 09/2768
Dean v Dean [1978] Fam. 161; [1978] 3 W.L.R. 288; [1978] 3 All E.R. 758; (1978) 8 Fam. Law 171; (1978) 122 S.J. 211, Fam Div .... *Digested,* 78/**806**:
Approved 82/1490: *Considered* 83/1841, 17/1029: *Followed* 02/1676
Dean v Secretary of State for Business, Energy and Industrial Strategy see R. (on the application of Dean) v Secretary of State for Business, Energy and Industrial Strategy
Dean (Zain Taj) v Lord Advocate; *sub nom* Lord Advocate v Dean [2016] HCJAC 83; 2016 S.L.T. 1105; 2016 S.C.L. 864; 2016 S.C.C.R. 499; 2016 G.W.D. 33-594, HCJ .... *Digested,* 16/**2634**:
Reversed 17/905
Dean (Zain Taj) v Lord Advocate; *sub nom* Lord Advocate v Dean [2017] UKSC 44; [2017] 1 W.L.R. 2721; [2018] 1 All E.R. 995; 2018 S.C. (U.K.S.C.) 1; 2017 S.L.T. 773; 2017 S.C.C.R. 388; 2017 G.W.D. 21-345, SC .... *Digested,* 17/**905**
Debtor (No.32/SD/1991) (No.1), Re [1993] 1 W.L.R. 314; [1993] 2 All E.R. 991, Ch D . *Digested,* 93/**237**:
Applied 15/1410, 17/1290: *Considered* 95/424, 05/2277
Debtor (No.259 of 1990), Re [1992] 1 W.L.R. 226; [1992] 1 All E.R. 641, Ch D .... *Digested,* 92/**234**:
Applied 17/1302: *Followed* 98/3354
Decadent Vapours Ltd v Bevan see Denton v TH White Ltd
Dechert LLP v Eurasian Natural Resources Corp Ltd see Eurasian Natural Resources Corp Ltd v Dechert LLP
Dee Valley Group Plc, Re [2017] EWHC 184 (Ch); [2018] Ch. 55; [2017] 3 W.L.R. 767; [2017] 2 B.C.L.C. 328; Times, March 21, 2017, Ch D (Companies Ct) .... *Digested,* 17/**405**
Deed Poll Services Ltd v Revenue and Customs Commissioners see Multimedia Computing Ltd v Revenue and Customs Commissioners
Deep Purple (Overseas) Ltd (In Administration), Re see Gillan v HEC Enterprises Ltd
Deer v University of Oxford see Ittihadieh v 5-11 Cheyne Gardens RTM Co Ltd
Deezer Ltd v Revenue and Customs Commissioners [2017] UKFTT 203 (TC); [2017] S.T.I. 873, FTT (Tax)
DEG-Deutsche Investitions und Entwicklungsgesellschaft mbH v Koshy (Account of Profits: Limitations); *sub nom* Gwembe Valley Development Co Ltd (In Receivership) v Koshy (Account of Profits: Limitations) [2003] EWCA Civ 1048; [2004] 1 B.C.L.C. 131; [2004] W.T.L.R. 97; Times, September 9, 2003; (2003) 147 S.J.L.B. 1086, CA (Civ Div) .... *Digested,* 03/**519**:
Applied 07/471, 17/321: *Considered* 06/4076, 06/470: *Followed* 13/433, 17/2192
Degorce v Revenue and Customs Commissioners [2017] EWCA Civ 1427; [2017] S.T.C. 2226; [2017] B.T.C. 26; [2017] S.T.I. 2180, CA (Civ Div) .... *Digested,* 17/**2147**
Degorce v Revenue and Customs Commissioners [2015] UKUT 447 (TCC); [2016] S.T.C. 542; [2015] B.T.C. 528, UT (Tax) .... *Digested,* 15/**2484**:
Affirmed 17/2147
Delaney v Secretary of State for Transport [2015] EWCA Civ 172; [2015] 1 W.L.R. 5177; [2015] 3 All E.R. 329; [2015] C.P. Rep. 25; [2015] R.T.R. 19; [2015] 2 C.M.L.R. 30; [2015] Lloyd's Rep. I.R. 441; [2015] P.I.Q.R. P17, CA (Civ Div)..... *Digested,* 15/**1469**:
Applied 17/1349, 17/1815
Delaney v Staples (t/a De Montfort Recruitment) [1991] 2 Q.B. 47; [1991] 2 W.L.R. 627; [1991] 1 All E.R. 609; [1991] I.C.R. 331; [1991] I.R.L.R. 112; (1991) 141 N.L.J. 581, CA (Civ Div) .... *Digested,* 91/**1708**:
Affirmed 92/2028: *Applied* 97/2294: *Considered* 98/5827: *Followed* 17/853
Dell Products Ltd v General State Administration 19 I.T.L. Rep. 633, Trib Sup (Sp)
Demarco Almeida v Opportunity Equity Partners Ltd [2006] UKPC 44, PC (Cl)
Considered 17/1100
Demir v Turkey (34503/97) [2009] I.R.L.R. 766; (2009) 48 E.H.R.R. 54, ECHR .... *Digested,* 09/**1938**:
Applied 13/1057, 16/736: *Considered* 11/4384, 12/1155, 14/1016, 14/1627, 17/766
Dennard v Plant see Lagden v O'Connor
Denney v John Hudson & Co Ltd see SA&D Wright Ltd, Re
Denning v Greenhalgh Financial Services Ltd [2017] EWHC 143 (QB); [2017] 2 B.C.L.C. 526; [2017] P.N.L.R. 19, QBD .... *Digested,* 17/**1567**

Dennis v McDonald [1982] Fam. 63; [1982] 2 W.L.R. 275; [1982] 1 All E.R. 590; (1982) 12 Fam. Law 84; (1982) 126 S.J. 16, CA (Civ Div) .... *Digested,* 82/**1524**: *Applied* 08/3064: *Considered* 84/1696, 93/1920, 17/1826: *Disapproved* 82/2674

Dennis & Robinson Ltd v Kiossos Establishment (1987) 54 P. & C.R. 282; [1987] 1 E.G.L.R. 133; (1987) 282 E.G. 857, CA (Civ Div) .... *Digested,* 88/**2068**: *Followed* 17/1461

Denso Manufacturing UK Ltd v Great Lakes Reinsurance (UK) Plc; *sub nom* Mploy Group Ltd v Denso Manufacturing UK Ltd [2017] EWHC 391 (Comm); [2017] Lloyd's Rep. I.R. 240, QBD (Comm) .... *Digested,* 17/**1338**

Dent (In Administration), Re; *sub nom* McLean v Berry [2016] EWHC 2650 (Ch); [2017] Ch. 422; [2017] 3 W.L.R. 198; [2017] B.P.I.R. 164, Ch D (Leeds) .... *Digested,* 17/**891**

Denton v TH White Ltd; *joined cases* Decadent Vapours Ltd v Bevan; Utilise TDS Ltd v Cranstoun Davies [2014] EWCA Civ 906; [2014] 1 W.L.R. 3926; [2015] 1 All E.R. 880; [2014] C.P. Rep. 40; [2014] B.L.R. 547; 154 Con. L.R. 1; [2014] 4 Costs L.R. 752; [2014] C.I.L.L. 3568; (2014) 164(7614) N.L.J. 17, CA (Civ Div) . *Digested,* 14/**454**: *Applied* 14/453, 15/1352, 15/1401, 15/2602, 15/2620, 15/285, 15/295, 15/298, 15/352, 16/1104, 16/1601, 16/2204, 16/324, 17/278, 17/375, 17/383: *Considered* 14/2983, 14/838, 15/1146, 15/292, 15/370, 16/65, 17/339: *Explained* 17/2182: *Followed* 14/330, 15/210, 15/247, 15/299, 15/317, 15/350, 15/351, 15/354, 15/355, 15/373, 16/1034, 16/1245, 16/171, 16/241, 16/283, 16/304, 16/305, 16/307, 16/308, 16/323, 17/1506, 17/1508, 17/264, 17/271, 17/297, 17/348, 17/349, 17/350

Department for Business, Energy and Industrial Strategy v Information Commissioner [2017] EWCA Civ 844; [2017] P.T.S.R. 1644; [2018] 1 C.M.L.R. 8; [2018] Env. L.R. 3, CA (Civ Div)

Department for Work and Pensions v Information Commissioner [2016] EWCA Civ 758; [2017] 1 W.L.R. 1; Times, October 17, 2016, CA (Civ Div) .... *Digested,* 16/**33**

Department of Constitutional Affairs v O'Brien; *sub nom* Ministry of Justice v O'Brien; O'Brien v Ministry of Justice; O'Brien v Department of Constitutional Affairs [2013] UKSC 6; [2013] 1 W.L.R. 522; [2013] 2 All E.R. 1; [2013] I.C.R. 499; [2013] I.R.L.R. 315; [2013] Pens. L.R. 129; Times, February 22, 2013, SC .... *Digested,* 13/**998**: *Applied* 14/2021: *Considered* 16/2622: *Distinguished* 17/790

Department of Health v Information Commissioner [2017] EWCA Civ 374; [2017] 1 W.L.R. 3330, CA (Civ Div) .... *Digested,* 17/**36**

Derby & Co Ltd v Weldon (No.1) [1990] Ch. 48; [1989] 2 W.L.R. 276; [1989] 1 All E.R. 469; [1989] 1 Lloyd's Rep. 122; [1989] E.C.C. 283; Times, August 2, 1988; (1988) 138 N.L.J. Rep. 236; (1989) 133 S.J. 83, CA (Civ Div) .... *Digested,* 89/**3042**: *Applied* 92/3547, 97/474, 17/300

Derbyshire Dales DC v Secretary of State for Communities and Local Government [2009] EWHC 1729 (Admin); [2010] 1 P. & C.R. 19; [2010] J.P.L. 341; [2009] N.P.C. 96, QBD (Admin) .... *Digested,* 10/**2595**: *Applied* 13/1969, 16/1742, 17/1761: *Considered* 17/1772

Derbyshire Waste Ltd v Blewett see R. (on the application of Blewett) v Derbyshire CC

Dereci v Bundesministerium fur Inneres (C-256/11) EU:C:2011:734; [2011] E.C.R. I-11315; [2012] 1 C.M.L.R. 45; [2012] All E.R. (EC) 373; [2012] Imm. A.R. 230; [2012] I.N.L.R. 151, ECJ (Grand Chamber) *Applied* 15/1318: *Considered* 12/1775, 13/1597, 13/3783, 17/1239: *Followed* 15/1323

Derfshaw Ltd, Re [2011] EWHC 1565 (Ch); [2011] B.C.C. 631; [2012] 1 B.C.L.C. 814; [2011] B.P.I.R. 1289, Ch D .... *Digested,* 11/**1824**: *Applied* 11/1825: *Considered* 12/1804, 17/1268

Deripaska v Cherney [2012] EWCA Civ 1235; [2013] C.P. Rep. 1; (2012) 156(38) S.J.L.B. 31, CA (Civ Div) .... *Digested,* 13/**413**: *Applied* 17/353

Deroo-Blanquart v Sony Europe Ltd (C-310/15) EU:C:2016:633; [2016] 1 W.L.R. 4538; [2017] C.E.C. 513, ECJ (8th Chamber)

Detention Action v First-tier Tribunal (Immigration and Asylum Chamber) see R. (on the application of Detention Action) v First-tier Tribunal (Immigration and Asylum Chamber)

Deutsche Bahn AG v Mastercard Inc [2016] CAT 13; [2017] Comp. A.R. 1, CAT .... *Digested,* 17/**425**

Deutsche Bahn AG v Mastercard Inc; *sub nom* Peugeot Citroen Automobiles UK Ltd v Pilkington Group Ltd [2016] CAT 14; [2017] Bus. L.R. 63; [2017] Comp. A.R. 16, CAT .... *Digested,* 17/**418**

Deutsche Bank (Suisse) SA v Khan [2013] EWHC 482 (Comm), QBD (Comm) *Applied* 17/482

Deutsche Bank AG v Highland Crusader Offshore Partners LP; *sub nom* Highland Crusader Offshore Partners LP v Deutsche Bank AG [2009] EWCA Civ 725; [2010] 1 W.L.R. 1023; [2009] 2 All E.R. (Comm) 987; [2010] Bus. L.R. 515; [2009] 2 Lloyd's Rep. 617; [2009] C.P. Rep. 45; [2009] 2 C.L.C. 45; Times, October 15, 2009, CA (Civ Div) .... *Digested,* 10/**518**: *Applied* 15/2305, 15/445: *Considered* 17/2000: *Followed* 10/516

Deutsche Bank AG v Sebastian Holding Inc [2017] EWHC 913 (Comm); [2017] 6 Costs L.R. 1003, QBD (Comm)

Deutsche Bank AG v Sebastian Holdings Inc [2016] EWHC 3222 (Comm); [2017] 1 W.L.R. 1842, QBD (Comm) .... *Digested,* 17/**380**

Deutsche Bank AG v Sebastian Holdings Inc [2017] EWHC 459 (Comm); [2017] 1 W.L.R. 3056; [2017] I.L.Pr. 39, QBD (Comm) .... *Digested,* 17/**212**

Deutsche Bank AG v Sebastian Holdings Inc [2016] EWCA Civ 23; [2016] 4 W.L.R. 17; [2016] C.P. Rep. 17; Times, February 25, 2016, CA (Civ Div) .... *Digested,* 16/**286**: *Considered* 17/251: *Followed* 16/287, 17/252

Deutsche Bank AG v Unitech Global Ltd [2016] EWCA Civ 119; [2016] 1 W.L.R. 3598; [2017] 1 All E.R. 570; [2016] 2 All E.R. (Comm) 689; [2016] 1 C.L.C. 453, CA (Civ Div) .... *Digested,* 16/**130**

Deutsche Bank AG, London v CIMB Bank Berhad [2017] EWHC 1264 (Comm); [2017] Bus. L.R. 1671, QBD (Comm) .... *Digested,* 17/**166**

Deutsche Bank Group Services (UK) Ltd v Revenue and Customs Commissioners see UBS AG v Revenue and Customs Commissioners

Deutsche Parkinson Vereinigung eV v Zentrale zur Bekampfung unlauteren Wettbewerbs eV (C-148/15) EU:C:2016:776; [2017] 2 C.M.L.R. 1; [2017] C.E.C. 724, ECJ (1st Chamber)

Deutsche Telekom AG v European Commission (T-210/15) EU:T:2017:224; [2017] 4 C.M.L.R. 30, GC (6th Chamber)

Devani v Wells see Wells v Devani

Devaseelan v Secretary of State for the Home Department [2002] UKIAT 702; [2003] Imm. A.R. 1, IAT .... *Digested,* 04/**2013**: *Applied* 02/2577, 04/2009, 07/926, 08/1940, 08/2025, 13/1187: *Considered* 04/2015, 05/2152, 07/2283, 11/1716, 17/2672: *Not applied* 09/358

Devon CC v Kirk [2016] EWCA Civ 1221; [2017] 4 W.L.R. 36, CA (Civ Div) .... *Digested,* 17/**218**

Dexia Crediop SpA v Comune di Prato [2015] EWHC 1746 (Comm), QBD (Comm) *Disapproved* 17/163: *Not followed* 16/135

Dextra Accessories Ltd v MacDonald (Inspector of Taxes); *sub nom* MacDonald (Inspector of Taxes) v Dextra Accessories Ltd [2002] S.T.C. (S.C.D.) 413; [2003] W.T.L.R. 349; [2002] S.T.I. 1335, Sp Comm .... *Digested,* 03/**4233**: *Overruled* 17/2131

Dextra Bank & Trust Co Ltd v Bank of Jamaica [2002] 1 All E.R. (Comm) 193, PC (Jam) .... *Digested,* 02/**252**: *Applied* 04/3267, 17/466: *Considered* 04/3265: *Followed* 03/2418

DF v N B-F see F (A Child) (International Relocation Case), Re

DFC Group AS (Societe) v Calli Invest (Societes) [2017] I.L.Pr. 3, Cass (F)

DHL Express (Austria) GmbH v Post-Control-Kommission (C-2/15) EU:C:2016:880; [2017] 2 C.M.L.R. 10, ECJ (5th Chamber)

Dhunna v Creditsights Ltd; *sub nom* Creditsights Ltd v Dhunna [2014] EWCA Civ 1238; [2015] I.C.R. 105; [2014] I.R.L.R. 953, CA (Civ Div) .... *Digested,* 15/**881**: *Considered* 16/735: *Followed* 17/849

DI v Estate of A [2017] 2 C.M.L.R. 14, HR (DK)

Di Benedetto v Court of Palermo, Italy see Alexander v France

Di Benedetto v Italy see Alexander v France

Diag Human SE v Czech Republic [2013] EWHC 3190 (Comm); [2014] 1 All E.R. (Comm) 605; [2014] 1 Lloyd's Rep. 288, QBD (Comm) .... *Digested,* 14/**127**: *Applied* 17/361

Diamandis v Wills [2015] EWHC 312 (Ch), Ch D *Applied* 17/340

Dibden v France [2014] EWHC 3074 (Admin), QBD (Admin) *Applied* 17/901

Dickie v Khandani [2012] CSOH 122; 2012 G.W.D. 26-546, OH *Considered* 17/2757

Dickins v O2 Plc [2008] EWCA Civ 1144; [2009] I.R.L.R. 58; (2008) 105(41) L.S.G. 19, CA (Civ Div) .... *Digested,* 09/**2833**: *Doubted* 17/826

Dickinson v Cassillas [2017] EWCA Civ 1254; [2017] H.L.R. 43; [2018] 1 P. & C.R. 8; [2018] J.P.L. 144, CA (Civ Div)

Dickinson v NAL Realisations (Staffordshire) Ltd [2017] EWHC 28 (Ch); [2017] B.P.I.R. 611, Ch D (Birmingham) .... *Digested,* 17/**394**

Dickinson v Tesco Plc; *joined cases* Simmonds v Stewart Alexander Group Ltd; Verley v O'Neil; Moonsam v Axa Corporate Solutions Assurances SA [2013] EWCA Civ 36; [2013] C.P. Rep. 24; [2013] R.T.R. 27, CA (Civ Div) .... *Digested,* 13/**408**: *Considered* 17/644

Dickson v United Dominions Trust Ltd (No.4) 1988 S.L.T. 19, OH .... *Digested,* 87/**4913**: *Applied* 95/5485: *Considered* 17/2677: *Referred to* 95/6212

Didymi Corp v Atlantic Lines and Navigation Co Inc (The Didymi) [1988] 2 Lloyd's Rep. 108, CA (Civ Div) .... *Digested,* 89/**3402**: *Applied* 06/682: *Considered* 17/500

Digipos Store Solutions Group Ltd v Digi International Inc [2008] EWHC 3371 (Ch); [2008] Bus. L.R. 1621; [2008] R.P.C. 24, Ch D .... *Digested,* 08/**2397**: *Considered* 17/2690

Dimond v Lovell [2002] 1 A.C. 384; [2000] 2 W.L.R. 1121; [2000] 2 All E.R. 897; [2000] R.T.R. 243; [2000] C.C.L.R. 57; 2000 Rep. L.R. 62; Times, May 12, 2000; Independent, May 17, 2000; (2000) 97(22) L.S.G. 47; (2000) 150 N.L.J. 740, HL .... *Digested,* 00/**2566**: *Applied* 01/1527, 01/881, 01/900, 07/2497, 12/1898, 14/1852, 14/829: *Cited* 00/2574, 00/2593, 01/3830, 01/896, 01/899, 02/685: *Considered* 00/311, 01/885, 01/888, 01/890, 01/898, 06/702, 09/683, 09/970, 11/2258, 14/3473: *Distinguished* 00/2578, 00/2585, 01/893, 01/894, 02/932, 04/630: *Followed* 00/2565, 00/2577, 00/2579, 01/657, 01/887, 01/901, 04/628, 12/1902, 12/2812, 14/610, 15/681, 17/644: *Referred to* 01/1542

Dingle v Associated Newspapers Ltd see Associated Newspapers Ltd v Dingle

Dinsmore (Niall Brian) v HM Advocate [2017] HCJAC 11; 2017 S.L.T. 446; 2017 S.C.L. 411; 2017 G.W.D. 8-121, HCJ .... *Digested,* 17/**2810**

Directia Generala Regionala a Finantelor Publice Brasov v Toma (C-205/15) EU:C:2016:499; [2017] 1 C.M.L.R. 15, ECJ (2nd Chamber)

Director of Legal Aid Casework v Briggs see Briggs (Incapacitated Person), Re

Director of Legal Casework v IS see R. (on the application of S) v Director of Legal Aid Casework

Director of the Assets Recovery Agency v Jackson [2007] EWHC 2553 (QB), QBD *Applied* 10/271, 14/440, 17/209

Director of the Serious Fraud Office v A [2007] EWCA Crim 1927; [2008] Lloyd's Rep. F.C. 30; (2007) 151 S.J.L.B. 1058, CA (Crim Div) *Followed* 17/624

Director of the Serious Fraud Office v Eurasian Natural Resources Corp Ltd [2017] EWHC 1017 (QB); [2017] 1 W.L.R. 4205; [2017] 2 Cr. App. R. 24; [2017] Lloyd's Rep. F.C. 330; [2018] Crim. L.R. 63, QBD .... *Digested,* 17/**530**

Direktor na Direktsia 'Obzhalvane i danachno-osiguritelna praktika' - Sofia v 'Iberdrola Inmobiliaria Real Estate Investments' EOOD (C-132/16) EU:C:2017:683; [2017] B.V.C. 39; [2017] S.T.I. 2102, ECJ (1st Chamber)

Dispute over Option Contracts Following a Party's Insolvency, Re (IX ZR 314/14) [2017] I.L.Pr. 26, BGH (Ger)

Distinctive Care Ltd v Revenue and Customs Commissioners [2016] UKFTT 764 (TC); [2016] 6 Costs L.R. 1091, FTT (Tax) .... *Digested,* 17/**2153**

District Court in Legnica, Poland v Ciureja see Poland v Ciureja

Divine-Bortey v Brent LBC [1998] I.C.R. 886; [1998] I.R.L.R. 525; Times, May 20, 1998; Independent, May 20, 1998; (1998) 95(22) L.S.G. 29; (1998) 142 S.J.L.B. 152, CA (Civ Div) .... *Digested,* 98/**2163**: *Considered* 17/190: *Distinguished* 00/2236: *Doubted* 11/1077

Dixon v Blindley Heath Investments Ltd see Blindley Heath Investments Ltd v Bass

Dixon v Radley House Partnership (A Firm) [2016] EWHC 2511 (TCC); [2017] C.P. Rep. 4; [2016] T.C.L.R. 10; [2016] 5 Costs L.R. 979, QBD (TCC) .... *Digested,* 16/**273**

DJ v Secretary of State for Work and Pensions [2017] UKUT 83 (AAC); [2017] 2 F.C.R. 225, UT (AAC)

DJ&C Withers (Farms) Ltd v Ambic Equipment Ltd see English v Emery Reimbold & Strick Ltd

Djaba v West London Mental Health Trust [2017] EWCA Civ 436; [2018] 1 W.L.R. 1333; (2017) 20 C.C.L. Rep. 264; [2017] M.H.L.R. 345, CA (Civ Div) .... *Digested,* 17/**1541**

Djibouti v Boreh [2016] EWHC 405 (Comm), QBD (Comm) *Applied* 17/458

DK v Secretary of State for Work and Pensions see K v Secretary of State for Work and Pensions

DKH Retail Ltd v H Young Operations Ltd [2014] EWHC 4034 (IPEC); [2016] E.C.D.R. 9; [2015] F.S.R. 21, IPEC .... *Digested,* 15/**1489**: *Considered* 17/1363

DL v SL (Financial Remedy Proceedings: Privacy) [2015] EWHC 2621 (Fam); [2016] 1 W.L.R. 1259; [2016] 2 F.L.R. 552; [2015] Fam. Law 1474, Fam Div .... *Digested,* 16/**818**: *Applied* 16/894, 16/907: *Considered* 17/1029

DM v HM Advocate see M (D) v HM Advocate

DM v SJ (Surrogacy: Parental Order) see M v J

DM & DD MacPherson v Revenue and Customs Commissioners [2015] UKFTT 626 (TC); [2016] S.T.I. 157, FTT (Tax) *Affirmed* 17/2296

DMWSHNZ Ltd v Revenue and Customs Commissioners [2015] EWCA Civ 1036; [2017] S.T.C. 1076; [2015] B.T.C. 32; [2015] S.T.I. 3036, CA (Civ Div) .... *Digested,* 15/**2431**

DNB Banka AS v Valsts Ienemumu Dienests (C-326/15) EU:C:2017:719; [2017] B.V.C. 43, ECJ (4th Chamber)

Do v Immigration Appeal Tribunal see R. (on the application of Ullah) v Special Adjudicator

Do v Secretary of State for the Home Department see R. (on the application of Ullah) v Special Adjudicator

Dobbs v National Bank of Australia 53 C.L.R. 643 *Applied* 73/1546: *Considered* 11/204, 17/2010

Doberman v Watson [2017] EWHC 1708 (Ch); [2017] 4 W.L.R. 103; [2017] H.L.R. 41, Ch D .... *Digested,* 17/**1856**

Dobson v Thames Water Utilities Ltd [2007] EWHC 2021 (TCC); [2008] 2 All E.R. 362; [2007] B.L.R. 465; [2007] T.C.L.R. 7; 116 Con. L.R. 135; [2008] Env. L.R. 21; [2007] H.R.L.R. 45; [2007] C.I.L.L. 2518; [2007] N.P.C. 102, QBD (TCC) .... *Digested,* 07/**2961**: *Applied* 17/2297: *Considered* 11/2275, 13/3251: *Reversed in part* 09/2745

Docherty v Secretary of State for Business, Innovation and Skills [2017] CSOH 54; 2017 S.L.T. 671; 2017 G.W.D. 13-197, OH .... *Digested,* 17/**2448**

Doci v Court of Brescia, Italy see Doci v Italy

Doci v Italy; *sub nom* Motiu v Criminal Court Nowy of Santa Maria Capua Vetere, Italy; Doci v Court of Brescia, Italy; *joined case* Motiu v Italy [2016] EWHC 2100 (Admin); [2017] A.C.D. 21, DC

Dodd v Raebarn Estates Ltd [2017] EWCA Civ 439; [2017] H.L.R. 34; [2017] P.I.Q.R. P19; [2017] 2 P. & C.R. 14; [2017] L. & T.R. 27, CA (Civ Div) .... *Digested,* 17/**1563**

Dodd v Raebarn Estates Ltd [2016] EWHC 262 (QB); [2016] H.L.R. 12; [2016] P.I.Q.R. P16, QBD .... *Digested,* 16/**1536**: *Affirmed* 17/1563

Doe on the demise of Chadborn v Green 112 E.R. 1361; (1839) 9 Ad. & El. 658, KB *Applied* 17/1440

Dogan v Germany (C-138/13) EU:C:2014:2066; [2015] 1 C.M.L.R. 16; [2015] C.E.C. 130, ECJ (2nd Chamber) *Considered* 17/2668

Dogan v Turkey (62649/10) (2017) 64 E.H.R.R. 5, ECHR

Doherty v Fannigan Holdings Ltd [2016] EWHC 2098 (Ch); [2016] B.P.I.R. 1377, Ch D *Reversed* 17/1322

Dollar Financial UK Ltd v Revenue and Customs Commissioners [2016] UKFTT 598 (TC); [2016] S.F.T.D. 953; [2016] S.T.I. 2563, FTT (Tax) .... *Digested,* 17/**2267**

Dollar Land (Calthorpe House) v Customs and Excise Commissioners Ltd see Dollar Land (Feltham) Ltd v Customs and Excise Commissioners

Dollar Land (Cumbernauld) Ltd v CIN Properties Ltd 1998 S.C. (H.L.) 90; 1998 S.L.T. 992; 1998 S.C.L.R. 929; [1998] 3 E.G.L.R. 79; [1998] 51 E.G. 83; Times, August 24, 1998; 1998 G.W.D. 25-1268, HL .... *Digested,* 98/**6034**: *Applied* 17/2772: *Distinguished* 02/6152: *Followed* 00/6634

Dollar Land (Cumbernauld) Ltd v Customs and Excise Commissioners see Dollar Land (Feltham) Ltd v Customs and Excise Commissioners

Dollar Land (Feltham) Ltd v Customs and Excise Commissioners; *joined cases* Dollar Land (Cumbernauld) Ltd v Customs and Excise Commissioners; Dollar Land (Calthorpe House) v Customs and Excise Commissioners Ltd [1995] S.T.C. 414, QBD .... *Digested,* 95/**5011**: *Applied* 17/2170

Dollfus Mieg et Compagnie SA v Bank of England (No.1); *sub nom* United States v Dollfus Mieg et Cie SA [1952] A.C. 582; [1952] 1 All E.R. 572; [1952] 1 T.L.R. 541; (1952) 96 S.J. 180, HL .... *Digested,* 52/**2766**: *Applied* 54/2627, 56/6899, 56/6979, 57/2864, 61/8865, 63/3545, 75/364: *Considered* 08/341, 17/1426

Dolphin Maritime & Aviation Services Ltd v Sveriges Angartygs see Dolphin Maritime & Aviation Services Ltd v Sveriges Angfartygs Assurans Forening

Dolphin Maritime & Aviation Services Ltd v Sveriges Angfartygs Assurans Forening; *sub nom* Dolphin Maritime & Aviation Services Ltd v Sveriges Angartygs [2009] EWHC 716 (Comm); [2010] 1 All E.R. (Comm) 473; [2009] 2 Lloyd's Rep. 123; [2009] 1 C.L.C. 460; [2009] I.L.Pr. 52, QBD (Comm) .... *Digested,* 09/**618**: *Applied* 14/556: *Considered* 16/721, 17/2022: *Distinguished* 15/438

Domicrest Ltd v Swiss Bank Corp [1999] Q.B. 548; [1999] 2 W.L.R. 364; [1998] 3 All E.R. 577; [1999] 1 Lloyd's Rep. 80; [1998] C.L.C. 1451; [1999] I.L.Pr. 146; Times, July 16, 1998; Independent, July 20, 1998, QBD .... *Digested,* 98/**770**: *Applied* 07/672, 17/160: *Considered* 06/646, 16/2145

Donald Kenyon Ltd, Re see Kenyon (Donald), Re

Donaldson v Revenue and Customs Commissioners see Revenue and Customs Commissioners v Donaldson

Donnelly v Royal Bank of Scotland Plc [2017] SAC (Civ) 1; 2017 S.L.T. (Sh Ct) 41; [2017] B.P.I.R. 400; 2017 G.W.D. 2-22, SAC .... *Digested,* 17/**2678**

Donnelly v Royal Bank of Scotland Plc 2016 S.L.T. (Sh Ct) 307; [2016] B.P.I.R. 606; 2016 G.W.D. 8-159, Sh Ct (Glasgow) .... *Digested,* 16/**2694**: *Reversed in part* 17/2678

Donnelly (Brian) v HM Advocate 2000 S.C.C.R. 861, HCJ Appeal .... *Digested,* 01/**6391**: *Considered* 17/2505: *Overruled* 17/2559

Donoghue v Stevenson; *sub nom* McAlister v Stevenson [1932] A.C. 562; 1932 S.C. (H.L.) 31; 1932 S.L.T. 317; [1932] W.N. 139, HL
Applied 47-51/6681, 47-51/6693, 47-51/6761, 47-51/6881, 47-51/6897, 52/1563, 52/2362, 53/2422, 53/639, 56/904, 57/1415, 57/2371, 61/825, 62/2028, 62/2188, 63/2362, 64/1670, 65/2669, 65/416, 68/4511, 69/2403, 70/1493, 70/1850, 72/1104, 72/2350, 72/2352, 72/2408, 72/2409, 74/2579, 75/3994, 75/933, 77/2025, 78/2065, 78/3538, 81/1849, 82/2135, 85/2301, 87/2579, 88/3410, 89/1286, 01/4509, 04/2747, 07/5426, 14/3697: *Considered* 47-51/351, 47-51/6734, 47-51/9691, 54/2200, 55/1839, 57/2369, 62/2083, 62/3080, 63/2416, 65/2663, 65/2671, 69/1157, 70/1849, 72/2528, 74/363, 74/3638, 75/2343, 76/228, 78/2088, 87/2580, 88/2418, 88/2433, 88/3376, 88/3409, 91/2657, 91/2661, 93/2983, 93/2997, 94/5335, 95/3698, 95/4519, 98/3995, 99/3960, 00/4227, 17/2193: *Distinguished* 47-51/6584, 47-51/6705, 47-51/7886, 51/3988, 52/4290, 57/2366, 57/2639, 63/2360, 63/330, 64/2516, 66/6884, 72/2361, 83/2746: *Followed* 76/3296, 85/4437, 11/2270, 11/4487: *Referred to* 79/1866

Doolan v United Kingdom (30678/96) see Wilson v United Kingdom (30668/96)

Dooneen Ltd (t/a McGinnes Associates) v Mond [2016] CSOH 23; 2016 G.W.D. 5-122, OH
Affirmed 17/2845: *Followed* 17/2678

Dooneen Ltd (t/a McGinnes Associates) v Mond [2016] CSIH 59; 2017 S.C.L.R. 199; [2017] B.P.I.R. 380; 2016 G.W.D. 23-441, IH (2 Div) .... *Digested,* 17/**2845**: *Followed* 17/2678

Doran Bros (London) Ltd v Revenue and Customs Commissioners [2016] UKFTT 829 (TC); [2017] S.T.I. 171, FTT (Tax)

Dorr v Sicherheitsdirektion fur das Bundesland Karnten (C136/03); *joined case* Unal v Sicherheitsdirektion fur das Bundesland Vorarlberg (C136/03) EU:C:2005:340; [2005] E.C.R. I-4759; [2005] 3 C.M.L.R. 11, ECJ (3rd Chamber) .... *Digested,* 06/**1587**: *Applied* 17/1230

Dorset Healthcare NHS Foundation Trust v MH [2009] UKUT 4 (AAC); [2009] P.T.S.R. 1112; (2010) 11 B.M.L.R. 1; [2009] M.H.L.R. 102, UT (AAC)
Applied 17/1830

Dosanjh (Setting of Minimum Term), Re see Jones (Setting of Minimum Term), Re

Douglas v Hello! Ltd (No.1) [2001] Q.B. 967; [2001] 2 W.L.R. 992; [2001] 2 All E.R. 289; [2001] E.M.L.R. 9; [2001] 1 F.L.R. 982; [2002] 1 F.C.R. 289; [2001] H.R.L.R. 26; [2001] U.K.H.R.R. 223; 9 B.H.R.C. 543; [2001] F.S.R. 40; Times, January 16, 2001; Daily Telegraph, January 9, 2001, CA (Civ Div) .... *Digested,* 01/**567**: *Applied* 01/2583, 04/1391, 08/1992: *Considered* 01/1824, 03/2923, 03/2941, 03/4363, 17/342

Douglas v Hello! Ltd see OBG Ltd v Allan

Dove v Havering LBC [2017] EWCA Civ 156; [2017] P.T.S.R. 1233; [2017] H.L.R. 19; [2017] 2 P. & C.R. 18; [2017] 2 P. & C.R. DG7, CA (Civ Div) .... *Digested,* 17/**1465**

Dow Jones & Co Inc v Jameel see Jameel v Dow Jones & Co Inc

Dowden v Stack see Stack v Dowden

Dowding v Matchmove Ltd see Matchmove Ltd v Dowding

Dowling v Minister for Finance (C-41/15) EU:C:2016:836; [2017] Bus. L.R. 1083; [2017] 3 C.M.L.R. 27, ECJ (Grand Chamber)

Dowling v Promontoria (Arrow) Ltd [2017] B.P.I.R. 1477, Ch D (Bankruptcy Ct)

Dowsett Securities Ltd v United Kingdom (9405/81) see Lithgow v United Kingdom (A/102)

DP v General Dental Council see R. (on the application of P) v General Dental Council
DP Holding SA (In Provisional Liquidation), Re; *sub nom* Hellard v Chen [2017] B.P.I.R. 687, Ch D (Companies Ct) .... *Digested,* 17/**1312**
DPP v D [2017] EWHC 2244 (Admin); [2017] 4 W.L.R. 177; [2018] 1 Cr. App. R. 13; (2018) 182 J.P. 1; [2018] Crim. L.R. 170; [2017] A.C.D. 121, DC .... *Digested,* 17/**563**
DPP v Jones (Margaret) [1999] 2 A.C. 240; [1999] 2 W.L.R. 625; [1999] 2 All E.R. 257; [1999] 2 Cr. App. R. 348; (1999) 163 J.P. 285; 6 B.H.R.C. 513; Times, March 5, 1999; Independent, March 9, 1999; [1999] Crim. L.R. 672; (1999) 163 J.P.N. 355; [1999] E.G. 36 (C.S.); (1999) 96(13) L.S.G. 31; (1999) 96(11) L.S.G. 71; (1999) 143 S.J.L.B. 98; [1999] N.P.C. 31, HL .... *Digested,* 99/**965**: *Applied* 10/2770: *Followed* 17/1860
DPP v Kang see DPP v Vince
DPP v SK [2016] EWHC 837 (Admin); (2017) 181 J.P. 197; [2017] Crim. L.R. 226, DC
DPP v Smith [2017] EWHC 359 (Admin); (2017) 181 J.P. 258, DC
DPP v Vince; *sub nom* DPP v Kang; *joined case* Kang v DPP [2016] EWHC 3014 (Admin); [2017] 4 W.L.R. 3; (2018) 182 J.P. 154; [2017] R.T.R. 7; [2017] Crim. L.R. 307; [2017] A.C.D. 8, DC .... *Digested,* 17/**509**
DPP v Woods [2017] EWHC 1070 (Admin); (2017) 181 J.P. 395; [2017] A.C.D. 72, DC .... *Digested,* 17/**628**
Dr Jacek Trzaski Ltd v Revenue and Customs Commissioners see Christianuyi Ltd v Revenue and Customs Commissioners
Drake Insurance Plc (In Provisional Liquidation) v Provident Insurance Plc [2003] EWCA Civ 1834; [2004] Q.B. 601; [2004] 2 W.L.R. 530; [2004] 2 All E.R. (Comm) 65; [2004] 1 Lloyd's Rep. 268; [2004] 1 C.L.C. 574; [2004] R.T.R. 19; [2004] Lloyd's Rep. I.R. 277, CA (Civ Div) .... *Digested,* 04/**2228**: *Applied* 14/1850: *Considered* 04/192, 08/2386, 17/1354
Drew v Insure the Box Ltd (Unreported, August 3, 2017), CC (Bristol) [*Irwin Mitchell LLP, Riverside West, 1 Millsands, Sheffield*] .... *Digested,* 17/**1647**
Driver and Vehicle Standards Agency v Rowe [2017] EWHC 608 (Admin); [2018] R.T.R. 2; [2017] L.L.R. 444, QBD (Admin) .... *Digested,* 17/**1882**
Droma v Germany see Kandola v Germany
Droma v State Prosecutor Nurnburg-Furth, Bavaria see Kandola v Germany
Dronsfield v Reading University; *sub nom* Dronsfield v University of Reading [2016] I.C.R. 1107, EAT .... *Digested,* 17/**852**
Dronsfield v University of Reading see Dronsfield v Reading University
Drown v Revenue and Customs Commissioners [2017] UKUT 111 (TCC); [2017] B.T.C. 512, UT (Tax) .... *Digested,* 17/**2172**
Drown v Revenue and Customs Commissioners [2014] UKFTT 892 (TC); [2015] W.T.L.R. 775; [2014] S.T.I. 3707, FTT (Tax) .... *Digested,* 15/**2492**: *Reversed* 17/2172
Drummond v Revenue and Customs Commissioners [2016] UKUT 221 (TCC); [2017] 1 W.L.R. 2185; [2016] 4 All E.R. 884; [2016] S.T.C. 1870; [2016] C.P. Rep. 34; [2016] B.V.C. 517, UT (Tax) .... *Digested,* 16/**246**
Dry Log Bulk Carriers v Phaethon International Co SA [2016] EWHC 3798 (Comm); [2017] 2 Lloyd's Rep. 385, QBD (Comm) .... *Digested,* 17/**2004**
DS v HM Advocate see S (D) v HM Advocate
DSV Silo und Verwaltungsgesellschaft mbH v Owners of the Sennar (The Sennar) (No.2) [1985] 1 W.L.R. 490; [1985] 2 All E.R. 104; [1985] 1 Lloyd's Rep. 521; (1985) 82 L.S.G. 1863; (1985) 135 N.L.J. 316; (1985) 129 S.J. 248, HL .... *Digested,* 85/**1291**: *Applied* 90/2019, 95/3559, 10/1976, 17/346: *Considered* 86/3078, 00/785: *Followed* 11/139, 16/433
DTEK Finance Plc, Re [2016] EWHC 3562 (Ch); [2017] B.C.C. 165, Ch D (Companies Ct) .... *Digested,* 17/**1321**
Dtek Trading SA v Morozov [2017] EWHC 94 (Comm); [2017] Bus. L.R. 628; [2017] 1 Lloyd's Rep. 126; [2017] 1 C.L.C. 53, QBD (Comm) .... *Digested,* 17/**334**
DU PONT Trade Mark see ST Dupont v El du Pont de Nemours & Co
Dubai Aluminium Co Ltd v Amhurst Brown Martin & Nicholson see Dubai Aluminium Co Ltd v Salaam
Dubai Aluminium Co Ltd v Salaam; *joined case* Dubai Aluminium Co Ltd v Amhurst Brown Martin & Nicholson [2002] UKHL 48; [2003] 2 A.C. 366; [2002] 3 W.L.R. 1913; [2003] 1 All E.R. 97; [2003] 2 All E.R. (Comm) 451; [2003] 1 Lloyd's Rep. 65; [2003] 1 B.C.L.C. 32; [2003] 1 C.L.C. 1020; [2003] I.R.L.R. 608; [2003] W.T.L.R. 163; Times, December 6, 2002; Independent, December 10, 2002; (2003) 100(7) L.S.G. 36; (2002) 146 S.J.L.B. 280, HL .... *Digested,* 03/**3046**: *Applied* 03/3033, 03/3045, 05/4199, 05/4200, 06/1337, 06/2915, 06/543, 07/4248, 08/3897, 08/3906, 15/2531: *Considered* 08/3953, 12/3344, 14/2991: *Distinguished* 03/3613: *Followed* 09/265, 11/3476, 16/2146, 17/219

Dublin City Distillery Ltd v Doherty [1914] A.C. 823, HL (UK-Irl)
Followed 17/1997

Dubska v Czech Republic (28859/11); *joined case* Krejzova v Czech Republic (28473/12) (2017) 65 E.H.R.R. 5; 42 B.H.R.C. 654, ECHR (Grand Chamber)

Dudley MBC v Willetts [2018] I.C.R. 31; [2017] I.R.L.R. 870, EAT .... *Digested,* 17/**805**

Duggan v Revenue and Customs Commissioners [2015] UKFTT 125 (TC), FTT (Tax)
Affirmed 17/631

Duggan v Revenue and Customs Commissioners see McKeown v Revenue and Customs Commissioners

Dukali v Lamrani [2012] EWHC 1748 (Fam); [2012] 2 F.L.R. 1099; [2012] 2 F.C.R. 574; [2012] Fam. Law 1205, Fam Div .... *Digested,* 12/**1443**:
Approved 13/1299: *Considered* 14/2008, 17/1043

Dulas (Michael) v HM Advocate [2016] HCJAC 91; 2016 S.C.L. 994; 2016 G.W.D. 32-583, HCJ .... *Digested,* 17/**2796**

Dumez France SA v Hessische Landesbank (220/88) EU:C:1990:8; [1990] E.C.R. I-49; [1990] I.L.Pr. 299, ECJ (6th Chamber)
Applied 09/618, 10/3410, 14/556, 15/438, 17/2022: *Considered* 91/3931, 06/646, 16/191: *Explained* 14/542: *Followed* 17/430

Dumrul v Standard Chartered Bank [2010] EWHC 2625 (Comm); [2010] 2 C.L.C. 661, QBD (Comm) .... *Digested,* 11/**382**:
Applied 14/407: *Considered* 17/362

Dunbar Assets Plc v Dorcas Holdings Ltd [2013] EWCA Civ 864, CA (Civ Div)
Applied 17/1290

Duncan's Hotel (Glasgow) Ltd v J&A Ferguson Ltd 1974 S.C. 191, OH
Applied 17/2464: *Considered* 97/6073

Duncombe v Department for Education and Skills see Duncombe v Secretary of State for Children, Schools and Families

Duncombe v Secretary of State for Children, Schools and Families; *sub nom* Duncombe v Department for Education and Skills; Secretary of State for Children, Schools and Families v Fletcher UKEAT/0433/07/DM, EAT
Considered 17/850: *Reversed in part* 10/1036

Duncombe v Secretary of State for Children, Schools and Families [2011] UKSC 36; [2011] 4 All E.R. 1020; [2011] I.C.R. 1312; [2011] I.R.L.R. 840; Times, August 1, 2011, SC .... *Digested,* 11/**1134**:
Applied 13/1075, 16/673: *Considered* 12/1176: *Followed* 15/880, 15/881, 16/735, 17/849

Dunhill v Hughmans (A Firm) [2017] EWHC 2073 (Ch); [2017] 5 Costs L.O. 589; [2018] B.P.I.R. 59, Ch D .... *Digested,* 17/**269**

Dunlea v Cashwell [2017] SAC (Civ) 12; 2017 S.C.L.R. 675; 2017 G.W.D. 13-207, SAC .... *Digested,* 17/**2654**

Dunn v Parole Board for England and Wales [2008] EWCA Civ 374; [2009] 1 W.L.R. 728; [2008] H.R.L.R. 32; [2008] U.K.H.R.R. 711; [2009] Prison L.R. 67, CA (Civ Div) .... *Digested,* 08/**2680**:
Followed 17/299

Dunne v English (1874) L.R. 18 Eq. 524, Ct of Chancery
Considered 17/1585

Dunnett Investments Ltd v Secretary of State for Communities and Local Government [2017] EWCA Civ 192; [2017] J.P.L. 848, CA (Civ Div) .... *Digested,* 17/**1749**

Dunnett Investments Ltd v Secretary of State for Communities and Local Government [2016] EWHC 534 (Admin), QBD (Admin)
Affirmed 17/1749

Dunoon Developments v Secretary of State for the Environment and Poole BC (1993) 65 P. & C.R. 101; [1992] 2 P.L.R. 128; [1992] J.P.L. 936; [1992] E.G. 24 (C.S.); [1992] N.P.C. 22, CA (Civ Div) .... *Digested,* 93/**3943**:
Considered 14/2408, 17/1749

Dunsire (Lee) v HM Advocate [2017] HCJAC 30; 2017 S.C.L. 611; 2017 S.C.C.R. 348; 2017 G.W.D. 17-267, HCJ Appeal .... *Digested,* 17/**2476**

Dunthorne v Bentley [1996] R.T.R. 428; [1996] P.I.Q.R. P323; Times, March 11, 1996, CA (Civ Div) .... *Digested,* 96/**5652**:
Considered 12/1900, 16/1266, 17/1347: *Distinguished* 99/4070: *Followed* 13/1744, 17/1877

Duomatic Ltd, Re [1969] 2 Ch. 365; [1969] 2 W.L.R. 114; [1969] 1 All E.R. 161; (1968) 112 S.J. 922, Ch D .... *Digested,* 69/**412**:
Applied 74/321, 80/268, 80/269, 99/607, 00/654, 01/748, 03/540, 04/472, 07/572, 07/588, 11/409, 11/413, 14/510, 14/512, 15/409, 16/1583, 16/333: *Considered* 98/704, 02/556, 04/458, 05/470, 08/3792, 08/494, 17/387, 17/409: *Distinguished* 90/487, 07/321

Durant v Financial Services Authority (Disclosure) [2003] EWCA Civ 1746; [2004] F.S.R. 28; Times, January 2, 2004, CA (Civ Div) .... *Digested,* 04/**1551**: *Applied* 10/463, 16/1057, 17/1171: *Considered* 07/4889, 17/1165: *Followed* 17/1112

Durkin v HSBC Bank Plc [2016] CSIH 93; 2017 S.L.T. 125; 2017 S.C.L.R. 731; 2017 G.W.D. 1-3, IH (Ex Div) .... *Digested,* 17/**2412**

Durojaiye v Secretary of State for the Home Department [1991] Imm. A.R. 307, CA (Civ Div) .... *Digested,* 92/**2403**: *Applied* 17/1225: *Cited* 94/2498: *Followed* 98/3234

Durrant v Chief Constable of Avon and Somerset [2013] EWCA Civ 1624; [2014] 1 W.L.R. 4313; [2014] 2 All E.R. 757; [2014] C.P. Rep. 11; [2014] 1 Costs L.R. 130, CA (Civ Div) .... *Digested,* 14/**463**: *Applied* 14/462, 14/9: *Approved* 17/2182: *Considered* 14/451, 14/461, 16/324: *Followed* 14/457

Dutton v FDR Ltd; *sub nom* FDR Ltd v Dutton [2015] EWHC 2946 (Ch); [2015] Pens. L.R. 569, Ch D .... *Digested,* 16/**1579**: *Reversed* 17/1612

Dutton v FDR Ltd; *sub nom* FDR Ltd v Dutton [2017] EWCA Civ 200; [2017] Pens. L.R. 14, CA (Civ Div) .... *Digested,* 17/**1612**

Dutton v Minards [2015] EWCA Civ 984; [2015] 6 Costs L.R. 1047, CA (Civ Div) .... *Digested,* 16/**222**: *Followed* 17/258

DW v CG see W v G (Financial Provision: Conditional Order for Sale: Equitable Interest)

Dwr Cymru (Welsh Water) v Carmarthenshire CC [2004] EWHC 2991 (TCC), QBD (TCC) *Applied* 15/314: *Considered* 17/2219

Dwr Cymru Cyfyngedig (Welsh Water) v Barratt Homes Ltd; *sub nom* Barratt Homes Ltd v Dwr Cymru Cyfyngedig (Welsh Water) [2013] EWCA Civ 233; [2013] 1 W.L.R. 3486; 147 Con. L.R. 1; [2013] Env. L.R. 30, CA (Civ Div) .... *Digested,* 13/**3251**: *Distinguished* 17/2297

Dyer v Dorset CC [1989] Q.B. 346; [1988] 3 W.L.R. 213; (1988) 20 H.L.R. 490; 86 L.G.R. 686; [1989] R.V.R. 41; (1988) 152 L.G. Rev. 992; [1988] E.G. 75 (C.S.); (1988) 85(25) L.S.G. 43; (1988) 132 S.J. 934, CA (Civ Div) .... *Digested,* 88/**1758**: *Applied* 94/4335, 03/3378, 17/1737: *Considered* 92/2313, 95/4860, 00/4450, 00/4473

Dyer v Revenue and Customs Commissioners [2013] UKFTT 691 (TC), FTT (Tax) *Affirmed* 17/2096

Dyer v Revenue and Customs Commissioners [2016] UKUT 381 (TCC); [2017] S.T.C. 189; [2016] B.T.C. 518; [2016] S.T.I. 2543, UT (Tax) .... *Digested,* 17/**2096**

Dymocks Franchise Systems (NSW) Pty Ltd v Todd (Costs) [2004] UKPC 39; [2004] 1 W.L.R. 2807; [2005] 4 All E.R. 195; [2005] 1 Costs L.R. 52; (2004) 154 N.L.J. 1325; (2004) 148 S.J.L.B. 971, PC (NZ) .... *Digested,* 04/**328**: *Applied* 06/395, 07/379, 07/405, 07/420, 09/384, 10/327, 11/293, 12/376, 13/1928, 16/286, 17/254: *Considered* 06/374, 06/417, 07/387, 07/404, 07/421, 07/428, 08/327, 08/328, 11/292, 12/2083, 13/317, 13/318, 15/236, 16/287, 17/250, 17/336: *Referred to* 15/375

Dyna-Jet Pte Ltd v Wilson Taylor Asia Pacific Pte Ltd; *sub nom* Wilson Taylor Asia Pacific Pte Ltd v Dyna-Jet Pte Ltd [2017] SGCA 32; [2017] 2 Lloyd's Rep. 104, CA (Sing)

Dyna-Jet Pte Ltd v Wilson Taylor Asia Pacific Pte Ltd; *sub nom* Wilson Taylor Asia Pacific Pte Ltd v Dyna-Jet Pte Ltd [2016] SGHC 238; [2017] 1 Lloyd's Rep. 59, HC (Sing)

Dynamics Corp of America (In Liquidation) (No.2), Re [1976] 1 W.L.R. 757; [1976] 2 All E.R. 669; (1976) 120 S.J. 450, Ch D .... *Digested,* 76/**273**: *Applied* 16/1168: *Considered* 81/260, 15/1395: *Followed* 82/335: *Not applied* 17/1259

Dyson Ltd v Registrar of Trade Marks (C-321/03) EU:C:2007:51; [2007] Bus. L.R. 787; [2007] E.C.R. I-687; [2007] 2 C.M.L.R. 14; [2007] C.E.C. 223; [2007] E.T.M.R. 34; [2007] R.P.C. 27, ECJ (3rd Chamber) .... *Digested,* 07/**1580**: *Applied* 13/1758: *Considered* 14/1934, 17/1387

Dzhurayev v Russia (71386/10) (2013) 57 E.H.R.R. 22, ECHR *Considered* 14/3521, 15/101: *Not applied* 17/83

E v E; *sub nom* FE v YE [2017] EWHC 2165 (Fam); [2018] Fam. 24; [2018] 2 W.L.R. 200; [2018] 1 F.L.R. 689; [2017] 3 F.C.R. 331, Fam Div .... *Digested,* 17/**1036**

E v E (BIIA: Arts 16 and 19) see E v E (Jurisdiction: Lis Pendens)

E v E (Jurisdiction: Lis Pendens); *sub nom* E v E (BIIA: Arts 16 and 19) [2015] EWHC 3742 (Fam); [2017] 1 F.L.R. 658; [2016] Fam. Law 301, Fam Div

E v E see CE (Female Genital Mutilation), Re

E v HM Advocate; *sub nom* AJE v HM Advocate 2002 J.C. 215; 2002 S.L.T. 715; 2002 S.C.C.R. 341; 2002 G.W.D. 13-407, HCJ .... *Digested,* 02/**5526**: *Applied* 17/2532: *Considered* 03/5380, 10/4045, 16/2495: *Distinguished* 03/5379, 15/2943

E v Refugee Applications Commissioner (C-493/10) see R. (on the application of NS) v Secretary of State for the Home Department (C-411/10)

E v Secretary of State for the Home Department; *joined case* R v Secretary of State for the Home Department [2004] EWCA Civ 49; [2004] Q.B. 1044; [2004] 2 W.L.R. 1351; [2004] I.N.L.R. 268; [2004] B.L.G.R. 463; Times, February 9, 2004; Independent, February 4, 2004; (2004) 101(7) L.S.G. 35; (2004) 148 S.J.L.B. 180, CA (Civ Div) .... *Digested,* 04/**2030**: *Applied* 05/2208, 05/2213, 06/1216, 06/2269, 07/1256, 09/1789, 09/2083, 10/2594, 10/73, 13/2272, 17/1754: *Considered* 06/2212, 06/2225, 13/1594: *Followed* 05/2215, 05/2224, 15/1324

E (A Child) (Brussels II Revised: Vienna Convention: Reporting Restriction), Re see E (A Child) (Care Proceedings: European Dimension), Re

E (A Child) (Care Proceedings: European Dimension), Re; *sub nom* E (A Child) (Brussels II Revised: Vienna Convention: Reporting Restriction), Re; E (A Child) (Care Proceedings: Jurisdiction), Re [2014] EWHC 6 (Fam); [2014] 1 W.L.R. 2670; [2014] 2 F.L.R. 151; [2014] 2 F.C.R. 264; [2014] Fam. Law 425, Fam Div .... *Digested,* 14/**1344**: *Applied* 15/993, 16/850: *Considered* 15/1040, 17/960, 17/980: *Followed* 16/805

E (A Child) (Care Proceedings: Jurisdiction), Re see E (A Child) (Care Proceedings: European Dimension), Re

E (A Child) (Care Proceedings: Live Oral Evidence from Children), Re see E (A Child) (Family Proceedings: Evidence), Re

E (A Child) (Care Proceedings: Placement Outside Jurisdiction), Re; *sub nom* A Local Authority v Father [2017] 4 W.L.R. 99, Fam Div .... *Digested,* 17/**932**

E (A Child) (Family Proceedings: Evidence), Re; *sub nom* E (A Child) (Care Proceedings: Live Oral Evidence from Children), Re [2016] EWCA Civ 473; [2016] 4 W.L.R. 105; [2017] 1 F.L.R. 1675; [2016] 3 F.C.R. 499; [2016] Crim. L.R. 649; [2016] Fam. Law 953, CA (Civ Div) .... *Digested,* 16/**857**: *Considered* 17/1548

E (A Child) (Medical Treatment), Re [2016] EWHC 2267 (Fam); [2017] 1 F.L.R. 645; (2016) 152 B.M.L.R. 207; [2016] Fam. Law 1325, Fam Div .... *Digested,* 17/**968**

E (A Child) (Wardship Order: Child in Voluntary Accommodation), Re [2012] EWCA Civ 1773; [2013] 2 F.L.R. 63; [2013] Fam. Law 399, CA (Civ Div) .... *Digested,* 13/**1347**: *Considered* 17/1070

E (Family Assistance Order), Re [1999] 2 F.L.R. 512; [1999] 3 F.C.R. 700; [1999] Fam. Law 529; (2000) 164 J.P.N. 762, Fam Div .... *Digested,* 99/**2379**: *Considered* 17/1057

E Buyer UK Ltd v Revenue and Customs Commissioners; *joined case* Revenue and Customs Commissioners v Citibank NA [2016] UKUT 123 (TCC); [2016] S.T.C. 1533; [2016] Lloyd's Rep. F.C. 225; [2016] B.V.C. 510, UT (Tax) .... *Digested,* 16/**2169**: *Reversed* 17/2252

E-R (Children) (Child Arrangements), Re [2016] EWHC 805 (Fam); [2017] 2 F.L.R. 501; [2016] Fam. Law 665, Fam Div

E1 (OS Russia) v Secretary of State for the Home Department see R. (on the application of E (Russia)) v Secretary of State for the Home Department

Ealing LBC v R. (on the application of H) see R. (on the application of H) v Ealing LBC

Ealing LBC v Revenue and Customs Commissioners (C-633/15) EU:C:2017:544; [2017] 4 W.L.R. 174; [2017] S.T.C. 1598; [2017] B.V.C. 35; Times, September 8, 2017; [2017] S.T.I. 1721, ECJ (4th Chamber) .... *Digested,* 17/**2239**

Eames v Dacorum BC [2017] P.A.D. 30, Planning Inspector

Earlsferry Thistle Golf Club v Revenue and Customs Commissioners; *sub nom* Revenue and Customs Commissioners v Earlsferry Thistle Golf Club [2014] UKUT 250 (TCC); [2014] S.T.C. 2498; [2014] B.V.C. 520; [2014] S.T.I. 2221, UT (Tax) .... *Digested,* 15/**2577**: *Considered* 17/2269

Early (Gerald Patrick) v HM Advocate [2006] HCJAC 65; 2007 J.C. 50; 2006 S.L.T. 856; 2006 S.C.C.R. 583; 2006 G.W.D. 28-623, HCJ .... *Digested,* 06/**5205**: *Applied* 07/5046, 10/4078, 17/2521: *Cited* 08/4646: *Considered* 07/5068, 09/4798, 16/2535, 17/2520: *Followed* 09/4772

Ease Faith Ltd v Leonis Marine Management Ltd [2006] EWHC 232 (Comm); [2006] 2 All E.R. (Comm) 422; [2006] 1 Lloyd's Rep. 673; [2006] 1 C.L.C. 345, QBD (Comm) .... *Digested,* 06/**3940**: *Applied* 17/2008

East Hertfordshire DC v Secretary of State for Communities and Local Government [2017] EWHC 465 (Admin); [2017] P.T.S.R. 714; [2017] 2 P. & C.R. 13, QBD (Admin) .... *Digested,* 17/**1693**

East Lothian Council v S; *sub nom* East Lothian Council, Petitioner [2012] CSIH 3; 2012 Fam. L.R. 7; 2012 G.W.D. 7-125, IH (Ex Div) .... *Digested,* 12/**4025**: *Applied* 17/917

East Lothian Council, Petitioner see East Lothian Council v S

East Midlands SHA v Nottingham City Council see Peters v East Midlands SHA

East Northamptonshire DC v Secretary of State for Communities and Local Government; *joined case* Barnwell Manor Wind Energy Ltd v East Northamptonshire DC [2014] EWCA Civ 137; [2015] 1 W.L.R. 45; [2014] 1 P. & C.R. 22; [2014] 2 E.G.L.R. 85; [2014] J.P.L. 731; [2014] A.C.D. 80, CA (Civ Div) .... *Digested,* 14/**2388**: *Applied* 15/2043, 16/1743, 17/1759: *Explained* 16/1737: *Followed* 15/2018, 17/1721

East Renfrewshire Council, Appellant [2016] SAC (Civ) 14; 2017 Fam. L.R. 23; 2016 G.W.D. 38-679, SAC .... *Digested,* 17/**2606**

East Staffordshire BC v Secretary of State for Communities and Local Government; *sub nom* Barwood Strategic Land II LLP v East Staffordshire BC [2016] EWHC 2973 (Admin); [2017] P.T.S.R. 386, QBD (Admin) *Affirmed* 17/1779: *Applied* 17/1767, 17/1769

East Staffordshire BC v Secretary of State for Communities and Local Government; *sub nom* Barwood Strategic Land II LLP v East Staffordshire BC [2017] EWCA Civ 893; [2018] P.T.S.R. 88; [2018] 1 P. & C.R. 4; [2017] J.P.L. 1378, CA (Civ Div) .... *Digested,* 17/**1779**

East Sussex CC v TW; *sub nom* East Sussex CC v W [2016] UKUT 528 (AAC); [2017] P.T.S.R. 755; [2017] E.L.R. 119, UT (AAC) .... *Digested,* 17/**710**

East Sussex CC v W see East Sussex CC v TW

Eastbourne BC v Allen (Valuation Officer) [2001] R.A. 273, Lands Tr .... *Digested,* 02/**3799**: *Applied* 17/1526

Eastern European Engineering Ltd v Vijay Construction (Proprietary) Ltd [2017] EWHC 797 (Comm); [2018] 1 All E.R. (Comm) 410; [2017] Bus. L.R. 1261; [2017] 1 Lloyd's Rep. 661, QBD (Comm) .... *Digested,* 17/**82**

Eastern Power Networks Plc v Revenue and Customs Commissioners; *joined cases* UK Power Networks (Transport) Ltd v Revenue and Customs Commissioners; South Eastern Power Networks Plc v Revenue and Customs Commissioners; London Power Networks Plc v Revenue and Customs Commissioners [2017] UKFTT 494 (TC); [2017] S.T.I. 1723, FTT (Tax)

Eastman v Tesco Stores Ltd UKEAT/0143/12/SM, EAT *Not followed* 17/821

Eastwood (Deceased), Re; *sub nom* Lloyds Bank Ltd v Eastwood [1975] Ch. 112; [1974] 3 W.L.R. 454; [1974] 3 All E.R. 603; [1997] Costs L.R. (Core Vol.) 50; (1974) 118 S.J. 533, CA (Civ Div) .... *Digested,* 74/**2927**: *Applied* 76/2129, 81/837, 94/4556, 95/4019, 99/393, 00/390, 10/3986, 14/1073, 17/268: *Considered* 83/2915: *Followed* 16/1370

Easy Air Ltd (t/a Openair) v Opal Telecom Ltd see Easyair Ltd (t/a Openair) v Opal Telecom Ltd

Easyair Ltd (t/a Openair) v Opal Telecom Ltd; *sub nom* Easy Air Ltd (t/a Openair) v Opal Telecom Ltd [2009] EWHC 339 (Ch), Ch D (Manchester) *Applied* 16/1558, 17/371

Easynet Global Services Ltd, Re [2016] EWHC 2681 (Ch); [2017] B.C.C. 20, Ch D (Companies Ct) .... *Digested,* 17/**392**: *Considered* 17/396

Eatherley v Camden LBC; *sub nom* Eatherley v Camden LBC [2016] EWHC 3108 (Admin); [2017] P.T.S.R. 288; Times, January 19, 2017; [2017] J.P.L. 504, QBD (Admin) .... *Digested,* 17/**1735**

Eatherley v Camden LBC see Eatherley v Camden LBC

EB (Kosovo) v Secretary of State for the Home Department; *joined cases* JL (Sierra Leone) v Secretary of State for the Home Department; HB (Ethiopia) v Secretary of State for the Home Department; FI (Nigeria) v Secretary of State for the Home Department [2008] UKHL 41; [2009] 1 A.C. 1159; [2008] 3 W.L.R. 178; [2008] 4 All E.R. 28; [2008] H.R.L.R. 40; [2008] U.K.H.R.R. 1087; 25 B.H.R.C. 228; [2008] Imm. A.R. 713; [2008] I.N.L.R. 516; Times, June 30, 2008; (2008) 105(26) L.S.G. 21; (2008) 158 N.L.J. 968; (2008) 152(26) S.J.L.B. 30, HL .... *Digested,* 08/**2037**:
Applied 09/2141, 11/1770, 14/1671: *Considered* 10/1777, 10/1806, 11/1790, 13/3776, 14/1650, 15/1374: *Distinguished* 16/1118: *Followed* 09/2163, 10/1761, 10/1790, 11/1735, 11/1789, 13/1618, 17/1186, 17/1239

Eba v Advocate General for Scotland [2010] CSIH 78; [2010] S.T.C. 2689; 2011 S.C. 70; 2010 S.L.T. 1047; 2010 S.C.L.R. 759; Times, October 20, 2010; [2010] S.T.I. 2617; 2010 G.W.D. 31-634, IH (1 Div)
Affirmed 11/3958: *Considered* 17/2663

Ebbvale Ltd v Hosking [2013] UKPC 1; [2013] 2 B.C.L.C. 204; [2013] B.P.I.R. 219, PC (Bah)
Applied 17/1294: *Considered* 15/1436, 16/1195, 16/1198

Ecclesiastical Insurance Office Plc v Whitehouse-Grant-Christ [2017] CSIH 33; 2017 S.C. 684; 2017 S.L.T. 697; 2017 G.W.D. 19-292, IH (Ex Div) .... *Digested,* 17/**2712**

Eclipse Film Partners No.35 LLP v Revenue and Customs Commissioners; *sub nom* Revenue and Customs Commissioners v Eclipse Film Partners No.35 LLP [2016] UKSC 24; [2016] 1 W.L.R. 1939; [2016] 3 All E.R. 719; [2016] S.T.C. 1385; [2017] R.V.R. 105; [2016] B.T.C. 20; Times, May 18, 2016; [2016] S.T.I. 1531, SC .... *Digested,* 16/**2067**

Eclipse Film Partners No.35 LLP v Revenue and Customs Commissioners [2015] EWCA Civ 95; [2015] S.T.C. 1429; [2015] B.T.C. 10; [2015] S.T.I. 522, CA (Civ Div) .... *Digested,* 15/**2524**:
Applied 16/343: *Considered* 15/2484: *Followed* 17/2147, 17/2188

Eco-Emballages SA v Sphere France SAS (C-313/15) EU:C:2016:859; [2017] Env. L.R. 19, ECJ (3rd Chamber)

Ecolab USA Inc v European Union Intellectual Property Office (EUIPO) (T-150/16) EU:T:2017:490; [2017] E.T.M.R. 40, GC (7th Chamber)

Economou v de Freitas [2016] EWHC 1218 (QB), QBD
Applied 17/648

Economou v de Freitas [2016] EWHC 1853 (QB); [2017] E.M.L.R. 4, QBD .... *Digested,* 17/**651**

Eddie Rockets (Ireland) Ltd v Johnny Rockets Licensing Corp see Johnny Rockets Licensing Corp v Eddie Rockets (Ireland) Ltd

Edem v Information Commissioner [2014] EWCA Civ 92, CA (Civ Div)
Considered 17/1165

Eden (NI) Ltd v Mills Selig (A Firm) [2016] NIQB 71; [2017] P.N.L.R. 2, QBD (NI) .... *Digested,* 17/**2328**

Edenwest Ltd v CMS Cameron McKenna [2012] EWHC 1258 (Ch); [2013] B.C.C. 152; [2013] 1 B.C.L.C. 525; (2012) 109(22) L.S.G. 20, Ch D .... *Digested,* 13/**2096**:
Applied 13/1061: *Considered* 17/222

Edgeworth Capital (Luxembourg) Sarl v Ramblas Investments BV [2016] EWCA Civ 412; [2017] 1 All E.R. (Comm) 577, CA (Civ Div) .... *Digested,* 17/**170**

Edgeworth Capital (Luxembourg) Sarl v Ramblas Investments BV [2015] EWHC 150 (Comm); [2016] 1 All E.R. (Comm) 368, QBD (Comm) .... *Digested,* 16/**142**:
Reversed in part 17/170

Edilizia Industriale Siderurgica Srl (EDIS) v Ministero delle Finanze (C231/96) EU:C:1998:401; [1998] E.C.R. I-4951; [1999] 2 C.M.L.R. 995; [1999] C.E.C. 337, ECJ .... *Digested,* 99/**2276**:
Applied 17/2228

Edinburgh & District Tramways Co Ltd v Courtenay 1909 S.C. 99; (1908) 16 S.L.T. 548, IH (1 Div)
Applied 17/2772

Edinburgh and Lothians Greenspace Trust v Network Rail Infrastucture Ltd [2016] R.V.R. 369; 2016 G.W.D. 25-465, Lands Tr (Scot) .... *Digested,* 17/**2648**

Edinburgh City Council v Secretary of State for Scotland; *joined cases* Revival Properties Ltd v Edinburgh City Council; Secretary of State for Scotland v Revival Properties Ltd [1997] 1 W.L.R. 1447; [1998] 1 All E.R. 174; 1998 S.C. (H.L.) 33; 1998 S.L.T. 120; 1997 S.C.L.R. 1112; [1997] 3 P.L.R. 71; Times, October 31, 1997; [1998] J.P.L. 224; [1997] E.G. 140 (C.S.); (1997) 94(42) L.S.G. 31; (1997) 141 S.J.L.B. 228; [1997] N.P.C. 146; 1997 G.W.D. 33-1693, HL .... *Digested,* 97/**6350**:
Applied 99/4178, 06/3289, 06/3346, 07/5464, 11/2533, 11/2554, 11/2574, 17/1779: *Considered* 99/4218, 01/4743, 05/3295, 09/2989, 15/2031: *Followed* 97/4116, 99/6411, 17/1769, 17/1776

Edkins v Hopkins [2016] EWHC 2542 (Ch); [2017] W.T.L.R. 39, Ch D (Cardiff) .... *Digested,* 17/**2076**
Edwards v Environment Agency (C-260/11) see R. (on the application of Edwards) v Environment Agency (C-260/11)
Edwards v Flightline Ltd see Flightline Ltd v Edwards
Edwards v Kumarasamy [2016] UKSC 40; [2016] A.C. 1334; [2016] 3 W.L.R. 310; [2017] 2 All E.R. 624; [2016] H.L.R. 32; [2017] 1 P. & C.R. 2; [2016] L. & T.R. 25; Times, July 18, 2016, SC .... *Digested,* 16/**1382**
Edwards v Lowndes 118 E.R. 367; (1852) 1 El. & Bl. 81, QB
Considered 17/2219
Edwards v Panesar [2016] EWHC 1944 (Ch); [2017] B.P.I.R. 175, Ch D .... *Digested,* 17/**378**
Edwards v Roberts 19 T.C. 618, CA
Considered 17/2131
Edwards v Sutton LBC; *sub nom* Sutton LBC v Edwards [2016] EWCA Civ 1005; [2017] P.I.Q.R. P2, CA (Civ Div) .... *Digested,* 17/**2200**
Edwards v Sutton LBC; *sub nom* Sutton LBC v Edwards [2014] EWHC 4378 (QB), QBD
Reversed in part 17/2200
Edwards (Inspector of Taxes) v Bairstow; *joined case* Edwards (Inspector of Taxes) v Harrison [1956] A.C. 14; [1955] 3 W.L.R. 410; [1955] 3 All E.R. 48; 48 R. & I.T. 534; 36 T.C. 207; (1955) 34 A.T.C. 198; [1955] T.R. 209; (1955) 99 S.J. 558, HL .... *Digested,* 55/**417**:
Applied 56/4272, 59/1529, 62/1506, 66/6154, 67/1949, 71/3949, 71/999, 74/320, 76/250, 77/2446, 82/1617, 82/1647, 82/476, 83/1225, 83/1976, 84/460, 89/125, 89/3189, 90/2675, 90/754, 92/3364, 93/2274, 95/391, 95/876, 98/2137, 98/2140, 98/4622, 99/3066, 99/6471, 03/4251, 06/4189, 06/4278, 07/4068, 09/4532, 11/3390, 14/2849, 14/2981, 15/2624, 16/2200, 16/2202: *Cited* 17/2271: *Considered* 56/4853, 74/1834, 74/1873, 74/2097, 74/283.u, 74/485, 82/3282, 84/3218, 84/3253, 87/3193, 90/1864, 91/2373, 92/164, 94/357, 94/7, 95/155, 95/5020, 95/7, 95/896, 98/4604, 99/4660, 99/4663, 06/215, 06/4118, 07/4348, 08/160, 14/1453, 16/2187: *Followed* 03/4190, 10/3096, 10/3509, 14/3105, 15/2586: *Referred to* 74/1816
Edwards (Inspector of Taxes) v Harrison see Edwards (Inspector of Taxes) v Bairstow
Edwards-Tubb v JD Wetherspoon Plc [2011] EWCA Civ 136; [2011] 1 W.L.R. 1373; [2011] C.P. Rep. 27; [2011] P.I.Q.R. P16; (2011) 121 B.M.L.R. 70; (2011) 155(9) S.J.L.B. 31, CA (Civ Div) .... *Digested,* 11/**327**:
Applied 14/291: *Followed* 16/152, 16/154, 17/298
EE (Children) (Habitual Residence), Re; *sub nom* KE v SS-E [2016] EWHC 3363 (Fam); [2017] 1 F.C.R. 500, Fam Div
EE Ltd v Office of Communications [2016] EWHC 2134 (Admin); [2017] 1 C.M.L.R. 23; [2016] A.C.D. 111, QBD (Admin) .... *Digested,* 17/**2190**
Effort Shipping Co Ltd v Linden Management SA (The Giannis NK) [1998] A.C. 605; [1998] 2 W.L.R. 206; [1998] 1 All E.R. 495; [1998] 1 Lloyd's Rep. 337; [1998] C.L.C. 374; 1998 A.M.C. 1050; Times, January 29, 1998; Independent, January 27, 1998; (1998) 95(7) L.S.G. 32; (1998) 148 N.L.J. 121; (1998) 142 S.J.L.B. 54, HL .... *Digested,* 98/**4400**:
Applied 08/2261, 17/2003: *Considered* 98/4395, 09/3559, 09/4216
Efobi v Royal Mail Group Ltd [2018] I.C.R. 359; [2017] I.R.L.R. 956, EAT .... *Digested,* 17/**819**
EG v CA [2017] EWFC 52; [2017] 4 W.L.R. 140; [2017] 2 F.L.R. 1423, Fam Ct .... *Digested,* 17/**959**
EG v Secretary of State for the Home Department see EG (UT Rule 17: Withdrawal: Rule 24: Scope: Ethiopia), Re
EG (UT Rule 17: Withdrawal: Rule 24: Scope: Ethiopia), Re; *sub nom* Secretary of State for the Home Department v EG; EG v Secretary of State for the Home Department [2013] UKUT 143 (IAC); [2013] Imm. A.R. 670; [2013] I.N.L.R. 700, UT (IAC) .... *Digested,* 13/**1617**:
Applied 17/2280
Egeneonu v Egeneonu [2017] EWHC 43 (Fam); [2017] 4 W.L.R. 100; [2017] 2 F.L.R. 1181; [2017] 2 F.C.R. 130, Fam Div .... *Digested,* 17/**8**
Egiazaryan v OJSC OEK Finance [2015] EWHC 3532 (Comm); [2017] 1 All E.R. (Comm) 207; [2016] 1 Lloyd's Rep. 295; [2016] 1 C.L.C. 1, QBD (Comm) .... *Digested,* 16/**72**
Egon Zehnder Ltd v Tillman; *sub nom* Tillman v Egon Zehnder Ltd [2017] EWCA Civ 1054; [2018] I.C.R. 574; [2017] I.R.L.R. 906, CA (Civ Div) .... *Digested,* 17/**823**
Egon Zehnder Ltd v Tillman; *sub nom* Tillman v Egon Zehnder Ltd [2017] EWHC 1278 (Ch); [2017] I.R.L.R. 828, Ch D
Reversed 17/823
EH v Dorset Healthcare University NHS Foundation Trust see Henderson v Dorset Healthcare University NHS Foundation Trust

EH (Albania) v Secretary of State for the Home Department see EH (Blood Feuds: Albania), Re

EH (Blood Feuds: Albania), Re; *sub nom* EH (Albania) v Secretary of State for the Home Department [2012] UKUT 348 (IAC), UT (IAC)
Applied 17/1241: *Considered* 15/1351

EI du Pont de Nemours & Co v ST Dupont see ST Dupont v EI du Pont de Nemours & Co

Eiger Securities LLP v Korshunova [2017] I.C.R. 561; [2017] I.R.L.R. 115, EAT .... *Digested,* 17/**815**

Eight Representative Claimants v MGN Ltd [2016] EWHC 855 (Ch); [2016] 3 Costs L.O. 413, Ch D .... *Digested,* 16/**1403**: *Affirmed* 17/1478

El Dakkak v Administration des Douanes et des Droits Indirects (C-17/16) EU:C:2017:341; [2017] 4 W.L.R. 161; [2017] 3 C.M.L.R. 38; [2018] C.E.C. 33, ECJ (1st Chamber)

El Greco (Australia) Pty Ltd v Mediterranean Shipping Co SA [2004] FCAFC 202; [2004] 2 Lloyd's Rep. 537, Fed Ct (Aus) (Full Ct) .... *Digested,* 05/**3786**: *Considered* 17/2003, 17/2015

El Kaada v Germany (2130/10) 41 B.H.R.C. 552, ECHR

El Majjaoui v Netherlands (25525/03) (2008) 47 E.H.R.R. 23, ECHR .... *Digested,* 09/**1959**: *Applied* 17/1212

El Makdessi v Cavendish Square Holdings BV see Makdessi v Cavendish Square Holdings BV

EL Oldendorff & Co GmbH v Tradax Export SA (The Johanna Oldendorff) [1974] A.C. 479; [1973] 3 W.L.R. 382; [1973] 3 All E.R. 148; [1973] 2 Lloyd's Rep. 285; (1973) 117 S.J. 760, HL .... *Digested,* 73/**3100**: *Applied* 75/3181, 77/2728, 78/2720, 87/3405: *Considered* 85/3189: *Followed* 17/2005

El-Huseini v General Medical Council [2016] EWHC 2326 (Admin); [2016] Med. L.R. 647; (2016) 152 B.M.L.R. 133, QBD (Admin) .... *Digested,* 17/**202**

El-Masri v Macedonia (39630/09) (2013) 57 E.H.R.R. 25; 34 B.H.R.C. 313, ECHR (Grand Chamber)
Considered 15/101: *Not applied* 17/83

Elaph Publishing Ltd v Prince Moulay Hicham Ben Abdullah Al Alaoui of Morocco see Prince Moulay Hicham Ben Abdullah Al Alaoui of Morocco v Elaph Publishing Ltd

Elashmawy v Italy [2015] EWHC 28 (Admin), QBD (Admin)
Applied 17/904

Elbrook Cash and Carry Ltd v Revenue and Customs Commissioners; *sub nom* Revenue and Customs Commissioners v Elbrook (Cash & Carry) Ltd [2016] UKFTT 191 (TC); [2016] S.T.I. 1415, FTT (Tax)
Affirmed 17/2281

Elbrook Cash and Carry Ltd v Revenue and Customs Commissioners; *sub nom* Revenue and Customs Commissioners v Elbrook (Cash & Carry) Ltd [2017] UKUT 181 (TCC); [2017] B.V.C. 514, UT (Tax) .... *Digested,* 17/**2281**

Eleni Maritime Ltd v Heung-a Shipping Co Ltd [2017] 2 Lloyd's Rep. 263, CFI (HK)

Elgin Legal Ltd, Re; *sub nom* Stares v Elgin Legal Ltd [2016] EWHC 2523 (Ch); [2017] B.C.C. 43; [2017] B.P.I.R. 406, Ch D .... *Digested,* 17/**1269**: *Considered* 17/1268

Elguzouli-Daf v Commissioner of Police of the Metropolis; *joined case* McBrearty v Ministry of Defence [1995] Q.B. 335; [1995] 2 W.L.R. 173; [1995] 1 All E.R. 833; (1995) 7 Admin. L.R. 421; Times, November 23, 1994; (1995) 145 N.L.J. 151, CA (Civ Div) .... *Digested,* 95/**3652**: *Applied* 98/4778, 08/2641, 17/1240: *Considered* 12/2629

Eli Lilly & Co v Actavis UK Ltd see Actavis UK Ltd v Eli Lilly & Co

Elias v Secretary of State for Defence see R. (on the application of Elias) v Secretary of State for Defence

Elichaoff (Deceased), Re see Robert v Woodall

Elida Gibbs Ltd v Customs and Excise Commissioners (C-317/94) EU:C:1996:400; [1997] Q.B. 499; [1996] S.T.C. 1387; [1996] E.C.R. I-5339; [1996] C.E.C. 1022; [1997] B.V.C. 80; Times, November 12, 1996, ECJ (6th Chamber) .... *Digested,* 96/**5908**: *Applied* 07/4323, 09/4074, 12/3382, 13/3217: *Cited* 16/2202: *Considered* 01/5556, 03/4569, 04/3983, 04/4024, 08/4026, 08/4029, 09/4081, 11/1261, 11/3572, 12/3408, 15/2611: *Distinguished* 01/5614, 04/3981, 08/4028, 14/3809: *Followed* 09/4092, 17/2256

Elim Court RTM Co Ltd v Avon Freeholds Ltd; *joined cases* Sinclair Gardens Investments (Kensington) Ltd v Farnborough Road (Calloway House) RTM Co Ltd; Assethold Ltd v 369 Upland Road RTM Co Ltd [2017] EWCA Civ 89; [2018] Q.B. 571; [2017] 3 W.L.R. 876; [2017] H.L.R. 18; [2017] 2 P. & C.R. 8; [2017] L. & T.R. 15, CA (Civ Div) .... *Digested,* 17/**1463**

Elim Court RTM Co Ltd v Avon Freeholds Ltd; *joined cases* Sinclair Gardens Investments (Kensington) Ltd v Farnborough Road (Calloway House) RTM Co Ltd; Assethold Ltd v 369 Upland Road RTM Co Ltd [2014] UKUT 397 (LC); [2015] L. & T.R. 3, UT (Lands) .... *Digested,* 15/**1601**: *Reversed* 17/1463

Elkamet Kunststofftechnik GmbH v Saint-Gobain Glass France SA [2016] EWHC 3421 (Pat); [2017] F.S.R. 23, Ch D (Patents Ct) .... *Digested,* 17/**237**: *Considered* 17/231

Elkamet Kunststofftechnik GmbH v Saint-Gobain Glass France SA [2016] EWHC 3420 (Pat); [2017] F.S.R. 22, Ch D (Patents Ct) .... *Digested,* 17/**1373**

Ellenborough Park, Re; *sub nom* Powell v Maddison; Davies (Deceased), Re [1956] Ch. 131; [1955] 3 W.L.R. 892; [1955] 3 All E.R. 667; (1955) 99 S.J. 870, CA
Applied 16/1812, 17/1842: *Considered* 90/1279, 02/3817

Elliot v Flanagan [2016] NIQB 8; [2017] N.I. 264, QBD (NI)

Elliott v Grey [1960] 1 Q.B. 367; [1959] 3 W.L.R. 956; [1959] 3 All E.R. 733; (1960) 124 J.P. 58; 57 L.G.R. 357; (1959) 103 S.J. 921, QBD .... *Digested,* 59/**2903**:
Applied 64/3225, 64/3236, 73/2965, 75/2914, 75/2915, 75/3001, 88/4846: *Considered* 17/1347: *Distinguished* 63/3097, 74/3397, 86/2993, 87/3579: *Followed* 71/10361

Elliott Steam Tug Co Ltd v Shipping Controller [1922] 1 K.B. 127; (1921) 8 Ll. L. Rep. 462, CA
Applied 67/3608, 17/2455: *Considered* 85/2310

Ellon Car Clinic Ltd v Revenue and Customs Commissioners [2017] UKFTT 336 (TC); [2017] S.T.I. 1148, FTT (Tax)

Elmi v United Kingdom (11449/07) see Sufi v United Kingdom (8319/07)

Ely v Robson [2016] EWCA Civ 774; [2017] 1 F.L.R. 1704; [2016] W.T.L.R. 1383; 20 I.T.E.L.R. 428; [2016] Fam. Law 1221; [2017] 1 P. & C.R. DG1, CA (Civ Div) .... *Digested,* 16/**1795**

EM v AM see M v M

EM (Eritrea) v Secretary of State for the Home Department see R. (on the application of EM (Eritrea)) v Secretary of State for the Home Department

Emerald Meats (London) Ltd, Re see McCarthy v Tann

Emile Elias & Co Ltd v Pine Groves Ltd [1993] 1 W.L.R. 305; (1993) 66 P. & C.R. 1; [1993] E.G. 31 (C.S.); (1993) 137 S.J.L.B. 52; [1993] N.P.C. 30, PC (Trin) .... *Digested,* 93/**560**: *Applied* 17/1828: *Considered* 08/3112

Emilio Pucci Srl v H&M Hennes and Mauritz AB [2017] I.L.Pr. 4, Cass (F)

Eminence Property Developments Ltd v Heaney [2010] EWCA Civ 1168; [2011] 2 All E.R. (Comm) 223; [2010] 3 E.G.L.R. 165; [2010] 43 E.G. 99 (C.S.), CA (Civ Div) .... *Digested,* 11/**2678**:
Applied 11/1068, 15/1802: *Considered* 13/2434: *Followed* 11/1049, 17/2008

EML v University Hospitals of Morecambe Bay NHS Foundation Trust (Unreported, April 11, 2016), QBD (Manchester) [*Potter Rees Dolan, 12 Commercial Street, Manchester*] .... *Digested,* 17/**1659**

Emmanuel v Emmanuel [2016] SGCA 30; 19 I.T.E.L.R. 495, CA (Sing)

Emmanuel v Revenue and Customs Commissioners [2017] EWHC 1253 (Ch); [2017] 3 Costs L.R. 515; [2017] B.P.I.R. 1182, Ch D .... *Digested,* 17/**1292**

Emmott v Michael Wilson & Partners Ltd [2017] EWCA Civ 367; [2017] 1 W.L.R. 4330; [2017] C.P. Rep. 34, CA (Civ Div) .... *Digested,* 17/**315**: *Applied* 17/1314

Emmott v Michael Wilson & Partners Ltd [2016] EWHC 1152 (Comm), QBD (Comm)
Affirmed 17/315

Emmott v Michael Wilson and Partners [2016] EWHC 3010 (Comm); [2017] 2 All E.R. (Comm) 569; [2017] 1 Lloyd's Rep. 21, QBD .... *Digested,* 17/**200**

Emokpae v Chamberlin Solicitors see Wong v Igen Ltd (formerly Leeds Careers Guidance)

Empire Brent, The (1947-48) 81 Ll. L. Rep. 306, PDAD
Applied 17/2020

EMW Law LLP v Halborg [2017] EWHC 1014 (Ch); [2017] 3 Costs L.O. 281, Ch D ..... *Digested,* 17/**292**

EMW Law LLP v Halborg see Halborg v EMW Law LLP

ENEFI Energiahatekonysagi Nyrt v Directia Generala Regionala a Finantelor Publice Brasov (DGRFP) (C-212/15) EU:C:2016:841; [2017] I.L.Pr. 10, ECJ (5th Chamber)

Energy Solutions EU Ltd v Nuclear Decommissioning Authority; *sub nom* Nuclear Decommissioning Authority v ATK Energy EU Ltd (formerly Energy Solutions EU Ltd); Nuclear Decommissioning Authority v Energy Solutions EU Ltd [2017] UKSC 34; [2017] 1 W.L.R. 1373; [2017] 4 All E.R. 1; [2017] P.T.S.R. 539; [2017] B.L.R. 351; 171 Con. L.R. 16; [2017] 3 C.M.L.R. 13; Times, April 24, 2017, SC .... *Digested,* 17/**1813**

Energy Solutions EU Ltd v Nuclear Decommissioning Authority [2016] EWHC 3326 (TCC); [2017] B.L.R. 92, QBD (TCC) .... *Digested,* 17/**1815**

Energy Solutions EU Ltd v Nuclear Decommissioning Authority; *sub nom* Nuclear Decommissioning Authority v ATK Energy EU Ltd (formerly Energy Solutions EU Ltd); Nuclear Decommissioning Authority v Energy Solutions EU Ltd [2015] EWCA Civ 1262; [2016] P.T.S.R. 689; 163 Con. L.R. 27; [2016] 2 C.M.L.R. 6, CA (Civ Div) .... *Digested,* 16/**1792**: *Affirmed* 17/1813

EnergySolutions EU Ltd v Nuclear Decommissioning Authority [2016] EWHC 1988 (TCC); [2016] B.L.R. 625, QBD (TCC) .... *Digested,* 17/**1816**

Enfield LBC v Najim [2015] EWCA Civ 319; [2015] H.L.R. 19, CA (Civ Div) .... *Digested,* 15/**1268**: *Followed* 17/1159

Enfield LBC v SA [2010] EWHC 196 (Admin); [2010] 1 F.L.R. 1836; [2010] Fam. Law 457, CP .... *Digested,* 10/**2257**: *Applied* 17/1548

Engbers v Secretary of State for Communities and Local Government; *sub nom* Secretary of State for Communities and Local Government v Engbers [2015] EWHC 3541 (Admin), QBD (Admin) *Affirmed* 17/1763

Engbers v Secretary of State for Communities and Local Government; *sub nom* Secretary of State for Communities and Local Government v Engbers [2016] EWCA Civ 1183; [2017] J.P.L. 489, CA (Civ Div) .... *Digested,* 17/**1763**

Engel v Ministry of Justice [2017] I.C.R. 277, EAT

Engel v Netherlands (A/22) (1979-80) 1 E.H.R.R. 647, ECHR *Applied* 88/2973, 98/3119, 00/3235, 02/3349, 03/4604, 03/866, 03/925, 05/2909, 05/4164, 06/4640, 07/2172, 07/2226, 08/1956, 08/1958, 09/2008, 10/975, 12/2288, 12/3127, 17/633: *Considered* 01/98, 02/2470, 02/2619, 03/2141, 04/2777, 04/3144, 06/5128, 07/2171, 07/54, 07/953, 09/1098, 09/1934, 09/2033, 11/1691, 14/2657, 17/2537

England v Magill see Porter v Magill

England and Wales Cricket Board Ltd v Tixdaq Ltd [2016] EWHC 575 (Ch); [2016] Bus. L.R. 641; [2017] E.C.D.R. 2; [2016] R.P.C. 21, Ch D .... *Digested,* 16/**1283**

English v Emery Reimbold & Strick Ltd; *joined cases* Verrechia (t/a Freightmaster Commercials) v Commissioner of Police of the Metropolis; DJ&C Withers (Farms) Ltd v Ambic Equipment Ltd [2002] EWCA Civ 605; [2002] 1 W.L.R. 2409; [2002] 3 All E.R. 385; [2002] C.P.L.R. 520; [2003] I.R.L.R. 710; [2002] U.K.H.R.R. 957; Times, May 10, 2002; Independent, May 7, 2002; (2002) 99(22) L.S.G. 34; (2002) 152 N.L.J. 758; (2002) 146 S.J.L.B. 123, CA (Civ Div) *Digested,* 02/**301**: *Applied* 02/371, 04/2698, 05/1212, 05/1256, 05/950, 06/1335, 06/4090, 06/498, 07/1434, 07/249, 09/1747, 11/1107, 11/217, 12/1357, 12/2040, 15/817: *Considered* 03/1544, 03/847, 05/2213, 06/1817, 06/2226, 06/468, 07/2453, 07/466, 08/283, 13/1280, 13/1536, 13/312: *Distinguished* 05/1138: *Followed* 12/1347, 13/112, 13/1442, 14/3059, 15/300, 16/1511, 16/881, 17/2263, 17/2281, 17/918: *Referred to* 11/1142

English v O'Driscoll [2016] IEHC 584; [2017] P.N.L.R. 9, HC (Irl)

English v Thomas Sanderson Blinds Ltd [2008] EWCA Civ 1421; [2009] 2 All E.R. 468; [2009] 2 C.M.L.R. 18; [2009] I.C.R. 543; [2009] I.R.L.R. 206; Times, January 5, 2009; (2009) 153(1) S.J.L.B. 31, CA (Civ Div) .... *Digested,* 09/**1240**: *Considered* 11/1057, 17/777

English Electric Co Ltd v United Kingdom (9263/81) see Lithgow v United Kingdom (A/102)

English Holdings v Revenue and Customs Commissioners [2016] UKFTT 436 (TC); [2017] S.F.T.D. 20; [2016] S.T.I. 2549, FTT (Tax) .... *Digested,* 17/**2138**

Enka Insaat Ve Sanayi AS v Banca Popolare dell'Alto Adige SpA; *joined case* Enka Insaat Ve sanayi AS v Cassa di Risparmio di Bolzano SpA [2009] EWHC 2410 (Comm); [2009] C.I.L.L. 2777, QBD (Comm) *Applied* 17/167

Enka Insaat Ve sanayi AS v Cassa di Risparmio di Bolzano SpA see Enka Insaat Ve Sanayi AS v Banca Popolare dell'Alto Adige SpA

Enkler v Finanzamt Homburg (C-230/94) EU:C:1996:352; [1996] S.T.C. 1316; [1996] E.C.R. I-4517; [1997] 1 C.M.L.R. 881; [1996] C.E.C. 858; [1997] B.V.C. 24, ECJ (4th Chamber)
Applied 07/4305, 10/3531: *Followed* 17/2295

Ensign Tankers (Leasing) Ltd v Stokes (Inspector of Taxes) [1992] 1 A.C. 655; [1992] 2 W.L.R. 469; [1992] 2 All E.R. 275; [1992] S.T.C. 226; 64 T.C. 617; Times, March 17, 1992; Independent, April 2, 1992; [1992] S.T.I. 364; Financial Times, March 17, 1992; (1992) 89(17) L.S.G. 49; (1992) 136 S.J.L.B. 89, HL .... *Digested,* 92/**611**:
Applied 08/4019, 11/3277: *Considered* 93/2254, 94/2569, 15/2524, 17/2180:
Distinguished 10/3390: *Followed* 03/4190: *Not followed* 02/4457

Enta Technologies Ltd v Revenue and Customs Commissioners see Enta Technologies Ltd, Re

Enta Technologies Ltd, Re; *sub nom* Enta Technologies Ltd v Revenue and Customs Commissioners; Revenue and Customs Commissioners v Changtel Solutions UK Ltd (formerly Enta Technologies Ltd); Changtel Solutions UK Ltd (formerly Enta Technologies Ltd) v Revenue and Customs Commissioners [2015] EWCA Civ 29; [2015] 1 W.L.R. 3911; [2015] S.T.C. 931; [2015] B.C.C. 317; [2015] 2 B.C.L.C. 586; [2015] B.P.I.R. 327; [2015] B.V.C. 8; Times, March 5, 2015; [2015] S.T.I. 248, CA (Civ Div) .... *Digested,* 15/**1456**:
Applied 17/1327

Enterprise Holdings Inc v Europcar Group UK Ltd [2015] EWHC 17 (Ch); [2017] E.C.C. 11; [2015] E.T.M.R. 16; [2015] F.S.R. 22, Ch D .... *Digested,* 15/**1533**:
Applied 15/1525, 16/1289, 16/1337

Entidad de Gestion de Derechos de los Productores Audiovisuales (EGEDA) v Administracion del Estado (C-470/14) EU:C:2016:418; [2017] C.E.C. 111, ECJ (4th Chamber)

Entry Clearance Officer, Nicosia v Papajorgji see Papajorgji (EEA Spouse: Marriage of Convenience: Greece), Re

Entry Clearance Officer, United States v MW [2016] EWCA Civ 1273; [2017] 1 W.L.R. 1556; Times, February 24, 2017, CA (Civ Div) .... *Digested,* 17/**1227**

Enviroflow Management Ltd v Redhill Works (Nottingham) Ltd [2017] EWHC 2159 (TCC); 174 Con. L.R. 13; [2017] C.I.L.L. 4061, QBD (TCC)

Environment Agency v Barrass [2017] EWHC 548 (Admin); [2017] P.T.S.R. 985; [2017] L.L.R. 301, DC .... *Digested,* 17/**2016**

Environment Agency v Churngold Recycling Ltd [2014] EWCA Civ 909; [2015] Env. L.R. 13, CA (Civ Div) .... *Digested,* 15/**2533**:
Applied 17/768

Envis v Thakkar [1997] B.P.I.R. 189; Times, May 2, 1995, CA (Civ Div) .... *Digested,* 95/**4012**:
Followed 17/363

EO (Ghana) v Secretary of State for the Home Department see GS (India) v Secretary of State for the Home Department

Epoch Co Ltd v Character Options Ltd [2017] EWHC 556 (IPEC); [2017] F.S.R. 42, IPEC .... *Digested,* 17/**1380**

Epshtein v Comptroller General of Patents Designs and Trade Marks [2016] EWHC 1511 (Ch); [2017] R.P.C. 11, Ch D (Patents Ct)

Eqiom SAS v Ministre des Finances et des Comptes Publics (C-6/16) EU:C:2017:641; [2017] S.T.I. 1974, ECJ (6th Chamber)

Equal Opportunities Commission v Secretary of State for Trade and Industry; *sub nom* R. (on the application of Equal Opportunities Commission) v Secretary of State for Communities and Local Government [2007] EWHC 483 (Admin); [2007] 2 C.M.L.R. 49; [2007] I.C.R. 1234; [2007] I.R.L.R. 327; [2007] A.C.D. 74; (2007) 104(13) L.S.G. 25, QBD (Admin) .... *Digested,* 07/**1405**:
Applied 08/1190: *Considered* 17/840

Equitas Ltd v Walsham Bros & Co Ltd [2013] EWHC 3264 (Comm); [2014] Lloyd's Rep. I.R. 398; [2014] P.N.L.R. 8; [2014] Bus. L.R. D7, QBD (Comm) .... *Digested,* 14/**1840**:
Applied 17/412

Equiticorp International Plc, Re [1989] 1 W.L.R. 1010; (1989) 5 B.C.C. 599; [1989] B.C.L.C. 597; (1989) 86(41) L.S.G. 36; (1989) 133 S.J. 1405, Ch D .... *Digested,* 89/**290**:
Considered 11/1816, 17/409

Erdenet Mining Corp LLC v ICBC Standard Bank Plc [2017] EWHC 1090 (Comm); [2018] 1 All E.R. (Comm) 691; [2017] 2 Lloyd's Rep. 25, QBD (Comm) .... *Digested,* 17/**70**

ERGO Insurance SE v If P&C Insurance AS (C-359/14); *joined case* Gjensidige Baltic AAS v PZU Lietuva UAB DK (C□475/14) EU:C:2016:40; [2016] R.T.R. 14; [2017] C.E.C. 3; [2016] I.L.Pr. 20; [2016] Lloyd's Rep. I.R. 299, ECJ (4th Chamber)

Erikson v Carr (1945) 46 S.R. (N.S.W.) 9
Considered 17/1585

Erith Holdings Ltd v Murphy [2017] EWHC 1364 (TCC); 172 Con. L.R. 51, QBD (TCC) .... *Digested,* 17/**501**
Eroglu v Secretary of State for the Home Department see R. (on the application of Buer) v Secretary of State for the Home Department
Erridge v Revenue and Customs Commissioners [2015] UKFTT 89 (TC), FTT (Tax) *Approved* 17/2144
Erskine 1948 Trust, Re; *sub nom* Gregg v Pigott [2012] EWHC 732 (Ch); [2013] Ch. 135; [2012] 3 W.L.R. 913; [2012] 3 All E.R. 532; [2012] 2 F.L.R. 725; [2012] 3 F.C.R. 114; [2012] W.T.L.R. 953; 14 I.T.E.L.R. 890; Times, July 10, 2012; [2012] Fam. Law 809; (2012) 109(16) L.S.G. 22; (2012) 162 N.L.J. 577, Ch D .. *Digested,* 12/**3366**: *Not followed* 17/2074
Erste Group Bank AG (London) v JSC (VMZ Red October) [2015] EWCA Civ 379; [2015] 1 C.L.C. 706, CA (Civ Div) *Applied* 17/371, 17/377: *Considered* 16/1539, 17/1382: *Followed* 15/365, 17/2194, 17/369, 17/426
ERY v Associated Newspapers Ltd [2016] EWHC 2760 (QB); [2017] E.M.L.R. 9; [2017] Lloyd's Rep. F.C. 40, QBD .... *Digested,* 17/**214**: *Applied* 17/2199
ES v Romania (60281/11) (2017) 65 E.H.R.R. 15, ECHR
ESAB AB/Re-establishment of Rights (J23/14) [2017] E.P.O.R. 23, EPO (Legal Bd App)
Eschenbrenner v Bundesagentur fur Arbeit (C-496/15) EU:C:2017:152; [2017] 3 C.M.L.R. 12; [2017] Env. L.R. D4, ECJ (2nd Chamber)
Eslame v Public Prosecutor in Kortrijk, Belgium see Purcell v Belgium
Esporta Ltd v Revenue and Customs Commissioners; *sub nom* Revenue and Customs Commissioners v Esporta Ltd [2014] EWCA Civ 155; [2014] S.T.C. 1548; [2014] B.V.C. 28; [2014] L.L.R. 483; [2014] S.T.I. 741, CA (Civ Div) .... *Digested,* 14/**3090**: *Applied* 16/2176: *Distinguished* 17/2264: *Followed* 16/2187
Essar Oilfield Services Ltd v Norscot Rig Management Pvt Ltd [2016] EWHC 2361 (Comm); [2017] Bus. L.R. 227; [2016] 2 Lloyd's Rep. 481; [2016] 2 C.L.C. 419, QBD (Comm) .... *Digested,* 17/**66**
Essence Bars (London) Ltd (t/a Essence) v Wimbledon Magistrates' Court; *sub nom* R. (on the application of Essence Bars (London) Ltd (t/a Essence Ltd)) v Wimbledon Magistrates' Court [2016] EWCA Civ 63; [2016] 1 W.L.R. 3265; [2016] C.P. Rep. 18; (2017) 181 J.P. 297; [2016] L.L.R. 330, CA (Civ Div) .... *Digested,* 16/**1424**
Essent Belgium NV v Vlaams Gewest (C-492/14) EU:C:2016:732; [2017] 1 C.M.L.R. 39, ECJ (2nd Chamber)
Esso Petroleum Co Ltd v Scottish Ministers [2015] CSOH 21; 2015 G.W.D. 7-134, OH *Applied* 17/2740
Esso Petroleum Co Ltd v Scottish Ministers [2016] CSOH 15; 2016 S.C.L.R. 539; 2016 G.W.D. 4-98, OH .... *Digested,* 17/**2464**
Essop v Home Office (UK Border Agency); *sub nom* Home Office (UK Border Agency) v Essop; *joined case* Naeem v Secretary of State for Justice [2017] UKSC 27; [2017] 1 W.L.R. 1343; [2017] 3 All E.R. 551; [2017] I.C.R. 640; [2017] I.R.L.R. 558; Times, April 18, 2017, SC .... *Digested,* 17/**783**
Essop v Home Office (UK Border Agency); *sub nom* Home Office (UK Border Agency) v Essop; *joined case* Naeem v Secretary of State for Justice [2015] EWCA Civ 609; [2016] 3 All E.R. 137; [2015] I.C.R. 1063; [2015] I.R.L.R. 724, CA (Civ Div) .... *Digested,* 15/**835**: *Applied* 16/710: *Reversed* 17/783
Estasis Salotti di Colzani Aimo e Gianmario Colzani v RUWA Polstereimaschinen GmbH (24/76); *sub nom* Colzani v RUWA Polstereimaschinen GmbH (24/76) EU:C:1976:177; [1976] E.C.R. 1831; [1977] 1 C.M.L.R. 345; Times, December 20, 1976, ECJ .... *Digested,* 77/**1242**: *Applied* 85/1452, 89/4512, 01/3838, 01/800, 07/364, 07/659, 13/362, 16/434, 17/153: *Considered* 96/1097, 09/623, 17/295: *Followed* 10/502, 10/637, 11/472
Estmanco (Kilner House) Ltd v Greater London Council [1982] 1 W.L.R. 2; [1982] 1 All E.R. 437; 80 L.G.R. 464; (1981) 125 S.J. 790, QBD .... *Digested,* 82/**330**: *Considered* 13/353, 17/287
Estor Ltd v Multifit (UK) Ltd [2009] EWHC 2108 (TCC); 126 Con. L.R. 40, QBD (TCC) *Digested,* 10/**561**: *Applied* 17/494
Estrada Juffali v Juffali; *sub nom* Juffali v Juffali [2016] EWHC 1684 (Fam); [2016] 4 W.L.R. 119; [2017] 1 F.L.R. 729; [2016] Fam. Law 1086, Fam Div .... *Digested,* 16/**904**
Estrada Juffali v Juffali; *sub nom* Estrada v Al-Juffali; W v H [2016] EWCA Civ 176; [2017] Fam. 35; [2016] 3 W.L.R. 243; [2017] 1 All E.R. 790; [2017] 1 F.L.R. 702; [2016] 2 F.C.R. 477; Times, May 11, 2016; [2016] Fam. Law 673, CA (Civ Div) .... *Digested,* 16/**891**

Estrada Juffali v Juffali; *sub nom* Estrada v Al-Juffali; W v H [2016] EWHC 213 (Fam); [2017] 1 F.L.R. 669; [2016] Fam. Law 294, Fam Div
Affirmed 16/891

ETB (2014) Ltd v Revenue and Customs Commissioners; *sub nom* ETB (214) Ltd v Revenue and Customs Commissioners [2016] UKUT 424 (TCC); [2016] B.V.C. 540; [2016] S.T.I. 2654, UT (Tax) .... *Digested,* 17/**2273**

ETB (2014) Ltd v Revenue and Customs Commissioners; *sub nom* ETB (214) Ltd v Revenue and Customs Commissioners [2015] UKFTT 569 (TC), FTT (Tax)
Reversed 17/2273

EUI Ltd v Bristol Alliance Ltd Partnership see Bristol Alliance Ltd Partnership v Williams

Eurasian Natural Resources Corp Ltd v Dechert LLP; *sub nom* Dechert LLP v Eurasian Natural Resources Corp Ltd [2016] EWCA Civ 375; [2016] 1 W.L.R. 5027; [2017] 3 All E.R. 1084; [2016] C.P. Rep. 31; [2016] 3 Costs L.O. 327, CA (Civ Div) .... *Digested,* 16/**248**

Euro Park Service v Ministre des Finances et des Comptes publics (C-14/16) EU:C:2017:177; [2017] 3 C.M.L.R. 17; [2017] B.T.C. 5, ECJ (1st Chamber)

Euro Tyre - Sucursal em Portugal v Autoridade Tributaria e Aduaneira (C-21/16) EU:C:2017:106; [2017] B.V.C. 9, ECJ (9th Chamber)

Euro Wines (C&C) Ltd v Revenue and Customs Commissioners [2016] UKUT 359 (TCC), UT (Tax)
Applied 17/633

Euro-Asian Oil SA v Abilo (UK) Ltd; *joined case* Euro-Asian Oil SA v Credit Suisse AG [2016] EWHC 3340 (Comm); [2017] 1 Lloyd's Rep. 287, QBD (Comm) .... *Digested,* 17/**1998**

Euro-Asian Oil SA v Credit Suisse AG see Euro-Asian Oil SA v Abilo (UK) Ltd

European Commission v Aer Lingus Ltd (C-164/15 P); *joined case* European Commission v Ryanair Designated Activity Co (C-165/15 P) EU:C:2016:990; [2017] 2 C.M.L.R. 23, ECJ (3rd Chamber)

European Commission v Germany (C-616/15) EU:C:2017:721; [2017] B.V.C. 41, ECJ (4th Chamber)

European Commission v Kadi (C-584/10 P) EU:C:2013:518; [2014] 1 C.M.L.R. 24; [2014] All E.R. (EC) 123; (2013) 163(7578) N.L.J. 20, ECJ (Grand Chamber)
Applied 16/1157: *Followed* 17/1250

European Commission v Keramag Keramische Werke GmbH (C-613/13 P); *sub nom* Keramag Keramische Werke GmbH v European Commission (C-613/13 P) EU:C:2017:49; [2017] 4 C.M.L.R. 18, ECJ (1st Chamber)

European Commission v Luxembourg (C-274/15) EU:C:2017:333; [2017] B.V.C. 24, ECJ (4th Chamber)

European Commission v Netherlands (C-233/14) EU:C:2016:396; [2017] 1 C.M.L.R. 5; Times, June 21, 2016, ECJ (1st Chamber)

European Commission v Portugal (C-557/14) EU:C:2016:471; [2017] Env. L.R. 4, ECJ (3rd Chamber)

European Commission v Ryanair Designated Activity Co (C-165/15 P) see European Commission v Aer Lingus Ltd (C-164/15 P)

European Commission v Stichting Greenpeace Nederland (C-673/13 P) EU:C:2016:889; [2017] 2 C.M.L.R. 16, ECJ (5th Chamber)

European Commission v United Kingdom (C-304/15) EU:C:2016:706; [2017] Env. L.R. 6, ECJ (7th Chamber)

European Commission v United Kingdom (C-308/14) EU:C:2016:436; [2016] 1 W.L.R. 5049; [2016] 3 C.M.L.R. 41, ECJ (1st Chamber)
Followed 17/1796

European Commission v United Kingdom (C-530/11) EU:C:2014:67; [2014] Q.B. 988; [2014] 3 W.L.R. 853; [2014] 3 C.M.L.R. 6; [2014] Env. L.R. D2, ECJ (2nd Chamber) .... *Digested,* 14/**1222**:
Applied 17/280: *Considered* 16/2451

European Commission v World Duty Free Group SA (C-20/15 P) EU:C:2016:981; [2017] 2 C.M.L.R. 22, ECJ (Grand Chamber)

European Federation for Cosmetic Ingredients v Secretary of State for Business, Innovation and Skills (C-592/14) EU:C:2016:703; [2017] C.E.C. 585, ECJ (1st Chamber)

European Food SA v EUIPO (T-476/15) EU:T:2016:568; [2017] E.T.M.R. 2, GC (6th Chamber)

European Parliament v Council of the European Union (C-263/14) EU:C:2016:435; [2016] Q.B. 1123; [2016] 3 W.L.R. 1075; [2017] 1 C.M.L.R. 10, ECJ (Grand Chamber) .... *Digested,* 17/**892**

European Union Intellectual Property Office (EUIPO) v Instituto dos Vinhos do Douro e do PortoIP (C-56/16 P) EU:C:2017:693; [2017] E.T.M.R. 41, ECJ (2nd Chamber)

Eurosteel Ltd v Stinnes AG [2000] 1 All E.R. (Comm) 964; [2000] C.L.C. 470, QBD (Comm) .... *Digested,* 00/**736**: *Applied* 05/89: *Followed* 17/77

EV (A Child), Re see West Lothian Council v B

EV (Philippines) v Secretary of State for the Home Department [2014] EWCA Civ 874, CA (Civ Div)
Applied 16/1127, 17/1242: *Followed* 17/1235

Evans v Evans; *sub nom* Evans (Deceased), Re [1986] 1 W.L.R. 101; [1985] 3 All E.R. 289; [1986] 1 F.L.R. 319; [1986] Fam. Law 103; (1985) 82 L.S.G. 3530; (1985) 135 N.L.J. 1008, CA (Civ Div) .... *Digested,* 85/**1513**: *Applied* 08/3942: *Considered* 11/3253: *Distinguished* 08/3946: *Followed* 17/2216

Evans v Jones; *sub nom* Rococo Developments Ltd (In Liquidation), Re [2016] EWCA Civ 660; [2017] Ch. 1; [2016] 3 W.L.R. 1480; [2017] 1 B.C.L.C. 184; [2016] B.P.I.R. 1207, CA (Civ Div) .... *Digested,* 16/**1233**

Evans v Motor Insurers Bureau see White v White

Evans v Secretary of State for the Environment, Transport and the Regions (C-63/01) EU:C:2003:650; [2003] E.C.R. I-14447; [2004] R.T.R. 32; [2004] 1 C.M.L.R. 47; [2005] All E.R. (EC) 763; [2004] Lloyd's Rep. I.R. 391; Times, December 9, 2003, ECJ (5th Chamber) .... *Digested,* 04/**2230**: *Applied* 07/2469, 07/2496, 08/2212: *Considered* 09/2292, 11/1923: *Followed* 17/1348

Evans v Serious Fraud Office; *sub nom* R. v Evans (Eric) [2015] EWHC 263 (QB); [2015] 1 W.L.R. 3595; [2015] Lloyd's Rep. F.C. 223, QBD .... *Digested,* 15/**612**: *Applied* 17/620

Evans v Serious Fraud Office [2015] EWHC 1525 (QB); [2015] 3 Costs L.R. 557; [2015] Lloyd's Rep. F.C. 496, QBD
Applied 17/620

Evans (Deceased), Re see Evans v Evans

Evans (Michael) v Inspector of the Serious Fraud Office see R. (on the application of Evans) v Director of the Serious Fraud Office

Evans Construction Co Ltd v Bass Holdings Ltd see Evans Construction Co Ltd v Charrington & Co Ltd

Evans Construction Co Ltd v Charrington & Co Ltd; *joined case* Evans Construction Co Ltd v Bass Holdings Ltd [1983] Q.B. 810; [1983] 2 W.L.R. 117; [1983] 1 All E.R. 310; (1982) 264 E.G. 347; (1982) 79 L.S.G. 1138, CA (Civ Div) .... *Digested,* 83/**3025**: *Applied* 90/480, 17/195: *Considered* 89/2104, 90/2770, 91/2214, 91/3204: *Followed* 98/374

Evonik Degussa GmbH v European Commission (C-162/15 P) EU:C:2017:205; [2017] 4 C.M.L.R. 28, ECJ (Grand Chamber)

Evonik Degussa UK Holdings Ltd v Revenue and Customs Commissioners see Test Claimants in the FII Group Litigation v Revenue and Customs Commissioners

Ewart v Cochranes (1861) 23 D. (H.L.) 3, HL
Applied 17/2655

Eweida v United Kingdom (48420/10); *joined cases* McFarlane v United Kingdom (36516/10); Ladele v United Kingdom (51671/10); Chaplin v United Kingdom (59842/10) [2013] I.R.L.R. 231; (2013) 57 E.H.R.R. 8; 34 B.H.R.C. 519; [2013] Eq. L.R. 264; Times, February 4, 2013; (2013) 163 N.L.J. 70, ECHR .... *Digested,* 13/**1548**: *Applied* 16/711, 17/822: *Considered* 14/3099: *Followed* 13/1568

Ewing v Inverclyde Council 2016 Hous. L.R. 121; 2016 G.W.D. 32-576, Sh Ct (North Strathclyde) (Greenock)
Applied 17/2656

Ex p. the Debtor v Official Receiver see Baron, Re

Excalibur Ventures LLC v Texas Keystone Inc; *sub nom* Psari Holdings Ltd v Association of Litigation Funders of England and Wales; *joined case* Texas Keystone Inc v Psari Holdings Ltd [2014] EWHC 3436 (Comm); [2014] 6 Costs L.O. 975, QBD (Comm) .... *Digested,* 15/**282**: *Affirmed* 17/253

Excalibur Ventures LLC v Texas Keystone Inc; *sub nom* Psari Holdings Ltd v Association of Litigation Funders of England and Wales; *joined case* Texas Keystone Inc v Psari Holdings Ltd [2016] EWCA Civ 1144; [2017] 1 W.L.R. 2221; [2017] C.P. Rep. 13; [2016] 6 Costs L.O. 999; [2017] C.I.L.L. 3919, CA (Civ Div) .... *Digested,* 17/**253**

Excelsior Commercial & Industrial Holdings Ltd v Salisbury Hamer Aspden & Johnson (Costs); *sub nom* Excelsior Commercial & Industrial Holdings Ltd v Salisbury Hammer Aspden & Johnson [2002] EWCA Civ 879; [2002] C.P. Rep. 67; [2002] C.P.L.R. 693; Independent, June 18, 2002, CA (Civ Div) .... *Digested,* 02/**353**: *Applied* 07/399, 09/373, 10/1283, 11/285, 11/288, 13/309, 16/210, 17/263: *Considered* 06/380, 07/398, 08/318, 09/374, 10/290: *Followed* 14/1337, 15/233, 15/236, 16/207, 17/246

Excelsior Commercial & Industrial Holdings Ltd v Salisbury Hammer Aspden & Johnson see Excelsior Commercial & Industrial Holdings Ltd v Salisbury Hamer Aspden & Johnson (Costs)

Execution of a European Arrest Warrant against Aranyosi (C-404/15 PPU) see Criminal Proceedings against Aranyosi (C-404/15 PPU)

Execution of a European Arrest Warrant against Bob-Dogi (C-241/15) see Criminal Proceedings against Bob-Dogi (C-241/15)

Executors of Lady Fox v Inland Revenue Commissioners see Gray v Inland Revenue Commissioners

Exler (Deceased), Re see Keeling v Keeling

EXP v Barker [2017] EWCA Civ 63; [2017] Med. L.R. 121; (2017) 155 B.M.L.R. 18, CA (Civ Div) .... *Digested,* 17/**185**

EXP v Barker [2015] EWHC 1289 (QB), QBD *Affirmed* 17/185

Express Electrical Distributors Ltd v Beavis [2016] EWCA Civ 765; [2016] 1 W.L.R. 4783; [2016] B.C.C. 566; [2016] B.P.I.R. 1386, CA (Civ Div) .... *Digested,* 17/**1330**: *Applied* 17/1334

Express Newspapers Plc v News (UK) Ltd [1990] 1 W.L.R. 1320; [1990] 3 All E.R. 376; [1991] F.S.R. 36; [1990] F.S.R. 359; Times, February 13, 1990; Independent, February 14, 1990; Guardian, March 14, 1990; (1990) 87(35) L.S.G. 41, Ch D .... *Digested,* 91/**2978**: *Applied* 09/983, 16/1403: *Considered* 98/3422, 17/433

Exsus Travel Ltd v Baker Tilly [2016] EWHC 2818 (Ch), Ch D *Applied* 17/328

EY (Turkey) v Secretary of State for the Home Department; *sub nom* Y v Secretary of State for the Home Department [2011] CSIH 3; 2011 S.C. 388; 2011 S.L.T. 508; 2011 S.C.L.R. 202; 2011 G.W.D. 3-115, IH (Ex Div) .... *Digested,* 11/**4386**: *Applied* 11/4390: *Considered* 17/2663

Eynsham Cricket Club v Revenue and Customs Commissioners [2017] S.T.I. 1901, FTT (Tax)

Ezsias v North Glamorgan NHS Trust [2007] EWCA Civ 330; [2007] 4 All E.R. 940; [2007] I.C.R. 1126; [2007] I.R.L.R. 603; Times, March 19, 2007; (2007) 104(12) L.S.G. 34, CA (Civ Div) .... *Digested,* 07/**1428**: *Applied* 16/701: *Considered* 12/3988: *Followed* 13/1053, 17/821

Ezsias v Welsh Ministers 6CF90111, QBD (Cardiff) *Considered* 17/1171

F v Birmingham City Council [2006] EWCA Civ 1427; [2007] H.L.R. 18; (2006) 103(45) L.S.G. 29; (2006) 150 S.J.L.B. 1466; [2006] N.P.C. 119, CA (Civ Div) .. *Digested,* 07/**2135**: *Considered* 09/1904, 17/1159

F v F (MMR Vaccine); *sub nom* F v F (Welfare of Children: Immunisation) [2013] EWHC 2683 (Fam); [2014] 1 F.L.R. 1328; (2014) 136 B.M.L.R. 105; [2014] Fam. Law 29, Fam Div .... *Digested,* 14/**1304**: *Applied* 17/923

F v F (Welfare of Children: Immunisation) see F v F (MMR Vaccine)

F v L (Child Arrangements Order: Relocation) see D (A Child), Re

F v L (Permission to Relocate: Appeal) see D (A Child), Re

F v M [2017] EWHC 949 (Fam); [2018] Fam. 1; [2018] 2 W.L.R. 178; [2017] 3 F.C.R. 467, Fam Div *Applied* 17/1036

F v M [2015] EWHC 3601 (Fam); [2016] Fam. Law 291, Fam Div *Applied* 17/1055

F (A Child) (Care Proceedings: Failures of Expert), Re [2016] EWHC 2149 (Fam); [2017] 1 F.L.R. 1304; [2016] Fam. Law 1326, Fam Div .... *Digested,* 17/**992**

F (A Child) (Care Proceedings: Habitual Residence), Re [2014] EWCA Civ 789; [2015] 1 F.C.R. 88; [2014] Fam. Law 1244, CA (Civ Div) .... *Digested,* 15/**1023**: *Considered* 17/1066

F (A Child) (Financial Provision: Legal Costs Funding), Re; *sub nom* BC v DE (Proceedings under Children Act 1989: Legal Costs Funding) [2016] EWHC 1806 (Fam); [2016] 1 W.L.R. 4720; [2017] 1 F.L.R. 1521; [2016] Fam. Law 1219, Fam Div .... *Digested,* 17/**1017**

F (A Child) (International Relocation Case), Re; *sub nom* F (A Child) (International Relocation: Welfare Analysis), Re; DF v N B-F [2015] EWCA Civ 882; [2017] 1 F.L.R. 979; [2016] 2 F.C.R. 368; [2016] Fam. Law 565, CA (Civ Div) .... *Digested,* 16/**859**: *Applied* 16/858, 16/999, 17/1123, 17/913: *Considered* 16/883

F (A Child) (International Relocation: Welfare Analysis), Re see F (A Child) (International Relocation Case), Re

F (A Child) (Permission to Relocate), Re; *sub nom* F (Relocation), Re [2012] EWCA Civ 1364; [2013] 1 F.L.R. 645; [2012] 3 F.C.R. 443; [2013] Fam. Law 37; (2012) 156(41) S.J.L.B. 31, CA (Civ Div) .... *Digested,* 13/**1248**: *Applied* 16/858: *Followed* 16/859, 17/970

F (A Child) (Return Order: Power to Revoke), Re; *sub nom* TF v PJ (Reversal of Judgment) [2014] EWHC 1780 (Fam); [2014] 1 W.L.R. 4375; [2015] 1 F.L.R. 861; [2014] Fam. Law 1226, Fam Div .... *Digested,* 15/**1079**: *Applied* 15/1048: *Considered* 17/1039

F (Children) (Adoption: Natural Parents), Re [2006] EWCA Civ 1345; [2007] 1 F.L.R. 363; Times, November 16, 2006; [2006] Fam. Law 1015; (2006) 150 S.J.L.B. 1394, CA (Civ Div) .... *Digested,* 07/**1683**: *Applied* 17/917

F (Children) (Return Order: Appeal), Re; *sub nom* F (Children) (Setting Aside Return Orders), Re [2016] EWCA Civ 1253; [2017] 4 W.L.R. 4; [2017] 1 F.L.R. 1535; [2017] 1 F.C.R. 163, CA (Civ Div) .... *Digested,* 17/**1039**

F (Children) (Setting Aside Return Orders), Re see F (Children) (Return Order: Appeal), Re

F (Children) (Thai Surrogacy: Enduring Family Relationship), Re; *sub nom* P v Z [2016] EWHC 1594 (Fam); [2016] 4 W.L.R. 126; [2017] 2 F.L.R. 168; [2016] Fam. Law 1098, Fam Ct .... *Digested,* 16/**940**

F (Children), Re [2016] EWCA Civ 546; [2016] 3 F.C.R. 255, CA (Civ Div) *Considered* 17/929

F (Relocation), Re see F (A Child) (Permission to Relocate), Re

F Hoffmann La Roche & Co AG v Commission of the European Communities (85/76) EU:C:1979:36; [1979] E.C.R. 461; [1979] 3 C.M.L.R. 211; [1980] F.S.R. 13, ECJ .... *Digested,* 79/**1204**: *Applied* 03/5306, 07/1547, 07/1548, 09/562: *Considered* 05/575, 07/2723, 10/460, 10/463, 10/483, 17/410: *Followed* 07/616, 09/546

F Privatstiftung v HB (40 b 36/16x) [2017] E.C.C. 14; [2017] E.C.D.R. 27, OGH (A)

F&C Alternative Investments (Holdings) Ltd v Barthelemy; *sub nom* F&C Partners LLP, Re; *joined case* Barthelemy v F&C Alternative Investments (Holdings) Ltd [2011] EWHC 1731 (Ch); [2012] Ch. 613; [2012] 3 W.L.R. 10; [2012] Bus. L.R. 891, Ch D .... *Digested,* 12/**2319**: *Considered* 17/2067

F&C Alternative Investments (Holdings) Ltd v Barthelemy (Costs); *sub nom* Barthelemy v F&C Alternative Investments (Holdings) Ltd; *joined case* F&C Partners LLP, Re [2012] EWCA Civ 843; [2013] 1 W.L.R. 548; [2012] 4 All E.R. 1096; [2013] Bus. L.R. 186; [2013] 1 Costs L.R. 35, CA (Civ Div) .... *Digested,* 13/**320**: *Applied* 14/371, 16/194, 17/225, 17/272: *Considered* 14/445: *Distinguished* 13/323: *Followed* 13/349, 16/227

F&C Partners LLP, Re see F&C Alternative Investments (Holdings) Ltd v Barthelemy

F&C Partners LLP, Re see F&C Alternative Investments (Holdings) Ltd v Barthelemy (Costs)

F-K v Poland see R. (on the application of HH) v Westminster City Magistrates' Court

F-T v Hampton Dene Primary School Governors [2016] UKUT 468 (AAC); [2017] E.L.R. 38, UT (AAC)

FA & AB Ltd v Lupton (Inspector of Taxes) see Lupton (Inspector of Taxes) v FA & AB Ltd

Fagan v Knowsley MBC 83 L.G.R. 782; (1985) 50 P. & C.R. 363; [1985] 2 E.G.L.R. 39; (1985) 275 E.G. 717; [1985] R.V.R. 176; [1986] J.P.L. 355, CA (Civ Div) ..... *Digested,* 86/**358**: *Applied* 17/1514: *Considered* 89/2160

Fage UK Ltd v Chobani UK Ltd [2014] EWCA Civ 5; [2014] E.T.M.R. 26; [2014] F.S.R. 29; [2014] C.T.L.C. 49, CA (Civ Div) .... *Digested,* 14/**1889**: *Applied* 16/2171, 17/2253: *Considered* 15/1545: *Followed* 16/1019

Fahimian v Germany (C-544/15) EU:C:2017:255; [2017] 1 W.L.R. 4143; [2017] 3 C.M.L.R. 28; [2018] C.E.C. 3, ECJ (Grand Chamber)

Fairhold Freeholds No.2 Ltd v Moody [2016] UKUT 311 (LC); [2017] L. & T.R. 16, UT (Lands) .... *Digested,* 17/**1442**

Fairstar Heavy Transport NV v Adkins [2013] EWCA Civ 886; [2013] 2 C.L.C. 272; [2014] E.M.L.R. 12; [2014] F.S.R. 8; [2014] Bus. L.R. D2, CA (Civ Div) .... *Digested,* 14/**80**: *Considered* 17/768

Fairway Lakes Ltd v Revenue and Customs Commissioners [2016] UKUT 340 (TCC); [2016] B.V.C. 530; [2016] S.T.I. 2634, UT (Tax) .... *Digested,* 17/**2232**
Fairway Lakes Ltd v Revenue and Customs Commissioners [2015] UKFTT 605 (TC); [2016] S.T.I. 104, FTT (Tax)
Affirmed 17/2232
Falconbridge Nickel Mines Ltd v Chimo Shipping Ltd [1973] 2 Lloyd's Rep. 469, Sup Ct (Can) .... *Digested,* 74/**3545**:
Considered 74/3543, 17/2003: *Distinguished* 79/2434
Falgor Commercial SA v Alsabahia Inc (1986) 18 H.L.R. 123; [1986] 1 E.G.L.R. 41; (1985) 277 E.G. 185; Times, November 22, 1985, CA (Civ Div) .... *Digested,* 86/**1880**:
Considered 17/1443
Falkirk Council v Gillies 2016 Hous. L.R. 104, Sh Ct (Tayside) (Falkirk)
Reversed 17/2709
Falkirk Council v Gillies [2016] CSIH 90; 2017 S.C. 230; 2016 G.W.D. 40-724, IH (Ex Div) .... *Digested,* 17/**2709**
Falmouth House Freehold Co Ltd v Morgan Walker LLP [2010] EWHC 3092 (Ch); [2011] 2 Costs L.R. 292, Ch D .... *Digested,* 11/**2127**:
Considered 17/288
Family X v Air Canada (Societe) [2017] I.L.Pr. 19, Cass (F)
Fannigan Holdings Ltd v Doherty [2017] B.P.I.R. 980, Ch D .... *Digested,* 17/**1322**
Fanning Social Care Ltd v Revenue and Customs Commissioners see Christianuyi Ltd v Revenue and Customs Commissioners
Farenco Shipping Co Ltd v Daebo Shipping Co Ltd (The Bremen Max) [2008] EWHC 2755 (Comm); [2009] 1 All E.R. (Comm) 423; [2009] 1 Lloyd's Rep. 81, QBD (Comm) .... *Digested,* 09/**3560**:
Considered 17/1999
Farkas v Nemzeti Ado- es Vamhivatal Del-alfoldi Regionalis Ado Foigazgatosaga (C-564/15) EU:C:2017:302; [2017] B.V.C. 17, ECJ (4th Chamber)
Farmah v Birmingham City Council; *joined cases* Callaghan v Birmingham City Council; Fenton v Asda Stores Ltd; Asda Stores Ltd v Brierley; Sainsbury's Supermarket Ltd v Ahmed [2017] I.R.L.R. 785, EAT .... *Digested,* 17/**799**
Farmer v Heart of Birmingham Teaching Primary Care Trust [2016] I.C.R. 1088, EAT . *Digested,* 17/**792**
Farn v Loosley [2017] NZHC 317; 20 I.T.E.L.R. 69, HC (NZ)
Farnborough Airport Properties Co v Revenue & Customs Commissioners [2017] UKUT 394 (TCC); [2017] S.T.C. 2293; [2017] B.T.C. 532, UT (Tax) .... *Digested,* 17/**2109**
Farnborough Airport Properties Co Ltd v Revenue and Customs Commissioners [2016] UKFTT 431 (TC); [2016] S.F.T.D. 826, FTT (Tax) .... *Digested,* 16/**2059**:
Affirmed 17/2109
Farren v United Lincolnshire Hospitals NHS Foundation Trust 2600417/2015, ET
Reversed 17/851
FAS v Secretary of State for the Home Department; *sub nom* SAS v Bradford MDC [2015] EWCA Civ 951; [2016] 1 W.L.R. 407; [2016] 2 All E.R. 251; [2016] 2 F.L.R. 1035; [2016] 1 F.C.R. 191; Times, December 17, 2015; [2015] Fam. Law 1449, CA (Civ Div) .... *Digested,* 16/**811**:
Followed 17/1034
Fast Drinks Ltd v Cetyl International Group Inc [2016] EWHC 3501 (QB); [2017] L. & T.R. 17, QBD .... *Digested,* 17/**1451**
Fastrack Contractors Ltd v Morrison Construction Ltd [2000] B.L.R. 168; 75 Con. L.R. 33; (2000) 16 Const. L.J. 273, QBD (TCC) .... *Digested,* 00/**227**:
Applied 10/847, 16/395, 17/465: *Considered* 01/858, 06/671, 12/586, 15/463
Father v Mother; *sub nom* A (Letter to a Young Person), Re [2017] EWFC 48; [2017] 3 F.C.R. 323, Fam Ct .... *Digested,* 17/**969**
Fathollahipour v Aliabadibenisi see R. (on the application of Hysaj) v Secretary of State for the Home Department
Fatnani v General Medical Council; *sub nom* R. (on the application of Fatnani) v General Medical Council; *joined case* Raschid v General Medical Council [2007] EWCA Civ 46; [2007] 1 W.L.R. 1460; [2007] I.C.R. 811; (2007) 104(5) L.S.G. 29; (2007) 151 S.J.L.B. 127, CA (Civ Div) .... *Digested,* 07/**1943**:
Applied 08/1804, 08/966, 09/1750, 10/1540, 10/1545, 17/1111:
Considered 10/1539, 15/2068: *Followed* 09/1749
Faulkner v Revenue and Customs Commissioners [2017] UKFTT 693 (TC); [2017] S.T.I. 2071, FTT (Tax)
Faulkner v United Kingdom (68909/13) (2017) 64 E.H.R.R. 18, ECHR
Fazenda Publica v Camara Municipal do Porto (C446/98) EU:C:2000:691; [2001] S.T.C. 560; [2000] E.C.R. I-11435; [2001] B.T.C. 5414; [2001] B.V.C. 493; [2000] S.T.I. 1736, ECJ (5th Chamber) .... *Digested,* 01/**5561**:
Applied 03/4333, 17/2268
FB v Princess Alexandra Hospital NHS Trust see FB v Rana

FB v PS [2015] EWHC 2797 (Fam); [2016] 2 F.L.R. 697; [2016] Fam. Law 156, Fam Div .... *Digested,* 17/**1009**

FB v Rana; *sub nom* FB v Princess Alexandra Hospital NHS Trust [2017] EWCA Civ 334; [2017] P.I.Q.R. P17; [2017] Med. L.R. 279; (2017) 156 B.M.L.R. 152, CA (Civ Div) .... *Digested,* 17/**1559**

FB v Rana; *sub nom* FB v Princess Alexandra Hospital NHS Trust [2015] EWHC 1536 (Admin), QBD (Admin)
Reversed 17/1559

FD (Inherent Jurisdiction: Power of Arrest), Re see D (Vulnerable Adult) (Injunction: Power of Arrest), Re

FDR Ltd v Dutton see Dutton v FDR Ltd

FE v YE see E v E

Fecitt v NHS Manchester [2011] EWCA Civ 1190; [2012] I.C.R. 372; [2012] I.R.L.R. 64; (2011) 108(43) L.S.G. 20, CA (Civ Div) .... *Digested,* 12/**1117**:
Followed 16/705, 17/815

Federacion de Servicios Privados del sindicato Comisiones obreras (CC OO) v Tyco Integrated Security SL (C-266/14) EU:C:2015:578; [2016] 1 C.M.L.R. 22; [2016] C.E.C. 433; [2015] I.C.R. 1159; [2015] I.R.L.R. 935; Times, October 7, 2015, ECJ (3rd Chamber)
Considered 17/856

Federated Homes Ltd v Mill Lodge Properties Ltd [1980] 1 W.L.R. 594; [1980] 1 All E.R. 371; (1980) 39 P. & C.R. 576; (1979) 254 E.G. 39; (1980) 124 S.J. 412, CA (Civ Div) .... *Digested,* 80/**2251**:
Applied 08/3110: *Considered* 84/2956, 89/473, 04/3250: *Distinguished* 85/1882:
Followed 17/1857

Federatie Nederlandse Vakvereniging v Smallsteps BV (C-126/16) EU:C:2017:489; [2017] B.C.C. 540; [2018] 1 C.M.L.R. 19; [2017] I.C.R. 1316; [2017] I.R.L.R. 852, ECJ (3rd Chamber)

Federation of Independent Practitioner Organisations v Competition and Markets Authority [2016] EWCA Civ 777; [2017] U.K.C.L.R. 1, CA (Civ Div) .... *Digested,* 17/**413**

Federation of Independent Practitioner Organisations v Competition and Markets Authority [2015] CAT 8; [2015] Comp. A.R. 214, CAT .... *Digested,* 15/**411**:
Affirmed 17/413

Fee (Rachel) v HM Advocate; *sub nom* Trelfa (Rachel) v HM Advocate [2017] HCJAC 13; 2017 S.L.T. 469; 2017 S.C.L. 376; 2017 S.C.C.R. 166; 2017 G.W.D. 10-137, HCJ .... *Digested,* 17/**2545**

Feeney (Mark) v HM Advocate [2017] HCJAC 16; 2017 S.C.L. 485; 2017 G.W.D. 11-164, HCJ .... *Digested,* 17/**2803**

Fehily v Atkinson [2016] EWHC 3069 (Ch); [2017] Bus. L.R. 695; [2017] B.P.I.R. 21, Ch D .... *Digested,* 17/**1307**

Feilen v Finanzamt Fulda (C-123/15) EU:C:2016:496; [2016] 4 W.L.R. 151; [2017] S.T.C. 480; [2017] 1 C.M.L.R. 16; [2016] S.T.I. 2197, ECJ (2nd Chamber)

Feldarol Foundry Plc v Amari Sant Agata Classics see Feldarol Foundry Plc v Hermes Leasing (London) Ltd

Feldarol Foundry Plc v Hermes Leasing (London) Ltd; *sub nom* Feldaroll Foundry Plc v Hermes Leasing (London) Ltd; *joined case* Feldarol Foundry Plc v Amari Sant Agata Classics [2004] EWCA Civ 747; (2004) 101(24) L.S.G. 32; (2004) 148 S.J.L.B. 630, CA (Civ Div)
Applied 17/657

Feldaroll Foundry Plc v Hermes Leasing (London) Ltd see Feldarol Foundry Plc v Hermes Leasing (London) Ltd

Fellowes International Holdings Ltd v Kyrgyz Mobil Tel Ltd see AK Investment CJSC v Kyrgyz Mobil Tel Ltd

Fenice Investments Inc v Jerram Falkus Construction Ltd [2011] EWHC 1678 (TCC); 141 Con. L.R. 206; [2011] C.I.L.L. 3068, QBD (TCC) .... *Digested,* 12/**585**:
Applied 17/657

Fenton v Asda Stores Ltd see Farmah v Birmingham City Council

Feralpi Holding SpA v European Commission (C-85/15 P) EU:C:2017:709; [2017] 5 C.M.L.R. 23, ECJ (9th Chamber)

Ferguson v Lacey (Unreported, April 24, 2017), CC (Yeovil) [*Irwin Mitchell LLP, Riverside West, 1 Millsands, Sheffield*] .... *Digested,* 17/**1663**

Ferguson (Derek Charles) v HM Advocate [2008] HCJAC 71; 2009 S.L.T. 67; 2009 S.C.L. 250; 2009 S.C.C.R. 78; 2008 G.W.D. 40-595, HCJ .... *Digested,* 09/**4828**:
Applied 15/2998, 16/2565: *Considered* 09/4805, 10/4113, 13/3602, 15/2987, 15/2999, 17/2558

Ferguson (James Douglas) v HM Advocate; *joined cases* Nolan (Thomas) v HM Advocate; Balfour (Bruce James) v HM Advocate; Cameron (Stuart) v HM Advocate [2014] HCJAC 19; 2014 S.L.T. 431; 2014 S.C.C.R. 244; 2014 G.W.D. 10-194, HCJ .... *Digested,* 14/**3778**: *Applied* 17/2808: *Considered* 17/2809

Fern Computer Consultancy Ltd v Intergraph Cadworx & Analysis Solutions Inc [2014] EWHC 2908 (Ch); [2014] Bus. L.R. 1397; [2015] 1 Lloyd's Rep. 1; [2014] 2 C.L.C. 326, Ch D .... *Digested,* 15/**56**: *Considered* 17/45

Fernhill Primary School Ltd v Revenue and Customs Commissioners [2016] UKFTT 220 (TC); [2016] S.F.T.D. 875; [2016] S.T.I. 1672, FTT (Tax) .... *Digested,* 17/**2170**

Ferreira v HM Senior Coroner for Inner South London see R. (on the application of Ferreira) v HM Senior Coroner for Inner South London

Ferriera Valsabbia SpA v European Commission (C-86/15 P); *sub nom* Alfa Acciai SpA v European Commission (C-87/15 P) EU:C:2017:717; [2017] 5 C.M.L.R. 24, ECJ (9th Chamber)

Ferriere Nord SpA v European Commission (C-88/15) EU:C:2017:716; [2017] 5 C.M.L.R. 25, ECJ (9th Chamber)

Ferryways NV v Associated British Ports (The Humber Way) [2008] EWHC 225 (Comm); [2008] 2 All E.R. (Comm) 504; [2008] 1 Lloyd's Rep. 639; [2008] 1 C.L.C. 117, QBD (Comm) .... *Digested,* 08/**3464**: *Applied* 17/505

FF v KF [2017] EWHC 1093 (Fam); [2017] 2 F.C.R. 509, Fam Div .... *Digested,* 17/**1022**

FG v Sweden (43611/11) 41 B.H.R.C. 595, ECHR (Grand Chamber)

FG Minter Ltd v Welsh Health Technical Services Organisation 13 B.L.R. 1, CA (Civ Div) .... *Digested,* 81/**187**: *Applied* 84/225: *Approved* 94/5413: *Followed* 17/468

FHR European Ventures LLP v Cedar Capital Partners LLC; *sub nom* FHR European Ventures LLP v Mankarious [2014] UKSC 45; [2015] A.C. 250; [2014] 3 W.L.R. 535; [2014] 4 All E.R. 79; [2014] 2 All E.R. (Comm) 425; [2014] 2 Lloyd's Rep. 471; [2014] 2 B.C.L.C. 145; [2014] Lloyd's Rep. F.C. 617; [2014] 3 E.G.L.R. 119; [2014] W.T.L.R. 1135; 10 A.L.R. Int'l 635; [2015] 1 P. & C.R. DG1, SC .... *Digested,* 14/**79**: *Followed* 17/321

FHR European Ventures LLP v Mankarious see FHR European Ventures LLP v Cedar Capital Partners LLC

FI (Nigeria) v Secretary of State for the Home Department see EB (Kosovo) v Secretary of State for the Home Department

Fidelidade-Companhia de Seguros SA v Caisse Suisse de Compensation (C-287/16) EU:C:2017:575; [2017] R.T.R. 26; [2017] Lloyd's Rep. I.R. 540, ECJ

Fidex Ltd v Revenue and Customs Commissioners [2016] EWCA Civ 385; [2016] 4 All E.R. 1063; [2016] S.T.C. 1920; [2016] B.T.C. 16, CA (Civ Div) .... *Digested,* 16/**2053**: *Considered* 17/2101: *Followed* 17/2113

Fielding v Hunt see Burnden Group Ltd, Re

FIH Holding A/S v European Commission (T-386/14) EU:T:2016:474; [2017] 1 C.M.L.R. 43, GC (6th Chamber)

Finance and Business Training Ltd v Revenue and Customs Commissioners [2016] EWCA Civ 7; [2016] 4 W.L.R. 47; [2017] 1 All E.R. 758; [2016] S.T.C. 2190; [2016] B.V.C. 6; [2016] S.T.I. 211, CA (Civ Div) .... *Digested,* 16/**2173**

Financial Conduct Authority v Macris see Macris v Financial Conduct Authority

Finch v Lloyds TSB Bank Plc; *joined case* Promontoria Holding 87 BV v Finch [2016] EWHC 1236 (QB); [2017] 1 B.C.L.C. 34, QBD (Merc) .... *Digested,* 17/**172**

Findcharm Ltd v Churchill Group Ltd [2017] EWHC 1108 (TCC); 172 Con. L.R. 117; [2017] 3 Costs L.O. 263; [2017] C.I.L.L. 3980, QBD (TCC) .... *Digested,* 17/**275**

Findlay v Secretary of State for the Home Department see Findlay, Re

Findlay, Re; *sub nom* Findlay v Secretary of State for the Home Department [1985] A.C. 318; [1984] 3 W.L.R. 1159; [1984] 3 All E.R. 801; [1985] Crim. L.R. 154; (1985) 82 L.S.G. 38; (1984) 128 S.J. 816, HL .... *Digested,* 84/**2756**: *Applied* 94/4983, 99/5221, 00/4490, 07/4378, 16/1479: *Cited* 94/2469: *Considered* 87/20, 87/3617, 94/43, 95/3098, 95/3099, 95/3252, 99/2684, 06/2224, 10/2595: *Followed* 97/3934, 14/2234, 17/1772

Findmypast Ltd (formerly Brightsolid Online Technology Ltd) v Revenue and Customs Commissioners see Findmypast Ltd (formerly DC Thomson Family History Ltd) v Revenue and Customs Commissioners

Findmypast Ltd (formerly DC Thomson Family History Ltd) v Revenue and Customs Commissioners; *sub nom* Findmypast Ltd (formerly Brightsolid Online Technology Ltd) v Revenue and Customs Commissioners [2016] UKUT 17 (TCC); [2016] S.T.C. 1107; [2016] B.V.C. 503; [2016] S.T.I. 241, UT (Tax) .... *Digested,* 16/**2208**: *Affirmed* 17/2848

Finger v Bulgaria (37346/05) (2017) 64 E.H.R.R. 9, ECHR

Finlayson Media Communications Ltd v Revenue and Customs Commissioners [2017] UKFTT 491 (TC); [2017] S.T.I. 1421, FTT (Tax)

Finmeccanica Global Services SpA v Revenue and Customs Commissioners see Finmeccanica Group Services SpA v Revenue and Customs Commissioners

Finmeccanica Group Services SpA v Revenue and Customs Commissioners; *sub nom* Revenue and Customs Commissioners v Finmeccanica Group Services SpA; Finmeccanica Global Services SpA v Revenue and Customs Commissioners [2015] UKUT 378 (TCC); [2016] S.T.C. 916; [2015] B.V.C. 525; [2015] S.T.I. 2535, UT (Tax) .... *Digested,* 15/**2617**: *Affirmed* 17/2278

Finmeccanica Group Services SpA v Revenue and Customs Commissioners; *sub nom* Revenue and Customs Commissioners v Finmeccanica Group Services SpA; Finmeccanica Global Services SpA v Revenue and Customs Commissioners [2016] EWCA Civ 1105; [2017] S.T.C. 1017; [2016] B.V.C. 41; [2016] S.T.I. 3055, CA (Civ Div) .... *Digested,* 17/**2278**

Finnegan (Harry) v HM Advocate [2016] HCJAC 88; 2016 S.L.T. 1139; 2016 S.C.L. 1003; 2016 G.W.D. 31-557, HCJ .... *Digested,* 17/**2793**

Finnish Society of Social Rights v Finland (106/2014) (2017) 65 E.H.R.R. SE15, ECSR

Finnish Society of Social Rights v Finland (107/2014) (2017) 65 E.H.R.R. SE4, ECSR

Fiona Trust & Holding Corp v Privalov [2010] EWHC 3199 (Comm); (2011) 108(3) L.S.G. 17, QBD (Comm)
Applied 15/390: *Considered* 17/179

Fiona Trust & Holding Corp v Privalov; *sub nom* Premium Nafta Products Ltd v Fili Shipping Co Ltd [2007] UKHL 40; [2007] 4 All E.R. 951; [2007] 2 All E.R. (Comm) 1053; [2007] Bus. L.R. 1719; [2008] 1 Lloyd's Rep. 254; [2007] 2 C.L.C. 553; 114 Con. L.R. 69; Times, October 25, 2007; [2007] C.I.L.L. 2528; (2007) 104(42) L.S.G. 34; (2007) 151 S.J.L.B. 1364, HL .... *Digested,* 07/**792**: *Applied* 08/154, 09/620, 10/371, 11/75, 12/481, 15/366, 15/506, 16/398, 16/72, 17/1377: *Considered* 08/249, 08/425, 08/670, 09/607, 09/733, 10/173, 10/351, 10/563, 11/873, 13/2803, 13/99, 14/557, 15/430, 17/375, 17/377, 17/65: *Followed* 10/353, 10/420, 12/105, 12/114, 13/250, 13/96, 14/133

Fiona Trust and Holding Corp v Privalov [2016] EWHC 2163 (Comm); [2017] 2 All E.R. 570; [2017] 2 All E.R. (Comm) 57, QBD (Comm) .... *Digested,* 17/**302**

Fiona Trust Holdings Corp v Privalov [2007] EWHC 39 (Comm), QBD (Comm)
Applied 17/78

Fire Nymph Products Ltd v Heating Centre Pty Ltd (1992) 7 A.C.S.R. 365, CA (NSW)
Considered 17/159

First Independent Factors and Finance Ltd v Mountford [2008] EWHC 835 (Ch); [2008] B.C.C. 598; [2008] 2 B.C.L.C. 297; [2008] B.P.I.R. 515, Ch D (Birmingham) .... *Digested,* 08/**2146**: *Applied* 17/1297

First Subsea Ltd (formerly BSW Ltd) v Balltec Ltd [2017] EWCA Civ 186; [2018] Ch. 25; [2017] 3 W.L.R. 896; [2018] 1 B.C.L.C. 20; [2017] F.S.R. 37; Times, May 12, 2017, CA (Civ Div) .... *Digested,* 17/**321**

First Subsea Ltd (formerly BSW Ltd) v Balltec Ltd [2014] EWHC 866 (Ch), Ch D
Affirmed 17/321

First Time Ltd v Liquidator of Denmore Investments Ltd [2016] SAC (Civ) 9; 2016 S.L.T. (Sh Ct) 430; 2016 G.W.D. 32-568, SAC .... *Digested,* 17/**2451**

First Tower Trustees Ltd v CDS (Superstores International) Ltd [2017] EWHC 891 (Ch); [2017] 4 W.L.R. 73; [2017] 2 P. & C.R. 16, Ch D .... *Digested,* 17/**1446**

FirstGroup Plc v Paulley see Paulley v FirstGroup Plc

Firstpost Homes Ltd v Johnson [1995] 1 W.L.R. 1567; [1995] 4 All E.R. 355; [1996] 1 E.G.L.R. 175; [1996] 13 E.G. 125; Times, August 14, 1995; (1995) 92(28) L.S.G. 30; (1995) 139 S.J.L.B. 187; [1995] N.P.C. 135, CA (Civ Div) .... *Digested,* 96/**5025**: *Explained* 17/497

Fish & Fish Ltd v Sea Shepherd UK; *sub nom* Sea Shepherd UK v Fish & Fish Ltd [2015] UKSC 10; [2015] A.C. 1229; [2015] 2 W.L.R. 694; [2015] 4 All E.R. 247; [2015] 2 All E.R. (Comm) 867; [2015] 1 Lloyd's Rep. 593, SC .... *Digested,* 15/**2538**: *Followed* 17/1364, 17/1403

Fitzgerald v Lloyd Williams see Fitzgerald v Williams

Fitzgerald v Williams; *sub nom* Fitzgerald v Lloyd Williams; *joined case* O'Regan v Williams [1996] Q.B. 657; [1996] 2 W.L.R. 447; [1996] 2 All E.R. 171; [1996] C.L.C. 646; [1996] I.L.Pr. 275; Times, January 3, 1996; Independent, February 12, 1996, CA (Civ Div) .... *Digested,* 96/**726**: *Applied* 00/439: *Considered* 17/362: *Distinguished* 99/5701: *Followed* 96/731

FKB 1, Re see Fujifilm Kyowa Kirin Biologics Co Ltd v Abbvie Biotechnology Ltd

FKI Engineering Ltd v Stribog Ltd; *sub nom* Stribog Ltd v FKI Engineering Ltd [2011] EWCA Civ 622; [2011] 1 W.L.R. 3264; [2012] 1 All E.R. (Comm) 549; [2011] Bus. L.R. 1410; [2011] 2 Lloyd's Rep. 387; [2011] C.P. Rep. 33; [2011] 1 C.L.C. 1005; (2011) 108(23) L.S.G. 17, CA (Civ Div) ... *Digested,* 11/**392**:
Applied 16/363: *Considered* 13/442, 14/565, 17/428

Flamagas SA v EUIPO (T-580/15) EU:T:2017:433; [2017] E.T.M.R. 33, GC (4th Chamber)

Flannery v Halifax Estate Agencies Ltd (t/a Colleys Professional Services) [2000] 1 W.L.R. 377; [2000] 1 All E.R. 373; [2000] C.P. Rep. 18; [1999] B.L.R. 107; (1999) 11 Admin. L.R. 465; Times, March 4, 1999; Independent, February 26, 1999; (1999) 15 Const. L.J. 313; (1999) 96(13) L.S.G. 32; (1999) 149 N.L.J. 284; [1999] N.P.C. 22, CA (Civ Div) ... *Digested,* 99/**37**:
Applied 00/1476, 01/559, 05/950: *Considered* 01/50, 10/2115, 10/996: *Followed* 16/881, 17/2251: *Referred to* 00/3457

Flaxmode Ltd v Revenue and Customs Commissioners [2008] S.T.C. (S.C.D.) 666, Sp Comm ... *Digested,* 08/**3824**:
Applied 16/2119: *Considered* 17/2129

Fleming (t/a Bodycraft) v Customs and Excise Commissioners; *sub nom* Fleming (t/a Bodycraft) v Revenue and Customs Commissioners; *joined case* Conde Nast Publications Ltd v Revenue and Customs Commissioners [2008] UKHL 2; [2008] 1 W.L.R. 195; [2008] 1 All E.R. 1061; [2008] S.T.C. 324; [2008] 1 C.M.L.R. 48; [2008] Eu. L.R. 455; [2008] B.T.C. 5096; [2008] B.V.C. 221; Times, January 25, 2008; [2008] S.T.I. 181; (2008) 158 N.L.J. 182; (2008) 152(5) S.J.L.B. 30; [2008] N.P.C. 5, HL ... *Digested,* 08/**4016**:
Applied 10/3507, 12/3381: *Cited* 12/3430, 17/2246: *Considered* 08/3676, 09/4070, 10/2672, 10/3491, 14/3038: *Followed* 11/3519, 16/2191, 16/2192, 17/2177: *Referred to* 15/2582, 17/2271

Fleming (t/a Bodycraft) v Revenue and Customs Commissioners see Fleming (t/a Bodycraft) v Customs and Excise Commissioners

Fletcher v Midland Bank Plc (No.2) see Preston v Wolverhampton Healthcare NHS Trust (No.2)

Fletcher Estates (Harlescott) Ltd v Secretary of State for the Environment, Transport and the Regions; *sub nom* Secretary of State for the Environment, Transport and the Regions v Newell; Secretary of State for the Environment, Transport and the Regions v Fletcher Estates (Harlescott) Ltd; *joined case* Newell v Secretary of State for the Environment, Transport and the Regions [2000] 2 A.C. 307; [2000] 2 W.L.R. 438; [2000] 1 All E.R. 929; [2000] B.L.G.R. 240; (2000) 80 P. & C.R. 95; [2000] 1 P.L.R. 93; [2000] 1 E.G.L.R. 13; [2000] 11 E.G. 141; [2000] R.V.R. 215; Times, February 23, 2000; Independent, February 24, 2000; [2000] J.P.L. 923; [2000] E.G. 24 (C.S.); (2000) 97(9) L.S.G. 41; (2000) 144 S.J.L.B. 110; [2000] N.P.C. 14, HL ... *Digested,* 00/**4427**:
Applied 02/6031, 10/2543, 10/2551: *Considered* 04/3032: *Followed* 13/2276, 17/1698

FlibTravel International SA v AAL Renting SA (C-253/16) EU:C:2017:211; [2017] R.T.R. 18, ECJ (3rd Chamber)

Flightline Ltd v Edwards; *sub nom* Edwards v Flightline Ltd; Swissair Schweizerische Luftverkehr AG, Re [2003] EWCA Civ 63; [2003] 1 W.L.R. 1200; [2003] 3 All E.R. 1200; [2003] B.C.C. 361; [2003] 1 B.C.L.C. 427; [2003] B.P.I.R. 549; Times, February 13, 2003; Independent, February 21, 2003; (2003) 100(13) L.S.G. 28; (2003) 147 S.J.L.B. 178, CA (Civ Div) ... *Digested,* 03/**2426**:
Applied 05/709, 12/483: *Considered* 17/357: *Followed* 11/2128

Flint v Eastern Electricity Board [1975] I.C.R. 395; [1975] I.R.L.R. 277; [1975] I.T.R. 152, QBD ... *Digested,* 76/**1008**:
Applied 17/811: *Considered* 85/1174, 10/1098

Floridienne SA v Belgium (C-142/99) EU:C:2000:623; [2000] S.T.C. 1044; [2000] E.C.R. I-9567; [2001] 1 C.M.L.R. 26; [2001] All E.R. (EC) 37; [2001] C.E.C. 11; [2001] B.T.C. 5003; [2001] B.V.C. 76; [2000] S.T.I. 1633, ECJ (1st Chamber) ... *Digested,* 01/**5578**:
Considered 15/2606: *Followed* 02/4763, 17/2295

Flowers v Linstone Chine Management Co Ltd [2016] EWCA Civ 674; [2017] R.V.R. 6, CA (Civ Div) ... *Digested,* 17/**1855**

Fluss v Queensbridge Terrace Residents Ltd; *sub nom* 3-15 Queensbridge Road, Haggeston, London, E2 8NP; 1-6 Dunloe Passage, London, E2 8JS [2011] UKUT 285 (LC), UT (Lands)
Applied 15/2104, 17/1830

Flynn Pharma Ltd v Competition and Markets Authority [2017] CAT 13; [2017] Comp. A.R. 366, CAT

Flynn Pharma Ltd v Competition and Markets Authority [2017] CAT 7; [2017] Comp. A.R. 234, CAT

Flynn Pharma Ltd v Competition and Markets Authority [2017] CAT 1; [2017] Comp. A.R. 76, CAT .... *Digested,* 17/**427**
Flynn Pharma Ltd v Drugsrus Ltd [2017] EWCA Civ 226; [2017] Bus. L.R. 1874; [2017] 3 C.M.L.R. 11; [2017] E.T.M.R. 25; [2017] R.P.C. 18; (2017) 156 B.M.L.R. 124, CA (Civ Div) .... *Digested,* 17/**1401**
Flynn Pharma Ltd v Drugsrus Ltd [2015] EWHC 2759 (Ch); [2016] E.C.C. 4; [2016] E.T.M.R. 4; [2016] R.P.C. 8; (2016) 147 B.M.L.R. 100, Ch D .... *Digested,* 16/**1336**: *Affirmed* 17/1401
FM v KAH see SU (Children) (Passports), Re
Focus Care Agency Ltd v Roberts; *joined cases* Royal Mencap Society v Tomlinson-Blake; Frudd v Partington Group Ltd [2017] I.C.R. 1186; [2017] I.R.L.R. 588, EAT .... *Digested,* 17/**812**
Folien Fischer AG v Ritrama SpA (C-133/11) EU:C:2012:664; [2013] Q.B. 523; [2013] 2 W.L.R. 373; [2014] 1 All E.R. (Comm) 569; [2013] C.E.C. 727; [2013] I.L.Pr. 1, ECJ (1st Chamber) *Followed* 17/430
Folk v Unabhangiger Verwaltungssenat fur die Steiermark (C-529/15) see Proceedings Brought by Folk (C-529/15)
Fomento de Construcciones y Contratas SA v Black Diamond Offshore Ltd see Black Diamond Offshore Ltd v Fomento de Construcciones y Contratas SA
Fomento de Construcciones y Contratas SA v Black Diamond Offshore Ltd see Black Diamond Offshore Ltd v Fomento de Construcciones y Contratas SA
Fonecomp Ltd v Revenue and Customs Commissioners [2015] EWCA Civ 39; [2015] S.T.C. 2254; [2015] Lloyd's Rep. F.C. 149; [2015] B.V.C. 9; [2015] S.T.I. 355, CA (Civ Div) .... *Digested,* 15/**2592**: *Applied* 17/2250: *Considered* 17/2252: *Followed* 16/2169
Football Association Premier League Ltd v British Sky Broadcasting Ltd [2013] EWHC 2058 (Ch); [2013] E.C.D.R. 14, Ch D .... *Digested,* 13/**1763**: *Applied* 14/1868, 15/1476, 17/1358
Football Association Premier League Ltd v British Telecommunications Plc [2017] EWHC 480 (Ch); [2017] E.C.C. 17; [2017] E.C.D.R. 17, Ch D .... *Digested,* 17/**1358**
Football Association Premier League Ltd v Luxton [2014] EWHC 253 (Ch), Ch D *Affirmed* 17/1361
Football Association Premier League Ltd v Luxton [2016] EWCA Civ 1097; [2017] E.C.D.R. 7; [2017] F.S.R. 21; [2017] L.L.R. 102, CA (Civ Div) .... *Digested,* 17/**1361**
Football Association Premier League Ltd v O'Donovan [2017] EWHC 152 (Ch); [2017] F.S.R. 31, Ch D .... *Digested,* 17/**197**
Football Association Premier League Ltd v QC Leisure (C-403/08); *joined case* Murphy v Media Protection Services Ltd (C-429/08) EU:C:2011:631; [2012] Bus. L.R. 1321; [2011] E.C.R. I-9083; [2012] 1 C.M.L.R. 29; [2012] All E.R. (EC) 629; [2012] C.E.C. 242; [2012] E.C.D.R. 8; [2012] F.S.R. 1; Times, November 23, 2011; (2011) 108(40) L.S.G. 22; (2011) 161 N.L.J. 1415, ECJ (Grand Chamber) .... *Digested,* 12/**1924**: *Applied* 12/1920, 12/1925, 13/1769: *Considered* 13/1762, 13/3542, 14/1860, 14/3349, 14/3354: *Followed* 12/1928, 17/1361: *Referred to* 15/297
Forbes (David Landells) v HM Advocate see Steele (Kevin Munro) v HM Advocate
Force India Formula One Team Ltd v 1 Malaysia Racing Team Sdn Bhd; *sub nom* Force India Formula One Team Ltd v Aerolab Srl [2013] EWCA Civ 780; [2013] R.P.C. 36, CA (Civ Div) .... *Digested,* 14/**624**: *Considered* 14/2989: *Followed* 17/2197
Force India Formula One Team Ltd v 1 Malaysia Racing Team Sdn Bhd; *sub nom* Force India Formula One Team Ltd v Aerolab Srl [2012] EWHC 616 (Ch); [2012] R.P.C. 29, Ch D .... *Digested,* 13/**1776**: *Affirmed* 14/624: *Applied* 14/247, 14/2989, 15/1477, 17/2197
Force India Formula One Team Ltd v Aerolab Srl see Force India Formula One Team Ltd v 1 Malaysia Racing Team Sdn Bhd
Forcelux Ltd v Binnie [2009] EWCA Civ 854; [2010] C.P. Rep. 7; [2009] 5 Costs L.R. 825; [2010] H.L.R. 20, CA (Civ Div) .... *Digested,* 10/**2077**: *Applied* 17/265: *Considered* 12/461: *Explained* 11/367
Forcelux Ltd v Binnie (Costs) [2009] EWCA Civ 1077; [2009] 5 Costs L.R. 825; [2010] H.L.R. 20, CA (Civ Div) .... *Digested,* 10/**318**: *Distinguished* 17/235
Forcelux Ltd v Sweetman [2001] 2 E.G.L.R. 173, Lands Tr .... *Digested,* 03/**2785**: *Considered* 17/1470
Ford v Financial Conduct Authority [2016] UKUT 41 (TCC), UT (Tax) *Applied* 17/1073

Forest of Dean DC v Secretary of State for Communities and Local Government [2016] EWHC 421 (Admin); [2016] P.T.S.R. 1031; [2016] J.P.L. 918, QBD (Admin) ... *Digested,* 16/**1705**: *Applied* 17/1770

Forge Care Homes Ltd v Cardiff and Vale University Health Board see R. (on the application of Forge Care Homes Ltd) v Cardiff and Vale University Health Board

Forkner v Zas Ventures Ltd; *sub nom* Zas Ventures Ltd v Forkner [2016] EWCA Civ 1062; [2017] H.L.R. 2; [2017] 1 P. & C.R. DG7, CA (Civ Div) ... *Digested,* 17/**1852**

Forman (ss 117A-C Considerations: United States); *sub nom* Secretary of State for the Home Department v Forman [2015] UKUT 412 (IAC); [2015] Imm. A.R. 1231, UT (IAC) *Considered* 17/1235

Formula One World Championship Ltd v Commissioner of Income Tax, International 19 I.T.L. Rep. 542, HC (Ind)

Formula One World Championship Ltd v Commissioner of Income Tax, International 19 I.T.L. Rep. 784, Sup Ct (Ind)

Forster v Secretary of State for Communities and Local Government [2016] EWCA Civ 609; [2017] L.L.R. 116; [2016] J.P.L. 1220, CA (Civ Div) ... *Digested,* 16/**1728**

Fort Gilkicker Ltd, Re; *sub nom* Universal Project Management Services Ltd v Fort Gilkicker Ltd [2013] EWHC 348 (Ch); [2013] Ch. 551; [2013] 3 W.L.R. 164; [2013] 3 All E.R. 546; [2013] B.C.C. 365; (2013) 163 N.L.J. 268, Ch D (Companies Ct) ... *Digested,* 13/**353**: *Considered* 17/287

Forte's (Manufacturing) Ltd, Re see Stanhope Pension Trust Ltd v Registrar of Companies

Forthright Finance Ltd v Ingate [1997] 4 All E.R. 99; [1997] C.C.L.R. 95, CA (Civ Div) . *Digested,* 97/**957**: *Applied* 15/504: *Followed* 17/480

Fortis Bank SA/NV v Indian Overseas Bank [2009] EWHC 2303 (Comm); [2010] 1 Lloyd's Rep. 227; [2009] 2 C.L.C. 550, QBD (Comm) ... *Digested,* 10/**227**: *Affirmed* 11/215: *Applied* 17/166

Fortisbank SA v Trenwick International Ltd [2005] EWHC 399 (Comm); [2005] Lloyd's Rep. I.R. 464, QBD (Comm) ... *Digested,* 05/**705**: *Applied* 17/493

Fortyseven Park Street Ltd v Revenue and Customs Commissioners [2016] UKFTT 569 (TC); [2017] S.F.T.D. 35; [2016] S.T.I. 2557, FTT (Tax) ... *Digested,* 17/**2264**

Foss v Harbottle 67 E.R. 189; (1843) 2 Hare 461, Ct of Chancery *Applied* 56/1149, 64/465, 78/241, 78/366, 82/330, 16/345: *Cited* 01/6300: *Considered* 47-51/10390, 68/445, 82/331, 85/3514, 85/3534, 91/414, 92/3560, 94/421, 96/1213, 96/5732, 02/619, 06/2324, 07/435, 09/510, 13/353, 17/2423, 17/287: *Distinguished* 63/411, 66/1409, 72/3459: *Followed* 10/826

Foster Wheeler Ltd v Hanley [2009] EWCA Civ 651; [2009] 3 C.M.L.R. 49; [2010] I.C.R. 374; [2009] Pens. L.R. 229; (2009) 153(27) S.J.L.B. 30, CA (Civ Div) ... *Digested,* 09/**2798**: *Applied* 17/1612

Foundry Miniatures Ltd, Re; *sub nom* Pinfold v Ansell [2017] EWHC 889 (Ch); [2017] 2 B.C.L.C. 489, Ch D (Birmingham)

Fourie v Le Roux; *sub nom* Herlan Edmunds Engineering (Pty) Ltd, Re [2007] UKHL 1; [2007] 1 W.L.R. 320; [2007] 1 All E.R. 1087; [2007] 1 All E.R. (Comm) 571; [2007] Bus. L.R. 925; [2007] B.P.I.R. 24; Times, January 25, 2007; (2007) 157 N.L.J. 178, HL ... *Digested,* 07/**453**: *Applied* 15/306, 17/219: *Followed* 15/1520, 16/1200, 16/1325, 17/308

Fowler v Revenue and Customs Commissioners [2016] UKFTT 338 (TC); [2016] S.F.T.D. 930, FTT (Tax) ... *Digested,* 17/**2133**

Fowler v Revenue and Customs Commissioners [2016] UKFTT 234 (TC); [2016] S.F.T.D. 535; 18 I.T.L. Rep. 644; [2016] S.T.I. 1718, FTT (Tax) ... *Digested,* 16/**2081**: *Reversed* 17/2130

Fowler v Revenue and Customs Commissioners see Revenue and Customs Commissioners v Fowler

Fox v Foundation Piling Ltd [2011] EWCA Civ 790; [2011] C.P. Rep. 41; [2011] 6 Costs L.R. 961, CA (Civ Div) ... *Digested,* 12/**352**: *Applied* 14/371, 15/255: *Considered* 12/353, 13/339, 17/248, 17/643: *Followed* 13/290

Fox (Victor) v Patterson 1948 J.C. 104; 1948 S.L.T. 547; 1948 S.L.T. (Notes) 48, HCJ Appeal ... *Digested,* 48/**4167**: *Applied* 54/750: *Considered* 52/795, 54/3697, 90/4943, 17/2501

Fox Strategic Land & Property Ltd v Secretary of State for Communities and Local Government; *sub nom* R. (on the application of Fox Strategic Land & Property Ltd) v Secretary of State for Communities and Local Government [2012] EWCA Civ 1198; [2013] 1 P. & C.R. 6, CA (Civ Div) .... *Digested,* 13/**2349**: *Distinguished* 17/1731

Fox-Davies v Burberry Plc see Burberry Group Plc v Fox-Davies

Frade v Radford [2017] EWCA Civ 1010; [2017] 4 Costs L.R. 583, CA (Civ Div) .... *Digested,* 17/**213**

France v Kensington and Chelsea RLBC; *sub nom* R. (on the application of France) v Kensington and Chelsea RLBC [2017] EWCA Civ 429; [2017] 1 W.L.R. 3206; Times, August 30, 2017; [2017] J.P.L. 1256, CA (Civ Div) .... *Digested,* 17/**1717**

France v Kensington and Chelsea RLBC; *sub nom* R. (on the application of France) v Kensington and Chelsea RLBC [2015] EWHC 3437 (Admin); [2016] J.P.L. 387, QBD (Admin) .... *Digested,* 16/**1668**: *Reversed in part* 17/1717

Francia Properties Ltd v Aristou [2017] L. & T.R. 5, CC (Central London) .... *Digested,* 17/**1436**

Francis v Trustees of the Phillimore Kensington Estate see Mosley v Hickman

Francis (Angus) v HM Advocate [2017] HCJAC 63; 2017 S.C.L. 909; 2017 G.W.D. 29-459, HCJ .... *Digested,* 17/**2488**

Francovich v Italy (C-6/90); *joined case* Bonifacti v Italy (C-9/90) EU:C:1991:428; [1991] E.C.R. I-5357; [1993] 2 C.M.L.R. 66; [1995] I.C.R. 722; [1992] I.R.L.R. 84; Times, November 20, 1991, ECJ .... *Digested,* 92/**4815**: *Applied* 98/2570, 98/3396, 99/3620, 08/2208, 13/1581, 16/2428: *Cited* 00/2380: *Considered* 92/2904, 94/3046, 94/4842, 95/2031, 96/2566, 96/2596, 96/2597, 96/2629, 96/2792, 96/2803, 97/4627, 07/2490, 14/2987, 15/2526: *Distinguished* 09/1379: *Followed* 97/2265, 02/1571, 11/1717, 17/1813, 17/1815

Fraser (Nat Gordon) v HM Advocate [2013] HCJAC 117; 2014 J.C. 115; 2013 S.C.L. 1031; 2013 S.C.C.R. 674; 2013 G.W.D. 33-652, HCJ .... *Digested,* 14/**3448**: *Applied* 17/2529, 17/2567: *Considered* 15/3018

Freeman v Hambrook [1947] V.L.R. 70
Considered 17/1456

French v Barcham; *sub nom* Barcham, Re [2008] EWHC 1505 (Ch); [2009] 1 W.L.R. 1124; [2009] 1 All E.R. 145; [2008] 2 F.C.R. 643; [2008] B.P.I.R. 857; [2008] 3 E.G.L.R. 51; [2008] 39 E.G. 126; [2008] W.T.L.R. 1813; (2008-09) 11 I.T.E.L.R. 507; Times, July 24, 2008; [2008] 28 E.G. 112 (C.S.); [2008] N.P.C. 80; [2008] 2 P. & C.R. DG20, Ch D .... *Digested,* 08/**3064**: *Applied* 10/1853: *Considered* 17/1826

French v Groupama Insurance Co Ltd [2011] EWCA Civ 1119; [2012] C.P. Rep. 2; [2011] 4 Costs L.O. 547, CA (Civ Div) .... *Digested,* 12/**387**: *Applied* 17/242: *Considered* 16/222: *Followed* 15/262

French v Revenue and Customs Commissioners [2014] UKFTT 940 (TC); [2015] S.T.I. 159, FTT (Tax)
Considered 17/2144

French's (Wine Bar) Ltd, Re (1987) 3 B.C.C. 173; [1987] B.C.L.C. 499, Ch D (Companies Ct) .... *Digested,* 87/**384**: *Followed* 17/1276

FREP (Belle Vale) Ltd (In Administration), Re see Thomas v Frogmore Real Estate Partners GP1 Ltd

FREP (Ellesmere Port) Ltd (In Administration), Re see Thomas v Frogmore Real Estate Partners GP1 Ltd

FREP (Knowle) Ltd (In Administration), Re see Thomas v Frogmore Real Estate Partners GP1 Ltd

Frew (Laura) v HM Advocate see Cafferkey (Daniel) v HM Advocate

Frey v Labrouche; *sub nom* Labrouche v Frey [2012] EWCA Civ 881; [2012] 1 W.L.R. 3160; (2012) 162 N.L.J. 934, CA (Civ Div) .... *Digested,* 13/**41**: *Applied* 15/996, 17/1290

Fries v Lufthansa CityLine GmbH (C-190/16) EU:C:2017:513; [2017] I.R.L.R. 1003, ECJ (1st Chamber)

Frisby v Birmingham City Council see Hounslow LBC v Powell

Frogmore Real Estate Partners GP1 Ltd v Thomas see Thomas v Frogmore Real Estate Partners GP1 Ltd

Frosdick v Fox [2017] EWHC 1737 (Ch); [2018] 1 W.L.R. 38; [2017] B.P.I.R. 1194, Ch D .... *Digested,* 17/**1296**

Frosh v Revenue and Customs Commissioners [2016] UKFTT 558 (TC), FTT (Tax)
Affirmed 17/2176

Frosh v Revenue and Customs Commissioners [2017] UKUT 320 (TCC); [2017] S.T.C. 1941; [2017] B.T.C. 530; [2017] S.T.I. 1859, UT (Tax) .... *Digested,* 17/**2176**

Frost v MGN Ltd see Gulati v MGN Ltd

Frost v MGN Ltd see Times Newspapers Ltd v Flood

Frudd v Partington Group Ltd see Focus Care Agency Ltd v Roberts
FSL Holdings NV v European Commission (C-469/15 P) EU:C:2017:308; [2017] 4 C.M.L.R. 29, ECJ (1st Chamber)
Fuglers LLP v Solicitors Regulation Authority; *sub nom* Fuglers LLP v Solicitors Regulatory Authority [2014] EWHC 179 (Admin); [2014] B.P.I.R. 610, QBD (Admin) .... *Digested,* 14/**2056**: *Applied* 17/1489
Fuglers LLP v Solicitors Regulatory Authority see Fuglers LLP v Solicitors Regulation Authority
Fujifilm Kyowa Kirin Biologics Co Ltd v Abbvie Biotechnology Ltd; *sub nom* FKB 1, Re; *joined case* Samsung Bioepis UK Ltd v Abbvie Biotechnology Ltd [2016] EWHC 3383 (Ch); [2017] R.P.C. 8, Ch D (Patents Ct) .... *Digested,* 17/**1372**
Fujifilm Kyowa Kirin Biologics Co Ltd v Abbvie Biotechnology Ltd [2016] EWHC 2204 (Pat); [2017] Bus. L.R. 333; [2017] R.P.C. 7, Ch D (Patents Ct) *Affirmed* 17/1371
Fujifilm Kyowa Kirin Biologics Co Ltd v Abbvie Biotechnology Ltd [2016] EWHC 425 (Pat); [2017] R.P.C. 6, Ch D (Patents Ct) *Affirmed* 17/1371
Fujifilm Kyowa Kirin Biologics Co Ltd v Abbvie Biotechnology Ltd [2017] EWCA Civ 1; [2018] Bus. L.R. 228; [2017] C.P. Rep. 16; [2017] R.P.C. 9, CA (Civ Div) .... *Digested,* 17/**1371**
Fulfilment Logistics Ltd v May (Valuation Officer) see Total Fulfilment Logistics Ltd v May (Valuation Officer)
Fulham Leisure Holdings Ltd v Nicholson Graham & Jones [2006] EWHC 158 (Ch); [2006] 2 All E.R. 599; [2006] P.N.L.R. 23; Times, February 23, 2006, Ch D .... *Digested,* 06/**429**: *Considered* 17/355
Fuller v Kitzing [2017] EWHC 810 (Ch); [2017] Ch. 485; [2017] 3 W.L.R. 615, Ch D (Manchester) .... *Digested,* 17/**1854**
Fulton Shipping Inc of Panama v Globalia Business Travel SAU (formerly Travelplan SAU) of Spain; *sub nom* Fulton Shipping Inc of Panama v Globalia Business Travel SAU (formerly Travelplan SAU) of Spain [2015] EWCA Civ 1299; [2016] 1 W.L.R. 2450; [2016] 4 All E.R. 77; [2016] 2 All E.R. (Comm) 366; [2016] 1 Lloyd's Rep. 383; [2016] 1 C.L.C. 215, CA (Civ Div) .... *Digested,* 16/**573**: *Reversed* 17/642
Fulton Shipping Inc of Panama v Globalia Business Travel SAU (formerly Travelplan SAU) of Spain [2017] UKSC 43; [2017] 1 W.L.R. 2581; [2018] 1 All E.R. 45; [2018] 1 All E.R. (Comm) 95; [2017] 2 Lloyd's Rep. 177; 173 Con. L.R. 20; Times, July 12, 2017, SC .... *Digested,* 17/**642**
Fulton Shipping Inc of Panama v Globalia Business Travel SAU (formerly Travelplan SAU) of Spain see Fulton Shipping Inc of Panama v Globalia Business Travel SAU (formerly Travelplan SAU) of Spain
Furness v B&S Massey Ltd see Gammell v Wilson
FV (Italy) v Secretary of State for the Home Department see Secretary of State for the Home Department v Vomero
Fyfe v Council of the Law Society of Scotland [2017] CSIH 6; 2017 S.C. 283; 2017 S.L.T. 254; 2017 S.C.L.R. 464; 2017 G.W.D. 5-73, IH (2 Div) .... *Digested,* 17/**2713**
FZ v SZ (Ancillary Relief: Conduct: Valuations) [2010] EWHC 1630 (Fam); [2011] 1 F.L.R. 64; [2010] Fam. Law 1259, Fam Div .... *Digested,* 11/**1289**: *Applied* 11/1296, 11/1298: *Considered* 10/1280, 17/1024
FZ (Democratic Republic of Congo) v Secretary of State for the Home Department; *sub nom* Zoumbas v Secretary of State for the Home Department [2013] UKSC 74; [2013] 1 W.L.R. 3690; [2014] 1 All E.R. 638; 2014 S.C. (U.K.S.C.) 75; [2014] 1 F.C.R. 141; [2014] Imm. A.R. 479; [2014] I.N.L.R. 262, SC .... *Digested,* 14/**1650**: *Applied* 14/1651, 15/3147, 17/1242: *Considered* 15/1353: *Followed* 17/1235

G v de Visser (C-292/10) EU:C:2012:142; [2013] Q.B. 168; [2012] 3 W.L.R. 1523; Times, June 22, 2012, ECJ (1st Chamber) *Applied* 17/294
G v G 2017 S.L.T. (Sh Ct) 169; 2017 G.W.D. 20-317, Sh Ct (Grampian) (Aberdeen) ... *Digested,* 17/**2617**
G v G (Maintenance Pending Suit: Legal Costs) [2002] EWHC 306 (Fam); [2003] 2 F.L.R. 71; [2002] 3 F.C.R. 339; [2003] Fam. Law 393, Fam Div .... *Digested,* 03/**1586**: *Applied* 02/1680: *Considered* 17/1017

G v G (Minors: Custody Appeal) [1985] 1 W.L.R. 647; [1985] 2 All E.R. 225; [1985] F.L.R. 894; [1985] Fam. Law 321; (1985) 82 L.S.G. 2010; (1985) 83 L.S.G. 2010; (1985) 135 N.L.J. 439; (1985) 129 S.J. 315, HL .... *Digested,* 85/**2594**: *Applied* 86/2145, 86/2196, 87/1773, 87/2489, 87/2490, 87/2519, 87/2527, 91/2553, 92/3032, 95/3372, 95/3390, 95/3469, 95/3486, 95/3489, 95/3493, 95/3561, 96/563, 96/604, 96/607, 96/614, 96/6976, 02/3270, 02/498, 06/1670, 07/1800, 08/2128, 09/1572, 09/1639, 10/1310, 14/1323: *Approved* 98/2398: *Considered* 86/2142, 86/2182, 88/2357, 88/2952, 89/2410, 89/2459, 90/3125, 95/3386, 95/3498, 95/3532, 95/67, 96/608, 97/384, 00/2489, 04/2134, 07/4550: *Distinguished* 88/2935, 09/2217: *Explained* 87/2439: *Followed* 86/1099, 86/2068, 86/2201, 96/560, 96/609, 09/1226, 10/1308, 10/1437, 11/1379, 16/1452, 16/237, 17/274: *Referred to* 86/3641, 94/3220

G v G see Magiera v Magiera

G v R (Pre-Nuptial Contract) see Radmacher v Granatino

G v S (Children Act 1989: Schedule 1) [2017] EWHC 365 (Fam); [2017] 2 F.L.R. 1207; [2017] 2 F.C.R. 307, Fam Div .... *Digested,* 17/**1003**

G v Scottish Criminal Cases Review Commission; *sub nom* Gordon v Scottish Criminal Cases Review Commission [2013] CSIH 101; 2013 G.W.D. 40-755, IH (Ex Div) *Affirmed* 17/623

G v Scottish Criminal Cases Review Commission; *sub nom* Gordon v Scottish Criminal Cases Review Commission [2017] UKSC 20; 2017 S.C. (U.K.S.C.) 86; 2017 S.L.T. 365; 2017 S.C.C.R. 214; 2017 G.W.D. 11-144, SC .... *Digested,* 17/**623**

G v Secretary of State for the Home Department [2016] EWHC 3232 (Admin); [2017] Imm. A.R. 918, QBD (Admin) .... *Digested,* 17/**1234**

G v Stirling Council [2016] CSOH 121; 2016 Hous. L.R. 64; 2016 G.W.D. 26-483, OH . *Digested,* 17/**2657**

G (A Child) (Custody Rights: Article 13 Defence); *sub nom* JZ v TG [2017] EWHC 514 (Fam); [2017] 4 W.L.R. 142, Fam Div .... *Digested,* 17/**1038**

G (An Adult) v Associated Newspapers Ltd see G (An Adult) (Costs), Re

G (An Adult) (Costs), Re; *sub nom* G (An Adult) v Associated Newspapers Ltd [2014] EWCOP 5; [2014] C.O.P.L.R. 432, CP .... *Digested,* 14/**346**: *Affirmed* 15/238: *Considered* 17/243

G (Children) (Foreign Contact Order: Enforcement), Re; *sub nom* G (Children) (Restoration of Custody Rights), Re [2003] EWCA Civ 1607; [2004] 1 W.L.R. 521; [2004] 1 F.L.R. 378; [2004] 1 F.C.R. 266; Times, November 19, 2003; [2004] Fam. Law 98; (2004) 101(2) L.S.G. 27; (2003) 147 S.J.L.B. 1364, CA (Civ Div) .... *Digested,* 04/**1532**: *Considered* 04/1485, 05/1590, 17/1057: *Followed* 15/1105

G (Children) (Restoration of Custody Rights), Re see G (Children) (Foreign Contact Order: Enforcement), Re

G (Foreign Adoption: Consent), Re [1995] 2 F.L.R. 534; [1995] Fam. Law 664, Fam Div .... *Digested,* 96/**467**: *Applied* 06/1617, 17/1034

G (Human Fertilisation and Embryology Act 2008), Re [2016] EWHC 729 (Fam); [2016] 4 W.L.R. 65; [2017] 1 F.L.R. 299; [2016] Fam. Law 677, Fam Div .... *Digested,* 16/**925**: *Applied* 17/1055

G (Wardship) (Jurisdiction: Power of Arrest), Re (1983) 4 F.L.R. 538, CA (Civ Div) *Applied* 17/1050

G and R (Wards) (Police Interviews), Re see R and G (Minors) (Wardship), Re

G Lawrence Wholesale Meat Co Ltd v Citigen (London) Ltd see City of London v Reeve & Co Ltd

G Percy Trentham Ltd v Archital Luxfer Ltd [1993] 1 Lloyd's Rep. 25; 63 B.L.R. 44, CA (Civ Div) .... *Digested,* 93/**294**: *Applied* 07/811, 09/667, 16/427, 17/469: *Considered* 00/812, 09/726, 09/727, 10/631: *Distinguished* 09/676: *Followed* 12/2102

G Scammell and Nephew Ltd v HC&JG Ouston [1941] A.C. 251; [1941] 1 All E.R. 14, HL *Applied* 53/660, 68/35, 11/545: *Considered* 00/837, 12/158: *Distinguished* 53/661: *Followed* 17/74

G-Tech Construction Ltd, Re [2007] B.P.I.R. 1275, Ch D .... *Digested,* 08/**2118**: *Applied* 11/1824, 11/1825, 12/1802, 12/1804, 16/1255, 17/1268: *Considered* 11/1873, 12/1796, 17/1269: *Not followed* 12/1803

Gaafar v Secretary of State for the Home Department see Januzi v Secretary of State for the Home Department

Gabriel v Little; *joined cases* Hughes-Holland v BPE Solicitors; Gabriel v Little (t/a High Tech Design & Build Ltd); BPE Solicitors v Gabriel [2013] EWCA Civ 1513; 16 I.T.E.L.R. 567, CA (Civ Div) .... *Digested,* 14/**2195**: *Affirmed* 17/641: *Followed* 15/1789

Gabriel v Little; *joined cases* Hughes-Holland v BPE Solicitors; Gabriel v Little (t/a High Tech Design & Build Ltd); BPE Solicitors v Gabriel [2017] UKSC 21; [2017] 2 W.L.R. 1029; [2017] 3 All E.R. 969; 171 Con. L.R. 46; [2017] P.N.L.R. 23, SC .... *Digested,* 17/**641**: *Followed* 17/1571

Gabriel v Little (t/a High Tech Design & Build Ltd) see Gabriel v Little

Gadd v Law Society [2012] EWHC 2843 (QB), QBD
Followed 17/1323

Gaffoor (Abdul) Trustees v Ceylon Commissioner of Income Tax see Caffoor (Trustees of the Abdul Gaffoor Trust) v Income Tax Commissioner (Colombo)

Gaind v Dunbar Assets Plc [2016] EWHC 3187 (Ch); [2017] B.P.I.R. 667, Ch D (Bankruptcy Ct) .... *Digested,* 17/**1325**

Gala 1 Ltd v Revenue and Customs Commissioners see Gala Leisure Ltd v Revenue and Customs Commissioners

Gala Leisure Ltd v Revenue and Customs Commissioners; *sub nom* Gala 1 Ltd v Revenue and Customs Commissioners [2015] UKFTT 516 (TC); [2016] S.F.T.D. 56; [2015] S.T.I. 3258, FTT (Tax)
Affirmed 17/2290

Gala Leisure Ltd v Revenue and Customs Commissioners; *sub nom* Gala 1 Ltd v Revenue and Customs Commissioners [2016] UKUT 564 (TCC); [2017] S.T.C. 437; [2017] B.V.C. 501, UT (Tax) .... *Digested,* 17/**2290**

Galbraith v Whitehead, &c (1863) 1 M. 644, IH (2 Div)
Applied 17/2677

Gale v Serious Organised Crime Agency see Serious Organised Crime Agency v Gale

Galea v Malta (Admissibility) (77209/16) (2017) 65 E.H.R.R. SE14, ECHR

Galino v Paraguay see Serra v Paraguay

Gall (Daniel Campbell) v HM Advocate 1992 J.C. 115; 1993 S.L.T. 290; 1992 S.C.C.R. 447, HCJ .... *Digested,* 92/**5519**: *Considered* 17/2571

Gallacher (Edward William) v HM Advocate see M v HM Advocate

Gallagher Homes Ltd v Solihull MBC; *sub nom* Solihull MBC v Gallagher Homes Ltd [2014] EWCA Civ 1610; [2015] J.P.L. 713, CA (Civ Div) .... *Digested,* 15/**1985**: *Followed* 15/1981, 17/1780

Gallaher Group Ltd v Competition and Markets Authority see R. (on the application of Gallaher Group Ltd) v Competition and Markets Authority

Gallaher Ltd v Gallaher Pensions Ltd [2005] EWHC 42 (Ch); [2005] O.P.L.R. 57; [2005] Pens. L.R. 103, Ch D .... *Digested,* 05/**2990**: *Applied* 17/1626: *Considered* 08/2743

Gallemos Ltd (In Receivership) v Barratt Falkirk Ltd 1989 S.C. 239; 1990 S.L.T. 98, IH (Ex Div) .... *Digested,* 89/**4878**: *Applied* 17/2610

Galliford Try Building Ltd v Estura Ltd [2015] EWHC 412 (TCC); [2015] B.L.R. 321; 159 Con. L.R. 10, QBD (TCC) .... *Digested,* 15/**459**: *Applied* 17/471: *Considered* 16/391, 16/405, 16/582, 17/454, 17/462

Gamatronic (UK) Ltd v Hamilton [2016] EWHC 2225 (QB); [2017] B.C.C. 670, QBD

Gambling Commission v Greene King Brewing and Retailing Ltd; *sub nom* Greene King Brewing and Retailing Ltd v Gambling Commission [2016] UKUT 50 (AAC); [2016] L.L.R. 502, UT (AAC)
Affirmed 17/1494

Gameart sp z o o v European Commission (T-264/15) EU:T:2017:290; [2017] 3 C.M.L.R. 33, GC (4th Chamber)

Gammell v Wilson; *joined case* Furness v B&S Massey Ltd [1982] A.C. 27; [1981] 2 W.L.R. 248; [1981] 1 All E.R. 578; (1981) 125 S.J. 116, HL .... *Digested,* 81/**581**: *Applied* 84/1030: *Considered* 82/772, 08/892, 15/1890: *Followed* 16/1607, 17/638

Gangar v General Medical Council [2003] H.R.L.R. 24, PC (UK) .... *Digested,* 03/**1732**: *Considered* 17/1108

Gangway Ltd v Caledonian Park Investments (Jersey) Ltd [2001] 2 Lloyd's Rep. 715, QBD (Comm) .... *Digested,* 02/**440**: *Doubted* 17/303

Gannon (Anthony) v HM Advocate [2017] HCJAC 58; 2017 S.L.T. 1034; 2017 S.C.L. 892; 2017 G.W.D. 26-432, HCJ .... *Digested,* 17/**2560**

Gantner Electronic GmbH v Basch Exploitatie Maatschappij BV (C-111/01) EU:C:2003:257; [2003] E.C.R. I-4207; [2003] I.L.Pr. 37; Times, May 14, 2003, ECJ (5th Chamber) .... *Digested,* 03/**614**: *Applied* 07/682, 08/565: *Considered* 17/428: *Distinguished* 10/505

Garcia v BIH (UK) Ltd [2017] EWHC 739 (Admlty); [2017] 2 Lloyd's Rep. 310, QBD (Admlty) .... *Digested,* 17/**371**

Gard v United Kingdom (Admissibility) (39793/17) [2017] 2 F.L.R. 773; (2017) 157 B.M.L.R. 59; (2017) 65 E.H.R.R. SE9, ECHR .... *Digested,* 17/**1170**
Gard (A Child) (Child on Life Support: Withdrawal of Treatment), Re see Great Ormond Street Hospital for Children NHS Foundation Trust v Yates
Gard Marine & Energy Ltd v China National Chartering Co Ltd; *joined cases* Daiichii Chuo Kisen Kaisha v Gard Marine & Energy Ltd; China National Chartering Co Ltd v Daiichii Chuo Kisen Kaisha [2015] EWCA Civ 16; [2015] 2 All E.R. (Comm) 894; [2015] 1 Lloyd's Rep. 381; [2015] 1 C.L.C. 72; [2015] Lloyd's Rep. I.R. 295, CA (Civ Div) .... *Digested,* 15/**2325**: *Affirmed* 17/2017: *Considered* 16/1277
Gard Marine & Energy Ltd v China National Chartering Co Ltd; *joined cases* Daiichii Chuo Kisen Kaisha v Gard Marine & Energy Ltd; China National Chartering Co Ltd v Daiichii Chuo Kisen Kaisha [2017] UKSC 35; [2017] 1 W.L.R. 1793; [2018] 1 All E.R. 832; [2018] 1 All E.R. (Comm) 1; [2017] 1 Lloyd's Rep. 521; [2017] Lloyd's Rep. I.R. 291; 2017 A.M.C. 1336; Times, May 22, 2017, SC ...... *Digested,* 17/**2017**
Gard Shipping AS v Clearlake Shipping Pte Ltd [2017] EWHC 1091 (Comm); [2017] 2 All E.R. (Comm) 179; [2017] 2 Lloyd's Rep. 38, QBD (Comm) .... *Digested,* 17/**2024**
Gardiner v Revenue and Customs Commissioners [2014] UKFTT 421 (TC), FTT (Tax) *Considered* 17/2088
Gareddu v London Underground Ltd 2201116/2015, ET *Affirmed* 17/822
Gareddu v London Underground Ltd [2017] I.R.L.R. 404, EAT .... *Digested,* 17/**822**
Garfield v Maddocks [1974] Q.B. 7; [1973] 2 W.L.R. 888; [1973] 2 All E.R. 303; (1973) 57 Cr. App. R. 372; [1973] Crim. L.R. 231; (1973) 117 S.J. 145, QBD .... *Digested,* 73/**470**: *Applied* 79/2293, 79/2313, 86/539, 90/861, 94/943, 17/902: *Considered* 79/392, 85/2095, 89/680, 14/785
Garforth (Inspector of Taxes) v Newsmith Stainless Ltd [1979] 1 W.L.R. 409; [1979] 2 All E.R. 73; [1979] S.T.C. 129; 52 T.C. 522; [1978] T.R. 477; (1978) 122 S.J. 828, Ch D .... *Digested,* 79/**1440**: *Applied* 13/3095: *Considered* 17/2131: *Distinguished* 08/3671
Garland v Revenue and Customs Commissioners [2016] UKUT 431 (TCC); [2016] B.T.C. 520, UT (Tax) .... *Digested,* 17/**2169**
Garland v Revenue and Customs Commissioners [2015] UKFTT 417 (TC); [2015] S.T.I. 3331, FTT (Tax) *Affirmed* 17/2169
Garlsson Real Estate SA v Consob (C-537/16) EU:C:2017:668; [2017] Lloyd's Rep. F.C. 648, AGO
Garner (Inspector of Taxes) v Pounds see Garner (Inspector of Taxes) v Pounds Shipowners & Shipbreakers Ltd
Garner (Inspector of Taxes) v Pounds Shipowners & Shipbreakers Ltd; *sub nom* Pounds Shipowners & Shipbreakers Ltd v Garner (Inspector of Taxes); *joined case* Garner (Inspector of Taxes) v Pounds [2000] 1 W.L.R. 1107; [2000] 3 All E.R. 218; [2000] S.T.C. 420; [2000] 2 E.G.L.R. 69; [2000] 34 E.G. 84; 72 T.C. 561; [2000] B.T.C. 190; Times, May 19, 2000; Independent, May 24, 2000; [2000] S.T.I. 783; [2000] E.G. 62 (C.S.); (2000) 97(23) L.S.G. 41; [2000] N.P.C. 58, HL .... *Digested,* 00/**4922**: *Applied* 02/4357: *Considered* 12/3233, 14/2852: *Followed* 17/2097
Garnett's Executor, Applicant 2017 S.L.T. (Sh Ct) 50; 2016 G.W.D. 40-729, Sh Ct (Glasgow) .... *Digested,* 17/**2838**
Garritt-Critchley v Ronnan [2014] EWHC 1774 (Ch); [2015] 3 Costs L.R. 453, Ch D *Applied* 17/246
Gartside v Inland Revenue Commissioners; *sub nom* Gartside's Will Trusts, Re [1968] A.C. 553; [1968] 2 W.L.R. 277; [1968] 1 All E.R. 121; (1967) 46 A.T.C. 323; [1967] T.R. 309; Times, December 14, 1967; (1967) 111 S.J. 982, HL .... *Digested,* 68/**1207**: *Applied* 69/1061, 69/1063: *Considered* 68/1208, 80/228, 82/1581, 89/2124, 17/1637: *Distinguished* 79/232
Gartside's Will Trusts, Re see Gartside v Inland Revenue Commissioners
Gascogne Sack Deutschland GmbH v European Union (T-577/14) EU:T:2017:1; [2017] 5 C.M.L.R. 10, GC (3rd Chamber)
Gascoigne v MGN Ltd see Gulati v MGN Ltd
Gaspar v Zaleski [2017] EWHC 1770 (Ch); [2017] 3 F.C.R. 787, Ch D
Gate Gourmet Luxembourg IV Sarl v Morby see Morby v Gate Gourmet Luxembourg IV Sarl
Gater v Wellington Real Estate Ltd [2014] UKUT 561 (LC); [2015] L. & T.R. 19, UT (Lands) *Approved* 17/1472
Gateshead MBC v JM see M-W (A Child) (Care Proceedings: Expert Evidence), Re

Gay (Grant) v HM Advocate [2017] HCJAC 62; 2017 S.C.L. 913; 2017 G.W.D. 28-448, HCJ .... *Digested*, 17/**2794**

Gazdasagi Versenyhivatal v Siemens Aktiengesellschaft Osterreich (C-102/15) EU:C:2016:607; [2016] 5 C.M.L.R. 14; [2017] C.E.C. 489; [2016] I.L.Pr. 33, ECJ (2nd Chamber)

GB Building Solutions Ltd (In Administration) v SFS Fire Services Ltd (t/a Central Fire Protection) [2017] EWHC 1289 (TCC); 172 Con. L.R. 18; [2017] C.I.L.L. 3993, QBD (TCC) .... *Digested*, 17/**474**

GB Housley Ltd v Revenue and Customs Commissioners see Revenue and Customs Commissioners v GB Housley Ltd

GD v Wakefield MDC see D (Children) v Wakefield MDC

GD (Ghana) v Secretary of State for the Home Department see Secretary of State for the Home Department v GD (Ghana)

GD SpA/Tobacco flow (T416/12) [2017] E.P.O.R. 2, EPO (Technical Bd App)

GDF Suez Teesside Ltd (formerly Teesside Power Ltd) v Revenue and Customs Commissioners [2017] UKUT 68 (TCC); [2017] S.T.C. 1622; [2017] B.T.C. 507, UT (Tax) .... *Digested*, 17/**2111**: *Applied* 17/2187

GDF Suez Teesside Ltd (formerly Teesside Power Ltd) v Revenue and Customs Commissioners [2015] UKFTT 413 (TC); [2015] S.T.I. 3280, FTT (Tax) *Affirmed* 17/2111

GE MA TA SpA/Petition for review (R7/13) [2017] E.P.O.R. 9, EPO (Enlarged Bd App)

Gedrimas v Lithuania (21048/12) (2017) 64 E.H.R.R. 14, ECHR

Gekko and Co Ltd v Revenue and Customs Commissioners [2017] UKFTT 586 (TC); [2017] S.T.I. 1835, FTT (Tax)

Geller v Yeshurun Hebrew Congregation [2016] I.C.R. 1028, EAT .... *Digested*, 17/**828**

Gem Environmental Building Services Ltd v Tower Hamlets LBC [2016] EWHC 3045 (TCC); 169 Con. L.R. 100, QBD (TCC) .... *Digested*, 17/**1811**

Gemeente Borsele v Staatssecretaris van Financien (C-520/14) EU:C:2016:334; [2016] S.T.C. 1570; [2016] B.V.C. 18; [2016] S.T.I. 1659, ECJ (5th Chamber) *Considered* 17/2262

Gemmell (James Kelly) v HM Advocate; *joined cases* Robertson (Paul) v HM Advocate; Gibson (David Alexander) v HM Advocate; McCourt (Peter Stephen) v HM Advocate; Ross v Richardson; Hart v Brown; Nisbet v Ogilvie [2011] HCJAC 129; 2012 J.C. 223; 2012 S.L.T. 484; 2012 S.C.L. 385; 2012 S.C.C.R. 176; 2012 G.W.D. 4-78, HCJ .... *Digested*, 12/**4277**: *Applied* 16/2808, 17/2814: *Cited* 12/3912: *Considered* 13/3972, 13/3990, 14/3771, 16/2779, 16/2821: *Followed* 16/2813

Gencor Ltd v Commission of the European Communities (T-102/96) EU:T:1999:65; [1999] E.C.R. II-753; [1999] B.C.C. 877; [1999] 4 C.M.L.R. 971; [1999] All E.R. (EC) 289; [1999] C.E.C. 395, CFI (5th Chamber) .... *Digested*, 99/**692**: *Applied* 05/582, 06/607, 17/416: *Distinguished* 05/542

Gencor Ltd v Commission of the European Communities (T102/96) (Applications to Intervene) EU:T:1997:82; [1997] E.C.R. II-879; [1998] 1 C.M.L.R. 142; [1997] 5 C.M.L.R. 290, CFI (5th Chamber) .... *Digested*, 99/**2231**: *Applied* 17/426

Genentech Inc v Hoechst GmbH (C-567/14) EU:C:2016:526; [2016] Bus. L.R. 1016; [2016] 5 C.M.L.R. 9; [2017] C.E.C. 192, ECJ (1st Chamber)

General Healthcare Group Ltd v Revenue and Customs Commissioners [2014] UKFTT 1087 (TC), FTT (Tax) *Affirmed* 17/2294

General Healthcare Group Ltd v Revenue and Customs Commissioners [2016] UKUT 315 (TCC); [2016] S.T.C. 2520; [2016] B.V.C. 528, UT (Tax) .... *Digested*, 17/**2294**

General Medical Council v Jagjivan [2017] EWHC 1247 (Admin); [2017] 1 W.L.R. 4438; [2017] Med. L.R. 380; (2017) 158 B.M.L.R. 146, DC .... *Digested*, 17/**1105**

General Medical Council v Michalak; *sub nom* Michalak v General Medical Council [2016] EWCA Civ 172; [2017] 2 All E.R. 534; [2016] I.C.R. 628; [2016] I.R.L.R. 458; [2016] Med. L.R. 211; (2016) 150 B.M.L.R. 90; Times, April 28, 2016, CA (Civ Div) .... *Digested*, 16/**676**

General Medical Council v Nwachuku; *joined case* R. (on the application of Nwachuku) v General Medical Council [2017] EWHC 2085 (Admin); (2017) 158 B.M.L.R. 161, QBD (Admin)

General Medical Council v Stone [2017] EWHC 2534 (Admin); [2017] Med. L.R. 530; [2017] A.C.D. 133, QBD (Admin)

General Medical Council v Theodoropoulos [2017] EWHC 1984 (Admin); [2017] 1 W.L.R. 4794, QBD (Admin)

General Motors UK Ltd v Manchester Ship Canal Co Ltd [2017] EWHC 21 (Ch); [2017] 1 Costs L.O. 71, Ch D

General Municipal and Boilermakers Union v Henderson see Henderson v General Municipal and Boilermakers Union

General Tire & Rubber Co Ltd v Firestone Tyre & Rubber Co Ltd (No.2) [1975] 1 W.L.R. 819; [1975] 2 All E.R. 173; [1975] F.S.R. 273; [1976] R.P.C. 197; (1975) 119 S.J. 389, HL .... *Digested,* 75/**2503**:
Applied 86/2496, 86/972, 00/3523, 03/944, 11/1997: *Considered* 90/3474, 94/3433, 94/3437, 94/4489, 95/3756, 97/1032, 02/2769, 17/1357: *Followed* 15/1477: *Referred to* 98/3496

Generali France Assurances v Marshall see Pickard v Marshall

Generics (UK) Ltd v Competition and Markets Authority; *joined cases* Merck KGAA v Competition and Markets Authority; Actavis UK Ltd v Competition and Markets Authority; Xellia Pharmaceuticals APS v Competition and Markets Authority; Glaxosmithkline Plc v Competition and Markets Authority [2016] CAT 24; [2017] Comp. A.R. 74, CAT

Generics (UK) Ltd v European Commission (T-469/13) EU:T:2016:454; [2017] 4 C.M.L.R. 2, GC (9th Chamber)

Generics (UK) Ltd (t/a Mylan) v Warner-Lambert Co LLC; *sub nom* Warner-Lambert Co LLC v Generics (UK) Ltd (t/a Mylan); Actavis Group PTC EHF v Warner-Lambert Co LLC [2016] EWCA Civ 1006; [2017] R.P.C. 1; (2017) 153 B.M.L.R. 28, CA (Civ Div) .... *Digested,* 17/**1375**

Generics (UK) Ltd (t/a Mylan) v Warner-Lambert Co LLC; *sub nom* Warner-Lambert Co LLC v Generics (UK) Ltd (t/a Mylan); Actavis Group PTC EHF v Warner-Lambert Co LLC [2015] EWHC 2548 (Pat); [2016] R.P.C. 3, Ch D (Patents Ct) . *Digested,* 16/**1310**:
Affirmed 17/1375: *Applied* 16/1317

Genovese v Malta (53124/09) [2012] 1 F.L.R. 10; (2014) 58 E.H.R.R. 25; [2011] Eq. L.R. 1282; [2012] Fam. Law 20, ECHR
Applied 17/1182

Genport Ltd, Re [1996] IEHC 34, HC (Irl)
Considered 17/1294

Gentoo Group Ltd (formerly Sunderland Housing Co Ltd) v Hanratty [2008] EWHC 627 (QB), QBD
Applied 17/327

Gentry v Miller [2016] EWCA Civ 141; [2016] 1 W.L.R. 2696; [2016] C.P. Rep. 25; Times, April 21, 2016, CA (Civ Div) .... *Digested,* 16/**305**:
Followed 17/350

Genzyme Ltd v Office of Fair Trading (Interim Relief) [2003] CAT 8; [2003] Comp. A.R. 290, CAT .... *Digested,* 04/**530**:
Applied 17/427: *Considered* 08/500

Geodesign Barriers Ltd v Environment Agency [2015] EWHC 1121 (TCC), QBD (TCC)
Considered 17/215

Geophysical Service Centre Co v Dowell Schlumberger (ME) Inc [2013] EWHC 147 (TCC); 147 Con. L.R. 240, QBD (TCC) .... *Digested,* 13/**421**:
Applied 17/358: *Considered* 15/357

George (Matthew Strannigan Smith) v HM Advocate [2011] HCJAC 88; 2012 S.C.L. 54; 2011 S.C.C.R. 568; 2011 G.W.D. 29-645, HCJ .... *Digested,* 12/**4260**:
Considered 17/2797

George East Housewares Ltd v Fackelmann GmbH & Co KG [2016] EWHC 2476 (IPEC); [2017] E.T.M.R. 4, IPEC .... *Digested,* 17/**1365**

George Wimpey UK Ltd v Tewkesbury BC see MA Holdings Ltd v George Wimpey UK Ltd

Georgiou (t/a Marios Chippery) v Customs and Excise Commissioners; *sub nom* Marios Chippery, Re [1996] S.T.C. 463, CA (Civ Div) .... *Digested,* 96/**5905**:
Applied 07/4283, 11/3533, 13/779, 14/3065, 17/2274: *Cited* 17/2271: *Complaint dismissed* 01/3522: *Considered* 10/3469: *Followed* 10/3496

Germany v Conrath see Puceviciene v Lithuania

Gesamtbetriebsrat der Kuhne & Nagel AG & Co KG v Kuhne & Nagel AG & Co KG (C-440/00) EU:C:2004:16; [2004] E.C.R. I-787; [2004] 2 C.M.L.R. 54; [2004] I.R.L.R. 332, ECJ .... *Digested,* 04/**1262**:
Applied 17/801

Gestmin SGPS SA v Credit Suisse (UK) Ltd [2013] EWHC 3560 (Comm), QBD (Comm)
Applied 17/320, 17/984, 17/993

Geys v Societe Generale; *sub nom* Societe Generale (London Branch) v Geys [2012] UKSC 63; [2013] 1 A.C. 523; [2013] 2 W.L.R. 50; [2013] 1 All E.R. 1061; [2013] I.C.R. 117; [2013] I.R.L.R. 122; Times, January 28, 2013, SC .... *Digested,* 13/**1056**: *Considered* 14/1026, 14/952, 15/855, 17/344, 17/803: *Followed* 16/423

GFN SA v Bancredit Cayman Ltd (In Liquidation) [2009] UKPC 39; [2010] Bus. L.R. 587; [2010] B.P.I.R. 344, PC (CI) *Considered* 17/361

GH v Catholic Child Welfare Society (Diocese of Middlesbrough) [2016] EWHC 3337 (QB); [2017] E.L.R. 136, QBD .... *Digested,* 17/**320**

Ghaidan v Godin-Mendoza; *sub nom* Mendoza v Ghaidan; Ghaidan v Mendoza; Godin-Mendoza v Ghaidan [2004] UKHL 30; [2004] 2 A.C. 557; [2004] 3 W.L.R. 113; [2004] 3 All E.R. 411; [2004] 2 F.L.R. 600; [2004] 2 F.C.R. 481; [2004] H.R.L.R. 31; [2004] U.K.H.R.R. 827; 16 B.H.R.C. 671; [2004] H.L.R. 46; [2005] 1 P. & C.R. 18; [2005] L. & T.R. 3; [2004] 2 E.G.L.R. 132; Times, June 24, 2004; [2004] Fam. Law 641; [2004] 27 E.G. 128 (C.S.); (2004) 101(27) L.S.G. 30; (2004) 154 N.L.J. 1013; (2004) 148 S.J.L.B. 792; [2004] N.P.C. 100; [2004] 2 P. & C.R. DG17, HL .... *Digested,* 04/**2538**: *Applied* 04/1889, 05/2118, 05/2641, 06/4484, 07/3293, 07/4358, 08/3137, 09/2528, 09/4294, 10/1049, 11/594, 13/1629, 14/1016, 14/1063, 14/2008, 14/823, 16/937, 17/804: *Considered* 04/707, 05/2129, 06/1004, 06/1649, 06/4470, 06/871, 07/5431, 09/2106, 09/3765, 13/1868, 16/1374: *Followed* 13/947, 13/991, 14/1123, 14/1262, 14/2864, 16/2326

Ghaidan v Mendoza see Ghaidan v Godin-Mendoza

Ghezelbash v Staatssecretaris van Veiligheid en Justitie (C-63/15) EU:C:2016:409; [2016] 1 W.L.R. 3969; [2017] 1 C.M.L.R. 6; [2016] Imm. A.R. 1246; [2017] I.N.L.R. 165, ECJ (Grand Chamber)

Ghosh v General Medical Council [2001] UKPC 29; [2001] 1 W.L.R. 1915; [2001] U.K.H.R.R. 987; [2001] Lloyd's Rep. Med. 433; Times, June 25, 2001, PC (UK) *Digested,* 01/**2894**: *Applied* 02/5954, 07/1943: *Considered* 02/1837, 09/2587, 17/1807

Gibbon v Manchester City Council; *joined case* LG Blower Specialist Bricklayer Ltd v Reeves [2010] EWCA Civ 726; [2010] 1 W.L.R. 2081; [2011] 2 All E.R. 258; [2010] C.P. Rep. 40; [2010] 5 Costs L.R. 828; [2010] P.I.Q.R. P16; [2010] 3 E.G.L.R. 85; [2010] 36 E.G. 120; [2010] 27 E.G. 84 (C.S.), CA (Civ Div) .... *Digested,* 10/**387**: *Applied* 11/359, 14/371, 15/255: *Considered* 13/401, 16/226, 17/373: *Followed* 11/297, 13/290, 13/295

Gibbons v Wright 91 C.L.R. 423, HC (Aus) .... *Digested,* 56/**5244**: *Applied* 78/1538, 17/1307: *Considered* 10/2751

Gibbs v Gibbs [2017] EWHC 1700 (Fam); [2017] 2 F.C.R. 746, Fam Div .... *Digested,* 17/**1065**

Gibraltar Betting & Gaming Association Ltd v Secretary of State for Culture, Media and Sport [2014] EWHC 3236 (Admin); [2015] 1 C.M.L.R. 28; [2015] L.L.R. 6; [2015] A.C.D. 10, QBD (Admin) .... *Digested,* 15/**1262**: *Considered* 17/1816

Gibson v Douglas [2016] EWCA Civ 1266; [2017] H.L.R. 11; [2017] 1 P. & C.R. DG21, CA (Civ Div) .... *Digested,* 17/**1449**

Gibson v Pride Mobility Products Ltd [2017] CAT 9; [2017] Comp. A.R. 257; [2017] 4 C.M.L.R. 33, CAT .... *Digested,* 17/**417**

Gibson (David Alexander) v HM Advocate see Gemmell (James Kelly) v HM Advocate

Giele v General Medical Council [2005] EWHC 2143 (Admin); [2006] 1 W.L.R. 942; [2005] 4 All E.R. 1242; (2006) 87 B.M.L.R. 34, QBD (Admin) .... *Digested,* 06/**1810**: *Applied* 17/1116: *Considered* 17/1111

Gilchrist v McPherson [2016] SAC (Crim) 28; 2016 S.C.L. 1022; 2016 G.W.D. 33-606, SAC .... *Digested,* 17/**2814**

Gilchrist v Revenue and Customs Commissioners [2014] UKUT 169 (TCC); [2015] Ch. 183; [2015] 2 W.L.R. 1; [2014] 4 All E.R. 943; [2014] S.T.C. 1713; [2014] B.T.C. 513; [2014] W.T.L.R. 1209; [2014] S.T.I. 1875, UT (Tax) .... *Digested,* 14/**2939**: *Applied* 15/2500, 17/1830

Gilham v Kent CC (No.2) [1985] I.C.R. 233; [1985] I.R.L.R. 18, CA (Civ Div) .... *Digested,* 85/**1259**: *Applied* 86/1278, 00/2239, 00/2240, 12/3975: *Followed* 17/788

Gilham v Ministry of Justice [2017] I.C.R. 404; [2017] I.R.L.R. 23, EAT .... *Digested,* 17/**790**

Gilje v Charlegrove Securities Ltd [2003] EWHC 1284 (Ch); [2004] 1 All E.R. 91; [2004] H.L.R. 1; [2004] L. & T.R. 3; [2003] 3 E.G.L.R. 9; [2003] 36 E.G. 110, Ch D .... *Digested,* 03/**2790**: *Considered* 12/2065: *Followed* 11/2072: *Not applied* 17/1468

Gill v Lewis [1956] 2 Q.B. 1; [1956] 2 W.L.R. 962; [1956] 1 All E.R. 844; (1956) 100 S.J. 299, CA .... *Digested,* 56/**4743**: *Applied* 62/1698, 65/2237, 17/1447: *Considered* 82/152.u, 85/1877, 88/2030, 06/2674, 07/2725: *Distinguished* 62/2478

Gill v RSPCA see Gill v Woodall
Gill v Woodall; *sub nom* Gill v RSPCA [2010] EWCA Civ 1430; [2011] Ch. 380; [2011] 3 W.L.R. 85; [2011] W.T.L.R. 251; Times, February 1, 2011; [2010] N.P.C. 126, CA (Civ Div) .... *Digested,* 11/**3268**:
Applied 13/2985, 14/2843: *Considered* 14/2840, 17/2077: *Followed* 14/2841
Gillan v HEC Enterprises Ltd; *sub nom* HEC Enterprises Ltd (In Administration), Re; Gillan v HEC Enterprises Ltd (In Administration); *joined case* Deep Purple (Overseas) Ltd (In Administration), Re [2016] EWHC 3179 (Ch); [2017] 1 B.C.L.C. 340, Ch D (Companies Ct) .... *Digested,* 17/**1272**
Gillan v HEC Enterprises Ltd (In Administration) see Gillan v HEC Enterprises Ltd
Gillan v United Kingdom (4158/05) (2010) 50 E.H.R.R. 45; 28 B.H.R.C. 420; Times, January 15, 2010; [2010] Crim. L.R. 415; (2010) 160 N.L.J. 104, ECHR .... *Digested,* 10/**1746**:
Applied 12/2663, 16/1776: *Considered* 14/2461, 14/701, 15/580, 17/1209
Gillan (Shaun Christopher) v HM Advocate 2002 S.L.T. 551; 2002 S.C.C.R. 502; 2002 G.W.D. 10-305, HCJ Appeal .... *Digested,* 02/**5440**:
Applied 17/2490
Gillette Safety Razor Co v Anglo-American Trading Ltd (1913) 30 R.P.C. 465
Applied 96/4568: *Considered* 83/2782: *Referred to* 17/1372
Gillick v West Norfolk and Wisbech AHA [1986] A.C. 112; [1985] 3 W.L.R. 830; [1985] 3 All E.R. 402; [1986] Crim. L.R. 113; (1985) 82 L.S.G. 3531; (1985) 135 N.L.J. 1055; (1985) 129 S.J. 738, HL .... *Digested,* 85/**2230**:
Applied 87/2483, 92/35, 93/2845, 04/1924, 17/1090: *Cited* 92/2919:
Considered 86/19, 91/2512, 94/3234, 95/4105, 99/2681, 08/210, 15/1129:
Distinguished 92/3135: *Followed* 06/1848, 15/1643, 17/966: *Referred to* 94/3229
Gilmour (John) v HM Advocate [2014] HCJAC 2; 2014 S.C.L. 162; 2014 G.W.D. 3-61, HCJ .... *Digested,* 14/**3379**:
Distinguished 17/2477
Girls Day School Trust v GDST Pension Trustees Ltd [2016] EWHC 1254 (Ch); [2016] Pens. L.R. 181, Ch D .... *Digested,* 16/**1578**:
Applied 17/1627: *Considered* 17/1626
Gisda Cyf v Barratt [2010] UKSC 41; [2010] 4 All E.R. 851; [2010] I.C.R. 1475; [2010] I.R.L.R. 1073; Times, October 19, 2010; (2010) 160 N.L.J. 1457; (2010) 154(39) S.J.L.B. 30, SC .... *Digested,* 10/**1142**:
Applied 13/987: *Considered* 11/1122, 14/3506, 17/344, 17/845:
Distinguished 15/878: *Followed* 17/830
GJ v Secretary of State for the Home Department [2013] UKUT 319 (IAC), UT (IAC)
Applied 17/1208: *Considered* 15/1310
Gjensidige Baltic AAS v PZU Lietuva UAB DK (C□475/14) see ERGO Insurance SE v If P&C Insurance AS (C-359/14)
GL v JL [2017] CSOH 60; 2017 Fam. L.R. 54; 2017 G.W.D. 14-219, OH .... *Digested,* 17/**2619**
Gladman Developments Ltd v Daventry District Council see Daventry DC v Secretary of State for Communities and Local Government
Gladman Developments Ltd v Suffolk Coastal DC [2017] P.A.D. 24, Planning Inspector
Gladman Developments Ltd v West Oxfordshire DC [2017] P.A.D. 3, Planning Inspector
Gladstone F1 Ltd v Revenue and Customs Commissioners [2017] UKFTT 541 (TC); [2017] S.T.I. 1670, FTT (Tax)
Gladwin v Bogescu [2017] EWHC 1287 (QB); [2017] 4 Costs L.O. 437, QBD (Liverpool) .... *Digested,* 17/**352**
Glasgow City Council v M (Transfer of Parental Rights: Jurisdiction) 2001 S.C. 415; 2001 S.L.T. 396; 2001 G.W.D. 3-107, IH (Ex Div) .... *Digested,* 01/**6511**:
Applied 17/2601
Glasgow City Council v Unison Claimants [2017] CSIH 34; 2017 S.C. 611; 2017 S.L.T. 729; [2017] I.R.L.R. 739; 2017 G.W.D. 19-300, IH (2 Div) .... *Digested,* 17/**2585**
Glaxo Wellcome UK Ltd (t/a Allen & Hanburys) v Sandoz Ltd [2016] EWHC 2743 (Ch); [2017] Bus. L.R. 397, Ch D
Reversed 17/1364
Glaxo Wellcome UK Ltd (t/a Allen & Hanburys) v Sandoz Ltd [2016] EWHC 1537 (Ch); [2016] F.S.R. 36, Ch D .... *Digested,* 16/**1327**:
Affirmed 17/1387
Glaxo Wellcome UK Ltd (t/a Allen & Hanburys) v Sandoz Ltd [2017] EWCA Civ 335; [2017] E.T.M.R. 27; [2017] F.S.R. 33, CA (Civ Div) .... *Digested,* 17/**1387**
Glaxo Wellcome UK Ltd (t/a Allen & Hanburys) v Sandoz Ltd [2017] EWCA Civ 227; [2017] F.S.R. 32, CA (Civ Div) .... *Digested,* 17/**1364**
Glaxosmithkline Plc v Competition and Markets Authority see Generics (UK) Ltd v Competition and Markets Authority

Gleeds Retirement Benefits Scheme, Re; *sub nom* Gleeds (Head Office) v Briggs; Briggs v Gleeds [2016] EWCA Civ 1284; [2017] Pens. L.R. 4, CA (Civ Div) .... *Digested,* 17/**1603**

Gleeson v J Wippell & Co Ltd [1977] 1 W.L.R. 510; [1977] 3 All E.R. 54; [1977] F.S.R. 301; (1977) 121 S.J. 157, Ch D .... *Digested,* 77/**2399**: *Applied* 98/3385, 98/618, 08/2125, 13/419, 14/1878, 17/500: *Cited* 00/346: *Considered* 82/2514, 93/3153

Glen International Ltd v Triplerose Ltd [2007] EWCA Civ 388; [2007] L. & T.R. 28; [2007] 2 E.G.L.R. 81; [2007] 26 E.G. 164, CA (Civ Div) .... *Digested,* 07/**2755**: *Applied* 17/1514

Glen Lyn Generations Ltd v Revenue and Customs Commissioners [2016] UKFTT 795 (TC); [2017] S.T.I. 116, FTT (Tax)

Glencore Agriculture Hungary Kft v Nemzeti Ado- es Vamhivatal Fellebbviteli Igazgatosag (C-254/16) EU:C:2017:522; [2017] B.V.C. 33; [2017] S.T.I. 1612, ECJ (1st Chamber)

Glencore Energy UK Ltd v Revenue and Customs Commissioners [2017] EWHC 1476 (Admin); [2017] S.T.C. 1824; [2017] B.T.C. 20, QBD (Admin) .... *Digested,* 17/**39**

Glencore Energy UK Ltd v Revenue and Customs Commissioners (Permissions) [2017] EWHC 1587 (Admin); [2017] B.T.C. 21; [2017] A.C.D. 98, QBD (Admin) *Digested,* 17/**316**

Glencore International AG v MSC Mediterranean Shipping Co SA; *sub nom* MSC Mediterranean Shipping Co SA v Glencore International AG [2017] EWCA Civ 365; [2017] 2 All E.R. (Comm) 881; [2018] Bus. L.R. 1; [2017] 2 Lloyd's Rep. 186, CA (Civ Div) .... *Digested,* 17/**1997**

Glencore International AG v MSC Mediterranean Shipping Co SA; *sub nom* MSC Mediterranean Shipping Co SA v Glencore International AG [2015] EWHC 1989 (Comm); [2015] 2 Lloyd's Rep. 508; [2015] 2 C.L.C. 253, QBD (Comm) ... *Digested,* 16/**1944**: *Affirmed* 17/1997

Glenmorie Wind Farm Ltd v Scottish Ministers [2016] CSOH 34; 2016 S.C.L.R. 619; 2016 G.W.D. 8-161, OH .... *Digested,* 17/**2765**

Glenn v Watson; *sub nom* Spartan Capital Ltd, Re; *joined cases* Kea Investments Ltd v Novatrust Ltd; Novatrust Ltd v Kea Investments Ltd [2016] EWHC 3259 (Ch); [2017] 4 W.L.R. 48, Ch D .... *Digested,* 17/**216**

Glenn & Co (Essex) Ltd v Revenue and Customs Commissioners see R. (on the application of Glenn & Co (Essex) Ltd) v Revenue and Customs Commissioners

Global Asset Capital Inc v Aabar Block Sarl [2017] EWCA Civ 37; [2017] 4 W.L.R. 163, CA (Civ Div) .... *Digested,* 17/**496**

Global Asset Capital Inc v Aabar Block Sarl [2016] EWHC 298 (Comm), QBD (Comm) *Reversed* 17/496

Global Container Lines Ltd v Bonyad Shipping Co (No.2) [1999] 1 Lloyd's Rep. 287; [1998] C.L.C. 1324; Times, July 14, 1998, QBD (Comm) .... *Digested,* 98/**376**: *Followed* 17/77

Global Foods Ltd v Revenue and Customs Commissioners [2017] UKFTT 577 (TC); [2017] S.T.I. 1832, FTT (Tax)

Global Gaming Ventures (Southampton) Ltd v Southampton City Council [2017] EWHC 165 (Admin); [2017] L.L.R. 317, QBD (Admin)

Global Garden Products Italy SpA, Re [2016] EWHC 1884 (Ch); [2017] B.C.C. 637, Ch D (Companies Ct) *Considered* 17/1321

Globe Motors Inc v TRW LucasVarity Electric Steering Ltd [2014] EWHC 3718 (Comm), QBD (Comm) *Reversed* 17/488

Globe Motors Inc v TRW LucasVarity Electric Steering Ltd [2016] EWCA Civ 396; [2017] 1 All E.R. (Comm) 601; [2016] 1 C.L.C. 712; 168 Con. L.R. 59, CA (Civ Div) .... *Digested,* 17/**488**: *Applied* 16/402, 17/1334: *Considered* 16/442

Gloucester Place Music Ltd v Le Bon [2016] EWHC 3091 (Ch); [2017] F.S.R. 27, Ch D .... *Digested,* 17/**490**

Gloucestershire CC v EH [2017] UKUT 85 (AAC); [2017] E.L.R. 193, UT (AAC) .... *Digested,* 17/**706**

Gloucestershire CC v K see K (A Child) (Disposal of Body: Court's Power to Authorise), Re

Glyn Mills Currie & Co v East and West India Dock Co (1882) 7 App. Cas. 591, HL *Followed* 17/1997

GM (India) v Secretary of State for the Home Department see GS (India) v Secretary of State for the Home Department

GMAC UK Plc v Revenue and Customs Commissioners see Revenue and Customs Commissioners v GMAC UK Plc

GN v MA (Child Maintenance: Children Act Sch.1) [2015] EWHC 3939 (Fam); [2017] 1 F.L.R. 285; [2016] Fam. Law 439, Fam Div

Godfrey v McCormick [2017] NZHC 420; 20 I.T.E.L.R. 138, HC (NZ)

Godfrey Morgan Solicitors v Armes see Armes v Godfrey Morgan Solicitors Ltd

Godin-Mendoza v Ghaidan see Ghaidan v Godin-Mendoza

Gogova v Iliev (C-215/15) EU:C:2015:710; [2017] I.L.Pr. 1; [2016] 1 F.L.R. 158; [2016] Fam. Law 22, ECJ (4th Chamber)

Gohil v Gohil [2015] UKSC 61; [2016] A.C. 849; [2015] 3 W.L.R. 1085; [2016] 1 All E.R. 685; [2015] 2 F.L.R. 1289; [2015] 3 F.C.R. 497; Times, November 3, 2015; [2015] Fam. Law 1459, SC .... *Digested,* 15/**1089**: *Considered* 15/1090: *Followed* 17/977

Gold Nuts Ltd v Revenue and Customs Commissioners [2017] UKFTT 354 (TC); [2017] S.T.I. 1326, FTT (Tax)

Golden Endurance Shipping SA v RMA Watanya SA [2016] EWHC 2110 (Comm); [2017] 1 All E.R. (Comm) 438, QBD (Comm) .... *Digested,* 17/**433**

Golden Endurance Shipping SA v RMA Watanya SA [2014] EWHC 3917 (Comm); [2015] 2 All E.R. (Comm) 435; [2015] 1 Lloyd's Rep. 266; [2014] 2 C.L.C. 867, QBD (Comm) .... *Digested,* 15/**2305**: *Considered* 17/2000

Golden Ocean Assurance and World Mariner Shipping SA v Martin (The Goldean Mariner) [1990] 2 Lloyd's Rep. 215; Times, June 20, 1990, CA (Civ Div) .... *Digested,* 91/**2958**: *Applied* 08/420: *Considered* 10/416, 17/366, 17/371: *Distinguished* 93/3317

Golden Ocean Group Ltd v Humpuss Intermoda Transportasi Tbk Ltd [2013] EWHC 1240 (Comm); [2013] 2 All E.R. (Comm) 1025; [2013] 2 Lloyd's Rep. 421; [2013] 1 C.L.C. 929, QBD (Comm) .... *Digested,* 13/**429**: *Applied* 17/377, 17/74

Goldman Sachs International v Novo Banco SA; *joined case* Guardians of New Zealand Superannuation Fund v Novo Banco SA [2016] EWCA Civ 1092; [2017] 2 B.C.L.C. 277; [2016] 2 C.L.C. 690, CA (Civ Div) .... *Digested,* 17/**153**

Goldman Sachs International v Novo Banco SA; *joined case* Guardians of New Zealand Superannuation Fund v Novo Banco SA [2015] EWHC 2371 (Comm); [2015] 2 C.L.C. 475, QBD (Comm) *Reversed* 17/153

Goldman Sachs International v Revenue and Customs Commissioners; *joined case* Goldman Sachs Services Ltd v Revenue and Customs Commissioners [2009] UKUT 290 (TCC); [2010] S.T.C. 763; [2010] B.T.C. 1501; [2010] S.T.I. 433, UT (Tax) .... *Digested,* 10/**3095**: *Applied* 11/3544, 17/2275

Goldman Sachs International v Videocon Global Ltd see Videocon Global Ltd v Goldman Sachs International

Goldman Sachs Services Ltd v Revenue and Customs Commissioners see Goldman Sachs International v Revenue and Customs Commissioners

Goldsmiths (Jewellers) Ltd v Customs and Excise Commissioners (C-330/95) EU:C:1997:339; [1997] S.T.C. 1073; [1997] E.C.R. I-3801; [1997] 3 C.M.L.R. 978; [1997] B.T.C. 5380; [1997] B.V.C. 494; Times, July 25, 1997, ECJ (6th Chamber) .... *Digested,* 97/**4974**: *Applied* 11/3519, 12/3381, 14/3038, 17/2230: *Considered* 07/4323

Goldtrail Travel Ltd (In Liquidation) v Aydin; *sub nom* Goldtrail Travel Ltd (In Liquidation) v Onur Air Tasimacilik AS [2017] UKSC 57; [2017] 1 W.L.R. 3014; [2018] 1 All E.R. 721; [2017] 2 B.C.L.C. 425, SC .... *Digested,* 17/**203**

Goldtrail Travel Ltd (In Liquidation) v Aydin; *sub nom* Goldtrail Travel Ltd (In Liquidation) v Onur Air Tasimacilik AS [2016] EWCA Civ 20, CA (Civ Div) *Reversed* 17/203

Golstein v Bishop [2016] EWHC 2187 (Ch); [2017] B.P.I.R. 51, Ch D .... *Digested,* 17/**1305**

Golstein v Bishop [2016] EWHC 2804 (Ch); [2017] B.P.I.R. 51, Ch D .... *Digested,* 17/**1306**

Goluchowski v District Court in Elblag, Poland see Goluchowski v Poland

Goluchowski v Poland; *sub nom* Goluchowski v District Court in Elblag, Poland; Sas v Zielona Gora, Poland; *joined case* Sas v Poland [2016] UKSC 36; [2016] 1 W.L.R. 2665; [2017] 2 All E.R. 887; [2016] 3 C.M.L.R. 39, SC .... *Digested,* 16/**789**

Gomes v Trinidad and Tobago; *joined case* Goodyer v Trinidad and Tobago [2009] UKHL 21; [2009] 1 W.L.R. 1038; [2009] 3 All E.R. 549; [2009] Extradition L.R. 243; Times, May 5, 2009; (2009) 159 N.L.J. 673; (2009) 153(18) S.J.L.B. 28, HL .... *Digested,* 09/**1474**: *Applied* 11/1277, 16/788: *Considered* 11/4265: *Followed* 13/1177, 17/899

Good (Deceased), Re; *sub nom* Carapeto v Good; Brennan v Good [2002] EWHC 640 (Ch); [2002] W.T.L.R. 801; [2002] W.T.L.R. 1305; Times, May 22, 2002; (2002) 99(23) L.S.G. 27, Ch D .... *Digested,* 02/**4334**: *Considered* 12/3185, 12/398, 17/2077

Goode v Martin [2001] 3 All E.R. 562, QBD (Admlty) .... *Digested,* 01/**421**:
Distinguished 01/419: *Followed* 17/648: *Reversed* 02/487
Goode v Martin [2001] EWCA Civ 1899; [2002] 1 W.L.R. 1828; [2002] 1 All E.R. 620; [2002] C.P. Rep. 16; [2002] C.P.L.R. 74; [2002] C.L.C. 420; [2002] P.I.Q.R. P24; Times, January 24, 2002; Independent, January 16, 2002; (2002) 152 N.L.J. 109, CA (Civ Div) .... *Digested,* 02/**487**:
Applied 07/350, 07/491: *Considered* 02/486: *Followed* 14/426, 17/211
Goode Concrete (In Receivership), Re [2012] IEHC 439, HC (Irl)
Applied 16/1198: *Considered* 17/1294
Goodlife Foods Ltd v Hall Fire Protection Ltd [2017] EWHC 767 (TCC); [2017] B.L.R. 389; 172 Con. L.R. 73, QBD (TCC) .... *Digested,* 17/**1566**
Goodman v Goodman [2013] EWHC 758 (Ch); [2014] Ch. 186; [2013] 3 W.L.R. 1551; [2013] 3 All E.R. 490; [2013] W.T.L.R. 1181, Ch D .... *Digested,* 13/**2961**:
Applied 17/401
Goodman v Transport for London [2016] UKUT 126 (LC); [2017] R.V.R. 50, UT (Lands) .... *Digested,* 17/**1839**
Goodman Logistics Developments (UK) Ltd v Secretary of State for Communities and Local Government [2017] EWHC 947 (Admin); [2017] J.P.L. 1115, QBD (Admin) .... *Digested,* 17/**1757**
Goodwin v United Kingdom (17488/90) (1996) 22 E.H.R.R. 123; 1 B.H.R.C. 81; Times, March 28, 1996, ECHR .... *Digested,* 96/**3145**:
Applied 98/3089, 98/3090, 10/1726, 17/356: *Considered* 96/23, 97/2780, 98/3422, 08/408, 17/290
Goodwood Recoveries Ltd v Breen; *joined case* Breen v Slater [2005] EWCA Civ 414; [2006] 1 W.L.R. 2723; [2006] 2 All E.R. 533; [2007] 2 Costs L.R. 147, CA (Civ Div) .... *Digested,* 06/**374**:
Applied 06/395, 15/282: *Considered* 07/387, 07/404, 11/292: *Followed* 17/250
Goodyer v Trinidad and Tobago see Gomes v Trinidad and Tobago
Google France Sarl v Centre National de Recherche en Relations Humaines (CNRRH) Sarl (C-238/08) see Google France Sarl v Louis Vuitton Malletier SA (C-236/08)
Google France Sarl v Louis Vuitton Malletier SA (C-236/08); *joined cases* Google France Sarl v Centre National de Recherche en Relations Humaines (CNRRH) Sarl (C-238/08); Google France Sarl v Viaticum SA (C-237/08) EU:C:2010:159; [2011] Bus. L.R. 1; [2010] E.C.R. I-2417; [2011] All E.R. (EC) 411; [2010] E.T.M.R. 30; [2010] R.P.C. 19; 3 A.L.R. Int'l 867; Times, June 8, 2010, ECJ (Grand Chamber) .... *Digested,* 10/**2005**:
Applied 12/1973, 13/1831, 15/1531: *Followed* 14/1927, 17/1403
Google France Sarl v Viaticum SA (C-237/08) see Google France Sarl v Louis Vuitton Malletier SA (C-236/08)
Gordon v National Grid Gas Plc [2017] R.V.R. 138; 2016 G.W.D. 30-535, Lands Tr (Scot) .... *Digested,* 17/**2644**
Gordon v Scottish Criminal Cases Review Commission see G v Scottish Criminal Cases Review Commission
Gore v Naheed [2017] EWCA Civ 369; [2017] 3 Costs L.R. 509; [2018] 1 P. & C.R. 1; [2017] 2 P. & C.R. DG17, CA (Civ Div) .... *Digested,* 17/**1840**
Goring-on-Thames Parish Council v South Oxfordshire DC [2016] EWHC 2898 (Admin); [2017] Env. L.R. D2, QBD (Admin)
Gorjat v Gorjat [2010] EWHC 1537 (Ch); 13 I.T.E.L.R. 312, Ch D .... *Digested,* 11/**3255**:
Applied 15/2406, 17/2071
Gorry v Wiltshire CC see Burnip v Birmingham City Council
Gottrup-Klim Grovvareforeninger v Dansk Landsbrugs Grovvareselskab AmbA (C-250/92) EU:C:1994:413; [1994] E.C.R. I-5641; [1996] 4 C.M.L.R. 191, ECJ (5th Chamber) .... *Digested,* 95/**617**:
Applied 17/411: *Considered* 97/855, 06/583: *Referred to* 99/3498
Gough v McFadyen see Robertson (Stewart) v HM Advocate
Gough (Stephen Peter) v HM Advocate see Robertson (Stewart) v HM Advocate
Gould v Advent Computer Training Ltd; *sub nom* Advent Computer Training Ltd, Re [2010] EWHC 459 (Ch); [2011] B.C.C. 44, Ch D (Birmingham) .... *Digested,* 11/**1884**:
Applied 17/311
Government Insurance Office of NSW v RJ Green and Lloyd Pty Ltd [1966] HCA 6, HC (Aus)
Considered 17/1877
Government Legal Service v Brookes [2017] I.R.L.R. 780, EAT .... *Digested,* 17/**780**
Govia Thameslink Railway Ltd v Associated Society of Locomotive Engineers and Firemen [2016] EWCA Civ 1309; [2017] 4 All E.R. 982; [2017] 2 C.M.L.R. 24; [2017] I.C.R. 497; [2017] I.R.L.R. 246, CA (Civ Div) .... *Digested,* 17/**807**

Govia Thameslink Railway Ltd v Associated Society of Locomotive Engineers and Firemen [2017] EWHC 3178 (Comm), QBD (Comm)
Affirmed 17/807
Goyal v Goyal [2017] EWFC 1; [2017] 4 W.L.R. 31; [2017] 2 F.C.R. 159, Fam Ct
Goyal v Goyal [2016] EWCA Civ 792; [2016] 4 W.L.R. 140; [2017] 2 F.L.R. 223; [2017] 1 F.C.R. 174; [2016] Fam. Law 1220, CA (Civ Div) .... *Digested,* 16/**906**
Goyal v Goyal [2016] EWFC 50; [2016] 4 W.L.R. 170; [2017] 2 F.L.R. 236; [2017] 1 F.C.R. 188, Fam Ct .... *Digested,* 17/**1026**
GP (Wrongful Removal), Re [2017] EWHC 1480 (Fam); [2017] 3 F.C.R. 631, Fam Div
GP Aviation Group International Ltd (In Liquidation), Re; *sub nom* Williams v Glover [2017] B.P.I.R. 95, Ch D
GR v Wirral MBC see B v Nugent Care Society
Grace Electrical Engineering Pte Ltd v EQ Insurance Co Ltd [2016] SGHC 233; [2017] Lloyd's Rep. I.R. 323, HC (Sing)
Grafton Group (UK) Plc v Secretary of State for Transport [2016] EWCA Civ 561; [2017] 1 W.L.R. 373; [2016] C.P. Rep. 37, CA (Civ Div) .... *Digested,* 16/**1677**
Graham v Commercial Bodyworks Ltd [2015] EWCA Civ 47; [2015] I.C.R. 665; [2015] P.I.Q.R. P15, CA (Civ Div) .... *Digested,* 15/**1800**: *Followed* 17/2205
Graham v Mackenzie (1871) 9 M. 798, IH (2 Div)
Applied 17/2677
Graham (Charles) v HM Advocate [2017] HCJAC 71; 2017 S.C.L. 963; 2017 S.C.C.R. 497; 2017 G.W.D. 30-479, HCJ .... *Digested,* 17/**2546**
Graham Joint Stock Shipping Co Ltd v Merchants Marine Insurance Co Ltd (The Ioanna) (No.1); *sub nom* Graham Joint Stock Shipping Co v Motor Union Insurance Co (1922) 12 Ll. L. Rep. 38, KBD
Applied 17/2021
Graham-York v York [2015] EWCA Civ 72; [2016] 1 F.L.R. 407; [2015] H.L.R. 26; 18 I.T.E.L.R. 525; [2015] Fam. Law 528; [2015] 2 P. & C.R. DG1, CA (Civ Div) ...... *Digested,* 15/**2092**: *Considered* 17/890
Grahame v Secretary of State for Scotland 1951 S.C. 368; 1951 S.L.T. 312; 1951 S.L.C.R. 35, IH (1 Div) .... *Digested,* 51/**4362**: *Applied* 00/5938: *Considered* 17/2412
Graico Property Co Ltd (In Administration), Re [2016] EWHC 2827 (Ch); [2017] B.C.C. 15, Ch D (Leeds) .... *Digested,* 17/**1336**
Grainger v North East London NHS Foundation Trust [2017] EWHC 2254 (QB); [2017] I.R.L.R. 981, QBD .... *Digested,* 17/**773**
Gram Engineering Pty Ltd, Re BL O/275/08, IPO
Considered 17/1380
Grampian RC v Aberdeen DC see Grampian RC v City of Aberdeen DC
Grampian RC v City of Aberdeen DC; *sub nom* Grampian RC v Aberdeen DC; Grampian RC v Secretary of State for Scotland 1984 S.C. (H.L.) 58; 1984 S.L.T. 197; (1984) 47 P. & C.R. 633; [1984] J.P.L. 590, HL .... *Digested,* 84/**4734**: *Considered* 91/3524, 99/4240, 02/6031, 06/3355, 17/1763: *Followed* 96/7257: *Referred to* 89/3636, 91/5757, 00/4509
Grampian RC v Secretary of State for Scotland see Grampian RC v City of Aberdeen DC
Gran Gelato Ltd v Richcliff (Group) Ltd [1992] Ch. 560; [1992] 2 W.L.R. 867; [1992] 1 All E.R. 865; [1992] 1 E.G.L.R. 297; Times, December 19, 1991; Independent, December 18, 1991; [1991] E.G. 136 (C.S.); (1992) 142 N.L.J. 51, Ch D .... *Digested,* 92/**4085**: *Applied* 98/3939, 17/44: *Considered* 93/3789, 01/871, 17/285
Granada Group Ltd v Law Debenture Pension Trust Corp Plc [2016] EWCA Civ 1289; [2017] Bus. L.R. 870; [2017] B.C.C. 57; [2017] 2 B.C.L.C. 1; [2017] Pens. L.R. 5, CA (Civ Div) .... *Digested,* 17/**1637**
Granada Group Ltd v Law Debenture Pension Trust Corp Plc [2015] EWHC 1499 (Ch); [2015] Bus. L.R. 1119; [2015] 2 B.C.L.C. 604, Ch D .... *Digested,* 16/**1572**: *Affirmed* 17/1637
Granarolo SpA v Ambrosi Emmi France SA (C-196/15) EU:C:2016:559; [2017] C.E.C. 473; [2016] I.L.Pr. 32, ECJ (2nd Chamber)
Grand China Logistics Holding (Group) Co Ltd v Spar Shipping AS see Spar Shipping AS v Grand China Logistics Holding (Group) Co Ltd
Grande Stevens v Italy (18640/10) (Unreported, July 7, 2014), ECHR
Applied 17/633
Grange v Abellio London Ltd [2017] I.C.R. 287; [2017] I.R.L.R. 108, EAT .... *Digested,* 17/**855**
Grange Shipping Ltd v Revenue and Customs Commissioners [2017] UKFTT 142 (TC); [2017] S.T.I. 306, FTT (Tax)
Grant v Asda [2017] I.C.R. D17, EAT

Grant v Baker [2016] EWHC 1782 (Ch); [2017] 2 F.L.R. 646; [2016] B.P.I.R. 1409; [2016] Fam. Law 1215, Ch D .... *Digested,* 17/**1288**
Grant v Ralls; *sub nom* Ralls Builders Ltd (In Liquidation), Re [2016] EWHC 1812 (Ch); [2016] 1 W.L.R. 5190; [2016] B.C.C. 581, Ch D .... *Digested,* 17/**1298**
Gravel Road Records Ltd v Revenue and Customs Commissioners [2017] UKFTT 80 (TC); [2017] S.T.I. 224, FTT (Tax)
Gray v Advocate General for Scotland [2016] CSOH 166; 2016 S.L.T. 1287; 2017 Rep. L.R. 14; 2016 G.W.D. 39-688, OH .... *Digested,* 17/**2443**
Gray v Boreh see Boreh v Djibouti
Gray v Inland Revenue Commissioners; *sub nom* Lady Fox's Executors v Inland Revenue Commissioners; Executors of Lady Fox v Inland Revenue Commissioners [1994] S.T.C. 360; [1994] 2 E.G.L.R. 185; [1994] 38 E.G. 156; [1994] R.V.R. 129; Times, February 24, 1994; [1994] S.T.I. 208; [1994] E.G. 32 (C.S.); [1994] N.P.C. 15, CA (Civ Div) .... *Digested,* 95/**534**:
Applied 96/443, 06/4240, 11/3393, 17/1461: *Considered* 06/4245, 07/4066, 09/3859, 12/3316: *Followed* 16/1362
Gray v MacNeil's Executor 2016 S.L.T. (Sh Ct) 250; 2016 G.W.D. 5-119, Sh Ct (Grampian) (Lochmaddy) .... *Digested,* 16/**2487**:
Reversed 17/2470
Gray v MacNeil's Executor [2017] SAC (Civ) 9; 2017 S.L.T. (Sh Ct) 83; 2017 S.C.L.R. 666; 2017 Hous. L.R. 47; 2017 G.W.D. 11-149, SAC .... *Digested,* 17/**2470**
Gray v Taylor [1998] 1 W.L.R. 1093; [1998] 4 All E.R. 17; (1999) 31 H.L.R. 262; [1998] L. & T.R. 50; Times, April 24, 1998; [1998] E.G. 62 (C.S.); (1998) 95(20) L.S.G. 34; (1998) 142 S.J.L.B. 141; [1998] N.P.C. 60, CA (Civ Div) .... *Digested,* 98/**3599**:
Followed 17/1448
Gray v Thames Trains Ltd [2009] UKHL 33; [2009] 1 A.C. 1339; [2009] 3 W.L.R. 167; [2009] 4 All E.R. 81; [2009] P.I.Q.R. P22; [2009] LS Law Medical 409; (2009) 108 B.M.L.R. 205; [2009] M.H.L.R. 73; [2009] Po. L.R. 229; Times, June 19, 2009; (2009) 159 N.L.J. 925; (2009) 153(24) S.J.L.B. 33, HL .... *Digested,* 09/**2836**:
Applied 12/2415, 13/2195: *Considered* 10/2293, 10/3411, 13/1797, 14/2994, 14/3718, 15/1881, 15/1892, 15/1893, 16/1542: *Followed* 10/2285, 12/2417, 17/2202
Gray v Work; *sub nom* W v G; Work v Gray [2015] EWHC 834 (Fam); [2015] Fam. Law 1045, Fam Div
Affirmed 17/1032: *Applied* 17/1021
Gray v Work; *sub nom* W v G; Work v Gray [2017] EWCA Civ 270; [2018] Fam. 35; [2017] 3 W.L.R. 535; [2017] 2 F.L.R. 1297; [2017] 2 F.C.R. 810; Times, June 20, 2017, CA (Civ Div) .... *Digested,* 17/**1032**
Gray (James) v HM Advocate 1999 S.L.T. 528; 1999 S.C.C.R. 24; 1999 G.W.D. 1-17, HCJ Appeal .... *Digested,* 99/**5915**:
Considered 17/2505: *Overruled* 17/2559
Gray Aitken Partnership Ltd v Link Housing Association Ltd see Link Housing Association Ltd v PBL Construction Ltd
Gray's Inn Construction Co Ltd, Re [1980] 1 W.L.R. 711; [1980] 1 All E.R. 814; (1980) 124 S.J. 463, CA (Civ Div) .... *Digested,* 80/**290**:
Applied 15/1447, 17/1334: *Considered* 87/380, 92/2583, 92/2645, 03/2418, 06/4077: *Distinguished* 00/3465: *Followed* 16/1221, 17/1330
Great Estates Group Ltd v Digby [2011] EWCA Civ 1120; [2012] 2 All E.R. (Comm) 361; [2011] 3 E.G.L.R. 101; [2011] 43 E.G. 104 (C.S.); [2011] N.P.C. 102; [2012] 1 P. & C.R. DG7, CA (Civ Div) .... *Digested,* 12/**58**:
Considered 17/47
Great Lakes Reinsurance (UK) SE v Western Trading Ltd see Western Trading Ltd v Great Lakes Reinsurance (UK) Plc
Great Ormond Street Hospital for Children Foundation NHS Trust v NO [2017] EWHC 241 (Fam); (2017) 155 B.M.L.R. 119, Fam Div .... *Digested,* 17/**1125**
Great Ormond Street Hospital for Children NHS Foundation Trust v Yates [2017] EWHC 1909 (Fam); [2017] 4 W.L.R. 131; [2018] 1 All E.R. 623; [2017] 2 F.L.R. 802; (2017) 157 B.M.L.R. 88, Fam Div .... *Digested,* 17/**1121**
Great Ormond Street Hospital for Children NHS Foundation Trust v Yates; *joined case* Yates v Great Ormond Street Hospital [2017] EWHC 972 (Fam), Fam Div
Affirmed 17/967
Great Ormond Street Hospital for Children NHS Foundation Trust v Yates; *sub nom* Gard (A Child) (Child on Life Support: Withdrawal of Treatment), Re; *joined case* Yates v Great Ormond Street Hospital [2017] EWCA Civ 410; [2018] 4 W.L.R. 5; [2018] 1 All E.R. 569; [2017] 2 F.L.R. 739; [2017] Med. L.R. 417; (2017) 157 B.M.L.R. 1; Times, July 11, 2017, CA (Civ Div) .... *Digested,* 17/**967**

Great Peace Shipping Ltd v Tsavliris Salvage (International) Ltd [2002] EWCA Civ 1407; [2003] Q.B. 679; [2002] 3 W.L.R. 1617; [2002] 4 All E.R. 689; [2002] 2 All E.R. (Comm) 999; [2002] 2 Lloyd's Rep. 653; [2003] 2 C.L.C. 16; Times, October 17, 2002; Independent, October 22, 2002; (2002) 99(43) L.S.G. 34; (2002) 152 N.L.J. 1616; [2002] N.P.C. 127, CA (Civ Div) ..... *Digested,* 02/**720**: *Applied* 04/383, 04/472, 08/2743, 12/1285: *Considered* 05/516, 08/360, 09/3565, 10/2748: *Followed* **14**/619, 17/504

Great Wealth Telecom Ltd v Simtel Communications Ltd [2007] EWHC 95 (Ch), Ch D *Disapproved* 17/313

Greater Glasgow and Clyde Health Board v Revenue and Customs Commissioners [2015] UKFTT 119 (TC), FTT (Tax) *Affirmed* 17/2271

Greathead v Greathead [2017] EWHC 1154 (Ch); [2017] W.T.L.R. 939, Ch D (Bristol)

Grecu v Cornetu Court, Romania see Grecu v Romania

Grecu v Romania; *sub nom* Grecu v Cornetu Court, Romania; Bagarea v Caras Severin Tribunal, Romania; *joined case* Bagarea v Romania [2017] EWHC 1427 (Admin); [2017] 4 W.L.R. 139, DC ..... *Digested,* 17/**906**

Greece v Nikiforidis (C-135/15) EU:C:2016:774; [2017] C.E.C. 658; [2016] I.L.Pr. 39; [2017] I.C.R. 147; Times, January 11, 2017, ECJ (Grand Chamber) *Applied* 17/163

Green v Adams [2017] EWFC 24; [2017] 2 F.L.R. 1413; [2017] 3 F.C.R. 79, Fam Ct ..... *Digested,* 17/**1006**

Green v Chalmers [2017] SAC (Civ) 8; 2017 S.L.T. (Sh Ct) 69; 2017 G.W.D. 7-94, SAC ..... *Digested,* 17/**2432**

Green v Chalmers 2016 S.C.L.R. 413; 2016 G.W.D. 32-565, Sh Ct (Tayside) (Perth) *Reversed in part* 17/2432

Green v Marston see Sports Management Group Ltd (In Liquidation), Re

Green v SIG Trading Ltd [2017] I.C.R. 1274, EAT ..... *Digested,* 17/**850**

Green v Wright [2017] EWCA Civ 111; [2017] Bus. L.R. 1070; [2017] B.P.I.R. 430, CA (Civ Div) ..... *Digested,* 17/**1301**

Green v Wright [2015] EWHC 993 (Ch); [2015] B.P.I.R. 806, Ch D (Manchester) ..... *Digested,* 15/**1424**: *Reversed* 17/1301

Green (Steven) v HM Advocate [2017] HCJAC 51; 2017 S.C.L. 771; 2017 G.W.D. 21-338, HCJ Appeal ..... *Digested,* 17/**2544**

Greene King Brewing and Retailing Ltd v Gambling Commission [2017] EWCA Civ 372; [2017] 1 W.L.R. 3611; [2017] L.L.R. 460, CA (Civ Div) ..... *Digested,* 17/**1494**

Greene King Brewing and Retailing Ltd v Gambling Commission see Gambling Commission v Greene King Brewing and Retailing Ltd

Greene King Plc v Revenue and Customs Commissioners [2014] UKUT 178 (TCC); [2014] S.T.C. 2439; [2014] B.T.C. 515, UT (Tax) ..... *Digested,* 14/**2883**: *Applied* 15/2447: *Reversed in part* 17/2112

Greene King Plc v Revenue and Customs Commissioners [2016] EWCA Civ 782; [2017] 4 W.L.R. 190; [2017] 2 All E.R. 947; [2017] S.T.C. 615; [2016] B.T.C. 35; [2016] S.T.I. 2441, CA (Civ Div) ..... *Digested,* 17/**2112**: *Applied* 17/2108

Greener Solutions Ltd v Revenue and Customs Commissioners; *sub nom* Revenue and Customs Commissioners v Greener Solutions Ltd [2012] UKUT 18 (TCC); [2012] S.T.C. 1056; [2012] Lloyd's Rep. F.C. 235; [2012] B.V.C. 1551, UT (Tax) ..... *Digested,* 12/**3401**: *Not followed* 17/2276

Greenhaven Motors Ltd, Re [1999] B.C.C. 463; [1999] 1 B.C.L.C 635, CA (Civ Div) ..... *Digested,* 99/**3352**: *Applied* 02/2684, 06/2356, 16/1231: *Followed* 17/1315

Greenway v Johnson Matthey Plc [2016] EWCA Civ 408; [2016] 1 W.L.R. 4487; [2017] I.C.R. 43; [2016] I.R.L.R. 526, CA (Civ Div) ..... *Digested,* 16/**2136**

Gregg v Pigott see Erskine 1948 Trust, Re

Gribben v Hall (Unreported, February 14, 2017), CC (Penrith) [*IMe Law Ltd, Riverside West, 1 Millsands, Sheffield*] ..... *Digested,* 17/**1649**

Griffin v Griffin [2000] C.P.L.R. 452; [2000] 2 F.L.R. 44; [2000] 2 F.C.R. 302; Times, April 28, 2000; [2000] Fam. Law 531; (2000) 97(20) L.S.G. 42; (2000) 144 S.J.L.B. 213, CA (Civ Div) ..... *Digested,* 00/**2506**: *Applied* 17/380

Griffin v Wainwright [2017] EWHC 2122 (Ch), Ch D ..... *Digested,* 17/**408**

Griffiths v Secretary of State for Justice see R. (on the application of Coll) v Secretary of State for Justice

Griffiths v Secretary of State for Work and Pensions [2015] EWCA Civ 1265; [2017] I.C.R. 160; [2016] I.R.L.R. 216, CA (Civ Div) ..... *Digested,* 16/**667**

Grimes v Essex Farmers and Union Hunt Trustees [2017] EWCA Civ 361; [2017] L. & T.R. 28; [2017] 2 P. & C.R. DG15, CA (Civ Div) ..... *Digested,* 17/**1455**

Grint v Revenue and Customs Commissioners [2016] UKFTT 537 (TC); [2017] S.F.T.D. 144; [2016] S.T.I. 2829, FTT (Tax) .... *Digested,* 17/**2185**

Grissell's Case see Overend Gurney & Co, Re

Grocon Constructors (Victoria) Pty Ltd v APN DF2 Project 2 Pty Ltd [2015] VSCA 190; (2017) 33 Const. L.J. 120, CA (Vic)

Gromax Plasticulture Ltd v Don & Low Nonwovens Ltd [1999] R.P.C. 367; (1998) 21(9) I.P.D. 21098, Ch D .... *Digested,* 99/**3592**: *Applied* 01/4062, 03/2649, 03/2650, 05/2575, 08/2235, 08/2366, 13/1832: *Considered* 17/1395: *Followed* 01/4047: *Referred to* 01/4024

Gross v Hauptzollamt Braunschweig (C-165/13) EU:C:2014:2042, ECJ *Applied* 17/632

Grosvenor (Mayfair) Estate v Merix [2017] EWCA Civ 190; [2017] L. & T.R. 18; [2017] R.V.R. 286, CA (Civ Div) .... *Digested,* 17/**1843**

Grosvenor Estates Ltd v Prospect Estates Ltd; *sub nom* Prospect Estates Ltd v Grosvenor Estates Ltd [2008] EWCA Civ 1281; [2009] 1 W.L.R. 1313; [2009] H.L.R. 32; [2009] 2 P. & C.R. 10; [2009] L. & T.R. 11; [2009] 1 E.G.L.R. 47; [2009] 2 E.G. 86; (2008) 152(46) S.J.L.B. 30; [2008] N.P.C. 126; [2009] 1 P. & C.R. DG6, CA (Civ Div) .... *Digested,* 09/**3158**: *Approved* 13/2439: *Distinguished* 10/2716: *Followed* 17/1843

Groupement des cartes bancaires (CB) v European Commission (C-67/13 P) EU:C:2014:2204; [2014] 5 C.M.L.R. 22, ECJ (3rd Chamber) *Followed* 17/412

Grove v Sharp see Caudle v Sharp

Grove Developments Ltd v Balfour Beatty Regional Construction Ltd; *sub nom* Balfour Beatty Regional Construction Ltd v Grove Developments Ltd [2016] EWCA Civ 990; [2017] 1 W.L.R. 1893; [2017] 1 All E.R. (Comm) 729; [2017] Bus. L.R. 824; [2017] B.L.R. 1; 168 Con. L.R. 1; (2018) 34 Const. L.J. 47, CA (Civ Div) ... *Digested,* 17/**464**: *Followed* 17/478

Grove Developments Ltd v Balfour Beatty Regional Construction Ltd; *sub nom* Balfour Beatty Regional Construction Ltd v Grove Developments Ltd [2016] EWHC 168 (TCC); [2016] Bus. L.R. 480; 165 Con. L.R. 153, QBD (TCC) .... *Digested,* 16/**406**: *Affirmed* 17/464

Grundig Italiana SpA v Ministero delle Finanze (C-255/00) EU:C:2002:525; [2002] E.C.R. I-8003; [2003] 1 C.M.L.R. 36; [2003] All E.R. (EC) 176; [2003] C.E.C. 178, ECJ (6th Chamber) .... *Digested,* 03/**1454**: *Applied* 05/4377: *Considered* 05/4367, 08/4016, 14/2885: *Distinguished* 06/4470: *Followed* 17/2177

Grundt v Great Boulder Proprietary Gold Mines Ltd 59 C.L.R. 641, HC (Aus) *Considered* 17/406

Grundza v Krajska prokuratura Presov (C-289/15) see Criminal Proceedings against Grundza (C-289/15)

Gruszka v Poland; *sub nom* Gruszka v Regional Court in Opole, Poland [2015] EWHC 2564 (Admin), QBD (Admin) *Considered* 17/2597

Gruszka v Regional Court in Opole, Poland see Gruszka v Poland

Gryc (Lech) v Lord Advocate [2017] HCJAC 1; 2017 S.C.L. 260; 2017 G.W.D. 2-18, HCJ .... *Digested,* 17/**2598**

GS (India) v Secretary of State for the Home Department; *joined cases* BA (Ghana) v Secretary of State for the Home Department; PL (Jamaica) v Secretary of State for the Home Department; GM (India) v Secretary of State for the Home Department; EO (Ghana) v Secretary of State for the Home Department; KK (DRC) v Secretary of State for the Home Department [2015] EWCA Civ 40; [2015] 1 W.L.R. 3312; [2015] Imm. A.R. 608; [2015] I.N.L.R. 446; (2015) 143 B.M.L.R. 79; Times, March 9, 2015, CA (Civ Div) .... *Digested,* 15/**1373**: *Applied* 17/1198, 17/1201

GS Media BV v Sanoma Media Netherlands BV (C-160/15) EU:C:2016:644; [2016] Bus. L.R. 1231; [2017] 1 C.M.L.R. 30; [2017] C.E.C. 442; [2016] E.C.D.R. 25, ECJ (2nd Chamber) *Applied* 17/1358

GSO Credit v Barclays Bank Plc [2016] EWHC 146 (Comm); [2017] 1 All E.R. (Comm) 421, QBD (Comm)

Guardian Europe Sarl v European Union (T-673/15) EU:T:2017:377; [2017] 5 C.M.L.R. 8, GC (3rd Chamber)

Guardian News and Media Ltd v City of Westminster Magistrates' Court see R. (on the application of Guardian News and Media Ltd) v City of Westminster Magistrates' Court

Guardian News and Media Ltd v Incedal; *sub nom* Guardian News and Media Ltd, Re [2016] EWCA Crim 11; [2016] 1 W.L.R. 1767; [2017] 2 All E.R. 121; [2016] 1 Cr. App. R. 33; (2016) 180 J.P. 233; [2016] E.M.L.R. 14; [2016] H.R.L.R. 9; Times, March 30, 2016; [2016] Crim. L.R. 433, CA (Crim Div) .... *Digested,* 16/**550**

Guardian News and Media Ltd v United States see R. (on the application of Guardian News and Media Ltd) v City of Westminster Magistrates' Court

Guardian News and Media Ltd, Re; *sub nom* HM Treasury v Youssef; Al-Ghabra v HM Treasury; Ahmed v HM Treasury [2010] UKSC 1; [2010] 2 A.C. 697; [2010] 2 W.L.R. 325; [2010] 2 All E.R. 799; [2010] E.M.L.R. 15; [2010] H.R.L.R. 14; [2010] U.K.H.R.R. 181; Times, January 28, 2010; (2010) 107(6) L.S.G. 18; (2010) 154(4) S.J.L.B. 29; [2010] N.P.C. 8, SC .... *Digested,* 10/**4**: *Applied* 11/4, 11/599, 15/1015, 15/824, 17/1015, 17/332, 17/353: *Considered* 10/1068, 10/1716, 11/373, 13/246, 16/172: *Followed* 11/1733, 11/868, 13/757, 14/790

Guardian News and Media Ltd, Re see Guardian News and Media Ltd v Incedal

Guardians of New Zealand Superannuation Fund v Novo Banco SA see Goldman Sachs International v Novo Banco SA

Gubinas (Justinas) v HM Advocate; *joined case* Radavicius (Nerijus) v HM Advocate [2017] HCJAC 59; 2018 J.C. 45; 2017 S.L.T. 1017; 2017 S.C.L. 828; 2017 S.C.C.R. 463; 2017 G.W.D. 26-431, HCJ .... *Digested,* 17/**2559**: *Applied* 17/2560

Gubinas (Justinas) v HM Advocate; *joined case* Radadvicius (Nerijus) v HM Advocate [2017] HCJAC 25; 2017 S.L.T. 663; 2017 S.C.L. 556; 2017 G.W.D. 16-257, HCJ .... *Digested,* 17/**2505**

Gubisch Maschinenfabrik KG v Palumbo (144/86) EU:C:1987:528; [1987] E.C.R. 4861; [1989] E.C.C. 420; Times, January 12, 1988, ECJ (6th Chamber) .... *Digested,* 91/**3934**: *Applied* 17/1042: *Considered* 96/7098, 00/5442, 11/1951: *Distinguished* 92/4436

Guccio Gucci SpA v EUIPO (T-753/15) EU:T:2016:604; [2017] E.T.M.R. 3, GC (3rd Chamber)

Gudanaviciene v Director of Legal Aid Casework see R. (on the application of Gudanaviciene) v Director of Legal Aid Casework

Gulati v MGN Ltd; *sub nom* Representative Claimants v MGN Ltd; *joined cases* Taggart v MGN Ltd; Yentob v MGN Ltd; Alcorn v MGN Ltd; Roche v MGN Ltd; Gascoigne v MGN Ltd; Ashworth v MGN Ltd; Frost v MGN Ltd [2015] EWCA Civ 1291; [2017] Q.B. 149; [2016] 2 W.L.R. 1217; [2016] 3 All E.R. 799; [2016] E.M.L.R. 9; [2016] F.S.R. 13, CA (Civ Div) .... *Digested,* 16/**571**: *Followed* 17/2198

Gulati v MGN Ltd; *sub nom* Representative Claimants v MGN Ltd; *joined cases* Taggart v MGN Ltd; Yentob v MGN Ltd; Alcorn v MGN Ltd; Roche v MGN Ltd; Gascoigne v MGN Ltd; Ashworth v MGN Ltd; Frost v MGN Ltd [2015] EWHC 1482 (Ch); [2016] F.S.R. 12, Ch D .... *Digested,* 16/**2141**: *Affirmed* 16/571: *Applied* 17/2198

Gulf International Bank v Al Ittefaq Steel Products Co; *joined case* Gulf International Bank v Al-Tuwairqi [2010] EWHC 2601 (QB), QBD
Applied 17/264

Gulf International Bank v Al-Tuwairqi see Gulf International Bank v Al Ittefaq Steel Products Co

Gunewardena v Conran Holdings Ltd [2016] EWHC 2983 (Ch); [2017] Bus. L.R. 301; [2017] B.C.C. 135, Ch D .... *Digested,* 17/**387**

Gunn v Diaz [2017] EWHC 157 (QB); [2017] 2 All E.R. (Comm) 129; [2017] 1 Lloyd's Rep. 165; [2017] R.T.R. 24; [2017] Lloyd's Rep. I.R. 139, QBD .... *Digested,* 17/**369**

Gunsbourg, Re [1920] 2 K.B. 426, CA
Applied 96/3452: *Considered* 94/280: *Followed* 17/1276

Gunton v Richmond upon Thames LBC [1981] Ch. 448; [1980] 3 W.L.R. 714; [1980] 3 All E.R. 577; [1980] I.C.R. 755; [1980] I.R.L.R. 321; 79 L.G.R. 241; (1980) 124 S.J. 792, CA (Civ Div) .... *Digested,* 80/**895**: *Applied* 85/1181, 86/1279, 87/1419, 93/1734, 98/2098, 13/952: *Considered* 96/2522, 99/2013, 13/1056, 17/803: *Followed* 98/2242, 10/1153, 11/1122

Guntrip v Parole Board for England and Wales [2014] EWHC 4180 (Admin); [2015] A.C.D. 67, QBD (Admin)
Applied 17/1595

Gupta v Partridge see Partridge v Gupta

GUS Merchandise Corp Ltd v Customs and Excise Commissioners (No.2); *joined case* Customs and Excise Commissioners v Gus Merchandise Corp Ltd (No.2) [1995] S.T.C. 279; Independent, October 24, 1994, CA (Civ Div) .... *Digested,* 95/**5086**: *Applied* 17/2246: *Followed* 10/3509

Gutierrez Naranjo v Cajasur Banco SAU (C-154/15); *joined cases* Palacios Martinez v Banco Bilbao Vizcaya Argentaria SA (BBVA) (C□307/15); Banco Popular Espamol SA v Irles Lopez (C-308/15) EU:C:2016:980; [2017] 2 C.M.L.R. 25, ECJ (2nd Chamber)
Gutsanovi v Bulgaria (34529/10) (2017) 64 E.H.R.R. 22, ECHR
GW v Gloucestershire CC [2016] UKUT 499 (AAC); [2017] M.H.L.R. 80, UT (AAC) ..... *Digested,* 17/**1547**
GW v GW [2016] EWHC 3000 (Fam); [2017] 4 W.L.R. 13; [2017] 2 F.L.R. 114; [2017] 1 F.C.R. 99, Fam Div ..... *Digested,* 17/**1023**
GW v RW (Financial Provision: Departure from Equality) [2003] EWHC 611 (Fam); [2003] 2 F.L.R. 108; [2003] 2 F.C.R. 289; [2003] Fam. Law 386, Fam Div ..... *Digested,* 03/**1587**: *Applied* 04/4216, 17/1001: *Considered* 14/1360: *Doubted* 03/1571: *Overruled* 11/1300
Gwembe Valley Development Co Ltd (In Receivership) v Koshy (Account of Profits: Limitations) see DEG-Deutsche Investitions und Entwicklungsgesellschaft mbH v Koshy (Account of Profits: Limitations)
Gye v McIntyre [1991] HCA 60; 171 C.L.R. 609, HC (Aus) *Considered* 17/1259

H v B (Wardship: Jurisdiction); *sub nom* H (Children) (Abduction: Jurisdiction: Habitual Residence), Re [2014] EWCA Civ 1101; [2015] 1 W.L.R. 863; [2015] 1 F.L.R. 1132; [2014] 3 F.C.R. 405; Times, August 8, 2014; [2014] Fam. Law 1523, CA (Civ Div) ..... *Digested,* 14/**1381**: *Applied* 15/1021: *Considered* 17/1040
H v Council of the European Union (C-455/14 P) EU:C:2016:569; [2017] 1 C.M.L.R. 24, ECJ (Grand Chamber)
H v Craven; *sub nom* OH v Craven; AKB v Willerton; *joined case* B v Willerton [2016] EWHC 3146 (QB); [2017] 4 W.L.R. 25, QBD (Manchester) ..... *Digested,* 17/**2217**
H v D (Appeal: Failure of Case Management: Cross-examination by Alleged Abuser); *sub nom* D (Appeal: Failure of Case Management), Re [2017] EWHC 1907 (Fam); [2017] 4 W.L.R. 176; [2017] 3 F.C.R. 451, Fam Div ..... *Digested,* 17/**986**
H v H; *sub nom* AH v CH [2016] CSOH 152; 2016 Fam. L.R. 186; 2016 G.W.D. 34-616, OH ..... *Digested,* 17/**2614**
H v Ishmail [2017] I.C.R. 486; [2017] I.R.L.R. 228, EAT ..... *Digested,* 17/**796**
H v Ismail 3304712/2011, ET *Reversed* 17/796
H v L [2017] EWHC 137 (Comm); [2017] 1 W.L.R. 2280; [2017] 2 All E.R. (Comm) 1097; [2017] 1 Lloyd's Rep. 553; [2017] 1 C.L.C. 112, QBD (Comm) ..... *Digested,* 17/**4**
H v Lancashire CC see Hammersmith and Fulham LBC v L
H v Lord Advocate; *sub nom* BH v Lord Advocate; Howes, Re; *joined case* KAS v Lord Advocate [2012] UKSC 24; [2013] 1 A.C. 413; [2012] 3 W.L.R. 151; [2012] 4 All E.R. 600; 2012 S.C. (U.K.S.C.) 308; 2012 S.L.T. 799; 2012 S.C.L. 635; 2012 S.C.C.R. 562; [2012] H.R.L.R. 24; Times, July 3, 2012; (2012) 109(27) L.S.G. 19; 2012 G.W.D. 21-432, SC ..... *Digested,* 12/**1289**: *Applied* 13/1187, 16/2633, 17/1242: *Considered* 14/1650
H v Special Educational Needs and Disability Tribunal see R. (on the application of MH) v Special Educational Needs and Disability Tribunal
H v Suffolk CC see A v Hoare
H (A Child) (Hair Strand Testing), Re; *sub nom* Barnet LBC v T [2017] EWFC 64; [2017] 4 W.L.R. 179; [2018] 1 F.L.R. 762; [2018] 1 F.C.R. 125, Fam Ct
H (A Child) (International Abduction: Asylum and Welfare), Re [2016] EWCA Civ 988; [2017] 2 F.L.R. 527; [2017] 1 F.C.R. 121, CA (Civ Div) ..... *Digested,* 17/**939**
H (A Child) (Placement Order: Judge's Understanding of Earlier Proceedings), Re see W (Adoption Application: Reunification with Family of Origin), Re
H (A Child), Re [2014] EWCA Civ 989, CA (Civ Div) *Followed* 15/1072, 17/1061
H (A Debtor) (No.38-SD of 1997), Re see Regional Collection Services Ltd v Heald
H (A Minor) v Northamptonshire CC [2017] EWHC 282 (Fam); [2018] 1 F.L.R. 499, Fam Div *Applied* 17/975
H (Article 9: Freedom of Religion), Re; *sub nom* KH v Secretary of State for the Home Department [2016] UKUT 286 (IAC); [2016] Imm. A.R. 1111, UT (IAC) ..... *Digested,* 17/**1212**
H (Care Order : Designated Local Authority), Re [2016] EWFC 39; [2017] 1 F.C.R. 389, Fam Ct ..... *Digested,* 17/**925**
H (Child Abduction: Mother's Asylum), Re [2003] EWHC 1820 (Fam); [2003] 2 F.L.R. 1105; Times, August 8, 2003; [2003] Fam. Law 712, Fam Div *Not followed* 17/939
H (Children) (Abduction: Jurisdiction: Habitual Residence), Re see H v B (Wardship: Jurisdiction)

H (In Bankruptcy), Re see Regional Collection Services Ltd v Heald

HA (Afghanistan) v Secretary of State for the Home Department; *joined case* TD (Nigeria) v Secretary of State for the Home Department [2010] CSIH 28; 2010 S.C. 457; [2010] Imm. A.R. 599; 2010 G.W.D. 14-267, IH (Ex Div) .... *Digested,* 10/**4333**: *Considered* 17/2768

HA (Iraq) v Secretary of State for the Home Department see Ali v Secretary of State for the Home Department

Hackney LBC v Findlay [2011] EWCA Civ 8; [2011] P.T.S.R. 1356; [2011] C.P. Rep. 18; [2011] H.L.R. 15; Times, April 13, 2011; [2011] N.P.C. 7, CA (Civ Div) .... *Digested,* 11/**367**: *Applied* 17/265: *Considered* 12/461: *Followed* 16/322

Hackney LBC v Haque; *sub nom* Haque v Hackney LBC [2017] EWCA Civ 4; [2017] P.T.S.R. 769; [2017] H.L.R. 14, CA (Civ Div) .... *Digested,* 17/**1160**

Hackney LBC v Williams see Williams v Hackney LBC

Haddassah Ltd v Revenue and Customs Commissioners see Christianuyi Ltd v Revenue and Customs Commissioners

Hadkinson v Hadkinson [1952] P. 285; [1952] 2 All E.R. 567; [1952] 2 T.L.R. 416, CA . *Digested,* 52/**2648**: *Applied* 65/3225, 84/2660, 85/3504, 85/3513, 97/2484, 05/1645, 05/1664, 08/1572, 11/1287, 11/1434: *Cited* 17/1010: *Considered* 82/2936, 84/1671, 84/2593, 86/2835, 90/3581, 07/1698, 09/1501, 15/214: *Distinguished* 79/1399: *Referred to* 17/1011, 17/1062

Hadlee and Sydney Bridge Nominees v Inland Revenue Commissioners [1993] A.C. 524; [1993] 2 W.L.R. 696; [1993] S.T.C. 294; (1993) 137 S.J.L.B. 81; [1993] N.P.C. 40, PC (NZ) .... *Digested,* 93/**3018**: *Applied* 16/2829: *Considered* 17/2131

Hadley Design Associates Ltd v Westminster City Council [2003] EWHC 1617 (TCC); [2004] T.C.L.R. 1; [2004] Masons C.L.R. 3, QBD (TCC) .... *Digested,* 04/**682**: *Approved* 17/508

Hagan v Trustees of the Phillimore Kensington Estate see Mosley v Hickman

Haggerty (Barry) v HM Advocate [2009] HCJAC 31; 2009 S.C.L. 810; 2009 G.W.D. 12-187, HCJ .... *Digested,* 10/**4101**: *Considered* 17/2556

Haider (Rehman) v Procurator Fiscal, Glasgow [2017] SAC (Crim) 9; 2017 S.L.T. (Sh Ct) 137; 2017 S.C.L. 822; 2017 G.W.D. 21-354, SAC .... *Digested,* 17/**2816**

Haigh v Charles W Ireland Ltd [1974] 1 W.L.R. 43; [1973] 3 All E.R. 1137; 1974 S.C. (H.L.) 1; 1974 S.L.T. 34; (1973) 15 K.I.R. 283; Times, November 23, 1973; (1973) 117 S.J. 939, HL .... *Digested,* 74/**2612**: *Considered* 17/2679

Hair Division Ltd v MacMillan [2013] Eq. L.R. 18, EAT (SC) .... *Digested,* 13/**3681**: *Considered* 17/829

Hajigeorgiou v Vasiliou see Vasiliou v Hajigeorgiou

Hakeem v Enfield LBC [2016] EWCA Civ 756; [2017] R.V.R. 40, CA (Civ Div) .... *Digested,* 17/**181**

Halabi (A Bankrupt), Re see Revenue and Customs Commissioners v Ariel

Halabi (In Bankruptcy), Re see Revenue and Customs Commissioners v Ariel

Halborg v EMW Law LLP; *sub nom* EMW Law LLP v Halborg [2017] EWCA Civ 793; [2018] 1 W.L.R. 52; [2017] C.P. Rep. 30; [2017] 2 B.C.L.C. 442; [2017] 3 Costs L.R. 553, CA (Civ Div) .... *Digested,* 17/**245**

Halborg v EMW Law LLP [2015] EWHC 2005 (Ch); [2015] 4 Costs L.O. 427, Ch D ..... *Digested,* 15/**252**: *Affirmed* 17/245

Halcrow Group Ltd v Blackpool BC [2016] EWHC 3596 (TCC); 172 Con. L.R. 224, QBD (TCC)

Hall v Bull; *sub nom* Bull v Hall; Preddy v Bull [2013] UKSC 73; [2013] 1 W.L.R. 3741; [2014] 1 All E.R. 919; [2014] H.R.L.R. 4; 36 B.H.R.C. 190; [2014] Eq. L.R. 76; (2013) 157(46) S.J.L.B. 37, SC .... *Digested,* 14/**1639**: *Considered* 16/708, 17/2324

Hall v Leeds City Council see Hounslow LBC v Powell

Hallam Estates Ltd v Baker [2014] EWCA Civ 661; [2014] C.P. Rep. 38; [2014] 4 Costs L.R. 660; (2014) 164(7608) N.L.J. 19, CA (Civ Div) .... *Digested,* 14/**397**: *Followed* 17/1292

Hallamshire Industrial Finance Trust v Inland Revenue Commissioners [1979] 1 W.L.R. 620; [1979] 2 All E.R. 433; [1979] S.T.C. 237; 53 T.C. 631; [1978] T.R. 341; (1979) 123 S.J. 389, Ch D .... *Digested,* 79/**1436**: *Applied* 84/1773: *Considered* 17/2133

Hallen Co v Brabantia (UK) Ltd (No.1) [1991] R.P.C. 195; Independent, October 26, 1990; Financial Times, October 24, 1990, CA (Civ Div) .... *Digested,* 92/**3318**: *Applied* 98/3453, 09/2396, 16/1312: *Considered* 95/3750, 95/3780, 02/2845, 09/2335: *Distinguished* 95/3778: *Followed* 01/3967, 17/1376: *Referred to* 94/3438

Halliburton Manufacturing & Services Ltd v Ravat see Ravat v Halliburton Manufacturing & Services Ltd

Halsall v Champion Consulting Ltd [2017] EWHC 1079 (QB); [2017] S.T.C. 1958; [2017] P.N.L.R. 32; [2017] B.T.C. 19, QBD (Merc) .... *Digested,* 17/**1568**

Halsey v Milton Keynes General NHS Trust; *joined case* Steel v Joy [2004] EWCA Civ 576; [2004] 1 W.L.R. 3002; [2004] 4 All E.R. 920; [2004] C.P. Rep. 34; [2004] 3 Costs L.R. 393; (2005) 81 B.M.L.R. 108; Times, May 27, 2004; Independent, May 21, 2004; (2004) 101(22) L.S.G. 31; (2004) 154 N.L.J. 769; (2004) 148 S.J.L.B. 629, CA (Civ Div) .... *Digested,* 04/**291**:
Applied 06/393, 06/397, 09/391, 11/295, 13/291, 14/1403, 15/231, 17/238:
Considered 04/255, 04/266, 05/356, 08/1084, 08/307, 12/2304, 12/382, 13/1364:
Followed 14/345, 14/375, 16/1609

Halton International Inc (Holdings) Sarl v Guernroy Ltd [2006] EWCA Civ 801; [2006] W.T.L.R. 1241, CA (Civ Div) .... *Digested,* 06/**470**:
Applied 17/321

Halva v SOS-Lapsikyla ry (C-175/16) EU:C:2017:617; [2017] I.C.R. 1408; [2017] I.R.L.R. 942, ECJ (4th Chamber)

Halvanon Insurance Co Ltd v Central Reinsurance Corp [1988] 1 W.L.R. 1122; [1988] 3 All E.R. 857; (1988) 138 N.L.J. Rep. 276; (1988) 132 S.J. 1356, QBD (Comm) .... *Digested,* 89/**3493**:
Considered 02/387, 02/471, 02/472, 12/2100, 17/1314

Hamid v Secretary of State for the Home Department see Januzi v Secretary of State for the Home Department

Hamilton v Brown; *sub nom* C&MB Holdings Ltd, Re [2016] EWHC 191 (Ch); [2017] B.C.C. 457; [2017] 1 B.C.L.C. 269; [2016] B.P.I.R. 531, Ch D (Companies Ct) .. *Digested,* 16/**1249**

Hamilton v Hamilton [2016] EWHC 1132 (Ch); [2016] W.T.L.R. 1699, Ch D .... *Digested,* 17/**2071**

Hamilton v Law Debenture Trustees Ltd see Barings Plc (In Liquidation) (No.1), Re

Hamlin v Hamlin [1986] Fam. 11; [1985] 3 W.L.R. 629; [1985] 2 All E.R. 1037; [1986] 1 F.L.R. 61; [1985] Fam. Law 321; (1985) 82 L.S.G. 3173; (1985) 135 N.L.J. 582; (1985) 129 S.J. 700, CA (Civ Div) .... *Digested,* 85/**1055**:
Applied 17/1026: *Considered* 12/1440

Hammersmith and Fulham LBC v F see Hammersmith and Fulham LBC v L

Hammersmith and Fulham LBC v L; *joined cases* H v Lancashire CC; O v Lancashire CC; Hammersmith and Fulham LBC v F [2015] UKUT 523 (AAC); [2015] E.L.R. 528, UT (AAC) .... *Digested,* 16/**621**:
Applied 17/712: *Considered* 17/713

Hammerton v United Kingdom (6287/10) [2017] 1 F.L.R. 835; (2016) 63 E.H.R.R. 23; Times, April 20, 2016; [2016] Fam. Law 676, ECHR

Hammond Suddards Solicitors v Agrichem International Holdings Ltd [2001] EWCA Civ 2065; [2002] C.P. Rep. 21, CA (Civ Div) .... *Digested,* 02/**383**:
Applied 02/303, 02/381, 14/432: *Considered* 09/443, 12/477:
Disapproved 17/203: *Distinguished* 03/306: *Followed* 10/412, 16/291

Hammonds (A Firm) v Danilunas; *sub nom* Hammonds (A Firm) v Jones [2009] EWCA Civ 1400; Times, January 4, 2010; (2010) 154(1) S.J.L.B. 29; [2010] Bus. L.R. D85, CA (Civ Div) .... *Digested,* 10/**2304**:
Distinguished 17/2130

Hammonds (A Firm) v Jones see Hammonds (A Firm) v Danilunas

Hamnett v Essex CC [2017] EWCA Civ 6; [2017] 1 W.L.R. 1155; [2017] R.T.R. 13; [2017] L.L.R. 328; Times, February 16, 2017, CA (Civ Div) .... *Digested,* 17/**29**

Hamnett v Essex CC [2014] EWHC 246 (Admin); [2014] 1 W.L.R. 2562; [2014] R.T.R. 22; [2014] A.C.D. 83, QBD (Admin) .... *Digested,* 14/**2580**:
Affirmed 17/29

Hampshire v Liverpool Victoria (Unreported, November 29, 2016), CC (Newport, Gwent) [*Irwin Mitchell LLP, Riverside West, 1 Millsands, Sheffield*] .... *Digested,* 17/**1670**

Hampshire CC v Beer (t/a Hammer Trout Farm) see R. (on the application of Beer (t/a Hammer Trout Farm)) v Hampshire Farmers Markets Ltd

Hanak v Green [1958] 2 Q.B. 9; [1958] 2 W.L.R. 755; [1958] 2 All E.R. 141; 1 B.L.R. 1; (1958) 102 S.J. 329, CA .... *Digested,* 58/**2734**:
Applied 73/3103, 80/1627, 85/2604, 91/2965, 10/505, 17/1334:
Considered 60/2563, 79/1633, 94/2797, 95/4214

Hanbury v Hogan see Cadmus Management Ltd, Re

Hancock v DHL Supply Chain Ltd (Unreported, April 27, 2017), CC (Bristol) [*Adam Griffiths, Pupil Barrister, Queen Square Chambers, Bristol*] .... *Digested,* 17/**1671**

Hancock v Revenue and Customs Commissioners [2017] EWCA Civ 198; [2017] 1 W.L.R. 4717; [2017] S.T.C. 1496; [2017] B.T.C. 14; [2017] S.T.I. 1325, CA (Civ Div) .... *Digested,* 17/**2095**

Hancock v Revenue and Customs Commissioners [2016] UKUT 81 (TCC); [2016] S.T.C. 1433; [2016] B.T.C. 503; [2016] S.T.I. 432, UT (Tax) .... *Digested,* 16/**2048**:
Affirmed 17/2095

Hand v George [2017] EWHC 533 (Ch); [2017] Ch. 449; [2017] 3 W.L.R. 559; [2017] 2 F.L.R. 1565; [2017] W.T.L.R. 495, Ch D .... *Digested,* 17/**2074**

Handy (William Thomas) v HM Advocate [2017] HCJAC 20; 2017 S.C.L. 521; 2017 G.W.D. 12-177, HCJ .... *Digested,* 17/**2500**

Hanif v Middleweeks (A Firm) [2000] Lloyd's Rep. P.N. 920, CA (Civ Div) .... *Digested,* 01/**4536**: *Applied* 09/966: *Considered* 10/832: *Followed* 17/1572

Hanningfield v Chief Constable of Essex [2013] EWHC 243 (QB); [2013] 1 W.L.R. 3632, QBD .... *Digested,* 14/**2458**: *Considered* 17/1802

Hannon v 169 Queens Gate Ltd [2000] 1 E.G.L.R. 40; [2000] 09 E.G. 179; Times, November 23, 1999, Ch D .... *Digested,* 99/**3697**: *Applied* 07/2729: *Followed* 17/1436

Hannon v Hillingdon Homes Ltd [2012] EWHC 1437 (QB); [2012] P.T.S.R. D37, QBD *Doubted* 17/1563

Hansa Metallwerke AG v European Commission (C-611/13 P) EU:C:2017:47; [2017] 4 C.M.L.R. 23, ECJ (1st Chamber)

HanseYachts AG v Port D'Hiver Yachting SARL (C-29/16) EU:C:2017:343; [2017] C.E.C. 1212; [2017] I.L.Pr. 25, ECJ (2nd Chamber)

Hanson v Revenue and Customs Commissioners [2012] UKFTT 314 (TC); [2012] W.T.L.R. 1769, FTT (Tax) .... *Digested,* 13/**3133**: *Applied* 15/2520, 16/2125, 17/2088

Hanssen Beleggingen v Prast-Knipping (C-341/16) EU:C:2017:738; [2018] C.E.C. 240; [2017] I.L.Pr. 36, ECJ (2nd Chamber)

Haque v Hackney LBC see Hackney LBC v Haque

Harazin (Grzegorz) v Lord Advocate [2010] HCJAC 65; [2011] Eu. L.R. 88; 2010 G.W.D. 26-496, HCJ .... *Digested,* 11/**4262**: *Applied* 17/2597

Harb v Aziz [2017] EWHC 258 (Ch); [2017] 2 Costs L.O. 157, Ch D .... *Digested,* 17/**351**

Harb v Aziz (No.2); *sub nom* Harb v King Fahd Bin Abdul Aziz (No.2) [2005] EWCA Civ 1324; [2006] 1 W.L.R. 578; [2006] 1 F.L.R. 825; [2006] W.T.L.R. 609; Times, November 21, 2005; [2006] Fam. Law 96; (2005) 102(45) L.S.G. 28, CA (Civ Div) .... *Digested,* 06/**1624**: *Applied* 16/1191, 17/2072: *Followed* 17/1282

Harb v King Fahd Bin Abdul Aziz (No.2) see Harb v Aziz (No.2)

Harding v Secretary of State for Transport [2017] UKUT 135 (LC); [2017] R.A. 271, UT (Lands) .... *Digested,* 17/**1851**

Harding (t/a MJ Harding Contractors) v Paice [2015] EWCA Civ 1231; [2016] 1 W.L.R. 4068; [2016] 2 All E.R. 819; [2016] 2 All E.R. (Comm) 656; [2016] C.P. Rep. 10; [2015] 2 C.L.C. 1003; [2016] B.L.R. 85; 163 Con. L.R. 299; [2016] C.I.L.L. 3785, CA (Civ Div) .... *Digested,* 16/**582**: *Applied* 16/583: *Considered* 17/462: *Followed* 17/454, 17/658

Hardy v Revenue and Customs Commissioners [2015] UKFTT 250 (TC); [2015] S.T.I. 2576, FTT (Tax) *Affirmed* 17/2092

Hardy v Revenue and Customs Commissioners [2016] UKUT 332 (TCC); [2016] B.T.C. 514; [2016] S.T.I. 2590, UT (Tax) .... *Digested,* 17/**2092**

Hare v Attwood (Unreported, February 7, 2017), CC (Bristol) [*Charlotte Robinson-Jones, Barrister, No.5 Chambers, 38 Queen Square*] .... *Digested,* 17/**1690**

Hargreaves v Revenue and Customs Commissioners [2016] EWCA Civ 174; [2016] 1 W.L.R. 2981; [2017] 1 All E.R. 129; [2016] S.T.C. 1652; [2016] B.T.C. 13; [2016] S.T.I. 1154, CA (Civ Div) .... *Digested,* 16/**2080**

Haringey LBC v Brown see Brown v Haringey LBC

Harlequin Property (SVG) Ltd v Wilkins Kennedy [2016] EWHC 3233 (TCC); [2016] 6 Costs L.R. 1201, QBD (TCC) .... *Digested,* 17/**643**: *Considered* 17/248

Harlequin Property (SVG) Ltd v Wilkins Kennedy (A Firm) [2016] EWHC 3188 (TCC); [2017] 4 W.L.R. 30; 170 Con. L.R. 86, QBD (TCC) .... *Digested,* 17/**458**

Harmon CFEM Facades (UK) Ltd v Corporate Officer of the House of Commons 67 Con. L.R. 1; (2000) 2 L.G.L.R. 372, QBD (TCC) .... *Digested,* 00/**824**: *Applied* 11/2632: *Considered* 09/4438, 13/2395: *Not applied* 17/1816

Harper v Letley [2016] CSOH 39; 2017 S.C.L.R. 1; 2016 Fam. L.R. 50; 2016 G.W.D. 9-165, OH .... *Digested,* 17/**2421**

Harraway v North Somerset Council [2017] P.A.D. 10, Planning Inspector

Harries v Church Commissioners for England; *sub nom* Lord Bishop of Oxford v Church Commissioners of England [1992] 1 W.L.R. 1241; [1993] 2 All E.R. 300; [1991] Pens. L.R. 185; Times, October 30, 1991; Independent, October 29, 1991; Guardian, October 30, 1991; (1991) 135 S.J.L.B. 180, Ch D .... *Digested,* 93/**344**: *Applied* 17/1090: *Considered* 15/1839

Harris v Conway see Berkeley Applegate (Investment Consultants) Ltd (No.1), Re
Harris v Flower & Sons (1905) 74 L.J. Ch. 127; (1904) 91 L.T. 816, CA
Applied 87/1233, 00/4635, 02/3820: *Considered* 03/3558, 03/3600, 17/1840: *Distinguished* 79/796, 84/1153, 99/4367: *Followed* 97/205, 12/2752
Harris v Hounslow LBC [2017] EWCA Civ 1476; [2017] H.L.R. 46, CA (Civ Div)
Harris v Microfusion 2003-2 LLP; *sub nom* Microfusion 2003-2 LLP v Harris [2016] EWCA Civ 1212; [2017] C.P. Rep. 15; [2017] 1 B.C.L.C. 305, CA (Civ Div) .... *Digested,* 17/**287**
Harris v Official Receiver [2016] EWHC 3433 (Ch); [2017] B.P.I.R. 444, Ch D (Bankruptcy Ct) .... *Digested,* 17/**1280**
Harris v Scholfield Roberts & Hall see Arthur JS Hall & Co v Simons
Harrison v University Hospitals Coventry and Warwickshire NHS Trust [2017] EWCA Civ 792; [2017] 1 W.L.R. 4456; [2017] C.P. Rep. 35; [2017] 3 Costs L.R. 425, CA (Civ Div) .... *Digested,* 17/**276**
Harrod v Chief Constable of West Midlands; *sub nom* Chief Constable of West Midlands v Harrod; *joined case* Chief Constable of West Midlands v Fowkes [2015] I.C.R. 1311; [2015] I.R.L.R. 790, EAT .... *Digested,* 15/**784**: *Affirmed* 17/1800
Harrod v Chief Constable of West Midlands; *sub nom* Chief Constable of West Midlands v Harrod; *joined case* Chief Constable of West Midlands v Fowkes [2017] EWCA Civ 191; [2017] I.C.R. 869; [2017] I.R.L.R. 539; [2017] Pens. L.R. 11, CA (Civ Div) .... *Digested,* 17/**1800**
Harrow LBC v Jackson (Valuation Officer) [2017] R.V.R. 278, VT .... *Digested,* 17/**1820**
Hart v Brown see Gemmell (James Kelly) v HM Advocate
Hart v Hart [2017] EWCA Civ 1306; [2018] Fam. 93; [2018] 2 W.L.R. 509; [2017] 3 F.C.R. 343, CA (Civ Div) .... *Digested,* 17/**1024**
Hartley v Birmingham City Council [1992] 1 W.L.R. 968; [1992] 2 All E.R. 213; Independent, August 16, 1991, CA (Civ Div) .... *Digested,* 92/**2811**: *Applied* 00/527, 09/420, 17/320: *Considered* 97/667, 99/476, 00/512
Hartley v King Edward VI College [2017] UKSC 39; [2017] 1 W.L.R. 2110; [2017] 4 All E.R. 637; [2017] I.C.R. 774; [2017] I.R.L.R. 763; [2017] E.L.R. 395; Times, May 31, 2017, SC .... *Digested,* 17/**808**
Hartley v King Edward VI College [2015] EWCA Civ 455; [2015] I.C.R. 1143; [2015] I.R.L.R. 650; [2015] E.L.R. 513, CA (Civ Div) .... *Digested,* 15/**863**: *Reversed* 17/808
Hartley v Magill see Porter v Magill
Hartshorne v Gardner [2008] 2 F.L.R. 1681; [2013] Inquest L.R. 1; [2008] W.T.L.R. 837; [2008] Fam. Law 985, Ch D (Birmingham) .... *Digested,* 08/**3606**: *Applied* 17/961
Harvey v Dunbar Assets Plc [2015] EWHC 3355 (Ch); [2015] Bus. L.R. 1383; [2016] B.P.I.R. 48, Ch D (Leeds) .... *Digested,* 16/**1239**: *Affirmed* 17/1324
Harvey v Dunbar Assets Plc [2017] EWCA Civ 60; [2017] Bus. L.R. 784; [2017] B.P.I.R. 450, CA (Civ Div) .... *Digested,* 17/**1324**: *Considered* 17/1290
Harvey Shopfitters Ltd v ADI Ltd [2003] EWCA Civ 1757; [2004] 2 All E.R. 982; [2004] C.P. Rep. 26; 91 Con. L.R. 71; Times, November 26, 2003; (2004) 20 Const. L.J. 291; (2003) 100(48) L.S.G. 18, CA (Civ Div) .... *Digested,* 04/**603**: *Applied* 06/677: *Followed* 17/473
Harvie v Robertson (1903) 5 F. 338; (1903) 10 S.L.T. 581, IH (1 Div)
Considered 17/2740
Hasan v Bulgaria (30985/96) (2002) 34 E.H.R.R. 55; 10 B.H.R.C. 646, ECHR .... *Digested,* 01/**3486**: *Applied* 06/1239, 07/2192, 10/1746: *Considered* 09/2046, 13/619, 17/1212
Hashimi v Hashimi [2016] EWHC 3112 (Fam); [2017] 4 W.L.R. 21; [2017] 1 F.C.R. 336, Fam Div .... *Digested,* 17/**989**
Hashwani v Jivraj [2015] EWHC 998 (Comm), QBD (Comm)
Applied 17/493
Hashwani v Jivraj see Jivraj v Hashwani
Hassan v Barnet LBC see R. (on the application of Mei Ling Lin) v Barnet LBC
Hassan v United Kingdom (29750/09) 38 B.H.R.C. 358; Times, October 16, 2014, ECHR
Applied 15/101, 15/1559, 17/1407, 17/83
Hassan Khan & Co v Al-Rawas see Al-Rawas v Hassan Khan & Co
Hassan Khan & Co v v Al-Shanfari see Al-Rawas v Hassan Khan & Co
Hastings BC v Manolete Partners Plc see Manolete Partners Plc v Hastings BC
Hatton v Revenue and Customs Commissioners [2010] UKUT 195 (LC); [2011] R.V.R. 63; [2017] W.T.L.R. 57, UT (Lands) .... *Digested,* 11/**3392**
Hatton v Sutherland see Barber v Somerset CC

Haugesund Kommune v Depfa ACS Bank [2011] EWCA Civ 33; [2011] 3 All E.R. 655; [2012] 1 All E.R. (Comm) 65; [2012] Bus. L.R. 230; [2011] 1 C.L.C. 166; 134 Con. L.R. 51; [2011] P.N.L.R. 14; (2011) 108(6) L.S.G. 19, CA (Civ Div) .... *Digested,* 11/**536**: *Approved* 17/641

Havenridge (Stevenage) Ltd v Revenue and Customs Commissioners [2017] UKFTT 490 (TC); [2017] S.T.I. 1420, FTT (Tax)

Havering LBC v Masters [2017] EWHC 848 (Admin); (2017) 181 J.P. 436, QBD (Admin) .... *Digested,* 17/**484**

Haward v Fawcetts (A Firm) [2006] UKHL 9; [2006] 1 W.L.R. 682; [2006] 3 All E.R. 497; [2006] P.N.L.R. 25; Times, March 3, 2006; [2006] 10 E.G. 154 (C.S.); [2006] N.P.C. 25, HL .... *Digested,* 06/**472**: *Considered* 07/475, 08/381, 11/2633, 15/320, 17/329: *Followed* 11/352, 13/391, 14/2212

Hawes v Burgess see Burgess v Hawes

Hawes & Curtis Ltd v Arfan [2012] I.C.R. 1244, EAT .... *Digested,* 13/**987**: *Considered* 17/845

Hawk Insurance Co Ltd, Re [2001] EWCA Civ 241; [2002] B.C.C. 300; [2001] 2 B.C.L.C. 480, CA (Civ Div) .... *Digested,* 02/**2714**: *Applied* 02/2715, 03/2440, 07/2448, 14/1820, 15/403, 16/350: *Considered* 06/2362, 06/2381: *Followed* 05/2333, 16/349, 17/404

Hawk Recovery Ltd v Hall HC-2014-000531, Ch D *Reversed* 17/1853

Hawk Recovery Ltd v Hall [2016] EWHC 1307 (Ch); [2016] B.P.I.R. 1169; [2016] 2 P. & C.R. DG19, Ch D .... *Digested,* 17/**1858**

Hawk Recovery Ltd v Hall [2016] EWHC 3260 (Ch); [2017] 4 W.L.R. 40; [2017] B.P.I.R. 675, Ch D .... *Digested,* 17/**1853**

Hawkes v County Leasing Asset Management Ltd see County Leasing Asset Management Ltd v Hawkes

Hay v Richardson see Hay (Ian Morris) v HM Advocate

Hay (Ian Morris) v HM Advocate; *joined case* Hay v Richardson [2012] HCJAC 28; 2014 J.C. 19; 2012 S.L.T. 569; 2012 S.C.L. 492; 2012 S.C.C.R. 281; 2012 G.W.D. 8-142, HCJ .... *Digested,* 12/**4271**: *Applied* 15/3243, 16/2782, 17/2798

Hayatleh v Modfy [2017] EWCA Civ 70; [2017] 3 F.C.R. 92, CA (Civ Div) .... *Digested,* 17/**1045**

Hayes v Chief Constable of Merseyside [2011] EWCA Civ 911; [2012] 1 W.L.R. 517; [2011] 2 Cr. App. R. 30; Times, August 19, 2011; [2012] Crim. L.R. 35, CA (Civ Div) .... *Digested,* 11/**2597**: *Applied* 14/2458: *Followed* 17/1802

Hayes v Dowding [1996] P.N.L.R. 578, Ch D .... *Digested,* 97/**469**: *Considered* 17/216: *Not applied* 09/333

Hayes v Willoughby [2013] UKSC 17; [2013] 1 W.L.R. 935; [2013] 2 All E.R. 405; [2013] 2 Cr. App. R. 11; [2013] E.M.L.R. 19; Times, May 28, 2013; (2013) 163(7554) N.L.J. 25, SC .... *Digested,* 13/**642**: *Considered* 17/2515

Hays Plc v Hartley [2010] EWHC 1068 (QB), QBD *Considered* 17/651

Haysport Properties Ltd v Ackerman [2016] EWHC 393 (Ch); [2016] B.C.C. 676; [2016] 2 B.C.L.C. 522, Ch D .... *Digested,* 17/**2192**

Hayter v L [1998] 1 W.L.R. 854; Times, February 3, 1998; Independent, February 4, 1998, QBD .... *Digested,* 98/**1078**: *Applied* 05/918: *Considered* 06/973, 17/621

Hayward v Zurich Insurance Co Plc; *sub nom* Zurich Insurance Co Plc v Hayward [2016] UKSC 48; [2017] A.C. 142; [2016] 3 W.L.R. 637; [2016] 4 All E.R. 628; [2016] 2 All E.R. (Comm) 755; [2016] 2 C.L.C. 246; [2017] Lloyd's Rep. I.R. 84; Times, September 5, 2016; [2016] C.I.L.L. 3865, SC .... *Digested,* 16/**2138**

Hayward (Deceased), Re [1997] Ch. 45; [1996] 3 W.L.R. 674; [1997] 1 All E.R. 32; [1997] B.P.I.R. 456, Ch D .... *Digested,* 96/**1111**: *Considered* 10/500, 12/563, 17/1849: *Distinguished* 01/3736

Haywood v Newcastle upon Tyne NHS Foundation Trust see Newcastle upon Tyne NHS Foundation Trust v Haywood

Hazelwood v RSA (Unreported, January 30, 2017), CC (Oldham) [*Irwin Mitchell LLP, Riverside West, 1 Millsands, Sheffield*] .... *Digested,* 17/**1668**

HB v A Local Authority (Wardship: Costs Funding Order) [2017] EWHC 524 (Fam); [2017] 1 W.L.R. 4289; [2018] 1 F.L.R. 538, Fam Div *Considered* 17/997

HB (Ethiopia) v Secretary of State for the Home Department see EB (Kosovo) v Secretary of State for the Home Department

HBJ Claimants v Glasgow City Council; *sub nom* Armstrong v Glasgow City Council; McDonald v Glasgow City Council; *joined case* Unison Claimants v Glasgow City Council [2017] CSIH 56; 2017 S.L.T. 1135; [2017] I.R.L.R. 993; 2017 G.W.D. 27-439, IH (2 Div) .... *Digested,* 17/**2584**

HC Trading Malta Ltd v Tradeland Commodities SL [2016] EWHC 1279 (Comm); [2016] 1 W.L.R. 3120; [2017] 2 All E.R. (Comm) 259; [2016] 2 Lloyd's Rep. 130; [2016] 2 C.L.C. 27; 166 Con. L.R. 94, QBD (Comm) .... *Digested,* 16/**61**

Health and Safety Executive v Wolverhampton City Council; *sub nom* R. (on the application of Health and Safety Executive) v Wolverhampton City Council [2012] UKSC 34; [2012] 1 W.L.R. 2264; [2012] 4 All E.R. 429; [2012] P.T.S.R. 1362; [2012] B.L.G.R. 843; Times, July 24, 2012; [2013] J.P.L. 43; [2012] 30 E.G. 74 (C.S.); (2012) 162 N.L.J. 1000; (2012) 156(29) S.J.L.B. 27, SC .... *Digested,* 12/**2603**: *Applied* 17/1784

Health Service Executive of Ireland v Z see Z (A Child) (Recognition of Foreign Order), Re

Healthwatch Hampshire CIC v Revenue and Customs Commissioners [2017] UKFTT 325 (TC); [2017] S.T.I. 1145, FTT (Tax)

Healy & Young's Trustee v Mair's Trustees see Craig v Mair's Trustees

Heard v Broadland DC [2012] EWHC 344 (Admin); [2012] Env. L.R. 23; [2012] P.T.S.R. D25, QBD (Admin) .... *Digested,* 12/**2535**: *Applied* 16/1704, 17/1730

Heather Capital Ltd (in Liquidation) v Burness Paull & Williamsons LLP [2015] CSOH 150; 2015 G.W.D. 38-599, OH
Reversed 17/2449

Heather Capital Ltd (In Liquidation) v Burness Paull LLP see Heather Capital Ltd (In Liquidation) v Levy & McRae

Heather Capital Ltd (In Liquidation) v Levy & McRae; *joined case* Heather Capital Ltd (In Liquidation) v Burness Paull LLP [2017] CSIH 19; 2017 S.L.T. 376; 2017 G.W.D. 9-127, IH (Ex Div) .... *Digested,* 17/**2449**: *Considered* 17/2697

Heather Capital Ltd (In Liquidation) v Levy & McRae [2016] CSOH 107; 2017 S.C.L.R. 317; 2016 G.W.D. 25-457, OH
Reversed 17/2449

Heatherington (UK) Ltd v Secretary of State for the Environment (1995) 69 P. & C.R. 374; [1994] 2 P.L.R. 9; [1994] E.G. 118 (C.S.), QBD .... *Digested,* 95/**4832**: *Applied* 17/1759: *Considered* 07/3266

Heaton v Axa Equity & Law Life Assurance Society Plc [2002] UKHL 15; [2002] 2 A.C. 329; [2002] 2 W.L.R. 1081; [2002] 2 All E.R. 961; [2002] C.P. Rep. 52; [2002] C.P.L.R. 475; [2003] 1 C.L.C. 37; Times, May 15, 2002, HL .... *Digested,* 02/**482**: *Applied* 16/1534: *Considered* 09/395: *Followed* 17/217, 17/2201

Heaton (Inspector of Taxes) v Bell [1970] A.C. 728; [1969] 2 W.L.R. 735; [1969] 2 All E.R. 70; (1969) 48 A.T.C. 73; [1969] T.R. 77; (1969) 113 S.J. 245, HL .... *Digested,* 69/**1743**: *Applied* 90/2659, 14/2912: *Considered* 15/2481: *Followed* 17/2131

Heatons Transport (St Helens) Ltd v Transport and General Workers Union; *joined cases* Craddock Bros v Transport and General Workers Union (Non-Payment of Fine: Accountability of Union); Panalpina Services Ltd v Transport and General Workers Union [1973] A.C. 15; [1972] 3 W.L.R. 431; [1972] 3 All E.R. 101; [1972] I.C.R. 308; [1972] I.R.L.R. 25; 14 K.I.R. 48; (1972) 116 S.J. 598, HL .... *Digested,* 72/**3463**: *Applied* 85/3534, 87/3768, 92/4144, 96/5732: *Considered* 75/1095, 95/4962, 17/840: *Distinguished* 74/3870, 75/3454, 85/3509: *Followed* 74/3872

HEC Enterprises Ltd (In Administration), Re see Gillan v HEC Enterprises Ltd

Heer v Singha see Singha v Heer

Heesom v Public Services Ombudsman for Wales [2014] EWHC 1504 (Admin); [2014] 4 All E.R. 269; [2015] P.T.S.R. 222; [2014] B.L.G.R. 509, QBD (Admin) .... *Digested,* 14/**2102**: *Considered* 17/1513

Heidelberger Bauchemie GmbH's Trade Mark Application (C-49/02) EU:C:2004:384; [2004] E.C.R. I-6129; [2004] E.T.M.R. 99, ECJ (2nd Chamber) .... *Digested,* 05/**2529**: *Applied* 16/1328: *Considered* 13/1758, 17/1387: *Followed* 16/1327

Hejduk v EnergieAgentur.NRW GmbH (C-441/13) EU:C:2015:28; [2015] Bus. L.R. 560; [2015] E.C.D.R. 10; [2017] I.L.Pr. 9, ECJ (4th Chamber)

Helden v Strathmore Ltd [2011] EWCA Civ 542; [2011] Bus. L.R. 1592; [2011] 2 B.C.L.C. 665; [2011] 3 Costs L.O. 289; [2011] H.L.R. 41; [2011] 2 E.G.L.R. 39; [2011] 33 E.G. 64; [2011] C.T.L.C. 158; Times, June 24, 2011; [2011] 20 E.G. 112 (C.S.); [2011] N.P.C. 48; [2011] 2 P. & C.R. DG12, CA (Civ Div) .... *Digested,* 11/**219**: *Considered* 15/1409: *Followed* 17/1836

Hellard v Chen see DP Holding SA (In Provisional Liquidation), Re

Hellawell v Eastwood 155 E.R. 554; (1851) 6 Ex. 295, Ex Ct
Applied 17/1474

Hellenic Capital Investments Ltd v Trainfx Ltd see Trainfx Ltd, Re

Hemisphere Freight Services Ltd v Revenue and Customs Commissioners [2017] UKFTT 740 (TC); [2017] S.T.I. 2136, FTT (Tax)

Hemming v Westminster City Council (C-316/15) see R. (on the application of Hemming (t/a Simply Pleasure Ltd)) v Westminster City Council (C-316/15)

Henderson v Crown Prosecution Service; *sub nom* Henderson v DPP [2016] EWHC 464 (Admin); [2016] 1 W.L.R. 1990; [2016] 2 Cr. App. R. 7; (2016) 180 J.P. 405; [2016] Crim. L.R. 422, DC .... *Digested,* 16/**492**: *Applied* 17/615

Henderson v Dorset Healthcare University Foundation NHS Trust [2016] EWHC 3032 (QB); [2017] Med. L.R. 57; [2017] M.H.L.R. 89, QBD .... *Digested,* 17/**343**

Henderson v Dorset Healthcare University NHS Foundation Trust; *sub nom* EH v Dorset Healthcare University NHS Foundation Trust [2016] EWHC 3275 (QB); [2017] 1 W.L.R. 2673; [2017] Med. L.R. 69; (2017) 154 B.M.L.R. 67, QBD .... *Digested,* 17/**2202**

Henderson v DPP see Henderson v Crown Prosecution Service

Henderson v Foxworth Investments Ltd; *sub nom* Liquidator of Letham Grange Development Co Ltd v Foxworth Investments Ltd [2014] UKSC 41; [2014] 1 W.L.R. 2600; 2014 S.C. (U.K.S.C.) 203; 2014 S.L.T. 775; 2014 S.C.L.R. 692; (2014) 158(27) S.J.L.B. 37; 2014 G.W.D. 23-437, SC .... *Digested,* 14/**1579**: *Applied* 15/2910, 15/3076, 17/2440, 17/2616: *Considered* 15/3133

Henderson v General Municipal and Boilermakers Union; *joined case* General Municipal and Boilermakers Union v Henderson [2016] EWCA Civ 1049; [2017] I.R.L.R. 340, CA (Civ Div) .... *Digested,* 17/**785**

Henderson v General Municipal and Boilermakers Union; *joined case* General Municipal and Boilermakers Union v Henderson [2015] I.R.L.R. 451, EAT
Affirmed 17/785

Henderson v Henderson [1843-60] All E.R. Rep. 378; 67 E.R. 313; (1843) 3 Hare 100, Ct of Chancery
Applied 65/100, 67/1498, 91/1736, 97/461, 97/997, 98/2162, 98/2163, 98/3454, 98/80, 99/3313, 99/4025, 00/5111, 01/4678, 02/419, 03/470, 04/264, 05/2505, 06/2531, 09/2742, 09/431, 14/368, 16/159: *Considered* 75/2463, 82/946, 84/2704, 89/1534, 94/3285, 94/3746, 95/3894, 96/1105, 98/244, 98/4067, 98/518, 98/618, 99/3732, 99/620, 00/604, 00/785, 01/410, 01/6474, 03/466, 04/425, 06/1319, 08/271, 10/458, 11/1077, 11/1136, 14/1449, 14/1790, 16/1292, 16/1313, 16/72, 17/1856, 17/425: *Distinguished* 47-51/3681, 99/4384, 99/549, 00/2605, 00/349: *Followed* 99/3952, 00/2322, 05/329, 14/2865: *Not applied* 99/1376: *Referred to* 99/4014

Henderson v Novo Banco SA (C-354/15) EU:C:2017:157; [2017] 4 W.L.R. 75, ECJ (10th Chamber)

Henderson v Revenue and Customs Commissioners [2017] UKFTT 556 (TC); [2017] W.T.L.R. 949; [2017] S.T.I. 2044, FTT (Tax)

Henderson (Colin) v HM Advocate [2017] HCJAC 43; 2017 S.C.L. 703; 2017 G.W.D. 20-319, HCJ Appeal .... *Digested,* 17/**2504**

Henderson Investment Funds Ltd v Revenue and Customs Commissioners [2015] UKFTT 505 (TC), FTT (Tax)
Affirmed 17/2178

Henderson Investment Funds Ltd v Revenue and Customs Commissioners [2017] UKUT 225 (TCC); [2017] S.T.C. 1403; [2017] B.T.C. 521, UT (Tax) .... *Digested,* 17/**2178**

Hendrickson v Revenue and Customs Commissioners [2017] UKFTT 563 (TC); [2017] S.T.I. 1733, FTT (Tax)

Hendry v Chartsearch Ltd [1998] C.L.C. 1382; (2000) 2 T.C.L.R. 115; Times, September 16, 1998, CA (Civ Div) .... *Digested,* 98/**401**: *Applied* 16/319: *Considered* 02/486, 17/306

Henia Investments Inc v Beck Interiors Ltd [2015] EWHC 2433 (TCC); [2015] B.L.R. 704; 161 Con. L.R. 51; [2015] C.I.L.L. 3727, QBD (TCC) .... *Digested,* 15/**483**: *Applied* 17/475

Henn v DPP see R. v Henn (Maurice Donald)

Henry v News Group Newspapers Ltd [2013] EWCA Civ 19; [2013] 2 All E.R. 840; [2013] C.P. Rep. 20; [2013] 2 Costs L.R. 334; (2013) 163 N.L.J. 140; (2013) 157(5) S.J.L.B. 31, CA (Civ Div) .... *Digested,* 13/**352**: *Applied* 17/279: *Considered* 13/296, 13/342, 17/277: *Followed* 13/288

Henry, Re; *sub nom* Horton v Henry [2016] EWCA Civ 989; [2017] 1 W.L.R. 391; [2017] 3 All E.R. 735; [2016] B.P.I.R. 1426; [2016] Pens. L.R. 311; Times, January 18, 2017, CA (Civ Div) .... *Digested,* 16/**1185**

Hepatitis C Litigation (No.1), Re see A v National Blood Authority (No.1)

HEPC (Mayfair Properties) v Department of the Environment see Town Investments Ltd v Department of the Environment
Herbert v Doyle [2010] EWCA Civ 1095; [2011] 1 E.G.L.R. 119; [2015] W.T.L.R. 1573; 13 I.T.E.L.R. 561; [2010] N.P.C. 100, CA (Civ Div) .... *Digested,* 11/**2710**: *Considered* 16/1795: *Explained* 17/1837
Herbosch-Kiere Marine Contractors Ltd v Dover Harbour Board [2012] EWHC 84 (TCC); [2012] B.L.R. 177; 140 Con. L.R. 97; [2012] C.I.L.L. 3148, QBD (TCC) .. *Digested,* 12/**871**: *Applied* 13/520: *Considered* 13/523, 17/453
Hereford and Worcester CC v Lane see White v Ealing LBC
Herlan Edmunds Engineering (Pty) Ltd, Re see Fourie v Le Roux
Hernandez v Trinidad and Tobago see Pitman v Trinidad and Tobago
Hernandez Zamora SA v European Union Intellectual Property Office (EUIPO) (T-369/15) EU:T:2017:106; [2017] E.T.M.R. 20, GC (9th Chamber)
Heron Bros Ltd v Central Bedfordshire Council [2015] EWHC 604 (TCC); [2015] P.T.S.R. 1146; [2015] B.L.R. 362; 160 Con. L.R. 199, QBD (TCC) .... *Digested,* 15/**2071**: *Considered* 17/368
Herring v Shorts Financial Services LLP [2016] W.T.L.R. 1203, CC (Leeds) .... *Digested,* 17/**1569**
Herry v Dudley MBC see Herry v Dudley Metropolitan Council
Herry v Dudley Metropolitan Council; *joined case* Herry v Dudley MBC [2017] I.C.R. 610; [2017] B.P.I.R. 1209, EAT .... *Digested,* 17/**795**
Hertfordshire CC v Davies [2017] EWHC 1488 (QB); [2017] 1 W.L.R. 4395; [2017] H.L.R. 33, QBD .... *Digested,* 17/**1473**
HETTLING-DENKER/Translucent Building Materials (T686/90) [2004] E.P.O.R. 5, EPO (Technical Bd App) .... *Digested,* 04/**2324**: *Considered* 17/1380
Hewlett Packard Enterprise Co v Sage; *sub nom* Sage v Hewlett Packard Enterprise Co [2017] EWCA Civ 973; [2017] 1 W.L.R. 4599, CA (Civ Div)
Heythrop Zoological Gardens Ltd (t/a Amazing Animals) v Captive Animals Protection Society [2016] EWHC 1370 (Ch); [2017] E.C.D.R. 22; [2017] F.S.R. 10, IPEC .. *Digested,* 17/**342**
HG Construction Ltd v Ashwell Homes (East Anglia) Ltd [2007] EWHC 144 (TCC); [2007] B.L.R. 175; 112 Con. L.R. 128; [2007] C.I.L.L. 2453, QBD (TCC) .... *Digested,* 07/**725**: *Applied* 16/582: *Considered* 17/476
HH v Italy see R. (on the application of HH) v Westminster City Magistrates' Court
Hicken v Ellison [2016] EWHC 2791 (Ch); [2017] B.P.I.R. 109, Ch D .... *Digested,* 17/**6**
Hickman v Trustees of the Phillimore Kensington Estate see Mosley v Hickman
Hicks v Gulliver [2002] B.P.I.R. 518, Ch D .... *Digested,* 03/**2365**: *Applied* 17/1294: *Followed* 16/1198
Higgins v Revenue and Customs Commissioners [2017] UKFTT 236 (TC); [2017] S.F.T.D. 814; [2017] S.T.I. 1176, FTT (Tax) .... *Digested,* 17/**2094**
Higgins Construction Plc v Aspect Contracts (Asbestos) Ltd see Aspect Contracts (Asbestos) Ltd v Higgins Construction Plc
High Commissioner for Pakistan in the United Kingdom v Prince Mukkaram Jah [2016] EWHC 1465 (Ch); [2016] W.T.L.R. 1763, Ch D .... *Digested,* 17/**379**
Higham v Stena Sealink Ltd [1996] 1 W.L.R. 1107; [1996] 3 All E.R. 660; [1996] 2 Lloyd's Rep. 26; [1996] C.L.C. 1193; [1996] P.I.Q.R. P351; Times, February 26, 1996, CA (Civ Div) .... *Digested,* 96/**825**: *Considered* 16/2454, 17/2436
Higherdelta Ltd v Covea Insurance Plc [2017] CSOH 84; [2017] Lloyd's Rep. I.R. 650; 2017 G.W.D. 21-349, OH
Highland Crusader Offshore Partners LP v Deutsche Bank AG see Deutsche Bank AG v Highland Crusader Offshore Partners LP
HIH Casualty & General Insurance Ltd v Chase Manhattan Bank; *joined case* Chase Manhattan Bank v HIH Casualty & General Insurance Ltd [2003] UKHL 6; [2003] 1 All E.R. (Comm) 349; [2003] 2 Lloyd's Rep. 61; [2003] 1 C.L.C. 358; [2003] Lloyd's Rep. I.R. 230; (2003) 147 S.J.L.B. 264, HL .... *Digested,* 03/**2461**: *Applied* 09/715, 09/735, 13/574, 13/587: *Considered* 16/1259: *Followed* 17/308
Hilden Park LLP v Revenue and Customs Commissioners [2017] UKFTT 217 (TC); [2017] S.T.I. 875, FTT (Tax)
Hill v Stewart Milne Group Ltd [2016] CSIH 65; 2016 S.C. 892; 2016 G.W.D. 24-444, IH (Ex Div) .... *Digested,* 17/**2426**
Hill v Stewart Milne Group Ltd [2016] CSIH 35; 2017 S.C.L.R. 92; 2016 G.W.D. 16-297, IH (Ex Div) .... *Digested,* 17/**2463**
Hillingdon LBC v DS [2016] EWHC 1858 (Fam); [2017] 1 F.C.R. 21, Fam Ct .... *Digested,* 17/**964**
Hillingdon LBC v Holley see Holley v Hillingdon LBC
Hillingdon LBC v Neary [2011] EWHC 3522 (Fam), CP *Considered* 17/243
Hillingdon LBC v Secretary of State for Transport see R. (on the application of Hillingdon LBC) v Secretary of State for Transport

Hills v Revenue and Customs Commissioners [2016] UKUT 266 (TCC); [2017] S.T.C. 173; [2016] 5 Costs L.O. 815; [2016] B.V.C. 523, UT (Tax) .... *Digested,* 17/**2269**

Hilton v Baker Booth & Eastwood see Hilton v Barker Booth & Eastwood

Hilton v Barker Booth & Eastwood; *sub nom* Hilton v Bariker Booth & Eastwood; Hilton v Baker Booth & Eastwood [2005] UKHL 8; [2005] 1 W.L.R. 567; [2005] 1 All E.R. 651; [2005] P.N.L.R. 23; [2006] Pens. L.R. 1; Times, February 4, 2005; [2005] 6 E.G. 141 (C.S.); (2005) 102(14) L.S.G. 27; (2005) 155 N.L.J. 219; (2005) 149 S.J.L.B. 179; [2005] N.P.C. 14, HL .... *Digested,* 05/**2881**: *Considered* 06/1042, 13/70: *Distinguished* 17/458

Hindawi v Secretary of State for the Home Department see R. (on the application of Clift) v Secretary of State for the Home Department

Hindcastle Ltd v Barbara Attenborough Associates Ltd [1997] A.C. 70; [1996] 2 W.L.R. 262; [1996] 1 All E.R. 737; [1996] B.C.C. 636; [1996] 2 B.C.L.C. 234; [1996] B.P.I.R. 595; [1996] 1 E.G.L.R. 94; [1996] 15 E.G. 103; Times, February 23, 1996; [1996] E.G. 32 (C.S.); (1996) 93(12) L.S.G. 29; (1996) 140 S.J.L.B. 84; [1996] N.P.C. 28, HL .... *Digested,* 96/**3704**: *Applied* 98/3650, 98/3651, 04/2194, 04/2511, 06/3469: *Considered* 17/1275: *Distinguished* 98/3620: *Followed* 09/2514, 14/1972

Hindley v AXA Insurance Plc (Unreported, October 19, 2016), CC (Norwich) [*Irwin Mitchell LLP, Riverside West, 1 Millsands, Sheffield*] .... *Digested,* 17/**1669**

His Royal Highness Okpabi v Royal Dutch Shell Plc; *joined case* Alame v Royal Dutch Shell Plc [2017] EWHC 89 (TCC); [2017] Bus. L.R. 1335; [2017] B.L.R. 136, QBD (TCC) .... *Digested,* 17/**2194**

Hitch v Stone (Inspector of Taxes); *sub nom* Stone (Inspector of Taxes) v Hitch [2001] EWCA Civ 63; [2001] S.T.C. 214; 73 T.C. 600; [2001] B.T.C. 78; Times, February 21, 2001; [2001] S.T.I. 104; [2001] N.P.C. 19, CA (Civ Div) .... *Digested,* 01/**5319**: *Applied* 04/3954, 05/1657, 08/1433, 08/4019: *Considered* 17/2180

Hives v Machin [2017] EWHC 1414 (Ch); [2017] W.T.L.R. 983, Ch D

HJ Glawe Spiel- und Unterhaltungsgerate Aufstellungsgesellschaft mbH & Co KG v Finanzamt Hamburg-Barmbek-Uhlenhorst (C-38/93) EU:C:1994:188; [1994] S.T.C. 543; [1994] E.C.R. I-1679; [1995] 1 C.M.L.R. 70; Times, May 26, 1994, ECJ (6th Chamber) .... *Digested,* 94/**4960**: *Considered* 97/4973, 97/4978, 98/4891, 04/3977, 17/2262: *Followed* 17/2256

HJ Heinz Co Ltd v EFL Inc [2010] EWHC 1203 (Comm); [2010] 2 Lloyd's Rep. 727; [2010] 1 C.L.C. 868, QBD (Comm) .... *Digested,* 10/**174**: *Applied* 17/80

HJB v MK (Declaration as to Marital Status) [2017] 2 F.C.R. 644, Fam Ct .... *Digested,* 17/**1044**

HL v United Kingdom (45508/99); *sub nom* L v United Kingdom (45508/99) (2005) 40 E.H.R.R. 32; 17 B.H.R.C. 418; (2004) 7 C.C.L. Rep. 498; [2005] Lloyd's Rep. Med. 169; (2005) 81 B.M.L.R. 131; [2004] M.H.L.R. 236; Times, October 19, 2004, ECHR .... *Digested,* 05/**2109**: *Applied* 07/3913, 14/2189: *Cited* 16/1482: *Considered* 11/3225, 12/2280, 17/1546

HLB Kidsons (A Firm) v Lloyd's Underwriters (Costs) [2007] EWHC 2699 (Comm); [2008] 3 Costs L.R. 427, QBD (Comm) .... *Digested,* 09/**389**: *Applied* 13/311, 13/338, 15/257, 17/241: *Considered* 09/374, 10/290

HM v Mar-Dive (Unreported, 1997) *Considered* 17/2019

HM v Switzerland (39187/98) (2004) 38 E.H.R.R. 17; [2002] M.H.L.R. 209, ECHR ...... *Digested,* 04/**1971**: *Applied* 17/19: *Considered* 03/2960, 07/3316, 09/2033

HM (A Child), Re; *sub nom* SM v HM [2012] Med. L.R. 449; [2014] Med. L.R. 40; [2012] W.T.L.R. 281, CP .... *Digested,* 12/**2287**: *Considered* 17/1549

HM Advocate v Al-Megrahi (Abdelbaset Ali) (No.4); *sub nom* HM Advocate v Megrahi (Abdelbaset Ali) (No.4); Megrahi (Abdelbaset Ali) v HM Advocate (No.4) 2002 J.C. 99; 2002 S.L.T. 1433; 2002 S.C.C.R. 509; 2002 G.W.D. 11-335, HCJ Appeal .... *Digested,* 03/**5384**: *Applied* 08/4627, 08/4632, 09/4732, 09/4740, 09/4768, 14/3389, 17/2473: *Considered* 06/5236

HM Advocate v Alongi (Margo Robertson); *sub nom* HM Advocate v Alongi (Margot Robertson) [2017] HCJAC 18; 2017 S.C.L. 455; 2017 S.C.C.R. 287; 2017 G.W.D. 12-176, HCJ .... *Digested,* 17/**2474**

HM Advocate v Alongi (Margot Robertson) see HM Advocate v Alongi (Margo Robertson)

HM Advocate v Ball (Ginette) [2016] HCJAC 109; 2017 S.L.T. 520; 2017 S.C.L. 4; 2017 S.C.C.R. 23; 2016 G.W.D. 40-706, HCJ .... *Digested,* 17/**2540**

HM Advocate v Bell (James Cunningham) 1995 S.L.T. 350; 1995 S.C.C.R. 244, HCJ Appeal .... *Digested,* 95/**5797**: *Applied* 96/6833, 96/6849, 11/4569, 17/2802: *Considered* 96/6862, 08/5054: *Followed* 10/4531

HM Advocate v Chung (Mark) [2017] HCJAC 48; 2017 S.C.L. 758, HCJ .... *Digested,* 17/**2490**

HM Advocate v Collins (Gordon); *sub nom* Collins (Gordon) v HM Advocate [2016] HCJAC 102; 2017 J.C. 99; 2017 S.L.T. 23; 2017 S.C.L. 202; 2017 S.C.C.R. 31; 2016 G.W.D. 38-685, HCJ .... *Digested,* 17/**2797**

HM Advocate v Cordiner (Jennifer) [2017] HCJAC 53; 2017 S.C.L. 748; 2017 G.W.D. 23-390, HCJ Appeal .... *Digested,* 17/**2528**

HM Advocate v Coulter (Andrew Alexander Marshall) see HM Advocate v Coulter (Ronnie)

HM Advocate v Coulter (Ronnie); *joined cases* HM Advocate v Coulter (Andrew Alexander Marshall); HM Advocate v Montgomery (David Shields) [2016] HCJAC 96; 2017 J.C. 115; 2016 S.L.T. 1276; 2017 S.C.L. 14; 2016 S.C.C.R. 464; 2016 G.W.D. 34-614, HCJ .... *Digested,* 17/**2523**

HM Advocate v Donaldson (Francis Jude) [2017] HCJAC 29; 2017 S.C.L. 672; 2017 G.W.D. 17-272, HCJ Appeal .... *Digested,* 17/**2563**

HM Advocate v ER see HM Advocate v R

HM Advocate v Graham (David William) [2010] HCJAC 50; 2011 J.C. 1; 2010 S.L.T. 715; 2010 S.C.L. 789; 2010 S.C.C.R. 641; 2010 G.W.D. 19-384, HCJ .... *Digested,* 10/**4523**: *Applied* 17/2805: *Considered* 16/2587: *Followed* 14/3772

HM Advocate v Grier (David Henry) see HM Advocate v Withey (Gary Martin)

HM Advocate v IP see HM Advocate v P

HM Advocate v JM see HM Advocate v V

HM Advocate v KS see HM Advocate v V

HM Advocate v Lisek (Miroslaw Aleksander) [2017] HCJAC 15; 2017 J.C. 223; 2017 S.L.T. 613; 2017 S.C.L. 469; 2017 S.C.C.R. 185; 2017 G.W.D. 11-155, HCJ .... *Digested,* 17/**2597**

HM Advocate v M (C) [2016] HCJAC 79; 2017 S.L.T. 795; 2017 S.C.L. 595; 2017 G.W.D. 18-283, HCJ .... *Digested,* 17/**2481**

HM Advocate v M see HM Advocate v V

HM Advocate v Mac Mowat; *sub nom* HM Advocate v MacMowat 2001 S.L.T. 738; 2001 S.C.C.R. 242; 2001 G.W.D. 12-408, HCJ .... *Digested,* 01/**6302**: *Applied* 17/2476

HM Advocate v MacMowat see HM Advocate v Mac Mowat

HM Advocate v McGuigan (John) 1936 J.C. 16; 1936 S.L.T. 161, HCJ *Cited* 17/2478: *Followed* 17/2472

HM Advocate v Megrahi (Abdelbaset Ali) (No.4) see HM Advocate v Al-Megrahi (Abdelbaset Ali) (No.4)

HM Advocate v Montgomery (David Shields) see HM Advocate v Coulter (Ronnie)

HM Advocate v O see HM Advocate v V

HM Advocate v P; *sub nom* HM Advocate v IP [2017] HCJAC 56; 2017 S.C.L. 877; 2017 S.C.C.R. 447; 2017 G.W.D. 23-391, HCJ .... *Digested,* 17/**2534**

HM Advocate v PO see HM Advocate v V

HM Advocate v R; *sub nom* HM Advocate v ER [2016] HCJ 98; 2016 S.L.T. 1267; 2017 S.C.L. 46; 2016 S.C.C.R. 490; 2016 G.W.D. 34-612, HCJ .... *Digested,* 17/**2493**

HM Advocate v RV see HM Advocate v V

HM Advocate v S see HM Advocate v V

HM Advocate v Steven (Andrew) [2017] HCJAC 7; 2017 S.C.L. 395; 2017 G.W.D. 4-59, HCJ Appeal .... *Digested,* 17/**2802**

HM Advocate v Swift (James Aloysius) 1984 J.C. 83; 1985 S.L.T. 26; 1984 S.C.C.R. 216, HCJ .... *Digested,* 84/**3906**: *Applied* 88/3921, 97/5801, 98/5594, 09/4798, 10/4078, 13/3622, 14/3415, 14/3416, 14/3420, 15/2969, 15/2971, 17/2519: *Considered* 97/5861, 97/5862, 06/5205, 07/5068, 08/4646, 13/3621, 14/3417, 17/2522, 17/2564: *Followed* 97/5803, 01/6344, 03/5378: *Referred to* 92/5423, 93/4935

HM Advocate v V; *sub nom* HM Advocate v RV; HM Advocate v PO; HM Advocate v JM; HM Advocate v KS; *joined cases* HM Advocate v O; HM Advocate v M; HM Advocate v S [2016] HCJAC 103; 2017 S.C.L. 29; 2017 S.C.C.R. 7; 2016 G.W.D. 37-663, HCJ .... *Digested,* 17/**2568**

HM Advocate v W [2016] HCJAC 111; 2017 S.C.L. 145; 2016 G.W.D. 38-670, HCJ .... *Digested,* 17/**2480**

HM Advocate v Withey (Gary Martin); *joined case* HM Advocate v Grier (David Henry) [2017] HCJAC 47; 2017 J.C. 249; 2017 S.C.L. 657; 2017 S.C.C.R. 325; 2017 G.W.D. 21-340, HCJ .... *Digested,* 17/**2527**

HM Land Registry v Benson [2012] I.C.R. 627; [2012] I.R.L.R. 373; [2012] Eq. L.R. 300, EAT .... *Digested,* 12/**1036**: *Applied* 15/784: *Considered* 17/1800

HM Treasury v Youssef see Guardian News and Media Ltd, Re

HMA v Secretary of State for the Home Department; *sub nom* A v Secretary of State for the Home Department [2016] CSIH 85; 2017 S.C. 186; 2017 S.L.T. 8; 2016 G.W.D. 37-667, IH (Ex Div) .... *Digested,* 17/**2674**
Ho v Welwyn Hatfield BC [2016] UKUT 151 (LC); [2016] R.V.R. 322, UT (Lands) .... *Digested,* 17/**1835**
Ho Tung v Man On Insurance Co Ltd [1902] A.C. 232, PC (HK)
Considered 11/409, 17/387
Hoare v Vale of White Horse DC [2017] EWHC 1711 (Admin); [2018] P.T.S.R. 210; [2017] J.P.L. 1406, QBD (Admin) .... *Digested,* 17/**1728**
Hoare (Valuation Officer) v National Trust for Places of Historic Interest or Natural Beauty; *sub nom* National Trust for Places of Historic Interest or Natural Beauty v Hoare; *joined case* National Trust for Places of Historic Interest or Natural Beauty v Spratling (Valuation Officer) (1999) 77 P. & C.R. 366; [1999] 1 E.G.L.R. 155; [1998] R.A. 391; Times, October 16, 1998; Independent, October 19, 1998; [1998] E.G. 141 (C.S.); [1998] N.P.C. 139, CA (Civ Div) .... *Digested,* 98/**4335**:
Applied 17/1461: *Considered* 09/3104, 17/1526
Hobbs v Gidman (Valuation Officer) [2017] UKUT 63 (LC); [2017] R.A. 123, UT (Lands) .... *Digested,* 17/**1523**
Hobson (Setting of Minimum Term), Re see Jones (Setting of Minimum Term), Re
Hoburne Ltd, Re see Burry & Knight Ltd, Re
Hochstrasser (Inspector of Taxes) v Mayes; *joined case* Jennings v Kinder (Inspector of Taxes) [1960] A.C. 376; [1960] 2 W.L.R. 63; [1959] 3 All E.R. 817; 53 R. & I.T. 12; 38 T.C. 673; (1959) 38 A.T.C. 360; [1959] T.R. 355, HL .... *Digested,* 59/**1543**:
Applied 64/1836, 76/1441, 78/1675, 82/1636, 89/2028, 90/2646, 91/2092, 99/4729, 05/4071, 10/3290: *Considered* 65/1946, 87/2034, 95/2766, 10/3323, 11/3326, 11/3359, 12/3299, 14/2908: *Distinguished* 76/1438, 86/1762:
Followed 16/2099, 17/2131
Hockin v Marsden; *sub nom* London & Westcountry Estates Ltd, Re [2014] EWHC 763 (Ch); [2014] Bus. L.R. 441; [2017] B.C.C. 433; [2014] 2 B.C.L.C. 531; [2014] B.P.I.R. 637, Ch D (Companies Ct) .... *Digested,* 14/**1750**
Hockley v Essex CC [2013] EWHC 4051 (Admin); [2014] Env. L.R. 24, QBD (Admin) . *Digested,* 14/**2427**:
Applied 15/2041, 17/1778
Hoe International Ltd v Andersen [2016] CSOH 33; 2016 G.W.D. 7-142, OH
Reversed 17/2471
Hoe International Ltd v Andersen [2017] CSIH 9; 2017 S.C. 313; 2017 G.W.D. 6-83, IH (2 Div) .... *Digested,* 17/**2471**
Hoffmann (C-144/00) see Criminal Proceedings against Hoffmann (C-144/00)
Hogg v Dover College [1990] I.C.R. 39, EAT .... *Digested,* 90/**1963**:
Applied 05/1204, 17/830: *Followed* 96/2657
Hok Ltd v Revenue and Customs Commissioners; *sub nom* Revenue and Customs Commissioners v Hok Ltd [2012] UKUT 363 (TCC); [2013] S.T.C. 225; 81 T.C. 540; [2012] B.T.C. 1711; [2012] S.T.I. 3402, UT (Tax) .... *Digested,* 13/**3073**:
Applied 13/3199, 17/2150: *Followed* 13/3218
Holder v Gedling BC [2016] EWHC 3095 (Admin); [2017] A.C.D. 11, QBD (Admin)
Holders Investment Trust, Re [1971] 1 W.L.R. 583; [1971] 2 All E.R. 289; (1970) 115 S.J. 202, Ch D .... *Digested,* 71/**1238**:
Applied 17/405
Holdsworth v Luton and Dunstable University Hospital NHS Foundation Trust [2016] EWHC 3347 (QB); (2017) 154 B.M.L.R. 172, QBD .... *Digested,* 17/**1643**
Holiday Extras Ltd v Crawley BC [2016] EWHC 3247 (Admin); [2017] Env. L.R. 21, QBD (Admin) .... *Digested,* 17/**1694**
Holland v Oxford City Council [2016] EWHC 2545 (Ch); [2017] 1 P. & C.R. DG5, Ch D *Digested,* 17/**1457**
Holley v Hillingdon LBC; *sub nom* Hillingdon LBC v Holley [2016] EWCA Civ 1052; [2017] P.T.S.R. 127; [2017] H.L.R. 3, CA (Civ Div) .... *Digested,* 17/**1163**
Hollicourt (Contracts) Ltd (In Liquidation) v Bank of Ireland; *sub nom* Bank of Ireland v Hollicourt (Contracts) Ltd; Claughton (Liquidator of Hollicourt (Contracts) Ltd) v Bank of Ireland [2001] Ch. 555; [2001] 2 W.L.R. 290; [2001] 1 All E.R. 289; [2001] 1 All E.R. (Comm) 357; [2001] Lloyd's Rep. Bank. 6; [2000] B.C.C. 1210; [2001] 1 B.C.L.C. 233; [2001] B.P.I.R. 47; Times, November 1, 2000; Independent, October 24, 2000; (2000) 97(45) L.S.G. 41, CA (Civ Div) .... *Digested,* 00/**3464**:
Considered 16/1188: *Distinguished* 07/2419: *Followed* 17/1276
Hollington v F Hewthorn & Co Ltd [1943] K.B. 587; [1943] 2 All E.R. 35, CA
Applied 67/759, 84/1531, 87/1669, 93/2525, 03/509, 11/2165, 14/1787, 15/688: *Approved* 66/11738: *Considered* 47-51/6522, 58/957, 67/1608, 67/3246, 69/2418, 70/1018, 70/1024, 80/2609, 93/3153, 96/1410, 04/192, 06/2926, 07/339, 09/336, 14/288, 17/191: *Disapproved* 07/826: *Distinguished* 56/2546, 93/3038:
Followed 66/7003: *Not applied* 15/1189
Holman Fenwick Willan LLP v Orr see Holman Fenwick Willan LLP v Procurator Fiscal, Glasgow

Holman Fenwick Willan LLP v Procurator Fiscal, Glasgow; *sub nom* Holman Fenwick Willan LLP v Orr [2017] HCJAC 38; 2017 J.C. 239; 2017 S.L.T. 899; 2017 S.C.L. 676; 2017 S.C.C.R. 309; 2017 G.W.D. 19-298, HCJ .... *Digested,* 17/**2566**
Holman Fenwick Willan LLP v Procurator Fiscal, Glasgow [2017] HCJAC 39; 2017 S.C.L. 687; 2017 G.W.D. 19-297, HCJ Appeal .... *Digested,* 17/**2535**
HOLMATRO/Coaxial Coupling (T2561/11) [2017] E.P.O.R. 13, EPO (Technical Bd App)
Holship Norge AS v Norsk Transport Arbeiderforbund (E-14/15) see Holship Norge AS v Norsk Transportarbeiderforbund (E-14/15)
Holship Norge AS v Norsk Transportarbeiderforbund (E-14/15); *sub nom* Holship Norge AS v Norsk Transport Arbeiderforbund (E-14/15) [2016] 4 C.M.L.R. 29, EFTA
Considered 17/807
Holtham v Arnold (1986) 2 B.M.L.R. 123
Considered 17/661
Holy Trinity, Freckleton, Re [1994] 1 W.L.R. 1588; Times, October 7, 1994; Independent, September 14, 1994, Cons Ct .... *Digested,* 95/**1862**: *Considered* 17/661
Holyoake v Candy [2016] EWHC 3065 (Ch); [2016] 6 Costs L.R. 1157, Ch D .... *Digested,* 17/**365**
Holyoake v Candy; *sub nom* Candy v Holyoake [2016] EWHC 970 (Ch); [2016] 3 W.L.R. 357; [2016] 2 All E.R. (Comm) 711, Ch D .... *Digested,* 16/**263**: *Reversed* 17/308
Holyoake v Candy; *sub nom* Candy v Holyoake [2017] EWCA Civ 92; [2017] 3 W.L.R. 1131; [2017] 2 All E.R. (Comm) 513, CA (Civ Div) .... *Digested,* 17/**308**
Home Credit Slovakia AS v Biroova (C-42/15) EU:C:2016:842; [2017] Bus. L.R. 573; [2017] 2 C.M.L.R. 8; [2017] C.E.C. 777; [2017] C.T.L.C. 31, ECJ (3rd Chamber)
Home Office v Lownds see Lownds v Home Office
Home Office (UK Border Agency) v Essop see Essop v Home Office (UK Border Agency)
Home Retail Group Plc, Re [2016] EWHC 2072 (Ch); [2017] B.C.C. 39, Ch D (Companies Ct) .... *Digested,* 17/**403**
Homes and Communities Agency v JS Bloor (Wilmslow) Ltd see JS Bloor (Wilmslow) Ltd v Homes and Communities Agency
Honda Motor Co Ltd v David Silver Spares Ltd [2010] EWHC 1973 (Ch); [2010] F.S.R. 40, Ch D .... *Digested,* 11/**1996**: *Considered* 17/1392
Hood v Council of the Law Society of Scotland [2017] CSIH 21; 2017 S.C. 386; 2017 S.C.L.R. 799; 2017 G.W.D. 9-132, IH (2 Div) .... *Digested,* 17/**2714**
Hood v Revenue and Customs Commissioners [2016] UKFTT 59 (TC); [2016] S.F.T.D. 351; [2016] W.T.L.R. 835; [2016] S.T.I. 1159, FTT (Tax)
Affirmed 17/2155
Hood v Revenue and Customs Commissioners [2017] UKUT 276 (TCC); [2017] S.T.C. 1707; [2017] B.T.C. 525; [2017] W.T.L.R. 999; [2017] S.T.I. 1773, UT (Tax) .... *Digested,* 17/**2155**
Hoodless v Financial Services Authority (Unreported, October 3, 2003), FSMT
Applied 17/1490: *Considered* 17/1491
Hooley Ltd v Ganges Jute Private Ltd; *sub nom* Hooley Ltd, Petitioner; Hooley Ltd v Titaghur Plc; Hooley Ltd v Samnuggur Jute Factory Ltd; Hooley Ltd v Victoria Jute Co Ltd [2016] CSOH 141; 2017 S.L.T. 58; [2016] B.C.C. 826; 2016 G.W.D. 33-584, OH .... *Digested,* 17/**2447**
Hooley Ltd v Samnuggur Jute Factory Ltd see Hooley Ltd v Ganges Jute Private Ltd
Hooley Ltd v Titaghur Plc see Hooley Ltd v Ganges Jute Private Ltd
Hooley Ltd v Victoria Jute Co Ltd see Hooley Ltd v Ganges Jute Private Ltd
Hooley Ltd, Petitioner see Hooley Ltd v Ganges Jute Private Ltd
Hooper v Secretary of State for Work and Pensions see R. (on the application of Hooper) v Secretary of State for Work and Pensions
Hope v Revenue and Customs Commissioners [2017] EWHC 812 (Ch); [2017] B.P.I.R. 992; [2017] B.V.C. 23, Ch D (Bankruptcy Ct) .... *Digested,* 17/**1303**
Hopkins Developments Ltd v Secretary of State for Communities and Local Government; *joined case* Secretary of State for Communities and Local Government v Hopkins Development Ltd [2013] EWHC 1783 (Admin), QBD (Admin)
Followed 17/1763: *Reversed* 14/2411
Hopkins Homes Ltd v Secretary of State for Communities and Local Government see Secretary of State for Communities and Local Government v Hopkins Homes Ltd

Horada v Secretary of State for Communities and Local Government [2016] EWCA Civ 169; [2017] 2 All E.R. 86; [2016] P.T.S.R. 1271; Times, May 12, 2016, CA (Civ Div) .... *Digested,* 16/**1678**: *Considered* 17/2763

Hormann Reisen GmbH v Stadt Augsburg (C-292/15) EU:C:2016:817; [2017] P.T.S.R. 181; [2017] R.T.R. 3, ECJ (4th Chamber)

Horton v Henry see Henry, Re

Hosebay Ltd v Day see Day v Hosebay Ltd

Hosking v Marathon Asset Management LLP [2016] EWHC 2418 (Ch); [2017] Ch. 157; [2017] 2 W.L.R. 746, Ch D .... *Digested,* 17/**1585**

Hospira UK Ltd v Cubist Pharmaceuticals LLC [2016] EWHC 1285 (Pat); [2017] R.P.C. 10, Ch D (Patents Ct) .... *Digested,* 17/**1378**

Hospira UK Ltd v Genentech Inc [2014] EWHC 3857 (Pat), Ch D (Patents Ct) *Affirmed* 17/1376

Hospira UK Ltd v Genentech Inc [2015] EWHC 1796 (Pat); [2016] R.P.C. 1, Ch D (Patents Ct) .... *Digested,* 16/**1311**: *Affirmed* 17/1374: *Applied* 16/1310

Hospira UK Ltd v Genentech Inc [2016] EWCA Civ 1185; [2017] R.P.C. 14, CA (Civ Div) .... *Digested,* 17/**1374**

Hospira UK Ltd v Genentech Inc [2016] EWCA Civ 780; [2017] R.P.C. 13; (2016) 152 B.M.L.R. 62, CA (Civ Div) .... *Digested,* 17/**1376**

Hossain v Secretary of State for the Home Department see R. (on the application of W) v Secretary of State for the Home Department

Hotak v Southwark LBC; *joined cases* Johnson v Solihull MBC; Kanu v Southwark LBC [2015] UKSC 30; [2016] A.C. 811; [2015] 2 W.L.R. 1341; [2015] 3 All E.R. 1053; [2015] P.T.S.R. 1189; [2015] H.L.R. 23; [2015] B.L.G.R. 530; Times, May 25, 2015, SC .... *Digested,* 15/**1277**: *Followed* 17/1160

Houghton v Donoghue (t/a Haulage and Plant Hire Ltd) [2017] EWHC 1738 (Ch); [2017] 5 Costs L.R. 857, Ch D .... *Digested,* 17/**259**

Houldsworth v Yorkshire Woolcombers Association Ltd see Illingworth v Houldsworth

Hounslow LBC v Powell; *sub nom* Mullen v Salford City Council; Mushin v Manchester City Council; Frisby v Birmingham City Council; Hall v Leeds City Council; Powell v Hounslow LBC; *joined cases* Birmingham City Council v Frisby; Leeds City Council v Hall; Salford City Council v Mullen [2011] UKSC 8; [2011] 2 A.C. 186; [2011] 2 W.L.R. 287; [2011] 2 All E.R. 129; [2011] P.T.S.R. 512; [2011] H.R.L.R. 18; [2011] U.K.H.R.R. 548; [2011] H.L.R. 23; [2011] B.L.G.R. 363; [2011] 1 P. & C.R. 20; Times, March 1, 2011; [2011] 9 E.G. 164 (C.S.); (2011) 155(8) S.J.L.B. 31; [2011] N.P.C. 24, SC .... *Digested,* 11/**2069**: *Applied* 14/1997, 14/3635: *Considered* 13/1892, 14/1625, 15/1290, 17/1168: *Followed* 12/1645, 12/2055, 13/1562, 13/1890, 13/3806, 14/2524, 15/339: *Not applied* 15/1592

Hounslow LBC v Waaler see Waaler v Hounslow LBC

Hourani v Thomson [2017] EWHC 173 (QB); [2017] 1 W.L.R. 933; [2017] E.M.L.R. 14, QBD .... *Digested,* 17/**290**

Housemaker Services Ltd v Cole [2017] EWHC 924 (Ch); [2017] Bus. L.R. 1935; [2017] 3 Costs L.R. 417, Ch D (Bristol) .... *Digested,* 17/**252**

Howard De Walden Estates Ltd v Accordway Ltd; *sub nom* Kateb v Howard de Walden Estates Ltd [2016] EWCA Civ 1176; [2017] 1 W.L.R. 1761; [2017] H.L.R. 5; [2017] 1 P. & C.R. 11; [2017] L. & T.R. 6; [2017] 1 P. & C.R. DG12, CA (Civ Div) .... *Digested,* 17/**1453**

Howard De Walden Estates Ltd v Accordway Ltd; *sub nom* Kateb v Howard de Walden Estates Ltd [2014] UKUT 486 (LC); [2015] L. & T.R. 5, UT (Lands) *Affirmed* 17/1453

Howard de Walden Estates Ltd v Lexgorge Ltd see Day v Hosebay Ltd

Howd v Bar Standards Board see Bar Standards Board v Howd

Howden (John) v HM Advocate 1994 S.C.C.R. 19, HCJ Appeal .... *Digested,* 94/**5531**: *Applied* 17/2490: *Cited* 16/2514: *Considered* 96/6722, 02/5440, 10/4103, 15/2993, 16/2518: *Distinguished* 14/3371

Howe v Motor Insurers' Bureau [2017] EWCA Civ 932; [2018] 1 W.L.R. 923; [2017] 4 Costs L.O. 473; [2018] R.T.R. 7; [2018] 1 C.M.L.R. 14; [2017] Lloyd's Rep. I.R. 576; [2017] P.I.Q.R. P20, CA (Civ Div) .... *Digested,* 17/**347**

Howe v Motor Insurers' Bureau [2016] EWHC 884 (QB); [2016] 1 W.L.R. 2751; [2016] 3 Costs L.O. 377, QBD .... *Digested,* 16/**1269**: *Considered* 17/262: *Reversed* 17/347

Howe v Motor Insurers' Bureau [2017] EWCA Civ 302; [2017] Lloyd's Rep. I.R. 570, CA (Civ Div)

Howell v Secretary of State for Communities and Local Government [2015] EWCA Civ 1189, CA (Civ Div)
Followed 17/1721

Howes, Re see H v Lord Advocate

Howgate Shopping Centre Ltd v Catercraft Services Ltd 2004 S.L.T. 231; 2004 S.C.L.R. 739; 2004 G.W.D. 4-76, OH .... *Digested,* 04/**4990**: *Applied* 17/2704

Howmet Ltd v Economy Devices Ltd [2014] EWHC 3933 (TCC); 157 Con. L.R. 1, QBD (TCC) .... *Digested,* 15/**1763**: *Affirmed* 17/2193

Howmet Ltd v Economy Devices Ltd [2016] EWCA Civ 847; [2016] B.L.R. 555; 168 Con. L.R. 27, CA (Civ Div) .... *Digested,* 17/**2193**

Hoyle v Rogers see Rogers v Hoyle

HR Trustees Ltd v German see IMG Pension Plan, Re

Hrabkova v Secretary of State for Work and Pensions [2017] EWCA Civ 794; [2017] P.T.S.R. 1624; [2018] 1 C.M.L.R. 5, CA (Civ Div)

HRH Prince Jefri Bolkiah v KPMG see Bolkiah v KPMG

HRH Prince of Wales v Associated Newspapers Ltd; *sub nom* Associated Newspapers Ltd v HRH Prince of Wales [2006] EWCA Civ 1776; [2008] Ch. 57; [2007] 3 W.L.R. 222; [2007] 2 All E.R. 139; [2008] E.M.L.R. 4; [2007] Info. T.L.R. 267; Times, December 28, 2006; (2007) 104(2) L.S.G. 30; (2007) 157 N.L.J. 106; (2007) 151 S.J.L.B. 63, CA (Civ Div) .... *Digested,* 07/**2510**: *Followed* 17/333

HSBC Bank Plc v Alder 19 I.T.E.L.R. 821, HC (IoM)

HSBC Holdings Plc v Revenue and Customs Commissioners [2012] UKFTT 163 (TC); 81 T.C. 663; [2012] S.F.T.D. 913, FTT (Tax) .... *Digested,* 12/**3330**: *Referred to* 17/2177

HSBC Holdings Plc v Revenue and Customs Commissioners (C-569/07) EU:C:2009:594; [2010] S.T.C. 58; [2009] E.C.R. I-9047; [2010] 1 C.M.L.R. 23; [2010] C.E.C. 336; [2010] B.T.C. 13; [2009] S.T.I. 2712, ECJ (2nd Chamber)
Applied 12/3330: *Referred to* 17/2177

HSBC Plc, Re see Barclays Bank Plc, Re

HTC Corp v Gemalto NV see HTC Corp v Gemalto SA

HTC Corp v Gemalto SA; *joined case* HTC Corp v Gemalto NV [2014] EWCA Civ 1335; [2014] Info. T.L.R. 337; [2015] R.P.C. 17, CA (Civ Div) .... *Digested,* 15/**1508**: *Followed* 17/1381

Hua Wang Bank Berhad v Commissioner of Taxation see Bywater Investments Ltd v Commissioner of Taxation

Huang v Secretary of State for the Home Department; *joined cases* Abu-Qulbain v Secretary of State for the Home Department; Kashmiri v Secretary of State for the Home Department [2007] UKHL 11; [2007] 2 A.C. 167; [2007] 2 W.L.R. 581; [2007] 4 All E.R. 15; [2007] 1 F.L.R. 2021; [2007] H.R.L.R. 22; [2007] U.K.H.R.R. 759; 24 B.H.R.C. 74; [2007] Imm. A.R. 571; [2007] I.N.L.R. 314; Times, March 22, 2007; [2007] Fam. Law 587; (2007) 151 S.J.L.B. 435, HL .... *Digested,* 07/**2340**: *Applied* 08/2039, 08/2075, 09/2102, 09/2132, 10/765, 11/1762, 11/1770, 12/1655, 12/1775, 12/3593, 14/1703, 14/2444, 17/1200, 17/1232: *Considered* 08/2052, 09/2101, 10/1266, 10/1821, 10/356, 10/795, 11/1778, 12/1004, 12/1767, 12/2330, 15/1336, 15/3243: *Followed* 08/2036, 09/4361, 10/1761, 10/1790, 13/1618, 14/1678, 14/1715, 14/1718, 17/1239

Hudson v Crown Prosecution Service [2017] EWHC 841 (Admin); [2017] 4 W.L.R. 108; [2017] 2 Cr. App. R. 21; [2017] 2 Cr. App. R. (S.) 23; (2017) 181 J.P. 346; [2017] R.V.R. 241; Times, June 13, 2017; [2017] Crim. L.R. 703; [2017] A.C.D. 79; [2017] 2 P. & C.R. DG10, DC .... *Digested,* 17/**535**

Hudson v Hudson see Hudson, Re

Hudson v Leigh; *joined case* Leigh v Hudson [2009] EWHC 1306 (Fam); [2013] Fam. 77; [2013] 2 W.L.R. 632; [2009] 2 F.L.R. 1129; [2009] 3 F.C.R. 401; Times, July 17, 2009; [2009] Fam. Law 810, Fam Div .... *Digested,* 09/**1617**: *Applied* 10/1406, 12/1444, 12/1446, 13/1322, 14/2190: *Considered* 17/1043

Hudson, Re; *sub nom* Hudson v Hudson [1966] Ch. 209; [1966] 2 W.L.R. 398; [1966] 1 All E.R. 110; (1966) 110 S.J. 149, Ch D .... *Digested,* 66/**9978**: *Applied* 17/160: *Considered* 97/2721, 16/2145

Huggins v Trinidad and Tobago; *joined case* Phillip v Trinidad and Tobago [2008] UKPC 32, PC (Trin)
Applied 17/2529

Hughes v Bourne [2012] EWHC 2232 (Ch); [2012] W.T.L.R. 1333, Ch D .... *Digested,* 12/**3369**: *Considered* 17/972

Hughes v Pendragon Sabre Ltd (t/a Porsche Centre Bolton) [2016] EWCA Civ 18; [2017] 1 All E.R. (Comm) 173; [2016] 1 Lloyd's Rep. 311; [2016] C.T.L.C. 91, CA (Civ Div) .... *Digested,* 16/**1844**

Hughes v Pump House Hotel Co Ltd (No.1) [1902] 2 K.B. 190, CA
Applied 17/449: *Distinguished* 55/2036: *Followed* 83/3413

Hughes (Valuation Officer) v York Museums and Gallery Trust [2017] UKUT 200 (LC); [2017] R.A. 302, UT (Lands)

Hughes-Holland v BPE Solicitors see Gabriel v Little

Hughmans Solicitors v Central Stream Services Ltd (In Liquidation) [2012] EWCA Civ 1720; [2013] B.P.I.R. 322; [2013] 1 E.G.L.R. 27; [2013] 12 E.G. 80; [2013] W.T.L.R. 239; [2013] 3 E.G. 86 (C.S.); (2013) 163 N.L.J. 20; [2013] 1 P. & C.R. DG15, CA (Civ Div) .... *Digested,* 13/**2426**: *Applied* 17/1846

Huitson v Revenue and Customs Commissioners [2017] UKUT 75 (TCC); [2017] B.T.C. 508, UT (Tax) .... *Digested,* 17/**2189**

Hull & Holderness Magistrates' Court v Darroch see Darroch v Football Association Premier League Ltd

Hull and Holderness Magistrates' Court v Darroch; *sub nom* Darroch v Football Association Premier League Ltd [2014] EWHC 4184 (Admin); (2015) 179 J.P. 64, DC .... *Digested,* 15/**375**: *Affirmed* 17/270

Human Fertilisation and Embryology Act 2008, Re see A (Human Fertilisation and Embryology Act 2008: Assisted Reproduction: Parent), Re

Hummel Holding A/S v Nike Inc (C-617/15) EU:C:2017:390; [2017] Bus. L.R. 1864, ECJ (2nd Chamber)

Humphrey v Aegis Defence Services Ltd [2014] EWHC 989 (QB), QBD
Affirmed 17/1564

Humphrey v Aegis Defence Services Ltd [2016] EWCA Civ 11; [2017] 1 W.L.R. 2937; [2017] 2 All E.R. 235, CA (Civ Div) .... *Digested,* 17/**1564**

Humphreys v Parking and Traffic Appeals Service see R. (on the application of Humphreys) v Parking and Traffic Appeals Service

Humphreys v Revenue and Customs Commissioners [2012] UKSC 18; [2012] 1 W.L.R. 1545; [2012] 4 All E.R. 27; [2012] P.T.S.R. 1024; [2012] 3 F.C.R. 403; [2012] H.R.L.R. 21; [2012] Eq. L.R. 714; Times, May 26, 2012; [2012] S.T.I. 1664; (2012) 162 N.L.J. 712; (2012) 156(20) S.J.L.B. 31, SC .... *Digested,* 12/**3093**: *Applied* 14/2757, 16/1975: *Considered* 15/2342: *Followed* 13/2885, 15/1214, 16/1397, 17/2026, 17/2030

Hunston Properties Ltd v Secretary of State for Communities and Local Government; *sub nom* St Albans City and District Council v Hunston Properties Ltd [2013] EWCA Civ 1610; [2014] 1 E.G.L.R. 79; [2014] J.P.L. 599, CA (Civ Div) .... *Digested,* 14/**2432**: *Applied* 16/1696: *Considered* 14/2430, 17/1762: *Followed* 15/1985

Hunter v Chief Constable of the West Midlands; *joined cases* Power v Chief Constable of Lancashire; Walker v Chief Constable of the West Midlands; McIlkenny v Chief Constable of the West Midlands [1982] A.C. 529; [1981] 3 W.L.R. 906; [1981] 3 All E.R. 727; Times, November 26, 1981; (1981) 125 S.J. 829, HL .... *Digested,* 82/**2382**: *Applied* 83/1128, 89/3073, 90/3542, 93/623, 94/3517, 94/4572, 94/663, 95/2857, 95/3699, 95/688, 96/4496, 00/2250, 00/4269, 02/3301, 17/190: *Considered* 90/2857, 91/1737, 91/894, 92/3844, 93/2525, 96/853, 97/628, 99/4021, 00/597, 01/5, 03/509, 07/339, 08/272, 08/2986, 12/3287, 13/249: *Distinguished* 88/2610, 93/3084, 99/313, 06/896: *Explained* 99/485: *Followed* 96/3912, 96/4490, 97/1107, 98/4865, 11/243, 11/739, 15/385, 17/191, 17/313, 17/372: *Referred to* 95/3882, 97/3355

Hunter v Hanley 1955 S.C. 200; 1955 S.L.T. 213; [1955-95] P.N.L.R. 1, IH (1 Div) ...... *Digested,* 55/**3451**: *Applied* 83/2548, 83/3962, 84/2322, 90/3264, 97/6302, 00/6588, 03/5826, 04/5055, 13/3857, 14/3688, 15/3230: *Considered* 86/3608, 89/2558, 03/5825, 17/1561: *Distinguished* 00/6585, 17/2389: *Followed* 90/5498: *Not applied* 88/4930, 89/4195: *Referred to* 00/6603

Hurstanger Ltd v Wilson [2007] EWCA Civ 299; [2007] 1 W.L.R. 2351; [2007] 4 All E.R. 1118; [2007] 2 All E.R. (Comm) 1037; [2008] Bus. L.R. 216; [2007] C.T.L.C. 59; Times, May 11, 2007; (2007) 104(16) L.S.G. 23; (2007) 157 N.L.J. 555; (2007) 151 S.J.L.B. 467; [2007] N.P.C. 41, CA (Civ Div) .... *Digested,* 07/**765**: *Applied* 14/138, 15/498: *Considered* 16/415, 17/482: *Followed* 12/57

Huscroft v P&O Ferries Ltd [2010] EWCA Civ 1483; [2011] 1 W.L.R. 939; [2011] 2 All E.R. 762; [2011] C.P. Rep. 16; Times, February 11, 2011; (2011) 161 N.L.J. 28, CA (Civ Div) .... *Digested,* 11/**363**: *Applied* 13/406: *Approved* 17/68: *Considered* 11/1978: *Followed* 15/341

Hussain v Chartis Insurance UK Ltd [2013] EWHC 4740 (QB); [2017] 5 Costs L.O. 555, QBD

Hussain v Glasgow City Council [2017] CSOH 1; 2017 S.L.T. 231; 2017 Hous. L.R. 8; 2017 G.W.D. 2-19, OH .... *Digested,* 17/**2660**

Hussain v Sandwell Metropolitan BC [2017] EWHC 1641 (Admin); [2018] P.T.S.R. 142; [2017] L.L.R. 713; [2017] A.C.D. 97, QBD (Admin)

Hussain (Muzaffar) v Procurator Fiscal, Glasgow [2017] SAC (Crim) 1; 2017 S.C.L. 421; 2017 G.W.D. 1-5, SAC .... *Digested,* 17/**2502**

Hussey v Eels [1990] 2 Q.B. 227; [1990] 2 W.L.R. 234; [1990] 1 All E.R. 449; [1990] 19 E.G. 77; [1989] E.G. 168 (C.S.); (1990) 140 N.L.J. 53, CA (Civ Div) .... *Digested,* 90/**1565**: *Applied* 03/938, 14/827, 17/1838: *Considered* 91/1503, 01/4152: *Followed* 97/3843

Hussey v Horne-Payne (1879) 4 App. Cas. 311, HL
Applied 71/1347, 89/2153, 17/496: *Considered* 65/680

Hutcheson (formerly WER) v Popdog Ltd (formerly REW) [2011] EWCA Civ 1580; [2012] 1 W.L.R. 782; [2012] 2 All E.R. 711; [2012] C.P. Rep. 13; [2012] E.M.L.R. 13, CA (Civ Div) .... *Digested,* 12/**2**: *Applied* 17/29

Hutchinson v United Kingdom (57592/08) 43 B.H.R.C. 667; Times, January 27, 2017, ECHR (Grand Chamber)

Hutchison (Alexander Wilson) v HM Advocate 1984 S.L.T. 233; 1983 S.C.C.R. 504, HCJ Appeal .... *Digested,* 84/**3943**: *Considered* 17/2571

Huttenwerke Krupp Mannesmann GmbH v Hauptzollamt Duisburg (C-465/15) EU:C:2017:640; [2017] S.T.I. 1976, ECJ (9th Chamber)

Hutton v Criminal Injuries Compensation Authority [2016] EWCA Civ 1305; [2017] A.C.D. 20, CA (Civ Div)

Hutton Construction Ltd v Wilson Properties (London) Ltd [2017] EWHC 517 (TCC); [2018] 1 All E.R. (Comm) 524; [2017] Bus. L.R. 908; [2017] B.L.R. 344; 171 Con. L.R. 228; [2017] C.I.L.L. 3949, QBD (TCC) .... *Digested,* 17/**452**

Hyde v Milton Keynes Hospital NHS Foundation Trust; *sub nom* Milton Keynes NHS Foundation Trust v Hyde [2017] EWCA Civ 399; [2018] 1 W.L.R. 597; [2017] C.P. Rep. 36; [2017] 3 Costs L.O. 391; Times, July 21, 2017, CA (Civ Div) .... *Digested,* 17/**1477**

Hyde v Milton Keynes Hospital NHS Foundation Trust; *sub nom* Milton Keynes NHS Foundation Trust v Hyde [2016] EWHC 72 (QB); [2016] 4 All E.R. 874; [2016] 1 Costs L.R. 1, QBD .... *Digested,* 16/**1402**: *Affirmed* 17/1477

Hydraulic Engineering Co Ltd v Spencer (1886) 2 T.L.R. 554, CA
Applied 17/472

Hydrogen Peroxide SA v Akzo Nobel NV (C-352/13) see Cartel Damage Claims (CDC) Hydrogen Peroxide SA v Akzo Nobel NV (C-352/13)

Hyland v Dundalk Racing Ltd [2017] L.L.R. 481, CA (Irl)

I (A Child) (Contact Application: Jurisdiction), Re; *sub nom* Y v I [2009] UKSC 10; [2010] 1 A.C. 319; [2009] 3 W.L.R. 1299; [2010] 1 All E.R. 445; [2010] I.L.Pr. 19; [2010] 1 F.L.R. 361; [2010] 1 F.C.R. 200; Times, December 4, 2009; [2010] Fam. Law 237; (2009) 159 N.L.J. 1736; (2009) 153(46) S.J.L.B. 32, SC .... *Digested,* 10/**1413**: *Applied* 14/1381, 16/826: *Considered* 11/1402: *Followed* 13/1282, 13/1335, 14/1287, 15/1026, 17/926

I (Human Fertilisation and Embryology Act 2008), Re [2016] EWHC 791 (Fam); [2017] 1 F.L.R. 998; [2016] Fam. Law 678, Fam Div .... *Digested,* 17/**1053**

I-A (Children) (Allegations of Sexual Abuse), Re [2012] EWCA Civ 582; [2012] 2 F.L.R. 837; [2012] Fam. Law 941, CA (Civ Div) .... *Digested,* 12/**1414**: *Followed* 17/952

Iansyst Ltd v Revenue and Customs Commissioners [2016] UKFTT 372 (TC); [2017] S.F.T.D. 361; [2016] S.T.I. 1679, FTT (Tax)

IBM United Kingdom Pensions Trust Ltd v IBM United Kingdom Holdings Ltd [2012] EWHC 3540 (Ch); [2013] Pens. L.R. 33, Ch D .... *Digested,* 13/**2169**: *Applied* 17/1627

Ibrahim v Birmingham City Council see Ali v Birmingham City Council

Ibrahim v Crown Prosecution Service [2016] EWHC 1750 (Admin); (2017) 181 J.P. 11, QBD (Admin) .... *Digested,* 17/**514**

Ibrahim v United Kingdom (50541/08) Times, December 19, 2016; [2017] Crim. L.R. 877, ECHR

ICAP Management Services Ltd v Berry [2017] EWHC 1321 (QB); [2017] 3 Costs L.R. 531; [2017] I.R.L.R. 811, QBD .... *Digested,* 17/**769**

Ice Rink Co Ltd v Revenue and Customs Commissioners [2017] UKFTT 698 (TC); [2018] S.F.T.D. 393; [2017] S.T.I. 2073, FTT (Tax)

Icebreaker 1 LLP v Revenue and Customs Commissioners [2010] UKUT 477 (TCC); [2011] S.T.C. 1078; [2011] B.T.C. 1579; [2011] S.T.I. 372, UT (Tax) .... *Digested,* 11/**3347**: *Followed* 14/2975, 17/2137

Iceland Foods Ltd v Berry (Valuation Officer) see Berry v Iceland Foods Ltd

Icescape Ltd v Ice-World International BV [2017] EWHC 42 (Pat); [2017] F.S.R. 38, Ch D (Patents Ct) .... *Digested,* 17/**1381**

ICU (Europe) Ltd v Ibrahim [2016] CSIH 62; 2016 S.L.T. 1182; 2016 G.W.D. 23-422, IH (2 Div) .... *Digested,* 17/**2423**

IFX Investment Co Ltd v Revenue and Customs Commissioners see Revenue and Customs Commissioners v IFX Investment Co Ltd

IG Index Ltd v Cloete [2014] EWCA Civ 1128; [2014] C.P. Rep. 44; [2015] I.C.R. 254; (2014) 158(32) S.J.L.B. 41, CA (Civ Div) .... *Digested,* 14/**380**: *Applied* 17/182

Igen Ltd (formerly Leeds Careers Guidance) v Wong see Wong v Igen Ltd (formerly Leeds Careers Guidance)

Igoe v Campbell see Courtney's Executors v Campbell

IH (Observance of Muslim Practice), Re [2017] EWCOP 9; [2017] C.O.P.L.R. 281, CP *Digested,* 17/**1110**

IHT Internationale Heiztechnik GmbH v Ideal Standard GmbH (C-9/93) EU:C:1994:261; [1994] E.C.R. I-2789; [1994] 3 C.M.L.R. 857; [1995] F.S.R. 59; Times, July 7, 1994; Financial Times, June 28, 1994, ECJ .... *Digested,* 94/**4870**: *Applied* 96/5713, 06/2606, 07/2686, 08/2391, 09/2441: *Considered* 04/2410, 17/1401: *Followed* 01/4029: *Referred to* 98/3506, 99/3572

Iiyama (UK) Ltd v Samsung Electronics Co Ltd [2016] EWHC 1980 (Ch); [2016] 5 C.M.L.R. 16, Ch D .... *Digested,* 17/**426**

Iiyama Benelux BV v Schott AG [2016] EWHC 1207 (Ch); [2017] U.K.C.L.R. 16; [2016] 5 C.M.L.R. 15, Ch D .... *Digested,* 17/**416**

Ijaz v Court of Milan see Kandola v Germany

Ijaz v Italy see Kandola v Germany

Ilkerler Otomotiv Sanayai ve Ticaret Anonim v Perkins Engines Co Ltd [2017] EWCA Civ 183; [2017] 4 W.L.R. 144; [2018] 1 All E.R. (Comm) 401; [2018] E.C.C. 1, CA (Civ Div) .... *Digested,* 17/**507**

Ilkerler Otomotiv Sanayai ve Ticaret Anonim v Perkins Engines Co Ltd [2015] EWHC 2006 (Comm), QBD (Comm) *Affirmed* 17/507

Illingworth v Houldsworth; *sub nom* Houldsworth v Yorkshire Woolcombers Association Ltd; Yorkshire Woolcombers Association Ltd, Re [1903] 2 Ch. 284, CA *Applied* 79/2389, 88/306: *Considered* 59/2597, 08/231: *Followed* 82/2177, 17/159

Ilott v Blue Cross see Ilott v Mitson

Ilott v Mitson; *sub nom* Ilott v Blue Cross [2015] EWCA Civ 797; [2016] 1 All E.R. 932; [2015] 2 F.L.R. 1409; [2015] 2 F.C.R. 547; [2015] W.T.L.R. 1399; [2015] Fam. Law 1196, CA (Civ Div) .... *Digested,* 15/**2413**: *Considered* 16/2031: *Reversed* 17/2073

Ilott v Mitson; *sub nom* Ilott v Blue Cross; Jackson (Deceased), Re [2017] UKSC 17; [2017] 2 W.L.R. 979; [2017] 4 All E.R. 545; [2017] 1 F.L.R. 1717; [2017] W.T.L.R. 533; 19 I.T.E.L.R. 1021, SC .... *Digested,* 17/**2073**

Imageview Management Ltd v Jack [2009] EWCA Civ 63; [2009] 2 All E.R. 666; [2009] 1 All E.R. (Comm) 921; [2009] Bus. L.R. 1034; [2009] 1 Lloyd's Rep. 436; [2009] 1 B.C.L.C. 724; Times, March 24, 2009, CA (Civ Div) .... *Digested,* 09/**86**: *Applied* 17/1585

Imerman v Imerman see Tchenguiz v Imerman

IMG Pension Plan, Re; *sub nom* International Management Group (UK) Ltd v German; HR Trustees Ltd v German [2010] EWCA Civ 1349; [2011] I.C.R. 329; [2011] Pens. L.R. 11, CA (Civ Div) .... *Digested,* 11/**2314**: *Applied* 17/1602: *Followed* 17/1603

IMI Plc v Delta Ltd see WH Newson Holding Ltd v IMI Plc

Impact Funding Solutions Ltd v AIG Europe Insurance Ltd (formerly Chartis Insurance UK) Ltd) see Impact Funding Solutions Ltd v Barrington Support Services Ltd (formerly Lawyers At Work Ltd)

Impact Funding Solutions Ltd v Barrington Support Services Ltd (formerly Lawyers At Work Ltd); *sub nom* Impact Funding Solutions Ltd v AIG Europe Insurance Ltd (formerly Chartis Insurance UK) Ltd) [2016] UKSC 57; [2017] A.C. 73; [2016] 3 W.L.R. 1422; [2017] 4 All E.R. 169; [2017] 2 All E.R. (Comm) 863; [2016] Bus. L.R. 1158; [2016] 6 Costs L.O. 903; [2017] Lloyd's Rep. I.R. 60; Times, November 7, 2016, SC .... *Digested,* 16/**1272**

Imperial Chemical Industries Ltd v Merit Merrell Technology Ltd [2017] EWHC 1763 (TCC); 173 Con. L.R. 137; [2017] C.I.L.L. 4025, QBD (TCC) .... *Digested,* 17/**462**

Imperial Chemical Industries Ltd v Merit Merrell Technology Ltd [2017] EWHC 2299 (QB); [2017] 5 Costs L.O. 631, QBD (TCC) .... *Digested,* 17/**263**

Imperial Chemical Industries Ltd v Merit Merrell Technology Ltd [2016] EWHC 3586 (TCC); 170 Con. L.R. 192; [2017] C.I.L.L. 3923, QBD (TCC) .... *Digested,* 17/**455**

Imperial Group Pension Trust Ltd v Imperial Tobacco Ltd [1991] 1 W.L.R. 589; [1991] 2 All E.R. 597; [1991] I.C.R. 524; [1991] I.R.L.R. 66; [1990] Pens. L.R. 263; [1990] P.L.R. 239; Independent, December 4, 1990; Financial Times, December 5, 1990; Guardian, December 11, 1990; (1991) 88(9) L.S.G. 39; (1991) 141 N.L.J. 55, Ch D .... *Digested,* 91/**2725**: *Applied* 13/2169: *Considered* 14/2263, 15/1832, 15/1850, 17/1602: *Followed* 97/3997

Imperial Loan Co Ltd v Stone [1892] 1 Q.B. 599, CA *Considered* 13/2199, 14/435, 14/625: *Followed* 17/1307

Improver Corp v Remington Consumer Products Ltd [1990] F.S.R. 181, Ch D (Patents Ct) .... *Digested,* 91/**2698**: *Applied* 95/3758, 96/4568, 99/3472, 02/2795, 02/2820, 04/2342: *Cited* 04/2339: *Considered* 00/3639, 00/3679, 05/2479, 15/1502: *Disapproved* 17/1366: *Followed* 95/3799, 97/3901, 98/3467: *Referred to* 99/3480

In Re A (Legal Parenthood: Written Consents) see A (Human Fertilisation and Embryology Act 2008: Assisted Reproduction: Parent), Re

In Re of St John the Baptist, Adel 16-88C (2016-002295), 16-105C (2016-003082), Cons Ct *Applied* 17/665

In Re St Peter Church, Lawford (Unreported, April 17, 2016), Cons Ct (Coventry) *Not applied* 17/665

Inco Europe Ltd v First Choice Distribution [2000] 1 W.L.R. 586; [2000] 2 All E.R. 109; [2000] 1 All E.R. (Comm) 674; [2000] 1 Lloyd's Rep. 467; [2000] C.L.C. 1015; [2000] B.L.R. 259; (2000) 2 T.C.L.R. 487; 74 Con. L.R. 55; Times, March 10, 2000; Independent, March 15, 2000; (2000) 97(12) L.S.G. 39; (2000) 144 S.J.L.B. 134; [2000] N.P.C. 22, HL .... *Digested,* 00/**220**: *Applied* 02/3792, 02/5549, 03/1962, 07/2810, 08/3316, 08/7, 12/7, 14/1063, 16/188, 17/2091: *Considered* 05/2742, 07/848, 11/4269, 11/4270, 11/4452, 12/2092: *Followed* 03/5952, 12/831, 13/2160, 14/799, 16/1580, 17/233

IndigoScott v Wandsworth LDC [2017] P.A.D. 14, Planning Inspector

Infineon Technologies AG v European Commission (T-758/14) EU:T:2016:737; [2017] 4 C.M.L.R. 14, GC (5th Chamber)

INFINEUM/Partial priority (G1/15) [2017] E.P.O.R. 14, EPO (Enlarged Bd App)

Infinis Energy Holdings Ltd v HM Treasury see R. (on the application of Drax Power Ltd) v HM Treasury

ING Bank NV v Canoptex Shipping Services Ltd [2017] 2 Lloyd's Rep. 270, CA (Can)

ING Intermediate Holdings Ltd v Revenue and Customs Commissioners [2016] UKUT 298 (TCC); [2017] S.T.C. 320; [2016] B.V.C. 525, UT (Tax) .... *Digested,* 17/**2258**

ING Intermediate Holdings Ltd v Revenue and Customs Commissioners [2014] UKFTT 938 (TC); [2015] S.F.T.D. 109; [2014] S.T.I. 3096, FTT (Tax) *Affirmed* 17/2258

Ingenious Games LLP v Revenue and Customs Commissioners [2016] UKFTT 521 (TC); [2017] S.F.T.D. 1158, FTT (Tax)

Ingenious Games LLP v Revenue and Customs Commissioners [2015] UKUT 105 (TCC); [2015] S.T.C. 1659; [2015] B.T.C. 508, UT (Tax) .... *Digested,* 15/**2473**: *Considered* 17/2275

Ingenious Games LLP v Revenue and Customs Commissioners [2017] UKFTT 429 (TC); [2017] S.F.T.D. 1443; [2017] S.T.I. 1655, FTT (Tax)

Ingram v Ahmed [2016] EWHC 1536 (Ch); [2016] B.P.I.R. 1087, Ch D .... *Digested,* 17/**1276**

Ingram v Inland Revenue Commissioners [2000] 1 A.C. 293; [1999] 2 W.L.R. 90; [1999] 1 All E.R. 297; [1999] S.T.C. 37; [1999] L. & T.R. 85; [1998] B.T.C. 8047; Times, December 16, 1998; Independent, December 15, 1998; [1998] E.G. 181 (C.S.); (1999) 96(3) L.S.G. 33; (1999) 143 S.J.L.B. 52; [1998] N.P.C. 160, HL .... *Digested,* 99/**4740**: *Applied* 14/2938: *Considered* 03/4270, 17/2287: *Distinguished* 15/2435: *Followed* 11/3394, 14/1809, 17/2155

Inland Revenue Commissioners v Ainsworth; *sub nom* Ainsworth v Inland Revenue Commissioners; Revenue and Customs Commissioners v Stringer; *joined cases* Inland Revenue Commissioners v Kilic; Inland Revenue Commissioners v Stringer; Inland Revenue Commissioners v Thwaites [2009] UKHL 31; [2009] 4 All E.R. 1205; [2009] I.C.R. 985; [2009] I.R.L.R. 677; Times, June 15, 2009, HL .... *Digested,* 09/**1187**: *Considered* 11/1750, 17/2228

Inland Revenue Commissioners v Bowater Property Developments Ltd see Craven (Inspector of Taxes) v White (Stephen)

Inland Revenue Commissioners v Guthrie 1952 S.C. 402; 1952 S.L.T. 376; 45 R. & I.T. 588; 33 T.C. 327; (1952) 31 A.T.C. 337; [1952] T.R. 315, IH (1 Div) .... *Digested,* 52/**4125**: *Applied* 17/2188: *Considered* 15/2466

Inland Revenue Commissioners v Kahn see Toshoku Finance UK Plc (In Liquidation), Re

Inland Revenue Commissioners v Kilic see Inland Revenue Commissioners v Ainsworth

Inland Revenue Commissioners v Royal Bank of Scotland Ltd see Lord Advocate v Royal Bank of Scotland Ltd

Inland Revenue Commissioners v Stringer see Inland Revenue Commissioners v Ainsworth

Inland Revenue Commissioners v Thwaites see Inland Revenue Commissioners v Ainsworth

Inland Revenue Commissioners v Wimbledon Football Club Ltd [2004] EWCA Civ 655; [2004] B.C.C. 638; [2005] 1 B.C.L.C. 66; [2004] B.P.I.R. 700; Independent, June 10, 2004; (2004) 148 S.J.L.B. 697, CA (Civ Div) .... *Digested,* 05/**2295**: *Applied* 06/2356: *Considered* 17/1302

Inntrepreneur Pub Co (CPC) Ltd v Langton; *joined case* Langton v Inntrepreneur Pub Co (CPC) Ltd [2000] 1 E.G.L.R. 34; [2000] 08 E.G. 169; Times, November 10, 1999; [1999] E.G. 124 (C.S.); (1999) 96(44) L.S.G. 39; (1999) 143 S.J.L.B. 268; (2000) 79 P. & C.R. D7, Ch D .... *Digested,* 99/**3665**: *Considered* 17/1447

Inquiry under the Company Securities (Insider Dealing) Act 1985 (No.1), Re; *sub nom* Lindsay v Warner [1988] A.C. 660; [1988] 2 W.L.R. 33; [1988] 1 All E.R. 203; (1988) 4 B.C.C. 35; [1988] B.C.L.C. 153; [1988] P.C.C. 133; Independent, December 11, 1987; (1988) 85(4) L.S.G. 33; (1987) 137 N.L.J. 1181; (1988) 132 S.J. 21, HL .... *Digested,* 88/**2784**: *Considered* 90/3581, 96/23, 17/1158

Insol Funding Co Ltd v Cowlam [2017] EWHC 1822 (Ch); [2017] B.P.I.R. 1489, Ch D

Inspired by Service Ltd v Revenue and Customs Commissioners [2016] UKFTT 812 (TC); [2017] S.T.I. 119, FTT (Tax)

Institute of Chartered Accountants in England and Wales v Customs and Excise Commissioners [1999] 1 W.L.R. 701; [1999] 2 All E.R. 449; [1999] S.T.C. 398; [1999] 2 C.M.L.R. 1333; [1999] B.T.C. 5165; [1999] B.V.C. 215; Times, March 29, 1999; Independent, April 14, 1999; (1999) 96(20) L.S.G. 40; (1999) 149 N.L.J. 559; (1999) 143 S.J.L.B. 131, HL .... *Digested,* 99/**4990**: *Applied* 03/4606, 05/4383, 09/5227, 14/3085, 17/2295: *Considered* 10/1139

Instrumentation Electrical Services Ltd, Re (1988) 4 B.C.C. 301; [1988] B.C.L.C. 550; [1989] P.C.C. 101, Ch D (Companies Ct) *Applied* 17/1263: *Considered* 89/290, 11/1816

Integral Petroleum SA v SCU-Finanz AG [2014] EWHC 702 (Comm), QBD (Comm) *Affirmed* 15/436: *Considered* 17/366

Intel Corp v European Commission (T-286/09) EU:T:2014:547; [2014] 5 C.M.L.R. 9, GC (7th Chamber) *Applied* 17/416

Intel Corp Inc v European Commission (C-413/14 P) EU:C:2017:632; [2017] 5 C.M.L.R. 18, ECJ (Grand Chamber)

Inter Lotto (UK) Ltd v Camelot Group Plc [2003] EWHC 1256 (Ch); [2004] 1 W.L.R. 955; [2003] 3 All E.R. 191; [2004] R.P.C. 8; [2003] L.L.R. 462, Ch D *Affirmed* 03/2647: *Applied* 17/386

Inter-Mark Group sp z oo sp komandytowa w Poznaniu v Minister Finansow (C-530/09) EU:C:2011:697; [2012] S.T.C. 156; [2011] E.C.R. I-10675, ECJ (1st Chamber) *Followed* 15/2617, 17/2278

Intercontinental Exchange Inc v Competition and Markets Authority [2017] CAT 6; [2017] Comp. A.R. 125, CAT .... *Digested,* 17/**414**

Intercontinental Exchange Inc v Competiton and Markets Authority [2017] CAT 8; [2017] Comp. A.R. 242, CAT

Interflora Inc v Marks & Spencer Plc; *sub nom* Marks & Spencer Plc v Interflora Inc [2012] EWCA Civ 1501; [2013] 2 All E.R. 663; [2013] E.T.M.R. 11; [2013] F.S.R. 21; [2013] Bus. L.R. D46, CA (Civ Div) .... *Digested,* 13/**1830**: *Applied* 14/1935, 15/1527, 16/1297: *Considered* 13/1793, 14/1936, 14/289: *Followed* 17/1390

Interflora Inc v Marks & Spencer Plc [2014] EWCA Civ 1403; [2015] Bus. L.R. 492; [2015] E.T.M.R. 5; [2015] F.S.R. 10; Times, January 5, 2015, CA (Civ Div) .... *Digested,* 15/**1531**: *Considered* 16/1340: *Followed* 16/1280, 17/1403

Interim Executive Board of X School v Chief Inspector of Education, Children's Services and Skills [2016] EWHC 2813 (Admin); [2017] I.R.L.R. 30; [2017] E.L.R. 54; [2017] A.C.D. 18, QBD (Admin) .... *Digested,* 17/**705**

International Antiques and Collectors Fairs Ltd v Revenue and Customs Commissioners [2015] UKFTT 354 (TC); [2015] S.F.T.D. 979; [2015] L.L.R. 718; [2015] S.T.I. 2463, FTT (Tax) .... *Digested,* 15/**2599**: *Approved* 17/2237

International Bank for Commerce and Development AD v Bulgaria (7031/05) (2017) 65 E.H.R.R. 16, ECHR

International Energy Group Ltd v Zurich Insurance Plc UK; *sub nom* Zurich Insurance Plc UK v International Energy Group Ltd [2015] UKSC 33; [2016] A.C. 509; [2015] 2 W.L.R. 1471; [2015] 4 All E.R. 813; [2016] 1 All E.R. (Comm) 114; [2015] Lloyd's Rep. I.R. 598, SC .... *Digested,* 15/**1458**: *Followed* 16/1526, 17/1338, 17/1342

International Management Group (UK) Ltd v German see IMG Pension Plan, Re

International Transport Workers' Federation v Viking Line ABP (C-438/05) EU:C:2007:772; [2007] E.C.R. I-10779; [2008] 1 C.M.L.R. 51; [2008] All E.R. (EC) 127; [2008] C.E.C. 332; [2008] I.C.R. 741; [2008] I.R.L.R. 143; Times, December 14, 2007, ECJ (Grand Chamber) .... *Digested,* 08/**1351**: *Applied* 17/807

Internetportal und Marketing GmbH v Schlicht (C-569/08) EU:C:2010:311; [2011] Bus. L.R. 726; [2010] E.T.M.R. 48, ECJ (2nd Chamber) *Considered* 17/1395

Interserve FM Ltd v Tuleikyte [2017] I.R.L.R. 615, EAT .... *Digested,* 17/**829**

Invensys Plc v Automotive Sealing Systems Ltd [2002] 1 All E.R. (Comm) 222, QBD (Comm) .... *Digested,* 02/**427**: *Applied* 17/407

Inventive Tax Strategies Ltd (In Administration) v Revenue and Customs Commissioners [2017] UKFTT 667 (TC); [2017] S.T.I. 2013, FTT (Tax)

Investec Trust (Guernsey) Ltd v Glenalla Properties Ltd [2017] W.T.L.R. 205; 18 I.T.E.L.R. 30, CA (Gue)

Investment Trust Companies (In Liquidation) v Revenue and Customs Commissioners; *sub nom* Revenue and Customs Commissioners v Investment Trust Companies (In Liquidation) [2017] UKSC 29; [2017] 2 W.L.R. 1200; [2017] 3 All E.R. 113; [2017] S.T.C. 985; [2017] B.V.C. 16; Times, April 26, 2017; [2017] S.T.I. 1041, SC .... *Digested,* 17/**2285**

Investment Trust Companies (In Liquidation) v Revenue and Customs Commissioners; *sub nom* Revenue and Customs Commissioners v Investment Trust Companies (In Liquidation) [2015] EWCA Civ 82; [2015] S.T.C. 1280; [2015] B.V.C. 10; [2015] S.T.I. 519, CA (Civ Div) .... *Digested,* 15/**2610**: *Considered* 15/2131: *Followed* 15/2615: *Reversed* 17/2285

Involnert Management Inc v Aprilgrange Ltd [2015] EWHC 2834 (Comm); [2015] 2 C.L.C. 405; [2015] 5 Costs L.R. 813, QBD (Comm) .... *Digested,* 15/**246**: *Applied* 17/231

Iona Hotels Ltd v Craig see Iona Hotels Ltd (In Receivership), Petitioners

Iona Hotels Ltd (In Receivership), Petitioners; *sub nom* Iona Hotels Ltd v Craig 1990 S.C. 330; 1991 S.L.T. 11; 1990 S.C.L.R. 614, IH (1 Div) .... *Digested,* 90/**4772**: *Considered* 16/2697, 17/2679

IOS Finance EFC SA v Servicio Murciano de Salud (C-555/14) EU:C:2017:121; [2017] 3 C.M.L.R. 5, ECJ (5th Chamber)

Iovita v Romania (Admissibility) (25698/10) (2017) 64 E.H.R.R. SE19, ECHR

IPCO (Nigeria) Ltd v Nigerian National Petroleum Corp; *sub nom* Nigerian National Petroleum Corp v IPCO (Nigeria) Ltd [2017] UKSC 16; [2017] 1 W.L.R. 970; [2018] 1 All E.R. 738; [2018] 1 All E.R. (Comm) 191; [2017] 1 Lloyd's Rep. 508; [2017] 1 C.L.C. 195, SC .... *Digested,* 17/**68**: *Followed* 17/82

IPCO (Nigeria) Ltd v Nigerian National Petroleum Corp [2015] EWCA Civ 1144; [2016] 1 Lloyd's Rep. 5; [2015] 2 C.L.C. 816, CA (Civ Div) .... *Digested,* 16/**64**: *Reversed* 17/68

IPCO (Nigeria) Ltd v Nigerian National Petroleum Corp; *sub nom* Nigerian National Petroleum Corp v IPCO (Nigeria) Ltd [2015] EWCA Civ 1145; [2016] 1 Lloyd's Rep. 36; [2015] 2 C.L.C. 816, CA (Civ Div) .... *Digested,* 16/**67**: *Reversed* 17/68

IPCom GmbH & Co KG v Nokia UK Ltd see Nokia GmbH v IPCom GmbH & Co KG

Ipswich Town Football Club Co Ltd v Chief Constable of Suffolk [2017] EWCA Civ 1484; [2017] 4 W.L.R. 195, CA (Civ Div)

Iqbal v Iqbal [2017] EWCA Civ 19; [2017] 2 F.C.R. 26, CA (Civ Div) .... *Digested,* 17/**1030**

Iraqi Civilian Litigation v Ministry of Defence; *sub nom* Iraqi Civilians v Ministry of Defence; Ministry of Defence v Iraqi Civilians; Ministry of Defence v Iraqi Civilian Litigation; Iraqi Civilian Litigation, Re [2016] UKSC 25; [2016] 1 W.L.R. 2001; [2017] 2 All E.R. 79, SC .... *Digested,* 16/**270**

Iraqi Civilian Litigation, Re see Iraqi Civilian Litigation v Ministry of Defence

Iraqi Civilians v Ministry of Defence see Iraqi Civilian Litigation v Ministry of Defence

Iraqi Civilians v Ministry of Defence see Mohammed v Secretary of State for Defence

Iraqi Civilians v Ministry of Defence see Rahmatullah v Ministry of Defence

Ireland v Health and Care Professions Council [2015] EWHC 846 (Admin); [2015] 1 W.L.R. 4643, QBD (Admin) .... *Digested,* 15/**1205**: *Considered* 17/1108

Irish Bank Resolution Corp Ltd (In Special Liquidation) v Camden Market Holdings Corp [2017] EWCA Civ 7; [2017] 2 All E.R. (Comm) 781, CA (Civ Div) .... *Digested,* 17/**486**

Irish Bank Resolution Corp Ltd (In Special Liquidation) v Revenue and Customs Commissioners [2017] UKFTT 702 (TC); [2017] S.F.T.D. 1135; [2017] S.T.I. 2207, FTT (Tax) .... *Digested,* 17/**2107**

Ironside (Joanne Mary) v HM Advocate see Copolo (John Murray) v HM Advocate

Ironside (Joanne Mary) (also known as Mitchell) v HM Advocate see Copolo (John Murray) v HM Advocate

Irvine v General Medical Council [2017] EWHC 2038 (Admin); [2017] Med. L.R. 482; (2017) 158 B.M.L.R. 194, QBD (Admin) .... *Digested,* 17/**1114**

Irvine v Talksport Ltd [2002] EWHC 367 (Ch); [2002] 1 W.L.R. 2355; [2002] 2 All E.R. 414; [2002] E.M.L.R. 32; [2002] F.S.R. 60; (2002) 25(6) I.P.D. 25039; (2002) 99(18) L.S.G. 38; (2002) 152 N.L.J. 553; (2002) 146 S.J.L.B. 85, Ch D .... *Digested,* 02/**2783**: *Applied* 14/1890, 15/1496, 17/1394: *Considered* 07/2674, 10/1990

IS v Director of Legal Aid Casework see R. (on the application of S) v Director of Legal Aid Casework

Isaghehi v Nursing and Midwifery Council [2014] EWHC 127 (Admin); [2014] A.C.D. 76, QBD (Admin) *Applied* 17/1116

ISG Construction Ltd v Seevic College [2014] EWHC 4007 (TCC); [2015] 2 All E.R. (Comm) 545; [2015] B.L.R. 233; 157 Con. L.R. 107; [2015] C.I.L.L. 3598, QBD (TCC) .... *Digested,* 15/**484**: *Applied* 17/471: *Considered* 16/582, 17/454, 17/462: *Explained* 15/459

Ishaq v Royal Mail Group Ltd [2017] I.R.L.R. 208, EAT .... *Digested,* 17/**770**

Isis Investments Ltd v Oscatello Investments Ltd [2013] EWCA Civ 1493; [2014] Bus. L.R. 341; [2014] C.P. Rep. 14, CA (Civ Div) .... *Digested,* 14/**495**: *Considered* 17/1332

Isis Investments Ltd v Oscatello Investments Ltd [2013] EWHC 7 (Ch), Ch D *Affirmed* 14/495: *Considered* 17/1332

Isle of Wight Council v Platt [2016] EWHC 1283 (Admin); (2016) 180 J.P. 349; [2016] E.L.R. 268, DC .... *Digested,* 16/**613**: *Reversed* 17/704

Isle of Wight Council v Platt [2017] UKSC 28; [2017] 1 W.L.R. 1441; [2017] 3 All E.R. 623; [2017] 2 Cr. App. R. 13; (2017) 181 J.P. 237; [2017] E.L.R. 413; Times, April 11, 2017, SC .... *Digested,* 17/**704**

Isle of Wight Council v Revenue and Customs Commissioners; *sub nom* Revenue and Customs Commissioners v Isle of Wight Council [2015] EWCA Civ 1303; [2017] 2 All E.R. 105; [2016] P.T.S.R. 620; [2016] S.T.C. 2152; [2016] R.T.R. 21; [2016] B.V.C. 3; [2016] S.T.I. 65, CA (Civ Div) .... *Digested,* 16/**2197**

Islington LBC v Dyer [2017] EWCA Civ 150; [2017] P.T.S.R. 731; [2017] H.L.R. 20; [2017] 2 P. & C.R. 17; Times, May 3, 2017; [2017] 2 P. & C.R. DG6, CA (Civ Div) .... *Digested,* 17/**1458**

Ismail v Choudhry [2016] EWCA Civ 17; [2017] 1 F.L.R. 522; [2016] 2 F.C.R. 270; [2016] Fam. Law 306, CA (Civ Div) .... *Digested,* 16/**922**

Ismail v Entry Clearance Officer see Mahad (Ethiopia) v Entry Clearance Officer

Ismail v News Group Newspapers Ltd [2012] EWHC 3056 (QB), QBD *Considered* 17/653

Ismail v Secretary of State for the Home Department; *sub nom* R. (on the application of Ismail) v Secretary of State for the Home Department [2016] UKSC 37; [2016] 1 W.L.R. 2814; [2017] 2 All E.R. 985; 42 B.H.R.C. 301; Times, July 11, 2016, SC .... *Digested,* 16/**41**

Ismail, Re [1999] 1 A.C. 320; [1998] 3 W.L.R. 495; [1998] 3 All E.R. 1007; (1999) 163 J.P. 154; (1999) 11 Admin. L.R. 37; Times, August 20, 1998; (1998) 95(35) L.S.G. 35; (1998) 148 N.L.J. 1302; (1998) 142 S.J.L.B. 246, HL .... *Digested,* 98/**2357**: *Applied* 01/5783, 05/1488, 05/1490, 06/1595, 08/1395, 10/1260: *Considered* 05/1486: *Followed* 11/1272, 17/907

Isteed v Redbridge LBC [2017] I.C.R. D1, EAT

Istituto di Ricovero e Cura a Carattere Scientifico (IRCCS) - Fondazione Santa Lucia v Cassa conguaglio per il settore elettrico (C-189/15) EU:C:2017:17; [2017] B.T.C. 1; [2017] S.T.I. 213, ECJ (9th Chamber)

Istituto Nazionale della Previdenza Sociale (INPS) v Bruno (C-395/08); *joined case* Istituto Nazionale della Previdenza Sociale (INPS) v Lotti (C-396/08) EU:C:2010:329; [2010] 3 C.M.L.R. 45; [2011] C.E.C. 352; [2010] I.R.L.R. 890, ECJ (2nd Chamber)
Applied 15/1858: *Considered* 14/1087, 17/1620

Istituto Nazionale della Previdenza Sociale (INPS) v Lotti (C-396/08) see Istituto Nazionale della Previdenza Sociale (INPS) v Bruno (C-395/08)

IT (Jamaica) v Secretary of State for the Home Department [2016] EWCA Civ 932; [2017] 1 W.L.R. 240; [2017] Imm. A.R. 414, CA (Civ Div) .... *Digested,* 17/**1190**

Itau BBA International Ltd, Re [2012] EWHC 1783 (Ch); [2013] Bus. L.R. 490; [2013] B.C.C. 225; Times, September 11, 2012, Ch D .... *Digested,* 12/**499**: *Considered* 14/503, 17/392

Iteshi v Bar Standards Board [2016] EWHC 2943 (Admin); [2017] I.R.L.R. 414; [2017] A.C.D. 15, QBD (Admin) .... *Digested,* 17/**1486**

ITouch Ltd, Re; *joined case* SMS Cosmos AS, Re [2016] EWHC 3448 (Ch); [2017] B.C.C. 96, Ch D .... *Digested,* 17/**391**

Ittihadieh v 5-11 Cheyne Gardens RTM Co Ltd; *joined cases* Deer v University of Oxford; University of Oxford v Deer [2017] EWCA Civ 121; [2018] Q.B. 256; [2017] 3 W.L.R. 811, CA (Civ Div) .... *Digested,* 17/**1165**

Ittihadieh v 5-11 Cheyne Gardens RTM Co Ltd [2015] EWHC 1491 (QB), QBD
Affirmed 17/1165

ITV Broadcasting Ltd v TV Catchup Ltd [2015] EWCA Civ 204; [2015] E.C.D.R. 16; [2015] Info. T.L.R. 335; [2015] F.S.R. 28, CA (Civ Div) .... *Digested,* 15/**1481**: *Preliminary ruling given* 17/893

ITV Broadcasting Ltd v TV Catchup Ltd (C-275/15); *sub nom* ITV Broadcasting Ltd v TVCatchup Ltd (C-275/15) EU:C:2017:144; [2017] Bus. L.R. 1208; [2017] 3 C.M.L.R. 16; [2017] E.C.D.R. 10; [2017] F.S.R. 39; Times, April 13, 2017, ECJ (4th Chamber) .... *Digested,* 17/**893**

ITV Broadcasting Ltd v TVCatchup Ltd (C-275/15) see ITV Broadcasting Ltd v TV Catchup Ltd (C-275/15)

ITV Network Ltd v Performing Right Society Ltd [2017] EWHC 234 (Ch); [2017] L.L.R. 341, Ch D .... *Digested,* 17/**1384**

ITV Network Ltd v Performing Right Society Ltd CT 127/14, Copyright Tr
Affirmed 17/1384

Ivanova v Bulgaria (46577/15) (2017) 65 E.H.R.R. 20; [2016] H.L.R. 21, ECHR

Ivey v Genting Casinos UK Ltd (t/a Crockfords Club) [2016] EWCA Civ 1093; [2017] 1 W.L.R. 679; [2017] 1 Cr. App. R. 16; [2017] L.L.R. 128, CA (Civ Div)
Affirmed 17/1145

Iwanowicz v Poland (Admissibility) (3148/14) (2017) 64 E.H.R.R. SE2, ECHR

J v B (Challenge to Arbitral Award); *sub nom* J v B (Family Law Arbitration: Award); DB v DLJ [2016] EWHC 324 (Fam); [2016] 1 W.L.R. 3319; [2016] 2 F.L.R. 1308; [2016] 3 F.C.R. 117; [2016] Fam. Law 562, Fam Div .... *Digested,* 16/**911**: *Followed* 17/959

J v B (Family Law Arbitration: Award) see J v B (Challenge to Arbitral Award)

J v B (Ultra-Orthodox Judaism: Transgender) see A (Children) (Contact: Ultra-Orthodox Judaism: Transgender Parent), Re

J v C (Child: Financial Provision) [1999] 1 F.L.R. 152; [1998] 3 F.C.R. 79; [1999] Fam. Law 78, Fam Div .... *Digested,* 98/**2474**: *Applied* 05/1666, 09/1487, 17/1003: *Followed* 05/1652

J v Crown Prosecution Service see Jennings v Crown Prosecution Service

J v DLA Piper UK LLP [2010] I.C.R. 1052; [2010] I.R.L.R. 936; [2010] Eq. L.R. 164; (2010) 115 B.M.L.R. 107; (2010) 154(24) S.J.L.B. 37, EAT .... *Digested,* 10/**1043**: *Applied* 14/1043, 17/795: *Considered* 17/777

J v J see Jones v Jones

J v R see B (A Child) (Welfare: Child Arrangement Order), Re

J v U (Child Arrangements Order: Jurisdiction) [2016] EWHC 2481 (Fam); [2017] Fam. 235; [2017] 2 W.L.R. 760; [2017] 1 F.C.R. 237, Fam Div .... *Digested,* 17/**941**

J v Worcestershire CC see A v Essex CC

J (A Child) (Child Returned Abroad: Convention Rights), Re see J (A Child) (Custody Rights: Jurisdiction), Re

J (A Child) (Custody Rights: Jurisdiction), Re; *sub nom* J (A Child) (Child Returned Abroad: Convention Rights), Re; J (A Child) (Return to Foreign Jurisdiction: Convention Rights), Re; J (Child Returned Abroad: Human Rights), Re [2005] UKHL 40; [2006] 1 A.C. 80; [2005] 3 W.L.R. 14; [2005] 3 All E.R. 291; [2005] 2 F.L.R. 802; [2005] 2 F.C.R. 381; Times, June 17, 2005; [2005] Fam. Law 689; (2005) 155 N.L.J. 972; (2005) 149 S.J.L.B. 773, HL .... *Digested,* 05/**1569**: *Applied* 07/1736: *Considered* 17/938: *Followed* 10/1343, 11/1360, 12/1369, 13/1325, 15/1042, 15/1111

J (A Child) (Finland: Habitual Residence), Re [2017] EWCA Civ 80; [2017] 2 F.C.R. 542, CA (Civ Div) .... *Digested,* 17/**962**

J (A Child) (Restrictions on Applications), Re [2007] EWCA Civ 906; [2008] 1 F.L.R. 369; [2007] 3 F.C.R. 123; [2007] Fam. Law 1071, CA (Civ Div) .... *Digested,* 07/**1781**: *Considered* 17/978

J (A Child) (Return to Foreign Jurisdiction: Convention Rights), Re see J (A Child) (Custody Rights: Jurisdiction), Re

J (A Child) (Vulnerable Witness: Sexual Abuse: Fact Finding), Re see A (A Child) (Vulnerable Witness: Fact Finding), Re

J (A Minor) (Adoption: Non-Patrial), Re [1998] 1 F.L.R. 225; [1998] 1 F.C.R. 125; [1998] I.N.L.R. 424; Independent, October 30, 1997; [1998] Fam. Law 130, CA (Civ Div) .... *Digested,* 97/**349**: *Applied* 04/2067, 17/1034

J (Care Proceedings: Procedure), Re see J (Children) (Care Proceedings: Issues Resolution Hearing), Re

J (Child Returned Abroad: Human Rights), Re see J (A Child) (Custody Rights: Jurisdiction), Re

J (Children) (Brussels II Revised: Article 15), Re; *sub nom* N (Children) (Adoption: Jurisdiction), Re [2015] EWCA Civ 1112; [2016] 2 W.L.R. 713; [2016] 1 All E.R. 1086; [2016] 1 F.L.R. 621; [2016] 1 F.C.R. 217; [2015] Fam. Law 1444, CA (Civ Div) .... *Digested,* 16/**824**: *Applied* 16/804: *Cited* 16/831: *Considered* 17/950: *Followed* 16/805, 17/913, 17/920: *Reversed* 16/826

J (Children) (Brussels II Revised: Article 15), Re see N (Children), Re

J (Children) (Care Proceedings: Issues Resolution Hearing), Re; *sub nom* A McC v Wandsworth LBC; J (Care Proceedings: Procedure), Re [2017] EWCA Civ 398; [2017] 4 W.L.R. 109; [2018] 1 F.L.R. 50; [2017] 2 F.C.R. 647, CA (Civ Div) .... *Digested,* 17/**924**

J (Children) (Care Proceedings: Past Possible Perpetrators in New Family Unit), Re see J (Children) (Care Proceedings: Threshold Criteria), Re

J (Children) (Care Proceedings: Threshold Criteria), Re; *sub nom* J (Children) (Non-Accidental Injury: Past Possible Perpetrator in New Family), Re; J (Children) (Care Proceedings: Past Possible Perpetrators in New Family Unit), Re [2013] UKSC 9; [2013] 1 A.C. 680; [2013] 2 W.L.R. 649; [2013] 3 All E.R. 1; [2013] 1 F.L.R. 1373; [2013] 2 F.C.R. 149; Times, February 26, 2013; [2013] Fam. Law 375; (2013) 157(8) S.J.L.B. 31, SC .... *Digested,* 13/**1216**: *Applied* 14/1405: *Considered* 15/2821: *Followed* 17/1063

J (Children) (Care Proceedings: Unaccompanied Child Refugees), Re [2017] EWFC 44; [2017] 4 W.L.R. 192; [2018] 1 F.L.R. 582, Fam Ct

J (Children) (Non-Accidental Injury: Past Possible Perpetrator in New Family), Re see J (Children) (Care Proceedings: Threshold Criteria), Re

J (Human Fertilisation and Embryology Act 2008), Re [2016] EWHC 1330 (Fam); [2017] 2 F.L.R. 1; [2016] Fam. Law 1088, Fam Div

J (Recognition of Foreign Adoption Order), Re [2012] EWHC 3353 (Fam); [2013] 2 F.L.R. 298; [2013] Fam. Law 670, Fam Div .... *Digested,* 13/**1195**: *Considered* 17/1034

J Leslie Engineers Co Ltd (In Liquidation), Re [1976] 1 W.L.R. 292; [1976] 2 All E.R. 85; (1976) 120 S.J. 146, Ch D .... *Digested,* 76/**274**: *Applied* 80/290, 15/1447, 17/1330: *Followed* 77/307

J Murphy & Sons Ltd v W Maher & Sons Ltd [2016] EWHC 1148 (TCC); [2017] Bus. L.R. 916; [2016] B.L.R. 435; 166 Con. L.R. 228; [2016] C.I.L.L. 3839, QBD (TCC) .... *Digested,* 16/**398**

J Sainsbury Plc v One in a Million Ltd see British Telecommunications Plc v One in a Million Ltd

J Varney & Sons Waste Management Ltd v Hertfordshire CC [2010] EWHC 1404 (QB); [2010] Eu. L.R. 669; [2010] B.L.G.R. 801, QBD *Affirmed* 11/2627: *Applied* 11/2631: *Considered* 11/2636, 17/1816

J&B Hopkins Ltd v Revenue and Customs Commissioners [2017] UKFTT 410 (TC); [2017] S.T.I. 1205, FTT (Tax)

J&R Builders (Norwich) Ltd (In Liquidation), Re see Kean v Lucas

J. & P. Coats, Ltd. v Brown. (1909) 6 Adam 19, HCJ
Distinguished 17/2530
J3 Building Solutions Ltd v Revenue and Customs Commissioners; *sub nom* Revenue and Customs Commissioners v J3 Building Solutions Ltd [2017] UKUT 253 (TCC); [2017] B.V.C. 519; [2017] S.T.I. 1650, UT (Tax) .... *Digested,* 17/**2292**
J3 Building Solutions Ltd v Revenue and Customs Commissioners; *sub nom* Revenue and Customs Commissioners v J3 Building Solutions Ltd [2016] UKFTT 318 (TC); [2016] S.T.I. 1608, FTT (Tax)
Reversed 17/2292
JA v Netherlands (214591/4) (Unreported, November 3, 2015), ECHR
Considered 17/1176
JA v TH (1996 Hague Convention: Request to Exercise Jurisdiction) see M (Children), Re
JA v WA [2017] CSOH 93; 2017 Fam. L.R. 94; 2017 G.W.D. 22-370, OH .... *Digested,* 17/**2609**
Jabang v Wadman [2017] EWHC 1993 (QB); [2017] 4 Costs L.R. 807, QBD .... *Digested,* 17/**223**
Jack v Jack [2015] CSOH 91; 2015 Fam. L.R. 95; 2015 G.W.D. 24-425, OH .... *Digested,* 15/**3079**: *Affirmed* 17/2610
Jack v Jack [2016] CSIH 75; 2016 Fam. L.R. 177; 2016 G.W.D. 33-595, IH (Ex Div) ... *Digested,* 17/**2610**
Jack Wills Ltd v House of Fraser (Stores) Ltd [2016] EWHC 626 (Ch), Ch D
Applied 17/1367
Jackson v Hall; *joined case* Williamson v Thompson [1980] A.C. 854; [1980] 2 W.L.R. 118; [1980] 1 All E.R. 177; (1980) 39 P. & C.R. 436; (1979) 253 E.G. 145; (1980) 124 S.J. 62, HL .... *Digested,* 80/**28**: *Considered* 17/1430: *Distinguished* 82/3400
Jackson (Deceased), Re see Ilott v Mitson
Jacobs v Coster (t/a Newington Commercials Service Station) [2000] Lloyd's Rep. I.R. 506, CA (Civ Div) .... *Digested,* 01/**3801**: *Applied* 15/1464: *Followed* 17/1346
Jacobs v Sesame Ltd [2014] EWCA Civ 1410; [2015] P.N.L.R. 6, CA (Civ Div) .... *Digested,* 15/**1773**: *Followed* 17/1568
Jacobs Douwe Egberts ES SLU v General State Administration 19 I.T.L. Rep. 425, Trib Sup (Sp)
Jacobs E&C Ltd v Laker Vent Engineering Ltd see Laker Vent Engineering Ltd v Jacobs E&C Ltd
Jacobs UK Ltd v Skanska Construction UK Ltd [2017] EWHC 2395 (TCC); [2017] B.L.R. 619; [2017] T.C.L.R. 9; 174 Con. L.R. 61; [2017] 5 Costs L.R. 865; [2017] C.I.L.L. 4044, QBD (TCC) .... *Digested,* 17/**656**
Jade Palace Ltd v Revenue and Customs Commissioners [2006] S.T.C. (S.C.D.) 419; [2006] S.T.I. 1623, Sp Comm .... *Digested,* 07/**4155**: *Applied* 07/4161, 17/2176
Jadebay Ltd v Clarke-Coles Ltd (t/a Feel Good UK) [2017] EWHC 1400 (IPEC); [2017] E.T.M.R. 34, IPEC .... *Digested,* 17/**1400**
Jafarov v Azerbaijan (69981/14) (2017) 64 E.H.R.R. 13; 42 B.H.R.C. 355, ECHR
Jafri v Lincoln College [2014] EWCA Civ 449; [2015] Q.B. 781; [2014] 3 W.L.R. 933; [2014] 3 All E.R. 709; [2014] I.C.R. 920; [2014] I.R.L.R. 544, CA (Civ Div) .... *Digested,* 14/**1061**: *Applied* 16/663: *Considered* 16/1414, 17/786: *Followed* 14/1059, 15/852, 15/880, 17/782, 17/785, 17/788
Jagoo v Bristol City Council [2017] EWHC 926 (Admin); [2017] P.T.S.R. 888; [2017] R.A. 159; [2017] A.C.D. 76, QBD (Admin) .... *Digested,* 17/**1504**
Jaguar Land Rover Ltd v Bombardier Recreational Products Inc [2016] EWHC 3266 (Ch); [2017] E.T.M.R. 11; [2017] F.S.R. 20, Ch D .... *Digested,* 17/**1395**
JAL Fish Ltd Small Self-Administered Pension Scheme Trustees v Robertson Construction Eastern Ltd [2017] CSOH 70; 2017 S.L.T. 577; 2017 G.W.D. 15-251, OH .... *Digested,* 17/**2771**
Jamadar v Bradford Teaching Hospitals NHS Foundation Trust [2016] EWCA Civ 1001; [2016] 5 Costs L.R. 809, CA (Civ Div) .... *Digested,* 16/**241**: *Applied* 17/278
Jamaica Mutual Life Assurance Society v Hillsborough [1989] 1 W.L.R. 1101; (1989) 133 S.J. 1032, PC (Jam) .... *Digested,* 91/**3550**: *Applied* 17/1828
Jameel v Dow Jones & Co Inc; *sub nom* Dow Jones & Co Inc v Jameel [2005] EWCA Civ 75; [2005] Q.B. 946; [2005] 2 W.L.R. 1614; [2005] E.M.L.R. 16; Times, February 14, 2005; Independent, February 10, 2005; (2005) 149 S.J.L.B. 181, CA (Civ Div) .... *Digested,* 05/**974**: *Applied* 09/975, 10/834, 10/838, 11/870, 13/792, 13/795, 14/841, 16/1281, 16/574: *Considered* 06/1041, 09/986, 11/869, 12/432, 12/864, 14/415: *Followed* 12/869, 13/800, 15/689, 15/693, 17/648: *Referred to* 17/646

Jameel v Wall Street Journal Europe SPRL (No.3) [2004] EWHC 37 (QB); [2004] E.M.L.R. 11, QBD .... *Digested,* 04/**935**: *Affirmed* 05/977: *Applied* 17/651

James v Aintree University Hospitals NHS Foundation Trust see Aintree University Hospitals NHS Foundation Trust v James

James v Buena Ventura Nitrate Grounds Syndicate Ltd [1896] 1 Ch. 456, CA *Considered* 17/409

James v United Kingdom (25119/09); *joined cases* Lee v United Kingdom (57877/09); Wells v United Kingdom (57715/09) (2013) 56 E.H.R.R. 12; 33 B.H.R.C. 617; (2012) 109(37) L.S.G. 20, ECHR .... *Digested,* 13/**1558**: *Approved* 17/1594: *Considered* 13/2112, 13/2113, 13/3878, 14/2234, 15/1813, 15/3242, 17/2745, 17/2746: *Followed* 14/3702: *Not applied* 15/1811

James H Donald (Darvel) Ltd v Revenue and Customs Commissioners [2017] UKFTT 446 (TC); [2017] S.T.I. 1400, FTT (Tax)

James Hall and Co (Property) Ltd v Maughan [2017] UKUT 240 (LC); [2017] 2 P. & C.R. DG22, UT (Lands)

Jameson v Central Electricity Generating Board (No.1) [2000] 1 A.C. 455; [1999] 2 W.L.R. 141; [1999] 1 All E.R. 193; [1999] 1 Lloyd's Rep. 573; [1999] P.I.Q.R. Q81; Times, December 17, 1998; (1999) 96(5) L.S.G. 37; (1999) 143 S.J.L.B. 29, HL .... *Digested,* 99/**1386**: *Applied* 00/598: *Considered* 00/377, 02/319, 17/2201: *Distinguished* 01/656: *Explained* 02/482: *Followed* 99/1640, 17/217: *Not applied* 00/5122

Jamieson (Brian) v HM Advocate (No.2) 1994 J.C. 251; 1995 S.L.T. 666; 1994 S.C.C.R. 610, HCJ .... *Digested,* 94/**5513**: *Considered* 09/4836, 12/3939, 14/3400: *Distinguished* 17/2492

Jan v Secretary of State for the Home Department see Jan (Upper Tribunal: Set-Aside Powers)

Jan (Upper Tribunal: Set-Aside Powers); *sub nom* Jan v Secretary of State for the Home Department [2016] UKUT 336 (IAC); [2016] Imm. A.R. 1437, UT (IAC) ... *Digested,* 17/**30**

Janecek v Freistaat Bayern (C-237/07) EU:C:2008:447; [2008] E.C.R. I-6221; [2009] Env. L.R. 12, ECJ (2nd Chamber) .... *Digested,* 09/**1351**: *Applied* 17/875

Janin Caribbean Construction Ltd v Wilkinson [2016] UKPC 26; [2017] P.N.L.R. 5, PC (Gren)

Januzi v Secretary of State for the Home Department; *joined cases* Mohammed v Secretary of State for the Home Department; Gaafar v Secretary of State for the Home Department; Hamid v Secretary of State for the Home Department [2006] UKHL 5; [2006] 2 A.C. 426; [2006] 2 W.L.R. 397; [2006] 3 All E.R. 305; 21 B.H.R.C. 65; [2006] Imm. A.R. 252; [2006] I.N.L.R. 118; Times, February 16, 2006; Independent, February 24, 2006; (2006) 103(11) L.S.G. 25; (2006) 150 S.J.L.B. 223, HL .... *Digested,* 06/**2232**: *Considered* 08/2079: *Followed* 08/2029, 17/1241

Janvey v Wastell see Stanford International Bank Ltd (In Receivership), Re

Japanese Taxation of Internet Sales, Re 19 I.T.L. Rep. 346

Jarvie v Greater Glasgow Primary Care NHS Trust 2006 G.W.D. 17-347, OH *Considered* 17/2428

Jasmine Trustees Ltd v L; *sub nom* Riviera Trust, Re; Piedmont Trust, Re [2015] JRC 196; 19 I.T.E.L.R. 210, Royal Ct (Jer)

Javed v Ageas Insurance (Unreported, November 8, 2016), CC (Luton) [*Irwin Mitchell LLP, Riverside West, 1 Millsands, Sheffield*] .... *Digested,* 17/**1655**

Jawaby Property Investment Ltd v Interiors Group Ltd [2016] EWHC 557 (TCC); [2016] B.L.R. 328, QBD (TCC) .... *Digested,* 16/**407**: *Considered* 17/475

Jazztel Plc v Revenue and Customs Commissioners [2017] EWHC 677 (Ch); [2017] 1 W.L.R. 3869; [2017] 4 All E.R. 470; [2017] S.T.C. 1422; [2017] B.T.C. 7, Ch D . *Digested,* 17/**2177**

JC v Bromley LBC [2016] UKUT 388 (AAC); [2016] E.L.R. 515, UT (AAC) .... *Digested,* 17/**708**

JC and A Solicitors Ltd v Iqbal [2017] EWCA Civ 355; [2017] C.P. Rep. 32; [2017] 3 Costs L.O. 377; [2017] P.I.Q.R. P18, CA (Civ Div) .... *Digested,* 17/**236**

JCAM Commercial Real Estate Property XV Ltd v Davis Haulage Ltd [2017] EWCA Civ 267; [2018] 1 W.L.R. 24; [2017] B.C.C. 222; [2018] 1 B.C.L.C. 165, CA (Civ Div) .... *Digested,* 17/**1261**

JD v East Berkshire Community Health NHS Trust; *sub nom* D v East Berkshire Community NHS Trust; MAK v Dewsbury Healthcare NHS Trust; *joined cases* RK v Oldham NHS Trust; K v Dewsbury Healthcare NHS Trust [2005] UKHL 23; [2005] 2 A.C. 373; [2005] 2 W.L.R. 993; [2005] 2 All E.R. 443; [2005] 2 F.L.R. 284; [2005] 2 F.C.R. 81; (2005) 8 C.C.L. Rep. 185; [2005] Lloyd's Rep. Med. 263; (2005) 83 B.M.L.R. 66; Times, April 22, 2005; Independent, April 27, 2005; [2005] Fam. Law 615; (2005) 155 N.L.J. 654, HL .... *Digested,* 05/**2848**: *Applied* 06/1662, 08/2643, 15/995: *Complaint upheld* 10/1744: *Considered* 06/2887, 07/2916, 07/2937, 10/3420, 15/1767, 17/1558: *Followed* 07/2934

JD v Lothian Health Board see D v Lothian Health Board

JD v West London Mental Health NHS Trust [2016] UKUT 496 (AAC); [2017] M.H.L.R. 66, UT (AAC)

JDI International Leasing Ltd v Revenue and Customs Commissioners [2017] UKFTT 329 (TC); [2017] S.F.T.D. 856; [2017] S.T.I. 1146, FTT (Tax)

Jeal (Country Estates Hampshire) v East Hampshire DC [2017] P.A.D. 9, Planning Inspector

JEB Recoveries LLP v Binstock [2016] EWCA Civ 1008; [2017] C.P. Rep. 5, CA (Civ Div) .... *Digested,* 17/**28**

JEB Recoveries LLP v Binstock [2015] EWHC 1063 (Ch), Ch D *Applied* 17/485

Jebsen v East and West India Dock Co (1874-75) L.R. 10 C.P. 300, CCP *Applied* 47-51/2554, 17/412

Jefferies v BMI Healthcare Ltd [2016] EWHC 2493 (Fam); [2017] 2 F.L.R. 664; [2016] Med. L.R. 656, Fam Div .... *Digested,* 17/**1141**

Jeffery v British Council [2016] I.R.L.R. 935, EAT .... *Digested,* 17/**849**

Jeffrey v Secretary of State for Work and Pensions see R. (on the application of Reilly) v Secretary of State for Work and Pensions

Jeffreys v Commissioner of Police for the Metropolis [2017] EWHC 1505 (QB); [2017] 4 Costs L.O. 409, QBD .... *Digested,* 17/**262**

Jellett v Brooke see Spire Healthcare Ltd v Brooke

Jemitus v Bank of Scotland Plc see Teasdale v HSBC Bank Plc

Jenks v Dickinson (Inspector of Taxes) [1997] S.T.C. 853; 69 T.C. 458; [1997] B.T.C. 286; Times, June 16, 1997, Ch D .... *Digested,* 97/**337**: *Applied* 17/2095

Jennings v Crown Prosecution Service; *sub nom* Crown Prosecution Service v J; J v Crown Prosecution Service [2005] EWCA Civ 746; [2006] 1 W.L.R. 182; [2005] 4 All E.R. 391; Times, July 12, 2005; Independent, June 30, 2005, CA (Civ Div) *Digested,* 05/**926**: *Affirmed* 08/858: *Applied* 07/3615, 09/932: *Considered* 08/3271: *Followed* 12/469, 17/624

Jennings v Kinder (Inspector of Taxes) see Hochstrasser (Inspector of Taxes) v Mayes

Jenyo v General Medical Council [2016] EWHC 1708 (Admin); (2016) 152 B.M.L.R. 122, QBD (Admin) .... *Digested,* 17/**1113**

Jerome v Kelly (Inspector of Taxes) [2004] UKHL 25; [2004] 1 W.L.R. 1409; [2004] 2 All E.R. 835; [2004] S.T.C. 887; 76 T.C. 147; [2004] B.T.C. 176; [2004] W.T.L.R. 681; Times, May 20, 2004; Independent, May 19, 2004; [2004] S.T.I. 1201; [2004] 21 E.G. 151 (C.S.); (2004) 101(23) L.S.G. 33; [2004] N.P.C. 75, HL .... *Digested,* 04/**3694**: *Followed* 17/1841, 17/2092, 17/2094

Jet Holdings Inc v Patel [1990] 1 Q.B. 335; [1988] 3 W.L.R. 295; [1989] 2 All E.R. 648, CA (Civ Div) .... *Digested,* 88/**400**: *Considered* 17/434

Jet2.com Ltd v Blackpool Airport Ltd [2012] EWCA Civ 417; [2012] 2 All E.R. (Comm) 1053; [2012] 1 C.L.C. 605; 142 Con. L.R. 1; [2012] C.I.L.L. 3165, CA (Civ Div) . *Digested,* 12/**158**: *Followed* 14/630, 17/74

Jetivia SA v Bilta (UK) Ltd (In Liquidation) see Bilta (UK) Ltd (In Liquidation) v Nazir

Jeunesse v Netherlands (12738/10) (2015) 60 E.H.R.R. 17, ECHR *Applied* 16/1079, 16/1125, 17/1200, 17/1207, 17/1239: *Considered* 17/2670: *Distinguished* 16/1118

Jewelcraft Ltd v Pressland [2015] EWCA Civ 1111; [2015] H.L.R. 48; [2016] 1 P. & C.R. 9; [2016] L. & T.R. 7, CA (Civ Div) .... *Digested,* 16/**1814**: *Considered* 17/1843

JFS (UK) Ltd v Dwr Cymru Cyf (No.1) [1999] 1 W.L.R. 231; [1999] B.L.R. 17; (1999) 1 T.C.L.R. 187; Times, October 10, 1998; (1998) 95(39) L.S.G. 40; (1998) 142 S.J.L.B. 256, CA (Civ Div) .... *Digested,* 98/**538**: *Considered* 17/329

JG v Lord Chancellor see JG (A Child) v Legal Services Commission

JG (A Child) v Legal Services Commission; *sub nom* JG v Lord Chancellor [2014] EWCA Civ 656; [2014] 5 Costs L.O. 708; [2014] 2 F.L.R. 1218; [2014] 3 F.C.R. 567; [2014] H.R.L.R. 18; [2014] Fam. Law 1097, CA (Civ Div) .... *Digested,* 14/**1342**: *Followed* 15/1072, 17/998

JG (Case No 12911940), Re; *sub nom* Public Guardian's Severance Applications, Re [2017] EWCOP 10; [2017] W.T.L.R. 1145, CP

JH (Zimbabwe) v Secretary of State for the Home Department; *joined case* R. (on the application of JH (Zimbabwe)) v Asylum and Immigration Tribunal [2009] EWCA Civ 78; [2009] Imm. A.R. 499; [2009] I.N.L.R. 385, CA (Civ Div) .... *Digested,* 10/**1804**: *Applied* 12/1737, 16/1136: *Followed* 17/1229

JH Rayner (Mincing Lane) Ltd v Department of Trade and Industry; *joined cases* Maclaine Watson & Co Ltd v Department of Trade and Industry; Maclaine Watson & Co Ltd v International Tin Council; TSB England and Wales v Department of Trade and Industry; Amalgamated Metal Trading Ltd v International Tin Council [1990] 2 A.C. 418; [1989] 3 W.L.R. 969; [1989] 3 All E.R. 523; (1989) 5 B.C.C. 872; [1990] B.C.L.C. 102; (1990) 87(4) L.S.G. 68; (1989) 139 N.L.J. 1559; (1989) 133 S.J. 1485, HL .... *Digested,* 90/**538**: *Applied* 90/614, 92/204, 06/2396, 16/973, 17/157: *Considered* 93/3805, 96/3659, 04/2088, 05/212: *Distinguished* 91/2200: *Followed* 89/149, 16/370: *Referred to* 95/2938

Jif Lemon case see Reckitt & Colman Products Ltd v Borden Inc (No.3)

Jigsaw Medical Services Ltd v Revenue and Customs Commissioners [2017] UKFTT 537 (TC); [2017] S.T.I. 1669, FTT (Tax)

JIH v News Group Newspapers Ltd [2011] EWCA Civ 42; [2011] 1 W.L.R. 1645; [2011] 2 All E.R. 324; [2011] C.P. Rep. 17; [2011] E.M.L.R. 15; [2011] 2 F.C.R. 95; Times, February 7, 2011; (2011) 108(7) L.S.G. 18; (2011) 161 N.L.J. 211, CA (Civ Div) .... *Digested,* 11/**373**: *Applied* 11/1302, 11/375, 12/331, 15/343, 15/4: *Distinguished* 12/15: *Followed* 14/790, 17/1028

Jirehouse Capital v Beller [2008] EWCA Civ 908; [2009] 1 W.L.R. 751; [2009] Bus. L.R. 404; [2008] C.P. Rep. 44; [2008] B.C.C. 636; [2008] B.P.I.R. 1498, CA (Civ Div) .... *Digested,* 08/**415**: *Applied* 16/311: *Followed* 15/358, 17/358

Jivraj v Hashwani; *sub nom* Hashwani v Jivraj [2011] UKSC 40; [2011] 1 W.L.R. 1872; [2012] 1 All E.R. 629; [2012] 1 All E.R. (Comm) 1177; [2011] Bus. L.R. 1182; [2011] 2 Lloyd's Rep. 513; [2011] 2 C.L.C. 427; [2012] 1 C.M.L.R. 12; [2011] I.C.R. 1004; [2011] I.R.L.R. 827; [2011] Eq. L.R. 1088; [2011] Arb. L.R. 28; Times, August 4, 2011; [2011] C.I.L.L. 3076; [2011] 32 E.G. 54 (C.S.), SC .... *Digested,* 11/**127**: *Followed* 15/822, 15/823, 17/840

JJ Food Service Ltd v Zulhayir [2013] EWCA Civ 1304; [2014] C.P. Rep. 15, CA (Civ Div) .... *Digested,* 14/**357**: *Followed* 17/786

JJ Gallagher Ltd v Cherwell DC; *sub nom* Woodfield v JJ Gallagher Ltd [2016] EWCA Civ 1007; [2016] 1 W.L.R. 5126; Times, December 6, 2016; [2017] J.P.L. 293, CA (Civ Div) .... *Digested,* 17/**1723**

JJ Gallagher Ltd v Cherwell DC; *sub nom* Woodfield v JJ Gallagher Ltd [2016] EWHC 290 (Admin), QBD (Birmingham)
Affirmed 17/1723

JJ Gallagher Ltd v Secretary of State for Transport, Local Government and the Regions [2002] EWHC 1812 (Admin); [2002] 4 P.L.R. 32; (2002) 99(36) L.S.G. 42, QBD (Admin)
Applied 13/2327, 17/1777

JK v Sweden (59166/12) (2017) 64 E.H.R.R. 15, ECHR

JKB Holdings Pty Ltd v de la Vega [2013] NSWSC 501
Considered 17/1314

JL v Bowen 11R72777, CC (Manchester)
Considered 16/1610: *Reversed* 17/2191

JL v Bowen [2017] EWCA Civ 82; [2017] P.I.Q.R. P11, CA (Civ Div) .... *Digested,* 17/**2191**

JL v HM Advocate see L v HM Advocate

JL v Secretary of State for the Home Department see JL (Medical Reports: Credibility: China), Re

JL v SL (Financial Remedies: Rehearing: Non-Matrimonial Property) [2015] EWHC 360 (Fam); [2015] 2 F.L.R. 1202; [2015] Fam. Law 519, Fam Div .... *Digested,* 15/**1091**: *Considered* 17/1024

JL (Babies Relinquished for Adoption), Re; *sub nom* A Western Circuit Local Authority v A Mother; A London Borough Council v JL [2016] EWHC 440 (Fam); [2016] 4 W.L.R. 40; [2017] 1 F.L.R. 1545; [2016] Fam. Law 556, Fam Div .... *Digested,* 16/**805**: *Applied* 16/804

JL (Medical Reports: Credibility: China), Re; *sub nom* JL v Secretary of State for the Home Department [2013] UKUT 145 (IAC); [2013] Imm. A.R. 727, UT (IAC) ..... *Digested,* 14/**1647**: *Approved* 17/1173

JL (Sierra Leone) v Secretary of State for the Home Department see EB (Kosovo) v Secretary of State for the Home Department

JLK Ltd v Ezekwe [2017] UKUT 277 (LC); [2017] L. & T.R. 29; [2017] 2 P. & C.R. DG26, UT (Lands) ..... *Digested,* 17/**1441**

JM v JW see M v W

JM (Liberia) v Secretary of State for the Home Department; *sub nom* JM (Rule 62(7): Human Rights Unarguable: Liberia), Re [2006] EWCA Civ 1402; [2007] Imm. A.R. 293; [2006] I.N.L.R. 548, CA (Civ Div) ..... *Digested,* 07/**2286**: *Applied* 08/2030: *Considered* 09/2105, 10/1807, 16/1144: *Distinguished* 16/1149, 17/1245: *Followed* 11/1777, 12/1759

JM (Rule 62(7): Human Rights Unarguable: Liberia), Re see JM (Liberia) v Secretary of State for the Home Department

JMN v Norway (Admissibility) (3145/16) (2017) 64 E.H.R.R. SE7, ECHR

JN v Staatssecretaris van Veiligheid en Justitie (C-601/15 PPU) see N v Staatssecretaris voor Veiligheid en Justitie (C-601/15 PPU)

JN v United Kingdom (37289/12) Times, June 3, 2016, ECHR *Applied* 17/1204

Jobcenter Berlin Neukolln v Alimanovic (C-67/14) EU:C:2015:597; [2016] Q.B. 308; [2016] 2 W.L.R. 208; [2016] 1 C.M.L.R. 29; [2016] C.E.C. 805, ECJ (Grand Chamber) *Applied* 16/1983: *Considered* 17/2658: *Followed* 16/1980

John Dee Ltd v Customs and Excise Commissioners [1995] S.T.C. 941; Times, July 20, 1995, CA (Civ Div) ..... *Digested,* 96/**5842**: *Applied* 08/3984, 08/885, 11/56, 15/2491, 15/2581: *Approved* 17/2229: *Considered* 00/5335, 03/4603, 10/3484, 12/3392: *Distinguished* 06/4454: *Followed* 17/2127

John Douglas v Alexander M'Cutcheon (Carson's Trustee) (1876) 3 R. 565, IH (2 Div) *Considered* 17/2781

JOHN HOPKINS/Factor-9 (T1329/04) [2006] E.P.O.R. 8, EPO (Technical Bd App) *Applied* 17/1375: *Considered* 08/2302, 08/2325

John Hudson & Co Ltd v Kirkness (Inspector of Taxes) see Kirkness (Inspector of Taxes) v John Hudson & Co Ltd

John Lyon's Charity v London Sephardi Trust see London Sephardi Trust v John Lyon's Charity

John Muir Trust v Scottish Ministers [2016] CSIH 33; 2016 S.C. 741; 2017 S.C.L.R. 261; 2016 G.W.D. 16-295, IH (Ex Div) ..... *Digested,* 17/**2430**

John Muir Trust v Scottish Ministers [2015] CSOH 163; 2016 G.W.D. 7-148, OH *Reversed* 17/2764

John Muir Trust v Scottish Ministers [2016] CSIH 61; 2017 S.C. 207; 2016 G.W.D. 24-453, IH (1 Div) ..... *Digested,* 17/**2764**

John Shaw & Sons (Salford) Ltd v Shaw [1935] 2 K.B. 113, CA *Applied* 17/390

John Thomas Witherington. (1881) 4 Coup. 475, HCJ *Considered* 17/2512

Johnny Rockets Licensing Corp v Eddie Rockets (Ireland) Ltd; *sub nom* Eddie Rockets (Ireland) Ltd v Johnny Rockets Licensing Corp [2017] E.C.C. 6; [2016] E.T.M.R. 37; [2017] F.S.R. 9, App Person ..... *Digested,* 17/**1393**

Johnson v Edwardian International Hotels [2010] EWCA Civ 466, CA (Civ Div) *Considered* 17/1173

Johnson v Gore Wood & Co (No.1); *sub nom* Johnson v Gore Woods & Co [2002] 2 A.C. 1; [2001] 2 W.L.R. 72; [2001] 1 All E.R. 481; [2001] C.P.L.R. 49; [2001] B.C.C. 820; [2001] 1 B.C.L.C. 313; [2001] P.N.L.R. 18; Times, December 22, 2000; Independent, February 7, 2001; (2001) 98(1) L.S.G. 24; (2001) 98(8) L.S.G. 46; (2000) 150 N.L.J. 1889; (2001) 145 S.J.L.B. 29, HL ..... *Digested,* 01/**410**: *Applied* 01/746, 02/280, 02/281, 02/3286, 02/3310, 03/291, 03/4600, 03/470, 04/265, 04/459, 05/2448, 05/2505, 05/520, 05/533, 06/2591, 06/320, 07/346, 08/271, 08/383, 09/2225, 09/2742, 09/696, 10/1889, 10/3225, 10/3528, 10/426, 11/1136, 11/1955, 13/1010, 13/1523, 14/1787, 15/179, 16/1303, 16/160, 17/1856, 17/190, 17/200: *Considered* 01/5710, 01/675, 01/708, 06/562, 07/2677, 10/458, 11/378, 12/1171, 13/266, 15/301, 17/322: *Distinguished* 02/565, 04/2338, 10/256, 10/425: *Followed* 04/2733, 04/425, 05/483, 10/1, 10/257, 10/826, 11/1077, 11/354, 13/1309, 13/434, 13/783, 14/1878, 15/445, 16/1292, 16/1313, 16/159, 16/568, 17/191, 17/206, 17/365

Johnson v Gore Woods & Co see Johnson v Gore Wood & Co (No.1)

Johnson v Havering LBC see L v Birmingham City Council

Johnson v Solihull MBC see Hotak v Southwark LBC
Johnson (Deportation: 4 Years' Imprisonment); *sub nom* Secretary of State for the Home Department v Johnson [2016] UKUT 282 (IAC); [2016] Imm. A.R. 1100, UT (IAC) .... *Digested,* 17/**1196**
Johnston v Ireland (9697/82) see Johnston v Ireland (A/112)
Johnston v Ireland (A/112); *sub nom* Johnston v Ireland (9697/82) (1987) 9 E.H.R.R. 203; Times, January 7, 1987, ECHR .... *Digested,* 87/**1912**: *Applied* 17/981: *Considered* 02/2510
Johnston v Secretary of State for Education [2016] EWHC 1871 (Admin); [2017] E.L.R. 163, QBD (Admin) .... *Digested,* 17/**717**
Johnston's Trustee v Baird [2012] CSOH 117; 2012 G.W.D. 25-514, OH *Applied* 17/2684
Johnstone v Attorney General for Northern Ireland see Johnstone's Application for Judicial Review, Re
Johnstone's Application for Judicial Review, Re; *sub nom* Johnstone v Attorney General for Northern Ireland [2017] NIQB 33; [2017] Inquest L.R. 134, QBD (NI)
Joint Administrators of Castlebridge Plant Ltd, Noters; *sub nom* Nimmo & Friar, Noters [2015] CSOH 165; [2017] B.C.C. 87; 2016 G.W.D. 1-17, OH
Joint Administrators of LB Holdings Intermediate 2 Ltd (In Administration) v Lomas see Lehman Brothers International (Europe) (In Administration), Re
Joint Administrators of Loanwell Ltd v Stonegale Ltd see Joint Administrators of Oceancrown Ltd v Stonegale Ltd
Joint Administrators of Oceancrown Ltd v Stonegale Ltd; *sub nom* Brown v Oceancrown Ltd; Brown v Stonegale Ltd; Brown v Pelosi; *joined cases* Joint Administrators of Loanwell Ltd v Stonegale Ltd; Joint Administrators of Questway Ltd v Pelosi [2015] CSIH 12; 2015 S.C.L.R. 619; 2015 G.W.D. 8-156, IH (Ex Div) .... *Digested,* 16/**2696**: *Affirmed* 17/1260
Joint Administrators of Oceancrown Ltd v Stonegale Ltd; *sub nom* Brown v Oceancrown Ltd; Brown v Stonegale Ltd; Brown v Pelosi; *joined cases* Joint Administrators of Loanwell Ltd v Stonegale Ltd; Joint Administrators of Questway Ltd v Pelosi [2016] UKSC 30; 2016 S.C. (U.K.S.C.) 91; 2016 G.W.D. 20-359, SC .... *Digested,* 17/**1260**
Joint Administrators of Questway Ltd v Pelosi see Joint Administrators of Oceancrown Ltd v Stonegale Ltd
Joint Stock Co Aeroflot - Russian Airlines v Leeds [2017] EWHC 150 (Ch); [2017] 1 W.L.R. 4537; [2018] 1 All E.R. 74; [2017] 1 Lloyd's Rep. 356, Ch D .... *Digested,* 17/**179**
Joint Stock Co Aeroflot Russian Airlines v Berezovsky see Aeroflot - Russian Airlines v Berezovsky
Jolley v Sutton LBC [2000] 1 W.L.R. 1082; [2000] 3 All E.R. 409; [2000] 2 Lloyd's Rep. 65; [2000] 2 F.C.R. 392; (2001) 3 L.G.L.R. 2; [2000] B.L.G.R. 399; [2000] P.I.Q.R. P136; Times, May 24, 2000; (2000) 97(23) L.S.G. 42, HL .... *Digested,* 00/**4239**: *Applied* 00/4214: *Considered* 05/4196: *Distinguished* 04/2716: *Referred to* 17/1564
Jolly (Andrew) v HM Advocate [2013] HCJAC 96; 2014 J.C. 171; 2013 S.L.T. 1100; 2013 S.C.L. 832; 2013 S.C.C.R. 511; 2013 G.W.D. 29-576, HCJ .... *Digested,* 13/**3564**: *Applied* 17/2477: *Considered* 15/2966: *Distinguished* 17/2481: *Overruled* 14/3410
Jones v Canal and River Trust; *sub nom* Canal and River Trust v Jones [2017] EWCA Civ 135; [2018] Q.B. 305; [2017] 3 W.L.R. 516; [2017] H.L.R. 25; [2017] 2 P. & C.R. 10; [2017] L.L.R. 353, CA (Civ Div) .... *Digested,* 17/**1168**
Jones v Chennell see Chennell, Re
Jones v Churcher [2009] EWHC 722 (QB); [2009] 2 Lloyd's Rep. 94, QBD (Bristol) ..... *Digested,* 09/**312**: *Considered* 17/379
Jones v IOS (RUK) Ltd (In Liquidation) [2012] EWHC 348 (Ch), Ch D *Considered* 17/2195
Jones v Jones [1977] 1 W.L.R. 438; [1977] 2 All E.R. 231; (1977) 33 P. & C.R. 147; (1976) 242 E.G. 371; Times, November 1, 1976; (1976) 120 S.J. 802, CA (Civ Div) .... *Digested,* 77/**2509**: *Applied* 08/3064: *Considered* 81/1344, 86/3034, 96/3781, 17/1826
Jones v Jones; *sub nom* J v J [2011] EWCA Civ 41; [2012] Fam. 1; [2011] 3 W.L.R. 582; [2011] 1 F.L.R. 1723; [2011] 1 F.C.R. 242; Times, March 28, 2011; [2011] Fam. Law 455; (2011) 161 N.L.J. 210, CA (Civ Div) .... *Digested,* 11/**1300**: *Applied* 15/1102: *Considered* 17/1024: *Followed* 11/1296, 11/64, 17/1023
Jones v Jones (Periodical Payments) [2001] Fam. 96; [2000] 3 W.L.R. 1505; [2000] 2 F.L.R. 307; [2000] 2 F.C.R. 201; Times, April 11, 2000; [2000] Fam. Law 607; (2000) 97(17) L.S.G. 34; (2000) 144 S.J.L.B. 203, CA (Civ Div) .... *Digested,* 00/**2533**: *Applied* 16/945, 17/1041

Jones v Lowe [1945] K.B. 73; [1945] 1 All E.R. 194, KBD
Approved 47-51/39: *Considered* 17/47: *Distinguished* 47-51/43, 47-51/45
Jones v Mordue; *sub nom* Mordue v Secretary of State for Communities and Local Government [2015] EWCA Civ 1243; [2016] 1 W.L.R. 2682; [2016] 1 P. & C.R. 12; [2016] J.P.L. 476, CA (Civ Div) .... *Digested,* 16/**1737**:
Followed 17/1721, 17/1751
Jones v Sandwell MBC see Barber v Somerset CC
Jones v Whalley [2006] UKHL 41; [2007] 1 A.C. 63; [2006] 3 W.L.R. 179; [2006] 4 All E.R. 113; [2007] 1 Cr. App. R. 2; Times, July 31, 2006; Independent, October 6, 2006; [2007] Crim. L.R. 74; (2006) 150 S.J.L.B. 1020, HL .... *Digested,* 06/**973**:
Considered 09/827, 09/900, 10/777, 14/798: *Followed* 17/621
Jones (Setting of Minimum Term), Re; *sub nom* R. v Jones (Neil); R. v Chandi (Amandeep Singh); R. v Multani (Hardeep Singh); R. v Khangura (Sukhjiwan Singh); R. v Dosanjh (Jaswinder Singh); R. v Ashman (Joseph Clifford); R. v Hobson (Mark); *joined cases* Chandi (Setting of Minimum Term), Re; Multani (Setting of Minimum Term), Re; Khangura (Setting of Minimum Term), Re; Dosanjh (Setting of Minimum Term), Re; Ashman (Setting of Minimum Term), Re; Hobson (Setting of Minimum Term), Re [2005] EWCA Crim 3115; [2006] 2 Cr. App. R. (S.) 19; [2006] Crim. L.R. 262, CA (Crim Div) .... *Digested,* 06/**3758**:
Applied 08/3336, 08/3431, 09/3432, 13/2680, 13/2701, 15/2298:
Considered 07/3694, 12/2962, 13/2682: *Distinguished* 17/1948: *Followed* 07/3689
Jonny Tooze Physiotherapy Services Ltd v Revenue and Customs Commissioners see Christianuyi Ltd v Revenue and Customs Commissioners
Jordan v MGN Ltd [2017] EWHC 1937 (Ch); [2017] 4 Costs L.R. 687, Ch D .... *Digested,* 17/**256**
Jordan, Re [2016] Inquest L.R. 309, QBD (NI) .... *Digested,* 17/**2299**
Joseph Gleave and Son Ltd v Secretary of State for Defence [2017] EWHC 238 (TCC); [2017] P.T.S.R. 607; [2017] B.L.R. 264, QBD (TCC) .... *Digested,* 17/**1809**
Joyce v Rigolli [2004] EWCA Civ 79; (2004) 148 S.J.L.B. 234; [2004] 1 P. & C.R. DG22, CA (Civ Div)
Considered 07/3365, 15/2541: *Explained* 17/1836: *Followed* 13/2423
JP v NP (Financial Remedies: Costs) see P v P (Divorce: Financial Remedy Order)
JP Morgan Chase Bank National Association v Director of the Serious Fraud Office [2012] EWHC 1674 (Admin); [2012] Lloyd's Rep. F.C. 655, QBD (Admin) .... *Digested,* 13/**737**:
Applied 17/597
JP Whitter (Waterwell Engineers) Ltd v Revenue and Customs Commissioners; *sub nom* Revenue and Customs Commissioners v JP Whitter (Waterwell Engineers) Ltd [2016] EWCA Civ 1160; [2017] S.T.C. 149; [2016] B.T.C. 45; [2016] S.T.I. 3058, CA (Civ Div) .... *Digested,* 17/**2103**
JP Whitter (Waterwell Engineers) Ltd v Revenue and Customs Commissioners; *sub nom* Revenue and Customs Commissioners v JP Whitter (Waterwell Engineers) Ltd [2015] UKUT 392 (TCC); [2016] S.T.C. 204; [2015] B.T.C. 524; [2015] S.T.I. 2555, UT (Tax) .... *Digested,* 16/**2050**:
Affirmed 17/2103
JQ v Mundell see Q (J) v Procurator Fiscal, Paisley
JR v HM Advocate see R (J) v HM Advocate
JR (A Protected Party) v Sheffield Teaching Hospitals NHS Foundation Trust [2017] EWHC 1245 (QB); [2017] 1 W.L.R. 4847; [2017] P.I.Q.R. Q3; (2017) 157 B.M.L.R. 148, QBD .... *Digested,* 17/**638**
JS v Children's Reporter see S v Children's Reporter
JS v M see JS (A Child) (Disposal of Body: Prospective Orders), Re
JS v RS [2017] EWCA Civ 408; [2017] 4 All E.R. 1046; [2017] 2 F.L.R. 1095; [2017] 2 F.C.R. 766; Times, July 26, 2017, CA (Civ Div) .... *Digested,* 17/**983**
JS v RS [2015] EWHC 2921 (Fam); [2016] 2 F.L.R. 839; [2016] Fam. Law 16, Fam Div
Reversed 17/983
JS (A Child) v DPP; *sub nom* S v DPP [2017] EWHC 1162 (Admin); [2017] 4 W.L.R. 102; [2017] 2 Cr. App. R. 17; [2017] Crim. L.R. 718; [2017] A.C.D. 90, DC .... *Digested,* 17/**532**
JS (A Child) (Disposal of Body: Prospective Orders), Re; *sub nom* JS v M [2016] EWHC 2859 (Fam); [2017] 4 W.L.R. 1; [2017] Med. L.R. 37; (2017) 153 B.M.L.R. 152; [2016] Inquest L.R. 259; [2017] W.T.L.R. 227, Fam Div .... *Digested,* 17/**972**
JS Bloor (Wilmslow) Ltd v Homes and Communities Agency; *sub nom* Homes and Communities Agency v JS Bloor (Wilmslow) Ltd [2017] UKSC 12; [2018] 1 All E.R. 817; [2017] 2 P. & C.R. 5; [2017] R.V.R. 110, SC .... *Digested,* 17/**1697**:
Followed 17/1698
JS Bloor (Wilmslow) Ltd v Homes and Communities Agency; *sub nom* Homes and Communities Agency v JS Bloor (Wilmslow) Ltd [2015] EWCA Civ 540; [2015] R.V.R. 292, CA (Civ Div) .... *Digested,* 15/**1948**:
Reversed 17/1697

JSB (A Child), Re; *sub nom* Chief Executive of Ministry of Social Development v TS (2009-10) 12 I.T.E.L.R. 773, HC (NZ)
Considered 17/972
JSC Bank of Moscow v Kekhman [2015] EWHC 396 (Ch); [2015] 1 W.L.R. 3737; [2015] 2 All E.R. (Comm) 1080; [2015] B.P.I.R. 513, Ch D .... *Digested,* 15/**1406**: *Applied* 17/1290
JSC BTA Bank v Ablyazov; *sub nom* Khrapunov v JSC BTA Bank [2016] EWHC 230 (Comm); [2016] 3 W.L.R. 659; [2016] 2 All E.R. (Comm) 218; [2016] 1 C.L.C. 267, QBD (Comm) .... *Digested,* 16/**2145**: *Reversed in part* 17/160
JSC BTA Bank v Ablyazov; *sub nom* Khrapunov v JSC BTA Bank [2017] EWCA Civ 40; [2017] Q.B. 853; [2017] 2 W.L.R. 1563; [2017] 2 All E.R. 918; [2017] 2 All E.R. (Comm) 1; [2017] C.P. Rep. 20; [2017] 1 C.L.C. 80, CA (Civ Div) .... *Digested,* 17/**160**
JSC BTA Bank v Ablyazov see Shalabayev v JSC BTA Bank
JSC BTA Bank v Solodchenko [2011] EWHC 1613 (Ch), Ch D
Applied 17/6
JSC Mezhdunarodniy Promyshlenniy Bank v Pugachev [2017] EWHC 1853 (Ch); [2017] 5 Costs L.R. 861, Ch D .... *Digested,* 17/**273**
JSC VTB Bank v Skurikhin [2014] EWHC 271 (Comm), QBD (Comm)
Considered 17/434
Juffali v Juffali see Estrada Juffali v Juffali
Julius Fillibeck Sohne GmbH & Co KG v Finanzamt Neustadt (C-258/95) EU:C:1997:491; [1998] 1 W.L.R. 697; [1998] S.T.C. 513; [1997] E.C.R. I-5577; [1998] All E.R. (EC) 466; [1998] C.E.C. 459; [1998] B.T.C. 5226; [1998] B.V.C. 206; Times, November 27, 1997, ECJ (5th Chamber) .... *Digested,* 97/**4972**: *Applied* 11/3568: *Considered* 17/2272: *Followed* 11/3539
Julius Samann Ltd v Tetrosyl Ltd [2006] EWHC 529 (Ch); [2006] E.T.M.R. 75; [2006] F.S.R. 42; (2006) 29(6) I.P.D. 29046, Ch D .... *Digested,* 06/**2598**: *Applied* 08/2387, 10/2004: *Considered* 12/1972, 16/1289, 17/2690
Jump v Lister [2016] EWHC 2160 (Ch); [2017] W.T.L.R. 61, Ch D (Manchester) .... *Digested,* 17/**2070**
Jyske Finans A/S v Ligebehandlingsnavnet (C-668/15) EU:C:2017:278; [2017] 1 W.L.R. 3031; [2017] 3 C.M.L.R. 29; [2017] I.R.L.R. 665, ECJ (1st Chamber)
JZ v TG see G (A Child) (Custody Rights: Article 13 Defence)

K v Dewsbury Healthcare NHS Trust see JD v East Berkshire Community Health NHS Trust
K v General Pharmaceutical Council see Khan v General Pharmaceutical Council
K v K (Children: Permanent Removal from Jurisdiction); *sub nom* K v K (Relocation: Shared Care Arrangement); MK v CK [2011] EWCA Civ 793; [2012] Fam. 134; [2012] 2 W.L.R. 941; [2012] 2 F.L.R. 880; [2011] 3 F.C.R. 111; [2011] Fam. Law 1078, CA (Civ Div) .... *Digested,* 11/**1382**: *Applied* 13/1248, 16/858: *Considered* 14/1311: *Followed* 16/859, 17/970
K v K (Family Proceedings: Costs) [2016] EWHC 2002 (Fam); [2016] 4 W.L.R. 143; [2016] 5 Costs L.O. 839; [2017] 1 F.C.R. 144, Fam Div .... *Digested,* 16/**875**
K v K (Financial Remedy: Final Order Prior to Decree Nisi); *sub nom* K (Husband) v K (Wife) [2016] EWFC 23; [2017] 1 F.L.R. 541; [2016] Fam. Law 804, Fam Ct...... *Digested,* 17/**1002**
K v K (Nullity: Bigamous Marriage) [2016] EWHC 3380 (Fam); [2017] 2 F.L.R. 1055, Fam Div .... *Digested,* 17/**1043**
K v K (Relocation: Shared Care Arrangement) see K v K (Children: Permanent Removal from Jurisdiction)
K v L (Ancillary Relief: Inherited Wealth); *sub nom* K v L (Non-Matrimonial Property: Special Contribution) [2011] EWCA Civ 550; [2012] 1 W.L.R. 306; [2011] 3 All E.R. 733; [2011] 2 F.L.R. 980; [2011] 2 F.C.R. 597; [2012] W.T.L.R. 153; [2011] Fam. Law 799; (2011) 108(21) L.S.G. 18; (2011) 161 N.L.J. 742, CA (Civ Div) .. *Digested,* 11/**1302**: *Applied* 16/818: *Considered* 15/1082: *Followed* 15/1091, 17/1015, 17/1023
K v L (Non-Matrimonial Property: Special Contribution) see K v L (Ancillary Relief: Inherited Wealth)
K v Marist Bros [2016] CSOH 54; 2016 G.W.D. 13-261, OH
Affirmed 17/2770
K v Marist Bros [2017] CSIH 2; 2017 S.C. 258; 2017 G.W.D. 2-24, IH (2 Div) .... *Digested,* 17/**2770**
K v S; *sub nom* Yegiazaryan v Smagin [2015] EWHC 1945 (Comm); [2015] 2 Lloyd's Rep. 363; [2015] 2 C.L.C. 231, QBD (Comm) .... *Digested,* 15/**95**: *Considered* 17/66
K v Secretary of State for Defence [2017] EWHC 830 (Admin); [2017] A.C.D. 75, DC
K v Secretary of State for Work and Pensions; *sub nom* DK v Secretary of State for Work and Pensions [2016] CSIH 84; 2017 S.C. 176; 2016 G.W.D. 36-650, IH (Ex Div) .... *Digested,* 17/**2825**

K (A Child) (International Relocation: Appeal against Judge's Findings of Fact), Re see K (A Child) (External Relocation: Judge's Evaluation), Re

K (A Child) (Brussels II Revised: Art.15), Re see T (A Child) (Care Proceedings: Request to Assume Jurisdiction), Re

K (A Child) (Care Proceedings: Jurisdiction), Re see T (A Child) (Care Proceedings: Request to Assume Jurisdiction), Re

K (A Child) (Disposal of Body: Court's Power to Authorise), Re; *sub nom* Gloucestershire CC v K [2017] EWHC 1083 (Fam); [2017] 4 W.L.R. 112; [2018] 1 F.L.R. 96, Fam Div .... *Digested,* 17/**961**

K (A Child) (External Relocation: Judge's Evaluation), Re; *sub nom* K (A Child) (International Relocation: Appeal against Judge's Findings of Fact), Re [2016] EWCA Civ 931; [2016] 4 W.L.R. 160; [2017] 1 F.L.R. 1459, CA (Civ Div) .... *Digested,* 16/**883**

K (A Child) (Private Law Proceedings: Consular Involvement), Re [2017] EWHC 2017 (Fam); [2017] 4 W.L.R. 150, Fam Ct .... *Digested,* 17/**960**

K (B) v HM Advocate [2017] HCJAC 68; 2017 S.C.L. 990; 2017 G.W.D. 30-477, HCJ . *Digested,* 17/**2532**

K (Children) (Contact: Failure to Consider Alternative Means), Re [2016] EWCA Civ 99; [2017] 1 F.L.R. 530; [2016] 2 F.C.R. 389; [2016] Fam. Law 440, CA (Civ Div) .... *Digested,* 16/**829**

K (Human Fertilisation and Embryology Act 2008) (No.2), Re [2017] EWHC 783 (Fam); [2017] 2 Costs L.R. 411, Fam Div .... *Digested,* 17/**261**

K (Husband) v K (Wife) see K v K (Financial Remedy: Final Order Prior to Decree Nisi)

K (Minors) (Wardship: Criminal Proceedings), Re [1988] Fam. 1; [1987] 3 W.L.R. 1233; [1988] 1 All E.R. 214; (1988) 152 J.P. 185; [1988] 1 F.L.R. 435; Times, September 10, 1987; [1988] Fam. Law 166; (1987) 84 L.S.G. 3501; (1988) 138 N.L.J. 388; (1987) 131 S.J. 1697, Fam Div .... *Digested,* 88/**0749**:
Applied 90/3189, 08/1514: *Approved* 91/2591: *Not followed* 17/1069

K (Pakistan) v Secretary of State for the Home Department see MAK (Pakistan) v Secretary of State for the Home Department

K (Reciprocal Enforcement of Maintenance Orders: Power of Magistrates to Issue Bench Warrant), Re see K (REMO: Power of Magistrates to Issue Bench Warrant), Re

K (REMO: Power of Magistrates to Issue Bench Warrant), Re; *sub nom* K (Reciprocal Enforcement of Maintenance Orders: Power of Magistrates to Issue Bench Warrant), Re [2017] EWFC 27; [2017] 1 W.L.R. 3605; [2017] 2 F.L.R. 1602, Fam Ct .... *Digested,* 17/**1007**

K (Wardship: Without Notice Return Order), Re see Surrey CC v NR

K Ltd v National Westminster Bank Plc [2006] EWCA Civ 1039; [2007] 1 W.L.R. 311; [2006] 4 All E.R. 907; [2006] 2 All E.R. (Comm) 655; [2007] Bus. L.R. 26; [2006] 2 Lloyd's Rep. 569; [2006] C.P. Rep. 45; Times, July 27, 2006; Independent, July 25, 2006; (2006) 103(31) L.S.G. 24; (2006) 150 S.J.L.B. 982, CA (Civ Div) .... *Digested,* 06/**260**:
Applied 07/1931: *Considered* 17/173: *Followed* 09/306, 10/205, 12/246

K&M Wholesale Suppliers Ltd Retirement Benefit Scheme Trustees v Meadowhead Christian Fellowship [2016] UKUT 31 (LC); [2017] R.V.R. 180, UT (Lands) .... *Digested,* 17/**1438**

K/S Norjarl A/S v Hyundai Heavy Industries Co Ltd [1992] Q.B. 863; [1991] 3 W.L.R. 1025; [1991] 3 All E.R. 211; [1991] 1 Lloyd's Rep. 524; Times, March 12, 1991; Independent, February 22, 1991; Financial Times, March 5, 1991; [1991] E.G. 20 (C.S.); (1991) 141 N.L.J. 343, CA (Civ Div) .... *Digested,* 91/**0186**:
Applied 96/355, 10/171, 17/78: *Considered* 97/266, 09/991

K/S Victoria Street v House of Fraser (Stores Management) Ltd [2011] EWCA Civ 904; [2012] Ch. 497; [2012] 2 W.L.R. 470; [2011] 2 P. & C.R. 15; [2011] L. & T.R. 28; [2011] 2 E.G.L.R. 11; [2011] 32 E.G. 56; Times, August 30, 2011; [2011] 31 E.G. 52 (C.S.); [2011] N.P.C. 93, CA (Civ Div) .... *Digested,* 11/**2050**:
Applied 15/1571, 17/463: *Followed* 16/1367

K2 v United Kingdom (Admissibility) (42387/13) (2017) 64 E.H.R.R. SE18, ECHR

KA Finanz AG v Sparkassen Versicherung AG Vienna Insurance Group (C-483/14) EU:C:2016:205; [2016] Q.B. 896; [2016] 3 W.L.R. 691; [2017] 1 All E.R. (Comm) 457; [2017] C.E.C. 62; [2016] I.L.Pr. 24, ECJ (3rd Chamber)

Kadhim v Brent LBC Housing Benefit Board see R. (on the application of Kadhim) v Brent LBC Housing Benefit Review Board

Kahn v Inland Revenue Commissioners see Toshoku Finance UK Plc (In Liquidation), Re

Kairos Shipping Ltd v ENKA & Co LLC [2016] EWHC 2412 (Admlty); [2016] 2 Lloyd's Rep. 525, QBD (Admlty) .... *Digested,* 17/**2021**

Kakis v Cyprus [1978] 1 W.L.R. 779; [1978] 2 All E.R. 634; [1978] Crim. L.R. 489; (1978) 122 S.J. 400, HL .... *Digested,* 78/**1451**: *Applied* 79/1295, 97/6050, 08/4770, 16/788, 17/899: *Considered* 96/1601, 97/2434, 10/1263: *Followed* 95/2288, 98/2344, 09/1474, 13/1177: *Referred to* 97/2433

Kalda v Estonia (17429/10) 42 B.H.R.C. 145, ECHR

Kalfelis v Bankhaus Schroder Munchmeyer Hengst & Co (t/a HEMA Beteiligungsgesellschaft mbH) (189/87) EU:C:1988:459; [1988] E.C.R. 5565; [1989] E.C.C. 407; Times, October 5, 1988, ECJ (5th Chamber) .... *Digested,* 91/**3936**: *Applied* 91/5161, 94/5038, 96/5344, 97/898, 03/484, 06/630, 06/640, 07/659, 10/3410, 16/361: *Considered* 93/450, 98/3466, 99/715, 05/427, 07/2584, 07/657, 12/556: *Distinguished* 96/7098: *Followed* 94/5036, 96/1085, 10/515, 17/430: *Referred to* 97/3890

Kallang Shipping SA Panama v AXA Assurances Senegal (The Kallang) [2008] EWHC 2761 (Comm); [2009] 1 Lloyd's Rep. 124, QBD (Comm) .... *Digested,* 09/**3557**: *Considered* 17/201: *Followed* 09/3558

Kamhi (Deceased), Re see Buzzoni v Revenue and Customs Commissioners

Kandola v Generalstaatwaltschaft Frankfurt see Kandola v Germany

Kandola v Germany; *sub nom* Ijaz v Court of Milan; Droma v State Prosecutor Nurnburg-Furth, Bavaria; Kandola v Generalstaatwaltschaft Frankfurt; *joined cases* Ijaz v Italy; Droma v Germany [2015] EWHC 619 (Admin); [2015] 1 W.L.R. 5097; [2016] 3 All E.R. 1037; [2015] A.C.D. 61, DC .... *Digested,* 16/**787**: *Not followed* 17/907

Kang v DPP see DPP v Vince

Kanthasamy v Canada (Citizenship and Immigration) 2015 SCC 61; 41 B.H.R.C. 679, Sup Ct (Can)

Kanu v Southwark LBC see Hotak v Southwark LBC

Kapoor v National Westminster Bank Plc see National Westminster Bank Plc v Kapoor

Kapri (Fatjon) v Lord Advocate [2014] HCJAC 63; 2014 G.W.D. 21-395, HCJ *Applied* 17/2440

Karacsony v Hungary (42461/13) (2017) 64 E.H.R.R. 10; 42 B.H.R.C. 1, ECHR (Grand Chamber)

Karanakaran v Secretary of State for the Home Department [2000] 3 All E.R. 449; [2000] Imm. A.R. 271; [2000] I.N.L.R. 122; Times, February 16, 2000; Independent, February 4, 2000; (2000) 97(5) L.S.G. 34; (2000) 97(10) L.S.G. 36; (2000) 144 S.J.L.B. 81, CA (Civ Div) .... *Digested,* 00/**3307**: *Applied* 03/2218, 03/2275, 03/5733: *Considered* 04/2043, 11/1714, 17/2825: *Followed* 02/5874, 02/5877, 05/2182

Kareda v Benko (C-249/16) EU:C:2017:472; [2018] Q.B. 445; [2018] 2 W.L.R. 232; [2017] C.E.C. 1394; [2017] I.L.Pr. 29, ECJ (3rd Chamber)

Kareem v Secretary of State for the Home Department see Kareem (Proxy Marriages: EU Law), Re

Kareem (Proxy Marriages: EU Law), Re; *sub nom* Kareem v Secretary of State for the Home Department [2014] UKUT 24 (IAC); [2014] Imm. A.R. 573, UT (IAC) *Overruled* 17/1247

Karim v Migrationsverket (C-155/15) EU:C:2016:410; [2017] 1 C.M.L.R. 7; [2016] Imm. A.R. 1264; [2017] I.N.L.R. 204, ECJ (Grand Chamber)

KAS v Lord Advocate see H v Lord Advocate

Kashmiri v Secretary of State for the Home Department see Huang v Secretary of State for the Home Department

Kasler v OTP Jelzalogbank Zrt (C-26/13) EU:C:2014:282; [2014] 2 All E.R. (Comm) 443; [2014] Bus. L.R. 664, ECJ (4th Chamber) *Considered* 17/485

Kasparov v Russia (53659/07) (2018) 66 E.H.R.R. 21; 42 B.H.R.C. 334, ECHR

Kateb v Howard de Walden Estates Ltd see Howard De Walden Estates Ltd v Accordway Ltd

Katib v Revenue and Customs Commissioners [2017] UKFTT 738 (TC); [2017] S.T.I. 2135, FTT (Tax)

Kats v Ukraine (29971/04) (2010) 51 E.H.R.R. 44; [2011] Inquest L.R. 189, ECHR *Applied* 16/1005: *Considered* 17/1593

Kaur v S Russell & Sons Ltd [1973] Q.B. 336; [1973] 2 W.L.R. 147; [1973] 1 All E.R. 617; Times, December 19, 1972; (1972) 117 S.J. 91, CA (Civ Div) .... *Digested,* 73/**1964**: *Applied* 73/1156, 82/2480, 94/393, 15/1964, 17/323, 17/327: *Considered* 07/477, 12/439: *Distinguished* 74/1321, 83/1311, 97/2914, 17/12: *Followed* 14/420: *Not followed* 82/1092: *Referred to* 13/2061

Kaur (Children's Best Interests: Public Interest Interface), Re [2017] UKUT 14 (IAC); [2017] Imm. A.R. 814; [2017] I.N.L.R. 757, UT (IAC) .... *Digested,* 17/**1235**

Kaverzin v Ukraine (23893/03) (2017) 64 E.H.R.R. 8, ECHR
Kazakhstan v Istil Group Inc [2005] EWCA Civ 1468; [2006] 1 W.L.R. 596; [2006] 2 All E.R. (Comm) 26; [2006] C.P. Rep. 12; Times, November 17, 2005, CA (Civ Div) .... *Digested,* 06/**502**: *Applied* 17/359
Kazakhstan v Istil Group Inc; *sub nom* Kazakhstan v Istil Group Ltd [2006] EWHC 448 (Comm); [2006] 2 Lloyd's Rep. 370, QBD (Comm) .... *Digested,* 06/**218**: *Affirmed* 07/240: *Followed* 17/77
Kazakhstan v Istil Group Ltd see Kazakhstan v Istil Group Inc
Kazakhstan Kagazy Plc v Arip see Kazakhstan Kagazy Plc v Zhunus
Kazakhstan Kagazy Plc v Zhunus [2016] EWHC 1048 (Comm); [2016] 4 W.L.R. 86, QBD (Comm) .... *Digested,* 16/**260**: *Reversed* 17/219
Kazakhstan Kagazy Plc v Zhunus [2016] EWCA Civ 1036; [2017] 1 W.L.R. 1360; [2017] C.P. Rep. 6; [2016] 2 C.L.C. 532, CA (Civ Div) .... *Digested,* 17/**219**
Kazakhstan Kagazy Plc v Zhunus [2016] EWHC 2363 (Comm); [2017] 1 W.L.R. 467, QBD (Comm) .... *Digested,* 17/**293**
Kazakhstan Kagazy Plc v Zhunus; *sub nom* Kazakhstan Kagazy Plc v Arip [2014] EWCA Civ 381; [2014] 1 C.L.C. 451, CA (Civ Div) .... *Digested,* 15/**301**: *Considered* 17/370
Kazic v Sweden (Admissibility) (41252/16) (2017) 64 E.H.R.R. SE12, ECHR
Kaziu v Secretary of State for the Home Department see R. (on the application of Kaziu) v Secretary of State for the Home Department
Kazmierczak v Poland see Krolik v Poland
KB v MS 2017 S.L.T. (Sh Ct) 160; 2017 Fam. L.R. 66; 2017 G.W.D. 13-204, Sh Ct (Tayside) (Dundee) .... *Digested,* 17/**2612**
KC v MGN Ltd see Cairns v Modi
KD (A Minor) (Ward: Termination of Access), Re [1988] A.C. 806; [1988] 2 W.L.R. 398; [1988] 1 All E.R. 577; [1988] 2 F.L.R. 139; [1988] F.C.R. 657; Times, February 19, 1988; Independent, February 19, 1988; [1988] Fam. Law 288; (1988) 152 J.P.N. 558; (1988) 132 S.J. 301, HL .... *Digested,* 88/**2294**: *Applied* 90/3138, 01/2598, 08/1502: *Considered* 91/2512, 95/3552, 95/4104, 02/1664: *Distinguished* 06/1695: *Followed* 95/3477, 02/1700, 17/1063
KE v SS-E see EE (Children) (Habitual Residence), Re
KE Entertainments Ltd v Revenue and Customs Commissioners [2016] UKFTT 508 (TC); [2016] S.T.I. 2878, FTT (Tax) *Affirmed* 17/2256
Kea Investments Ltd v Novatrust Ltd see Glenn v Watson
Kean v Lucas; *sub nom* J&R Builders (Norwich) Ltd (In Liquidation), Re [2016] EWHC 2684 (Ch); [2017] B.P.I.R. 128, Ch D (Companies Ct) .... *Digested,* 17/**1315**
Kean v Lucas [2017] EWHC 250 (Ch); [2017] B.C.C. 311; [2017] B.P.I.R. 702, Ch D (Companies Ct) .... *Digested,* 17/**1319**
Kearney v UP Global Sourcing (UK) Ltd (Unreported, February 24, 2017), CC (Oldham) [*Elahe Youshani, Barrister, 18-20 St John Street Chambers, Mancheste*] .... *Digested,* 17/**1664**
Keary Developments Ltd v Tarmac Construction Ltd [1995] 3 All E.R. 534; [1995] 2 B.C.L.C. 395; 73 B.L.R. 115, CA (Civ Div) .... *Digested,* 96/**724**: *Applied* 96/692, 96/704, 98/450, 07/416, 07/512, 09/443, 12/395, 12/523, 14/469: *Considered* 95/4009, 04/329, 14/468, 17/383: *Followed* 97/563, 10/412, 13/423
Kee v American International Assurance Co Ltd [2017] SGCA 10; [2017] Lloyd's Rep. I.R. 379, CA (Sing)
Keefe v Isle of Man Steam Packet Co Ltd [2010] EWCA Civ 683, CA (Civ Div) *Considered* 17/1555
Keeling v Keeling; *sub nom* Exler (Deceased), Re [2017] EWHC 1189 (Ch); [2017] 2 P. & C.R. DG18, Ch D
Keenan v Woking BC [2016] EWHC 427 (Admin), QBD (Admin) *Affirmed* 17/1746
Keenan v Woking BC [2017] EWCA Civ 438; Times, September 5, 2017, CA (Civ Div) *Digested,* 17/**1746**
Keith Langmead Ltd v Secretary of State for Communities and Local Government [2017] EWHC 788 (Admin); [2017] J.P.L. 1031, QBD (Admin) .... *Digested,* 17/**1769**
Kell (Scotland) Ltd v City of Glasgow Licensing Board 2010 S.L.T. (Sh Ct) 197; [2011] L.L.R. 59; 2010 G.W.D. 23-444, Sh Ct (Glasgow) .... *Digested,* 11/**4445**: *Applied* 17/2719
Kellar v Williams [2004] UKPC 30; [2005] 4 Costs L.R. 559; (2004) 148 S.J.L.B. 821, PC (TCI) .... *Digested,* 06/**2736**: *Considered* 16/200, 17/213

Kelly v Cooper [1993] A.C. 205; [1992] 3 W.L.R. 936; [1994] 1 B.C.L.C. 395; Times, November 5, 1992; [1992] E.G. 119 (C.S.); (1992) 136 S.J.L.B. 303; [1992] N.P.C. 134, PC (Ber) .... *Digested,* 93/**72**: *Applied* 17/458: *Considered* 12/1054, 13/70: *Distinguished* 00/2132

Kelly v GE Healthcare Ltd [2009] EWHC 181 (Pat); [2009] R.P.C. 12; Times, April 3, 2009; (2009) 32(5) I.P.D. 32035; [2010] Bus. L.R. D28, Ch D (Patents Ct) .... *Digested,* 09/**2311**: *Considered* 17/1379: *Followed* 15/1512

Kelly v Solari 152 E.R. 24; (1841) 9 M. & W. 54, Ex Ct *Applied* 89/900, 17/466: *Considered* 69/524, 83/447, 90/3918, 00/2331

Kelly (t/a Ludbrook Manor Partnership) v Revenue and Customs Commissioners [2017] UKUT 326 (TCC); [2017] B.V.C. 526; [2017] S.T.I. 1857, UT (Tax) .... *Digested,* 17/**2243**

Kelly (t/a Ludbrook Manor Partnership) v Revenue and Customs Commissioners [2015] UKFTT 632 (TC); [2016] S.T.I. 219, FTT (Tax) *Affirmed* 17/2243

Kemeh v Ministry of Defence see Ministry of Defence v Kemeh

Kenman Holdings Ltd v Comhairle Nan Eilean Siar [2015] CSOH 170; 2016 G.W.D. 1-28, OH *Reversed in part* 17/2773

Kenman Holdings Ltd v Comhairle Nan Eilean Siar [2017] CSIH 10; 2017 S.C. 339; 2017 S.L.T. 341; 2017 G.W.D. 6-78, IH (Ex Div) .... *Digested,* 17/**2773**

Kennedy v Charity Commission see Kennedy v Information Commissioner

Kennedy v Glenbelle Ltd 1996 S.C. 95; 1996 S.L.T. 1186; 1996 S.C.L.R. 411, IH (1 Div) .... *Digested,* 96/**7230**: *Applied* 13/3870, 17/2740, 17/2741

Kennedy v Information Commissioner; *sub nom* Kennedy v Charity Commission [2014] UKSC 20; [2015] A.C. 455; [2014] 2 W.L.R. 808; [2014] 2 All E.R. 847; [2014] E.M.L.R. 19; [2014] H.R.L.R. 14; Times, April 2, 2014; (2014) 158(13) S.J.L.B. 37, SC .... *Digested,* 14/**58**: *Considered* 15/1316, 15/418, 17/1787

Kennedy v Smith 2017 S.L.T. (Land Ct) 19; 2016 G.W.D. 30-539, Land Ct .... *Digested,* 17/**2402**

KENNEDY TRUST/Anti-TNK antibodies and methotrexate (T194/15) [2017] E.P.O.R. 4, EPO (Technical Bd App)

Kennemer Golf & Country Club v Inspecteur Belastingdienst Particulieren/Ondernemingen Haarlem (C-174/00) see Kennemer Golf & Country Club v Staatssecretaris van Financien (C-174/00)

Kennemer Golf & Country Club v Staatssecretaris van Financien (C-174/00); *sub nom* Kennemer Golf & Country Club v Inspecteur Belastingdienst Particulieren/Ondernemingen Haarlem (C-174/00) EU:C:2002:200; [2002] Q.B. 1252; [2002] 3 W.L.R. 829; [2002] S.T.C. 502; [2002] E.C.R. I-3293; [2002] 2 C.M.L.R. 12; [2002] All E.R. (EC) 480; [2002] C.E.C. 330; [2002] B.T.C. 5205; [2002] B.V.C. 395; Times, April 11, 2002; [2002] S.T.I. 354, ECJ (5th Chamber) .... *Digested,* 02/**4756**: *Applied* 07/4284, 07/4292, 13/3241, 14/3090, 15/2579, 17/2266: *Considered* 05/4358: *Distinguished* 17/2264: *Followed* 02/4758, 09/4107

Kensington and Chelsea RLBC v GG [2017] UKUT 141 (AAC); [2017] E.L.R. 367, UT (AAC)

Kensington Housing Trust v Oliver (1998) 30 H.L.R. 608; [1997] N.P.C. 119, CA (Civ Div) .... *Digested,* 97/**2721**: *Applied* 17/1008: *Considered* 06/523

Kent v Griffiths (No.3) [2001] Q.B. 36; [2000] 2 W.L.R. 1158; [2000] 2 All E.R. 474; [2000] P.I.Q.R. P57; [2000] Lloyd's Rep. Med. 109; Times, February 10, 2000; Independent, February 9, 2000; (2000) 97(7) L.S.G. 41; (2000) 150 N.L.J. 195; (2000) 144 S.J.L.B. 106, CA (Civ Div) .... *Digested,* 00/**4204**: *Considered* 02/3261, 11/4482, 15/2062: *Distinguished* 17/1565

Kent CC v B (A Child); *sub nom* B (A Child) (Disclosure), Re [2004] EWHC 411 (Fam); [2004] 2 F.L.R. 142; [2004] 3 F.C.R. 1; [2004] Lloyd's Rep. Med. 303; [2004] Fam. Law 493; (2004) 154 N.L.J. 498, Fam Div .... *Digested,* 04/**1459**: *Applied* 06/445, 07/1711, 07/1732, 08/1444: *Considered* 10/1299, 14/1436, 17/991

Kenyon v Gibson; *sub nom* Kenyon (Ria) v Procurator Fiscal, Hamilton [2016] HCJAC 116; 2017 S.C.L. 162; 2016 G.W.D. 38-673, HCJ .... *Digested,* 17/**2525**

Kenyon (Donald), Re; *sub nom* Donald Kenyon Ltd, Re [1956] 1 W.L.R. 1397; [1956] 3 All E.R. 596, Ch D .... *Digested,* 56/**1193**: *Considered* 69/396, 02/5373: *Distinguished* 69/399: *Doubted* 17/398

Kenyon (Ria) v Procurator Fiscal, Hamilton see Kenyon v Gibson

Kenyon-Brown v Desmond Banks & Co (Undue Influence) (No.2) see Royal Bank of Scotland Plc v Etridge (No.2)

Keramag Keramische Werke GmbH v European Commission (C-613/13 P) see European Commission v Keramag Keramische Werke GmbH (C-613/13 P)
Kerr v Secretary of State for the Home Department [2014] UKUT 493 (IAC), UT (IAC) *Approved* 17/1231
Kerry Ingredients (UK) Ltd v Bakkavor Group Ltd [2016] EWHC 2448 (Ch); [2017] 2 B.C.L.C. 74, Ch D (Bristol) ..... *Digested,* 17/**2197**
Kersfield Developments (Bridge Road) Ltd v Bray & Slaughter Ltd; *joined case* Bray & Slaughter Ltd v Kersfield Developments (Bridge Road) Ltd [2017] EWHC 15 (TCC); 170 Con. L.R. 40; [2017] C.I.L.L. 3929, QBD (TCC) ..... *Digested,* 17/**471**
Key v Key see Key (Deceased), Re
Key (Deceased), Re; *sub nom* Key v Key [2010] EWHC 408 (Ch); [2010] 1 W.L.R. 2020; [2010] M.H.L.R. 308; [2010] W.T.L.R. 623, Ch D ..... *Digested,* 10/**3214**: *Applied* 13/2982, 13/2984, 13/2986, 17/2078: *Considered* 15/2420, 16/2039
KH v Secretary of State for the Home Department see H (Article 9: Freedom of Religion), Re
Khachab v Subdelegacion del Gobierno en Alava (C-558/14) EU:C:2016:285; [2016] 3 C.M.L.R. 29; [2017] C.E.C. 87, ECJ (4th Chamber)
Khamtokhu v Russia (60367/08); *joined case* Aksenchik v Russia (961/11) (2017) 65 E.H.R.R. 6; 43 B.H.R.C. 79, ECHR (Grand Chamber)
Khan v Ali see Burridge v Stafford
Khan v General Pharmaceutical Council; *sub nom* K v General Pharmaceutical Council [2014] CSIH 61; 2014 G.W.D. 24-454, IH (Ex Div) *Reversed* 17/1807
Khan v General Pharmaceutical Council; *sub nom* K v General Pharmaceutical Council [2016] UKSC 64; [2017] 1 W.L.R. 169; [2017] 3 All E.R. 873; [2017] I.C.R. 223; [2017] Med. L.R. 49; (2017) 153 B.M.L.R. 1, SC ..... *Digested,* 17/**1807**
Khan v Inland Revenue Commissioners see Toshoku Finance UK Plc (In Liquidation), Re
Khan v McGee see Qader v Esure Services Ltd
Khan v Secretary of State for the Home Department see R. (on the application of Khan) v Secretary of State for the Home Department
Khan-Ghauri v Dunbar Bank Plc [2001] B.P.I.R. 618, Ch D ..... *Digested,* 01/**3739**: *Applied* 17/1296
Khangura (Setting of Minimum Term), Re see Jones (Setting of Minimum Term), Re
Kharlamov v Russia (27447/07) (2017) 65 E.H.R.R. 33; 40 B.H.R.C. 422, ECHR
Khouj v Acropolis Capital Partners Ltd [2016] EWHC 2120 (Comm); [2017] W.T.L.R. 83, QBD (Comm) ..... *Digested,* 17/**2067**
Khrapunov v JSC BTA Bank see JSC BTA Bank v Ablyazov
Khuja v Times Newspapers Ltd; *sub nom* M v Times Newspapers Ltd; PNM v Times Newspapers Ltd [2017] UKSC 49; [2017] 3 W.L.R. 351; [2018] 1 Cr. App. R. 1; [2017] E.M.L.R. 29; [2017] Crim. L.R. 998, SC ..... *Digested,* 17/**332**
Khuja v Times Newspapers Ltd see PNM v Times Newspapers Ltd
Kiam v MGN Ltd (Costs) [2002] EWCA Civ 66; [2002] 1 W.L.R. 2810; [2002] 2 All E.R. 242; [2002] C.P. Rep. 30; [2002] E.M.L.R. 26; Independent, March 25, 2002, CA (Civ Div) ..... *Digested,* 02/**347**: *Applied* 03/342, 05/2728, 06/381, 06/382, 10/1117, 10/399, 11/285, 13/309, 17/263: *Considered* 06/513, 11/288, 17/268
Kiani v Secretary of State for the Home Department; *sub nom* R. (on the application of Kiani) v Secretary of State for the Home Department [2015] EWCA Civ 776; [2016] Q.B. 595; [2016] 2 W.L.R. 788; [2016] 4 All E.R. 317; [2015] C.P. Rep. 43; [2016] 1 C.M.L.R. 15; [2015] I.C.R. 1179; [2015] I.R.L.R. 837; [2015] H.R.L.R. 18; Times, August 19, 2015, CA (Civ Div) ..... *Digested,* 15/**873**: *Followed* 17/1250
Kiko Srl v Wjcon Srl [2017] E.C.D.R. 4, Trib (Milano)
Kilker Projects Ltd v Purton (t/a Richwood Interiors) [2016] EWHC 2616 (TCC); [2017] Bus. L.R. 418; [2016] C.I.L.L. 3903, QBD (TCC) ..... *Digested,* 17/**454**
Kilraine v Wandsworth LBC [2016] I.R.L.R. 422, EAT ..... *Digested,* 16/**702**: *Applied* 17/815
Kimathi v Foreign and Commonwealth Office [2016] EWHC 3004 (QB); [2017] 1 W.L.R. 1067, QBD ..... *Digested,* 17/**385**
Kimathi v Foreign and Commonwealth Office [2016] EWHC 3005 (QB); [2017] 1 W.L.R. 1081, QBD ..... *Digested,* 17/**306**
Kimathi v Foreign and Commonwealth Office [2015] EWHC 3432 (QB), QBD *Applied* 17/352
King v Dorset CC [1997] 1 E.G.L.R. 245; [1998] R.V.R. 35, Lands Tr ..... *Digested,* 97/**4134**: *Applied* 11/2658, 17/1839

King v Udlaw Ltd [2008] L. & T.R. 28; [2008] 2 E.G.L.R. 99; [2008] 20 E.G. 138, Lands Tr .... *Digested,* 09/**2520**: *Not followed* 17/1441

King (A Child), Re; *sub nom* Portsmouth City Council v King [2014] EWHC 2964 (Fam); [2014] 2 F.L.R. 855; [2014] Fam. Law 1400, Fam Div .... *Digested,* 14/**1420**: *Explained* 17/967

King's Lynn and West Norfolk BC v Bunning [2016] EWCA Civ 1037; [2017] C.P. Rep. 7; [2016] 6 Costs L.O. 927; [2017] H.L.R. 9, CA (Civ Div) .... *Digested,* 17/**225**

King's Lynn and West Norfolk BC v Revenue and Customs Commissioners [2012] UKFTT 671 (TC); [2012] S.T.I. 3181, FTT (Tax) *Overruled* 17/2262

Kingfisher Plc v Customs and Excise Commissioners [2000] S.T.C. 992; [2000] B.T.C. 5420; [2001] B.V.C. 49; [2000] S.T.I. 1610, Ch D .... *Digested,* 01/**5614**: *Applied* 15/2621: *Considered* 11/3572, 17/2283: *Distinguished* 01/5598

Kings Court Trust Ltd v Lancashire Cleaning Services Ltd [2017] EWHC 1094 (Ch); [2017] Bus. L.R. 1255, Ch D (Manchester) .... *Digested,* 17/**401**

Kingsbridge Pension Fund Trust v Downs [2017] UKUT 237 (LC); [2017] L. & T.R. 31; [2017] 2 P. & C.R. DG19, UT (Lands) .... *Digested,* 17/**1430**

Kingston Maurward College v Revenue and Customs Commissioners [2017] UKFTT 502 (TC); [2017] S.T.I. 1666, FTT (Tax)

Kingston Miller & Co Ltd v Thomas Kingston & Co Ltd [1912] 1 Ch. 575, Ch D *Followed* 17/1394

Kinloch v Coral Racing Ltd [2017] CSOH 43; 2017 S.L.T. 856; [2017] L.L.R. 513; 2017 G.W.D. 10-136, OH .... *Digested,* 17/**2469**

Kirk v Devon CC see MM (A Patient), Re

Kirk (Carol) v Procurator Fiscal, Stirling [2017] HCJAC 66; 2017 S.C.L. 982; 2017 G.W.D. 30-475, HCJ .... *Digested,* 17/**2508**

Kirklees MBC v Radecki see Radecki v Kirklees MBC

Kirkness (Inspector of Taxes) v John Hudson & Co Ltd; *sub nom* John Hudson & Co Ltd v Kirkness (Inspector of Taxes) [1955] A.C. 696; [1955] 2 W.L.R. 1135; [1955] 2 All E.R. 345; 48 R. & I.T. 352; 36 T.C. 28; (1955) 34 A.T.C. 142; [1955] T.R. 145; (1955) 99 S.J. 368, HL .... *Digested,* 55/**1257**: *Considered* 57/280, 59/1549, 62/2916, 95/525, 99/4669, 15/2482, 17/2673

Kiss Cards Ltd, Re; *sub nom* Smith v Lawson [2016] EWHC 2176 (Ch); [2017] B.C.C. 489; [2016] B.P.I.R. 1450, Ch D (Birmingham) .... *Digested,* 17/**1317**

Kitcatt v MMS UK Holdings Ltd [2017] EWHC 786 (Comm); [2017] 2 B.C.L.C. 352, QBD (Comm) .... *Digested,* 17/**312**

Kitcatt v MMS UK Holdings Ltd [2017] EWHC 675 (Comm); [2017] 2 B.C.L.C. 352, QBD (Comm) .... *Digested,* 17/**491**

Kittel v Belgium (C-439/04); *joined case* Belgium v Recolta Recycling SPRL (C-440/04) EU:C:2006:446; [2008] S.T.C. 1537; [2006] E.C.R. I-6161; [2008] B.T.C. 5439; [2008] B.V.C. 559; [2006] S.T.I. 1851, ECJ (3rd Chamber) .... *Digested,* 08/**4052**: *Applied* 07/4317, 07/4318, 09/4061, 09/4063, 09/4064, 09/4078, 10/3495, 11/3533, 11/3556, 12/3402, 12/3405, 14/3066, 14/3070, 15/2589, 15/2590, 16/2169, 16/2180: *Considered* 07/4312, 09/4077, 09/4126, 09/4131, 10/3497, 12/3404, 14/3810, 15/2592, 17/2252, 17/2277: *Followed* 10/3502, 12/3401, 14/3065, 14/3067, 14/3069, 14/3071, 14/3092, 15/2609: *Referred to* 09/4079

KJ v Poland (30813/14) [2017] 1 F.L.R. 1006; [2016] 2 F.C.R. 539; [2016] Fam. Law 554, ECHR

KJ (Angola) v Secretary of State for the Home Department see NA (Pakistan) v Secretary of State for the Home Department

KK v DPP [2016] EWHC 1976 (Admin); [2016] 4 W.L.R. 162; [2016] Crim. L.R. 868, DC .... *Digested,* 17/**629**

KK (DRC) v Secretary of State for the Home Department see GS (India) v Secretary of State for the Home Department

KL v Sunday Newspapers Ltd [2015] NIQB 88; [2017] N.I. 229, QBD (NI)

KL (Algeria) v Secretary of State for the Home Department; *sub nom* L (Algeria) v Secretary of State for the Home Department [2016] CSIH 14; 2016 S.C. 543; 2016 G.W.D. 9-176, IH (1 Div) .... *Digested,* 17/**2669**

Kleinwort Benson Ltd v Glasgow City Council (No.2) [1999] 1 A.C. 153; [1997] 3 W.L.R. 923; [1997] 4 All E.R. 641; [1998] Lloyd's Rep. Bank. 10; [1997] C.L.C. 1609; [1998] I.L.Pr. 350; (1997) 9 Admin. L.R. 721; Times, October 31, 1997; (1997) 94(44) L.S.G. 36; (1997) 147 N.L.J. 1617; (1997) 141 S.J.L.B. 237, HL .. *Digested,* 97/**904**: *Applied* 07/659, 08/559: *Considered* 99/427, 00/739, 00/767: *Distinguished* 06/5161: *Followed* 98/747, 17/429

Kleinwort Benson Ltd v Glasgow City Council (No.3) 2002 S.L.T. 1190; 2002 S.C.L.R. 714; 2002 G.W.D. 16-544, OH .... *Digested,* 02/**5344**: *Applied* 17/2448

KMI v SMO 2017 Fam. L.R. 73; 2017 G.W.D. 13-196, Sh Ct (South Strathclyde) (Hamilton) .... *Digested,* 17/**2608**

KMO (section 117: Unduly Harsh: Nigeria), Re; *sub nom* Secretary of State for the Home Department v O; MM (Uganda) v Secretary of State for the Home Department; KO (Nigeria) v Secretary of State for the Home Department [2016] EWCA Civ 617; [2016] Imm. A.R. 954; [2017] I.N.L.R. 15, CA (Civ Div) .... *Digested,* 16/**1090**: *Applied* 17/1242: *Considered* 17/1190

Knapper v Francis [2017] UKUT 3 (LC); [2017] L. & T.R. 20; [2017] 1 P. & C.R. DG20, UT (Lands) .... *Digested,* 17/**1471**

Knight Frank LLP v Du Haney [2011] EWCA Civ 404; [2011] 16 E.G. 78 (C.S.); (2011) 108(17) L.S.G. 15; [2011] N.P.C. 40, CA (Civ Div) *Considered* 17/44

Knights v Parole Board for England and Wales; *sub nom* Knights v Secretary of State for Justice; R. (on the application of Knights) v Secretary of State for Justice [2015] EWHC 136 (Admin); [2015] A.C.D. 68, QBD (Admin) *Affirmed* 17/1588

Knights v Parole Board for England and Wales; *sub nom* Knights v Secretary of State for Justice; R. (on the application of Knights) v Secretary of State for Justice [2017] EWCA Civ 1053; [2017] 4 W.L.R. 134, CA (Civ Div) .... *Digested,* 17/**1588**

Knights v Secretary of State for Justice see Knights v Parole Board for England and Wales

Knights v Seymour Pierce Ellis Ltd (formerly Ellis & Partners Ltd); *sub nom* Taylor Sinclair (Capital) Ltd (In Liquidation), Re [2001] 2 B.C.L.C. 176; [2002] B.P.I.R. 203, Ch D (Companies Ct) .... *Digested,* 02/**2690**: *Applied* 13/1707: *Considered* 17/1317: *Distinguished* 10/1898

KO (Nigeria) v Secretary of State for the Home Department see KMO (section 117: Unduly Harsh: Nigeria), Re

Kodros Shipping Corp of Monrovia v Empresa Cubana de Fletes (The Evia) [1983] 1 A.C. 736; [1982] 3 W.L.R. 637; [1982] 3 All E.R. 350; [1982] 2 Lloyd's Rep. 307; [1982] Com. L.R. 199; (1982) 126 S.J. 656, HL .... *Digested,* 82/**2898**: *Applied* 92/3939, 93/3595: *Approved* 17/2017: *Considered* 07/815: *Distinguished* 93/3596: *Followed* 84/3218, 15/2325

Koksal (t/a Arcis Management Consultancy) v Financial Conduct Authority [2016] UKUT 192 (TCC); [2017] B.P.I.R. 1517, UT (Tax)

Koksal (t/a Arcis Management Consultancy) v Financial Conduct Authority [2016] UKUT 478 (TCC); [2016] C.T.L.C. 201, UT (Tax) .... *Digested,* 17/**1079**

Kolassa v Barclays Bank Plc (C-375/13) EU:C:2015:37; [2016] 1 All E.R. (Comm) 733; [2015] C.E.C. 753; [2015] I.L.Pr. 14, ECJ (4th Chamber) *Followed* 17/430

Komarek v Ramco Energy Plc HQ01X01631, QBD *Applied* 17/648

Komu v Komu (C-605/14) EU:C:2015:833; [2016] 4 W.L.R. 26; [2016] C.E.C. 1065; [2016] I.L.Pr. 8, ECJ (7th Chamber) *Applied* 17/1849

Konczak v BAE Systems (Operations) Ltd see BAE Systems (Operations) Ltd v Konczak

Konica Minolta Business Solutions (UK) Ltd v Applegate [2013] EWHC 2536 (Ch), Ch D *Followed* 17/1626

Konigsberg (A Bankrupt), Re [1989] 1 W.L.R. 1257; [1989] 3 All E.R. 289; [1990] Fam. Law 94; (1989) 86(40) L.S.G. 44; (1989) 139 N.L.J. 1302; (1989) 133 S.J. 1337, Ch D .... *Digested,* 90/**3666**: *Doubted* 17/1286

Koninklijke Philips Electronics NV v European Commission (C-622/15 P) see LG Electronics Inc v European Commission (C-588/15 P)

Koninklijke Philips Electronics NV v Remington Consumer Products Ltd (C-299/99); *sub nom* Philips Electronics NV v Remington Consumer Products Ltd (C-299/99) EU:C:2002:377; [2003] Ch. 159; [2003] 2 W.L.R. 294; [2002] E.C.R. I-5475; [2002] 2 C.M.L.R. 52; [2002] All E.R. (EC) 634; [2002] C.E.C. 525; [2002] E.T.M.R. 81; [2003] R.P.C. 2; Times, June 20, 2002; (2002) 25(9) I.P.D. 25060; Daily Telegraph, June 27, 2002, ECJ .... *Digested,* 02/**2903**: *Applied* 03/2632, 05/2438, 07/1580, 07/2637, 08/2402, 09/2437: *Considered* 03/2613, 03/2631, 05/2533, 06/2598, 14/1932: *Followed* 05/2548, 06/2610, 09/2411, 17/1389

Koninklijke Philips NV v European Commission (T-762/14) EU:T:2016:738; [2017] 4 C.M.L.R. 15, GC (5th Chamber)

Konstatinov v Netherlands (16351/03) [2007] 2 F.C.R. 194, ECHR .... *Digested,* 07/**2259**: *Applied* 17/1207

Kookmin Bank v Rainy Sky SA see Rainy Sky SA v Kookmin Bank
Kopecky v Slovakia (44912/98) (2005) 41 E.H.R.R. 43, ECHR (Grand Chamber) .... *Digested,* 06/**2120**: *Applied* 08/1952, 11/2338, 15/2512, 17/40: *Considered* 06/2395
Korcala v Poland [2017] EWHC 167 (Admin); [2017] 1 W.L.R. 1543; [2017] 4 All E.R. 882; [2017] A.C.D. 40, DC
Korneykova v Ukraine (56660/12) (2017) 64 E.H.R.R. 24, ECHR
Kornhaas v Dithmar (C-594/14) EU:C:2015:806; [2016] B.C.C. 116; [2017] C.E.C. 137; [2016] I.L.Pr. 25, ECJ (6th Chamber)
Kortas v Poland; *sub nom* Kortas v Regional Court in Bydgoszcz; Cortas v Poland [2017] EWHC 1356 (Admin); [2017] A.C.D. 88, DC
Kortas v Regional Court in Bydgoszcz see Kortas v Poland
Kossowski v Generalstaatsanwaltschaft Hamburg (C-486/14) see Criminal Proceedings against Kossowski (C-486/14)
Kostanjevec v F&S Leasing GmbH (C-185/15) EU:C:2016:763; [2017] 4 W.L.R. 7; [2016] I.L.Pr. 38, ECJ (3rd Chamber)
Kotnik v Drzavni zbor Republike Slovenije (C-526/14) EU:C:2016:570; [2017] 1 C.M.L.R. 26, ECJ (Grand Chamber)
Applied 17/153
Kotonou v National Westminster Bank Plc [2015] EWCA Civ 1106; [2017] 1 All E.R. (Comm) 350, CA (Civ Div) .... *Digested,* 17/**190**
Kotonou v National Westminster Bank Plc [2010] EWHC 1659 (Ch); [2011] 1 All E.R. (Comm) 1164, Ch D .... *Digested,* 11/**243**: *Affirmed* 17/190
KP v HM Advocate see P v HM Advocate
KP (A Child) (Abduction: Child's Objections), Re see A (Abduction: Child's Objections to Return), Re
KP (A Child) (Abduction: Judge Meeting Child: Conduct of Interview), Re see A (Abduction: Child's Objections to Return), Re
KP (A Child) (Abduction: Rights of Custody), Re see A (Abduction: Child's Objections to Return), Re
KP TWELVE/Certifying transmission of electronic documents (T540/13) [2017] E.P.O.R. 22, EPO (Technical Bd App)
KR v Bryn Alyn Community (Holdings) Ltd (In Liquidation); *sub nom* Various Claimants v Bryn Alyn Community (Holdings) Ltd (In Liquidation); Various Claimants v BACHL [2003] EWCA Civ 85; [2003] Q.B. 1441; [2003] 3 W.L.R. 107; [2004] 2 All E.R. 716; [2003] 1 F.L.R. 1203; [2003] 1 F.C.R. 385; [2003] Lloyd's Rep. Med. 175; Times, February 17, 2003; [2003] Fam. Law 482, CA (Civ Div) .... *Digested,* 03/**432**: *Applied* 05/2859, 08/2644: *Considered* 07/5096, 08/385, 09/425, 10/379, 11/353: *Doubted* 07/473, 07/483: *Followed* 06/476, 17/2191: *Not followed* 13/393
KR v Stirling Council see R v Stirling Council
Kratzer v R+V Allgemeine Versicherung AG (C-423/15) EU:C:2016:604; [2017] 1 C.M.L.R. 27; [2016] I.C.R. 967; [2016] I.R.L.R. 888; Times, October 12, 2016, ECJ (1st Chamber)
Krejzova v Czech Republic (28473/12) see Dubska v Czech Republic (28859/11)
Kretztechnik AG v Finanzamt Linz (C-465/03) EU:C:2005:320; [2005] 1 W.L.R. 3755; [2005] S.T.C. 1118; [2005] E.C.R. I-4357; [2005] 2 C.M.L.R. 46; [2005] B.T.C. 5823; [2006] B.V.C. 66; Times, June 21, 2005; [2005] S.T.I. 1020, ECJ (1st Chamber) .... *Digested,* 05/**4363**: *Applied* 08/4021, 15/2593: *Considered* 05/4371, 06/4471, 07/4314, 16/2176: *Followed* 10/3498, 16/2181, 17/2241: *Referred to* 15/2582
Krijgsman v Surinaamse Luchtvaart Maatschappij NV (C-302/16) EU:C:2017:359; [2017] Bus. L.R. 1194; [2017] 3 C.M.L.R. 41; [2018] C.E.C. 96, ECJ (8th Chamber)
Krolik v Poland; *joined cases* Walachowski v Poland; Soltan v Poland; Lachowski v Poland; Zwolinski v Poland; Kazmierczak v Poland [2012] EWHC 2357 (Admin); [2013] 1 W.L.R. 490; (2012) 162 N.L.J. 1125, DC .... *Digested,* 13/**1181**: *Applied* 17/904
Kroll v Commissioner of Police of the Metropolis see R. (on the application of P) v Secretary of State for the Home Department
Kronhofer v Maier (C168/02) EU:C:2004:364; [2004] 2 All E.R. (Comm) 759; [2005] 1 Lloyd's Rep. 284; [2004] E.C.R. I-6009; [2004] All E.R. (EC) 939; [2004] I.L.Pr. 27, ECJ (2nd Chamber) .... *Digested,* 05/**603**: *Applied* 14/556: *Considered* 17/2022
Kubicka (C-218/16) see Proceedings Brought by Kubicka (C-218/16)
Kukanauza (Ruslanas) v HM Advocate [2017] HCJAC 26; 2017 S.C.L. 629; 2017 S.C.C.R. 290; 2017 G.W.D. 16-258, HCJ Appeal .... *Digested,* 17/**2558**

Kulemesin v HKSAR [2013] 2 Lloyd's Rep. 367, CA (HK)
Applied 17/2020

Kulkarni v NHS Education Scotland [2013] Eq. L.R. 34, EAT (SC) .... *Digested,* 13/**3682**:
Applied 17/784

Kunicki v Hayward [2016] EWHC 3199 (Ch); [2017] 4 W.L.R. 32, Ch D .... *Digested,* 17/**2077**

Kupeli v Atlasjet Havacilik Anonim Sirketi see Kupeli v Cyprus Turkish Airlines

Kupeli v Cyprus Turkish Airlines; *sub nom* Kupeli v Atlasjet Havacilik Anonim Sirketi [2017] EWCA Civ 1037; [2017] 4 Costs L.O. 517; [2017] C.T.L.C. 145, CA (Civ Div) .... *Digested,* 17/**479**

Kuppinger v Germany (62198/11) (2017) 65 E.H.R.R. 13, ECHR

Kurt v Turkey (24276/94) (1999) 27 E.H.R.R. 373; 5 B.H.R.C. 1; [1998] H.R.C.D. 576, ECHR .... *Digested,* 99/**3115**:
Applied 99/3117, 17/83: *Considered* 06/2125: *Distinguished* 01/3569

Kuwait Airways Corp v Iraq Airways Co (No.6) see Kuwait Airways Corp v Iraqi Airways Co (No.6)

Kuwait Airways Corp v Iraqi Airways Co (No.5) see Kuwait Airways Corp v Iraqi Airways Co (No.6)

Kuwait Airways Corp v Iraqi Airways Co (No.6); *sub nom* Kuwait Airways Corp v Iraq Airways Co (No.6); *joined case* Kuwait Airways Corp v Iraqi Airways Co (No.5) [2002] UKHL 19; [2002] 2 A.C. 883; [2002] 2 W.L.R. 1353; [2002] 3 All E.R. 209; [2002] 1 All E.R. (Comm) 843; [2003] 1 C.L.C. 183; Times, May 21, 2002, HL .... *Digested,* 02/**4540**:
Applied 04/1277, 09/3578, 09/615, 10/2392, 15/1566: *Considered* 04/2249, 04/734, 05/212, 06/2451, 10/2016, 10/3414, 11/1071, 12/120, 12/1290, 14/825: *Followed* 04/427, 10/3409, 15/1710, 15/2533, 16/1963, 17/2196

Kuwait Petroleum (GB) Ltd v Customs and Excise Commissioners (C-48/97) EU:C:1999:203; [1999] S.T.C. 488; [1999] E.C.R. I-2323; [1999] 2 C.M.L.R. 651; [1999] All E.R. (EC) 450; [1999] C.E.C. 201; [1999] B.T.C. 5203; [1999] B.V.C. 250; Times, May 14, 1999, ECJ .... *Digested,* 99/**4967**:
Applied 08/4025, 08/4028: *Considered* 04/3981, 07/4290: *Distinguished* 07/4323, 17/2258

Kuwait Petroleum (GB) Ltd v Customs and Excise Commissioners see Lex Services Plc v Customs and Excise Commissioners

Kuwait Rocks Co v AMN Bulkcarriers Inc [2013] EWHC 865 (Comm); [2013] 2 All E.R. (Comm) 689; [2013] 2 Lloyd's Rep. 69; [2013] 1 C.L.C. 819, QBD (Comm) .... *Digested,* 13/**2839**:
Not applied 15/2334: *Overruled in part* 17/2023

Kuzel v Roche Products Ltd [2008] EWCA Civ 380; [2008] I.C.R. 799; [2008] I.R.L.R. 530; (2008) 152(17) S.J.L.B. 30, CA (Civ Div) .... *Digested,* 08/**1217**:
Applied 17/763: *Considered* 11/1128, 16/704

Kuznetsov v Royal Bank of Scotland [2017] EWCA Civ 43; [2017] C.P. Rep. 18; [2017] I.R.L.R. 350, CA (Civ Div) .... *Digested,* 17/**786**

Kuznetsov v Royal Bank of Scotland UKEAT/0089/15/BA, EAT
Affirmed 17/786

KV v Secretary of State for the Home Department [2014] UKUT 230 (IAC), UT (IAC)
Reversed 17/1178

KV (Sri Lanka) v Secretary of State for the Home Department [2017] EWCA Civ 119; [2017] 4 W.L.R. 88; [2017] Imm. A.R. 1009, CA (Civ Div) .... *Digested,* 17/**1178**

Kyaw v Claassen [2015] EWHC 3337 (Ch), Ch D
Applied 17/1847

Kyokuyo Co Ltd v AP Moller-Maersk A/S (t/a Maersk Line) [2017] EWHC 654 (Comm); [2017] 2 All E.R. (Comm) 922; [2017] Bus. L.R. 1270; [2017] 1 Lloyd's Rep. 580; [2017] 1 C.L.C. 253, QBD (Comm) .... *Digested,* 17/**2015**

Kyrian v Celni urad Tabor (C-233/08) EU:C:2010:11, ECJ
Applied 17/1284

L v Birmingham City Council; *sub nom* R. (on the application of Johnson) v Havering LBC; Johnson v Havering LBC; *joined case* YL v Birmingham City Council [2007] UKHL 27; [2008] 1 A.C. 95; [2007] 3 W.L.R. 112; [2007] 3 All E.R. 957; [2007] H.R.L.R. 32; [2008] U.K.H.R.R. 346; [2007] H.L.R. 44; [2008] B.L.G.R. 273; (2007) 10 C.C.L. Rep. 505; [2007] LS Law Medical 472; (2007) 96 B.M.L.R. 1; Times, June 21, 2007; (2007) 104(27) L.S.G. 29; (2007) 157 N.L.J. 938; (2007) 151 S.J.L.B. 860; [2007] N.P.C. 75, HL .... *Digested,* 07/**3912**:
Applied 17/1077: *Considered* 08/2483, 12/3158: *Followed* 09/2549

L v Board of State Hospital [2011] CSOH 21; 2011 S.L.T. 233; (2011) 121 B.M.L.R. 1; [2011] M.H.L.R. 290; 2011 G.W.D. 4-120, OH .... *Digested,* 11/**4479**:
Applied 17/1118: *Considered* 14/3573

L v DPP; *joined case* Pratt v Crown Prosecution Service (Northumbria) [2013] EWHC 1752 (Admin); (2013) 177 J.P. 502; [2013] A.C.D. 108, QBD (Admin) .... *Digested,* 13/**723**: *Applied* 17/571: *Considered* 17/38

L v HM Advocate; *sub nom* JL v HM Advocate [2016] HCJAC 61; 2016 S.C.L. 715; 2016 S.C.C.R. 365; 2016 G.W.D. 22-393, HCJ .... *Digested,* 16/**2498**: *Applied* 17/2552: *Cited* 16/2496

L v HM Advocate [2016] HCJAC 120; 2017 S.C.L. 166; 2016 G.W.D. 38-676, HCJ ...... *Digested,* 17/**2485**

L v L [2006] EWHC 956 (Fam); [2008] 1 F.L.R. 26; [2008] Fam. Law 306, Fam Div ...... *Digested,* 08/**1420**: *Applied* 17/1008, 17/1016: *Considered* 15/1094

L v L (Anticipatory Child Arrangements Order) see L v L (Child: Arrangements following Treatment)

L v L (Child: Arrangements following Treatment); *sub nom* L v L (Anticipatory Child Arrangements Order) [2017] EWHC 1212 (Fam); [2018] 1 F.L.R. 108; [2017] 2 F.C.R. 659, Fam Div

L v L (Financial Provision: Contributions) see Lambert v Lambert

L v L see TL (Human Rights: Relevant Person's Representative), Re

L v United Kingdom (45508/99) see HL v United Kingdom (45508/99)

L (A Child) (Procedure: Bundles: Translation), Re [2015] EWFC 15; [2015] 1 F.L.R. 1417; [2015] Fam. Law 378, Fam Ct .... *Digested,* 15/**1081**: *Followed* 17/998

L (A Child), Re; *sub nom* Oddin, Re; Uddin, Re [2016] EWCA Civ 173; [2017] 1 F.L.R. 1135; [2016] Fam. Law 668, CA (Civ Div) *Followed* 17/1065

L (A Child: Jurisdiction: Contact), Re [2016] EWCA Civ 1297; [2017] 2 F.L.R. 361; [2017] 1 F.C.R. 578, CA (Civ Div) .... *Digested,* 17/**942**

L (Algeria) v Secretary of State for the Home Department see KL (Algeria) v Secretary of State for the Home Department

L (Care Proceedings: Human Rights Claims), Re [2003] EWHC 665 (Fam); [2003] 2 F.L.R. 160; [2004] 1 F.C.R. 289; [2003] Fam. Law 466, Fam Div .... *Digested,* 03/**1519**: *Applied* 04/1460, 14/2182, 17/975: *Approved* 04/1461: *Considered* 08/1438

L (Children) (Care Proceedings: Judge's Reasons), Re [2017] EWCA Civ 1137; [2017] 4 W.L.R. 141, CA (Civ Div) .... *Digested,* 17/**922**

L (Children) (Interim Care Order), Re [2016] EWCA Civ 1110; [2017] 2 F.L.R. 547, CA (Civ Div)

L (Children) (Preliminary Finding: Power to Reverse), Re see L-B (Children) (Care Proceedings: Power to Revise Judgment), Re

L (Children) (Specific Issues: Temporary Leave to Remove from the Jurisdiction: Circumcision), Re [2016] EWHC 849 (Fam); [2017] 1 F.L.R. 1316; [2016] Fam. Law 690, Fam Div

L (Children), Re see Z (Foreign Surrogacy: Allocation of Work: Guidance on Parental Order Reports), Re

L'Office Cherifien des Phosphates Unitramp SA v Yamashita-Shinnihon Steamship Co Ltd (The Boucraa) [1994] 1 A.C. 486; [1994] 2 W.L.R. 39; [1994] 1 All E.R. 20; [1994] 1 Lloyd's Rep. 251; Times, December 20, 1993; Independent, January 19, 1994; (1994) 138 S.J.L.B. 19, HL .... *Digested,* 94/**221**: *Applied* 95/2038, 96/3566, 13/1619: *Considered* 97/1075, 97/82, 09/2137, 14/3344: *Followed* 99/5471, 00/105, 17/1104

L'Oreal SA v eBay International AG (C-324/09) EU:C:2011:474; [2012] Bus. L.R. 1369; [2012] All E.R. (EC) 501; [2011] E.T.M.R. 52; [2012] E.M.L.R. 6; [2011] R.P.C. 27; Times, July 19, 2011, ECJ (Grand Chamber) *Applied* 12/1922, 13/1772, 13/1829, 17/1398: *Considered* 16/1325: *Followed* 14/1927

L, Petitioners (No.3) 1996 S.L.T. 928, IH (1 Div) .... *Digested,* 96/**7129**: *Considered* 02/5935, 17/2426: *Followed* 01/6758

L-B (Children) (Care Proceedings: Power to Revise Judgment), Re; *sub nom* L-B (Children) (Reversal of Judgment), Re; L (Children) (Preliminary Finding: Power to Reverse), Re [2013] UKSC 8; [2013] 1 W.L.R. 634; [2013] 2 All E.R. 294; [2013] 2 F.L.R. 859; [2013] 2 F.C.R. 19; [2013] Fam. Law 664, SC .... *Digested,* 13/**1231**: *Applied* 17/2135: *Considered* 16/1121: *Explained* 14/427: *Followed* 15/1079, 15/1597, 15/315, 15/356

L-B (Children) (Reversal of Judgment), Re see L-B (Children) (Care Proceedings: Power to Revise Judgment), Re

LAB v KB (Abduction: Brussels II Revised) [2009] EWHC 2243 (Fam); [2010] 2 F.L.R. 1664; [2010] Fam. Law 933, Fam Div .... *Digested,* 11/**1359**: *Approved* 13/1284: *Considered* 15/1137, 17/1057

LABORATOIRE DE LA MER Trade Mark (No.1) see Laboratoires Goemar SA's Trade Mark (No.1)

Laboratoires Goemar SA's Trade Mark (No.1); *sub nom* Laboratories Goemar SA's Trade Mark; LABORATOIRE DE LA MER Trade Mark (No.1) [2002] E.T.M.R. 34; [2002] F.S.R. 51, Ch D .... *Digested,* 02/**2924**: *Applied* 05/2575: *Considered* 17/1395
Laboratories Goemar SA's Trade Mark see Laboratoires Goemar SA's Trade Mark (No.1)
Labrouche v Frey see Frey v Labrouche
Lachaux v AOL (UK) Ltd see Lachaux v Independent Print Ltd
Lachaux v Evening Standard Ltd see Lachaux v Independent Print Ltd
Lachaux v Independent Print Ltd; *joined cases* Lachaux v AOL (UK) Ltd; Lachaux v Evening Standard Ltd [2015] EWHC 2242 (QB); [2016] Q.B. 402; [2016] 2 W.L.R. 437; [2016] 4 All E.R. 140; [2015] E.M.L.R. 28, QBD .... *Digested,* 15/**689**: *Considered* 17/646, 17/649
Lachaux v Lachaux [2017] EWHC 385 (Fam); [2017] 4 W.L.R. 57; [2018] 1 F.L.R. 380; [2017] 2 F.C.R. 678, Fam Div .... *Digested,* 17/**984**
Lachowski v Poland see Krolik v Poland
Ladbroke Group Plc v One in a Million Ltd see British Telecommunications Plc v One in a Million Ltd
Laddingford Enclosures Ltd v Forsyth see Ruxley Electronics v Forsyth
Ladele v United Kingdom (51671/10) see Eweida v United Kingdom (48420/10)
Lady & Kid A/S v Skatteministeriet (C-398/09) EU:C:2011:540; [2012] S.T.C. 854; [2012] 1 C.M.L.R. 14; [2012] All E.R. (EC) 410; [2012] C.E.C. 517; [2012] B.V.C. 83, ECJ (Grand Chamber) *Applied* 14/3079, 17/2289: *Followed* 14/2874
Lady Fox's Executors v Inland Revenue Commissioners see Gray v Inland Revenue Commissioners
Lafayette Electronics Europe Ltd, Re [2006] EWHC 1005 (Ch); [2007] B.C.C. 890, Ch D .... *Digested,* 08/**2120**: *Applied* 17/1269
Lagden v O'Connor; *sub nom* Clark v Tull (t/a Ardington Electrical Services); *joined cases* Burdis v Livsey; Sen v Steelform Engineering Co Ltd; Dennard v Plant; Clark v Ardington Electrical Services [2002] EWCA Civ 510; [2003] Q.B. 36; [2002] 3 W.L.R. 762; [2003] R.T.R. 3; [2002] Lloyd's Rep. I.R. 524, CA (Civ Div) .... *Digested,* 02/**690**: *Affirmed* 04/630: *Applied* 08/896, 14/829, 15/681: *Cited* 02/687: *Considered* 17/644: *Followed* 06/1033, 11/858, 12/1902, 12/2812
Lagos v Grunwaldt [1910] 1 K.B. 41, CA *Considered* 13/392, 17/2219
Lahey v Pirelli Tyres Ltd [2007] EWCA Civ 91; [2007] 1 W.L.R. 998; [2007] C.P. Rep. 21; [2007] 3 Costs L.R. 462; [2007] P.I.Q.R. P20; Times, February 19, 2007; (2007) 104(9) L.S.G. 30; (2007) 157 N.L.J. 294, CA (Civ Div) .... *Digested,* 07/**403**: *Applied* 17/238: *Approved* 11/278: *Considered* 10/283, 13/1788
Laidlaw v Richardson see Laidlaw (Robert) v Procurator Fiscal, Livingston
Laidlaw (Robert) v Procurator Fiscal, Livingston; *sub nom* Laidlaw v Richardson [2017] SAC (Crim) 8; 2017 S.C.L. 719; 2017 S.C.C.R. 359; 2017 G.W.D. 21-355, SAC .... *Digested,* 17/**2799**
Laing v Taylor Walton (A Firm); *sub nom* Taylor Walton (A Firm) v Laing [2007] EWCA Civ 1146; [2008] B.L.R. 65; [2008] P.N.L.R. 11; [2007] 47 E.G. 169 (C.S.); (2007) 104(46) L.S.G. 27, CA (Civ Div) .... *Digested,* 08/**272**: *Applied* 14/1842, 17/191: *Followed* 14/2209
Laker Vent Engineering Ltd v Jacobs E&C Ltd; *joined case* Jacobs E&C Ltd v Laker Vent Engineering Ltd [2014] EWHC 1058 (TCC); 154 Con. L.R. 77, QBD (TCC) .... *Digested,* 14/**114**: *Considered* 17/451
Lakhani v Mahmud [2017] EWHC 1713 (Ch); [2017] 1 W.L.R. 3482; [2017] 4 Costs L.O. 453, Ch D .... *Digested,* 17/**278**
Lalana Hans Place Ltd v Michael Barclay Partnership LLP [2017] EWHC 29 (TCC); [2017] T.C.L.R. 3, QBD (TCC) .... *Digested,* 17/**355**
Lam v Inland Revenue Commissioners [2005] EWHC 592 (Ch); [2006] S.T.C. 893; [2009] B.P.I.R. 301; [2005] S.T.I. 652, Ch D .... *Digested,* 06/**2347**: *Applied* 15/2601, 17/1327: *Considered* 09/2222, 11/3579
Lambert v Lambert; *sub nom* L v L (Financial Provision: Contributions) [2002] EWCA Civ 1685; [2003] Fam. 103; [2003] 2 W.L.R. 631; [2003] 4 All E.R. 342; [2003] 1 F.L.R. 139; [2002] 3 F.C.R. 673; Times, November 27, 2002; Independent, November 21, 2002; [2003] Fam. Law 16, CA (Civ Div) .... *Digested,* 02/**1690**: *Applied* 03/1581, 06/1621, 13/1298: *Considered* 04/4216, 06/1633: *Distinguished* 03/1587: *Followed* 17/1031, 17/1032

Lambert v Lewis; *sub nom* Lexmead (Basingstoke) Ltd v Lewis [1982] A.C. 225; [1981] 2 W.L.R. 713; [1981] 1 All E.R. 1185; [1981] 2 Lloyd's Rep. 17; [1981] R.T.R. 346; (1981) 125 S.J. 310, HL .... *Digested,* 81/**1841**: *Applied* 85/2331, 17/2193: *Considered* 14/617: *Referred to* 88/3408

Lambeth LBC v Secretary of State for Communities and Local Government [2017] EWHC 2412 (Admin); [2017] P.T.S.R. 1494; [2018] J.P.L. 329, QBD (Admin)

Lamont v Burton [2007] EWCA Civ 429; [2007] 1 W.L.R. 2814; [2007] 3 All E.R. 173; [2007] C.P. Rep. 33; [2007] 4 Costs L.R. 574; [2008] R.T.R. 4; [2007] P.I.Q.R. Q8; Times, June 7, 2007; (2007) 104(21) L.S.G. 26; (2007) 157 N.L.J. 706; (2007) 151 S.J.L.B. 670, CA (Civ Div) .... *Digested,* 07/**418**: *Applied* 08/335, 17/235

Lamont v Kennedy 2010 S.L.C.R. 76, Land Ct *Considered* 17/2402

Lamont-Perkins v RSPCA [2012] EWHC 1002 (Admin); (2012) 176 J.P. 369; [2012] A.C.D. 64, DC .... *Digested,* 12/**92**: *Applied* 17/617

Lancefield v Lancefield [2002] B.P.I.R. 1108, Ch D .... *Digested,* 03/**2445**: *Applied* 13/1715, 16/1252, 17/1336

Lancer Scott Ltd v Revenue and Customs Commissioners [2012] UKUT 10 (TCC); [2012] S.T.C. 928; [2012] B.T.C. 1549; (2012) 109(28) L.S.G. 21, UT (Tax) .... *Digested,* 12/**3328**: *Applied* 17/794

Land Baden-Wurttemberg v Tsakouridis (C-145/09) EU:C:2010:708; [2011] 2 C.M.L.R. 11; [2013] All E.R. (EC) 183; [2011] C.E.C. 714; [2011] Imm. A.R. 276; [2011] I.N.L.R. 415, ECJ (Grand Chamber) *Considered* 13/1647, 17/1195: *Followed* 12/1708, 13/1595, 14/1675, 14/1676

Landau v Big Bus Co Ltd 1403806, Sen Cts Costs Office *Considered* 17/226

Landelijke Vereniging tot Behoud van de Waddenzee v Staatssecretaris van Landbouw, Natuurbeheer en Visserij (C-127/02) EU:C:2004:482; [2004] E.C.R. I-7405; [2005] 2 C.M.L.R. 31; [2005] All E.R. (EC) 353; [2005] Env. L.R. 14; [2004] N.P.C. 136, ECJ .... *Digested,* 05/**1439**: *Applied* 09/1353, 10/1189, 14/1197, 16/1759: *Considered* 08/2967, 10/1227, 14/1188, 17/1775

Landesanstalt fur Landwirtschaft v Gotz (C-408/06) EU:C:2007:789; [2007] E.C.R. I-11295, ECJ *Followed* 17/2295

Landeskrankenanstalten-Betriebsgesellschaft - KABEG v Mutuelles du Mans assurances - IARD SA (C-340/16) EU:C:2017:576; [2018] C.E.C. 114; [2017] I.L.Pr. 31, ECJ (3rd Chamber)

Lanes Group Plc v Galliford Try Infrastructure Ltd (t/a Galliford Try Rail) [2011] EWCA Civ 1617; [2012] Bus. L.R. 1184; [2012] 1 C.L.C. 129; [2012] B.L.R. 121; 141 Con. L.R. 46; [2012] 1 E.G.L.R. 27; [2012] 13 E.G. 92; [2012] C.I.L.L. 3116, CA (Civ Div) .... *Digested,* 12/**581**: *Considered* 14/577, 16/31, 16/390: *Followed* 17/656

Langley v Bradford MDC see M v Secretary of State for Work and Pensions

Langman v Lake District National Park Authority [2017] P.A.D. 17, Planning Inspector

Langton v Inntrepreneur Pub Co (CPC) Ltd see Inntrepreneur Pub Co (CPC) Ltd v Langton

Languard New Homes Ltd v Revenue and Customs Commissioners; *sub nom* Revenue and Customs Commissioners v Languard New Homes Ltd; *joined case* MacPherson v Revenue and Customs Commissioners [2016] UKFTT 129 (TC); [2016] S.T.I. 1196, FTT (Tax) *Reversed* 17/2296

Languard New Homes Ltd v Revenue and Customs Commissioners; *sub nom* Revenue and Customs Commissioners v Languard New Homes Ltd; *joined case* MacPherson v Revenue and Customs Commissioners [2017] UKUT 307 (TCC); [2017] S.T.C. 1925; [2017] B.V.C. 522; [2017] S.T.I. 1769, UT (Tax) .... *Digested,* 17/**2296**

Lansforsakringar AB v Matek A/S (C-654/15) EU:C:2016:998; [2017] Bus. L.R. 806; [2017] E.T.M.R. 10, ECJ (2nd Chamber)

Lantic Sugar Ltd v Baffin Investments Ltd [2009] EWHC 3325 (Comm); [2010] 2 All E.R. (Comm) 1170; [2010] 2 Lloyd's Rep. 141, QBD (Comm) .... *Digested,* 10/**168**: *Applied* 10/575, 16/60, 17/1514: *Considered* 16/62

Lauchlan v United Kingdom (75702/13) see O'Neill v United Kingdom (41516/10)

Laufen Austria AG v European Commission (C-637/13 P) EU:C:2017:51; [2017] 4 C.M.L.R. 26, ECJ (1st Chamber)

Laughlan v Harrower [2016] SAC (Crim) 30; 2017 S.C. (S.A.C.) 17; 2016 S.L.T. (Sh Ct) 427; 2017 S.C.L. 108; 2016 S.C.C.R. 544; 2016 G.W.D. 32-570, SAC .... *Digested,* 17/**2526**

Lauzikas v Secretary of State for the Home Department see R. (on the application of Lauzikas) v Secretary of State for the Home Department

Laval v Byggnads (C-341/05) see Laval un Partneri Ltd v Svenska Byggnadsarbetareforbundet (C-341/05)

Laval un Partneri Ltd v Svenska Byggnadsarbetareforbundet (C-341/05); *sub nom* Laval v Byggnads (C-341/05) EU:C:2007:809; [2007] E.C.R. I-11767; [2008] 2 C.M.L.R. 9; [2008] All E.R. (EC) 166; [2008] C.E.C. 438; [2008] I.R.L.R. 160, ECJ (Grand Chamber) .... *Digested,* 08/**1352**: *Applied* 17/807

Laverie v Scottish Ministers [2017] CSOH 45; 2017 S.L.T. 640; 2017 G.W.D. 11-145, OH .... *Digested,* 17/**2575**

Law Debenture Trust Corp v Ural Caspian Oil Corp Ltd [1995] Ch. 152; [1994] 3 W.L.R. 1221; [1995] 1 All E.R. 157; [1994] C.L.C. 299; Independent, March 10, 1994, CA (Civ Div) .... *Digested,* 95/**2192**: *Considered* 17/314: *Distinguished* 02/538

Law Debenture Trust Corp Plc v Ukraine [2017] EWHC 655 (Comm); [2017] Q.B. 1249; [2017] 3 W.L.R. 667; [2017] 2 B.C.L.C. 616; [2017] 1 C.L.C. 298, QBD (Comm) .... *Digested,* 17/**157**

Law Society v Kordowski [2011] EWHC 3185 (QB); [2014] E.M.L.R. 2; [2011] Info. T.L.R. 221; (2012) 109(1) L.S.G. 13, QBD *Applied* 17/647

Law Society v Pathania [2017] EWHC 2496 (Ch); [2017] 1 W.L.R. 4813; [2018] 1 P. & C.R. DG8, Ch D

Law Society v Sephton & Co [2006] UKHL 22; [2006] 2 A.C. 543; [2006] 2 W.L.R. 1091; [2006] 3 All E.R. 401; [2006] P.N.L.R. 31; Times, May 11, 2006; (2006) 156 N.L.J. 844; (2006) 150 S.J.L.B. 669; [2006] N.P.C. 56, HL .... *Digested,* 06/**474**: *Applied* 08/384, 13/391: *Considered* 07/2490, 08/382, 09/2735, 14/2523, 14/591: *Distinguished* 08/2651, 10/2284, 17/319: *Explained* 09/426: *Followed* 07/479, 13/2087

Law Society of England and Wales v Schubert Murphy (A Firm) see Schubert Murphy v Law Society

Lawless v Ireland (No.3) (A/3) (1979-80) 1 E.H.R.R. 15, ECHR .... *Digested,* 79/**1172**: *Applied* 17/1803: *Considered* 14/2464

Lawrence v Coventry (t/a RDC Promotions) see Coventry (t/a RDC Promotions) v Lawrence

Lawrence v Fen Tigers Ltd see Coventry (t/a RDC Promotions) v Lawrence

Lawrie (Jeanie) v Muir 1950 J.C. 19; 1950 S.L.T. 37; 1949 S.L.T. (Notes) 58, HCJ Appeal .... *Digested,* 47-51/**2075**: *Applied* 47-51/2076, 01/6303, 05/5088, 17/2495: *Considered* 94/5508, 15/2952: *Referred to* 01/6385

Lawrie (Joshua) v HM Advocate see McDowall (Luke) v HM Advocate

Lawson v Serco Ltd; *sub nom* Serco Ltd v Lawson; *joined cases* Botham v Ministry of Defence; Crofts v Veta Ltd [2006] UKHL 3; [2006] 1 All E.R. 823; [2006] I.C.R. 250; [2006] I.R.L.R. 289; Times, January 27, 2006; (2006) 103(6) L.S.G. 36; (2006) 156 N.L.J. 184; (2006) 150 S.J.L.B. 131, HL .... *Digested,* 06/**1390**: *Applied* 07/1355, 08/1171, 08/1214, 10/1146, 11/1134, 12/1181, 16/1582, 16/673: *Considered* 08/1201, 08/17, 11/4227, 12/1143, 12/1176, 13/1075, 14/1077: *Followed* 09/1264, 10/1036, 10/1145, 11/1070, 15/880, 15/881, 16/735, 17/849, 17/850

Lawson Builders Ltd v Secretary of State for Communities and Local Government [2015] EWCA Civ 122; [2015] P.T.S.R. 1324; [2015] J.P.L. 896, CA (Civ Div) ... *Digested,* 15/**2039**: *Considered* 17/1748

Lay v Ackerman [2004] EWCA Civ 184; [2004] H.L.R. 40; [2004] L. & T.R. 29; [2005] 1 E.G.L.R. 139; Times, March 24, 2004; (2004) 101(15) L.S.G. 28; (2004) 148 S.J.L.B. 299; [2004] N.P.C. 37, CA (Civ Div) .... *Digested,* 04/**2497**: *Considered* 17/1432

Layher Ltd v Lowe 58 Con. L.R. 42; [2000] Lloyd's Rep. I.R. 510; Times, January 8, 1997; (1997) 73 P. & C.R. D37, CA (Civ Div) .... *Digested,* 97/**3124**: *Applied* 15/1464: *Considered* 98/3374: *Followed* 01/3801, 17/1346

Layne (A Bankrupt), Re see Sands v Layne

Layne (Deceased), Re see Sands v Layne

Lazar v Allianz SpA (C-350/14) EU:C:2015:586, AGO *Considered* 17/431

LB Holdings Intermediate 2 Ltd (In Administration), Re see Lehman Brothers International (Europe) (In Administration), Re

LBG Capital No.1 Plc v BNY Mellon Corporate Trustee Services Ltd see BNY Mellon Corporate Trustee Services Ltd v LBG Capital No.1 Plc

LBI HF v Stanford [2014] EWHC 3921 (Ch), Ch D
Considered 17/1332
LC (Albania) v Secretary of State for the Home Department [2017] EWCA Civ 351; [2017] 1 W.L.R. 4173, CA (Civ Div)
LC (China) v Secretary of State for the Home Department [2014] EWCA Civ 1310; [2015] Imm. A.R. 227; [2015] I.N.L.R. 302, CA (Civ Div) .... *Digested,* 15/**1327**:
Applied 15/1318, 16/1081, 16/1084: *Considered* 17/1200: *Followed* 16/1090
LC IK v Valsts ienemumu dienests (C-288/16) EU:C:2017:502; [2017] B.V.C. 31; [2017] S.T.I. 1614, ECJ (1st Chamber)
Le Guevel-Mouly v AIG Europe Ltd [2016] EWHC 1794 (QB), QBD
Applied 17/375
Lea Valley Developments Ltd v Derbyshire [2017] EWHC 1353 (TCC); [2017] 4 W.L.R. 120; [2017] 2 P. & C.R. DG21, QBD (TCC) .... *Digested,* 17/**1850**
Lea Valley Developments Ltd v Derbyshire [2017] EWHC 1243 (TCC); 174 Con. L.R. 71, QBD (TCC)
Leach v Fleming (Unreported, February 14, 2017), CC (Preston) [*Irwin Mitchell LLP, Riverside West, 1 Millsands, Sheffield*] .... *Digested,* 17/**1665**
Leach v Linderman see Leach (Deceased), Re
Leach (Deceased), Re; *sub nom* Leach v Linderman [1986] Ch. 226; [1985] 3 W.L.R. 413; [1985] 2 All E.R. 754; [1985] Fam. Law 319; (1985) 82 L.S.G. 2081; (1985) 135 N.L.J. 392; (1985) 129 S.J. 318, CA (Civ Div) .... *Digested,* 85/**3644**:
Considered 17/2443
Learning Centre (Romford) Ltd v Revenue and Customs Commissioners [2017] UKFTT 492 (TC); [2017] S.F.T.D. 1100; [2017] S.T.I. 1422, FTT (Tax)
Leaseholders of Foundling Court and O'Donnell Court v Camden LBC [2016] UKUT 366 (LC); [2017] L. & T.R. 7, UT (Lands) .... *Digested,* 17/**1435**
Leathem (John) v HM Advocate [2017] HCJAC 10; 2017 J.C. 214; 2017 S.L.T. 215; 2017 S.C.L. 401; 2017 S.C.C.R. 157; 2017 G.W.D. 6-89, HCJ .... *Digested,* 17/**2807**
Leather Goods Case, Re 11 E.R. 1435; (1865) 11 H.L. Cas. 523
Followed 17/1394
Lebara Ltd v Revenue and Customs Commissioners (C-520/10) EU:C:2012:264; [2012] S.T.C. 1536; [2012] B.V.C. 219, ECJ (3rd Chamber)
Applied 16/2208: *Considered* 17/2848: *Followed* 16/2187
Lebek v Domino (C-70/15) EU:C:2016:524; [2016] 1 W.L.R. 4221; [2017] C.E.C. 393; [2016] I.L.Pr. 31, ECJ (2nd Chamber)
Ledra Advertising Ltd v European Commission (C-8/15 P) EU:C:2016:701; [2017] 1 C.M.L.R. 35, ECJ (Grand Chamber)
Lee v Cardiff CC see Cardiff CC v Lee
Lee v Lee (A Bankrupt); *sub nom* Lee (A Bankrupt), Re [2000] B.C.C. 500; [2000] 1 F.L.R. 92; [1999] B.P.I.R. 926; Times, September 22, 1999; [1999] Fam. Law 808, CA (Civ Div) .... *Digested,* 99/**3260**:
Considered 17/1275
Lee v McArthur [2016] NICA 39; [2017] I.R.L.R. 69; [2016] H.R.L.R. 22, CA (NI) .... *Digested,* 17/**2324**
Lee v Revenue and Customs Commissioners; *joined case* Bunter v Revenue and Customs Commissioners [2017] UKFTT 279 (TC); [2017] S.F.T.D. 826; 19 I.T.L. Rep. 741, FTT (Tax) .... *Digested,* 17/**2089**
Lee v United Kingdom (57877/09) see James v United Kingdom (25119/09)
Lee (A Bankrupt), Re see Lee v Lee (A Bankrupt)
Lee-Hirons v Secretary of State for Justice see R. (on the application of Lee-Hirons) v Secretary of State for Justice
Leeds v Lemos; *sub nom* Lemos, Re [2017] EWHC 1825 (Ch); [2018] Ch. 81; [2018] 2 W.L.R. 73; [2018] 1 All E.R. 313; [2017] B.P.I.R. 1223, Ch D .... *Digested,* 17/**1286**
Leeds Beckett University (formerly Leeds Metropolitan University) v Travelers Insurance Co Ltd [2017] EWHC 558 (TCC); [2017] Bus. L.R. 2022; [2017] Lloyd's Rep. I.R. 417, QBD (TCC) .... *Digested,* 17/**1353**
Leeds City Council v Broadley [2016] EWCA Civ 1213; [2017] 1 W.L.R. 738; [2017] H.L.R. 7; [2017] 1 P. & C.R. 13; [2017] L. & T.R. 21; [2017] R.A. 21; Times, December 22, 2016; [2017] 1 P. & C.R. DG15, CA (Civ Div) .... *Digested,* 17/**1440**
Leeds City Council v Broadley [2016] EWHC 1839 (Admin); [2016] 4 W.L.R. 137; [2016] H.L.R. 38; [2017] L. & T.R. 8; [2016] R.A. 300; [2016] A.C.D. 109, QBD (Admin) .... *Digested,* 16/**1438**:
Affirmed 17/1440
Leeds City Council v C [1993] 1 F.L.R. 269; [1993] 1 F.C.R. 585; [1993] Fam. Law 73, Fam Div .... *Digested,* 93/**2826**:
Considered 95/3496, 17/1057: *Distinguished* 95/3578
Leeds City Council v Hall see Hounslow LBC v Powell

Leeds City Council v Revenue and Customs Commissioners [2015] EWCA Civ 1293; [2016] S.T.C. 2256; [2016] B.V.C. 2; [2016] S.T.I. 142, CA (Civ Div) .... *Digested,* 16/**2191**: *Followed* 17/2177

Leeds Shipping Co v Societe Francaise Bunge SA (The Eastern City) [1958] 2 Lloyd's Rep. 127, CA .... *Digested,* 58/**3144**: *Applied* 77/2760, 95/4517: *Approved* 79/2445, 17/2017: *Considered* 69/3301, 78/2723, 07/3817, 10/3045: *Followed* 14/2726

Legal & General Assurance Society Ltd v Expeditors International (UK) Ltd [2006] EWHC 1008 (Ch); [2007] 1 P. & C.R. 5; [2006] L. & T.R. 22; [2006] 18 E.G. 151 (C.S.); (2006) 150 S.J.L.B. 573, Ch D *Affirmed* 07/2720: *Applied* 17/1474

Legends Live Ltd v Harrison [2016] EWHC 1938 (QB); [2017] I.R.L.R. 59, QBD .... *Digested,* 17/**825**

Legg v Burton [2017] EWHC 2088 (Ch); [2017] 4 W.L.R. 186; [2017] W.T.L.R. 1017, Ch D (Bristol)

Lehman Brothers International (Europe) (In Administration) v Exxonmobil Financial Services BV [2016] EWHC 2699 (Comm); [2017] 2 All E.R. (Comm) 959; [2016] 2 C.L.C. 578, QBD (Comm)

Lehman Brothers International (Europe) (In Administration), Re; *sub nom* Lomas v Revenue and Customs Commissioners [2016] EWHC 2492 (Ch); [2017] Bus. L.R. 520; [2016] B.T.C. 42; [2016] S.T.I. 2782, Ch D (Companies Ct) .... *Digested,* 16/**1171**

Lehman Brothers International (Europe) (In Administration), Re; *sub nom* Lomas v Burlington Loan Management Ltd; Waterfall II, Re [2016] EWHC 2417 (Ch); [2017] 2 All E.R. (Comm) 275; [2017] Bus. L.R. 1475, Ch D (Companies Ct) ..... *Digested,* 17/**1265**

Lehman Brothers International (Europe) (In Administration), Re; *sub nom* Joint Administrators of LB Holdings Intermediate 2 Ltd (In Administration) v Lomas; *joined cases* Lehman Brothers Ltd (In Administration), Re; LB Holdings Intermediate 2 Ltd (In Administration), Re [2015] EWCA Civ 485; [2016] Ch. 50; [2015] 3 W.L.R. 1205; [2016] 2 All E.R. 836; [2016] 1 All E.R. (Comm) 1079; [2015] B.C.C. 431; [2015] 2 B.C.L.C. 433; [2015] B.P.I.R. 1035, CA (Civ Div) .... *Digested,* 15/**1395**: *Reversed* 17/1259

Lehman Brothers International (Europe) (In Administration), Re; *sub nom* Joint Administrators of LB Holdings Intermediate 2 Ltd (In Administration) v Lomas; *joined cases* Lehman Brothers Ltd (In Administration), Re; LB Holdings Intermediate 2 Ltd (In Administration), Re [2017] UKSC 38; [2017] 2 W.L.R. 1497; [2018] 1 All E.R. 205; [2018] 1 All E.R. (Comm) 629; [2017] B.C.C. 235; [2017] 2 B.C.L.C. 149, SC .... *Digested,* 17/**1259**

Lehman Brothers International (Europe) (In Administration), Re; *sub nom* Lomas v Burlington Loan Management Ltd [2016] EWHC 2131 (Ch); [2017] B.C.C. 1, Ch D (Companies Ct) .... *Digested,* 17/**1262**

Lehman Brothers International (Europe) (In Administration), Re see Bloom v Pensions Regulator

Lehman Brothers Ltd (In Administration), Re see Lehman Brothers International (Europe) (In Administration), Re

Lehman Brothers Luxembourg Investments Sarl v Lehman Brothers UK Holdings Ltd [2016] EWHC 617 (Ch); [2017] 1 All E.R. (Comm) 393; [2016] 2 B.C.L.C. 244, Ch D (Companies Ct) .... *Digested,* 16/**1169**

Lehman Companies, Re see Bloom v Pensions Regulator

Leicester City Council v T [2016] EWFC 20; [2017] 1 F.L.R. 1585; [2016] Fam. Law 952, Fam Ct .... *Digested,* 17/**948**

Leichenich v Peffekoven (C-532/11) EU:C:2012:720; [2013] S.T.C. 846; [2013] C.E.C. 903; [2012] S.T.I. 3400, ECJ (3rd Chamber) *Followed* 17/2238

Leichhardt Municipal Council v Montgomery [2007] HCA 6, HC (Aus) *Applied* 17/470

Leigh v Hudson see Hudson v Leigh

Leigh Estates (UK) Ltd, Re [1994] B.C.C. 292; [1994] R.A. 57; [1993] E.G. 212 (C.S.), Ch D (Companies Ct) .... *Digested,* 94/**2635**: *Applied* 15/1436, 17/1294

Lejonvarn v Burgess see Burgess v Lejonvarn

LELY ENTERPRISES AG/Underpayment (T2554/11) [2017] E.P.O.R. 5, EPO (Technical Bd App)

Lemon v Chawda see Chawda, Re

Lemos v Lemos [2016] EWCA Civ 1181; [2017] B.P.I.R. 716; [2017] 1 P. & C.R. 12; [2017] 1 P. & C.R. DG11, CA (Civ Div) .... *Digested,* 17/**304**

Lemos, Re see Leeds v Lemos

Lenderink-Woods v Zurich Assurance Ltd [2016] EWHC 3287 (Ch); [2017] P.N.L.R. 15, Ch D (Manchester) .... *Digested,* 17/**1570**

Lendore v Attorney General of Trinidad and Tobago [2017] UKPC 25; [2017] 1 W.L.R. 3369, PC (Trin)

Leno Merken BV v Hagelkruis Beheer BV (C-149/11) EU:C:2012:816; [2013] Bus. L.R. 928; [2013] E.T.M.R. 16, ECJ (2nd Chamber)
Considered 17/386: *Explained* 15/1524: *Followed* 16/1289, 17/1391

Leopold Walford (LONDON) Ltd v Les Affreteurs Reunis SA see Les Affreteurs Reunis SA v Leopold Walford (London) Ltd

Leppard v Excess Insurance Co Ltd [1979] 1 W.L.R. 512; [1979] 2 All E.R. 668; [1979] 2 Lloyd's Rep. 91; (1979) 250 E.G. 751; (1978) 122 S.J. 182, CA (Civ Div) .... *Digested,* 79/**1509**:
Applied 09/2275: *Followed* 17/1343

Les Affreteurs Reunis SA v Leopold Walford (London) Ltd; *sub nom* Leopold Walford (LONDON) Ltd v Les Affreteurs Reunis SA [1919] A.C. 801, HL
Considered 17/2022

Les Laboratoires Servier v Apotex Inc [2008] EWHC 2347 (Ch); [2009] F.S.R. 3, Ch D *Digested,* 09/**2312**:
Approved 15/1510: *Considered* 13/783, 15/680, 17/302

Leslie v Farrar Construction Ltd [2016] EWCA Civ 1041; [2017] B.L.R. 21; 169 Con. L.R. 1; [2016] C.I.L.L. 3906, CA (Civ Div) .... *Digested,* 17/**466**

Leslie v Farrar Construction Ltd [2015] EWHC 58 (TCC), QBD (TCC)
Affirmed 17/466

Lesotho Highlands Development Authority v Impregilo SpA [2005] UKHL 43; [2006] 1 A.C. 221; [2005] 3 W.L.R. 129; [2005] 3 All E.R. 789; [2005] 2 All E.R. (Comm) 265; [2005] 2 Lloyd's Rep. 310; [2005] 2 C.L.C. 1; [2005] B.L.R. 351; 101 Con. L.R. 1; Times, July 6, 2005; [2005] 27 E.G. 220 (C.S.); (2005) 155 N.L.J. 1046, HL .... *Digested,* 05/**207**:
Applied 07/250, 07/253, 08/564, 09/184, 10/176: *Considered* 10/175, 10/509, 15/92: *Distinguished* 06/203: *Followed* 11/141, 12/114, 12/115, 13/112, 16/430, 17/66, 17/67

Letherbarrow v Warwickshire CC [2014] EWHC 4820 (Admin); (2015) 179 J.P. 307; [2015] C.T.L.C. 273, DC .... *Digested,* 15/**648**:
Applied 17/617

Level One Residential (Jersey) Ltd, Re; *sub nom* Special Opportunity Holdings Ltd, Re; O'Keefe v Caner [2017] EWHC 1105 (Ch); [2017] W.T.L.R. 615, Ch D (Companies Ct) .... *Digested,* 17/**324**

Leventis v Malcon Navigation Co Ltd (C-436/16) EU:C:2017:497; [2018] 1 W.L.R. 80; [2017] I.L.Pr. 32, ECJ (7th Chamber)

Lever Bros Ltd v Bell see Bell v Lever Brothers Ltd

Levez v TH Jennings (Harlow Pools) Ltd (C-326/96) EU:C:1998:577; [1998] E.C.R. I-7835; [1999] 2 C.M.L.R. 363; [1999] All E.R. (EC) 1; [1999] C.E.C. 3; [1999] I.C.R. 521; [1999] I.R.L.R. 36; Times, December 10, 1998, ECJ (1st Chamber) *Digested,* 99/**2067**:
Applied 00/2162, 12/1184, 15/15: *Considered* 17/2228: *Followed* 04/401

Levob Verzekeringen BV v Staatssecretaris van Financien (C-41/04) EU:C:2005:649; [2006] S.T.C. 766; [2005] E.C.R. I-9433; [2006] 2 C.M.L.R. 8; [2006] C.E.C. 424; [2007] B.T.C. 5186; [2007] B.V.C. 155; [2005] S.T.I. 1777, ECJ (1st Chamber) .... *Digested,* 06/**4501**:
Applied 07/4332, 07/4341, 08/4035, 08/4048, 09/4098, 09/4099, 09/4106, 13/3229, 16/2177: *Considered* 12/3420: *Distinguished* 12/3438: *Followed* 08/4041, 09/4100, 10/3519, 13/3221, 14/3050, 17/2294

LEVSI/Olanzapine (T1936/13) [2017] E.P.O.R. 31, EPO (Technical Bd App)

Levy v ABN AMRO Bank NV see Norglen Ltd (In Liquidation) v Reeds Rains Prudential Ltd

Lewis v Warner; *joined case* Warner v Lewis [2016] EWHC 1787 (Ch); [2017] Ch. 13; [2016] 3 W.L.R. 1545; [2017] 2 F.L.R. 133; [2016] W.T.L.R. 1399; [2016] Fam. Law 1091; [2016] Fam. Law 1322, Ch D .... *Digested,* 16/**2031**

Lewisham Hospital NHS Trust v Hamuth see University Hospital Lewisham NHS Trust v Hamuth

Lewisham LBC v Malcolm see Malcolm v Lewisham LBC

Lex Services Plc v Customs and Excise Commissioners; *sub nom* Customs and Excise Commissioners v Lex Services Plc; *joined cases* Littlewoods Organisation Plc v Customs and Excise Commissioners; Bugeja v Customs and Excise Commissioners (No.2); Kuwait Petroleum (GB) Ltd v Customs and Excise Commissioners [2003] UKHL 67; [2004] 1 W.L.R. 1; [2004] 1 All E.R. 434; [2004] S.T.C. 73; [2004] R.T.R. 18; [2003] B.T.C. 5658; [2004] B.V.C. 53; Times, December 5, 2003; [2003] S.T.I. 2274; (2004) 101(3) L.S.G. 34; (2003) 147 S.J.L.B. 1430, HL .... *Digested,* 04/**4016**:
Applied 08/4028: *Considered* 11/3572, 14/3081, 17/2258

Lexgorge Ltd v Howard de Walden Estates Ltd see Day v Hosebay Ltd

Lexmead (Basingstoke) Ltd v Lewis see Lambert v Lewis

Leyland Cars (BL Cars Ltd) v Vyas see Science Research Council v Nasse

LG (A Child) (Adoption: Leave to Oppose), Re; *sub nom* A v Local Authority [2015] EWFC 52; [2016] 1 F.L.R. 607; [2017] 1 F.C.R. 251; [2015] Fam. Law 1039, Fam Ct .... *Digested,* 16/**807**

LG Blower Specialist Bricklayer Ltd v Reeves see Gibbon v Manchester City Council

LG DISPLAY/Right to be heard (R12/14) [2017] E.P.O.R. 15, EPO (Enlarged Bd App)

LG Electronics Inc v European Commission (C-588/15 P); *joined case* Koninklijke Philips Electronics NV v European Commission (C-622/15 P) EU:C:2017:679; [2017] 5 C.M.L.R. 20, ECJ (8th Chamber)

Liability Under A Collateral Promise, Re (5 AZR 767/14) [2017] I.L.Pr. 17, BAG (Ger)

Libertel Groep BV v Benelux-Merkenbureau (C-104/01) EU:C:2003:244; [2004] Ch. 83; [2004] 2 W.L.R. 1081; [2003] E.C.R. I-3793; [2005] 2 C.M.L.R. 45; [2003] E.T.M.R. 63; [2004] F.S.R. 4; Times, May 12, 2003, ECJ .... *Digested,* 03/**2599**: *Applied* 04/2370, 05/2529, 05/2533, 16/1328: *Considered* 05/2532, 07/2673, 13/1758, 17/1387: *Explained* 14/1933: *Followed* 05/2553, 13/1821, 16/1327

Liberty v Government Communications Headquarters [2015] 3 All E.R. 142; [2015] 1 Cr. App. R. 24; [2015] H.R.L.R. 2; [2014] Info. T.L.R. 255, IPT .... *Digested,* 15/**1388**: *Applied* 17/25

Liberty Holdings Unlimited, Re; *sub nom* Owen v Secretary of State for Business, Innovation and Skills [2017] B.C.C. 298, Ch D (Companies Ct)

Lickiss v Milestone Motor Policies at Lloyds see Barrett Bros (Taxis) Ltd v Davies

Lictor Anstalt v Mir Steel UK Ltd; *sub nom* Mir Steel UK Ltd v Morris [2012] EWCA Civ 1397; [2013] 2 All E.R. (Comm) 54; [2013] C.P. Rep. 7; [2013] 2 B.C.L.C. 76, CA (Civ Div) .... *Digested,* 13/**574**: *Applied* 17/463

Liddle v Liddle [2017] EWHC 2261 (Ch); [2017] B.P.I.R. 1538, Ch D (Leeds)

Liden v Burton see Burton v Liden

Lifestyle Equities CV v Sportsdirect.com Retail Ltd [2016] EWHC 2092 (Ch); [2017] F.S.R. 12, Ch D .... *Digested,* 17/**282**

Lin v Commissioner of Inland Revenue [2017] NZHC 969; 19 I.T.L. Rep. 840, HC (NZ)

Linden Gardens Trust Ltd v Lenesta Sludge Disposal Ltd; *joined case* St Martins Property Corp Ltd v Sir Robert McAlpine & Sons [1994] 1 A.C. 85; [1993] 3 W.L.R. 408; [1993] 3 All E.R. 417; 63 B.L.R. 1; 36 Con. L.R. 1; Times, July 23, 1993; Independent, July 30, 1993; [1993] E.G. 139 (C.S.); (1993) 143 N.L.J. 1152; (1993) 137 S.J.L.B. 183, HL .... *Digested,* 93/**303**: *Applied* 95/3701, 95/487, 98/809, 99/832, 02/3042, 05/2372, 06/5150, 13/1709, 13/2097: *Cited* 99/1417: *Considered* 95/4162, 95/771, 99/440, 00/864, 02/726, 06/268, 08/649, 17/637: *Followed* 98/401, 00/5980, 00/859, 03/2753

Lindsay v Ironsides Ray & Vials [1994] I.C.R. 384; [1994] I.R.L.R. 318, EAT .... *Digested,* 94/**1964**: *Applied* 17/811: *Considered* 10/1098

Lindsay v O'Loughnane [2010] EWHC 529 (QB); [2012] B.C.C. 153, QBD *Applied* 17/312: *Considered* 11/324

Lindsay v Warner see Inquiry under the Company Securities (Insider Dealing) Act 1985 (No.1), Re

Lines Bros (In Liquidation), Re [1983] Ch. 1; [1982] 2 W.L.R. 1010; [1982] 2 All E.R. 183; [1982] Com. L.R. 81; (1982) 126 S.J. 197, CA (Civ Div) .... *Digested,* 82/**335**: *Applied* 04/2192, 16/1168: *Considered* 84/323, 87/365, 93/2626, 14/1752: *Distinguished* 15/1395: *Not applied* 17/1259

Link Housing Association Ltd v Gray Aitken Partnership Ltd see Link Housing Association Ltd v PBL Construction Ltd

Link Housing Association Ltd v PBL Construction Ltd; *sub nom* Gray Aitken Partnership Ltd v Link Housing Association Ltd; Link Housing Association Ltd v Gray Aitken Partnership Ltd [2007] CSIH 4; 2007 S.C. 294; 2007 S.C.L.R. 343; 2007 G.W.D. 17-305, IH (1 Div) .... *Digested,* 08/**4591**: *Distinguished* 08/4593, 16/2475, 17/2454

Link Lending Ltd v Bustard see Link Lending Ltd v Hussein

Link Lending Ltd v Hussein; *joined case* Link Lending Ltd v Bustard [2010] EWCA Civ 424; [2010] 2 E.G.L.R. 55; [2010] 28 E.G. 86; [2010] 18 E.G. 98 (C.S.); (2010) 154(17) S.J.L.B. 28; [2010] N.P.C. 49; [2010] 2 P. & C.R. DG15, CA (Civ Div) .. *Digested,* 10/**2724**: *Followed* 17/1841

Linnett v Halliwells LLP [2009] EWHC 319 (TCC); [2009] 1 C.L.C. 157; [2009] B.L.R. 312; 123 Con. L.R. 104; [2009] C.I.L.L. 2704; (2009) 159 N.L.J. 396; [2009] N.P.C. 32, QBD (TCC) .... *Digested,* 09/**991**: *Applied* 13/524, 14/577, 17/657

Lion Laboratories Ltd v Evans [1985] Q.B. 526; [1984] 3 W.L.R. 539; [1984] 2 All E.R. 417; (1984) 81 L.S.G. 2000; (1984) 81 L.S.G. 1233; (1984) 128 S.J. 533, CA (Civ Div) .... *Digested,* 84/**1325**: *Applied* 17/333: *Considered* 86/2646, 88/2859, 00/3573, 01/3850

Liquidator of Letham Grange Development Co Ltd v Foxworth Investments Ltd see Henderson v Foxworth Investments Ltd
Lismore v Davey see Davey (A Bankrupt), Re
Lissenden v CAV Bosch Ltd [1940] A.C. 412; [1940] 1 All E.R. 425, HL
Considered 91/202, 09/609, 17/1850
Litdana UAB v Valstybine mokesciu inspekcija prie Lietuvos Respublikos finansu ministerijos (C-624/15) EU:C:2017:389; [2017] B.V.C. 26, ECJ (9th Chamber)
Lithgow v United Kingdom (9006/80) see Lithgow v United Kingdom (A/102)
Lithgow v United Kingdom (A/102); *sub nom* Lithgow v United Kingdom (9006/80); Vosper Plc v United Kingdom (9262/81); English Electric Co Ltd v United Kingdom (9263/81); Banstonian Co v United Kingdom (9265/81); Yarrow Plc v United Kingdom (9266/81); Vickers Plc v United Kingdom (9313/81); Dowsett Securities Ltd v United Kingdom (9405/81) (1986) 8 E.H.R.R. 329; Times, July 7, 1986, ECHR .... *Digested,* 86/**1415**:
Applied 02/2458, 10/211: *Considered* 09/440, 13/3417, 17/1453
Lithuania v Rizleriene see Wolkowicz v Poland
Littaur v Steggles Palmer [1986] 1 W.L.R. 287; [1986] 1 All E.R. 780; (1986) 83 L.S.G. 1138; (1985) 130 S.J. 225, CA (Civ Div) .... *Digested,* 86/**1968**:
Applied 90/2887, 96/3858: *Followed* 17/1477
Little Rascals Pets Ltd v Revenue and Customs Commissioners [2017] UKFTT 334 (TC); [2017] S.F.T.D. 1001; [2017] S.T.I. 1147, FTT (Tax)
Littlewood v Morley [2017] W.T.L.R. 591, HC (IoM)
Littlewoods Organisation Plc v Customs and Excise Commissioners see Lex Services Plc v Customs and Excise Commissioners
Littlewoods Retail Ltd v Revenue and Customs Commissioners [2015] EWCA Civ 515; [2016] Ch. 373; [2015] 3 W.L.R. 1748; [2015] S.T.C. 2014; [2015] B.V.C. 26; [2015] S.T.I. 1791, CA (Civ Div) .... *Digested,* 15/**2613**:
Followed 16/2191, 17/2080
Littlewoods Retail Ltd v Revenue and Customs Commissioners (C-591/10) EU:C:2012:478; [2012] S.T.C. 1714; [2012] S.T.I. 2359, ECJ (Grand Chamber)
Applied 15/2516: *Considered* 13/3219, 17/2255: *Explained* 15/2613:
Followed 14/2874, 14/3079, 17/2228
Litton and Thorner's Community Hall v Revenue and Customs Commissioners [2017] UKFTT 674 (TC); [2017] S.T.I. 2015, FTT (Tax)
Liverpool City Council v Secretary of State for Health see R. (on the application of Liverpool City Council) v Secretary of State for Health
Livingstone v Rawyards Coal Co (1880) 5 App. Cas. 25; (1880) 7 R. (H.L.) 1, HL
Applied 79/2776, 87/3551, 89/1199, 90/1522, 91/1322, 92/1533, 03/3023, 05/962, 08/2659, 09/2726, 16/572: *Cited* 01/4593: *Considered* 90/1567, 94/2771, 94/3928, 96/4483, 15/1891, 17/636: *Referred to* 94/3437
Lizanec v Procurator Fiscal, Edinburgh see Lizanec v Richardson
Lizanec v Richardson; *sub nom* Lizanec v Procurator Fiscal, Edinburgh [2016] SAC (Crim) 33; 2017 S.C.L. 417; 2016 G.W.D. 37-660, SAC .... *Digested,* 17/**2517**
LL v Lord Chancellor (Liability) [2017] EWCA Civ 237; [2017] 4 W.L.R. 162; [2017] 2 F.L.R. 1429, CA (Civ Div) .... *Digested,* 17/**307**
LL v Lord Chancellor (Liability) [2015] EWHC 3273 (QB), QBD
Reversed 17/307
Llewellyn v Kasintoe Rubber Estates Ltd [1914] 2 Ch. 670, CA
Applied 70/289: *Considered* 61/1146, 17/409
Lloyd v McMahon Times, August 1, 1986, DC
Followed 17/1590
Lloyd's Syndicate 102 for 2001 Year of Account, Re see Simmonds v Gammell
Lloyds Bank Ltd v Eastwood see Eastwood (Deceased), Re
Lloyds Bank Plc v Carrick [1996] 4 All E.R. 630; [1996] 2 F.L.R. 600; [1996] 2 F.C.R. 771; (1996) 28 H.L.R. 707; (1997) 73 P. & C.R. 314; [1997] 1 E.G.L.R. 160; [1997] 11 E.G. 155; Times, March 13, 1996; [1997] Fam. Law 94; (1996) 93(14) L.S.G. 30; (1996) 146 N.L.J. 405; (1996) 140 S.J.L.B. 101; [1996] N.P.C. 32, CA (Civ Div) .... *Digested,* 96/**4950**:
Considered 17/1841
Lloyds Bank Plc v McBains Cooper [2017] EWHC 30 (TCC); [2017] T.C.L.R. 2; [2017] 1 Costs L.O. 95, QBD (TCC) .... *Digested,* 17/**242**
Lloyds Bank Plc v McBains Cooper Consulting Ltd [2016] EWHC 2045 (TCC); [2017] P.N.L.R. 11, QBD (TCC) .... *Digested,* 17/**640**
Lloyds Bank Plc v Wojcik Independent, January 19, 1998, CA (Civ Div) .... *Digested,* 98/**537**:
Considered 17/329
Lloyds Bank Plc, Re see Barclays Bank Plc, Re
Lloyds Banking Group Plc v Revenue and Customs Commissioners see Revenue and Customs Commissioners v MG Rover Group Ltd

Lloyds Banking Group Plc v Revenue and Customs Commissioners see Standard Chartered Plc v Revenue and Customs Commissioners
Lloyds Investment (Scandinavia) Ltd v Ager-Hanssen [2003] EWHC 1740 (Ch), Ch D
Applied 05/420, 07/387, 09/392, 17/265: *Approved* 12/443: *Considered* 11/345, 12/416, 15/316
Lloyds Trust Co (Channel Islands) Ltd v Fragoso [2017] W.T.L.R. 103, Royal Ct (Jer)
Lloyd's Syndicate 994 for 2001 Year of Account, Re see Simmonds v Gammell
LO v N [2017] CSIH 14; 2017 Fam. L.R. 44; 2017 G.W.D. 7-101, IH (Ex Div) .... *Digested,* 17/**2600**
Lobler v Revenue and Customs Commissioners [2015] UKUT 152 (TCC); [2015] S.T.C. 1893; [2015] B.T.C. 515; [2015] S.T.I. 1398, UT (Tax) .... *Digested,* 15/**2486**:
Applied 16/2077, 17/2091
Lobo v Corich; *sub nom* Corich v Lobo [2017] EWHC 1438 (TCC); 174 Con. L.R. 46; (2018) 34 Const. L.J. 104, QBD (TCC)
Locabail (UK) Ltd v Bayfield Properties Ltd (Leave to Appeal); *joined cases* R. v Bristol Betting and Gaming Licensing Committee Ex p. O'Callaghan; Williams v Inspector of Taxes; Timmins v Gormley; Locabail (UK) Ltd v Waldorf Investment Corp (Leave to Appeal) [2000] Q.B. 451; [2000] 2 W.L.R. 870; [2000] 1 All E.R. 65; [2000] I.R.L.R. 96; [2000] H.R.L.R. 290; [2000] U.K.H.R.R. 300; 7 B.H.R.C. 583; Times, November 19, 1999; Independent, November 23, 1999; (1999) 149 N.L.J. 1793; [1999] N.P.C. 143, CA (Civ Div) .... *Digested,* 99/**38**:
Applied 00/52, 00/53, 01/13, 01/2268, 04/30, 05/890, 06/19, 06/2803, 06/30, 06/5206, 07/1351, 07/31, 09/658, 10/27, 13/48, 15/28, 16/680, 17/78:
Considered 00/4140, 00/6092, 01/334, 02/4828, 03/5169, 06/2755, 06/961, 07/2558, 10/2144, 15/2843, 17/668: *Followed* 10/768, 11/282, 15/93, 17/1560
Locabail (UK) Ltd v Waldorf Investment Corp (Leave to Appeal) see Locabail (UK) Ltd v Bayfield Properties Ltd (Leave to Appeal)
Local Authority X v B see B (Children) (Sexual Abuse: Standard of Proof), Re
Local Authority X v HI [2016] EWHC 1123 (Fam); [2017] 1 F.L.R. 1362; [2016] Fam. Law 802, Fam Div .... *Digested,* 17/**928**
Loch Hill Windfarm (Scotland) Ltd v Scottish Ministers [2015] CSIH 37; 2015 G.W.D. 17-294, IH (Ex Div)
Considered 17/2765
Loch Lomond and Trossachs National Park Authority v Anstalt [2017] SAC (Civ) 11; 2017 S.L.T. (Sh Ct) 138; 2017 G.W.D. 13-206, SAC .... *Digested,* 17/**2643**
Lock v British Gas Trading Ltd; *sub nom* British Gas Trading Ltd v Lock [2016] EWCA Civ 983; [2017] 4 All E.R. 291; [2017] 1 C.M.L.R. 25; [2017] I.C.R. 1; [2016] I.R.L.R. 946; Times, December 14, 2016, CA (Civ Div) .... *Digested,* 17/**804**
Lock v British Gas Trading Ltd; *sub nom* British Gas Trading Ltd v Lock [2016] 2 C.M.L.R. 40; [2016] I.C.R. 503; [2016] I.R.L.R. 316, EAT .... *Digested,* 16/**652**:
Affirmed 17/804
Lock v British Gas Trading Ltd (C-539/12) EU:C:2014:351; [2014] 3 C.M.L.R. 53; [2014] All E.R. (EC) 1194; [2014] I.C.R. 813; [2014] I.R.L.R. 648, ECJ (1st Chamber) .... *Digested,* 15/**792**:
Applied 15/2679, 15/833: *Considered* 17/805
Lockett v A&M Charles Ltd [1938] 4 All E.R. 170, KBD
Applied 17/1883
Lodwick v Southwark LBC [2004] EWCA Civ 306; [2004] I.C.R. 884; [2004] I.R.L.R. 554; Times, April 9, 2004; (2004) 148 S.J.L.B. 385, CA (Civ Div)
Applied 07/1343, 13/969: *Considered* 05/1220: *Followed* 17/5
Logicrose Ltd v Southend United Football Club Ltd (No.2) [1988] 1 W.L.R. 1256; Times, August 4, 1988; [1988] E.G. 114 (C.S.), Ch D .... *Digested,* 89/**55**:
Considered 17/504
Lokhova v Longmuir [2016] EWHC 2579 (QB); [2017] E.M.L.R. 7, QBD .... *Digested,* 17/**648**
Lomas v Burlington Loan Management Ltd see Lehman Brothers International (Europe) (In Administration), Re
Lomas v Pensions Regulator see Bloom v Pensions Regulator
Lomas v Revenue and Customs Commissioners see Lehman Brothers International (Europe) (In Administration), Re
Lombard Ingatlan Lizing Zrt v Nemzeti Ado- es Vamhivatal Fellebbviteli Igazgatosag (C-404/16) EU:C:2017:759; [2017] B.V.C. 48; [2017] S.T.I. 2205, ECJ (6th Chamber)
London & Westcountry Estates Ltd, Re see Hockin v Marsden
London Corp, The [1935] P. 70; (1935) 51 Ll. L. Rep. 67, CA
Applied 67/1021, 14/829, 17/459: *Followed* 99/2504
London County Freehold and Leasehold Properties v Department of the Environment see Town Investments Ltd v Department of the Environment
London Power Networks Plc v Revenue and Customs Commissioners see Eastern Power Networks Plc v Revenue and Customs Commissioners

London Russian Ballet School v Lambeth LBC [2017] P.A.D. 19, Planning Inspector
London Scottish Benefit Society v Chester see London Scottish Benefit Society v Chorley
London Scottish Benefit Society v Chorley; *joined cases* London Scottish Benefit Society v Crawford; London Scottish Benefit Society v Chester (1884) 13 Q.B.D. 872, CA
Applied 69/2820, 87/2947, 87/3010, 01/527, 02/391, 03/323, 16/1414, 17/268: *Considered* 15/1651: *Distinguished* 52/2668: *Followed* 17/245
London Scottish Benefit Society v Crawford see London Scottish Benefit Society v Chorley
London Sephardi Trust v John Lyon's Charity; *sub nom* John Lyon's Charity v London Sephardi Trust [2015] UKUT 619 (LC), UT (Lands)
Affirmed 17/1845
London Sephardi Trust v John Lyon's Charity; *sub nom* John Lyon's Charity v London Sephardi Trust [2017] EWCA Civ 846; [2018] 2 W.L.R. 1016; [2017] H.L.R. 36; [2018] 1 P. & C.R. 2; [2017] L. & T.R. 30; [2017] R.V.R. 295, CA (Civ Div) .... *Digested,* 17/**1845**
London Steam-Ship Owners' Mutual Insurance Association Ltd v Jordan International Insurance Co see Aline Tramp SA v Jordan International Insurance Co
London Taxi Corp Ltd (t/a London Taxi Co) v Fraser-Nash Research Ltd [2016] EWHC 52 (Ch); [2016] E.T.M.R. 18; [2016] F.S.R. 20, Ch D .... *Digested,* 16/**1289**:
Applied 17/1391, 17/1393
Long v Farrer & Co [2004] EWHC 1774 (Ch); [2004] B.P.I.R. 1218, Ch D .... *Digested,* 05/**2294**:
Applied 14/1787, 17/1320
Long Wellesley's Case see Wellesley v Duke of Beaufort
Longmeade Ltd (In Administration), Re; *sub nom* Allen (Joint Liquidator), Re [2016] EWHC 356 (Ch); [2017] 2 All E.R. 244; [2016] Bus. L.R. 506; [2017] B.C.C. 203; [2017] 1 B.C.L.C. 605; [2016] B.P.I.R. 666, Ch D (Companies Ct) .... *Digested,* 16/**1231**
Longridge on the Thames v Revenue and Customs Commissioners; *sub nom* Revenue and Customs Commissioners v Longridge on the Thames [2014] UKUT 504 (TCC); [2015] S.T.C. 672; [2014] B.V.C. 546; [2014] S.T.I. 3428, UT (Tax) .... *Digested,* 15/**2628**:
Reversed 17/2295
Longridge on the Thames v Revenue and Customs Commissioners; *sub nom* Revenue and Customs Commissioners v Longridge on the Thames [2016] EWCA Civ 930; [2017] 1 W.L.R. 1497; [2016] S.T.C. 2362; [2016] B.V.C. 33; [2016] S.T.I. 2541, CA (Civ Div) .... *Digested,* 17/**2295**
Lonsdale (t/a Lonsdale Agencies) v Howard & Hallam Ltd [2007] UKHL 32; [2007] 1 W.L.R. 2055; [2007] 4 All E.R. 1; [2007] 2 All E.R. (Comm) 621; [2008] Bus. L.R. 788; [2008] 1 Lloyd's Rep. 78; [2007] 2 C.L.C. 1; [2008] E.C.C. 11; [2007] Eu. L.R. 799; [2007] I.C.R. 1338; [2007] I.R.L.R. 825; Times, July 10, 2007; (2007) 151 S.J.L.B. 922, HL .... *Digested,* 07/**68**:
Applied 15/57, 17/45: *Considered* 09/87: *Followed* 17/46
Loose v Lynn Shellfish Ltd; *sub nom* Lynn Shellfish Ltd v Loose [2016] UKSC 14; [2017] A.C. 599; [2016] 2 W.L.R. 1126; [2017] 1 All E.R. 677; Times, April 22, 2016, SC .... *Digested,* 16/**966**
Lopez v Ayuntamiento de Vitoria (C-197/15) see Martinez Andres v Servicio Vasco de Salud (C-184/15)
Lord Advocate v Dean (Zain Taj) [2016] HCJAC 117; 2017 S.L.T. 121; 2017 S.C.L. 170; 2017 S.C.C.R. 17; 2016 G.W.D. 38-672, HCJ .... *Digested,* 17/**2440**
Lord Advocate v Dean see Dean (Zain Taj) v Lord Advocate
Lord Advocate v Royal Bank of Scotland Ltd; *sub nom* Inland Revenue Commissioners v Royal Bank of Scotland Ltd 1977 S.C. 155; 1978 S.L.T. 38, IH (1 Div) .... *Digested,* 78/**3157**:
Distinguished 90/4772: *Followed* 83/4001, 16/2697: *Not followed* 17/2679
Lord Bernstein v Skyviews and General Ltd [1978] Q.B. 479; [1977] 3 W.L.R. 136; [1977] 2 All E.R. 902; (1977) 241 E.G. 917; (1977) 121 S.J. 157; (1977) 121 S.J. 437, QBD .... *Digested,* 77/**3101**:
Considered 17/92
Lord Bishop of Oxford v Church Commissioners of England see Harries v Church Commissioners for England
Lord Carlile of Berriew v Secretary of State for the Home Department see R. (on the application of Lord Carlile of Berriew QC) v Secretary of State for the Home Department
Lord Chancellor v Detention Action see R. (on the application of Detention Action) v First-tier Tribunal (Immigration and Asylum Chamber)
Lord Chancellor v Edward Hayes LLP [2017] EWHC 138 (QB); [2017] 1 Costs L.R. 147, QBD .... *Digested,* 17/**1482**:
Applied 17/1481

Lord Chancellor v SVS Solicitors; *sub nom* Secretary of State for Justice v SVS Solicitors [2017] EWHC 1045 (QB); [2017] 4 W.L.R. 87; [2017] 3 Costs L.O. 331; [2017] Lloyd's Rep. F.C. 404, QBD .... *Digested,* 17/**1481**
Lord Fisher DSC v Customs and Excise Commissioners see Customs and Excise Commissioners v Lord Fisher
Lornamead Acquisitions Ltd v Kaupthing Bank HF [2011] EWHC 2611 (Comm); [2013] 1 B.C.L.C. 73, QBD (Comm)
Applied 15/310: *Approved* 17/1332
Loterie Nationale - Nationale Loterij NV van Publiek Recht v Adriaensen (C-667/15) EU:C:2016:958; [2017] Bus. L.R. 609, ECJ (6th Chamber)
Lothian NHS Health Board v Revenue and Customs Commissioners see NHS Lothian Health Board v Revenue and Customs Commissioners
Loughborough Students Union v Revenue and Customs Commissioners [2017] UKFTT 518 (TC); [2017] S.T.I. 1667, FTT (Tax)
Louis Dreyfus Commodities Suisse SA v MT Maritime Management BV [2015] EWHC 2505 (Comm); [2017] 1 All E.R. (Comm) 99; [2016] 1 Lloyd's Rep. 197; [2015] 2 C.L.C. 508, QBD (Comm) .... *Digested,* 16/**1972**
Love v Dunn see Paterson v Harvie
LowCost Holidays Ltd (t/a Lowcost Beds) v Revenue and Customs Commissioners [2017] UKFTT 463 (TC); [2017] S.T.I. 1331, FTT (Tax)
Lowe v First Secretary of State; *sub nom* Lowe v Secretary of State for the Environment, Food and Rural Affairs [2003] EWHC 537 (Admin); [2003] 2 P. & C.R. 24; [2003] 1 P.L.R. 81; [2003] J.P.L. 1281; [2003] 8 E.G. 129 (C.S.), QBD (Admin) .... *Digested,* 03/**3378**:
Applied 06/3301, 17/1737
Lowe v Secretary of State for the Environment, Food and Rural Affairs see Lowe v First Secretary of State
Lowenthal v United Kingdom (41008/09) see Austin v United Kingdom (39692/09)
Lower Mill Estates Ltd v Revenue and Customs Commissioners [2010] UKUT 463 (TCC); [2011] S.T.C. 636; [2011] B.V.C. 1554; [2011] S.T.I. 345, UT (Tax) .... *Digested,* 11/**3561**:
Applied 15/2605, 17/2248
Lowick Rose LLP (In Liquidation) v Swynson Ltd see Swynson Ltd v Lowick Rose LLP (In Liquidation) (formerly Hurst Morrison Thomson LLP)
Lowin v W Portsmouth and Co Ltd [2016] EWHC 2301 (QB); [2017] C.P. Rep. 1; [2016] 5 Costs L.O. 719, QBD .... *Digested,* 16/**236**
Lownds v Home Office; *sub nom* Lownds v Secretary of State for the Home Department; Home Office v Lownds [2002] EWCA Civ 365; [2002] 1 W.L.R. 2450; [2002] 4 All E.R. 775; [2002] C.P. Rep. 43; [2002] C.P.L.R. 328; [2002] 2 Costs L.R. 279; Times, April 5, 2002; (2002) 99(19) L.S.G. 28; (2002) 146 S.J.L.B. 86, CA (Civ Div) .... *Digested,* 02/**333**:
Applied 03/259, 03/347, 04/293, 04/301, 04/303, 04/316, 04/320, 05/331, 05/372, 06/2421, 11/284, 12/388, 15/229, 16/211, 16/244: *Considered* 04/319, 06/556, 07/389, 10/283, 10/284, 14/331, 17/229: *Followed* 08/336, 11/270, 13/299
Lownds v Secretary of State for the Home Department see Lownds v Home Office
Loyalty Management UK Ltd v Revenue and Customs Commissioners see Revenue and Customs Commissioners v Loyalty Management UK Ltd
LP (Sri Lanka) v Secretary of State for the Home Department [2007] UKAIT 76, AIT
Applied 09/2085: *Considered* 10/1762: *Superseded* 17/1208
LSREF III Wight Ltd v Millvalley Ltd [2016] EWHC 466 (Comm); 165 Con. L.R. 58, QBD (Comm) .... *Digested,* 16/**137**:
Applied 17/1817
LTE Scientific Ltd v Thomas [2004] EWCA Civ 1622, CA (Civ Div)
Applied 17/308
Lucas v Security Service [2017] 1 All E.R. 283, IPT
Lucasfilm Ltd v Ainsworth [2011] UKSC 39; [2012] 1 A.C. 208; [2011] 3 W.L.R. 487; [2011] 4 All E.R. 817; [2012] 1 All E.R. (Comm) 1011; [2011] Bus. L.R. 1211; [2011] E.C.D.R. 21; [2012] E.M.L.R. 3; [2011] F.S.R. 41; 7 A.L.R. Int'l 711; Times, August 3, 2011; (2011) 161 N.L.J. 1098, SC .... *Digested,* 11/**1944**:
Considered 12/120, 16/1324: *Followed* 17/1377
Luckhurst v Harrower see Luckhurst v Procurator Fiscal, Forfar
Luckhurst v Procurator Fiscal, Forfar; *sub nom* Luckhurst v Harrower [2016] SAC (Crim) 29; 2017 S.L.T. (Sh Ct) 7; 2017 S.C.L. 104; 2016 G.W.D. 31-543, SAC .. *Digested,* 17/**2511**
Ludlow v Commissioner of Police of the Metropolis; *sub nom* Ludlow v Metropolitan Police Commissioner; R. v Ludlow (Edward Alexander) [1971] A.C. 29; [1970] 2 W.L.R. 521; [1970] 1 All E.R. 567; (1970) 54 Cr. App. R. 233; (1970) 114 S.J. 148, HL .... *Digested,* 70/**458**:
Applied 80/1744, 80/520, 80/559, 91/683, 17/602: *Considered* 81/388, 86/624, 94/935, 96/1566: *Followed* 14/774

Ludlow v Metropolitan Police Commissioner see Ludlow v Commissioner of Police of the Metropolis
Luisi v Ministero del Tesoro (286/82) EU:C:1984:35; [1984] E.C.R. 377; [1985] 3 C.M.L.R. 52, ECJ .... *Digested,* 85/**1458**: *Considered* 17/807
Lumba v Secretary of State for the Home Department see R. (on the application of Lumba) v Secretary of State for the Home Department
Lumsden (Paul William) v HM Advocate [2011] HCJAC 89; 2012 J.C. 133; 2012 S.C.L. 175; 2011 S.C.C.R. 648; 2011 G.W.D. 33-693, HCJ .... *Digested,* 12/**3936**: *Considered* 17/2556
Lund v Taylor (1976) 31 P. & C.R. 167; 239 E.G. 199, CA (Civ Div) .... *Digested,* 76/**2298**: *Considered* 08/3112: *Followed* 17/1828
Lungowe v Vedanta Resources Plc [2017] EWCA Civ 1528; [2017] B.C.C. 787; [2017] B.L.R. 585, CA (Civ Div)
Lungowe v Vedanta Resources Plc [2016] EWHC 975 (TCC); [2016] B.C.C. 774; [2016] B.L.R. 461, QBD (TCC) .... *Digested,* 16/**1539**: *Applied* 17/371: *Considered* 17/2194
Lupton (Inspector of Taxes) v FA & AB Ltd; *sub nom* FA & AB Ltd v Lupton (Inspector of Taxes) [1972] A.C. 634; [1971] 3 W.L.R. 670; [1971] 3 All E.R. 948; 47 T.C. 580; [1971] T.R. 284; (1971) 115 S.J. 849, HL .... *Digested,* 71/**1919**: *Applied* 03/4190, 16/2097: *Considered* 77/1600, 92/611, 12/3249, 12/3324, 13/3044, 13/3086, 17/2180: *Followed* 82/485
Luton BC v B; *sub nom* Luton BC v SB; RS (Capacity to Consent to Sexual Intercourse and Marriage), Re [2015] EWHC 3534 (Fam); [2017] 4 W.L.R. 61; [2017] 1 F.L.R. 141; [2016] 1 F.C.R. 461; [2016] Fam. Law 276, Fam Div .... *Digested,* 16/**1503**
Luton BC v PW see W (Children) (Convention Rights Claim: Procedure), Re
Luton BC v SB see Luton BC v B
Luxim Corp v Ceravision Ltd [2007] EWHC 1624 (Ch); [2007] Bus. L.R. 1534; [2007] R.P.C. 33; (2007) 30(9) I.P.D. 30057, Ch D (Patents Ct) .... *Digested,* 08/**2275**: *Applied* 17/1369
Luxor (Eastbourne) Ltd v Cooper [1941] A.C. 108; [1941] 1 All E.R. 33, HL
Applied 47-51/10604, 47-51/46, 47-51/49, 47-51/5218, 47-51/5506, 47-51/59, 47-51/63, 47-51/7870, 52/19, 53/18, 56/57, 56/62, 60/17, 70/22, 74/37, 74/40, 81/17, 86/35, 92/314: *Considered* 58/19, 69/35, 69/37, 78/317, 80/17, 87/60, 90/108, 93/70, 94/2367: *Distinguished* 47-51/43, 47-51/45, 08/430: *Followed* 47-51/39, 47-51/40, 02/68, 17/47: *Referred to* 76/452.u
Lyell v Kennedy (No.3) (1884) 27 Ch. D. 1, CA
Applied 74/2941, 81/1191, 84/1528, 17/186: *Considered* 93/3219, 10/338: *Distinguished* 01/553
Lynch's Application for Judicial Review, Re [2016] NIQB 4; [2017] N.I. 281, QBD (NI)
Lynn Shellfish Ltd v Loose see Loose v Lynn Shellfish Ltd
Lyons v Fraser [2016] HCJAC 92; 2017 S.C.L. 44; 2016 G.W.D. 32-571, HCJ .... *Digested,* 17/**2536**

M v A Hospital see M (Withdrawal of Treatment : Need for Proceedings), Re
M v Aviva Insurance UK Ltd; *sub nom* CM v Aviva Insurance UK Ltd 2017 Rep. L.R. 32; 2016 G.W.D. 40-704, Sh Ct (Lothian) (Edinburgh) .... *Digested,* 17/**2445**
M v Croatia (10161/13) [2016] 2 F.L.R. 18; (2017) 65 E.H.R.R. 9; [2015] Fam. Law 1337, ECHR
M v Croydon LBC; *sub nom* R. (on the application of M) v Croydon LBC [2012] EWCA Civ 595; [2012] 1 W.L.R. 2607; [2012] 3 All E.R. 1237; [2012] 4 Costs L.R. 689; [2012] 3 F.C.R. 179; [2012] B.L.G.R. 822, CA (Civ Div) .... *Digested,* 12/**343**: *Applied* 16/235, 17/239: *Considered* 12/399, 17/255: *Explained* 14/64, 17/232: *Followed* 13/1963, 13/329, 13/330, 16/1063, 16/201, 17/261
M v F [2017] EWHC 2176 (Fam); [2017] 3 F.C.R. 511, Fam Div
M v F (Removal from Jurisdiction: Practice) see M (Children) (Temporary Relocation), Re
M v F see A (Children) (Restrictions on Parental Responsibility: Extremism and Radicalisation in Private Law), Re
M v HM Advocate; *joined case* Gallacher (Edward William) v HM Advocate [2012] HCJAC 121; 2012 S.C.L. 1037; 2012 G.W.D. 32-644, HCJ .... *Digested,* 13/**3645**: *Considered* 17/623
M v HM Advocate (No.2); *sub nom* CJM v HM Advocate [2013] HCJAC 22; 2013 S.L.T. 380; 2013 S.C.L. 361; 2013 S.C.C.R. 215; 2013 G.W.D. 8-170, HCJ .... *Digested,* 13/**3558**: *Applied* 16/2489: *Considered* 13/3561, 14/3371, 17/2480: *Followed* 15/2953
M v J; *sub nom* DM v SJ (Surrogacy: Parental Order) [2016] EWHC 270 (Fam); [2017] 1 F.L.R. 514; [2016] Fam. Law 456, Fam Ct
M v M; *sub nom* EM v AM [2016] CSIH 2; 2016 S.C.L.R. 571; 2016 Fam. L.R. 2; 2016 G.W.D. 3-75, IH (Ex Div) .... *Digested,* 17/**2616**

M v M; *sub nom* WM v HM (Financial Remedies: Sharing Principle: Special Contribution) [2017] EWFC 25; [2018] 1 F.L.R. 313; [2017] 3 F.C.R. 198, Fam Ct .... *Digested,* 17/**1021**
M v M (Short Marriage: Clean Break) see Miller v Miller
M v Minister for Justice and Equality (C-560/14) EU:C:2017:101; [2017] 1 W.L.R. 1631; [2017] 3 C.M.L.R. 2, ECJ (3rd Chamber)
M v N [2015] EWCOP 76; [2016] C.O.P.L.R. 88; (2015) 18 C.C.L. Rep. 603; (2016) 148 B.M.L.R. 116, CP .... *Digested,* 16/**999**: *Applied* 16/998: *Considered* 17/1123, 17/1124
M v Nursing and Midwifery Council [2016] CSIH 86; 2017 S.C. 224; 2017 S.L.T. 53; 2016 G.W.D. 39-696, IH (Ex Div) .... *Digested,* 17/**2640**
M v Press Association [2016] EWCOP 34; [2016] C.O.P.L.R. 592, CP .... *Digested,* 17/**353**
M v Secretary of State for Work and Pensions; *sub nom* Secretary of State for Work and Pensions v M; *joined case* Langley v Bradford MDC [2006] UKHL 11; [2006] 2 A.C. 91; [2006] 2 W.L.R. 637; [2006] 4 All E.R. 929; [2006] 2 F.L.R. 56; [2006] 1 F.C.R. 497; [2006] H.R.L.R. 19; [2006] U.K.H.R.R. 799; 21 B.H.R.C. 254; Times, March 14, 2006; [2006] Fam. Law 524; (2006) 150 S.J.L.B. 363, HL .... *Digested,* 06/**1649**: *Applied* 06/1714, 07/3875, 08/2596, 09/1560, 09/1737: *Complaint upheld* 11/1676: *Considered* 06/1706, 08/2767, 10/4426: *Distinguished* 17/976: *Followed* 15/1954, 17/1645
M v State Hospitals Board for Scotland see McCann v State Hospitals Board for Scotland
M v Times Newspapers Ltd see Khuja v Times Newspapers Ltd
M v Times Newspapers Ltd see PNM v Times Newspapers Ltd
M v W; *sub nom* JM v JW [2017] SAC (Civ) 3; 2017 Fam. L.R. 50; 2017 G.W.D. 4-43, SAC .... *Digested,* 17/**2413**
M (A Child) v McDonalds Restaurants Ltd (Unreported, August 11, 2016), CC (Boston) [*Freeths Solicitors, 5000 Oxford Business Park South, Oxford*] .... *Digested,* 17/**1677**
M (A Child) v Ministry of Justice [2009] EWCA Civ 419; (2009) 159 N.L.J. 860, CA (Civ Div) *Considered* 17/299
M (A Child), Re see Z (A Child) (Surrogacy Agreements: Child Arrangements Orders), Re
M (Application for Certificate of Inadequacy), Re see McKinsley v Crown Prosecution Service
M (Brussels II Revised: Art.15), Re see D (A Child) (Transfer of Proceedings), Re
M (Children) (Abduction: Hague Convention: Article 13(b)), Re [2016] EWCA Civ 942; [2017] 2 F.L.R. 556; [2016] Fam. Law 1397, CA (Civ Div)
M (Children) (Care Proceedings: Adoption Support), Re [2016] EWCA Civ 61; [2017] 1 F.L.R. 548; [2016] Fam. Law 280, CA (Civ Div)
M (Children) (Care Proceedings: Passport Order), Re [2017] EWCA Civ 69; [2017] 4 W.L.R. 41; [2017] 2 F.C.R. 318, Fam Div .... *Digested,* 17/**931**
M (Children) (Contact: Enforcement of Foreign Order), Re [2017] EWCA Civ 891; [2018] 2 W.L.R. 860; [2018] 1 F.L.R. 589; [2017] 3 F.C.R. 369, CA (Civ Div) .... *Digested,* 17/**1057**
M (Children) (Jurisdicition: Wardship), Re [2016] EWCA Civ 937; [2017] 2 F.L.R. 153; [2016] 3 F.C.R. 463; [2016] Fam. Law 1323, CA (Civ Div) .... *Digested,* 17/**1070**
M (Children) (Relocation), Re [2016] EWCA Civ 1059; [2017] 2 F.L.R. 562, CA (Civ Div) .... *Digested,* 17/**970**
M (Children) (Specific Issue Order: Guardian's Application to Enforce), Re [2017] EWFC 49; [2017] 4 W.L.R. 151, Fam Ct .... *Digested,* 17/**1060**
M (Children) (Temporary Relocation), Re; *sub nom* M v F (Removal from Jurisdiction: Practice); AM v DF (Temporary Removal) [2017] EWHC 2034 (Fam); [2017] 4 W.L.R. 149; [2018] 1 F.L.R. 481, Fam Div .... *Digested,* 17/**1061**
M (Children), Re; *sub nom* A v H; JA v TH (1996 Hague Convention: Request to Exercise Jurisdiction) [2016] EWHC 2535 (Fam); [2017] 2 F.L.R. 250; [2017] 1 F.C.R. 33, Fam Div .... *Digested,* 17/**980**
M (Children), Re [2013] EWCA Civ 1170, CA (Civ Div) *Considered* 17/335, 17/999
M (Children), Re; *sub nom* A Local Authority v M [2009] EWHC 3172 (Fam); [2010] 1 F.L.R. 1355; [2010] Fam. Law 236, Fam Div .... *Digested,* 10/**1318**: *Applied* 17/930
M (D) v HM Advocate; *sub nom* DM v HM Advocate [2017] HCJAC 19; 2017 S.C.L. 535; 2017 S.C.C.R. 235; 2017 G.W.D. 12-180, HCJ .... *Digested,* 17/**2552**
M (Incapacitated Person: Withdrawal of Treatment), Re see M (Withdrawal of Treatment : Need for Proceedings), Re

M (Notification of Step-parent Adoption), Re; *sub nom* A v P Council [2014] EWHC 1128 (Fam); [2014] Fam. Law 1085, Fam Div
Applied 17/930: *Considered* 16/824

M (Restraint Order: External Confiscation Order), Re see United States v Montgomery (No.1)

M (Withdrawal of Treatment : Need for Proceedings), Re; *sub nom* M (Incapacitated Person: Withdrawal of Treatment), Re; M v A Hospital [2017] EWCOP 19; [2018] 1 W.L.R. 465; [2018] 2 All E.R. 551; [2017] C.O.P.L.R. 398; [2017] Med. L.R. 558, CP

M Najib & Sons Ltd v Revenue and Customs Commissioners [2017] UKFTT 147 (TC); [2017] S.F.T.D. 536; [2017] S.T.I. 796, FTT (Tax) .... *Digested,* 17/**2121**

M Young Legal Associates Ltd v Lees see M Young Legal Associates Ltd v Zahid (A Firm)

M Young Legal Associates Ltd v Zahid (A Firm); *sub nom* M Young Legal Associates Ltd v Lees [2006] EWCA Civ 613; [2006] 1 W.L.R. 2562; (2006) 103(22) L.S.G. 26; [2006] N.P.C. 57, CA (Civ Div) .... *Digested,* 06/**2925**:
Applied 09/2750, 11/1076, 12/1081: *Considered* 10/2303, 17/1585

M&G Securities Ltd v Inland Revenue Commissioners; *joined case* Schroder Unit Trusts Ltd v Inland Revenue Commissioners [1999] S.T.C. 315; [1999] B.T.C. 8003; Times, February 2, 1999; Independent, February 1, 1999, Ch D .... *Digested,* 99/**4763**:
Distinguished 17/2178

M&M Management Ltd v Revenue and Customs Commissioners [2017] UKFTT 156 (TC); [2017] S.T.I. 362, FTT (Tax)

M, Petitioner [2016] CSOH 115; 2016 S.L.T. 911; 2016 G.W.D. 23-435, OH .... *Digested,* 16/**2417**:
Affirmed 17/2386

M-W (A Child) (Care Proceedings: Expert Evidence), Re; *sub nom* Gateshead MBC v JM [2010] EWCA Civ 12; [2010] 2 F.L.R. 46; [2010] 1 F.C.R. 427; [2010] Fam. Law 340, CA (Civ Div) .... *Digested,* 10/**1315**:
Applied 17/1049

MA (Eritrea) v Secretary of State for the Home Department see R. (on the application of EM (Eritrea)) v Secretary of State for the Home Department

MA Holdings Ltd v George Wimpey UK Ltd; *sub nom* R. (on the application of George Wimpey UK Ltd) v Tewkesbury BC; George Wimpey UK Ltd v Tewkesbury BC [2008] EWCA Civ 12; [2008] 1 W.L.R. 1649; [2008] 3 All E.R. 859; [2008] C.P. Rep. 19; 127 Con. L.R. 17; (2008) 105(5) L.S.G. 28; [2008] N.P.C. 6, CA (Civ Div) .... *Digested,* 08/**397**:
Applied 17/999: *Followed* 15/1110

MA Lloyd and Son Ltd (In Administration) v PPC International Ltd (t/a Professional Powercraft) [2016] EWHC 2162 (QB); [2016] 5 Costs L.R. 853; [2017] P.N.L.R. 1, QBD .... *Digested,* 16/**232**

Mabbutt v Revenue and Customs Commissioners; *sub nom* Revenue and Customs Commissioners v Mabbutt [2016] UKFTT 306 (TC), FTT (Tax)
Considered 17/2111: *Reversed* 17/2187

Mabbutt v Revenue and Customs Commissioners; *sub nom* Revenue and Customs Commissioners v Mabbutt [2017] UKUT 289 (TCC); [2017] S.T.C. 1873; [2017] B.T.C. 528; [2017] S.T.I. 1868, UT (Tax) .... *Digested,* 17/**2187**

Mabon v Mabon [2005] EWCA Civ 634; [2005] Fam. 366; [2005] 3 W.L.R. 460; [2005] 2 F.L.R. 1011; [2005] 2 F.C.R. 354; [2005] H.R.L.R. 29; [2006] U.K.H.R.R. 421; (2005) 8 C.C.L. Rep. 412; Times, June 2, 2005; [2005] Fam. Law 696, CA (Civ Div) .... *Digested,* 05/**1634**:
Applied 15/1050: *Considered* 15/985: *Followed* 15/1039, 17/929, 17/966

Macadam, Re; *joined case* Dallow and Moscrop v Codd [1946] Ch. 73; [1945] 2 All E.R. 664, Ch D
Applied 47-51/9426, 53/1392, 64/3345, 17/2221: *Considered* 47-51/9423:
Distinguished 47-51/9431

Macallans v W Burrell Homes Ltd 2017 S.L.T. (Sh Ct) 1; 2016 G.W.D. 37-652, Sh Ct (Glasgow) .... *Digested,* 17/**2437**

Macari, Re [2017] NICh 5; [2017] I.L.Pr. 35; [2017] B.P.I.R. 515, Ch D (NI) .... *Digested,* 17/**2325**

Maccaferri Ltd v Zurich Insurance Plc; *sub nom* Zurich Insurance Plc v Maccaferri Ltd [2015] EWHC 1708 (Comm); [2015] 2 C.L.C. 77; [2016] E.C.C. 22; [2015] Lloyd's Rep. I.R. 594, QBD (Comm) .... *Digested,* 15/**1464**:
Affirmed 17/1346

Maccaferri Ltd v Zurich Insurance Plc; *sub nom* Zurich Insurance Plc v Maccaferri Ltd [2016] EWCA Civ 1302; [2018] 1 All E.R. (Comm) 112; [2017] Lloyd's Rep. I.R. 200, CA (Civ Div) .... *Digested,* 17/**1346**:
Considered 17/1338

Macclesfield v Parker see Parker v Parker

MacDonald v Aberdeenshire Council [2013] CSIH 83; 2014 S.C. 114; 2014 S.L.T. 2; 2014 S.C.L.R. 111; 2014 Rep. L.R. 2; 2013 G.W.D. 36-709, IH (Ex Div) .... *Digested,* 14/**3690**: *Applied* 17/2738: *Considered* 17/2739

MacDonald (Inspector of Taxes) v Dextra Accessories Ltd see Dextra Accessories Ltd v MacDonald (Inspector of Taxes)

MacDonald Dickens & Macklin v Costello; *sub nom* Costello v MacDonald [2011] EWCA Civ 930; [2012] Q.B. 244; [2011] 3 W.L.R. 1341; [2012] 1 All E.R. (Comm) 357; [2011] B.L.R. 544; 137 Con. L.R. 55; [2011] 3 E.G.L.R. 87; [2011] 47 E.G. 106; [2011] C.I.L.L. 3081, CA (Civ Div) .... *Digested,* 11/**543**: *Followed* 17/501

MacDonald Estate v Martin (Unreported, 1994) *Considered* 17/1585

Macdonald Resorts Ltd v Revenue and Customs Commissioners (C-270/09) EU:C:2010:780; [2011] S.T.C. 412; [2011] B.V.C. 171; [2011] S.T.I. 137, ECJ (1st Chamber) .... *Digested,* 11/**3569**: *Applied* 17/2236, 17/2264: *Considered* 12/3410, 17/2258

Macguire v Grant & Wilson Property Management Ltd [2017] SAC (Civ) 20; 2017 S.L.T. (Sh Ct) 107; 2017 G.W.D. 16-254, SAC .... *Digested,* 17/**2439**

MacInnes v Gross [2017] EWHC 127 (QB); [2017] 4 W.L.R. 49; [2017] 2 Costs L.R. 243, QBD .... *Digested,* 17/**231**: *Applied* 17/277: *Considered* 17/276

MacKay (Scott Henry) v HM Advocate [2017] HCJAC 44; 2017 J.C. 311; 2017 S.L.T. 1127; 2017 S.C.L. 761; 2017 S.C.C.R. 364; 2017 G.W.D. 21-344, HCJ Appeal *Digested,* 17/**2551**

Mackie v Maxi Construction Ltd 2017 S.L.T. (Sh Ct) 97; 2017 G.W.D. 9-130, Sh Ct (Lothian) (Livingston) .... *Digested,* 17/**2688**

Macklin (Paul Alexander) v HM Advocate [2015] UKSC 77; [2017] 1 All E.R. 32; 2016 S.C. (U.K.S.C.) 47; 2016 S.L.T. 1; 2016 S.C.L. 80; 2016 S.C.C.R. 119; Times, January 25, 2016; 2016 G.W.D. 1-6, SC .... *Digested,* 16/**524**

Maclaine Watson & Co Ltd v Department of Trade and Industry see JH Rayner (Mincing Lane) Ltd v Department of Trade and Industry

Maclaine Watson & Co Ltd v International Tin Council see JH Rayner (Mincing Lane) Ltd v Department of Trade and Industry

Macleod and Mitchell Contractors Ltd v Revenue and Customs Commissioners; *sub nom* Mitchell v Revenue and Customs Commissioners [2017] UKFTT 139 (TC); [2017] S.T.I. 1007, FTT (Tax)

MacLeod's Legal Representatives v Highland Health Board [2016] CSIH 25; 2016 S.C. 647; 2017 S.C.L.R. 115; 2016 G.W.D. 12-241, IH (Ex Div) .... *Digested,* 17/**2736**

Maclurcan v Maclurcan (1897) 77 L.T. 474 *Applied* 47-51/3034, 02/2676, 17/1846

MacMillan v MacKenzie 1995 S.L.T. (Land Ct) 7, Land Ct (Full Ct) .... *Digested,* 95/**6416**: *Considered* 17/2402

MacMillan v T Leith Developments Ltd (In Receivership and Liquidation) [2016] CSOH 19; 2016 S.L.T. 477; 2016 G.W.D. 7-146, OH .... *Digested,* 16/**2697**: *Reversed in part* 17/2679

MacMillan v T Leith Developments Ltd (In Receivership and Liquidation) [2017] CSIH 23; 2017 S.C. 642; 2017 S.L.T. 415; 2017 S.C.L.R. 477; 2017 G.W.D. 10-141, IH (1 Div) .... *Digested,* 17/**2679**

Macob Civil Engineering Ltd v Morrison Construction Ltd [1999] C.L.C. 739; [1999] B.L.R. 93; (1999) 1 T.C.L.R. 113; 64 Con. L.R. 1; [1999] 3 E.G.L.R. 7; [1999] 37 E.G. 173; Times, March 11, 1999; Independent, March 1, 1999; (1999) 15 Const. L.J. 300; (1999) 96(10) L.S.G. 28, QBD (TCC) .... *Digested,* 99/**794**: *Applied* 02/662, 03/643, 03/667, 06/333, 10/560, 11/487, 13/1719, 14/130, 14/581, 17/451, 17/452: *Approved* 00/806: *Considered* 11/131, 16/59: *Distinguished* 00/807: *Referred to* 99/795

MacPherson v Revenue and Customs Commissioners see Languard New Homes Ltd v Revenue and Customs Commissioners

Macrae v KPMG LLP; *sub nom* Primeo Fund (In Liquidation), Re [2016] EWHC 2432 (Ch); [2017] Bus. L.R. 726, Ch D (Companies Ct)

Macris v Financial Conduct Authority; *sub nom* Financial Conduct Authority v Macris [2015] EWCA Civ 490; [2016] 2 All E.R. 265; [2015] Bus. L.R. 1141; [2015] Lloyd's Rep. F.C. 445, CA (Civ Div) .... *Digested,* 15/**1154**: *Cited* 16/959: *Reversed* 17/1074

Macris v Financial Conduct Authority; *sub nom* Financial Conduct Authority v Macris [2017] UKSC 19; [2017] 1 W.L.R. 1095; [2017] 4 All E.R. 1027; [2017] Bus. L.R. 643; Times, March 23, 2017, SC .... *Digested,* 17/**1074**

Madami v Secretary of State for the Home Department see R. (on the application of Lumba) v Secretary of State for the Home Department

Madarassy v Nomura International Plc [2007] EWCA Civ 33; [2007] I.C.R. 867; [2007] I.R.L.R. 246, CA (Civ Div) .... *Digested,* 07/**1401**: *Applied* 07/1184, 09/4267, 11/1119, 12/1125, 17/819: *Approved* 12/1072: *Considered* 12/1033, 13/1032, 17/2308: *Followed* 10/1122, 14/1100: *Referred to* 13/986

Madhewoo v Mauritius [2016] UKPC 30; [2016] 4 W.L.R. 167; 42 B.H.R.C. 290, PC (Mau)

Magee v United Kingdom (28135/95) (2001) 31 E.H.R.R. 35; 8 B.H.R.C. 646; [2000] Po. L.R. 188; Times, June 20, 2000; [2000] Crim. L.R. 681, ECHR .... *Digested,* 00/**3223**: *Applied* 04/4153: *Considered* 10/2322, 17/1095

Magellan Spirit ApS v Vitol SA [2016] EWHC 454 (Comm); [2017] 1 All E.R. (Comm) 241; [2016] 2 Lloyd's Rep. 1; [2016] 1 C.L.C. 480, QBD (Comm) .... *Digested,* 16/**1969**

Magiera v Magiera; *sub nom* G v G [2015] EWHC 2101 (Fam); [2016] 4 W.L.R. 22; [2016] Fam. Law 454, Fam Div .... *Digested,* 16/**898**: *Reversed in part* 17/1849

Magiera v Magiera; *sub nom* G v G [2016] EWCA Civ 1292; [2017] Fam. 327; [2017] 3 W.L.R. 41; [2017] B.P.I.R. 472; [2017] W.T.L.R. 245; 20 I.T.E.L.R. 47, CA (Civ Div) .... *Digested,* 17/**1849**

Magill v Panel Systems (DB Ltd) [2017] EWHC 1517 (QB); [2017] Med. L.R. 440, QBD .... *Digested,* 17/**1553**

Magill v Porter see Porter v Magill

Magill v Weeks see Porter v Magill

Magnesium Elektron Ltd v Molycorp Chemicals and Oxides (Europe) Ltd [2015] EWHC 3596 (Pat); [2016] R.P.C. 18, Ch D (Patents Ct) .... *Digested,* 17/**1382**

Magyar Kereszteny Mennonita Egyhaz v Hungary (70945/11) (2015) 61 E.H.R.R. 23; (2017) 64 E.H.R.R. 12; 37 B.H.R.C. 187, ECHR

Magyar Tartalomszolgaltatok Egyesulete v Hungary (22947/13) 42 B.H.R.C. 52, ECHR

Magyarorszagi Evangeliumi Testverkozosseg v Hungary (54977/12) (2017) 65 E.H.R.R. SE1, ECHR

Mahad (Ethiopia) v Entry Clearance Officer; *sub nom* Ali v Entry Clearance Officer; Ismail v Entry Clearance Officer; Sakthivel v Entry Clearance Officer; Muhumed v Entry Clearance Officer; *joined cases* AM (Ethiopia) v Entry Clearance Officer; SA (Somalia) v Entry Clearance Officer; MB (Pakistan) v Entry Clearance Officer; VS (Sri Lanka) v Entry Clearance Officer; MI (Somalia) v Entry Clearance Officer [2008] EWCA Civ 1082; [2009] Imm. A.R. 254; (2008) 105(41) L.S.G. 19, CA (Civ Div) .... *Digested,* 09/**2166**: *Applied* 10/1781, 10/1782, 11/1744, 12/1741, 13/1649, 17/1207: *Considered* 14/1703: *Reversed* 10/1822

Mahadervan v Mahadervan; *sub nom* Mahadevan v Mahadevan [1964] P. 233; [1963] 2 W.L.R. 271; [1962] 3 All E.R. 1108; (1962) 106 S.J. 533, PDAD .... *Digested,* 63/**1684**: *Applied* 01/2611: *Considered* 74/1069, 99/3734, 17/1045: *Distinguished* 64/1732

Mahadevan v Mahadevan see Mahadervan v Mahadervan

Maier v ASOS Plc [2015] EWCA Civ 220; [2016] 2 All E.R. 738; [2016] Bus. L.R. 1063; [2015] E.T.M.R. 26; [2015] F.S.R. 20, CA (Civ Div) .... *Digested,* 15/**1536**: *Applied* 15/1539, 16/1340, 17/1402: *Considered* 17/1395: *Followed* 16/1289

Maierhofer v Finanzamt Augsburg-Land (C-315/00) EU:C:2003:23; [2003] S.T.C. 564; [2003] E.C.R. I-563; [2003] 2 C.M.L.R. 37; [2003] C.E.C. 192; [2003] B.T.C. 5269; [2003] B.V.C. 325; [2003] S.T.I. 88, ECJ (5th Chamber) .... *Digested,* 03/**4532**: *Applied* 05/4421, 14/3052: *Considered* 05/4403: *Followed* 12/3414, 13/3194, 17/2238

Mailbox (Birmingham) Ltd v Galliford Construction Ltd [2017] EWHC 67 (TCC); [2017] B.L.R. 180; 170 Con. L.R. 219; [2017] C.I.L.L. 3967, QBD (TCC) .... *Digested,* 17/**449**

Mailbox (Birmingham) Ltd v Galliford Try Building Ltd (formerly Galliford Construction Ltd) [2017] EWHC 1405 (TCC); [2017] Bus. L.R. 2103; [2017] B.L.R. 443; 172 Con. L.R. 198; [2017] C.I.L.L. 3999, QBD (TCC) .... *Digested,* 17/**658**

Mainstream Properties Ltd v Young see OBG Ltd v Allan

Majorowski v Guy's and St Thomas's NHS Trust see Majrowski v Guy's and St Thomas's NHS Trust

Majrowski v Guy's and St Thomas's NHS Trust; *sub nom* Majorowski v Guy's and St Thomas's NHS Trust [2006] UKHL 34; [2007] 1 A.C. 224; [2006] 3 W.L.R. 125; [2006] 4 All E.R. 395; [2006] I.C.R. 1199; [2006] I.R.L.R. 695; (2006) 91 B.M.L.R. 85; Times, July 13, 2006; Independent, July 14, 2006; (2006) 156 N.L.J. 1173; (2006) 150 S.J.L.B. 986, HL .... *Digested,* 06/**1337**: *Applied* 06/2916, 07/1377, 07/1437, 11/658, 12/1117, 15/311: *Considered* 09/3959, 11/335, 11/775, 12/3901, 12/855, 13/3862, 16/871: *Followed* 10/3413, 17/645

Majumder v Secretary of State for the Home Department see SM v Secretary of State for the Home Department

MAK v Dewsbury Healthcare NHS Trust see JD v East Berkshire Community Health NHS Trust

MAK (Pakistan) v Secretary of State for the Home Department; *sub nom* K (Pakistan) v Secretary of State for the Home Department [2016] CSIH 13; 2016 S.C. 536; 2016 G.W.D. 9-175, IH (1 Div) .... *Digested,* 17/**2670**: *Applied* 17/2669: *Considered* 17/2665

Makdessi v Cavendish Square Holdings BV; *sub nom* Cavendish Square Holding BV v Makdessi; El Makdessi v Cavendish Square Holdings BV; *joined case* ParkingEye Ltd v Beavis [2015] UKSC 67; [2016] A.C. 1172; [2015] 3 W.L.R. 1373; [2016] 2 All E.R. 519; [2016] 2 All E.R. (Comm) 1; [2016] 1 Lloyd's Rep. 55; [2015] 2 C.L.C. 686; [2016] B.L.R. 1; 162 Con. L.R. 1; [2016] R.T.R. 8; Times, November 23, 2015; [2016] C.I.L.L. 3769, SC .... *Digested,* 16/**437**: *Considered* 16/2481, 17/395: *Followed* 17/1444, 17/170: *Referred to* 16/860

Makhlouf v Secretary of State for the Home Department see Makhlouf's Application, Re

Makhlouf's Application, Re; *sub nom* Makhlouf v Secretary of State for the Home Department [2016] UKSC 59; [2017] 3 All E.R. 1; [2017] N.I. 127; [2017] Imm. A.R. 538; [2017] I.N.L.R. 222, SC .... *Digested,* 17/**1191**

Makhlouf's Application, Re; *sub nom* Makhlouf v Secretary of State for the Home Department [2014] NICA 86, CA (NI)
Affirmed 17/1191

Mal Bower's Macquarie Electrical Centre Pty Ltd (In Liquidation), Re [1974] 1 N.S.W.L.R. 254
Applied 00/3465: *Considered* 17/1334

Malcolm v Dundee City Council [2017] CSIH 32; 2017 S.L.T. 1008; 2017 G.W.D. 18-288, IH (2 Div) .... *Digested,* 17/**2583**

Malcolm v Lewisham LBC; *sub nom* Lewisham LBC v Malcolm [2008] UKHL 43; [2008] 1 A.C. 1399; [2008] 3 W.L.R. 194; [2008] 4 All E.R. 525; [2008] I.R.L.R. 700; [2008] H.L.R. 41; [2008] B.L.G.R. 549; (2008) 11 C.C.L. Rep. 573; (2008) 102 B.M.L.R. 170; [2008] 2 P. & C.R. 18; [2008] L. & T.R. 29; Times, June 26, 2008; [2008] 26 E.G. 117 (C.S.); (2008) 105(26) L.S.G. 23; (2008) 152(26) S.J.L.B. 29; [2008] N.P.C. 76, HL .... *Digested,* 08/**2466**: *Applied* 09/1095, 09/1172, 09/1173, 11/1057, 11/1851, 11/2070: *Considered* 09/1178, 12/3111, 13/968, 15/808, 17/2308: *Followed* 10/1045, 11/1055: *Not followed* 16/667: *Referred to* 10/1046

Malik v Manchester Crown Court see R. (on the application of Malik) v Manchester Crown Court

Malins v Solicitors Regulation Authority [2017] EWHC 835 (Admin); [2017] 4 W.L.R. 85, QBD (Admin) .... *Digested,* 17/**1491**

Malkinson v Trim [2002] EWCA Civ 1273; [2003] 1 W.L.R. 463; [2003] 2 All E.R. 356; [2003] C.P. Rep. 11; [2003] C.P.L.R. 99; [2002] 3 Costs L.R. 515; Times, October 11, 2002; (2002) 99(40) L.S.G. 33; (2002) 152 N.L.J. 1484; (2002) 146 S.J.L.B. 207; [2002] N.P.C. 116, CA (Civ Div) .... *Digested,* 02/**391**: *Applied* 17/268: *Considered* 03/371, 13/3522: *Followed* 03/323, 17/245

Mallalieu v Drummond (Inspector of Taxes) [1983] 2 A.C. 861; [1983] 3 W.L.R. 409; [1983] 2 All E.R. 1095; [1983] S.T.C. 665; 57 T.C. 330; (1983) 80 L.S.G. 2368; (1983) 133 N.L.J. 869; (1983) 127 S.J. 538, HL
Applied 85/1784, 13/3027, 14/2870, 14/2932, 17/2145: *Considered* 90/2667, 99/4701: *Distinguished* 97/2945: *Followed* 96/3356, 13/3080, 14/2975, 15/2429

Mallett & Sons (Antiques) Ltd v Grosvenor West End Properties Ltd see Boss Holdings Ltd v Grosvenor West End Properties Ltd

Mallis v European Commission (C-105/15 P) EU:C:2016:702; [2017] 1 C.M.L.R. 36, ECJ (Grand Chamber)

Malloch v Aberdeen Corp (No.1) [1971] 1 W.L.R. 1578; [1971] 2 All E.R. 1278; 1971 S.C. (H.L.) 85; 1971 S.L.T. 245; (1971) 115 S.J. 756, HL .... *Digested,* 71/**3866**: *Applied* 83/15: *Considered* 75/3760, 76/3084, 77/3072, 80/99, 87/3162, 92/5290, 95/5443, 04/466, 17/2768: *Distinguished* 84/14, 93/5405, 98/2242, 03/3475: *Followed* 83/24, 96/3961

Malpas v Fife Council 1999 S.L.T. 499; 1999 S.C.L.R. 550; 1999 G.W.D. 6-308, OH ... *Digested,* 99/**5688**: *Considered* 17/2428

Malvern Fishing Co Ltd v Ailsa Craig Fishing Co Ltd (The Strathallan) see Ailsa Craig Fishing Co Ltd v Malvern Fishing Co Ltd (The Strathallan)

Malyon v Plummer [1964] 1 Q.B. 330; [1963] 2 W.L.R. 1213; [1963] 2 All E.R. 344; (1963) 107 S.J. 270, CA .... *Digested,* 63/**918**: *Followed* 17/634

Mama Milla Ltd (In Creditors' Voluntary Liquidation), Re see Top Brands Ltd v Sharma
Mamazhonov v Russia (17239/13) (2017) 64 E.H.R.R. 26, ECHR
Mamidoil-Jetoil Greek Petroleum Co SA v Okta Crude Oil Refinery AD (No.1) [2001] EWCA Civ 406; [2001] 2 All E.R. (Comm) 193; [2001] 2 Lloyd's Rep. 76, CA (Civ Div) .... *Digested,* 01/**956**:
Applied 06/682, 13/566: *Followed* 17/500, 17/74
Mamola Challenger Shipping Co v Omak Maritime Ltd see Omak Maritime Ltd v Mamola Challenger Shipping Co Ltd
Management Corp Strata Title Plan No 3322 v Tiong Aik Construction Pte Ltd [2016] SGCA 40; 167 Con. L.R. 160, CA (Sing) .... *Digested,* 17/**470**
Manchester and District Housing Association v Roberts see City West Housing Trust v Massey
Manchester City Council v JW [2014] UKUT 168 (AAC); [2014] E.L.R. 304, UT (AAC) . *Digested,* 14/**941**:
Applied 17/707
Manchester City Council v Pinnock; *sub nom* Pinnock v Manchester City Council [2010] UKSC 45; [2011] 2 A.C. 104; [2010] 3 W.L.R. 1441; [2011] 1 All E.R. 285; [2011] P.T.S.R. 61; [2011] H.R.L.R. 3; [2010] U.K.H.R.R. 1213; 31 B.H.R.C. 670; [2011] H.L.R. 7; [2010] B.L.G.R. 909; [2011] L. & T.R. 2; [2010] 3 E.G.L.R. 113; Times, November 4, 2010; [2010] 45 E.G. 93 (C.S.); (2010) 107(44) L.S.G. 16; (2011) 108(8) L.S.G. 20; (2010) 154(42) S.J.L.B. 30; [2010] N.P.C. 109, SC .... *Digested,* 11/**2066**:
Applied 11/2069, 14/1997, 14/3635: *Considered* 13/1892, 14/1625, 15/1290, 16/1374, 17/1168: *Distinguished* 12/2599: *Followed* 12/1301, 12/1645, 12/2055, 13/1562, 13/1890, 14/2000, 17/1730, 17/562: *Not applied* 15/1592
Mandalia v Secretary of State for the Home Department; *joined case* Secretary of State for the Home Department v Rodriguez [2015] UKSC 59; [2015] 1 W.L.R. 4546; [2016] 4 All E.R. 189; [2016] Imm. A.R. 180; [2016] I.N.L.R. 184; Times, October 26, 2015, SC .... *Digested,* 15/**1359**:
Considered 16/2686: *Followed* 17/1209
Mann v Mann [2016] EWHC 314 (Fam); [2016] Fam. 281; [2016] 3 W.L.R. 67; [2017] 1 F.L.R. 559; [2016] Fam. Law 448, Fam Div .... *Digested,* 16/**892**
Manna v Central Manchester University Hospitals NHS Foundation Trust [2015] EWHC 2279 (QB), QBD
Affirmed 17/639
Manna v Central Manchester University Hospitals NHS Foundation Trust [2017] EWCA Civ 12; [2017] 1 Costs L.O. 89; [2017] P.I.Q.R. Q2; [2017] Med. L.R. 132; (2017) 157 B.M.L.R. 134, CA (Civ Div) .... *Digested,* 17/**639**
Mannai Investment Co Ltd v Eagle Star Life Assurance Co Ltd [1997] A.C. 749; [1997] 2 W.L.R. 945; [1997] 3 All E.R. 352; [1997] C.L.C. 1124; [1997] 1 E.G.L.R. 57; [1997] 25 E.G. 138; [1997] 24 E.G. 122; (1997) 16 Tr. L.R. 432; Times, May 26, 1997; [1997] E.G. 82 (C.S.); (1997) 94(30) L.S.G. 30; (1997) 147 N.L.J. 846; (1997) 141 S.J.L.B. 130; [1997] N.P.C. 81, HL .... *Digested,* 97/**3256**:
Applied 98/3598, 00/5612, 01/4156, 01/4182, 02/3008, 03/2723, 04/2243, 04/2497, 04/670, 05/2646, 05/523, 06/284, 07/2728, 07/807, 08/2438, 11/2060, 12/3364, 14/1996, 14/2970, 16/2060, 17/2111: *Considered* 03/2758, 05/475, 07/2754, 09/5040, 10/4356, 12/4124, 16/2707, 17/1432: *Distinguished* 98/3033, 98/3608, 00/3910, 04/2488, 08/2437, 12/2022: *Explained* 06/2703: *Followed* 00/3885, 00/4421, 10/2049, 14/1970, 14/2226, 15/2847, 17/2471: *Overruled* 99/3660
Manning v King's College Hospital NHS Trust [2008] EWHC 3008 (QB), QBD
Considered 17/634
Manolete Partners Plc v Hastings BC; *sub nom* Hastings BC v Manolete Partners Plc [2016] UKSC 50; [2016] 1 W.L.R. 3059; [2017] 2 All E.R. 611; [2016] B.L.R. 503; [2016] R.V.R. 301; Times, August 23, 2016, SC .... *Digested,* 16/**1449**
Mansel Oil Ltd v Troon Storage Tankers SA [2008] EWHC 1269 (Comm); [2008] 2 All E.R. (Comm) 898; [2008] 2 Lloyd's Rep. 384; [2008] 1 C.L.C. 945, QBD (Comm) .... *Digested,* 08/**3465**:
Affirmed 09/3581: *Considered* 17/503
Manson v Henry Robb Ltd [2017] CSOH 126; 2017 S.L.T. 1173; 2017 Rep. L.R. 118; 2017 G.W.D. 31-498, OH .... *Digested,* 17/**2572**
Mansworth (Inspector of Taxes) v Jelley [2002] EWCA Civ 1829; [2003] S.T.C. 53; 75 T.C. 1; [2003] B.T.C. 3; Times, December 20, 2002; [2002] S.T.I. 1808; (2003) 100(10) L.S.G. 29, CA (Civ Div) .... *Digested,* 03/**4161**:
Applied 16/2049: *Considered* 07/3990, 17/2087
Maoudis (t/a Montana Debt Management) v Financial Conduct Authority [2016] UKUT 548 (TCC); [2017] B.P.I.R. 1555, UT (Tax)

Maple Leaf Macro Volatility Master Fund v Rouvroy [2009] EWCA Civ 1334; [2010] 2 All E.R. (Comm) 788, CA (Civ Div) ... *Digested,* 11/**525**: *Followed* 17/499

Marathon Asset Management LLP v Seddon [2017] EWHC 300 (Comm); [2017] I.C.R. 791; [2017] I.R.L.R. 503; [2017] F.S.R. 36, QBD (Comm) ... *Digested,* 17/**2196**: *Applied* 17/217

Marathon Asset Management LLP v Seddon [2017] EWHC 479 (Comm); [2017] 2 Costs L.R. 255, QBD (Comm) ... *Digested,* 17/**247**

Marchday Holdings Ltd v Customs and Excise Commissioners see Customs and Excise Commissioners v Marchday Holdings Ltd

Marchon Germany GmbH v Karaszkiewicz (C-315/14) EU:C:2016:211; [2016] 2 All E.R. (Comm) 851; [2016] Bus. L.R. 694; [2016] 1 Lloyd's Rep. 531; [2016] 3 C.M.L.R. 18; [2017] C.E.C. 252, ECJ (4th Chamber)

Marcic v Thames Water Utilities Ltd; *sub nom* Thames Water Utilities Ltd v Marcic [2003] UKHL 66; [2004] 2 A.C. 42; [2003] 3 W.L.R. 1603; [2004] 1 All E.R. 135; [2004] B.L.R. 1; 91 Con. L.R. 1; [2004] Env. L.R. 25; [2004] H.R.L.R. 10; [2004] U.K.H.R.R. 253; Times, December 5, 2003; Independent, December 9, 2003; [2003] 50 E.G. 95 (C.S.); (2004) 101(4) L.S.G. 32; (2003) 153 N.L.J. 1869; (2003) 147 S.J.L.B. 1429; [2003] N.P.C. 150, HL ... *Digested,* 04/**2763**: *Applied* 05/2893, 07/2961, 09/1560, 09/4031: *Cited* 10/297: *Considered* 06/1482, 07/3990, 07/4276, 11/2275, 13/3251, 16/1723: *Distinguished* 04/1373, 06/4417, 07/3973, 17/1832: *Followed* 17/2297

Marcu v Agentia Nationala de Administrare Fiscala (ANAF) - Directia Generala Regionala a Finantelor Publice Bucuresti (C-392/16) EU:C:2017:519; [2017] B.V.C. 32, ECJ (9th Chamber)

Marex Financial Ltd v Sevilleja Garcia [2017] EWHC 918 (Comm); [2017] 4 W.L.R. 105; [2018] 1 All E.R. (Comm) 761, QBD (Comm) ... *Digested,* 17/**314**

Margarit Panicello v Hernandez Martinez (C-503/15); *sub nom* Panicello v Martinez (C-503/15) EU:C:2017:126; [2017] 3 C.M.L.R. 7, ECJ (3rd Chamber)

Maridive & Oil Services SAE v CNA Insurance Co (Europe) Ltd [2002] EWCA Civ 369; [2002] 1 All E.R. (Comm) 653; [2002] 2 Lloyd's Rep. 9; [2002] C.P. Rep. 45; [2002] C.L.C. 972, CA (Civ Div) ... *Digested,* 02/**486**: *Applied* 07/2920, 12/268: *Considered* 17/306

Marinari v Lloyds Bank Plc (C-364/93) EU:C:1995:289; [1996] Q.B. 217; [1996] 2 W.L.R. 159; [1995] E.C.R. I-2719; [1996] 5 Bank. L.R. 84; [1996] All E.R. (E.C.) 84; [1996] C.E.C. 14; [1995] I.L.Pr. 737; Times, October 19, 1995, ECJ ... *Digested,* 95/**705**: *Applied* 08/418, 14/556, 15/438: *Considered* 06/646: *Followed* 17/160, 17/430

Marine A v Judge Advocate General see R. v Marine A

Marine Trade SA v Pioneer Freight Futures Co Ltd BVI [2009] EWHC 2656 (Comm); [2010] 1 Lloyd's Rep. 631; [2009] 2 C.L.C. 657, QBD (Comm) ... *Digested,* 10/**3015**: *Considered* 11/199, 11/200, 11/222, 11/526, 17/2177: *Not followed* 12/254: *Overruled* 12/259

Marios Chippery, Re see Georgiou (t/a Marios Chippery) v Customs and Excise Commissioners

Markem Corp v Zipher Ltd; *joined case* Markem Technologies Ltd v Buckby [2005] EWCA Civ 267; [2005] R.P.C. 31; (2005) 28(6) I.P.D. 28042, CA (Civ Div) ... *Digested,* 05/**2448**: *Applied* 06/2522: *Considered* 17/1320: *Overruled* 07/2557

Markem Technologies Ltd v Buckby see Markem Corp v Zipher Ltd

Marketing Force Ltd v Alexander (Valuation Officer) [2016] R.V.R. 290, VT ... *Digested,* 17/**1529**

Markovic v Italy (1398/03) (2007) 44 E.H.R.R. 52; 22 B.H.R.C. 641, ECHR ... *Digested,* 07/**2212**: *Applied* 17/1425

Marks & Spencer Plc v Asda Stores Ltd [2016] EWHC 2081 (Pat); [2016] 5 Costs L.R. 837; [2017] F.S.R. 11, Ch D (Patents Ct) ... *Digested,* 16/**242**

Marks & Spencer Plc v BNP Paribas Securities Services Trust Co (Jersey) Ltd [2015] UKSC 72; [2016] A.C. 742; [2015] 3 W.L.R. 1843; [2016] 4 All E.R. 441; 163 Con. L.R. 1; [2016] 1 P. & C.R. 13; [2016] L. & T.R. 8; Times, December 12, 2015; [2016] C.I.L.L. 3779, SC ... *Digested,* 16/**1377**: *Applied* 16/1803, 16/721: *Considered* 17/854: *Followed* 16/1265, 16/1272, 16/1333, 16/423, 16/440, 17/2024, 17/399, 17/47, 17/486, 17/500

Marks & Spencer Plc v Customs and Excise Commissioners (C-62/00) EU:C:2002:435; [2003] Q.B. 866; [2003] 2 W.L.R. 665; [2002] S.T.C. 1036; [2002] E.C.R. I-6325; [2002] 3 C.M.L.R. 9; [2002] C.E.C. 572; [2002] B.T.C. 5477; [2002] B.V.C. 622; Times, July 20, 2002; [2002] S.T.I. 1009, ECJ (5th Chamber) ... *Digested,* 02/**4775**: *Applied* 04/3987, 05/4377, 06/4442, 06/4470, 09/3771, 10/3483, 11/3570, 13/3244, 14/3038: *Cited* 15/955: *Considered* 05/4367, 06/4460, 06/4487, 08/4016, 08/4065, 09/4070, 10/3507, 14/2885: *Followed* 17/2177

Marks & Spencer Plc v Customs and Excise Commissioners (No.1) [1999] S.T.C. 205; [1999] 1 C.M.L.R. 1152; [1999] Eu. L.R. 450; [1999] B.T.C. 5073; [1999] B.V.C. 107; Times, January 19, 1999, QBD .... *Digested,* 99/**5001**: *Applied* 03/4569, 17/2228: *Considered* 11/56: *Reversed in part* 00/5317

Marks & Spencer Plc v Interflora Inc see Interflora Inc v Marks & Spencer Plc

Marks & Spencer Plc v One in a Million Ltd see British Telecommunications Plc v One in a Million Ltd

Marks & Spencer Plc v Williams-Ryan [2005] EWCA Civ 470; [2005] I.C.R. 1293; [2005] I.R.L.R. 562, CA (Civ Div) .... *Digested,* 05/**1336**: *Considered* 08/1220: *Followed* 17/847

Marlbray Ltd v Laditi see Rabiu v Marlbray Ltd

Marley v Rawlings [2014] UKSC 2; [2015] A.C. 129; [2014] 2 W.L.R. 213; [2014] 1 All E.R. 807; [2014] 2 F.L.R. 555; [2015] 1 F.C.R. 187; [2014] W.T.L.R. 299; 16 I.T.E.L.R. 642; Times, January 28, 2014; [2014] Fam. Law 466; (2014) 158(4) S.J.L.B. 49, SC .... *Digested,* 14/**2835**: *Applied* 16/925: *Cited* 15/3154: *Followed* 14/2833, 14/2834, 15/2418, 16/2034, 16/2037, 17/2075

Marlon Insurance Co Ltd, Re see Copenhagen Reinsurance Co (UK) Ltd, Re

Marme Inversiones 2007 SL v Royal Bank of Scotland Plc; *joined case* Royal Bank of Scotland Plc v Marme Inversiones 2007 Sl [2016] EWHC 1570 (Comm); [2017] B.P.I.R. 138, QBD (Comm) .... *Digested,* 17/**435**

Marr v Collie [2017] UKPC 17; [2017] 3 W.L.R. 1507; [2017] 2 F.L.R. 674; [2018] 1 P. & C.R. 5; 20 I.T.E.L.R. 602, PC (Bah)

Marrakesh Treaty, Re (Opinion 3/15) EU:C:2016:657; [2017] 3 C.M.L.R. 4; [2018] E.C.D.R. 6, ECJ (Grand Chamber)

Marriott Rewards LLC v Revenue and Customs Commissioners; *joined case* Whitbread Group Plc v Revenue and Customs Commissioners [2017] UKFTT 140 (TC); [2017] S.F.T.D. 489; [2017] S.T.I. 305, FTT (Tax) .... *Digested,* 17/**2260**

Marsden v Barclays Bank Plc [2016] EWHC 1601 (QB); [2016] 2 Lloyd's Rep. 420, QBD (Merc) (London) .... *Digested,* 17/**164**

Marshall v Benjamin Cope & Sons Ltd see Benjamin Cope & Sons Ltd, Re

Marshall v Marshall 2007 Fam. L.R. 48; 2007 G.W.D. 10-188, OH .... *Digested,* 07/**5188**: *Applied* 17/2610

Marshall (Inspector of Taxes) v Kerr [1993] S.T.C. 360; 67 T.C. 73; Times, March 8, 1993; Independent, April 26, 1993; [1993] S.T.I. 353; (1993) 90(14) L.S.G. 45, CA (Civ Div) .... *Digested,* 93/**335**: *Applied* 13/3130, 16/2097, 17/2095: *Considered* 07/3988, 09/3847: *Reversed* 94/359

Marson (Inspector of Taxes) v Morton [1986] 1 W.L.R. 1343; [1986] S.T.C. 463; 59 T.C. 381; (1986) 83 L.S.G. 3161; (1986) 130 S.J. 731, Ch D .... *Digested,* 87/**2022**: *Applied* 12/3320, 13/3086: *Considered* 15/2484, 17/2147

Martell v Consett Iron Co Ltd [1955] Ch. 363; [1955] 2 W.L.R. 463; [1955] 1 All E.R. 481; (1955) 99 S.J. 211; (1955) 99 S.J. 148, CA .... *Digested,* 55/**2680**: *Applied* 81/298: *Considered* 70/2935, 98/411: *Followed* 67/128, 67/3776, 17/1570

Marten v Flight Refuelling Ltd [1962] Ch. 115; [1961] 2 W.L.R. 1018; [1961] 2 All E.R. 696; (1962) 13 P. & C.R. 389; (1961) 105 S.J. 442, Ch D .... *Digested,* 61/**7524**: *Applied* 72/2911, 74/3130, 17/1857

Martin v Williams [2017] EWHC 491 (Ch); [2018] 1 F.L.R. 125; [2017] W.T.L.R. 1041, Ch D

Martin (Matthew) v HM Advocate [2016] HCJAC 42; 2016 S.C.L. 524; 2016 S.C.C.R. 276; 2016 G.W.D. 15-282, HCJ .... *Digested,* 16/**2514**: *Applied* 17/2490

Martin (Ronald O'Neill) v HM Advocate [2006] HCJAC 86; 2007 J.C. 70; 2006 S.C.C.R. 683; 2006 G.W.D. 37-740, HCJ .... *Digested,* 07/**5518**: *Applied* 16/2802: *Considered* 17/2812

Martin McColl Ltd v West Dunbartonshire Licensing Board [2017] L.L.R. 551; 2017 G.W.D. 14-226, Sh Ct (North Strathclyde) (Dumbarton) .... *Digested,* 17/**2719**

Martinez Andres v Servicio Vasco de Salud (C-184/15); *joined case* Lopez v Ayuntamiento de Vitoria (C-197/15) EU:C:2016:680; [2017] 1 C.M.L.R. 32, ECJ (2nd Chamber)

Maruko v Versorgungsanstalt der Deutschen Buhnen (C-267/06) EU:C:2008:179; [2008] E.C.R. I-1757; [2008] 2 C.M.L.R. 32; [2008] All E.R. (EC) 977; [2008] I.R.L.R. 450; [2008] Pens. L.R. 223, ECJ (Grand Chamber) .... *Digested,* 08/**2732**: *Applied* 13/2146: *Considered* 15/1858: *Followed* 17/1610

Maryland v Kulbicki 41 B.H.R.C. 567, US Court

Marzillier, Dr Meier & Dr Guntner Rechtsanwaltsgesellschaft mbH v AMT Futures Ltd see AMT Futures Ltd v Marzillier, Dr Meier & Dr Guntner Rechtsanwaltsgesellschaft mbH

Masala Zone Ltd v Golding (Valuation Officer) [2016] UKUT 328 (LC); [2017] R.A. 33, UT (Lands) .... *Digested,* 17/**1522**

Maschek v Magistratsdirektion der Stadt Wien (C-341/15) EU:C:2016:576; [2017] C.E.C. 218; [2016] I.R.L.R. 801, ECJ (10th Chamber)

Masco Corp v European Commission (C-614/13 P) EU:C:2017:63; [2017] 4 C.M.L.R. 24, ECJ (1st Chamber)

Maslov v Austria (1638/03) [2009] I.N.L.R. 47, ECHR (Grand Chamber) .... *Digested,* 09/**2070**: *Applied* 10/1772, 10/1773, 11/1731, 11/1734, 12/1676, 13/1566, 13/1596, 14/1678, 17/1198: *Considered* 12/1677, 12/1775, 13/1620, 14/1717, 16/1079

Masocha (Walter) v HM Advocate [2016] HCJAC 15; 2016 S.C.L. 369; 2016 G.W.D. 7-144, HCJ Appeal .... *Digested,* 16/**2563**: *Considered* 17/2555

Masri v Consolidated Contractors International Co SAL [2009] UKHL 43; [2010] 1 A.C. 90; [2009] 3 W.L.R. 385; [2009] 4 All E.R. 847; [2010] 1 All E.R. (Comm) 220; [2009] Bus. L.R. 1269; [2009] 2 Lloyd's Rep. 473; [2009] C.P. Rep. 47; [2010] B.C.C. 25; [2009] 2 B.C.L.C. 382; [2009] 2 C.L.C. 366; [2009] B.P.I.R. 1029; Times, August 13, 2009; (2009) 159 N.L.J. 1137; (2009) 159 N.L.J. 1250, HL ... *Digested,* 09/**408**: *Considered* 10/268, 10/404, 14/3345, 17/380: *Distinguished* 14/305, 15/220

Massey v Boulden [2002] EWCA Civ 1634; [2003] 1 W.L.R. 1792; [2003] 2 All E.R. 87; [2003] 1 P. & C.R. 22; [2003] 1 E.G.L.R. 24; [2003] 11 E.G. 154; Times, November 27, 2002; [2002] 48 E.G. 139 (C.S.); (2003) 100(3) L.S.G. 34; (2002) 146 S.J.L.B. 264; [2002] N.P.C. 143; [2003] 1 P. & C.R. DG13, CA (Civ Div) .... *Digested,* 03/**3600**: *Considered* 17/1840: *Followed* 03/3558: *Overruled* 04/3224

Massive Bionics SL v EUIPO (T-223/16) EU:T:2017:500; [2017] E.T.M.R. 38, GC (2nd Chamber)

Master Wishmakers Ltd v Revenue and Customs Commissioners [2017] UKFTT 130 (TC); [2017] S.T.I. 303, FTT (Tax)

Mastercard Inc v Deutsche Bahn AG [2017] EWCA Civ 272; [2017] C.P. Rep. 26, CA (Civ Div) .... *Digested,* 17/**211**

MasterCard Inc v European Commission (C-382/12 P) EU:C:2014:2201; [2014] 5 C.M.L.R. 23, ECJ (3rd Chamber) *Applied* 17/411: *Considered* 17/412

Mastercigars Direct Ltd v Hunters & Frankau Ltd; *joined case* Corporacion Habanos SA v Mastercigars Direct Ltd [2007] EWCA Civ 176; [2008] E.C.C. 14; [2007] E.T.M.R. 44; [2007] R.P.C. 24; (2007) 30(4) I.P.D. 30026; (2007) 104(12) L.S.G. 32, CA (Civ Div) .... *Digested,* 08/**2391**: *Applied* 15/1528: *Followed* 17/1392

Masterman-Lister v Brutton & Co see Masterman-Lister v Jewell

Masterman-Lister v Jewell; *joined case* Masterman-Lister v Brutton & Co [2002] EWCA Civ 1889; [2003] 1 W.L.R. 1511; [2003] 3 All E.R. 162; [2003] C.P. Rep. 29; (2004) 7 C.C.L. Rep. 5; [2003] P.I.Q.R. P20; [2003] Lloyd's Rep. Med. 244; (2003) 73 B.M.L.R. 1; [2003] M.H.L.R. 166; [2003] W.T.L.R. 259; Times, December 28, 2002; (2003) 147 S.J.L.B. 60, CA (Civ Div) .... *Digested,* 03/**311**: *Applied* 06/482, 06/483, 07/811, 08/2468, 08/3568, 09/2737, 12/319, 17/975: *Approved* 14/435: *Considered* 07/484, 09/2200, 13/2055, 13/2199: *Followed* 05/473, 15/1729, 17/1307

Matalia v Warwickshire CC see Warwickshire CC v Matalia

Matchmove Ltd v Dowding; *sub nom* Dowding v Matchmove Ltd [2016] EWCA Civ 1233; [2017] 1 W.L.R. 749; [2017] W.T.L.R. 265, CA (Civ Div) .... *Digested,* 17/**1837**

Matei v SC Volksbank Romania SA (C-143/13) EU:C:2015:127; [2015] 1 W.L.R. 2385, ECJ (9th Chamber) *Considered* 17/485

MATHWORKS/Modelling a multiprocessor system (T1630/11) [2017] E.P.O.R. 17, EPO (Technical Bd App)

Matra Communications SA v Home Office [1999] 1 W.L.R. 1646; [1999] 3 All E.R. 562; [1999] B.L.R. 112; [1999] 1 C.M.L.R. 1454; [1999] Eu. L.R. 635; (1999) 1 L.G.L.R. 877; (1999) 11 Admin. L.R. 478; Times, March 8, 1999; (1999) 163 J.P.N. 854; (1999) 143 S.J.L.B. 104, CA (Civ Div) .... *Digested,* 99/**482**: *Applied* 10/2672, 16/1792: *Considered* 10/4484, 11/1750: *Doubted* 17/1813

Mattis v Pollock (t/a Flamingos Nightclub) [2003] EWCA Civ 887; [2003] 1 W.L.R. 2158; [2004] 4 All E.R. 85; [2003] I.C.R. 1335; [2003] I.R.L.R. 603; [2004] P.I.Q.R. P3; [2003] L.L.R. 718; Times, July 16, 2003; (2003) 147 S.J.L.B. 816, CA (Civ Div) .... *Digested,* 03/**3033**: *Applied* 08/3906: *Considered* 12/3344, 14/3000: *Followed* 17/2205

Maud v Aabar Block Sarl; *sub nom* Aabar Block Sarl v Maud [2016] EWHC 2175 (Ch); [2016] Bus. L.R. 1243; [2016] B.P.I.R. 1486, Ch D (Bankruptcy Ct) .... *Digested,* 17/**1294**

Mauger v Chief Constable of the Police Service of Scotland [2016] CSIH 44; 2017 S.C. 20; 2016 G.W.D. 20-355, IH (1 Div) .... *Digested,* 17/**2768**

Mauger v Chief Constable of the Police Service of Scotland [2016] CSOH 22; 2016 G.W.D. 9-164, OH
Affirmed 17/2768

Mawer v Bland [2013] EWHC 3122 (Ch); [2015] B.P.I.R. 66, Ch D
Applied 17/1300

Mawer v Moore see Moore (A Bankrupt), Re

Maximov v Open Joint Stock Co [2017] EWHC 1911 (Comm); [2017] 2 Lloyd's Rep. 519, QBD (Comm)

Maxwell (Ivan Keith David) v HM Advocate [2017] HCJAC 64; 2017 S.C.L. 947; 2017 G.W.D. 29-462, HCJ .... *Digested,* 17/**2542**

May v Robinson see R. (on the application of Hysaj) v Secretary of State for the Home Department

Mayflower Theatre Trust Ltd v Revenue and Customs Commissioners [2007] EWCA Civ 116; [2007] S.T.C. 880; [2007] B.T.C. 5221; [2007] B.V.C. 190; [2007] S.T.I. 413; (2007) 104(10) L.S.G. 30; (2007) 151 S.J.L.B. 294; [2007] N.P.C. 24, CA (Civ Div) .... *Digested,* 08/**4013**:
Considered 14/3089, 17/2272: *Distinguished* 08/4012

Mayhew-Lewis v Westminster Scaffolding Group Plc see Norglen Ltd (In Liquidation) v Reeds Rains Prudential Ltd

Maynard v Oliver [2003] 3 Q.R. 6; [2002] 5 Q.R. 5, CC (Lincoln) [*Irwin Mitchell Solicitors, St. Peter's House, Hartshead, Sheffield*] .... *Digested,* 03/**3183**:
Considered 17/2757

Maynard v West Midlands AHA see Maynard v West Midlands RHA

Maynard v West Midlands RHA; *sub nom* Maynard v West Midlands AHA [1984] 1 W.L.R. 634; [1985] 1 All E.R. 635; Times, May 9, 1983; (1984) 81 L.S.G. 1926; (1983) 133 N.L.J. 641; (1984) 128 S.J. 317, HL .... *Digested,* 84/**2324**:
Applied 85/135, 90/3264, 99/3997: *Considered* 84/2282, 88/2453, 89/2558, 17/1561: *Distinguished* 96/4469: *Referred to* 92/3247, 92/5658

Mayor v Mahendru see Chandra v Mayor

MB v GK [2017] EWHC 16 (Fam); [2017] 2 F.C.R. 38, Fam Div .... *Digested,* 17/**973**

MB v KB; *sub nom* B v B [2007] EWHC 789 (Fam); [2007] 2 F.L.R. 586; [2007] Fam. Law 801, Fam Div .... *Digested,* 07/**1685**:
Applied 13/1308, 17/1000

MB v Secretary of State for Work and Pensions [2016] UKSC 53; [2017] 1 All E.R. 338; [2017] 1 C.M.L.R. 13, SC .... *Digested,* 17/**1634**

MB (Pakistan) v Entry Clearance Officer see Mahad (Ethiopia) v Entry Clearance Officer

McAlister v Stevenson see Donoghue v Stevenson

McAllister (Lesley) v Procurator Fiscal, Aberdeen [2017] SAC (Crim) 15; 2017 S.L.T. (Sh Ct) 243; 2017 S.C.L. 1058; 2017 G.W.D. 31-494, SAC .... *Digested,* 17/**2516**

McAteer (Conor) v HM Advocate [2016] HCJAC 90; 2016 S.C.L. 1009; 2016 G.W.D. 31-558, HCJ .... *Digested,* 17/**2800**

McBrearty v Ministry of Defence see Elguzouli-Daf v Commissioner of Police of the Metropolis

McBrearty (Samuel) v HM Advocate 2004 J.C. 122; 2004 S.L.T. 917; 2004 S.C.C.R. 337; 2004 G.W.D. 15-329, HCJ .... *Digested,* 04/**4679**:
Considered 17/2797: *Followed* 13/3558

McBride v Scottish Police Services Authority see Scottish Police Services Authority v McBride

McBride v UK Insurance Ltd; *joined case* Clayton v EUI Ltd (t/a Admiral Insurance) [2017] EWCA Civ 144; [2017] R.T.R. 27; [2017] Lloyd's Rep. I.R. 352, CA (Civ Div) .... *Digested,* 17/**644**

McCallum v City of Edinburgh Council [2017] CSIH 24; 2017 S.L.T. 466; 2017 Hous. L.R. 42; 2017 G.W.D. 11-162, IH (Ex Div) .... *Digested,* 17/**2705**

McCallum v City of Edinburgh Council 2017 S.L.T. (Lands Tr) 9; 2016 G.W.D. 24-450, Lands Tr (Scot)
Affirmed 17/2705

McCann v State Hospitals Board for Scotland; *sub nom* CM, Petitioner; CM v State Hospitals Board for Scotland; M v State Hospitals Board for Scotland [2014] CSIH 71; 2015 S.C. 112; 2014 S.L.T. 905; 2014 S.C.L.R. 817; [2015] M.H.L.R. 458; 2014 G.W.D. 27-534, IH (2 Div) .... *Digested,* 14/**3573**:
Reversed in part 17/1118

McCann v State Hospitals Board for Scotland; *sub nom* CM, Petitioner; CM v State Hospitals Board for Scotland; M v State Hospitals Board for Scotland [2017] UKSC 31; [2017] 1 W.L.R. 1455; [2017] 4 All E.R. 449; 2017 S.C. (U.K.S.C.) 121; 2017 S.L.T. 451; 43 B.H.R.C. 1; (2017) 156 B.M.L.R. 35; [2017] M.H.L.R. 306; Times, April 25, 2017; 2017 G.W.D. 12-169, SC .... *Digested,* 17/**1118**

McCartan Turkington Breen v Times Newspapers Ltd; *sub nom* Turkington v Times Newspapers Ltd [2001] 2 A.C. 277; [2000] 3 W.L.R. 1670; [2000] 4 All E.R. 913; [2000] N.I. 410; [2001] E.M.L.R. 1; [2001] U.K.H.R.R. 184; 9 B.H.R.C. 497; Times, November 3, 2000; Independent, November 7, 2000; (2000) 97(47) L.S.G. 40; (2000) 150 N.L.J. 1657; (2000) 144 S.J.L.B. 287, HL (NI) ...... *Digested,* 00/**5491**: *Considered* 07/1070, 07/2217: *Followed* 17/650

McCarthy v Tann; *sub nom* Emerald Meats (London) Ltd, Re [2016] EWHC 542 (Ch); [2017] 2 B.C.L.C. 60, Ch D (Companies Ct)

McCarthy (A Bankrupt), Re; *sub nom* Trustee Ex p. v McCarthy [1975] 1 W.L.R. 807; [1975] 2 All E.R. 857; (1975) 119 S.J. 391, Ch D .... *Digested,* 75/**171**: *Applied* 17/1275

McClurg v Chief Constable of the Royal Ulster Constabulary [2009] NICA 37, CA (NI) *Followed* 17/2327

McCord's Application for Judicial Review, Re; *joined case* Agnew's Application for Judicial Review, Re [2016] NIQB 85; [2017] 2 C.M.L.R. 7, QBD (NI) *Affirmed* 17/441

McCord's Application for Judicial Review, Re see R. (on the application of Miller) v Secretary of State for Exiting the European Union

McCormick (Adam) v HM Advocate [2016] HCJAC 50; 2016 S.L.T. 793; 2016 S.C.L. 651; 2016 S.C.C.R. 308; 2016 G.W.D. 18-334, HCJ .... *Digested,* 16/**2795**: *Considered* 17/2817

McCorry v McKeith [2016] NICA 47; [2017] I.R.L.R. 253, CA (NI) .... *Digested,* 17/**2308**

McCourt (Peter Stephen) v HM Advocate see Gemmell (James Kelly) v HM Advocate

McCrae (Kyle) v HM Advocate [2017] HCJAC 27; 2017 S.C.L. 637; 2017 G.W.D. 16-256, HCJ Appeal .... *Digested,* 17/**2491**

McCrone v Boots Farm Sales Ltd 1981 S.C. 68; 1981 S.L.T. 103, OH .... *Digested,* 81/**3608**: *Applied* 93/504: *Approved* 17/508

McCue v Scottish Daily Record & Sunday Mail Ltd (No.1) 1998 S.C. 811; 1998 S.L.T. 983; 1998 S.C.L.R. 742; 1998 G.W.D. 23-1153, IH (Ct of 5 judges) .... *Digested,* 98/**5493**: *Considered* 99/5680, 17/2435: *Distinguished* 00/5940: *Followed* 12/3831

McDonald v Glasgow City Council see HBJ Claimants v Glasgow City Council

McDonald v Horn [1995] 1 All E.R. 961; [1995] I.C.R. 685; [1994] Pens. L.R. 155; Times, August 10, 1994; Independent, August 8, 1994; (1994) 144 N.L.J. 1515, CA (Civ Div) .... *Digested,* 95/**3836**: *Applied* 02/378, 02/4696, 08/3942, 10/321, 17/2216: *Considered* 98/481, 98/482, 01/3803, 01/506, 02/379, 12/389: *Followed* 97/3952

McDonald v McDonald; *sub nom* McDonald v Newton [2017] UKSC 52; 2017 S.C. (U.K.S.C.) 142; 2017 S.L.T. 837; 2018 S.C.L.R. 26; 2017 Fam. L.R. 78; 2017 G.W.D. 23-395, SC .... *Digested,* 17/**1014**

McDonald v McDonald [2016] UKSC 28; [2017] A.C. 273; [2016] 3 W.L.R. 45; [2017] 1 All E.R. 961; [2016] H.R.L.R. 18; [2017] B.P.I.R. 728; [2016] H.L.R. 28; [2017] L. & T.R. 9; Times, June 29, 2016; [2016] 2 P. & C.R. DG22, SC .... *Digested,* 16/**1374**

McDonald v McDonald [2015] CSIH 61; 2016 S.C. 118; 2015 S.L.T. 587; 2015 Fam. L.R. 112; 2015 G.W.D. 27-473, IH (Ex Div) .... *Digested,* 15/**3080**: *Reversed* 17/1014

McDonald v Newton see McDonald v McDonald

McDonald v Revenue and Customs Commissioners [2017] UKFTT 265 (TC); [2017] S.F.T.D. 993, FTT (Tax)

McDonald's Trustee v Aberdeen City Council 2000 S.C. 185; 2000 S.L.T. 985; 2000 Hous. L.R. 30; 2000 G.W.D. 1-24, IH (Ex Div) .... *Digested,* 00/**6465**: *Distinguished* 17/2694

McDonnell v HM Assistant Coroner for West London [2016] EWHC 3078 (Admin); (2017) 154 B.M.L.R. 188; [2016] Inquest L.R. 312; [2017] A.C.D. 1, DC .... *Digested,* 17/**11**

McDonough v O'Keeffe [2015] UKUT 74 (LC); [2015] R.V.R. 385, UT (Lands) .... *Digested,* 16/**1460**: *Considered* 17/1515

McDowall (Luke) v HM Advocate; *joined cases* Lawrie (Joshua) v HM Advocate; Scott (Jordan) v HM Advocate [2016] HCJAC 105; 2017 S.C.L. 158; 2016 G.W.D. 37-659, HCJ .... *Digested,* 17/**2501**

McFadden v Sony Music Entertainment Germany GmbH (C-484/14) EU:C:2016:689; [2017] Bus. L.R. 430; [2017] 1 C.M.L.R. 38; [2016] E.C.D.R. 26, ECJ (3rd Chamber)

McFarlane v McFarlane see Miller v Miller

McFarlane v United Kingdom (36516/10) see Eweida v United Kingdom (48420/10)
McGee Group Ltd v Galliford Try Building Ltd [2017] EWHC 87 (TCC); 170 Con. L.R. 203; [2017] C.I.L.L. 3935, QBD (TCC) .... *Digested,* 17/**468**
McGeoch v Lord President of the Council [2011] CSOH 65; 2011 S.L.T. 633; 2011 G.W.D. 14-320, OH
Affirmed 12/3970: *Considered* 17/2773
McGill v Sports and Entertainment Media Group [2016] EWCA Civ 1063; [2017] 1 W.L.R. 989, CA (Civ Div) .... *Digested,* 17/**2201**
McGill v Sports and Entertainment Media Group [2014] EWHC 3000 (QB), QBD (Merc) (Manchester)
Reversed 17/2201
McGlinn v Waltham Contractors Ltd [2007] EWHC 149 (TCC); [2008] Bus. L.R. 233; 111 Con. L.R. 1; Times, March 20, 2007; [2007] C.I.L.L. 2441, QBD (TCC) .... *Digested,* 08/**894**: *Considered* 15/278, 17/355
McGraddie v McGraddie [2013] UKSC 58; [2013] 1 W.L.R. 2477; 2014 S.C. (U.K.S.C.) 12; 2013 S.L.T. 1212; 2015 S.C.L.R. 109; 2013 G.W.D. 25-471, SC *Digested,* 13/**6**: *Applied* 17/2440: *Considered* 15/300, 15/3133: *Followed* 14/1579
McGuinness v Norwich and Peterborough Building Society [2011] EWCA Civ 1286; [2012] 2 All E.R. (Comm) 265; [2012] 2 B.C.L.C. 233; [2012] B.P.I.R. 145; Times, December 21, 2011; [2011] N.P.C. 117, CA (Civ Div) .... *Digested,* 12/**1819**: *Applied* 13/1690, 15/1413: *Considered* 17/1323: *Followed* 12/1817, 15/1437, 17/1322, 17/162
McGurk v Spain [2016] EWHC 536 (Admin), DC
Applied 17/899
McHale (Joseph Francis) v HM Advocate; *joined case* Schruyers (Kevin Charles) v HM Advocate [2017] HCJAC 35; 2018 J.C. 11; 2017 S.C.L. 866; 2017 S.C.C.R. 427; 2017 G.W.D. 27-438, HCJ .... *Digested,* 17/**2503**
McHugh v Harvie [2015] HCJAC 86; 2015 S.C.L. 987; 2015 S.C.C.R. 430; 2015 G.W.D. 34-556, HCJ .... *Digested,* 16/**2818**: *Distinguished* 17/2798
McIlkenny v Chief Constable of the West Midlands see Hunter v Chief Constable of the West Midlands
McInally (John Francis) v HM Advocate [2006] HCJAC 48; 2006 J.C. 224; 2006 S.C.C.R. 391; 2006 G.W.D. 23-503, HCJ
Applied 17/2482
McKay v Hamlani see Cain v Francis
McKechnie v Murray [2016] CSIH 4; 2016 S.C. 339; 2016 G.W.D. 9-167, IH (Ex Div) .. *Digested,* 17/**2452**
McKenna v O'Hare [2017] SAC (Civ) 16; 2017 S.C. (S.A.C.) 33; 2017 S.L.T. (Sh Ct) 117; 2017 G.W.D. 14-228, SAC .... *Digested,* 17/**2741**
McKeown v Revenue and Customs Commissioners; *joined cases* Duggan v Revenue and Customs Commissioners; McPolin v Revenue and Customs Commissioners [2016] UKUT 479 (TCC); [2017] S.T.C. 294, UT (Tax) .... *Digested,* 17/**631**
McKerr's Application for Judicial Review, Re; *sub nom* McKerr, Re [2004] UKHL 12; [2004] 1 W.L.R. 807; [2004] 2 All E.R. 409; [2004] N.I. 212; [2004] H.R.L.R. 26; [2004] U.K.H.R.R. 385; 17 B.H.R.C. 68; [2004] Lloyd's Rep. Med. 263; [2004] Inquest L.R. 35; Times, March 12, 2004; (2004) 101(13) L.S.G. 33; (2004) 148 S.J.L.B. 355, HL (NI) .... *Digested,* 04/**1976**: *Applied* 06/17, 06/2932, 06/4528, 16/45: *Considered* 05/17, 08/1975, 10/3545, 12/2336: *Doubted* 11/1695: *Followed* 07/27, 14/62, 17/1484
McKerr, Re see McKerr's Application for Judicial Review, Re
McKie v Scottish Ministers [2006] CSOH 54; 2006 S.C. 528; 2006 S.L.T. 668; 2006 G.W.D. 20-437, OH .... *Digested,* 06/**5105**: *Applied* 17/2427
McKinsley v Crown Prosecution Service; *sub nom* M (Application for Certificate of Inadequacy), Re; McKinsley, Re [2006] EWCA Civ 1092; [2006] 1 W.L.R. 3420; Times, August 22, 2006; Independent, October 12, 2006, CA (Civ Div) .... *Digested,* 06/**907**: *Considered* 09/849, 17/578
McKinsley, Re see McKinsley v Crown Prosecution Service
McLaughlin v Duffill [2008] EWCA Civ 1627; [2010] Ch. 1; [2009] 3 W.L.R. 1139; [2009] 2 E.G.L.R. 71; [2009] 34 E.G. 80, CA (Civ Div) .... *Digested,* 09/**3148**: *Applied* 11/219, 15/2541: *Followed* 17/1836
McLean v Berry see Dent (In Administration), Re
McLean (Darryl) v HM Advocate see Wood (Kenneth) v HM Advocate
McLeish v Lothian NHS Board [2017] CSOH 71; 2017 Rep. L.R. 90; 2017 G.W.D. 15-248, OH .... *Digested,* 17/**2642**
McLeod v Cedar Holdings Ltd 1989 S.L.T. 620, IH (2 Div) .... *Digested,* 89/**4794**: *Applied* 17/2677: *Distinguished* 93/5393: *Referred to* 94/5914

McLocklin v Revenue and Customs Commissioners [2014] UKFTT 42 (TC), FTT (Tax)
Applied 17/2142

McLuckie v Coroner for Northern Ireland [2011] NICA 34; [2011] Inquest L.R. 65, CA (NI)
Applied 17/384

McMaster v Scottish Ministers [2017] CSOH 46; 2017 S.L.T. 586; 2017 G.W.D. 11-143, OH .... *Digested,* 17/**2693**

McMillan v Mundell see McMillan (Graham) v Procurator Fiscal, Paisley

McMillan (Graham) v Procurator Fiscal, Paisley; *sub nom* McMillan v Mundell [2017] SAC (Crim) 2; 2017 S.L.T. (Sh Ct) 80; 2017 S.C.L. 489; 2017 S.C.C.R. 96; 2017 G.W.D. 4-44, SAC .... *Digested,* 17/**2570**

McMultan (Christopher) v HM Advocate [2016] HCJAC 89; 2016 S.C.L. 973; 2016 S.C.C.R. 496; 2016 G.W.D. 31-544, HCJ .... *Digested,* 17/**2541**

McNair (Ryan) v HM Advocate [2017] HCJAC 6; 2017 S.L.T. 229; 2017 S.C.L. 312; 2017 G.W.D. 4-58, HCJ .... *Digested,* 17/**2804**

McNeil v Tesco Plc see Cook v Virgin Media Ltd

McNicholas Construction Co Ltd v Customs and Excise Commissioners [2000] S.T.C. 553; [2000] B.T.C. 5225; [2000] B.V.C. 255; Independent, July 24, 2000; [2000] S.T.I. 889, QBD .... *Digested,* 00/**5348**:
Applied 05/2307, 08/2648: *Approved* 03/4601: *Considered* 02/4732, 14/1807:
Doubted 17/2276: *Followed* 12/3401

McNulty v McNulty 2016 Fam. L.R. 145; 2016 G.W.D. 36-646, Sh Ct (Tayside) (Dunfermline) .... *Digested,* 17/**2611**

McPhail v Lanarkshire CC (No.2) 1951 S.C. 301; 1951 S.L.T. 167, IH (1 Div) .... *Digested,* 51/**3988**:
Considered 17/2448

McPhee v Queen, The [2016] UKPC 29; [2016] 4 W.L.R. 166; [2017] 1 Cr. App. R. 10; Times, December 23, 2016, PC (Bah)

McPherson v BNP Paribas SA (London Branch) [2004] EWCA Civ 569; [2004] 3 All E.R. 266; [2004] 4 Costs L.R. 596; [2004] I.C.R. 1398; [2004] I.R.L.R. 558; Times, May 31, 2004; Independent, May 20, 2004, CA (Civ Div) .... *Digested,* 04/**1314**:
Applied 05/1220, 13/969, 17/1460: *Considered* 12/1091, 14/946:
Followed 11/1097

McPhilemy v Times Newspapers Ltd (Costs) [2001] EWCA Civ 933; [2002] 1 W.L.R. 934; [2001] 4 All E.R. 861; [2002] C.P. Rep. 9; [2001] 2 Costs L.R. 295; [2001] E.M.L.R. 35; Times, July 3, 2001, CA (Civ Div) .... *Digested,* 01/**484**:
Applied 02/349, 03/355, 10/388, 11/294, 17/231: *Considered* 02/347, 05/369,
08/390, 10/2401, 17/339

McPhilemy v Times Newspapers Ltd (Re-Amendment: Justification) [1999] 3 All E.R. 775; [1999] C.P.L.R. 533; [1999] E.M.L.R. 751; Times, May 26, 1999; Independent, June 9, 1999, CA (Civ Div) .... *Digested,* 99/**1635**:
Applied 00/568, 00/605, 03/953: *Considered* 99/312, 17/286: *Followed* 00/1757,
12/866

McPolin v Director of Border Revenue [2015] UKFTT 243 (TC), FTT (Tax)
Affirmed 17/631

McPolin v Revenue and Customs Commissioners see McKeown v Revenue and Customs Commissioners

McQuade v Clarke see Stewart v Payne

McQuillan v Revenue and Customs Commissioners [2016] UKFTT 305 (TC); [2017] S.F.T.D. 353; [2016] S.T.I. 2227, FTT (Tax) .... *Digested,* 17/**2119**

McTier v Secretary of State for Education [2017] EWHC 212 (Admin); [2017] P.T.S.R. 815; [2017] E.L.R. 327; [2017] A.C.D. 46, QBD (Admin) .... *Digested,* 17/**719**

McTigue v University Hospital Bristol NHS Foundation Trust [2016] I.C.R. 1155; [2016] I.R.L.R. 742, EAT .... *Digested,* 16/**651**:
Considered 17/818

McVey v Friel 1996 S.C.C.R. 768, HCJ Appeal .... *Digested,* 97/**5789**:
Considered 17/557: *Distinguished* 98/5587

McWilliam v Gibson see McWilliam v Harvie

McWilliam v Harvie; *sub nom* McWilliam v Gibson [2016] HCJAC 29; 2017 J.C. 31; 2016 S.L.T. 648; 2016 S.C.L. 434; 2016 G.W.D. 13-254, HCJ .... *Digested,* 16/**2588**:
Applied 17/2570

MD (Jamaica) v Secretary of State for the Home Department [2010] EWCA Civ 213; [2010] Imm. A.R. 526; [2010] I.N.L.R. 580; (2010) 160 N.L.J. 422, CA (Civ Div) *Digested,* 10/**1799**:
Considered 17/1232

MDS's Application, Re [2016] QSC 61; 19 I.T.E.L.R. 922, Sup Ct (Qld)

ME v Refugee Applications Commissioner (C-493/10) see R. (on the application of NS) v Secretary of State for the Home Department (C-411/10)

ME v Southwark LBC [2017] UKUT 73 (AAC); [2017] E.L.R. 209, UT (AAC) .... *Digested,* 17/**709**

Mears Ltd v Leeds City Council [2011] EWHC 40 (QB); [2011] B.L.R. 155; [2011] Eu. L.R. 596; [2011] P.T.S.R. D31, QBD ..... *Digested,* 11/**2631**: *Considered* 17/215
Mechkarov v Citibank NA [2016] I.C.R. 1121, EAT ..... *Digested,* 17/**821**
MedImmune Ltd v Novartis Pharmaceuticals UK Ltd; *joined case* Novartis Pharmaceuticals UK Ltd v MedImmune Ltd [2012] EWCA Civ 1234; [2013] R.P.C. 27, CA (Civ Div)
Applied 13/1801, 15/1501, 16/1320, 16/1322: *Considered* 16/1298: *Followed* 13/1807, 14/1897, 16/1311, 17/1381
Mediterranean Feeders LP v Schiffahrts SLJ 97/6074/B, CA
Considered 17/308
Mediterranean Shipping Co v Sotramon Ltd [2017] UKPC 23; [2017] B.L.R. 558, PC (Mau)
Medway Council v JB [2015] EWHC 3064 (Fam); [2016] 2 F.L.R. 1360; [2016] Fam. Law 23, Fam Div ..... *Digested,* 17/**926**
Medway Council v Kent CC see W (A Child) (Designation of Local Authority), Re
Medway Council v M see T (A Child), Re
Mee v Jones see Select Car Rentals (North West) Ltd v Esure Services Ltd
Meek v Birmingham City Council see Meek v Birmingham DC
Meek v Birmingham DC; *sub nom* Meek v Birmingham City Council [1987] I.R.L.R. 250, CA (Civ Div) ..... *Digested,* 87/**1399**: *Applied* 03/1224, 06/1384, 06/4090, 07/1424, 12/1090, 12/926, 13/904: *Considered* 09/1178, 12/1149: *Followed* 05/1333, 17/2251
Meerza v Al Baho [2015] EWHC 3154 (Ch), Ch D
Not applied 17/306
Meeth v Glacetal Sarl (C23/78) EU:C:1978:198; [1978] E.C.R. 2133; [1979] 1 C.M.L.R. 520, ECJ ..... *Digested,* 79/**1169**: *Applied* 03/613, 17/436: *Considered* 96/1219
Meghnagi v Hackney LBC; *sub nom* 24 Lea Bridge Road, Re [2008] R.V.R. 122, Lands Tr ..... *Digested,* 08/**3079**: *Considered* 13/2282, 17/1835
Megji and Co Ltd v Revenue and Customs Commissioners [2017] UKFTT 573 (TC); [2017] S.T.I. 1831, FTT (Tax)
Megrahi (Abdelbaset Ali) v HM Advocate (No.4) see HM Advocate v Al-Megrahi (Abdelbaset Ali) (No.4)
Megtian Ltd (In Administration) v Revenue and Customs Commissioners [2010] EWHC 18 (Ch); [2010] S.T.C. 840; [2010] B.V.C. 314; Times, February 2, 2010; [2010] S.T.I. 232; [2010] Bus. L.R. D93, Ch D ..... *Digested,* 10/**3496**: *Applied* 14/3071, 16/2169, 17/2274: *Considered* 14/3065
Mehanne v Westminster Housing Benefit Review Board see R. (on the application of Mehanne) v Westminster Housing Benefit Review Board
Meikle v Nottinghamshire CC; *sub nom* Nottinghamshire CC v Meikle [2004] EWCA Civ 859; [2004] 4 All E.R. 97; [2005] I.C.R. 1; [2004] I.R.L.R. 703; (2004) 80 B.M.L.R. 129; Times, July 15, 2004; Independent, July 14, 2004; (2004) 148 S.J.L.B. 908, CA (Civ Div) ..... *Digested,* 04/**1193**: *Applied* 05/1227, 06/1282, 08/1122, 10/1034, 14/3500, 17/770: *Considered* 06/1300: *Followed* 14/1023
Melis v Comune di Loiri Porto San Paolo (C□67/15) see Promoimpresa srl v Consorzio dei comuni della Sponda Bresciana del Lago di Garda e del Lago di Idro (C-458/14)
Melzer v MF Global UK Ltd (C-228/11) EU:C:2013:305; [2013] Q.B. 1112; [2013] 3 W.L.R. 883; [2013] C.E.C. 1023; [2013] I.L.Pr. 30, ECJ (1st Chamber)
Followed 17/430
Mena Energy DMCC v Hascol Petroleum Ltd [2017] EWHC 262 (Comm); [2017] 2 All E.R. (Comm) 1058; [2017] 1 Lloyd's Rep. 607, QBD (Comm) ..... *Digested,* 17/**2007**
Mendoza v Ghaidan see Ghaidan v Godin-Mendoza
Menelaou v Bank of Cyprus Plc; *sub nom* Bank of Cyprus UK Ltd v Menelaou; Menelaou v Bank of Cyprus UK Ltd [2015] UKSC 66; [2016] A.C. 176; [2015] 3 W.L.R. 1334; [2016] 2 All E.R. 913; [2016] 2 All E.R. (Comm) 259; [2015] 2 Lloyd's Rep. 585; [2016] 1 B.C.L.C. 335, SC ..... *Digested,* 15/**2131**: *Applied* 17/1826: *Considered* 17/637
Menelaou v Bank of Cyprus Plc; *sub nom* Bank of Cyprus UK Ltd v Menelaou; Menelaou v Bank of Cyprus UK Ltd [2013] EWCA Civ 1960; [2014] 1 W.L.R. 854; [2013] 2 P. & C.R. 21, CA (Civ Div) ..... *Digested,* 13/**2472**: *Affirmed* 15/2131: *Applied* 15/2610, 17/2285
Menelaou v Bank of Cyprus UK Ltd see Menelaou v Bank of Cyprus Plc
Mengesteab v Germany (C-670/16) EU:C:2017:587; [2018] 1 W.L.R. 865; [2017] Imm. A.R. 1484, ECJ (Grand Chamber)

Mengozzi v European Union Intellectual Property Office (EUIPO) (T-510/15) EU:T:2017:54; [2017] E.T.M.R. 15, GC (7th Chamber)

Mental Health Trust v DD [2014] EWCOP 11; [2015] 1 F.L.R. 1430; (2014) 140 B.M.L.R. 118; [2014] Fam. Law 1380, CP .... *Digested,* 15/**1729**: *Considered* 17/1544

Mentmore Towers Ltd v Packman Lucas Ltd [2010] EWHC 457 (TCC); [2010] C.P. Rep. 34; [2010] B.L.R. 393; [2010] C.I.L.L. 2846; [2010] Bus. L.R. D114, QBD (TCC) .... *Digested,* 10/**849**: *Applied* 17/656: *Considered* 14/3360, 15/2924

Mercedes Benz Italia SpA v Agenzia delle Entrate Direzione Provinciale Roma 3 (C-378/15) EU:C:2016:950; [2017] S.T.C. 352; [2017] B.V.C. 2; [2017] S.T.I. 103, ECJ (3rd Chamber)

Mercer Ltd v Ballinger see Bellinger v Mercer Ltd

Merck KGAA v Competition and Markets Authority see Generics (UK) Ltd v Competition and Markets Authority

Merck KGaA v European Commission (T-470/13) EU:T:2016:452; [2017] 4 C.M.L.R. 3, GC (9th Chamber)

Merck Sharp & Dohme Corp v Comptroller-General of Patents, Designs and Trade Marks [2016] EWHC 1896 (Pat); [2017] R.P.C. 2, Ch D (Patents Ct) .... *Digested,* 17/**1385**

Meredith v King's Lynn and West Norfolk BC [2017] UKUT 2 (LC); [2017] R.V.R. 221, UT (Lands)

MERIAL/Language of the Proceedings (G4/08) [2017] E.P.O.R. 27, EPO (Enlarged Bd App)

Meridian Global Funds Management Asia Ltd v Securities Commission [1995] 2 A.C. 500; [1995] 3 W.L.R. 413; [1995] 3 All E.R. 918; [1995] B.C.C. 942; [1995] 2 B.C.L.C. 116; Times, June 29, 1995; (1995) 92(28) L.S.G. 39; (1995) 139 S.J.L.B. 152, PC (NZ) .... *Digested,* 96/**969**: *Applied* 04/456, 07/2485, 07/439, 09/4064, 11/1139, 12/687, 13/1798, 16/961, 17/2193: *Considered* 00/980, 05/2307, 10/446

Merit Holdings Ltd v Michael J Lonsdale Ltd [2017] EWHC 2450 (TCC); [2018] B.L.R. 14; 174 Con. L.R. 92; [2017] C.I.L.L. 4047, QBD (TCC)

Meroni v Recoletos Ltd (C-559/14) EU:C:2016:349; [2017] Q.B. 85; [2016] 3 W.L.R. 949; [2017] C.E.C. 369; [2016] I.L.Pr. 29, ECJ (1st Chamber) *Considered* 16/261

Merricks v Mastercard Inc [2017] CAT 16; [2018] Comp. A.R. 1; [2017] 5 C.M.L.R. 16, CAT

Merrix v Heart of England NHS Foundation Trust [2017] EWHC 346 (QB); [2017] 1 W.L.R. 3399; [2017] 1 Costs L.R. 91, QBD (Birmingham) .... *Digested,* 17/**277**: *Approved* 17/276

Merrygold v Bates see Anderson Owen Ltd (In Liquidation), Re

Merthyr Tydfil Car Auction Ltd v Thomas see Thomas v Merthyr Tydfil Car Auction Ltd

Merton LBC v Stanley Hugh Leach Ltd 32 B.L.R. 51; (1986) 2 Const. L.J. 189, Ch D ... *Digested,* 86/**222**: *Applied* 89/217: *Considered* 13/531, 17/468: *Explained* 92/3375: *Followed* 09/717

Method Development v Jones [1971] 1 W.L.R. 168; [1971] 1 All E.R. 1027; (1971) 22 P. & C.R. 141; (1970) 115 S.J. 13, CA (Civ Div) .... *Digested,* 71/**6588**: *Considered* 87/2124, 90/2772: *Followed* 17/1454

Metinvest BV, Re [2016] EWHC 79 (Ch); [2016] I.L.Pr. 19, Ch D (Companies Ct) .... *Digested,* 16/**349**: *Considered* 17/1321

Metlife Insurance Ltd v RGA Reinsurance Co of Australia Ltd [2016] NSWSC 980; [2017] Lloyd's Rep. I.R. 160, Sup Ct (NSW)

Metropol Spielstatten Unternehmergesellschaft (haftungsbeschrankt) v Finanzamt Hamburg-Bergedorf (C-440/12) EU:C:2013:687; [2014] S.T.C. 505; [2013] B.V.C. 514; [2013] S.T.I. 3398, ECJ (1st Chamber) *Considered* 17/2262

Metropole Television (M6) v Commission of the European Communities (T112/99) EU:T:2001:215; [2001] E.C.R. II-2459; [2001] 5 C.M.L.R. 33; [2002] All E.R. (EC) 1, CFI (3rd Chamber) .... *Digested,* 02/**607**: *Applied* 06/583: *Considered* 17/411

Metropolitan Housing Trust Ltd v Taylor [2015] EWHC 2897 (Ch), Ch D *Considered* 17/308

Meux's Brewery Co v City of London Electric Lighting Co see Shelfer v City of London Electric Lighting Co (No.1)

MF v SF (Financial Remedy: Financial Conduct) [2015] EWHC 1273 (Fam); [2016] 2 F.L.R. 622; [2016] Fam. Law 157, Fam Div .... *Digested,* 17/**1018**

MF (Nigeria) v Secretary of State for the Home Department [2013] EWCA Civ 1192; [2014] 1 W.L.R. 544; [2014] 2 All E.R. 543; [2014] Imm. A.R. 211; [2014] I.N.L.R. 18; Times, December 17, 2013, CA (Civ Div) .... *Digested,* 14/**1669**: *Applied* 14/1678, 14/1710, 15/1318, 15/1319, 15/1336, 16/1081, 16/1084, 16/1092, 17/1187, 17/1190, 17/1198, 17/1209, 17/1227: *Considered* 15/1317, 16/1075, 16/2754, 17/1197, 17/1200, 17/1239: *Followed* 15/1325, 15/1327, 17/1186

MG v Cambridgeshire CC [2017] UKUT 172 (AAC); [2017] E.L.R. 351, UT (AAC)

MG v FG (Schedule 1: Application to Strike out: Estoppel: Legal Costs Funding) [2016] EWHC 1964 (Fam); [2016] 3 F.C.R. 480, Fam Div .... *Digested,* 17/**1000**

MG Rover Group Ltd (In Creditors Voluntary Liquidation) v Revenue and Customs Commissioners [2014] UKFTT 327 (TC); [2014] S.F.T.D. 1218, FTT (Tax) *Reversed* 17/2289

MGN Ltd v United Kingdom (39401/04); *sub nom* Mirror Group Newspapers Ltd v United Kingdom (39401/04) [2011] 1 Costs L.O. 84; [2011] E.M.L.R. 20; (2011) 53 E.H.R.R. 5; 29 B.H.R.C. 686; Times, January 20, 2011, ECHR .... *Digested,* 11/**1680**: *Considered* 14/2221, 15/229, 16/579, 17/1478: *Not applied* 16/1403

MH v MH (C-173/16) EU:C:2016:542; [2017] I.L.Pr. 23; [2017] 1 F.C.R. 538, ECJ (6th Chamber)

MH (Bangladesh) v Secretary of State for the Home Department [2014] CSOH 143; 2014 G.W.D. 30-597, OH *Considered* 17/2663

MI (Somalia) v Entry Clearance Officer see Mahad (Ethiopia) v Entry Clearance Officer

MIAB v Secretary of State for the Home Department; *sub nom* B v Secretary of State for the Home Department [2016] CSIH 64; 2016 S.C. 871; 2016 S.L.T. 1220; 2017 S.C.L.R. 557; 2016 G.W.D. 28-509, IH (1 Div) .... *Digested,* 17/**2663**: *Applied* 17/2671

Miah v Revenue and Customs Commissioners [2016] UKFTT 644 (TC); [2016] S.T.I. 2644, FTT (Tax) *Considered* 17/2291

Miah v Secretary of State for the Home Department [2012] EWCA Civ 261; [2013] Q.B. 35; [2012] 3 W.L.R. 492; [2012] Imm. A.R. 702; [2013] I.N.L.R. 50; Times, June 6, 2012, CA (Civ Div) .... *Digested,* 12/**1767**: *Applied* 17/1232

Michael v Salford City Council [2016] UKUT 370 (LC); [2017] R.V.R. 323, UT (Lands)

Michael Wilson & Partners Ltd v Emmott [2015] EWCA Civ 1285; [2016] 1 W.L.R. 857; [2016] 4 All E.R. 484; [2017] 1 All E.R. (Comm) 152; [2016] 1 Lloyd's Rep. 577; [2016] 1 C.L.C. 58, CA (Civ Div) .... *Digested,* 16/**292**: *Applied* 16/69

Michael Wilson & Partners Ltd v Sinclair [2012] EWHC 2560 (Comm); [2013] 1 All E.R. (Comm) 476, QBD (Comm) .... *Digested,* 13/**249**: *Reversed* 17/191

Michael Wilson & Partners Ltd v Sinclair [2017] EWCA Civ 55; [2017] 1 W.L.R. 3069; [2017] 1 C.L.C. 161; [2017] B.L.R. 125; Times, March 24, 2017, CA (Civ Div) ... *Digested,* 17/**376**

Michael Wilson & Partners Ltd v Sinclair [2017] EWHC 2424 (Comm); [2017] 5 Costs L.R. 877, QBD (Comm) .... *Digested,* 17/**381**

Michael Wilson & Partners Ltd v Sinclair [2017] EWCA Civ 3; [2017] 1 W.L.R. 2646; [2017] 4 All E.R. 216; [2017] 2 All E.R. (Comm) 30; [2017] 1 Lloyd's Rep. 136, CA (Civ Div) .... *Digested,* 17/**191**

Michael Wilson & Partners Ltd v Sinclair [2015] EWHC 2847 (QB), QBD *Reversed* 17/376

Michalak v General Medical Council see General Medical Council v Michalak

Michalak v Wandsworth LBC see Wandsworth LBC v Michalak

Micro Leisure Ltd v County Properties & Developments Ltd (No.1) 1999 S.C. 501; 1999 S.L.T. 1307; 1999 G.W.D. 7-320, OH .... *Digested,* 99/**5728**: *Considered* 17/1637

Microfusion 2003-2 LLP v Harris see Harris v Microfusion 2003-2 LLP

Microsoft Corp v Commission of the European Communities (T-201/04) EU:T:2007:289; [2007] E.C.R. II-3601; [2007] 5 C.M.L.R. 11, CFI .... *Digested,* 08/**505**: *Applied* 17/410

Microsoft Mobile Oy (Ltd) v Sony Europe Ltd [2017] EWHC 374 (Ch); [2018] 1 All E.R. (Comm) 419; [2017] 2 Lloyd's Rep. 119; [2017] 5 C.M.L.R. 5, Ch D .... *Digested,* 17/**377**

Micula v Romania [2017] EWHC 31 (Comm); [2017] Bus. L.R. 1147; [2017] 3 C.M.L.R. 6, QBD (Comm) .... *Digested,* 17/**69**

Mid Suffolk DC v Clarke [2006] EWCA Civ 71; [2007] 1 W.L.R. 980; [2006] Env. L.R. 38; [2006] L.L.R. 284; Times, March 10, 2006; [2006] 8 E.G. 174 (C.S.); [2006] N.P.C. 15, CA (Civ Div) .... *Digested,* 06/**523**: *Applied* 17/1008: *Considered* 08/1420

Midland Bank Plc v Wallace see Royal Bank of Scotland Plc v Etridge (No.2)

Midland Expressway Ltd v Carillion Construction Ltd (No.3) [2006] EWHC 1505 (TCC); [2006] B.L.R. 325; 107 Con. L.R. 205; [2006] C.I.L.L. 2386, QBD (TCC) *Digested,* 06/**674**: *Applied* 14/586, 17/656

Midlothian Council v Bracewell Stirling Architects [2017] CSOH 87; [2017] P.N.L.R. 33; 2017 G.W.D. 21-330, OH .... *Digested,* 17/**2468**

Midtown Acquisitions LP v Essar Global Fund Ltd [2017] EWHC 519 (Comm); [2017] 1 W.L.R. 3083, QBD (Comm) .... *Digested,* 17/**434**

Mighell v Reading see White v White

Mighty v Secretary of State for the Home Department see R. (on the application of Lumba) v Secretary of State for the Home Department

Migros-Genossenschafts-Bund v EUIPO (T-189/16) EU:T:2017:488; [2017] E.T.M.R. 36, GC (5th Chamber)

Mikki v Duncan [2017] EWCA Civ 57; [2017] 1 W.L.R. 2907; [2017] B.P.I.R. 490; Times, February 23, 2017, CA (Civ Div) .... *Digested,* 17/**1281**

Mikolajczyk v Czarnecka (C-294/15) EU:C:2016:772; [2017] Fam. 119; [2017] 2 W.L.R. 1; [2017] C.E.C. 641, ECJ (2nd Chamber)

Milebush Properties Ltd v Tameside MBC [2011] EWCA Civ 270; [2011] P.T.S.R. 1654; [2012] 1 P. & C.R. 3; [2011] 2 E.G.L.R. 143; [2011] 12 E.G. 114 (C.S.); [2011] N.P.C. 31; [2011] 2 P. & C.R. DG5, CA (Civ Div) .... *Digested,* 12/**2612**: *Applied* 17/1343: *Considered* 14/2224, 15/525: *Followed* 15/1400

Miles v Linkage Community Trust Ltd [2008] I.R.L.R. 602, EAT .... *Digested,* 08/**1222**: *Not followed* 17/855

Miles v Public Guardian; *sub nom* Beattie v Public Guardian [2015] EWHC 2960 (Ch); [2015] C.O.P.L.R. 676, Ch D .... *Digested,* 16/**1497**: *Considered* 17/1122

Milev (C-439/16 PPU) see Criminal Proceedings against Milev (C-439/16 PPU)

Miley v Friends Life Ltd [2017] EWHC 2415 (QB); [2017] 5 Costs L.R. 895, QBD .... *Digested,* 17/**1341**

Miliangos v George Frank (Textiles) Ltd [1976] A.C. 443; [1975] 3 W.L.R. 758; [1975] 3 All E.R. 801; [1976] 1 Lloyd's Rep. 201; [1975] 2 C.M.L.R. 585; (1975) 119 S.J. 774, HL .... *Digested,* 75/**2657**: *Applied* 77/194, 77/735, 78/2709, 78/710, 87/365, 05/330: *Considered* 76/327, 77/1602, 77/2728, 77/3735, 77/731, 79/155, 81/260, 84/323, 00/1467, 17/237: *Distinguished* 78/3691: *Followed* 77/2334, 77/3625, 15/1395: *Not applied* 17/1259: *Not followed* 76/273, 82/335

Milkova v Izpalnitelen direktor na Agentsiata za privatizatsia i sledprivatizatsionen control (C-406/15) EU:C:2017:198; [2017] I.R.L.R. 566, ECJ (2nd Chamber)

Millar v Criminal Injuries Compensation Board see P's Curator Bonis v Criminal Injuries Compensation Board

Millburn-Snell v Evans [2011] EWCA Civ 577; [2012] 1 W.L.R. 41; [2011] C.P. Rep. 37; [2011] W.T.L.R. 1213; Times, June 17, 2011; (2011) 155(21) S.J.L.B. 31, CA (Civ Div) .... *Digested,* 11/**394**: *Considered* 17/306: *Followed* 16/2025

Millen v Karen Millen Fashions Ltd [2016] EWHC 2104 (Ch); [2016] E.T.M.R. 44; [2017] F.S.R. 7, Ch D .... *Digested,* 17/**1404**

Miller v Associated Newspapers Ltd [2016] EWHC 397 (QB); [2016] 2 Costs L.R. 195, QBD .... *Digested,* 16/**579**: *Affirmed* 17/1478: *Applied* 16/1403

Miller v Associated Newspapers Ltd see Times Newspapers Ltd v Flood

Miller v Bain (Director's Breach of Duty); *sub nom* Pantone 485 Ltd, Re [2002] 1 B.C.L.C. 266, Ch D (Companies Ct) .... *Digested,* 02/**552**: *Applied* 16/272, 17/2192: *Considered* 10/1892

Miller v Chivas Brothers Ltd [2014] CSIH 65; 2015 S.C. 85; 2014 G.W.D. 24-452, IH (Ex Div) .... *Digested,* 15/**2895**: *Applied* 17/2426: *Considered* 16/2445

Miller v Miller [2017] UKPC 21; [2017] 2 P. & C.R. DG24, PC (Jam)

Miller v Miller; *sub nom* M v M (Short Marriage: Clean Break); *joined case* McFarlane v McFarlane [2006] UKHL 24; [2006] 2 A.C. 618; [2006] 2 W.L.R. 1283; [2006] 3 All E.R. 1; [2006] 1 F.L.R. 1186; [2006] 2 F.C.R. 213; Times, May 25, 2006; Independent, May 26, 2006; [2006] Fam. Law 629; (2006) 103(23) L.S.G. 28; (2006) 156 N.L.J. 916; (2006) 150 S.J.L.B. 704, HL .... *Digested,* 06/**1629**: *Applied* 07/1695, 07/1700, 08/1419, 08/1434, 08/1564, 09/1488, 09/1495, 09/1510, 12/3188, 13/1310, 15/1086, 15/1102, 17/1009: *Cited* 07/1694, 08/1423, 12/1316: *Considered* 06/1627, 07/1691, 07/1697, 07/1704, 08/1422, 10/1296, 11/1290, 11/1297, 11/1309, 11/1311, 12/1427, 12/1440, 15/1091, 17/1024: *Distinguished* 06/1717, 14/1367: *Followed* 07/1706, 10/1297, 11/1300, 11/1302, 13/1309, 15/1082, 15/1119, 17/1019, 17/1032, 17/983: *Referred to* 08/1552

Miller's Executor v Miller 2016 S.L.T. (Sh Ct) 399; 2016 G.W.D. 23-431, Sh Ct (Lothian) (Livingston) .... *Digested,* 17/**2683**

Mills v Marks and Spencer Financial Services Plc see Teasdale v HSBC Bank Plc

Mills v Revenue and Customs Commissioners [2017] UKFTT 378 (TC); [2017] S.F.T.D. 872; [2017] S.T.I. 1457, FTT (Tax)

Mills (Kenneth Anthony) v HM Advocate (No.1) 1999 J.C. 216; 1999 S.L.T. 680; 1999 S.C.C.R. 202; 1999 G.W.D. 11-495, HCJ .... *Digested,* 99/**5857**: *Applied* 17/2532

MILLSTONE A/S/Prefilled packing usable as baking tin (T2094/12) [2017] E.P.O.R. 21, EPO (Technical Bd App)

Milne v Harrower [2016] SAC (Crim) 26; 2017 S.C. (S.A.C.) 1; 2016 S.C.L. 1011; 2016 S.C.C.R. 392; 2016 G.W.D. 29-519, SAC .... *Digested,* 17/**2515**

Milton Keynes BC v Nulty see Nulty v Milton Keynes BC

Milton Keynes BC v Viridor (Community Recycling MK) Ltd [2016] EWHC 2764 (TCC); [2017] B.L.R. 47; [2016] 6 Costs L.R. 1041, QBD (TCC) .... *Digested,* 17/**196**

Milton Keynes BC v Viridor (Community Recycling MK) Ltd [2017] EWHC 239 (TCC); [2017] B.L.R. 216; 170 Con. L.R. 147, QBD (TCC) .... *Digested,* 17/**1817**

Milton Keynes NHS Foundation Trust v Hyde see Hyde v Milton Keynes Hospital NHS Foundation Trust

Minister Finansow v Aviva Towarzystwo Ubezpieczen na Zycie SA w Warszawie (C-605/15) EU:C:2017:718; [2017] B.V.C. 42; [2017] S.T.I. 2004, ECJ (4th Chamber)

Minister Finansow v Posnania Investment SA (C-36/16) EU:C:2017:361; [2017] S.T.C. 1764; [2018] C.E.C. 279; [2017] B.V.C. 22; [2017] S.T.I. 1195, ECJ (2nd Chamber)

Minister Finansow v RR Donnelley Global Turnkey Solutions Poland sp z oo (C-155/12) EU:C:2013:434; [2014] S.T.C. 131; [2013] B.V.C. 342; [2013] S.T.I. 2473, ECJ (1st Chamber)
Followed 17/2260

Minister Finansow v Stowarzyszenie Artystow Wykonawcow Utworow Muzycznych i Slowno-Muzycznych SAWP (SAWP) (C-37/16) EU:C:2017:22; [2017] B.V.C. 6; [2017] S.T.I. 166, ECJ (8th Chamber)

Minister of Health v Bellotti; *joined case* Minister of Health v Holliday [1944] K.B. 298; [1944] 1 All E.R. 238, CA
Applied 54/618: *Considered* 71/1838, 76/1549, 80/1073, 97/2654, 17/1449: *Distinguished* 88/446: *Followed* 47-51/1535

Minister of Health v Holliday see Minister of Health v Bellotti

Minister voor Immigratie, Integratie en Asiel v B (C-456/12) see O v Minister voor Immigratie, Integratie en Asiel (C-456/12)

Ministre Charge de l'Economie v Galec-Groupement d'Achats des Centres Leclerc [2017] E.C.C. 21, Cass (F)

Ministre de l'Economie, des Finances et de l'Industrie v Gillan Beach Ltd (C114/05) EU:C:2006:169; [2006] S.T.C. 1080; [2006] E.C.R. I-2427; [2006] B.T.C. 5292; [2006] B.V.C. 361; [2006] S.T.I. 585, ECJ (6th Chamber) .... *Digested,* 06/**4500**: *Followed* 15/2617, 17/2278

Ministry of Defence v Iraqi Civilian Litigation see Iraqi Civilian Litigation v Ministry of Defence

Ministry of Defence v Kemeh; *sub nom* Kemeh v Ministry of Defence [2014] EWCA Civ 91; [2014] I.C.R. 625; [2014] I.R.L.R. 377; [2014] Eq. L.R. 259; Times, March 11, 2014, CA (Civ Div) .... *Digested,* 14/**1099**: *Considered* 17/840

Ministry of Justice v Burton [2016] EWCA Civ 714; [2017] 4 All E.R. 603; [2016] I.C.R. 1128, CA (Civ Div) .... *Digested,* 17/**811**

Ministry of Justice v Burton [2016] I.R.L.R. 100, EAT .... *Digested,* 16/**698**: *Affirmed* 17/811

Ministry of Justice v O'Brien see Department of Constitutional Affairs v O'Brien

Ministry of Justice v O'Brien see O'Brien v Ministry of Justice

Ministry of Justice v Prison Officers' Association [2017] EWHC 1839 (QB); [2018] I.C.R. 181; [2017] I.R.L.R. 1121; Times, September 20, 2019, QBD

Ministry of Justice v Prison Officers' Association; *sub nom* Secretary of State for Justice v Prison Officers' Association [2017] EWHC 699 (QB); [2017] I.R.L.R. 621; [2017] I.C.R. D14, QBD .... *Digested,* 17/**810**

Minmar (929) Ltd v Khalatschi [2011] EWHC 1159 (Ch); [2011] B.C.C. 485; [2012] 1 B.C.L.C. 798, Ch D .... *Digested,* 11/**1816**: *Applied* 11/1824, 12/1805, 17/409: *Considered* 12/1796, 12/1800, 12/1804, 12/1807, 12/1809: *Followed* 12/1799

Minmetals Germany GmbH v Ferco Steel Ltd [1999] 1 All E.R. (Comm.) 315; [1999] C.L.C. 647; Times, March 1, 1999; Independent, February 2, 1999, QBD (Comm) .... *Digested,* 99/**237**: *Considered* 17/80

Minnesota Mining & Manufacturing Co v Johnson & Johnson Ltd (No.3) [1976] F.S.R. 139; [1976] R.P.C. 671, CA (Civ Div) .... *Digested,* 76/**344.u**: *Applied* 10/1965, 17/309: *Followed* 14/1885

Minter v United Kingdom (Admissiblity) (62964/14) (2017) 65 E.H.R.R. SE6, ECHR

Mionis v Democratic Press SA [2017] EWCA Civ 1194; [2018] 2 W.L.R. 565; [2018] E.M.L.R. 4; Times, September 12, 2017, CA (Civ Div) .... *Digested,* 17/**650**

Mionis v Democratic Press SA [2014] EWHC 4104 (QB), QBD *Reversed* 17/650

Mir Steel UK Ltd v Morris see Lictor Anstalt v Mir Steel UK Ltd

Mirga v Secretary of State for Work and Pensions; *joined case* Samin v Westminster City Council [2016] UKSC 1; [2016] 1 W.L.R. 481; [2016] 2 All E.R. 447; [2016] 2 C.M.L.R. 31; [2016] H.L.R. 7; Times, February 8, 2016, SC .... *Digested,* 16/**1983**: *Considered* 17/2658

Mirror Group Newspapers Ltd v United Kingdom (39401/04) see MGN Ltd v United Kingdom (39401/04)

Mirza v Bevandorlasi es Allampolgarsagi Hivatal (C-695/15 PPU) EU:C:2016:188; [2016] 3 C.M.L.R. 24; [2017] C.E.C. 31; [2017] I.L.Pr. 18, ECJ (4th Chamber)

Mirza v Newham LBC; *sub nom* R. v Mirza (Nuzhat) [2017] EWCA Crim 924; [2018] 1 W.L.R. 619; [2017] 2 Cr. App. R. 29; [2017] J.P.L. 1397, CA (Crim Div) .... *Digested,* 17/**1711**

Mitchell v Harrower see Mitchell (Fraser) v Procurator Fiscal, Kirkcaldy

Mitchell v James (Costs) [2002] EWCA Civ 997; [2004] 1 W.L.R. 158; [2003] 2 All E.R. 1064; [2002] C.P. Rep. 72; [2002] C.P.L.R. 764; Times, July 20, 2002; Independent, July 18, 2002; (2002) 99(36) L.S.G. 38; (2002) 146 S.J.L.B. 202, CA (Civ Div) .... *Digested,* 02/**352**: *Applied* 03/342, 06/487, 17/257: *Considered* 12/387, 16/222

Mitchell v News Group Newspapers Ltd [2013] EWCA Civ 1537; [2014] 1 W.L.R. 795; [2014] 2 All E.R. 430; [2014] B.L.R. 89; [2013] 6 Costs L.R. 1008; [2014] E.M.L.R. 13; [2014] C.I.L.L. 3452; (2013) 163(7587) N.L.J. 20, CA (Civ Div) ..... *Digested,* 14/**445**: *Applied* 14/1757, 14/292, 14/341, 14/379, 14/395, 14/448, 14/449, 14/450, 14/451, 14/462, 14/475, 14/9, 15/1079, 15/1352, 15/285, 15/295, 15/298, 15/352, 16/170, 16/2204, 16/324, 17/1013, 17/278: *Approved* 17/2182: *Cited* 15/351: *Considered* 14/2983, 14/330, 14/397, 14/446, 15/1146, 15/2602, 15/296, 15/299, 15/828, 16/241, 16/65, 17/349: *Distinguished* 14/456: *Explained* 14/454: *Followed* 14/299, 14/353, 14/391, 14/447, 14/452, 14/455, 14/457, 14/460, 14/461, 14/463, 15/205, 15/210, 15/331, 15/354, 15/373, 16/171, 16/304, 16/305, 16/307, 16/308, 17/297: *Not applied* 14/398: *Referred to* 14/343

Mitchell v News Group Newspapers Ltd [2013] EWHC 2355 (QB), QBD *Affirmed* 14/445: *Followed* 17/1506

Mitchell v Revenue and Customs Commissioners see Macleod and Mitchell Contractors Ltd v Revenue and Customs Commissioners

Mitchell (Darrell) v HM Advocate [2017] HCJAC 60; 2018 J.C. 67; 2017 S.C.L. 896; 2017 S.C.C.R. 485; 2017 G.W.D. 26-430, HCJ .... *Digested,* 17/**2554**

Mitchell (Fraser) v Procurator Fiscal, Kirkcaldy; *sub nom* Mitchell v Harrower [2017] SAC (Crim) 14; 2017 S.L.T. (Sh Ct) 207; 2017 S.C.L. 1066; 2017 S.C.C.R. 512; 2017 G.W.D. 29-460, SAC .... *Digested,* 17/**2477**

Mitsui & Co Ltd v Beteiligungsgesellschaft LPG Tankerflotte mbH & Co KG [2016] EWCA Civ 708; [2017] 1 All E.R. (Comm) 264; [2016] Bus. L.R. 1285; [2016] 2 Lloyd's Rep. 375; [2016] 2 C.L.C. 127, CA (Civ Div) .... *Digested,* 16/**1956**

Mitsui & Co Ltd v Novorossiysk Shipping Co (The Gudermes) [1993] 1 Lloyd's Rep. 311, CA (Civ Div) .... *Digested,* 93/**3583**: *Applied* 17/507

Mittal v RP Capital Explorer Master Fund [2014] B.P.I.R. 1537, Ch D .... *Digested,* 15/**1437**: *Considered* 17/1322

MJ Hickey Plant Hire and Contracts Ltd v Revenue and Customs Commissioners [2017] UKUT 308 (TCC); [2017] B.V.C. 523, UT (Tax) .... *Digested,* 17/**2291**

MJ Hickey Plant Hire and Contracts Ltd v Revenue and Customs Commissioners [2016] UKFTT 61 (TC); [2016] S.T.I. 554, FTT (Tax)
Reversed 17/2291
MK v CK see K v K (Children: Permanent Removal from Jurisdiction)
ML v ANS see S v L
ML Tiles Ltd v Revenue and Customs Commissioners [2017] UKFTT 687 (TC); [2017] S.T.I. 2070, FTT (Tax)
MM v WL Clinic [2015] UKUT 644 (AAC); [2016] M.H.L.R. 198, UT (AAC) .... *Digested,* 17/**1552**
MM (A Patient), Re; *sub nom* Kirk v Devon CC [2017] EWCA Civ 260; [2017] 2 Costs L.R. 403, CA (Civ Div) .... *Digested,* 17/**224**
MM (Uganda) v Secretary of State for the Home Department see KMO (section 117: Unduly Harsh: Nigeria), Re
MM (Zimbabwe) v Secretary of State for the Home Department [2017] EWCA Civ 797; [2017] 4 W.L.R. 132, CA (Civ Div) .... *Digested,* 17/**1201**
MM (Zimbabwe) v Secretary of State for the Home Department [2012] EWCA Civ 279, CA (Civ Div)
Applied 17/1201: *Followed* 15/1373
MMF (UK) Ltd v Secretary of State for Communities and Local Government [2010] EWHC 3686 (Admin); [2011] J.P.L. 1067, QBD (Admin) .... *Digested,* 11/**2558**:
Considered 17/1734
MN v Hackney LBC see R. (on the application of MN) v Hackney LBC
MN (An Adult), Re see N (An Adult) (Court of Protection: Jurisdiction), Re
Mobile Sourcing Ltd v Revenue and Customs Commissioners [2016] UKUT 274 (TCC); [2016] B.V.C. 524, UT (Tax) .... *Digested,* 17/**2276**
Mobile Sourcing Ltd v Revenue and Customs Commissioners [2014] UKFTT 1089 (TC), FTT (Tax)
Affirmed 17/2276
Mobilx Ltd (In Administration) v Revenue and Customs Commissioners; *joined cases* Calltel Telecom Ltd v Revenue and Customs Commissioners; Revenue and Customs Commissioners v Blue Sphere Global Ltd [2010] EWCA Civ 517; [2010] S.T.C. 1436; [2010] Lloyd's Rep. F.C. 445; [2010] B.V.C. 638; Times, June 2, 2010; [2010] S.T.I. 1589, CA (Civ Div) .... *Digested,* 10/**3502**:
Applied 11/3533, 14/3066, 14/3070, 15/2589, 15/2590: *Considered* 11/3538, 11/3556, 12/3398, 14/3071, 14/3810, 17/2167, 17/2252, 17/2277: *Followed* 11/3554, 12/3401, 12/3402, 12/3404, 12/3405, 14/3065, 14/3067, 14/3069, 14/3092, 15/2592, 15/2609, 16/2169
MOC (Scotland) Ltd v Revenue and Customs Commissioners [2017] S.T.I. 364, FTT (Tax)
Mockiene v Lithuania (Admissibility) (75916/13) (2017) 65 E.H.R.R. SE13, ECHR
Modi v Clarke [2011] EWCA Civ 937, CA (Civ Div)
Considered 17/647
Mohammadi v Shellpoint Trustees Ltd [2009] EWHC 1098 (Ch); [2010] 1 All E.R. 433; [2009] 3 Costs L.R. 486; [2009] 23 E.G. 92 (C.S.); (2009) 159 N.L.J. 823; (2009) 153(22) S.J.L.B. 31, Ch D .... *Digested,* 10/**2121**:
Applied 17/1477
Mohammed v Advocate General for Scotland [2017] L.L.R. 570; 2017 G.W.D. 14-217, Sh Ct (Lothian) (Livingston) .... *Digested,* 17/**2666**
Mohammed v Ministry of Defence see Rahmatullah v Ministry of Defence
Mohammed v Newcastle City Council [2016] UKUT 415 (LC); [2017] R.V.R. 75, UT (Lands)
Mohammed v Secretary of State for Defence; *sub nom* Qasim v Ministry of Defence; Iraqi Civilians v Ministry of Defence; *joined cases* Al-Waheed v Ministry of Defence; Rahmatullah v Ministry of Defence [2015] EWCA Civ 843; [2016] 2 W.L.R. 247; [2015] H.R.L.R. 20; Times, September 10, 2015, CA (Civ Div) .... *Digested,* 15/**1558**:
Reversed in part 17/1407, 17/1425
Mohammed v Secretary of State for Defence; *sub nom* Qasim v Ministry of Defence; Iraqi Civilians v Ministry of Defence; *joined cases* Al-Waheed v Ministry of Defence; Rahmatullah v Ministry of Defence [2017] UKSC 2; [2017] A.C. 821; [2017] 2 W.L.R. 327; [2017] 3 All E.R. 215; [2017] H.R.L.R. 1; 43 B.H.R.C. 137, SC .... *Digested,* 17/**1407**
Mohammed v Secretary of State for the Home Department see Januzi v Secretary of State for the Home Department
Mohamud v Wm Morrison Supermarkets Plc [2016] UKSC 11; [2016] A.C. 677; [2016] 2 W.L.R. 821; [2017] 1 All E.R. 15; [2016] I.C.R. 485; [2016] I.R.L.R. 362; [2016] P.I.Q.R. P11; Times, March 14, 2016, SC .... *Digested,* 16/**2146**:
Considered 17/2205: *Referred to* 16/1553
Moir v Memsie 2017 Rep. L.R. 78; 2017 G.W.D. 12-173, Sh Ct (Lothian) (Edinburgh) . *Digested,* 17/**2444**
Moir v Wallersteiner (No.1) see Wallersteiner v Moir (No.1)

Monarch Financial Services Ltd, Re; *sub nom* Cooper v Monarch Financial Services Ltd [2017] EWHC 2324 (Ch); [2017] B.C.C. 570, Ch D

Mond v Synergi Partners Ltd see Synergi Partners Ltd, Re

Monde Petroleum SA v WesternZagros Ltd [2016] EWHC 1472 (Comm); [2017] 1 All E.R. (Comm) 1009; [2016] 2 Lloyd's Rep. 229; 167 Con. L.R. 15, QBD (Comm) *Digested,* 16/**423**

Mondelez UK Holdings & Services Ltd v EUIPO (T-112/13) EU:T:2016:735; [2017] E.T.M.R. 13, GC (5th Chamber)

Moneybarn No.1 Ltd v Bell 2016 S.L.T. (Sh Ct) 419; 2016 G.W.D. 32-569, Sh Ct (South Strathclyde) (Dumfries) .... *Digested,* 17/**2456**

Monk v Warbey [1935] 1 K.B. 75; (1934) 50 Ll. L. Rep. 33, CA
Applied 47-51/9111: *Considered* 70/206, 71/3138, 00/3544, 05/2843, 16/1257, 17/1349: *Distinguished* 71/11235, 95/2901, 15/3166

Monroe v Hopkins [2017] EWHC 645 (QB); [2017] 1 W.L.R. 3587, QBD

Monroe v Hopkins [2017] EWHC 433 (QB); [2017] 4 W.L.R. 68; [2017] E.M.L.R. 16, QBD .... *Digested,* 17/**652**

Monte Developments Ltd (In Administration) v Court Management Consultants Ltd [2010] EWHC 3071 (Ch); [2011] 1 W.L.R. 1579; [2011] 1 B.C.L.C. 368; [2011] 2 Costs L.O. 163, Ch D (Companies Ct) .... *Digested,* 11/**253**: *Applied* 17/1849

Montgomery v Lanarkshire Health Board; *sub nom* NM v Lanarkshire Health Board [2015] UKSC 11; [2015] A.C. 1430; [2015] 2 W.L.R. 768; [2015] 2 All E.R. 1031; 2015 S.C. (U.K.S.C.) 63; 2015 S.L.T. 189; 2015 S.C.L.R. 315; [2015] P.I.Q.R. P13; [2015] Med. L.R. 149; (2015) 143 B.M.L.R. 47; 2015 G.W.D. 10-179, SC .... *Digested,* 15/**1769**:
Applied 17/1640: *Considered* 16/1404, 16/2477, 17/1558: *Followed* 15/1768, 17/1556, 17/1560, 17/1642

Montis Design BV v Goossens Meubelen BV (C-169/15) EU:C:2016:790; [2017] Bus. L.R. 510; [2017] E.C.D.R. 11, ECJ (3rd Chamber)

Montpelier Business Reorganisation Ltd v Armitage Jones LLP [2017] EWHC 2273 (QB); [2017] 5 Costs L.O. 659, QBD (Leeds) .... *Digested,* 17/**336**

Moon v Atherton [1972] 2 Q.B. 435; [1972] 3 W.L.R. 57; [1972] 3 All E.R. 145; (1972) 116 S.J. 374, CA (Civ Div) .... *Digested,* 72/**2793**: *Not applied* 17/354

Moon v Garrett [2006] EWCA Civ 1121; [2006] C.P. Rep. 46; [2006] B.L.R. 402; [2007] 1 Costs L.R. 41; [2007] I.C.R. 95; [2007] P.I.Q.R. P3; Times, September 1, 2006, CA (Civ Div)
Considered 17/223

Moonsam v Axa Corporate Solutions Assurances SA see Dickinson v Tesco Plc

Moore v President of the Methodist Conference; *sub nom* Preston v President of the Methodist Church; President of the Methodist Conference v Preston (formerly Moore) [2013] UKSC 29; [2013] 2 A.C. 163; [2013] 2 W.L.R. 1350; [2013] 4 All E.R. 477; [2013] I.C.R. 833; [2013] I.R.L.R. 646; Times, June 11, 2013; (2013) 157(20) S.J.L.B. 35, SC .... *Digested,* 13/**994**:
Considered 17/178: *Followed* 15/821, 17/790

Moore v United Kingdom (3896/10) see Vinter v United Kingdom (66069/09)

Moore (A Bankrupt), Re; *sub nom* Mawer v Moore [2017] EWHC 1242 (Ch); [2017] 3 Costs L.R. 571, Ch D .... *Digested,* 17/**310**

Moran v Freyssinet Ltd [2014] CSOH 173; 2015 Rep. L.R. 15; 2015 G.W.D. 1-7, OH .. *Digested,* 15/**2912**:
Affirmed 16/2461: *Applied* 17/2445

Moran v Manchester City Council see Ali v Birmingham City Council

Moran Yacht & Ship Inc v Pisarev [2016] EWCA Civ 317; [2017] 1 All E.R. (Comm) 62; [2016] 1 Lloyd's Rep. 625, CA (Civ Div) .... *Digested,* 16/**1965**

Moray Council v Scottish Ministers [2006] CSIH 41; 2006 S.C. 691; 2007 S.C.L.R. 55; 2006 G.W.D. 25-578, IH (2 Div) .... *Digested,* 07/**5464**: *Considered* 17/2765

Morby v Gate Gourmet Luxembourg IV Sarl; *sub nom* Gate Gourmet Luxembourg IV Sarl v Morby [2016] EWHC 74 (Ch); [2016] Bus. L.R. 218; [2016] B.P.I.R. 414, Ch D .... *Digested,* 16/**1205**: *Considered* 17/1295

Mordue v Secretary of State for Communities and Local Government see Jones v Mordue

Moreno v Motor Insurers' Bureau [2016] UKSC 52; [2016] 1 W.L.R. 3194; [2017] 4 All E.R. 28; [2016] R.T.R. 26; [2017] Lloyd's Rep. I.R. 99; [2017] P.I.Q.R. P3; Times, September 13, 2016, SC .... *Digested,* 16/**1639**

Morey v Ghataura (Unreported, May 10, 2017), CC (Coventry) [*Irwin Mitchell LLP, Riverside West, 1 Millsands, Sheffield*] .... *Digested,* 17/**1653**

Morgan v DPP [2016] EWHC 3414 (Admin); [2017] A.C.D. 23, DC

Morgan & Morgan Srl International Insurance Brokers v European Union Intellectual Property Office (EUIPO) (T-399/15) EU:T:2017:17; [2017] E.T.M.R. 17, GC (7th Chamber)

Morgan Grenfell & Co Ltd v Welwyn Hatfield DC [1995] 1 All E.R. 1; Times, June 1, 1993, QBD .... *Digested,* 95/**789**: *Approved* 17/171

Morning Star Inc v European Commission (T-76/14) see Morningstar Inc v European Commission (T-76/14)

Morningstar Inc v European Commission (T-76/14); *sub nom* Morning Star Inc v European Commission (T-76/14) EU:T:2016:481; [2017] 4 C.M.L.R. 5, GC (8th Chamber)

Moroni v Collo GmbH (C-110/91) see Ten Oever v Stichting Bedrijfspensioenfonds voor het Glazenwassers- en Schoonmaakbedrijf (C-109/91)

Morris v Agrichemicals Ltd see Bank of Credit and Commerce International SA (In Liquidation) (No.8), Re

Morris v Morris [2016] EWCA Civ 812; [2017] 1 W.L.R. 554; [2016] 3 F.C.R. 224, CA (Civ Div) .... *Digested,* 16/**901**

Morris v Rayners Enterprises Inc see Bank of Credit and Commerce International SA (In Liquidation) (No.8), Re

Morris-Garner v One Step (Support) Ltd see One Step (Support) Ltd v Morris-Garner

Morrow v Attorney General for Northern Ireland [2015] NICA 69; [2017] N.I. 254, CA (NI)

Mortgage Business Plc v Cook see North East Property Buyers Litigation, Re

Mortgage Business Plc v O'Shaughnessy see North East Property Buyers Litigation, Re

Mortgage Express v Lambert [2016] EWCA Civ 555; [2017] Ch. 93; [2016] 3 W.L.R. 1582; [2016] H.L.R. 34; [2016] 2 P. & C.R. 13, CA (Civ Div) .... *Digested,* 16/**1820**

Mortgage Express Ltd v Bowerman & Partners [1996] 2 All E.R. 836; [1996] E.C.C. 228; [1996] P.N.L.R. 62; [1996] 1 E.G.L.R. 126; [1996] 04 E.G. 126; Times, August 1, 1995; [1995] E.G. 129 (C.S.); [1995] N.P.C. 129, CA (Civ Div) .... *Digested,* 96/**4497**: *Applied* 98/4027, 99/4379, 16/2327: *Considered* 97/3373, 97/3829, 98/4020, 98/4026, 99/4037, 00/4271: *Followed* 16/1549, 17/2328

Morton (Henry) v HM Advocate [2017] HCJAC 21; 2017 S.C.L. 513; 2017 G.W.D. 13-211, HCJ .... *Digested,* 17/**2811**

Mosley v Hickman; *sub nom* Hickman v Trustees of the Phillimore Kensington Estate; *joined cases* Hagan v Trustees of the Phillimore Kensington Estate; Francis v Trustees of the Phillimore Kensington Estate (1986) 18 H.L.R. 292; (1986) 52 P. & C.R. 248; [1986] 1 E.G.L.R. 161; (1986) 278 E.G. 728; [1986] R.V.R. 102; (1986) 83 L.S.G. 1058; (1986) 130 S.J. 245, CA (Civ Div) .... *Digested,* 86/**1869**: *Applied* 17/1845

Mosson v Spousal (London) Ltd [2016] EWHC 53 (QB); [2016] 4 W.L.R. 28, QBD .... *Digested,* 16/**1607**: *Applied* 17/1553: *Considered* 17/1658

Motiu v Criminal Court Nowy of Santa Maria Capua Vetere, Italy see Doci v Italy

Motiu v Italy see Doci v Italy

Moto Hospitality Ltd v Secretary of State for Transport [2007] EWCA Civ 764; [2008] 1 W.L.R. 2822; [2008] 2 All E.R. 718; [2007] R.V.R. 247; [2008] J.P.L. 358; (2007) 157 S.J.L.B. 1426; [2007] N.P.C. 95, CA (Civ Div) .... *Digested,* 08/**3074**: *Followed* 09/2734, 17/1832

Motorola Ltd v Davidson [2001] I.R.L.R. 4, EAT .... *Digested,* 01/**6467**: *Applied* 17/825

Mott v Long [2017] EWHC 2130 (TCC); [2017] B.L.R. 566; [2017] 4 Costs L.R. 817, QBD (TCC) .... *Digested,* 17/**348**

Motto v Trafigura Ltd [2011] EWCA Civ 1150; [2012] 1 W.L.R. 657; [2012] 2 All E.R. 181; [2011] 6 Costs L.R. 1028; Times, November 22, 2011, CA (Civ Div) .... *Digested,* 12/**388**: *Considered* 14/331, 17/229

Moulai v France see Mucelli v Albania

Moulton Parish Council v Secretary of State for Communities and Local Government [2017] EWHC 1047 (Admin); [2017] J.P.L. 1144, QBD (Admin) .... *Digested,* 17/**1777**

Mounsey v Ismay 159 E.R. 621; (1865) 3 Hurl. & C. 486, Ex Ct
Applied 55/882: *Considered* 87/316, 16/1812: *Not applied* 17/1842

Mount Cook Land Ltd v Westminster City Council see R. (on the application of Mount Cook Land Ltd) v Westminster City Council

Mountney v Treharne; *sub nom* Mountney, Re [2002] EWCA Civ 1174; [2003] Ch. 135; [2002] 3 W.L.R. 1760; [2002] 2 F.L.R. 930; [2002] 3 F.C.R. 97; [2002] B.P.I.R. 1126; Times, September 9, 2002; [2002] Fam. Law 809; (2002) 99(39) L.S.G. 38, CA (Civ Div) .... *Digested,* 02/**2676**: *Applied* 14/3199, 17/1846: *Considered* 09/2208: *Followed* 04/2129

Mountney, Re see Mountney v Treharne

Mowbray v Sanders see Mowbray (A Bankrupt), Re
Mowbray (A Bankrupt), Re; *sub nom* Mowbray v Sanders [2015] EWHC 296 (Ch); [2015] B.P.I.R. 665, Ch D .... *Digested,* 15/**1405**: *Applied* 17/1290
Mowlem Plc (t/a Mowlem Marine) v Scrabster Harbour Trust see Scrabster Harbour Trust v Mowlem Plc (t/a Mowlem Marine)
Moynihan (Sean Barry) v HM Advocate [2016] HCJAC 85; 2017 J.C. 71; 2016 S.C.L. 977; 2016 S.C.C.R. 548; 2016 G.W.D. 31-546, HCJ .... *Digested,* 17/**2556**: *Considered* 17/2555
MP (Sri Lanka) v Secretary of State for the Home Department [2016] UKSC 32; [2017] 2 All E.R. 155, SC .... *Digested,* 17/**1249**
Mploy Group Ltd v Denso Manufacturing UK Ltd see Denso Manufacturing UK Ltd v Great Lakes Reinsurance (UK) Plc
MPT Group Ltd v Peel [2017] EWHC 1222 (Ch); [2017] I.R.L.R. 1092, Ch D (Manchester)
MR v SR [2016] EWCOP 54; [2017] 1 Costs L.R. 71, Fam Div .... *Digested,* 17/**243**
MR (Iran) v Secretary of State for the Home Department see NA (Sudan) v Secretary of State for the Home Department
MRI Trading AG v Erdenet Mining Corp LLC [2013] EWCA Civ 156; [2013] 1 Lloyd's Rep. 638; [2013] 1 C.L.C. 423, CA (Civ Div) .... *Digested,* 13/**566**: *Applied* 14/112: *Followed* 17/74
Mrs Maggie Brack Ferguson and Others v Andrew Paul (1885) 12 R. 1222, IH (2 Div) *Considered* 17/2710: *Followed* 16/2709
MS v PS (C-283/16); *sub nom* S v S (C-283/16) EU:C:2017:104; [2017] 4 W.L.R. 72; [2017] I.L.Pr. 24; [2017] 1 F.L.R. 1163, ECJ (6th Chamber) .... *Digested,* 17/**896**
MS v PS see S v S
MS v Secretary of State for the Home Department [2016] EWHC 3162 (Admin); [2017] A.C.D. 25, QBD (Admin) *Applied* 17/1234: *Reversed* 17/1209
MS (India) v Secretary of State for the Home Department [2013] CSIH 52; 2013 G.W.D. 23-441, IH (Ex Div) *Applied* 15/3149, 15/3157: *Considered* 17/2665
MS (India) v Secretary of State for the Home Department; *sub nom* Secretary of State for the Home Department v MS; *joined cases* MT (Tunisia) v Secretary of State for the Home Department; MS (India) v Secretary of State for the Home Department [2017] EWCA Civ 1190; [2018] 1 W.L.R. 389; [2018] Imm. A.R. 117; Times, September 14, 2017, CA (Civ Div) .... *Digested,* 17/**1209**
MS (India) v Secretary of State for the Home Department see MS (India) v Secretary of State for the Home Department
MS (Uganda) v Secretary of State for the Home Department [2016] UKSC 33; [2016] 1 W.L.R. 2615; [2017] 3 All E.R. 709; [2016] Imm. A.R. 1330; [2016] I.N.L.R. 577, SC .... *Digested,* 16/**1059**
MSC Mediterranean Shipping Co SA v Cottonex Anstalt [2015] EWHC 283 (Comm); [2015] 2 All E.R. (Comm) 614; [2015] 1 Lloyd's Rep. 359; [2015] 1 C.L.C. 143, QBD (Comm) .... *Digested,* 15/**2318**: *Reversed in part* 17/2011
MSC Mediterranean Shipping Co SA v Cottonex Anstalt [2016] EWCA Civ 789; [2017] 1 All E.R. (Comm) 483; [2016] 2 Lloyd's Rep. 494; [2016] 2 C.L.C. 272, CA (Civ Div) .... *Digested,* 17/**2011**
MSC Mediterranean Shipping Co SA v Glencore International AG see Glencore International AG v MSC Mediterranean Shipping Co SA
MT v Gerry see T v Locality Reporter
MT v Sweden (1412/12) (2017) 65 E.H.R.R. 28; [2015] Imm. A.R. 756, ECHR
MT (Tunisia) v Secretary of State for the Home Department see MS (India) v Secretary of State for the Home Department
MT Hojgaard A/S v E.ON Climate and Renewables UK Robin Rigg East Ltd [2017] UKSC 59; [2018] 2 All E.R. 22; [2017] Bus. L.R. 1610; [2017] B.L.R. 477; 173 Con. L.R. 1; Times, August 21, 2017; [2017] C.I.L.L. 4032, SC .... *Digested,* 17/**472**
MT Hojgaard A/S v E.ON Climate and Renewables UK Robin Rigg East Ltd [2015] EWCA Civ 407; [2015] B.L.R. 431; 160 Con. L.R. 1; [2015] C.I.L.L. 3661, CA (Civ Div) .... *Digested,* 15/**470**: *Reversed* 17/472
MTM Construction Ltd v William Reid Engineering Ltd 1998 S.L.T. 211; 1997 S.C.L.R. 778; 1997 Rep. L.R. 27; Times, April 22, 1997; 1997 G.W.D. 7-260, OH .... *Digested,* 97/**6073**: *Applied* 17/2464

Mucelli v Albania; *joined case* Moulai v France [2009] UKHL 2; [2009] 1 W.L.R. 276; [2009] 3 All E.R. 1035; [2009] Extradition L.R. 122; Times, January 27, 2009; (2009) 153(4) S.J.L.B. 28, HL .... *Digested,* 09/**1472**: *Applied* 09/354, 11/1276, 12/2269, 12/2541, 12/317, 12/439, 17/323: *Considered* 10/3974, 17/12: *Followed* 12/1287, 16/799: *Not followed* 12/1291: *Referred to* 13/2061

Muhumed v Entry Clearance Officer see Mahad (Ethiopia) v Entry Clearance Officer

Muldoon (John Scott) v Herron 1970 J.C. 30; 1970 S.L.T. 228, HCJ .... *Digested,* 70/**3070**: *Applied* 90/4852, 91/4586, 94/5513, 17/2492

Mulholland's Will Trusts, Re; *sub nom* Bryan v Westminster Bank [1949] 1 All E.R. 460; [1949] W.N. 103; [1949] L.J.R. 1078, Ch D .... *Digested,* 47-51/**9426**: *Applied* 93/2442, 17/2221: *Considered* 91/557

Mull Shellfish Ltd v Golden Sea Produce Ltd 1992 S.L.T. 703; Times, October 17, 1991; Scotsman, August 28, 1991, IH (2 Div) .... *Digested,* 91/**5457**: *Considered* 17/2455

Mullan v Anderson 1993 S.L.T. 835; 1993 S.C.L.R. 506, IH (Ct of 5 judges) .... *Digested,* 93/**5815**: *Applied* 04/4564: *Considered* 03/5293, 13/3728, 17/2779: *Followed* 96/6627, 09/5044: *Referred to* 08/5003

Mullan (t/a Grange Road Car Sales) v Revenue and Customs Commissioners [2017] UKFTT 193 (TC); [2017] S.T.I. 870, FTT (Tax)

Mullen v Salford City Council see Hounslow LBC v Powell

Muller v King's College Hospital NHS Foundation Trust [2017] EWHC 128 (QB); [2017] Q.B. 987; [2017] 2 W.L.R. 1595; [2017] P.I.Q.R. P10; [2017] Med. L.R. 142, QBD .... *Digested,* 17/**1561**

Muller v Linsley & Mortimer [1996] P.N.L.R. 74; Times, December 8, 1994; (1995) 92(3) L.S.G. 38; (1995) 139 S.J.L.B. 43, CA (Civ Div) .... *Digested,* 94/**3674**: *Applied* 99/349, 01/1536, 09/764: *Considered* 04/260, 08/357, 09/329, 17/292

Multani (Setting of Minimum Term), Re see Jones (Setting of Minimum Term), Re

Multimedia Computing Ltd v Revenue and Customs Commissioners; *joined case* Deed Poll Services Ltd v Revenue and Customs Commissioners [2016] UKFTT 779 (TC); [2017] S.T.I. 78, FTT (Tax)

Munatsi Logistics Ltd v Revenue and Customs Commissioners [2017] UKFTT 617 (TC); [2017] Lloyd's Rep. F.C. 549, FTT (Tax)

Munir v Secretary of State for the Home Department see R. (on the application of Abbassi) v Secretary of State for the Home Department

Munjaz v Mersey Care NHS Trust see R. (on the application of Munjaz) v Mersey Care NHS Trust

Munks v Munks [1985] F.L.R. 576; [1985] Fam. Law 131; (1985) 82 L.S.G. 43; (1985) 129 S.J. 65, CA (Civ Div) .... *Digested,* 85/**2722**: *Applied* 87/1731, 04/1521, 16/1193: *Followed* 17/1002

Munnoch v Tay-Forth Foundries Ltd 2008 S.C.L.R. 232; 2007 G.W.D. 31-530, OH *Considered* 17/2757

Munton v Greater London Council; *sub nom* Munton v Newham LBC [1976] 1 W.L.R. 649; [1976] 2 All E.R. 815; 74 L.G.R. 416; (1976) 32 P. & C.R. 269; (1976) 239 E.G. 43; (1976) 120 S.J. 149, CA (Civ Div) .... *Digested,* 76/**2850**: *Applied* 82/356, 01/598: *Considered* 17/2075

Munton v Newham LBC see Munton v Greater London Council

Mur Joint Ventures Bv v Compagnie Monegasque de Banque [2016] EWHC 3107 (Comm); [2017] 1 Lloyd's Rep. 186, QBD (Comm) .... *Digested,* 17/**161**

Mures Court v Zagrean see Romania v Zagrean

Murphy v Media Protection Services Ltd [2012] EWHC 529 (Admin); [2013] 1 Costs L.R. 16; [2012] 3 C.M.L.R. 3; [2012] F.S.R. 13; [2013] L.L.R. 400, DC .... *Digested,* 12/**360**: *Considered* 14/1861, 15/375, 17/270

Murphy v Media Protection Services Ltd (C-429/08) see Football Association Premier League Ltd v QC Leisure (C-403/08)

Murphy (Charles) v HM Advocate [2016] HCJAC 118; 2017 S.L.T. 143; 2017 S.C.L. 176; 2016 G.W.D. 39-691, HCJ .... *Digested,* 17/**2538**

Murray v Associated Newspapers Ltd; *sub nom* Associated Newspapers Ltd v Murray [2015] EWCA Civ 488; [2015] E.M.L.R. 21, CA (Civ Div) .... *Digested,* 15/**694**: *Followed* 17/374

Murray v Legal & General Assurance Society [1970] 2 Q.B. 495; [1970] 2 W.L.R. 465; [1969] 3 All E.R. 794; [1969] 2 Lloyd's Rep. 405; (1969) 113 S.J. 720, QBD ...... *Digested,* 69/**1825**: *Applied* 17/1338

Murray v Netherlands (10511/10) (2017) 64 E.H.R.R. 3; [2017] M.H.L.R. 1, ECHR

Murray Group Holdings Ltd v Revenue and Customs Commissioners; *sub nom* RFC 2012 Plc (In Liquidation) (formerly Rangers Football Club Plc) v Advocate General for Scotland; Revenue and Customs Commissioners v Murray Group Holdings Ltd; Advocate General for Scotland v Murray Group Holdings Ltd [2015] CSIH 77; [2016] S.T.C. 468; 2016 S.C. 201; 2015 S.L.T. 765; 2016 S.C.L.R. 485; [2015] B.T.C. 36; 2015 G.W.D. 36-583, IH (2 Div) .... *Digested,* 16/**2829**:
Affirmed 17/2131: *Applied* 17/2132, 17/2238

Murray Group Holdings Ltd v Revenue and Customs Commissioners see RFC 2012 Plc (In Liquidation) (formerly Rangers Football Club Plc) v Advocate General for Scotland

Murray, Petitioner 2012 S.L.T. (Sh Ct) 57; 2012 G.W.D. 14-300, Sh Ct (Tayside) (Kirkcaldy) .... *Digested,* 12/**4294**:
Considered 17/2839

Murray-Hession v Revenue and Customs Commissioners [2016] UKFTT 612 (TC); [2017] S.F.T.D. 299; [2016] S.T.I. 3024, FTT (Tax) .... *Digested,* 17/**2142**

Murrell v Secretary of State for Communities and Local Government; *sub nom* R. (on the application of Murrell) v Secretary of State for Communities and Local Government [2010] EWCA Civ 1367; [2012] 1 P. & C.R. 6; [2011] J.P.L. 739; [2010] N.P.C. 120, CA (Civ Div) .... *Digested,* 11/**2539**:
Applied 11/2541: *Considered* 17/1746

Mursic v Croatia (7334/13) (2017) 65 E.H.R.R. 1; 42 B.H.R.C. 439, ECHR (Grand Chamber)
Applied 17/903, 17/906

Mushin v Manchester City Council see Hounslow LBC v Powell

Musion Systems Ltd v Activ8-3D Ltd [2012] EWPCC 5, PCC
Applied 17/381

Musisi v Secretary of State for the Home Department see Bugdaycay v Secretary of State for the Home Department

Mustafic-Mujic v Netherlands (49037/15) (2017) 64 E.H.R.R. SE5, ECHR

Mutch v Mutch [2016] EWCA Civ 370; [2017] 1 F.L.R. 408; [2016] Fam. Law 674, CA (Civ Div) .... *Digested,* 17/**1041**:
Applied 16/945

MV Yorke Motors v Edwards [1982] 1 W.L.R. 444; [1982] 1 All E.R. 1024; (1982) 126 S.J. 245, HL .... *Digested,* 82/**2398**:
Applied 96/811, 97/874, 00/316, 00/543: *Considered* 85/2731, 96/724, 96/854, 97/1376, 97/4516, 00/509, 17/203: *Explained* 84/2723

MVF 3 Aps (formerly Vestergaard Frandsen A/S) v Bestnet Europe Ltd see Vestergaard Frandsen A/S (now called MVF 3 Aps) v Bestnet Europe Ltd

MVM Magyar Villamos Muvek Zrt v Nemzeti Ado- es Vamhivatal Fellebbviteli Igazgatosag (C-28/16) EU:C:2017:7; [2017] S.T.C. 452, ECJ (6th Chamber)

MWB Business Exchange Centres Ltd v Rock Advertising Ltd [2016] EWCA Civ 553; [2017] Q.B. 604; [2016] 3 W.L.R. 1519; [2016] 2 Lloyd's Rep. 391; [2016] L. & T.R. 27; Times, July 22, 2016, CA (Civ Div) .... *Digested,* 16/**442**:
Applied 16/402

MY (Kenya) v Secretary of State for the Home Department see NA (Pakistan) v Secretary of State for the Home Department

Myall v Tower Insurance Ltd [2017] NZHC 251; [2017] Lloyd's Rep. I.R. 546, HC (NZ)

Myers v Queen, The; *joined cases* Brangman v Queen, The; Cox v Queen, The [2015] UKPC 40; [2016] A.C. 314; [2015] 3 W.L.R. 1145; [2016] 1 Cr. App. R. 11; Times, October 20, 2015; [2017] Crim. L.R. 125, PC (Ber)

Myrie v Secretary of State for the Home Department see Caroopen v Secretary of State for the Home Department

N v A Clinical Commissioning Group see N (An Adult) (Court of Protection: Jurisdiction), Re

N v ACCG see N (An Adult) (Court of Protection: Jurisdiction), Re

N v F (Financial Orders: Pre-Acquired Wealth) [2011] EWHC 586 (Fam); [2011] 2 F.L.R. 533; [2012] 1 F.C.R. 139; [2011] Fam. Law 686, Fam Div .... *Digested,* 11/**1296**:
Considered 15/1091, 17/1024: *Followed* 12/1425, 12/1427

N v Royal Bank of Scotland Plc see National Crime Agency v N

N v S [2015] EWHC 3248 (Comm), QBD (Comm)
Reversed 17/173

N v Staatssecretaris voor Veiligheid en Justitie (C-601/15 PPU); *sub nom* JN v Staatssecretaris van Veiligheid en Justitie (C-601/15 PPU) EU:C:2016:84; [2016] 1 W.L.R. 3027; [2017] 1 C.M.L.R. 42, ECJ (Grand Chamber)
Considered 17/1202

N (A Child) (Adoption: Foreign Guardianship), Re; *sub nom* AGN (Adoption: Foreign Adoption), Re [2000] 2 F.L.R. 431; [2000] 2 F.C.R. 512; Times, June 27, 2000; [2000] Fam. Law 694, Fam Div .... *Digested,* 00/**2434**: *Applied* 17/1034: *Considered* 03/1474

N (A Child) (Care Proceedings: Adoption), Re [2012] EWCA Civ 1563; [2013] 1 F.L.R. 1244; [2013] Fam. Law 142, CA (Civ Div) .... *Digested,* 13/**1218**: *Followed* 17/924

N (A Child) (Recognition of Foreign Adoption), Re; *sub nom* S v S [2016] EWHC 3085 (Fam); [2018] 2 W.L.R. 449; [2017] 2 F.L.R. 297, Fam Div .... *Digested,* 17/**1034**

N (An Adult) (Court of Protection: Jurisdiction), Re; *sub nom* N v ACCG; ACCG v MN; N v A Clinical Commissioning Group; MN (An Adult), Re [2015] EWCA Civ 411; [2016] Fam. 87; [2015] 3 W.L.R. 1585; [2015] C.O.P.L.R. 505; (2015) 18 C.C.L. Rep. 521; [2015] Med. L.R. 287, CA (Civ Div) .... *Digested,* 15/**1741**: *Affirmed* 17/1536: *Applied* 16/1481, 16/1521

N (An Adult) (Court of Protection: Jurisdiction), Re; *sub nom* N v ACCG; ACCG v MN; N v A Clinical Commissioning Group; MN (An Adult), Re [2017] UKSC 22; [2017] A.C. 549; [2017] 2 W.L.R. 1011; [2017] 3 All E.R. 719; [2017] C.O.P.L.R. 200; (2017) 20 C.C.L. Rep. 133; (2017) 155 B.M.L.R. 1; Times, March 29, 2017, SC .... *Digested,* 17/**1536**

N (Children) (Adoption: Jurisdiction), Re see J (Children) (Brussels II Revised: Article 15), Re

N (Children) (Adoption: Jurisdiction), Re see N (Children), Re

N (Children), Re; *sub nom* N (Children) (Adoption: Jurisdiction), Re; J (Children) (Brussels II Revised: Article 15), Re [2016] UKSC 15; [2017] A.C. 167; [2016] 2 W.L.R. 1103; [2017] 1 All E.R. 527; [2016] 1 F.L.R. 1082; [2016] 3 F.C.R. 394; Times, April 18, 2016; [2016] Fam. Law 681, SC .... *Digested,* 16/**826**: *Applied* 17/940: *Followed* 17/913

N (Children: Welfare Decision), Re; *sub nom* A London Borough v M [2016] EWFC 44; [2017] 1 F.C.R. 203, Fam Ct

N (Hague Convention: Habitual Residence), Re [2017] EWHC 63 (Fam); [2017] 1 F.C.R. 413, Fam Div .... *Digested,* 17/**1037**

N (Human Fertilisation and Embryology Act 2008), Re [2016] EWHC 1329 (Fam); [2017] 2 F.L.R. 6; [2016] Fam. Law 1090, Fam Div .... *Digested,* 17/**1055**

N-A (Children), Re [2017] EWCA Civ 230; [2017] 2 F.C.R. 169, CA (Civ Div) .... *Digested,* 17/**971**

N-S (Children) (Care and Placement Orders: Judge's Reasons), Re [2017] EWCA Civ 1121; [2017] 4 W.L.R. 133; [2017] 3 F.C.R. 137, CA (Civ Div) .... *Digested,* 17/**918**

NA v Nottinghamshire CC; *sub nom* Armes v Nottinghamshire CC [2014] EWHC 4005 (QB); [2015] P.T.S.R. 653; [2015] 2 F.L.R. 671; [2015] Fam. Law 133, QBD (Nottingham) .... *Digested,* 15/**1113**: *Affirmed* 16/909: *Applied* 17/320

NA (Libya) v Secretary of State for the Home Department [2017] EWCA Civ 143; [2017] Imm. A.R. 1200, CA (Civ Div)

NA (Pakistan) v Secretary of State for the Home Department; *sub nom* Secretary of State for the Home Department v KJ (Angola); Secretary of State for the Home Department v MY (Kenya); Secretary of State for the Home Department v WM (Afghanistan); *joined cases* KJ (Angola) v Secretary of State for the Home Department; MY (Kenya) v Secretary of State for the Home Department; WM (Afghanistan) v Secretary of State for the Home Department [2016] EWCA Civ 662; [2017] 1 W.L.R. 207; [2017] Imm. A.R. 1; [2016] I.N.L.R. 587, CA (Civ Div) .... *Digested,* 17/**1198**

NA (Sudan) v Secretary of State for the Home Department; *sub nom* MR (Iran) v Secretary of State for the Home Department [2016] EWCA Civ 1060; [2017] 3 All E.R. 885; [2017] Imm. A.R. 592, CA (Civ Div) .... *Digested,* 17/**1176**

Nacap Ltd v Moffat Plant Ltd 1987 S.L.T. 221, IH (1 Div) .... *Digested,* 87/**4767**: *Considered* 17/2455: *Followed* 03/5772: *Referred to* 91/5457

Nadaf (Allabaksh) v HM Advocate [2017] HCJAC 37; 2017 S.C.L. 699; 2017 G.W.D. 19-296, HCJ Appeal .... *Digested,* 17/**2497**

Nadarajah v Secretary of State for the Home Department see R. (on the application of Nadarajah) v Secretary of State for the Home Department

Naeem v Secretary of State for Justice [2015] EWCA Civ 1264; [2016] I.C.R. 289; [2016] I.R.L.R. 118; Times, February 4, 2016, CA (Civ Div) .... *Digested,* 16/**710**: *Reversed* 17/783

Naeem v Secretary of State for Justice see Essop v Home Office (UK Border Agency)

Nagarajan v London Regional Transport; *sub nom* Swiggs v Nagarajan (No.2); *joined case* Nagarajan v Swiggs (No.2) [2000] 1 A.C. 501; [1999] 3 W.L.R. 425; [1999] 4 All E.R. 65; [1999] I.C.R. 877; [1999] I.R.L.R. 572; Times, July 19, 1999; Independent, October 11, 1999; (1999) 96(31) L.S.G. 36; (1999) 149 N.L.J. 1109; (1999) 143 S.J.L.B. 219, HL .... *Digested,* 99/**2093**:
Applied 02/1332, 02/1415, 05/1290, 05/2162, 06/1368, 07/1402, 08/1190: *Cited* 07/1404: *Considered* 01/2301, 07/266, 09/1210, 09/1228, 09/1229, 12/1150, 15/788: *Followed* 03/1354, 11/1103, 14/1104, 17/828

Nagarajan v Swiggs (No.2) see Nagarajan v London Regional Transport

Nagiub v General Medical Council [2013] EWHC 1766 (Admin), QBD (Admin)
Applied 17/202

Nahajec v Fowle see Nahajec (Deceased), Re

Nahajec (Deceased), Re; *sub nom* Nahajec v Fowle [2017] W.T.L.R. 1071, Ch D (Leeds)

Nan v Romania (Admissibility) (52920/13) (2017) 64 E.H.R.R. SE17, ECHR

NAP Anglia Ltd v Sun-Land Development Co Ltd (Costs) [2012] EWHC 51 (TCC); [2012] B.L.R. 195; 141 Con. L.R. 247; [2012] 4 Costs L.O. 485, QBD (TCC) ..... *Digested,* 12/**349**:
Applied 14/359, 17/220

Napp Pharmaceutical Holdings Ltd v Dr Reddy's Laboratories (UK) Ltd [2017] EWHC 1433 (Pat); [2017] 4 Costs L.R. 647, Ch D .... *Digested,* 17/**341**

Napp Pharmaceutical Holdings Ltd v Dr Reddy's Laboratories (UK) Ltd [2016] EWCA Civ 1053; [2017] R.P.C. 5, CA (Civ Div) .... *Digested,* 17/**1370**

Napp Pharmaceutical Holdings Ltd v Dr Reddy's Laboratories (UK) Ltd [2016] EWHC 1517 (Pat); [2017] R.P.C. 4, Ch D (Patents Ct)
Affirmed 17/1370

Napp Pharmaceutical Holdings Ltd v Sandoz Ltd see Ratiopharm GmbH v Napp Pharmaceutical Holdings Ltd

Nasse v Science Research Council see Science Research Council v Nasse

Nasser v United Bank of Kuwait (Security for Costs) [2001] EWCA Civ 556; [2002] 1 W.L.R. 1868; [2002] 1 All E.R. 401; [2001] C.P. Rep. 105, CA (Civ Div) .... *Digested,* 02/**385**:
Applied 04/330, 05/465: *Considered* 02/384, 04/274, 10/411, 12/393, 13/421, 17/358: *Distinguished* 17/362: *Explained* 14/433: *Followed* 11/382, 12/392

Nasseri v Secretary of State for the Home Department see R. (on the application of Nasseri) v Secretary of State for the Home Department

Nathan v Smilovitch (Application to Set Aside Permission to Appeal) [2002] EWCA Civ 759, CA (Civ Div)
Applied 03/305: *Followed* 17/1282

National Aids Trust v NHS Commissioning Board (NHS England); *sub nom* R. (on the application of National Aids Trust) v NHS Commissioning Board (NHS England) [2016] EWCA Civ 1100; [2017] 1 W.L.R. 1477; [2017] 3 All E.R. 993; [2017] P.T.S.R. 366; (2017) 20 C.C.L. Rep. 30; (2016) 152 B.M.L.R. 1; Times, January 23, 2017, CA (Civ Div) .... *Digested,* 17/**1096**

National Aids Trust v NHS Commissioning Board (NHS England); *sub nom* R. (on the application of National Aids Trust) v NHS Commissioning Board (NHS England) [2016] EWHC 2005 (Admin); [2016] P.T.S.R. 1093; (2016) 19 C.C.L. Rep. 459; [2016] Med. L.R. 487; Times, October 18, 2016; [2016] A.C.D. 132, QBD (Admin) .... *Digested,* 16/**981**:
Affirmed 17/1096

National Asset Loan Management Ltd v Cahillane; *sub nom* Cahillane, Re [2015] EWHC 62 (Ch); [2016] 1 W.L.R. 45; [2015] 4 All E.R. 380; [2016] 1 All E.R. (Comm) 310; [2015] B.P.I.R. 1433, Ch D .... *Digested,* 16/**1204**:
Considered 17/1310

National Bank of Greece and Athens SA v Metliss [1958] A.C. 509; [1957] 3 W.L.R. 1056; [1957] 3 All E.R. 608; (1957) 101 S.J. 972, HL .... *Digested,* 57/**505**:
Applied 60/477, 92/3559, 00/736: *Considered* 58/492, 59/476, 69/1733, 71/1572: *Followed* 17/77

National Bank of Greece and Athens SA v Metliss [1957] 2 Q.B. 33; [1957] 2 W.L.R. 570; [1957] 2 All E.R. 1; (1957) 101 S.J. 301, CA
Affirmed 57/505: *Followed* 17/77

National Car Parks Ltd v Revenue and Customs Commissioners [2017] UKUT 247 (TCC); [2017] S.T.C. 1859; [2017] B.V.C. 518, UT (Tax) .... *Digested,* 17/**2262**

National Car Parks Ltd v Revenue and Customs Commissioners [2015] UKFTT 666 (TC); [2016] S.T.I. 256, FTT (Tax)
Affirmed 17/2262

National Crime Agency v Abacha; *sub nom* Abacha v National Crime Agency; Blue Holdings (1) Pte Ltd v National Crime Agency [2016] EWCA Civ 760; [2016] 1 W.L.R. 4375; [2016] C.P. Rep. 43; [2016] Lloyd's Rep. F.C. 497; Times, September 29, 2016, CA (Civ Div) .... *Digested,* 16/**266**: *Followed* 17/291

National Crime Agency v Jardine see National Crime Agency v Simkus

National Crime Agency v Khan [2017] EWHC 27 (QB); [2017] Lloyd's Rep. F.C. 153, QBD

National Crime Agency v Khan see National Crime Agency v Simkus

National Crime Agency v N; *sub nom* N v Royal Bank of Scotland Plc [2017] EWCA Civ 253; [2017] 1 W.L.R. 3938; [2017] Lloyd's Rep. F.C. 232; Times, June 6, 2017, CA (Civ Div) .... *Digested,* 17/**173**

National Crime Agency v Simkus; *joined cases* National Crime Agency v Khan; National Crime Agency v Jardine [2016] EWHC 255 (Admin); [2016] 1 W.L.R. 3481; [2016] Lloyd's Rep. F.C. 195; [2016] A.C.D. 63, QBD (Admin) .... *Digested,* 16/**174**: *Applied* 17/559: *Not followed* 16/547

National Crime Agency v Wong [2016] EWHC 142 (QB); [2016] Lloyd's Rep. F.C. 588, QBD .... *Digested,* 17/**209**

National Exhibition Centre Ltd v Revenue and Customs Commissioners; *sub nom* Revenue and Customs Commissioners v National Exhibition Centre Ltd [2015] UKUT 23 (TCC); [2015] S.T.C. 1185; [2015] B.V.C. 506; [2015] L.L.R. 331; [2015] S.T.I. 250, UT (Tax) .... *Digested,* 15/**2600**: *Doubted* 17/2289

National Exhibition Centre Ltd v Revenue and Customs Commissioners (C-130/15) see Revenue and Customs Commissioners v National Exhibition Centre Ltd (C-130/15)

National Infrastructure Development Co Ltd v Banco Santander SA [2017] EWCA Civ 27; [2018] 1 All E.R. (Comm) 156; [2017] 1 Lloyd's Rep. 361; [2017] 1 C.L.C. 37; [2017] C.I.L.L. 3939, CA (Civ Div) .... *Digested,* 17/**167**

National Infrastructure Development Co Ltd v Banco Santander SA [2016] EWHC 2990 (Comm), QBD (Comm) *Affirmed* 17/167

National Insurance and Guarantee Corp Ltd v Nulty's Estate see Nulty v Milton Keynes BC

National Iranian Oil Co v Crescent Petroleum Co International Ltd [2016] EWHC 1900 (Comm); [2017] 1 All E.R. (Comm) 566, QBD (Comm) .... *Digested,* 17/**72**

National Iranian Oil Co v Crescent Petroleum Co International Ltd [2016] EWHC 510 (Comm); [2016] 2 Lloyd's Rep. 146; [2016] 1 C.L.C. 508; [2017] Lloyd's Rep. F.C. 53, QBD (Comm) .... *Digested,* 16/**430**: *Considered* 17/81

National Justice Compania Naviera SA v Prudential Assurance Co Ltd (The Ikarian Reefer) (No.1) [1995] 1 Lloyd's Rep. 455, CA (Civ Div) .... *Digested,* 96/**3609**: *Applied* 17/2021: *Considered* 00/3517

National Justice Compania Naviera SA v Prudential Assurance Co Ltd (The Ikarian Reefer) (No.2); *sub nom* Comninos v Prudential Assurance Co Ltd [2000] 1 W.L.R. 603; [2000] 1 All E.R. 37; [1999] 2 All E.R. (Comm) 673; [2000] 1 Lloyd's Rep. 129; [2000] C.P. Rep. 13; [2000] C.L.C. 22; [2000] 1 Costs L.R. 37; [2000] I.L.Pr. 490; [2000] Lloyd's Rep. I.R. 230; Times, October 15, 1999; Independent, October 20, 1999; Independent, November 22, 1999; (1999) 96(41) L.S.G. 35; (1999) 96(42) L.S.G. 40; (1999) 149 N.L.J. 1561; (1999) 143 S.J.L.B. 255, CA (Civ Div) .... *Digested,* 99/**749**: *Applied* 08/371: *Considered* 00/455: *Distinguished* 09/408: *Followed* 17/1571

National Roads Authority v Revenue Commissioners (C-344/15) EU:C:2017:28; [2017] B.V.C. 8; [2017] S.T.I. 164, ECJ (6th Chamber)

National Trust for Places of Historic Interest or Natural Beauty v Hoare see Hoare (Valuation Officer) v National Trust for Places of Historic Interest or Natural Beauty

National Trust for Places of Historic Interest or Natural Beauty v Spratling (Valuation Officer) see Hoare (Valuation Officer) v National Trust for Places of Historic Interest or Natural Beauty

National Trust for Places of Historic Interest or Natural Beauty v White [1987] 1 W.L.R. 907; (1987) 84 L.S.G. 2119; (1987) 131 S.J. 915, Ch D .... *Digested,* 87/**1233**: *Considered* 02/3820, 17/1840

National Westminster Bank Plc v Gill see Royal Bank of Scotland Plc v Etridge (No.2)

National Westminster Bank Plc v Inland Revenue Commissioners; *joined case* Barclays Bank Plc v Inland Revenue Commissioners [1995] 1 A.C. 119; [1994] 3 W.L.R. 159; [1994] 3 All E.R. 1; [1994] S.T.C. 580; [1994] 2 B.C.L.C. 239; 67 T.C. 38; Times, June 24, 1994; Independent, July 25, 1994; [1994] S.T.I. 756; (1994) 91(32) L.S.G. 44; (1994) 138 S.J.L.B. 139, HL .... *Digested,* 94/**2538**: *Followed* 17/2140

National Westminster Bank Plc v Kapoor; *sub nom* Kapoor v National Westminster Bank Plc [2011] EWCA Civ 1083; [2012] 1 All E.R. 1201; [2011] B.P.I.R. 1680; [2011] N.P.C. 97; [2012] Bus. L.R. D25, CA (Civ Div) .... *Digested,* 12/**1864**: *Applied* 16/1817: *Followed* 17/1302

National Westminster Bank Plc v Spectrum Plus Ltd (In Creditors Voluntary Liquidation) see Spectrum Plus Ltd (In Liquidation), Re

Nationaldemokratische Partei Deutschlands (NPD) v Germany (55977/13) (2017) 64 E.H.R.R. SE8, ECHR

Natt v Osman; *sub nom* Osman v Natt [2014] EWCA Civ 1520; [2015] 1 W.L.R. 1536; [2015] H.L.R. 11; [2015] 1 P. & C.R. 11, CA (Civ Div) .... *Digested,* 15/**1576**: *Followed* 16/1386, 17/1463

Nautical Challenge Ltd v Evergreen Marine (UK) Ltd [2017] EWHC 453 (Admlty); [2018] 1 All E.R. (Comm) 775; [2017] 1 Lloyd's Rep. 666; [2017] 1 C.L.C. 217, QBD (Admlty) .... *Digested,* 17/**2020**

Navalmar UK Ltd v Kalemaden Hammeddeler Sanayi ve Ticaret As [2017] EWHC 116 (Comm); [2017] 2 All E.R. (Comm) 1033; [2017] Bus. L.R. 1186; [2017] 1 Lloyd's Rep. 370; [2017] 1 C.L.C. 71, QBD (Comm) .... *Digested,* 17/**2005**

Navalnyy v Russia (46632/13) 41 B.H.R.C. 520, ECHR

Nayif v High Commission of Brunei Darussalam [2014] EWCA Civ 1521; [2015] 4 All E.R. 159; [2015] C.P. Rep. 11; [2015] I.C.R. 517; [2015] I.R.L.R. 134, CA (Civ Div) .... *Digested,* 15/**313**: *Considered* 17/425

NC v Leicestershire CC [2012] UKUT 85 (AAC); [2012] E.L.R. 365, UT (AAC) .... *Digested,* 12/**995**: *Applied* 13/904, 14/943: *Considered* 14/941: *Explained* 17/707

NCL Investments Ltd v Revenue and Customs Commissioners [2017] UKFTT 495 (TC); [2018] S.F.T.D. 92; [2017] S.T.I. 1744, FTT (Tax)

ND v SD [2017] EWHC 1507 (Fam); [2017] 3 F.C.R. 809, Fam Div

Ndole Assets Ltd v Designer M&E Services UK Ltd [2017] EWHC 1148 (TCC); [2017] 1 W.L.R. 4367; [2017] C.I.L.L. 3982, QBD (TCC)

NE-A (Nigeria) v Secretary of State for the Home Department; *joined case* Secretary of State for the Home Department v HM (Uganda) [2017] EWCA Civ 239; [2017] Imm. A.R. 1077; [2018] I.N.L.R. 88, CA (Civ Div) .... *Digested,* 17/**1197**

Neary v Dean of Westminster [1999] I.R.L.R. 288, Visitor (Westminster) .... *Digested,* 00/**2132**: *Applied* 10/1152, 17/803

Neath v Hugh Steeper Ltd (C-152/91) see Ten Oever v Stichting Bedrijfspensioenfonds voor het Glazenwassers- en Schoonmaakbedrijf (C-109/91)

Nederlandsche Banden Industrie Michelin NV v Commission of the European Communities (322/81) EU:C:1983:313; [1983] E.C.R. 3461; [1985] 1 C.M.L.R. 282; [1985] F.S.R. 250, ECJ .... *Digested,* 85/**1319**: *Applied* 02/597, 07/1547, 07/1548, 07/636: *Considered* 05/571, 05/575, 06/605, 10/460, 17/410: *Followed* 00/715, 09/546

NEF Telecom Co BV, Re [2012] EWHC 2944 (Ch); [2014] B.C.C. 417, Ch D (Companies Ct) *Considered* 16/349, 17/1321

Nelidow Santis v Secretary of State for the Home Department see Bugdaycay v Secretary of State for the Home Department

Nelmes v Nram Plc [2016] EWCA Civ 491; [2016] C.T.L.C. 106, CA (Civ Div) .... *Digested,* 16/**415**: *Considered* 17/482

Nelson's Yard Management Co v Eziefula [2013] EWCA Civ 235; [2013] C.P. Rep. 29; [2013] B.L.R. 289; [2013] 14 E.G. 87 (C.S.), CA (Civ Div) .... *Digested,* 13/**303**: *Applied* 17/1373

Nemcova v Fairfield Rents Ltd [2016] UKUT 303 (LC); [2017] 1 P. & C.R. 4; [2017] L. & T.R. 10, UT (Lands) .... *Digested,* 17/**1443**

Neon Shipping Inc v Foreign Economic & Technical Corp Co of China [2016] EWHC 399 (Comm); [2017] 1 All E.R. (Comm) 964; [2016] 2 Lloyd's Rep. 158; [2016] 1 C.L.C. 418, QBD (Comm) .... *Digested,* 16/**1968**

Neptune (Europe) Ltd v Devol Kitchens Ltd [2017] EWHC 2172 (Pat); [2017] E.C.D.R. 25; [2018] F.S.R. 3, Ch D (Patents Ct)

Neshanthan v Immigration Officer (Heathrow Airport) see Neshanthan (Cancellation or Revocation of ILR), Re

Neshanthan (Cancellation or Revocation of ILR), Re; *sub nom* Neshanthan v Immigration Officer (Heathrow Airport) [2017] UKUT 77 (IAC); [2017] Imm. A.R. 833, UT (IAC)

NESTEC/EPO (Communication with Parties) (T1691/15) [2017] E.P.O.R. 18, EPO (Technical Bd App)

Netley v Revenue and Customs Commissioners [2017] UKFTT 442 (TC); [2017] S.F.T.D. 1044, FTT (Tax)

Network Rail Infrastructure Ltd v Secretary of State for the Environment, Food and Rural Affairs see R. (on the application of Network Rail Infrastructure Ltd) v Secretary of State for the Environment, Food and Rural Affairs

Neuberger v York 19 I.T.E.L.R. 378, CA (Ont)

New Age Alzarooni 2 Ltd v Range Energy Natural Resources Inc [2014] EWHC 4358 (Comm), QBD (Comm) *Applied* 17/66, 17/67

New Cap Reinsurance Corp Ltd (In Liquidation) v Grant see Rubin v Eurofinance SA

New Milton Town Council v Gidman (Valuation Officer) [2017] R.A. 111, VT .... *Digested,* 17/**1822**

New Valmar BVBA v Global Pharmacies Partner Health Srl (C-15/15) EU:C:2016:464; [2017] C.E.C. 293, ECJ (Grand Chamber)

NEW WAVE CZ as v ALLTOYS spol s r o (C-427/15) EU:C:2017:18; [2017] Bus. L.R. 1201; [2017] E.T.M.R. 16, ECJ (9th Chamber)

New Zealand Forest Products Ltd v New Zealand Insurance Co Ltd [1997] 1 W.L.R. 1237, PC (NZ) .... *Digested,* 97/**3133**: *Followed* 17/1342

New Zealand Railways v Progressive Engineering Co Ltd [1968] N.Z.L.R. 1053, HC (NZ) *Considered* 17/2003

Newbigin (Valuation Officer) v SJ&J Monk (A Firm) see SJ&J Monk (A Firm) v Newbigin (Valuation Officer)

Newbold v Coal Authority [2016] UKUT 432 (LC); [2017] R.V.R. 7, UT (Lands) .... *Digested,* 17/**1859**

Newbury v Sun Microsystems Ltd [2013] EWHC 2180 (QB); [2013] C.I.L.L. 3425, QBD *Applied* 17/2066

Newcastle upon Tyne NHS Foundation Trust v Haywood; *sub nom* Haywood v Newcastle upon Tyne NHS Foundation Trust [2017] EWCA Civ 153; [2017] I.C.R. 1370; [2017] I.R.L.R. 629, CA (Civ Div) .... *Digested,* 17/**344**

Newcastle upon Tyne University v Revenue and Customs Commissioners [2017] UKFTT 145 (TC); [2017] S.T.I. 307, FTT (Tax)

Newell v Secretary of State for the Environment, Transport and the Regions see Fletcher Estates (Harlescott) Ltd v Secretary of State for the Environment, Transport and the Regions

Newell-Austin v Solicitors Regulatory Authority [2017] EWHC 411 (Admin); [2017] Med. L.R. 194, QBD (Admin) .... *Digested,* 17/**1490**

Newey v Revenue and Customs Commissioners (C-653/11) see Revenue and Customs Commissioners v Newey (t/a Ocean Finance) (C-653/11)

Newham LBC v Miah [2016] EWHC 1043 (Admin); [2016] P.T.S.R. 1082; [2016] C.T.L.C. 51, QBD (Admin) .... *Digested,* 16/**1687**: *Considered* 17/1733

Newman v Clarke [2016] EWHC 2959 (Ch); [2017] 4 W.L.R. 26; [2017] W.T.L.R. 599, Ch D .... *Digested,* 17/**2221**

Newman v HM Advocate [2016] HCJAC 46; 2016 J.C. 165; 2016 S.C.L. 602; 2016 G.W.D. 16-299, HCJ .... *Digested,* 16/**2495**: *Considered* 17/2797

News International v Shepherd (Inspector of Taxes) see Shepherd (Inspector of Taxes) v Lyntress

Newton v Secretary of State for Business, Energy and Industrial Strategy see Newtons Coaches Ltd, Re

Newtons Coaches Ltd, Re; *joined case* Newton v Secretary of State for Business, Energy and Industrial Strategy [2016] EWHC 3068 (Ch); [2017] B.C.C. 34; [2018] 1 B.C.L.C. 285, Ch D (Companies Ct) .... *Digested,* 17/**1297**

NGPOD Global Ltd v Aspirate N Go Ltd [2016] EWHC 3124 (Pat); [2017] F.S.R. 25, Ch D .... *Digested,* 17/**1369**

NHS Acute Trust v C [2016] EWCOP 17; (2016) 152 B.M.L.R. 193, CP .... *Digested,* 17/**1542**

NHS Business Services Authority v Williams; *sub nom* Williams v NHS Business Services Authority [2016] EWHC 1952 (Ch); [2017] I.C.R. 327, Ch D .... *Digested,* 17/**1608**

NHS Business Services Authority v Young see Young v NHS Business Services Authority

NHS Greater Glasgow and Clyde Health Board v Revenue and Customs Commissioners [2017] UKUT 19 (TCC); [2017] B.V.C. 502, UT (Tax) .... *Digested,* 17/**2271**

NHS Lothian Health Board v Revenue and Customs Commissioners; *sub nom* Lothian NHS Health Board v Revenue and Customs Commissioners [2015] UKUT 264 (TCC); [2015] S.T.C. 2221; [2015] B.V.C. 519, UT (Tax) .... *Digested,* 15/**2585**: *Considered* 17/2271

NHS Trust v FG; *sub nom* NHS Trust 1 v G [2014] EWCOP 30; [2015] 1 W.L.R. 1984; [2014] C.O.P.L.R. 598; (2014) 17 C.C.L. Rep. 365; [2014] Med. L.R. 470; (2015) 142 B.M.L.R. 209, CP .... *Digested,* 15/**1752**: *Considered* 17/1544

NHS Trust 1 v G see NHS Trust v FG

Nicholas-Pillai v General Medical Council [2009] EWHC 1048 (Admin), QBD (Admin) *Considered* 17/1111

Nichols v Inland Revenue Commissioners see Nichols (Deceased), Re

Nichols (Deceased), Re; *sub nom* Nichols v Inland Revenue Commissioners [1975] 1 W.L.R. 534; [1975] 2 All E.R. 120; [1975] S.T.C. 278; [1974] T.R. 411; (1974) 119 S.J. 257, CA (Civ Div) .... *Digested,* 75/**937**: *Considered* 95/2764, 96/3433: *Distinguished* 76/1407: *Followed* 11/3394, 17/2155

Nicholson v Thames Water Utilities Ltd [2014] EWHC 4249 (QB), QBD *Not applied* 17/2297

Nicklinson v Ministry of Justice see R. (on the application of Nicklinson) v Ministry of Justice

Nicola v Zenith Marque Insurance Ltd (Unreported, February 10, 2017), CC (Edmonton) [*Irwin Mitchell LLP, Riverside West, 1 Millsands, Sheffield*] .... *Digested,* 17/**1672**

Nicolson v Grant Thornton UK LLP [2016] EWHC 710 (Admin); [2016] 2 Costs L.R. 211; [2017] R.V.R. 43, DC

Nielsen v Denmark (10929/84) see Nielsen v Denmark (A/144)

Nielsen v Denmark (A/144); *sub nom* Nielsen v Denmark (10929/84) (1989) 11 E.H.R.R. 175, ECHR *Applied* 17/19: *Considered* 03/2960, 09/2033

Nigerian National Petroleum Corp v IPCO (Nigeria) Ltd see IPCO (Nigeria) Ltd v Nigerian National Petroleum Corp

Nigerian National Petroleum Corp v IPCO (Nigeria) Ltd see IPCO (Nigeria) Ltd v Nigerian National Petroleum Corp

Nike European Operations Netherlands BV v Sportland Oy (C-310/14) EU:C:2015:690; [2015] Bus. L.R. 1547; [2017] B.C.C. 446; [2016] 1 B.C.L.C. 297; [2016] C.E.C. 845; [2016] I.L.Pr. 1, ECJ (6th Chamber)

Nike Innovate CV v Intermar Simanto; *sub nom* Nike Innovate CV's Trade Mark Application [2017] F.S.R. 8, App Person .... *Digested,* 17/**1391**

Nike Innovate CV's Trade Mark Application see Nike Innovate CV v Intermar Simanto

Nimmo & Friar, Noters see Joint Administrators of Castlebridge Plant Ltd, Noters

Ninemia Maritime Corp v Trave Schiffahrts GmbH & Co KG (The Niedersachsen) [1983] 1 W.L.R. 1412; [1984] 1 All E.R. 398; [1983] 2 Lloyd's Rep. 600; (1984) 81 L.S.G. 198, CA (Civ Div) .... *Digested,* 84/**2646**: *Applied* 93/3284, 02/714, 09/407, 16/263: *Considered* 16/2440, 17/308

Nisbet v Ogilvie see Gemmell (James Kelly) v HM Advocate

Nissan v Attorney General see Attorney General v Nissan

NISSAN/Exhaust Manifold for Internal Combustion Engine (T792/12) [2017] E.P.O.R. 12, EPO (Technical Bd App)

Nizam of Hyderabad v Jung see Rahimtoola v Nizam of Hyderabad

NJ Rickard Ltd v Holloway [2015] EWCA Civ 1631; [2017] 1 Costs L.R. 1, CA (Civ Div) .... *Digested,* 17/**272**

NKT Cables A/S v SP Power Systems Ltd [2017] CSOH 38; 2017 S.L.T. 494; 172 Con. L.R. 121; 2017 G.W.D. 10-135, OH .... *Digested,* 17/**2461**

NM v Lanarkshire Health Board see Montgomery v Lanarkshire Health Board

NML Capital Ltd v Argentina; *sub nom* Argentina v NML Capital Ltd [2011] UKSC 31; [2011] 2 A.C. 495; [2011] 3 W.L.R. 273; [2011] 4 All E.R. 1191; [2012] 1 All E.R. (Comm) 1081; [2011] 2 Lloyd's Rep. 628; [2011] 2 C.L.C. 373; 9 A.L.R. Int'l 595; Times, July 8, 2011; (2011) 155(27) S.J.L.B. 39, SC .... *Digested,* 11/**331**: *Applied* 16/256: *Followed* 17/369

NN/Language of Proceedings (J13/14) [2017] E.P.O.R. 26, EPO (Legal Bd App)

No.1 West India Quay (Residential) Ltd v East Tower Apartments Ltd [2016] EWHC 2438 (Ch); [2017] 1 P. & C.R. 8, Ch D .... *Digested,* 17/**1445**

Noble Denton Middle East v Noble Denton International Ltd [2010] EWHC 2574 (Comm); [2011] 1 Lloyd's Rep. 387, QBD (Comm) .... *Digested,* 11/**134**: *Applied* 14/134, 17/64: *Considered* 15/79

Noble's Trustees v Economic Forestry (Scotland) Ltd 1988 S.L.T. 662, OH .... *Digested,* 88/**4578**: *Applied* 01/6826, 17/2464: *Followed* 93/4761

Noell v Kensington and Chelsea RLBC [2017] P.A.D. 8, Planning Inspector

Nokia GmbH v IPCom GmbH & Co KG; *joined case* IPCom GmbH & Co KG v Nokia UK Ltd [2011] EWCA Civ 6; [2011] Bus. L.R. 1488; [2011] F.S.R. 15, CA (Civ Div) .... *Digested,* 11/**1955**: *Followed* 17/1375

Nolan (Thomas) v HM Advocate see Ferguson (James Douglas) v HM Advocate

Noor v Revenue and Customs Commissioners; *sub nom* Revenue and Customs Commissioners v Noor [2013] UKUT 71 (TCC); [2013] S.T.C. 998; [2013] B.V.C. 1571; [2013] S.T.I. 481, UT (Tax) .... *Digested,* 13/**3199**: *Applied* 14/2926, 17/2105, 17/2150

Nordic Trustee ASA v OGX Petroleo e Gas SA see OGX Petroleo e Gas SA, Re

Norglen Ltd (In Liquidation) v Reeds Rains Prudential Ltd; *joined cases* Circuit Systems Ltd (In Liquidation) v Zuken-Redac (UK) Ltd; Levy v ABN AMRO Bank NV; Mayhew-Lewis v Westminster Scaffolding Group Plc [1999] 2 A.C. 1; [1997] 3 W.L.R. 1177; [1998] 1 All E.R. 218; [1998] B.C.C. 44; [1998] 1 B.C.L.C. 176; 87 B.L.R. 1; Times, December 1, 1997; (1997) 94(48) L.S.G. 29; (1997) 147 N.L.J. 1773; (1998) 142 S.J.L.B. 26; (1998) 75 P. & C.R. D21, HL .. *Digested,* 98/**375**: *Applied* 02/363, 07/4301: *Considered* 06/323: *Distinguished* 03/339, 15/1432: *Followed* 98/401, 17/358

Norman v Norman [2017] EWCA Civ 120; [2017] 1 W.L.R. 2554, CA (Civ Div) .... *Digested,* 17/**1013**

Norman v Norman [2017] EWCA Civ 49; [2017] 1 W.L.R. 2523; [2018] 1 All E.R. 769; [2018] E.M.L.R. 3; [2018] 1 F.L.R. 426; [2017] 2 F.C.R. 270; Times, March 13, 2017, CA (Civ Div) .... *Digested,* 17/**1015**

Norman v Secretary of State for the Home Department see Bugdaycay v Secretary of State for the Home Department

Normans Bay Ltd (formerly Illingworth Morris Ltd) v Coudert Bros; *sub nom* Coudert Bros v Normans Bay Ltd (formerly Illingworth Morris) [2004] EWCA Civ 215; Times, March 24, 2004; (2004) 101(13) L.S.G. 36; (2004) 148 S.J.L.B. 296, CA (Civ Div) *Applied* 05/1319: *Considered* 17/211

Norris v United States [2010] UKSC 9; [2010] 2 A.C. 487; [2010] 2 W.L.R. 572; [2010] 2 All E.R. 267; [2010] H.R.L.R. 20; [2010] U.K.H.R.R. 523; [2010] Lloyd's Rep. F.C. 325; Times, February 25, 2010, SC .... *Digested,* 10/**1266**: *Considered* 12/1289, 12/1293, 16/2633: *Followed* 12/1282, 16/797, 17/901

Norris, Re [2001] UKHL 34; [2001] 1 W.L.R. 1388; [2001] 3 All E.R. 961; [2001] 3 F.C.R. 97; Times, June 29, 2001; Daily Telegraph, July 3, 2001; (2001) 98(30) L.S.G. 37; (2001) 151 N.L.J. 1094, HL .... *Digested,* 01/**5**: *Applied* 08/782, 17/191: *Considered* 06/907, 06/911, 12/465: *Followed* 17/313

Nortel Companies, Re see Bloom v Pensions Regulator

Nortel GmbH (In Administration), Re see Bloom v Pensions Regulator

Nortel Group, Re; *sub nom* Nortel Networks UK Ltd (No.2), Re [2016] EWHC 2769 (Ch); [2017] Bus. L.R. 590; [2017] 2 B.C.L.C. 572, Ch D (Companies Ct) .... *Digested,* 17/**1264**

Nortel Networks UK Ltd (No.2), Re see Nortel Group, Re

Nortel Networks UK Ltd (No.536 of 2009), Re [2015] EWHC 2506 (Ch); [2017] 2 B.C.L.C. 555, Ch D (Companies Ct)

Nortel Networks UK Ltd, Re [2017] EWHC 1429 (Ch); [2018] Bus. L.R. 206; [2017] B.C.C. 325; [2017] 2 B.C.L.C. 592, Ch D (Companies Ct) .... *Digested,* 17/**1258**

Nortel Networks UK Pension Trust Ltd, Re see Bloom v Pensions Regulator

North East Property Buyers Litigation, Re; *sub nom* Mortgage Business Plc v O'Shaughnessy; Cook v Mortgage Business Plc; Tweddle v Southern Pacific Mortgages Ltd; Taylor v Southern Pacific Mortgages Ltd; Southern Pacific Mortgages Ltd v Scott; Mortgage Business Plc v Cook; Scott v Southern Pacific Mortgages Ltd [2014] UKSC 52; [2015] A.C. 385; [2014] 3 W.L.R. 1163; [2015] 1 All E.R. 277; [2014] H.L.R. 48; [2015] W.T.L.R. 1067; Times, October 28, 2014, SC .... *Digested,* 14/**2505**: *Followed* 17/1841

North Eastern Properties Ltd v Coleman & Quinn Conveyancing [2010] EWCA Civ 277; [2010] 1 W.L.R. 2715; [2010] 3 All E.R. 528; [2010] 2 All E.R. (Comm) 494; [2010] B.L.R. 579; [2010] T.C.L.R. 4; [2011] 1 P. & C.R. 3; [2010] 2 E.G.L.R. 161; [2010] 12 E.G. 97 (C.S.); [2010] N.P.C. 39, CA (Civ Div) .... *Digested,* 10/**2710**: *Applied* 11/1875: *Considered* 12/2726, 17/497

North Lanarkshire Council v Scottish Ministers [2016] CSIH 69; 2017 S.C. 88; 2016 G.W.D. 28-514, IH (Ex Div) .... *Digested,* 17/**2763**

North Lanarkshire Council v Stewart and Shields Ltd [2017] CSOH 76; 2017 S.L.T. 741; 2017 G.W.D. 15-233, OH .... *Digested,* 17/**2409**

North Midland Building Ltd v Cyden Homes Ltd [2017] EWHC 2414 (TCC); [2017] B.L.R. 605; 174 Con. L.R. 1; (2018) 34 Const. L.J. 117; [2017] C.I.L.L. 4051, QBD (TCC)

North Shore Ventures Ltd v Anstead Holdings Inc [2011] EWCA Civ 230; [2012] Ch. 31; [2011] 3 W.L.R. 628; [2011] 2 All E.R. (Comm) 1024; [2011] Bus. L.R. 1036; [2011] 2 Lloyd's Rep. 45; [2011] B.L.R. 757, CA (Civ Div) .... *Digested,* 11/**204**: *Considered* 17/2010

North Wiltshire DC v Secretary of State for the Environment (1993) 65 P. & C.R. 137; [1992] 3 P.L.R. 113; Times, April 21, 1992; [1992] J.P.L. 955; [1992] E.G. 65 (C.S.); [1992] N.P.C. 57, CA (Civ Div) .... *Digested,* 93/**3930**: *Applied* 00/4519, 14/2397: *Considered* 94/4437, 94/4464, 95/4875, 07/3276, 07/3283, 11/2165: *Distinguished* 96/4702, 17/1731: *Followed* 12/2602, 12/2751, 13/2349, 16/1700

Northampton CC v Islington LBC see Northamptonshire CC v Islington LBC

Northamptonshire CC v Entwhistle [2010] I.R.L.R. 740, EAT *Considered* 17/847

Northamptonshire CC v Islington LBC; *sub nom* Northampton CC v Islington LBC [2001] Fam. 364; [2000] 2 W.L.R. 193; [1999] 2 F.L.R. 881; [1999] 3 F.C.R. 385; [2000] B.L.G.R. 125; Times, August 17, 1999; [1999] Fam. Law 687; (2000) 164 J.P.N. 166, CA (Civ Div) .... *Digested,* 99/**2312**: *Applied* 04/1456: *Considered* 04/1455, 13/1210: *Followed* 00/2461, 12/1356, 17/925

Northamptonshire CC v M [2017] EWHC 997 (Fam); [2017] 2 F.L.R. 1250, Fam Div ... *Digested,* 17/**965**

Northsea Base Investment Ltd, Re; *joined cases* Baltic Tankers Holding Ltd, Re; B Endeavour Shipping Co Ltd, Re; B Force Shipping Co Ltd, Re; B Faith Shipping Co Ltd, Re; B Marshall Shipping Co Ltd, Re; B Ambition Shipping Co Ltd, Re; B Merchant Shipping Co Ltd, Re [2015] EWHC 121 (Ch); [2015] 1 B.C.L.C. 539, Ch D .... *Digested,* 15/**1393**: *Applied* 17/1257

Northumberland CC v Z see X (A Child), Re

Norwegian American Cruises A/S v Paul Mundy Ltd (The Vistafjord) [1988] 2 Lloyd's Rep. 343; Times, April 22, 1988, CA (Civ Div) .... *Digested,* 89/**1531**: *Applied* 05/538: *Considered* 17/406

Norwich and Peterborough Building Society v Steed (No.2) [1993] Ch. 116; [1992] 3 W.L.R. 669; [1993] 1 All E.R. 330; Times, March 18, 1992; Independent, March 10, 1992; [1992] N.P.C. 33, CA (Civ Div) .... *Digested,* 92/**2638**: *Applied* 06/3487: *Considered* 03/3606: *Followed* 17/1848

Nossen's Letter Patent, Re; *sub nom* Nossen's Patent, Re [1969] 1 W.L.R. 638; [1969] 1 All E.R. 775; [1968] F.S.R. 617; (1969) 113 S.J. 445, Ch D .... *Digested,* 69/**2826**: *Applied* 02/341, 17/268

Nossen's Patent, Re see Nossen's Letter Patent, Re

Nottingham City Council v Calverton Parish Council; *sub nom* Calverton Parish Council v Nottingham City Council [2015] EWHC 503 (Admin); [2015] P.T.S.R. 1130; [2015] A.C.D. 97, QBD (Admin) .... *Digested,* 15/**1964**: *Applied* 17/12

Nottingham City Council v LM see D (A Child) (Transfer of Proceedings), Re

Nottingham City Council v Parr [2017] EWCA Civ 188; [2017] P.T.S.R. 879; [2017] H.L.R. 22; [2017] L.L.R. 585, CA (Civ Div) .... *Digested,* 17/**1152**

Nottingham City Council v Parr [2016] UKUT 71 (LC); [2016] L.L.R. 601, UT (Lands) *Affirmed* 17/1152

Nottinghamshire CC v Meikle see Meikle v Nottinghamshire CC

Novartis Pharmaceuticals UK Ltd v MedImmune Ltd see MedImmune Ltd v Novartis Pharmaceuticals UK Ltd

Novatrust Ltd v Kea Investments Ltd see Glenn v Watson

Novruk v Russia (31039/11) (2016) 63 E.H.R.R. 19; 41 B.H.R.C. 212, ECHR

Novus Aviation Ltd v Alubaf Arab International Bank BSC(c) [2016] EWHC 1575 (Comm); [2017] 1 B.C.L.C. 414, QBD (Comm) .... *Digested,* 17/**499**

NR v AB (Financial Remedies) [2016] EWHC 277 (Fam); [2017] 1 F.L.R. 1030; [2016] Fam. Law 445, Fam Div

NRAM v Cordiner [2017] SAC (Civ) 27; 2017 S.L.T. (Sh Ct) 217; 2017 Hous. L.R. 100; 2017 G.W.D. 29-457, SAC .... *Digested,* 17/**2420**

NRAM Ltd v Evans [2017] EWCA Civ 1013; [2018] 1 W.L.R. 639; [2017] B.P.I.R. 1273; [2018] 1 P. & C.R. 3; [2017] 2 P. & C.R. DG27, CA (Civ Div) .... *Digested,* 17/**1848**

NRAM Ltd v Evans [2015] EWHC 1543 (Ch); [2015] B.P.I.R. 888; [2015] 2 P. & C.R. DG18, Ch D (Cardiff) .... *Digested,* 15/**2122**: *Affirmed in part* 17/1848

NRC Holding Ltd v Danilitskiy [2017] EWHC 1431 (Ch); [2017] 2 P. & C.R. DG20, Ch D

NS v Secretary of State for the Home Department (C-411/10) see R. (on the application of NS) v Secretary of State for the Home Department (C-411/10)

NS (Sri Lanka) v Secretary of State for the Home Department see R. (on the application of MA (Pakistan)) v Upper Tribunal (Immigration and Asylum Chamber)

NSK/Rolling Bearing Apparatus with Sensor (T1903/13) [2017] E.P.O.R. 28, EPO (Technical Bd App)

NT Advisors Partnership v Revenue and Customs Commissioners [2017] UKFTT 625 (TC); [2018] S.F.T.D. 206; [2017] S.T.I. 1904, FTT (Tax)

NT Gallagher & Son Ltd, Re; *sub nom* Shierson v Tomlinson; NT Gallagher & Sons Ltd v Howard [2002] EWCA Civ 404; [2002] 1 W.L.R. 2380; [2002] 3 All E.R. 474; [2002] B.C.C. 867; [2002] 2 B.C.L.C. 133; [2002] B.P.I.R. 565; Times, April 11, 2002; Independent, April 16, 2002; (2002) 99(19) L.S.G. 29, CA (Civ Div) .... *Digested,* 02/**2710**:
Applied 03/2443, 09/2229, 10/1865: *Considered* 06/1, 06/2354, 15/1424: *Followed* 17/1301

NT Gallagher & Sons Ltd v Howard see NT Gallagher & Son Ltd, Re

NTS v Georgia (71776/12) [2017] 1 F.L.R. 898; [2016] Fam. Law 450, ECHR

NTS Specialised Equipment Ltd v Revenue and Customs Commissioners see BTS Specialised Equipment Ltd v Revenue and Customs Commissioners

Nuclear Decommissioning Authority v ATK Energy EU Ltd (formerly Energy Solutions EU Ltd) see Energy Solutions EU Ltd v Nuclear Decommissioning Authority

Nuclear Decommissioning Authority v Energy Solutions EU Ltd see Energy Solutions EU Ltd v Nuclear Decommissioning Authority

Nuffield Health v Revenue and Customs Commissioners [2013] UKFTT 291 (TC); [2014] S.F.T.D. 164; [2013] S.T.I. 2004, FTT (Tax) .... *Digested,* 14/**3050**:
Approved 17/2294

Nulty v Milton Keynes BC; *sub nom* Milton Keynes BC v Nulty; *joined case* National Insurance and Guarantee Corp Ltd v Nulty's Estate [2012] EWHC 730 (QB), QBD (TCC)
Considered 17/259

Nussberger v Phillips see Phillips v Symes (A Bankrupt)

Nutrivet DOOEL v Orszagos Kornyezetvedelmi es Termeszetvedelmi Fofelugyeloseg (C-69/15) EU:C:2016:425; [2017] Env. L.R. 5, ECJ (4th Chamber)

Nvidia Corp v Hardware Labs Performance Systems Inc [2016] EWHC 3135 (Ch); [2017] Bus. L.R. 549; [2017] F.S.R. 28, Ch D .... *Digested,* 17/**1397**

NW v Sanofi Pasteur MSD SNC (C-621/15) see W v Sanofi Pasteur MSD SNC (C-621/15)

Nykredit Mortgage Bank Plc v Edward Erdman Group Ltd (Interest on Damages) [1997] 1 W.L.R. 1627; [1998] 1 All E.R. 305; [1998] Lloyd's Rep. Bank. 39; [1998] C.L.C. 116; [1998] 1 Costs L.R. 108; [1998] P.N.L.R. 197; [1998] 1 E.G.L.R. 99; [1998] 05 E.G. 150; Times, December 3, 1997; (1998) 95(1) L.S.G. 24; (1998) 142 S.J.L.B. 29; [1997] N.P.C. 165; (1998) 75 P. & C.R. D28, HL .... *Digested,* 98/**1432**:
Applied 99/4053, 01/4532, 02/465, 03/3003, 08/384, 16/1550, 16/276, 16/570: *Considered* 98/3917, 99/477, 99/557, 01/946, 06/474, 08/382, 09/2735, 09/426, 10/238, 12/2306, 14/2523, 16/567: *Distinguished* 98/1472, 01/4527, 08/2651: *Followed* 98/4021, 98/4029, 02/3276, 10/2284, 13/2087, 13/2093, 14/2217, 15/344, 16/1551, 17/641

Nykredit Mortgage Bank Plc v Edward Erdman Group Ltd see South Australia Asset Management Corp v York Montague Ltd

Nzolameso v Westminster City Council [2015] UKSC 22; [2015] 2 All E.R. 942; [2015] P.T.S.R. 549; [2015] H.L.R. 22; [2015] B.L.G.R. 215; (2015) 18 C.C.L. Rep. 201, SC .... *Digested,* 15/**1272**:
Applied 17/675: *Followed* 17/1154

O v Aberdeen City Council [2017] CSOH 9; 2017 S.L.T. 181; 2017 G.W.D. 4-47, OH .. *Digested,* 17/**2658**

O v Lancashire CC see Hammersmith and Fulham LBC v L

O v Minister voor Immigratie, Integratie en Asiel (C-456/12); *sub nom* Minister voor Immigratie, Integratie en Asiel v B (C-456/12) EU:C:2014:135; [2014] Q.B. 1163; [2014] 3 W.L.R. 799; [2014] 3 C.M.L.R. 17; [2014] All E.R. (EC) 843; [2014] Imm. A.R. 828; [2014] I.N.L.R. 748, ECJ (Grand Chamber)
Applied 17/2673

O v Nursing and Midwifery Council [2015] EWHC 2949 (Admin); [2016] A.C.D. 16, QBD (Admin)
Applied 17/1116

O v P see SO (A Child) (Wardship: Extension of Protective Injunction Orders), Re

O Palomo SA v Turner & Co see Turner & Co v O Palomo SA

O'Brien v Bolton St Catherine's Academy see Bolton St Catherine's Academy v O'Brien

O'Brien v Department of Constitutional Affairs see Department of Constitutional Affairs v O'Brien

O'Brien v Ministry of Justice; *sub nom* Ministry of Justice v O'Brien [2017] UKSC 46; [2017] 4 All E.R. 997; [2017] I.C.R. 1101; [2017] I.R.L.R. 939, SC .... *Digested,* 17/**1620**

O'Brien v Ministry of Justice; *joined case* Walker v Innospec Ltd [2015] EWCA Civ 1000; [2017] 1 All E.R. 1078; [2016] 1 C.M.L.R. 28; [2016] I.C.R. 182; [2015] I.R.L.R. 1005; [2015] Pens. L.R. 543; Times, November 10, 2015, CA (Civ Div) *Digested,* 15/**1858**: *Reversed* 17/1610

O'Brien v Ministry of Justice see Department of Constitutional Affairs v O'Brien

O'Brien v Quigley (Inspector of Taxes) [2013] IEHC 398; 19 I.T.L. Rep. 605, HC (Irl)

O'Brien v Scottish Ministers [2017] CSOH 96; 2017 S.L.T. 1113; 2017 G.W.D. 23-385, OH .... *Digested,* 17/**2391**

O'Brien (Inspector of Taxes) v Benson's Hosiery (Holdings) Ltd [1980] A.C. 562; [1979] 3 W.L.R. 572; [1979] 3 All E.R. 652; [1979] S.T.C. 735; 53 T.C. 241; [1979] T.R. 335; (1979) 123 S.J. 752, HL .... *Digested,* 82/**1574**: *Applied* 17/2092: *Considered* 87/2039, 09/3749, 13/3012: *Followed* 85/238

O'Flynn v Adjudication Officer (C237/94) EU:C:1996:206; [1996] E.C.R. I-2617; [1996] 3 C.M.L.R. 103; [1996] All E.R. (EC) 541; [1998] I.C.R. 608; (1997) 33 B.M.L.R. 54; Times, June 7, 1996; Independent, July 8, 1996, ECJ (5th Chamber) .... *Digested,* 96/**5517**: *Applied* 06/4010: *Considered* 05/3827, 15/15, 17/2091

O'Hara (Patrick) v HM Advocate [2016] HCJAC 107; 2017 S.L.T. 71; 2017 S.C.L. 84; 2016 G.W.D. 37-669, HCJ .... *Digested,* 17/**2817**

O'Keefe v Caner see Level One Residential (Jersey) Ltd, Re

O'Neill v Harvie [2014] HCJAC 136; 2015 S.L.T. 55; 2015 S.C.L. 292; 2015 G.W.D. 1-15, HCJ .... *Digested,* 15/**3009**: *Considered* 17/2478

O'Neill v United Kingdom (41516/10); *joined case* Lauchlan v United Kingdom (75702/13) 2016 S.C.C.R. 337; (2017) 64 E.H.R.R. 16; Times, July 21, 2016, ECHR .... *Digested,* 16/**1050**

O'Neill (Patrick) v HM Advocate [2016] HCJAC 86; 2017 J.C. 79; 2017 S.L.T. 74; 2016 S.C.L. 987; 2016 S.C.C.R. 558; 2016 G.W.D. 31-545, HCJ .... *Digested,* 17/**2555**

O'Regan v Williams see Fitzgerald v Williams

O'Rourke (Mark) v HM Advocate [2017] HCJAC 70; 2017 S.L.T. 1101; 2017 S.C.L. 929; 2017 S.C.C.R. 411; 2017 G.W.D. 30-480, HCJ *Reversed* 17/537

O2 (Germany) GmbH & Co OHG v Commission of the European Communities (T-328/03) EU:T:2006:116; [2006] E.C.R. II-1231; [2006] 5 C.M.L.R. 5, CFI (4th Chamber) .... *Digested,* 07/**618**: *Applied* 10/467, 17/211

Oadby and Wigston BC v Secretary of State for Communities and Local Government [2016] EWCA Civ 1040; [2017] J.P.L. 358, CA (Civ Div) .... *Digested,* 17/**1762**

Oadby and Wigston BC v Secretary of State for Communities and Local Government [2015] EWHC 1879 (Admin), QBD (Birmingham) *Affirmed* 17/1762

Oak Tree Motor Homes Ltd v Revenue and Customs Commissioners [2015] UKFTT 251 (TC); [2015] S.T.I. 1968, FTT (Tax) *Affirmed* 17/2286

Oak Tree Motor Homes Ltd v Revenue and Customs Commissioners [2017] UKUT 27 (TCC); [2017] B.V.C. 504, UT (Tax) .... *Digested,* 17/**2286**

Oakley v North Ayrshire Council 2017 Hous. L.R. 13; 2017 G.W.D. 1-10, Lands Tr (Scot) .... *Digested,* 17/**2706**

Oakley v South Cambridgeshire DC [2017] EWCA Civ 71; [2017] 1 W.L.R. 3765; [2017] 2 P. & C.R. 4; [2017] J.P.L. 703, CA (Civ Div) .... *Digested,* 17/**1764**

Oakley v South Cambridgeshire DC [2016] EWHC 570 (Admin), QBD (Admin) *Reversed* 17/1764

Obergefell v Hodges 41 B.H.R.C. 160, US Court

OBG Ltd v Allan; *sub nom* OBG Ltd v Allen; *joined cases* Mainstream Properties Ltd v Young; Douglas v Hello! Ltd [2007] UKHL 21; [2008] 1 A.C. 1; [2007] 2 W.L.R. 920; [2007] 4 All E.R. 545; [2008] 1 All E.R. (Comm) 1; [2007] Bus. L.R. 1600; [2007] I.R.L.R. 608; [2007] E.M.L.R. 12; [2007] B.P.I.R. 746; Times, May 3, 2007; Times, May 4, 2007; (2007) 30(6) I.P.D. 30037; [2007] 19 E.G. 165 (C.S.); (2007) 151 S.J.L.B. 674; [2007] N.P.C. 54, HL .... *Digested,* 07/**4190**: *Applied* 09/3557, 09/3558, 10/1034, 10/3410, 13/488, 14/2528, 14/415, 15/1909, 15/684: *Considered* 10/4134, 12/3347: *Followed* 08/3902, 11/369, 15/2533, 16/187, 17/314

OBG Ltd v Allen see OBG Ltd v Allan

Obukofe v General Medical Council [2014] EWHC 408 (Admin), QBD (Admin) *Considered* 17/1807

Occidental Petroleum Corp v Buttes Gas & Oil Co (No.2) see Buttes Gas & Oil Co v Hammer (No.3)
Occidental Petroleum Corp v Buttes Gas & Oil Co (No.2) see Buttes Gas & Oil Co v Hammer (No.3)
Ocensa Pipeline Group Litigation, Re see Arroyo v BP Exploration Co (Colombia) Ltd
Octagon Overseas Ltd v Coates; *sub nom* Coates v Octagon Overseas Ltd [2017] EWHC 877 (Ch); [2017] 4 W.L.R. 91; [2017] H.L.R. 26; [2017] L. & T.R. 32, Ch D .... *Digested,* 17/**1450**
Octoesse LLP v Trak Special Projects Ltd [2016] EWHC 3180 (TCC); [2017] B.L.R. 82; 169 Con. L.R. 70; [2016] 6 Costs L.R. 1187, QBD (TCC) .... *Digested,* 17/**220**
Ocular Sciences Ltd v Aspect Vision Care Ltd (No.2) [1997] R.P.C. 289; (1997) 20(3) I.P.D. 20022, Ch D (Patents Ct) .... *Digested,* 97/**3894**:
Applied 02/1311, 17/1357: *Considered* 99/3462, 04/2265, 10/1937, 15/1489:
Explained 17/286: *Followed* 97/1035: *Referred to* 01/3863, 03/2509
Oddin, Re see L (A Child), Re
Odyssey Re (London) Ltd v OIC Run-Off Ltd (formerly Orion Insurance Co Plc) (Unreported, February 11, 1999), QBD
Applied 13/368: *Considered* 17/194
Office of Fair Trading v Abbey National Plc; *sub nom* Abbey National Plc v Office of Fair Trading [2009] UKSC 6; [2010] 1 A.C. 696; [2009] 3 W.L.R. 1215; [2010] 1 All E.R. 667; [2010] 2 All E.R. (Comm) 945; [2010] 1 Lloyd's Rep. 281; [2010] 1 C.M.L.R. 44; [2010] Eu. L.R. 309; Times, November 26, 2009; (2009) 159 N.L.J. 1702; (2009) 153(45) S.J.L.B. 28, SC .... *Digested,* 10/**609**:
Followed 17/485
Officeserve Technologies Ltd (In Liquidation) v Anthony-Mike [2017] EWHC 1920 (Ch); [2017] B.C.C. 574; [2017] B.P.I.R. 1291, Ch D (Bristol) .... *Digested,* 17/**1334**
Officeserve Technologies Ltd, Re [2017] EWHC 906 (Ch); [2017] B.C.C. 363, Ch D (Birmingham) .... *Digested,* 17/**1266**
Official Liquidator v Molleson see Phosphate Sewage Co Ltd v Molleson (Res Judicata)
Official Receiver, Ex p. see Arthur Williams & Co, Re
Offshore Marine Services Alliance Pty Ltd v Leighton Contractors Pty Ltd [2017] FCA 333; [2017] 2 Lloyd's Rep. 79, Fed Ct (Aus) (Sgl judge)
OGX Petroleo e Gas SA, Re; *sub nom* Nordic Trustee ASA v OGX Petroleo e Gas SA [2016] EWHC 25 (Ch); [2017] 2 All E.R. 217; [2017] 1 All E.R. (Comm) 910; [2016] Bus. L.R. 121, Ch D .... *Digested,* 16/**301**:
Applied 17/361
OH v Craven see H v Craven
Okon v Lewisham LBC [2017] EWHC 1933 (Admin); [2017] B.P.I.R. 1568; [2018] R.V.R. 158, QBD (Admin)
Olayemi v Athena Medical Centre [2016] I.C.R. 1074, EAT .... *Digested,* 17/**827**
Old & Campbell Ltd v Liverpool Victoria Friendly Society see Taylor Fashions Ltd v Liverpool Victoria Trustees Co Ltd
Old Co-operative Day Nursery Ltd v Chief Inspector of Education, Children's Services and Skills (Ofsted) [2016] EWHC 1126 (Admin); (2016) 19 C.C.L. Rep. 507; [2016] A.C.D. 75, QBD (Admin) .... *Digested,* 17/**698**
Oldcorn v Southern Water Services Ltd [2017] EWHC 62 (TCC); [2017] Env. L.R. 25, QBD (TCC) .... *Digested,* 17/**2297**
Oldcorn v Southern Water Services Ltd [2017] EWHC 460 (TCC); [2017] 2 Costs L.O. 227, QBD (TCC) .... *Digested,* 17/**248**
Oldendorff GmbH & Co KG v Sea Powerful II Special Maritime Enterprises [2016] EWHC 3212 (Comm); [2017] 1 Lloyd's Rep. 194, QBD (Comm) .... *Digested,* 17/**1999**
Oldham MBC v Tanna [2017] EWCA Civ 50; [2017] 1 W.L.R. 1970; [2017] 2 P. & C.R. 11; [2017] R.V.R. 174; [2017] J.P.L. 696, CA (Civ Div) .... *Digested,* 17/**1733**
Oldham MBC v Worldwide Marketing Solutions Ltd [2014] EWHC 1910 (QB); [2014] P.T.S.R. 1072; [2014] B.L.G.R. 733, QBD .... *Digested,* 14/**497**:
Applied 17/619
Oliari v Italy (18766/11) (2017) 65 E.H.R.R. 26; 40 B.H.R.C. 549, ECHR
Considered 16/1132, 17/976
Oliver v Secretary of State for the Environment see Thrasyvoulou v Secretary of State for the Environment
Oliver v Sheffield City Council [2015] UKUT 229 (LC), UT (Lands)
Affirmed 17/1472
Oliver v Sheffield City Council; *sub nom* Sheffield City Council v Oliver [2017] EWCA Civ 225; [2017] 1 W.L.R. 4473; [2017] H.L.R. 23; [2017] L. & T.R. 35, CA (Civ Div) .... *Digested,* 17/**1472**
Olson v Gullo C13150, CA (Ont)
Considered 17/1585

Olympus UK Ltd, Re [2014] EWHC 1350 (Ch); [2014] Bus. L.R. 816; [2014] 2 B.C.L.C. 402, Ch D (Companies Ct) .... *Digested,* 14/**503**: *Applied* 17/392

Omak Maritime Ltd v Mamola Challenger Shipping Co Ltd; *joined case* Mamola Challenger Shipping Co v Omak Maritime Ltd [2010] EWHC 2026 (Comm); [2011] 2 All E.R. (Comm) 155; [2011] Bus. L.R. 212; [2011] 1 Lloyd's Rep. 47; [2010] 2 C.L.C. 194; 132 Con. L.R. 196; Times, September 21, 2010, QBD (Comm) .... *Digested,* 11/**538**: *Applied* 17/502

Omar v Chief Constable of Bedfordshire see R. (on the application of Omar) v Chief Constable of Bedfordshire

Omega Engineering Inc v Omega SA; *sub nom* Omega SA v Omega Engineering Inc [2010] EWHC 1211 (Ch); [2010] E.C.C. 18; [2010] E.T.M.R. 49; [2010] F.S.R. 26, Ch D .... *Digested,* 10/**2012**: *Affirmed* 11/1935: *Applied* 17/1405

Omega SA v Omega Engineering Inc see Omega Engineering Inc v Omega SA

Omielan v Omielan [1996] 2 F.L.R. 306; [1996] 3 F.C.R. 329; Times, July 30, 1996; [1996] Fam. Law 608, CA (Civ Div) .... *Digested,* 96/**2890**: *Applied* 15/1094: *Disapproved* 17/1008

OMV Petrom SA v Glencore International AG [2017] EWCA Civ 195; [2017] 1 W.L.R. 3465; [2018] 1 All E.R. 703; [2018] 1 All E.R. (Comm) 210; [2017] 2 Lloyd's Rep. 93; [2017] C.P. Rep. 24; [2017] 2 Costs L.R. 287; Times, May 10, 2017, CA (Civ Div) .... *Digested,* 17/**339**: *Followed* 17/256

OMV Petrom SA v Glencore International AG [2015] EWHC 666 (Comm), QBD (Comm) *Affirmed* 17/636

OMV Petrom SA v Glencore International AG [2016] EWCA Civ 778; [2017] 3 All E.R. 157; [2017] 2 All E.R. (Comm) 409; [2016] 2 Lloyd's Rep. 432; [2016] 2 C.L.C. 651, CA (Civ Div) .... *Digested,* 17/**636**

One Step (Support) Ltd v Morris-Garner; *sub nom* Morris-Garner v One Step (Support) Ltd [2016] EWCA Civ 180; [2017] Q.B. 1; [2016] 3 W.L.R. 1281; [2017] 2 All E.R. 262; [2016] I.R.L.R. 435, CA (Civ Div) .... *Digested,* 16/**564**

Onesavings Bank Plc v Burns 2017 S.L.T. (Sh Ct) 129; 2017 Hous. L.R. 55; 2017 G.W.D. 12-184, Sh Ct (Grampian) (Banff) .... *Digested,* 17/**2652**

Onix Asigurari SA v Istituto per la Vigilanza Sulle Assicurazioni (IVASS) (C-559/15) EU:C:2017:316; [2017] 3 C.M.L.R. 31, ECJ (3rd Chamber)

Onu v Akwiwu see Taiwo v Olaigbe

Onyx of Leicester Ltd v Revenue and Customs Commissioners [2017] UKFTT 297 (TC); [2017] S.T.I. 1144, FTT (Tax)

Oomerjee v Revenue and Customs Commissioners [2017] UKFTT 505 (TC); [2017] S.T.I. 1664, FTT (Tax)

OOO Abbott v Design and Display Ltd [2017] EWHC 932 (IPEC); [2017] F.S.R. 43, IPEC .... *Digested,* 17/**1367**

OOO Abbott v Design and Display Ltd [2014] EWHC 3234 (IPEC), IPEC *Applied* 17/1359

OOO Abbott v Econowall UK Ltd [2016] EWHC 660 (IPEC); [2017] F.S.R. 1, IPEC ..... *Digested,* 17/**367**

Open Safety Equipment Ltd v Revenue and Customs Commissioners [2017] UKFTT 261 (TC); [2017] S.T.I. 1049, FTT (Tax)

Optician v Ophthalmologist (4 Ob 133/16m) [2017] E.C.C. 20, OGH (A)

Oracle America Inc v M-Tech Data Ltd see Sun Microsystems Inc v M-Tech Data Ltd

Oraki v Bramston [2017] EWCA Civ 403; [2017] B.P.I.R. 1021, CA (Civ Div) .... *Digested,* 17/**1328**

Oraki v Bramston [2015] EWHC 2046 (Ch); [2016] 3 W.L.R. 1231; [2016] 2 All E.R. 1065; [2015] B.P.I.R. 1238, Ch D .... *Digested,* 16/**1244**: *Affirmed* 17/1328

Oraki v Dean and Dean see Oraki, Re

Oraki, Re; *sub nom* Oraki v Dean and Dean [2017] EWHC 11 (Ch); [2017] Bus. L.R. 545; [2017] B.P.I.R. 750, Ch D (Bankruptcy Ct) .... *Digested,* 17/**1291**

Ordem dos Tecnicos Oficiais de Contas v Autoridade da Concorrencia (C-1/12) EU:C:2013:127; [2013] 4 C.M.L.R. 20, ECJ (2nd Chamber) *Considered* 17/410

Orientfield Holdings Ltd v Bird & Bird LLP [2017] EWCA Civ 348; [2017] P.N.L.R. 31, CA (Civ Div)

Orland Ltd v Hackney LBC [2017] P.A.D. 26, Planning Inspector

Orleans v Vlaams Gewest (C-387/15) EU:C:2016:583; [2017] Env. L.R. 12, ECJ (7th Chamber)

Ornua Co-operative Ltd v Tindale & Stanton Ltd Espana SL (C-93/16) EU:C:2017:571; [2018] Bus. L.R. 319; [2017] E.T.M.R. 37, ECJ (2nd Chamber)

Oroville Reman & Reload Inc v R. 2016 TCC 75; 19 I.T.L. Rep. 259, Tax Ct (Can)
Orozco v Attorney General 41 B.H.R.C. 135, Sup Ct (Bze)
Osborn v Parole Board see Reilly's Application for Judicial Review, Re
Osborne v Automatic Bottle Makers Ltd see Automatic Bottle Makers Ltd, Re
Osborne v Follett Stock (A Firm) [2017] EWHC 1811 (QB); [2017] P.N.L.R. 35, QBD (Bristol) .... *Digested,* 17/**319**
Osborne v Matthan (No.2) 1998 G.W.D. 9-424, IH (Ex Div)
Applied 17/2616
Osborne-Tulloch v Admiral Insurance (Unreported, December 9, 2016), CC (Central London) [*Irwin Mitchell LLP, Riverside West, 1 Millsands, Sheffield*] .... *Digested,* 17/**1666**
Osman v Natt see Natt v Osman
Ostendorf v Germany (15598/08) 34 B.H.R.C. 738; [2013] Crim. L.R. 601, ECHR
Considered 14/2464: *Not applied* 17/1803
OT Africa Line Ltd v Magic Sportswear Corp [2005] EWCA Civ 710; [2006] 1 All E.R. (Comm) 32; [2005] 2 Lloyd's Rep. 170; [2005] 1 C.L.C. 923; 2005 A.M.C. 2179; Times, June 21, 2005; Independent, June 16, 2005, CA (Civ Div) .... *Digested,* 05/**627**:
Considered 06/639, 15/2305, 16/367, 17/2000
Otgon v Moldova (22743/07) (2016) 19 C.C.L. Rep. 618, ECHR .... *Digested,* 17/**1169**
Othman v United Kingdom (8139/09); *sub nom* Abu Qatada v United Kingdom (8139/09) (2012) 55 E.H.R.R. 1; 32 B.H.R.C. 62; Times, January 25, 2012, ECHR .... *Digested,* 12/**1664**:
Applied 14/3521: *Considered* 13/1187, 16/2634, 16/794, 16/796, 17/2440, 17/903
Otkritie Capital International Ltd v Threadneedle Asset Management Ltd [2017] EWCA Civ 274; [2017] C.P. Rep. 27; [2017] 2 Costs L.R. 375, CA (Civ Div) .... *Digested,* 17/**206**
Otkritie Capital International Ltd v Threadneedle Asset Management Ltd [2015] EWHC 2329 (Comm); [2015] 2 C.L.C. 459, QBD (Comm)
Affirmed 17/206
Otkritie International Investment Management Ltd v Urumov [2014] EWCA Civ 1315; [2015] C.P. Rep. 6, CA (Civ Div) .... *Digested,* 15/**28**:
Followed 17/1560
Otuo v Watchtower Bible and Tract Society of Britain [2017] EWCA Civ 136; [2017] C.P. Rep. 22; [2017] E.M.L.R. 15, CA (Civ Div) .... *Digested,* 17/**327**
Otuo v Watchtower Bible and Tract Society of Britain [2015] EWHC 509 (QB), QBD
Reversed 17/327
Outasight VB Ltd v Brown [2015] I.C.R. D11, EAT
Applied 17/811
Outlook Finance Ltd v Lindsay's Executor Nominate 2016 Hous. L.R. 75; 2016 G.W.D. 28-508, Sh Ct (South Strathclyde) (Lanark) .... *Digested,* 17/**2780**
Oval Estates (Bath) Ltd v Revenue and Customs Commissioners [2017] UKFTT 403 (TC); [2017] S.T.I. 1204, FTT (Tax)
Overend Gurney & Co, Re; *sub nom* Grissell's Case (1865-66) L.R. 1 Ch. App. 528, CA in Chancery
Considered 17/1259
Overseas Plastic Import Export Ltd v Greater London Authority [2016] UKUT 113 (LC); [2017] R.V.R. 177, UT (Lands) .... *Digested,* 17/**1833**
Overseas Union Insurance Ltd v New Hampshire Insurance Co (C-351/89) EU:C:1991:279; [1992] Q.B. 434; [1992] 2 W.L.R. 586; [1992] 2 All E.R. 138; [1992] 1 Lloyd's Rep. 204; [1991] E.C.R. I-3317; [1991] I.L.Pr. 495; Times, August 20, 1991; Financial Times, July 19, 1991, ECJ (6th Chamber) .... *Digested,* 91/**3931**:
Applied 01/827, 03/600, 09/404, 17/1042
Overy v Paypal (Europe) Ltd [2012] EWHC 2659 (QB); [2013] Bus. L.R. D1, QBD (Manchester)
Applied 17/1340
Owda v Court of Appeals Thessaloniki (Greece) see Owda v Greece
Owda v Greece; *sub nom* Owda v Court of Appeals Thessaloniki (Greece) [2017] EWHC 1174 (Admin), DC
Considered 17/906
Owen v Secretary of State for Business, Innovation and Skills see Liberty Holdings Unlimited, Re
Owens v Owens [2017] EWCA Civ 182; [2017] 4 W.L.R. 74; [2018] 1 F.L.R. 1002; [2017] 2 F.C.R. 569, CA (Civ Div) .... *Digested,* 17/**981**
Owens (Hugh) v HM Advocate 1946 J.C. 119; 1946 S.L.T. 227, HCJ Appeal
Considered 17/2482: *Disapproved* 73/3603: *Followed* 63/785, 82/683, 90/4891:
Referred to 93/5031
Owens Bank Ltd v Bracco [1992] 2 A.C. 443; [1992] 2 W.L.R. 621; [1992] 2 All E.R. 193; [1993] I.L.Pr. 24; Times, April 3, 1992; Independent, May 6, 1992; Financial Times, April 8, 1992, HL .... *Digested,* 92/**464**:
Followed 17/372: *Preliminary ruling given* 94/4801

Owens Bank Ltd v Etoile Commerciale SA [1995] 1 W.L.R. 44, PC (StV) .... *Digested,* 95/**688**: *Applied* 17/372

OWENS-BROCKWAY/Measurement of Hot Container Wall Thickness (T2092/13) [2017] E.P.O.R. 30, EPO (Technical Bd App)

Owners and/or Bareboat Charterers of the Samco Europe v Owners of the MSC Prestige (Costs) [2011] EWHC 1656 (Admlty); [2011] 2 C.L.C. 679; [2012] B.L.R. 267; (2011) 161 N.L.J. 988, QBD (Admlty) .... *Digested,* 12/**3050**: *Considered* 17/266

Owners and/or Demise Charterers of the Nordlake v Owners of the SeaEagle (now named Elbella) [2015] EWHC 3605 (Admlty); [2016] 2 All E.R. (Comm) 449; [2016] 1 Lloyd's Rep. 656; [2016] 1 C.L.C. 353, QBD (Admlty) .... *Digested,* 16/**1952**: *Considered* 17/2020

Owners of Cargo Lately Laden on Board the River Gurara v Nigerian National Shipping Line Ltd [1996] 2 Lloyd's Rep. 53; [1996] C.L.C. 927; Times, March 6, 1996, QBD (Admlty) .... *Digested,* 96/**5306**: *Affirmed* 98/4405: *Applied* 17/2003: *Followed* 05/3786

Owners of Cargo Lately Laden on Board the River Gurara v Nigerian National Shipping Line Ltd [1998] Q.B. 610; [1997] 3 W.L.R. 1128; [1997] 4 All E.R. 498; [1998] 1 Lloyd's Rep. 225; [1997] C.L.C. 1322; Times, July 29, 1997; (1997) 94(33) L.S.G. 27; (1997) 141 S.J.L.B. 175, CA (Civ Div) .... *Digested,* 98/**4405**: *Applied* 17/2015

Owners of Steamship Enterprises of Panama Inc v Owners of SS Ousel (The Liverpool) (No.2) [1963] P. 64; [1960] 3 W.L.R. 597; [1960] 3 All E.R. 307; [1960] 2 Lloyd's Rep. 66; Times, July 29, 1960; (1960) 104 S.J. 824, CA .... *Digested,* 60/**2987**: *Applied* 83/1074, 09/2834: *Considered* 11/536: *Followed* 17/285

Owners of the Eleftherotria v Owners of the Despina R; *sub nom* Services Europe Atlantique Sud (SEAS) v Stockholms Rederi AB Svea (The Folias); Canadian Transport, The [1979] A.C. 685; [1978] 3 W.L.R. 804; [1979] 1 All E.R. 421; [1979] 1 Lloyd's Rep. 1; (1978) 122 S.J. 758, HL .... *Digested,* 78/**710**: *Applied* 79/155, 79/334, 82/776, 85/379, 95/4507: *Considered* 81/97, 88/166: *Followed* 85/100, 93/5165, 04/656, 17/643

Owusu v Jackson (t/a Villa Holidays Bal Inn Villas) (C-281/02) EU:C:2005:120; [2005] Q.B. 801; [2005] 2 W.L.R. 942; [2005] 2 All E.R. (Comm) 577; [2005] 1 Lloyd's Rep. 452; [2005] E.C.R. I-1383; [2005] 1 C.L.C. 246; [2005] I.L.Pr. 25; Times, March 9, 2005, ECJ .... *Digested,* 05/**604**: *Applied* 09/455, 09/511, 10/371, 10/421, 14/560: *Considered* 06/329, 08/559, 10/1943, 10/501, 10/503, 11/469, 12/557, 13/1274, 14/1326, 15/1103, 17/2194: *Distinguished* 05/2406, 09/621: *Explained* 11/1402: *Followed* 15/437, 16/1539: *Referred to* 17/371

Oxfam v Revenue and Customs Commissioners [2009] EWHC 3078 (Ch); [2010] S.T.C. 686; [2010] B.V.C. 108; Times, December 31, 2009; [2010] A.C.D. 50; [2010] S.T.I. 556, Ch D .... *Digested,* 10/**3488**: *Applied* 11/3573, 17/2150: *Considered* 11/56, 12/3334, 13/3073, 15/2516, 16/2124: *Not applied* 16/2177: *Not followed* 13/3199: *Referred to* 11/9

Oxford Legal Group Ltd v Sibbasbridge Services Plc [2008] EWCA Civ 387; [2008] Bus. L.R. 1244; [2008] B.C.C. 558; [2008] 2 B.C.L.C. 381; Times, May 15, 2008, CA (Civ Div) .... *Digested,* 08/**483**: *Applied* 17/1575: *Followed* 15/407

Oxfordshire CC v Oxford City Council [2004] EWHC 12 (Ch); [2004] Ch. 253; [2004] 2 W.L.R. 1291; [2004] 2 P. & C.R. 19; [2004] 2 P.L.R. 65; [2004] 1 E.G.L.R. 105; Times, January 30, 2004; [2004] 6 E.G. 144 (C.S.); (2004) 101(6) L.S.G. 32; [2004] N.P.C. 6, Ch D .... *Digested,* 04/**3203**: *Applied* 17/1860: *Considered* 04/3262: *Reversed in part* 05/3440

P v A Local Authority [2016] EWHC 2779 (Fam); [2016] 4 W.L.R. 180; [2017] 1 F.L.R. 1589, Fam Div .... *Digested,* 17/**1485**: *Not followed* 17/995

P v Cheshire West and Chester Council see Cheshire West and Chester Council v P

P v HM Advocate; *sub nom* KP v HM Advocate [2017] HCJAC 57; 2018 J.C. 33; 2017 S.C.L. 729; 2017 S.C.C.R. 451; 2017 G.W.D. 24-406, HCJ Appeal .... *Digested,* 17/**2529**

P v Home Office [2017] EWHC 663 (QB); [2017] 1 W.L.R. 3189, QBD .... *Digested,* 17/**192**

P v P (Divorce: Financial Remedy Order); *sub nom* JP v NP (Financial Remedies: Costs) [2014] EWHC 1101 (Fam); [2014] 1 W.L.R. 4607; [2015] 1 F.L.R. 659; [2014] Fam. Law 1106, Fam Div .... *Digested,* 15/**1097**: *Applied* 17/1002

P v P (Removal of Child to New Zealand) see Payne v Payne

P v Q [2017] EWHC 194 (Comm); [2017] 1 W.L.R. 3823, QBD (Comm) .... *Digested,* 17/**79**

P v Q [2017] EWHC 148 (Comm); [2017] 1 W.L.R. 3800, QBD (Comm) .... *Digested,* 17/**78**

P v Scottish Ministers [2017] CSOH 33; 2017 S.L.T. 271; 2017 G.W.D. 8-110, OH ...... *Digested,* 17/**2749**

P v Surrey CC see Cheshire West and Chester Council v P

P v Worcestershire CC [2016] UKUT 120 (AAC); [2016] E.L.R. 194, UT (AAC) .... *Digested,* 17/**713**

P v Z see F (Children) (Thai Surrogacy: Enduring Family Relationship), Re

P (A Child) (Care Proceedings: Appeal), Re [2016] EWCA Civ 3; [2017] 1 F.L.R. 417; [2016] Fam. Law 282, CA (Civ Div) .... *Digested,* 17/**934**

P (Children) (Adoption: Parental Consent), Re see P (Children) (Placement Orders: Parental Consent), Re

P (Children) (Child Abduction: Anticipatory Breach), Re see C (Children) (Abduction), Re

P (Children) (Placement Orders: Parental Consent), Re; *sub nom* B v X CC; P (Children) (Adoption: Parental Consent), Re [2008] EWCA Civ 535; [2009] P.T.S.R. 150; [2008] 2 F.L.R. 625; [2008] 2 F.C.R. 185; Times, May 29, 2008, CA (Civ Div) .... *Digested,* 08/**1575**:
Applied 10/1272, 10/1425, 12/1297, 14/1341, 16/812: *Considered* 11/1283, 11/4275, 14/1244, 14/1253: *Explained* 15/991: *Followed* 12/1296, 14/1243, 17/932

P (Human Fertilisation and Embryology Act 2008) (No.2), Re see P (Legal Parenthood: Written Consents), Re

P (Incapacitated Person) (Representatives and Advocates: Duties and Powers), Re see D (Incapacitated Person) (Representatives and Advocates: Duties and Powers), Re

P (Legal Parenthood: Written Consents), Re; *sub nom* P (Human Fertilisation and Embryology Act 2008) (No.2), Re [2017] EWHC 2532 (Fam); [2017] 4 W.L.R. 183, Fam Div

P Resources Ltd v Prest see Petrodel Resources Ltd v Prest

P&A Swift Investments v Combined English Stores Group Plc [1989] A.C. 632; [1988] 3 W.L.R. 313; [1988] 2 All E.R. 885; (1989) 57 P. & C.R. 42; [1988] 43 E.G. 73; [1988] E.G. 104 (C.S.); (1988) 138 N.L.J. Rep. 202, HL .... *Digested,* 88/**2002**:
Applied 89/2201, 95/2974, 04/3222: *Followed* 17/1857

P&J Macrae Ltd, Re; *sub nom* Credit Enterprise v Woodcocks Sussex [1961] 1 W.L.R. 229; [1961] 1 All E.R. 302; (1961) 105 S.J. 108, CA .... *Digested,* 61/**1186**:
Applied 65/487, 17/1294

P&O Nedlloyd BV v Arab Metals Co (No.2) see P&O Nedlloyd BV v Arab Metals Co (The UB Tiger)

P&O Nedlloyd BV v Arab Metals Co (The UB Tiger); *sub nom* P&O Nedlloyd BV v Arab Metals Co (No.2) [2006] EWCA Civ 1717; [2007] 1 W.L.R. 2288; [2007] 2 All E.R. (Comm) 401; [2007] 2 Lloyd's Rep. 231; [2006] 2 C.L.C. 985; 116 Con. L.R. 200; Times, January 15, 2007, CA (Civ Div) .... *Digested,* 07/**472**:
Applied 17/1324: *Considered* 10/2748: *Followed* 14/1393

P&P Property Ltd v Owen White and Catlin LLP [2016] EWHC 2276 (Ch); [2016] Bus. L.R. 1337; [2017] P.N.L.R. 3; [2017] 1 P. & C.R. DG6, Ch D .... *Digested,* 17/**44**

P's C B v Criminal Injuries Compensation Board see P's Curator Bonis v Criminal Injuries Compensation Board

P's Curator Bonis v Criminal Injuries Compensation Board; *sub nom* Millar v Criminal Injuries Compensation Board; A's Curator Bonis v Criminal Injuries Compensation Board; P's C B v Criminal Injuries Compensation Board 1997 S.L.T. 1180; 1997 S.C.L.R. 69; (1998) 44 B.M.L.R. 70; 1997 Rep. L.R. 3; Times, January 24, 1997, OH .... *Digested,* 97/**5783**:
Applied 17/1644

PA v Criminal Court Coimbra (Portugal) [2017] EWHC 331 (Admin), QBD (Admin)
Not followed 17/910

PA Thomas & Co v Mould [1968] 2 Q.B. 913; [1968] 2 W.L.R. 737; [1968] 1 All E.R. 963; (1967) 112 S.J. 216, QBD .... *Digested,* 68/**3066**:
Applied 17/286: *Referred to* 99/583

Pablo Star Ltd, Re; *sub nom* Price v Registrar of Companies [2016] EWHC 2640 (Ch); [2017] 1 W.L.R. 299, Ch D .... *Digested,* 17/**402**

Pablo Star Media Ltd v Bowen [2017] EWHC 2541 (IPEC); [2017] 5 Costs L.R. 909, IPEC .... *Digested,* 17/**1362**

Pacitti v Manganiello 1995 S.C.L.R. 557, Sh Pr .... *Digested,* 95/**6058**:
Applied 17/2704

Pacol Ltd v Trade Lines Ltd (The Henrik Sif) [1982] 1 Lloyd's Rep. 456; [1982] Com. L.R. 92; (1982) 126 S.J. 312, QBD (Comm) .... *Digested,* 82/**1145**:
Considered 17/493: *Distinguished* 97/983: *Followed* 94/4047

Paczkowski v Sieradzka [2017] I.C.R. 62, EAT .... *Digested,* 17/**847**

Padden v Arbuthnot Pensions & Investments Ltd; *sub nom* Arbuthnot Pensions & Investments Ltd v Padden [2004] EWCA Civ 582; [2004] C.P. Rep. 36; (2004) 101(24) L.S.G. 32; (2004) 148 S.J.L.B. 631, CA (Civ Div) .... *Digested,* 05/**1237**: *Followed* 15/1400, 17/1343

Page v Champion Financial Management Ltd [2014] EWHC 1778 (QB), QBD *Considered* 17/350

Page v Hewetts Solicitors [2013] EWHC 2845 (Ch); [2014] W.T.L.R. 479, Ch D .... *Digested,* 14/**420**: *Applied* 17/282: *Considered* 14/577: *Not applied* 16/179

Page v Smith [1996] A.C. 155; [1995] 2 W.L.R. 644; [1995] 2 All E.R. 736; [1995] 2 Lloyd's Rep. 95; [1995] R.T.R. 210; [1995] P.I.Q.R. P329; Times, May 12, 1995; Independent, May 12, 1995; Lloyd's List, May 25, 1995; (1995) 92(23) L.S.G. 33; (1995) 145 N.L.J. 723; (1995) 139 S.J.L.B. 173, HL .... *Digested,* 95/**3682**: *Applied* 99/3978, 00/6582, 04/4901: *Considered* 96/4426, 96/4478, 96/4862, 98/3954, 98/3981, 99/4059, 00/4220, 00/6598, 02/3275, 02/3307, 04/1277, 06/2877, 09/2835, 15/3026: *Distinguished* 07/2919, 09/4426: *Followed* 99/3980, 13/2185, 17/1638

Paget v Paget [1898] 1 Ch. 470, CA *Considered* 85/162: *Followed* 17/890

Pagnan SpA v Tradax Ocean Transportation SA; *sub nom* Tradax Ocean Transportation SA v Pagnan [1987] 3 All E.R. 565; [1987] 2 Lloyd's Rep. 342, CA (Civ Div) .... *Digested,* 88/**3174**: *Applied* 15/186: *Considered* 12/3072: *Followed* 05/2867, 10/3047, 15/2168, 17/175

Palacios Martinez v Banco Bilbao Vizcaya Argentaria SA (BBVA) (C□307/15) see Gutierrez Naranjo v Cajasur Banco SAU (C-154/15)

Palanisami v Hindu Community in General and Citizens of Gobichettipalayam 20 I.T.E.L.R. 106, Sup Ct (Ind)

Pallot v Douglas 2017 BCCA 254; 20 I.T.E.L.R. 144, CA (BC)

Palmer v Herefordshire Council see R. (on the application of Palmer) v Herefordshire Council

Palmer v Nightingale (t/a Andover Pest Control) [2016] EWHC 2800 (TCC); 170 Con. L.R. 19, QBD (TCC)

Palmer v United Kingdom (30671/96) see Wilson v United Kingdom (30668/96)

Pan Oceanic Chartering Inc v UNIPEC UK Co Ltd [2016] EWHC 2774 (Comm); [2017] 2 All E.R. (Comm) 196, QBD (Comm) .... *Digested,* 17/**2022**

Panalpina Services Ltd v Transport and General Workers Union see Heatons Transport (St Helens) Ltd v Transport and General Workers Union

Panama & South Pacific Telegraph Co v India Rubber, Gutta Percha & Telegraph Works Co (1874-75) L.R. 10 Ch. App. 515, CA in Chancery *Considered* 89/55, 17/504

Panasonic Corp v European Commission (C-608/15 P) EU:C:2016:538; [2017] 4 C.M.L.R. 8, ECJ (8th Chamber)

Panayiotou v Chief Constable of Hampshire see Panayiotou v Kernaghan

Panayiotou v Kernaghan; *sub nom* Panayiotou v Chief Constable of Hampshire [2014] I.R.L.R. 500; [2014] I.C.R. D23, EAT .... *Digested,* 14/**1093**: *Applied* 17/815

Pandey v Revenue and Customs Commissioners [2017] UKFTT 216 (TC); [2017] S.F.T.D. 928, FTT (Tax)

Panicello v Martinez (C-503/15) see Margarit Panicello v Hernandez Martinez (C-503/15)

Pannullo v France (37794/97) (2003) 36 E.H.R.R. 42; [2006] Inquest L.R. 136, ECHR *Digested,* 03/**2181**: *Applied* 17/1645

Pantone 485 Ltd, Re see Miller v Bain (Director's Breach of Duty)

Papajorgji v Entry Clearance Officer, Nicosia see Papajorgji (EEA Spouse: Marriage of Convenience: Greece), Re

Papajorgji (EEA Spouse: Marriage of Convenience: Greece), Re; *sub nom* Papajorgji v Entry Clearance Officer, Nicosia; Entry Clearance Officer, Nicosia v Papajorgji [2012] UKUT 38 (IAC); [2012] Imm. A.R. 447; [2012] I.N.L.R. 617, UT (IAC) .... *Digested,* 12/**1717**: *Applied* 16/1151, 17/1248: *Approved* 16/1156

Paponette v Attorney General of Trinidad and Tobago [2010] UKPC 32; [2012] 1 A.C. 1; [2011] 3 W.L.R. 219; Times, December 15, 2010, PC (Trin) *Considered* 12/999, 16/2206, 17/2126

Paposhvili v Belgium (41738/10) [2017] Imm. A.R. 867; [2017] I.N.L.R. 497, ECHR (Grand Chamber)

Parabola Investments Ltd v Browallia Cal Ltd (formerly Union Cal Ltd) [2010] EWCA Civ 486; [2011] Q.B. 477; [2010] 3 W.L.R. 1266; [2011] 1 All E.R. (Comm) 210; [2010] Bus. L.R. 1446; [2011] 1 B.C.L.C. 26; [2010] 19 E.G. 108 (C.S.); (2010) 107(20) L.S.G. 20, CA (Civ Div) .... *Digested,* 11/**857**: *Considered* 16/1544: *Distinguished* 16/567: *Followed* 17/302

Paradiso v Italy (25358/12) (2017) 65 E.H.R.R. 22, ECHR

Paradiso v Italy (25358/12) (2017) 65 E.H.R.R. 2, ECHR

Paragon Finance Plc v DB Thakerar & Co; *joined case* Paragon Finance Plc v Thimbleby & Co [1999] 1 All E.R. 400; Times, August 7, 1998; (1998) 95(35) L.S.G. 36; (1998) 142 S.J.L.B. 243, CA (Civ Div) .... *Digested,* 98/**536**: *Applied* 00/1452, 00/513, 03/519, 04/380, 06/470, 06/543, 06/561, 07/476, 07/491, 08/897, 14/426, 17/321, 17/325: *Considered* 98/383, 99/501, 00/520, 01/5505, 01/626, 07/4258, 10/394, 13/433, 14/2991: *Followed* 99/458

Paragon Finance Plc v Thimbleby & Co see Paragon Finance Plc v DB Thakerar & Co

Paragon Finance Plc (formerly National Home Loans Corp) v Freshfields [1999] 1 W.L.R. 1183; [2000] C.P. Rep. 81; [1999] Lloyd's Rep. P.N. 446; Times, March 22, 1999; Independent, March 16, 1999; (1999) 96(20) L.S.G. 40; (1999) 143 S.J.L.B. 136; [1999] N.P.C. 33, CA (Civ Div) .... *Digested,* 99/**4024**: *Applied* 06/429, 09/333, 16/248: *Considered* 13/244, 15/342: *Explained* 17/216

Parakou Shipping Pte Ltd v Jinhui Shipping and Transportation Ltd (Unreported, September 30, 2010), HC (HK)
Considered 17/191

Parissis v Matthias Gentle Page Hassan LLP [2017] EWHC 761 (QB); [2017] 3 Costs L.O. 269, QBD .... *Digested,* 17/**288**

Park v Cho [2014] EWHC 55 (Ch); [2014] P.T.S.R. 769; [2017] W.T.L.R. 279, Ch D

Parker v Butler [2016] EWHC 1251 (QB); [2016] 3 Costs L.R. 435, QBD .... *Digested,* 16/**229**: *Considered* 17/262

Parker v Parham LRX/35/2002, Lands Tr
Considered 17/1471

Parker v Parker; *sub nom* Macclesfield v Parker [2003] EWHC 1846 (Ch); [2003] N.P.C. 94, Ch D
Considered 17/1449

Parker (t/a NBC Services) v Rasalingham (t/a Micro Tec) (Inquiry into Damages) Times, July 25, 2000, Ch D .... *Digested,* 00/**494**: *Applied* 17/160

Parkes v Wilkes [2017] EWHC 1556 (Ch); [2017] 4 W.L.R. 123; [2017] 2 P. & C.R. 15; [2017] L. & T.R. 33, Ch D .... *Digested,* 17/**1847**

ParkingEye Ltd v Beavis [2015] EWCA Civ 402; [2015] R.T.R. 27; [2015] C.T.L.C. 82, CA (Civ Div) .... *Digested,* 15/**2153**: *Affirmed* 16/437: *Considered* 17/2467

ParkingEye Ltd v Beavis see Makdessi v Cavendish Square Holdings BV

Parkinson v St James and Seacroft University Hospital NHS Trust [2001] EWCA Civ 530; [2002] Q.B. 266; [2001] 3 W.L.R. 376; [2001] 3 All E.R. 97; [2001] 2 F.L.R. 401; [2002] 2 F.C.R. 65; [2001] P.I.Q.R. Q12; [2001] Lloyd's Rep. Med. 309; (2001) 61 B.M.L.R. 100; [2001] P.N.L.R. 43; Times, April 24, 2001; [2001] Fam. Law 592; Daily Telegraph, April 17, 2001; (2001) 98(22) L.S.G. 35; (2001) 145 S.J.L.B. 118, CA (Civ Div) .... *Digested,* 01/**1509**: *Applied* 02/1683, 02/3255, 02/927, 03/3124: *Considered* 03/3129, 17/1644: *Followed* 03/3120

Parklane UK Investments Ltd v Revenue and Customs Commissioners [2017] S.T.I. 118, FTT (Tax)

Parkwood Landfill Ltd v Customs and Excise Commissioners; *sub nom* Customs and Excise Commissioners v Parkwood Landfill Ltd [2002] EWCA Civ 1707; [2003] 1 W.L.R. 697; [2003] 1 All E.R. 579; [2002] S.T.C. 1536; [2003] Env. L.R. 19; [2002] B.T.C. 8045; Times, December 4, 2002; [2003] J.P.L. 861; [2002] S.T.I. 1653; (2003) 100(6) L.S.G. 26; (2002) 146 S.J.L.B. 278; [2002] N.P.C. 155, CA (Civ Div) .... *Digested,* 03/**4278**: *Applied* 17/2164: *Considered* 08/3818: *Distinguished* 14/2946

Parris v Trinity College Dublin (C-443/15) EU:C:2016:897; [2017] 2 C.M.L.R. 17; [2017] I.C.R. 313; [2017] I.R.L.R. 173; [2017] Pens. L.R. 3, ECJ (1st Chamber)

Parry v Revenue and Customs Commissioners; *sub nom* Revenue and Customs Commissioners v Parry [2014] UKFTT 419 (TC); [2014] W.T.L.R. 1265; [2014] S.T.I. 2415, FTT (Tax)
Reversed in part 17/2159

Parry v Revenue and Customs Commissioners; *sub nom* Revenue and Customs Commissioners v Parry [2017] UKUT 4 (TCC); [2017] S.T.C. 574; [2017] B.T.C. 504, UT (Tax) .... *Digested,* 17/**2159**

Parsons Corp v CV Scheepvaartonderneming Happy Ranger [2002] EWCA Civ 694; [2002] 2 All E.R. (Comm) 24; [2002] 2 Lloyd's Rep. 357; [2003] 1 C.L.C. 122, CA (Civ Div) .... *Digested,* 02/**4090**: *Applied* 14/2706, 17/2015: *Considered* 02/4098, 16/1945: *Followed* 03/3897

Partners of Proteus v Revenue and Customs Commissioners see Samarkand Film Partnership No.3 v Revenue and Customs Commissioners

Partners of Samarkand v Revenue and Customs Commissioners see Samarkand Film Partnership No.3 v Revenue and Customs Commissioners

Partridge v Gupta; *sub nom* Gupta v Partridge [2017] EWHC 2110 (QB); [2018] 1 W.L.R. 1; [2017] H.L.R. 44; [2018] L. & T.R. 8, QBD

Patel v Brent LBC (No.3) [2004] EWHC 763 (Ch); [2005] 1 P. & C.R. 20; [2004] 3 P.L.R. 74; [2004] 17 E.G. 129 (C.S.); (2004) 101(16) L.S.G. 29, Ch D *Applied* 17/503: *Reversed in part* 05/3289

Patel v Mirza [2016] UKSC 42; [2017] A.C. 467; [2016] 3 W.L.R. 399; [2017] 1 All E.R. 191; [2016] 2 Lloyd's Rep. 300; [2016] Lloyd's Rep. F.C. 435; 19 I.T.E.L.R. 627; [2016] L.L.R. 731; Times, August 25, 2016, SC .... *Digested,* 16/**431**: *Considered* 17/2202, 17/337: *Followed* 17/174

Patel v Patel 19 I.T.E.L.R. 958, Royal Ct (Gue)

Patel v Secretary of State for the Home Department [2015] EWCA Civ 1175; [2016] C.P. Rep. 9; [2016] Imm. A.R. 444; [2016] I.N.L.R. 289, CA (Civ Div) .... *Digested,* 16/**1121**: *Followed* 17/30

Paterson v Harvie; *joined cases* Bow v Harvie; Love v Dunn [2014] HCJAC 87; 2015 J.C. 118; 2014 S.L.T. 857; 2014 S.C.L. 606; 2014 S.C.C.R. 521; 2014 G.W.D. 26-517, HCJ .... *Digested,* 14/**3410**: *Applied* 16/2508, 17/2494

Patersons of Greenoakhill Ltd v Revenue and Customs Commissioners [2014] UKUT 225 (TCC); [2014] S.T.C. 2178; [2015] Env. L.R. 8; [2014] B.T.C. 517; [2014] S.T.I. 2232, UT (Tax) .... *Digested,* 14/**2946**: *Affirmed* 17/2164

Patersons of Greenoakhill Ltd v Revenue and Customs Commissioners [2016] EWCA Civ 1250; [2017] 1 W.L.R. 1210; [2017] S.T.C. 225; [2017] Env. L.R. 24; [2017] S.T.I. 33, CA (Civ Div) .... *Digested,* 17/**2164**

Patley Wood Farm LLP v Brake; *sub nom* Brake (t/a Stay in Style), Re [2016] EWHC 1688 (Ch); [2017] 1 W.L.R. 343; [2017] B.P.I.R. 1357, Ch D .... *Digested,* 17/**1263**

Patrick v Patrick 2017 Fam. L.R. 128; 2017 G.W.D. 27-440, Sh Ct (Glasgow) .... *Digested,* 17/**2613**

Patterson v Spencer [2014] EWHC 1878 (Ch), Ch D *Reversed* 17/349

Patterson v Spencer [2017] EWCA Civ 140; [2017] B.P.I.R. 754, CA (Civ Div) .... *Digested,* 17/**349**

Pattinson v Finningley Internal Drainage Board [1970] 2 Q.B. 33; [1970] 2 W.L.R. 622; [1970] 1 All E.R. 790; 68 L.G.R. 420; (1970) 114 S.J. 109, QBD .... *Digested,* 70/**1496**: *Applied* 03/4613: *Considered* 17/884

Pattni v Ali; *sub nom* Ali v Pattni [2006] UKPC 51; [2007] 2 A.C. 85; [2007] 2 W.L.R. 102; [2007] 2 All E.R. (Comm) 427, PC (IoM) .... *Digested,* 07/**448**: *Applied* 17/346: *Considered* 11/2165, 13/361

Pattni v First Leicester Buses Ltd; *sub nom* Bent v Highways and Utilities Construction [2011] EWCA Civ 1384; [2012] R.T.R. 17; [2012] Lloyd's Rep. I.R. 577; [2012] P.I.Q.R. Q1, CA (Civ Div) .... *Digested,* 12/**2812**: *Applied* 15/681: *Considered* 14/3474, 17/644: *Followed* 13/2528

Paulley v First Group Plc see Paulley v FirstGroup Plc

Paulley v FirstGroup Plc; *sub nom* FirstGroup Plc v Paulley; Paulley v First Group Plc [2017] UKSC 4; [2017] 1 W.L.R. 423; [2017] 2 All E.R. 1; [2017] R.T.R. 19; [2017] I.R.L.R. 258; Times, January 24, 2017, SC .... *Digested,* 17/**2206**

Paulley v FirstGroup Plc; *sub nom* FirstGroup Plc v Paulley; Paulley v First Group Plc [2014] EWCA Civ 1573; [2015] 1 W.L.R. 3384; [2015] R.T.R. 22, CA (Civ Div) .. *Digested,* 15/**2543**: *Reversed* 17/2206

Pavlou (A Bankrupt), Re [1993] 1 W.L.R. 1046; [1993] 3 All E.R. 955; [1993] 2 F.L.R. 751; [1993] Fam. Law 629, Ch D .... *Digested,* 93/**1920**: *Applied* 03/3542, 07/3432, 08/3064, 17/1826: *Considered* 03/3604, 06/4391, 08/2124

Paxton v North Ayrshire Council [2017] SAC (Civ) 14; 2017 Rep. L.R. 87; 2017 G.W.D. 13-202, SAC .... *Digested,* 17/**2756**

Payne v Payne; *sub nom* P v P (Removal of Child to New Zealand) [2001] EWCA Civ 166; [2001] Fam. 473; [2001] 2 W.L.R. 1826; [2001] 1 F.L.R. 1052; [2001] 1 F.C.R. 425; [2001] H.R.L.R. 28; [2001] U.K.H.R.R. 484; Times, March 9, 2001; Independent, February 22, 2001; (2001) 165 J.P.N. 466; Daily Telegraph, February 27, 2001; (2001) 98(10) L.S.G. 41; (2001) 145 S.J.L.B. 61, CA (Civ Div) .... *Digested,* 01/**2596**:
Applied 01/2597, 03/1545, 05/1590, 06/1626, 06/1688, 06/5363, 07/1794, 10/1359, 11/1373, 11/1380, 12/1389, 13/1248, 13/1252: *Considered* 05/1572, 05/1574, 05/1635, 06/1691, 07/1795, 11/1378, 11/1382, 12/4010, 14/1311, 16/858, 16/859, 16/883, 17/970: *Distinguished* 05/1575, 08/4780: *Followed* 11/1360, 11/1379, 13/1249, 17/943: *Referred to* 08/1515

PayPal Inc v EUIPO (T-132/16) EU:T:2017:316; [2017] E.T.M.R. 30, GC (8th Chamber)

Paypoint Collections Ltd v Revenue and Customs Commissioners [2017] UKFTT 424 (TC); [2017] S.F.T.D. 1016; [2017] S.T.I. 1214, FTT (Tax)

Payzu Ltd v Saunders [1919] 2 K.B. 581, CA
Applied 53/3775: *Distinguished* 75/3518: *Followed* 17/285

Pazpena de Vire v Pazpena de Vire [2001] 1 F.L.R. 460; [2001] Fam. Law 95, Fam Div .... *Digested,* 01/**2611**:
Considered 17/1045

PD (Article 8: Conjoined Family Claims: Sri Lanka); *sub nom* PD (Sri Lanka) v Secretary of State for the Home Department [2016] UKUT 108 (IAC); [2016] Imm. A.R. 797; [2017] I.N.L.R. 26, UT (IAC) .... *Digested,* 16/**1127**

PD (Sri Lanka) v Secretary of State for the Home Department see PD (Article 8: Conjoined Family Claims: Sri Lanka)

PDHL Ltd v Financial Conduct Authority [2016] UKUT 130 (TCC); [2017] B.P.I.R. 1623, UT (Tax)

PDHL Ltd v Financial Conduct Authority [2016] UKUT 129 (TCC); [2017] B.P.I.R. 1592, UT (Tax)

PE (Cameroon) v Secretary of State for the Home Department see R. (on the application of PE (Cameroon)) v Secretary of State for the Home Department

Peacock v Custin see Peacock v Custins

Peacock v Custins; *sub nom* Custins v Peacock; Peacock v Custin [2002] 1 W.L.R. 1815; [2001] 2 All E.R. 827; (2001) 81 P. & C.R. 34; [2001] 1 E.G.L.R. 87; [2001] 13 E.G. 152; Times, December 15, 2000; Independent, November 24, 2000; [2000] E.G. 132 (C.S.); (2000) 97(48) L.S.G. 36; [2000] N.P.C. 124, CA (Civ Div) .... *Digested,* 00/**4635**:
Considered 03/3600, 17/1840: *Followed* 03/3558

Peak Hotels and Resorts Ltd, Re; *sub nom* Crumpler v Candey Ltd [2017] EWHC 1511 (Ch); [2017] Bus. L.R. 1765, Ch D (Companies Ct) .... *Digested,* 17/**1314**

Pearson v Naydler [1977] 1 W.L.R. 899; [1977] 3 All E.R. 531; (1977) 121 S.J. 304, Ch D .... *Digested,* 77/**2393**:
Applied 92/3443: *Considered* 92/3442, 17/383: *Followed* 86/2696, 95/5929

Pearson v Primeo Fund [2017] UKPC 19; [2017] B.C.C. 552, PC (CI)

Peek v Barclay see Peek v Gurney

Peek v Birkbeck see Peek v Gurney

Peek v Gibb see Peek v Gurney

Peek v Gordon see Peek v Gurney

Peek v Gurney; *joined cases* Peek v Birkbeck; Peek v Barclay; Peek v Gordon; Peek v Rennie; Peek v Gibb; Peek v Overend & Gurney Co; Peek v Turquand; Peek v Harding (1873) L.R. 6 H.L. 377; [1861-1873] All E.R. Rep. 116, HL
Applied 69/1532, 91/2650: *Considered* 72/173: *Followed* 17/169

Peek v Harding see Peek v Gurney

Peek v Overend & Gurney Co see Peek v Gurney

Peek v Rennie see Peek v Gurney

Peek v Turquand see Peek v Gurney

Peekay Intermark Ltd v Australia & New Zealand Banking Group Ltd [2006] EWCA Civ 386; [2006] 2 Lloyd's Rep. 511; [2006] 1 C.L.C. 582, CA (Civ Div) .... *Digested,* 06/**766**:
Considered 10/619, 10/641, 11/193, 17/1568: *Followed* 11/186, 11/566, 17/1583

Peel Port Shareholder Finance Co Ltd v Dornoch Ltd [2017] EWHC 876 (TCC); [2017] 2 All E.R. (Comm) 1024; [2017] Bus. L.R. 1663; [2017] B.L.R. 382; [2017] Lloyd's Rep. I.R. 374, QBD (TCC) .... *Digested,* 17/**188**

Peeters Landbouwmachines BV v Office for Harmonisation in the Internal Market (Trade Marks and Designs) (OHIM) (T-33/11) EU:T:2012:77, GC
Considered 17/1395

Pegasus Birds Ltd v Customs and Excise Commissioners; *sub nom* Customs and Excise Commissioners v Pegasus Birds Ltd [2004] EWCA Civ 1015; [2004] S.T.C. 1509; [2004] B.T.C. 5729; [2004] B.V.C. 788; Times, August 2, 2004; [2004] S.T.I. 1759; (2004) 101(36) L.S.G. 35; (2004) 148 S.J.L.B. 945, CA (Civ Div) .... *Digested,* 04/**3972**:
Applied 10/3469, 11/3517, 11/3573, 14/3037: *Cited* 06/4427: *Considered* 06/4425: *Explained* 17/2245: *Followed* 15/2601, 17/2261

Pegasus Birds Ltd v Customs and Excise Commissioners [2000] S.T.C. 91; [2000] B.T.C. 5036; [2000] B.V.C. 68; Times, February 10, 2000; [2000] S.T.I. 82, CA (Civ Div) .... *Digested,* 00/**5351**:
Followed 17/2261

Pegasus Birds Ltd v Customs and Excise Commissioners [1999] S.T.C. 95; [1999] B.T.C. 5003; [1999] B.V.C. 56; Independent, December 7, 1998, QBD .... *Digested,* 99/**5021**:
Affirmed 00/5351: *Applied* 12/3379, 15/2491, 17/2261

Peires v Bickerton's Aerodromes Ltd [2016] EWCA Civ 1019; [2017] Env. L.R. D1, CA (Civ Div) .... *Digested,* 17/**309**

Peires v Bickerton's Aerodromes Ltd [2017] EWCA Civ 273; [2017] 1 W.L.R. 2865; [2017] 2 Lloyd's Rep. 330; [2017] Env. L.R. 32; [2017] L.L.R. 594, CA (Civ Div) *Digested,* 17/**92**

Pemberton v Inwood [2017] I.C.R. 929; [2017] I.R.L.R. 211, EAT .... *Digested,* 17/**784**

Pemberton v Pemberton [2016] EWHC 2345 (Ch); [2016] W.T.L.R. 1817, Ch D .... *Digested,* 17/**2222**

Peng v Chai see Chai v Peng

Pengal v Court of First Instance Antwerp, Belgium see Purcell v Belgium

Pengel v Prosecutor of the Court of First Instance Antwerp, Belgium see Purcell v Belgium

Peninsula Business Service Ltd v Baker; *sub nom* Peninsula Business Services Ltd v Baker [2017] I.C.R. 714; [2017] I.R.L.R. 394, EAT .... *Digested,* 17/**777**

Peninsula Business Services Ltd v Baker see Peninsula Business Service Ltd v Baker

Peninsular & Oriental Steam Navigation Co v Revenue and Customs Commissioners [2016] EWCA Civ 468; [2017] 1 W.L.R. 4489; [2017] 2 All E.R. 190; [2016] S.T.C. 2001; [2016] B.T.C. 21, CA (Civ Div) .... *Digested,* 16/**2056**

Penn v Bristol & West Building Society; *sub nom* Brill & Co v Penn [1997] 1 W.L.R. 1356; [1997] 3 All E.R. 470; [1997] 3 F.C.R. 789; [1997] P.N.L.R. 607; (1997) 74 P. & C.R. 210; Times, April 24, 1997; [1997] E.G. 54 (C.S.); (1997) 94(18) L.S.G. 32; (1997) 141 S.J.L.B. 105; [1997] N.P.C. 58, CA (Civ Div) .... *Digested,* 97/**1023**:
Applied 98/4027, 99/4379: *Considered* 17/44: *Followed* 99/4036

Penney v East Kent HA [2000] Lloyd's Rep. Med. 41; (2000) 55 B.M.L.R. 63; [2000] P.N.L.R. 323; Times, November 25, 1999; Independent, November 24, 1999; (1999) 96(47) L.S.G. 32; (1999) 143 S.J.L.B. 269, CA (Civ Div) .... *Digested,* 99/**3995**:
Applied 17/1561

Penrose v Official Receiver; *sub nom* Penrose v Secretary of State for Trade and Industry [1996] 1 W.L.R. 482; [1996] 2 All E.R. 96; [1995] B.C.C. 311; [1996] 1 B.C.L.C. 389; Times, December 19, 1995, Ch D .... *Digested,* 96/**3462**:
Applied 17/1297

Penrose v Secretary of State for Trade and Industry see Penrose v Official Receiver

Pensions Regulator v Dalriada Trustees Ltd see Bovey Cranbrook RBS, Re

Pensionsversicherungsanstalt v Brey (C-140/12) EU:C:2013:565; [2014] 1 W.L.R. 1080; [2014] 1 C.M.L.R. 37; [2014] All E.R. (EC) 534, ECJ (3rd Chamber)
Applied 14/1739: *Considered* 17/2658

Penten Group Ltd v Spartafield Ltd [2016] EWHC 317 (TCC); 165 Con. L.R. 97, QBD (TCC) .... *Digested,* 16/**584**:
Explained 17/494

Pentikainen v Finland (11882/10) (2017) 65 E.H.R.R. 21, ECHR (Grand Chamber)

Pepper v Hart see Pepper (Inspector of Taxes) v Hart

Pepper (Inspector of Taxes) v Hart; *sub nom* Pepper v Hart [1993] A.C. 593; [1992] 3 W.L.R. 1032; [1993] 1 All E.R. 42; [1992] S.T.C. 898; [1993] I.C.R. 291; [1993] I.R.L.R. 33; [1993] R.V.R. 127; Times, November 30, 1992; Independent, November 26, 1992; (1993) 143 N.L.J. 17; [1992] N.P.C. 154, HL .... *Digested,* 93/**459**:
Applied 93/3714, 94/2514, 98/321, 98/966, 01/4489, 03/3600, 05/4063, 09/3847, 10/2068: *Cited* 00/5239, 15/3150: *Considered* 93/1866, 93/2260, 93/3860, 93/426, 94/3413, 94/3900, 96/1297, 96/3928, 01/5174, 04/628, 05/2742, 06/635, 07/3064, 11/484, 12/2360, 13/1588: *Distinguished* 95/181, 95/2520, 97/4657, 00/2122, 01/4284: *Followed* 96/4190, 10/2755, 11/2667, 12/3127, 17/2138: *Not applied* 01/4206: *Referred to* 93/486, 94/2723, 94/2729, 94/353, 94/5459, 94/5899, 95/522, 95/861

Percy v Hall [1997] Q.B. 924; [1997] 3 W.L.R. 573; [1996] 4 All E.R. 523; Times, May 31, 1996; (1996) 160 J.P. Rep. 788; (1996) 93(23) L.S.G. 36; (1996) 140 S.J.L.B. 130; [1996] N.P.C. 74, CA (Civ Div) .... *Digested,* 96/**5688**:
Applied 97/4856, 13/253, 14/386, 15/1333, 15/1568, 17/1172:
Considered 14/3344: *Followed* 16/2149

Pereira v Secretary of State for the Home Department see R. (on the application of MA (Pakistan)) v Upper Tribunal (Immigration and Asylum Chamber)

Pereira de Souza v Vinci Construction UK Ltd; *sub nom* De Souza v Vinci Construction UK Ltd [2017] EWCA Civ 879; [2018] I.C.R. 433; [2017] I.R.L.R. 844, CA (Civ Div) .... *Digested,* 17/**782**

Pereira de Souza v Vinci Construction UK Ltd; *sub nom* De Souza v Vinci Construction UK Ltd [2015] I.C.R. 1034; [2015] I.R.L.R. 536, EAT .... *Digested,* 15/**804**:
Doubted 16/671: *Reversed* 17/782

Perez Lopez v Servicio Madrileno de Salud (Comunidad de Madrid) (C-16/15) EU:C:2016:679; [2017] 1 C.M.L.R. 33; [2016] I.C.R. 1168; [2016] I.R.L.R. 970, ECJ (10th Chamber)

Perinatal Institute v Healthcare Quality Improvement Partnership [2016] EWHC 2626 (TCC); 170 Con. L.R. 128, QBD (TCC) .... *Digested,* 17/**1810**

Perrins v Dooney see Perrins v Holland

Perrins v Holland; *sub nom* Perrins (Deceased), Re; *joined case* Perrins v Dooney [2010] EWCA Civ 840; [2011] Ch. 270; [2011] 2 W.L.R. 1086; [2011] 2 All E.R. 174; [2010] W.T.L.R. 1415; 13 I.T.E.L.R. 405; (2010) 160 N.L.J. 1076; (2010) 154(29) S.J.L.B. 34, CA (Civ Div) .... *Digested,* 11/**3267**:
Followed 17/2078

Perrins (Deceased), Re see Perrins v Holland

Perry v Raleys Solicitors [2017] EWCA Civ 314; [2017] P.N.L.R. 27, CA (Civ Div) .... *Digested,* 17/**1572**

Perry v Suffields Ltd [1916] 2 Ch. 187, CA
Applied 47-51/9262, 62/3110: *Considered* 95/3947, 17/496

Persimmon Homes (Thames Valley) Ltd v Stevenage BC; *sub nom* Persimmon Homes (Thames Valley) Ltd v Taylor Woodrow Homes Ltd [2005] EWCA Civ 1365; [2006] 1 W.L.R. 334; [2006] 1 P. & C.R. 31; [2006] J.P.L. 526; [2005] N.P.C. 136, CA (Civ Div) .... *Digested,* 06/**3304**:
Followed 17/1727

Persimmon Homes (Thames Valley) Ltd v Taylor Woodrow Homes Ltd see Persimmon Homes (Thames Valley) Ltd v Stevenage BC

Persimmon Homes Ltd v Ove Arup and Partners Ltd [2017] EWCA Civ 373; [2017] B.L.R. 417; 172 Con. L.R. 1; [2017] P.N.L.R. 29; [2017] C.I.L.L. 4005, CA (Civ Div) .... *Digested,* 17/**463**

Persimmon Homes Ltd v Ove Arup and Partners Ltd [2015] EWHC 3573 (TCC); [2016] B.L.R. 112; 163 Con. L.R. 191, QBD (TCC) .... *Digested,* 16/**403**:
Affirmed 17/463

Perth and Kinross Council v Scottish Water Ltd [2015] CSOH 138; 2015 S.L.T. 788; 2015 G.W.D. 34-547, OH .... *Digested,* 16/**2475**:
Affirmed 17/2454

Perth and Kinross Council v Scottish Water Ltd [2016] CSIH 83; 2017 S.C. 164; 2016 S.L.T. 1251; 2016 G.W.D. 35-627, IH (Ex Div) .... *Digested,* 17/**2454**:
Considered 17/2448

Peskova v Travel Service as (C-315/15) EU:C:2017:342; [2017] Bus. L.R. 1134, ECJ (3rd Chamber)

Petchey Islington Ltd v Islington LBC [2017] P.A.D. 22, Planning Inspector

Peters v East Midlands SHA; *joined case* East Midlands SHA v Nottingham City Council [2009] EWCA Civ 145; [2010] Q.B. 48; [2009] 3 W.L.R. 737; (2009) 12 C.C.L. Rep. 299; [2009] P.I.Q.R. Q1; [2009] LS Law Medical 229; Times, March 16, 2009; (2009) 153(9) S.J.L.B. 30, CA (Civ Div) .... *Digested,* 09/**2834**:
Applied 11/1619, 11/244, 15/1887: *Considered* 10/2252, 15/1743, 17/1540

Petit v Bradford Bulls (Northern) Ltd (In Administration) see Pettit v Bradford Bulls (Northern) Ltd (In Administration)

Petroalliance Services Co Ltd v Yukos Oil Co see Dardana Ltd v Yukos Oil Co (No.1)

Petrochemical Industries Co (KSC) v Dow Chemical Co [2012] EWHC 2739 (Comm); [2012] 2 Lloyd's Rep. 691; [2013] 2 C.L.C. 864; [2012] C.I.L.L. 3269, QBD (Comm) .... *Digested,* 13/**111**:
Applied 14/118, 17/73

Petrodel Resources Ltd v Prest; *sub nom* Prest v Petrodel Resources Ltd; P Resources Ltd v Prest; Prest v Prest [2013] UKSC 34; [2013] 2 A.C. 415; [2013] 3 W.L.R. 1; [2013] 4 All E.R. 673; [2013] B.C.C. 571; [2014] 1 B.C.L.C. 30; [2013] 2 F.L.R. 732; [2013] 3 F.C.R. 210; [2013] W.T.L.R. 1249; Times, June 24, 2013; [2013] Fam. Law 953; (2013) 163(7565) N.L.J. 27; (2013) 157(24) S.J.L.B. 37, SC .... *Digested,* 13/**1300**: *Applied* 13/362, 13/685, 16/507: *Considered* 14/1372, 14/1388, 16/342: *Followed* 15/601, 16/1823, 16/433, 16/503, 16/902, 17/1004

Petropavlovskis v Latvia (44230/06) (2017) 65 E.H.R.R. 7, ECHR

Petrotrade Inc v Texaco Ltd [2002] 1 W.L.R. 947 (Note); [2001] 4 All E.R. 853; [2001] C.P. Rep. 29; [2000] C.L.C. 1341; [2002] 1 Costs L.R. 60; Times, June 14, 2000; Independent, July 10, 2000, CA (Civ Div) .... *Digested,* 00/**539**: *Applied* 01/484, 02/346, 02/349, 10/388: *Considered* 02/347, 05/369, 07/343, 10/2401, 17/339

Petruhhin (C-182/15) see Criminal Proceedings against Petruhhin (C-182/15)

Petschulies v Germany (6281/13) [2017] M.H.L.R. 153, ECHR

Petter v EMC Europe Ltd [2015] EWCA Civ 828; [2015] C.P. Rep. 47; [2015] 2 C.L.C. 178; [2016] I.L.Pr. 3; [2015] I.R.L.R. 847, CA (Civ Div) .... *Digested,* 15/**208**: *Considered* 17/2000: *Followed* 16/366

Pettigrew v Edwards [2017] EWHC 8 (Ch); [2017] W.T.L.R. 675; [2017] 1 P. & C.R. DG19, Ch D .... *Digested,* 17/**2216**

Pettigrew v River Clyde Homes 2017 Hous. L.R. 15; 2017 G.W.D. 12-189, Lands Tr (Scot) .... *Digested,* 17/**2708**

Pettit v Bradford Bulls (Northern) Ltd (In Administration); *sub nom* Petit v Bradford Bulls (Northern) Ltd (In Administration); Bates v Green [2016] EWHC 3557 (Ch); [2017] B.C.C. 50; [2017] 2 B.C.L.C. 519, Ch D .... *Digested,* 17/**1268**

Peugeot Citroen Automobiles UK Ltd v Pilkington Group Ltd [2016] CAT 16; [2017] Comp. A.R. 43, CAT

Peugeot Citroen Automobiles UK Ltd v Pilkington Group Ltd see Deutsche Bahn AG v Mastercard Inc

Peugeot SA v NSK Ltd [2017] CAT 2; [2017] Comp. A.R. 103, CAT .... *Digested,* 17/**415**

PF v CF [2016] EWHC 3117 (Fam); [2017] 1 F.C.R. 266, Fam Div .... *Digested,* 17/**987**

Pfannenstiehl v Pfannenstiehl 19 I.T.E.L.R. 351, US Court

Pfeiffer v Deutsches Rotes Kreuz Kreisverband Waldshut eV (C-397/01) EU:C:2004:584; [2004] E.C.R. I-8835; [2005] 1 C.M.L.R. 44; [2005] I.C.R. 1307; [2005] I.R.L.R. 137, ECJ .... *Digested,* 05/**1275**: *Applied* 05/358, 07/1330, 07/1370, 09/1382, 15/832, 17/804: *Considered* 09/2292, 09/3032, 10/2352, 15/56: *Followed* 12/2679: *Referred to* 16/740

PGF II SA v OMFS Co 1 Ltd [2013] EWCA Civ 1288; [2014] 1 W.L.R. 1386; [2014] 1 All E.R. 970; [2014] C.P. Rep. 6; [2014] B.L.R. 1; 152 Con. L.R. 72; [2013] 6 Costs L.R. 973; [2013] 3 E.G.L.R. 16; [2013] 44 E.G. 98 (C.S.); (2013) 157(42) S.J.L.B. 37, CA (Civ Div) .... *Digested,* 14/**375**: *Applied* 17/1840, 17/272: *Considered* 15/231, 15/331, 17/266

PH v Italy see R. (on the application of HH) v Westminster City Magistrates' Court

Pham v Secretary of State for the Home Department; *sub nom* B2 v Secretary of State for the Home Department [2015] UKSC 19; [2015] 1 W.L.R. 1591; [2015] 3 All E.R. 1015; [2015] 2 C.M.L.R. 49; [2015] Imm. A.R. 950; [2015] I.N.L.R. 593; Times, April 9, 2015, SC .... *Digested,* 15/**1316**: *Considered* 16/2756, 17/1787: *Followed* 16/1094

Pharmacists' Defence Association Union v Boots Management Services Ltd see R. (on the application of Boots Management Services Ltd) v Central Arbitration Committee

Phensrisai v Yutikan [2017] CSOH 48; 2017 S.L.T. 631; 2017 G.W.D. 12-181, OH ...... *Digested,* 17/**2757**

PHI Group Ltd v Robert West Consulting Ltd see Carillion JM Ltd v PHI Group Ltd

Philex Plc v Golban see Ridehalgh v Horsefield

Philip Morris Brands Sarl v Secretary of State for Health (C-547/14) see R. (on the application of Philip Morris Brands Sarl) v Secretary of State for Health (C-547/14)

Philips Electronics NV v Remington Consumer Products Ltd (C-299/99) see Koninklijke Philips Electronics NV v Remington Consumer Products Ltd (C-299/99)

Philis v Greece (No.1) (A/209) (1991) 13 E.H.R.R. 741; Times, December 23, 1991, ECHR *Considered* 97/2810, 17/1453: *Distinguished* 05/1553

Phillip v Trinidad and Tobago see Huggins v Trinidad and Tobago

Phillips v Camden LBC see Cramp v Hastings BC

Phillips v Francis [2010] L. & T.R. 28; [2010] 2 E.G.L.R. 31; [2010] 24 E.G. 118, QBD (Truro) .... *Digested,* 10/**2090**: *Applied* 17/1441

Phillips v Magill see Porter v Magill

Phillips v Nussberger see Phillips v Symes (A Bankrupt)

Phillips v Peace [1996] 2 F.L.R. 230; [1996] 2 F.C.R. 237; [1996] Fam. Law 603, Fam Div .... *Digested,* 96/**2854**: *Applied* 09/1487, 17/1006: *Approved* 07/1767: *Considered* 01/2636

Phillips v Symes (A Bankrupt); *sub nom* Nussberger v Phillips; Phillips v Nussberger [2008] UKHL 1; [2008] 1 W.L.R. 180; [2008] 2 All E.R. 537; [2008] 1 All E.R. (Comm) 918; [2008] 1 Lloyd's Rep. 344; [2008] 1 C.L.C. 29; [2008] I.L.Pr. 21; Times, January 28, 2008; (2008) 152(4) S.J.L.B. 28, HL .... *Digested,* 08/**420**: *Applied* 08/419: *Considered* 10/416, 15/362, 16/286, 17/366

Phillips v Willis [2016] EWCA Civ 401; [2016] C.P. Rep. 28; [2016] 3 Costs L.R. 473; [2017] R.T.R. 4, CA (Civ Div) .... *Digested,* 16/**281**

Phillips & Co v Bath Housing Co-operative Ltd [2012] EWCA Civ 1591; [2013] 1 W.L.R. 1479; [2013] 2 All E.R. 475; [2013] C.P. Rep. 12; [2013] 1 Costs L.R. 163; [2013] B.P.I.R. 102; [2013] 1 E.G. 48 (C.S.), CA (Civ Div) .... *Digested,* 13/**392**: *Considered* 17/2219

Phillips Petroleum Co (UK) Ltd v Enron (Europe) Ltd [1997] C.L.C. 329, CA (Civ Div) .. *Digested,* 97/**4951**: *Applied* 06/683, 12/639: *Considered* 08/2966, 09/719, 12/158, 17/500: *Followed* 14/630

Phillips Petroleum Co (UK) Ltd v Snamprogetti Ltd; *sub nom* Snamprogetti Ltd v Phillips Petroleum Co (UK) Ltd [2001] EWCA Civ 889; 79 Con. L.R. 80, CA (Civ Div) .... *Digested,* 02/**706**: *Considered* 17/1817

Phoenix House Ltd v Stockman [2017] I.C.R. 84; [2016] I.R.L.R. 848, EAT .... *Digested,* 16/**729**

Phonographic Performance Ltd v CGK Trading Ltd [2016] EWHC 2642 (Ch); [2017] L.L.R. 161, Ch D .... *Digested,* 17/**1360**

Phonographic Performance Ltd v Hagan (t/a Lower Ground Bar and Brent Tavern) [2016] EWHC 3076 (IPEC); [2017] F.S.R. 24, IPEC .... *Digested,* 17/**1359**

Phononet (Unauthorised Use of DVD on Internet Website without Performer's Consent) (I ZR 88/13) [2017] E.C.C. 15; [2017] E.C.D.R. 24, BGH (Ger)

Phosphate Sewage Co Ltd v Molleson (Res Judicata); *joined case* Official Liquidator v Molleson (1879) 4 App. Cas. 801; (1879) 6 R. (H.L.) 113, HL *Applied* 80/2609, 82/2382, 90/3542, 08/1432, 08/272, 14/2209: *Considered* 17/2412: *Followed* 17/372

PHP Tobacco Carib Sarl v BAT Caribbean SA; *sub nom* BAT Caribbean SA v PHP Tobacco Carib Sarl [2016] EWHC 3377 (Comm), QBD (Comm) *Affirmed* 17/295

PHP Tobacco Carib Sarl v BAT Caribbean SA; *sub nom* BAT Caribbean SA v PHP Tobacco Carib Sarl [2017] EWCA Civ 1131; [2017] C.P. Rep. 44, CA (Civ Div) . *Digested,* 17/**295**

PI Consulting (Trustee Services) Ltd v Pensions Regulator; *sub nom* Dalriada Trustees Ltd v Nidd Vale Trustees Ltd [2013] EWHC 3181 (Ch); [2013] Pens. L.R. 433, Ch D .... *Digested,* 14/**2265**: *Applied* 17/1609

Pickard v Marshall; *sub nom* Pickard v Motor Insurers' Bureau; *joined case* Generali France Assurances v Marshall [2017] EWCA Civ 17; [2017] R.T.R. 20, CA (Civ Div) .... *Digested,* 17/**431**

Pickard v Motor Insurers' Bureau see Pickard v Marshall

Pickering v Davy see Davy v Pickering

Pickett v British Rail Engineering Ltd; *sub nom* Ralph Henry Pickett (Deceased), Re [1980] A.C. 136; [1978] 3 W.L.R. 955; [1979] 1 All E.R. 774; [1979] 1 Lloyd's Rep. 519; (1978) 122 S.J. 778, HL .... *Digested,* 79/**656**: *Applied* 79/2367, 81/581, 82/771, 82/791, 84/1030, 85/1036, 89/2195, 07/3071, 17/638: *Considered* 79/2150, 79/663, 79/669, 79/702, 80/633, 80/748, 82/772, 82/774, 83/976, 08/360, 08/892, 15/1890: *Distinguished* 84/1042: *Followed* 96/2126

Piedmont Trust, Re see Jasmine Trustees Ltd v L

Pierce v Bemis (The Lusitania) [1986] Q.B. 384; [1986] 2 W.L.R. 501; [1986] 1 All E.R. 1011; [1986] 1 Lloyd's Rep. 132; Times, November 30, 1985; (1986) 130 S.J. 202, QBD (Admlty) .... *Digested,* 86/**3101**: *Applied* 17/2019

Pieretti v Enfield LBC [2010] EWCA Civ 1104; [2011] 2 All E.R. 642; [2011] P.T.S.R. 565; [2010] Eq. L.R. 312; [2011] H.L.R. 3; [2010] B.L.G.R. 944; (2010) 13 C.C.L. Rep. 650; [2010] N.P.C. 98, CA (Civ Div) .... *Digested,* 11/**1648**: *Applied* 14/1601, 17/1146: *Considered* 11/2168, 14/1596, 14/2017

Piglowska v Piglowski [1999] 1 W.L.R. 1360; [1999] 3 All E.R. 632; [1999] 2 F.L.R. 763; [1999] 2 F.C.R. 481; Times, June 25, 1999; [1999] Fam. Law 617; (1999) 96(27) L.S.G. 34; (1999) 143 S.J.L.B. 190, HL .... *Digested,* 99/**2421**: *Applied* 06/1633, 07/1766, 11/1344, 14/1283, 15/1073: *Considered* 00/2489, 01/2632, 01/4450, 09/603, 13/1280, 13/6, 14/1254, 17/1049: *Followed* 11/1332, 13/1224, 15/980, 17/944

Pihl v Sweden (Admissibility) (74742/14) (2017) 64 E.H.R.R. SE20, ECHR

Pilecki v Circuit Court of Legnica see Pilecki v Poland

Pilecki v Poland; *sub nom* Pilecki v Circuit Court of Legnica [2008] UKHL 7; [2008] 1 W.L.R. 325; [2008] 4 All E.R. 445; [2008] Extradition L.R. 78; Times, February 14, 2008; (2008) 152(6) S.J.L.B. 29, HL .... *Digested,* 08/**1397**: *Considered* 12/1282: *Distinguished* 17/908: *Followed* 08/1398

Pilkington UK Ltd v CGU Insurance Plc [2004] EWCA Civ 23; [2005] 1 All E.R. (Comm) 283; [2004] 1 C.L.C. 1059; [2004] B.L.R. 97; [2004] T.C.L.R. 5; [2004] Lloyd's Rep. I.R. 891; [2004] N.P.C. 10, CA (Civ Div) .... *Digested,* 05/**2378**: *Applied* 13/1733, 17/1338: *Considered* 07/2482

Pilon Ltd v Breyer Group Plc [2010] EWHC 837 (TCC); [2010] B.L.R. 452; 130 Con. L.R. 90; [2010] C.I.L.L. 2865; [2011] Bus. L.R. D42, QBD (TCC) .... *Digested,* 10/**845**: *Applied* 11/871, 13/523, 16/389: *Considered* 13/3550, 15/463, 17/453

Pimlico Plumbers Ltd v Smith UKEAT/0495/12/DM, EAT *Affirmed* 17/793

Pimlico Plumbers Ltd v Smith [2017] EWCA Civ 51; [2017] I.C.R. 657; [2017] I.R.L.R. 323; Times, March 9, 2017, CA (Civ Div) .... *Digested,* 17/**793**: *Followed* 17/788

Pindos Shipping Corp v Raven (The Mata Hari) [1983] 2 Lloyd's Rep. 449, QBD (Comm) .... *Digested,* 83/**3454**: *Applied* 08/2196: *Considered* 09/2278, 17/1817

Pineport Ltd v Grangeglen Ltd [2016] EWHC 1318 (Ch); [2016] L. & T.R. 28, Ch D ...... *Digested,* 17/**1447**

Pinfold v Ansell see Foundry Miniatures Ltd, Re

Pinisetty v Manikonda [2017] EWHC 838 (QB); [2017] 5 Costs L.O. 565, QBD

Pinnock v Manchester City Council see Manchester City Council v Pinnock

Pinterest Inc v Premium Interest Ltd [2015] EWHC 738 (Ch); [2015] E.C.C. 14; [2015] E.T.M.R. 30; [2015] F.S.R. 27, Ch D .... *Digested,* 15/**1526**: *Applied* 17/386

Piotrowski v Poland (Admissibility) (8923/12) (2017) 64 E.H.R.R. SE6, ECHR

PIP Breast Implant Litigation, Re see XYZ v Various Companies

Pipe v Revenue and Customs Commissioners [2008] EWHC 646 (Ch); [2008] S.T.C. 1911; [2008] Lloyd's Rep. F.C. 364; [2008] B.T.C. 558; [2008] S.T.I. 1151, Ch D .... *Digested,* 08/**3873**: *Applied* 17/2082: *Considered* 10/3363, 17/2187

Piscarreta Ricardo v Portimao Urbis EM SA (C-416/16) EU:C:2017:574; [2017] I.C.R. 1451, ECJ (8th Chamber)

Pitman v Trinidad and Tobago; *joined case* Hernandez v Trinidad and Tobago [2017] UKPC 6; [2018] A.C. 35; [2017] 3 W.L.R. 790, PC (Trin)

Pittalis v Grant [1989] Q.B. 605; [1989] 3 W.L.R. 139; [1989] 2 All E.R. 622; (1989) 21 H.L.R. 368; [1989] 28 E.G. 126; [1989] E.G. 37 (C.S.); (1989) 139 N.L.J. 578; (1989) 133 S.J. 752, CA (Civ Div) .... *Digested,* 89/**2890**: *Applied* 92/2755, 13/1738, 16/432: *Considered* 92/1553, 95/3082, 97/3332, 07/3989, 13/2427, 13/439: *Distinguished* 92/4507: *Followed* 17/1876: *Not followed* 97/3334

Pittville Ltd v Hunters & Frankau Ltd [2016] EWHC 2683 (Ch); [2016] 6 Costs L.R. 1059, Ch D .... *Digested,* 17/**383**

Pizzo v CRGT Srl (C-27/15) EU:C:2016:404; [2017] 1 C.M.L.R. 1, ECJ (6th Chamber)

PJ (A Patient) v A Local Health Board; *sub nom* Secretary of State for Justice v MM; Welsh Ministers v PJ [2015] UKUT 480 (AAC); [2015] C.O.P.L.R. 756; [2016] M.H.L.R. 178, UT (AAC) .... *Digested,* 16/**1480**: *Reversed* 17/1538

PJ (A Patient) v Local Health Board; *sub nom* Secretary of State for Justice v MM; Welsh Ministers v PJ [2017] EWCA Civ 194; [2017] 1 W.L.R. 4681; [2017] C.O.P.L.R. 319; (2017) 20 C.C.L. Rep. 282; [2017] Med. L.R. 230; [2017] M.H.L.R. 282, CA (Civ Div) .... *Digested,* 17/**1538**: *Applied* 17/1541

PJS v News Group Newspapers Ltd [2016] UKSC 26; [2016] A.C. 1081; [2016] 2 W.L.R. 1253; [2016] 4 All E.R. 554; [2016] E.M.L.R. 21; [2016] 2 F.L.R. 251; [2016] H.R.L.R. 13; 42 B.H.R.C. 111; [2016] F.S.R. 33; [2016] Fam. Law 963, SC .... *Digested,* 16/**284**: *Followed* 17/1028, 17/3, 17/342

PJSC Tatneft v Bogolyubov [2016] EWHC 2816 (Comm); [2017] 1 All E.R. (Comm) 833, QBD (Comm) .... *Digested,* 17/**370**

PL (Jamaica) v Secretary of State for the Home Department see GS (India) v Secretary of State for the Home Department

Pla v Andorra (69498/01) [2004] 2 F.C.R. 630; (2006) 42 E.H.R.R. 25; 18 B.H.R.C. 120, ECHR .... *Digested,* 05/**2126**: *Applied* 12/3366, 17/2074

Plant Force (Leeds) Ltd v Revenue and Customs Commissioners [2017] UKFTT 349 (TC); [2017] S.T.I. 1177, FTT (Tax)

Plantiflor Ltd v Customs and Excise Commissioners see Customs and Excise Commissioners v Plantiflor Ltd

Plasticos Espanoles SA (ASPLA) v European Union (T-40/15) EU:T:2017:105; [2017] 5 C.M.L.R. 12, GC (3rd Chamber)

Platform Funding Ltd v Bank of Scotland Plc (formerly Halifax Plc) [2008] EWCA Civ 930; [2009] Q.B. 426; [2009] 2 W.L.R. 1016; [2009] 2 All E.R. 344; [2009] 2 All E.R. (Comm) 143; 120 Con. L.R. 201; [2009] P.N.L.R. 4; [2008] 3 E.G.L.R. 83; [2008] 42 E.G. 168; Times, October 6, 2008; [2008] 32 E.G. 83 (C.S.), CA (Civ Div) .... *Digested,* 08/**656**: *Applied* 10/88: *Considered* 12/622, 17/44

Platt v London Underground Ltd [2001] 2 E.G.L.R. 121; Times, March 13, 2001; Independent, April 2, 2001; [2001] 20 E.G. 227 (C.S.); (2001) 98(17) L.S.G. 37, Ch D .... *Digested,* 01/**4152**: *Applied* 09/3184: *Followed* 17/1436

Platt v Platt (1976) 6 Fam. Law 107; (1976) 120 S.J. 199, CA (Civ Div) .... *Digested,* 76/**158**: *Followed* 17/1282

Playboy Club London Ltd v Banca Nazionale del Lavoro SpA [2016] EWCA Civ 457; [2016] 1 W.L.R. 3169; [2017] 1 All E.R. (Comm) 309; [2016] 2 B.C.L.C. 442, CA (Civ Div) .... *Digested,* 16/**1537**

Plevin v Paragon Personal Finance Ltd; *joined case* Conlon v Black Horse Ltd [2014] UKSC 61; [2014] 1 W.L.R. 4222; [2015] 1 All E.R. 625; [2015] 1 All E.R. (Comm) 1007; [2014] Bus. L.R. 1257; [2015] E.C.C. 2; [2015] Lloyd's Rep. I.R. 247, SC .... *Digested,* 15/**492**: *Applied* 16/420: *Considered* 15/505: *Followed* 17/481

Plevin v Paragon Personal Finance Ltd [2017] UKSC 23; [2017] 1 W.L.R. 1249; [2018] 1 All E.R. 292; [2017] 2 Costs L.O. 247; Times, April 6, 2017, SC .... *Digested,* 17/**221**: *Considered* 17/310: *Followed* 17/226, 17/240

Plewa v Chief Adjudication Officer [1995] 1 A.C. 249; [1994] 3 W.L.R. 317; [1994] 3 All E.R. 323; Times, July 9, 1994; Independent, July 29, 1994; (1994) 91(30) L.S.G. 32; (1994) 138 S.J.L.B. 152, HL .... *Digested,* 94/**4179**: *Applied* 97/2241, 17/2772

Plockl v Finanzamt Schrobenhausen (C-24/15) EU:C:2016:791; [2017] S.T.C. 379; [2016] B.V.C. 38; [2016] S.T.I. 2825, ECJ (4th Chamber)

Ploski v Poland (26761/95) [2003] Prison L.R. 120, ECHR *Applied* 17/1645

Plummer v Johnstone (Unreported, March 20, 2017), CC (Bolton) [*Irwin Mitchell LLP, 1 Millsands, Sheffield*] .... *Digested,* 17/**1686**

Pluss Organisation Ltd v Gidman (Valuation Officer) [2017] R.A. 265, VT .... *Digested,* 17/**1516**

PML Accounting Ltd v Revenue and Customs Commissioners [2017] EWHC 733 (Admin); [2017] S.T.C. 1091; [2017] B.T.C. 10; [2017] S.T.I. 1101, QBD (Admin) .... *Digested,* 17/**2125**

PN (A Child) (Care Proceedings: Flawed Assessments), Re; *sub nom* Cheshire East BC v NA [2017] EWFC 20; [2017] 4 W.L.R. 56, Fam Ct .... *Digested,* 17/**937**

PNM v Times Newspapers Ltd; *sub nom* M v Times Newspapers Ltd; Khuja v Times Newspapers Ltd [2014] EWCA Civ 1132; [2014] C.P. Rep. 48; [2015] 1 Cr. App. R. 1; [2014] E.M.L.R. 30, CA (Civ Div) .... *Digested,* 14/**790**: *Affirmed* 17/332: *Applied* 17/2199

PNM v Times Newspapers Ltd see Khuja v Times Newspapers Ltd

Pocock v Highland Council [2017] CSOH 40; 2017 Rep. L.R. 69; 2017 G.W.D. 10-142, OH .... *Digested,* 17/**2739**

Pointstar Shipping & Finance Ltd v 7 Strathray Gardens Ltd see 7 Strathray Gardens Ltd v Pointstar Shipping & Finance Ltd

Poland v Biskup see Wolkowicz v Poland

Poland v Celinski; *joined cases* Poland v Pawelec; Poland v Ciemiega; Poland v Nida; Slovakia v Cambal; R. (on the application of Inglot) v Secretary of State for the Home Deparment [2015] EWHC 1274 (Admin); [2016] 1 W.L.R. 551; [2016] 3 All E.R. 71; [2015] A.C.D. 125, DC .... *Digested,* 16/**797**: *Applied* 16/801: *Considered* 16/2633, 16/798: *Followed* 17/901

Poland v Ciemiega see Poland v Celinski

Poland v Ciureja; *sub nom* District Court in Legnica, Poland v Ciureja [2016] EWHC 2931 (Admin); [2017] A.C.D. 5, QBD (Admin)
Poland v Nida see Poland v Celinski
Poland v Pawelec see Poland v Celinski
Poland v Ulatowski [2010] EWHC 2673 (Admin); [2011] Lloyd's Rep. F.C. 18, QBD (Admin) .... *Digested,* 11/**1274**: *Followed* 17/909
Poland v Wolkowicz see Wolkowicz v Poland
Pole v Peake Times, July 22, 1998; [1998] E.G. 125 (C.S.); [1998] N.P.C. 121, CA (Civ Div) .... *Digested,* 98/**4373**: *Applied* 17/1854
Pole 2 Pole Scaffolding Ltd v Sqibb Group Ltd see Squibb Group Ltd v Pole 2 Pole Scaffolding Ltd
Poletan v Macedonia (26711/07) (2017) 65 E.H.R.R. 25, ECHR
Policie CR,Krajske Reditelstvi Policie Usteckeho Kraje, Odbor Cizinecke Policie v Al Chodor (C-528/15) EU:C:2017:213; [2017] 4 W.L.R. 125; [2017] 3 C.M.L.R. 24, ECJ (2nd Chamber)
Followed 17/1226
Pollard v Ashurst see Ashurst v Pollard
Pollard v University Hospitals of North Midlands NHS Trust [2017] 1 Costs L.R. 45, QBD (Birmingham)
Polo Club v EUIPO (T-67/15) EU:T:2016:657; [2017] E.T.M.R. 7, GC (9th Chamber)
Pompa's Trustees v Edinburgh Burgh Council 1942 S.C. 119; 1942 S.L.T. 118, IH (2 Div)
Applied 63/4108, 83/4964, 90/5395, 08/4591: *Considered* 91/5470, 08/4593, 17/2454: *Distinguished* 61/10496
Popandopulo v Russia (4512/09) (2017) 64 E.H.R.R. 21, ECHR
Poplar Housing and Regeneration Community Association Ltd v Begum [2017] EWHC 2040 (QB); [2017] H.L.R. 42; [2018] 1 P. & C.R. DG4, QBD
Poplawski v Openbaar Ministerie (C-579/15) EU:C:2017:503; [2017] 4 W.L.R. 173, ECJ (5th Chamber)
Popperl v Land Nordrhein-Westfalen (C-187/15) EU:C:2016:550; [2017] 1 C.M.L.R. 21; [2017] C.E.C. 1095, ECJ (1st Chamber)
Port of London Authority v Mendoza [2017] UKUT 146 (TCC); [2017] 2 P. & C.R. DG12, UT (Tax)
Porteous v West Dorset DC [2004] EWCA Civ 244; [2004] H.L.R. 30; [2004] B.L.G.R. 577; Independent, March 12, 2004; (2004) 148 S.J.L.B. 300, CA (Civ Div) .... *Digested,* 04/**1893**: *Applied* 15/1192, 17/1149: *Followed* 14/1493
Porter v Magill; *sub nom* Magill v Porter; Magill v Weeks; *joined cases* Phillips v Magill; England v Magill; Hartley v Magill; Weeks v Magill [2001] UKHL 67; [2002] 2 A.C. 357; [2002] 2 W.L.R. 37; [2002] 1 All E.R. 465; [2002] H.R.L.R. 16; [2002] H.L.R. 16; [2002] B.L.G.R. 51; Times, December 14, 2001; Independent, February 4, 2002; Daily Telegraph, December 20, 2001; (2001) 151 N.L.J. 1886; [2001] N.P.C. 184, HL .... *Digested,* 02/**3185**:
Applied 03/1251, 03/1261, 03/319, 04/2652, 04/30, 05/13, 05/2153, 05/2908, 05/3279, 05/894, 06/207, 06/2755, 06/3339, 06/3346, 06/3987, 06/967, 07/1343, 07/1428, 07/31, 07/3252, 07/3264, 08/370, 08/834, 09/2456, 10/1722, 10/2144, 10/2805, 11/4221, 12/749, 13/760, 16/1725, 17/1486: *Considered* 02/294, 02/451, 05/646, 08/2935, 09/24, 12/2095, 12/970, 16/2226, 16/924: *Followed* 03/5397, 04/1904, 04/4467, 10/1691, 10/768, 11/3598, 12/581, 13/262, 14/42, 15/2014, 15/219, 15/373, 15/825, 15/876, 15/93, 16/2237, 16/388, 17/1560, 17/210, 17/5
Portman Building Society v Bevan Ashford [2000] Lloyd's Rep. Bank. 96; [2000] Lloyd's Rep. P.N. 354; [2000] P.N.L.R. 344; (2000) 80 P. & C.R. 239; [2000] 1 E.G.L.R. 81; [2000] 07 E.G. 131; [2000] E.G. 2 (C.S.); (2000) 79 P. & C.R. D25, CA (Civ Div)
Considered 15/1792: *Distinguished* 11/2259: *Followed* 13/1950: *Overruled* 17/641
Portman Estate Nominees (One) Ltd v Starlight Headlease Ltd [2016] UKUT 467 (LC); [2017] 1 P. & C.R. 10; [2017] L. & T.R. 11, UT (Lands) .... *Digested,* 17/**1844**
Portman Insurance Plc, Re [2016] EWHC 2994 (Ch); [2017] B.C.C. 30, Ch D (Companies Ct) .... *Digested,* 17/**396**
Porton Capital Technology Funds (A Body Corporate) v 3M UK Holdings Ltd [2010] EWHC 114 (Comm), QBD (Comm)
Applied 17/216
Portsmouth City Council v King see King (A Child), Re
Porzelack KG v Porzelack (UK) Ltd [1987] 1 W.L.R. 420; [1987] 1 All E.R. 1074; [1987] 2 C.M.L.R. 333; [1987] E.C.C. 407; [1987] F.S.R. 353, Ch D .... *Digested,* 87/**2954**: *Applied* 90/3607, 90/3609: *Approved* 90/3608: *Considered* 89/3042, 17/78

Poshteh v Kensington and Chelsea RLBC [2015] EWCA Civ 711; [2015] H.L.R. 36, CA (Civ Div) .... *Digested,* 15/**1271**: *Affirmed* 17/1147

Poshteh v Kensington and Chelsea RLBC [2017] UKSC 36; [2017] A.C. 624; [2017] 2 W.L.R. 1417; [2017] 3 All E.R. 1065; [2017] H.L.R. 28; Times, May 16, 2017, SC .... *Digested,* 17/**1147**

Post Office v Norwich Union Fire Insurance Society Ltd [1967] 2 Q.B. 363; [1967] 2 W.L.R. 709; [1967] 1 All E.R. 577; [1967] 1 Lloyd's Rep. 216; (1967) 111 S.J. 71, CA (Civ Div) .... *Digested,* 67/**2038**: *Applied* 98/6113, 08/2225, 12/1889: *Approved* 89/2064: *Considered* 69/1825, 74/1887, 74/1904, 74/266.u, 85/2013, 94/2067, 96/3508, 03/2455, 17/1338: *Followed* 11/1927

Potts v Gibson [2016] SAC (Crim) 25; 2016 S.C.L. 819; 2016 S.C.C.R. 412; 2016 G.W.D. 29-520, SAC .... *Digested,* 16/**2583**: *Affirmed* 17/2564

Potts v Gibson see Potts (Donnie Daniel) v Procurator Fiscal, Hamilton

Potts (Donnie Daniel) v Procurator Fiscal, Hamilton; *sub nom* Potts v Gibson [2017] HCJAC 8; 2017 J.C. 194; 2017 S.L.T. 313; 2017 S.C.L. 222; 2017 S.C.C.R. 109; 2017 G.W.D. 7-98, HCJ .... *Digested,* 17/**2564**

Pounds v Pounds [1994] 1 W.L.R. 1535; [1994] 4 All E.R. 777; [1994] 1 F.L.R. 775; Times, March 17, 1994; Independent, March 3, 1994; [1994] Fam. Law 436; (1994) 144 N.L.J. 459, CA (Civ Div) .... *Digested,* 95/**2337**: *Applied* 15/1097: *Considered* 17/1002

Pounds Shipowners & Shipbreakers Ltd v Garner (Inspector of Taxes) see Garner (Inspector of Taxes) v Pounds Shipowners & Shipbreakers Ltd

Poundstretcher v Secretary of State for the Environment [1988] 3 P.L.R. 69; [1989] J.P.L. 90; [1988] E.G. 89 (C.S.) .... *Digested,* 89/**3560**: *Applied* 03/3414: *Considered* 00/4506, 01/4736: *Followed* 17/1772: *Referred to* 96/4819

Pour v Secretary of State for the Home Department [2016] EWHC 401 (Admin); [2016] 2 C.M.L.R. 47; [2016] Imm. A.R. 721; [2016] A.C.D. 65, QBD (Admin) .... *Digested,* 16/**1066**: *Applied* 17/1177

Powell v Hounslow LBC see Hounslow LBC v Powell

Powell v Maddison see Ellenborough Park, Re

Powell Duffryn Plc v Petereit (C-214/89) EU:C:1992:115; [1992] E.C.R. I-1745; [1992] I.L.Pr. 300; Times, April 15, 1992, ECJ .... *Digested,* 92/**4826**: *Applied* 13/362, 16/434: *Considered* 09/608, 13/509, 17/295

Power v Chief Constable of Lancashire see Hunter v Chief Constable of the West Midlands

Power Curber International Ltd v National Bank of Kuwait SAK [1981] 1 W.L.R. 1233; [1981] 3 All E.R. 607; [1981] 2 Lloyd's Rep. 394; [1981] Com. L.R. 224, CA (Civ Div) .... *Digested,* 81/**149**: *Disapproved* 17/165: *Explained* 91/510: *Followed* 15/189, 17/167: *Referred to* 95/399

Powertrain Ltd, Re [2015] EWHC 3998 (Ch); [2016] B.C.C. 216; [2017] 1 B.C.L.C. 95; [2016] B.P.I.R. 456, Ch D (Birmingham) .... *Digested,* 16/**1227**

Powles v Reeves [2016] EWCA Civ 1375; [2017] 1 Costs L.R. 19, CA (Civ Div)

Powlson v Welbeck Securities Ltd see Welbeck Securities Ltd v Powlson (Inspector of Taxes)

Powys CC v Price see Price v Powys CC

Pozzoli SpA v BDMO SA [2007] EWCA Civ 588; [2007] F.S.R. 37; (2007) 30(8) I.P.D. 30051; [2007] Bus. L.R. D117, CA (Civ Div) .... *Digested,* 07/**2634**: *Applied* 08/2332, 09/2396, 09/2406, 09/2407, 10/1966, 10/1968, 10/1969, 10/1973, 10/1974, 10/1981, 10/2014, 11/1972, 11/1979, 15/1501, 16/1322: *Considered* 15/1517, 16/1298, 16/1312: *Followed* 10/1980, 11/1956, 12/1940, 14/1897, 16/1311, 16/1318: *Not followed* 17/1368

PR Hardman & Partners v Greenwood [2015] UKUT 587 (LC), UT (Lands) *Affirmed* 17/1467

PR Hardman & Partners v Greenwood [2017] EWCA Civ 52; [2017] 4 W.L.R. 59; [2017] H.L.R. 17; [2017] 2 P. & C.R. DG3, CA (Civ Div) .... *Digested,* 17/**1467**

Practice Direction (CA (Crim Div): Criminal Proceedings: General Matters); *sub nom* Criminal Practice Directions 2015 [2015] EWCA Crim 1567, CA (Crim Div) *Considered* 17/624

Practice Direction (CA: Citation of Authorities) [2001] 1 W.L.R. 1001; [2001] 2 All E.R. 510; [2001] 1 Lloyd's Rep. 725; [2001] C.P.L.R. 301; [2001] 1 F.C.R. 764; Times, May 1, 2001; (2001) 145 S.J.L.B. 132, CA (Civ Div) .... *Digested,* 01/**623**: *Cited* 10/297: *Considered* 02/483, 17/570: *Followed* 12/1840

Practice Direction (Fam Div: Wards: Witness in Criminal Proceedings) [1988] 1 W.L.R. 989; [1988] 2 All E.R. 1015; [1988] Fam. Law 394, Fam Div .... *Digested*, 88/**639**: *Considered* 91/2591: *Referred to* 17/1069

Practice Direction (Fam Div: Wards: Witness in Criminal Proceedings) [1987] 1 W.L.R. 1739; [1988] 1 All E.R. 223; [1988] 1 F.L.R. 183; (1987) 131 S.J. 1542, Fam Div .... *Digested*, 87/**654**: *Applied* 91/2591: *Considered* 90/3193: *Referred to* 17/1069

Practice Direction: Insolvency Proceedings [2014] B.C.C. 502; [2014] B.P.I.R. 1286, Ch D .... *Digested*, 15/**1426**: *Applied* 15/1414, 16/1225: *Cited* 17/1292: *Considered* 17/1327, 17/345: *Referred to* 17/1330

Practice Guidance (Fam Ct: Duration of Ex Parte (Without Notice) Orders [2014] 3 F.C.R. 402, Fam Ct .... *Digested*, 15/**1145**: *Superseded* 17/1051

Practice Guidance (Fam Ct: Duration of Ex Parte (Without Notice) Orders) see Practice Guidance (Family Courts: Without Notice Orders)

Practice Guidance (Family Courts: Radicalisation Cases); *sub nom* President's Guidance: Radicalisation Cases in the Family Courts [2017] 1 W.L.R. 4452; [2016] 1 F.C.R. 617, Fam Div

Practice Guidance (Family Courts: Serious Case Reviews) [2017] 1 W.L.R. 1779, Fam Div

Practice Guidance (Family Courts: Without Notice Orders); *sub nom* Practice Guidance (Fam Ct: Duration of Ex Parte (Without Notice) Orders) [2017] 1 W.L.R. 478, Fam Div .... *Digested*, 17/**1051**

Practice Guidance (HC: Interim Non-Disclosure Orders) [2012] 1 W.L.R. 1003; [2012] E.M.L.R. 5, Sen Cts .... *Digested*, 12/**436**: *Applied* 17/353: *Cited* 12/2: *Considered* 13/377, 15/343

Practice Note (Ch D: Relating to the Insolvency Proceedings Practice Direction) [2017] B.C.C. 221, Ch D .... *Digested*, 17/**345**

Practice Note (HL: Judicial Precedent) see Practice Statement (HL: Judicial Precedent)

Practice Statement (HL: Judicial Precedent); *sub nom* Practice Note (HL: Judicial Precedent) [1966] 1 W.L.R. 1234; [1966] 3 All E.R. 77; [1966] 2 Lloyd's Rep. 151; (1986) 83 Cr. App. R. 191 (Note); (1966) 110 S.J. 584, HL .... *Digested*, 66/**9921**: *Applied* 75/2657, 16/1606: *Considered* 78/1590, 83/1908, 86/482, 08/385, 17/1595

Practice Surgeries Ltd v Srivatsa UKEAT/0212/15/RN UKEAT/0213/15/RN UKEAT/0214/15/RN UKEAT/0215/15, EAT
Considered 17/797

Prankl v Zollamt Wien (C-175/14) EU:C:2015:142; [2015] S.T.C. 1375, ECJ (6th Chamber)
Applied 17/631

Pratt v Crown Prosecution Service (Northumbria) see L v DPP

Pratt v Smith HQ0000539, QBD
Applied 17/1671

Prattley Enterprises Ltd v Vero Insurance New Zealand Ltd [2017] Lloyd's Rep. I.R. 175, Sup Ct (NZ)

Preddy v Bull see Hall v Bull

Prekopp (Valuation Officer) v GPS (Great Britain) Ltd (t/a Gap) [2016] UKUT 127 (LC); [2017] R.V.R. 271, UT (Lands) .... *Digested*, 17/**1524**

Premier Motorauctions Ltd (In Liquidation) v PricewaterhouseCoopers LLP [2016] EWHC 2610 (Ch); [2017] 4 All E.R. 243; [2017] 2 All E.R. (Comm) 681; [2017] Bus. L.R. 490; [2017] B.P.I.R. 182; [2017] Lloyd's Rep. I.R. 186, Ch D .... *Digested*, 17/**358**

Premium Nafta Products Ltd v Fili Shipping Co Ltd see Fiona Trust & Holding Corp v Privalov

Presbyterian Support (Upper South Island) v New Zealand Guardian Trust Co Ltd [2016] NZCA 556; 19 I.T.E.L.R. 856, CA (NZ)

Prescott v University of St Andrews [2016] CSOH 3; 2016 G.W.D. 4-99, OH
Considered 17/2429

President of the Methodist Conference v Preston (formerly Moore) see Moore v President of the Methodist Conference

President's Guidance: Radicalisation Cases in the Family Courts see Practice Guidance (Family Courts: Radicalisation Cases)

Press v Ageas Insurance Ltd (Unreported, January 30, 2017), CC (Derby) [*IMe Law Ltd, Riverside West, 1 Millsands, Sheffield*] .... *Digested*, 17/**1682**

Presslie v Cochrane McGregor Group Ltd (No.1) 1996 S.C. 289; 1996 S.L.T. 988, IH (2 Div) .... *Digested*, 96/**6570**: *Considered* 17/2696

Prest v Petrodel Resources Ltd see Petrodel Resources Ltd v Prest
Prest v Prest; *sub nom* Prest v Prest (Judgment Summons: Appeal) [2015] EWCA Civ 714; [2016] 1 F.L.R. 773; [2015] Fam. Law 1047, CA (Civ Div) .... *Digested,* 16/**896**: *Considered* 16/890: *Followed* 17/1030
Prest v Prest (Judgment Summons: Appeal) see Prest v Prest
Prest v Prest see Petrodel Resources Ltd v Prest
Preston v President of the Methodist Church see Moore v President of the Methodist Conference
Preston v Wolverhampton Healthcare NHS Trust (No.2); *joined case* Fletcher v Midland Bank Plc (No.2) [2001] UKHL 5; [2001] 2 A.C. 455; [2001] 2 W.L.R. 448; [2001] 3 All E.R. 947; [2001] 1 C.M.L.R. 46; [2001] I.C.R. 217; [2001] I.R.L.R. 237; [2001] Emp. L.R. 256; [2001] O.P.L.R. 1; [2001] Pens. L.R. 39; Times, February 9, 2001; (2001) 98(10) L.S.G. 41; (2001) 145 S.J.L.B. 55, HL . *Digested,* 01/**2279**: *Applied* 05/1263, 06/1326, 07/2496: *Considered* 11/1086, 11/1750, 13/1013, 17/2228
Preston New Road Action Group v Secretary of State for Communities and Local Government [2017] EWHC 808 (Admin); [2017] Env. L.R. 33; [2017] J.P.L. 963, QBD (Manchester) .... *Digested,* 17/**1756**
Price v Powys CC; *sub nom* Powys CC v Price [2016] EWHC 2596 (QB), QBD (Cardiff) .... *Digested,* 17/**872**
Price v Registrar of Companies see Pablo Star Ltd, Re
Price v United Kingdom (15602/07) (2017) 64 E.H.R.R. 17, ECHR
PricewaterhouseCoopers v Saad Investments Co Ltd [2014] UKPC 35; [2014] 1 W.L.R. 4482; [2015] B.C.C. 53; [2014] 2 B.C.L.C. 583; Times, December 16, 2014, PC (Ber) *Applied* 17/1291
PricewaterhouseCoopers v SAAD Investments Co Ltd (In Official Liquidation); *joined case* Singularis Holdings Ltd (In Official Liquidation) v PricewaterhouseCoopers [2016] UKPC 33; [2017] 1 W.L.R. 953; [2017] 2 B.C.L.C. 216; Times, December 20, 2016, PC (Ber)
Priebe's Estate, Re see Royal Trust Corp of Canada v University of Western Ontario
Primary Group (UK) Ltd v Royal Bank of Scotland Plc [2014] EWHC 1082 (Ch); [2014] 2 All E.R. (Comm) 1121; [2014] R.P.C. 26, Ch D .... *Digested,* 14/**247**: *Applied* 17/2195
Primeo Fund (In Liquidation), Re see Macrae v KPMG LLP
Prince Abdulaziz v Apex Global Management Ltd; *sub nom* Apex Global Management Ltd v Fi Call Ltd [2014] UKSC 64; [2014] 1 W.L.R. 4495; [2015] 2 All E.R. 206; [2015] 1 All E.R. (Comm) 1183; [2015] 1 Costs L.O. 79; Times, December 8, 2014, SC .... *Digested,* 15/**353**: *Applied* 15/295, 17/2182
Prince Moulay Hicham Ben Abdullah Al Alaoui of Morocco v Elaph Publishing Ltd; *sub nom* Elaph Publishing Ltd v Prince Moulay Hicham Ben Abdullah Al Alaoui of Morocco [2017] EWCA Civ 29; [2017] 4 W.L.R. 28; [2017] E.M.L.R. 13, CA (Civ Div) .... *Digested,* 17/**647**
Prince Moulay Hicham Ben Abdullah Al Alaoui of Morocco v Elaph Publishing Ltd; *sub nom* Elaph Publishing Ltd v Prince Moulay Hicham Ben Abdullah Al Alaoui of Morocco [2015] EWHC 2021 (QB), QBD *Reversed* 17/647
Principal Reporter v LZ [2017] CSIH 51; 2017 S.L.T. 961; 2017 G.W.D. 24-403, IH (Ex Div) .... *Digested,* 17/**2601**
Principal Reporter, Applicant 2017 S.L.T. (Sh Ct) 21; 2017 G.W.D. 3-35, Sh Ct (Glasgow) *Reversed* 17/2601
Printeos SA v European Commission (T-95/15) EU:T:2016:722; [2017] 4 C.M.L.R. 9, GC (4th Chamber)
Privacy International v Secretary of State for Foreign and Commonwealth Affairs [2017] 3 All E.R. 647; [2016] H.R.L.R. 21, IPT .... *Digested,* 17/**25**
Private Equity Insurance Group SIA v Swedbank AS (C-156/15) EU:C:2016:851; [2017] 1 W.L.R. 1602; [2017] 1 B.C.L.C. 207, ECJ (4th Chamber)
Priya Properties Ltd v Inverclyde Council 2017 Hous. L.R. 19; 2016 G.W.D. 40-718, Sh Ct (North Strathclyde) (Greenock) .... *Digested,* 17/**2656**
Proceedings Brought by A Oy (C-33/16); *sub nom* A Oy v Veronsaajien oikeudenvalvontayksikko (C-33/16) EU:C:2017:339; [2017] B.V.C. 21, ECJ (8th Chamber)
Proceedings Brought by Folk (C-529/15); *sub nom* Folk v Unabhangiger Verwaltungssenat fur die Steiermark (C-529/15) EU:C:2017:419; [2018] 1 C.M.L.R. 6; [2017] Env. L.R. 35, ECJ (1st Chamber)

Proceedings Brought by Kubicka (C-218/16); *sub nom* Kubicka (C-218/16) EU:C:2017:755; [2017] I.L.Pr. 40, ECJ (2nd Chamber)
Proceedings on the Constitutional Complaint of R, Re (2BVR 2735/14) [2017] 2 C.M.L.R. 2, BverfG (Ger)
Proceedings relating to Piringer (C-342/15) EU:C:2017:196; [2017] 3 C.M.L.R. 19, ECJ (5th Chamber)
Procter v Raleys Solicitors [2015] EWCA Civ 400; [2015] P.N.L.R. 24, CA (Civ Div) .... *Digested,* 15/**1790**: *Applied* 17/1576
Procter & Gamble Co v Svenska Cellulosa Aktiebolaget SCA [2012] EWHC 2839 (Ch); [2013] 1 W.L.R. 1464; [2013] 1 Costs L.R. 97, Ch D .... *Digested,* 13/**323**: *Doubted* 17/272
Procter & Gamble UK v Revenue and Customs Commissioners; *sub nom* Revenue and Customs Commissioners v Procter & Gamble UK [2009] EWCA Civ 407; [2009] S.T.C. 1990; [2009] B.T.C. 5462; [2009] B.V.C. 461; [2009] S.T.I. 1722, CA (Civ Div) .... *Digested,* 09/**4129**: *Applied* 10/61, 13/3205, 14/2910, 17/2251: *Considered* 16/2197: *Distinguished* 10/3509
Procter (Inspector of Taxes) v Zim Properties see Zim Properties Ltd v Procter (Inspector of Taxes)
Procter and Gamble International Operations SA v Star Global Trading Ltd [2016] EWHC 734 (Ch); [2016] R.P.C. 19, Ch D .... *Digested,* 17/**1392**
Procurator Fiscal, Forfar v B (D) 2017 S.L.T. (Sh Ct) 44; 2017 G.W.D. 4-54, Sh Ct (Tayside) (Forfar) .... *Digested,* 17/**2533**
Procurator Fiscal, Peterhead v Elrick (Lyn) 2017 S.L.T. (Sh Ct) 157; 2017 S.C.L. 1072; 2017 G.W.D. 18-285, Sh Ct (Grampian) (Peterhead) .... *Digested,* 17/**2518**
Procurator Fiscal, Peterhead v Elrick (Lyn) 2017 S.L.T. (Sh Ct) 67; 2017 G.W.D. 12-179, Sh Ct (Grampian) (Peterhead) .... *Digested,* 17/**2514**
Professional Standards Authority v Health and Care Professions Council [2016] EWHC 1237 (Admin); [2016] Med. L.R. 591, QBD (Admin) .... *Digested,* 17/**1109**
Professional Standards Authority v Health and Care Professions Council [2015] EWHC 822 (Admin), QBD (Admin) *Affirmed* 17/1108
Professional Standards Authority v Health and Care Professions Council [2017] EWCA Civ 319; [2017] Med. L.R. 301, CA (Civ Div) .... *Digested,* 17/**1108**
Professional Standards Authority for Health and Social Care v General Dental Council [2016] CSIH 58; 2017 S.C.L.R. 185; 2016 G.W.D. 24-445, IH (Ex Div) .... *Digested,* 17/**2635**
Professional Standards Authority for Health and Social Care v General Medical Council [2015] EWHC 1304 (Admin); [2015] Med. L.R. 327, QBD (Admin) .... *Digested,* 15/**1203**: *Considered* 17/2638
Professional Standards Authority for Health and Social Care v Nursing and Midwifery Council [2017] EWHC 817 (Admin); (2017) 157 B.M.L.R. 191, QBD (Admin) .... *Digested,* 17/**1115**
Professional Standards Authority for Health and Social Care v Nursing and Midwifery Council [2015] EWHC 764 (Admin), QBD (Admin) *Considered* 17/1108
Professional Standards Authority for Health and Social Care v Nursing and Midwifery Council [2017] CSIH 29; 2017 S.C. 542; 2017 S.L.T. 625; 2017 G.W.D. 16-262, IH (Ex Div) .... *Digested,* 17/**2638**
Project Blue Ltd (formerly Project Blue (Guernsey Ltd)) v Revenue and Customs Commissioners [2016] EWCA Civ 485; [2018] 1 W.L.R. 368; [2017] 2 All E.R. 549; [2016] S.T.C. 2168; [2016] B.T.C. 22; [2016] S.T.I. 1795, CA (Civ Div) .... *Digested,* 16/**2109**
Promo International Ltd v Revenue and Customs Commissioners [2017] UKFTT 161 (TC); [2017] S.T.I. 363, FTT (Tax)
Promoimpresa srl v Consorzio dei comuni della Sponda Bresciana del Lago di Garda e del Lago di Idro (C-458/14); *joined case* Melis v Comune di Loiri Porto San Paolo (C□67/15) EU:C:2016:558; [2017] 1 C.M.L.R. 22; [2017] C.E.C. 325, ECJ (5th Chamber)
Promontoria Holding 87 BV v Finch see Finch v Lloyds TSB Bank Plc
Property Alliance Group Ltd v Royal Bank of Scotland Plc [2015] EWHC 1557 (Ch); [2016] 1 W.L.R. 361; [2015] 2 B.C.L.C. 401, Ch D .... *Digested,* 15/**198**: *Applied* 17/216
Property Alliance Group Ltd v Royal Bank of Scotland Plc [2015] EWHC 3187 (Ch); [2016] 1 W.L.R. 992, Ch D .... *Digested,* 16/**155**: *Explained* 17/530
Property Edge Lettings Ltd, Re see SAW (SW) 2010 Ltd v Wilson
Property Renaissance Ltd (t/a Titanic Spa) v Stanley Dock Hotel Ltd (t/a Titanic Hotel) [2016] EWHC 3103 (Ch); [2017] Bus. L.R. 464; [2017] E.T.M.R. 12; [2017] R.P.C. 12, Ch D .... *Digested,* 17/**1402**

Prospect Estates Ltd v Grosvenor Estates Ltd see Grosvenor Estates Ltd v Prospect Estates Ltd
Prospective Adopters v Brighton and Hove City Council see W (Adoption Application: Reunification with Family of Origin), Re
Proteus Film Partnership No.1 v Revenue and Customs Commissioners see Samarkand Film Partnership No.3 v Revenue and Customs Commissioners
Proto Glazing Ltd, Re 13410, V&DTr (London)
Disapproved 17/2289
Proxima GR Properties Ltd v McGhee [2014] UKUT 59 (LC); [2014] 2 E.G.L.R. 27, UT (Lands)
Applied 17/1445
Prudential Assurance Co Ltd v London Residuary Body [1992] 2 A.C. 386; [1992] 3 W.L.R. 279; [1992] 3 All E.R. 504; (1992) 64 P. & C.R. 193; [1992] 36 E.G. 129; Times, July 23, 1992; Independent, August 14, 1992; [1992] E.G. 100 (C.S.); (1992) 142 N.L.J. 1087; [1992] N.P.C. 105, HL .... *Digested,* 92/**2688**:
Applied 11/2056: *Cited* 93/2477: *Considered* 94/2765, 96/3764, 10/2086:
Followed 12/2035, 17/1440
Prudential Assurance Co Ltd v Revenue and Customs Commissioners [2016] EWCA Civ 376; [2017] 1 W.L.R. 4031; [2017] 1 All E.R. 815; [2016] S.T.C. 1798; [2016] B.T.C. 15; [2016] S.T.I. 1430, CA (Civ Div) .... *Digested,* 16/**2057**:
Followed 17/2080
PS v Greenwich RLBC [2016] EWHC 1967 (Admin); [2017] J.P.L. 165, QBD (Admin) . *Digested,* 17/**1753**
Psari Holdings Ltd v Association of Litigation Funders of England and Wales see Excalibur Ventures LLC v Texas Keystone Inc
PST Energy 7 Shipping LLC v OW Bunker Malta Ltd [2016] UKSC 23; [2016] A.C. 1034; [2016] 2 W.L.R. 1193; [2016] 3 All E.R. 879; [2017] 1 All E.R. (Comm) 1; [2016] 1 Lloyd's Rep. 589; [2016] 2 C.L.C. 1; [2016] B.P.I.R. 973; Times, May 17, 2016, SC .... *Digested,* 16/**1846**:
Not applied 17/1883
Psytech International Ltd v Office for Harmonisation in the Internal Market (Trade Marks and Designs) (OHIM) (T-507/08) EU:T:2011:253; [2011] E.T.M.R. 46, GC (2nd Chamber)
Considered 17/1395
PT Transportasi Gas Indonesia v ConocoPhillips (Grissik) Ltd [2016] EWHC 2834 (Comm); [2017] 1 All E.R. (Comm) 634; [2016] 2 Lloyd's Rep. 600, QBD (Comm) .... *Digested,* 17/**73**
Public and Commercial Services Union v Advisory, Concilation and Arbitration Service [2017] I.R.L.R. 680, CAC .... *Digested,* 17/**809**
Public and Commercial Services Union v Minister for the Cabinet Office see R. (on the application of Public and Commercial Services Union) v Minister for the Cabinet Office
Public Guardian v Matrix Deputies Ltd [2017] EWCOP 14; [2017] C.O.P.L.R. 415, CP
Public Guardian's Severance Applications, Re see JG (Case No 12911940), Re
Public Law Project v Lord Chancellor see R. (on the application of Public Law Project) v Secretary of State for Justice
Public Trustee v Cooper [2001] W.T.L.R. 901, Ch D .... *Digested,* 01/**5527**:
Applied 02/4708, 16/2122, 17/972: *Considered* 10/3205, 12/3191
Puceviciene v Lithuania; *sub nom* Germany v Conrath; *joined cases* Conrath v Germany; Savov v Czech Republicy [2016] EWHC 1862 (Admin); [2016] 1 W.L.R. 4937; [2017] 4 All E.R. 678; [2016] A.C.D. 106, DC .... *Digested,* 17/**907**
Pugh v RT Electrics Ltd [2017] I.C.R. D3, EAT
Pula Parking doo v Tederahn (C-551/15) EU:C:2017:193; [2017] C.E.C. 1036; [2017] I.L.Pr. 15, ECJ (2nd Chamber)
Puligienica Facility Esco SpA (PFE) v Airgest SpA (C-689/13) EU:C:2016:199; [2017] P.T.S.R. 13, ECJ (Grand Chamber)
Puma SE v European Union Intellectual Property Office (EUIPO) (T-104/16) EU:T:2017:153; [2017] E.T.M.R. 23, GC (9th Chamber)
Pumbien v Vines [1996] R.T.R. 37; Times, June 14, 1995, DC
Considered 17/1347
Purcell v Belgium; *sub nom* Eslame v Public Prosecutor in Kortrijk, Belgium; Pengal v Court of First Instance Antwerp, Belgium; Purcell v Public Prosecutor of Antwerp, Belgium [2017] EWHC 1328 (Admin); [2017] A.C.D. 95, DC
Purcell v Belgium; *sub nom* Purcell v Public Prosecutor of Antwerp, Belgium; Pengel v Prosecutor of the Court of First Instance Antwerp, Belgium [2017] EWHC 1981 (Admin); [2017] 3 C.M.L.R. 34, DC .... *Digested,* 17/**904**
Purcell v Public Prosecutor of Antwerp, Belgium see Purcell v Belgium

Purkiss Application, Re [1962] 1 W.L.R. 902; [1962] 2 All E.R. 690; 60 L.G.R. 349; (1962) 13 P. & C.R. 277; [1962] R.V.R. 455; (1962) 106 S.J. 308, CA .... *Digested,* 62/**2595**: *Applied* 17/1856: *Considered* 71/9933, 90/709, 08/3076

Purton (t/a Richwood Interiors) v Kilker Projects Ltd [2015] EWHC 2624 (TCC); [2015] B.L.R. 754; [2015] C.I.L.L. 3741, QBD (TCC) .... *Digested,* 16/**387**: *Applied* 16/399: *Considered* 17/494

Pusinskas (t/a Sigito Ekspreso Transportas) v Border Force [2017] UKFTT 172 (TC); [2017] S.T.I. 919, FTT (Tax)

PW v Luton BC see W (Children) (Convention Rights Claim: Procedure), Re

Pye v Stodday Land Ltd see Stodday Land Ltd v Pye

Pyke v Law Society [2006] EWHC 3489 (Ch), Ch D *Not followed* 17/1323

Pyle Works (No.1), Re (1890) 44 Ch. D. 534, CA *Applied* 17/1259

Pyrene Co Ltd v Scindia Steam Navigation Co Ltd [1954] 2 Q.B. 402; [1954] 2 W.L.R. 1005; [1954] 2 All E.R. 158; [1954] 1 Lloyd's Rep. 321; (1954) 98 S.J. 354, QBD .... *Digested,* 54/**3197**: *Applied* 57/3300, 59/3031, 79/2434, 81/215, 82/389, 93/3573, 17/2015: *Considered* 59/3029, 74/3545, 80/2667, 81/2538, 05/3787: *Followed* 84/3160

Q v Q (Contact: Undertakings) [2016] EWFC 5; [2017] 1 F.L.R. 438; [2016] Fam. Law 286, Fam Ct .... *Digested,* 17/**978**

Q (A Child) (Implacable Contact Dispute), Re [2015] EWCA Civ 991; [2016] 2 F.L.R. 287; [2015] Fam. Law 1454, CA (Civ Div) .... *Digested,* 16/**868**: *Applied* 17/978: *Followed* 16/829

Q (J) v Procurator Fiscal, Paisley; *sub nom* JQ v Mundell [2017] HCJAC 9; 2017 J.C. 201; 2017 S.L.T. 398; 2017 S.C.L. 332; 2017 S.C.C.R. 116; 2017 G.W.D. 5-65, HCJ .... *Digested,* 17/**2537**

Qader v Esure Services Ltd; *joined case* Khan v McGee [2016] EWCA Civ 1109; [2017] 1 W.L.R. 1924; [2017] 4 All E.R. 865; [2017] C.P. Rep. 10; [2016] 6 Costs L.O. 973; [2017] R.T.R. 14; [2017] P.I.Q.R. P5, CA (Civ Div) .... *Digested,* 17/**233**

Qadir v Associated Newspapers Ltd [2012] EWHC 2606 (QB); [2013] E.M.L.R. 15, QBD .... *Digested,* 13/**799**: *Considered* 17/653

Qasim v Ministry of Defence see Mohammed v Secretary of State for Defence

QBE Management Services (UK) Ltd v Dymoke [2012] EWHC 116 (QB); [2012] I.R.L.R. 458, QBD .... *Digested,* 12/**430**: *Applied* 17/769

QN Hotels (Aylesbury) Ltd v Revenue and Customs Commissioners see Swanfield Ltd v Revenue and Customs Commissioners

QN Hotels (Wrexham) Ltd v Revenue and Customs Commissioners see Swanfield Ltd v Revenue and Customs Commissioners

QN Hotels Ltd v Revenue and Customs Commissioners see Swanfield Ltd v Revenue Revenue and Customs Commissioners

QQ, Re [2016] EWCOP 22; (2017) 153 B.M.L.R. 175, CP

QS v RS see S v S (Foreign Adoption Order: Recognition)

Quah v Goldman Sachs International [2015] EWHC 759 (Comm), QBD (Comm) *Applied* 16/2156: *Considered* 17/263

Quan v Bray [2017] EWCA Civ 405; [2017] 3 F.C.R. 648, CA (Civ Div)

Queen's Club Ltd v Revenue and Customs Commissioners [2017] UKFTT 700 (TC); [2017] S.T.I. 2074, FTT (Tax)

Queens Moat Houses Plc, Re see Secretary of State for Trade and Industry v Bairstow

Quenon K SPRL v Beobank SA (C-338/14) EU:C:2015:795; [2016] Bus. L.R. 264; [2016] 2 C.M.L.R. 41; [2017] C.E.C. 231, ECJ (4th Chamber)

Quick v Taff Ely BC [1986] Q.B. 809; [1985] 3 W.L.R. 981; [1985] 3 All E.R. 321; (1986) 18 H.L.R. 66; [1985] 2 E.G.L.R. 50; (1985) 276 E.G. 452, CA (Civ Div) .. *Digested,* 85/**1610**: *Applied* 87/2141, 98/2987, 13/540, 16/1536: *Considered* 91/2228, 93/2462, 95/3062, 02/3059, 02/3066, 07/2738, 11/2071: *Distinguished* 98/3628: *Explained* 17/1563: *Followed* 01/4203, 16/1392: *Referred to* 87/2140

Quietfield Ltd v Vascroft Construction Ltd see Quietfield Ltd v Vascroft Contractors Ltd

Quietfield Ltd v Vascroft Contractors Ltd; *sub nom* Quietfield Ltd v Vascroft Construction Ltd [2006] EWCA Civ 1737; [2007] B.L.R. 67; 114 Con. L.R. 81; [2007] C.I.L.L. 2425; [2007] Bus. L.R. D1, CA (Civ Div) .... *Digested,* 07/**723**: *Applied* 07/725, 13/521, 15/458, 16/583: *Considered* 16/582, 17/476: *Followed* 15/697, 17/658

Quila v Secretary of State for the Home Department see R. (on the application of Aguilar Quila) v Secretary of State for the Home Department
Quilter v Hodson Developments Ltd [2016] EWCA Civ 1125; [2017] P.N.L.R. 7; [2017] 2 P. & C.R. 2; [2017] 1 P. & C.R. DG10, CA (Civ Div) .... *Digested,* 17/**1838**
Quinn v Scottish Ministers [2017] CSIH 53; 2017 S.L.T. 1036; 2017 Rep. L.R. 98; 2017 G.W.D. 25-427, IH (Ex Div) .... *Digested,* 17/**2745**
Quinn v Scottish Ministers [2016] CSOH 67; 2017 Rep. L.R. 104; 2016 G.W.D. 17-303, OH
Reversed 17/2745
Quinton v Peirce [2009] EWHC 912 (QB); [2009] F.S.R. 17, QBD .... *Digested,* 10/**3416**: *Considered* 11/3473, 17/647
Quitie Ltd v Revenue and Customs Commissioners [2017] UKFTT 206 (TC); [2017] S.T.I. 873, FTT (Tax)

R v A University [2017] CSIH 11; 2017 S.L.T. 284; 2017 S.C.L.R. 762; 2017 G.W.D. 7-100, IH (2 Div) .... *Digested,* 17/**2580**
R v Andrews see R. v Andrews (Donald Joseph)
R v B [2017] EWFC 33; [2017] 3 F.C.R. 519, Fam Ct
R v Brimecome (Steven Anthony) see R. v Martin (Dwain Ashley)
R v Denbigh Justices Ex p. Evans see R. v Denbigh Justices Ex p. Williams
R v E [2016] EWHC 3113 (Fam); [2017] 1 F.C.R. 283, Fam Div
R v HM Advocate [2016] HCJAC 94; 2017 S.L.T. 177; 2017 S.C.L. 77; 2016 G.W.D. 32-582, HCJ .... *Digested,* 17/**2792**
R v N see R, Petitioner
R v R (Jurisdiction and Acquiescence) see R (Children) (Children Act Proceedings: Foreign Dimension), Re
R v Secretary of State for the Home Department see E v Secretary of State for the Home Department
R v Solomon (Michael Herbert) see R. v Conaghan (Terence)
R v Stirling Council; *sub nom* KR v Stirling Council [2016] CSIH 36; 2016 S.L.T. 689; 2016 S.C.L.R. 557; 2016 Fam. L.R. 108; 2016 G.W.D. 17-313, IH (Ex Div) .... *Digested,* 16/**2653**: *Applied* 17/1063
R v Wirral MBC see B v Nugent Care Society
R (A Child) v DPP [2001] EWHC 17 (Admin); (2001) 165 J.P. 349; Times, February 20, 2001; Independent, March 5, 2001; [2001] Crim. L.R. 396; [2002] A.C.D. 50; (2001) 165 J.P.N. 267, DC .... *Digested,* 01/**1049**: *Applied* 17/550
R (A Child) (Adoption: Judicial Approach), Re; *sub nom* R (A Child) (Placement: Realistic Options), Re [2014] EWCA Civ 1625; [2015] 1 W.L.R. 3273; [2015] 1 F.L.R. 715; [2015] 2 F.C.R. 499; [2015] Fam. Law 119, CA (Civ Div) .... *Digested,* 15/**975**: *Applied* 16/805: *Followed* 16/819, 17/934
R (A Child) (Internal Relocation: Appeal), Re [2016] EWCA Civ 1016; [2017] 2 F.L.R. 921; [2016] 3 F.C.R. 532; [2016] Fam. Law 1401, CA (Civ Div) .... *Digested,* 17/**938**
R (A Child) (Placement: Realistic Options), Re see R (A Child) (Adoption: Judicial Approach), Re
R (A Child) (Prohibited Steps Order), Re; *sub nom* A (Prohibited Steps Order), Re [2013] EWCA Civ 1115; [2014] 1 F.L.R. 643; [2014] 1 F.C.R. 113; [2013] Fam. Law 1532, CA (Civ Div) .... *Digested,* 14/**1313**: *Applied* 15/1038, 15/1130: *Followed* 15/1072, 17/1061
R (A Child) (Recognition of Indian Adoption), Re [2012] EWHC 2956 (Fam); [2013] 1 F.L.R. 1487; [2013] Fam. Law 274, Fam Div .... *Digested,* 13/**1194**: *Applied* 14/1242, 17/914: *Considered* 17/1034
R (A Minor) (Wardship: Criminal Proceedings), Re [1991] Fam. 56; [1991] 2 W.L.R. 912; [1991] 2 All E.R. 193; [1991] 2 F.L.R. 95; [1991] F.C.R. 642; Times, January 24, 1991; Independent, February 13, 1991; [1991] Fam. Law 315; Daily Telegraph, January 31, 1991; (1991) 141 N.L.J. 164; (1991) 135 S.J.L.B. 164, CA (Civ Div) .... *Digested,* 91/**2591**: *Applied* 08/1514: *Considered* 94/1060: *Not applied* 17/1069
R (Children) (Children Act Proceedings: Foreign Dimension), Re; *sub nom* R v R (Jurisdiction and Acquiescence) [2016] EWHC 1339 (Fam); [2018] 1 W.L.R. 350; [2017] 1 F.L.R. 1750; [2016] Fam. Law 1093, Fam Div
R (Children), Re see R, Petitioner
R (Closed Material Procedure: Special Advocates: Funding), Re [2017] EWHC 1793 (Fam); [2018] 1 W.L.R. 163; [2017] 4 Costs L.R. 653; [2018] 1 F.L.R. 460; [2017] 3 F.C.R. 309, Fam Div .... *Digested,* 17/**997**
R (J) v HM Advocate; *sub nom* JR v HM Advocate [2017] HCJAC 49; 2017 S.C.L. 814; 2017 S.C.C.R. 402; 2017 G.W.D. 22-383, HCJ Appeal .... *Digested,* 17/**2809**

R and G (Minors) (Wardship), Re; *sub nom* G and R (Wards) (Police Interviews), Re [1990] 2 All E.R. 633; [1990] 2 F.L.R. 347; [1990] F.C.R. 495; [1991] Fam. Law 64, Fam Div .... *Digested,* 91/**2593**: *Applied* 17/1069

R&B Customs Brokers Co Ltd v United Dominions Trust Ltd [1988] 1 W.L.R. 321; [1988] 1 All E.R. 847; [1988] R.T.R. 134; (1988) 85(11) L.S.G. 42; (1988) 132 S.J. 300, CA (Civ Div) .... *Digested,* 88/**3168**: *Applied* 91/3183, 93/504, 17/657: *Considered* 99/4406, 03/723: *Distinguished* 95/775: *Referred to* 00/3570

R&S Fire and Security Services Ltd v Fire Defence Plc [2013] EWHC 4222 (Ch); [2013] 2 B.C.L.C. 92; [2013] B.L.R. 500; [2013] B.P.I.R. 1085, Ch D .... *Digested,* 13/**1720**: *Considered* 17/1333

R+V Versicherung AG v Robertson & Co SA [2016] EWHC 1243 (QB); [2016] 4 W.L.R. 106; [2017] 2 All E.R. 676; [2017] 1 All E.R. (Comm) 995; [2016] Lloyd's Rep. I.R. 612, QBD (Merc) .... *Digested,* 16/**434**

R, v Richards (Tyrone) see R. v Odegbune (Samson)

R, Petitioner; *sub nom* AR v RN; AR, Petitioner; R (Children), Re; R v N [2015] UKSC 35; [2016] A.C. 76; [2015] 2 W.L.R. 1583; [2015] 3 All E.R. 749; 2015 S.C. (U.K.S.C.) 129; 2015 S.L.T. 392; 2015 S.C.L.R. 471; [2015] 2 F.L.R. 503; [2015] 2 F.C.R. 570; 2015 Fam. L.R. 54; [2015] Fam. Law 777; 2015 G.W.D. 17-289, SC .... *Digested,* 15/**1021**: *Applied* 17/1040: *Followed* 15/1037, 16/853

R-B (A Patient) v Official Solicitor see A (Mental Patient: Sterilisation), Re

R-R Realisations, Re [1980] 1 W.L.R. 805; [1980] 1 All E.R. 1019; (1980) 124 S.J. 326, Ch D .... *Digested,* 80/**292**: *Considered* 13/1705, 17/1258

R. v A [2014] EWCA Crim 567; [2014] 2 Cr. App. R. 7; Times, April 8, 2014, CA (Crim Div) .... *Digested,* **14/718**: *Considered* 17/586

R. v A [2015] EWCA Crim 177; [2015] 2 Cr. App. R. (S.) 12; [2015] Crim. L.R. 555, CA (Crim Div) .... *Digested,* 15/**2235**: *Applied* 17/1897

R. v A (Complainant's Sexual History); *sub nom* R. v A (No.2); R. v Y (Sexual Offence: Complainant's Sexual History) [2001] UKHL 25; [2002] 1 A.C. 45; [2001] 2 W.L.R. 1546; [2001] 3 All E.R. 1; [2001] 2 Cr. App. R. 21; (2001) 165 J.P. 609; [2001] H.R.L.R. 48; [2001] U.K.H.R.R. 825; 11 B.H.R.C. 225; Times, May 24, 2001; Independent, May 22, 2001; [2001] Crim. L.R. 908; (2001) 165 J.P.N. 750; Daily Telegraph, May 29, 2001, HL [*likelihood*] .... *Digested,* 01/**977**: *Applied* 02/487, 11/1686: *Considered* 02/753, 03/5019, 05/799: *Followed* 17/513

R. v A (No.2) see R. v A (Complainant's Sexual History)

R. v A Ltd [2016] EWCA Crim 1469; [2016] 4 W.L.R. 176; [2017] 1 Cr. App. R. 1; [2017] Lloyd's Rep. F.C. 1, CA (Crim Div) .... *Digested,* 17/**511**

R. v A see R. v RH

R. v AA see R. v Joseph (Verna Sermanfure)

R. v AB see R. v B

R. v ABC see R. v Chapman (Scott Derek)

R. v Abdallah (Abdalraouf); *joined cases* Attorney General's Reference (No.323 of 2016); R. v Gray (Stephen); R. v Khan (Junead); R. v Khan (Shazib); R. v Shaukat (Ayman); R. v Moore (Lorna) [2016] EWCA Crim 1868; [2017] 1 W.L.R. 1699; [2017] 2 All E.R. 795; [2017] 1 Cr. App. R. (S.) 29; [2017] Crim. L.R. 246, CA (Crim Div) .... *Digested,* 17/**1987**

R. v Abdi (Hassan) see R. v Lang (Stephen Howard)

R. v Abdin (Joynal) see Attorney General's Reference (Nos 128 to 141 of 2015 and 8 to 10 of 2016)

R. v Abi-Khalil (Tannous); *joined case* R. Porja (Arben) [2017] EWCA Crim 17; [2017] 4 W.L.R. 76; [2017] 2 Cr. App. R. 4; [2017] Crim. L.R. 471, CA (Crim Div) .... *Digested,* 17/**546**

R. v Abu Hamza [2006] EWCA Crim 2918; [2007] Q.B. 659; [2007] 2 W.L.R. 226; [2007] 3 All E.R. 451; [2007] 1 Cr. App. R. 27; Times, November 30, 2006; [2007] Crim. L.R. 320, CA (Crim Div) .... *Digested,* 07/**923**: *Applied* 11/812, 17/529: *Considered* 08/3404, 09/3339, 11/795

R. v Adams (Terence George) see Adams v Crown Prosecution Service

R. v Adams (Terence George) see Adams, Re

R. v Adomako (John Asare); *joined cases* R. v Sullman (Barry); R. v Holloway (Stephen John); R. v Prentice (Michael Charles) [1995] 1 A.C. 171; [1994] 3 W.L.R. 288; [1994] 3 All E.R. 79; (1994) 99 Cr. App. R. 362; (1994) 158 J.P. 653; [1994] 5 Med. L.R. 277; Times, July 4, 1994; Independent, July 1, 1994; [1994] Crim. L.R. 757; (1994) 158 J.P.N. 507; (1994) 144 N.L.J. 936, HL .... *Digested,* 94/**1124**: *Applied* 95/875, 05/804, 08/10, 09/795: *Considered* 96/1644, 96/47, 05/805: *Distinguished* 95/923: *Followed* 01/1052, 17/553: *Referred to* 12/25

R. v Advertising Standards Authority Ltd Ex p. Vernons Organisation Ltd [1992] 1 W.L.R. 1289; [1993] 2 All E.R. 202; Times, November 23, 1992, QBD .... *Digested,* 93/**3253**: *Considered* 17/697

R. v Afrisib (Sarkhel) [2016] EWCA Crim 2123; [2017] 1 Cr. App. R. (S.) 25, CA (Crim Div) .... *Digested,* 17/**1916**

R. v Afshar (Saeideh) see R. v Mateta (Koshi Pitshou)

R. v Agera (Stephen); *joined case* R. v Lansana (Stephen) [2017] EWCA Crim 740; [2017] 4 W.L.R. 115; [2017] 2 Cr. App. R. 22, CA (Crim Div) .... *Digested,* 17/**610**

R. v Ahmad (Goran Kamal) see Attorney General's Reference (No.27 of 2013)

R. v Ahmadi (Reshad) see R. v Safi (Ali Ahmed)

R. v Ahmed (Hussein) see R. v Goodwin (Gary William)

R. v Ahmed (Jakir) [2017] EWCA Crim 1158; [2017] 2 Cr. App. R. (S.) 44, CA (Crim Div)

R. v Ahmed (Saber Mohammed) [2016] EWCA Crim 670; [2016] M.H.L.R. 282; [2017] Crim. L.R. 150, CA (Crim Div) .... *Digested,* 16/**1900**

R. v AIL (A Company) [2016] EWCA Crim 2; [2016] Q.B. 763; [2016] 2 W.L.R. 1287; [2017] 1 All E.R. 268; [2016] 1 Cr. App. R. 21; [2016] Lloyd's Rep. F.C. 80, CA (Crim Div) .... *Digested,* 16/**464**

R. v Aitchison (Lee James) [2016] EWCA Crim 739; [2017] M.H.L.R. 187, CA (Crim Div)

R. v Aitken (Tony) see R. v Needham (Paul Maurice)

R. v Akbar (Yusuf) see R. v McLeod (Ralph)

R. v Akhtar (Itzaz Nafeez) [2015] EWCA Crim 176; [2015] 1 W.L.R. 3046; [2015] 2 Cr. App. R. 7, CA (Crim Div) .... *Digested,* 15/**650**: *Applied* 17/615

R. v Akhtar (Siddiqua) [2016] EWCA Crim 390; [2017] M.H.L.R. 189, CA (Crim Div)

R. v Akinsete (Marcel); *joined case* R. v Prempeh (Gabriel) [2012] EWCA Crim 2377, CA (Crim Div) *Considered* 17/546

R. v Akra (Adonis Junior) see R. v Odegbune (Samson)

R. v Alderson (Georgina) [2017] EWCA Crim 1050; [2017] 2 Cr. App. R. (S.) 53, CA (Crim Div) .... *Digested,* 17/**1957**

R. v Alford (Dean) see R. v Brandford (Olivia)

R. v Ali [2017] 4 Costs L.O. 533, Sen Cts Costs Office

R. v Ali (Mudassir Mohammed) see R. v Lambert (Steven)

R. v Ali (Sajid Pasha) see R. v Graham (Hemamali Krishna)

R. v Ali (Shafiq) see R. v Needham (Paul Maurice)

R. v Alshateri (Majid) [2016] EWCA Crim 1266; [2017] 1 Cr. App. R. (S.) 3, CA (Crim Div) .... *Digested,* 17/**1903**

R. v AM; *joined cases* R. v MN; R. v RM; R. v MV [2010] EWCA Crim 2400; [2011] 1 Cr. App. R. 35, CA (Crim Div) .... *Digested,* 11/**681**: *Considered* 13/656, 17/612: *Followed* 14/696

R. v AM see R. v PW

R. v Amjad (Adeel) [2016] EWCA Crim 1618; [2017] 1 Cr. App. R. 22, CA (Crim Div) .. *Digested,* 17/**515**

R. v Amoah (Enoch Charles) see R. v Odegbune (Samson)

R. v Andrews (Donald Joseph); *sub nom* R v Andrews [1987] A.C. 281; [1987] 2 W.L.R. 413; [1987] 1 All E.R. 513; (1987) 84 Cr. App. R. 382; [1987] Crim. L.R. 487; (1987) 151 J.P.N. 254, HL .... *Digested,* 87/**659**: *Applied* 93/652: *Considered* 88/552, 91/649: *Followed* 15/536, 17/514

R. v Andukwa (Simon Ebunji) see R. v Mateta (Koshi Pitshou)

R. v Anigbugu (Michael) see Attorney General's Reference (Nos 3, 73 and 75 of 2010)

R. v Anwar (Umar); *joined cases* R. v Stockley (David); R. v Celaire (Ramone); R. v Knight (Carl); R. v Richards (Jiovaughni); R. v Scott (Taylor) [2016] EWCA Crim 551; [2016] 4 W.L.R. 127; [2016] 2 Cr. App. R. 23, CA (Crim Div) .... *Digested,* 17/**552**

R. v Appleby (Declan Paul) see Attorney General's Reference (Nos 60, 62 and 63 of 2009)

R. v Appulonappa 2015 SCC 59; 41 B.H.R.C. 313, Sup Ct (Can)

R. v Armel (Jude Michael) see R. v Kitchener (Matthew David)

R. v Armitage (Lewis) see R. v Lang (Stephen Howard)

R. v Asfaw (Fregenet) [2008] UKHL 31; [2008] 1 A.C. 1061; [2008] 2 W.L.R. 1178; [2008] 3 All E.R. 775; 25 B.H.R.C. 87; [2008] I.N.L.R. 378; 4 A.L.R. Int'l 649; Times, May 26, 2008; (2008) 105(22) L.S.G. 25; (2008) 158 N.L.J. 788; (2008) 152(22) S.J.L.B. 30, HL .... *Digested,* 08/**735**: *Applied* 11/681: *Followed* 09/2160, 14/696: *Referred to* 17/612

R. v Ashman (Joseph Clifford) see Jones (Setting of Minimum Term), Re

R. v Asmelash (Dawit) [2013] EWCA Crim 157; [2014] Q.B. 103; [2013] 3 W.L.R. 1056; [2013] 1 Cr. App. R. 33; [2013] Crim. L.R. 599, CA (Crim Div) .... *Digested,* 13/**652**: *Considered* 17/517

R. v Atkinson (David) see R. v Ogden (Neil)

R. v Avis (Tony); *joined cases* R. v Thomas (Richard Bartgerald); R. v Torrington (Richard Edward); R. v Marquez (Shaun); R. v Goldsmith (Harold Egan) [1998] 1 Cr. App. R. 420; [1998] 2 Cr. App. R. (S.) 178; Times, December 19, 1997; [1998] Crim. L.R. 428, CA (Crim Div) .... *Digested,* 98/**1214**: *Applied* 01/1299, 01/1308, 02/3873, 04/3350, 04/3409, 04/876, 06/3719, 09/3388, 09/3389, 09/3390, 11/2871, 11/2872, 12/2900, 12/2904, 12/2906, 13/2724, 14/2633, 15/2218, 15/2220, 16/448: *Considered* 99/1158, 99/1160, 99/1161, 99/1162, 99/1164, 99/1165, 00/1242, 00/1244, 00/1245, 00/1247, 00/1250, 00/1252, 00/1253, 01/1298, 01/1304, 01/1312, 01/1313, 02/3941, 02/3947, 02/3948, 02/4057, 04/3411, 05/3690, 05/3692, 05/3696, 05/3759, 06/3716, 06/3718, 08/3295, 09/3387, 10/2878, 10/2882, 12/2903, 12/2905, 14/2634, 17/1919, 17/1920: *Followed* 99/1168, 05/3675: *Referred to* 99/1110, 11/2868

R. v Awoyemi (Toby); *joined cases* R. v Toto (Randy); R. v Thomas (Victor) [2016] EWCA Crim 668; [2016] 4 W.L.R. 114; [2016] 2 Cr. App. R. 22; [2017] Crim. L.R. 131, CA (Crim Div) .... *Digested,* 16/**444**

R. v Aylesbury Vale DC Ex p. Chaplin (1998) 76 P. & C.R. 207; [1997] 3 P.L.R. 55; Times, August 19, 1997; Independent, October 6, 1997; [1998] J.P.L. 49, CA (Civ Div) .... *Digested,* 97/**4107**: *Followed* 17/1764

R. v Aziz (Qaiser) [2016] EWCA Crim 1945; [2017] 1 Cr. App. R. (S.) 28; [2017] Crim. L.R. 414, CA (Crim Div) .... *Digested,* 17/**1966**

R. v B; *sub nom* R. v AB [2017] EWCA Crim 534; [2017] 1 W.L.R. 4071; [2017] 2 Cr. App. R. 25; [2017] Lloyd's Rep. F.C. 297; [2017] L.L.R. 607; [2017] Crim. L.R. 989, CA (Crim Div) .... *Digested,* 17/**619**

R. v B; *sub nom* B, Re [2006] EWCA Crim 2692; [2007] E.M.L.R. 5; [2007] H.R.L.R. 1; [2007] U.K.H.R.R. 577; Times, November 6, 2006, CA (Crim Div) .... *Digested,* 07/**1018**: *Applied* 11/808, 11/812, 17/529: *Considered* 11/795: *Followed* 13/757

R. v B [2017] EWCA Crim 35; [2017] 1 W.L.R. 4545; [2017] 1 Cr. App. R. 31; (2017) 181 J.P. 205, CA (Crim Div) .... *Digested,* 17/**518**

R. v Babiak (Tomasz); *joined case* R. v Flynn (Tarique Samuel) [2017] EWCA Crim 160; [2017] 1 Cr. App. R. (S.) 52, CA (Crim Div) .... *Digested,* 17/**1992**

R. v Bala (Mehmet) [2017] EWCA Crim 1460; [2017] M.H.L.R. 375, CA (Crim Div)

R. v Bala (Yilkyes Finok); *sub nom* R. v Ekwugha (Casmir); R. v Bala-Tonglele (Giwo) [2016] EWCA Crim 560; [2017] Q.B. 430; [2016] 3 W.L.R. 1379; [2016] 2 Cr. App. R. 14, CA (Crim Div) .... *Digested,* 16/**467**

R. v Bala-Tonglele (Giwo) see R. v Bala (Yilkyes Finok)

R. v Barkshire (Unreported, May 21, 2010), Crown Ct *Doubted* 17/542

R. v Barnes (Carl) see R. v Vowles (Lucinda)

R. v Barnet LBC Ex p. Shah; *joined cases* Akbarali v Brent LBC; Abdullah v Shropshire CC; Shabpar v Barnet LBC; Shah (Jitendra) v Barnet LBC; Ablack v Inner London Education Authority; R. v Shropshire CC Ex p. Abdullah [1983] 2 A.C. 309; [1983] 2 W.L.R. 16; [1983] 1 All E.R. 226; 81 L.G.R. 305; (1983) 133 N.L.J. 61; (1983) 127 S.J. 36, HL .... *Digested,* 83/**1157**: *Applied* 84/3033, 85/1074, 85/1737, 86/1692, 86/703, 87/3489, 98/3007, 01/2612, 01/2617, 03/1127, 03/1556, 05/1627, 07/3910, 09/1541, 09/1802, 10/1041, 10/3333, 11/3371, 12/1371, 12/2278, 12/3416: *Considered* 82/973, 84/1173, 84/1178, 84/1645, 85/1107, 85/1108, 85/1127, 85/1771, 85/2165, 86/1136, 86/1703, 91/2372, 95/3206, 99/4564, 00/2778, 08/1692, 13/1250, 13/1645, 13/2956, 15/2393, 15/2394, 16/2827: *Distinguished* 83/1800, 04/1885, 17/160: *Followed* 87/1928, 09/3829, 10/3179, 10/3332, 12/1392, 13/3011, 14/1729: *Not applied* 13/2058: *Referred to* 91/2373

R. v Bashir (Yasin) see R. v Mateta (Koshi Pitshou)

R. v Baverstock (Stephen Alan) [2013] EWCA Crim 1502; [2014] 1 Cr. App. R. (S.) 64, CA (Crim Div) .... *Digested,* 14/**2628**: *Followed* 17/1918

R. v Bawa-Garba (Hadiza) [2016] EWCA Crim 1841; [2016] Inquest L.R. 320, CA (Crim Div) .... *Digested,* 17/**606**

R. v BC see R. v PW
R. v BD see R. v Forbes (Stephen John)
R. v Beale (Jemma) [2017] EWCA Crim 1012; [2017] E.M.L.R. 26, CA (Crim Div) .... *Digested,* 17/**33**
R. v Beaman (Paul) see R. v Rogers (Georgina)
R. v Beech (Dean Colin); *joined cases* R. v Bowman (Darren) (also known as Bowman (Darren William)); R. v Hadley (Jason Lee); R. v Taylor-Powell (Pedro George) [2016] EWCA Crim 1746; [2016] 4 W.L.R. 182; [2017] R.T.R. 8; [2017] Crim. L.R. 238, CA (Crim Div) .... *Digested,* 17/**1910**
R. v Bell (Mark Julian) see R. v Rogers (Bradley David)
R. v Belmarsh Magistrates' Court Ex p. Watts [1999] 2 Cr. App. R. 188, QBD .... *Digested,* 99/**485**: *Applied* 13/3072, 17/620: *Considered* 08/2986
R. v Bertram (Robert Leslie) [2003] EWCA Crim 2026; [2004] 1 Cr. App. R. (S.) 27, CA (Crim Div) .... *Digested,* 04/**3395**: *Considered* 11/2934, 11/2969: *Followed* 17/1972
R. v Bianco (Leonardo) [2001] EWCA Crim 2516, CA (Crim Div) *Followed* 17/547
R. v Billington (Jason Leon) [2017] EWCA Crim 618; [2017] 4 W.L.R. 114; [2017] 2 Cr. App. R. (S.) 22; [2017] Crim. L.R. 816, CA (Crim Div) .... *Digested,* 17/**1953**
R. v Birmingham City Council Ex p. Equal Opportunities Commission (No.1); *sub nom* Birmingham City Council v Equal Opportunities Commission (No.1) [1989] A.C. 1155; [1989] 2 W.L.R. 520; [1989] 1 All E.R. 769; [1989] I.R.L.R. 173; 87 L.G.R. 557; Times, February 24, 1989; Independent, February 24, 1989; Guardian, February 24, 1989; (1989) 86(15) L.S.G. 36; (1989) 139 N.L.J. 292; (1989) 133 S.J. 322, HL .... *Digested,* 89/**1371**: *Applied* 10/969, 17/1587: *Considered* 89/2342, 90/2565, 93/1685, 95/2028, 96/6121, 00/2187: *Followed* 99/2093: *Referred to* 89/1923
R. v Blackledge (William Stuart) see Attorney General v Newspaper Publishing Plc
R. v Blackman (Alexander Wayne) [2017] EWCA Crim 326; [2017] E.M.L.R. 17, CA (Crim Div) .... *Digested,* 17/**1533**
R. v Blackman (Alexander Wayne) [2017] EWCA Crim 190; [2017] Crim. L.R. 557, CMAC
R. v Blakemore (Luke) [2016] EWCA Crim 1396; [2017] 1 Cr. App. R. (S.) 5, CA (Crim Div) .... *Digested,* 17/**1986**
R. v Bolton (Mark) see R. v Healey (Robert)
R. v Boothman (Richard) see R. v Twist (Andrew Terence)
R. v Botcher (Henrik) see R. v Greaves (Claude Clifford)
R. v Bow Street Metropolitan Stipendiary Magistrate Ex p. Pinochet Ugarte (No.3) [2000] 1 A.C. 147; [1999] 2 W.L.R. 827; [1999] 2 All E.R. 97; 6 B.H.R.C. 24; Times, March 25, 1999; (1999) 96(17) L.S.G. 24; (1999) 149 N.L.J. 497, HL ..... *Digested,* 99/**2292**: *Applied* 06/2200, 14/1949: *Considered* 04/3849, 06/2644, 12/1290, 16/1356: *Followed* 17/379
R. v Bowker (Anthony) [2007] EWCA Crim 1608; [2008] 1 Cr. App. R. (S.) 72; [2007] Crim. L.R. 904, CA (Crim Div) .... *Digested,* 08/**3423**: *Considered* 14/2680, 17/1980
R. v Bowman (Darren) (also known as Bowman (Darren William)) see R. v Beech (Dean Colin)
R. v Boyer (George Kenneth) (1981) 3 Cr. App. R. (S.) 35, CA (Crim Div) *Considered* 96/1996, 97/1618: *Followed* 17/1972
R. v Bradshaw (Wayne Martin); *joined case* R. v Waters (Paul Anthony) [2001] R.T.R. 4; Times, December 31, 1994, CA (Crim Div) .... *Digested,* 95/**1304**: *Considered* 14/2691, 17/1910: *Followed* 00/1126
R. v Bramich (David) see R. v Graham (Hemamali Krishna)
R. v Brandford (Olivia); *sub nom* R. v Karemera (Michael); R. v Alford (Dean) [2016] EWCA Crim 1794; [2017] 4 W.L.R. 17; [2017] 2 All E.R. 43; [2017] 1 Cr. App. R. 14; [2017] Crim. L.R. 554, CA (Crim Div) .... *Digested,* 17/**547**
R. v Brearley (Gary) see R. v Healey (Robert)
R. v Brent LBC Ex p. Gunning 84 L.G.R. 168; Times, April 30, 1985, QBD .... *Digested,* 86/**1127**: *Applied* 08/52, 12/3163, 14/2149, 16/989: *Considered* 91/94, 93/3679, 95/30, 96/2483, 96/2487, 11/2093, 11/52, 12/2105, 16/615, 17/89
R. v Brent LBC Housing Benefit Review Board Ex p. Khadim see R. (on the application of Kadhim) v Brent LBC Housing Benefit Review Board
R. v Bristol Betting and Gaming Licensing Committee Ex p. O'Callaghan see Locabail (UK) Ltd v Bayfield Properties Ltd (Leave to Appeal)
R. v Bromell (Jerome) (aka Henry) see R. v Samuriwo (Michael Tatenda)
R. v Brough (Kevin) see R. v Ogden (Neil)
R. v Brown (Milton) [1998] 2 Cr. App. R. 364; Times, May 7, 1998; Independent, May 8, 1998, CA (Crim Div) .... *Digested,* 98/**887**: *Applied* 15/1075: *Considered* 17/594

R. v Browne-Morgan (Samuel) [2016] EWCA Crim 1903; [2017] 4 W.L.R. 118; [2017] 1 Cr. App. R. (S.) 33, CA (Crim Div) ... *Digested,* 17/**589**
R. v Brownlee (Raymond) [2015] NICA 39; [2017] N.I. 71, CA (Crim Div) (NI)
R. v Brownlee (Raymond) [2015] NICA 58; [2017] N.I. 83, CA (NI)
R. v Bryan (Thomas) see Attorney General's Reference (Nos 60, 62 and 63 of 2009)
R. v Bryon (Michael David) [2015] EWCA Crim 997; [2015] 2 Cr. App. R. 21, CA (Crim Div) ... *Digested,* 15/**540**: *Considered* 17/524: *Doubted* 16/460
R. v BT see R. v LM
R. v Bullen (David Frederick) see R. v Soneji (Kamlesh Kumar)
R. v Burgess (Daniel James) [2017] EWCA Crim 495; [2017] 2 Cr. App. R. (S.) 25; [2017] Crim. L.R. 899, CA (Crim Div) ... *Digested,* 17/**1944**
R. v Burinskas (Gintas) see Attorney General's Reference (No.27 of 2013)
R. v Burton (Tyler Winston) see R. v Johnson (Lewis)
R. v Bush (Anthony) [2017] EWCA Crim 137; [2017] 1 Cr. App. R. (S.) 49, CA (Crim Div) ... *Digested,* 17/**1984**
R. v Byrne (Jason) [2016] EWCA Crim 2124; [2017] Crim. L.R. 801, CA (Crim Div)
R. v Byrne (Patrick Joseph) [1960] 2 Q.B. 396; [1960] 3 W.L.R. 440; [1960] 3 All E.R. 1; (1960) 44 Cr. App. R. 246; (1960) 104 S.J. 645, CCA ... *Digested,* 60/**741**: *Applied* 61/1938, 65/858, 66/2637, 85/638, 86/830, 92/798: *Considered* 61/1939, 82/650, 94/835, 11/647, 17/544: *Followed* 16/454: *Referred to* 09/786
R. v C; *joined cases* R. v T; R. v M [2016] EWCA Crim 1617; [2017] 1 Cr. App. R. 20; (2017) 181 J.P. 143; [2017] E.C.C. 24; [2017] Lloyd's Rep. F.C. 9; [2017] F.S.R. 19; [2016] C.T.L.C. 240; [2017] L.L.R. 176, CA (Crim Div) *Affirmed* 17/565
R. v C [2014] EWCA Crim 343, CA (Crim Div) *Applied* 17/1963
R. v C; *joined cases* R. v T; R. v M [2017] UKSC 58; [2017] 1 W.L.R. 3006; [2018] 1 All E.R. 304; [2017] 2 Cr. App. R. 30; (2017) 181 J.P. 465; [2018] E.C.C. 3; [2017] E.T.M.R. 39; [2017] Lloyd's Rep. F.C. 513; [2017] C.T.L.C. 207; Times, August 16, 2017, SC ... *Digested,* 17/**565**
R. v C [2012] EWCA Crim 3062, CA (Crim Div) *Considered* 15/2220, 17/1920
R. v C [2009] UKHL 42; [2009] 1 W.L.R. 1786; [2009] 4 All E.R. 1033; [2010] 1 Cr. App. R. 7; [2009] M.H.L.R. 189; Times, August 7, 2009; [2010] Crim. L.R. 75; (2009) 153(31) S.J.L.B. 30, HL ... *Digested,* 09/**806**: *Considered* 11/2204, 14/2175: *Followed* 16/1504, 17/1307
R. v C [2017] EWCA Crim 557; [2017] Lloyd's Rep. F.C. 531, CA (Crim Div) ... *Digested,* 17/**529**
R. v C (Peter Charles) see Attorney General's Reference (No.75 of 2007)
R. v C see Attorney General's Reference (No.27 of 2013)
R. v Camelo (Joseph Nicholas David) see R. v Turnbull (Raymond)
R. v Campbell (Jermain) [2017] EWCA Crim 213; [2017] 1 Cr. App. R. (S.) 57, CA (Crim Div) ... *Digested,* 17/**1884**
R. v Canavan (Darren Anthony); *joined cases* R. v Shaw (Dennis); R. v Kidd (Philip Richard) [1998] 1 W.L.R. 604; [1998] 1 All E.R. 42; [1998] 1 Cr. App. R. 79; [1998] 1 Cr. App. R. (S.) 243; (1997) 161 J.P. 709; Times, July 21, 1997; [1997] Crim. L.R. 766; (1997) 161 J.P.N. 838; (1997) 94(35) L.S.G. 33; (1997) 147 N.L.J. 1457; (1997) 141 S.J.L.B. 169, CA (Crim Div) ... *Digested,* 97/**1492**: *Applied* 04/3376, 05/3742, 07/3723, 13/2680, 15/2235, 17/1897: *Considered* 98/1387, 99/1351, 99/1352, 07/3606, 09/831, 13/2586: *Distinguished* 03/3826: *Followed* 15/2282, 17/601: *Referred to* 12/794
R. v Carasco (Charles) see R. v Lang (Stephen Howard)
R. v Carter (Hayley Claire) [2016] EWCA Crim 2114; [2017] 1 Cr. App. R. (S.) 40, CA (Crim Div) ... *Digested,* 17/**1956**
R. v Cassell (Warren) see Cassell v Queen, The
R. v Celaire (Ramone) see R. v Anwar (Umar)
R. v Chamberlain (William Andrew) (1992) 13 Cr. App. R. (S.) 525; (1992) 156 J.P. 440; Times, December 19, 1991; [1992] Crim. L.R. 380; (1992) 156 J.P.N. 172, CA (Crim Div) ... *Digested,* 93/**1287**: *Explained* 17/1973
R. v Chamberlin (Jackie) [2017] EWCA Crim 39; [2017] 4 W.L.R. 70; [2017] 1 Cr. App. R. (S.) 46; [2017] Crim. L.R. 416, CA (Crim Div) ... *Digested,* 17/**1990**
R. v Chan Wing Siu see Chan Wing Siu v R.
R. v Chandi (Amandeep Singh) see Jones (Setting of Minimum Term), Re
R. v Chapman (Helen) [2013] EWCA Crim 1370; [2014] 1 W.L.R. 1376; [2013] Lloyd's Rep. F.C. 683; [2014] Crim. L.R. 611, CA (Crim Div) ... *Digested,* 14/**794**: *Considered* 17/610

R. v Chapman (Scott Derek); *sub nom* R. v ABC; *joined cases* R. v Sabey (Ryan); R. v Gaffney (Lynn); R. v Panton (Lucy Rebecca) [2015] EWCA Crim 539; [2015] Q.B. 883; [2015] 3 W.L.R. 726; [2016] 1 All E.R. 1065; [2015] 2 Cr. App. R. 10; [2015] Crim. L.R. 633, CA (Crim Div) .... *Digested,* 15/**569**: *Followed* 17/522, 17/604

R. v Chief Adjudication Officer Ex p. Remelien see Secretary of State for Social Security v Remilien

R. v Chief Constable of Nottinghamshire Ex p. Sunderland see R. v Chief Constable of the West Midlands Ex p. Wiley

R. v Chief Constable of the West Midlands Ex p. Wiley; *joined case* R. v Chief Constable of Nottinghamshire Ex p. Sunderland [1995] 1 A.C. 274; [1994] 3 W.L.R. 433; [1994] 3 All E.R. 420; [1995] 1 Cr. App. R. 342; Times, July 15, 1994; Independent, July 15, 1994; [1994] C.O.D. 520; (1994) 91(40) L.S.G. 35; (1994) 144 N.L.J. 1008; (1994) 138 S.J.L.B. 156, HL .... *Digested,* 96/**876**: *Applied* 00/5464: *Considered* 95/4123, 95/4124, 10/370, 13/247, 14/294: *Followed* 17/933

R. v Choudary (Anjem); *joined case* R. v Rahman (Mohammed Mizanur) [2016] EWCA Crim 1436; [2018] 1 W.L.R. 695; [2017] 3 All E.R. 459, CA (Crim Div)

R. v Chowdhury (Saleh) [2016] EWCA Crim 1341; [2016] 2 Cr. App. R. (S.) 41; [2017] Crim. L.R. 68, CA (Crim Div) .... *Digested,* 17/**1977**

R. v Churchill (Kristian); *joined case* R. v Ward (Damian) [2017] EWCA Crim 841; [2017] 2 Cr. App. R. (S.) 34; [2017] Crim. L.R. 1003, CA (Crim Div) .... *Digested,* 17/**1922**

R. v Cipriani (Danny) (Unreported, June 24, 2016), MC *Approved* 17/570

R. v Civil Service Appeal Board Ex p. Cunningham [1991] 4 All E.R. 310; [1992] I.C.R. 817; [1992] I.C.R. 816; [1991] I.R.L.R. 297; Times, March 11, 1991; Independent, March 19, 1991; [1991] C.O.D. 478; Guardian, March 13, 1991; Daily Telegraph, March 18, 1991; (1991) 141 N.L.J. 455, CA (Civ Div) .... *Digested,* 91/**18**: *Applied* 93/1213: *Considered* 94/6012, 95/2534, 95/42, 96/2117, 02/3234: *Distinguished* 94/5948: *Followed* 17/1454

R. v Clark (John Eric) see R. v Forbes (Stephen John)

R. v Clarke (Andrew James); *joined case* R. v Sheppard (Geoffrey Brian) [2017] EWCA Crim 37; [2017] 1 W.L.R. 2886; [2017] 1 Cr. App. R. 28, CA (Crim Div) .. *Digested,* 17/**596**

R. v Clarke (Antwon) see R. v Huggins (Kaneel)

R. v Clarke (Paul) see R. v Paywand (Azmari)

R. v Clarke (Ralph); *joined case* R. v Cooper (Peter) [2017] EWCA Crim 393; [2017] 1 W.L.R. 3851; [2018] 2 All E.R. 333; [2017] 2 Cr. App. R. (S.) 18; [2017] Crim. L.R. 572, CA (Crim Div) .... *Digested,* 17/**1981**

R. v Clarke (Wayne) see R. v Smith (Steven)

R. v Clayton-Wright (Derek) [1948] 2 All E.R. 763; (1948-49) 82 Ll. L. Rep. 7; 64 T.L.R. 543; (1949) 33 Cr. App. R. 22; (1948) 112 J.P. 428; 47 L.G.R. 48; [1948] W.N. 392; [1949] L.J.R. 380; (1948) 92 S.J. 648, CCA .... *Digested,* 47-51/**2167**: *Applied* 69/673, 17/602: *Considered* 70/458, 94/935

R. v Cockshott [1898] 1 Q.B. 582, QBD *Applied* 52/2125, 54/2035: *Considered* 17/573: *Followed* 47-51/6143, 68/2402

R. v Coleman (Danielle) see R. v Vowles (Lucinda)

R. v Coleman (John) [2016] EWCA Crim 1665; [2017] 4 W.L.R. 29, CA (Crim Div) ...... *Digested,* 17/**585**

R. v Collier (Edward) see R. v Lang (Stephen Howard)

R. v Collins (David) see R. v Hyde (Daniel)

R. v Conaghan (Terence); *joined cases* R. v James (Thomas William Henry); R. v Ramchaitar (David Noel); R v Solomon (Michael Herbert) [2017] EWCA Crim 597; [2018] 4 W.L.R. 58; [2017] 2 Cr. App. R. 19; [2017] Crim. L.R. 1009, CA (Crim Div) .... *Digested,* 17/**587**

R. v Connor (Michael) [2007] EWCA Crim 2591; [2008] 1 Cr. App. R. (S.) 89, CA (Crim Div) .... *Digested,* 08/**3336**: *Distinguished* 17/1948

R. v Conroy (Jason John) [2017] EWCA Crim 81; [2017] 2 Cr. App. R. 26, CA (Crim Div) .... *Digested,* 17/**544**

R. v Cooper (Martin Francis); *joined cases* R. v Ferry (Jonathan Paul); R. v Darby (Jamie Alan); R. v Higgs (Adam Lee); R. v Hull (Paul James); R. v Frazier (Stuart Andrew); R. v Sly (Tyrone); R. v Straw (James Robert) [2017] EWCA Crim 558; [2017] 2 Cr. App. R. (S.) 14, CA (Crim Div) .... *Digested,* 17/**1913**

R. v Cooper (Peter) see R. v Clarke (Ralph)

R. v Cooper (Roger Andrew) [2017] EWCA Crim 419; [2017] 4 W.L.R. 165, CA (Crim Div) .... *Digested,* 17/**1951**

R. v Cordle (John William) [2016] EWCA Crim 1793; [2017] 1 Cr. App. R. (S.) 36, CA (Crim Div) .... *Digested,* 17/**1961**

R. v Cornish (Errol) [2016] EWHC 779 (QB); [2016] Crim. L.R. 560, QBD
Applied 17/620

R. v Cornwall CC Ex p. Hardy [2001] Env. L.R. 25; [2001] J.P.L. 786, QBD .... *Digested,* 01/**2390**:
Applied 17/1755: *Approved* 03/3420: *Distinguished* 04/3027

R. v Cottrell (Steven); *joined case* R. v Fletcher (Joseph) [2007] EWCA Crim 2016; [2007] 1 W.L.R. 3262; [2008] 1 Cr. App. R. 7; Times, September 5, 2007; [2008] Crim. L.R. 50, CA (Crim Div) .... *Digested,* 07/**970**:
Applied 17/551: *Considered* 13/691

R. v Cowles (Ben Kevin) see Attorney General's Reference (Nos 60, 62 and 63 of 2009)

R. v Cowles (Tom Andew) see Attorney General's Reference (Nos 60, 62 and 63 of 2009)

R. v Craciunescu (Alexandra Dorina) see R. v Joseph (Verna Sermanfure)

R. v Criminal Injuries Compensation Board Ex p. A [1999] 2 A.C. 330; [1999] 2 W.L.R. 974; Times, March 26, 1999; Independent, April 15, 1999; [1999] C.O.D. 244; (1999) 96(17) L.S.G. 25; (1999) 149 N.L.J. 522; (1999) 143 S.J.L.B. 120, HL .... *Digested,* 99/**918**:
Applied 03/3429, 10/2594, 17/1754: *Considered* 04/2030

R. v Criminal Injuries Compensation Board Ex p. Warner; *joined case* R. v Criminal Injuries Compensation Board Ex p. Webb [1987] Q.B. 74; [1986] 3 W.L.R. 251; [1986] 2 All E.R. 478; (1986) 136 N.L.J. 536; (1986) 130 S.J. 468, CA (Civ Div) *Digested,* 86/**535**:
Applied 01/1022, 08/821, 11/2369: *Considered* 00/28, 17/1644:
Followed 92/5537, 93/5068, 98/927, 14/54

R. v Criminal Injuries Compensation Board Ex p. Webb see R. v Criminal Injuries Compensation Board Ex p. Warner

R. v Customs and Excise Commissioners Ex p. Allied Domecq Plc see R. v Customs and Excise Commissioners Ex p. Kay & Co Ltd

R. v Customs and Excise Commissioners Ex p. Association of Optometrists see R. v Customs and Excise Commissioners Ex p. Kay & Co Ltd

R. v Customs and Excise Commissioners Ex p. Building Societies Ombudsman Co Ltd see R. (on the application of Building Societies Ombudsman Co Ltd) v Customs and Excise Commissioners

R. v Customs and Excise Commissioners Ex p. Colaingrove Ltd see R. v Customs and Excise Commissioners Ex p. Kay & Co Ltd

R. v Customs and Excise Commissioners Ex p. Greenlee Group Plc see R. v Customs and Excise Commissioners Ex p. Kay & Co Ltd

R. v Customs and Excise Commissioners Ex p. Kay & Co Ltd; *joined cases* R. v Customs and Excise Commissioners Ex p. Association of Optometrists; R. v Customs and Excise Commissioners Ex p. National Provident Institution; R. v Customs and Excise Commissioners Ex p. Greenlee Group Plc; R. v Customs and Excise Commissioners Ex p. Colaingrove Ltd; R. v Customs and Excise Commissioners Ex p. Wardens and Commonality of the Mystery of Mercers of the City of London; R. v Customs and Excise Commissioners Ex p. Allied Domecq Plc; R. v Customs and Excise Commissioners Ex p. Rayner and Keeler [1996] S.T.C. 1500; [1997] B.T.C. 5010; [1997] B.V.C. 128; Times, December 10, 1996; Independent, January 13, 1997, QBD .... *Digested,* 97/**5028**:
Considered 03/4567, 17/2125: *Followed* 00/5310

R. v Customs and Excise Commissioners Ex p. National Provident Institution see R. v Customs and Excise Commissioners Ex p. Kay & Co Ltd

R. v Customs and Excise Commissioners Ex p. Rayner and Keeler see R. v Customs and Excise Commissioners Ex p. Kay & Co Ltd

R. v Customs and Excise Commissioners Ex p. Wardens and Commonality of the Mystery of Mercers of the City of London see R. v Customs and Excise Commissioners Ex p. Kay & Co Ltd

R. v D [2017] EWCA Crim 355; [2017] 2 Cr. App. R. (S.) 1, CA (Crim Div) .... *Digested,* 17/**1921**

R. v D see R. v Lang (Stephen Howard)

R. v Dan see R. v H

R. v Daniels (Antonio Eval) see R. v Powell (Anthony Glassford)

R. v Darby (Jamie Alan) see R. v Cooper (Martin Francis)

R. v Darby (John Frederick) see R. v Henn (Maurice Donald)

R. v Darrigan (Christopher) [2017] EWCA Crim 169; [2017] 1 Cr. App. R. (S.) 50; [2017] Crim. L.R. 565, CA (Crim Div) .... *Digested,* 17/**1995**

R. v Deakin (Lloyd) see R. v Needham (Paul Maurice)

R. v Deitschmann (Anthony) see R. v Dietschmann (Anthony)

R. v Denbigh Justices Ex p. Williams; *joined case* R v Denbigh Justices Ex p. Evans [1974] Q.B. 759; [1974] 3 W.L.R. 45; [1974] 2 All E.R. 1052; [1974] Crim. L.R. 442; (1974) 118 S.J. 478, QBD .... *Digested,* 74/**2270**:
Applied 17/18: *Considered* 95/2012

R. v Denham (John); *joined case* R. v Stansfield (Matthew) [2016] EWCA Crim 1048; [2017] 1 Cr. App. R. 7; [2017] Crim. L.R. 213, CA (Crim Div) .... *Digested,* 17/**510**
R. v DG see R. v LM
R. v Dhnoay (Gurdev Singh) see R. v Knights (Richard Michael)
R. v Diaby (Sanissi Jean) [2017] EWCA Crim 125; [2017] 1 Cr. App. R. (S.) 58, CA (Crim Div) .... *Digested,* 17/**1968**
R. v Dietschmann (Anthony); *sub nom* R. v Deitschmann (Anthony) [2003] UKHL 10; [2003] 1 A.C. 1209; [2003] 2 W.L.R. 613; [2003] 1 All E.R. 897; [2003] 2 Cr. App. R. 4; [2003] M.H.L.R. 333; Times, February 28, 2003; Independent, March 4, 2003; (2003) 100(14) L.S.G. 27; (2003) 147 S.J.L.B. 265, HL .... *Digested,* 03/**799**: *Applied* 08/839: *Considered* 06/960: *Followed* 17/545
R. v Dillon (Paul) [2015] EWCA Crim 3; [2015] 1 Cr. App. R. (S.) 62; [2015] Crim. L.R. 383, CA (Crim Div) .... *Digested,* 15/**2248**: *Considered* 17/1938
R. v Dobby (Joshua Mark) [2017] EWCA Crim 775; [2017] 4 W.L.R. 145; [2017] 2 Cr. App. R. (S.) 27; [2017] R.T.R. 28, CA (Crim Div) .... *Digested,* 17/**1945**
R. v Docherty (Shaun Kevin) [2014] EWCA Crim 1197; [2014] 2 Cr. App. R. (S.) 76, CA (Crim Div) .... *Digested,* 15/**2232**: *Affirmed* 17/1934
R. v Docherty (Shaun Kevin) [2016] UKSC 62; [2017] 1 W.L.R. 181; [2017] 4 All E.R. 263; [2017] 1 Cr. App. R. (S.) 31, SC .... *Digested,* 17/**1934**: *Followed* 17/1588, 17/1933
R. v Dodd (Jonathan) see R. v Smith (Steven)
R. v Doe (Henry) see R. v Smith (William)
R. v Donegan (David) see Attorney General's Reference (No.27 of 2013)
R. v Donovan (Mark) [2009] EWCA Crim 1258, CA (Crim Div) *Not followed* 17/1991
R. v Dosanjh (Jaswinder Singh) see Jones (Setting of Minimum Term), Re
R. v Dowse (Adrian); *joined case* R. v White (Kevin) [2017] EWCA Crim 598; [2017] 2 Cr. App. R. (S.) 26, CA (Crim Div) .... *Digested,* 17/**1960**
R. v DPP Ex p. Boukemiche (Farid) see R. v DPP Ex p. Kebeline
R. v DPP Ex p. Kebelene see R. v DPP Ex p. Kebeline
R. v DPP Ex p. Kebeline; *sub nom* R. v DPP Ex p. Kebelene; R. v DPP Ex p. Kebilene; *joined cases* R. v DPP Ex p. Boukemiche (Farid); R. v DPP Ex p. Souidi (Sofiane); R. v DPP Ex p. Rechachi (Fatah) [2000] 2 A.C. 326; [1999] 3 W.L.R. 972; [1999] 4 All E.R. 801; [2000] 1 Cr. App. R. 275; [2000] H.R.L.R. 93; [2000] U.K.H.R.R. 176; (2000) 2 L.G.L.R. 697; (1999) 11 Admin. L.R. 1026; Times, November 2, 1999; [2000] Crim. L.R. 486; (1999) 96(43) L.S.G. 32, HL . *Digested,* 99/**1045**: *Applied* 00/5473, 00/921, 01/5291, 01/564, 01/5879, 02/3079, 03/1938, 03/2171, 04/2088, 07/53: *Considered* 02/5866, 02/795, 02/849, 03/2676, 03/761, 08/1661: *Followed* 17/384
R. v DPP Ex p. Kebilene see R. v DPP Ex p. Kebeline
R. v DPP Ex p. Rechachi (Fatah) see R. v DPP Ex p. Kebeline
R. v DPP Ex p. Souidi (Sofiane) see R. v DPP Ex p. Kebeline
R. v Ducram (Fitzroy) see Attorney General's Reference (Nos 128 to 141 of 2015 and 8 to 10 of 2016)
R. v Duncan (Christopher) [2006] EWCA Crim 1576; [2007] 1 Cr. App. R. (S.) 26, CA (Crim Div) .... *Digested,* 07/**3693**: *Considered* 17/1938
R. v Dunn (Brett Walter) [2017] EWCA Crim 520; [2017] 2 Cr. App. R. (S.) 21, CA (Crim Div) .... *Digested,* 17/**1918**
R. v Dunstan (David) [2016] EWCA Crim 2098; [2017] 1 Cr. App. R. (S.) 24, CA (Crim Div) .... *Digested,* 17/**1948**
R. v Eckersley (Anthony) [2003] EWCA Crim 2361, CA (Crim Div) *Considered* 17/518
R. v Edmonson (Andrew) see R. v Quillan (Gary)
R. v Edwards (Kim Rose) see R. v Markham (Stan Lucas)
R. v Edwards (Kyle Frederick) see R. v Lang (Stephen Howard)
R. v Effionayi (Collins) see R. v Effionayi (Grace)
R. v Effionayi (Grace); *sub nom* R. v Efionayi (Grace); *joined case* R. v Effionayi (Collins) (1995) 16 Cr. App. R. (S.) 380; [1994] Crim. L.R. 870, CA (Crim Div) *Explained* 17/1972
R. v Efionayi (Grace) see R. v Effionayi (Grace)
R. v Egginton (Luke) [2016] EWCA Crim 1775; [2017] 1 Cr. App. R. (S.) 20, CA (Crim Div) .... *Digested,* 17/**568**
R. v Ekwugha (Casmir) see R. v Bala (Yilkyes Finok)

R. v Elliott (Trevor) (1985) 81 Cr. App. R. 115; Times, December 13, 1984; [1985] Crim. L.R. 310, CA (Crim Div) .... *Digested,* 85/**597**: *Considered* 92/843, 10/729, 12/1039, 17/593: *Explained* 16/496: *Followed* 95/2379

R. v Ellis (Benjamin) [2016] EWCA Crim 1398; [2017] 1 Cr. App. R. (S.) 4, CA (Crim Div) .... *Digested,* 17/**1967**

R. v Ellis (James) (1973) 57 Cr. App. R. 571; [1973] Crim. L.R. 389, CA (Crim Div) ..... *Digested,* 73/**588**: *Applied* 90/957, 95/1045: *Considered* 17/573: *Distinguished* 77/453

R. v English (Philip) see R. v Powell (Anthony Glassford)

R. v Eshati (Abdurraouf) see R. v Kahar (Mohammed Abdul)

R. v Etherington (Samuel) [2014] EWCA Crim 1867; [2015] 1 Cr. App. R. (S.) 7, CA (Crim Div) .... *Digested,* 15/**2265**: *Considered* 17/1945

R. v Evans (Chedwyn) [2016] EWCA Crim 452; [2016] 4 W.L.R. 169; [2017] 1 Cr. App. R. 13; [2017] Crim. L.R. 406, CA (Crim Div) .... *Digested,* 17/**513**

R. v Evans (Eric) see Evans v Serious Fraud Office

R. v Evans (Wayne) [2017] EWCA Crim 139; [2017] 1 Cr. App. R. (S.) 56, CA (Crim Div) .... *Digested,* 17/**1902**

R. v Exeter City Council Ex p. Tranckle (1994) 26 H.L.R. 244, CA (Civ Div) .... *Digested,* 94/**2327**: *Considered* 96/3050: *Followed* 17/1159

R. v F (David) see R. v Forbes (Stephen John)

R. v F see R. v H

R. v Farnish (Malcolm) see R. v Reynolds (Stephen)

R. v Farnish (Valerie) see R. v Reynolds (Stephen)

R. v Fedar (Mohammed) see Attorney General's Reference (Nos 128 to 141 of 2015 and 8 to 10 of 2016)

R. v Feihn (Steven) see R. v Lang (Stephen Howard)

R. v Ferizi (Orhan); *joined case* R. v Timmerman (Ramis) [2016] EWCA Crim 2022; [2017] 1 Cr. App. R. (S.) 26, CA (Crim Div) .... *Digested,* 17/**1919**

R. v Ferry (Jonathan Paul) see R. v Cooper (Martin Francis)

R. v Finnerty (Daniel Mark) [2016] EWCA Crim 1513; [2017] 1 Cr. App. R. (S.) 9, CA (Crim Div) .... *Digested,* 17/**1886**

R. v FK (Alan Charles) see R. v Forbes (Stephen John)

R. v Flack (Perry) [2013] EWCA Crim 115; [2013] 2 Cr. App. R. (S.) 56; [2013] Crim. L.R. 521, CA (Crim Div) .... *Digested,* 13/**680**: *Followed* 17/535

R. v Fletcher (Joseph) see R. v Cottrell (Steven)

R. v Flynn (Tarique Samuel) see R. v Babiak (Tomasz)

R. v FNC [2015] EWCA Crim 1732; [2016] 1 W.L.R. 980; [2016] 1 Cr. App. R. 12; [2016] Crim. L.R. 275, CA (Crim Div) .... *Digested,* 16/**460**: *Followed* 17/524

R. v Forbes (Stephen John); *joined cases* R. v F (David); R. v FK (Alan Charles); R. v T (Dean); Rouse (Mark David); R. v BD; R. v McCallen (Anthony John); R. v Clark (John Eric); R. v Warren (Barry James) [2016] EWCA Crim 1388; [2017] 1 W.L.R. 53; [2016] 2 Cr. App. R. (S.) 44; [2016] Crim. L.R. 946, CA (Crim Div) *Digested,* 17/**1979**: *Followed* 17/1980

R. v Foster (Billy Tom) see R. v Loveridge (Wayne)

R. v Foye (Lee Robert) [2013] EWCA Crim 475; (2013) 177 J.P. 449; [2013] M.H.L.R. 182; [2013] Crim. L.R. 839, CA (Crim Div) .... *Digested,* 13/**634**: *Followed* 17/517

R. v France (Anthony Jonathan) [2016] EWCA Crim 1588; [2016] 4 W.L.R. 175; [2017] 1 Cr. App. R. 19, CA (Crim Div) .... *Digested,* 17/**604**

R. v Frazier (Stuart Andrew) see R. v Cooper (Martin Francis)

R. v French (Geraldine) see R. v Rogers (Bradley David)

R. v Fuller [2016] EWCA Crim 1867; [2017] M.H.L.R. 228, CA (Crim Div) .... *Digested,* 17/**1906**

R. v Fulton (Gary Peter); *joined case* R. v Wood (Daniel) [2017] EWCA Crim 308; [2018] 4 W.L.R. 25; [2017] 2 Cr. App. R. (S.) 11, CA (Crim Div) .... *Digested,* 17/**1947**

R. v Furniss (Michael); *joined cases* R. v Stacey (James); R. v Hall (Stuart) [2015] 1 Costs L.R. 151, Crown Ct (Nottingham) .... *Digested,* 15/**1641**: *Applied* 17/1481: *Doubted* 16/1407

R. v G; *sub nom* R. v SG [2017] EWCA Crim 617; [2017] 4 W.L.R. 119; [2017] 2 Cr. App. R. 20; (2017) 181 J.P. 363; [2017] Crim. L.R. 733, CA (Crim Div) .... *Digested,* 17/**520**

R. v G [2016] EWCA Crim 541; [2016] 4 W.L.R. 124; [2016] 2 Cr. App. R. (S.) 17; [2016] Crim. L.R. 784, CA (Crim Div) .... *Digested,* 16/**1855**: *Followed* 17/1993

R. v G [2008] UKHL 37; [2009] 1 A.C. 92; [2008] 1 W.L.R. 1379; [2008] 3 All E.R. 1071; [2009] 1 Cr. App. R. 8; [2008] H.R.L.R. 36; [2009] U.K.H.R.R. 72; Times, June 20, 2008; [2008] Crim. L.R. 818; (2008) 152(25) S.J.L.B. 31, HL .... *Digested,* 08/**722**: *Applied* 14/1646, 14/674: *Considered* 09/4824: *Followed* 17/1896

R. v G (Germaine) [2016] EWCA Crim 1633; [2016] 4 W.L.R. 185; [2017] 1 Cr. App. R. 27, CA (Crim Div) .... *Digested,* 17/**519**

R. v Gaffney (Lynn) see R. v Chapman (Scott Derek)

R. v Gard (Christopher Richard) [2017] EWCA Crim 21; [2017] 1 Cr. App. R. (S.) 45, CA (Crim Div) .... *Digested,* 17/**1965**

R. v Garland (Jason) [2016] EWCA Crim 1743; [2017] 4 W.L.R. 117; [2017] Crim. L.R. 402, CA (Crim Div) .... *Digested,* 17/**523**

R. v Garrett (Gregory) see R. v Quillan (Gary)

R. v Garrett (Peter) see R. v Quillan (Gary)

R. v Garwood (Reece); *sub nom* R. v Miah (Javed Ruhel); R. v Hall (Michael) [2017] EWCA Crim 59; [2017] 1 W.L.R. 3182; [2018] 1 All E.R. 388; [2017] 1 Cr. App. R. 30, CA (Crim Div) .... *Digested,* 17/**572**

R. v Garwood (Reece) see R. v Johnson (Lewis)

R. v George-Davies (Stephen) [2010] EWCA Crim 919; [2011] 1 Cr. App. R. (S.) 13, CA (Crim Div)
Distinguished 17/1948

R. v Geraghty (Anthony) [2016] EWCA Crim 1523; [2017] 1 W.L.R. 657; [2017] 1 Cr. App. R. (S.) 10; [2017] Crim. L.R. 158, CA (Crim Div) .... *Digested,* 17/**609**

R. v Ghalib (Amar) see Attorney General's Reference (Nos 128 to 141 of 2015 and 8 to 10 of 2016)

R. v Ghavami (Amir) see R. v Mateta (Koshi Pitshou)

R. v Ghayur (Abdul) see R. v Safi (Ali Ahmed)

R. v Ghosh (Deb Baran) [1982] Q.B. 1053; [1982] 3 W.L.R. 110; [1982] 2 All E.R. 689; (1982) 75 Cr. App. R. 154; [1982] Crim. L.R. 608; (1982) 126 S.J. 429, CA (Crim Div) .... *Digested,* 82/**659**: *Applied* 84/677, 88/841, 90/1140, 90/910, 03/4592, 14/2829, 15/1184: *Cited* 93/771, 94/838, 17/1114: *Considered* 86/608, 87/783, 90/909, 90/911, 91/753, 91/762, 92/652, 92/789, 93/780, 97/3828, 01/2343, 11/3495: *Distinguished* 92/806: *Followed* 96/1512, 16/468: *Overruled in part* 17/1145

R. v Glasson (Davin) see R. v Thorsby (Adrian Kenneth)

R. v Glave (Heathcliffe) see R. v Lang (Stephen Howard)

R. v Golds (Mark Richard) [2014] EWCA Crim 748; [2015] 1 W.L.R. 1030; [2014] 4 All E.R. 64; [2014] 2 Cr. App. R. 17; [2015] M.H.L.R. 427; [2014] Crim. L.R. 744, CA (Crim Div) .... *Digested,* 14/**778**: *Affirmed* 17/555

R. v Golds (Mark Richard) [2016] UKSC 61; [2016] 1 W.L.R. 5231; [2017] 1 All E.R. 1055; [2017] 1 Cr. App. R. 18; [2017] M.H.L.R. 99; [2017] Crim. L.R. 316, SC ... *Digested,* 17/**555**: *Considered* 17/606

R. v Goldsmith (Harold Egan) see R. v Avis (Tony)

R. v Gomez (Jason George) see R. v Wadkin (Paul)

R. v Goodwin (Gary William); *joined case* R. v Ahmed (Hussein) [2017] EWCA Crim 90; [2017] 1 Cr. App. R. (S.) 53, CA (Crim Div) .... *Digested,* 17/**1907**

R. v Gor (Kaushikial) [2017] EWCA Crim 3; [2017] Lloyd's Rep. F.C. 73, CA (Crim Div) .... *Digested,* 17/**580**

R. v Gordon (Khianni) see R. v Huggins (Kaneel)

R. v Governor of Whitemoor Prison Ex p. Main see R. v Secretary of State for the Home Department Ex p. Simms

R. v Graham (Garry Allan) see R. v Graham (Hemamali Krishna)

R. v Graham (Hemamali Krishna); *joined cases* R. v Bramich (David); R. v Price (Paul Graham); R. v Graham (Garry Allan); R. v Marsh (Terence Colin); R. v Ali (Sajid Pasha); R. v Kansal (Rupe Lal) [1997] 1 Cr. App. R. 302; Times, October 28, 1996; Independent, October 30, 1996; [1997] Crim. L.R. 340; (1996) 93(44) L.S.G. 29; (1996) 140 S.J.L.B. 253, CA (Crim Div) .... *Digested,* 96/**1532**: *Applied* 97/1228, 98/892, 02/809, 11/652, 11/822, 12/795, 16/532, 17/551: *Approved* 00/5480: *Considered* 97/1224, 97/1226, 97/1227, 97/1249, 07/971, 13/717, 14/772, 15/550: *Distinguished* 07/869: *Followed* 97/1126: *Referred to* 97/1225, 97/1229, 97/1230, 97/1231, 97/1304

R. v Graham (Paul Anthony) [1982] 1 W.L.R. 294; [1982] 1 All E.R. 801; (1982) 74 Cr. App. R. 235; [1982] Crim. L.R. 365; (1982) 126 S.J. 117, CA (Crim Div) .... *Digested,* 82/**556**: *Applied* 86/649, 89/827, 95/1257, 03/877: *Approved* 87/800: *Considered* 95/4430, 96/1454: *Followed* 17/547

R. v Grant (Lemar) see R. v McLeod (Ralph)

R. v Grant (Ricardo) see R. v McLeod (Ralph)

R. v Gray (Stephen) see R. v Abdallah (Abdalraouf)

R. v Greaves (Claude Clifford); *joined cases* R. v Jenkins (Fraser); R. v Botcher (Henrik) [2010] EWCA Crim 709; [2011] 1 Cr. App. R. (S.) 8; [2010] Lloyd's Rep. F.C. 423; [2010] Crim. L.R. 650, CA (Crim Div) .... *Digested,* 10/**2876**: *Applied* 11/2857, 17/1960: *Considered* 14/2655

R. v Green (Jerome) see R. v Johnson (Lewis)

R. v Green (Victoria) [2016] EWCA Crim 1888; [2017] 1 Cr. App. R. (S.) 22, CA (Crim Div) .... *Digested,* 17/**1926**

R. v Greenwood (Andrew Philip) [2004] EWCA Crim 1388; [2005] 1 Cr. App. R. 7; [2005] Crim. L.R. 59; (2004) 148 S.J.L.B. 788, CA (Crim Div) .... *Digested,* 05/**735**: *Considered* 17/516

R. v Gribby (Brendan Clifford) [2016] EWCA Crim 1847; [2017] 1 Cr. App. R. (S.) 18; [2017] Crim. L.R. 411, CA (Crim Div) .... *Digested,* 17/**1896**

R. v Griffin (Craig) [2008] EWCA Crim 119; [2008] 2 Cr. App. R. (S.) 61, CA (Crim Div) .... *Digested,* 08/**3318**: *Followed* 17/1972

R. v Guidera (Michael) see R. v Lang (Stephen Howard)

R. v Gul (Rowan) see Attorney General's Reference (Nos 128 to 141 of 2015 and 8 to 10 of 2016)

R. v Guraj (Lodvik) [2015] EWCA Crim 305; [2015] 1 W.L.R. 4149; [2016] 2 All E.R. 33; [2015] 2 Cr. App. R. (S.) 21, CA (Crim Div) .... *Digested,* 15/**606**: *Reversed* 17/583

R. v Guraj (Lodvik) [2016] UKSC 65; [2017] 1 W.L.R. 22; [2017] 4 All E.R. 848; [2017] 1 Cr. App. R. (S.) 32; [2017] Lloyd's Rep. F.C. 117; Times, January 6, 2017; [2017] Crim. L.R. 320, SC .... *Digested,* 17/**583**

R. v H; *joined cases* R. v P; R. v Robertson; R. v S; R. v Dan; R. v Walker (P); R. v W; R. v F [2011] EWCA Crim 2753; [2012] 1 W.L.R. 1416; [2012] 2 All E.R. 340; [2012] 2 Cr. App. R. (S.) 21; Times, December 9, 2011; [2012] Crim. L.R. 149, CA (Crim Div) .... *Digested,* 12/**3016**: *Applied* 15/2181, 15/2254, 16/1854, 16/1899, 17/1979: *Cited* 16/1857: *Considered* 17/1980: *Followed* 12/3011, 15/2282

R. v H see Attorney General's Reference (No.126 of 2006)

R. v H see R. v RH

R. v Hackett (Adam Steve) [2017] EWCA Crim 250; [2017] 2 Cr. App. R. (S.) 10; [2017] Crim. L.R. 725, CA (Crim Div) .... *Digested,* 17/**1898**

R. v Hackett (Sean) [2015] NICA 57; [2017] M.H.L.R. 171, CA (NI)

R. v Hadley (Jason Lee) see R. v Beech (Dean Colin)

R. v Halim (Akim); *sub nom* R. v Halmin [2017] EWCA Crim 33; [2017] Lloyd's Rep. F.C. 186, CA (Crim Div) .... *Digested,* 17/**582**

R. v Hall (Bryan) see R. v Smith (Steven)

R. v Hall (Daniel Patrick) [2013] EWCA Crim 82; [2013] 2 Cr. App. R. (S.) 68; [2013] Crim. L.R. 426, CA (Crim Div) .... *Digested,* 13/**2605**: *Considered* 15/2209, 17/1925

R. v Hall (Michael) see R. v Garwood (Reece)

R. v Hall (Michael) see R. v Johnson (Lewis)

R. v Hall (Stuart) see R. v Furniss (Michael)

R. v Halmin see R. v Halim (Akim)

R. v Hamberger (Martin) [2017] EWCA Crim 273; [2017] 4 W.L.R. 77; [2017] 2 Cr. App. R. 9; (2017) 181 J.P. 449; [2017] Crim. L.R. 708, CA (Crim Div) .... *Digested,* 17/**521**

R. v Hamer (Robert) [2017] EWCA Crim 192; [2017] 2 Cr. App. R. (S.) 13, CA (Crim Div) .... *Digested,* 17/**1983**

R. v Hammersmith and Fulham LBC Ex p. Lusi (1991) 23 H.L.R. 260; (1992) 4 Admin. L.R. 277; Times, March 25, 1991; [1991] C.O.D. 290; (1992) 156 L.G. Rev. 202; Guardian, March 14, 1991, QBD .... *Digested,* 91/**1903**: *Applied* 17/1159: *Considered* 92/2257, 93/2056, 09/1904

R. v Hammersmith and Fulham LBC Ex p. O'Brian (1985) 17 H.L.R. 471; 84 L.G.R. 202, QBD .... *Digested,* 86/**1627**: *Overruled in part* 93/2050: *Superseded* 17/1148

R. v Hamza (Mohammed) [2017] EWCA Crim 1217; [2017] 2 Cr. App. R. (S.) 47, CA (Crim Div) .... *Digested,* 17/**1946**

R. v Handford (Mark Timothy) [2016] EWCA Crim 1838; [2017] 1 Cr. App. R. (S.) 19, CA (Crim Div) .... *Digested,* 17/**1912**

R. v Hanson (John) see Attorney General's Reference (No.27 of 2013)

R. v Harrak (Musa) see Attorney General's Reference (No.105 of 2014)

R. v Harris (John) [1969] 1 W.L.R. 745; [1969] 2 All E.R. 599 (Note); (1969) 53 Cr. App. R. 376; (1969) 133 J.P. 422; (1969) 113 S.J. 363, CA (Crim Div) .... *Digested,* 69/**668**: *Explained* 17/615: *Followed* 96/1517

R. v Harrison (John) [2017] EWCA Crim 888; [2017] 2 Cr. App. R. (S.) 37, CA (Crim Div)

R. v Harrow LBC Ex p. Cobham see R. (on the application of Stennett) v Manchester City Council

R. v Harrow LBC Ex p. Fahia [1998] 1 W.L.R. 1396; [1998] 4 All E.R. 137; [1998] 3 F.C.R. 363; (1998) 30 H.L.R. 1124; Times, July 24, 1998; (1998) 95(35) L.S.G. 38; (1998) 148 N.L.J. 1354; (1998) 142 S.J.L.B. 226; [1998] N.P.C. 122, HL ..... *Digested,* 98/**3014**: *Applied* 05/1986, 05/1988: *Followed* 16/1036, 17/1148, 17/1157

R. v Hartley (John) [2011] EWCA Crim 1299; [2012] 1 Cr. App. R. 7; [2012] 1 Cr. App. R. (S.) 28; [2011] Crim. L.R. 726, CA (Crim Div) ..... *Digested,* 12/**794**: *Applied* 15/2235, 17/1897, 17/601: *Considered* 13/2586

R. v Harvey (Jack Frederick) [2015] UKSC 73; [2017] A.C. 105; [2016] 2 W.L.R. 37; [2016] 4 All E.R. 521; [2016] 1 Cr. App. R. (S.) 60; [2016] Lloyd's Rep. F.C. 41; [2016] Crim. L.R. 356, SC ..... *Digested,* 16/**499**: *Considered* 16/506

R. v Hasa (Ilir) see R. v Mula (Gazmend)

R. v Hasan (Aytach); *sub nom* R. v Z [2005] UKHL 22; [2005] 2 A.C. 467; [2005] 2 W.L.R. 709; [2005] 4 All E.R. 685; [2005] 2 Cr. App. R. 22; Times, March 21, 2005; Independent, March 22, 2005; [2006] Crim. L.R. 142; (2005) 149 S.J.L.B. 360, HL ..... *Digested,* 05/**765**: *Considered* 05/772, 12/721: *Followed* 17/547

R. v Havering BC [2017] EWCA Crim 242; [2017] 2 Cr. App. R. (S.) 9, CA (Crim Div)

R. v Hawkins (Paul Nigel) [1997] 1 Cr. App. R. 234; Times, August 6, 1996; [1997] Crim. L.R. 134; (1996) 93(36) L.S.G. 35; (1996) 140 S.J.L.B. 214, CA (Crim Div) ..... *Digested,* 96/**1548**: *Applied* 05/859, 11/652, 17/551: *Considered* 01/1113: *Followed* 97/1260

R. v Haymer (Matthew Phillip) [2012] EWCA Crim 2200; [2013] 1 Cr. App. R. (S.) 115, CA (Crim Div) ..... *Digested,* 13/**2719**: *Considered* 17/1954

R. v Haywood (Nigel) see R. v Hyde (Daniel)

R. v Healey (Robert); *joined cases* R. v Bolton (Mark); R. v McGregor (Alexander); R. v Brearley (Gary); R. v Taylor (Matthew) [2012] EWCA Crim 1005; [2013] 1 Cr. App. R. (S.) 33; [2012] Crim. L.R. 640, CA (Crim Div) ..... *Digested,* 13/**2623**: *Applied* 13/2615, 13/2791: *Considered* 13/2616, 17/1912, 17/1923

R. v Heggarty (David John) [2017] EWCA Crim 988; [2017] 2 Cr. App. R. (S.) 48, CA (Crim Div) ..... *Digested,* 17/**1994**

R. v Hemmings (David Christopher) [2007] EWCA Crim 2413; [2008] 1 Cr. App. R. (S.) 106, CA (Crim Div) ..... *Digested,* 09/**3360**: *Considered* 10/2862, 17/1904: *Doubted* 12/2867

R. v Henderson (Christopher) [2016] EWCA Crim 965; [2016] 4 W.L.R. 172; [2017] 1 Cr. App. R. 4; (2017) 181 J.P. 229; [2017] Crim. L.R. 233, CA (Crim Div) ..... *Digested,* 17/**557**

R. v Henley (Clifford James) (Appeal against Conviction) [2000] Crim. L.R. 582, CA (Crim Div) *Followed* 17/550

R. v Henn (Maurice Donald); *sub nom* Henn v DPP; *joined case* R. v Darby (John Frederick) [1981] A.C. 850; (1980) 71 Cr. App. R. 44; [1980] 2 C.M.L.R. 229; [1980] F.S.R. 382; (1980) 124 S.J. 290, HL *Applied* 82/560: *Considered* 98/3574: *Followed* 17/2240

R. v Henry (Jose) see R. v Hyde (Daniel)

R. v Hereford Corp Ex p. Harrower [1970] 1 W.L.R. 1424; [1970] 3 All E.R. 460; 69 L.G.R. 28; (1970) 114 S.J. 705, DC ..... *Digested,* 70/**1608**: *Applied* 79/2646: *Considered* 81/1626, 17/1814

R. v Herrington (Wayne) [2017] EWCA Crim 889; [2018] 4 W.L.R. 35; [2017] 2 Cr. App. R. (S.) 38, CA (Crim Div) ..... *Digested,* 17/**1962**

R. v Hertfordshire CC Ex p. Cheung; *joined case* R. v Sefton MBC Ex p. Pau Times, April 4, 1986, CA (Civ Div) ..... *Digested,* 86/**1135**: *Applied* 14/787: *Considered* 10/1432, 17/2711

R. v Hester-Wox (Jack) [2016] EWCA Crim 1397; [2016] 2 Cr. App. R. (S.) 43; (2017) 181 J.P. 132; [2017] Crim. L.R. 154, CA (Crim Div) ..... *Digested,* 17/**1973**

R. v Higgs (Adam Lee) see R. v Cooper (Martin Francis)

R. v Hill-Trevor (Mark Charles) see Attorney General's Reference (Nos 3 and 5 of 1989)

R. v Hillingdon LBC Ex p. London Regional Transport [1999] B.L.G.R. 543; Times, August 31, 1999; [1999] N.P.C. 112, CA (Civ Div) ..... *Digested,* 99/**4883**: *Considered* 17/870

R. v Hirani (Amin Mohammed) [2008] EWCA Crim 1463, CA (Crim Div) *Applied* 12/760: *Followed* 17/576

R. v HM Coroner for North Humberside and Scunthorpe Ex p. Jamieson [1995] Q.B. 1; [1994] 3 W.L.R. 82; [1994] 3 All E.R. 972; (1994) 158 J.P. 1011; [1994] 5 Med. L.R. 217; Times, April 28, 1994; Independent, April 27, 1994; [1994] C.O.D. 455, CA (Civ Div) .... *Digested,* 94/**631**: *Applied* 00/50, 01/26, 02/26, 03/13, 04/36, 06/16, 07/27, 09/41, 11/30, 13/37, 14/35: *Considered* 95/872, 95/873, 96/42, 96/44, 96/49, 97/39, 00/49, 01/27, 02/25, 04/12, 04/38, 05/17, 06/17, 06/4528, 09/21, 09/2567, 16/8, 17/11: *Disapproved* 04/37: *Followed* 11/3599

R. v HM Coroner for Western Somerset Ex p. Middleton see R. (on the application of Middleton) v HM Coroner for Western Somerset

R. v Hoang Mai see R. v van Dao (Vinh)

R. v Hobson (Mark) see Jones (Setting of Minimum Term), Re

R. v Hockey (Terence John) [2017] EWCA Crim 742; [2018] 1 W.L.R. 343; [2017] 2 Cr. App. R. 23; [2017] 2 Cr. App. R. (S.) 31; [2017] Crim. L.R. 785, CA (Crim Div) .... *Digested,* 17/**588**

R. v Holloway (Adrian) [2016] EWCA Crim 2175; [2017] 1 W.L.R. 1660; [2017] 1 Cr. App. R. 26; [2017] M.H.L.R. 236, CA (Crim Div) .... *Digested,* 17/**594**

R. v Holloway (Stephen John) see R. v Adomako (John Asare)

R. v Hoole (Christopher) see R. v Quillan (Gary)

R. v Hore (John Derek) see R. v Johnson (Lewis)

R. v Howard (Gary Alan) [2016] EWCA Crim 1511; [2017] 1 Cr. App. R. (S.) 8; [2017] Crim. L.R. 72, CA (Crim Div) .... *Digested,* 17/**1899**

R. v Hudson (Linda); *joined case* R. v Taylor (Elaine) [1971] 2 Q.B. 202; [1971] 2 W.L.R. 1047; [1971] 2 All E.R. 244; (1972) 56 Cr. App. R. 1; (1971) 115 S.J. 303, CA (Crim Div) .... *Digested,* 71/**2528**: *Applied* 17/547: *Considered* 93/732, 95/1256, 98/944

R. v Huggins (Kaneel); *sub nom* R. v Clarke (Antwon); *joined case* R. v Gordon (Khianni) [2016] EWCA Crim 1715; [2017] 1 Cr. App. R. (S.) 21, CA (Crim Div) *Digested,* 17/**1941**

R. v Hughes (James Francis) [2009] EWCA Crim 841; [2010] 1 Cr. App. R. (S.) 25; [2010] M.H.L.R. 183; Times, June 1, 2009; [2009] Crim. L.R. 672, CA (Crim Div) .... *Digested,* 09/**819**: *Applied* 17/609

R. v Hughes (Robert) (1985) 81 Cr. App. R. 344, CA (Crim Div) .... *Digested,* 86/**640**: *Applied* 15/562: *Considered* 17/546

R. v Hull (Paul James) see R. v Cooper (Martin Francis)

R. v Hunter (Nigel); *joined cases* R. v Saruwu (Joseph); R. v Johnstone (Ian); R. v Walker (Alan); R. v Lonsdale (Paul) [2015] EWCA Crim 631; [2015] 1 W.L.R. 5367; [2016] 2 All E.R. 1021; [2015] 2 Cr. App. R. 9; (2015) 179 J.P. 487, CA (Crim Div) .... *Digested,* 15/**627**: *Applied* 17/518

R. v Hussain (Ifran) see Attorney General's Reference (Nos 128 to 141 of 2015 and 8 to 10 of 2016)

R. v Hussain (Kabeer) see R. v Woodward (Robert)

R. v Hussain (Mohammed Naqi) see R. v Hyde (Daniel)

R. v Hussain (Mohammed Sajjaad) see R. v Johnson (Lewis)

R. v Hussain (Usman) see Attorney General's Reference (Nos 128 to 141 of 2015 and 8 to 10 of 2016)

R. v Hussein (Kazam) see R. v Woodward (Robert)

R. v HVN see R. v L

R. v Hyde (Daniel); *joined cases* R. v Jesuthansan (Jesurajan); R. v Stokes (Christy); R. v McGinley (Bernard); R. v Williams (Michael); R. v Collins (David); R. v Haywood (Nigel); R. v Henry (Jose); R. v Hussain (Mohammed Naqi) [2016] EWCA Crim 1031; [2016] 1 W.L.R. 4020; [2017] 3 All E.R. 580; [2016] 2 Cr. App. R. (S.) 39; [2016] Crim. L.R. 790, CA (Crim Div) .... *Digested,* 16/**494**

R. v Immigration Appeal Tribunal Ex p. Antonissen (C-292/89) EU:C:1991:80; [1991] E.C.R. I-745; [1991] 2 C.M.L.R. 373; Times, February 27, 1991; Guardian, March 7, 1991; (1991) 135 S.J. 6, ECJ .... *Digested,* 91/**4007**: *Applied* 96/3164, 06/2041: *Considered* 95/52, 98/4539, 06/1589, 08/2094, 17/2658: *Followed* 11/1794

R. v Immigration Appeal Tribunal Ex p. Secretary of State for the Home Department (C370/90) EU:C:1992:296; [1992] 3 All E.R. 798; [1992] E.C.R. I-4265; [1992] 3 C.M.L.R. 358; [1993] 1 F.L.R. 798; [1992] Imm. A.R. 565; Times, August 31, 1992; Independent, July 17, 1992; [1993] Fam. Law 294; Guardian, July 15, 1992, ECJ .... *Digested,* 92/**4802**: *Applied* 95/2715: *Cited* 17/2673: *Considered* 97/2919, 98/3250, 06/1573: *Followed* 04/2071

R. v Imray (Barry) see R. v Mills (Julie Lillian)

R. v Ineos Chlorvinyls Ltd [2016] EWCA Crim 607; [2017] Env. L.R. 7, CA (Crim Div) .. *Digested,* 17/**1917**

R. v Inhabitants of Chawton 113 E.R. 1123; (1841) 1 Q.B. 247, QB
Applied 17/1440

R. v Inland Revenue Commissioners Ex p. Matteson's Walls Ltd see R. v Inland Revenue Commissioners Ex p. Unilever Plc

R. v Inland Revenue Commissioners Ex p. Morgan Grenfell & Co Ltd see R. (on the application of Morgan Grenfell & Co Ltd) v Special Commissioners of Income Tax

R. v Inland Revenue Commissioners Ex p. Unilever Plc; *joined case* R. v Inland Revenue Commissioners Ex p. Matteson's Walls Ltd [1996] S.T.C. 681; 68 T.C. 205; [1996] C.O.D. 421, CA (Civ Div)
Applied 00/4072, 11/3573, 13/853, 16/1830, 16/2069: *Considered* 01/5605, 06/4198, 07/45, 08/2019, 09/1738, 16/2106: *Distinguished* 04/3786, 05/4121, 08/70: *Followed* 17/2087

R. v Insurance Ombudsman Bureau Ex p. Aegon Life Assurance Ltd [1995] L.R.L.R. 101; [1994] C.L.C. 88; Times, January 7, 1994; Independent, January 11, 1994; [1994] C.O.D. 426, DC .... *Digested,* 95/**55**:
Applied 02/52, 17/1077: *Considered* 97/4851

R. v International Stock Exchange of the United Kingdom and the Republic of Ireland Ltd Ex p. Else (1982) Ltd; *joined case* R. v International Stock Exchange of the United Kingdom and the Republic of Ireland Ltd Ex p. Thomas [1993] Q.B. 534; [1993] 2 W.L.R. 70; [1993] 1 All E.R. 420; [1993] B.C.C. 11; [1993] B.C.L.C. 834; [1993] 2 C.M.L.R. 677; (1994) 6 Admin. L.R. 67; Times, November 2, 1992; Independent, November 24, 1992; [1993] C.O.D. 236, CA (Civ Div) .... *Digested,* 95/**614**:
Applied 01/2332, 06/5739, 15/2606, 15/2882: *Considered* 94/4, 96/3164, 96/5906, 00/4404: *Followed* 12/1185, 17/2240: *Referred to* 08/5104

R. v International Stock Exchange of the United Kingdom and the Republic of Ireland Ltd Ex p. Thomas see R. v International Stock Exchange of the United Kingdom and the Republic of Ireland Ltd Ex p. Else (1982) Ltd

R. v Iqbal (Quisar) [2017] EWCA Crim 449; [2017] 2 Cr. App. R. (S.) 20, CA (Crim Div) .... *Digested,* 17/**1920**

R. v Irving (David Stuart) see R. v Vowles (Lucinda)

R. v Islam (Samsul) [2009] UKHL 30; [2009] 1 A.C. 1076; [2009] 3 W.L.R. 1; [2010] 1 All E.R. 493; [2010] 1 Cr. App. R. (S.) 42; [2009] Lloyd's Rep. F.C. 513; Times, June 12, 2009; [2009] Crim. L.R. 751; (2009) 106(25) L.S.G. 16, HL .... *Digested,* 09/**843**:
Applied 14/729, 16/505: *Considered* 10/733, 17/580: *Followed* 15/605

R. v James (Mark George); *sub nom* R. v Selby (James Alec) [2016] EWCA Crim 1639; [2017] Crim. L.R. 228, CA (Crim Div)

R. v James (Thomas William Henry) see R. v Conaghan (Terence)

R. v Jawad (Mohid) [2013] EWCA Crim 644; [2013] 1 W.L.R. 3861; [2014] 1 Cr. App. R. (S.) 16; (2013) 177 J.P. 436; [2013] Crim. L.R. 698, CA (Crim Div) .... *Digested,* 13/**691**:
Applied 14/794: *Considered* 16/500, 16/506, 17/581

R. v Jefferson (Andrew Paul) [2016] EWCA Crim 2023; [2017] 1 Cr. App. R. (S.) 38, CA (Crim Div) .... *Digested,* 17/**1937**

R. v Jenkin (John) see Attorney General's Reference (No.34 of 2014)

R. v Jenkins (Fraser) see R. v Greaves (Claude Clifford)

R. v Jesuthansan (Jesurajan) see R. v Hyde (Daniel)

R. v Jogee (Ameen Hassan); *joined case* Ruddock v Queen, The [2016] UKSC 8; [2017] A.C. 387; [2016] 2 W.L.R. 681; [2016] 2 All E.R. 1; [2016] 1 Cr. App. R. 31; (2016) 180 J.P. 313; Times, March 2, 2016, SC .... *Digested,* 16/**482**:
Considered 17/572: *Followed* 17/551, 17/552, 17/610, 17/612

R. v Johal (Jaswinder Singh) [2013] EWCA Crim 647; [2014] 1 W.L.R. 146, CA (Crim Div) .... *Digested,* 14/**742**:
Considered 15/606: *Followed* 17/582

R. v Johnson (Asher) see R. v Johnson (Lewis)

R. v Johnson (Billy) see R. v Noble (Charles)

R. v Johnson (Brian) see R. v Sinclair (James)

R. v Johnson (Charlotte Elizabeth May) see R. v Jurecka (Aniela Halina)

R. v Johnson (Costs) [2017] 1 Costs L.O. 125, Sen Cts Costs Office

R. v Johnson (Lewis); *joined cases* R. v Johnson (Asher); R. v Green (Jerome); R. v Garwood (Reece); R. v Burton (Tyler Winston); R. v Terrelonge (Nicholas); R. v Moises (Queba); R. v Hore (John Derek); R. v Miah (Javed Ruhel); R. v Hussain (Mohammed Sajjaad); R. v Khan (Fahim); R. v Miah (Rubel); R. v Hall (Michael) [2016] EWCA Crim 1613; [2017] 4 W.L.R. 104; [2017] 4 All E.R. 769; [2017] 1 Cr. App. R. 12; [2017] Crim. L.R. 216, CA (Crim Div) .... *Digested,* 17/**551**:
Applied 17/610: *Followed* 17/612

R. v Johnson (Wayne) [2017] EWCA Crim 189; [2018] 1 W.L.R. 19; [2017] 2 Cr. App. R. 6; [2017] Crim. L.R. 483, CA (Crim Div) .... *Digested,* 17/**540**

R. v Johnstone (Ian) see R. v Hunter (Nigel)

R. v Jones (Margaret); *joined cases* Swain v DPP; Ayliffe v DPP; R. v Richards (Josh); R. v Pritchard (Philip); R. v Olditch (Toby); R. v Milling (Arthur Paul) [2006] UKHL 16; [2007] 1 A.C. 136; [2006] 2 W.L.R. 772; [2006] 2 All E.R. 741; [2006] 2 Cr. App. R. 9; Times, March 30, 2006; [2007] Crim. L.R. 66; [2006] A.C.D. 52; (2006) 170 J.P.N. 263; (2006) 103(15) L.S.G. 20; (2006) 156 N.L.J. 600, HL .... *Digested,* 06/**835**: *Applied* 06/2622, 07/2234, 12/668: *Followed* 14/667, 17/542

R. v Jones (Neil) see Jones (Setting of Minimum Term), Re

R. v Jordan (Shirley) see R. v Lambert (Steven)

R. v Joseph (Verna Sermanfure); *joined cases* R. v Craciunescu (Alexandra Dorina); R. v VCL; R. v NTN; R. v Nguyen (Dong); R. v AA [2017] EWCA Crim 36; [2017] 1 W.L.R. 3153; [2017] 1 Cr. App. R. 33; [2017] Crim. L.R. 817, CA (Crim Div) .... *Digested,* 17/**548**

R. v Joyce (Trevor); *joined case* R. v Kay (Robert) [2017] EWCA Crim 647; [2017] 4 W.L.R. 121; [2018] 1 All E.R. 881; [2017] 2 Cr. App. R. 16; [2017] 2 Cr. App. R. (S.) 24; [2017] M.H.L.R. 338; [2017] Crim. L.R. 881, CA (Crim Div) .... *Digested,* 17/**545**

R. v JP see R. v PW

R. v Jurecka (Aniela Halina); *joined cases* R. v Smith (David Edward); R. v Johnson (Charlotte Elizabeth May) [2017] EWCA Crim 1007; [2017] 4 W.L.R. 205, CA (Crim Div)

R. v K [2017] EWCA Crim 486; [2017] Crim. L.R. 716, CA (Crim Div)

R. v Kahar (Mohammed Abdul); *joined cases* R. v Ziamani (Brusthom); R. v Eshati (Abdurraouf); R. v Rashid (Yahya); R. v Ozcelik (Silhan); R. v Khan (Sana) [2016] EWCA Crim 568; [2016] 1 W.L.R. 3156; [2017] 2 All E.R. 782; [2016] 2 Cr. App. R. (S.) 32; [2016] Crim. L.R. 670, CA (Crim Div) .... *Digested,* 16/**1933**: *Followed* 17/1987

R. v Kahn (Shagufta) see R. v Khan (Rehman)

R. v Kansal (Rupe Lal) see R. v Graham (Hemamali Krishna)

R. v Karemera (Michael) see R. v Brandford (Olivia)

R. v Kassa (Tadeusz) see R. v Saw (Rebecca)

R. v Kay (Robert) see R. v Joyce (Trevor)

R. v Kazin (Mohammed) see R. v Safi (Ali Ahmed)

R. v Keane (Daniel); *joined case* R. v McGrath (Katherine Rosa) [2010] EWCA Crim 2514; [2011] Crim. L.R. 393, CA (Crim Div) *Applied* 17/21: *Followed* 15/2540

R. v Kelly (Lewis Bradley) see R. v Twist (Andrew Terence)

R. v Kelsey (Alan) (1982) 74 Cr. App. R. 213; [1982] R.T.R. 135; [1982] Crim. L.R. 435; (1982) 126 S.J. 97, CA (Crim Div) .... *Digested,* 82/**598**: *Considered* 87/570: *Distinguished* 94/714: *Followed* 17/531

R. v Kensington and Chelsea RLBC Ex p. Bayani (1990) 22 H.L.R. 406; Times, June 1, 1990; Guardian, June 7, 1990, CA (Civ Div) .... *Digested,* 91/**1897**: *Applied* 92/2247, 00/3144: *Considered* 95/2556, 06/2022: *Followed* 96/3068, 17/239

R. v Kent Justices Ex p. Machin (Peter Laurence) [1952] 2 Q.B. 355; [1952] 1 All E.R. 1123; [1952] 1 T.L.R. 1197; (1952) 36 Cr. App. R. 23; (1952) 116 J.P. 242; (1952) 96 S.J. 297, QBD .... *Digested,* 52/**2125**: *Considered* 17/573: *Distinguished* 82/1933: *Followed* 52/844

R. v Khan (Adil) see R. v Khan (Yasar)

R. v Khan (Fahim) see R. v Johnson (Lewis)

R. v Khan (Imran) see R. v Khan (Yasar)

R. v Khan (Junead) see R. v Abdallah (Abdalraouf)

R. v Khan (Mohammed Tahmid); *sub nom* R. v Khan (Mohammid Tahmid) [2017] EWCA Crim 440; [2017] 2 Cr. App. R. (S.) 19; [2017] Crim. L.R. 813, CA (Crim Div) .... *Digested,* 17/**1970**

R. v Khan (Mohammed) [2016] EWCA Crim 2162; [2017] 1 Cr. App. R. (S.) 34, CA (Crim Div) .... *Digested,* 17/**1996**

R. v Khan (Mohammid Tahmid) see R. v Khan (Mohammed Tahmid)

R. v Khan (Rehman); *joined case* R. v Kahn (Shagufta) [2016] EWCA Crim 1292; [2016] 2 Cr. App. R. (S.) 42; [2017] Crim. L.R. 70, CA (Crim Div) .... *Digested,* 17/**1925**

R. v Khan (Saddiq) see R. v Needham (Paul Maurice)

R. v Khan (Sana) see R. v Kahar (Mohammed Abdul)

R. v Khan (Shazib) see R. v Abdallah (Abdalraouf)

R. v Khan (Uzma) [2009] EWCA Crim 2; [2009] 1 W.L.R. 2036; [2009] 4 All E.R. 544; [2009] 1 Cr. App. R. 28; [2009] 3 F.C.R. 484; [2009] Crim. L.R. 348, CA (Crim Div) .... *Digested,* 09/**905**: *Considered* 17/536

R. v Khan (Yasar); *joined cases* R. v Khan (Adil); R. v Liquat (Yasser); R. v Khan (Imran) [2013] EWCA Crim 802, CA (Crim Div) *Considered* 17/1903

R. v Khangura (Sukhjiwan Singh) see Jones (Setting of Minimum Term), Re
R. v Khellaf (Bilal) [2016] EWCA Crim 1297; [2017] 1 Cr. App. R. (S.) 1, CA (Crim Div) .... *Digested,* 17/**1963**
R. v Kidd (Philip Richard) see R. v Canavan (Darren Anthony)
R. v King (Dwayne) [2017] EWCA Crim 128; [2017] 4 W.L.R. 95; [2017] 2 Cr. App. R. (S.) 6; [2017] Crim. L.R. 497, CA (Crim Div) .... *Digested,* 17/**1972**
R. v Kitchener (Matthew David); *sub nom* R. v Armel (Jude Michael) [2017] EWCA Crim 937; [2017] 4 W.L.R. 159; [2017] M.H.L.R. 355, CA (Crim Div) .... *Digested,* 17/**1949**
R. v Knight (Carl) see R. v Anwar (Umar)
R. v Knights (James) [2017] EWCA Crim 1052; [2017] 4 W.L.R. 215; [2017] 2 Cr. App. R. (S.) 33; [2017] Crim. L.R. 904, CA (Crim Div) .... *Digested,* 17/**1933**
R. v Knights (Richard Michael); *joined cases* R. v Sekhon (Daljit Singh); R. v McFaul (Kevin); R. v Maguire (Kevin); R. v Dhnoay (Gurdev Singh); R. v Singh (Satnam); R. v Singh (Shangara) [2005] UKHL 50; [2006] 1 A.C. 368; [2005] 3 W.L.R. 330; [2005] 4 All E.R. 347; [2006] 1 Cr. App. R. (S.) 80; Times, July 27, 2005; Independent, July 27, 2005; [2006] Crim. L.R. 171; (2005) 155 N.L.J. 1316, HL .... *Digested,* 05/**841**:
Applied 15/606: *Followed* 11/719, 17/583
R. v L [2017] EWCA Crim 43; [2017] 1 Cr. App. R. (S.) 51; [2017] Crim. L.R. 567, CA (Crim Div) .... *Digested,* 17/**1980**
R. v L; *joined cases* R. v T; R. v THN; R. v HVN [2013] EWCA Crim 991; [2014] 1 All E.R. 113; [2013] 2 Cr. App. R. 23; Times, October 03, 2013; [2014] Crim. L.R. 150, CA (Crim Div) .... *Digested,* 13/**671**:
Considered 17/548
R. v L see R. v Twist (Andrew Terence)
R. v LA see R. v RH
R. v Lama (Kumar) [2014] EWCA Crim 1729; [2017] Q.B. 1171; [2017] 3 W.L.R. 469, CA (Crim Div)
R. v Lambert (Goldan) [2009] EWCA Crim 700; [2010] 1 W.L.R. 898; [2009] 2 Cr. App. R. 32, CA (Crim Div) .... *Digested,* 10/**729**:
Applied 16/496: *Considered* 17/593: *Followed* 16/497
R. v Lambert (Steven); *joined cases* R. v Jordan (Shirley); R. v Ali (Mudassir Mohammed) [2001] UKHL 37; [2002] 2 A.C. 545; [2001] 3 W.L.R. 206; [2001] 3 All E.R. 577; [2002] 1 All E.R. 2; [2001] 2 Cr. App. R. 28; [2001] H.R.L.R. 55; [2001] U.K.H.R.R. 1074; Times, July 6, 2001; Independent, July 19, 2001; [2001] Crim. L.R. 806; Daily Telegraph, July 17, 2001; (2001) 98(33) L.S.G. 29; (2001) 145 S.J.L.B. 174, HL .... *Digested,* 01/**3504**:
Applied 01/2315, 03/4064, 03/780, 05/875: *Considered* 02/785, 02/795, 03/761, 03/802, 04/4066, 04/707, 04/800, 05/5111, 09/2698, 13/658: *Distinguished* 02/813, 03/814: *Followed* 01/1193, 01/5271, 02/1526, 02/2663, 02/844, 02/849, 08/4694, 17/1484
R. v Lang (Stephen Howard); *joined cases* R. v D; R. v Edwards (Kyle Frederick); R. v Guidera (Michael); R. v Sheppard (James); R. v Collier (Edward); R. v Glave (Heathcliffe); R. v Armitage (Lewis); R. v Smith (Gary); R. v Wright (Robert); R. v Feihn (Steven); R. v Carasco (Charles); R. v Winters (Keith); R. v Abdi (Hassan) [2005] EWCA Crim 2864; [2006] 1 W.L.R. 2509; [2006] 2 All E.R. 410; [2006] 2 Cr. App. R. (S.) 3; Times, November 10, 2005; [2006] Crim. L.R. 174, CA (Crim Div) .... *Digested,* 06/**3836**:
Applied 06/3669, 06/3681, 06/3719, 06/3749, 06/3872, 06/3886, 06/3902, 07/3623, 07/3640, 07/3656, 07/3658, 07/3663, 07/3675, 07/3742, 07/3788, 08/3314, 08/3321, 08/3322, 15/2276, 16/1882: *Considered* 06/3709, 06/3755, 06/3756, 06/3829, 06/3830, 06/3883, 06/3890, 06/993, 07/3622, 07/3657, 07/3662, 07/3729, 07/3751, 08/3318, 08/3330, 08/3377, 10/2887, 11/2935, 13/772: *Explained* 09/3406: *Followed* 17/1897
R. v Lansana (Stephen) see R. v Agera (Stephen)
R. v Lansley (Robert Brian) [2017] EWCA Crim 476; [2017] 2 Cr. App. R. (S.) 16, CA (Crim Div) .... *Digested,* 17/**1954**
R. v Lashley (Estelle Jenna) [2017] EWCA Crim 260; [2017] 2 Cr. App. R. (S.) 4, CA (Crim Div) .... *Digested,* 17/**1927**
R. v Lawrence (Nicole) see R. v Mills (Julie Lillian)
R. v Lawson (Joel) see R. v Lintott (Mark James)
R. v LD see R. v PW
R. v Lea (Nicholas) [2011] EWCA Crim 487, CA (Crim Div)
Applied 17/1975: *Considered* 12/3019
R. v Leathem (Aaron); *joined case* R. v Mallett (James) [2017] EWCA Crim 42; [2017] Crim. L.R. 788, CA (Crim Div)

R. v Legris (Piere Jean Alain); *sub nom* R. v Legris (Piere Jean Alain) (also known as Baron (Alain)) [2017] EWCA Crim 196; [2017] 1 Cr. App. R. (S.) 55, CA (Crim Div) .... *Digested,* 17/**1950**

R. v Legris (Piere Jean Alain) (also known as Baron (Alain)) see R. v Legris (Piere Jean Alain)

R. v Lewandowski (Artur) see R. v Woodward (Robert)

R. v Lewis (Justin) [2016] EWCA Crim 1020; [2017] 1 Cr. App. R. (S.) 2; [2017] Crim. L.R. 147, CA (Crim Div) .... *Digested,* 17/**1975**

R. v Lewis (Kenny Martyn) [2010] EWCA Crim 579; [2010] 2 Cr. App. R. (S.) 104, CA (Crim Div) .... *Digested,* 10/**2902**: *Considered* 12/2952, 12/2953, 14/2652, 17/1946

R. v Licensing Authority Ex p. Generics (UK) Ltd (C-368/96); *joined cases* R. v Licensing Authority Ex p. Wellcome Foundation Ltd (C-368/96); R. v Licensing Authority Ex p. Glaxo Operations UK Ltd (C-368/96) EU:C:1998:583; [1998] E.C.R. I-7967; [1999] 2 C.M.L.R. 181; (1999) 48 B.M.L.R. 161; Times, January 4, 1999, ECJ (5th Chamber) .... *Digested,* 99/**2695**: *Applied* 04/1697, 06/2466, 17/1137

R. v Licensing Authority Ex p. Glaxo Operations UK Ltd (C-368/96) see R. v Licensing Authority Ex p. Generics (UK) Ltd (C368/96)

R. v Licensing Authority Ex p. Wellcome Foundation Ltd (C-368/96) see R. v Licensing Authority Ex p. Generics (UK) Ltd (C-368/96)

R. v Lindley (David) [2016] EWCA Crim 1980; [2017] 1 Cr. App. R. (S.) 39, CA (Crim Div) .... *Digested,* 17/**1890**

R. v Lintott (Mark James); *sub nom* R. v Lawson (Joel) [2017] EWCA Crim 986; [2017] 2 Cr. App. R. (S.) 50, CA (Crim Div) .... *Digested,* 17/**1943**

R. v Liquat (Yasser) see R. v Khan (Yasar)

R. v LM; *joined cases* R. v YT; R. v BT; R. v DG; R. v MB [2010] EWCA Crim 2327; [2011] 1 Cr. App. R. 12; [2011] Crim. L.R. 425, CA (Crim Div) .... *Digested,* 11/**635**: *Applied* 12/725, 13/671: *Considered* 17/548

R. v Lockton (Robert John) see R. v Whale (Geoffrey)

R. v Logan (Gavin) see R. v Ogden (Neil)

R. v Lonsdale (Paul) see R. v Hunter (Nigel)

R. v Lord Chancellor's Department Ex p. Nangle [1992] 1 All E.R. 897; [1991] I.C.R. 743; [1991] I.R.L.R. 343; [1991] C.O.D. 484, QBD .... *Digested,* 91/**1624**: *Considered* 17/790: *Distinguished* 98/4785

R. v Loveridge (Wayne); *joined case* R. v Foster (Billy Tom) [2016] EWCA Crim 1884; [2017] 1 Cr. App. R. (S.) 35, CA (Crim Div) .... *Digested,* 17/**1989**

R. v Ludlow (Edward Alexander) see Ludlow v Commissioner of Police of the Metropolis

R. v Lundt-Smith [1964] 2 Q.B. 167; [1964] 2 W.L.R. 1063; [1964] 3 All E.R. 225 (Note); (1964) 128 J.P. 534; 62 L.G.R. 376; (1964) 108 S.J. 425, Assizes .... *Digested,* 64/**3194**: *Approved* 71/10171: *Considered* 69/3177, 98/1365, 16/2793: *Distinguished* 17/2516

R. v Lunn (Christopher) [2017] EWCA Crim 34; [2017] 4 W.L.R. 214; [2017] 2 Cr. App. R. 5; [2017] Lloyd's Rep. F.C. 139; [2017] Crim. L.R. 478, CA (Crim Div) .... *Digested,* 17/**601**

R. v Luvaglio (Michael) (No.1) see R. v Stafford (Dennis) (No.1)

R. v Lyons (Isidore Jack) (No.3); *joined cases* R. v Parnes (Anthony Keith) (No.3); R. v Ronson (Gerald Maurice) (No.3); R. v Saunders (Ernest Walter) (No.3) [2002] UKHL 44; [2003] 1 A.C. 976; [2002] 3 W.L.R. 1562; [2002] 4 All E.R. 1028; [2002] B.C.C. 968; [2003] 1 Cr. App. R. 24; [2003] H.R.L.R. 6; Times, November 15, 2002; Independent, November 20, 2002; [2003] Crim. L.R. 623; (2002) 146 S.J.L.B. 264, HL .... *Digested,* 02/**844**: *Applied* 05/875, 13/1307: *Considered* 03/2676, 04/2088, 14/3642: *Followed* 16/522, 17/1484

R. v M see Crown Prosecution Service v M

R. v M see R. v C

R. v Mackle (Benedict) see R. v Mackle (Plunkett Jude)

R. v Mackle (Patrick) see R. v Mackle (Plunkett Jude)

R. v Mackle (Plunkett Jude); *joined cases* R. v McLaughlin (Henry); R. v Mackle (Patrick); R. v Mackle (Benedict) [2014] UKSC 5; [2014] A.C. 678; [2014] 2 W.L.R. 267; [2014] 2 All E.R. 170; [2014] N.I. 292; [2014] 2 Cr. App. R. (S.) 33; [2014] Lloyd's Rep. F.C. 253; Times, February 10, 2014, SC .... *Digested,* 14/**727**: *Distinguished* 17/576: *Followed* 14/728

R. v Magee (William) [2017] EWCA Crim 972; [2017] 2 Cr. App. R. (S.) 40, CA (Crim Div) .... *Digested,* 17/**1964**

R. v Maguire (Kevin) see R. v Knights (Richard Michael)

R. v Malhi (Hardip Singh) [2016] EWCA Crim 2025; [2017] 4 W.L.R. 27, CA (Crim Div) .... *Digested,* 17/**579**

R. v Maling (Andrew James) [2016] EWCA Crim 1740; [2017] 1 Cr. App. R. (S.) 14, CA (Crim Div) .... *Digested,* 17/**1940**
R. v Mallett (James) see R. v Leathem (Aaron)
R. v Manchester City Council Ex p. Stennett see R. (on the application of Stennett) v Manchester City Council
R. v Marine A; *joined case* Marine A v Judge Advocate General [2013] EWCA Crim 2367; [2014] 1 W.L.R. 3326; [2014] 1 Cr. App. R. 26; [2014] E.M.L.R. 10; [2014] Crim. L.R. 536, CMAC .... *Digested,* 14/**664**: *Applied* 17/1533
R. v Markham (Stan Lucas); *sub nom* R. v Edwards (Kim Rose) [2017] EWCA Crim 739; [2017] 2 Cr. App. R. (S.) 30; [2017] E.M.L.R. 23; [2017] Crim. L.R. 727; [2017] Crim. L.R. 895, CA (Crim Div) .... *Digested,* 17/**1952**
R. v Marquez (Shaun) see R. v Avis (Tony)
R. v Marsh (Terence Colin) see R. v Graham (Hemamali Krishna)
R. v Martin (Daniel Jeffrey) [2017] EWCA Crim 648; [2017] 2 Cr. App. R. (S.) 28, CA (Crim Div) .... *Digested,* 17/**1974**
R. v Martin (Dwain Ashley); *joined case* R v Brimecome (Steven Anthony) [2014] EWCA Crim 1940; [2015] 1 W.L.R. 588; [2015] 1 Cr. App. R. 11; [2015] Crim. L.R. 83, CA (Crim Div) .... *Digested,* 15/**562**: *Applied* 17/546
R. v Martin (Glen) see R. v Ogden (Neil)
R. v Massey (James) [2001] EWCA Crim 531; [2001] 2 Cr. App. R. (S.) 80, CA (Crim Div) .... *Digested,* 01/**1220**: *Followed* 17/535
R. v Mateta (Koshi Pitshou); *joined cases* R. v Ghavami (Amir); R. v Afshar (Saeideh); R. v Bashir (Yasin); R. v Andukwa (Simon Ebunji) [2013] EWCA Crim 1372; [2014] 1 W.L.R. 1516; [2014] 1 All E.R. 152; [2013] 2 Cr. App. R. 35; [2014] Crim. L.R. 227, CA (Crim Div) .... *Digested,* 14/**696**: *Considered* 17/612
R. v Mathews (Michael Richard) see Attorney General's Reference (No.27 of 2013)
R. v Mattu (Joga Singh) see Attorney General's Reference (Nos 128 to 141 of 2015 and 8 to 10 of 2016)
R. v MB see R. v LM
R. v MC see R. v PW
R. v McCallen (Anthony John) see R. v Forbes (Stephen John)
R. v McCleary (Jake Simon) [2014] EWCA Crim 302, CA (Crim Div) *Considered* 15/2220, 17/1920
R. v McCook (Jason Trevor) [2014] EWCA Crim 734; [2016] 2 Cr. App. R. 30; [2015] Crim. L.R. 350, CA (Crim Div) .... *Digested,* 17/**586**: *Followed* 17/567
R. v McDermott (Louis Junior) see Attorney General's Reference (Nos 128 to 141 of 2015 and 8 to 10 of 2016)
R. v McDermott-Mullane (Danielle) [2016] EWCA Crim 2239; [2017] 4 W.L.R. 127, CA (Crim Div) .... *Digested,* 17/**592**
R. v McDonald (Michael Christopher) [2004] EWCA Crim 2614; Times, November 8, 2004; (2004) 148 S.J.L.B. 1218, CA (Crim Div) .... *Digested,* 05/**860**: *Distinguished* 17/596
R. v McDougall (Gordon) see R. v Vowles (Lucinda)
R. v McDowell (Christopher James); *joined case* R. v Singh (Harjit Sarana) [2015] EWCA Crim 173; [2015] 2 Cr. App. R. (S.) 14; [2015] Crim. L.R. 623, CA (Crim Div) .... *Digested,* 15/**601**: *Considered* 16/502, 16/507, 17/577
R. v McFaul (Kevin) see R. v Knights (Richard Michael)
R. v McGee (Mark Stuart) see Attorney General's Reference (Nos 3, 73 and 75 of 2010)
R. v McGinley (Bernard) see R. v Hyde (Daniel)
R. v McGlade (Peter) (1990-91) 12 Cr. App. R. (S.) 105; Times, March 14, 1990; [1990] Crim. L.R. 527, CA (Crim Div) .... *Digested,* 90/**1307**: *Cited* 93/827: *Followed* 17/1972
R. v McGrath (Katherine Rosa) see R. v Keane (Daniel)
R. v McGregor (Alexander) see R. v Healey (Robert)
R. v McInerney (Michael) see R. v Rollins (Neil)
R. v McLaughlin (Henry) see R. v Mackle (Plunkett Jude)
R. v McLeod (Anthony) see R. v McLeod (Ralph)
R. v McLeod (Ralph); *sub nom* R. v Poyser (Lewis); R. v Akbar (Yusuf); R. v Grant (Ricardo); R. v McLeod (Anthony); R. v Poyser (Kofi); R. v Grant (Lemar) [2017] EWCA Crim 800; [2017] 2 Cr. App. R. (S.) 39, CA (Crim Div) .... *Digested,* 17/**1930**
R. v McLoughlin (Ian) see Attorney General's Reference (No.69 of 2013)

R. v McPhee (Colin) see R. v Saw (Rebecca)
R. v Mealey (Jeremiah); *joined case* R. v Sheridan (Philip Michael) (1974) 60 Cr. App. R. 59; [1974] Crim. L.R. 710, CA (Crim Div) .... *Digested,* 74/**541**: *Applied* 17/572: *Approved* 79/448
R. v Mee (Jason David) [2004] EWCA Crim 629; [2004] 2 Cr. App. R. (S.) 81; Times, April 1, 2004; [2004] Crim. L.R. 487; (2004) 148 S.J.L.B. 267, CA (Crim Div) .... *Digested,* 04/**3458**: *Applied* 12/3026: *Considered* 05/3588, 07/3635: *Followed* 06/3858: *Not applied* 17/574
R. v Melim (Virgilio) [2014] EWCA Crim 1915, CA (Crim Div) *Considered* 17/1985
R. v Mendip DC Ex p. Fabre [2017] P.T.S.R. 1112; (2000) 80 P. & C.R. 500; [2000] J.P.L. 810; [2000] C.O.D. 372, QBD .... *Digested,* 00/**4508**: *Applied* 09/3041, 16/1684, 16/1752: *Considered* 17/1785
R. v Mentore (Darren) see Attorney General's Reference (Nos 128 to 141 of 2015 and 8 to 10 of 2016)
R. v Miah (Javed Ruhel) see R. v Garwood (Reece)
R. v Miah (Javed Ruhel) see R. v Johnson (Lewis)
R. v Miah (Mohammed Selu) see Attorney General's Reference (Nos 128 to 141 of 2015 and 8 to 10 of 2016)
R. v Miah (Rubel) see R. v Johnson (Lewis)
R. v Midmore (Billy Nathan) [2017] EWCA Crim 533; [2017] 4 W.L.R. 107; [2017] 2 Cr. App. R. 8; (2017) 181 J.P. 354; [2017] Crim. L.R. 793, CA (Crim Div) .... *Digested,* 17/**512**
R. v Mildenhall Magistrates' Court Ex p. Forest Heath DC see R. v North West Suffolk (Mildenhall) Magistrates' Court Ex p. Forest Heath DC
R. v Milling (Arthur Paul) see R. v Jones (Margaret)
R. v Mills (Julie Lillian); *sub nom* R. v Imray (Barry); R. v Lawrence (Nicole) [2017] EWCA Crim 559; [2017] 2 Cr. App. R. (S.) 7; [2017] Crim. L.R. 644, CA (Crim Div) .... *Digested,* 17/**1893**
R. v Mincher (Sharon) [2016] EWCA Crim 1528; [2017] 1 Cr. App. R. (S.) 12, CA (Crim Div) .... *Digested,* 17/**1891**
R. v Mirza (Nuzhat) see Mirza v Newham LBC
R. v Misra (Amit); *joined case* R. v Srivastava (Rajeev) [2004] EWCA Crim 2375; [2005] 1 Cr. App. R. 21; Times, October 13, 2004; [2005] Crim. L.R. 234; (2004) 101(41) L.S.G. 35; (2004) 148 S.J.L.B. 1213, CA (Crim Div) .... *Digested,* 05/**804**: *Applied* 06/873: *Considered* 17/605
R. v Mitchell (Alvin Lorenzo) [1977] 1 W.L.R. 753; [1977] 2 All E.R. 168; (1977) 65 Cr. App. R. 185; [1977] Crim. L.R. 626; (1977) 121 S.J. 252, CA (Crim Div) *Considered* 96/1548, 01/1113: *Distinguished* 78/545: *Followed* 17/612
R. v Mitchell (Angeline) [2016] UKSC 55; [2017] A.C. 571; [2016] 3 W.L.R. 1405; [2017] 1 All E.R. 1037; [2017] N.I. 108; [2017] 1 Cr. App. R. 9; (2017) 181 J.P. 77; Times, October 27, 2016; [2017] Crim. L.R. 310, SC .... *Digested,* 16/**452**
R. v MN see R. v AM
R. v Modhwadia (Dipa) [2017] EWCA Crim 501; [2017] 2 Cr. App. R. (S.) 15, CA (Crim Div) .... *Digested,* 17/**1888**
R. v Mohammed (Janed) see Attorney General's Reference (Nos 128 to 141 of 2015 and 8 to 10 of 2016)
R. v Mohammidy (Nazamuddin) see R. v Safi (Ali Ahmed)
R. v Moises (Queba) see R. v Johnson (Lewis)
R. v Moore (Lorna) see R. v Abdallah (Abdalraouf)
R. v Morfitt (John Robert) [2017] EWCA Crim 669; [2017] Lloyd's Rep. F.C. 383, CA (Crim Div) .... *Digested,* 17/**576**
R. v Moulden (Leslie James); *sub nom* R. v Mouldon (Leslie James) [2004] EWCA Crim 2715; [2005] 1 Cr. App. R. (S.) 121, CA (Crim Div) .... *Digested,* 05/**3593**: *Applied* 17/572: *Not applied* 13/689
R. v Mouldon (Leslie James) see R. v Moulden (Leslie James)
R. v Mula (Gazmend); *joined cases* R. v Hasa (Ilir); R. v Nezaj (Saimir) [2017] EWCA Crim 32; [2017] 4 W.L.R. 124, CA (Crim Div) .... *Digested,* 17/**1936**
R. v Mulindwa (Trevor William) [2017] EWCA Crim 416; [2017] 4 W.L.R. 157; [2017] 2 Cr. App. R. 10; (2018) 182 J.P. 75; [2017] Crim. L.R. 979, CA (Crim Div)
R. v Muliswela (Stewart Kudzai) see R. v Samuriwo (Michael Tatenda)
R. v Mullen (Nicholas Robert) [2000] Q.B. 520; [1999] 3 W.L.R. 777; [1999] 2 Cr. App. R. 143; Times, February 15, 1999; [1999] Crim. L.R. 561, CA (Crim Div) .... *Digested,* 99/**972**: *Applied* 00/1026, 00/1056, 01/5733, 02/904, 09/816, 11/709, 14/298: *Considered* 00/1025, 05/3343, 05/838, 15/554, 17/1073: *Distinguished* 05/875, 13/285
R. v Multani (Hardeep Singh) see Jones (Setting of Minimum Term), Re
R. v Muoi Thi NGuyen see R. v van Dao (Vinh)

R. v Murray (Joel James) [2017] EWCA Crim 299; [2017] 2 Cr. App. R. (S.) 8; [2017] Crim. L.R. 723, CA (Crim Div) .... *Digested,* 17/**1915**
R. v MV see R. v AM
R. v Myrie (Owen Anthony) see Attorney General's Reference (No.68 of 2008)
R. v Nazran (Sundish Singh) see Attorney General's Reference (Nos 128 to 141 of 2015 and 8 to 10 of 2016)
R. v NC [2016] EWCA Crim 1448; [2017] 1 Cr. App. R. (S.) 13; [2017] Crim. L.R. 334, CA (Crim Div) .... *Digested,* 17/**1976**
R. v Needham (Paul Maurice); *joined cases* R. v Ali (Shafiq); R. v Williams (Michael); R. v Smythe (Lee); R. v Deakin (Lloyd); R. v Aitken (Tony); R. v Khan (Saddiq) [2016] EWCA Crim 455; [2016] 1 W.L.R. 4449; [2016] 2 Cr. App. R. (S.) 26; (2016) 180 J.P. 361; [2016] R.T.R. 23; [2016] Crim. L.R. 585, CA (Crim Div) ..... *Digested,* 16/**1871**: *Followed* 17/1909, 17/1967
R. v Nelson (Scott); *joined case* R. v Shaibu (Mubarak) [2016] EWCA Crim 1517; [2017] 1 W.L.R. 491; [2017] 1 Cr. App. R. 11; [2017] 1 Cr. App. R. (S.) 11; [2017] Crim. L.R. 161, CA (Crim Div) .... *Digested,* 17/**615**
R. v Neuberg (Karen) [2016] EWCA Crim 1927; [2017] 4 W.L.R. 58; [2017] Lloyd's Rep. F.C. 129; [2017] Crim. L.R. 327, CA (Crim Div) .... *Digested,* 17/**577**
R. v Nevitt (Raymond Andrew) [2017] EWCA Crim 421; [2017] 4 W.L.R. 82, CA (Crim Div) .... *Digested,* 17/**575**
R. v Newbury DC Ex p. Chieveley Parish Council Times, July 22, 1997; [1997] J.P.L. 1137; [1997] E.G. 105 (C.S.); [1997] N.P.C. 106, QBD *Affirmed in part* 98/4226: *Considered* 99/4259, 12/2594, 17/1734
R. v Newell (Lee William) see Attorney General's Reference (No.69 of 2013)
R. v Newton (John Robert) [2017] EWCA Crim 874; [2017] 2 Cr. App. R. (S.) 41, CA (Crim Div) .... *Digested,* 17/**1978**
R. v Nezaj (Saimir) see R. v Mula (Gazmend)
R. v Nguyen (Dong) see R. v Joseph (Verna Sermanfure)
R. v Noble (Charles); *joined case* R. v Johnson (Billy) [2016] EWCA Crim 2219; [2017] Crim. L.R. 473, CA (Crim Div)
R. v Nodjoumi (Benham) (1985) 7 Cr. App. R. (S.) 183, CA (Crim Div) .... *Digested,* 86/**864**: *Cited* 90/1259: *Considered* 99/1343: *Disapproved* 17/1993: *Not followed* 16/1855
R. v Norman (Robert) [2016] EWCA Crim 1564; [2017] 4 W.L.R. 16; [2017] 1 Cr. App. R. 8, CA (Crim Div) .... *Digested,* 17/**522**
R. v North and East Devon HA Ex p. Coughlan [2001] Q.B. 213; [2000] 2 W.L.R. 622; [2000] 3 All E.R. 850; (2000) 2 L.G.L.R. 1; [1999] B.L.G.R. 703; (1999) 2 C.C.L. Rep. 285; [1999] Lloyd's Rep. Med. 306; (2000) 51 B.M.L.R. 1; Times, July 20, 1999; Independent, July 20, 1999; [1999] C.O.D. 340; (1999) 96(31) L.S.G. 39; (1999) 143 S.J.L.B. 213, CA (Civ Div) .... *Digested,* 99/**2643**: *Applied* 00/4526, 01/5879, 02/4293, 02/46, 03/1917, 03/2837, 03/3399, 03/4101, 03/4713, 04/1905, 04/2643, 04/3859, 05/1837, 06/1927, 06/40, 07/3937, 07/716, 08/4302, 08/52, 08/70, 09/1770, 10/2184, 11/2138, 13/2935, 13/2947, 15/2376, 16/1479: *Considered* 05/2154, 06/1163, 06/1436, 06/2224, 07/1946, 07/45, 07/57, 10/2162, 10/3488, 14/2087, 15/1210, 15/1636, 16/38, 16/991, 17/1136, 17/2126: *Distinguished* 03/4091, 05/4121: *Followed* 99/3931, 00/1915, 09/4130, 12/2542, 14/2106, 14/2794
R. v North West Suffolk (Mildenhall) Magistrates' Court Ex p. Forest Heath DC; *sub nom* R. v Mildenhall Magistrates' Court Ex p. Forest Heath DC (1997) 161 J.P. 401; [1998] Env. L.R. 9; [2013] L.L.R. 69; Times, May 16, 1997; [1997] C.O.D. 352; (1997) 161 J.P.N. 602, CA (Civ Div) .... *Digested,* 97/**510**: *Followed* 17/542
R. v Nsumbu (Michael) [2017] EWCA Crim 1046; [2017] 2 Cr. App. R. (S.) 51, CA (Crim Div) .... *Digested,* 17/**1971**
R. v NTN see R. v Joseph (Verna Sermanfure)
R. v Nwokeh (Obi) see R. v Odegbune (Samson)
R. v Nyokanhete (Chen Constantine) [2016] EWCA Crim 1406; [2017] 1 Cr. App. R. (S.) 6; [2017] Crim. L.R. 156, CA (Crim Div) .... *Digested,* 17/**1908**
R. v Odegbune (Samson); *joined cases* R, v Richards (Tyrone); R. v Amoah (Enoch Charles); R. v Akra (Adonis Junior); R. v Omoregi (Christopher); R. v Oderinwale (Femi); R. v Nwokeh (Obi); R. v Roberts (Samuel Junior) [2013] EWCA Crim 711, CA (Crim Div) *Followed* 17/1941
R. v Oderinwale (Femi) see R. v Odegbune (Samson)
R. v Odesanyi (Akinwumi) [2005] EWCA Crim 2260, CA (Crim Div) *Explained* 17/609
R. v Odiowei (Justin Obuza) see R. v Vowles (Lucinda)
R. v Officer (Clinton) see Attorney General's Reference (Nos 128 to 141 of 2015 and 8 to 10 of 2016)

R. v Ogden (Neil); *joined cases* R. v Logan (Gavin); R. v Wilson (Dean); R. v Martin (Glen); R. v Atkinson (David); R. v Brough (Kevin); R. v Ogden (Stephen) [2016] EWCA Crim 6; [2017] 1 W.L.R. 1224; [2016] 1 Cr. App. R. 29; [2016] Crim. L.R. 573, CA (Crim Div) .... *Digested,* 16/**466**: *Followed* 17/1884

R. v Ogden (Stephen) see R. v Ogden (Neil)

R. v Olditch (Toby) see R. v Jones (Margaret)

R. v Omoregi (Christopher) see R. v Odegbune (Samson)

R. v Opuku (David Swire) [2017] EWCA Crim 1110; [2017] 2 Cr. App. R. (S.) 49, CA (Crim Div)

R. v Ordu (Mehmet) [2017] EWCA Crim 4; [2017] 1 Cr. App. R. 21; [2017] Crim. L.R. 396, CA (Crim Div) .... *Digested,* 17/**612**

R. v Oxfordshire CC Ex p. Sunningwell Parish Council [2000] 1 A.C. 335; [1999] 3 W.L.R. 160; [1999] 3 All E.R. 385; [1999] B.L.G.R. 651; (2000) 79 P. & C.R. 199; [1999] 2 E.G.L.R. 94; [1999] 31 E.G. 85; Times, June 25, 1999; Independent, June 29, 1999; [2000] J.P.L. 384; [1999] E.G. 91 (C.S.); (1999) 96(29) L.S.G. 29; (1999) 149 N.L.J. 1038; (1999) 143 S.J.L.B. 205; [1999] N.P.C. 74, HL .... *Digested,* 99/**4393**: *Applied* 04/3205, 08/3116, 09/3191, 13/2469, 14/2526: *Considered* 04/3203, 05/3440, 10/2754, 13/2468: *Followed* 12/2729, 17/1860

R. v Ozcelik (Silhan) see R. v Kahar (Mohammed Abdul)

R. v P (Anthony) see Attorney General's Reference (No.27 of 2013)

R. v P see R. v H

R. v Pacurar (Adrian) [2016] EWCA Crim 569; [2016] 1 W.L.R. 3913; [2016] 2 Cr. App. R. 26; (2017) 181 J.P. 186, CA (Crim Div) .... *Digested,* 16/**481**

R. v Palmer (Keith Anthony) [2016] EWCA Crim 1049; [2017] 4 W.L.R. 15; [2016] Lloyd's Rep. F.C. 541; [2016] C.T.L.C. 173; [2016] L.L.R. 811; [2016] Crim. L.R. 856, CA (Crim Div) .... *Digested,* 16/**502**

R. v Panel on Takeovers and Mergers Ex p. Datafin Plc [1987] Q.B. 815; [1987] 2 W.L.R. 699; [1987] 1 All E.R. 564; (1987) 3 B.C.C. 10; [1987] B.C.L.C. 104; [1987] 1 F.T.L.R. 181; (1987) 131 S.J. 23, CA (Civ Div) .... *Digested,* 87/**21**: *Applied* 91/83, 92/13, 01/5140, 03/68, 06/4713, 07/55, 17/1077: *Considered* 86/2054, 90/30, 90/3912, 91/76, 92/12, 92/38, 92/4, 93/31, 93/32, 93/33, 95/47, 95/55

R. v Panton (Lucy Rebecca) see R. v Chapman (Scott Derek)

R. v Parke (Russel) [2017] EWCA Crim 301; [2017] 2 Cr. App. R. (S.) 3, CA (Crim Div) .... *Digested,* 17/**1924**

R. v Parkinson (Matthew) [2015] EWCA Crim 1448; [2016] 1 Cr. App. R. (S.) 6; [2015] Crim. L.R. 991, CA (Crim Div) .... *Digested,* 16/**501**: *Followed* 17/581

R. v Parnes (Anthony Keith) (No.3) see R. v Lyons (Isidore Jack) (No.3)

R. v Parveaz (Mohsin) [2017] EWCA Crim 873; [2017] Crim. L.R. 891, CA (Crim Div)

R. v Patel (Hitendra) [2016] EWCA Crim 2001; [2017] 1 Costs L.R. 77, CA (Crim Div) . *Digested,* 17/**584**

R. v Paywand (Azmari); *joined case* R. v Clarke (Paul) [2017] EWCA Crim 885; [2017] 2 Cr. App. R. (S.) 35; [2017] Crim. L.R. 1005, CA (Crim Div) .... *Digested,* 17/**1911**

R. v PC see R. v PW

R. v Pereira-Lee (Cheyenn) [2016] EWCA Crim 1705; [2017] 1 Cr. App. R. (S.) 17; [2017] Crim. L.R. 243, CA (Crim Div) .... *Digested,* 17/**1904**

R. v Petherick (Rosie Lee) [2012] EWCA Crim 2214; [2013] 1 W.L.R. 1102; [2013] 1 Cr. App. R. (S.) 116; (2013) 177 J.P. 94; [2013] Crim. L.R. 80, CA (Crim Div) ... *Digested,* 13/**2749**: *Applied* 17/1887: *Considered* 15/2224: *Followed* 16/1873

R. v Pidgeon (Stephen Paul); *sub nom* R. v Pidgeon (Stephen Paul) (also known as Smith) [2017] EWCA Crim 538; [2017] 2 Cr. App. R. (S.) 43, CA (Crim Div) ...... *Digested,* 17/**1969**

R. v Pidgeon (Stephen Paul) (also known as Smith) see R. v Pidgeon (Stephen Paul)

R. v Pilkington (Keith Robert) see R. v Thorsby (Adrian Kenneth)

R. v Pinkerton (Jon) [2017] EWCA Crim 38; [2017] 4 W.L.R. 65; [2017] 1 Cr. App. R. (S.) 47; [2017] Crim. L.R. 493, CA (Crim Div) .... *Digested,* 17/**1935**

R. v Powell (Anthony Glassford); *joined cases* R. v Daniels (Antonio Eval); R. v English (Philip) [1999] 1 A.C. 1; [1997] 3 W.L.R. 959; [1997] 4 All E.R. 545; [1998] 1 Cr. App. R. 261; (1998) 162 J.P. 1; Times, October 31, 1997; Independent, November 11, 1997; [1998] Crim. L.R. 48; (1998) 162 J.P.N. 26; (1997) 161 J.P.N. 1100; (1997) 147 N.L.J. 1654, HL .... *Digested,* 97/**1220**: *Applied* 00/5468, 00/5481, 06/1606, 06/862, 08/743, 11/674: *Considered* 98/959, 04/855, 17/551, 17/610: *Followed* 98/1035, 07/877, 10/701, 11/676: *Superseded* 16/482

R. v Powell (Jacqueline); *sub nom* R. v Westwood (Jonathan) [2016] EWCA Crim 1043; [2017] Env. L.R. 11; [2016] Lloyd's Rep. F.C. 546; [2016] C.T.L.C. 137; [2016] Crim. L.R. 852, CA (Crim Div) .... *Digested,* 16/**503**

R. v Poyser (Kofi) see R. v McLeod (Ralph)
R. v Poyser (Lewis) see R. v McLeod (Ralph)
R. v PQ see R. v PW
R. v Prempeh (Gabriel) see R. v Akinsete (Marcel)
R. v Prentice (Michael Charles) see R. v Adomako (John Asare)
R. v Price (Paul Graham) see R. v Graham (Hemamali Krishna)
R. v Pritchard (John) [2017] EWCA Crim 1267; [2018] 1 W.L.R. 1631; [2017] 2 Cr. App. R. (S.) 54; [2017] Lloyd's Rep. F.C. 590; [2017] Crim. L.R. 993, CA (Crim Div) .... *Digested,* 17/**574**
R. v Pritchard (Philip) see R. v Jones (Margaret)
R. v PW; *sub nom* R. v W; *joined cases* R. v PQ; R. v JP; R. v AM; R. v MC; R. v BC; R. v LD; R. v PC [2016] EWCA Crim 745; [2017] 4 W.L.R. 79; [2016] 2 Cr. App. R. 27; [2016] Crim. L.R. 844, CA (Crim Div) .... *Digested,* 16/**480**
R. v Pyo (Hyung-Woo) see Attorney General's Reference (Nos 3, 73 and 75 of 2010)
R. v Qosja (Robert) [2016] EWCA Crim 1543; [2017] 1 W.L.R. 311; [2017] 1 Cr. App. R. 17, CA (Crim Div) .... *Digested,* 17/**550**
R. v Quick (George) [2017] EWCA Crim 66; [2017] 1 Cr. App. R. (S.) 54, CA (Crim Div) .... *Digested,* 17/**1914**
R. v Quillan (Gary); *joined cases* R. v Hoole (Christopher); R. v Garrett (Peter); R. v Garrett (Gregory); R. v Edmonson (Andrew); R. v Thomson (Neal) [2015] EWCA Crim 538; [2015] 1 W.L.R. 4673; [2016] 2 All E.R. 653; [2015] 2 Cr. App. R. 3; [2015] Lloyd's Rep. F.C. 321; [2015] B.T.C. 16; [2015] Crim. L.R. 618, CA (Crim Div) .... *Digested,* 15/**644**: *Referred to* 17/2071
R. v Rahman (Mohammed Mizanur) see R. v Choudary (Anjem)
R. v Rakib (Mohammed) [2011] EWCA Crim 870; [2012] 1 Cr. App. R. (S.) 1; [2011] Crim. L.R. 570, CA (Crim Div) .... *Digested,* 12/**2867**: *Considered* 17/1904
R. v Ramchaitar (David Noel) see R. v Conaghan (Terence)
R. v Ramzan (Rauf Mohammed) [2012] EWCA Crim 2891; [2013] 2 Cr. App. R. (S.) 33; [2013] Crim. L.R. 526, CA (Crim Div) .... *Digested,* 13/**2637**: *Considered* 15/2220, 17/1920
R. v Rashid (Yahya) [2017] EWCA Crim 2; [2017] 1 W.L.R. 2449; [2017] 1 Cr. App. R. 25; [2017] Crim. L.R. 418, CA (Crim Div) .... *Digested,* 17/**525**
R. v Rashid (Yahya) see R. v Kahar (Mohammed Abdul)
R. v Ray (Stephen Jason) see R. v Ray (Steven Jason)
R. v Ray (Steven Jason); *sub nom* R. v Ray (Stephen Jason) [2017] EWCA Crim 1391; [2018] 2 W.L.R. 1148; [2018] 1 Cr. App. R. 4; (2017) 181 J.P. 493; [2018] Crim. L.R. 342, CA (Crim Div)
R. v Rayworth (Paul Michael) [2003] EWCA Crim 2887; [2004] 1 Cr. App. R. (S.) 75, CA (Crim Div) .... *Digested,* 04/**3406**: *Applied* 07/3714, 17/1955
R. v Recycled Materials Supplies Ltd [2017] EWCA Crim 58; [2017] P.T.S.R. 837; [2017] Env. L.R. 29, CA (Crim Div) .... *Digested,* 17/**549**
R. v Redcar and Cleveland BC Ex p. Armstrong see R. (on the application of Stennett) v Manchester City Council
R. v Rehinsi (Amarjit) [2017] EWCA Crim 157; [2017] 1 Cr. App. R. (S.) 59, CA (Crim Div) .... *Digested,* 17/**1892**
R. v Rehman (Zakir); *joined case* R. v Wood (Gary Dominic) [2005] EWCA Crim 2056; [2006] 1 Cr. App. R. (S.) 77; Times, September 27, 2005; [2005] Crim. L.R. 878, CA (Crim Div) .... *Digested,* 05/**3693**: *Applied* 06/3717, 08/3292, 09/3544, 10/2879, 10/2880, 11/2867, 11/2869, 12/2901, 14/2634, 14/2637, 15/2220, 16/1908, 17/1921: *Considered* 07/3718, 09/3384, 11/2864, 13/2637, 14/2636: *Distinguished* 07/3791: *Followed* 14/2638: *Referred to* 08/3289
R. v Renouf (John William) [1986] 1 W.L.R. 522; [1986] 2 All E.R. 449; (1986) 82 Cr. App. R. 344; [1986] R.T.R. 191; [1986] Crim. L.R. 408, CA (Crim Div) .... *Digested,* 86/**2970**: *Considered* 92/1310, 17/542: *Distinguished* 88/3137
R. v Reynolds (Anna Maria) see R. v Reynolds (Stephen)
R. v Reynolds (Jacqueline) [2017] EWCA Crim 57; 2017 S.C.L. 324, CA (Crim Div) .... *Digested,* 17/**581**
R. v Reynolds (Jamie); *joined case* R. v Rosser (Anwar) [2014] EWCA Crim 2205; [2015] 1 Cr. App. R. (S.) 24, CA (Crim Div) .... *Digested,* 15/**2298**: *Applied* 17/1938
R. v Reynolds (Naomi Donna) [2016] EWCA Crim 2217; [2017] 1 Cr. App. R. (S.) 42, CA (Crim Div) .... *Digested,* 17/**1901**
R. v Reynolds (Stephen); *joined cases* R. v Reynolds (Anna Maria); R. v Farnish (Valerie); R. v Farnish (Malcolm) [2017] EWCA Crim 1455; [2018] 4 W.L.R. 33; [2017] Lloyd's Rep. F.C. 579; [2018] Crim. L.R. 163, CA (Crim Div)

R. v RH; *sub nom* R. v H; R. v A; *joined case* R. v LA [2016] EWCA Crim 1754; [2017] 4 W.L.R. 81; [2017] 1 Cr. App. R. (S.) 23, CA (Crim Div) ..... *Digested,* 17/**1894**
R. v Richards (David James) [2014] EWCA Crim 1302, CA (Crim Div) *Not followed* 17/585
R. v Richards (Jiovaughni) see R. v Anwar (Umar)
R. v Richards (Josh) see R. v Jones (Margaret)
R. v Richmond LBC Ex p. Watson see R. (on the application of Stennett) v Manchester City Council
R. v Riddell (Tracey) [2017] EWCA Crim 413; [2017] 1 W.L.R. 3593; [2018] 1 All E.R. 62; [2017] 2 Cr. App. R. 3; (2017) 181 J.P. 284; [2017] R.T.R. 29; [2017] Crim. L.R. 637, CA (Crim Div) ..... *Digested,* 17/**543**
R. v RM see R. v AM
R. v Roberts (Graham Francis) see R. v Turnbull (Raymond)
R. v Roberts (Peter Jason) see Attorney General's Reference (Nos 60, 62 and 63 of 2009)
R. v Roberts (Samuel Junior) see R. v Odegbune (Samson)
R. v Robertson see R. v H
R. v Robinson (Zoe Marie) see R. v Thorsby (Adrian Kenneth)
R. v Rochdale MBC Ex p. Milne (No.2) [2001] Env. L.R. 22; (2001) 81 P. & C.R. 27; [2001] J.P.L. 229 (Note); [2001] J.P.L. 470; [2000] E.G. 103 (C.S.), QBD ..... *Digested,* 01/**4680**: *Applied* 03/3416, 07/1500, 16/1681, 17/1755: *Approved* 03/3420
R. v Rodmell (Daniel Michael) 9704724/Y3, CA (Crim Div) *Followed* 17/535
R. v Rogers (Bradley David); *joined cases* R. v Bell (Mark Julian); R. v French (Geraldine); R. v Samuels (Colin Martin) [2014] EWCA Crim 1680; [2015] 1 W.L.R. 1017; [2014] 2 Cr. App. R. 32; [2014] Lloyd's Rep. F.C. 638; [2014] Crim. L.R. 910; (2014) 158(32) S.J.L.B. 41, CA (Crim Div) ..... *Digested,* 14/**788**: *Followed* 17/900
R. v Rogers (Georgina); *joined cases* R. (on the application of the Environment Agency) v Tapecrown Ltd; R. v Beaman (Paul) [2016] EWCA Crim 801; [2017] 1 W.L.R. 481; [2016] 2 Cr. App. R. (S.) 36; [2016] Crim. L.R. 787, CA (Crim Div) ..... *Digested,* 16/**448**
R. v Rollins (Neil); *joined case* R. v McInerney (Michael) [2009] EWCA Crim 1941; [2010] 1 All E.R. 1183; [2010] Bus. L.R. 734; [2010] 1 Cr. App. R. 14; [2010] Lloyd's Rep. F.C. 16; [2010] L.L.R. 340; Times, October 20, 2009; [2010] Crim. L.R. 772, CA (Crim Div) *Affirmed* 10/777: *Distinguished* 17/619
R. v Roman (Ana-Maria) [2017] EWCA Crim 6; [2017] 1 Cr. App. R. (S.) 43, CA (Crim Div) ..... *Digested,* 17/**1887**
R. v Ronson (Gerald Maurice) (No.3) see R. v Lyons (Isidore Jack) (No.3)
R. v Rose (Honey Maria) [2017] EWCA Crim 1168; [2018] Q.B. 328; [2017] 3 W.L.R. 1461; [2018] 2 All E.R. 430; [2017] 2 Cr. App. R. 28; [2017] Med. L.R. 465; [2018] Crim. L.R. 76, CA (Crim Div) ..... *Digested,* 17/**553**
R. v Rosser (Anwar) see R. v Reynolds (Jamie)
R. v Rudling (Joanne) [2016] EWCA Crim 741; (2016) 151 B.M.L.R. 79, CA (Crim Div) ..... *Digested,* 16/**483**: *Applied* 17/553
R. v S [2016] EWCA Crim 2058; [2017] 1 Cr. App. R. (S.) 41; [2017] Crim. L.R. 340, CA (Crim Div) ..... *Digested,* 17/**1958**
R. v S [2016] EWCA Crim 1908; [2018] 4 W.L.R. 24; [2017] Crim. L.R. 982, CA (Crim Div)
R. v S [2008] EWCA Crim 2177; [2009] 1 W.L.R. 1489; [2009] 1 All E.R. 716; [2009] 1 Cr. App. R. 18; Times, October 15, 2008; [2009] Crim. L.R. 191; (2008) 158 N.L.J. 1459, CA (Crim Div) ..... *Digested,* 08/**711**: *Followed* 12/413, 17/291
R. v S see Attorney General's Reference (No.58 of 2007)
R. v S see Attorney General's Reference (No.103 of 2015)
R. v S see R. v H
R. v Sabey (Ryan) see R. v Chapman (Scott Derek)
R. v Safarzadeh-Markhali 2016 SCC 14; 42 B.H.R.C. 426, Sup Ct (Can)
R. v Safi (Ali Ahmed); *joined cases* R. v Ghayur (Abdul); R. v Shah (Taimur); R. v Showaib (Mohammed); R. v Mohammidy (Nazamuddin); R. v Shohab (Abdul); R. v Ahmadi (Reshad); R. v Safi (Mahammad Nasir); R. v Kazin (Mohammed) [2003] EWCA Crim 1809; [2004] 1 Cr. App. R. 14; Times, June 10, 2003; Independent, June 12, 2003; [2003] Crim. L.R. 721; (2003) 100(31) L.S.G. 31, CA (Crim Div) ..... *Digested,* 03/**877**: *Applied* 17/547
R. v Safi (Mahammad Nasir) see R. v Safi (Ali Ahmed)

R. v Samuels (Colin Martin) see R. v Rogers (Bradley David)
R. v Samuriwo (Michael Tatenda); *sub nom* R. v Bromell (Jerome) (aka Henry); R. v Muliswela (Stewart Kudzai) [2016] EWCA Crim 1948; [2017] 1 Cr. App. R. (S.) 30, CA (Crim Div) .... *Digested,* 17/**1923**
R. v Sandhu (Amandeep) [2017] EWCA Crim 908; [2017] 4 W.L.R. 160, CA (Crim Div) .... *Digested,* 17/**1959**
R. v Sardar (Anis Abid) [2016] EWCA Crim 1616; [2017] 1 W.L.R. 917; [2017] 1 Cr. App. R. 15; [2017] 1 Cr. App. R. (S.) 16; [2017] Crim. L.R. 500, CA (Crim Div) .. *Digested,* 17/**516**
R. v Saruwu (Joseph) see R. v Hunter (Nigel)
R. v Saunders (Ernest Walter) (No.3) see R. v Lyons (Isidore Jack) (No.3)
R. v Saw (Rebecca); *joined cases* R. v McPhee (Colin); R. v Younis (Naveed); R. v Kassa (Tadeusz); R. v Smith (Martin); R. v Tete-Djawu (Andrew) [2009] EWCA Crim 1; [2009] 2 All E.R. 1138; [2009] 2 Cr. App. R. (S.) 54; Times, January 26, 2009; [2009] Crim. L.R. 295, CA (Crim Div) .... *Digested,* 09/**3346**:
Applied 09/3342, 09/3343, 09/3344, 12/2846: *Considered* 10/2848, 10/2961, 11/2784, 11/2785, 12/2842, 12/2843, 12/2847: *Followed* 17/535
R. v Scott (Taylor) see R. v Anwar (Umar)
R. v Secretary of State for Foreign and Commonwealth Affairs Ex p. Lord Rees-Mogg [1994] Q.B. 552; [1994] 2 W.L.R. 115; [1994] 1 All E.R. 457; [1993] 3 C.M.L.R. 101; Times, July 31, 1993; Independent, August 3, 1993; [1994] C.O.D. 119; Guardian, August 2, 1993; (1993) 143 N.L.J. 1153; (1993) 137 S.J.L.B. 195, DC .... *Digested,* 94/**76**:
Applied 95/140: *Considered* 16/370, 17/441
R. v Secretary of State for Scotland Ex p. Greenpeace Ltd (Unreported, May 24, 1995), QBD
Distinguished 17/317
R. v Secretary of State for Social Security Ex p. Remelien see Secretary of State for Social Security v Remilien
R. v Secretary of State for Social Security Ex p. Wolke see Secretary of State for Social Security v Remilien
R. v Secretary of State for the Environment Ex p. Bolton MDC see Bolton MBC v Secretary of State for the Environment
R. v Secretary of State for the Environment Ex p. Slough BC; *sub nom* Slough BC v Secretary of State for the Environment 94 L.G.R. 376; (1995) 70 P. & C.R. 560; [1995] 3 P.L.R. 28; Times, May 24, 1995; Independent, June 14, 1995; [1995] J.P.L. 1128; [1996] C.O.D. 174; (1995) 159 L.G. Rev. 969; [1995] E.G. 95 (C.S.); (1995) 92(23) L.S.G. 32; (1995) 139 S.J.L.B. 130; [1995] N.P.C. 96, CA (Civ Div) .... *Digested,* 95/**4867**:
Applied 96/4835, 99/4249: *Considered* 17/1734: *Followed* 98/4224
R. v Secretary of State for the Environment, Transport and the Regions Ex p. Holdings & Barnes Plc see R. (on the application of Holding & Barnes Plc) v Secretary of State for the Environment, Transport and the Regions
R. v Secretary of State for the Home Department Ex p. Bentley [1994] Q.B. 349; [1994] 2 W.L.R. 101; [1993] 4 All E.R. 442; Times, July 8, 1993; Independent, July 8, 1993; [1994] C.O.D. 65; (1993) 143 N.L.J. 1025; (1993) 137 S.J.L.B. 194, DC .... *Digested,* 94/**75**:
Applied 09/915: *Considered* 17/1905
R. v Secretary of State for the Home Department Ex p. Bugdaycay see Bugdaycay v Secretary of State for the Home Department
R. v Secretary of State for the Home Department Ex p. Doody; *joined cases* R. v Secretary of State for the Home Department Ex p. Pierson; R. v Secretary of State for the Home Department Ex p. Smart; R. v Secretary of State for the Home Department Ex p. Pegg [1994] 1 A.C. 531; [1993] 3 W.L.R. 154; [1993] 3 All E.R. 92; (1995) 7 Admin. L.R. 1; Times, June 29, 1993; Independent, June 25, 1993; (1993) 143 N.L.J. 991, HL .... *Digested,* 93/**1213**:
Applied 94/3848, 95/960, 97/1335, 97/3929, 99/5437, 03/2058, 04/2772, 05/1785, 05/4967, 06/4534, 07/2173, 11/1779, 14/2162, 14/70, 17/1764: *Considered* 95/162, 95/2534, 95/2617, 96/1954, 96/1975, 96/4579, 96/6855, 97/1595, 97/2443, 98/4079, 00/3334, 00/4326, 02/3234, 04/1904, 11/3204, 17/2126: *Distinguished* 15/1365: *Followed* 95/81, 96/1953, 96/3981, 97/1626, 97/2672, 97/2678, 99/5212, 15/1819, 15/49: *Referred to* 95/1314
R. v Secretary of State for the Home Department Ex p. Duggan [1994] 3 All E.R. 277; Times, December 9, 1993; Independent, January 28, 1994; [1994] C.O.D. 258; Guardian, December 13, 1993, DC .... *Digested,* 94/**3848**:
Applied 10/2315, 17/1480: *Cited* 00/4329: *Considered* 97/3927, 14/2162: *Followed* 97/3928
R. v Secretary of State for the Home Department Ex p. Main see R. v Secretary of State for the Home Department Ex p. Simms

R. v Secretary of State for the Home Department Ex p. O'Brien see R. v Secretary of State for the Home Department Ex p. Simms
R. v Secretary of State for the Home Department Ex p. Pegg see R. v Secretary of State for the Home Department Ex p. Doody
R. v Secretary of State for the Home Department Ex p. Pierson see R. v Secretary of State for the Home Department Ex p. Doody
R. v Secretary of State for the Home Department Ex p. Salem [1999] 1 A.C. 450; [1999] 2 W.L.R. 483; [1999] 2 All E.R. 42; (1999) 11 Admin. L.R. 194; Times, February 12, 1999; [1999] C.O.D. 486; (1999) 96(9) L.S.G. 32; (1999) 143 S.J.L.B. 59, HL .... *Digested,* 99/**8**:
Applied 11/1722, 16/1035: *Considered* 13/1533: *Followed* 17/29: *Not applied* 15/1720: *Overruled* 03/2223
R. v Secretary of State for the Home Department Ex p. Shingara (No.2); *sub nom* Shingara v Secretary of State for the Home Department [1999] Imm. A.R. 257; [1999] I.N.L.R. 99, CA (Civ Div) .... *Digested,* 99/**3196**:
Considered 16/1835, 17/192
R. v Secretary of State for the Home Department Ex p. Simms; *sub nom* R. v Secretary of State for the Home Department Ex p. Main; *joined cases* R. v Governor of Whitemoor Prison Ex p. Main; R. v Secretary of State for the Home Department Ex p. O'Brien [2000] 2 A.C. 115; [1999] 3 W.L.R. 328; [1999] 3 All E.R. 400; [1999] E.M.L.R. 689; 7 B.H.R.C. 411; (1999) 11 Admin. L.R. 961; [1999] Prison L.R. 82; Times, July 9, 1999; [1999] C.O.D. 520; (1999) 96(30) L.S.G. 28; (1999) 149 N.L.J. 1073; (1999) 143 S.J.L.B. 212, HL .... *Digested,* 99/**4105**:
Applied 02/4505, 06/2096, 07/2318, 08/1444, 09/4216, 10/2031, 10/282, 12/2280, 13/665, 16/2075, 17/1289: *Considered* 99/335, 03/2223, 08/358: *Distinguished* 05/2914: *Followed* 11/3518, 15/1826
R. v Secretary of State for the Home Department Ex p. Smart see R. v Secretary of State for the Home Department Ex p. Doody
R. v Secretary of State for the Home Department Ex p. T; *sub nom* T (Political Asylum), Re; *joined case* T v Aberash [1995] 1 F.L.R. 293; [1995] 3 F.C.R. 1; [1994] Imm. A.R. 368; Times, April 8, 1994; Independent, May 2, 1994; [1995] Fam. Law 124, CA (Civ Div) .... *Digested,* 95/**2721**:
Applied 17/1034: *Considered* 96/3255, 09/1647
R. v Secretary of State for the Home Department Ex p. Turgut; *sub nom* Turgut v Secretary of State for the Home Department [2001] 1 All E.R. 719; [2000] H.R.L.R. 337; [2000] U.K.H.R.R. 403; [2000] Imm. A.R. 306; [2000] I.N.L.R. 292; Times, February 15, 2000; [2001] A.C.D. 12; (2000) 97(7) L.S.G. 40; (2000) 150 N.L.J. 131, CA (Civ Div) .... *Digested,* 00/**3297**:
Applied 00/3344, 01/5879: *Considered* 00/3392, 17/1231: *Distinguished* 14/68: *Followed* 17/37
R. v Secretary of State for Transport Ex p. Factortame Ltd (No.5) [2000] 1 A.C. 524; [1999] 3 W.L.R. 1062; [1999] 4 All E.R. 906; [1999] 3 C.M.L.R. 597; [2000] Eu. L.R. 40; Times, November 3, 1999; (1999) 96(43) L.S.G. 32; [1999] N.P.C. 126, HL .... *Digested,* 99/**2259**:
Applied 01/1092, 10/3278, 14/1853, 16/2428: *Considered* 15/951: *Followed* 17/1815
R. v Sefton MBC Ex p. Pau see R. v Hertfordshire CC Ex p. Cheung
R. v Sekhon (Daljit Singh) see R. v Knights (Richard Michael)
R. v Selby (James Alec) see R. v James (Mark George)
R. v Selby DC Ex p. Oxton Farms [2017] P.T.S.R. 1103; [1997] E.G. 60 (C.S.), CA (Civ Div) .... *Digested,* 97/**4114**:
Applied 05/3279, 07/3291, 09/3041, 14/2397, 16/1684, 16/1766: *Followed* 16/1700
R. v Sellu (David) [2016] EWCA Crim 1716; [2017] 4 W.L.R. 64; [2017] 1 Cr. App. R. 24; [2016] Inquest L.R. 267; [2017] Crim. L.R. 799, CA (Crim Div) .... *Digested,* 17/**605**
R. v Semanshia (Frederick) [2015] EWCA Crim 2479; [2016] M.H.L.R. 425, CA (Crim Div)
Considered 17/1906
R. v SG see R. v G
R. v Shah (Taimur) see R. v Safi (Ali Ahmed)
R. v Shahadat (Zaydene) [2017] EWCA Crim 822; [2017] 4 W.L.R. 212; [2017] 2 Cr. App. R. (S.) 32; [2017] Crim. L.R. 902, CA (Crim Div) .... *Digested,* 17/**1985**
R. v Shaibu (Mubarak) see R. v Nelson (Scott)
R. v Shaukat (Ayman) see R. v Abdallah (Abdalraouf)
R. v Shaw (Dennis) see R. v Canavan (Darren Anthony)
R. v Sheppard (Geoffrey Brian) see R. v Clarke (Andrew James)
R. v Sheppard (James) see R. v Lang (Stephen Howard)
R. v Sheridan (Philip Michael) see R. v Mealey (Jeremiah)

R. v Sherwood Ex p. Telegraph Group Plc see R. (on the application of Telegraph Group Plc) v Sherwood
R. v Shohab (Abdul) see R. v Safi (Ali Ahmed)
R. v Showaib (Mohammed) see R. v Safi (Ali Ahmed)
R. v Shropshire CC Ex p. Abdullah see R. v Barnet LBC Ex p. Shah
R. v Sinclair (James); *joined cases* R. v Johnson (Brian); R. v Smith (Ian) (1998) 148 N.L.J. 1353, CA (Crim Div)
Considered 05/805, 09/795, 17/606
R. v Singh (Gurphal) Times, April 17, 1999; [1999] Crim. L.R. 582, CA (Crim Div) .... *Digested,* 99/**945**:
Applied 17/553: *Considered* 05/805
R. v Singh (Harjit Sarana) see R. v McDowell (Christopher James)
R. v Singh (Kunwar Ajit) [2017] EWCA Crim 466; [2018] 1 W.L.R. 1425; [2017] 2 Cr. App. R. 15; [2017] Crim. L.R. 634, CA (Crim Div) .... *Digested,* 17/**567**
R. v Singh (Satnam) see R. v Knights (Richard Michael)
R. v Singh (Shangara) see R. v Knights (Richard Michael)
R. v Sly (Tyrone) see R. v Cooper (Martin Francis)
R. v Smith (David Edward) see R. v Jurecka (Aniela Halina)
R. v Smith (Gary) see R. v Lang (Stephen Howard)
R. v Smith (Ian) see R. v Sinclair (James)
R. v Smith (Jamal Shaka) see Attorney General's Reference (Nos 128 to 141 of 2015 and 8 to 10 of 2016)
R. v Smith (Kathryn Helen) [2017] EWCA Crim 1174; [2017] 2 Cr. App. R. (S.) 42, CA (Crim Div) .... *Digested,* 17/**603**
R. v Smith (Lonnie Augustus) [2015] EWCA Crim 333, CA (Crim Div)
Applied 17/1947
R. v Smith (Martin) see R. v Saw (Rebecca)
R. v Smith (Patrick) (1988) 87 Cr. App. R. 393; (1988) 10 Cr. App. R. (S.) 271; Times, July 2, 1988; Independent, July 11, 1988; [1988] Crim. L.R. 769; Daily Telegraph, July 8, 1988, CA (Crim Div) .... *Digested,* 89/**1006**:
Considered 97/1636, 12/2919, 17/629: *Followed* 11/583
R. v Smith (Paul Simon) see Attorney General's Reference (No.27 of 2013)
R. v Smith (Steven); *joined cases* R. v Clarke (Wayne); R. v Hall (Bryan); R. v Dodd (Jonathan) [2011] EWCA Crim 1772; [2012] 1 W.L.R. 1316; [2012] 1 All E.R. 451; [2012] 1 Cr. App. R. (S.) 82; [2011] Crim. L.R. 967, CA (Crim Div) .... *Digested,* 12/**3019**:
Applied 13/2776, 14/2687, 15/1826, 16/1926, 17/1975, 17/1976, 17/1983:
Considered 13/2580, 14/2685, 14/2686, 14/3461: *Followed* 13/2125, 14/775
R. v Smith (Terry) [2017] EWCA Crim 252; [2017] 2 Cr. App. R. (S.) 2; [2017] Crim. L.R. 641, CA (Crim Div) .... *Digested,* 17/**1895**
R. v Smith (William); *joined case* R. v Doe (Henry) (1987) 85 Cr. App. R. 197; Times, December 3, 1986; [1987] Crim. L.R. 267, CA (Crim Div) .... *Digested,* 88/**651**:
Applied 17/603
R. v Smythe (Lee) see R. v Needham (Paul Maurice)
R. v Solomon (Paul); *joined case* R. v Triumph (Gary Martin) (1984) 6 Cr. App. R. (S.) 120; [1984] Crim. L.R. 433, CA (Crim Div) .... *Digested,* 85/**863**:
Cited 89/1003: *Followed* 17/1972
R. v Soneiji (Kamalesh Kumar) see R. v Soneji (Kamlesh Kumar)
R. v Soneji (Kamlesh Kumar); *sub nom* R. v Soneiji (Kamalesh Kumar); *joined case* R. v Bullen (David Frederick) [2005] UKHL 49; [2006] 1 A.C. 340; [2005] 3 W.L.R. 303; [2005] 4 All E.R. 321; [2006] 2 Cr. App. R. 20; [2006] 1 Cr. App. R. (S.) 79; Times, July 22, 2005; Independent, July 26, 2005; [2006] Crim. L.R. 167; (2005) 102(31) L.S.G. 26; (2005) 155 N.L.J. 1315; (2005) 149 S.J.L.B. 924, HL *Digested,* 05/**842**:
Applied 06/3679, 06/912, 06/950, 08/1394, 09/2685, 09/3578, 09/845, 10/2240, 12/1803, 12/1806, 13/1623, 13/3283, 14/2011, 14/742, 15/605, 15/606:
Cited 10/740: *Complaint upheld* 09/2012: *Considered* 07/3059, 08/3355, 08/589, 09/4031, 11/4480, 12/2334, 12/4196, 13/736, 15/1127: *Followed* 05/841, 10/1774, 11/2747, 11/719, 11/733, 12/981, 13/1672, 17/582, 17/583
R. v Southwark LBC Ex p. Dagou (1996) 28 H.L.R. 72; [1995] N.P.C. 20, QBD .... *Digested,* 95/**75**:
Applied 17/1149
R. v Spearing (Barry Charles) [2010] EWCA Crim 2169; [2011] 1 Cr. App. R. (S.) 101; [2011] Crim. L.R. 71, CA (Crim Div) .... *Digested,* 11/**721**:
Followed 17/575
R. v Special Commissioners of Income Tax Ex p. Morgan Grenfell & Co Ltd see R. (on the application of Morgan Grenfell & Co Ltd) v Special Commissioners of Income Tax
R. v Special Commissioners of Income Tax Ex p. Morgan Grenfell & Co Ltd see R. (on the application of Morgan Grenfell & Co Ltd) v Special Commissioners of Income Tax
R. v Srivastava (Rajeev) see R. v Misra (Amit)

R. v Stacey (James) see R. v Furniss (Michael)
R. v Stafford (Dennis) (No.1); *joined case* R. v Luvaglio (Michael) (No.1) [1968] 3 All E.R. 752 (Note); (1969) 53 Cr. App. R. 1, CA (Crim Div) .... *Digested,* 69/**622**: *Applied* 17/572
R. v Stansfield (Matthew) see R. v Denham (John)
R. v Steele see Steele (Kevin Munro) v HM Advocate
R. v Stephenson (Nosakhere) see Attorney General's Reference (Nos 128 to 141 of 2015 and 8 to 10 of 2016)
R. v Stewart (James) [2009] EWCA Crim 593; [2009] 1 W.L.R. 2507; [2010] 1 All E.R. 260; [2009] 2 Cr. App. R. 30; Times, July 20, 2009; [2009] Crim. L.R. 807, CA (Crim Div) .... *Digested,* 09/**786**: *Applied* 14/680: *Followed* 17/545
R. v Stewart (William Anthony) [2016] EWCA Crim 2238; [2017] 1 Cr. App. R. (S.) 48; [2017] R.T.R. 30; [2017] Crim. L.R. 490, CA (Crim Div) .... *Digested,* 17/**1889**
R. v Sticklen (Daniel John) [2013] EWCA Crim 615, CA (Crim Div) *Considered* 17/535
R. v Stockley (David) see R. v Anwar (Umar)
R. v Stoker (Graham) [2013] EWCA Crim 1431; [2014] 1 Cr. App. R. (S.) 47, CA (Crim Div) .... *Digested,* 14/**2634**: *Considered* 17/1920
R. v Stokes (Christy) see R. v Hyde (Daniel)
R. v Stosiek (Andrew) (1982) 4 Cr. App. R. (S.) 205; [1982] Crim. L.R. 615, CA (Crim Div) .... *Digested,* 83/**824**: *Applied* 04/3395: *Considered* 94/1260: *Not followed* 17/1972
R. v Straw (James Robert) see R. v Cooper (Martin Francis)
R. v Sullman (Barry) see R. v Adomako (John Asare)
R. v Sumal & Sons (Properties) Ltd see Sumal & Sons (Properties) Ltd v Newham LBC
R. v Sumner (Peter Anthony) see Attorney General's Reference (Nos 3 and 5 of 1989)
R. v Susorovs (Sergejs) [2016] EWCA Crim 1856; [2017] 1 Cr. App. R. (S.) 15; [2017] Crim. L.R. 337, CA (Crim Div) .... *Digested,* 17/**1982**
R. v Szrajber (Jozef Michael) (1994) 15 Cr. App. R. (S.) 821; Independent, March 21, 1994; [1994] Crim. L.R. 543, CA (Crim Div) .... *Digested,* 95/**1335**: *Applied* 11/732: *Considered* 96/1868, 12/761, 17/585
R. v T [2010] EWCA Crim 2703, CA (Crim Div) *Considered* 14/742: *Followed* 17/582
R. v T (Dean) see R. v Forbes (Stephen John)
R. v T see R. v C
R. v T see R. v L
R. v Tahir (Mohammed Akhtar) [2006] EWCA Crim 792, CA (Crim Div) *Followed* 17/575
R. v Talebi (Javad) [2012] EWCA Crim 3040; [2013] 2 Cr. App. R. (S.) 49, CA (Crim Div) .... *Digested,* 13/**2618**: *Applied* 17/1916
R. v Tata Steel UK Ltd [2017] EWCA Crim 704; [2017] 2 Cr. App. R. (S.) 29, CA (Crim Div) .... *Digested,* 17/**1931**
R. v Tatham (Philip) [2014] EWCA Crim 226; [2014] Lloyd's Rep. F.C. 354; [2014] Crim. L.R. 672, CA (Crim Div) .... *Digested,* 14/**739**: *Followed* 17/631
R. v Taylor (David) [2016] NICA 10; [2017] N.I. 294, CA (NI)
R. v Taylor (Elaine) see R. v Hudson (Linda)
R. v Taylor (Matthew) see R. v Healey (Robert)
R. v Taylor-Powell (Pedro George) see R. v Beech (Dean Colin)
R. v Terrelonge (Nicholas) see R. v Johnson (Lewis)
R. v Tete-Djawu (Andrew) see R. v Saw (Rebecca)
R. v Tharmaratnam (Tharmathasan) [2017] EWCA Crim 887; [2017] 2 Cr. App. R. (S.) 36, CA (Crim Div) .... *Digested,* 17/**1929**
R. v Thelwall (Kenneth) [2016] EWCA Crim 1755; [2016] C.T.L.C. 180; [2017] Crim. L.R. 240, CA (Crim Div) .... *Digested,* 17/**1932**: *Applied* 17/1959
R. v THN see R. v L
R. v Thomas (Richard Bartgerald) see R. v Avis (Tony)
R. v Thomas (Victor) see R. v Awoyemi (Toby)
R. v Thomson (Neal) see R. v Quillan (Gary)
R. v Thornley (James William) [2011] EWCA Crim 153; [2011] 2 Cr. App. R. (S.) 62; [2011] Crim. L.R. 415, CA (Crim Div) .... *Digested,* 11/**2939**: *Applied* 17/1942

R. v Thorsby (Adrian Kenneth); *joined cases* R. v Robinson (Zoe Marie); R. v Pilkington (Keith Robert); R. v Glasson (Davin) [2015] EWCA Crim 1; [2015] 1 W.L.R. 2901; [2015] 1 Cr. App. R. (S.) 63; Times, March 2, 2015, CA (Crim Div) .... *Digested,* 15/**2200**: *Followed* 16/1863, 17/1949

R. v Tibbits; *sub nom* R. v Tibbits and Windust [1902] 1 K.B. 77, Crown Cases Reserved
Considered 76/2117, 17/8

R. v Tibbits and Windust see R. v Tibbits

R. v Timmerman (Ramis) see R. v Ferizi (Orhan)

R. v Tomlinson (Rhys) see R. v Twist (Andrew Terence)

R. v Torrington (Richard Edward) see R. v Avis (Tony)

R. v Toto (Randy) see R. v Awoyemi (Toby)

R. v Triumph (Gary Martin) see R. v Solomon (Paul)

R. v Troninas (Paulias) see Attorney General's Reference (No.5 of 2011)

R. v Tsekiri (Jonathan) [2017] EWCA Crim 40; [2017] 1 W.L.R. 2879; [2018] 1 All E.R. 394; [2017] 1 Cr. App. R. 32; [2017] Crim. L.R. 628, CA (Crim Div) .... *Digested,* 17/**524**

R. v Tunney (Reynolds Thomas) [2006] EWCA Crim 2066; [2007] 1 Cr. App. R. (S.) 91, CA (Crim Div) .... *Digested,* 07/**3714**: *Applied* 10/2834, 10/2835, 17/1955: *Considered* 11/2983, 13/2712, 13/2713, 13/2716: *Followed* 17/1954, 17/1956

R. v Turk (Darren) [2017] EWCA Crim 391; [2017] 1 W.L.R. 2919; [2017] 2 Cr. App. R. 2; (2017) 181 J.P. 277; [2017] Crim. L.R. 649, CA (Crim Div) .... *Digested,* 17/**630**

R. v Turnbull (Raymond); *joined cases* R. v Whitby (Christopher John); R. v Roberts (Graham Francis); R. v Camelo (Joseph Nicholas David) [1977] Q.B. 224; [1976] 3 W.L.R. 445; [1976] 3 All E.R. 549; (1976) 63 Cr. App. R. 132; [1976] Crim. L.R. 565; (1976) 120 S.J. 486, CA (Crim Div) .... *Digested,* 76/**451**: *Applied* 78/480, 79/461, 81/431, 83/654, 88/650, 90/944, 91/1119, 92/861, 93/785, 94/5047, 94/911, 95/1060, 95/1127, 95/1128, 95/1131, 96/1383, 97/1152, 03/1055, 17/629: *Considered* 77/541, 78/481, 78/482, 83/628, 83/655, 85/582, 88/576, 91/745, 91/764, 91/767, 91/768, 94/913, 94/919, 94/924, 94/925, 94/926, 94/927, 95/1041, 95/1059, 95/1062, 95/1130, 96/1377, 96/1379, 96/1382, 96/1385, 97/1153, 97/1155, 04/772: *Distinguished* 83/656, 86/556, 92/794: *Explained* 80/2333: *Followed* 80/487, 88/558, 16/537: *Not applied* 82/579

R. v Turner (Jennifer) [2015] EWCA Crim 1249; [2017] M.H.L.R. 180; [2015] Crim. L.R. 920, CA (Crim Div)
Followed 17/1949

R. v Turner (Mark Simon) see Attorney General's Reference (No.68 of 2009)

R. v Twist (Andrew Terence); *joined cases* R. v Boothman (Richard); R. v Tomlinson (Rhys); R. v Kelly (Lewis Bradley); R. v L [2011] EWCA Crim 1143; [2011] 3 All E.R. 1055; [2011] 2 Cr. App. R. 17; (2011) 175 J.P. 257; [2011] Crim. L.R. 793, CA (Crim Div) .... *Digested,* 11/**584**: *Followed* 17/512

R. v Uddin (Tohel) [2017] EWCA Crim 1072; [2017] 1 W.L.R. 4739; [2018] 1 All E.R. 1073; [2017] 2 Cr. App. R. 31; [2017] Crim. L.R. 976, CA (Crim Div) .... *Digested,* 17/**536**

R. v Ulhaqdad (Rashid) [2017] EWCA Crim 1216; [2018] 4 W.L.R. 65; [2017] 2 Cr. App. R. (S.) 46; [2017] Crim. L.R. 1007, CA (Crim Div)

R. v van Dao (Vinh); *joined cases* R. v Muoi Thi NGuyen; R. v Hoang Mai [2012] EWCA Crim 1717; [2013] Crim. L.R. 234, CA (Crim Div)
Considered 17/548

R. v VCL see R. v Joseph (Verna Sermanfure)

R. v Vowles (Lucinda); *sub nom* R. (on the application of Vowles) v Secretary of State for Justice; *joined cases* R. v Barnes (Carl); R. v Coleman (Danielle); R. v Odiowei (Justin Obuza); R. v Irving (David Stuart); R. v McDougall (Gordon) [2015] EWCA Crim 45; [2015] 1 W.L.R. 5131; [2015] 2 Cr. App. R. (S.) 6; [2016] M.H.L.R. 66; [2015] Crim. L.R. 542, CA (Civ Div) .... *Digested,* 15/**2234**: *Applied* 16/1900: *Followed* 16/1898, 17/1545, 17/1906, 17/1937, 17/1949

R. v W [2016] EWCA Crim 2115; [2017] 1 Cr. App. R. (S.) 37, CA (Crim Div) .... *Digested,* 17/**1900**

R. v W see Attorney General's Reference (No.1 of 2003)

R. v W see R. v H

R. v W see R. v PW

R. v Wadkin (Paul); *joined case* R. v Gomez (Jason George) [2016] EWCA Crim 1047; [2016] 2 Cr. App. R. (S.) 40, CA (Crim Div) .... *Digested,* 17/**1938**

R. v Walker (Alan) see R. v Hunter (Nigel)

R. v Walker (Lee David) [2016] EWCA Crim 2053; [2017] 1 Cr. App. R. (S.) 27, CA (Crim Div) .... *Digested,* 17/**1955**

R. v Walker (P) see R. v H

R. v Walker (Triston) [2016] EWCA Crim 751; [2016] 4 W.L.R. 131; [2016] 2 Cr. App. R. 24; [2016] Crim. L.R. 848, CA (Crim Div) .... *Digested,* 17/**593**

R. v Waltham Forest LBC Ex p. Baxter [1988] Q.B. 419; [1988] 2 W.L.R. 257; [1987] 3 All E.R. 671; 86 L.G.R. 254; [1988] R.V.R. 6; (1987) 137 N.L.J. 947; (1988) 132 S.J. 227, CA (Civ Div) .... *Digested,* 88/**2187**: *Considered* 91/54, 95/3252, 12/2189, 17/1814: *Followed* 07/2867

R. v Wandsworth LBC Ex p. Rose (1984) 11 H.L.R. 105, QBD .... *Digested,* 84/**1640**: *Applied* 17/1159

R. v Ward (Damian) see R. v Churchill (Kristian)

R. v Warren (Barry James) see R. v Forbes (Stephen John)

R. v Warren (Connor) [2017] EWCA Crim 1086; [2017] 2 Cr. App. R. (S.) 45, CA (Crim Div)

R. v Warren (Davis Lewis) [2017] EWCA Crim 226; [2017] 4 W.L.R. 71; [2017] 2 Cr. App. R. (S.) 5; [2017] Crim. L.R. 569, CA (Crim Div) .... *Digested,* 17/**1993**

R. v Waters (Oliver Frederic); *joined case* R. v Westminster Recliners Ltd [2016] EWCA Crim 1112; (2016) 180 J.P. 459; [2017] E.C.C. 5; [2016] C.T.L.C. 147, CA (Crim Div) .... *Digested,* 17/**533**

R. v Waters (Paul Anthony) see R. v Bradshaw (Wayne Martin)

R. v Watts (Lewis) [2017] EWCA Crim 1009; [2017] 2 Cr. App. R. (S.) 52, CA (Crim Div) .... *Digested,* 17/**1991**

R. v Waya (Terry); *sub nom* R. v Waya Solicitors [2012] UKSC 51; [2013] 1 A.C. 294; [2012] 3 W.L.R. 1188; [2013] 1 All E.R. 889; [2013] 2 Cr. App. R. (S.) 20; [2013] H.R.L.R. 5; [2013] Lloyd's Rep. F.C. 187; 35 B.H.R.C. 293; Times, December 10, 2012; [2013] Crim. L.R. 256, SC .... *Digested,* 13/**689**: *Applied* 13/685, 14/736, 14/794, 15/595, 16/176, 16/499, 17/577: *Considered* 14/1631, 14/730, 14/731, 14/738, 15/599, 15/605, 16/506, 17/580: *Followed* 13/686, 13/690, 13/691, 13/749, 14/728, 14/729, 14/733, 14/734, 14/741, 14/743, 14/773, 14/798, 15/601, 16/504, 16/505

R. v Waya Solicitors see R. v Waya (Terry)

R. v Welsh (Christopher Mark) [2015] EWCA Crim 1516; [2016] 4 W.L.R. 13; [2016] 1 Cr. App. R. 9; [2016] Crim. L.R. 43, CA (Crim Div) .... *Digested,* 16/**496**: *Considered* 17/593

R. v Westminster City Council Ex p. Jaafer (1998) 30 H.L.R. 698, QBD .... *Digested,* 98/**3008**: *Considered* 17/2052

R. v Westminster City Council Ex p. Obeid (1997) 29 H.L.R. 389; Times, July 16, 1996, QBD .... *Digested,* 96/**3050**: *Applied* 17/1159: *Considered* 00/3144

R. v Westminster Housing Benefit Review Board Ex p. Mehanne see R. (on the application of Mehanne) v Westminster Housing Benefit Review Board

R. v Westminster Recliners Ltd see R. v Waters (Oliver Frederic)

R. v Westwood (Jonathan) see R. v Powell (Jacqueline)

R. v Whale (Geoffrey); *joined case* R. v Lockton (Robert John) Times, May 9, 1991; [1991] Crim. L.R. 692, CA (Crim Div) .... *Digested,* 92/**843**: *Considered* 10/729, 17/593: *Explained* 16/496: *Followed* 95/2379

R. v Whitby (Christopher John) see R. v Turnbull (Raymond)

R. v White (Kevin) see R. v Dowse (Adrian)

R. v Wickens (Ian David) [2016] EWCA Crim 2077; [2017] R.T.R. 15, CA (Crim Div) ... *Digested,* 17/**1909**

R. v Wicks (Derek John) [2013] EWCA Crim 1414; [2014] 1 Cr. App. R. (S.) 57, CA (Crim Div) *Considered* 17/1912

R. v Wicks (Peter Edward) [1998] A.C. 92; [1997] 2 W.L.R. 876; [1997] 2 All E.R. 801; (1997) 161 J.P. 433; (1997) 9 Admin. L.R. 349; [1997] 2 P.L.R. 97; Times, May 26, 1997; Independent, June 4, 1997; [1997] J.P.L. 1049; (1997) 161 J.P.N. 628; (1997) 94(35) L.S.G. 34; (1997) 147 N.L.J. 883; (1997) 141 S.J.L.B. 127; [1997] N.P.C. 85, HL .... *Digested,* 97/**4065**: *Applied* 98/3222, 06/4869, 08/2921, 15/1667: *Considered* 13/2301, 17/549: *Distinguished* 02/3708, 03/776: *Followed* 98/4203, 01/81, 12/2544, 14/717

R. v Wiggan (Theodore Junior) see Attorney General's Reference (Nos 128 to 141 of 2015 and 8 to 10 of 2016)

R. v Wiggins (Jamie Mark) (2001) 165 J.P. 210; [2001] R.T.R. 3; Times, June 23, 2000, CA (Crim Div) .... *Digested,* 00/**1126**: *Considered* 17/1910

R. v Wilcocks (Callum Paul) [2016] EWCA Crim 2043; [2017] 4 W.L.R. 39; [2017] 1 Cr. App. R. 23; [2017] Crim. L.R. 706, CA (Crim Div) .... *Digested,* 17/**517**

R. v Willett (Tommy) [2011] EWCA Crim 2710; [2012] 2 Cr. App. R. (S.) 18; Times, March 9, 2012, CA (Crim Div) .... *Digested,* 12/**821**: *Considered* 17/1939

R. v Williams (Clayton Ronald) [2017] EWCA Crim 305; [2017] 4 W.L.R. 78; [2017] 2 Cr. App. R. (S.) 12; [2017] Crim. L.R. 647, CA (Crim Div) .... *Digested,* 17/**1939**: *Considered* 17/1943, 17/1945
R. v Williams (Malachi Lloyd) [2017] EWCA Crim 281; [2017] 4 W.L.R. 93; [2017] 2 Cr. App. R. 7; [2017] Crim. L.R. 581, CA (Crim Div) .... *Digested,* 17/**602**
R. v Williams (Michael) see R. v Hyde (Daniel)
R. v Williams (Michael) see R. v Needham (Paul Maurice)
R. v Williams (Roy Brian) [1978] Q.B. 373; [1977] 2 W.L.R. 400; [1977] 1 All E.R. 874; (1977) 64 Cr. App. R. 106; [1977] Crim. L.R. 305; (1977) 121 S.J. 135, CA (Crim Div) .... *Digested,* 77/**453**: *Considered* 17/573
R. v Wilson (Dean) see R. v Ogden (Neil)
R. v Wilson (Kevin) [2016] EWCA Crim 1555; [2017] 1 Cr. App. R. (S.) 7, CA (Crim Div) .... *Digested,* 17/**1928**
R. v Winters (Keith) see R. v Lang (Stephen Howard)
R. v Wolverhampton MBC Ex p. Watters [1997] 3 F.C.R. 747; (1997) 29 H.L.R. 931; Times, March 4, 1997; Independent, March 18, 1997; [1997] C.O.D. 285, CA (Civ Div) .... *Digested,* 97/**2696**: *Considered* 17/1154
R. v Wood (Clive) [2009] EWCA Crim 651; [2010] 1 Cr. App. R. (S.) 2; Times, April 8, 2009; [2009] Crim. L.R. 543, CA (Crim Div) .... *Digested,* 09/**3418**: *Applied* 11/2930, 11/2937, 11/582, 17/1939: *Considered* 10/2893, 11/2927, 11/2933, 12/2942, 12/2945, 13/2688, 15/2239: *Followed* 12/2943
R. v Wood (Daniel) see R. v Fulton (Gary Peter)
R. v Wood (Gary Dominic) see R. v Rehman (Zakir)
R. v Woodward (Robert see R. v Woodward (Robert)
R. v Woodward (Robert); *joined cases* R. v Woodward (Robert; R. v Hussain (Kabeer); R. v Hussein (Kazam); R. v Lewandowski (Artur) [2017] EWHC 1008 (Admin); (2017) 181 J.P. 405; [2017] Crim. L.R. 884; [2017] A.C.D. 77, DC .... *Digested,* 17/**617**
R. v Wright (Robert) see R. v Lang (Stephen Howard)
R. v Y (Sexual Offence: Complainant's Sexual History) see R. v A (Complainant's Sexual History)
R. v Yasain (Mohammed Abdullah) [2015] EWCA Crim 1277; [2016] Q.B. 146; [2015] 3 W.L.R. 1571; [2016] 2 All E.R. 686; [2015] 2 Cr. App. R. 28; [2016] 1 Cr. App. R. (S.) 7; [2016] Crim. L.R. 131, CA (Crim Div) .... *Digested,* 15/**616**: *Explained* 17/588: *Followed* 17/609
R. v Younas (Muhammad Anees) [2017] EWCA Crim 1; [2017] 1 Cr. App. R. (S.) 44, CA (Crim Div) .... *Digested,* 17/**1897**
R. v Young (Allen) [2016] EWCA Crim 1321; [2016] 4 W.L.R. 154; [2017] 1 Cr. App. R. 2; [2017] Crim. L.R. 144, CA (Crim Div) .... *Digested,* 16/**476**
R. v Younis (Naveed) see R. v Saw (Rebecca)
R. v YT see R. v LM
R. v Z; *sub nom* Z (Attorney General for Northern Ireland's Reference), Re [2005] UKHL 35; [2005] 2 A.C. 645; [2005] 2 W.L.R. 1286; [2005] 3 All E.R. 95; [2005] N.I. 468; Times, May 20, 2005; Independent, May 25, 2005; [2005] Crim. L.R. 985, HL (NI) .... *Digested,* 05/**823**: *Followed* 17/384
R. v Z see R. v Hasan (Aytach)
R. v Zaredar (Arash) [2016] EWCA Crim 877; [2017] Crim. L.R. 57, CA (Crim Div)
R. v Ziamani (Brusthom) see R. v Kahar (Mohammed Abdul)
R. v Zinga (Munaf Ahmed); *sub nom* R. (on the application of Virgin Media Ltd) v Zinga [2014] EWCA Crim 52; [2014] 1 W.L.R. 2228; [2014] 3 All E.R. 90; [2014] 1 Cr. App. R. 27; [2014] 2 Cr. App. R. (S.) 30; (2014) 178 J.P. 105, CA (Crim Div) .... *Digested,* 14/**798**: *Followed* 17/620
R. (on the application of A (A Child)) v Secretary of State for Health [2017] UKSC 41; [2017] 1 W.L.R. 2492; [2017] 4 All E.R. 353; [2017] H.R.L.R. 9; [2017] Med. L.R. 347; (2017) 156 B.M.L.R. 1; Times, June 19, 2017, SC .... *Digested,* 17/**1095**
R. (on the application of A (A Child)) v Secretary of State for Health [2015] EWCA Civ 771; [2016] 1 W.L.R. 331; [2016] 2 F.L.R. 502; (2015) 146 B.M.L.R. 107; Times, July 28, 2015; [2015] Fam. Law 1175, CA (Civ Div) .... *Digested,* 15/**1177**: *Affirmed* 17/1095
R. (on the application of A) v Central Criminal Court; *joined case* C v Central Criminal Court [2017] EWHC 70 (Admin); [2017] 1 W.L.R. 3567, DC

R. (on the application of A) v Croydon LBC; *joined case* R. (on the application of M) v Lambeth LBC [2009] UKSC 8; [2009] 1 W.L.R. 2557; [2010] 1 All E.R. 469; [2010] P.T.S.R. 106; [2010] 1 F.L.R. 959; [2009] 3 F.C.R. 607; [2010] H.R.L.R. 9; [2010] U.K.H.R.R. 63; [2010] B.L.G.R. 183; (2009) 12 C.C.L. Rep. 552; Times, November 30, 2009; [2010] Fam. Law 137; (2009) 159 N.L.J. 1701; (2009) 153(46) S.J.L.B. 34, SC .... *Digested,* 10/**2197**: *Applied* 11/1803, 16/1068: *Considered* 10/1694, 10/975, 11/2165, 11/3194, 12/1625, 12/4159, 17/1203: *Followed* 10/2208, 11/1709, 12/3161, 15/2388, 15/41: *Referred to* 12/343

R. (on the application of A) v Director of Establishments of the Security Service see A v B (Investigatory Powers Tribunal: Jurisdiction)

R. (on the application of A) v DPP [2017] EWHC 714 (Admin); [2017] 2 Costs L.R. 323, QBD (Admin) .... *Digested,* 17/**265**

R. (on the application of A) v Enfield LBC; *sub nom* A v Enfield LBC [2016] EWHC 567 (Admin); [2017] 1 F.L.R. 203; [2016] H.L.R. 33; (2016) 19 C.C.L. Rep. 236; [2016] A.C.D. 89; [2016] Fam. Law 688, QBD (Admin) .... *Digested,* 16/**2007**

R. (on the application of A) v Haringey LBC [2016] EWHC 3054 (Admin); (2017) 20 C.C.L. Rep. 60, QBD (Admin) .... *Digested,* 17/**2053**

R. (on the application of A) v Oxfordshire CC [2016] EWHC 2419 (Admin); (2017) 20 C.C.L. Rep. 539; (2017) 20 C.C.L. Rep. 539, QBD (Admin)

R. (on the application of A) v Secretary of State for the Home Department [2017] EWHC 1233 (Admin); [2017] A.C.D. 71, QBD (Admin)

R. (on the application of A) v Secretary of State for Work and Pensions see R. (on the application of Carmichael) v Secretary of State for Work and Pensions

R. (on the application of A) v Secretary of State for Work and Pensions see Rutherford v Secretary of State for Work and Pensions

R. (on the application of AA (Afghanistan)) v Secretary of State for the Home Department [2013] UKSC 49; [2013] 1 W.L.R. 2224; [2013] 4 All E.R. 140; [2013] 3 F.C.R. 515; [2013] H.R.L.R. 34; [2014] I.N.L.R. 51; Times, August 2, 2013; (2013) 163(7569) N.L.J. 15, SC .... *Digested,* 13/**1601**: *Considered* 16/1068: *Superseded in part* 17/1203

R. (on the application of AA (Sudan)) v Secretary of State for the Home Department [2017] EWCA Civ 138; [2017] 1 W.L.R. 2894; [2017] 4 All E.R. 964; [2017] I.N.L.R. 896, CA (Civ Div) .... *Digested,* 17/**1203**

R. (on the application of AA (Sudan)) v Secretary of State for the Home Department [2016] EWHC 1453 (Admin); [2017] 1 W.L.R. 145; (2016) 19 C.C.L. Rep. 267, QBD (Admin) .... *Digested,* 16/**1068**: *Affirmed* 17/1203

R. (on the application of AB) v Secretary of State for the Home Department [2017] EWCA Civ 59; [2017] Imm. A.R. 1154, CA (Civ Div)

R. (on the application of AB) v Secretary of State for the Home Department [2016] EWHC 2751 (Admin); [2017] Imm. A.R. 680; [2017] A.C.D. 19, QBD (Admin) ... *Digested,* 17/**1174**

R. (on the application of Abbas) v Secretary of State for the Home Department [2017] EWHC 78 (Admin); [2017] 4 W.L.R. 34; [2017] A.C.D. 35, QBD (Admin) .... *Digested,* 17/**1225**

R. (on the application of Abbassi) v Secretary of State for the Home Department; *sub nom* R. (on the application of Rahman) v Secretary of State for the Home Department; R. (on the application of Munir) v Secretary of State for the Home Department; Secretary of State for the Home Department v Rahman; *joined case* Munir v Secretary of State for the Home Department [2012] UKSC 32; [2012] 1 W.L.R. 2192; [2012] 4 All E.R. 1025; [2012] Imm. A.R. 1038; [2012] I.N.L.R. 546; Times, August 6, 2012, SC .... *Digested,* 12/**1735**: *Considered* 13/1648, 16/1129: *Followed* 17/1209

R. (on the application of Abdi) v Secretary of State for the Home Department see R. (on the application of Nadarajah) v Secretary of State for the Home Department

R. (on the application of Abdulrahman) v Hillingdon LBC [2016] EWHC 2647 (Admin); [2017] H.L.R. 1, QBD (Admin) .... *Digested,* 17/**1157**

R. (on the application of Accident Exchange Ltd) v Broom [2017] EWHC 1530 (Admin); [2017] A.C.D. 96, QBD (Admin)

R. (on the application of Adesina) v Nursing and Midwifery Council see Adesina v Nursing and Midwifery Council

R. (on the application of AE (Eritrea)) v Secretary of State for the Home Department see R. (on the application of EM (Eritrea)) v Secretary of State for the Home Department

R. (on the application of AF) v Secretary of State for the Home Department see R. (on the application of MM (Lebanon)) v Secretary of State for the Home Department

R. (on the application of Aguilar Quila) v Secretary of State for the Home Department; *sub nom* Quila v Secretary of State for the Home Department; Aguilar Quila v Secretary of State for the Home Department; Bibi v Secretary of State for the Home Department; *joined case* R. (on the application of Bibi) v Secretary of State for the Home Department [2011] UKSC 45; [2012] 1 A.C. 621; [2011] 3 W.L.R. 836; [2012] 1 All E.R. 1011; [2012] 1 F.L.R. 788; [2011] 3 F.C.R. 575; [2012] H.R.L.R. 2; [2011] U.K.H.R.R. 1347; 33 B.H.R.C. 381; [2012] Imm. A.R. 135; [2011] I.N.L.R. 698; Times, October 20, 2011; [2012] Fam. Law 21; (2011) 108(41) L.S.G. 15; (2011) 155(39) S.J.L.B. 31, SC .... *Digested,* 11/**1762**:
Applied 12/1720, 14/1703, 17/1207: *Considered* 12/2330: *Followed* 13/1625, 14/1715, 15/1307, 17/1231

R. (on the application of Agyarko) v Secretary of State for the Home Department; *joined cases* R. (on the application of Evans) v Secretary of State for the Home Department; R. (on the application of Ikuga) v Secretary of State for the Home Department [2017] UKSC 11; [2017] 1 W.L.R. 823; [2017] 4 All E.R. 575; [2017] 3 C.M.L.R. 3; [2017] Imm. A.R. 764; [2017] I.N.L.R. 548; Times, March 1, 2017, SC .... *Digested,* 17/**1239**:
Considered 17/2665

R. (on the application of Agyarko) v Secretary of State for the Home Department; *joined cases* R. (on the application of Evans) v Secretary of State for the Home Department; R. (on the application of Ikuga) v Secretary of State for the Home Department [2015] EWCA Civ 440; [2016] 1 W.L.R. 390; [2015] Imm. A.R. 1201; [2016] I.N.L.R. 198, CA (Civ Div) .... *Digested,* 16/**1141**:
Affirmed 17/1239: *Considered* 17/1200, 17/2670

R. (on the application of Ahmad) v Newham LBC [2009] UKHL 14; [2009] 3 All E.R. 755; [2009] P.T.S.R. 632; [2009] H.L.R. 31; [2009] B.L.G.R. 627; Times, March 6, 2009; (2009) 153(9) S.J.L.B. 29; [2009] N.P.C. 36, HL .... *Digested,* 09/**1910**:
Considered 11/3220, 16/1040: *Followed* 17/1154, 17/1155

R. (on the application of AI) v Secretary of State for the Home Department see R. (on the application of XH) v Secretary of State for the Home Department

R. (on the application of Aitjilal) v Secretary of State for the Home Department [2016] UKUT 563 (IAC); [2017] Imm. A.R. 552, UT (IAC)

R. (on the application of Akarcay) v Chief Constable of West Yorkshire [2017] EWHC 159 (Admin); [2017] A.C.D. 39, DC

R. (on the application of Akturk) v Secretary of State for the Home Department; *sub nom* R. (on the application of Arturk) v Secretary of State for the Home Department [2017] EWHC 297 (Admin); [2017] 4 W.L.R. 62; [2017] 2 C.M.L.R. 37; [2018] I.N.L.R. 18; [2017] A.C.D. 52, QBD (Admin) .... *Digested,* 17/**1230**

R. (on the application of Al Rabbat) v Westminster Magistrates' Court [2017] EWHC 1969 (Admin); [2018] 1 W.L.R. 2009; [2017] 4 All E.R. 1084, DC

R. (on the application of Al-Jedda) v Secretary of State for Defence [2007] UKHL 58; [2008] 1 A.C. 332; [2008] 2 W.L.R. 31; [2008] 3 All E.R. 28; [2008] H.R.L.R. 13; [2008] U.K.H.R.R. 244; 24 B.H.R.C. 569; Times, December 13, 2007; (2008) 152(1) S.J.L.B. 22, HL .... *Digested,* 08/**1964**:
Applied 10/2031: *Complaint upheld* 11/1692: *Considered* 15/1559, 17/1407

R. (on the application of Al-Saadoon) v Secretary of State for Defence; *sub nom* R. (on the application of Rahmatullah) v Secretary of State for Defence); *joined cases* Rahmatullah v Secretary of State for Defence; Al-Saadoon v Secretary of State for Defence [2016] EWCA Civ 811; [2017] Q.B. 1015; [2017] 2 W.L.R. 219; [2017] 2 All E.R. 453; [2016] H.R.L.R. 20, CA (Civ Div) .... *Digested,* 17/**83**

R. (on the application of Al-Saadoon) v Secretary of State for Defence; *sub nom* Al-Saadoon v Secretary of State for Defence; *joined case* R. (on the application of Rahmatullah) v Secretary of State for Defence [2015] EWHC 715 (Admin); [2015] 3 W.L.R. 503; [2015] A.C.D. 49, QBD (Admin) .... *Digested,* 15/**101**:
Reversed in part 17/83

R. (on the application of Alconbury Developments Ltd) v Secretary of State for the Environment, Transport and the Regions see R. (on the application of Holding & Barnes Plc) v Secretary of State for the Environment, Transport and the Regions

R. (on the application of Alemi) v Westminster City Council [2015] EWHC 1765 (Admin); [2015] P.T.S.R. 1339, QBD (Admin) .... *Digested,* 15/**1283**:
Distinguished 17/1154

R. (on the application of Ali) v Secretary of State for the Home Department; *joined case* R. (on the application of Mehmood) v Secretary of State for the Home Department [2015] EWCA Civ 744; [2016] 1 W.L.R. 461; [2016] 3 All E.R. 398; [2016] Imm. A.R. 25; [2015] I.N.L.R. 827, CA (Civ Div) .... *Digested,* 16/**1124**:
Followed 16/1147, 17/1243

R. (on the application of Ali) v Secretary of State for the Home Department see R. (on the application of Bibi) v Secretary of State for the Home Department

R. (on the application of Alvi) v Secretary of State for the Home Department [2012] UKSC 33; [2012] 1 W.L.R. 2208; [2012] 4 All E.R. 1041; [2012] Imm. A.R. 998; [2012] I.N.L.R. 504, SC .... *Digested,* 12/**1755**: *Applied* 13/1648, 14/1688, 14/1716, 15/1347, 16/1145, 17/1230: *Considered* 14/1653, 16/1129, 16/2683, 17/2668: *Followed* 17/1209

R. (on the application of AM (Pakistan)) v Secretary of State for the Home Department see R. (on the application of MM (Lebanon)) v Secretary of State for the Home Department

R. (on the application of AM) v DPP see R. (on the application of Nicklinson) v Ministry of Justice

R. (on the application of Antonio) v Secretary of State for the Home Department; *sub nom* Secretary of State for the Home Department v R. (on the application of Antonio) [2014] EWHC 3894 (Admin), QBD (Admin) *Reversed* 17/1185

R. (on the application of Antonio) v Secretary of State for the Home Department; *sub nom* Secretary of State for the Home Department v R. (on the application of Antonio) [2017] EWCA Civ 48; [2017] 1 W.L.R. 3431; [2018] I.N.L.R. 259; Times, March 22, 2017, CA (Civ Div) .... *Digested,* 17/**1185**

R. (on the application of AR (Pakistan)) v Secretary of State for the Home Department; *sub nom* AR (Pakistan) v Secretary of State for the Home Department [2016] EWCA Civ 807; [2017] 1 W.L.R. 255; [2017] I.N.L.R. 1, CA (Civ Div) .... *Digested,* 17/**41**: *Considered* 17/1202

R. (on the application of AR) v Secretary of State for the Home Department see AR (Bail: Conditions: Variation: Article 9 ECHR)

R. (on the application of Archer) v Revenue and Customs Commissioners [2017] EWHC 296 (Admin); [2017] 1 W.L.R. 2066; [2017] 3 All E.R. 524; [2017] S.T.C. 1037; [2017] B.T.C. 3; [2017] A.C.D. 70; [2017] S.T.I. 328, QBD (Admin) .... *Digested,* 17/**2100**

R. (on the application of Ardagh Glass Ltd) v Cheshire West and Chester Council see Ardagh Glass Ltd v Chester City Council

R. (on the application of Ariemuguvbe) v Islington LBC [2009] EWCA Civ 1308; [2010] H.L.R. 14, CA (Civ Div) .... *Digested,* 10/**1701**: *Followed* 17/1154

R. (on the application of Armstrong) v Redcar and Cleveland BC see R. (on the application of Stennett) v Manchester City Council

R. (on the application of Arturk) v Secretary of State for the Home Department see R. (on the application of Akturk) v Secretary of State for the Home Department

R. (on the application of ASK) v Secretary of State for the Home Department [2017] EWHC 196 (Admin); [2017] A.C.D. 42, QBD (Admin)

R. (on the application of Assisted Reproduction and Gynaecology Centre) v Human Fertilisation and Embryology Authority [2017] EWHC 659 (Admin); [2017] A.C.D. 63, QBD (Admin)

R. (on the application of Association of British Insurers) v Lord Chancellor [2017] EWHC 106 (Admin); [2017] A.C.D. 34, QBD (Admin)

R. (on the application of Aviva Life and Pensions (UK) Ltd) v Financial Ombudsman Service [2017] EWHC 352 (Admin); [2017] Lloyd's Rep. I.R. 404; [2017] A.C.D. 53, QBD (Admin) .... *Digested,* 17/**35**

R. (on the application of AW) v Secretary of State for the Home Department see R. (on the application of T) v Chief Constable of Greater Manchester

R. (on the application of Aweys) v Birmingham City Council see Ali v Birmingham City Council

R. (on the application of AZ) v Secretary of State for the Home Department; *sub nom* AZ (Syria) v Secretary of State for the Home Department [2017] EWCA Civ 35; [2017] 4 W.L.R. 94; Times, March 16, 2017, CA (Civ Div) .... *Digested,* 17/**1250**

R. (on the application of AZ) v Secretary of State for the Home Department; *sub nom* AZ (Syria) v Secretary of State for the Home Department [2015] EWHC 3695 (Admin); [2016] 4 W.L.R. 12, QBD (Admin) .... *Digested,* 16/**1157**: *Affirmed* 17/1250

R. (on the application of B) v Calderdale MBC; *sub nom* B v Calderdale MBC [2004] EWCA Civ 134; [2004] 1 W.L.R. 2017; [2004] H.L.R. 19; Times, February 26, 2004; (2004) 101(8) L.S.G. 30, CA (Civ Div) .... *Digested,* 04/**2653**

R. (on the application of B) v Director of Legal Aid Casework see R. (on the application of Gudanaviciene) v Director of Legal Aid Casework

R. (on the application of B) v Secretary of State for Justice [2017] EWHC 1694 (Admin); [2017] 4 W.L.R. 153; [2017] A.C.D. 101, QBD (Admin) .... *Digested,* 17/**1598**

R. (on the application of B) v Secretary of State for the Home Department see R. (on the application of T) v Chief Constable of Greater Manchester

R. (on the application of BA (Nigeria)) v Secretary of State for the Home Department see R. (on the application of PE (Cameroon)) v Secretary of State for the Home Department

R. (on the application of Bagdanavicius) v Secretary of State for the Home Department [2005] UKHL 38; [2005] 2 A.C. 668; [2005] 2 W.L.R. 1359; [2005] 4 All E.R. 263; [2005] H.R.L.R. 24; [2005] U.K.H.R.R. 907; [2005] Imm. A.R. 430; [2005] I.N.L.R. 422; Times, May 30, 2005; Independent, June 15, 2005, HL ...... *Digested,* 05/**2167**: *Considered* 08/4873: *Distinguished* 06/2246: *Followed* 17/905

R. (on the application of Baker) v Secretary of State for Communities and Local Government; *sub nom* Baker v Secretary of State for Communities and Local Government [2008] EWCA Civ 141; [2009] P.T.S.R. 809; [2008] B.L.G.R. 239; [2008] 2 P. & C.R. 6; [2008] J.P.L. 1469; [2008] A.C.D. 62; (2008) 105(10) L.S.G. 27; (2008) 152(10) S.J.L.B. 31; [2008] N.P.C. 26, CA (Civ Div) .... *Digested,* 08/**2934**: *Applied* 08/920, 10/1548, 12/2611, 12/3156, 13/2356, 15/2395, 17/1160: *Considered* 14/2106: *Distinguished* 11/2563: *Followed* 12/2209, 12/2586

R. (on the application of Bakijasi) v Secretary of State for the Home Department see R. (on the application of Kaziu) v Secretary of State for the Home Department

R. (on the application of Bancoult) v Secretary of State for Foreign and Commonwealth Affairs [2016] UKSC 35; [2017] A.C. 300; [2016] 3 W.L.R. 157; [2017] 1 All E.R. 403; [2016] H.R.L.R. 16, SC .... *Digested,* 16/**40**

R. (on the application of Banerjee) v General Medical Council [2015] EWHC 2263 (Admin), QBD (Admin)
Affirmed 17/1100

R. (on the application of Banerjee) v General Medical Council [2017] EWCA Civ 78; (2017) 156 B.M.L.R. 199, CA (Civ Div) .... *Digested,* 17/**1100**

R. (on the application of BAPIO Action Ltd) v Secretary of State for the Home Department [2007] EWCA Civ 1139; [2008] A.C.D. 7, CA (Civ Div)
Affirmed 08/1670: *Applied* 10/356, 17/1717: *Considered* 08/2068, 09/1598, 11/178, 16/673: *Distinguished* 08/70: *Followed* 11/3518, 16/615

R. (on the application of Barking and Dagenham LBC) v Secretary of State for Health [2017] EWHC 2449 (Admin); (2017) 20 C.C.L. Rep. 505, QBD (Admin) .... *Digested,* 17/**2056**

R. (on the application of Bateman) v South Cambridgeshire DC [2011] EWCA Civ 157; [2011] N.P.C. 22, CA (Civ Div)
Applied 15/2049: *Considered* 12/2548, 14/1188, 14/2425: *Distinguished* 16/1763: *Followed* 14/2420, 14/2427, 14/2434, 15/2044, 16/1701, 16/1745, 17/1778

R. (on the application of Beer (t/a Hammer Trout Farm)) v Hampshire Farmers Markets Ltd; *sub nom* Hampshire CC v Beer (t/a Hammer Trout Farm) [2003] EWCA Civ 1056; [2004] 1 W.L.R. 233; [2004] U.K.H.R.R. 727; [2003] L.L.R. 681; Times, August 25, 2003; Independent, July 30, 2003; [2003] 31 E.G. 67 (C.S.); (2003) 100(36) L.S.G. 40; (2003) 147 S.J.L.B. 1085; [2003] N.P.C. 93, CA (Civ Div) .... *Digested,* 03/**68**: *Applied* 04/2652, 17/1077: *Considered* 06/4044, 07/3912

R. (on the application of Behary) v Secretary of State for the Home Department; *joined case* R. (on the application of Ullah) v Secretary of State for the Home Department [2013] EWHC 3575 (Admin), QBD (Admin)
Affirmed 16/1126: *Considered* 17/1232

R. (on the application of Bermingham) v Director of the Serious Fraud Office; *joined case* Bermingham v United States [2006] EWHC 200 (Admin); [2007] Q.B. 727; [2007] 2 W.L.R. 635; [2006] 3 All E.R. 239; [2006] U.K.H.R.R. 450; [2006] Extradition L.R. 52; Times, February 24, 2006; [2006] A.C.D. 55, DC .... *Digested,* 06/**1605**: *Applied* 06/1608, 10/1265: *Considered* 07/1671, 11/1277, 17/38: *Distinguished* 09/1475

R. (on the application of Bewley Homes Plc) v Waverley BC [2017] EWHC 1776 (Admin); [2018] P.T.S.R. 423; [2017] 2 P. & C.R. 19, QBD (Admin) .... *Digested,* 17/**1727**

R. (on the application of Bhandal) v Revenue and Customs Commissioners; *sub nom* Bhandal, Re [2016] EWHC 3387 (Admin); [2017] 3 Costs L.R. 449, QBD (Admin) .... *Digested,* 17/**264**

R. (on the application of Bhatt Murphy (A Firm)) v Independent Assessor see R. (on the application of Niazi) v Secretary of State for the Home Department

R. (on the application of Bibi) v Secretary of State for the Home Department; *sub nom* R. (on the application of Ali) v Secretary of State for the Home Department [2015] UKSC 68; [2015] 1 W.L.R. 5055; [2016] 2 All E.R. 193; [2016] H.R.L.R. 4; 40 B.H.R.C. 606; [2016] Imm. A.R. 270; [2016] I.N.L.R. 314; Times, December 16, 2015, SC .... *Digested,* 16/**1125**: *Applied* 17/1207: *Followed* 17/562

R. (on the application of Bibi) v Secretary of State for the Home Department see R. (on the application of Aguilar Quila) v Secretary of State for the Home Department

R. (on the application of Biffa Waste Services Ltd) v Revenue and Customs Commissioners [2016] EWHC 1444 (Admin); [2017] Env. L.R. 10; [2016] B.T.C. 25, QBD (Admin) .... *Digested,* 17/**2165**

R. (on the application of Birchall Gardens LLP) v Hertfordshire CC [2016] EWHC 2794 (Admin); [2017] Env. L.R. 17, QBD (Admin) .... *Digested,* 17/**1785**

R. (on the application of Black) v Secretary of State for Justice see R. (on the application of Black) v Secretary of State for the Home Department

R. (on the application of Black) v Secretary of State for the Home Department; *sub nom* R. (on the application of Black) v Secretary of State for Justice [2009] UKHL 1; [2009] 1 A.C. 949; [2009] 2 W.L.R. 282; [2009] 4 All E.R. 1; [2009] H.R.L.R. 15; [2009] U.K.H.R.R. 382; 26 B.H.R.C. 664; [2009] Prison L.R. 395; Times, January 30, 2009; (2009) 153(4) S.J.L.B. 27, HL .... *Digested,* 09/**2768**: *Applied* 11/2286: *Considered* 13/2124, 14/2233: *Distinguished* 17/1595: *Followed* 10/2874

R. (on the application of Blewett) v Derbyshire CC; *sub nom* Derbyshire Waste Ltd v Blewett; Blewitt v Derbyshire Waste Ltd [2003] EWHC 2775 (Admin); [2004] Env. L.R. 29; [2004] J.P.L. 751, QBD (Admin) .... *Digested,* 04/**3088**: *Affirmed* 05/1402: *Applied* 17/1755: *Approved* 08/1263: *Followed* 05/3298

R. (on the application of Blue Green London Plan) v Secretary of State for the Environment, Food and Rural Affairs; *joined case* R. (on the application of Southwark LBC) v Secretary of State for Communities and Local Government [2015] EWHC 495 (Admin), QBD (Admin) *Applied* 15/1960: *Cited* 17/1726

R. (on the application of Boot) v Elmbridge BC [2017] EWHC 12 (Admin); [2017] 2 P. & C.R. 6, QBD (Admin) .... *Digested,* 17/**1758**

R. (on the application of Booth) v Parole Board see Reilly's Application for Judicial Review, Re

R. (on the application of Boots Management Services Ltd) v Central Arbitration Committee; *sub nom* Pharmacists' Defence Association Union v Boots Management Services Ltd [2014] EWHC 2930 (Admin); [2014] I.R.L.R. 887; (2014) 158(37) S.J.L.B. 37, QBD (Admin) .... *Digested,* 14/**1017**: *Affirmed* 17/766

R. (on the application of Boots Management Services Ltd) v Central Arbitration Committee; *sub nom* Pharmacists' Defence Association Union v Boots Management Services Ltd [2017] EWCA Civ 66; [2017] I.R.L.R. 355, CA (Civ Div) .... *Digested,* 17/**766**

R. (on the application of Bourgass) v Secretary of State for Justice see R. (on the application of King) v Secretary of State for Justice

R. (on the application of Bracking) v Secretary of State for Work and Pensions; *joined case* Bracking v Secretary of State for Work and Pensions [2013] EWCA Civ 1345; [2014] Eq. L.R. 60; (2013) 16 C.C.L. Rep. 479, CA (Civ Div) .... *Digested,* 14/**2804**: *Applied* 16/1399, 16/673: *Followed* 15/1214, 17/1160

R. (on the application of Brady) v Lord Chancellor [2017] EWHC 410 (Admin); [2017] M.H.L.R. 274, QBD (Admin)

R. (on the application of Britcits) v Secretary of State for the Home Department [2017] EWCA Civ 368; [2017] 1 W.L.R. 3345; Times, July 27, 2017, CA (Civ Div) .... *Digested,* 17/**1223**

R. (on the application of Britcits) v Secretary of State for the Home Department [2016] EWHC 956 (Admin), QBD (Admin) *Affirmed* 17/1223

R. (on the application of British American Tobacco UK Ltd) v Secretary of State for Health; *joined cases* R. (on the application of Imperial Tobacco Ltd) v Secretary of State for Health; R. (on the application of Philip Morris Brands Sarl) v Secretary of State for Health; R. (on the application of JT International SA) v Secretary of State for Health; R. (on the application of Tann UK Ltd) v Secretary of State for Health [2016] EWCA Civ 1182; [2018] Q.B. 149; [2017] 3 W.L.R. 225; [2017] 2 All E.R. 691; [2017] E.T.M.R. 9; [2017] R.P.C. 16; [2017] L.L.R. 1, CA (Civ Div) .... *Digested,* 17/**386**

R. (on the application of British American Tobacco UK Ltd) v Secretary of State for Health; *joined cases* R. (on the application of Imperial Tobacco Ltd) v Secretary of State for Health; R. (on the application of Philip Morris Brands Sarl) v Secretary of State for Health; R. (on the application of JT International SA) v Secretary of State for Health; R. (on the application of Tann UK Ltd) v Secretary of State for Health [2016] EWHC 1169 (Admin); [2016] E.T.M.R. 38; [2016] R.P.C. 22, QBD (Admin) .... *Digested,* 16/**326**: *Affirmed* 17/386

R. (on the application of Brown) v Secretary of State for Work and Pensions [2008] EWHC 3158 (Admin); [2009] P.T.S.R. 1506, DC
Applied 10/1537, 10/2199, 13/2356, 13/2947, 17/1160: *Considered* 10/992, 12/914, 14/1509: *Followed* 11/64

R. (on the application of Bruton) v Secretary of State for Justice [2017] EWHC 1967 (Admin); [2017] 4 W.L.R. 152; [2017] A.C.D. 110, QBD (Admin) .... *Digested,* 17/**1590**

R. (on the application of Buer) v Secretary of State for the Home Department; *joined cases* Eroglu v Secretary of State for the Home Department; R. (on the application of KP (Turkey) v Secretary of State for the Home Department [2014] EWCA Civ 1109; [2015] 1 C.M.L.R. 3; [2015] Imm. A.R. 82, CA (Civ Div) .... *Digested,* 15/**959**: *Considered* 17/2668

R. (on the application of Building Societies Ombudsman Co Ltd) v Customs and Excise Commissioners; *sub nom* R. v Customs and Excise Commissioners Ex p. Building Societies Ombudsman Co Ltd [2000] S.T.C. 892; [2000] B.T.C. 5384; [2001] B.V.C. 3; Times, November 8, 2000; [2000] S.T.I. 1516, CA (Civ Div) .... *Digested,* 00/**5318**: *Applied* 02/4776, 15/2614, 16/2190: *Considered* 14/3076, 17/2125

R. (on the application of Bunnvale Ltd) v Central Criminal Court see R. (on the application of Merida Oil Traders Ltd) v Central Criminal Court

R. (on the application of Bushell) v Newcastle upon Tyne Licensing Justices [2006] UKHL 7; [2006] 1 W.L.R. 496; [2006] 2 All E.R. 161; (2006) 170 J.P. 132; [2006] L.L.R. 303; Times, February 20, 2006; Independent, February 21, 2006; (2006) 170 J.P.N. 216; (2006) 103(10) L.S.G. 27; (2006) 156 N.L.J. 329; (2006) 150 S.J.L.B. 225; [2006] N.P.C. 17, HL .... *Digested,* 06/**2781**: *Considered* 17/29

R. (on the application of Butt) v Secretary of State for the Home Department; *sub nom* Butt v Secretary of State for the Home Department [2017] EWHC 1930 (Admin); [2017] 4 W.L.R. 154; [2017] H.R.L.R. 12; [2017] E.L.R. 537; [2017] A.C.D. 109, QBD (Admin) .... *Digested,* 17/**558**

R. (on the application of Byczek) v Secretary of State for the Home Department [2014] EWHC 4298 (Admin); [2015] 2 C.M.L.R. 7, QBD (Admin) .... *Digested,* 15/**1321**: *Applied* 17/1189

R. (on the application of Byndloss) v Secretary of State for the Home Department; *sub nom* R. (on the application of Kiarie) v Secretary of State for the Home Department [2017] UKSC 42; [2017] 1 W.L.R. 2380; [2017] 4 All E.R. 811; [2017] H.R.L.R. 7; [2017] Imm. A.R. 1299; [2017] I.N.L.R. 909, SC .... *Digested,* 17/**1184**

R. (on the application of Byndloss) v Secretary of State for the Home Department; *sub nom* R. (on the application of Kiarie) v Secretary of State for the Home Department [2015] EWCA Civ 1020; [2016] 1 W.L.R. 1961; [2016] 3 All E.R. 741; [2016] Imm. A.R. 209; [2016] I.N.L.R. 212; Times, July 10, 2017, CA (Civ Div) .... *Digested,* 16/**1076**: *Applied* 17/1231: *Followed* 16/1086: *Reversed* 17/1184

R. (on the application of C) v Chief Constable of A [2006] EWHC 2352 (Admin); [2008] Po. L.R. 23, QBD (Admin)
Considered 17/38

R. (on the application of C) v Financial Services Authority; *sub nom* R. (on the application of Willford) v Financial Services Authority [2013] EWCA Civ 677, CA (Civ Div)
Applied 17/1633: *Considered* 15/372

R. (on the application of C) v Islington LBC [2017] EWHC 1288 (Admin); [2017] H.L.R. 32, QBD (Admin) .... *Digested,* 17/**1153**

R. (on the application of C) v Secretary of State for Justice see C v Secretary of State for Justice

R. (on the application of Cable & Wireless Services UK Ltd) v Central Arbitration Committee [2008] EWHC 115 (Admin); [2008] I.C.R. 693; [2008] I.R.L.R. 425, QBD (Admin) .... *Digested,* 08/**1192**: *Considered* 17/765

R. (on the application of Campaign Against Arms Trade) v Secretary of State for International Trade [2017] EWHC 1754 (Admin); [2017] H.R.L.R. 8; [2017] A.C.D. 103, DC .... *Digested,* 17/**1408**

R. (on the application of Campaign to Protect Rural England) v Dover DC; *sub nom* R. (on the application of CPRE Kent) v Dover DC [2016] EWCA Civ 936; [2017] J.P.L. 180, CA (Civ Div) .... *Digested,* 17/**1765**

R. (on the application of Campaign to Protect Rural England) v Dover DC; *sub nom* R. (on the application of CPRE Kent) v Dover DC [2015] EWHC 3808 (Admin), QBD (Admin)
Reversed 17/1765

R. (on the application of Campbell) v Bromley Magistrates' Court see R. (on the application of Campbell) v Independent Police Complaints Commission

R. (on the application of Campbell) v Commissioner of Police of the Metropolis see R. (on the application of Campbell) v Independent Police Complaints Commission

R. (on the application of Campbell) v Independent Police Complaints Commission; *sub nom* Campbell v Commissioner of Police of the Metropolis; Campbell v Bromley Magistrates' Court; *joined cases* R. (on the application of Campbell) v Bromley Magistrates' Court; R. (on the application of Campbell) v Commissioner of Police of the Metropolis [2017] EWCA Civ 1161; [2017] Lloyd's Rep. F.C. 598; [2017] Crim. L.R. 987, CA (Civ Div)

R. (on the application of Cardin) v Birmingham Crown Court [2017] EWHC 2101 (Admin); [2018] 1 Cr. App. R. 3; (2017) 181 J.P. 421; [2017] Crim. L.R. 969, DC .... *Digested,* 17/**616**

R. (on the application of Carman) v Secretary of State for the Home Department [2004] EWHC 2400 (Admin); [2005] 2 Prison L.R. 172; Times, October 11, 2004, QBD (Admin) .... *Digested,* 04/**2785**: *Applied* 17/1589

R. (on the application of Carmichael) v Secretary of State for Work and Pensions; *sub nom* R. (on the application of MA) v Secretary of State for Work and Pensions; *joined cases* R. (on the application of Rutherford) v Secretary of State for Work and Pensions; R. (on the application of A) v Secretary of State for Work and Pensions; R. (on the application of Daly) v Secretary of State for Work and Pensions [2016] UKSC 58; [2016] 1 W.L.R. 4550; [2017] 1 All E.R. 869; [2016] P.T.S.R. 1422; [2016] H.R.L.R. 24; [2016] H.L.R. 46; (2017) 20 C.C.L. Rep. 103; Times, November 22, 2016, SC .... *Digested,* 17/**2030**: *Considered* 17/2824: *Followed* 17/2026

R. (on the application of Carson) v Secretary of State for Work and Pensions; *sub nom* Carson v Secretary of State for Work and Pensions; *joined case* R. (on the application of Reynolds) v Secretary of State for Work and Pensions [2005] UKHL 37; [2006] 1 A.C. 173; [2005] 2 W.L.R. 1369; [2005] 4 All E.R. 545; [2005] H.R.L.R. 23; [2005] U.K.H.R.R. 1185; 18 B.H.R.C. 677; Times, May 27, 2005, HL .... *Digested,* 05/**3835**: *Applied* 06/2277, 07/2327, 07/3256, 08/2024, 17/1466: *Complaint dismissed* 09/2827: *Considered* 06/3381, 08/3527, 10/4537, 11/3159, 13/240, 17/1182: *Followed* 13/2885, 15/1954, 15/3159, 16/1397

R. (on the application of Cart) v Upper Tribunal; *joined case* R. (on the application of MR (Pakistan)) v Upper Tribunal [2011] UKSC 28; [2012] 1 A.C. 663; [2011] 3 W.L.R. 107; [2011] 4 All E.R. 127; [2011] P.T.S.R. 1053; [2011] S.T.C. 1659; [2012] 1 F.L.R. 997; [2011] Imm. A.R. 704; [2011] M.H.L.R. 196; Times, June 23, 2011; [2012] Fam. Law 398; [2011] S.T.I. 1943; (2011) 161 N.L.J. 916; (2011) 155(25) S.J.L.B. 35, SC .... *Digested,* 11/**48**: *Applied* 12/1770, 12/457: *Considered* 11/3958, 13/350, 14/2939, 15/1378, 16/30: *Explained* 14/50: *Followed* 13/455, 15/337, 17/1243: *Referred to* 14/41

R. (on the application of Cart) v Upper Tribunal; *joined case* R. (on the application of MR (Pakistan)) v Upper Tribunal [2010] EWCA Civ 859; [2011] Q.B. 120; [2011] 2 W.L.R. 36; [2010] 4 All E.R. 714; [2011] P.T.S.R. 42; [2010] S.T.C. 2556; [2010] M.H.L.R. 353; [2011] A.C.D. 1; [2010] S.T.I. 2272; (2010) 160 N.L.J. 1115; [2010] N.P.C. 86, CA (Civ Div) *Affirmed* 11/48: *Applied* 11/59: *Considered* 16/2111, 17/26

R. (on the application of Catt) v Association of Chief Police Officers of England, Wales and Northern Ireland; *sub nom* R. (on the application of Catt) v Commissioner of Police of the Metropolis; *joined case* R. (on the application of T) v Commissioner of Police of the Metropolis [2015] UKSC 9; [2015] A.C. 1065; [2015] 2 W.L.R. 664; [2015] 2 All E.R. 727; [2015] H.R.L.R. 4; 41 B.H.R.C. 108, SC .... *Digested,* 15/**1298**: *Considered* 15/1013, 16/1782, 17/558: *Followed* 15/1301

R. (on the application of Catt) v Commissioner of Police of the Metropolis see R. (on the application of Catt) v Association of Chief Police Officers of England, Wales and Northern Ireland

R. (on the application of Champion) v North Norfolk DC; *sub nom* Champion v North Norfolk DC [2015] UKSC 52; [2015] 1 W.L.R. 3710; [2015] 4 All E.R. 169; [2016] Env. L.R. 5; [2015] B.L.G.R. 593; [2016] 1 P. & C.R. 19, SC .... *Digested,* 15/**2027**: *Applied* 16/1681: *Followed* 16/1747, 17/1775

R. (on the application of Chandler) v Secretary of State for Children, Schools and Families; *sub nom* Chandler v Camden LBC [2009] EWCA Civ 1011; [2010] P.T.S.R. 749; [2010] 1 C.M.L.R. 19; [2010] Eu. L.R. 232; [2010] B.L.G.R. 1; [2010] E.L.R. 192; [2010] A.C.D. 7, CA (Civ Div) .... *Digested,* 10/**2671**: *Applied* 17/1814

R. (on the application of Charles) v Criminal Cases Review Commission [2017] EWHC 1219 (Admin); [2017] 2 Cr. App. R. 14; [2017] Crim. L.R. 972, DC

R. (on the application of Chaudhry) v DPP; *sub nom* R. (on the application of Chaudry) v DPP [2016] EWHC 2447 (Admin); [2017] Crim. L.R. 231; [2016] A.C.D. 120, DC

R. (on the application of Chaudry) v DPP see R. (on the application of Chaudhry) v DPP

R. (on the application of Chief Constable of Cleveland) v Police Appeals Tribunal [2017] EWHC 1286 (Admin); [2017] I.C.R. 1212, QBD (Admin)

R. (on the application of Chief Constable of Dorset) v Police Appeals Tribunal [2012] EWCA Civ 1047, CA (Civ Div) *Followed* 17/1790

R. (on the application of Chief Constable of Sussex) v Police Appeals Tribunal [2017] EWHC 2333 (Admin); [2017] A.C.D. 120, QBD (Admin)

R. (on the application of Chief Constable of West Yorkshire) v Independent Police Complaints Commission [2014] EWCA Civ 1367; [2015] P.T.S.R. 72; [2015] I.C.R. 184, CA (Civ Div) .... *Digested,* 15/**2055**: *Applied* 17/1795

R. (on the application of Chief Executive of the Independent Police Complaints Commission) v Independent Police Complaints Commission [2016] EWHC 2993 (Admin); [2016] Inquest L.R. 302; [2017] A.C.D. 7, DC .... *Digested,* 17/**1795**

R. (on the application of Child Poverty Action Group) v Secretary of State for Work and Pensions [2010] UKSC 54; [2011] 2 A.C. 15; [2011] 2 W.L.R. 1; [2011] 1 All E.R. 729; [2011] P.T.S.R. 185; Times, December 13, 2010; (2010) 108(2) L.S.G. 19; (2010) 154(47) S.J.L.B. 30, SC .... *Digested,* 11/**3157**: *Applied* 13/397, 14/1542: *Considered* 16/1835, 17/2772

R. (on the application of Citizens UK) v Secretary of State for the Home Department; *sub nom* Citizens UK v Secretary of State for the Home Department [2017] EWHC 2301 (Admin); [2018] 2 All E.R. 573; [2018] Imm. A.R. 209; [2017] A.C.D. 127, QBD (Admin)

R. (on the application of City College Birmingham) v Office for Standards in Education, Children Services and Skills [2009] EWHC 2373 (Admin); [2009] E.L.R. 500, QBD (Admin) .... *Digested,* 10/**959**: *Considered* 17/697

R. (on the application of Clarke) v Revenue and Customs Commissioners [2017] UKUT 379 (TCC); [2017] S.T.C. 2438; [2017] B.V.C. 530, UT (Tax)

R. (on the application of Clift) v Secretary of State for the Home Department; *sub nom* Hindawi v Secretary of State for the Home Department; Secretary of State for the Home Department v Hindawi; Secretary of State for the Home Department v Headley; *joined cases* R. (on the application of Headley) v Secretary of State for the Home Department; R. (on the application of Hindawi) v Secretary of State for the Home Department [2006] UKHL 54; [2007] 1 A.C. 484; [2007] 2 W.L.R. 24; [2007] 2 All E.R. 1; [2007] H.R.L.R. 12; [2007] U.K.H.R.R. 348; 21 B.H.R.C. 704; [2007] Prison L.R. 125; Times, December 21, 2006; [2007] A.C.D. 27, HL .... *Digested,* 07/**2975**: *Applied* 07/3867, 08/3527, 09/1737, 12/2970, 17/1645: *Considered* 07/2300, 07/2981, 08/2690, 09/2761, 09/2768: *Followed* 14/2234, 14/2682, 15/2232, 17/1588: *Not applied* 17/976

R. (on the application of CN) v Lewisham LBC see R. (on the application of N) v Lewisham LBC

R. (on the application of Cobham) v Harrow LBC see R. (on the application of Stennett) v Manchester City Council

R. (on the application of Coll) v Secretary of State for Justice; *sub nom* Coll v Secretary of State for Justice; *joined case* Griffiths v Secretary of State for Justice [2017] UKSC 40; [2017] 1 W.L.R. 2093; [2018] 1 All E.R. 31; 43 B.H.R.C. 65, SC .... *Digested,* 17/**1587**

R. (on the application of Coll) v Secretary of State for Justice; *sub nom* Coll v Secretary of State for Justice; *joined case* Griffiths v Secretary of State for Justice [2015] EWCA Civ 328; [2015] 1 W.L.R. 3781; Times, April 27, 2015, CA (Civ Div) .... *Digested,* 15/**1808**: *Reversed* 17/1587

R. (on the application of Colonel M) v Ashworth Hospital Authority (now Mersey Care NHS Trust) see R. (on the application of Munjaz) v Mersey Care NHS Trust

R. (on the application of Community Against Dean Super Quarry Ltd) v Cornwall Council [2017] EWHC 74 (Admin); [2017] Env. L.R. 26, QBD (Admin) .... *Digested,* 17/**1784**

R. (on the application of Connell) v Secretary of State for the Home Department [2017] EWHC 100 (Admin); [2017] 4 W.L.R. 38, QBD (Admin) .... *Digested,* 17/**1189**

R. (on the application of Conville) v Richmond upon Thames LBC; *sub nom* Conville v Richmond upon Thames LBC [2005] EWHC 1430 (Admin); [2006] H.L.R. 1, QBD (Admin)
Applied 17/1151: *Reversed* 06/2021

R. (on the application of Conway) v Secretary of State for Justice [2017] EWHC 640 (Admin); (2017) 156 B.M.L.R. 169; [2017] A.C.D. 62, QBD (Admin) .... *Digested,* 17/**564**

R. (on the application of Conway) v Secretary of State for Justice [2017] EWCA Civ 275; (2017) 156 B.M.L.R. 169, CA (Civ Div)

R. (on the application of Conway) v Secretary of State for Justice [2017] EWHC 2447 (Admin); [2018] 2 W.L.R. 322; [2018] 2 All E.R. 250; [2017] H.R.L.R. 14; [2017] Med. L.R. 507; (2018) 159 B.M.L.R. 14; [2017] A.C.D. 130, QBD (Admin)

R. (on the application of Cooper) v Ashford BC [2016] EWHC 1525 (Admin); [2016] P.T.S.R. 1455, QBD (Admin) .... *Digested,* 17/**1772**:
Doubted 17/1766

R. (on the application of Corner House Research) v BAE Systems Plc see R. (on the application of Corner House Research) v Director of the Serious Fraud Office

R. (on the application of Corner House Research) v Director of the Serious Fraud Office; *sub nom* R. (on the application of Corner House Research) v BAE Systems Plc [2008] EWHC 246 (Admin); [2008] C.P. Rep. 20; [2008] A.C.D. 63, QBD (Admin) .... *Digested,* 08/**388**:
Applied 17/1772

R. (on the application of Corner House Research) v Director of the Serious Fraud Office [2008] UKHL 60; [2009] 1 A.C. 756; [2008] 3 W.L.R. 568; [2008] 4 All E.R. 927; [2008] Lloyd's Rep. F.C. 537; Times, July 31, 2008; [2009] Crim. L.R. 46; (2008) 158 N.L.J. 1149; (2008) 152(32) S.J.L.B. 29, HL .... *Digested,* 08/**1661**:
Considered 10/370, 17/38: *Followed* 11/802, 12/783

R. (on the application of Countryside Alliance) v Attorney General; *joined cases* R. (on the application of Derwin) v Attorney General; R. (on the application of Friend) v Attorney General [2007] UKHL 52; [2008] 1 A.C. 719; [2007] 3 W.L.R. 922; [2008] 2 All E.R. 95; [2008] Eu. L.R. 359; [2008] H.R.L.R. 10; [2008] U.K.H.R.R. 1; Times, November 29, 2007; (2007) 104(48) L.S.G. 23; (2007) 157 N.L.J. 1730; (2007) 151 S.J.L.B. 1564; [2007] N.P.C. 127, HL .... *Digested,* 07/**204**:
Applied 15/899, 17/1118: *Considered* 09/2717, 11/117, 12/4151:
Followed 16/1773

R. (on the application of CPRE Kent) v Dover DC see R. (on the application of Campaign to Protect Rural England) v Dover DC

R. (on the application of Crompton) v South Yorkshire Police and Crime Commissioner [2017] EWHC 1349 (Admin); [2018] 1 W.L.R. 131; Times, June 27, 2017, DC .... *Digested,* 17/**1787**

R. (on the application of Cronin) v Sheffield Justices; *sub nom* R. (on the application of Cronin) v Sheffield Magistrates' Court [2002] EWHC 2568 (Admin); [2003] 1 W.L.R. 752; (2002) 166 J.P. 777; Times, November 28, 2002; (2003) 167 J.P.N. 133; (2003) 100(4) L.S.G. 31, DC .... *Digested,* 03/**3457**:
Applied 17/624: *Considered* 12/824

R. (on the application of Cronin) v Sheffield Magistrates' Court see R. (on the application of Cronin) v Sheffield Justices

R. (on the application of Crownhall Estates Ltd) v Chichester DC [2016] EWHC 73 (Admin), QBD (Admin)
Applied 17/1727, 17/1730

R. (on the application of Cuns) v Hammersmith Magistrates' Court [2016] EWHC 748 (Admin); (2017) 181 J.P. 111; [2016] Crim. L.R. 580, QBD (Admin) .... *Digested,* 17/**541**

R. (on the application of CXF) v Central Bedfordshire Council [2017] EWHC 2311 (Admin); (2017) 20 C.C.L. Rep. 466; (2018) 160 B.M.L.R. 187; [2017] M.H.L.R. 366; [2017] A.C.D. 123, QBD (Admin)

R. (on the application of D) v DPP [2017] EWHC 1768 (Admin); [2017] Crim. L.R. 907; [2017] A.C.D. 106, DC

R. (on the application of D) v Southwark LBC; *sub nom* R. (on the application of ED) v Southwark LBC; D v Southwark LBC [2007] EWCA Civ 182; [2007] 1 F.L.R. 2181; [2007] 1 F.C.R. 788; (2007) 10 C.C.L. Rep. 280; [2007] Fam. Law 701, CA (Civ Div) .... *Digested,* 07/**1777**:
Applied 09/3695, 09/3696, 09/3698: *Considered* 07/3940, 17/2057:
Distinguished 08/3590: *Explained* 10/3159: *Followed* 10/1306, 12/3172, 16/2016:
Not followed 15/2388

R. (on the application of DA) v Secretary of State for Work and Pensions [2017] EWHC 1446 (Admin); [2017] P.T.S.R. 1266; [2017] H.L.R. 35, QBD (Admin) .... *Digested,* 17/**2026**

R. (on the application of Daly) v Secretary of State for Work and Pensions see R. (on the application of Carmichael) v Secretary of State for Work and Pensions

R. (on the application of Dari) v Secretary of State for the Home Department (C-16/05) see Tum v Secretary of State for the Home Department (C-16/05)

R. (on the application of Das) v Secretary of State for the Home Department [2013] EWHC 682 (Admin), QBD (Admin)
Applied 17/1772: *Reversed* 14/1681

R. (on the application of Davey) v Oxfordshire CC [2017] EWHC 354 (Admin); [2017] P.T.S.R. 904, QBD (Admin)
Affirmed 17/2047

R. (on the application of Davey) v Oxfordshire CC [2017] EWCA Civ 1308; [2018] P.T.S.R. 281; (2017) 20 C.C.L. Rep. 303; Times, December 5, 2017, CA (Civ Div) .... *Digested,* 17/**2047**

R. (on the application of Davies) v Birmingham Deputy Coroner (Costs) see R. (on the application of Davies) v HM Deputy Coroner for Birmingham (Costs)

R. (on the application of Davies) v Financial Services Authority; *sub nom* R. (on the application of Davis) v Financial Services Authority [2003] EWCA Civ 1128; [2004] 1 W.L.R. 185; [2003] 4 All E.R. 1196; [2004] 1 All E.R. (Comm) 88; [2005] 1 B.C.L.C. 286; Times, October 6, 2003; [2003] A.C.D. 83; (2003) 100(38) L.S.G. 34, CA (Civ Div) .... *Digested,* 03/**1630**:
Applied 17/1633

R. (on the application of Davies) v HM Deputy Coroner for Birmingham (Costs); *sub nom* R. (on the application of Davies) v Birmingham Deputy Coroner (Costs) [2004] EWCA Civ 207; [2004] 1 W.L.R. 2739; [2004] 3 All E.R. 543; [2004] 4 Costs L.R. 545; (2004) 80 B.M.L.R. 48; [2004] Inquest L.R. 96; Times, March 10, 2004; Independent, March 18, 2004; (2004) 148 S.J.L.B. 297, CA (Civ Div) *Digested,* 04/**300**:
Applied 05/387, 17/255: *Considered* 11/2745: *Followed* 12/400, 17/232

R. (on the application of Davies) v Revenue and Customs Commissioners; *joined case* R. (on the application of Gaines-Cooper) v Revenue and Customs Commissioners [2010] EWCA Civ 83; [2010] S.T.C. 860; [2010] B.T.C. 198; [2010] W.T.L.R. 681; Times, February 23, 2010; [2010] S.T.I. 485; (2010) 107(9) L.S.G. 17, CA (Civ Div) .... *Digested,* 10/**3371**:
Affirmed 11/3419: *Considered* 11/3375: *Distinguished* 17/2087

R. (on the application of Davis) v Financial Services Authority see R. (on the application of Davies) v Financial Services Authority

R. (on the application of Davis) v Secretary of State for the Home Department; *sub nom* Secretary of State for the Home Department v Davis [2015] EWCA Civ 1185; [2017] 1 All E.R. 62; [2016] 1 C.M.L.R. 48; [2016] H.R.L.R. 1; [2015] Info. T.L.R. 293, CA (Civ Div) .... *Digested,* 16/**1161**:
Preliminary ruling given 17/894

R. (on the application of de Silva) v Revenue and Customs Commissioners [2016] EWCA Civ 40; [2016] S.T.C. 1333; [2016] B.T.C. 6; [2016] S.T.I. 303, CA (Civ Div) .... *Digested,* 16/**2092**:
Applied 17/2129

R. (on the application of Dean) v Secretary of State for Business, Energy and Industrial Strategy; *sub nom* Dean v Secretary of State for Business, Energy and Industrial Strategy [2017] EWHC 1998 (Admin); [2017] 4 W.L.R. 158; [2017] A.C.D. 117, QBD (Admin) .... *Digested,* 17/**870**

R. (on the application of Derrin Brother Properties Ltd) v Judge of the First-tier Tribunal (Tax Chamber) see R. (on the application of Derrin Brothers Properties Ltd) v Revenue and Customs Commissioners

R. (on the application of Derrin Brothers Properties Ltd) v Revenue and Customs Commissioners; *sub nom* R. (on the application of Derrin Brother Properties Ltd) v Judge of the First-tier Tribunal (Tax Chamber) [2016] EWCA Civ 15; [2016] 1 W.L.R. 2423; [2016] 4 All E.R. 203; [2016] S.T.C. 1081; [2016] B.T.C. 10; 18 I.T.L. Rep. 472; [2016] S.T.I. 209, CA (Civ Div) .... *Digested,* 16/**2118**:
Applied 16/1190, 17/2152

R. (on the application of Derry) v Revenue and Customs Commissioners [2017] EWCA Civ 435; [2017] S.T.C. 1723; [2017] B.T.C. 16; [2017] S.T.I. 1718, CA (Civ Div) .... *Digested,* 17/**2141**

R. (on the application of Derry) v Revenue and Customs Commissioners [2015] UKUT 416 (TCC); [2016] S.T.C. 334; [2015] B.T.C. 525; [2015] S.T.I. 2557, UT (Tax)
Reversed in part 17/2141

R. (on the application of Derwin) v Attorney General see R. (on the application of Countryside Alliance) v Attorney General

R. (on the application of Detention Action) v First-tier Tribunal (Immigration and Asylum Chamber); *sub nom* Detention Action v First-tier Tribunal (Immigration and Asylum Chamber); Lord Chancellor v Detention Action [2015] EWCA Civ 840; [2015] 1 W.L.R. 5341; [2016] 3 All E.R. 626; [2015] Imm. A.R. 1349; [2016] I.N.L.R. 79; Times, September 9, 2015, CA (Civ Div) .... *Digested,* 15/**1305**: *Applied* 16/1076, 16/1117, 16/973: *Considered* 17/1539: *Followed* 17/1172

R. (on the application of DHL International (UK) Ltd) v Office of Communications [2016] EWHC 938 (Admin); [2016] 1 W.L.R. 4274, QBD (Admin) .... *Digested,* 17/**1805**

R. (on the application of Dickinson) v Revenue and Customs Commissioners [2017] EWHC 1705 (Admin); [2017] 4 W.L.R. 126; [2017] S.T.C. 2129; [2017] B.T.C. 23; [2017] S.T.I. 1648, QBD (Admin) .... *Digested,* 17/**2126**

R. (on the application of Dickinson) v Revenue and Customs Commissioners [2017] EWHC 1004 (Admin); [2017] B.T.C. 18, QBD (Admin) .... *Digested,* 17/**198**

R. (on the application of DLA Delivery Ltd) v Lewes DC [2015] EWHC 2311 (Admin), QBD (Admin) *Affirmed* 17/1729

R. (on the application of DLA Delivery Ltd) v Lewes DC [2017] EWCA Civ 58; [2017] P.T.S.R. 949; [2017] Env. L.R. 18; [2017] 2 P. & C.R. 7; [2017] J.P.L. 721, CA (Civ Div) .... *Digested,* 17/**1729**: *Followed* 17/1727

R. (on the application of Donnachie) v Cardiff Magistrates' Court [2009] EWHC 489 (Admin); [2009] C.T.L.C. 51; [2009] L.L.R. 523, DC *Applied* 17/619

R. (on the application of DPP) v Stratford Magistrates' Court [2017] EWHC 1794 (Admin); [2018] 4 W.L.R. 47; [2017] 2 Cr. App. R. 32; (2017) 181 J.P. 474; [2018] Crim. L.R. 157; [2017] A.C.D. 104, DC .... *Digested,* 17/**542**

R. (on the application of Draga) v Secretary of State for the Home Department [2012] EWCA Civ 842, CA (Civ Div) *Applied* 17/1172: *Followed* 15/1378, 16/1147

R. (on the application of Drax Power Ltd) v HM Treasury; *sub nom* R. (on the application of Drax Power Ltd) v Revenue and Customs Commissioners; Infinis Energy Holdings Ltd v HM Treasury [2016] EWCA Civ 1030; [2017] Q.B. 1221; [2017] 2 W.L.R. 194; [2017] S.T.C. 414; [2017] 2 C.M.L.R. 12; Times, December 8, 2016; [2016] S.T.I. 2777, CA (Civ Div) .... *Digested,* 17/**871**

R. (on the application of Drax Power Ltd) v HM Treasury; *sub nom* R. (on the application of Drax Power Ltd) v Revenue and Customs Commissioners; Infinis Energy Holdings Ltd v HM Treasury [2016] EWHC 228 (Admin); [2016] 2 C.M.L.R. 33; [2016] B.V.C. 8; [2016] A.C.D. 51; [2016] S.T.I. 394, QBD (Admin) .... *Digested,* 16/**765**: *Affirmed* 17/871

R. (on the application of Drax Power Ltd) v Revenue and Customs Commissioners see R. (on the application of Drax Power Ltd) v HM Treasury

R. (on the application of DS (A Child)) v Wolverhampton City Council [2017] EWHC 1660 (Admin); [2017] E.L.R. 630; [2017] A.C.D. 99, QBD (Admin)

R. (on the application of Duggan) v Assistant Deputy Coroner for the Northern District of Greater London [2017] EWCA Civ 142; [2017] 1 W.L.R. 2199; [2017] 4 All E.R. 104; [2017] Inquest L.R. 142; Times, April 21, 2017, CA (Civ Div) .... *Digested,* 17/**21**

R. (on the application of Duggan) v Assistant Deputy Coroner for the Northern District of Greater London [2014] EWHC 3343 (Admin); [2016] 1 W.L.R. 525; [2015] 3 All E.R. 237; (2015) 179 J.P. 1; (2015) 179 J.P. 361; [2014] Inquest L.R. 232; [2015] A.C.D. 3, DC .... *Digested,* 15/**20**: *Affirmed* 17/21

R. (on the application of Dunn) v Governor of Frankland Prison [2015] EWHC 858 (Admin), QBD (Admin) *Applied* 17/1591

R. (on the application of Durand Academy Trusts) v Office for Standards in Education, Children's Services and Skills (Ofsted) [2017] EWHC 2097 (Admin); [2017] E.L.R. 444; [2017] A.C.D. 116, QBD (Admin) .... *Digested,* 17/**695**

R. (on the application of Durham Co Ltd (t/a Max Recycle)) v Revenue and Customs Commissioners [2016] UKUT 417 (TCC); [2017] S.T.C. 264; [2016] B.V.C. 539; [2016] S.T.I. 2632, UT (Tax) .... *Digested,* 17/**2268**

R. (on the application of Dyer) v Watford Magistrates' Court [2013] EWHC 547 (Admin); (2013) 177 J.P. 265; [2013] A.C.D. 47, DC .... *Digested,* 13/**697**: *Applied* 16/492, 17/615

R. (on the application of E (Russia)) v Secretary of State for the Home Department; *sub nom* E1 (OS Russia) v Secretary of State for the Home Department [2012] EWCA Civ 357; [2012] 1 W.L.R. 3198; [2013] I.N.L.R. 191, CA (Civ Div) .... *Digested,* 13/**1623**: *Considered* 13/1598: *Followed* 17/1229

R. (on the application of E) v DPP [2011] EWHC 1465 (Admin); [2012] 1 Cr. App. R. 6; [2012] Crim. L.R. 39; (2011) 155(24) S.J.L.B. 43, DC .... *Digested,* 12/**783**: *Applied* 17/571: *Considered* 13/753

R. (on the application of E) v Islington LBC [2017] EWHC 1440 (Admin); [2018] P.T.S.R. 349; [2017] E.L.R. 458; (2017) 20 C.C.L. Rep. 148, QBD (Admin) .... *Digested,* 17/**675**

R. (on the application of E) v JFS Governing Body [2009] UKSC 1; [2009] 1 W.L.R. 2353; [2010] 1 All E.R. 1; [2009] 4 Costs L.R. 695; Times, October 19, 2009; (2009) 153(40) S.J.L.B. 37, SC .... *Digested,* 09/**2559**: *Applied* 12/1733: *Considered* 17/255

R. (on the application of E) v JFS Governing Body; *joined case* R. (on the application of E) v Office of the Schools Adjudicator [2009] UKSC 15; [2010] 2 A.C. 728; [2010] 2 W.L.R. 153; [2010] 1 All E.R. 319; [2010] P.T.S.R. 147; [2010] I.R.L.R. 136; 27 B.H.R.C. 656; [2010] E.L.R. 26; Times, December 17, 2009; (2010) 160 N.L.J. 29; (2009) 153(48) S.J.L.B. 32, SC .... *Digested,* 10/**969**: *Applied* 14/1639, 14/2444: *Followed* 11/1063, 15/844, 17/829

R. (on the application of E) v Office of the Schools Adjudicator see R. (on the application of E) v JFS Governing Body

R. (on the application of ED) v Southwark LBC see R. (on the application of D) v Southwark LBC

R. (on the application of Edgehill) v Director of Legal Aid Casework see R. (on the application of Gudanaviciene) v Director of Legal Aid Casework

R. (on the application of Edwards) v Environment Agency (C-260/11); *sub nom* Edwards v Environment Agency (C-260/11) EU:C:2013:221; [2013] 1 W.L.R. 2914; [2013] 3 C.M.L.R. 18; [2014] All E.R. (EC) 207, ECJ (4th Chamber) .... *Digested,* 14/**1183**: *Applied* 14/333, 14/339, 17/280: *Considered* 14/3338, 17/2430: *Followed* 14/442

R. (on the application of EH (Iran)) v Secretary of State for the Home Department see R. (on the application of EM (Eritrea)) v Secretary of State for the Home Department

R. (on the application of Ehsan) v Secretary of State for the Home Department see R. (on the application of Iqbal) v Secretary of State for the Home Department

R. (on the application of Eisa) v Secretary of State for the Home Department [2017] UKUT 261 (IAC); [2017] Imm. A.R. 1289, UT (IAC)

R. (on the application of EL) v Essex CC; *sub nom* R. (on the application of L) v Essex CC [2017] EWHC 1041 (Admin); [2017] P.T.S.R. 1000; [2018] 1 F.L.R. 802; [2017] A.C.D. 87, QBD (Admin)

R. (on the application of Elias) v Secretary of State for Defence; *sub nom* Elias v Secretary of State for Defence; Secretary of State for the Home Department v Elias [2006] EWCA Civ 1293; [2006] 1 W.L.R. 3213; [2006] I.R.L.R. 934; Times, October 17, 2006; Independent, October 18, 2006, CA (Civ Div) .... *Digested,* 06/**44**: *Applied* 08/3582, 09/1207, 13/1929, 14/2044, 15/747: *Considered* 07/1399, 08/920, 09/1163, 15/806: *Followed* 17/1459

R. (on the application of ELS Group Ltd) v Revenue and Customs Commissioners [2015] UKUT 48 (TCC); [2015] S.T.C. 1386; [2015] B.V.C. 508, UT (Tax) .... *Digested,* 15/**2618**: *Affirmed* 17/2259

R. (on the application of ELS Group Ltd) v Revenue and Customs Commissioners [2016] EWCA Civ 663; [2016] S.T.C. 2417; [2016] B.V.C. 26, CA (Civ Div) .... *Digested,* 17/**2259**

R. (on the application of EM (Eritrea)) v Secretary of State for the Home Department; *sub nom* MA (Eritrea) v Secretary of State for the Home Department; EM (Eritrea) v Secretary of State for the Home Department; *joined cases* R. (on the application of MA (Eritrea)) v Secretary of State for the Home Department; R. (on the application of AE (Eritrea)) v Secretary of State for the Home Department; R. (on the application of EH (Iran)) v Secretary of State for the Home Department [2014] UKSC 12; [2014] A.C. 1321; [2014] 2 W.L.R. 409; [2014] 2 All E.R. 192; [2014] H.R.L.R. 8; [2014] Imm. A.R. 640; [2014] I.N.L.R. 635; Times, February 27, 2014, SC .... *Digested,* 14/**1652**: *Applied* 14/1651: *Considered* 16/1063: *Followed* 15/966, 16/1060, 17/1176

R. (on the application of Equal Opportunities Commission) v Secretary of State for Communities and Local Government see Equal Opportunities Commission v Secretary of State for Trade and Industry

R. (on the application of Essence Bars (London) Ltd (t/a Essence Ltd)) v Wimbledon Magistrates' Court see Essence Bars (London) Ltd (t/a Essence) v Wimbledon Magistrates' Court

R. (on the application of Evans) v Director of the Serious Fraud Office; *sub nom* Evans (Michael) v Inspector of the Serious Fraud Office [2002] EWHC 2304 (Admin); [2003] 1 W.L.R. 299; Times, November 15, 2002; (2002) 99(45) L.S.G. 34, DC .... *Digested,* 02/**754**: *Applied* 17/291

R. (on the application of Evans) v Secretary of State for Communities and Local Government [2013] EWCA Civ 114; [2013] J.P.L. 1027, CA (Civ Div) .... *Digested,* 13/**2365**: *Applied* 15/1987: *Followed* 14/2427, 17/1778

R. (on the application of Evans) v Secretary of State for the Home Department see R. (on the application of Agyarko) v Secretary of State for the Home Department

R. (on the application of FA) v Ealing LBC (2017) 20 C.C.L. Rep. 383, UT (IAC) .... *Digested,* 17/**2049**

R. (on the application of Faraday Development Ltd) v West Berkshire Council [2016] EWHC 2166 (Admin); 168 Con. L.R. 131, QBD (Admin) .... *Digested,* 17/**1812**: *Applied* 17/1464

R. (on the application of Fatnani) v General Medical Council see Fatnani v General Medical Council

R. (on the application of Faulkner) v Director of Legal Aid Casework [2016] EWHC 717 (Admin); [2016] 4 W.L.R. 178; [2016] 2 Costs L.R. 237, QBD (Admin) .... *Digested,* 16/**1410**: *Distinguished* 17/1485

R. (on the application of Fawcett Society) v Chancellor of the Exchequer [2010] EWHC 3522 (Admin); [2011] Eq. L.R. 297, QBD (Admin) *Applied* 12/3178, 17/1539

R. (on the application of Feller) v Cambridge City Council [2011] EWHC 1252 (Admin); [2011] R.A. 321, QBD (Admin) .... *Digested,* 11/**2153**: *Applied* 17/1504

R. (on the application of Ferreira) v HM Senior Coroner for Inner South London; *sub nom* R. (on the application of LF) v HM Senior Coroner for Inner South London; Ferreira v HM Senior Coroner for Inner South London [2015] EWHC 2990 (Admin); [2016] 1 W.L.R. 2385; (2016) 180 J.P. 85; [2016] C.O.P.L.R. 119; [2015] Inquest L.R. 293; Times, January 18, 2016; [2016] A.C.D. 14, DC .... *Digested,* 16/**14**: *Affirmed* 17/19: *Applied* 17/1552

R. (on the application of Ferreira) v HM Senior Coroner for Inner South London; *sub nom* R. (on the application of LF) v HM Senior Coroner for Inner South London; Ferreira v HM Senior Coroner for Inner South London [2017] EWCA Civ 31; [2018] Q.B. 487; [2017] 3 W.L.R. 382; [2017] C.O.P.L.R. 172; [2017] Med. L.R. 161; [2017] Inquest L.R. 118; [2017] M.H.L.R. 258, CA (Civ Div) .... *Digested,* 17/**19**: *Followed* 17/1534

R. (on the application of Fisher) v Chief Constable of Northumbria [2017] EWHC 455 (Admin); [2017] I.C.R. 1106; [2017] A.C.D. 55, QBD (Admin) .... *Digested,* 17/**1630**

R. (on the application of Flint) v South Gloucestershire Council [2016] EWHC 2180 (Admin); [2016] L.L.R. 818; [2017] J.P.L. 310, QBD (Admin) .... *Digested,* 17/**1696**

R. (on the application of Forge Care Homes Ltd) v Cardiff and Vale University Health Board; *sub nom* Forge Care Homes Ltd v Cardiff and Vale University Health Board [2016] EWCA Civ 26; [2016] P.T.S.R. 908; (2016) 19 C.C.L. Rep. 62; (2016) 149 B.M.L.R. 98, CA (Civ Div) .... *Digested,* 16/**996**: *Reversed* 17/1136

R. (on the application of Forge Care Homes Ltd) v Cardiff and Vale University Health Board; *sub nom* Forge Care Homes Ltd v Cardiff and Vale University Health Board [2017] UKSC 56; [2018] 1 All E.R. 449; [2017] P.T.S.R. 1140; (2017) 20 C.C.L. Rep. 324; (2017) 158 B.M.L.R. 1; Times, August 24, 2017, SC .... *Digested,* 17/**1136**

R. (on the application of Forsey) v Northern Derbyshire Magistrates' Court [2017] EWHC 1152 (QB); [2017] I.C.R. 1161, DC .... *Digested,* 17/**618**

R. (on the application of Fox Strategic Land & Property Ltd) v Secretary of State for Communities and Local Government see Fox Strategic Land & Property Ltd v Secretary of State for Communities and Local Government

R. (on the application of FR (Albania)) v Secretary of State for the Home Department; *joined case* R. (on the application of KL (Albania)) v Secretary of State for the Home Department [2016] EWCA Civ 605; [2016] Imm. A.R. 1341, CA (Civ Div) *Digested,* 17/**1241**

R. (on the application of Frack Free Balcombe Residents Association) v West Sussex CC [2014] EWHC 4108 (Admin), QBD (Admin) *Considered* 17/1756

R. (on the application of France) v Kensington and Chelsea RLBC see France v Kensington and Chelsea RLBC

R. (on the application of Friend) v Attorney General see R. (on the application of Countryside Alliance) v Attorney General

R. (on the application of Friends of Finsbury Park) v Haringey LBC [2016] EWHC 1454 (Admin); [2016] P.T.S.R. 1299; [2016] L.L.R. 831, QBD (Admin) .... *Digested,* 17/**89**

R. (on the application of Friends of Hethel Ltd) v South Norfolk DC [2010] EWCA Civ 894; [2011] 1 W.L.R. 1216; [2011] P.T.S.R. 630; [2011] B.L.G.R. 19; [2011] J.P.L. 192; [2010] N.P.C. 90, CA (Civ Div) .... *Digested,* 11/**2552**: *Followed* 17/1721

R. (on the application of Friends of the Earth England, Wales and Northern Ireland Ltd) v Welsh Ministers [2015] EWHC 776 (Admin); [2016] Env. L.R. 1; [2015] P.T.S.R. D28, QBD (Admin) .... *Digested,* 16/**1704**: *Considered* 17/1694

R. (on the application of Friends of the Earth Ltd) v North Yorkshire CC [2016] EWHC 3303 (Admin); [2017] Env. L.R. 22; [2017] J.P.L. 518, QBD (Admin) .... *Digested,* 17/**1755**: *Considered* 17/1756

R. (on the application of G) v Chief Constable of Surrey; *joined case* R. (on the application of G) v Secretary of State for the Home Department [2016] EWHC 295 (Admin); [2016] 4 W.L.R. 94; [2016] 2 Cr. App. R. 2; [2016] A.C.D. 64, QBD (Admin) .... *Digested,* 16/**1770**: *Affirmed* 17/1586

R. (on the application of G) v Mental Health Review Tribunal [2004] EWHC 2193 (Admin); [2004] M.H.L.R. 265; [2005] A.C.D. 74, QBD (Admin) *Applied* 17/1538: *Considered* 11/24

R. (on the application of G) v Secretary of State for Justice [2010] EWHC 3407 (Admin), QBD (Admin) *Applied* 17/1135

R. (on the application of G) v Secretary of State for the Home Department see R. (on the application of G) v Chief Constable of Surrey

R. (on the application of G) v Secretary of State for the Home Department see R. (on the application of P) v Secretary of State for the Home Department

R. (on the application of Gaines-Cooper) v Revenue and Customs Commissioners see R. (on the application of Davies) v Revenue and Customs Commissioners

R. (on the application of Gallaher Group Ltd) v Competition and Markets Authority; *sub nom* Gallaher Group Ltd v Competition and Markets Authority; *joined case* R. (on the application of Somerfield Stores Ltd) v Competition and Markets Authority [2016] EWCA Civ 719; [2016] Bus. L.R. 1200; Times, September 22, 2016, CA (Civ Div) .... *Digested,* 16/**355**: *Followed* 17/2087

R. (on the application of Garner) v Elmbridge BC [2010] EWCA Civ 1006; [2011] 3 All E.R. 418; [2012] P.T.S.R. 250; [2011] 1 Costs L.R. 48; [2011] Env. L.R. 10; [2010] 3 E.G.L.R. 137; [2011] J.P.L. 289; [2011] A.C.D. 7, CA (Civ Div) .... *Digested,* 11/**279**: *Applied* 17/280: *Cited* 14/339: *Considered* 11/278, 14/1222, 14/333, 16/56: *Followed* 11/2561, 14/442

R. (on the application of Gazi (Bangladesh)) v Secretary of State for the Home Department [2015] UKUT 327 (IAC); [2015] Imm. A.R. 1127, UT (IAC) .... *Digested,* 16/**1146**: *Approved* 17/1243

R. (on the application of Gedi) v Secretary of State for the Home Department [2016] EWCA Civ 409; [2016] 4 W.L.R. 93, CA (Civ Div) .... *Digested,* 16/**1110**: *Applied* 17/1234

R. (on the application of George Wimpey UK Ltd) v Tewkesbury BC see MA Holdings Ltd v George Wimpey UK Ltd

R. (on the application of Gibraltar Betting & Gaming Association Ltd) v Revenue and Customs Commissioners [2015] EWHC 1863 (Admin); [2016] S.T.C. 151; [2015] L.L.R. 829, QBD (Admin) .... *Digested,* 16/**2108**: *Preliminary ruling given* 17/895

R. (on the application of Gibraltar Betting and Gaming Association Ltd) v Revenue and Customs Commissioners (C-591/15) EU:C:2017:449; [2017] 4 W.L.R. 167; [2017] S.T.C. 1300; [2018] 1 C.M.L.R. 13; [2018] C.E.C. 165; Times, July 19, 2017, ECJ (Grand Chamber) .... *Digested,* 17/**895**

R. (on the application of Gibson) v Secretary of State for Justice [2015] EWCA Civ 1148; [2017] 1 W.L.R. 1115; [2016] 4 All E.R. 244; [2016] Lloyd's Rep. F.C. 11, CA (Civ Div) .... *Digested,* 16/**188**

R. (on the application of Glenn & Co (Essex) Ltd) v Revenue and Customs Commissioners; *sub nom* Glenn & Co (Essex) Ltd v Revenue and Customs Commissioners [2011] EWHC 2998 (Admin); [2012] 1 Cr. App. R. 22; (2012) 176 J.P. 65; [2012] Lloyd's Rep. F.C. 115; [2012] Crim. L.R. 464; [2012] A.C.D. 5, DC .... *Digested,* 12/**824**: *Applied* 15/652, 17/624, 17/625

R. (on the application of Gottlieb) v Winchester City Council [2015] EWHC 231 (Admin); [2015] A.C.D. 74, QBD (Admin) *Not applied* 17/1814

R. (on the application of Gourlay) v Parole Board [2017] EWCA Civ 1003; [2017] 1 W.L.R. 4107; [2017] 4 Costs L.O. 489; Times, July 28, 2017, CA (Civ Div) .... *Digested,* 17/**255**

R. (on the application of Grace Bay II Holdings Sarl) v Pensions Regulator [2017] EWHC 7 (Admin); [2017] Pens. L.R. 7; [2017] A.C.D. 32; [2017] I.C.R. D13, QBD (Admin) .... *Digested,* 17/**1633**

R. (on the application of Graham) v Revenue and Customs Commissioners [2016] EWHC 1197 (Admin); [2017] S.T.C. 1; [2016] B.T.C. 23; [2016] S.T.I. 1653, QBD (Admin) .... *Digested,* 16/**2117**

R. (on the application of Greenwich LBC) v Secretary of State for Health [2006] EWHC 2576 (Admin); (2007) 10 C.C.L. Rep. 60, QBD (Admin) .... *Digested,* 07/**3910**: *Considered* 13/2956, 15/2393, 17/2056

R. (on the application of Griggs) v Financial Services Authority [2008] EWHC 2587 (Admin); [2009] A.C.D. 28, QBD (Admin) *Applied* 17/1633

R. (on the application of GS) v Camden LBC [2016] EWHC 1762 (Admin); [2017] P.T.S.R. 140; [2016] H.L.R. 43; (2016) 19 C.C.L. Rep. 398, QBD (Admin) .... *Digested,* 16/**2002**

R. (on the application of Guardian News and Media Ltd) v City of Westminster Magistrates' Court; *sub nom* Guardian News and Media Ltd v City of Westminster Magistrates' Court; *joined case* Guardian News and Media Ltd v United States [2012] EWCA Civ 420; [2013] Q.B. 618; [2012] 3 W.L.R. 1343; [2012] 3 All E.R. 551; [2012] C.P. Rep. 30; [2012] E.M.L.R. 22; Times, July 12, 2012; (2012) 109(16) L.S.G. 22; (2012) 162 N.L.J. 619, CA (Civ Div) .... *Digested,* 12/**660**: *Applied* 14/664, 17/1533: *Considered* 17/189: *Followed* 14/1791

R. (on the application of Guardian News and Media Ltd) v City of Westminster Magistrates' Court [2011] EWCA Civ 1188; [2011] 1 W.L.R. 3253; [2012] C.P. Rep. 5; [2012] E.M.L.R. 11; (2011) 108(43) L.S.G. 21, CA (Civ Div) .... *Digested,* 12/**1285**: *Applied* 16/188: *Considered* 12/3920, 17/270: *Followed* 15/630

R. (on the application of Gudanaviciene) v Director of Legal Aid Casework; *sub nom* Gudanaviciene v Director of Legal Aid Casework; *joined cases* R. (on the application of S) v Director of Legal Aid Casework; R. (on the application of Reis) v Director of Legal Aid Casework; R. (on the application of B) v Director of Legal Aid Casework; R. (on the application of Edgehill) v Director of Legal Aid Casework [2014] EWCA Civ 1622; [2015] 1 W.L.R. 2247; [2015] 3 All E.R. 827, CA (Civ Div) .... *Digested,* 15/**1626**: *Applied* 16/973, 17/1480: *Considered* 16/1408, 16/2713

R. (on the application of Gudanaviciene) v Immigration and Asylum First Tier Tribunal [2017] EWCA Civ 352; [2017] 1 W.L.R. 4095; [2017] C.P. Rep. 31; [2017] 3 Costs L.O. 361; [2017] Inquest L.R. 154, CA (Civ Div) .... *Digested,* 17/**232**: *Considered* 17/255

R. (on the application of Guest) v DPP [2009] EWHC 594 (Admin); [2009] 2 Cr. App. R. 26; (2009) 173 J.P. 511; [2009] Crim. L.R. 730, DC .... *Digested,* 09/**827**: *Applied* 09/900, 17/621

R. (on the application of H (A Child)) v Newham LBC see R. (on the application of N) v Lewisham LBC

R. (on the application of H) v Ealing LBC; *sub nom* Ealing LBC v R. (on the application of H) [2016] EWHC 841 (Admin); [2016] P.T.S.R. 1546; [2016] H.L.R. 20, QBD (Admin) .... *Digested,* 16/**1040**: *Applied* 17/1155

R. (on the application of H) v National Probation Service see R. (on the application of X) v National Probation Service

R. (on the application of H) v Secretary of State for the Home Department; *sub nom* Secretary of State for the Home Department v H [2015] EWHC 1725 (Admin); [2015] A.C.D. 121, QBD (Admin) *Reversed* 17/1222

R. (on the application of H) v Secretary of State for the Home Department; *sub nom* Secretary of State for the Home Department v H [2016] EWCA Civ 565; [2016] Imm. A.R. 1272; [2017] I.N.L.R. 267, CA (Civ Div) .... *Digested,* 17/**1222**

R. (on the application of HA) v Ealing LBC [2015] EWHC 2375 (Admin); [2016] P.T.S.R. 16; [2015] B.L.G.R. 954; [2015] A.C.D. 145, QBD (Admin) .... *Digested,* 16/**1039**: *Applied* 16/1040: *Distinguished* 17/1154

R. (on the application of Hagos) v Secretary of State for the Home Department [2015] UKUT 271 (IAC); [2015] Imm. A.R. 1070, UT (IAC) *Applied* 17/1177

R. (on the application of Haigh) v City of Westminster Magistrates' Court [2017] EWHC 232 (Admin); [2017] 1 Costs L.R. 175; (2017) 181 J.P. 325; [2017] Lloyd's Rep. F.C. 193; [2017] A.C.D. 47, DC .... *Digested,* 17/**620**

R. (on the application of Hakeem) v Enfield LBC [2013] EWHC 1026 (Admin), QBD (Admin) *Applied* 17/1504

R. (on the application of Hallam) v Secretary of State for Justice see R. (on the application of Nealon) v Secretary of State for Justice

R. (on the application of Halvai) v Hammersmith and Fulham LBC [2017] EWHC 802 (Admin); (2017) 20 C.C.L. Rep. 517, QBD (Admin)

R. (on the application of Hamad) v Secretary of State for the Home Department [2015] EWHC 2511 (Admin), QBD (Admin)
Applied 17/1177

R. (on the application of Hamilton-Jackson) v Assistant Coroner for Mid Kent and Medway [2016] EWHC 1796 (Admin); [2016] Inquest L.R. 225, DC .... *Digested,* 17/**22**

R. (on the application of Hammersmith and Fulham LBC) v Judicial Conduct Investigations Office [2016] EWHC 2849 (Admin); [2017] A.C.D. 2, QBD (Admin)

R. (on the application of Haney) v Secretary of State for Justice see R. (on the application of Kaiyam) v Secretary of State for Justice

R. (on the application of Harris) v Broads Authority [2016] EWHC 799 (Admin); [2017] 1 W.L.R. 567; Times, May 9, 2016, QBD (Admin) .... *Digested,* 16/**774**

R. (on the application of Hassan) v Secretary of State for the Home Department; *joined case* R. (on the application of Karada) v Secretary of State for the Home Department [2016] UKUT 452 (IAC); [2017] Imm. A.R. 258, UT (IAC) .... *Digested,* 17/**1177**

R. (on the application of Hassani) v West London Magistrates' Court [2017] EWHC 1270 (Admin); [2017] 3 Costs L.R. 477; (2017) 181 J.P. 253; [2017] Crim. L.R. 720; [2017] A.C.D. 73, DC .... *Digested,* 17/**570**

R. (on the application of Hassett) v Secretary of State for Justice [2017] EWCA Civ 331; [2017] 1 W.L.R. 4750, CA (Civ Div)
Followed 17/1590

R. (on the application of Hawksworth Securities Plc) v Peterborough City Council [2016] EWHC 1870 (Admin), QBD (Admin)
Considered 17/1765

R. (on the application of Hayes) v York City Council [2017] EWHC 1374 (Admin); [2017] P.T.S.R. 1587, QBD (Admin)

R. (on the application of Headcorn Parish Council) v Maidstone BC see R. (on the application of Headcorn Parish Council) v Secretary of State for Communities and Local Government

R. (on the application of Headcorn Parish Council) v Secretary of State for Communities and Local Government; *joined case* R. (on the application of Headcorn Parish Council) v Maidstone BC [2017] EWHC 970 (Admin); [2017] Env. L.R. 34, QBD (Admin) .... *Digested,* 17/**1778**

R. (on the application of Headley) v Secretary of State for the Home Department see R. (on the application of Clift) v Secretary of State for the Home Department

R. (on the application of Health and Safety Executive) v Wolverhampton City Council see Health and Safety Executive v Wolverhampton City Council

R. (on the application of Heather Moor & Edgecomb Ltd) v Financial Ombudsman Service [2008] EWCA Civ 642; [2008] Bus. L.R. 1486; (2008) 158 N.L.J. 897, CA (Civ Div) .... *Digested,* 09/**73**:
Applied 11/55, 14/1449: *Considered* 13/2080: *Followed* 17/35

R. (on the application of Helford Village Development Co Ltd) v Kerrier DC [2009] EWHC 400 (Admin), QBD (Admin)
Distinguished 17/1772

R. (on the application of Hely-Hutchinson) v Revenue and Customs Commissioners [2017] EWCA Civ 1075; [2018] 1 W.L.R. 1682; [2017] S.T.C. 2048; [2017] B.T.C. 24, CA (Civ Div) .... *Digested,* 17/**2087**

R. (on the application of Hely-Hutchinson) v Revenue and Customs Commissioners [2015] EWHC 3261 (Admin); [2016] S.T.C. 962; [2015] B.T.C. 37; [2016] A.C.D. 15, QBD (Admin) .... *Digested,* 16/**2049**:
Considered 16/2069: *Reversed* 17/2087

R. (on the application of Hemming (t/a Simply Pleasure Ltd)) v Westminster City Council [2017] UKSC 50; [2017] 3 W.L.R. 342; [2017] P.T.S.R. 1020; [2017] L.L.R. 835; Times, August 17, 2017, SC .... *Digested,* 17/**1493**

R. (on the application of Hemming (t/a Simply Pleasure Ltd)) v Westminster City Council [2015] UKSC 25; [2015] A.C. 1600; [2015] 2 W.L.R. 1271; [2015] 4 All E.R. 471; [2015] P.T.S.R. 643; [2015] 3 C.M.L.R. 9; [2015] B.L.G.R. 753; [2015] L.L.R. 564, SC .... *Digested,* 15/**1665**:
Preliminary ruling given 17/1495

R. (on the application of Hemming (t/a Simply Pleasure Ltd)) v Westminster City Council (C-316/15); *sub nom* Hemming v Westminster City Council (C-316/15) EU:C:2016:879; [2017] 3 W.L.R. 317; [2017] P.T.S.R. 325; [2017] C.E.C. 920; [2017] L.L.R. 189; Times, January 17, 2017, ECJ (3rd Chamber) .... *Digested,* 17/**1495**

R. (on the application of HH) v Westminster City Magistrates' Court; *sub nom* PH v Italy; HH v Italy; *joined case* F-K v Poland [2012] UKSC 25; [2013] 1 A.C. 338; [2012] 3 W.L.R. 90; [2012] 4 All E.R. 539; [2012] H.R.L.R. 25; Times, July 2, 2012; (2012) 156(25) S.J.L.B. 31, SC .... *Digested,* 12/**1293**: *Applied* 13/2652, 13/2749, 14/1596, 14/662, 17/1242: *Considered* 12/1289, 14/1650, 14/1668, 14/1704, 16/2633, 16/798, 17/901: *Followed* 16/797, 17/910

R. (on the application of Hicks) v Commissioner of Police of the Metropolis; *joined cases* R. (on the application of M) v Commissioner of Police of the Metropolis; R. (on the application of Pearce) v Commissioner of Police of the Metropolis; R. (on the application of Middleton) v Bromley Magistrates' Court [2017] UKSC 9; [2017] A.C. 256; [2017] 2 W.L.R. 824; [2018] 1 All E.R. 374; 43 B.H.R.C. 254; Times, February 20, 2017, SC .... *Digested,* 17/**1803**

R. (on the application of Hicks) v Commissioner of Police of the Metropolis; *joined cases* R. (on the application of M) v Commissioner of Police of the Metropolis; R. (on the application of Pearce) v Commissioner of Police of the Metropolis; R. (on the application of Middleton) v Bromley Magistrates' Court [2014] EWCA Civ 3; [2014] 1 W.L.R. 2152; [2014] 2 Cr. App. R. 4; [2014] H.R.L.R. 11; [2014] Crim. L.R. 681, CA (Civ Div) .... *Digested,* 14/**2464**: *Affirmed* 17/1803

R. (on the application of Hicks) v Inner North London Senior Coroner [2016] EWHC 1726 (Admin); (2017) 181 J.P. 1; [2016] Inquest L.R. 219, DC .... *Digested,* 17/**20**

R. (on the application of Higham) v Cornwall Council [2015] EWHC 2191 (Admin), QBD (Admin) *Applied* 17/1721

R. (on the application of Hillingdon LBC) v Lord Chancellor [2008] EWHC 2683 (Admin); [2009] C.P. Rep. 13; [2009] 1 F.L.R. 39; [2009] 1 F.C.R. 1; [2009] B.L.G.R. 554; [2009] Fam. Law 13; (2008) 158 N.L.J. 1602; [2009] P.T.S.R. (C.S.) 20, DC .... *Digested,* 09/**1598**: *Applied* 15/15: *Considered* 17/1539

R. (on the application of Hillingdon LBC) v Secretary of State for Transport; *sub nom* Hillingdon LBC v Secretary of State for Transport [2017] EWHC 121 (Admin); [2017] 1 W.L.R. 2166; [2017] J.P.L. 610; [2017] A.C.D. 38, QBD (Admin) .... *Digested,* 17/**1726**

R. (on the application of Hindawi) v Secretary of State for the Home Department see R. (on the application of Clift) v Secretary of State for the Home Department

R. (on the application of Hockerill Anglo-European College Academy Trust) v Schools Adjudicator [2016] EWHC 1642 (Admin); [2017] E.L.R. 187, QBD (Admin) .... *Digested,* 17/**703**

R. (on the application of Holding & Barnes Plc) v Secretary of State for the Environment, Transport and the Regions; *sub nom* R. v Secretary of State for the Environment, Transport and the Regions Ex p. Holdings & Barnes Plc; *joined cases* Secretary of State for the Environment, Transport and the Regions v Legal & General Assurance Society Ltd; R. (on the application of Alconbury Developments Ltd) v Secretary of State for the Environment, Transport and the Regions; R. (on the application of Premier Leisure UK Ltd) v Secretary of State for the Environment, Transport and the Regions [2001] UKHL 23; [2003] 2 A.C. 295; [2001] 2 W.L.R. 1389; [2001] 2 All E.R. 929; [2002] Env. L.R. 12; [2001] H.R.L.R. 45; [2001] U.K.H.R.R. 728; (2001) 3 L.G.L.R. 38; (2001) 82 P. & C.R. 40; [2001] 2 P.L.R. 76; Times, May 10, 2001; Independent, June 25, 2001; [2001] J.P.L. 920; Daily Telegraph, May 15, 2001; [2001] 20 E.G. 228 (C.S.); (2001) 98(24) L.S.G. 45; (2001) 151 N.L.J. 727; (2001) 145 S.J.L.B. 140; [2001] N.P.C. 90, HL .... *Digested,* 01/**4761**: *Applied* 02/2337, 02/3700, 02/4191, 05/1410, 09/3019, 12/2599, 14/2864, 15/899, 17/1725: *Cited* 01/6853, 02/1647: *Considered* 02/3696, 02/3699, 03/55, 04/1529, 04/790, 08/2935, 13/350: *Distinguished* 08/1955, 10/1052: *Followed* 02/1526, 03/3446, 16/1707

R. (on the application of Holdsworth) v Secretary of State for Justice [2016] EWHC 3405 (Admin); [2017] A.C.D. 22, QBD (Admin)

R. (on the application of Holmcroft Properties Ltd) v KPMG LLP [2016] EWHC 323 (Admin); [2017] Bus. L.R. 932; [2016] 2 B.C.L.C. 545; [2016] A.C.D. 67, DC ..... *Digested,* 17/**1077**

R. (on the application of Hooper) v Secretary of State for Work and Pensions; *sub nom* Hooper v Secretary of State for Work and Pensions; *joined cases* R. (on the application of Martin) v Secretary of State for Work and Pensions; R. (on the application of Naylor) v Secretary of State for Work and Pensions; R. (on the application of Withey) v Secretary of State for Work and Pensions [2005] UKHL 29; [2005] 1 W.L.R. 1681; [2006] 1 All E.R. 487; [2005] 2 F.C.R. 183; [2005] H.R.L.R. 21; [2005] U.K.H.R.R. 717; [2005] Pens. L.R. 337; Times, May 6, 2005; Independent, May 10, 2005, HL .... *Digested,* 05/**3926**: *Applied* 06/2010, 17/1466, 17/976: *Considered* 08/3860

R. (on the application of Hope & Glory Public House Ltd) v City of Westminster Magistrates' Court [2011] EWCA Civ 31; [2011] 3 All E.R. 579; [2011] P.T.S.R. 868; (2011) 175 J.P. 77; [2011] 2 E.G.L.R. 53; [2011] 18 E.G. 110; [2011] L.L.R. 105, CA (Civ Div) .... *Digested,* 11/**2136**: *Applied* 16/1452, 17/1200

R. (on the application of Hossain) v Secretary of State for the Home Department see R. (on the application of W) v Secretary of State for the Home Department

R. (on the application of Howard League for Penal Reform) v Lord Chancellor [2017] EWCA Civ 244; [2017] 4 W.L.R. 92; Times, May 23, 2017, CA (Civ Div) .... *Digested,* 17/**1480**

R. (on the application of Humphreys) v Parking and Traffic Appeals Service; *sub nom* Humphreys v Parking and Traffic Appeals Service; Camden LBC v Humphreys [2017] EWCA Civ 24; [2017] R.T.R. 22, CA (Civ Div) .... *Digested,* 17/**1876**

R. (on the application of Humphreys) v Parking and Traffic Appeals Service; *sub nom* Humphreys v Parking and Traffic Appeals Service; Camden LBC v Humphreys [2015] EWHC 713 (Admin), QBD (Admin) *Affirmed* 17/1876

R. (on the application of Hurley) v Secretary of State for Business, Innovation and Skills [2012] EWHC 201 (Admin); [2012] H.R.L.R. 13; [2012] Eq. L.R. 447; [2012] E.L.R. 297; [2012] A.C.D. 50, DC .... *Digested,* 12/**1004**: *Applied* 17/1160: *Considered* 14/1509, 16/1040

R. (on the application of Hussain) v Parole Board for England and Wales [2017] EWCA Civ 1074; [2017] 1 W.L.R. 3748, CA (Civ Div) .... *Digested,* 17/**1591**

R. (on the application of Hussain) v Parole Board for England and Wales [2016] EWHC 288 (Admin); [2016] 1 W.L.R. 4996; [2016] A.C.D. 68, QBD (Admin) *Reversed* 17/1591

R. (on the application of Hussain) v Secretary of State for Justice [2016] EWCA Civ 1111; [2017] 1 W.L.R. 761; [2017] C.P. Rep. 11, CA (Civ Div) .... *Digested,* 17/**37**

R. (on the application of Hussain) v Secretary of State for Justice see R. (on the application of King) v Secretary of State for Justice

R. (on the application of Hussein) v First-tier Tribunal [2016] UKUT 409 (IAC); [2017] Imm. A.R. 84, UT (IAC)

R. (on the application of Hysaj) v Secretary of State for the Home Department; *joined cases* Fathollahipour v Aliabadibenisi; May v Robinson [2014] EWCA Civ 1633; [2015] 1 W.L.R. 2472; [2015] C.P. Rep. 17; [2015] 2 Costs L.R. 191; Times, January 22, 2015, CA (Civ Div) .... *Digested,* 15/**295**: *Applied* 15/1000: *Approved* 17/2182: *Considered* 15/292, 17/2189: *Followed* 15/1352, 15/299, 16/283, 16/307, 17/296, 17/350

R. (on the application of Hysaj) v Secretary of State for the Home Department see R. (on the application of Kaziu) v Secretary of State for the Home Department

R. (on the application of IDT Card Services Ireland Ltd) v Customs and Excise Commissioners; *sub nom* Revenue and Customs Commissioners v IDT Card Services Ireland Ltd [2006] EWCA Civ 29; [2006] S.T.C. 1252; [2006] B.T.C. 5175; [2006] B.V.C. 244; [2006] S.T.I. 239, CA (Civ Div) .... *Digested,* 06/**4484**: *Applied* 09/4078, 10/1049, 14/823, 17/2266: *Considered* 09/3765, 13/2146: *Distinguished* 11/3519: *Followed* 09/4044, 11/3566

R. (on the application of Ikuga) v Secretary of State for the Home Department see R. (on the application of Agyarko) v Secretary of State for the Home Department

R. (on the application of IM) v Human Fertilisation and Embryology Authority see R. (on the application of M) v Human Fertilisation and Embryology Authority

R. (on the application of Imbeah) v Willesden Magistrates' Court [2016] EWHC 1760 (Admin); [2018] 4 W.L.R. 3; [2017] 1 Cr. App. R. 3, QBD (Admin) .... *Digested,* 17/**27**

R. (on the application of Imperial Tobacco Ltd) v Secretary of State for Health see R. (on the application of British American Tobacco UK Ltd) v Secretary of State for Health

R. (on the application of Ingenious Media Holdings Plc) v Revenue and Customs Commissioners [2016] UKSC 54; [2016] 1 W.L.R. 4164; [2017] 1 All E.R. 95; [2016] S.T.C. 2306; [2017] E.M.L.R. 6; [2016] B.T.C. 41; Times, October 28, 2016; [2016] S.T.I. 2746, SC .... *Digested,* 16/**2075**

R. (on the application of Inglot) v Secretary of State for the Home Deparment see Poland v Celinski

R. (on the application of Interim Executive Board of X) v Ofsted [2016] EWHC 2004 (Admin); [2017] E.M.L.R. 5; [2016] E.L.R. 519, QBD (Admin) .... *Digested,* 17/**697**

R. (on the application of Iqbal) v Secretary of State for the Home Department; *joined cases* R. (on the application of Mirza) v Secretary of State for the Home Department; R. (on the application of Ehsan) v Secretary of State for the Home Department [2015] EWCA Civ 838; [2016] 1 W.L.R. 582; [2016] 2 All E.R. 469; [2016] Imm. A.R. 77; [2016] I.N.L.R. 367, CA (Civ Div) .... *Digested,* 16/**1137**: *Affirmed* 17/1237

R. (on the application of Iqbal) v Secretary of State for the Home Department; *joined cases* R. (on the application of Mirza) v Secretary of State for the Home Department; R. (on the application of Ehsan) v Secretary of State for the Home Department [2016] UKSC 63; [2017] 1 W.L.R. 85; [2017] 3 All E.R. 824; [2017] Imm. A.R. 716; [2017] I.N.L.R. 325; Times, December 21, 2016, SC .... *Digested,* 17/**1237**

R. (on the application of Irving) v Mid-Sussex DC [2016] EWHC 1529 (Admin); [2016] P.T.S.R. 1365, QBD (Admin) .... *Digested,* 17/**1759**

R. (on the application of Islam) v Secretary of State for the Home Department [2016] EWHC 2491 (Admin); [2017] Imm. A.R. 565, QBD (Admin) .... *Digested,* 17/**1243**

R. (on the application of Ismail) v Secretary of State for the Home Department see Ismail v Secretary of State for the Home Department

R. (on the application of Jakimaviciute) v Hammersmith and Fulham LBC [2014] EWCA Civ 1438; [2015] 3 All E.R. 490; [2015] P.T.S.R. 822; [2015] H.L.R. 5; [2015] B.L.G.R. 306, CA (Civ Div) .... *Digested,* 15/**1282**: *Distinguished* 17/1154

R. (on the application of Javed) v Secretary of State for the Home Department see R. (on the application of MM (Lebanon)) v Secretary of State for the Home Department

R. (on the application of JB) v Secretary of State for the Home Department see R. (on the application of T) v Chief Constable of Greater Manchester

R. (on the application of Jewish Rights Watch (t/a Jewish Human Rights Watch)) v City and County of Swansea see R. (on the application of Jewish Rights Watch (t/a Jewish Human Rights Watch)) v Leicester City Council

R. (on the application of Jewish Rights Watch (t/a Jewish Human Rights Watch)) v Gwynedd Council see R. (on the application of Jewish Rights Watch (t/a Jewish Human Rights Watch)) v Leicester City Council

R. (on the application of Jewish Rights Watch (t/a Jewish Human Rights Watch)) v Leicester City Council; *joined cases* R. (on the application of Jewish Rights Watch (t/a Jewish Human Rights Watch)) v City and County of Swansea; R. (on the application of Jewish Rights Watch (t/a Jewish Human Rights Watch)) v Gwynedd Council [2016] EWHC 1512 (Admin); [2017] 3 All E.R. 505; [2017] P.T.S.R. 1433, DC

R. (on the application of JF) v Merton LBC [2017] EWHC 1519 (Admin); (2017) 20 C.C.L. Rep. 241, QBD (Admin) .... *Digested,* 17/**2058**

R. (on the application of JH (Zimbabwe)) v Asylum and Immigration Tribunal see JH (Zimbabwe) v Secretary of State for the Home Department

R. (on the application of JK (Burundi)) v Secretary of State for the Home Department [2017] EWCA Civ 433; [2017] 1 W.L.R. 4567; (2018) 21 C.C.L. Rep. 55, CA (Civ Div)

R. (on the application of JL) v Secretary of State for Justice see R. (on the application of JL) v Secretary of State for the Home Department

R. (on the application of JL) v Secretary of State for the Home Department; *sub nom* R. (on the application of JL) v Secretary of State for Justice [2008] UKHL 68; [2009] 1 A.C. 588; [2008] 3 W.L.R. 1325; [2009] 2 All E.R. 521; [2009] H.R.L.R. 9; [2009] U.K.H.R.R. 415; 27 B.H.R.C. 24; [2008] Inquest L.R. 88; Times, December 2, 2008; (2008) 158 N.L.J. 1719; (2008) 152(46) S.J.L.B. 31, HL ...... *Digested,* 09/**2754**: *Considered* 14/47: *Followed* 09/2037, 10/17, 11/1682, 15/1643, 17/1593

R. (on the application of JM (Zimbabwe)) v Secretary of State for the Home Department [2016] EWHC 1773 (Admin); [2017] 1 W.L.R. 268, QBD (Admin) ... *Digested,* 17/**1205**

R. (on the application of Johnson) v Havering LBC see L v Birmingham City Council

R. (on the application of Johnson) v Secretary of State for the Home Department [2016] UKSC 56; [2017] A.C. 365; [2016] 3 W.L.R. 1267; [2017] 4 All E.R. 91; 41 B.H.R.C. 711; [2017] Imm. A.R. 306; [2017] I.N.L.R. 235; Times, October 26, 2016, SC .... *Digested,* 16/**1083**: *Considered* 17/1182

R. (on the application of Jones) v Denbighshire CC [2016] EWHC 2074 (Admin); (2017) 20 C.C.L. Rep. 362; [2016] A.C.D. 113, DC

R. (on the application of Jones) v Liverpool and Knowsley Magistrates' Court [2016] EWHC 3520 (Admin); [2017] A.C.D. 24, DC

R. (on the application of Jones) v Mansfield DC [2003] EWCA Civ 1408; [2004] Env. L.R. 21; [2004] 2 P. & C.R. 14; Times, October 31, 2003; (2003) 147 S.J.L.B. 1209; [2003] N.P.C. 119, CA (Civ Div) .... *Digested,* 03/**3421**: *Applied* 05/3270, 05/3298, 08/2967, 10/2601, 11/2530: *Considered* 04/3084: *Followed* 14/2431, 14/2434, 17/1785

R. (on the application of Joseph) v Director of Legal Aid Casework [2015] EWHC 2749 (Admin); [2017] Inquest L.R. 51, QBD (Admin)

R. (on the application of JS) v Secretary of State for Work and Pensions; *sub nom* R. (on the application of SG) v Secretary of State for Work and Pensions [2015] UKSC 16; [2015] 1 W.L.R. 1449; [2015] 4 All E.R. 939; [2015] P.T.S.R. 471; [2015] H.R.L.R. 5; [2015] H.L.R. 21; (2015) 18 C.C.L. Rep. 215; Times, April 2, 2015, SC .... *Digested,* 15/**2338**: *Considered* 16/1040, 17/2026: *Followed* 16/1975

R. (on the application of JT International SA) v Secretary of State for Health see R. (on the application of British American Tobacco UK Ltd) v Secretary of State for Health

R. (on the application of Justice for Health Ltd) v Secretary of State for Health [2016] EWHC 2338 (Admin); [2016] Med. L.R. 599; [2016] A.C.D. 119, QBD (Admin) .. *Digested,* 17/**1099**

R. (on the application of K) v Secretary of State for Defence [2016] EWCA Civ 1149; [2017] 1 W.L.R. 1671, CA (Civ Div) .... *Digested,* 17/**180**

R. (on the application of K) v Secretary of State for Defence [2016] EWHC 1261 (Admin); [2016] A.C.D. 74, DC

Reversed 17/180

R. (on the application of Kadhim) v Brent LBC Housing Benefit Review Board; *sub nom* Kadhim v Brent LBC Housing Benefit Board; R. v Brent LBC Housing Benefit Review Board Ex p. Khadim; R. (on the application of Khadim) v Brent LBC Housing Benefit Review Board [2001] Q.B. 955; [2001] 2 W.L.R. 1674; (2001) 33 H.L.R. 79; Times, March 27, 2001; [2001] A.C.D. 35; (2001) 98(14) L.S.G. 40; [2001] N.P.C. 7, CA (Civ Div) .... *Digested,* 01/**5021**: *Applied* 17/1595: *Considered* 14/294

R. (on the application of Kaiyam) v Secretary of State for Justice; *sub nom* R. (on the application of Haney) v Secretary of State for Justice; R. (on the application of Massey) v Secretary of State for Justice; *joined case* R. (on the application of Robinson) v Governor of Whatton Prison [2014] UKSC 66; [2015] A.C. 1344; [2015] 2 W.L.R. 76; [2015] 2 All E.R. 822; 38 B.H.R.C. 313; Times, December 15, 2014, SC .... *Digested,* 15/**1811**: *Applied* 17/2745: *Considered* 15/3242, 16/2750, 16/2751, 17/1588, 17/2746, 17/2747: *Followed* 17/1591: *Superseded* 17/1594

R. (on the application of Karada) v Secretary of State for the Home Department see R. (on the application of Hassan) v Secretary of State for the Home Department

R. (on the application of Kardi) v Secretary of State for the Home Department [2014] EWCA Civ 934, CA (Civ Div)

Followed 17/1209

R. (on the application of Kathro) v Rhondda Cynon Taff CBC [2001] EWHC 527 (Admin); [2002] Env. L.R. 15; [2001] 4 P.L.R. 83; [2002] J.P.L. 304, QBD (Admin) .... *Digested,* 02/**3699**: *Applied* 17/1814

R. (on the application of Kaur) v Secretary of State for the Home Department [2017] EWCA Civ 821; [2017] C.P. Rep. 37; [2017] 5 Costs L.O. 615, CA (Civ Div) ..... *Digested,* 17/**318**

R. (on the application of Kaziu) v Secretary of State for the Home Department; *sub nom* Kaziu v Secretary of State for the Home Department; *joined cases* R. (on the application of Bakijasi) v Secretary of State for the Home Department; R. (on the application of Hysaj) v Secretary of State for the Home Department [2015] EWCA Civ 1195; [2016] 1 W.L.R. 673; [2017] 1 All E.R. 380; [2016] Imm. A.R. 329; [2016] I.N.L.R. 343; Times, January 26, 2016, CA (Civ Div) ...... *Digested,* 16/**1071**

R. (on the application of Kemball) v Secretary of State for Communities and Local Government [2015] EWHC 3338 (Admin); [2016] J.P.L. 359, QBD (Admin) .... *Digested,* 16/**1667**: *Considered* 17/1780

R. (on the application of Kensington and Chelsea RLBC) v Ealing LBC [2017] EWHC 24 (Admin); [2017] P.T.S.R. 1029; [2017] H.L.R. 13, QBD (Admin) .... *Digested,* 17/**1148**

R. (on the application of Khadim) v Brent LBC Housing Benefit Review Board see R. (on the application of Kadhim) v Brent LBC Housing Benefit Review Board

R. (on the application of Khaled Salim Saleem) v Secretary of State for the Home Department (Unreported)

Not followed 17/1226

R. (on the application of Khan) v HM Coroner for West Hertfordshire [2002] EWHC 302 (Admin); [2008] Inquest L.R. 200, QBD (Admin)

Considered 17/606

R. (on the application of Khan) v Secretary of State for the Home Department; *sub nom* Khan v Secretary of State for the Home Department [2017] EWCA Civ 424; [2017] 4 W.L.R. 156; [2017] Imm. A.R. 1409, CA (Civ Div) .... *Digested,* 17/**1229**

R. (on the application of Khodari) v Kensington and Chelsea RLBC [2015] EWHC 4084 (Admin), QBD (Admin)

Affirmed 17/1750

R. (on the application of Khodari) v Kensington and Chelsea RLBC [2017] EWCA Civ 333; [2018] 1 W.L.R. 584; [2018] R.T.R. 5; [2017] J.P.L. 1105, CA (Civ Div) ..... *Digested,* 17/**1750**

R. (on the application of Kiani) v Secretary of State for the Home Department see Kiani v Secretary of State for the Home Department

R. (on the application of Kiarie) v Secretary of State for the Home Department see R. (on the application of Byndloss) v Secretary of State for the Home Department

R. (on the application of Kides) v South Cambridgeshire DC [2002] EWCA Civ 1370; [2003] 1 P. & C.R. 19; [2002] 4 P.L.R. 66; Times, October 15, 2002; Independent, October 16, 2002; [2003] J.P.L. 431; [2002] 42 E.G. 160 (C.S.); (2002) 99(43) L.S.G. 35; (2002) 146 S.J.L.B. 230; [2002] N.P.C. 121, CA (Civ Div) ..... *Digested,* 02/**3662**: *Applied* 16/1684: *Considered* 07/3264, 10/2602, 11/2546, 15/1982, 16/1743: *Followed* 10/2590, 12/2590, 14/2428, 16/1742, 17/1770

R. (on the application of Kigen) v Secretary of State for the Home Department [2015] EWCA Civ 1286; [2016] 1 W.L.R. 723; [2016] C.P. Rep. 15; [2016] Imm. A.R. 390; [2016] I.N.L.R. 645; Times, February 16, 2016, CA (Civ Div) ..... *Digested,* 16/**283**: *Applied* 17/299

R. (on the application of King) v Parole Board for England and Wales [2016] EWCA Civ 51; [2016] 1 W.L.R. 1947; [2017] 2 All E.R. 176; Times, March 29, 2016, CA (Civ Div) ..... *Digested,* 16/**1568**

R. (on the application of King) v Secretary of State for Environment Food and Rural Affairs [2016] EWHC 1692 (Admin); [2017] P.T.S.R. 62, QBD (Admin) ..... *Digested,* 17/**57**

R. (on the application of King) v Secretary of State for Justice; *sub nom* R. (on the application of Hussain) v Secretary of State for Justice; R. (on the application of Bourgass) v Secretary of State for Justice [2015] UKSC 54; [2016] A.C. 384; [2015] 3 W.L.R. 457; [2016] 1 All E.R. 1033, SC ..... *Digested,* 15/**1819**: *Considered* 16/2756: *Followed* 17/1596

R. (on the application of Kingston upon Hull City Council) v Secretary of State for Business, Innovation and Skills [2016] EWHC 1064 (Admin); [2016] P.T.S.R. 967; (2017) 181 J.P. 20; [2016] C.T.L.C. 63; [2016] A.C.D. 94, QBD (Admin) .... *Digested,* 16/**1474**

R. (on the application of KL (Albania)) v Secretary of State for the Home Department see R. (on the application of FR (Albania)) v Secretary of State for the Home Department

R. (on the application of KM (Jamaica)) v Secretary of State for the Home Department see R. (on the application of Lumba) v Secretary of State for the Home Department

R. (on the application of Knight) v Secretary of State for Transport [2017] EWHC 1722 (Admin); [2017] 2 Lloyd's Rep. 453; [2017] A.C.D. 102, QBD (Admin)

R. (on the application of Knights) v Secretary of State for Justice see Knights v Parole Board for England and Wales

R. (on the application of KP (Turkey)) v Secretary of State for the Home Department see R. (on the application of Buer) v Secretary of State for the Home Department

R. (on the application of Krol) v Commissioner of Police of the Metropolis [2014] EWHC 4552 (Admin), QBD (Admin) *Affirmed* 17/1586

R. (on the application of L) v Chief Constable of Surrey; *sub nom* R. (on the application of TL) v Chief Constable of Surrey [2017] EWHC 129 (Admin); [2017] 1 W.L.R. 2047; [2017] 1 Cr. App. R. 29; [2017] Crim. L.R. 576, DC ..... *Digested,* 17/**1802**

R. (on the application of L) v Essex CC see R. (on the application of EL) v Essex CC

R. (on the application of L) v Secretary of State for the Home Department; *sub nom* R. (on the application of ZL) v Secretary of State for the Home Department; *joined case* R. (on the application of VL) v Secretary of State for the Home Department [2003] EWCA Civ 25; [2003] 1 W.L.R. 1230; [2003] 1 All E.R. 1062; [2003] Imm. A.R. 330; [2003] I.N.L.R. 224; Times, January 30, 2003; Independent, January 28, 2003; (2003) 100(11) L.S.G. 33, CA (Civ Div) ..... *Digested,* 03/**2263**: *Applied* 17/1241

R. (on the application of L) v West London Mental Health NHS Trust [2014] EWCA Civ 47; [2014] 1 W.L.R. 3103; (2014) 137 B.M.L.R. 76; [2014] M.H.L.R. 361; [2014] A.C.D. 79; (2014) 158(6) S.J.L.B. 37, CA (Civ Div) ..... *Digested,* 14/**2162**: *Followed* 17/1545

R. (on the application of L) v Westminster City Council see R. (on the application of SL) v Westminster City Council

R. (on the application of Laing Homes Ltd) v Buckinghamshire CC [2003] EWHC 1578 (Admin); [2004] 1 P. & C.R. 36; [2003] 3 P.L.R. 60; [2003] 3 E.G.L.R. 69; [2004] J.P.L. 319; [2003] 29 E.G. 119 (C.S.); [2003] N.P.C. 86, QBD (Admin) ..... *Digested,* 04/**3206**: *Applied* 09/3191: *Considered* 17/1860: *Doubted* 10/2754

R. (on the application of Lamb) v Ministry of Justice see R. (on the application of Nicklinson) v Ministry of Justice

R. (on the application of Lauzikas) v Secretary of State for the Home Department; *sub nom* Lauzikas v Secretary of State for the Home Department [2016] EWHC 3215 (Admin); [2017] 1 W.L.R. 1683; [2017] 2 C.M.L.R. 20, QBD (Admin) .... *Digested,* 17/**1202**

R. (on the application of LB) v Independent Appeal Panel of Newport City Council [2017] EWHC 2216 (Admin); [2017] E.L.R. 646, QBD (Admin)

R. (on the application of Leckhampton Green Land Action Group Ltd) v Tewkesbury BC [2017] EWHC 198 (Admin); [2017] Env. L.R. 28, QBD (Admin) .... *Digested,* 17/**1770**

R. (on the application of Lee Valley Regional Park Authority) v Epping Forest DC [2016] EWCA Civ 404; [2016] Env. L.R. 30; [2016] J.P.L. 1009, CA (Civ Div) .... *Digested,* 16/**1735**: *Followed* 17/1758

R. (on the application of Lee-Hirons) v Secretary of State for Justice; *sub nom* Lee-Hirons v Secretary of State for Justice [2016] UKSC 46; [2017] A.C. 52; [2016] 3 W.L.R. 590; [2017] 3 All E.R. 97; (2016) 19 C.C.L. Rep. 383; [2016] Med. L.R. 551; (2016) 151 B.M.L.R. 1; [2017] M.H.L.R. 57; Times, September 1, 2016, SC .... *Digested,* 16/**1507**

R. (on the application of Lensbury Ltd) v Richmond Upon Thames LBC [2016] EWCA Civ 814; [2017] J.P.L. 96, CA (Civ Div) .... *Digested,* 17/**1760**

R. (on the application of Lensbury Ltd) v Richmond Upon Thames LBC [2016] EWHC 980 (Admin); [2016] Env. L.R. 29, QBD (Admin) .... *Digested,* 16/**1684**: *Reversed* 17/1760

R. (on the application of Lewis) v Redcar and Cleveland BC [2010] UKSC 11; [2010] 2 A.C. 70; [2010] 2 W.L.R. 653; [2010] 2 All E.R. 613; [2010] B.L.G.R. 295; [2010] 2 P. & C.R. 16; [2010] 1 E.G.L.R. 153; Times, March 4, 2010; [2010] J.P.L. 1135; [2010] 10 E.G. 116 (C.S.); (2010) 160 N.L.J. 390; (2010) 154(9) S.J.L.B. 30; [2010] N.P.C. 27, SC .... *Digested,* 10/**2754**: *Applied* 14/2526: *Followed* 12/2729, 17/1860

R. (on the application of Lewisham LBC) v Assessment and Qualifications Alliance (AQA) [2013] EWHC 211 (Admin); [2013] E.L.R. 281; [2013] A.C.D. 52; [2013] P.T.S.R. D18, QBD (Admin) .... *Digested,* 13/**853**: *Applied* 17/2087

R. (on the application of LF) v HM Senior Coroner for Inner South London see R. (on the application of Ferreira) v HM Senior Coroner for Inner South London

R. (on the application of Lidl Ltd) v Central Arbitration Committee [2016] EWHC 2040 (Admin); [2016] I.R.L.R. 756, QBD (Admin) .... *Digested,* 16/**655**: *Affirmed* 17/765

R. (on the application of Lidl Ltd) v Central Arbitration Committee [2017] EWCA Civ 328; [2017] I.C.R. 1145; [2017] I.R.L.R. 646, CA (Civ Div) .... *Digested,* 17/**765**

R. (on the application of Lim) v Secretary of State for the Home Department [2006] EWHC 3004 (Admin), QBD (Admin) *Followed* 17/1243: *Reversed* 08/2091

R. (on the application of Lin) v Barnet LBC see R. (on the application of Mei Ling Lin) v Barnet LBC

R. (on the application of Lisle-Mainwaring) v Kensington and Chelsea RLBC [2017] EWHC 904 (Admin); [2017] P.T.S.R. 850; [2017] J.P.L. 940; [2017] A.C.D. 74, QBD (Admin) .... *Digested,* 17/**1747**

R. (on the application of Liverpool City Council) v Hillingdon LBC [2009] EWCA Civ 43; [2009] P.T.S.R. 1067; [2009] 1 F.L.R. 1536; [2009] 3 F.C.R. 46; [2009] B.L.G.R. 289; (2009) 12 C.C.L. Rep. 286; Times, February 13, 2009; [2009] Fam. Law 394, CA (Civ Div) .... *Digested,* 09/**2653**: *Applied* 14/2148, 17/2053

R. (on the application of Liverpool City Council) v Secretary of State for Health; *sub nom* Liverpool City Council v Secretary of State for Health [2017] EWHC 986 (Admin); [2017] P.T.S.R. 1564; [2017] C.O.P.L.R. 295; (2017) 20 C.C.L. Rep. 391; [2017] A.C.D. 80, QBD (Admin) .... *Digested,* 17/**1539**

R. (on the application of Loader) v Rother DC [2016] EWCA Civ 795; [2017] J.P.L. 25, CA (Civ Div) .... *Digested,* 17/**1768**

R. (on the application of Loader) v Rother DC [2015] EWHC 1877 (Admin), QBD (Admin) *Reversed* 17/1768

R. (on the application of Loader) v Secretary of State for Communities and Local Government [2012] EWCA Civ 869; [2013] P.T.S.R. 406; [2012] 3 C.M.L.R. 29; [2013] Env. L.R. 7; [2012] B.L.G.R. 862; [2012] J.P.L. 1509, CA (Civ Div) .... *Digested,* 12/**2548**: *Applied* 15/1987: *Considered* 13/2344, 13/2365: *Followed* 14/2431, 14/2434, 15/2041, 17/1778

R. (on the application of Lonnie) v National College for Teaching and Leadership [2014] EWHC 4351 (Admin), QBD (Admin)
Applied 17/718

R. (on the application of Lord Carlile of Berriew QC) v Secretary of State for the Home Department; *sub nom* Lord Carlile of Berriew v Secretary of State for the Home Department [2014] UKSC 60; [2015] A.C. 945; [2014] 3 W.L.R. 1404; [2015] 2 All E.R. 453; [2015] H.R.L.R. 1; 38 B.H.R.C. 193, SC .... *Digested,* 15/**1295**:
Applied 16/1123, 16/631: *Considered* 17/1231: *Followed* 16/1076

R. (on the application of Lord) v Secretary of State for the Home Department [2003] EWHC 2073 (Admin); [2004] Prison L.R. 65, QBD (Admin)
Applied 17/1171: *Considered* 14/2162

R. (on the application of Lowden) v Gateshead Magistrates' Court [2016] EWHC 3536 (Admin); [2017] 4 W.L.R. 43; [2017] 2 Cr. App. R. 1; [2017] Crim. L.R. 487, DC *Digested,* 17/**621**

R. (on the application of Lucas) v Oldham MBC [2017] EWHC 349 (Admin); [2017] J.P.L. 804, QBD (Admin) .... *Digested,* 17/**1761**

R. (on the application of Lumba) v Secretary of State for the Home Department; *sub nom* Abdi v Secretary of State for the Home Department; Ashori v Secretary of State for the Home Department; Madami v Secretary of State for the Home Department; Mighty v Secretary of State for the Home Department; Lumba v Secretary of State for the Home Department; R. (on the application of WL (Congo)) v Secretary of State for the Home Department; R. (on the application of KM (Jamaica)) v Secretary of State for the Home Department; *joined case* R. (on the application of Mighty) v Secretary of State for the Home Department [2011] UKSC 12; [2012] 1 A.C. 245; [2011] 2 W.L.R. 671; [2011] 4 All E.R. 1; [2011] U.K.H.R.R. 437; Times, March 24, 2011; (2011) 108(14) L.S.G. 20; (2011) 155(12) S.J.L.B. 30, SC .... *Digested,* 11/**1727**:
Applied 11/1733, 14/1680, 14/2766, 15/1737, 16/1100, 17/192:
Considered 14/1682, 15/3151, 16/1101, 16/1409, 16/2141: *Followed* 12/1712, 13/1601, 13/1602, 14/2234, 14/842, 15/1307, 15/1331, 15/1332, 15/1735, 16/1097, 16/1507, 17/1560, 17/2087, 17/571

R. (on the application of M (A Child)) v Secretary of State for the Home Department (Unaccompanied Children: Art.17 Dublin Regulation: Remedies) [2017] UKUT 124 (IAC); [2017] Imm. A.R. 1097, UT (IAC)

R. (on the application of M) v Commissioner of Police of the Metropolis see R. (on the application of Hicks) v Commissioner of Police of the Metropolis

R. (on the application of M) v Croydon LBC see M v Croydon LBC

R. (on the application of M) v Hammersmith Magistrates' Court [2017] EWHC 1359 (Admin); [2017] A.C.D. 86, DC

R. (on the application of M) v Human Fertilisation and Embryology Authority; *sub nom* R. (on the application of IM) v Human Fertilisation and Embryology Authority [2016] EWCA Civ 611; [2017] 4 W.L.R. 130; [2017] 3 All E.R. 77; [2017] 1 F.L.R. 452; (2016) 151 B.M.L.R. 18; [2016] Fam. Law 1094, CA (Civ Div) .... *Digested,* 16/**946**

R. (on the application of M) v Lambeth LBC see R. (on the application of A) v Croydon LBC

R. (on the application of M) v Secretary of State for Work and Pensions [2008] UKHL 63; [2009] 1 A.C. 311; [2008] 3 W.L.R. 1023; [2009] 2 All E.R. 556; [2009] P.T.S.R. 336; [2009] H.R.L.R. 5; [2009] U.K.H.R.R. 117; 26 B.H.R.C. 587; Times, October 27, 2008, HL .... *Digested,* 08/**3527**:
Applied 09/1737, 09/2544: *Considered* 15/2342, 16/2417, 16/736, 17/1182:
Followed 10/2314, 13/2885, 17/1645

R. (on the application of M) v Slough BC [2008] UKHL 52; [2008] 1 W.L.R. 1808; [2008] 4 All E.R. 831; [2008] H.L.R. 44; [2008] B.L.G.R. 871; (2008) 11 C.C.L. Rep. 733; Times, September 5, 2008; (2008) 152(32) S.J.L.B. 30; [2008] N.P.C. 94, HL .... *Digested,* 08/**2090**:
Applied 12/3175: *Considered* 16/2002, 17/2047: *Followed* 10/3186, 11/3213, 13/2951, 16/2012

R. (on the application of MA (Eritrea)) v Secretary of State for the Home Department see R. (on the application of EM (Eritrea)) v Secretary of State for the Home Department

R. (on the application of MA (Pakistan)) v Upper Tribunal (Immigration and Asylum Chamber); *joined cases* AZ (Pakistan) v Secretary of State for the Home Department; CW (Sri Lanka) v Secretary of State for the Home Department; AR (Sri Lanka) v Secretary of State for the Home Department; NS (Sri Lanka) v Secretary of State for the Home Department; Pereira v Secretary of State for the Home Department [2016] EWCA Civ 705; [2016] 1 W.L.R. 5093; [2017] Imm. A.R. 53; [2017] I.N.L.R. 47, CA (Civ Div) .... *Digested,* 17/**1242**:
Followed 17/1235

R. (on the application of MA) v Secretary of State for Work and Pensions [2014] EWCA Civ 13; [2014] P.T.S.R. 584; [2014] Eq. L.R. 426; [2014] H.L.R. 19, CA (Civ Div) .... *Digested,* 14/**2757**:
Applied 15/2343: *Considered* 15/3159: *Followed* 16/1982: *Reversed in part* 17/2030

R. (on the application of MA) v Secretary of State for Work and Pensions see R. (on the application of Carmichael) v Secretary of State for Work and Pensions

R. (on the application of Mackay) v Secretary of State for Justice see R. (on the application of McLuckie) v Secretary of State for Justice

R. (on the application of Maguire) v Assistant Coroner for West Yorkshire (Eastern Area) [2017] EWHC 2039 (Admin); [2017] A.C.D. 118, QBD (Admin)

R. (on the application of Majid) v Secretary of State for the Home Department see R. (on the application of MM (Lebanon)) v Secretary of State for the Home Department

R. (on the application of Malik) v Manchester Crown Court; *sub nom* Malik v Manchester Crown Court [2008] EWHC 1362 (Admin); [2008] 4 All E.R. 403; [2008] E.M.L.R. 19; [2008] U.K.H.R.R. 1151, DC .... *Digested,* 08/**408**:
Applied 10/418, 10/763, 14/799, 16/1776, 17/356: *Considered* 09/2489, 17/291

R. (on the application of Mandic-Bozic) v British Association for Counselling and Psychotherapy [2016] EWHC 3134 (Admin); (2017) 154 B.M.L.R. 159, QBD (Admin) .... *Digested,* 17/**1806**

R. (on the application of Mann) v Somerset CC [2017] 4 W.L.R. 170, QBD (Admin)
Applied 16/1833

R. (on the application of Martin) v Secretary of State for Work and Pensions see R. (on the application of Hooper) v Secretary of State for Work and Pensions

R. (on the application of Massey) v Secretary of State for Justice see R. (on the application of Kaiyam) v Secretary of State for Justice

R. (on the application of Master AF) v Secretary of State for the Home Department see R. (on the application of MM (Lebanon)) v Secretary of State for the Home Department

R. (on the application of Mauritius Hindu Association) v Durham CC [2016] EWHC 3130 (Admin); [2017] R.V.R. 109, QBD (Admin)

R. (on the application of Maxwell) v Wiltshire Council [2011] EWHC 1840 (Admin), QBD (Admin)
Applied 17/1748

R. (on the application of Mazarona Properties Ltd) v Financial Ombudsman Service [2017] EWHC 1135 (Admin); [2017] A.C.D. 94, QBD (Admin)

R. (on the application of McLuckie) v Secretary of State for Justice; *joined case* R. (on the application of Mackay) v Secretary of State for Justice [2011] EWCA Civ 522, CA (Civ Div)
Applied 12/2324, 17/1480

R. (on the application of Medical Justice) v Secretary of State for the Home Department [2017] EWHC 2461 (Admin); [2017] 4 W.L.R. 198; [2018] 1 All E.R. 400; [2017] A.C.D. 131, QBD (Admin)

R. (on the application of Medical Justice) v Secretary of State for the Home Department [2010] EWHC 1925 (Admin), QBD (Admin)
Considered 17/1539

R. (on the application of Mehanne) v Westminster Housing Benefit Review Board; *sub nom* Mehanne v Westminster Housing Benefit Review Board; R. v Westminster Housing Benefit Review Board Ex p. Mehanne [2000] 1 W.L.R. 16; [1999] 2 All E.R. 317; (2000) 32 H.L.R. 35; Independent, January 11, 1999; [1999] N.P.C. 2, CA (Civ Div) .... *Digested,* 99/**4550**:
Affirmed 01/5016: *Considered* 17/2031

R. (on the application of Mehanne) v Westminster Housing Benefit Review Board; *sub nom* Mehanne v Westminster Housing Benefit Review Board; R. v Westminster Housing Benefit Review Board Ex p. Mehanne [2001] UKHL 11; [2001] 1 W.L.R. 539; [2001] 2 All E.R. 690; (2001) 33 H.L.R. 46; Independent, April 30, 2001; [2001] N.P.C. 51, HL .... *Digested,* 01/**5016**:
Followed 17/2031

R. (on the application of Mehmood) v Secretary of State for the Home Department see R. (on the application of Ali) v Secretary of State for the Home Department

R. (on the application of Mei Ling Lin) v Barnet LBC; *sub nom* R. (on the application of Lin) v Barnet LBC; *joined case* Hassan v Barnet LBC [2007] EWCA Civ 132; [2007] H.L.R. 30; [2007] B.L.G.R. 454; (2007) 104(10) L.S.G. 28; (2007) 151 S.J.L.B. 297, CA (Civ Div)
Followed 17/1153, 17/1154

R. (on the application of Merck Sharp & Dohme Ltd) v Licensing Authority [2005] EWHC 710 (Admin); [2005] Eu. L.R. 797, QBD (Admin) .... *Digested*, 06/**2466**: *Applied* 17/1137

R. (on the application of Merida Oil Traders Ltd) v Central Criminal Court; *sub nom* R. (on the application of Bunnvale Ltd) v Central Criminal Court [2017] EWHC 747 (Admin); [2017] 1 W.L.R. 3680; [2017] Lloyd's Rep. F.C. 313; [2017] A.C.D. 68, DC .... *Digested*, 17/**559**

R. (on the application of MH) v NHS [2015] EWHC 4243 (Admin); (2016) 19 C.C.L. Rep. 592, QBD (Admin) .... *Digested*, 17/**1097**

R. (on the application of MH) v Special Educational Needs and Disability Tribunal; *sub nom* H v Special Educational Needs and Disability Tribunal [2004] EWCA Civ 770; [2004] B.L.G.R. 844; [2004] E.L.R. 424; Times, July 8, 2004; (2004) 101(29) L.S.G. 29; (2004) 148 S.J.L.B. 792, CA (Civ Div) .... *Digested*, 04/**1079**: *Applied* 17/709: *Considered* 04/1085, 05/1145, 11/982: *Distinguished* 13/906

R. (on the application of Miah) v Independent Police Complaints Commission [2016] EWHC 3310 (Admin); [2017] A.C.D. 29, QBD (Admin)

R. (on the application of Miah) v Secretary of State for the Home Department [2016] UKUT 23 (IAC), UT (IAC) *Considered* 17/1243

R. (on the application of Middleton) v Bromley Magistrates' Court see R. (on the application of Hicks) v Commissioner of Police of the Metropolis

R. (on the application of Middleton) v HM Coroner for Western Somerset; *sub nom* R. v HM Coroner for Western Somerset Ex p. Middleton; R. (on the application of Middleton) v West Somerset Coroner [2004] UKHL 10; [2004] 2 A.C. 182; [2004] 2 W.L.R. 800; [2004] 2 All E.R. 465; (2004) 168 J.P. 329; [2004] H.R.L.R. 29; [2004] U.K.H.R.R. 501; 17 B.H.R.C. 49; [2004] Lloyd's Rep. Med. 288; (2004) 79 B.M.L.R. 51; [2004] Inquest L.R. 17; Times, March 12, 2004; Independent, March 16, 2004; (2004) 168 J.P.N. 479; (2004) 101(15) L.S.G. 27; (2004) 154 N.L.J. 417; (2004) 148 S.J.L.B. 354, HL .... *Digested*, 04/**37**: *Applied* 05/34, 06/18, 06/2108, 07/27, 08/17, 08/1975, 09/2041, 09/2754, 09/41, 10/1737, 10/19, 10/20, 10/23, 13/37, 14/47: *Considered* 05/17, 06/17, 07/13, 07/28, 07/2980, 09/21, 10/15, 11/2094, 11/29: *Followed* 04/38, 10/17, 15/853, 16/10, 16/13, 16/2228, 17/1593: *Referred to* 13/36

R. (on the application of Middleton) v West Somerset Coroner see R. (on the application of Middleton) v HM Coroner for Western Somerset

R. (on the application of Midlands Co-operative Society Ltd) v Birmingham City Council [2012] EWHC 620 (Admin); [2012] Eu. L.R. 640; [2012] B.L.G.R. 393, QBD (Admin) .... *Digested*, 12/**2563**: *Applied* 17/1812

R. (on the application of Mighty) v Secretary of State for the Home Department see R. (on the application of Lumba) v Secretary of State for the Home Department

R. (on the application of Miller Homes Ltd) v Leeds City Council [2014] EWHC 82 (Admin), QBD (Admin) *Considered* 17/1692

R. (on the application of Miller) v North Yorkshire CC [2009] EWHC 2172 (Admin), QBD (Admin) *Applied* 17/1721

R. (on the application of Miller) v Secretary of State for Exiting the European Union; *joined cases* Agnew's Application for Judicial Review, Re; McCord's Application for Judicial Review, Re [2016] EWHC 2768 (Admin); [2017] 1 All E.R. 158; [2017] 1 C.M.L.R. 34; [2016] H.R.L.R. 23; Times, November 9, 2016; [2016] A.C.D. 134, DC .... *Digested*, 16/**370**: *Affirmed* 17/441

R. (on the application of Miller) v Secretary of State for Exiting the European Union; *joined cases* Agnew's Application for Judicial Review, Re; McCord's Application for Judicial Review, Re [2017] UKSC 5; [2018] A.C. 61; [2017] 2 W.L.R. 583; [2017] 1 All E.R. 593; [2017] N.I. 141; [2017] 2 C.M.L.R. 15; [2017] H.R.L.R. 2; Times, January 25, 2017, SC .... *Digested*, 17/**441**

R. (on the application of Minton Morrill Solicitors) v Lord Chancellor [2017] EWHC 612 (Admin); [2017] H.R.L.R. 5, QBD (Admin) .... *Digested*, 17/**1484**

R. (on the application of Mirza) v Secretary of State for the Home Department see R. (on the application of Iqbal) v Secretary of State for the Home Department

R. (on the application of MK) v Secretary of State for the Home Department [2017] EWHC 1365 (Admin); [2017] Imm. A.R. 1425, QBD (Admin)

R. (on the application of MM (Lebanon)) v Secretary of State for the Home Department; *sub nom* R. (on the application of SJ (Pakistan)) v Secretary of State for the Home Department; R. (on the application of AM (Pakistan)) v Secretary of State for the Home Department; *joined cases* R. (on the application of AF) v Secretary of State for the Home Department; R. (on the application of Javed) v Secretary of State for the Home Department; R. (on the application of Majid) v Secretary of State for the Home Department [2017] UKSC 10; [2017] 1 W.L.R. 771; [2017] H.R.L.R. 6; [2017] Imm. A.R. 729; [2017] I.N.L.R. 575; Times, February 28, 2017, SC .... *Digested,* 17/**1207**: *Followed* 17/1223

R. (on the application of MM (Lebanon)) v Secretary of State for the Home Department; *sub nom* R. (on the application of SJ (Pakistan)) v Secretary of State for the Home Department; R. (on the application of AM (Pakistan)) v Secretary of State for the Home Department; *joined cases* R. (on the application of Master AF) v Secretary of State for the Home Department; R. (on the application of Javed) v Secretary of State for the Home Department; R. (on the application of Majid) v Secretary of State for the Home Department [2014] EWCA Civ 985; [2015] 1 W.L.R. 1073; [2014] Imm. A.R. 1207; [2015] I.N.L.R. 22; Times, July 18, 2014; (2014) 158(29) S.J.L.B. 37, CA (Civ Div) .... *Digested,* 14/**1703**: *Considered* 15/1352, 15/1362: *Reversed in part* 17/1207

R. (on the application of MN) v Hackney LBC; *sub nom* MN v Hackney LBC [2013] EWHC 1205 (Admin), QBD (Admin)
Applied 17/2051: *Considered* 14/2805

R. (on the application of Mohamed) v Secretary of State for Foreign and Commonwealth Affairs [2010] EWCA Civ 158; [2011] Q.B. 218; [2010] 3 W.L.R. 554; [2010] 4 All E.R. 177; [2010] C.P. Rep. 28, CA (Civ Div) .... *Digested,* 10/**361**: *Considered* 17/208

R. (on the application of Morgan Grenfell & Co Ltd) v Special Commissioners of Income Tax; *sub nom* R. v Inland Revenue Commissioners Ex p. Morgan Grenfell & Co Ltd; R. v Special Commissioners of Income Tax Ex p. Morgan Grenfell & Co Ltd [2002] UKHL 21; [2003] 1 A.C. 563; [2002] 2 W.L.R. 1299; [2002] 3 All E.R. 1; [2002] S.T.C. 786; [2002] H.R.L.R. 42; 74 T.C. 511; [2002] B.T.C. 223; 4 I.T.L. Rep. 809; Times, May 20, 2002; Independent, May 21, 2002; [2002] S.T.I. 806; (2002) 99(25) L.S.G. 35; (2002) 146 S.J.L.B. 126; [2002] N.P.C. 70, HL .... *Digested,* 02/**4505**: *Applied* 06/839, 08/3863, 11/2172, 17/1289: *Considered* 07/999, 09/4216, 11/2123: *Followed* 14/2973, 15/552

R. (on the application of Morgan Grenfell & Co Ltd) v Special Commissioners of Income Tax; *sub nom* R. v Inland Revenue Commissioners Ex p. Morgan Grenfell & Co Ltd; R. v Special Commissioners of Income Tax Ex p. Morgan Grenfell & Co Ltd [2001] EWCA Civ 329; [2002] 2 W.L.R. 255; [2002] 1 All E.R. 776; [2001] S.T.C. 497; Times, April 17, 2001; Independent, March 15, 2001; [2001] S.T.I. 281; (2001) 98(18) L.S.G. 45; [2000] N.P.C. 54, CA (Civ Div) .... *Digested,* 01/**5313**: *Applied* 06/4304, 17/2152: *Reversed* 02/4505

R. (on the application of Moseley) v Haringey LBC; *sub nom* R. (on the application of Stirling) v Haringey LBC [2014] UKSC 56; [2014] 1 W.L.R. 3947; [2015] 1 All E.R. 495; [2014] P.T.S.R. 1317; [2014] B.L.G.R. 823; [2015] R.V.R. 93; Times, November 5, 2014, SC .... *Digested,* 14/**2087**: *Applied* 16/2206, 16/608: *Considered* 16/1707: *Distinguished* 15/2397: *Followed* 15/1956, 16/615, 16/989, 17/1464, 17/1717

R. (on the application of Mott) v Environment Agency [2016] EWCA Civ 564; [2016] 1 W.L.R. 4338; [2017] Env. L.R. 1; [2016] L.L.R. 649, CA (Civ Div) .... *Digested,* 16/**967**

R. (on the application of Mount Cook Land Ltd) v Westminster City Council; *sub nom* Mount Cook Land Ltd v Westminster City Council [2003] EWCA Civ 1346; [2017] P.T.S.R. 1166; [2004] C.P. Rep. 12; [2004] 2 Costs L.R. 211; [2004] 2 P. & C.R. 22; [2004] 1 P.L.R. 29; Times, October 16, 2003; [2004] J.P.L. 470; [2003] 43 E.G. 137 (C.S.); (2003) 147 S.J.L.B. 1272; [2003] N.P.C. 117, CA (Civ Div) .... *Digested,* 04/**367**: *Applied* 04/1387, 09/3039, 14/366, 15/2022: *Considered* 05/3307, 06/417, 07/402, 07/489, 10/2611: *Distinguished* 08/321: *Followed* 17/10

R. (on the application of MR (Pakistan)) v Upper Tribunal see R. (on the application of Cart) v Upper Tribunal

R. (on the application of MR) v Secretary of State for the Home Department [2017] EWHC 469 (Admin); [2017] A.C.D. 58, DC

R. (on the application of MR) v Secretary of State for the Home Department [2016] EWHC 1622 (Admin); [2016] 3 C.M.L.R. 42, QBD (Admin) .... *Digested,* 17/**442**: *Applied* 16/35

R. (on the application of Munir) v Secretary of State for the Home Department see R. (on the application of Abbassi) v Secretary of State for the Home Department

R. (on the application of Munjaz) v Ashworth Hospital Authority (now Mersey Care NHS Trust) see R. (on the application of Munjaz) v Mersey Care NHS Trust

R. (on the application of Munjaz) v Mersey Care NHS Trust; *sub nom* Munjaz v Mersey Care NHS Trust; S v Airedale NHS Trust; R. (on the application of Colonel M) v Ashworth Hospital Authority (now Mersey Care NHS Trust); R. (on the application of Munjaz) v Ashworth Hospital Authority (now Mersey Care NHS Trust); *joined case* R. (on the application of S) v Airedale NHS Trust (Appeal) [2005] UKHL 58; [2006] 2 A.C. 148; [2005] 3 W.L.R. 793; [2006] 4 All E.R. 736; [2005] H.R.L.R. 42; [2006] Lloyd's Rep. Med. 1; (2005) 86 B.M.L.R. 84; [2005] M.H.L.R. 276; Times, October 18, 2005; Independent, October 18, 2005, HL .... *Digested,* 05/**2829**:
Applied 12/2337, 13/2023, 16/1118, 17/1596: *Considered* 15/3220:
Followed 13/2066, 17/1108

R. (on the application of Murrell) v Secretary of State for Communities and Local Government see Murrell v Secretary of State for Communities and Local Government

R. (on the application of Mynydd y Gwynt Ltd) v Secretary of State for Business, Energy and Industrial Strategy [2016] EWHC 2581 (Admin); [2017] Env. L.R. 14, QBD (Admin) .... *Digested,* 17/**1786**

R. (on the application of N) v Lewisham LBC; *sub nom* R. (on the application of CN) v Lewisham LBC; R. (on the application of ZH) v Newham LBC; *joined case* R. (on the application of H (A Child)) v Newham LBC [2014] UKSC 62; [2015] A.C. 1259; [2014] 3 W.L.R. 1548; [2015] 1 All E.R. 783; [2015] H.L.R. 6; [2014] B.L.G.R. 842; [2015] 1 P. & C.R. 13; Times, December 1, 2014; (2014) 158(45) S.J.L.B. 37, SC .... *Digested,* 15/**1290**:
Considered 17/2679: *Followed* 17/562

R. (on the application of N) v Secretary of State for the Home Department [2009] EWHC 1581 (Admin), QBD (Admin)
Explained 17/1209

R. (on the application of Nadarajah) v Secretary of State for the Home Department; *sub nom* Nadarajah v Secretary of State for the Home Department; Abdi v Secretary of State for the Home Department; *joined case* R. (on the application of Abdi) v Secretary of State for the Home Department [2005] EWCA Civ 1363; Times, December 14, 2005, CA (Civ Div) .... *Digested,* 06/**2224**:
Applied 07/57, 09/3052, 11/2138: *Considered* 12/999: *Followed* 17/2126

R. (on the application of Nadarajah) v Secretary of State for the Home Department see R. (on the application of Razgar) v Secretary of State for the Home Department (No.2)

R. (on the application of Napp Pharmaceuticals Ltd) v Secretary of State for Health [2016] EWHC 1982 (Admin); (2016) 152 B.M.L.R. 172; [2016] A.C.D. 110, QBD (Admin) .... *Digested,* 17/**1137**

R. (on the application of Nash) v Chelsea College of Art and Design [2001] EWHC 538 (Admin); Times, July 25, 2001, QBD (Admin) .... *Digested,* 01/**95**:
Applied 05/3281, 09/3038: *Approved* 17/1231: *Considered* 05/2910, 10/3180, 14/56

R. (on the application of Nasseri) v Secretary of State for the Home Department; *sub nom* Secretary of State for the Home Department v Nasseri; Nasseri v Secretary of State for the Home Department [2009] UKHL 23; [2010] 1 A.C. 1; [2009] 2 W.L.R. 1190; [2009] 3 All E.R. 774; [2009] H.R.L.R. 24; [2009] U.K.H.R.R. 1481; [2009] Imm. A.R. 772; [2009] I.N.L.R. 418; Times, May 7, 2009, HL .... *Digested,* 09/**2089**:
Considered 17/1231: *Followed* 15/1581

R. (on the application of National Aids Trust) v NHS Commissioning Board (NHS England) see National Aids Trust v NHS Commissioning Board (NHS England)

R. (on the application of National Union of Journalists) v Central Arbitration Committee [2005] EWCA Civ 1309; [2006] I.C.R. 1; [2006] I.R.L.R. 53; Times, July 29, 2005; [2006] A.C.D. 24, CA (Civ Div) .... *Digested,* 06/**1375**:
Distinguished 13/1057: *Followed* 17/766

R. (on the application of Naylor) v Secretary of State for Work and Pensions see R. (on the application of Hooper) v Secretary of State for Work and Pensions

R. (on the application of Nealon) v Secretary of State for Justice; *joined case* R. (on the application of Hallam) v Secretary of State for Justice [2016] EWCA Civ 355; [2017] Q.B. 571; [2016] 3 W.L.R. 329; [2016] 2 Cr. App. R. 11; Times, May 5, 2016; [2016] Crim. L.R. 772, CA (Civ Div) .... *Digested,* 16/**541**

R. (on the application of Network Rail Infrastructure Ltd) v Secretary of State for the Environment, Food and Rural Affairs; *sub nom* Network Rail Infrastructure Ltd v Secretary of State for the Environment, Food and Rural Affairs [2017] EWHC 2259 (Admin); [2017] P.T.S.R. 1662; (2018) 34 Const. L.J. 126, QBD (Admin)

R. (on the application of Newby Foods Ltd) v Food Standards Agency [2017] EWCA Civ 400; [2017] C.T.L.C. 157, CA (Civ Div)

R. (on the application of Newcastle United Football Club Ltd) v Revenue and Customs Commissioners [2017] EWHC 2402 (Admin); [2017] 4 W.L.R. 187; [2018] S.T.C. 103; [2017] Lloyd's Rep. F.C. 604; [2017] B.V.C. 44; [2017] A.C.D. 129; [2017] S.T.I. 2181, DC .... *Digested,* 17/**624**

R. (on the application of Newham LBC) v Stratford Magistrates' Court [2008] EWHC 125 (Admin); (2009) 172 J.P. 30; [2008] R.A. 108, QBD (Admin) .... *Digested,* 09/**2616**: *Considered* 17/1506

R. (on the application of Newhaven Port and Properties Ltd) v East Sussex CC; *sub nom* R. (on the application of Newhaven Port and Properties Ltd) v Secretary of State for the Environment, Food and Rural Affairs [2015] UKSC 7; [2015] A.C. 1547; [2015] 2 W.L.R. 601; [2015] 2 All E.R. 991; [2015] B.L.G.R. 232; [2015] 2 P. & C.R. 7, SC .... *Digested,* 15/**2128**: *Applied* 16/1834: *Followed* 16/1824, 17/1860

R. (on the application of Newhaven Port and Properties Ltd) v Secretary of State for the Environment, Food and Rural Affairs see R. (on the application of Newhaven Port and Properties Ltd) v East Sussex CC

R. (on the application of Newsmith Stainless Ltd) v Secretary of State for the Environment, Transport and the Regions [2001] EWHC 527 (Admin); [2017] P.T.S.R. 1126, QBD (Admin)
Applied 07/3223, 11/2551, 15/1989, 15/2050: *Considered* 15/1946, 16/1743

R. (on the application of NHS Property Services Ltd) v Surrey CC [2016] EWHC 1715 (Admin); [2016] 4 W.L.R. 130; [2017] J.P.L. 59, QBD (Admin) .... *Digested,* 16/**1834**

R. (on the application of Niazi) v Secretary of State for the Home Department; *joined case* R. (on the application of Bhatt Murphy (A Firm)) v Independent Assessor [2008] EWCA Civ 755; Times, July 21, 2008; (2008) 152(29) S.J.L.B. 29, CA (Civ Div) .... *Digested,* 08/**70**: *Applied* 11/2138, 12/2588, 13/853, 15/62, 16/2206: *Considered* 09/1598, 09/1738, 10/2162, 13/2016, 13/2393: *Followed* 11/63, 11/64, 12/914, 16/39, 17/2087

R. (on the application of Nicklinson) v Ministry of Justice; *sub nom* Nicklinson v Ministry of Justice; *joined cases* R. (on the application of Lamb) v Ministry of Justice; R. (on the application of AM) v DPP [2014] UKSC 38; [2015] A.C. 657; [2014] 3 W.L.R. 200; [2014] 3 All E.R. 843; [2014] 3 F.C.R. 1; [2014] H.R.L.R. 17; 36 B.H.R.C. 465; (2014) 139 B.M.L.R. 1; Times, June 26, 2014, SC .... *Digested,* 14/**672**: *Considered* 16/938, 17/564: *Explained* 16/463: *Followed* 15/1202

R. (on the application of Noble Organisation Ltd) v Thanet DC [2005] EWCA Civ 782; [2006] Env. L.R. 8; [2006] 1 P. & C.R. 13; Times, August 26, 2005; [2006] J.P.L. 60; [2005] N.P.C. 86, CA (Civ Div) .... *Digested,* 05/**3270**: *Applied* 06/3364: *Considered* 13/1964, 15/2041: *Followed* 17/1785

R. (on the application of Nottingham City Council) v Bus Lane Adjudicator [2017] EWHC 430 (Admin); [2017] A.C.D. 56, QBD (Admin)

R. (on the application of Novartis Pharmaceuticals UK Ltd) v Licensing Authority (C-106/01) EU:C:2004:245; [2004] E.C.R. I-4403; [2004] 2 C.M.L.R. 26; [2005] All E.R. (EC) 192; (2005) 81 B.M.L.R. 200, ECJ (6th Chamber) .... *Digested,* 04/**1697**: *Applied* 06/2466, 17/1137

R. (on the application of NS) v Secretary of State for the Home Department (C-411/10); *sub nom* ME v Refugee Applications Commissioner (C-493/10); NS v Secretary of State for the Home Department (C-411/10); *joined case* E v Refugee Applications Commissioner (C-493/10) EU:C:2011:865; [2013] Q.B. 102; [2012] 3 W.L.R. 1374; [2012] 2 C.M.L.R. 9; [2012] All E.R. (EC) 1011; (2012) 109(29) L.S.G. 26, ECJ (Grand Chamber) .... *Digested,* 12/**1698**: *Applied* 14/1672, 16/1066: *Considered* 13/1577, 17/2663: *Explained* 14/1652: *Followed* 13/1578

R. (on the application of Nwachuku) v General Medical Council see General Medical Council v Nwachuku

R. (on the application of O'Connor) v Aldershot Magistrates' Court [2016] EWHC 2792 (Admin); [2017] 1 W.L.R. 2833; (2017) 181 J.P. 117, DC .... *Digested,* 17/**18**

R. (on the application of O) v Lambeth LBC [2016] EWHC 937 (Admin); (2016) 19 C.C.L. Rep. 626; [2016] A.C.D. 96, QBD (Admin) .... *Digested,* 17/**2051**

R. (on the application of O) v Peterborough City Council [2016] EWHC 2717 (Admin); (2016) 19 C.C.L. Rep. 548, QBD (Admin) .... *Digested,* 17/**947**

R. (on the application of Omar) v Chief Constable of Bedfordshire; *sub nom* Omar v Chief Constable of Bedfordshire [2002] EWHC 3060 (Admin); [2002] Po. L.R. 413; Independent, February 24, 2003; [2003] A.C.D. 55, DC
Considered 17/621

R. (on the application of Omar) v Secretary of State for the Home Department [2012] EWHC 3448 (Admin); [2013] Imm. A.R. 601, QBD (Admin) .... *Digested,* 13/**1629**: *Considered* 17/1231

R. (on the application of Oriaku) v Nursing and Midwifery Council [2017] EWHC 235 (Admin); [2017] Med. L.R. 207, QBD (Admin) .... *Digested,* 17/**1135**

R. (on the application of Osborn) v Parole Board see Reilly's Application for Judicial Review, Re

R. (on the application of Owusu-Yianoma) v Chief Constable of Leicestershire [2017] EWHC 576 (Admin); [2017] A.C.D. 48, DC

R. (on the application of Oxfordshire and Buckinghamshire Mental Health NHS Foundation Trust) v Oxfordshire CC [2010] EWHC 530 (Admin); [2010] B.L.G.R. 631; [2010] 2 E.G.L.R. 171; [2010] J.P.L. 1106; [2010] 14 E.G. 108 (C.S.), QBD (Admin) .... *Digested,* 10/**2755**: *Applied* 17/1860

R. (on the application of P) v General Dental Council; *sub nom* DP v General Dental Council [2016] EWHC 3181 (Admin); [2017] 4 W.L.R. 14; (2017) 154 B.M.L.R. 217; [2017] A.C.D. 10, QBD (Admin) .... *Digested,* 17/**1104**

R. (on the application of P) v Mersey Care NHS Trust [2003] EWHC 994 (Admin); [2004] M.H.L.R. 107, QBD (Admin)
Approved 17/1545

R. (on the application of P) v Secretary of State for the Home Department; *joined cases* Kroll v Commissioner of Police of the Metropolis; R. (on the application of W) v Secretary of State for Justice; R. (on the application of G) v Secretary of State for the Home Department [2017] EWCA Civ 321; [2017] 2 Cr. App. R. 12, CA (Civ Div) .... *Digested,* 17/**1586**

R. (on the application of Pal) v General Medical Council [2009] EWHC 1061 (Admin), QBD (Admin)
Applied 17/1135

R. (on the application of Palestine Solidarity Campaign Ltd) v Secretary of State for Communities and Local Government [2017] EWHC 1502 (Admin); [2017] 1 W.L.R. 4611; [2017] Pens. L.R. 17, QBD (Admin) .... *Digested,* 17/**1090**

R. (on the application of Palmer) v Herefordshire Council; *sub nom* Palmer v Herefordshire Council [2016] EWCA Civ 1061; [2017] 1 W.L.R. 411, CA (Civ Div) .... *Digested,* 17/**1751**

R. (on the application of Palmer) v Herefordshire Council; *sub nom* Palmer v Herefordshire Council [2015] EWHC 2688 (Admin), QBD (Admin)
Affirmed 17/1751

R. (on the application of Parmak) v Secretary of State for the Home Department [2006] EWHC 244 (Admin); [2006] 2 C.M.L.R. 56, QBD (Admin) .... *Digested,* 06/**2279**: *Applied* 07/2282, 17/1230

R. (on the application of PC) v Hertfordshire CC see R. (on the application of T) v Hertfordshire CC

R. (on the application of PE (Cameroon)) v Secretary of State for the Home Department; *sub nom* PE (Cameroon) v Secretary of State for the Home Department; *joined case* R. (on the application of BA (Nigeria)) v Secretary of State for the Home Department [2009] UKSC 7; [2010] 1 A.C. 444; [2009] 3 W.L.R. 1253; [2010] 2 All E.R. 95; [2010] Imm. A.R. 363; [2010] I.N.L.R. 307; Times, December 1, 2009; (2009) 153(46) S.J.L.B. 33, SC .... *Digested,* 10/**1778**: *Considered* 11/1716, 14/1679, 17/1220

R. (on the application of Pearce) v Commissioner of Police of the Metropolis see R. (on the application of Hicks) v Commissioner of Police of the Metropolis

R. (on the application of Philip Morris Brands Sarl) v Secretary of State for Health (C-547/14); *sub nom* Philip Morris Brands Sarl v Secretary of State for Health (C-547/14) EU:C:2016:325; [2017] Q.B. 327; [2016] 3 W.L.R. 973; [2016] E.T.M.R. 36, ECJ (2nd Chamber) .... *Digested,* 16/**783**: *Followed* 16/326

R. (on the application of Philip Morris Brands Sarl) v Secretary of State for Health see R. (on the application of British American Tobacco UK Ltd) v Secretary of State for Health

R. (on the application of Pitt) v General Pharmaceutical Council [2017] EWHC 809 (Admin); (2017) 156 B.M.L.R. 222, QBD (Admin) .... *Digested,* 17/**1138**

R. (on the application of Pitts) v Commissioner of Police of the Metropolis [2017] EWHC 646 (Admin); [2017] A.C.D. 61, QBD (Admin)

R. (on the application of PJSC Rosneft Oil Co) v HM Treasury (C-72/15) EU:C:2017:236; [2018] Q.B. 1; [2017] 3 W.L.R. 1031; [2017] 3 C.M.L.R. 23; [2017] Lloyd's Rep. F.C. 447, ECJ (Grand Chamber)

R. (on the application of Plant) v Lambeth LBC [2016] EWHC 3324 (Admin); [2017] P.T.S.R. 453; [2017] H.L.R. 12; [2017] A.C.D. 30, QBD (Admin) .... *Digested,* 17/**1464**

R. (on the application of Powell) v Marine Management Organisation [2017] EWHC 1491 (Admin); [2017] L.L.R. 808, QBD (Admin)

R. (on the application of Premier Leisure UK Ltd) v Secretary of State for the Environment, Transport and the Regions see R. (on the application of Holding & Barnes Plc) v Secretary of State for the Environment, Transport and the Regions

R. (on the application of Preston) v Lord President of the Council see R. (on the application of Preston) v Wandsworth LBC

R. (on the application of Preston) v Wandsworth LBC; *sub nom* R. (on the application of Preston) v Lord President of the Council [2012] EWCA Civ 1378; [2013] Q.B. 687; [2013] 2 W.L.R. 733; [2013] 1 All E.R. 869; [2013] 1 C.M.L.R. 34; Times, January 11, 2013, CA (Civ Div) .... *Digested,* 13/**932**: *Considered* 16/636, 17/807: *Distinguished* 16/384: *Followed* 16/383

R. (on the application of Privacy International) v Investigatory Powers Tribunal [2017] EWHC 114 (Admin); [2017] 3 All E.R. 1127, DC .... *Digested,* 17/**26**

R. (on the application of Prokopp) v London Underground Ltd [2003] EWCA Civ 961; [2004] Env. L.R. 8; [2004] 1 P. & C.R. 31; Times, August 28, 2003; [2004] J.P.L. 44; (2003) 100(34) L.S.G. 30; (2003) 147 S.J.L.B. 870, CA (Civ Div) .... *Digested,* 03/**3402**: *Applied* 17/1784: *Considered* 15/347

R. (on the application of Proteus Film Partnership No 1) v Revenue and Customs Commissioners see Samarkand Film Partnership No.3 v Revenue and Customs Commissioners

R. (on the application of Proteus Film Partnership No.1) v Revenue and Customs Commissioners see Samarkand Film Partnership No.3 v Revenue and Customs Commissioners

R. (on the application of Prudential Assurance Co Ltd) v Revenue and Customs Commissioners [2017] EWHC 1484 (Admin); [2017] B.T.C. 17, QBD (Admin) ... *Digested,* 17/**2120**

R. (on the application of Public and Commercial Services Union) v Minister for the Cabinet Office; *sub nom* Public and Commercial Services Union v Minister for the Cabinet Office [2017] EWHC 1787 (Admin); [2018] 1 All E.R. 142; [2018] I.C.R. 269; [2017] I.R.L.R. 967; [2017] A.C.D. 105, DC .... *Digested,* 17/**40**

R. (on the application of Public Law Project) v Lord Chancellor see R. (on the application of Public Law Project) v Secretary of State for Justice

R. (on the application of Public Law Project) v Secretary of State for Justice; *sub nom* R. (on the application of Public Law Project) v Lord Chancellor; Public Law Project v Lord Chancellor [2016] UKSC 39; [2016] A.C. 1531; [2016] 3 W.L.R. 387; [2017] 2 All E.R. 423; [2016] H.R.L.R. 17; Times, July 27, 2016, SC .... *Digested,* 16/**1398**

R. (on the application of Purdy) v DPP [2009] UKHL 45; [2010] 1 A.C. 345; [2009] 3 W.L.R. 403; [2009] 4 All E.R. 1147; [2010] 1 Cr. App. R. 1; [2009] H.R.L.R. 32; [2009] U.K.H.R.R. 1104; 27 B.H.R.C. 126; (2009) 12 C.C.L. Rep. 498; [2009] LS Law Medical 479; (2009) 109 B.M.L.R. 153; Times, July 31, 2009; (2009) 179 N.L.J. 1175; (2009) 153(31) S.J.L.B. 28, HL .... *Digested,* 09/**2046**: *Applied* 15/2986: *Considered* 13/619, 14/672, 16/2541, 17/564: *Distinguished* 17/1730: *Followed* 12/1517, 14/799, 16/463

R. (on the application of Quintavalle) v Secretary of State for Health [2003] UKHL 13; [2003] 2 A.C. 687; [2003] 2 W.L.R. 692; [2003] 2 All E.R. 113; [2003] 1 F.C.R. 577; (2003) 71 B.M.L.R. 209; Times, March 14, 2003; Independent, March 18, 2003; (2003) 153 N.L.J. 439, HL .... *Digested,* 04/**3274**: *Applied* 05/823, 08/3840, 08/3921, 09/2604, 14/814: *Considered* 06/699, 09/1737, 13/2487, 14/3752: *Followed* 16/2019, 17/1534, 17/384

R. (on the application of Rahman) v Secretary of State for the Home Department see R. (on the application of Abbassi) v Secretary of State for the Home Department

R. (on the application of Rahmatullah) v Secretary of State for Defence see R. (on the application of Al-Saadoon) v Secretary of State for Defence

R. (on the application of Rahmatullah) v Secretary of State for Defence see Rahmatullah v Ministry of Defence

R. (on the application of Rahmatullah) v Secretary of State for Defence) see R. (on the application of Al-Saadoon) v Secretary of State for Defence

R. (on the application of Rahmdezfouli) v Wood Green Crown Court [2013] EWHC 2998 (Admin); [2014] 1 W.L.R. 1793; [2014] 1 All E.R. 567; [2014] 1 Cr. App. R. 20; (2013) 177 J.P. 677; [2014] Crim. L.R. 158; [2014] A.C.D. 31, DC .... *Digested,* 14/**783**: *Considered* 17/573

R. (on the application of Rathakrishnan) v Secretary of State for the Home Department [2011] EWHC 1406 (Admin), QBD (Admin)
Applied 14/68: *Considered* 17/1231

R. (on the application of Rawlinson and Hunter Trustees) v Central Criminal Court; *joined case* R. (on the application of Tchenguiz) v Director of Serious Fraud Office [2012] EWHC 2254 (Admin); [2013] 1 W.L.R. 1634; [2013] Lloyd's Rep. F.C. 132, DC .... *Digested,* 13/**211**:
Applied 13/764, 14/2467, 14/803, 16/511, 17/624: *Considered* 14/804

R. (on the application of Razgar) v Secretary of State for the Home Department (No.2); *sub nom* Secretary of State for the Home Department v Razgar; *joined cases* R. (on the application of Soumahoro) v Secretary of State for the Home Department; R. (on the application of Nadarajah) v Secretary of State for the Home Department [2004] UKHL 27; [2004] 2 A.C. 368; [2004] 3 W.L.R. 58; [2004] 3 All E.R. 821; [2004] H.R.L.R. 32; [2004] Imm. A.R. 381; [2004] I.N.L.R. 349; [2004] M.H.L.R. 218; Times, June 21, 2004; Independent, June 23, 2004; [2004] A.C.D. 83; (2004) 101(28) L.S.G. 33; (2004) 154 N.L.J. 986; (2004) 148 S.J.L.B. 761, HL .... *Digested,* 04/**2029**:
Applied 05/2181, 05/2192, 06/2229, 06/2233, 06/2244, 06/2245, 06/2286, 07/2301, 07/2307, 07/2340, 08/2036, 10/4329, 12/1293, 12/1707, 17/1212: *Cited* 09/2102: *Considered* 04/839, 05/2179, 05/2213, 05/5431, 07/2295, 10/1809, 10/2322, 11/1711, 12/4097, 15/1374, 15/3149, 15/3160: *Explained* 09/2163: *Followed* 07/2313, 09/2075, 10/1790, 11/1789, 14/1715, 15/1373, 16/1132

R. (on the application of Recycling with Skips Ltd) v Secretary of State for Rural Affairs [2017] EWHC 458 (Admin); [2017] Env. L.R. 27; [2017] A.C.D. 51, QBD (Admin) .... *Digested,* 17/**881**

R. (on the application of Refugee Legal Centre) v Secretary of State for the Home Department [2004] EWCA Civ 1481; [2005] 1 W.L.R. 2219; [2005] I.N.L.R. 236; Times, November 24, 2004; [2005] A.C.D. 52; (2005) 102(1) L.S.G. 16, CA (Civ Div) .... *Digested,* 05/**2155**:
Applied 15/1305, 15/15, 16/1408, 17/1480: *Considered* 14/658, 17/1539: *Followed* 15/1822

R. (on the application of Reilly) v Secretary of State for Work and Pensions; *sub nom* Reilly v Secretary of State for Work and Pensions; *joined case* Jeffrey v Secretary of State for Work and Pensions [2016] EWCA Civ 413; [2017] Q.B. 657; [2016] 3 W.L.R. 1641, CA (Civ Div) .... *Digested,* 17/**2033**:
Applied 17/417

R. (on the application of Reilly) v Secretary of State for Work and Pensions [2013] EWCA Civ 66; [2013] 1 W.L.R. 2239; [2013] 3 All E.R. 67; (2013) 163 N.L.J. 236, CA (Civ Div) .... *Digested,* 13/**2890**:
Followed 17/2033: *Reversed in part* 14/2766

R. (on the application of Reilly) v Secretary of State for Work and Pensions; *sub nom* Reilly v Secretary of State for Work and Pensions; *joined case* Jeffrey v Secretary of State for Work and Pensions [2014] EWHC 2182 (Admin); [2015] Q.B. 573; [2015] 2 W.L.R. 309, QBD (Admin) .... *Digested,* 15/**2348**:
Reversed 17/2033

R. (on the application of Reilly) v Secretary of State for Work and Pensions; *joined case* R. (on the application of Wilson) v Secretary of State for Work and Pensions [2013] UKSC 68; [2014] A.C. 453; [2013] 3 W.L.R. 1276; [2014] 1 All E.R. 505, SC .... *Digested,* 14/**2766**:
Followed 17/2033

R. (on the application of Reis) v Director of Legal Aid Casework *see* R. (on the application of Gudanaviciene) v Director of Legal Aid Casework

R. (on the application of Remedy UK Ltd) v General Medical Council [2010] EWHC 1245 (Admin); [2010] Med. L.R. 330; [2010] A.C.D. 72, DC .... *Digested,* 11/**1534**:
Applied 14/1497, 17/1135

R. (on the application of Reynolds) v Secretary of State for Work and Pensions *see* R. (on the application of Carson) v Secretary of State for Work and Pensions

R. (on the application of Rights of Women) v Lord Chancellor; *sub nom* R. (on the application of Rights of Women) v Secretary of State for Justice [2016] EWCA Civ 91; [2016] 1 W.L.R. 2543; [2016] 3 All E.R. 473; [2017] 1 F.L.R. 615; [2016] 2 F.C.R. 65; [2016] Fam. Law 453, CA (Civ Div) .... *Digested,* 16/**1396**

R. (on the application of Rights of Women) v Secretary of State for Justice *see* R. (on the application of Rights of Women) v Lord Chancellor

R. (on the application of River East Supplies Ltd) v Nottingham Crown Court [2017] EWHC 1942 (Admin); [2017] 4 W.L.R. 135; [2017] C.P. Rep. 43; [2017] 2 Cr. App. R. 27; [2017] Lloyd's Rep. F.C. 482; [2018] Crim. L.R. 172; [2017] A.C.D. 112, DC .... *Digested,* 17/**291**

R. (on the application of RK (Nepal)) v Secretary of State for the Home Department; *sub nom* RK (Nepal) v Secretary of State for the Home Department [2009] EWCA Civ 359; [2010] Imm. A.R. 21; [2010] I.N.L.R. 37; Times, May 11, 2009, CA (Civ Div) .... *Digested,* 09/**2115**:
Applied 16/1124, 17/1243: *Considered* 15/1377: *Followed* 10/1794, 15/1371, 15/1385

R. (on the application of RLT Built Environment Ltd) v Cornwall Council [2016] EWHC 2817 (Admin); [2017] J.P.L. 378; [2017] A.C.D. 16, QBD (Bristol) .... *Digested,* 17/**1730**

R. (on the application of Roberts) v Commissioner of Police of the Metropolis [2015] UKSC 79; [2016] 1 W.L.R. 210; [2016] 2 All E.R. 1005; [2016] 1 Cr. App. R. 19; [2016] H.R.L.R. 5; 41 B.H.R.C. 93; Times, January 4, 2016; [2016] Crim. L.R. 278, SC .... *Digested,* 16/**1785**

R. (on the application of Robinson) v Governor of Whatton Prison see R. (on the application of Kaiyam) v Secretary of State for Justice

R. (on the application of Robinson) v Secretary of State for the Home Department [2016] UKUT 133 (IAC), UT (IAC)
Affirmed 17/1220

R. (on the application of Robinson) v Secretary of State for the Home Department [2017] EWCA Civ 316; [2017] Imm. A.R. 1339; [2017] I.N.L.R. 613, CA (Civ Div) .... *Digested,* 17/**1220**

R. (on the application of Robson) v Crown Prosecution Service [2016] EWHC 2191 (Admin); [2018] 4 W.L.R. 27; [2017] 1 Cr. App. R. 5; (2017) 181 J.P. 37, DC ..... *Digested,* 17/**571**

R. (on the application of Rowe) v Revenue and Customs Commissioners [2015] EWHC 2293 (Admin); [2015] B.T.C. 27, QBD (Admin) .... *Digested,* 15/**2512**:
Applied 16/2115, 17/2079: *Considered* 16/2051, 17/2126: *Referred to* 16/2116

R. (on the application of Royal Society for the Protection of Birds) v Secretary of State for Justice; *sub nom* Royal Society for the Protection of Birds (RSPB) v Secretary of State for Justice [2017] EWHC 2309 (Admin); [2017] 5 Costs L.O. 691; [2018] Env. L.R. 13; [2018] J.P.L. 271; [2017] A.C.D. 126, QBD (Admin) ... *Digested,* 17/**280**

R. (on the application of Rutherford) v Secretary of State for Work and Pensions see R. (on the application of Carmichael) v Secretary of State for Work and Pensions

R. (on the application of Rutherford) v Secretary of State for Work and Pensions see Rutherford v Secretary of State for Work and Pensions

R. (on the application of RWE Npower Renewables Ltd) v Milton Keynes BC [2013] EWHC 751 (Admin), QBD (Admin)
Considered 17/1692

R. (on the application of S (A Child)) v NHS England; *sub nom* S (A Child) v NHS England [2016] EWHC 1395 (Admin); (2016) 19 C.C.L. Rep. 336; [2016] Med. L.R. 329; (2017) 154 B.M.L.R. 114; [2016] A.C.D. 103, QBD (Admin) .... *Digested,* 16/**991**

R. (on the application of S (Albania)) v Waltham Forest LBC [2016] EWHC 1240 (Admin); [2016] H.L.R. 41; [2016] A.C.D. 77, QBD (Admin) .... *Digested,* 17/**1151**

R. (on the application of S) v Airedale NHS Trust (Appeal) see R. (on the application of Munjaz) v Mersey Care NHS Trust

R. (on the application of S) v Chief Constable of the British Transport Police [2013] EWHC 2189 (Admin); [2014] 1 W.L.R. 1647; [2014] 1 All E.R. 268; (2014) 178 J.P. 221; [2014] A.C.D. 19, QBD (Admin) .... *Digested,* 14/**2466**:
Applied 17/624

R. (on the application of S) v Croydon LBC [2017] EWHC 265 (Admin); [2017] P.T.S.R. 744, QBD (Admin) .... *Digested,* 17/**2055**

R. (on the application of S) v Director of Legal Aid Casework; *sub nom* IS v Director of Legal Aid Casework; *joined case* Director of Legal Casework v IS [2016] EWCA Civ 464; [2016] 1 W.L.R. 4733; [2017] 2 All E.R. 642; [2016] 3 Costs L.R. 569; [2016] 2 F.L.R. 392; [2016] Fam. Law 959, CA (Civ Div) .... *Digested,* 16/**1408**

R. (on the application of S) v Director of Legal Aid Casework see R. (on the application of Gudanaviciene) v Director of Legal Aid Casework

R. (on the application of S) v Haringey LBC [2016] EWHC 2692 (Admin); (2016) 19 C.C.L. Rep. 527, QBD (Admin) .... *Digested,* 17/**2052**

R. (on the application of S) v Westminster City Council see R. (on the application of SL) v Westminster City Council

R. (on the application of Samarkand Film Partnership No 3) v Revenue and Customs Commissioners see Samarkand Film Partnership No.3 v Revenue and Customs Commissioners

R. (on the application of Samarkand Film Partnership No.3) v Revenue and Customs Commissioners see Samarkand Film Partnership No.3 v Revenue and Customs Commissioners

R. (on the application of Sambotin) v Brent LBC [2017] EWHC 1190 (Admin); [2017] P.T.S.R. 1154; [2017] H.L.R. 31, QBD (Admin) .... *Digested,* 17/**1149**

R. (on the application of Saunders) v Tendring DC [2003] EWHC 2977 (Admin), QBD (Admin) *Considered* 17/1734

R. (on the application of Savage) v Hillingdon LBC; *sub nom* Savage v Hillingdon LBC [2010] EWHC 88 (Admin); [2010] P.T.S.R. 1859, QBD (Admin) .... *Digested,* 11/**1661**: *Applied* 17/1151

R. (on the application of Save Britain's Heritage) v Liverpool City Council [2016] EWHC 48 (Admin), QBD (Admin) *Affirmed* 17/1773

R. (on the application of Save Britain's Heritage) v Liverpool City Council [2016] EWCA Civ 806; [2017] J.P.L. 39, CA (Civ Div) .... *Digested,* 17/**1773**

R. (on the application of SB) v NHS England [2017] EWHC 2000 (Admin); [2018] P.T.S.R. 576; (2017) 158 B.M.L.R. 117; [2017] A.C.D. 115, QBD (Admin)

R. (on the application of Scarfe) v Governor of Woodhill Prison [2017] EWHC 1194 (Admin); [2017] A.C.D. 92, DC

R. (on the application of Secerno Ltd) v Oxford Magistrates' Court; *sub nom* Secerno Ltd v Oxford Magistrates' Court [2011] EWHC 1009 (Admin); [2011] R.A. 247; [2011] 17 E.G. 71 (C.S.), QBD (Admin) .... *Digested,* 11/**2186**: *Applied* 17/1518

R. (on the application of Secretary of State for Transport) v HM Senior Coroner for Norfolk [2016] EWHC 2279 (Admin); (2017) 181 J.P. 59; [2016] Inquest L.R. 243; [2016] A.C.D. 118, DC .... *Digested,* 17/**90**

R. (on the application of Sehwerert) v Entry Clearance Officer; *sub nom* R. (on the application of Sehwerert) v Secretary of State for the Home Department [2015] EWCA Civ 1141; [2016] Imm. A.R. 253, CA (Civ Div) .... *Digested,* 16/**1123**: *Applied* 16/1060, 17/1227

R. (on the application of Sehwerert) v Secretary of State for the Home Department see R. (on the application of Sehwerert) v Entry Clearance Officer

R. (on the application of Seiont, Gwyrfai and Llyfni Anglers Society) v Natural Resources Wales [2016] EWCA Civ 797; [2018] 1 W.L.R. 228; [2017] 3 All E.R. 1106; [2018] P.T.S.R. 110; [2017] 1 C.M.L.R. 8; [2017] Env. L.R. 2, CA (Civ Div) .... *Digested,* 17/**880**

R. (on the application of Seiont, Gwyrfai and Llyfni Anglers' Society) v Natural Resources Wales [2015] EWHC 3578 (Admin); [2016] 2 All E.R. 396; [2016] P.T.S.R. 505; [2016] Env. L.R. 18; [2016] A.C.D. 31, QBD (Admin) .... *Digested,* 16/**769**: *Affirmed* 17/880

R. (on the application of SG) v Secretary of State for Work and Pensions see R. (on the application of JS) v Secretary of State for Work and Pensions

R. (on the application of Sharer) v City of London Magistrates' Court [2016] EWHC 1412 (Admin); (2017) 181 J.P. 48, DC .... *Digested,* 17/**625**

R. (on the application of Sharp) v North Essex Magistrates' Court see Sharp v North Essex Magistrates' Court

R. (on the application of Shasha) v Westminster City Council; *sub nom* Shasha v Westminster City Council [2016] EWHC 3283 (Admin); [2017] P.T.S.R. 306; [2017] J.P.L. 539, QBD (Admin) .... *Digested,* 17/**1766**

R. (on the application of Shields-McKinley) v Secretary of State for Justice and Lord Chancellor [2017] EWHC 658 (Admin); [2017] 1 W.L.R. 3705; [2017] 2 Cr. App. R. (S.) 17; [2017] Crim. L.R. 809; [2017] A.C.D. 64, QBD (Admin) .... *Digested,* 17/**1905**

R. (on the application of Shirley) v Secretary of State for Communities and Local Government [2017] EWHC 2306 (Admin); [2018] J.P.L. 298; [2017] A.C.D. 124, QBD (Admin)

R. (on the application of Shoesmith) v Ofsted [2011] EWCA Civ 642; [2011] P.T.S.R. 1459; [2011] I.C.R. 1195; [2011] I.R.L.R. 679; [2011] B.L.G.R. 649; (2011) 108(23) L.S.G. 16; (2011) 155(22) S.J.L.B. 35, CA (Civ Div) .... *Digested,* 11/**65**: *Applied* 17/1787: *Considered* 14/60

R. (on the application of SJ (Pakistan)) v Secretary of State for the Home Department see R. (on the application of MM (Lebanon)) v Secretary of State for the Home Department

R. (on the application of SK) v Croydon LBC see R. (on the application of ZM) v Croydon LBC

R. (on the application of Skipton Properties Ltd) v Craven DC [2017] EWHC 534 (Admin); [2017] J.P.L. 825; [2017] Env. L.R. D5, QBD (Leeds) .... *Digested,* 17/**1692**

R. (on the application of SL) v Westminster City Council; *sub nom* R. (on the application of S) v Westminster City Council; R. (on the application of L) v Westminster City Council; SL v Westminster City Council [2013] UKSC 27; [2013] 1 W.L.R. 1445; [2013] 3 All E.R. 191; [2013] P.T.S.R. 691; [2013] H.L.R. 30; [2013] B.L.G.R. 423; (2013) 16 C.C.L. Rep. 161, SC .... *Digested,* 13/**2951**: *Followed* 16/2012, 17/2056

R. (on the application of SM (Congo)) v Secretary of State for the Home Department see R. (on the application of ZA (Nigeria)) v Secretary of State for the Home Department

R. (on the application of Smith) v North Eastern Derbyshire Primary Care Trust see Smith v North Eastern Derbyshire Primary Care Trust

R. (on the application of Smith) v Oxfordshire Assistant Deputy Coroner; *sub nom* R. (on the application of Smith) v Secretary of State for Defence; *joined case* Secretary of State for Defence v Smith [2010] UKSC 29; [2011] 1 A.C. 1; [2010] 3 W.L.R. 223; [2010] 3 All E.R. 1067; [2010] H.R.L.R. 28; [2010] U.K.H.R.R. 1020; 29 B.H.R.C. 497; [2010] Inquest L.R. 119; Times, July 8, 2010; (2010) 107(28) L.S.G. 17; (2010) 160 N.L.J. 973; (2010) 154(26) S.J.L.B. 28, SC .... *Digested,* 10/**1737**: *Applied* 11/1745: *Considered* 14/47, 17/1593: *Followed* 12/128, 15/1643: *Not followed* 13/121

R. (on the application of Smith) v Parole Board for England and Wales; *sub nom* Smith v Parole Board for England and Wales; *joined case* R. (on the application of West) v Parole Board for England and Wales [2005] UKHL 1; [2005] 1 W.L.R. 350; [2005] 1 All E.R. 755; [2005] H.R.L.R. 8; 18 B.H.R.C. 267; [2005] 2 Prison L.R. 14; Times, January 28, 2005; Independent, February 2, 2005; (2005) 102(12) L.S.G. 26; (2005) 149 S.J.L.B. 145, HL .... *Digested,* 05/**2920**: *Applied* 06/2937, 06/345, 08/2678, 08/2689, 08/4957, 10/2317, 11/2291: *Considered* 05/2907, 07/2981, 09/2761, 09/2768, 13/2124: *Distinguished* 17/1595: *Followed* 11/2286, 11/2290, 13/2115, 15/1823: *Not followed* 14/2233: *Referred to* 08/2680

R. (on the application of Smith) v Secretary of State for Defence see R. (on the application of Smith) v Oxfordshire Assistant Deputy Coroner

R. (on the application of Soma Oil and Gas Ltd) v Director of the Serious Fraud Office [2016] EWHC 2471 (Admin); [2017] Lloyd's Rep. F.C. 18; [2017] Crim. L.R. 65; [2016] A.C.D. 130, DC .... *Digested,* 17/**38**

R. (on the application of Somerfield Stores Ltd) v Competition and Markets Authority see R. (on the application of Gallaher Group Ltd) v Competition and Markets Authority

R. (on the application of Soumahoro) v Secretary of State for the Home Department see R. (on the application of Razgar) v Secretary of State for the Home Department (No.2)

R. (on the application of South Staffordshire and Shropshire Healthcare NHS Foundation Trust) v St George's Hospital Managers [2016] EWHC 1196 (Admin); [2017] 1 W.L.R. 1528; (2016) 19 C.C.L. Rep. 253; [2016] Med. L.R. 283; [2016] M.H.L.R. 273, QBD (Admin) .... *Digested,* 16/**1495**

R. (on the application of Southwark LBC) v Secretary of State for Communities and Local Government see R. (on the application of Blue Green London Plan) v Secretary of State for the Environment, Food and Rural Affairs

R. (on the application of Spinks) v Secretary of State for the Home Department [2005] EWCA Civ 275; [2006] 1 Prison L.R. 166, CA (Civ Div) *Applied* 09/2762: *Considered* 11/2836, 15/3245: *Followed* 17/1590

R. (on the application of SS) v Secretary of State for the Home Department [2017] EWHC 1295 (Admin); [2017] 1 W.L.R. 3641, QBD (Admin) .... *Digested,* 17/**1226**

R. (on the application of SS) v Secretary of State for the Home Department ('self-serving' statements) [2017] UKUT 164 (IAC); [2017] Imm. A.R. 1049, UT (IAC) *Digested,* 17/**1208**

R. (on the application of Steinfeld) v Secretary of State for Education see Steinfeld v Secretary of State for Education

R. (on the application of Stennett) v Manchester City Council; *sub nom* R. v Redcar and Cleveland BC Ex p. Armstrong; R. v Harrow LBC Ex p. Cobham; R. v Manchester City Council Ex p. Stennett; R. v Richmond LBC Ex p. Watson; *joined cases* R. (on the application of Cobham) v Harrow LBC; R. (on the application of Armstrong) v Redcar and Cleveland BC [2002] UKHL 34; [2002] 2 A.C. 1127; [2002] 3 W.L.R. 584; [2002] 4 All E.R. 124; [2002] B.L.G.R. 557; (2002) 5 C.C.L. Rep. 500; (2002) 68 B.M.L.R. 247; [2002] M.H.L.R. 377; Times, August 29, 2002; Independent, July 30, 2002; (2002) 99(40) L.S.G. 33; (2002) 146 S.J.L.B. 202, HL .... *Digested,* 02/**3237**: *Considered* 10/2251: *Followed* 11/3205, 17/1540

R. (on the application of Stirling) v Haringey LBC see R. (on the application of Moseley) v Haringey LBC

R. (on the application of Stonegate Homes Ltd) v Horsham DC [2016] EWHC 2512 (Admin); [2017] Env. L.R. 8; [2017] J.P.L. 271, QBD (Admin) .... *Digested,* 17/**1731**

R. (on the application of Stott) v Secretary of State for Justice [2017] EWHC 214 (Admin), DC *Approved* 17/1588

R. (on the application of Suppiah) v Secretary of State for the Home Department [2011] EWHC 2 (Admin); (2011) 108(4) L.S.G. 18, QBD (Admin)
Considered 17/1539

R. (on the application of Swan Quay LLP) v Swale BC [2017] EWHC 420 (Admin), QBD (Admin)
Applied 17/1727

R. (on the application of Swiss International Air Lines AG) v Secretary of State for Energy and Climate Change (C-272/15) see Swiss International Air Lines AG v Secretary of State for Energy and Climate Change (C-272/15)

R. (on the application of Sword Services Ltd) v Revenue and Customs Commissioners; *sub nom* Sword Services Ltd v Revenue and Customs Commissioners [2016] EWHC 1473 (Admin); [2016] 4 W.L.R. 113; [2017] S.T.C. 596; [2016] B.T.C. 24; [2016] S.T.I. 1799, QBD (Admin) .... *Digested,* 16/**2119**:
Applied 17/2187: *Considered* 17/2129

R. (on the application of Syed) v Secretary of State for Justice [2017] EWHC 727 (Admin); [2017] 4 W.L.R. 101; [2017] A.C.D. 66, QBD (Admin) .... *Digested,* 17/**1596**

R. (on the application of T) v Chief Constable of Greater Manchester; *sub nom* R. (on the application of B) v Secretary of State for the Home Department; *joined cases* R. (on the application of JB) v Secretary of State for the Home Department; R. (on the application of AW) v Secretary of State for the Home Department; R. (on the application of T) v Secretary of State for the Home Department [2014] UKSC 35; [2015] A.C. 49; [2014] 3 W.L.R. 96; [2014] 4 All E.R. 159; [2014] 2 Cr. App. R. 24; 38 B.H.R.C. 505; Times, June 23, 2014, SC *Digested,* 14/**1637**:
Applied 16/1769: *Followed* 17/2749

R. (on the application of T) v Chief Constable of Greater Manchester; *sub nom* R. (on the application of B) v Secretary of State for the Home Department; *joined cases* R. (on the application of JB) v Secretary of State for the Home Department; R. (on the application of AW) v Secretary of State for the Home Department; R. (on the application of T) v Secretary of State for the Home Department [2013] EWCA Civ 25; [2013] 1 W.L.R. 2515; [2013] 2 All E.R. 813; [2013] 1 Cr. App. R. 27; [2013] H.R.L.R. 14, CA (Civ Div) .... *Digested,* 13/**1564**:
Explained 17/1586: *Reversed in part* 14/1637

R. (on the application of T) v Commissioner of Police of the Metropolis see R. (on the application of Catt) v Association of Chief Police Officers of England, Wales and Northern Ireland

R. (on the application of T) v Hertfordshire CC; *sub nom* R. (on the application of PC) v Hertfordshire CC [2015] EWHC 1936 (Admin); (2015) 18 C.C.L. Rep. 632, QBD (Admin) .... *Digested,* 16/**2016**:
Affirmed 17/2057

R. (on the application of T) v Hertfordshire CC; *sub nom* R. (on the application of PC) v Hertfordshire CC [2016] EWCA Civ 1108; [2017] 1 W.L.R. 2153; [2017] H.L.R. 10, CA (Civ Div) .... *Digested,* 17/**2057**

R. (on the application of T) v Secretary of State for the Home Department [2016] EWCA Civ 801; [2017] Imm. A.R. 330; Times, October 20, 2016, CA (Civ Div) .. *Digested,* 16/**1134**

R. (on the application of T) v Secretary of State for the Home Department see R. (on the application of T) v Chief Constable of Greater Manchester

R. (on the application of Tann UK Ltd) v Secretary of State for Health see R. (on the application of British American Tobacco UK Ltd) v Secretary of State for Health

R. (on the application of Tatham Homes Ltd) v First Secretary of State [2005] EWHC 3538 (Admin); [2008] J.P.L. 185, QBD (Admin) .... *Digested,* 08/**2936**:
Applied 17/1763: *Considered* 14/2411

R. (on the application of Taylor) v Honiton Town Council; *sub nom* Taylor v Honiton Town Council [2016] EWHC 3307 (Admin); [2017] P.T.S.R. 271; [2017] L.L.R. 372; [2017] A.C.D. 28, QBD (Admin) .... *Digested,* 17/**1513**

R. (on the application of TB (Jamaica)) v Secretary of State for the Home Department; *sub nom* Secretary of State for the Home Department v TB (Jamaica); TB (Jamaica) v Secretary of State for the Home Department [2008] EWCA Civ 977; [2009] I.N.L.R. 221; Times, September 9, 2008; [2009] A.C.D. 10, CA (Civ Div) .... *Digested,* 08/**2005**:
Applied 12/1709, 17/1192: *Considered* 11/1749: *Followed* 12/1748

R. (on the application of Tchenguiz) v Director of Serious Fraud Office see R. (on the application of Rawlinson and Hunter Trustees) v Central Criminal Court

R. (on the application of Telegraph Group Plc) v Sherwood; *sub nom* R. v Sherwood Ex p. Telegraph Group Plc; Telegraph Group Plc, Ex p. [2001] EWCA Crim 1075; [2001] 1 W.L.R. 1983; [2002] E.M.L.R. 10; Times, June 12, 2001; (2001) 98(28) L.S.G. 42; (2001) 145 S.J.L.B. 159, CA (Crim Div) .... *Digested,* 01/**1182**:
Applied 11/808: *Considered* 10/795: *Followed* 07/1018, 17/33

R. (on the application of the Environment Agency) v Tapecrown Ltd see R. v Rogers (Georgina)

R. (on the application of The Pharmaceutical Services Negotiating Committee) v Secretary of State for Health; *sub nom* R. (on the application of The Pharmacy Association) v Secretary of State for Health [2017] EWHC 1147 (Admin); [2017] P.T.S.R. 1451, QBD (Admin)

R. (on the application of The Pharmacy Association) v Secretary of State for Health see R. (on the application of The Pharmaceutical Services Negotiating Committee) v Secretary of State for Health

R. (on the application of the Saint John the Evangelist College in the University of Cambridge) v Cambridgeshire CC [2017] EWHC 1753 (Admin); [2017] P.T.S.R. 1353, QBD (Admin)

R. (on the application of Thomas) v Merthyr Tydfil CBC [2016] EWHC 972 (Admin); [2017] Env. L.R. 3; [2016] A.C.D. 79, QBD (Cardiff) .... *Digested,* 17/**1748**

R. (on the application of Tigere) v Secretary of State for Business, Innovation and Skills [2015] UKSC 57; [2015] 1 W.L.R. 3820; [2016] 1 All E.R. 191; [2015] H.R.L.R. 19; 40 B.H.R.C. 19; [2015] E.L.R. 455, SC .... *Digested,* 15/**758**: *Applied* 17/1645: *Considered* 16/1040, 16/2599: *Explained* 16/627

R. (on the application of Timmins) v Gedling BC see Timmins v Gedling BC

R. (on the application of TL) v Chief Constable of Surrey see R. (on the application of L) v Chief Constable of Surrey

R. (on the application of TN (Vietnam)) v Secretary of State for the Home Department; *joined case* R. (on the application of US (Pakistan)) v Secretary of State for the Home Department [2017] EWHC 59 (Admin); [2017] 1 W.L.R. 2595; [2017] 4 All E.R. 399, QBD (Admin) .... *Digested,* 17/**1172**

R. (on the application of ToTel Ltd) v First-tier Tribunal (Tax Chamber) [2012] EWCA Civ 1401; [2013] Q.B. 860; [2013] 2 W.L.R. 1136; [2013] S.T.C. 1557; [2012] B.V.C. 333; Times, December 27, 2012; [2012] S.T.I. 3230, CA (Civ Div) .... *Digested,* 13/**3184**: *Followed* 17/2281

R. (on the application of Trinity Mirror Plc) v Croydon Crown Court; *sub nom* Trinity Mirror Plc, Re [2008] EWCA Crim 50; [2008] Q.B. 770; [2008] 3 W.L.R. 51; [2008] 2 All E.R. 1159; [2008] 2 Cr. App. R. 1; [2009] E.M.L.R. 3; Times, February 13, 2008; [2008] Crim. L.R. 554, CA (Crim Div) .... *Digested,* 08/**14**: *Applied* 14/801, 17/3: *Followed* 08/855, 13/757

R. (on the application of Trivedi) v HM Coroner for Southwark see R. (on the application of Trivedi) v HM Senior Coroner for Inner South London

R. (on the application of Trivedi) v HM Senior Coroner for Inner South London; *sub nom* R. (on the application of Trivedi) v HM Coroner for Southwark [2016] EWHC 4166 (Admin); [2016] Inquest L.R. 252, QBD (Admin) .... *Digested,* 17/**10**

R. (on the application of Troitino) v National Crime Agency [2017] EWHC 931 (Admin); [2017] A.C.D. 78, DC

R. (on the application of Tum) v Secretary of State for the Home Department (C-16/05) see Tum v Secretary of State for the Home Department (C-16/05)

R. (on the application of Turley) v Wandsworth LBC [2017] EWCA Civ 189; [2017] H.L.R. 21; [2017] 2 P. & C.R. DG9, CA (Civ Div) .... *Digested,* 17/**1466**

R. (on the application of Turley) v Wandsworth LBC [2014] EWHC 4040 (Admin); [2015] P.T.S.R. D11, QBD (Admin) *Affirmed* 17/1466

R. (on the application of Uber London Ltd) v Transport for London [2017] EWHC 435 (Admin); [2018] L.L.R. 185; [2017] A.C.D. 54, QBD (Admin)

R. (on the application of UK Power Networks (Operations) Ltd) v Gas and Electricity Markets Authority [2017] EWHC 1175 (Admin); [2018] P.T.S.R. 262; [2017] A.C.D. 91, QBD (Admin)

R. (on the application of Ullah (Ahsan)) v Secretary of State for the Home Department see R. (on the application of Ullah) v Special Adjudicator

R. (on the application of Ullah) v Secretary of State for the Home Department [2017] EWHC 1999 (Admin); [2017] 4 W.L.R. 148, QBD (Admin) .... *Digested,* 17/**1244**

R. (on the application of Ullah) v Secretary of State for the Home Department see R. (on the application of Behary) v Secretary of State for the Home Department

R. (on the application of Ullah) v Special Adjudicator; *sub nom* Ullah (Ahsan) v Special Adjudicator; R. (on the application of Ullah (Ahsan)) v Secretary of State for the Home Department; Do v Secretary of State for the Home Department; *joined case* Do v Immigration Appeal Tribunal [2004] UKHL 26; [2004] 2 A.C. 323; [2004] 3 W.L.R. 23; [2004] 3 All E.R. 785; [2004] H.R.L.R. 33; [2004] U.K.H.R.R. 995; [2004] Imm. A.R. 419; [2004] I.N.L.R. 381; Times, June 18, 2004; Independent, June 22, 2004; (2004) 101(28) L.S.G. 33; (2004) 154 N.L.J. 985; (2004) 148 S.J.L.B. 762, HL .... *Digested,* 04/**2009**: *Applied* 05/401, 06/1598, 06/2223, 07/2309, 08/2038, 08/3056, 09/1473, 16/1772, 16/2637: *Considered* 04/839, 05/2140, 05/5431, 06/1605, 07/5169, 07/5432, 10/1265, 10/1266, 13/65, 15/3060, 17/1212: *Followed* 08/1940, 14/1725, 16/1132

R. (on the application of Unaenergy Group Holding Pte Ltd) v Director of the Serious Fraud Office [2017] EWHC 600 (Admin); [2017] 1 W.L.R. 3302; [2017] 2 Cr. App. R. 11; Times, May 11, 2017; [2017] A.C.D. 60, DC .... *Digested,* 17/**597**

R. (on the application of Underwritten Warranty Co Ltd (t/a Insurance Backed Guarantee Co)) v FENSA Ltd [2017] EWHC 2308 (Admin); [2017] A.C.D. 125, QBD (Admin)

R. (on the application of Unison) v Lord Chancellor [2017] UKSC 51; [2017] 3 W.L.R. 409; [2017] 4 All E.R. 903; [2017] 4 Costs L.R. 721; [2018] 1 C.M.L.R. 35; [2017] I.C.R. 1037; [2017] I.R.L.R. 911; [2017] H.R.L.R. 11, SC .... *Digested,* 17/**15**

R. (on the application of Unison) v Lord Chancellor [2015] EWCA Civ 935; [2016] 4 All E.R. 25; [2016] 1 C.M.L.R. 25; [2016] I.C.R. 1; [2015] I.R.L.R. 911; Times, September 28, 2015, CA (Civ Div) .... *Digested,* 15/**15**: *Reversed* 17/15

R. (on the application of UNISON) v NHS Wiltshire Primary Care Trust [2012] EWHC 624 (Admin); [2012] A.C.D. 84, QBD (Admin) *Applied* 13/2021, 17/1814

R. (on the application of US (Pakistan)) v Secretary of State for the Home Department see R. (on the application of TN (Vietnam)) v Secretary of State for the Home Department

R. (on the application of Veolia ES Landfill Ltd) v Revenue and Customs Commissioners; *joined case* R. (on the application of Viridor Waste Management Ltd) v Revenue and Customs Commissioners [2016] EWHC 1880 (Admin); [2017] Env. L.R. 15; [2016] B.T.C. 29; [2016] S.T.I. 2201, QBD (Admin) .... *Digested,* 16/**2106**: *Considered* 17/2126

R. (on the application of Virgin Media Ltd) v Zinga see R. v Zinga (Munaf Ahmed)

R. (on the application of Viridor Waste Management Ltd) v Revenue and Customs Commissioners see R. (on the application of Veolia ES Landfill Ltd) v Revenue and Customs Commissioners

R. (on the application of Vital Nut Co Ltd) v Revenue and Customs Commissioners [2016] EWHC 1128 (Admin), QBD (Admin) *Applied* 17/2079

R. (on the application of VL) v Secretary of State for the Home Department see R. (on the application of L) v Secretary of State for the Home Department

R. (on the application of Vowles) v Secretary of State for Justice see R. v Vowles (Lucinda)

R. (on the application of VVB Engineering Services Ltd) v Revenue and Customs Commissioners [2017] EWHC 506 (Admin); [2017] B.T.C. 8; [2017] S.T.I. 792, QBD (Admin) .... *Digested,* 17/**2079**

R. (on the application of W) v Secretary of State for Exiting the European Union see R. (on the application of Yalland) v Secretary of State for Exiting the European Union

R. (on the application of W) v Secretary of State for Justice [2015] EWHC 1952 (Admin); [2015] A.C.D. 139, QBD (Admin) *Reversed* 17/1586

R. (on the application of W) v Secretary of State for Justice see R. (on the application of P) v Secretary of State for the Home Department

R. (on the application of W) v Secretary of State for the Home Department; *sub nom* W v Secretary of State for the Home Department; Hossain v Secretary of State for the Home Department; *joined case* R. (on the application of Hossain) v Secretary of State for the Home Department [2016] EWCA Civ 82; [2016] 1 W.L.R. 2793; [2016] Imm. A.R. 585; [2016] I.N.L.R. 697; Times, April 4, 2016, CA (Civ Div) .... *Digested,* 16/**36**: *Considered* 16/178, 17/1241

R. (on the application of Wakil (t/a Orya Textiles)) v Hammersmith and Fulham LBC [2012] EWHC 1411 (QB); [2013] Env. L.R. 3; [2013] 1 P. & C.R. 13; [2012] J.P.L. 1334, QBD (Admin) .... *Digested,* 12/**2542**: *Applied* 17/1692

R. (on the application of Watson) v Secretary of State for the Home Department (C-698/15) see Tele2 Sverige AB v Post- och telestyrelsen (C-203/15)

R. (on the application of Watt) v Hackney LBC [2016] EWHC 1978 (Admin); [2017] J.P.L. 192; [2016] A.C.D. 115, QBD (Admin) .... *Digested,* 17/**1754**

R. (on the application of West Berkshire DC) v Secretary of State for Communities and Local Government; *sub nom* West Berkshire DC v Department for Communities and Local Government; Secretary of State for Communities and Local Government v West Berkshire DC [2016] EWCA Civ 441; [2016] 1 W.L.R. 3923; [2016] P.T.S.R. 982; [2016] 2 P. & C.R. 8; Times, June 6, 2016; [2016] J.P.L. 1034, CA (Civ Div) .... *Digested,* 16/**1708**: *Considered* 17/1725

R. (on the application of West) v Parole Board for England and Wales see R. (on the application of Smith) v Parole Board for England and Wales

R. (on the application of Westminster City Council) v National Asylum Support Service; *sub nom* Westminster City Council v National Asylum Support Services; R. (on the application of Westminster City Council) v Secretary of State for the Home Department [2002] UKHL 38; [2002] 1 W.L.R. 2956; [2002] 4 All E.R. 654; [2002] H.L.R. 58; [2003] B.L.G.R. 23; (2002) 5 C.C.L. Rep. 511; Times, October 18, 2002; (2002) 146 S.J.L.B. 241, HL .... *Digested,* 02/**4288**: *Applied* 04/2020, 07/2312, 11/236, 11/3186: *Considered* 03/4069, 08/2090, 12/3171, 13/2951, 13/3670, 14/2887, 17/819: *Distinguished* 10/3141: *Followed* 10/3186, 17/1534

R. (on the application of Westminster City Council) v Secretary of State for the Home Department see R. (on the application of Westminster City Council) v National Asylum Support Service

R. (on the application of Whiston) v Secretary of State for Justice [2014] UKSC 39; [2015] A.C. 176; [2014] 3 W.L.R. 436; [2014] 4 All E.R. 251; [2014] H.R.L.R. 19; Times, July 11, 2014, SC .... *Digested,* 14/**2233**: *Considered* 15/1823: *Followed* 17/1595

R. (on the application of Wilkinson) v Broadmoor Hospital; *sub nom* R. (on the application of Wilkinson) v Broadmoor Special Hospital Authority; R. (on the application of Wilkinson) v Responsible Medical Officer, Broadmoor Hospital [2001] EWCA Civ 1545; [2002] 1 W.L.R. 419; [2002] U.K.H.R.R. 390; (2002) 5 C.C.L. Rep. 121; [2002] Lloyd's Rep. Med. 41; (2002) 65 B.M.L.R. 15; [2001] M.H.L.R. 224; Times, November 2, 2001; Independent, December 10, 2001; [2002] A.C.D. 47; Daily Telegraph, October 30, 2001; (2001) 98(44) L.S.G. 36; (2001) 145 S.J.L.B. 247, CA (Civ Div) .... *Digested,* 01/**4431**: *Applied* 05/1837, 05/2830, 06/2861: *Considered* 02/3234, 02/51, 06/2860, 09/2714, 09/3955, 10/72: *Distinguished* 17/1545

R. (on the application of Wilkinson) v Broadmoor Special Hospital Authority see R. (on the application of Wilkinson) v Broadmoor Hospital

R. (on the application of Wilkinson) v Responsible Medical Officer, Broadmoor Hospital see R. (on the application of Wilkinson) v Broadmoor Hospital

R. (on the application of Willford) v Financial Services Authority see R. (on the application of C) v Financial Services Authority

R. (on the application of Williams) v Police Appeals Tribunal [2016] EWHC 2708 (Admin); [2017] I.C.R. 235; [2016] A.C.D. 138, QBD (Admin) .... *Digested,* 17/**1790**

R. (on the application of Williams) v Powys CC [2017] EWCA Civ 427; [2018] 1 W.L.R. 439; [2017] J.P.L. 1236, CA (Civ Div) .... *Digested,* 17/**1721**

R. (on the application of Williams) v Powys CC [2016] EWHC 480 (Admin), QBD (Admin) *Reversed* 17/1721

R. (on the application of Williams) v Secretary of State for the Home Department [2017] EWCA Civ 98; [2017] 1 W.L.R. 3283, CA (Civ Div) .... *Digested,* 17/**1182**

R. (on the application of Williams) v Secretary of State for the Home Department [2015] EWHC 1268 (Admin); [2015] A.C.D. 111, QBD (Admin) *Affirmed* 17/1182

R. (on the application of Williamson) v Secretary of State for Education and Employment; *sub nom* Williamson v Secretary of State for Education and Employment [2005] UKHL 15; [2005] 2 A.C. 246; [2005] 2 W.L.R. 590; [2005] 2 All E.R. 1; [2005] 2 F.L.R. 374; [2005] 1 F.C.R. 498; [2005] H.R.L.R. 14; [2005] U.K.H.R.R. 339; 19 B.H.R.C. 99; [2005] E.L.R. 291; Times, February 25, 2005; Independent, March 1, 2005; [2005] Fam. Law 456; (2005) 102(16) L.S.G. 27; (2005) 155 N.L.J. 324; (2005) 149 S.J.L.B. 266, HL .... *Digested,* 05/**1019**: *Applied* 08/1037, 09/1234, 09/1955, 10/1025, 12/2335, 14/1112: *Considered* 06/1145, 07/1400, 07/2194, 08/4867, 11/1425: *Followed* 16/662, 17/822

R. (on the application of Wilson) v Secretary of State for Work and Pensions see R. (on the application of Reilly) v Secretary of State for Work and Pensions

R. (on the application of Withey) v Secretary of State for Work and Pensions see R. (on the application of Hooper) v Secretary of State for Work and Pensions

R. (on the application of WL (Congo)) v Secretary of State for the Home Department see R. (on the application of Lumba) v Secretary of State for the Home Department

R. (on the application of Woolfe) v Islington LBC [2016] EWHC 1907 (Admin); [2016] H.L.R. 42, QBD (Admin) .... *Digested,* 17/**1154**

R. (on the application of Working Title Films Ltd) v Westminster City Council [2016] EWHC 1855 (Admin); [2017] J.P.L. 173, QBD (Admin)

R. (on the application of Wylde) v Waverley BC [2017] EWHC 466 (Admin); [2017] P.T.S.R. 1245; [2017] J.P.L. 861; [2017] A.C.D. 57, QBD (Admin) .... *Digested,* 17/**1814**

R. (on the application of X) v National Probation Service; *sub nom* R. (on the application of H) v National Probation Service; R. (on the application of ZX) v Secretary of State for Justice [2017] EWCA Civ 155; [2017] 4 W.L.R. 106, CA (Civ Div) .... *Digested,* 17/**1589**

R. (on the application of X) v National Probation Service; *sub nom* R. (on the application of H) v National Probation Service; R. (on the application of ZX) v Secretary of State for Justice [2015] EWHC 4074 (Admin), QBD (Admin) *Affirmed* 17/1589

R. (on the application of X) v Tower Hamlets LBC [2013] EWCA Civ 904; [2013] 4 All E.R. 237; [2014] 1 F.L.R. 1076; [2013] 3 F.C.R. 192; [2013] B.L.G.R. 721; [2013] Fam. Law 1384, CA (Civ Div) .... *Digested,* 13/**2023**: *Applied* 17/2055

R. (on the application of XC) v Southwark LBC [2017] EWHC 736 (Admin); [2017] H.L.R. 24; (2017) 20 C.C.L. Rep. 338; [2017] A.C.D. 65, QBD (Admin) .... *Digested,* 17/**1155**

R. (on the application of XH) v Secretary of State for the Home Department; *joined case* R. (on the application of AI) v Secretary of State for the Home Department [2016] EWHC 1898 (Admin); Times, October 10, 2016; [2016] A.C.D. 117, DC . *Digested,* 16/**35**: *Affirmed* 17/43

R. (on the application of XH) v Secretary of State for the Home Department; *sub nom* XH v Secretary of State for the Home Department; AI v Secretary of State for the Home Department; *joined case* R. (on the application of AI) v Secretary of State for the Home Department [2017] EWCA Civ 41; [2018] Q.B. 355; [2017] 2 W.L.R. 1437; [2017] 2 C.M.L.R. 33; [2017] I.N.L.R. 775; Times, February 27, 2017, CA (Civ Div) .... *Digested,* 17/**43**

R. (on the application of Y) v Croydon LBC see Croydon LBC v Y

R. (on the application of YA) v Secretary of State for the Home Department [2013] EWHC 3229 (Admin), QBD (Admin) *Considered* 17/1209

R. (on the application of Yalland) v Secretary of State for Exiting the European Union; *sub nom* Yalland v Secretary of State for Exiting the European Union [2017] EWHC 629 (Admin); [2017] A.C.D. 49, DC

R. (on the application of Yalland) v Secretary of State for Exiting the European Union; *sub nom* Y v Secretary of State for Exiting the European Union; R. (on the application of W) v Secretary of State for Exiting the European Union [2017] EWHC 630 (Admin); [2017] A.C.D. 50, DC

R. (on the application of Yam) v Central Criminal Court [2015] UKSC 76; [2016] A.C. 771; [2016] 2 W.L.R. 19; [2017] 1 All E.R. 462; [2016] 1 Cr. App. R. 17; [2016] H.R.L.R. 3; [2017] Crim. L.R. 235, SC .... *Digested,* 16/**522**

R. (on the application of Yavuz) v Chief Constable of West Yorkshire [2016] EWHC 2054 (Admin); [2017] P.T.S.R. 228, QBD (Admin) .... *Digested,* 17/**1794**

R. (on the application of Youngsam) v Parole Board [2017] EWHC 729 (Admin); [2017] 1 W.L.R. 2848; [2018] 1 All E.R. 800; [2017] A.C.D. 67, QBD (Admin) .... *Digested,* 17/**1595**

R. (on the application of YZ) v Oxleas NHS Foundation Trust; *sub nom* YZ v Oxleas NHS Foundation Trust [2017] EWCA Civ 203; [2017] 1 W.L.R. 3518; (2017) 155 B.M.L.R. 36; [2017] M.H.L.R. 293, CA (Civ Div) .... *Digested,* 17/**1545**

R. (on the application of YZ) v Oxleas NHS Foundation Trust see YZ v NHS Trust 1
R. (on the application of ZA (Nigeria)) v Secretary of State for the Home Department; *sub nom* R. (on the application of SM (Congo)) v Secretary of State for the Home Department [2010] EWCA Civ 926; [2011] Q.B. 722; [2011] 2 W.L.R. 16; [2010] Imm. A.R. 776; [2011] I.N.L.R. 78, CA (Civ Div)
Applied 13/1599: *Considered* 14/1679: *Followed* 17/1210, 17/1220
R. (on the application of Zahid) v University of Manchester; *sub nom* Zahid v University of Manchester [2017] EWHC 188 (Admin); [2017] E.L.R. 269; [2017] A.C.D. 44, QBD (Admin) .... *Digested,* 17/**723**
R. (on the application of ZAI Corporate Finance Ltd) v AIM Disciplinary Committee of the London Stock Exchange Plc; *sub nom* ZAI Corporate Finance Ltd v AIM Disciplinary Committee of the London Stock Exchange Plc [2017] EWCA Civ 1294; [2017] Bus. L.R. 2139, CA (Civ Div)
R. (on the application of ZH) v Newham LBC see R. (on the application of N) v Lewisham LBC
R. (on the application of ZL) v Secretary of State for the Home Department see R. (on the application of L) v Secretary of State for the Home Department
R. (on the application of ZM) v Croydon LBC; *joined case* R. (on the application of SK) v Croydon LBC [2016] UKUT 559 (IAC); [2017] Imm. A.R. 459, UT (IAC) .... *Digested,* 17/**2048**: *Applied* 17/2049
R. (on the application of ZT (Syria)) v Secretary of State for the Home Department see Secretary of State for the Home Department v ZAT (Syria)
R. (on the application of ZX) v Secretary of State for Justice see R. (on the application of X) v National Probation Service
R. (on the Prosecution of Hargraves) v Steel (1876) 2 Q.B.D. 37, CA
Applied 17/270
R. Porja (Arben) see R. v Abi-Khalil (Tannous)
RA (Baby Relinquished for Adoption), Re see A (Baby Relinquished for Adoption: Case Management), Re
Rabess v London Fire and Emergency Planning Authority [2016] EWCA Civ 1017; [2017] I.R.L.R. 147, CA (Civ Div) .... *Digested,* 17/**845**
Rabess v London Fire and Emergency Planning Authority UKEAT/0029/14/JOJ, EAT
Affirmed 17/845
Rabiu v Marlbray Ltd; *sub nom* Marlbray Ltd v Laditi [2016] EWCA Civ 476; [2016] 1 W.L.R. 5147; [2016] 2 P. & C.R. DG21, CA (Civ Div) .... *Digested,* 17/**497**
Rabiu v Marlbray Ltd; *sub nom* Marlbray Ltd v Laditi [2013] EWHC 3272 (Ch), Ch D
Reversed in part 17/497
Radadvicius (Nerijus) v HM Advocate see Gubinas (Justinas) v HM Advocate
Radecki v Kirklees MBC; *sub nom* Kirklees MBC v Radecki [2009] EWCA Civ 298; [2009] I.C.R. 1244; [2009] I.R.L.R. 555, CA (Civ Div) .... *Digested,* 09/**1265**: *Considered* 10/1142, 17/845: *Followed* 17/830
Radgen v Finanzamt Ettlingen (C-478/15) EU:C:2016:705; [2017] S.T.C. 30; [2016] S.T.I. 2751, ECJ (6th Chamber)
Radmacher v Granatino; *sub nom* G v R (Pre-Nuptial Contract) [2010] UKSC 42; [2011] 1 A.C. 534; [2010] 3 W.L.R. 1367; [2011] 1 All E.R. 373; [2010] 2 F.L.R. 1900; [2010] 3 F.C.R. 583; Times, October 22, 2010; [2010] Fam. Law 1263; (2010) 107(42) L.S.G. 18; (2010) 160 N.L.J. 1491; (2010) 154(40) S.J.L.B. 37, SC .... *Digested,* 11/**1311**: *Applied* 12/1437, 16/902, 17/1031: *Considered* 12/1316: *Followed* 12/1310, 12/1317, 14/1375, 15/1082, 17/1020
Radu v Germany (20084/07) [2017] M.H.L.R. 112, ECHR
Raduvha v Minister of Safety and Security 41 B.H.R.C. 723, Const Ct (SA)
Raeshaw Farms Ltd v Scottish Natural Heritage [2017] CSOH 50; 2017 S.L.T. 683; [2017] L.L.R. 632; 2017 G.W.D. 12-166, OH .... *Digested,* 17/**2408**: *Cited* 17/2407
Raggett v Society of Jesus Trust 1929 for Roman Catholic Purposes [2010] EWCA Civ 1002; [2010] C.P. Rep. 45; (2010) 160 N.L.J. 1228; (2010) 154(34) S.J.L.B. 30, CA (Civ Div) .... *Digested,* 11/**353**: *Considered* 17/2191
Rahhal v UK Insurance Ltd (Unreported, March 30, 2017), CC (Brentford) [*Glen Pearson, Riverside West, 1 Millsands, Sheffield*] .... *Digested,* 17/**1680**
Rahimtoola v Nizam of Hyderabad; *sub nom* Nizam of Hyderabad v Jung [1958] A.C. 379; [1957] 3 W.L.R. 884; [1957] 3 All E.R. 441; (1957) 101 S.J. 901, HL .... *Digested,* 57/**2864**: *Applied* 64/1931, 65/3226, 78/1736, 81/285: *Considered* 71/6115, 17/1426
Rahman v Arearose Ltd [2001] Q.B. 351; [2000] 3 W.L.R. 1184; (2001) 62 B.M.L.R. 84, CA (Civ Div)
Applied 04/2731, 07/2928, 11/2251, 16/1538, 17/1691: *Considered* 11/1071: *Followed* 17/1565, 17/826

Rahmatullah v Ministry of Defence; *sub nom* Iraqi Civilians v Ministry of Defence; *joined case* Mohammed v Ministry of Defence [2017] UKSC 1; [2017] A.C. 649; [2017] 2 W.L.R. 287; [2017] 3 All E.R. 179; [2017] H.R.L.R. 13, SC .... *Digested,* 17/**1425**

Rahmatullah v Ministry of Defence; *joined case* R. (on the application of Rahmatullah) v Secretary of State for Defence [2014] EWHC 3846 (QB), QBD

Affirmed 15/1558, 17/1426

Rahmatullah v Ministry of Defence see Belhaj v Straw

Rahmatullah v Ministry of Defence see Mohammed v Secretary of State for Defence

Rahmatullah v Secretary of State for Defence see R. (on the application of Al-Saadoon) v Secretary of State for Defence

Rai v Revenue and Customs Commissioners [2017] UKFTT 467 (TC); [2017] S.T.I. 1870, FTT (Tax)

Rainy Sky SA v Kookmin Bank; *sub nom* Kookmin Bank v Rainy Sky SA [2011] UKSC 50; [2011] 1 W.L.R. 2900; [2012] 1 All E.R. 1137; [2012] 1 All E.R. (Comm) 1; [2012] Bus. L.R. 313; [2012] 1 Lloyd's Rep. 34; [2011] 2 C.L.C. 923; [2012] B.L.R. 132; 138 Con. L.R. 1; Times, November 18, 2011; [2011] C.I.L.L. 3105, SC .... *Digested,* 12/**637**:

Applied 12/2057, 12/2372, 12/2389, 13/2154, 14/2714, 14/2739, 14/474, 15/1861, 15/368, 15/475, 16/142, 17/2468, 17/498: *Considered* 12/1053, 13/1893, 15/383: *Followed* 13/2840, 14/117, 14/1775, 15/1606, 15/2113, 15/517, 16/1947, 16/424, 17/474

Rainys v Lithuania (56213/08) see Sidabras v Lithuania (50421/08)

Ralls Builders Ltd (In Liquidation), Re see Grant v Ralls

Ralph Henry Pickett (Deceased), Re see Pickett v British Rail Engineering Ltd

Ralph Hume Garry (A Firm) v Gwillim [2002] EWCA Civ 1500; [2003] 1 W.L.R. 510; [2003] 1 All E.R. 1038; [2003] C.P. Rep. 16; [2003] 1 Costs L.R. 77; Times, November 4, 2002; Independent, October 30, 2002; (2002) 99(45) L.S.G. 35; (2002) 152 N.L.J. 1653; (2002) 146 S.J.L.B. 237, CA (Civ Div) .... *Digested,* 02/**3110**:

Followed 17/204

Ralston v HM Advocate 1987 S.C.C.R. 467, HCJ Appeal .... *Digested,* 88/**3890**:

Applied 89/3997: *Considered* 94/5656, 97/5765: *Distinguished* 97/5766: *Followed* 11/4093, 17/2492: *Referred to* 95/5625

Ramadan v Malta (76136/12) (2017) 65 E.H.R.R. 32; [2016] Imm. A.R. 1288, ECHR

Rampal v Rampal (Ancillary Relief); *sub nom* Rampal v Rampal (No.2) [2001] EWCA Civ 989; [2002] Fam. 85; [2001] 3 W.L.R. 795; [2001] 2 F.L.R. 1179; [2001] 2 F.C.R. 552; Times, July 24, 2001; Independent, June 29, 2001; [2001] Fam. Law 731; (2001) 98(29) L.S.G. 37; (2001) 151 N.L.J. 1006; (2001) 145 S.J.L.B. 165, CA (Civ Div) .... *Digested,* 01/**2545**:

Applied 17/1043: *Considered* 09/1489, 10/1803

Rampal v Rampal (No.2) see Rampal v Rampal (Ancillary Relief)

Ramphal v Department for Transport [2015] I.R.L.R. 985; [2015] I.C.R. D23, EAT .... *Digested,* 16/**669**:

Considered 17/844

Randall v Randall [2016] EWCA Civ 494; [2017] Ch. 77; [2016] 3 W.L.R. 1217; [2017] 2 F.L.R. 185; [2016] W.T.L.R. 1277; 19 I.T.E.L.R. 273; Times, June 28, 2016; [2016] Fam. Law 969, CA (Civ Div) .... *Digested,* 16/**2029**

Randall (Barry Victor) v Queen, The [2002] UKPC 19; [2002] 1 W.L.R. 2237; [2002] 2 Cr. App. R. 17; Times, April 24, 2002; [2002] Crim. L.R. 928, PC (CI) .... *Digested,* 02/**905**:

Applied 07/1027: *Considered* 06/958, 10/4093, 10/770: *Distinguished* 17/2529

Randhawa v Turpin see BW Estates Ltd, Re

Randhawa v Turpin see BW Estates Ltd, Re

Rankin v Meek 1995 S.L.T. 526, OH .... *Digested,* 95/**5554**:

Considered 17/2781

Rantsev v Cyprus (25965/04) (2010) 51 E.H.R.R. 1; 28 B.H.R.C. 313, ECHR

Applied 11/1684, 13/1543, 14/1728, 16/1064, 17/1222

Rapid Brickwork Ltd (In Liquidation) v Revenue and Customs Commissioners [2017] UKFTT 194 (TC); [2017] S.T.I. 871, FTT (Tax)

Rapp v Sarre [2016] EWCA Civ 93; [2017] 1 F.L.R. 782; [2016] 2 F.C.R. 403; [2016] Fam. Law 447, CA (Civ Div) .... *Digested,* 16/**905**

Ras Al Khaimah Investment Authority v Bestfort Development LLP [2017] EWCA Civ 1014; [2018] 1 W.L.R. 1099; [2017] C.P. Rep. 40, CA (Civ Div) .... *Digested,* 17/**300**

Ras Al Khaimah Investment Authority v Bestfort Development LLP [2015] EWHC 3383 (Ch), Ch D

Reversed in part 17/300

Raschid v General Medical Council see Fatnani v General Medical Council

Rasul v Revenue and Customs Commissioners [2017] UKUT 357 (TCC); [2017] S.T.C. 2261; [2017] B.V.C. 529; [2017] S.T.I. 2099, UT (Tax) .... *Digested,* 17/**2261**

Rasul v Revenue and Customs Commissioners [2016] S.T.I. 1474, FTT (Tax)

Affirmed 17/2261

Ratcliffe v Secretary of State for Defence [2009] EWCA Civ 39; [2009] I.C.R. 762; (2009) 153(5) S.J.L.B. 30, CA (Civ Div)
Applied 17/1466

Rathbone v Croydon LBC see Sim v Rotherham MBC

Ratiopharm GmbH v Napp Pharmaceutical Holdings Ltd; *sub nom* Napp Pharmaceutical Holdings Ltd v Sandoz Ltd [2008] EWHC 3070 (Pat); [2009] R.P.C. 11; (2009) 32(3) I.P.D. 32019, Ch D (Patents Ct)
Applied 17/1378: *Considered* 16/1317: *Reversed in part* 09/2335

Ravat v Halliburton Manufacturing & Services Ltd; *sub nom* Halliburton Manufacturing & Services Ltd v Ravat [2012] UKSC 1; [2012] 2 All E.R. 905; 2012 S.C. (U.K.S.C.) 265; 2012 S.L.T. 406; [2012] I.C.R. 389; [2012] I.R.L.R. 315; Times, February 15, 2012; (2012) 156(6) S.J.L.B. 31; 2012 G.W.D. 6-106, SC .... *Digested,* 12/**1176**:
Applied 13/1075, 13/945: *Considered* 14/1077: *Distinguished* 12/1181:
Followed 13/993, 15/880, 15/881, 16/735, 17/849

Ravat v Halliburton Manufacturing & Services Ltd; *sub nom* Halliburton Manufacturing & Services Ltd v Ravat UKEATS/0012/08/MT, EAT (SC)
Considered 17/850: *Reversed* 11/4227

Ravenscroft v Canal and River Trust [2017] EWHC 1874 (Ch); [2018] 1 W.L.R. 249; [2017] L.L.R. 842, Ch D

Rawlinson & Hunter Trustees SA v Director of the Serious Fraud Office see Tchenguiz v Director of the Serious Fraud Office

Raza v Orr see Raza (Ali) v Procurator Fiscal, Glasgow

Raza (Ali) v Procurator Fiscal, Glasgow; *sub nom* Raza v Orr [2017] SAC (Crim) 6; 2017 S.C.L. 649; 2017 S.C.C.R. 263; 2017 G.W.D. 13-199, SAC .... *Digested,* 17/**2483**

Razzakov v Russia (57519/09) (2017) 65 E.H.R.R. 10, ECHR

Razzaq (Mohammed) v HM Advocate [2017] HCJAC 45; 2018 J.C. 21; 2017 S.C.L. 786; 2017 S.C.C.R. 376; 2017 G.W.D. 21-339, HCJ Appeal .... *Digested,* 17/**2489**

RB v HM Advocate see B (R) v HM Advocate

RB v Hungary (64602/12) (2017) 64 E.H.R.R. 25, ECHR

RB (Male Patient: Sterilisation), Re see A (Mental Patient: Sterilisation), Re

RBC Trustees (CI) Ltd v Stubbs [2017] EWHC 180 (Ch); [2017] 2 P. & C.R. DG5, Ch D

RBS (Rights Issue Litigation), Re [2017] EWHC 1217 (Ch); [2017] 1 W.L.R. 4635, Ch D

RBS (Rights Issue Litigation), Re [2016] EWHC 3161 (Ch); [2017] 1 W.L.R. 1991; [2017] 1 B.C.L.C. 726; [2017] Lloyd's Rep. F.C. 83, Ch D .... *Digested,* 17/**186**:
Applied 17/530

RBS Rights Issue Litigation, Re [2017] EWHC 463 (Ch); [2017] 1 W.L.R. 3539, Ch D . *Digested,* 17/**205**

RC v HM Advocate see C v HM Advocate

RCI Europe v Revenue and Customs Commissioners (C-37/08) EU:C:2009:507; [2009] S.T.C. 2407; [2009] E.C.R. I-7533; [2010] B.V.C. 833; [2009] S.T.I. 2588, ECJ (1st Chamber) .... *Digested,* 10/**3518**:
Distinguished 17/2264

RCS Contractors Ltd v Conway see RSC Contractors Ltd v Conway

RD v Herefordshire Council see D (Incapacitated Person) (Representatives and Advocates: Duties and Powers), Re

RD (Duties and Powers of Relevant Person's Representatives and Section 39 IMCAs), Re see D (Incapacitated Person) (Representatives and Advocates: Duties and Powers), Re

RDS Driving Services Ltd v Revenue and Customs Commissioners [2017] UKFTT 660 (TC); [2018] S.F.T.D. 381; [2017] S.T.I. 1986, FTT (Tax)

RE v United Kingdom (62498/11) (2016) 63 E.H.R.R. 2; 41 B.H.R.C. 1; Times, January 8, 2016, ECHR .... *Digested,* 16/**1055**

RE (A Child) v Calderdale and Huddersfield NHS Foundation Trust [2017] EWHC 824 (QB); [2017] Med. L.R. 390; (2017) 156 B.M.L.R. 204, QBD .... *Digested,* 17/**1638**

Ready Rentals Ltd (In Liquidation) v Ahmed; *sub nom* Crown Prosecution Service v Ahmed [2016] EWHC 1996 (Ch); [2017] Lloyd's Rep. F.C. 30, Ch D (Birmingham) .... *Digested,* 17/**357**

Reckitt & Colman Products Ltd v Borden Inc (No.3); *sub nom* Jif Lemon case [1990] 1 W.L.R. 491; [1990] 1 All E.R. 873; [1990] R.P.C. 341; Times, February 9, 1990; Independent, March 13, 1990; Guardian, February 13, 1990; (1990) 134 S.J. 784, HL .... *Digested,* 90/**3465**:
Applied 93/3802, 00/3590, 02/2785, 07/2546, 08/2387, 08/2405, 09/2452, 10/1991, 11/2010, 16/1289: *Considered* 95/4739, 96/5715, 07/2674, 09/2317, 10/1990, 14/1887: *Distinguished* 95/4735: *Followed* 96/6663, 11/1962, 11/2000, 13/1791, 13/1793, 14/1889, 14/1890, 16/1339, 17/1400: *Referred to* 99/3593

Recovery of Medical Costs for Asbestos Diseases (Wales) Bill, Re [2015] UKSC 3; [2015] A.C. 1016; [2015] 2 W.L.R. 481; [2015] 2 All E.R. 899; [2015] H.R.L.R. 9; [2015] Lloyd's Rep. I.R. 474; (2015) 143 B.M.L.R. 1, SC .... *Digested,* 15/**1664**: *Considered* 17/417

Red Bull GmbH v Optimum Mark (R2037/2013) (Unreported, December 2, 2014), OHIM (1st Bd App) *Considered* 17/1387

Red Bull GmbH v Potters Ltd; *sub nom* RED KOOGA Trademark [2013] R.P.C. 15, App Person .... *Digested,* 13/**1836**: *Applied* 17/1405

Red Bull GmbH v Sun Mark Ltd [2012] EWHC 1929 (Ch); [2013] E.T.M.R. 53, Ch D *Applied* 16/1333, 16/1335: *Considered* 17/1395

RED KOOGA Trademark see Red Bull GmbH v Potters Ltd

Reda v Flag Ltd [2002] UKPC 38; [2002] I.R.L.R. 747, PC (Ber) .... *Digested,* 03/**1317**: *Applied* 17/486: *Considered* 06/1290: *Distinguished* 05/1212

Redbridge LBC v A; *sub nom* Redbridge LBC v SNA [2015] EWHC 2140 (Fam); [2015] Fam. 335; [2015] 3 W.L.R. 1617; [2016] 1 F.L.R. 994; [2015] Fam. Law 1187, Fam Div .... *Digested,* 16/**838**: *Considered* 17/961

Redbridge LBC v G [2014] EWCOP 17, CP *Considered* 17/1548

Redbridge LBC v SNA see Redbridge LBC v A

Redcar and Cleveland BC v B see B (A Child) (Looked After Child), Re

Redcar and Cleveland BC v Bainbridge; *joined case* Surtees v Middlesbrough BC [2008] EWCA Civ 885; [2009] I.C.R. 133; [2008] I.R.L.R. 776, CA (Civ Div) .... *Digested,* 08/**1156**: *Applied* 10/1020, 10/1082, 11/1116, 12/1097, 17/2585: *Considered* 09/1207, 10/1026

Redman v Revenue and Customs Commissioners [2017] UKFTT 199 (TC); [2017] S.T.I. 872, FTT (Tax)

Redman v Zurich Insurance Plc [2017] EWHC 1919 (QB); [2018] 1 W.L.R. 280; [2017] B.P.I.R. 1692; [2018] Lloyd's Rep. I.R. 45; [2018] P.I.Q.R. P2, QBD

Redrose Ltd v Thomas (Valuation Officer) [2014] UKUT 311 (LC); [2014] R.A. 538, UT (Lands) *Considered* 17/1517

Redwood Birkhill Ltd v Revenue and Customs Commissioners [2017] UKFTT 234 (TC); [2017] S.T.I. 1047, FTT (Tax)

Reed Employment Ltd v Revenue and Customs Commissioners [2011] UKFTT 200 (TC); [2011] S.F.T.D. 720; [2011] S.T.I. 1500, FTT (Tax) .... *Digested,* 11/**3558**: *Affirmed* 13/3220: *Referred to* 17/2254

REEF Trade Mark; *sub nom* Bessant v South Cone Inc; South Cone Inc v Bessant (t/a REEF) [2002] EWCA Civ 763; [2003] R.P.C. 5; Times, May 31, 2002, CA (Civ Div) .... *Digested,* 02/**2897**: *Applied* 05/2568, 07/2684, 12/1981: *Considered* 14/1938, 17/1356, 17/2690: *Followed* 08/2395

Reemtsma Cigarettenfabriken GmbH v Ministero delle Finanze (C-35/05) EU:C:2007:167; [2008] S.T.C. 3448; [2007] E.C.R. I-2425; [2007] 2 C.M.L.R. 34; [2010] B.V.C. 30; [2007] S.T.I. 543, ECJ (2nd Chamber) .... *Digested,* 08/**4044**: *Applied* 12/3430, 15/2610, 15/2615, 17/2289: *Followed* 15/2577

Reeve v Thomas Dykfs (1829) 7 S. 632, IH (1 Div) *Considered* 17/2431

Reeves v Revenue and Customs Commissioners [2017] UKFTT 192 (TC); [2017] S.F.T.D. 765; [2017] S.T.I. 1123, FTT (Tax) .... *Digested,* 17/**2091**

Regan v Williamson [1976] 1 W.L.R. 305; [1976] 2 All E.R. 241; (1976) 120 S.J. 217, QBD .... *Digested,* 76/**672**: *Applied* 77/733: *Considered* 88/1056, 17/1553

Regency Villas Title Ltd v Diamond Resorts (Europe) Ltd [2015] EWHC 3564 (Ch); [2016] 4 W.L.R. 61; [2016] 1 P. & C.R. DG19, Ch D (Birmingham) .... *Digested,* 16/**1812**: *Reversed in part* 17/1842

Regency Villas Title Ltd v Diamond Resorts (Europe) Ltd [2017] EWCA Civ 238; [2017] Ch. 516; [2017] 3 W.L.R. 644; Times, June 1, 2017; [2017] 2 P. & C.R. DG8, CA (Civ Div) .... *Digested,* 17/**1842**

Regeneron Pharmaceuticals Inc v Genentech Inc; *joined case* Bayer Pharma AG v Genentech Inc [2013] EWCA Civ 93; [2013] R.P.C. 28, CA (Civ Div) .... *Digested,* 13/**1807**: *Applied* 14/1900: *Followed* 16/1310, 17/1375

Regent Leisuretime Ltd v NatWest Finance Ltd (formerly County NatWest Ltd) [2003] EWCA Civ 391; [2003] B.C.C. 587; Independent, April 1, 2003; (2003) 147 S.J.L.B. 386, CA (Civ Div) .... *Digested,* 03/**505**: *Explained* 16/346: *Followed* 17/398

Regie communale autonome du stade Luc Varenne v Belgium (C-55/14) EU:C:2015:29; [2015] S.T.C. 922; [2015] B.V.C. 11; [2015] S.T.I. 247, ECJ (9th Chamber)
Applied 17/2236

Regie Dauphinoise-Cabinet A Forest Sarl v Ministre du Budget (C-306/94) EU:C:1996:290; [1996] S.T.C. 1176; [1996] E.C.R. I-3695; [1996] 3 C.M.L.R. 193; [1996] C.E.C. 817, ECJ (5th Chamber)
Applied 05/4345, 08/4021, 08/4055, 11/3527: *Considered* 17/2248

Regional Collection Services Ltd v Heald; *sub nom* H (In Bankruptcy), Re; H (A Debtor) (No.38-SD of 1997), Re [2000] B.P.I.R. 661; Times, May 10, 2000, CA (Civ Div) ..... *Digested,* 00/**3484**:
Followed 14/1778, 17/1292

Regulus Ship Services Pte Ltd v Lundin Services BV [2016] EWHC 2674 (Comm); [2017] 1 All E.R. (Comm) 686; [2016] 2 Lloyd's Rep. 612; [2016] 2 C.L.C. 544, QBD (Comm) ..... *Digested,* 17/**2008**

Regus Management (UK) Ltd v Jackson (Valuation Officer) [2017] R.V.R. 210, VT

Reha Training Gesellschaft fur Sport- und Unfallrehabilitation mbH v Gesellschaft fur musikalische Auffuhrungs- und mechanische (C-117/15) EU:C:2016:379; [2016] Bus. L.R. 933; [2016] 3 C.M.L.R. 40; [2017] C.E.C. 945; [2017] E.C.D.R. 1, ECJ (Grand Chamber)

Rehman v Ali [2015] EWHC 4056 (Ch), Ch D (Birmingham)
Applied 17/194

Rehman v Revenue and Customs Commissioners [2017] UKFTT 834 (TC); [2017] S.T.I. 174, FTT (Tax)

Reid v Bickerstaff [1909] 2 Ch. 305, CA
Applied 52/3582, 68/3334, 91/3550: *Considered* 70/2425, 08/3112:
Followed 76/2298, 17/1828

Reid v Buckinghamshire Healthcare NHS Trust HQ13X01778, Sen Cts Costs Office
Applied 17/246

Reid v Harrower see Reid v Murphy

Reid v Murphy; *sub nom* Reid v Harrower [2016] SAC (Crim) 27; 2016 S.C.L. 1019; 2016 G.W.D. 33-607, SAC ..... *Digested,* 17/**2821**

Reid v Scottish Ministers [2017] CSIH 20; 2017 S.C. 372; 2017 G.W.D. 9-123, IH (Ex Div) ..... *Digested,* 17/**2747**

Reid v Scottish Ministers [2015] CSOH 84; 2015 G.W.D. 21-357, OH
Affirmed 17/2747

Reigate and Banstead BC v Pawlowski [2017] EWHC 1764 (Admin); [2018] P.T.S.R. 1; [2018] R.T.R. 10; [2017] L.L.R. 875, QBD (Admin)

Reigate and Banstead BC v Secretary of State for Communities and Local Government [2017] EWHC 1562 (Admin); [2017] J.P.L. 1368, QBD (Admin) ..... *Digested,* 17/**1767**

Reilly v Secretary of State for Work and Pensions see R. (on the application of Reilly) v Secretary of State for Work and Pensions

Reilly (Andrew) v HM Advocate [2017] HCJAC 5; 2017 S.C.L. 347; 2017 S.C.C.R. 142; 2017 G.W.D. 6-84, HCJ ..... *Digested,* 17/**2484**

Reilly's Application for Judicial Review, Re; *sub nom* Booth v Parole Board; Osborn v Parole Board; *joined cases* R. (on the application of Booth) v Parole Board; R. (on the application of Osborn) v Parole Board [2013] UKSC 61; [2014] A.C. 1115; [2013] 3 W.L.R. 1020; [2014] 1 All E.R. 369; [2014] N.I. 154; [2014] H.R.L.R. 1; (2013) 157(39) S.J.L.B. 37, SC ..... *Digested,* 13/**2115**:
Applied 14/2162, 14/2444, 16/1518, 16/2268: *Considered* 14/2233, 16/615:
Followed 15/1819, 17/1480, 17/1590, 17/1595

Reinhard v Ondra LLP [2015] EWHC 26 (Ch); [2016] 2 B.C.L.C. 571, Ch D ..... *Digested,* 17/**1582**

Reinhard v Ondra LLP [2015] EWHC 1869 (Ch); [2016] 2 B.C.L.C. 571, Ch D ..... *Digested,* 17/**1583**

Reisner v Turkey (Admissibility) (46815/0) (2017) 64 E.H.R.R. SE11, ECHR

Relfo Ltd (In Liquidation) v Varsani [2014] EWCA Civ 360; [2015] 1 B.C.L.C. 14, CA (Civ Div) ..... *Digested,* 15/**2130**:
Applied 15/2610, 17/1277

Remia BV v Commission of the European Communities (42/84) EU:C:1985:327; [1985] E.C.R. 2545; [1987] 1 C.M.L.R. 1; [1987] F.S.R. 190, ECJ (5th Chamber) ..... *Digested,* 87/**1503**:
Applied 05/549, 07/1550, 17/411

Remilien v Secretary of State for Social Security see Secretary of State for Social Security v Remilien

Rendon Marin v Administracion del Estado (C-165/14) EU:C:2016:675; [2017] Q.B. 495; [2017] 2 W.L.R. 117; [2017] 1 C.M.L.R. 29; [2017] C.E.C. 527; [2017] Imm. A.R. 205; [2017] I.N.L.R. 338, ECJ (Grand Chamber)

Representative Claimants v MGN Ltd see Gulati v MGN Ltd

Residential Apartments Ltd v Billson see Billson v Residential Apartments Ltd

Resolution Chemicals Ltd v H Lundbeck A/S [2013] EWCA Civ 924; [2014] R.P.C. 5, CA (Civ Div) .... *Digested,* 14/**1878**: *Applied* 17/500

Restivo (EEA: Prisoner Transfer); *sub nom* Secretary of State for the Home Department v Restivo [2016] UKUT 449 (IAC); [2017] Imm. A.R. 188, UT (IAC)

Reveille Independent LLC v Anotech International (UK) Ltd [2016] EWCA Civ 443; 166 Con. L.R. 79, CA (Civ Div) .... *Digested,* 16/**427**: *Followed* 17/499

Revell v Revenue and Customs Commissioners [2016] UKFTT 97 (TC); [2016] S.F.T.D. 618; [2017] W.T.L.R. 695; [2016] S.T.I. 1435, FTT (Tax) .... *Digested,* 16/**2074**

Revenue and Customs Commissioners v ABL (Holding) Ltd [2017] UKFTT 220 (TC); [2017] S.F.T.D. 805; [2017] S.T.I. 1103, FTT (Tax)

Revenue and Customs Commissioners v Aimia Coalition Loyalty UK Ltd see Revenue and Customs Commissioners v Loyalty Management UK Ltd

Revenue and Customs Commissioners v Airtours Holiday Transport Ltd see Airtours Holiday Transport Ltd (formerly My Travel Group) v Revenue and Customs Commissioners

Revenue and Customs Commissioners v Anson see Anson v Revenue and Customs Commissioners

Revenue and Customs Commissioners v Apollo Fuels Ltd see Apollo Fuels Ltd v Revenue and Customs Commissioners

Revenue and Customs Commissioners v Ariel; *sub nom* Halabi (A Bankrupt), Re [2017] UKFTT 87 (TC); [2017] B.P.I.R. 295, FTT (Tax) .... *Digested,* 17/**2152**

Revenue and Customs Commissioners v Ariel; *sub nom* Ariel v Revenue and Customs Commissioners; Halabi (In Bankruptcy), Re [2016] EWHC 1674 (Ch); [2017] 1 W.L.R. 319; [2016] B.P.I.R. 1144; [2016] B.T.C. 27, Ch D .... *Digested,* 16/**1190**

Revenue and Customs Commissioners v Associated Newspapers Ltd see Associated Newspapers Ltd v Revenue and Customs Commissioners

Revenue and Customs Commissioners v Astral Construction Ltd see Astral Construction Ltd v Revenue and Customs Commissioners

Revenue and Customs Commissioners v Atlantic Electronics Ltd see Atlantic Electronics Ltd v Revenue and Customs Commissioners

Revenue and Customs Commissioners v B&M Retail Ltd see B&M Retail Ltd v Revenue and Customs Commissioners

Revenue and Customs Commissioners v Banerjee [2009] EWHC 1229 (Ch); [2009] 3 All E.R. 930; [2009] S.T.C. 1930; [2009] E.M.L.R. 24; 80 T.C. 625; [2009] B.T.C. 337; [2009] S.T.I. 1963, Ch D .... *Digested,* 09/**343**: *Applied* 13/2995, 17/199: *Considered* 12/331

Revenue and Customs Commissioners v Bank of Ireland Britain Holdings Ltd [2008] EWCA Civ 58; [2008] S.T.C. 398; [2008] B.T.C. 126; [2008] S.T.I. 252, CA (Civ Div) .... *Digested,* 08/**3687**: *Considered* 14/2883: *Not applied* 17/2112

Revenue and Customs Commissioners v Benchdollar Ltd [2009] EWHC 1310 (Ch); [2010] 1 All E.R. 174; [2009] S.T.C. 2342; 79 T.C. 668; [2011] B.T.C. 36; [2009] S.T.I. 2058, Ch D .... *Digested,* 10/**3358**: *Applied* 17/2066: *Considered* 15/1617

Revenue and Customs Commissioners v Benham (Specialist Cars) Ltd [2017] UKUT 389 (TCC); [2017] B.T.C. 533, UT (Tax)

Revenue and Customs Commissioners v Blackwell see Blackwell v Revenue and Customs Commissioners

Revenue and Customs Commissioners v Blue Sphere Global Ltd see Mobilx Ltd (In Administration) v Revenue and Customs Commissioners

Revenue and Customs Commissioners v Boyce [2017] UKUT 177 (TCC); [2017] B.V.C. 513, UT (Tax) .... *Digested,* 17/**2247**

Revenue and Customs Commissioners v Bridport and West Dorset Golf Club Ltd see Bridport and West Dorset Golf Club Ltd v Revenue and Customs Commissioners

Revenue and Customs Commissioners v Bristol & West Plc see Bristol & West Plc v Revenue and Customs Commissioners

Revenue and Customs Commissioners v British Film Institute (C-592/15); *sub nom* British Film Institute v Revenue and Customs Commissioners (C-592/15) EU:C:2017:117; [2017] S.T.C. 681; [2017] B.V.C. 11; Times, April 12, 2017; [2017] S.T.I. 293, ECJ (4th Chamber)

Revenue and Customs Commissioners v British Telecommunications Plc [2014] EWCA Civ 433; [2014] S.T.C. 1926; [2014] B.V.C. 24; [2014] S.T.I. 1760, CA (Civ Div) .... *Digested,* 14/**3038**: *Followed* 16/2192, 17/2230

Revenue and Customs Commissioners v Brockenhurst College (C-699/15); *sub nom* Brockenhurst College v Revenue and Customs Commissioners (C-699/15) EU:C:2017:344; [2017] 4 W.L.R. 96; [2017] S.T.C. 1112; [2017] B.V.C. 20; Times, June 21, 2017; [2017] S.T.I. 1174, ECJ (1st Chamber)

Revenue and Customs Commissioners v C Jenkin and Son Ltd see C Jenkin and Son Ltd v Revenue and Customs Commissioners

Revenue and Customs Commissioners v Chamberlin see Chamberlin v Revenue and Customs Commissioners

Revenue and Customs Commissioners v Changtel Solutions UK Ltd (formerly Enta Technologies Ltd) see Enta Technologies Ltd, Re

Revenue and Customs Commissioners v Charlton [2012] UKFTT 770 (TCC); [2013] S.T.C. 866; [2013] B.T.C. 1634; [2013] S.T.I. 259, UT (Tax) .... *Digested,* 13/**3006**: *Applied* 14/2891, 16/2043, 17/2088: *Considered* 16/2128

Revenue and Customs Commissioners v Citibank NA; *sub nom* Revenue and Customs Commissioners v E Buyer UK Ltd [2017] EWCA Civ 1416; [2018] 1 W.L.R. 1524; [2017] B.V.C. 47, CA (Civ Div) .... *Digested,* 17/**2252**

Revenue and Customs Commissioners v Citibank NA see E Buyer UK Ltd v Revenue and Customs Commissioners

Revenue and Customs Commissioners v CM Utilities Ltd [2017] UKUT 305 (TCC); [2017] B.T.C. 527, UT (Tax)

Revenue and Customs Commissioners v Coinstar Ltd see Coinstar Ltd v Revenue and Customs Commissioners

Revenue and Customs Commissioners v Colaingrove Ltd see Colaingrove Ltd v Revenue and Customs Commissioners

Revenue and Customs Commissioners v Cotter; *sub nom* Cotter v Revenue and Customs Commissioners [2013] UKSC 69; [2013] 1 W.L.R. 3514; [2014] 1 All E.R. 1; [2013] S.T.C. 2480; [2013] B.T.C. 837; [2013] S.T.I. 3450, SC .... *Digested,* 14/**2931**: *Considered* 14/2860, 17/2129, 17/2141: *Distinguished* 16/2092: *Followed* 14/2958

Revenue and Customs Commissioners v D'Arcy; *sub nom* D'Arcy v Revenue and Customs Commissioners [2006] S.T.C. (S.C.D.) 543; [2006] S.T.I. 1856, Sp Comm .... *Digested,* 06/**4184**: *Affirmed* 07/4102: *Applied* 08/3646, 09/3781: *Considered* 10/3390, 17/2133: *Distinguished* 09/3916

Revenue and Customs Commissioners v DCC Holdings (UK) Ltd see DCC Holdings (UK) Ltd v Revenue and Customs Commissioners

Revenue and Customs Commissioners v de Freitas [2016] EWHC 1433 (Ch); [2016] B.P.I.R. 1179, Ch D .... *Digested,* 17/**1293**

Revenue and Customs Commissioners v Donaldson; *sub nom* Donaldson v Revenue and Customs Commissioners [2016] EWCA Civ 761; [2016] 1 W.L.R. 4521; [2016] S.T.C. 2511; [2016] B.T.C. 28; Times, October 11, 2016; [2016] S.T.I. 2597, CA (Civ Div) .... *Digested,* 16/**2094**: *Applied* 17/2082

Revenue and Customs Commissioners v DPAS Ltd [2016] UKUT 373 (TCC); [2016] B.V.C. 536, UT (Tax) .... *Digested,* 17/**2233**

Revenue and Customs Commissioners v E Buyer UK Ltd see Revenue and Customs Commissioners v Citibank NA

Revenue and Customs Commissioners v Earlsferry Thistle Golf Club see Earlsferry Thistle Golf Club v Revenue and Customs Commissioners

Revenue and Customs Commissioners v Eclipse Film Partners No.35 LLP see Eclipse Film Partners No.35 LLP v Revenue and Customs Commissioners

Revenue and Customs Commissioners v Elbrook (Cash & Carry) Ltd see Elbrook Cash and Carry Ltd v Revenue and Customs Commissioners

Revenue and Customs Commissioners v Esporta Ltd see Esporta Ltd v Revenue and Customs Commissioners

Revenue and Customs Commissioners v Findmypast Ltd; *sub nom* Revenue and Customs Commissioners, Appellants [2017] CSIH 59; [2017] S.T.C. 2335; 2018 S.C. 24; 2017 S.L.T. 1071; [2017] B.V.C. 38; 2017 G.W.D. 30-488, IH (1 Div) .... *Digested,* 17/**2848**

Revenue and Customs Commissioners v Finmeccanica Group Services SpA see Finmeccanica Group Services SpA v Revenue and Customs Commissioners

Revenue and Customs Commissioners v Fowler; *sub nom* Fowler v Revenue and Customs Commissioners [2017] UKUT 219 (TCC); [2017] S.T.C. 1385; [2017] B.T.C. 518, UT (Tax) .... *Digested,* 17/**2130**

Revenue and Customs Commissioners v Garau [2017] I.C.R. 1121, EAT .... *Digested,* 17/**767**

Revenue and Customs Commissioners v GB Housley Ltd; *sub nom* GB Housley Ltd v Revenue and Customs Commissioners [2016] EWCA Civ 1299; [2017] S.T.C. 508; [2017] B.V.C. 4; [2017] S.T.I. 101, CA (Civ Div) .... *Digested,* 17/**2229**

Revenue and Customs Commissioners v GB Housley Ltd; *sub nom* GB Housley Ltd v Revenue and Customs Commissioners [2015] UKUT 71 (TCC); [2015] S.T.C. 1403; [2015] B.V.C. 509, UT (Tax) .... *Digested,* 15/**2581**: *Reversed* 17/2229

Revenue and Customs Commissioners v GMAC UK Plc; *sub nom* GMAC UK Plc v Revenue and Customs Commissioners; *joined case* British Telecommunications Plc v Revenue and Customs Commissioners [2016] EWCA Civ 1015; [2017] S.T.C. 1247; [2016] B.V.C. 39, CA (Civ Div) .... *Digested,* 17/**2230**

Revenue and Customs Commissioners v GMAC UK Plc; *sub nom* GMAC UK Plc v Revenue and Customs Commissioners; *joined case* British Telecommunications Plc v Revenue and Customs Commissioners [2012] UKUT 279 (TCC); [2012] S.T.C. 2349; [2012] B.V.C. 1804; [2012] S.T.I. 2558, UT (Tax) .... *Digested,* 12/**3381**: *Reversed in part* 14/3038, 17/2230

Revenue and Customs Commissioners v Greener Solutions Ltd see Greener Solutions Ltd v Revenue and Customs Commissioners

Revenue and Customs Commissioners v Hok Ltd see Hok Ltd v Revenue and Customs Commissioners

Revenue and Customs Commissioners v IDT Card Services Ireland Ltd see R. (on the application of IDT Card Services Ireland Ltd) v Customs and Excise Commissioners

Revenue and Customs Commissioners v IFX Investment Co Ltd; *sub nom* IFX Investment Co Ltd v Revenue and Customs Commissioners; 'Spotting the Ball' Partnership v Revenue and Customs Commissioners; Sportech Plc v Revenue and Customs Commissioners [2016] EWCA Civ 436; [2016] 1 W.L.R. 3952; [2017] 1 All E.R. 45; [2016] S.T.C. 1666; [2016] B.V.C. 14; [2016] L.L.R. 521; [2016] S.T.I. 1508, CA (Civ Div) .... *Digested,* 16/**2175**

Revenue and Customs Commissioners v Imperial College of Science, Technology and Medicine [2016] UKUT 278 (TCC); [2016] B.V.C. 521, UT (Tax) .... *Digested,* 17/**2246**

Revenue and Customs Commissioners v Imperial College of Science, Technology and Medicine [2015] UKFTT 33 (TC); [2015] S.T.I. 330, FTT (Tax) *Affirmed* 17/2246

Revenue and Customs Commissioners v Infinity Distribution Ltd (In Administration) [2016] EWCA Civ 1014; [2017] S.T.C. 915; [2016] B.V.C. 40, CA (Civ Div) .... *Digested,* 17/**2270**

Revenue and Customs Commissioners v Infinity Distribution Ltd (In Administration) [2015] UKUT 219 (TCC); [2015] S.T.C. 2374; [2015] B.V.C. 515, UT (Tax) .... *Digested,* 16/**2188**: *Reversed in part* 17/2270

Revenue and Customs Commissioners v Investment Trust Companies (In Liquidation) see Investment Trust Companies (In Liquidation) v Revenue and Customs Commissioners

Revenue and Customs Commissioners v Isle of Wight Council see Isle of Wight Council v Revenue and Customs Commissioners

Revenue and Customs Commissioners v J3 Building Solutions Ltd see J3 Building Solutions Ltd v Revenue and Customs Commissioners

Revenue and Customs Commissioners v Jackson Grundy Ltd [2017] UKUT 180 (TCC); [2017] Lloyd's Rep. F.C. 365; [2017] B.T.C. 517, UT (Tax) .... *Digested,* 17/**230**

Revenue and Customs Commissioners v JP Whitter (Waterwell Engineers) Ltd see JP Whitter (Waterwell Engineers) Ltd v Revenue and Customs Commissioners

Revenue and Customs Commissioners v KE Entertainments Ltd [2017] UKUT 328 (TCC); [2017] S.T.C. 1895; [2017] B.V.C. 528; [2018] L.L.R. 1; [2017] S.T.I. 1855, UT (Tax) .... *Digested,* 17/**2256**

Revenue and Customs Commissioners v Languard New Homes Ltd see Languard New Homes Ltd v Revenue and Customs Commissioners

Revenue and Customs Commissioners v Longridge on the Thames see Longridge on the Thames v Revenue and Customs Commissioners

Revenue and Customs Commissioners v Loyalty Management UK Ltd; *sub nom* Revenue and Customs Commissioners v Aimia Coalition Loyalty UK Ltd; Loyalty Management UK Ltd v Revenue and Customs Commissioners; Customs and Excise Commissioners v Loyalty Management UK Ltd [2013] UKSC 15; [2013] 2 All E.R. 719; [2013] S.T.C. 784; [2013] 2 C.M.L.R. 51; [2013] B.V.C. 67; [2013] S.T.I. 591, SC .... *Digested,* 13/**3204**: *Considered* 13/3209, 17/2249: *Followed* 17/2260

Revenue and Customs Commissioners v Mabbutt see Mabbutt v Revenue and Customs Commissioners

Revenue and Customs Commissioners v McCarthy and Stone (Developments) Ltd [2014] UKUT 196 (TCC); [2014] S.T.C. 973; [2014] B.V.C. 504; [2014] S.T.I. 626, UT (Tax) .... *Digested,* 14/**9**: *Approved* 16/2204, 17/2182: *Not followed* 14/2983, 15/2602

Revenue and Customs Commissioners v McQuillan [2017] UKUT 344 (TCC); [2017] S.T.C. 2192; [2017] B.T.C. 531; [2017] S.T.I. 1972, UT (Tax) .... *Digested,* 17/**2090**

Revenue and Customs Commissioners v Mercedes-Benz Financial Services UK (C-164/16) EU:C:2017:734; [2017] B.V.C. 46; [2017] S.T.I. 2127, ECJ (1st Chamber)

Revenue and Customs Commissioners v MG Rover Group Ltd; *joined cases* Standard Chartered Plc v Revenue and Customs Commissioners; Lloyds Banking Group Plc v Revenue and Customs Commissioners [2016] UKUT 434 (TCC); [2017] S.T.C. 41; [2016] B.V.C. 543, UT (Tax) .... *Digested,* 17/**2289**: *Considered* 17/2290

Revenue and Customs Commissioners v Murray Group Holdings Ltd see Murray Group Holdings Ltd v Revenue and Customs Commissioners

Revenue and Customs Commissioners v Murray Group Holdings Ltd see RFC 2012 Plc (In Liquidation) (formerly Rangers Football Club Plc) v Advocate General for Scotland

Revenue and Customs Commissioners v National Exhibition Centre Ltd (C-130/15); *sub nom* National Exhibition Centre Ltd v Revenue and Customs Commissioners (C-130/15) EU:C:2016:357; [2016] S.T.C. 2132; [2016] B.V.C. 19, ECJ (8th Chamber)
Considered 17/2233

Revenue and Customs Commissioners v National Exhibition Centre Ltd see National Exhibition Centre Ltd v Revenue and Customs Commissioners

Revenue and Customs Commissioners v Newey (t/a Ocean Finance) (C-653/11); *sub nom* Newey v Revenue and Customs Commissioners (C-653/11) EU:C:2013:409; [2013] S.T.C. 2432; [2013] B.V.C. 259; [2013] S.T.I. 2304, ECJ (3rd Chamber) .... *Digested,* 13/**3231**: *Applied* 14/3061, 14/3073, 17/2254, 17/2258: *Followed* 16/2186

Revenue and Customs Commissioners v Noor see Noor v Revenue and Customs Commissioners

Revenue and Customs Commissioners v Open University [2016] EWCA Civ 114; [2017] 4 W.L.R. 113; [2017] 2 All E.R. 390; [2016] S.T.C. 2273; [2016] B.V.C. 10; [2016] S.T.I. 519, CA (Civ Div) .... *Digested,* 16/**2198**

Revenue and Customs Commissioners v Pacific Computers Ltd [2016] UKUT 350 (TCC); [2016] B.V.C. 533; [2016] S.T.I. 2547, UT (Tax) .... *Digested,* 17/**2251**

Revenue and Customs Commissioners v Parry see Parry v Revenue and Customs Commissioners

Revenue and Customs Commissioners v Praesto Consulting UK Ltd [2017] UKUT 395 (TCC); [2017] B.V.C. 531, UT (Tax)

Revenue and Customs Commissioners v Procter & Gamble UK see Procter & Gamble UK v Revenue and Customs Commissioners

Revenue and Customs Commissioners v SAE Education Ltd see SAE Education Ltd v Revenue and Customs Commissioners

Revenue and Customs Commissioners v SDI (Brook EU) Ltd [2017] UKUT 327 (TCC); [2017] B.V.C. 527, UT (Tax) .... *Digested,* 17/**2257**

Revenue and Customs Commissioners v Secret Hotels2 Ltd (formerly Med Hotels Ltd) see Secret Hotels2 Ltd (formerly Med Hotels Ltd) v Revenue and Customs Commissioners

Revenue and Customs Commissioners v SiBCAS Ltd see SiBCAS Ltd v Revenue and Customs Commissioners

Revenue and Customs Commissioners v Sippchoice Ltd see Sippchoice Ltd v Revenue and Customs Commissioners

Revenue and Customs Commissioners v Smallwood see Smallwood v Revenue and Customs Commissioners

Revenue and Customs Commissioners v Smart [2016] B.P.I.R. 1329, Ch D .... *Digested,* 17/**1284**

Revenue and Customs Commissioners v Stolkin see Stolkin v Revenue and Customs Commissioners

Revenue and Customs Commissioners v Stringer see Inland Revenue Commissioners v Ainsworth

Revenue and Customs Commissioners v Tager [2017] UKUT 84 (TCC); [2017] B.T.C. 509, UT (Tax) .... *Digested,* 17/**2135**

Revenue and Customs Commissioners v Tager [2017] UKUT 161 (TCC); [2017] B.T.C. 515, UT (Tax) .... *Digested,* 17/**2151**

Revenue and Customs Commissioners v Temple Finance Ltd see Temple Finance Ltd v Revenue and Customs Commissioners

Revenue and Customs Commissioners v TGH (Commercial) Ltd [2017] UKUT 116 (TCC); [2017] B.V.C. 511, UT (Tax) .... *Digested,* 17/**2280**

Revenue and Customs Commissioners v Total Network SL see Customs and Excise Commissioners v Total Network SL

Revenue and Customs Commissioners v Tower MCashback LLP 1 see Tower MCashback LLP 1 v Revenue and Customs Commissioners

Revenue and Customs Commissioners v UK Storage Co (SW) Ltd see UK Storage Co (SW) Ltd v Revenue and Customs Commissioners

Revenue and Customs Commissioners v Vaccine Research LP see Vaccine Research LP v Revenue and Customs Commissioners

Revenue and Customs Commissioners v Volkswagen Financial Services (UK) Ltd see Volkswagen Financial Services (UK) Ltd v Revenue and Customs Commissioners

Revenue and Customs Commissioners v Walker see Walker v Revenue and Customs Commissioners

Revenue and Customs Commissioners v Wheels Private Hire Ltd see Wheels Private Hire Ltd v Revenue and Customs Commissioners

Revenue and Customs Commissioners v Zombory-Moldovan (t/a Craft Carnival) see Zombory-Moldovan (t/a Craft Carnival) v Revenue and Customs Commissioners

Revenue and Customs Commissioners, Appellants see Revenue and Customs Commissioners v Findmypast Ltd

Revival Properties Ltd v Edinburgh City Council see Edinburgh City Council v Secretary of State for Scotland

Rexha (S.117C: Earlier Offences); *sub nom* Secretary of State for the Home Department v Rexha [2016] UKUT 335 (IAC); [2016] Imm. A.R. 1426; [2017] I.N.L.R. 412, UT (IAC) .... *Digested,* 17/**1192**

Reynolds v CLFIS (UK) Ltd; *sub nom* CLFIS (UK) Ltd v Reynolds [2015] EWCA Civ 439; [2015] I.C.R. 1010; [2015] I.R.L.R. 562; Times, June 4, 2015, CA (Civ Div) *Digested,* 15/**788**: *Applied* 16/665: *Considered* 16/704: *Followed* 17/777, 17/840

Reynolds v Phoenix Assurance Co Ltd [1978] 2 Lloyd's Rep. 440, QBD .... *Digested,* 79/**1510**: *Considered* 17/1343

Reynolds v Times Newspapers Ltd [2001] 2 A.C. 127; [1999] 3 W.L.R. 1010; [1999] 4 All E.R. 609; [2000] E.M.L.R. 1; [2000] H.R.L.R. 134; 7 B.H.R.C. 289; Times, October 29, 1999; Independent, November 3, 1999; (1999) 96(45) L.S.G. 34; (1999) 149 N.L.J. 1697; (1999) 143 S.J.L.B. 270, HL .... *Digested,* 99/**1630**: *Applied* 00/1761, 00/1763, 01/1823, 01/1829, 01/1831, 02/953, 02/959, 04/935, 05/980, 06/1047, 06/1051, 07/1075, 07/1076, 08/904, 09/985, 12/868, 17/651: *Considered* 01/1824, 01/1832, 01/1834, 05/973, 05/977, 06/1049, 06/1050, 12/867: *Distinguished* 06/1044: *Followed* 02/960, 10/840: *Referred to* 11/865

Reynolds Porter Chamberlain LLP v Khan [2017] I.L.Pr. 13; [2016] B.P.I.R. 722, Ch D (Bankruptcy Ct) .... *Digested,* 16/**1186**

Rezmives v Romania (61467/12) (Unreported, April 25, 2017), ECJ *Applied* 17/906

RFC 2012 Plc (In Liquidation) (formerly Rangers Football Club Plc) v Advocate General for Scotland; *sub nom* Revenue and Customs Commissioners v Murray Group Holdings Ltd; Advocate General for Scotland v Murray Group Holdings Ltd; Murray Group Holdings Ltd v Revenue and Customs Commissioners [2017] UKSC 45; [2017] 1 W.L.R. 2767; [2017] 4 All E.R. 654; [2017] S.T.C. 1556; 2018 S.C. (U.K.S.C.) 15; 2017 S.L.T. 799; 2017 S.C.L.R. 517; [2017] B.T.C. 22; [2017] W.T.L.R. 1093; Times, July 17, 2017; [2017] S.T.I. 1610; 2017 G.W.D. 21-357, SC .... *Digested,* 17/**2131**

RFC 2012 Plc (In Liquidation) (formerly Rangers Football Club Plc) v Advocate General for Scotland see Murray Group Holdings Ltd v Revenue and Customs Commissioners

RG Kensington Management Co Ltd v Hutchinson IDH Ltd [2002] EWHC 1180 (Ch); [2003] 2 P. & C.R. 13, Ch D .... *Digested,* 03/**3552**: *Applied* 10/2591: *Considered* 17/497

RH Green & Silley Weir Ltd v British Railways Board [1985] 1 W.L.R. 570; [1985] 1 All E.R. 237, Ch D .... *Digested,* 85/**2013**: *Applied* 17/1342

RHM Bakeries (Scotland) Ltd v Strathclyde RC 1985 S.C. (H.L.) 17; 1985 S.L.T. 214; Times, January 29, 1985, HL .... *Digested,* 85/**4458**: *Applied* 13/3870, 17/2741: *Considered* 88/4575, 95/6164, 96/7230, 00/6600: *Followed* 95/6162, 12/4231

Rhuppiah v Secretary of State for the Home Department [2016] EWCA Civ 803; [2016] 1 W.L.R. 4203; [2017] Imm. A.R. 337; [2017] I.N.L.R. 248; Times, November 1, 2016, CA (Civ Div) .... *Digested,* 16/**1118**: *Followed* 17/1197, 17/1235

Rice v Connolly [1966] 2 Q.B. 414; [1966] 3 W.L.R. 17; [1966] 2 All E.R. 649; (1966) 130 J.P. 322; (1966) 110 S.J. 371, DC .... *Digested,* 66/**9240**: *Applied* 73/2870, 73/2994, 76/527, 81/2093, 82/2359, 83/3230, 83/726: *Approved* 70/2218: *Considered* 75/2566, 86/2974, 94/3491, 06/868, 15/2064, 17/1796: *Distinguished* 82/2358

Richard v BBC [2017] EWHC 1648 (Ch); [2017] E.M.L.R. 25, Ch D .... *Digested,* 17/**374**

Richards v IP Solutions Group Ltd [2016] EWHC 1835 (QB); [2017] I.R.L.R. 133, QBD .... *Digested,* 17/**395**

Richards v Vivendi SA [2017] EWHC 1581 (Ch); [2017] B.P.I.R. 1390, Ch D .... *Digested,* 17/**1290**

Richards v Worcestershire CC [2016] EWHC 1954 (Ch); [2017] P.T.S.R. 165; (2016) 19 C.C.L. Rep. 561; [2016] Med. L.R. 534; (2016) 152 B.M.L.R. 146; [2017] M.H.L.R. 72; [2017] W.T.L.R. 117, Ch D (Bristol) .... *Digested,* 16/**1835**

Richardson v Chief Constable of the West Midlands [2011] EWHC 773 (QB); [2011] 2 Cr. App. R. 1; Times, April 11, 2011; [2011] Crim. L.R. 903, QBD (Birmingham) *Digested,* 11/**2601**: *Applied* 14/2458: *Considered* 11/2597, 17/1802

Richardson v Facebook; *joined case* Richardson v Google (UK) Ltd [2015] EWHC 3154 (QB); [2015] Info. T.L.R. 69, QBD .... *Digested,* 17/**654**

Richardson v Google (UK) Ltd see Richardson v Facebook

Richardson v Howie [2004] EWCA Civ 1127; [2005] P.I.Q.R. Q3; Times, September 10, 2004; (2004) 101(37) L.S.G. 36; (2004) 154 N.L.J. 1361; (2004) 148 S.J.L.B. 1030, CA (Civ Div) .... *Digested,* 04/**914**: *Applied* 17/1560: *Considered* 08/891

Richardson v Richardson (No.1) [1994] 1 W.L.R. 186; [1994] 1 W.L.R. 187; [1993] 4 All E.R. 673; [1994] 1 F.L.R. 286; [1994] 1 F.C.R. 53; [1994] Fam. Law 188, Fam Div .... *Digested,* 93/**1906**: *Applied* 17/1041: *Considered* 95/2340

Richardson v Solihull MBC see White v Ealing LBC

Richborough Estates Partnership LLP v Cheshire East BC see Secretary of State for Communities and Local Government v Hopkins Homes Ltd

Richmond upon Thames LBC v AC [2017] UKUT 173 (AAC); [2017] E.L.R. 316, UT (AAC)

Ridehalgh v Horsefield; *joined cases* Watson v Watson (Wasted Costs Orders); Roberts v Coverite (Asphalters) Ltd; Philex Plc v Golban; Antonelli v Wade Gery Farr (A Firm); Allen v Unigate Dairies Ltd [1994] Ch. 205; [1994] 3 W.L.R. 462; [1994] 3 All E.R. 848; [1994] B.C.C. 390; [1997] Costs L.R. (Core Vol.) 268; [1994] 2 F.L.R. 194; [1955-95] P.N.L.R. 636; Times, January 28, 1994; Independent, February 4, 1994; [1994] Fam. Law 560; [1994] E.G. 15 (C.S.); (1994) 144 N.L.J. 231; [1994] N.P.C. 7, CA (Civ Div) .... *Digested,* 94/**3623**: *Applied* 95/4028, 95/4030, 95/4031, 95/4034, 96/3524, 96/936, 96/939, 97/602, 99/988, 00/4001, 00/470, 00/471, 01/4516, 02/408, 02/409, 03/382, 03/383, 04/323, 04/325, 05/496, 08/1173, 09/2737, 09/385, 09/386, 11/307, 11/311, 11/312, 12/1096, 13/1319, 13/457, 13/771, 15/1067, 17/1460, 17/1515, 17/222: *Approved* 00/469: *Considered* 94/3620, 95/2273, 95/4673, 96/3899, 96/4508, 97/1387, 97/1388, 97/605, 97/607, 97/610, 98/497, 99/422, 99/989, 00/2466, 01/537, 01/589, 04/324, 10/15, 14/946, 15/609, 17/1219: *Distinguished* 95/4032: *Followed* 98/496, 98/499, 00/1043, 12/2080, 16/232

RIGAKU/Method of setting measuring range (T1846/11) [2017] E.P.O.R. 25, EPO (Technical Bd App)

Riley v Crown Prosecution Service [2016] EWHC 2531 (Admin); [2017] 1 W.L.R. 505; (2017) 181 J.P. 96; [2016] C.T.L.C. 156; [2017] Crim. L.R. 222; [2016] A.C.D. 128, DC .... *Digested,* 17/**534**: *Applied* 17/617

Riley v Rollerteam Ltd see Rollerteam Ltd v Riley

Risk Management Partners Ltd v Brent LBC see Brent LBC v Risk Management Partners Ltd

Riskin v Belgium (C-176/15) EU:C:2016:488; [2016] 4 W.L.R. 149; [2017] S.T.C. 462; [2017] 1 C.M.L.R. 17; [2016] S.T.I. 2200, ECJ (6th Chamber)

Riva Fire SpA v European Commission (C-89/15 P) EU:C:2017:713; [2017] 5 C.M.L.R. 26, ECJ (9th Chamber)

Riverside Park Ltd v NHS Property Services Ltd [2016] EWHC 1313 (Ch); [2017] L. & T.R. 12, Ch D (Leeds) .... *Digested,* 17/**1474**

Riviera Trust, Re see Jasmine Trustees Ltd v L

Rizleriene v Lithuania see Wolkowicz v Poland

RK v Oldham NHS Trust see JD v East Berkshire Community Health NHS Trust

RK (Nepal) v Secretary of State for the Home Department see R. (on the application of RK (Nepal)) v Secretary of State for the Home Department

RMC Building & Civil Engineering Ltd v UK Construction Ltd [2016] EWHC 241 (TCC); [2016] B.L.R. 264, QBD (TCC) .... *Digested,* 16/**391**: *Applied* 17/471

Robert v Woodall; *sub nom* Elichaoff (Deceased), Re [2016] EWHC 2987 (Ch); [2017] 4 W.L.R. 11; [2017] B.P.I.R. 414, Ch D .... *Digested,* 17/**1282**

Robert Cort & Son Ltd v Charman [1981] I.C.R. 816; [1981] I.R.L.R. 437, EAT .... *Digested,* 82/**1099**: *Applied* 82/1132, 04/1208: *Approved* 17/845: *Considered* 82/1101, 87/1381, 00/2131: *Followed* 09/1265: *Not applied* 99/2145

Robert Lindley Ltd v East Riding of Yorkshire Council [2016] UKUT 6 (LC); [2017] R.V.R. 116, UT (Lands)

Roberts v Coverite (Asphalters) Ltd see Ridehalgh v Horsefield

Roberts v Fresco [2017] EWHC 283 (Ch); [2017] Ch. 433; [2017] 3 W.L.R. 209, Ch D . *Digested,* 17/**2072**

Roberts v Gill & Co [2010] UKSC 22; [2011] 1 A.C. 240; [2010] 2 W.L.R. 1227; [2010] 4 All E.R. 367; [2010] P.N.L.R. 30; [2010] W.T.L.R. 1223; Times, May 28, 2010; (2010) 154(20) S.J.L.B. 36, SC .... *Digested,* 10/**377**: *Applied* 13/2103, 17/329: *Followed* 12/1266

Roberts v Johnstone [1989] Q.B. 878; [1988] 3 W.L.R. 1247; Times, April 15, 1988; (1989) 86(5) L.S.G. 44; (1989) 132 S.J. 1672, CA (Civ Div) .... *Digested,* 89/**1202**: *Applied* 94/1542, 99/1415, 00/1515, 01/1554, 10/2397, 15/3254: *Cited* 94/1548, 05/5587: *Considered* 89/1185, 92/5639, 02/3412, 07/3071, 12/2408, 17/639: *Followed* 15/1878, 16/1602, 17/638: *Referred to* 90/1578

Roberts v Lawton [2016] UKUT 395 (TCC); [2017] 1 P. & C.R. 3, UT (Tax) .... *Digested,* 16/**1822**

Roberts v Soldiers, Sailors, Airmen and Families Association-Forces Help [2016] EWHC 2744 (QB); [2017] P.N.L.R. 10, QBD .... *Digested,* 17/**338**

Roberts v TUI UK Ltd (Unreported, April 4, 2017), CC (Birkenhead) [*Peter Harthan, Barrister, 7 Harrington Street, Liverpool*] .... *Digested,* 17/**1679**

Roberts v Wilsons Solicitors LLP [2017] 1 B.C.L.C. 138; [2016] I.C.R. 659; [2016] I.R.L.R. 586, EAT .... *Digested,* 16/**703**

Robertson v Dunn [2015] SAC (Crim) 1; 2016 S.L.T. (Sh Ct) 51; 2015 G.W.D. 40-641, SAC .... *Digested,* 16/**2802**: *Considered* 17/2812

Robertson v Muir [2016] SAC (Civ) 10; 2017 S.C. (S.A.C.) 9; 2016 Fam. L.R. 194; 2016 G.W.D. 34-615, SAC .... *Digested,* 17/**2425**

Robertson v Robertson [2016] EWHC 613 (Fam); [2017] 1 F.L.R. 1174; [2016] Fam. Law 805, Fam Div

Robertson (Paul) v HM Advocate see Gemmell (James Kelly) v HM Advocate

Robertson (Stewart) v HM Advocate; *sub nom* Robertson, Petitioner; Gough v McFadyen; *joined case* Gough (Stephen Peter) v HM Advocate [2007] HCJAC 63; 2008 J.C. 146; 2007 S.L.T. 1153; 2008 S.C.L. 80; 2008 S.C.C.R. 20; 2007 G.W.D. 37-643, HCJ .... *Digested,* 08/**4650**: *Applied* 15/2978, 16/19: *Considered* 17/2571: *Followed* 14/3427

Robertson, Petitioner see Robertson (Stewart) v HM Advocate

Robinson v Bird; *sub nom* Scott-Kilvert's Estate, Re; Robinson v Fernsby [2003] EWCA Civ 1820; [2004] W.T.L.R. 257; Times, January 20, 2004; (2004) 101(7) L.S.G. 36; (2004) 148 S.J.L.B. 59, CA (Civ Div) *Applied* 05/2693, 10/3217: *Considered* 10/361: *Followed* 10/2711, 17/49

Robinson v Fernsby see Robinson v Bird

Robinson v Hastings Direct Ltd (Unreported, April 20, 2017), CC (Romford) [*Irwin Mitchell, 1 Millsands, Riverside West, Sheffield*] .... *Digested,* 17/**1650**

Robinson v Revenue and Customs Commissioners [2017] UKUT 383 (TCC); [2017] B.V.C. 532, UT (Tax)

Robson v Hallett [1967] 2 Q.B. 939; [1967] 3 W.L.R. 28; [1967] 2 All E.R. 407; (1967) 51 Cr. App. R. 307; (1967) 131 J.P. 333; (1967) 111 S.J. 254, QBD .... *Digested,* 67/**3993**: *Applied* 75/3472, 90/1066: *Considered* 82/2367, 90/1073, 17/1449: *Distinguished* 68/632, 79/543

Roca Sanitario SA v European Commission (C-636/13 P) EU:C:2017:56; [2017] 4 C.M.L.R. 20, ECJ (1st Chamber)

Roche v MGN Ltd see Gulati v MGN Ltd

Roche Diagnostics Ltd v Mid Yorkshire Hospitals NHS Trust [2013] EWHC 933 (TCC); [2013] C.I.L.L. 3360; (2013) 163(7558) N.L.J. 17; [2013] P.T.S.R. D35, QBD (TCC) *Considered* 16/295, 17/1811

Rococo Developments Ltd (In Liquidation), Re see Evans v Jones

Rodger (Stephen) v HM Advocate [2017] HCJAC 65; 2017 S.C.L. 971; 2017 G.W.D. 29-461, HCJ .... *Digested,* 17/**2531**

Roe Brickwork Ltd v Wates Construction Ltd [2013] EWHC 3417 (TCC), QBD (TCC) *Applied* 16/393, 17/450

Rogers v Hoyle; *sub nom* Hoyle v Rogers [2014] EWCA Civ 257; [2015] Q.B. 265; [2014] 3 W.L.R. 148; [2014] 3 All E.R. 550; [2014] C.P. Rep. 30; [2014] 1 C.L.C. 316; [2014] Inquest L.R. 135, CA (Civ Div) .... *Digested,* 14/**288**: *Applied* 16/1400: *Considered* 17/191

Rogerson v Wigan MBC [2004] EWHC 1677 (QB); [2005] 2 All E.R. 1000; [2005] H.L.R. 10; [2005] B.L.G.R. 549; [2004] 2 P. & C.R. DG21, QBD .... *Digested,* 05/**2660**: *Applied* 17/1150

Rohde v Herefordshire Council [2016] EWHC 2407 (Admin); [2017] R.V.R. 69, QBD (Admin) .... *Digested,* 17/**296**

Rollerteam Ltd v Riley; *joined case* Riley v Rollerteam Ltd [2016] EWCA Civ 1291; [2017] Ch. 109; [2017] 2 W.L.R. 870; [2017] 1 P. & C.R. 14; Times, February 2, 2017, CA (Civ Div) .... *Digested,* 17/**1836**

Rollerteam Ltd v Riley; *joined case* Riley v Rollerteam Ltd [2015] EWHC 1545 (Ch), Ch D
Affirmed 17/1836

Rolls-Royce Plc v Unite the Union [2009] EWCA Civ 387; [2010] 1 W.L.R. 318; [2010] I.C.R. 1; [2009] I.R.L.R. 576; Times, May 27, 2009; (2009) 106(21) L.S.G. 15; (2009) 153(20) S.J.L.B. 38, CA (Civ Div) .... *Digested,* 09/**1162**: *Applied* 10/2591, 11/176, 11/1869, 14/2224, 16/1288, 17/1343: *Considered* 12/2612, 13/1730, 15/525: *Followed* 13/438, 15/801, 16/720, 17/8

Romania v Zagrean; *sub nom* Mures Court v Zagrean; Sunca v Iasi Court of Law; Chihaia v Bacau Court of Law; *joined cases* Sunca v Romania; Chihaia v Romania [2016] EWHC 2786 (Admin); [2016] A.C.D. 140, DC
Considered 17/908

Romein v Advocate General for Scotland [2016] CSIH 24; 2016 S.C. 629; 2016 S.L.T. 459; 2016 S.C.L.R. 789; [2016] Imm. A.R. 909; [2017] I.N.L.R. 76; 2016 G.W.D. 11-224, IH (Ex Div) .... *Digested,* 16/**2688**

Romer v Freie und Hansestadt Hamburg (C-147/08) EU:C:2011:286; [2013] 2 C.M.L.R. 11; [2011] Eq. L.R. 921, ECJ (Grand Chamber)
Applied 13/2146: *Considered* 14/1120, 15/1858: *Followed* 17/1610

Ronelp Marine Ltd v STX Offshore and Shipbuilding Co [2016] EWHC 2228 (Ch); [2017] B.P.I.R. 203, Ch D .... *Digested,* 17/**337**: *Considered* 17/453

Roocroft v Ball [2016] EWCA Civ 1009; [2017] 1 W.L.R. 1137; [2017] 2 F.L.R. 810; [2016] 3 F.C.R. 546; Times, December 13, 2016, CA (Civ Div) .... *Digested,* 17/**977**

Roshan v Singh [2017] EWHC 176 (Ch); [2017] 4 W.L.R. 46; [2017] 2 P. & C.R. DG2, Ch D .... *Digested,* 17/**194**

Ross v Richardson see Gemmell (James Kelly) v HM Advocate

Rotherham MBC v M [2016] EWHC 2660 (Fam); [2016] 4 W.L.R. 177; [2017] 2 F.L.R. 366, Fam Div .... *Digested,* 17/**951**

Rotronic Instruments (UK) Ltd v A One Distribution (UK) Ltd see ADVA Optical Networking Ltd v Optron Holding Ltd

Roult v North West SHA [2009] EWCA Civ 444; [2010] 1 W.L.R. 487; [2009] C.P. Rep. 37; [2009] P.I.Q.R. P18; [2009] LS Law Medical 383; Times, June 8, 2009; (2009) 106(22) L.S.G. 25, CA (Civ Div) .... *Digested,* 09/**392**: *Considered* 11/367, 12/404, 12/416, 12/443, 15/1048, 17/1013: *Followed* 11/1260, 11/345

Round v Round [2017] NZHC 428; 19 I.T.E.L.R. 987, HC (NZ)

Rouse (Mark David) see R. v Forbes (Stephen John)

Routier v Revenue and Customs Commissioners [2016] EWCA Civ 938; [2017] P.T.S.R. 73; [2016] S.T.C. 2218; [2016] B.T.C. 38; [2016] S.T.I. 2653, CA (Civ Div) .... *Digested,* 16/**2102**

Roxar v Jaledoust [2017] EWHC 977 (Fam); [2017] 2 F.C.R. 606, Fam Div

Royal Bank of Scotland Plc v Etridge (No.2); *joined cases* Barclays Bank Plc v Coleman; Barclays Bank Plc v Harris; Midland Bank Plc v Wallace; National Westminster Bank Plc v Gill; UCB Home Loans Corp Ltd v Moore; Bank of Scotland v Bennett; Kenyon-Brown v Desmond Banks & Co (Undue Influence) (No.2) [2001] UKHL 44; [2002] 2 A.C. 773; [2001] 3 W.L.R. 1021; [2001] 4 All E.R. 449; [2001] 2 All E.R. (Comm) 1061; [2002] 1 Lloyd's Rep. 343; [2001] 2 F.L.R. 1364; [2001] 3 F.C.R. 481; [2002] H.L.R. 4; Times, October 17, 2001; [2001] Fam. Law 880; Daily Telegraph, October 23, 2001; [2001] 43 E.G. 184 (C.S.); (2001) 151 N.L.J. 1538; [2001] N.P.C. 147; [2002] 1 P. & C.R. DG14, HL .... *Digested,* 01/**4880**:
Applied 03/2379, 03/3556, 03/3587, 03/3588, 03/3612, 03/4118, 03/4122, 03/4124, 04/3671, 05/1423, 05/2673, 05/3402, 05/3438, 05/3442, 05/3968, 06/4094, 07/2415, 08/3096, 08/474, 09/1362, 10/2119, 10/224, 10/2752, 10/3449, 11/204, 11/2711, 12/1824, 12/2301, 13/2467, 13/2979, 14/2836, 16/2249: *Considered* 02/3840, 02/3841, 02/5794, 03/233, 03/5680, 04/1526, 05/4291, 05/4301, 10/2750, 12/3185, 16/2250, 17/162, 17/504: *Followed* 04/3246, 10/2753, 11/1895, 11/3498, 12/273, 14/1965, 14/2844

Royal Bank of Scotland Plc v Highland Financial Partners LP [2013] EWCA Civ 328; [2013] 1 C.L.C. 596, CA (Civ Div) .... *Digested,* 13/**368**:
Applied 15/307, 16/305: *Considered* 17/1303: *Followed* 17/372

Royal Bank of Scotland Plc v Marme Inversiones 2007 Sl see Marme Inversiones 2007 SL v Royal Bank of Scotland Plc

Royal Bank of Scotland Plc v Mirza [2017] SAC (Civ) 13; 2017 S.L.T. (Sh Ct) 105; 2017 Hous. L.R. 45; 2017 G.W.D. 13-208, SAC .... *Digested,* 17/**2651**

Royal Bank of Scotland Plc v Wilson [2010] UKSC 50; 2011 S.C. (U.K.S.C.) 66; 2010 S.L.T. 1227; 2010 Hous. L.R. 88; 2010 G.W.D. 39-792, SC .... *Digested,* 11/**2717**:
Cited 12/4069: *Considered* 17/2781: *Followed* 13/3951

Royal Devon and Exeter NHS Foundation Trust v ATOS IT Services UK Ltd [2017] EWHC 2197 (TCC); [2017] B.L.R. 533; 174 Con. L.R. 24, QBD (TCC) .... *Digested,* 17/**502**

Royal Dornoch Golf Club v Crofters having Rights in Hilton of Embo Common Grazings 2017 S.L.T. (Land Ct) 14; 2016 G.W.D. 25-462, Land Ct .... *Digested,* 17/**2427**

Royal Insurance (UK) Ltd v Amec Construction Scotland Ltd [2007] CSOH 179; 2008 S.C. 201; 2008 S.L.T. 427; [2008] B.L.R. 53; 2008 G.W.D. 4-63, OH .... *Digested,* 08/**4587**:
Applied 17/2840

Royal Mencap Society v Tomlinson-Blake see Focus Care Agency Ltd v Roberts

Royal National Lifeboat Institution (RNLI) v Headley [2016] EWHC 1948 (Ch); [2016] W.T.L.R. 1433; [2017] 1 P. & C.R. DG4, Ch D .... *Digested,* 16/**2024**

Royal Society v Robinson [2015] EWHC 3442 (Ch); [2017] W.T.L.R. 299, Ch D

Royal Society for the Protection of Birds (RSPB) v Secretary of State for Justice see R. (on the application of Royal Society for the Protection of Birds) v Secretary of State for Justice

Royal Trust Corp of Canada v University of Western Ontario; *sub nom* Priebe's Estate, Re 19 I.T.E.L.R. 265, CJ (Gen Div) (Ont)

Royscot Trust Ltd v Rogerson; *sub nom* Royscott Trust v Maidenhead Honda Centre [1991] 2 Q.B. 297; [1991] 3 W.L.R. 57; [1991] 3 All E.R. 294; [1992] R.T.R. 99; (1992) 11 Tr. L.R. 23; [1991] C.C.L.R. 45; Times, April 3, 1991; Independent, April 10, 1991; Daily Telegraph, April 25, 1991; (1991) 141 N.L.J. 493; (1991) 135 S.J. 444, CA (Civ Div) .... *Digested,* 91/**1311**:
Applied 96/4975, 01/965, 04/920: *Cited* 01/3844: *Considered* 93/1398, 17/169: *Followed* 16/423

Royscott Trust v Maidenhead Honda Centre see Royscot Trust Ltd v Rogerson

RS (Capacity to Consent to Sexual Intercourse and Marriage), Re see Luton BC v B

RSC Contractors Ltd v Conway; *sub nom* RCS Contractors Ltd v Conway [2017] EWHC 715 (TCC); [2018] 1 All E.R. (Comm) 807; [2017] B.L.R. 376; 171 Con. L.R. 151; [2017] C.I.L.L. 3986, QBD (TCC) .... *Digested,* 17/**465**

RSP Architects Planners & Engineers v MCST Plan No.1075 [1999] SGCA 30, CA (Sing)
Considered 17/470

RSPCA v Johnson [2009] EWHC 2702 (Admin), DC
Applied 15/648, 17/534, 17/617

RT v Circuit Court in Tarnobrzeg, Poland see T v Poland

RT Coopers Solicitors v Revenue and Customs Commissioners [2017] UKFTT 440 (TC); [2017] S.T.I. 1330, FTT (Tax)

RTS Flexible Systems Ltd v Molkerei Alois Muller GmbH & Co KG [2010] UKSC 14; [2010] 1 W.L.R. 753; [2010] 3 All E.R. 1; [2010] 2 All E.R. (Comm) 97; [2010] Bus. L.R. 776; [2010] 1 C.L.C. 388; [2010] B.L.R. 337; 129 Con. L.R. 1; [2010] C.I.L.L. 2868; (2010) 107(12) L.S.G. 20; (2010) 160 N.L.J. 421; (2010) 154(11) S.J.L.B. 28, SC .... *Digested,* 10/**631**:
Applied 12/1053: *Considered* 16/1282: *Followed* 12/2102, 12/634, 13/448, 14/636, 15/464, 16/387, 17/2066, 17/469

Rubin v Eurofinance SA; *joined case* New Cap Reinsurance Corp Ltd (In Liquidation) v Grant [2012] UKSC 46; [2013] 1 A.C. 236; [2012] 3 W.L.R. 1019; [2013] 1 All E.R. 521; [2013] 1 All E.R. (Comm) 513; [2013] Bus. L.R. 1; [2012] 2 Lloyd's Rep. 615; [2013] B.C.C. 1; [2012] 2 B.C.L.C. 682; [2012] B.P.I.R. 1204; Times, November 9, 2012, SC .... *Digested,* 13/**1696**:
Applied 16/364: *Followed* 15/1420, 15/310, 17/314

Rubin v Rubin [2014] EWHC 611 (Fam); [2014] 1 W.L.R. 3289; [2014] 2 F.L.R. 1018; [2014] Fam. Law 797, Fam Div .... *Digested,* 14/**1362**:
Applied 17/1000: *Distinguished* 17/1017

Rubin & Partners v Cohen see Central A1 Ltd, Re

Ruddock v Queen, The see R. v Jogee (Ameen Hassan)

Ruddy v Chief Constable of Strathclyde [2012] UKSC 57; 2013 S.C. (U.K.S.C.) 126; 2013 S.L.T. 119; 2013 S.C.L.R. 110; [2013] H.R.L.R. 10; 2013 Rep. L.R. 67; 2012 G.W.D. 40-779, SC .... *Digested,* 13/**3527**:
Applied 13/3779: *Considered* 17/2773

Rupasinghe v West Hertfordshire Hospitals NHS Trust [2016] EWHC 2848 (QB); [2017] P.I.Q.R. Q1, QBD .... *Digested,* 17/**634**

Rupert Morgan Building Services (LLC) Ltd v Jervis [2003] EWCA Civ 1563; [2004] 1 W.L.R. 1867; [2004] 1 All E.R. 529; [2004] B.L.R. 18; [2004] T.C.L.R. 3; 91 Con. L.R. 81; Times, November 26, 2003; Independent, November 20, 2003; (2003) 153 N.L.J. 1761, CA (Civ Div) .... *Digested,* 04/**607**:
Applied 16/405, 16/582: *Distinguished* 05/198: *Followed* 12/592, 17/454

Ruscillo v Council for the Regulation of Health Care Professionals see Council for the Regulation of Health Care Professionals v General Medical Council

Rush Hair Ltd v Gibson-Forbes [2016] EWHC 2589 (QB); [2017] I.R.L.R. 48, QBD ...... *Digested,* 17/**495**

Russell v Cornwell [2014] EWHC 1509 (QB), QBD
Applied 17/319

Russell v McNair's Executrix 2017 S.L.T. (Sh Ct) 247; 2017 G.W.D. 26-436, Sh Ct (Glasgow) .... *Digested,* 17/**2839**

Russell v Russell (1956) [1956] P. 283; [1956] 2 W.L.R. 544; [1956] 1 All E.R. 466; (1956) 120 J.P. 140; (1956) 100 S.J. 149, CA .... *Digested,* 56/**2748**:
Applied 61/2729, 64/1144, 17/1008: *Followed* 97/2721

Russell v Stone [2017] EWHC 1555 (TCC); [2018] 1 All E.R. (Comm) 839; [2017] B.L.R. 429; 173 Con. L.R. 96; [2017] P.N.L.R. 34; [2017] C.I.L.L. 4018, QBD (TCC) .... *Digested,* 17/**328**

Russian Commercial & Industrial Bank v Comptoir d'Escompte de Mulhouse [1925] A.C. 112; (1924) 19 Ll. L. Rep. 63, HL
Applied 17/390

Rutherford v Secretary of State for Work and Pensions; *sub nom* R. (on the application of Rutherford) v Secretary of State for Work and Pensions; *joined case* R. (on the application of A) v Secretary of State for Work and Pensions [2016] EWCA Civ 29; [2016] H.L.R. 8, CA (Civ Div) .... *Digested,* 16/**1982**:
Reversed in part 17/2030

Rux Burton Associates Ltd v Revenue and Customs Commissioners [2017] UKFTT 709 (TC); [2017] S.T.I. 2133, FTT (Tax)

Ruxley Electronics v Forsyth; *joined case* Laddingford Enclosures Ltd v Forsyth [1996] A.C. 344; [1995] 3 W.L.R. 118; [1995] 3 All E.R. 268; [1995] C.L.C. 905; 73 B.L.R. 1; 45 Con. L.R. 61; (1995) 14 Tr. L.R. 541; Times, July 3, 1995; Independent, July 12, 1995; (1995) 11 Const. L.J. 381; [1995] E.G. 11 (C.S.); (1995) 145 N.L.J. 996; (1995) 139 S.J.L.B. 163, HL .... *Digested,* 95/**1561**:
Applied 01/4501, 03/5323, 03/943, 08/2659: *Considered* 03/670, 07/2948, 11/2053: *Distinguished* 07/794: *Followed* 96/1131, 17/1850

RW v HM Advocate see W (R) v HM Advocate

RWE npower Renewables Ltd v JN Bentley Ltd [2014] EWCA Civ 150; [2014] C.I.L.L. 3488, CA (Civ Div)
Applied 17/493

Ryanair Ltd v Esso Italiana Srl [2013] EWCA Civ 1450; [2015] 1 All E.R. (Comm) 152; [2013] 2 C.L.C. 950; [2014] U.K.C.L.R. 247, CA (Civ Div) .... *Digested,* 14/**557**:
Applied 17/377

Rynda (UK) Ltd v Rhijnsburger [2015] EWCA Civ 75; [2015] I.C.R. 1300; [2015] I.R.L.R. 394, CA (Civ Div) .... *Digested,* 15/**868**: *Applied* 17/841

Rysaffe Trustee Co (CI) Ltd v Customs and Excise Commissioners see Rysaffe Trustee Co (CI) Ltd v Inland Revenue Commissioners

Rysaffe Trustee Co (CI) Ltd v Inland Revenue Commissioners; *sub nom* Rysaffe Trustee Co (CI) Ltd v Customs and Excise Commissioners; Customs and Excise Commissioners v Rysaffe Trustee Co (CI) Ltd [2003] EWCA Civ 356; [2003] S.T.C. 536; [2003] B.T.C. 8021; [2003] W.T.L.R. 481; (2002-03) 5 I.T.E.L.R. 706; Times, April 29, 2003; [2003] S.T.I. 452; (2003) 100(22) L.S.G. 31; (2003) 147 S.J.L.B. 388; [2003] N.P.C. 39, CA (Civ Div) .... *Digested,* 03/**4271**: *Followed* 17/2157

Rzecznik Praw Obywatelskich (RPO) v Marszalek Sejmu Rzeczypospolitej Polskiej (C-390/15) EU:C:2017:174; [2017] B.V.C. 13, ECJ (Grand Chamber)

S v A [2016] EWHC 846 (Comm); [2017] 1 All E.R. (Comm) 121; [2016] 1 Lloyd's Rep. 604; [2016] 1 C.L.C. 638, QBD (Comm) .... *Digested,* 16/**65**

S v AG (Financial Orders: Lottery Prize) [2011] EWHC 2637 (Fam); [2012] 1 F.L.R. 651; [2011] 3 F.C.R. 523; Times, November 22, 2011; [2012] Fam. Law 18, Fam Div .... *Digested,* 12/**1313**: *Applied* 15/1091, 17/1009

S v Airedale NHS Trust see R. (on the application of Munjaz) v Mersey Care NHS Trust

S v Birmingham City Council; *sub nom* Birmingham City Council v SA; Birmingham City Council v SS; *joined case* A v Birmingham City Council [2016] EWCA Civ 1211; [2017] 1 W.L.R. 2251; [2017] H.L.R. 6, CA (Civ Div) .... *Digested,* 17/**2031**

S v C (Abduction: Art.13 Defence: Procedure) see S (A Child) (Abduction: Rights of Custody), Re

S v Children's Reporter; *sub nom* JS v Children's Reporter [2016] CSIH 74; 2017 S.C. 31; 2016 S.L.T. 1235; 2017 S.C.L.R. 539; 2016 Fam. L.R. 166; 2016 G.W.D. 31-547, IH (Ex Div) .... *Digested,* 17/**2603**

S v DPP see JS (A Child) v DPP

S v H (False Allegations of Abuse); *sub nom* AS v TH (False Allegations of Abuse) [2016] EWHC 532 (Fam); [2016] 3 F.C.R. 327, Fam Div .... *Digested,* 17/**952**

S v H (Jurisdiction to Make Final Orders) [2016] EWHC 2825 (Fam); [2016] 4 W.L.R. 179, Fam Div .... *Digested,* 17/**940**

S v Hertfordshire CC see A v Essex CC

S v K (Return to Wardship Jurisdiction: India) see S (Children) (Child Abduction: Asylum Appeal), Re

S v L; *sub nom* ML v ANS [2012] UKSC 30; 2013 S.C. (U.K.S.C.) 20; 2012 S.L.T. 961; [2012] H.R.L.R. 27; 2012 Fam. L.R. 108; Times, October 8, 2012; (2012) 156(28) S.J.L.B. 31; 2012 G.W.D. 24-488, SC .... *Digested,* 12/**1297**: *Considered* 17/2600: *Followed* 16/2653

S v NHS Trust (Unreported, November 22, 2016), CC (Barrow) [*Hill Dickinson LLP, No.1 St. Paul's Square, Liverpool*] .... *Digested,* 17/**1658**

S v O (Committal Proceedings in Absence of Respondents), Re see Sanchez v Oboz

S v S; *sub nom* CS v ACS [2015] EWHC 1005 (Fam); [2015] 1 W.L.R. 4592; [2016] 1 F.L.R. 131; [2015] Fam. Law 647, Fam Div .... *Digested,* 15/**1048**: *Applied* 17/1013

S v S; *sub nom* MS v PS [2016] EWHC 88 (Fam); [2017] 1 F.L.R. 394; [2016] Fam. Law 304, Fam Div *Preliminary ruling given* 17/896

S v S (C-283/16) see MS v PS (C-283/16)

S v S (Foreign Adoption Order: Recognition); *sub nom* QS v RS [2016] EWHC 2470 (Fam); [2017] Fam. 167; [2017] 2 W.L.R. 887; [2017] 2 F.L.R. 1456, Fam Div ... *Digested,* 17/**914**: *Considered* 17/1034

S v S see N (A Child) (Recognition of Foreign Adoption), Re

S v S see Sharland v Sharland

S v Secretary of State for the Home Department (C-304/14) see Secretary of State for the Home Department v CS (C-304/14)

S v Secretary of State for the Home Department see VS (India) v Secretary of State for the Home Department

S v SP [2016] EWHC 3673 (Fam); [2017] 2 F.L.R. 1079, Fam Div (Taunton) .... *Digested,* 17/**991**

S v Worcestershire CC [2017] UKUT 92 (AAC); [2017] E.L.R. 218, UT (AAC) .... *Digested,* 17/**712**

S (A Child) v Acromas Insurance Co Ltd (Unreported, February 10, 2017), CC (Coventry) [*Tim Jaques, Barrister, 85-87 Cornwall Street Chambers, Birmingham*] .... *Digested,* 17/**1675**

S (A Child) v NHS England see R. (on the application of S (A Child)) v NHS England

S (A Child) v Thomas Cook (Unreported, December 8, 2016), CC (Birmingham) [*Stephen Garner, Barrister, 10-11 Bedford Row, London*] ... *Digested,* 17/**1678**

S (A Child) (Abduction: Intolerable Situation), Re see S (A Child) (Abduction: Rights of Custody), Re

S (A Child) (Abduction: Rights of Custody), Re; *sub nom* S v C (Abduction: Art.13 Defence: Procedure); S (A Child) (Abduction: Intolerable Situation), Re [2012] UKSC 10; [2012] 2 A.C. 257; [2012] 2 W.L.R. 721; [2012] 2 All E.R. 603; [2012] 2 F.L.R. 442; [2012] 1 F.C.R. 493; Times, March 21, 2012; [2012] Fam. Law 639; (2012) 109(13) L.S.G. 23; (2012) 162 N.L.J. 424; (2012) 156(11) S.J.L.B. 31, SC ... *Digested,* 12/**1369**: *Applied* 15/1112: *Followed* 17/1038

S (A Child) (Identification: Restriction on Publication), Re see S (A Child) (Identification: Restrictions on Publication), Re

S (A Child) (Identification: Restrictions on Publication), Re; *sub nom* S (A Child) (Identification: Restriction on Publication), Re [2004] UKHL 47; [2005] 1 A.C. 593; [2004] 3 W.L.R. 1129; [2004] 4 All E.R. 683; [2005] E.M.L.R. 2; [2005] 1 F.L.R. 591; [2004] 3 F.C.R. 407; [2005] H.R.L.R. 5; [2005] U.K.H.R.R. 129; 17 B.H.R.C. 646; Times, October 29, 2004; Independent, November 2, 2004; [2005] Crim. L.R. 310; (2004) 154 N.L.J. 1654; (2004) 148 S.J.L.B. 1285, HL ... *Digested,* 05/**2121**: *Applied* 05/1686, 05/4191, 06/1665, 06/2853, 06/445, 07/1732, 07/1806, 07/2189, 08/1540, 09/1590, 10/1731, 10/1742, 11/599, 11/862, 12/331, 14/1279, 14/664, 14/790, 15/824, 16/309, 17/332: *Considered* 05/923, 06/1711, 08/1514, 08/1886, 09/1603, 10/1743, 11/2199, 12/3920, 13/246, 13/3510, 14/21: *Followed* 08/855, 09/929, 10/408, 11/1331, 12/15, 12/332, 13/2042, 14/801, 14/841, 16/888, 17/1028, 17/3

S (A Child), Re [2017] EWCA Civ 44; [2017] 2 F.C.R. 184, CA (Civ Div) ... *Digested,* 17/**994**

S (A) v HM Advocate; *sub nom* AS v HM Advocate; Sturrock v HM Advocate [2016] HCJAC 126; 2017 J.C. 180; 2017 S.L.T. 264; 2017 S.C.L. 290; 2017 S.C.C.R. 80; 2017 G.W.D. 1-4, HCJ ... *Digested,* 17/**2479**

S (A) v Procurator Fiscal, Kilmarnock [2017] SAC (Crim) 3; 2017 S.L.T. (Sh Ct) 89; 2017 S.C.L. 493; 2017 G.W.D. 9-128, SAC ... *Digested,* 17/**2790**

S (Brussels II (Revised): Enforcement of Contact Order), Re [2008] 2 F.L.R. 1358; [2008] Fam. Law 622, Fam Div ... *Digested,* 09/**1586**: *Considered* 17/1057

S (Brussels II: Recognition: Best Interests of Child) (No.2), Re; *sub nom* X v Y [2003] EWHC 2974 (Fam); [2004] 1 F.L.R. 582, Fam Div *Applied* 11/1359: *Considered* 17/1057

S (Care Proceedings: Case Management), Re see S (Children) (Abuse: Oral Evidence), Re

S (Child Abduction: Joinder of Sibling: Child's Objections), Re [2016] EWHC 1227 (Fam); [2017] 4 W.L.R. 216; [2017] 2 F.L.R. 384; [2016] Fam. Law 1075, Fam Div

S (Child Case: Intervener), Re see S (Minors) (Care: Residence: Intervener), Re

S (Children) (Abuse: Oral Evidence), Re; *sub nom* S (Care Proceedings: Case Management), Re [2016] EWCA Civ 83; [2017] 1 F.L.R. 1476; [2016] 3 F.C.R. 40; [2016] Fam. Law 441, CA (Civ Div) ... *Digested,* 16/**856**

S (Children) (Child Abduction: Asylum Appeal), Re; *sub nom* S v K (Return to Wardship Jurisdiction: India) [2002] EWCA Civ 843; [2002] 1 W.L.R. 2548; [2002] 2 F.L.R. 465; [2002] 2 F.C.R. 642; [2003] Imm. A.R. 52; [2002] I.N.L.R. 512; Times, June 3, 2002; [2002] Fam. Law 650; (2002) 99(27) L.S.G. 33; (2002) 146 S.J.L.B. 159, CA (Civ Div) ... *Digested,* 02/**1630**: *Distinguished* 17/939

S (Children), Re; *sub nom* C v P [2017] EWFC 23; [2017] 3 F.C.R. 417, Fam Ct

S (D) v HM Advocate; *sub nom* DS v HM Advocate [2017] HCJAC 12; 2017 S.C.L. 363; 2017 S.C.C.R. 129; 2017 G.W.D. 8-112, HCJ ... *Digested,* 17/**2801**

S (Minors) (Care: Residence: Intervener), Re; *sub nom* S (Child Case: Intervener), Re [1997] 1 F.L.R. 497; [1997] 2 F.C.R. 272; [1997] Fam. Law 232; (1997) 161 J.P.N. 458, CA (Civ Div) ... *Digested,* 97/**371**: *Applied* 17/999: *Considered* 00/2514

S (Minors) (Wardship: Police Investigation), Re [1987] Fam. 199; [1987] 3 W.L.R. 847; [1987] 3 All E.R. 1076; [1988] 1 F.L.R. 1; [1988] Fam. Law 90; (1987) 151 L.G. Rev. 712; (1987) 131 S.J. 1390, Fam Div ... *Digested,* 87/**2530**: *Applied* 97/378: *Considered* 90/3201: *Not followed* 17/1069

S Franses Ltd v Cavendish Hotel (London) Ltd [2017] EWHC 1670 (QB); [2017] Bus. L.R. 1941; [2018] 1 P. & C.R. 6; [2017] L. & T.R. 34, QBD ... *Digested,* 17/**1454**

S, Re 19 I.T.L. Rep. 534, Cons Const (F)

S-F (A Child), Re [2017] EWCA Civ 964; [2017] 2 F.C.R. 757, CA (Civ Div) ... *Digested,* 17/**1064**

S-G v Denbighshire CC [2016] UKUT 460 (AAC); [2017] E.L.R. 99, UT (AAC) ... *Digested,* 17/**714**

S-R (Contact: Jurisdiction), Re [2008] 2 F.L.R. 1741; [2008] Fam. Law 987, Fam Div .. *Digested,* 09/**1584**: *Applied* 11/1448: *Considered* 17/1057

S-W (Children) (Care Proceedings: Summary Disposal at Case Management Hearing), Re [2015] EWCA Civ 27; [2015] 1 W.L.R. 4099; [2015] 2 F.L.R. 136; [2015] 2 F.C.R. 173; [2015] Fam. Law 258, CA (Civ Div) .... *Digested,* 15/**996**: *Applied* 16/910: *Followed* 17/924

SA v FA see A v A (Setting aside Consent Order on Ground of Duress)

SA (Pakistan) v Secretary of State for the Home Department; *sub nom* SA (Section 82(2)(d): Interpretation and Effect: Pakistan), Re [2007] UKAIT 83; [2008] Imm. A.R. 124, AIT .... *Digested,* 08/**2009**: *Considered* 17/1229

SA (Section 82(2)(d): Interpretation and Effect: Pakistan), Re see SA (Pakistan) v Secretary of State for the Home Department

SA (Somalia) v Entry Clearance Officer see Mahad (Ethiopia) v Entry Clearance Officer

SA (Vulnerable Adult with Capacity: Marriage), Re; *sub nom* A Local Authority v MA [2005] EWHC 2942 (Fam); [2006] 1 F.L.R. 867; [2007] 2 F.C.R. 563; (2007) 10 C.C.L. Rep. 193; [2006] Fam. Law 268, Fam Div .... *Digested,* 07/**1832**: *Applied* 11/3212, 16/948: *Approved* 12/3173: *Considered* 07/1834, 10/303, 11/2218, 15/1719: *Followed* 11/3211: *Not applied* 17/1050

SA Consortium General Textiles v Sun & Sand Agencies [1978] Q.B. 279; [1978] 2 W.L.R. 1; [1978] 2 All E.R. 339; [1978] 1 Lloyd's Rep. 134; Times, July 7, 1977; (1977) 121 S.J. 662, CA (Civ Div) .... *Digested,* 78/**284**: *Applied* 17/432

SA&D Wright Ltd, Re; *sub nom* Denney v John Hudson & Co Ltd [1992] B.C.C. 503; [1992] B.C.L.C. 901; Financial Times, May 8, 1992, CA (Civ Div) .... *Digested,* 92/**2583**: *Applied* 02/2726, 17/1330: *Considered* 08/2189

Saadi v United Kingdom (13229/03) (2008) 47 E.H.R.R. 17; [2008] Imm. A.R. 368; [2008] I.N.L.R. 436; Times, February 4, 2008, ECHR (Grand Chamber) .... *Digested,* 08/**1960**: *Applied* 08/2047, 09/2028, 16/1104, 17/1588: *Considered* 09/2033, 10/1771

SABMiller Plc, Re [2016] EWHC 2153 (Ch); [2017] Ch. 173; [2017] 2 W.L.R. 837; [2017] B.C.C. 655, Ch D (Companies Ct) .... *Digested,* 17/**404**

Sadiq (Alam) v HM Advocate; *joined case* Sadiq (Omar) v HM Advocate [2017] HCJAC 67; 2017 S.C.L. 940; 2017 S.C.C.R. 421; 2017 G.W.D. 30-473, HCJ .... *Digested,* 17/**2472**

Sadiq (Omar) v HM Advocate see Sadiq (Alam) v HM Advocate

Sadovska v Secretary of State for the Home Department see VS (Lithuania) v Secretary of State for the Home Department

SAE Education Ltd v Revenue and Customs Commissioners; *sub nom* Revenue and Customs Commissioners v SAE Education Ltd [2016] UKUT 193 (TCC); [2016] S.T.C. 1837; [2016] B.V.C. 514, UT (Tax) .... *Digested,* 16/**2171**: *Affirmed* 17/2234

SAE Education Ltd v Revenue and Customs Commissioners; *sub nom* Revenue and Customs Commissioners v SAE Education Ltd [2017] EWCA Civ 1116; [2017] S.T.C. 2166; [2017] B.V.C. 37, CA (Civ Div) .... *Digested,* 17/**2234**

Saeed v Shine Motors (Unreported, February 7, 2017), CC (Stockport) [*Robert Skyner, Barrister, 39 Park Square Chambers, Leeds*] .... *Digested,* 17/**1684**

Safier v Wardell [2017] EWHC 20 (Ch); [2017] Bus. L.R. 564; [2017] B.P.I.R. 504, Ch D .... *Digested,* 17/**1283**

Safmar Property Ventures UK Ltd v Kensington and Chelsea RLBC [2017] P.A.D. 12, Planning Inspector

Saga Group Ltd v Paul [2016] EWHC 2344 (Ch); [2017] 4 W.L.R. 12; [2016] Pens. L.R. 329, Ch D .... *Digested,* 17/**1626**: *Applied* 17/1627

Sage v Double A Hydraulics Ltd; *joined case* Chambers v Starkings Times, April 2, 1992, CA (Civ Div) .... *Digested,* 92/**3630**: *Applied* 07/347: *Considered* 15/446: *Followed* 17/212

Sage v Hewlett Packard Enterprise Co see Hewlett Packard Enterprise Co v Sage

Sahin v Havard [2016] EWCA Civ 1202; [2017] 1 W.L.R. 1853; [2017] 4 All E.R. 157; [2017] 2 All E.R. (Comm) 851; [2017] R.T.R. 9; [2017] Lloyd's Rep. I.R. 110, CA (Civ Div) .... *Digested,* 17/**1348**: *Considered* 17/1878

Saif Ali v Sydney Mitchell & Co [1980] A.C. 198; [1978] 3 W.L.R. 849; [1978] 3 All E.R. 1033; [1955-95] P.N.L.R. 151; (1978) 122 S.J. 761, HL .... *Digested,* 78/**2323**: *Applied* 80/2609, 92/3499, 94/2687, 94/3623, 95/4033, 98/4011, 99/4034, 03/3008, 05/2870, 09/2737, 17/1568: *Considered* 90/3264, 93/2943, 96/3580, 96/4509, 98/4012, 99/4021, 09/2739: *Distinguished* 89/3073, 01/42: *Followed* 97/3815, 00/4001, 09/2738, 13/1020: *Referred to* 79/2110, 81/2184, 97/3825

Sainsbury's Supermarket Ltd v Ahmed see Farmah v Birmingham City Council
Sainsbury's Supermarket Ltd v Sykes [2017] UKUT 138 (LC); [2017] R.A. 211, UT (Lands)
Sainsbury's Supermarkets Ltd v Mastercard Inc [2016] CAT 11; [2016] Comp. A.R. 33, CAT .... *Digested,* 17/**412**: *Considered* 17/410
Sainsbury's Supermarkets Ltd v Mastercard Inc [2016] CAT 23; [2017] Comp. A.R. 70, CAT
Saint-Gobain Pam SA v Fusion Provida Ltd [2005] EWCA Civ 177; (2005) 28(6) I.P.D. 28043, CA (Civ Div) [*Peter Gibson, L.J., Scott Baker, L.J., Jacob, L.J.*] *Applied* 06/2503, 06/2601: *Considered* 17/1374: *Followed* 16/1318
Sakthivel v Entry Clearance Officer see Mahad (Ethiopia) v Entry Clearance Officer
Sala v Secretary of State for the Home Department see Sala (EFMs: Right of Appeal)
Sala (EFMs: Right of Appeal); *sub nom* Sala v Secretary of State for the Home Department [2016] UKUT 411 (IAC); [2017] Imm. A.R. 141, UT (IAC)
Salaberria Sorondo v Academia Vasca de Policia y Emergencias (C-258/15) EU:C:2016:873; [2017] C.E.C. 846; [2017] I.C.R. 302; [2017] I.R.L.R. 162, ECJ (Grand Chamber)
Saleh v Director of the Serious Fraud Office see Serious Fraud Office v Saleh
Salehabady v Eyre Estate Trustees [2017] UKUT 60 (LC); [2017] L. & T.R. 22; [2017] 2 P. & C.R. DG4, UT (Lands) .... *Digested,* 17/**1433**
Sales of Spectacle Frames, Re (VII ZR 328/12) [2017] E.C.C. 19, BGH (Ger)
Salford City Council v Mullen see Hounslow LBC v Powell
Salford Estates (No.2) Ltd v Altomart Ltd see Altomart Ltd v Salford Estates (No.2) Ltd
Salinger v Revenue and Customs Commissioners [2016] UKFTT 677 (TC); [2017] S.F.T.D. 316; [2016] W.T.L.R. 1833; [2017] S.T.I. 43, FTT (Tax) .... *Digested,* 17/**2156**
Salix River and Wetlands Ltd v City and County of Swansea Council [2017] P.A.D. 7, Planning Inspector
Salk Institute v Karo Bio AB T0609/02 *Applied* 17/1375
Salvation Army Trustee Co v Bahi [2017] I.R.L.R. 410, EAT .... *Digested,* 17/**843**
Salvesen v Riddell [2013] UKSC 22; 2013 S.C. (U.K.S.C.) 236; 2013 S.L.T. 863; 2014 S.C.L.R. 44; [2013] H.R.L.R. 23; 2013 G.W.D. 14-304, SC .... *Digested,* 13/**1865**: *Cited* 17/2693
Sam Purpose AS v Transnav Purpose Navigation Ltd [2017] EWHC 719 (Comm); [2018] 1 All E.R. (Comm) 711; [2017] 2 Lloyd's Rep. 50, QBD (Comm) .... *Digested,* 17/**201**
Samarkand Film Partnership No.3 v Revenue and Customs Commissioners; *joined cases* R. (on the application of Proteus Film Partnership No 1) v Revenue and Customs Commissioners; R. (on the application of Samarkand Film Partnership No 3) v Revenue and Customs Commissioners; Partners of Proteus v Revenue and Customs Commissioners; Partners of Samarkand v Revenue and Customs Commissioners; Proteus Film Partnership No.1 v Revenue and Customs Commissioners [2017] EWCA Civ 77; [2017] S.T.C. 926; [2017] B.T.C. 4, CA (Civ Div) .... *Digested,* 17/**2188**: *Followed* 17/2145, 17/2147
Samarkand Film Partnership No.3 v Revenue and Customs Commissioners; *joined cases* R. (on the application of Proteus Film Partnership No.1) v Revenue and Customs Commissioners; R. (on the application of Samarkand Film Partnership No.3) v Revenue and Customs Commissioners; Partners of Proteus v Revenue and Customs Commissioners; Partners of Samarkand v Revenue and Customs Commissioners; Proteus Film Partnership No.1 v Revenue and Customs Commissioners [2015] UKUT 211 (TCC); [2015] S.T.C. 2135; [2015] B.T.C. 517, UT (Tax) .... *Digested,* 15/**2466**: *Affirmed* 17/2188
Samin v Westminster City Council see Mirga v Secretary of State for Work and Pensions
Sampla v Rushmoor BC [2008] EWHC 2616 (TCC), QBD (TCC) *Considered* 17/259
Samsung Bioepis UK Ltd v Abbvie Biotechnology Ltd see Fujifilm Kyowa Kirin Biologics Co Ltd v Abbvie Biotechnology Ltd
Samsung SDI Co Ltd v European Commission (C-615/15 P) EU:C:2017:190; [2017] 4 C.M.L.R. 27, ECJ (8th Chamber)
Sanchez v Oboz; *sub nom* S v O (Committal Proceedings in Absence of Respondents), Re [2015] EWHC 235 (Fam); [2016] 1 F.L.R. 897; [2015] Fam. Law 380, Fam Div *Applied* 17/6

Sandhu v Revenue and Customs Commissioners [2017] EWHC 60 (QB); [2017] B.V.C. 5, QBD .... *Digested,* 17/**325**
Sandle v Adecco UK Ltd [2016] I.R.L.R. 941, EAT .... *Digested,* 17/**830**
Sandman v Panasonic UK Ltd [1998] F.S.R. 651; [1998] Masons C.L.R. 220; (1998) 21(4) I.P.D. 21038, Ch D .... *Digested,* 98/**3416**: *Considered* 17/1382: *Referred to* 99/3493
Sands v Layne; *sub nom* Layne (A Bankrupt), Re; Layne (Deceased), Re [2016] EWCA Civ 1159; [2017] 1 W.L.R. 1782; [2017] C.P. Rep. 14; [2017] B.P.I.R. 215, CA (Civ Div) .... *Digested,* 17/**1310**
Sands v Layne; *sub nom* Layne (A Bankrupt), Re; Layne (Deceased), Re [2014] EWHC 3665 (Ch); [2015] 2 All E.R. 332; [2015] B.P.I.R. 134, Ch D .... *Digested,* 15/**1410**: *Doubted* 16/1204: *Reversed in part* 17/1310
Sandvik Intellectual Property AB v Kennametal UK Ltd [2010] EWHC 3417 (Pat), Ch D (Patents Ct) *Considered* 17/1382
Sandwell MBC v Jones see Barber v Somerset CC
Sandyway Nurseries v Forest of Dean DC [2017] P.A.D. 23, Planning Inspector
Sangster (Stephen) v HM Advocate [2017] HCJAC 4; 2017 J.C. 204; 2017 S.C.L. 336; 2017 S.C.C.R. 119; 2017 G.W.D. 6-85, HCJ .... *Digested,* 17/**2492**
Sanguinetti v Fondaziona La Biennale di Venezia [2017] E.C.D.R. 5, Trib (I)
Sansom v Peay (Inspector of Taxes) [1976] 1 W.L.R. 1073; [1976] 3 All E.R. 375; [1976] S.T.C. 494; 52 T.C. 1; [1976] T.R. 205; (1976) 120 S.J. 571, Ch D .... *Digested,* 76/**1408**: *Considered* 96/439, 17/2094
Santander UK Plc, Re see Barclays Bank Plc, Re
Santogal M-Comercio e Reparacao de Automoveis v Autoridade Tributaria e Aduaneira (C-26/16) EU:C:2017:453; [2017] B.V.C. 29; [2017] S.T.I. 1397, ECJ (9th Chamber)
SAP/Audit trail (T1379/11) [2017] E.P.O.R. 16, EPO (Technical Bd App)
Sapor v Poland see Wisniewski v Poland
Sargaison v Roberts [1969] 1 W.L.R. 951; [1969] 3 All E.R. 1072; 45 T.C. 612; (1969) 48 A.T.C. 149; [1969] T.R. 149; (1969) 113 S.J. 470, Ch D .... *Digested,* 69/**1658**: *Considered* 12/2734, 17/2287
Sargent v Dewar see Sargent v Secretary of State for Scotland
Sargent v Secretary of State for Scotland; *sub nom* Sargent v Dewar 2001 S.C.L.R. 190; 2000 Rep. L.R. 118; 2000 G.W.D. 28-1089, OH .... *Digested,* 01/**6817**: *Considered* 17/2738
Sargsyan v Azerbaijan (40167/06) (2017) 64 E.H.R.R. 4, ECHR
Sarpd Oil International Ltd v Addax Energy SA [2016] EWCA Civ 120; [2016] C.P. Rep. 24; [2016] 1 C.L.C. 336; [2016] B.L.R. 301; [2016] 2 Costs L.O. 227, CA (Civ Div) .... *Digested,* 16/**311**: *Considered* 17/276, 17/277: *Followed* 17/358
SAS v Bradford MDC see FAS v Secretary of State for the Home Department
Sas v Poland see Goluchowski v Poland
Sas v Zielona Gora, Poland see Goluchowski v Poland
Sasea Finance Ltd (In Liquidation) v KPMG (formerly KPMG Peat Marwick McLintock) (No.2) [2000] 1 All E.R. 676; [2000] B.C.C. 989; [2000] 1 B.C.L.C. 236; [2000] Lloyd's Rep. P.N. 227, CA (Civ Div) .... *Digested,* 00/**4249**: *Applied* 17/458
Satnam Millennium Ltd v Warrington BC [2015] EWHC 370 (Admin); [2015] Env. L.R. 30, QBD (Admin) .... *Digested,* 15/**1986**: *Applied* 17/1780
Saunders v United Kingdom (19187/91); *sub nom* Saunders v United Kingdom (43/1994/490/572) [1997] B.C.C. 872; [1998] 1 B.C.L.C. 362; (1997) 23 E.H.R.R. 313; 2 B.H.R.C. 358; Times, December 18, 1996; Independent, January 14, 1997, ECHR .... *Digested,* 97/**2816**: *Applied* 01/1047, 05/2092, 09/2226, 14/701, 17/291: *Considered* 97/2818, 98/3150, 00/5473, 00/6043, 01/6319, 01/974, 02/2664, 02/849, 07/855, 09/2227, 09/764, 16/2124: *Distinguished* 00/2300, 00/667, 04/1951, 05/765: *Followed* 97/817: *Not applied* 98/682
Saunders v United Kingdom (43/1994/490/572) see Saunders v United Kingdom (19187/91)
Saunders v Vautier 41 E.R. 482; (1841) Cr. & Ph. 240, Ct of Chancery *Considered* 08/3787, 10/3337, 17/2156: *Distinguished* 09/3840
Savage v Hillingdon LBC see R. (on the application of Savage) v Hillingdon LBC
Savage v Saxena [1998] I.C.R. 357; [1998] I.R.L.R. 182; Times, February 11, 1998, EAT .... *Digested,* 98/**2226**: *Applied* 17/827

Save Britain's Heritage v Number 1 Poultry Ltd; *sub nom* Save Britain's Heritage v Secretary of State for the Environment [1991] 1 W.L.R. 153; [1991] 2 All E.R. 10; 89 L.G.R. 809; (1991) 3 Admin. L.R. 437; (1991) 62 P. & C.R. 105; [1991] 3 P.L.R. 17; Times, March 1, 1991; Independent, March 1, 1991; (1991) 155 L.G. Rev. 429; Guardian, March 1, 1991; [1991] E.G. 24 (C.S.); (1991) 88(15) L.S.G. 31; (1991) 135 S.J. 312, HL .... *Digested,* 91/**3494**: *Applied* 92/4157, 92/450, 93/3909, 97/4090, 99/4181, 99/4267, 01/4652, 01/4747, 12/1459, 16/1078, 16/1678, 16/1737: *Cited* 92/4319, 92/4354, 93/3810, 94/4349: *Considered* 93/3925, 96/4734, 96/4832, 96/4836, 97/4093, 17/1785: *Distinguished* 96/7151: *Followed* 95/3610, 96/4705, 96/4753, 97/4070, 98/6143, 99/6411, 00/4474, 01/4750, 17/1769: *Referred to* 95/2598

Save Britain's Heritage v Secretary of State for the Environment see Save Britain's Heritage v Number 1 Poultry Ltd

Savov v Czech Republicy see Puceviciene v Lithuania

SAW (SW) 2010 Ltd v Wilson; *sub nom* Property Edge Lettings Ltd, Re [2015] EWHC 4069 (Ch); [2017] 1 B.C.L.C. 401, Ch D (Manchester) .... *Digested,* 17/**158**

SAW (SW) 2010 Ltd v Wilson [2017] EWCA Civ 1001; [2018] 2 W.L.R. 636; [2017] B.C.C. 373; [2018] 1 B.C.L.C. 291, CA (Civ Div) .... *Digested,* 17/**159**

Sayer, Re [2014] UKUT 283 (LC), UT (Lands) *Applied* 17/1161

SBT Star Bulk and Tankers (Germany) GmbH Co KG v Cosmotrade SA [2016] EWHC 583 (Comm); [2017] 1 All E.R. (Comm) 231; [2016] 2 Lloyd's Rep. 170; [2016] 1 C.L.C. 562, QBD (Comm) .... *Digested,* 16/**1950**

SC v Worcestershire CC [2016] UKUT 267 (AAC); [2016] E.L.R. 537, UT (AAC) .... *Digested,* 17/**707**

SC Capoda Import-Export SRL v Registrul Auto Roman (C-354/14) EU:C:2015:658; [2016] R.T.R. 5; [2016] 2 C.M.L.R. 9; [2017] C.E.C. 355, ECJ (7th Chamber)

SC Casa Noastra SA v ISCTR (C-245/15) EU:C:2017:156; [2017] R.T.R. 21; [2017] I.C.R. 629, ECJ (10th Chamber)

SCA Packaging Ltd v Boyle; *sub nom* Boyle v SCA Packaging Ltd [2009] UKHL 37; [2009] 4 All E.R. 1181; [2009] N.I. 317; [2009] I.C.R. 1056; [2009] I.R.L.R. 746; (2009) 109 B.M.L.R. 53; Times, July 6, 2009; (2009) 153(26) S.J.L.B. 27, HL (NI) .... *Digested,* 09/**4260**: *Applied* 14/2890: *Considered* 17/781: *Followed* 16/2110

Scaddon v Morgan [2017] EWHC 1481 (QB); (2017) 158 B.M.L.R. 177, QBD

Scales (Inspector of Taxes) v George Thompson & Co Ltd (1927-28) 29 Ll. L. Rep. 176; 13 T.C. 83; (1927) 138 L.T. 331, KBD *Applied* 17/2146: *Considered* 09/3856

Scambler v Revenue and Customs Commissioners [2016] UKFTT 47 (TC), FTT (Tax) *Affirmed* 17/2144

Scambler v Revenue and Customs Commissioners [2017] UKUT 1 (TCC); [2017] S.T.C. 2108; [2017] B.T.C. 503, UT (Tax) .... *Digested,* 17/**2144**

Scancarriers A/S v Aotearoa International (The Barranduna and The Tarago) [1985] 2 Lloyd's Rep. 419; (1985) 135 N.L.J. 799, PC (NZ) .... *Digested,* 86/**3076**: *Applied* 17/47

Scarborough BC v Moore (Valuation Officer) [2017] R.A. 199, VT

Scatliffe v Scatliffe [2016] UKPC 36; [2017] A.C. 93; [2017] 2 W.L.R. 106; [2017] 2 F.L.R. 933, PC (BVI)

Scattolon v Ministero dell'Istruzione, dell'Universita e della Ricerca (C-108/10) EU:C:2011:542; [2012] 1 C.M.L.R. 17; [2012] C.E.C. 634; [2012] I.C.R. 740; [2011] I.R.L.R. 1020, ECJ (Grand Chamber) *Considered* 17/809

Schalit v Joseph Nadler Ltd [1933] 2 K.B. 79, KBD *Considered* 05/2657, 17/1456

Schalk v Austria (30141/04) [2011] 2 F.C.R. 650; (2011) 53 E.H.R.R. 20; 29 B.H.R.C. 396; [2010] Eq. L.R. 194, ECHR *Considered* 16/867, 17/976

Schatschaschwili v Germany (9154/10) (2016) 63 E.H.R.R. 14; 41 B.H.R.C. 474; [2017] Crim. L.R. 140, ECHR *Considered* 17/2603

Scheldebouw BV v St James Homes (Grosvenor Dock) Ltd [2006] EWHC 89 (TCC); [2006] B.L.R. 113; 105 Con. L.R. 90; (2006) 22 Const. L.J. 394, QBD (TCC) .... *Digested,* 06/**675**: *Applied* 06/203, 17/462

Schering Agrochemicals Ltd v Resibel NV SA (Unreported, November 26, 1992), CA (Civ Div) *Applied* 17/2193: *Considered* 14/617: *Distinguished* 98/4384: *Followed* 17/285: *Referred to* 96/1248

Schmidt v Schmidt (C-417/15) EU:C:2016:881; [2017] C.E.C. 870; [2017] I.L.Pr. 6, ECJ (2nd Chamber)

Schmitt v TUV Rheinland LGA Products GmbH (C-219/15) EU:C:2017:128; [2017] 3 C.M.L.R. 8; [2017] C.E.C. 1167; (2017) 155 B.M.L.R. 71, ECJ (1st Chamber)
School of Finance and Management (London) Ltd v Customs and Excise Commissioners; *sub nom* Customs and Excise Commissioners v School of Finance and Management (London) Ltd [2001] S.T.C. 1690; [2002] B.T.C. 5030; [2002] B.V.C. 158; [2001] S.T.I. 1663, Ch D .... *Digested,* 02/**4740**:
Considered 14/3041, 14/3045, 16/2171, 16/2173: *Overruled* 17/2234
Schotten & Hansen (UK) Ltd v Revenue and Customs Commissioners [2017] UKFTT 191 (TC); [2017] S.T.I. 1044, FTT (Tax)
Schroder Unit Trusts Ltd v Inland Revenue Commissioners see M&G Securities Ltd v Inland Revenue Commissioners
Schruyers (Kevin Charles) v HM Advocate see McHale (Joseph Francis) v HM Advocate
Schubert Murphy v Law Society; *sub nom* Law Society of England and Wales v Schubert Murphy (A Firm) [2017] EWCA Civ 1295; [2017] 4 W.L.R. 200; [2018] P.N.L.R. 4; Times, October 4, 2017, CA (Civ Div)
Schuh Ltd v Assessor for Glasgow [2013] CSIH 93; 2014 S.L.T. 184; [2014] R.V.R. 62; 2013 G.W.D. 39-754, LVAC .... *Digested,* 14/**3678**:
Applied 17/2726: *Cited* 14/3676
Schutzverband gegen Unlauteren Wettbewerb v X KG (40 b 95/16y) [2017] E.C.C. 13, OGH (A)
SCI Senior Home v Gemeinde Wedemark (C-195/15) EU:C:2016:804; [2017] C.E.C. 752; [2017] I.L.Pr. 2; [2018] B.P.I.R. 173, ECJ (5th Chamber)
Science Research Council v Nasse; *sub nom* Nasse v Science Research Council; Vyas v Leyland Cars; *joined case* Leyland Cars (BL Cars Ltd) v Vyas [1980] A.C. 1028; [1979] 3 W.L.R. 762; [1979] 3 All E.R. 673; [1979] I.C.R. 921; [1979] I.R.L.R. 465; (1979) 123 S.J. 768, HL .... *Digested,* 79/**940**:
Applied 82/2467, 91/2865, 94/3662, 10/347, 11/2631, 11/319, 17/798:
Considered 84/1243, 02/1387, 16/266: *Followed* 09/1226, 16/310
Scoppola v Italy (10249/03) (2010) 51 E.H.R.R. 12, ECHR
Considered 15/2232, 17/1934
Scordino v Italy (36813/97) (2007) 45 E.H.R.R. 7, ECHR (Grand Chamber) .... *Digested,* 08/**1925**:
Applied 07/2222, 09/2035, 17/1169: *Considered* 08/4653, 13/3417
Scotch Whisky Association v Lord Advocate [2013] CSOH 70; 2013 S.L.T. 776; [2013] 3 C.M.L.R. 34; [2013] L.L.R. 811; Times, June 13, 2013; 2013 G.W.D. 16-328, OH .... *Digested,* 13/**3750**:
Affirmed 17/2466
Scotch Whisky Association v Lord Advocate [2016] CSIH 77; 2017 S.C. 465; 2016 S.L.T. 1141; 2017 S.C.L.R. 410; [2017] 1 C.M.L.R. 41; 2016 G.W.D. 33-588, IH (1 Div) .... *Digested,* 17/**2466**
Scotch Whisky Association v Lord Advocate (C-333/14) EU:C:2015:845; [2016] 1 W.L.R. 2283; [2016] 2 C.M.L.R. 27, ECJ (2nd Chamber) .... *Digested,* 16/**784**:
Applied 16/326: *Considered* 17/386
Scott v Copenhagen Reinsurance Co (UK) Ltd [2003] EWCA Civ 688; [2003] 2 All E.R. (Comm) 190; [2003] 2 C.L.C. 431; [2003] Lloyd's Rep. I.R. 696; (2003) 147 S.J.L.B. 697, CA (Civ Div) .... *Digested,* 03/**2452**:
Applied 17/1351: *Considered* 12/1904, 13/1747, 17/1355
Scott v Revenue and Customs Commissioners [2017] UKFTT 385 (TC); [2018] S.F.T.D. 42; [2017] S.T.I. 1616, FTT (Tax)
Scott v Solicitors Regulation Authority [2016] EWHC 1256 (Admin), DC
Applied 17/1490: *Considered* 17/1491
Scott v Southern Pacific Mortgages Ltd see North East Property Buyers Litigation, Re
Scott (Jordan) v HM Advocate see McDowall (Luke) v HM Advocate
Scott-Kilvert's Estate, Re see Robinson v Bird
Scottbridge Construction Ltd v Wright; *sub nom* Wright v Scottbridge Construction Ltd 2003 S.C. 520; 2002 S.L.T. 1356; [2003] I.R.L.R. 21; 2002 G.W.D. 34-1150, IH (1 Div) .... *Digested,* 02/**5575**:
Applied 08/1177, 14/1091: *Considered* 11/1100, 12/1112, 16/696:
Distinguished 03/1286: *Followed* 17/812
Scottish & Newcastle Retail Ltd v Williams (Valuation Officer) see Williams (Valuation Officer) v Scottish & Newcastle Retail Ltd
Scottish Ambulance Service v Truslove UKEATS/0028/11/BI, EAT (SC)
Applied 17/855
Scottish Hydro Electric Transmission Plc v Auquhirie Land Co Ltd 2016 G.W.D. 32-575, Lands Tr (Scot)
Affirmed 17/2647

Scottish Hydro Electric Transmission Plc v Auquhirie Land Co Ltd [2017] CSIH 39; [2017] R.V.R. 315; 2017 G.W.D. 21-346, IH (Ex Div) ..... *Digested,* 17/**2647**

Scottish Ministers v Stirton [2014] CSIH 92; 2015 S.C.L.R. 350; 2014 G.W.D. 37-683, IH (2 Div) ..... *Digested,* 15/**3011**: *Considered* 17/2736

Scottish Parliamentary Corporate Body v Sovereign Indigenous Peoples of Scotland [2016] CSIH 81; 2016 S.L.T. 1307; 2016 Hous. L.R. 109; 2016 G.W.D. 34-610, IH (2 Div) ..... *Digested,* 17/**2662**

Scottish Parliamentary Corporate Body v Sovereign Indigenous Peoples of Scotland [2016] CSOH 113; 2016 S.L.T. 862; 2016 Hous. L.R. 87; 2016 G.W.D. 24-446, OH ..... *Digested,* 16/**2682**: *Affirmed* 17/2662

Scottish Police Services Authority v McBride; *sub nom* McBride v Scottish Police Authority; McBride v Scottish Police Services Authority; McBride v Strathclyde Police Joint Board [2016] UKSC 27; [2017] 2 All E.R. 875; 2017 S.C. (U.K.S.C.) 1; [2016] I.C.R. 788; [2016] I.R.L.R. 633; Times, June 22, 2016; 2016 G.W.D. 19-339, SC ..... *Digested,* 16/**738**: *Followed* 17/851

Scottish Power Generation Ltd v HM Advocate [2016] HCJAC 99; 2017 J.C. 85; 2016 S.L.T. 1296; 2017 S.C.L. 88; 2016 S.C.C.R. 569; 2016 G.W.D. 35-640, HCJ .... *Digested,* 17/**2641**

Scottish Solicitors Staff Pension Fund's Trustees v Pattison & Sim; *sub nom* Trustees of the Scottish Solicitors Staff Pension Fund v Pattison & Sim [2014] CSOH 119; 2014 G.W.D. 26-533, OH *Affirmed* 17/2844

Scottish Solicitors Staff Pension Fund's Trustees v Pattison & Sim; *sub nom* Trustees of the Scottish Solicitors Staff Pension Fund v Pattison & Sim [2015] CSIH 96; 2016 S.C. 284; 2016 G.W.D. 2-60, IH (Ex Div) ..... *Digested,* 17/**2844**

Scrabster Harbour Trust v Mowlem Plc (t/a Mowlem Marine); *joined case* Mowlem Plc (t/a Mowlem Marine) v Scrabster Harbour Trust [2006] CSIH 12; 2006 S.C. 469; 2006 S.L.T. 250; [2006] B.L.R. 207; 2006 G.W.D. 7-122, IH (1 Div) ..... *Digested,* 06/**5154**: *Cited* 17/2471

Scribes West Ltd v Anstalt (No.3) see Scribes West Ltd v Relsa Anstalt (No.3)

Scribes West Ltd v Relsa Anstalt (No.3); *sub nom* Scribes West Ltd v Anstalt (No.3) [2004] EWCA Civ 1744; [2005] 1 W.L.R. 1847; [2005] 2 All E.R. 690; [2005] 2 P. & C.R. 3; [2005] L. & T.R. 14; [2005] 1 E.G.L.R. 22; [2005] 09 E.G. 190; [2005] 2 E.G. 100 (C.S.); [2005] 1 P. & C.R. DG21, CA (Civ Div) ..... *Digested,* 05/**2657**: *Distinguished* 17/1456

SCT Finance Ltd v Bolton [2002] EWCA Civ 56; [2003] 3 All E.R. 434, CA (Civ Div) .... *Digested,* 04/**318**: *Followed* 12/375, 17/406

Scully UK Ltd v Lee [1998] I.R.L.R. 259, CA (Civ Div) ..... *Digested,* 98/**2192**: *Applied* 07/1328: *Considered* 17/823: *Distinguished* 98/727

Sea Assets Ltd v Perusahaan Perseroan (Persero) PT Perusahaan Penerbangan Garuda Indonesia [2001] EWCA Civ 1696, CA (Civ Div) *Considered* 17/404

Sea Shepherd UK v Fish & Fish Ltd see Fish & Fish Ltd v Sea Shepherd UK

Seahorse Maritime Ltd v Nautilus International (A Trade Union) [2017] I.C.R. 1463, EAT

Secerno Ltd v Oxford Magistrates' Court see R. (on the application of Secerno Ltd) v Oxford Magistrates' Court

SECIL - Companhia Geral de Cal e Cimento SA v Fazenda Publica (C-464/14) EU:C:2016:896; [2017] B.T.C. 2; [2016] S.T.I. 3218, ECJ (5th Chamber)

Secker v Fairhill Property Services Ltd [2017] EWHC 69 (QB); [2017] P.I.Q.R. P9, QBD ..... *Digested,* 17/**492**

Secret Hotels2 Ltd (formerly Med Hotels Ltd) v Revenue and Customs Commissioners; *sub nom* Revenue and Customs Commissioners v Secret Hotels2 Ltd (formerly Med Hotels Ltd) [2014] UKSC 16; [2014] 2 All E.R. 685; [2014] S.T.C. 937; [2014] B.V.C. 9; [2014] S.T.I. 864, SC ..... *Digested,* 14/**3073**: *Applied* 17/2258

Secretary of State for Business Innovation and Skills v New Horizon Energy Ltd [2015] EWHC 2961 (Ch); [2017] B.C.C. 629, Ch D

Secretary of State for Business, Innovation and Skills v PLT Anti-Marketing Ltd [2015] EWHC 3981 (Ch); [2016] B.C.C. 404; [2017] 1 B.C.L.C. 19, Ch D (Manchester) *Digested,* 16/**1252**

Secretary of State for Business, Innovation and Skills v Weston [2014] EWHC 2933 (Ch); [2014] B.C.C. 581; [2014] Lloyd's Rep. F.C. 648, Ch D (Birmingham) ..... *Digested,* 15/**385**: *Applied* 17/1806

Secretary of State for Children, Schools and Families v Fletcher see Duncombe v Secretary of State for Children, Schools and Families

Secretary of State for Communities and Local Government v BDW Trading Ltd (t/a David Wilson Homes (Central, Mercia and West Midlands)) see BDW Trading Ltd (t/a David Wilson Homes (Central, Mercia and West Midlands)) v Secretary of State for Communities and Local Government

Secretary of State for Communities and Local Government v Engbers see Engbers v Secretary of State for Communities and Local Government

Secretary of State for Communities and Local Government v Hopkins Development Ltd see Hopkins Developments Ltd v Secretary of State for Communities and Local Government

Secretary of State for Communities and Local Government v Hopkins Homes Ltd; *sub nom* Suffolk Coastal DC v Hopkins Homes Ltd; Hopkins Homes Ltd v Secretary of State for Communities and Local Government; Cheshire East BC v Secretary of State for Communities and Local Government; *joined case* Richborough Estates Partnership LLP v Cheshire East BC [2017] UKSC 37; [2017] 1 W.L.R. 1865; [2017] 4 All E.R. 938; [2017] P.T.S.R. 623; [2017] J.P.L. 1084, SC .... *Digested,* 17/**1725**: *Applied* 17/1767: *Followed* 17/1779

Secretary of State for Communities and Local Government v Hopkins Homes Ltd; *sub nom* Suffolk Coastal DC v Hopkins Homes Ltd; Hopkins Homes Ltd v Secretary of State for Communities and Local Government; Cheshire East BC v Secretary of State for Communities and Local Government; *joined case* Richborough Estates Partnership LLP v Cheshire East BC [2016] EWCA Civ 168; [2017] 1 All E.R. 1011; [2016] P.T.S.R. 1315; [2016] 2 P. & C.R. 1; [2016] J.P.L. 890, CA (Civ Div) .... *Digested,* 16/**1706**: *Affirmed* 17/1725: *Followed* 16/1748, 16/825, 17/1769

Secretary of State for Communities and Local Government v Wealden DC see Wealden DC v Secretary of State for Communities and Local Government

Secretary of State for Communities and Local Government v West Berkshire DC see R. (on the application of West Berkshire DC) v Secretary of State for Communities and Local Government

Secretary of State for Defence v Smith see R. (on the application of Smith) v Oxfordshire Assistant Deputy Coroner

Secretary of State for Education and Science v Tameside MBC [1977] A.C. 1014; [1976] 3 W.L.R. 641; [1976] 3 All E.R. 665; (1976) 120 S.J. 735, HL .... *Digested,* 76/**829**: *Applied* 78/861, 82/1453, 83/359, 83/3723, 94/4593, 98/1901, 00/3115, 00/5397, 07/1485, 10/2618, 10/491, 15/2397: *Considered* 79/198, 79/810, 81/1535, 87/31, 89/3586, 95/1911, 12/2105, 14/2744, 15/747: *Distinguished* 91/67, 99/4248: *Followed* 80/1378, 15/1332, 16/1747, 17/1408

Secretary of State for Health v Servier Laboratories Ltd [2016] EWHC 2381 (Ch); [2016] 5 C.M.L.R. 25, Ch D .... *Digested,* 17/**285**

Secretary of State for Health v Servier Laboratories Ltd [2017] EWHC 2006 (Ch); [2017] 5 C.M.L.R. 17, Ch D

Secretary of State for Justice v Betts [2017] I.C.R. 1130; [2017] I.R.L.R. 804, EAT .... *Digested,* 17/**789**

Secretary of State for Justice v KC [2015] UKUT 376 (AAC); [2015] C.O.P.L.R. 804; [2015] M.H.L.R. 369, UT (AAC) .... *Digested,* 16/**1494**: *Considered* 17/1552

Secretary of State for Justice v MM see PJ (A Patient) v A Local Health Board

Secretary of State for Justice v MM see PJ (A Patient) v Local Health Board

Secretary of State for Justice v Prison Officers' Association see Ministry of Justice v Prison Officers' Association

Secretary of State for Justice v RB [2011] EWCA Civ 1608; [2012] 1 W.L.R. 2043; (2012) 124 B.M.L.R. 13; [2012] M.H.L.R. 131; Times, January 19, 2012, CA (Civ Div) .... *Digested,* 12/**2280**: *Applied* 17/1541: *Considered* 17/1552: *Explained* 16/1494: *Followed* 17/1538

Secretary of State for Justice v RB [2010] UKUT 454 (AAC); [2011] M.H.L.R. 37, UT (AAC) .... *Digested,* 11/**2224**: *Applied* 14/2939, 17/1177: *Reversed* 12/2280

Secretary of State for Justice v Staffordshire CC see Staffordshire CC v K

Secretary of State for Justice v SVS Solicitors see Lord Chancellor v SVS Solicitors

Secretary of State for Justice v Windle see Windle v Secretary of State for Justice

Secretary of State for Scotland v Revival Properties Ltd see Edinburgh City Council v Secretary of State for Scotland

Secretary of State for Social Security v Remilien; *sub nom* Remilien v Secretary of State for Social Security; R. v Chief Adjudication Officer Ex p. Remelien; R. v Secretary of State for Social Security Ex p. Remelien; *joined cases* R. v Secretary of State for Social Security Ex p. Wolke; Chief Adjudication Officer v Wolke [1997] 1 W.L.R. 1640; [1998] 1 All E.R. 129; [1998] 1 F.L.R. 444; [1998] 1 F.C.R. 85; [1998] I.N.L.R. 238; Times, December 1, 1997; [1998] Fam. Law 193; (1997) 94(48) L.S.G. 30; (1998) 142 S.J.L.B. 21, HL .... *Digested,* 98/**4539**: *Considered* 00/3288, 17/1194

Secretary of State for the Environment, Transport and the Regions v Fletcher Estates (Harlescott) Ltd see Fletcher Estates (Harlescott) Ltd v Secretary of State for the Environment, Transport and the Regions

Secretary of State for the Environment, Transport and the Regions v Legal & General Assurance Society Ltd see R. (on the application of Holding & Barnes Plc) v Secretary of State for the Environment, Transport and the Regions

Secretary of State for the Environment, Transport and the Regions v Newell see Fletcher Estates (Harlescott) Ltd v Secretary of State for the Environment, Transport and the Regions

Secretary of State for the Environment, Transport and the Regions v Skerritts of Nottingham Ltd see Skerritts of Nottingham Ltd v Secretary of State for the Environment, Transport and the Regions (No.1)

Secretary of State for the Home Department v A (C-115/15); *sub nom* Secretary of State for the Home Department v NA (C-115/15) EU:C:2016:487; [2017] Q.B. 109; [2016] 3 W.L.R. 1439; [2017] 1 C.M.L.R. 12; [2017] Imm. A.R. 34; [2017] I.N.L.R. 642, ECJ (1st Chamber) .... *Digested,* 17/**898**: *Considered* 17/1246

Secretary of State for the Home Department v AJ (Angola); *joined case* Secretary of State for the Home Department v AJ (Gambia) [2014] EWCA Civ 1636, CA (Civ Div)
Applied 15/1318, 16/1081: *Considered* 17/1200

Secretary of State for the Home Department v AJ (Gambia) see Secretary of State for the Home Department v AJ (Angola)

Secretary of State for the Home Department v AJ (Zimbabwe); *joined case* Secretary of State for the Home Department v VH (Vietnam) [2016] EWCA Civ 1012; [2017] Imm. A.R. 442, CA (Civ Div) .... *Digested,* 17/**1199**

Secretary of State for the Home Department v Akbar; *sub nom* Akbar v Secretary of State for the Home Department [2017] EWCA Civ 16; [2017] 1 W.L.R. 1055; [2017] C.P. Rep. 17, CA (Civ Div) .... *Digested,* 17/**1221**

Secretary of State for the Home Department v Capparelli see Capparrelli (EEA Nationals: British Nationality)

Secretary of State for the Home Department v CS (C-304/14); *sub nom* S v Secretary of State for the Home Department (C-304/14) EU:C:2016:674; [2017] Q.B. 558; [2017] 2 W.L.R. 180; [2017] 1 C.M.L.R. 31; [2017] Imm. A.R. 429; [2017] I.N.L.R. 400; Times, November 18, 2016, ECJ (Grand Chamber) .... *Digested,* 17/**1193**: *Considered* 17/1239

Secretary of State for the Home Department v Davis see R. (on the application of Davis) v Secretary of State for the Home Department

Secretary of State for the Home Department v EG see EG (UT Rule 17: Withdrawal: Rule 24: Scope: Ethiopia), Re

Secretary of State for the Home Department v Elias see R. (on the application of Elias) v Secretary of State for Defence

Secretary of State for the Home Department v Forman see Forman (ss 117A-C Considerations: United States)

Secretary of State for the Home Department v GD (Ghana); *sub nom* GD (Ghana) v Secretary of State for the Home Department [2017] EWCA Civ 1126; [2018] Imm. A.R. 63; [2017] I.N.L.R. 882, CA (Civ Div)

Secretary of State for the Home Department v H see R. (on the application of H) v Secretary of State for the Home Department

Secretary of State for the Home Department v Headley see R. (on the application of Clift) v Secretary of State for the Home Department

Secretary of State for the Home Department v HF (Gambia) see Amirteymour (EEA Appeals: Human Rights: United States)

Secretary of State for the Home Department v Hindawi see R. (on the application of Clift) v Secretary of State for the Home Department

Secretary of State for the Home Department v HM (Uganda) see NE-A (Nigeria) v Secretary of State for the Home Department

Secretary of State for the Home Department v HM Senior Coroner for Surrey [2016] EWHC 3001 (Admin); [2017] 4 W.L.R. 191; [2017] 3 All E.R. 764; (2017) 181 J.P. 157; [2016] Inquest L.R. 289; [2017] A.C.D. 13, QBD (Admin) .... *Digested,* 17/**24**

Secretary of State for the Home Department v Izvira see Amirteymour (EEA Appeals: Human Rights: United States)
Secretary of State for the Home Department v Johnson see Johnson (Deportation: 4 Years' Imprisonment)
Secretary of State for the Home Department v JZ (Zambia) [2016] EWCA Civ 116; [2016] Imm. A.R. 781, CA (Civ Div) .... *Digested,* 16/**1075**: *Applied* 17/1198
Secretary of State for the Home Department v KG IA/07818/2014, UT (IAC) *Reversed* 17/1232
Secretary of State for the Home Department v KG (India) [2016] EWCA Civ 477; [2016] Imm. A.R. 1153, CA (Civ Div) .... *Digested,* 17/**1232**
Secretary of State for the Home Department v Khan [2016] EWCA Civ 137; [2016] 4 W.L.R. 56; [2017] 2 All E.R. 831; [2016] Imm. A.R. 853; [2017] I.N.L.R. 94; Times, April 14, 2016, CA (Civ Div) .... *Digested,* 16/**1136**
Secretary of State for the Home Department v KJ (Angola) see NA (Pakistan) v Secretary of State for the Home Department
Secretary of State for the Home Department v LG [2017] EWHC 1529 (Admin); [2017] A.C.D. 100, QBD (Admin)
Secretary of State for the Home Department v MG (Portugal) (C-400/12) EU:C:2014:9; [2014] 1 W.L.R. 2441; [2014] 2 C.M.L.R. 40; [2014] Imm. A.R. 561; [2014] I.N.L.R. 670, ECJ (2nd Chamber) .... *Digested,* 14/**1666**: *Applied* 16/1088: *Considered* 17/1195
Secretary of State for the Home Department v MS see MS (India) v Secretary of State for the Home Department
Secretary of State for the Home Department v MY (Kenya) see NA (Pakistan) v Secretary of State for the Home Department
Secretary of State for the Home Department v NA (C-115/15) see Secretary of State for the Home Department v A (C-115/15)
Secretary of State for the Home Department v NA (Pakistan) [2015] EWCA Civ 140, CA (Civ Div) *Preliminary ruling given* 17/898
Secretary of State for the Home Department v Nasseri see R. (on the application of Nasseri) v Secretary of State for the Home Department
Secretary of State for the Home Department v O see KMO (section 117: Unduly Harsh: Nigeria), Re
Secretary of State for the Home Department v R. (on the application of Antonio) see R. (on the application of Antonio) v Secretary of State for the Home Department
Secretary of State for the Home Department v Rahman see R. (on the application of Abbassi) v Secretary of State for the Home Department
Secretary of State for the Home Department v Razgar see R. (on the application of Razgar) v Secretary of State for the Home Department (No.2)
Secretary of State for the Home Department v Restivo see Restivo (EEA: Prisoner Transfer)
Secretary of State for the Home Department v Rexha see Rexha (S.117C: Earlier Offences)
Secretary of State for the Home Department v Rodriguez see Mandalia v Secretary of State for the Home Department
Secretary of State for the Home Department v Sheidu see Sheidu (Further Submissions: Appealable Decision)
Secretary of State for the Home Department v SU (Pakistan) [2017] EWCA Civ 1069; [2017] 4 W.L.R. 175, CA (Civ Div) .... *Digested,* 17/**1186**
Secretary of State for the Home Department v TB (Jamaica) see R. (on the application of TB (Jamaica)) v Secretary of State for the Home Department
Secretary of State for the Home Department v Treebhawon see Treebhawon (NIAA 2002 Part 5A: Compelling Circumstances Test), Re
Secretary of State for the Home Department v VH (Vietnam) see Secretary of State for the Home Department v AJ (Zimbabwe)
Secretary of State for the Home Department v VM (Jamaica); *joined case* VM (Jamaica) v Secretary of State for the Home Department [2017] EWCA Civ 255; [2017] Imm. A.R. 1237, CA (Civ Div)
Secretary of State for the Home Department v Vomero; *sub nom* FV (Italy) v Secretary of State for the Home Department [2016] UKSC 49; [2017] 1 All E.R. 999; [2017] 1 C.M.L.R. 3, SC .... *Digested,* 17/**1195**
Secretary of State for the Home Department v Watson (C-698/15) see Tele2 Sverige AB v Post- och telestyrelsen (C-203/15)
Secretary of State for the Home Department v WM (Afghanistan) see NA (Pakistan) v Secretary of State for the Home Department

Secretary of State for the Home Department v ZAT (Syria); *sub nom* R. (on the application of ZT (Syria)) v Secretary of State for the Home Department [2016] EWCA Civ 810; [2016] 1 W.L.R. 4894; [2017] 2 All E.R. 1024; [2017] Imm. A.R. 356; [2017] I.N.L.R. 422; Times, October 21, 2016, CA (Civ Div) .... *Digested,* 16/**1067**

Secretary of State for the Home Department v ZP (India) [2015] EWCA Civ 1197; [2016] 4 W.L.R. 35; [2016] Imm. A.R. 308; [2016] I.N.L.R. 381, CA (Civ Div) ..... *Digested,* 16/**1092**: *Applied* 17/1190: *Followed* 17/1186

Secretary of State for Trade and Industry v Bairstow; *sub nom* Queens Moat Houses Plc, Re [2003] EWCA Civ 321; [2004] Ch. 1; [2003] 3 W.L.R. 841; [2004] 4 All E.R. 325; [2003] C.P. Rep. 46; [2003] B.C.C. 682; [2003] 1 B.C.L.C. 696; Times, March 31, 2003; Independent, March 20, 2003; (2003) 100(18) L.S.G. 36; (2003) 153 N.L.J. 440, CA (Civ Div) .... *Digested,* 03/**509**: *Applied* 07/339, 07/345, 11/240, 14/297, 17/191: *Considered* 07/571, 08/266, 10/258: *Distinguished* 08/2125, 09/336: *Followed* 14/2209, 17/313

Secretary of State for Work and Pensions v City of Glasgow Council [2017] CSIH 35; 2017 S.C. 707; 2017 S.L.T. 783; 2017 Hous. L.R. 94; 2017 G.W.D. 19-314, IH (Ex Div) .... *Digested,* 17/**2824**

Secretary of State for Work and Pensions v G [2017] EWCA Civ 61; [2017] 1 W.L.R. 1956; (2017) 154 B.M.L.R. 100; Times, March 2, 2017, CA (Civ Div) .... *Digested,* 17/**2040**

Secretary of State for Work and Pensions v M; *sub nom* Secretary of State for Work and Pensions v MMcK [2017] CSIH 57; 2018 S.C. 1; 2017 S.L.T. 1045; 2017 G.W.D. 29-468, IH (Ex Div) .... *Digested,* 17/**2827**

Secretary of State for Work and Pensions v M see M v Secretary of State for Work and Pensions

Secretary of State for Work and Pensions v MMcK see Secretary of State for Work and Pensions v M

Secretary of State for Work and Pensions v Tolley (C-430/15); *sub nom* Tolley v Secretary of State for Work and Pensions (C-430/15) EU:C:2017:74; [2017] 1 W.L.R. 1261, ECJ (1st Chamber)

Secure Capital SA v Credit Suisse AG [2017] EWCA Civ 1486; [2017] 2 Lloyd's Rep. 599; [2018] 1 B.C.L.C. 325, CA (Civ Div)

Securenta Gottinger Immobilienanlagen und Vermogensmanagement AG v Finanzamt Gottingen (C-437/06) EU:C:2008:166; [2008] S.T.C. 3473; [2008] E.C.R. I-1597; [2010] B.V.C. 766; [2008] S.T.I. 939, ECJ (4th Chamber) .... *Digested,* 09/**4058**: *Distinguished* 16/2181: *Followed* 09/4052, 17/2241

Seddon Properties Ltd v Secretary of State for the Environment (1981) 42 P. & C.R. 26; (1978) 248 E.G. 951; [1978] J.P.L. 835, QBD .... *Digested,* 81/**2730**: *Applied* 83/3693, 05/3310, 17/1727: *Cited* 94/4427: *Considered* 86/3259, 88/3442: *Followed* 93/3925

Seechurn v Ace Insurance SA NV; *sub nom* Ace Insurance SA NV v Seechurn [2002] EWCA Civ 67; [2002] 2 Lloyd's Rep. 390; [2002] Lloyd's Rep. I.R. 489, CA (Civ Div) .... *Digested,* 02/**2734**: *Applied* 12/378, 17/493

Seery v Leathes Prior (A Firm) [2017] EWHC 80 (QB); [2017] P.N.L.R. 14, QBD .... *Digested,* 17/**1575**

Sefton BC v Wainwright [2015] I.C.R. 652; [2015] I.R.L.R. 90, EAT .... *Digested,* 15/**859**: *Considered* 17/829

Seldon v Clarkson Wright & Jakes [2012] UKSC 16; [2012] 3 All E.R. 1301; [2012] 2 C.M.L.R. 50; [2012] I.C.R. 716; [2012] I.R.L.R. 590; [2012] Eq. L.R. 579; [2012] Pens. L.R. 239; Times, May 2, 2012; (2012) 109(19) L.S.G. 18; (2012) 162 N.L.J. 653; (2012) 156(17) S.J.L.B. 31, SC .... *Digested,* 12/**1037**: *Considered* 15/783: *Followed* 15/806: *Not applied* 17/779

Select Car Rentals (North West) Ltd v Esure Services Ltd; *sub nom* Mee v Jones [2017] EWHC 1434 (QB); [2017] 1 W.L.R. 4426; [2017] 3 Costs L.R. 537; [2018] R.T.R. 8, QBD (Liverpool) .... *Digested,* 17/**251**

Sellars v IMI Yorkshire Imperial Ltd 1986 S.C. 235; 1986 S.L.T. 629, IH (2 Div) .... *Digested,* 86/**4228**: *Considered* 17/2454

Sempra Metals Ltd v Revenue and Customs Commissioners [2008] S.T.C. (S.C.D.) 1062; [2008] S.T.I. 1923, Sp Comm .... *Digested,* 08/**3671**: *Considered* 13/3095: *Overruled* 17/2131

Sempra Metals Ltd (formerly Metallgesellschaft Ltd) v Inland Revenue Commissioners [2007] UKHL 34; [2008] 1 A.C. 561; [2007] 3 W.L.R. 354; [2007] 4 All E.R. 657; [2008] Bus. L.R. 49; [2007] S.T.C. 1559; [2008] Eu. L.R. 1; [2007] B.T.C. 509; Times, July 25, 2007; [2007] S.T.I. 1865; (2007) 104(31) L.S.G. 25; (2007) 157 N.L.J. 1082; (2007) 151 S.J.L.B. 985, HL .... *Digested,* 07/**1052**: *Applied* 09/4081, 10/3506, 14/3079, 16/567: *Cited* 09/458: *Considered* 10/3512, 11/857, 12/2812, 15/1512, 15/2613: *Followed* 10/3268, 14/1892, 14/2874, 17/412: *Referred to* 11/2267

Sen v Steelform Engineering Co Ltd see Lagden v O'Connor

Senatex GmbH v Finanzamt Hannover-Nord (C-518/14) EU:C:2016:691; [2017] S.T.C. 205; [2016] B.V.C. 42, ECJ (4th Chamber)

Seprey-Hozo v Miercurea Ciuc Court see Seprey-Hozo v Romania

Seprey-Hozo v Romania; *sub nom* Seprey-Hozo v Miercurea Ciuc Court [2016] EWHC 2902 (Admin); [2016] 4 W.L.R. 181; [2017] A.C.D. 14, QBD (Admin) ..... *Digested,* 17/**908**

Serco Ltd v Dahou; *sub nom* Dahou v Serco Ltd [2015] I.R.L.R. 30, EAT .... *Digested,* 15/**872**: *Affirmed* 17/763

Serco Ltd v Dahou; *sub nom* Dahou v Serco Ltd [2016] EWCA Civ 832; [2017] I.R.L.R. 81, CA (Civ Div) .... *Digested,* 17/**763**

Serco Ltd v Lawson see Lawson v Serco Ltd

Serious Fraud Office v Rolls-Royce Plc [2017] Lloyd's Rep. F.C. 249, Crown Ct (Southwark) .... *Digested,* 17/**595**

Serious Fraud Office v Saleh; *sub nom* Saleh v Director of the Serious Fraud Office [2015] EWHC 2119 (QB); [2015] Lloyd's Rep. F.C. 629, QBD .... *Digested,* 16/**548**: *Affirmed* 17/346

Serious Fraud Office v Saleh; *sub nom* Saleh v Director of the Serious Fraud Office [2017] EWCA Civ 18; [2017] Lloyd's Rep. F.C. 177, CA (Civ Div) .... *Digested,* 17/**346**

Serious Fraud Office v Standard Bank Plc (now ICBC Standard Bank Plc) (Preliminary) [2016] Lloyd's Rep. F.C. 91, Crown Ct (Southwark) *Applied* 17/595: *Considered* 16/519

Serious Fraud Office v Wastell see Stanford International Bank Ltd (In Receivership), Re

Serious Organised Crime Agency v Gale; *sub nom* Gale v Serious Organised Crime Agency [2011] UKSC 49; [2011] 1 W.L.R. 2760; [2012] 2 All E.R. 1; [2012] 1 Costs L.R. 21; [2012] H.R.L.R. 5; [2012] Lloyd's Rep. F.C. 1; Times, November 17, 2011; (2011) 155(41) S.J.L.B. 31, SC .... *Digested,* 12/**329**: *Applied* 13/728: *Considered* 14/2954: *Followed* 12/467, 17/631

Serra v Paraguay; *joined case* Galino v Paraguay [2017] EWHC 2300 (Admin); [2017] Lloyd's Rep. F.C. 537; [2017] A.C.D. 122, DC .... *Digested,* 17/**903**

Services Europe Atlantique Sud (SEAS) v Stockholms Rederi AB Svea (The Folias) see Owners of the Eleftherotria v Owners of the Despina R

Seven Individuals v Revenue and Customs Commissioners [2017] UKUT 132 (TCC); [2017] S.T.C. 874; [2017] B.T.C. 513, UT (Tax) .... *Digested,* 17/**2145**

Seven Towns Ltd v Kiddiland [2017] F.S.R. 14, HC (Ind)

Seven Towns Ltd v Office for Harmonisation in the Internal Market (Trade Marks and Designs) (OHIM) (T-293/10) EU:T:2012:302, GC *Considered* 17/1387

Sexius v Attorney General of Saint Lucia [2017] UKPC 26; [2017] 1 W.L.R. 3236; [2018] 1 Cr. App. R. 2, PC (StL)

SF (Albania) v Secretary of State for the Home Department see SF (Guidance, post–2014 Act: Albania)

SF (Guidance, post–2014 Act: Albania); *sub nom* SF (Albania) v Secretary of State for the Home Department [2017] UKUT 120 (IAC); [2017] Imm. A.R. 1003, UT (IAC) .... *Digested,* 17/**1175**

Shabpar v Barnet LBC see R. v Barnet LBC Ex p. Shah

Shackleton and Associates Ltd v Al Shamsi; *sub nom* Shackleton and Associates Ltd v Shamsi [2017] EWHC 304 (Comm); [2017] 2 Costs L.O. 169, QBD (Comm) .. *Digested,* 17/**268**

Shackleton and Associates Ltd v Shamsi see Shackleton and Associates Ltd v Al Shamsi

Shah v Insafe International Ltd [2016] EWHC 1036 (Ch); [2017] S.T.C. 1538; [2016] B.T.C. 37; [2016] S.T.I. 1657, Ch D .... *Digested,* 17/**2132**

Shah (Jitendra) v Barnet LBC see R. v Barnet LBC Ex p. Shah

Shahid v Scottish Ministers [2015] UKSC 58; [2016] A.C. 429; [2015] 3 W.L.R. 1003; [2016] 4 All E.R. 363; 2016 S.C. (U.K.S.C.) 1; 2015 S.L.T. 707, SC .... *Digested,* 15/**1817**: *Considered* 16/2756: *Followed* 17/1596

Shakil-Ur-Rahman v ARY Network Ltd [2016] EWHC 3110 (QB); [2017] 4 W.L.R. 22; [2017] E.M.L.R. 10, QBD .... *Digested,* 17/**645**

Shalabayev v JSC BTA Bank; *sub nom* JSC BTA Bank v Ablyazov [2016] EWCA Civ 987; [2017] 1 W.L.R. 603, CA (Civ Div) .... *Digested,* 17/**313**

Shalabayev v JSC BTA Bank; *sub nom* JSC BTA Bank v Ablyazov [2013] EWHC 1836 (Comm), QBD (Comm) *Reversed* 17/313

Shamoon v Chief Constable of the Royal Ulster Constabulary [2003] UKHL 11; [2003] 2 All E.R. 26; [2003] N.I. 174; [2003] I.C.R. 337; [2003] I.R.L.R. 285; Times, March 4, 2003; (2003) 147 S.J.L.B. 268, HL (NI) .... *Digested,* 03/**4767**:
Applied 03/1297, 05/1337, 06/1303, 07/1388, 07/1402, 09/1172, 10/1137, 11/1055, 12/1126, 12/1153, 12/3527, 15/801: *Considered* 04/1275, 05/1291, 06/1349, 06/1365, 07/1401, 09/1180, 10/1021, 12/1121, 14/1024:
Followed 12/1060, 17/2324

Shanks v Unilever Plc [2014] EWHC 1647 (Pat); [2014] R.P.C. 29; (2014) 158(23) S.J.L.B. 41, Ch D (Patents Ct) .... *Digested,* 15/**1512**:
Affirmed 17/1379

Shanks v Unilever Plc [2017] EWCA Civ 2; [2017] Bus. L.R. 883; [2017] R.P.C. 15, CA (Civ Div) .... *Digested,* 17/**1379**

Shannon v Rampersad (t/a Clifton House Residential Home) [2015] I.R.L.R. 982, EAT *Digested,* 16/**696**:
Considered 17/812

Sharland v Sharland; *sub nom* S v S [2015] UKSC 60; [2016] A.C. 871; [2015] 3 W.L.R. 1070; [2016] 1 All E.R. 671; [2015] 2 F.L.R. 1367; [2015] 3 F.C.R. 481; Times, November 2, 2015; [2015] Fam. Law 1461, SC .... *Digested,* 15/**1090**:
Considered 16/336, 17/1013: *Followed* 16/895, 17/1023, 17/977

Sharma v Simposh Ltd [2011] EWCA Civ 1383; [2013] Ch. 23; [2012] 3 W.L.R. 503; [2012] 2 All E.R. (Comm) 288; [2012] 1 P. & C.R. 12; [2012] 1 E.G.L.R. 113; [2012] 6 E.G. 92; [2011] 48 E.G. 87 (C.S.); [2012] 1 P. & C.R. DG12, CA (Civ Div) .... *Digested,* 12/**2767**:
Applied 16/431: *Considered* 17/497

Sharma v Tendring DC [2017] P.A.D. 18, Planning Inspector

Sharma v Top Brands Ltd see Top Brands Ltd v Sharma

Sharp v Blank [2017] EWHC 141 (Ch); [2017] 4 W.L.R. 184, Ch D

Sharp v Blank [2015] EWHC 3220 (Ch); [2017] B.C.C. 187, Ch D

Sharp v Leeds City Council [2017] EWCA Civ 33; [2017] 4 W.L.R. 98; [2017] C.P. Rep. 19; [2017] 1 Costs L.R. 129, CA (Civ Div) .... *Digested,* 17/**234**

Sharp v North Essex Magistrates' Court; *sub nom* R. (on the application of Sharp) v North Essex Magistrates' Court [2017] EWCA Civ 1143; [2017] 1 W.L.R. 3789; [2018] Env. L.R. 4; [2018] 1 P. & C.R. 11; [2018] R.V.R. 121; Times, September 21, 2017, CA (Civ Div) .... *Digested,* 17/**884**

Sharp v North Essex Magistrates' Court; *sub nom* R. (on the application of Sharp) v North Essex Magistrates' Court [2015] EWHC 3957 (Admin); [2016] Env. L.R. 20, QBD (Admin) .... *Digested,* 16/**772**:
Affirmed 17/884

Sharpe v Bishop of Worcester see Sharpe v Worcester Diocesan Board of Finance Ltd

Sharpe v Worcester Diocesan Board of Finance Ltd; *sub nom* Sharpe v Bishop of Worcester [2015] EWCA Civ 399; [2015] I.C.R. 1241; [2015] I.R.L.R. 663, CA (Civ Div) .... *Digested,* 15/**821**:
Followed 17/790

Shasha v Westminster City Council see R. (on the application of Shasha) v Westminster City Council

Shaw v Grouby [2017] EWCA Civ 233; [2017] C.I.L.L. 3989, CA (Civ Div)

Shaw v Kovac; *sub nom* Shaw (Personal Representative of the Estate of Ewan (Deceased)) v Kovac [2015] EWHC 3335 (QB), QBD
Affirmed 17/1560

Shaw v Kovac [2017] EWCA Civ 1028; [2017] 1 W.L.R. 4773; [2018] 2 All E.R. 71; [2017] P.I.Q.R. Q4; [2017] Med. L.R. 403, CA (Civ Div) .... *Digested,* 17/**1560**

Shaw v Leigh Day (A Firm) [2017] EWHC 825 (QB); [2017] P.N.L.R. 26, QBD (Manchester) .... *Digested,* 17/**1574**

Shaw v Medtronic Corevalve LLC [2017] EWHC 1397 (QB); [2017] 3 Costs L.R. 491, QBD .... *Digested,* 17/**340**

Shaw v Solicitors Regulation Authority [2017] EWHC 2076 (Admin); [2017] 4 W.L.R. 143, QBD (Admin) .... *Digested,* 17/**1492**

Shaw v United States [2014] EWHC 4654 (Admin); [2015] A.C.D. 63, DC
Applied 17/901

Shaw v Webb see Brown Bear Foods Ltd, Re

Shaw (Inspector of Taxes) v Vicky Construction Ltd; *sub nom* Vicky Construction Ltd v Shaw (Inspector of Taxes) [2002] EWHC 2659 (Ch); [2002] S.T.C. 1544; 75 T.C. 26; [2003] B.T.C. 68; Times, December 27, 2002; [2002] S.T.I. 1689, Ch D .... *Digested,* 03/**4251**:
Applied 06/4136, 06/4209, 08/3859, 16/2050: *Considered* 05/4017, 17/2103:
Followed 05/4036

Shaw (Personal Representative of the Estate of Ewan (Deceased)) v Kovac see Shaw v Kovac

Sheffield City Council v Fairhall [2017] EWHC 2121 (QB); [2018] R.T.R. 11; [2018] Env. L.R. 12; [2017] L.L.R. 890, QBD (Leeds)
Sheffield City Council v Norouzi [2011] I.R.L.R. 897; [2011] Eq. L.R. 1039, EAT .... *Digested,* 11/**1107**: *Considered* 17/840
Sheffield City Council v Oliver see Oliver v Sheffield City Council
Sheffield Teaching Hospitals NHS Foundation Trust v TH [2014] EWCOP 4, CP
Considered 17/1124
Sheidu (Further Submissions: Appealable Decision); *sub nom* Secretary of State for the Home Department v Sheidu [2016] UKUT 412 (IAC); [2017] Imm. A.R. 179, UT (IAC) .... *Digested,* 17/**1210**
Shelfer v City of London Electric Lighting Co (No.1); *joined case* Meux's Brewery Co v City of London Electric Lighting Co [1895] 1 Ch. 287, CA
Applied 57/3609, 61/6344, 65/3985, 67/3170, 80/2251, 84/1150, 93/4040, 94/622, 95/4142, 07/3425, 09/2744, 17/2197: *Considered* 70/2290, 80/2007, 91/2676, 91/2976, 92/3602, 96/1267, 00/5127, 07/2962, 09/2318, 10/1937, 14/2223: *Distinguished* 69/2866, 70/2882, 82/2671: *Followed* 95/3766, 11/2682, 14/1895
Shelfside (Holdings) Ltd v Vale of White Horse DC [2016] UKUT 400 (LC); [2017] L.L.R. 199, UT (Lands)
Shendish Manor Ltd v Coleman [2001] EWCA Civ 913, CA (Civ Div)
Followed 17/649
Shephard Homes v Sandham (No.2) see Shepherd Homes Ltd v Sandham (No.2)
Shepherd (Inspector of Taxes) v Lyntress; *joined case* News International v Shepherd (Inspector of Taxes) [1989] S.T.C. 617; 62 T.C. 495; [1989] B.T.C. 346; Independent, July 10, 1989, DC
Not applied 17/2098
Shepherd Homes Ltd v Sandham (No.2); *sub nom* Shephard Homes v Sandham (No.2) [1971] 1 W.L.R. 1062; [1971] 2 All E.R. 1267; (1971) 22 P. & C.R. 835; (1971) 115 S.J. 487, Ch D .... *Digested,* 71/**9933**: *Applied* 04/576: *Considered* 17/1856
Sher v United Kingdom (5201/11) (2016) 63 E.H.R.R. 24; 41 B.H.R.C. 437; Times, January 15, 2016, ECHR
Sherlock Holmes International Society Ltd v Aidiniantz see Sherlock Holmes International Society Ltd, Re
Sherlock Holmes International Society Ltd, Re; *sub nom* Sherlock Holmes International Society Ltd v Aidiniantz; Aidiniantz v Sherlock Holmes International Society Ltd [2016] EWHC 1076 (Ch); [2017] 2 B.C.L.C. 14, Ch D (Companies Ct)
Sherlock Holmes International Society, Re; *sub nom* Aidiniantz v Sherlock Holmes International Society Ltd [2016] EWHC 1392 (Ch); [2016] 4 W.L.R. 173; [2017] 2 B.C.L.C. 38; [2016] P.N.L.R. 31, Ch D (Companies Ct) .... *Digested,* 16/**49**: *Applied* 17/48
Sherlock Systems CV v Apple Inc; *sub nom* 68 Applications by Entities Under the Control of Michael Gleissner to Revoke 68 Trade Marks Owned by Apple Inc for Non-Use [2017] F.S.R. 30, IPO
Shetland Islands Council, Applicant 2017 S.L.T. (Sh Ct) 59; 2017 G.W.D. 5-66, Sh Ct (Grampian) (Lerwick) .... *Digested,* 17/**2605**
Shetty v Al Rushaid Petroleum Investment Co; *joined case* Al Rushaid Parker Drilling Ltd v Shetty [2011] EWHC 1460 (Ch), Ch D
Applied 17/338
Shevill v Presse Alliance SA (C-68/93) EU:C:1995:61; [1995] 2 A.C. 18; [1995] 2 W.L.R. 499; [1995] E.C.R. I-415; [1995] All E.R. (E.C.) 289; [1995] I.L.Pr. 267; [1995] E.M.L.R. 543; Times, April 6, 1995; Financial Times, March 21, 1995, ECJ .... *Digested,* 95/**3127**: *Considered* 95/705, 99/715, 99/717, 05/5046: *Followed* 04/562, 17/160: *Referred to* 97/895
Shields & Sons Partnership v Revenue and Customs Commissioners [2016] UKUT 142 (TCC); [2016] B.V.C. 538, UT (Tax) .... *Digested,* 17/**2240**
Shields & Sons Partnership v Revenue and Customs Commissioners (C-262/16) EU:C:2017:756; [2017] 4 W.L.R. 208; [2017] S.T.C. 2205; [2017] B.V.C. 49, ECJ (3rd Chamber)
Shierson v Rastogi (A Bankrupt) [2007] EWHC 1266 (Ch); [2007] B.P.I.R. 891; (2007) 104(25) L.S.G. 39, Ch D (Bankruptcy Ct) .... *Digested,* 08/**2125**: *Applied* 14/1787, 14/1796, 17/1300: *Considered* 13/1700
Shierson v Tomlinson see NT Gallagher & Son Ltd, Re
Shilliday v Smith 1998 S.C. 725; 1998 S.L.T. 976; 1998 S.C.L.R. 502; 1998 G.W.D. 16-821, IH (1 Div) .... *Digested,* 98/**6215**: *Considered* 17/2846

Shimizu (UK) Ltd v Westminster City Council [1997] 1 W.L.R. 168; [1997] 1 All E.R. 481; [1997] R.V.R. 128; Times, February 11, 1997; [1997] J.P.L. 523; (1997) 94(10) L.S.G. 31; (1997) 147 N.L.J. 218; (1997) 141 S.J.L.B. 56; [1997] N.P.C. 11, HL .... *Digested,* 97/**4077**: *Applied* 03/3397: *Considered* 01/1845: *Not applied* 17/1702

Shimizu Europe Ltd v Automajor Ltd [2002] B.L.R. 113; (2002) 18 Const. L.J. 259, QBD (TCC) .... *Digested,* 02/**659**: *Applied* 10/558: *Considered* 04/592, 14/130, 17/451

Shindler v Chancellor of the Duchy of Lancaster [2016] EWCA Civ 469; [2017] Q.B. 226; [2016] 3 W.L.R. 1196; [2016] 3 C.M.L.R. 23; [2016] H.R.L.R. 14; Times, June 7, 2016, CA (Civ Div) .... *Digested,* 16/**384**: *Considered* 17/807

Shingara v Secretary of State for the Home Department see R. v Secretary of State for the Home Department Ex p. Shingara (No.2)

Shirley v Revenue and Customs Commissioners [2014] UKFTT 1023 (TC); [2015] S.F.T.D. 247; [2015] S.T.I. 360, FTT (Tax) .... *Digested,* 15/**2482**: *Approved* 17/2144

Shirley Children's Settlement Trustees v Crabtree [2007] EWHC 1532 (Admin); [2008] 1 W.L.R. 18; [2008] W.T.L.R. 133; Times, July 30, 2007; (2007) 157 N.L.J. 975, QBD (Admin) .... *Digested,* 08/**2436**: *Applied* 17/1430

Shlosberg v Avonwick Holdings Ltd; *sub nom* Avonwick Holdings Ltd v Shlosberg [2016] EWHC 1001 (Ch); [2016] 3 W.L.R. 1330; [2016] B.P.I.R. 1012, Ch D ..... *Digested,* 16/**1187**: *Affirmed* 17/1289

Shlosberg v Avonwick Holdings Ltd; *sub nom* Avonwick Holdings Ltd v Shlosberg [2016] EWCA Civ 1138; [2017] Ch. 210; [2017] 2 W.L.R. 1075; [2017] B.P.I.R. 1, CA (Civ Div) .... *Digested,* 17/**1289**: *Explained* 17/1286

Shop Direct Group v Revenue and Customs Commissioners [2016] UKSC 7; [2016] 1 W.L.R. 733; [2016] 2 All E.R. 725; [2016] S.T.C. 747; [2016] B.T.C. 8; Times, February 26, 2016; [2016] S.T.I. 393, SC .... *Digested,* 16/**2066**: *Considered* 17/2255

Short's Trustee v Chung (No.1) 1991 S.L.T. 472; 1991 S.C.L.R. 629, IH (2 Div) .... *Digested,* 91/**4415**: *Applied* 17/2684: *Considered* 96/7035: *Followed* 93/4825, 98/6001, 02/5891

Short's Trustee v Chung (No.2) 1999 S.C. 471; 1999 S.L.T. 751; 1999 S.C.L.R. 815; 1999 G.W.D. 12-537, IH (Ex Div) .... *Digested,* 99/**5709**: *Applied* 00/5938: *Considered* 17/2412

SI (India) v Secretary of State for the Home Department [2016] EWCA Civ 1255; Times, January 19, 2017, CA (Civ Div) .... *Digested,* 17/**1233**

SiBCAS Ltd v Revenue and Customs Commissioners; *sub nom* Revenue and Customs Commissioners v SiBCAS Ltd [2017] UKUT 298 (TCC); [2017] B.V.C. 521; [2017] S.T.I. 1771, UT (Tax) .... *Digested,* 17/**2238**

SiBCAS Ltd v Revenue and Customs Commissioners; *sub nom* Revenue and Customs Commissioners v SiBCAS Ltd [2016] UKFTT 502 (TC); [2016] S.T.I. 2250, FTT (Tax) *Reversed* 17/2238

Sidabras v Lithuania (50421/08); *joined case* Rainys v Lithuania (56213/08) (2017) 65 E.H.R.R. 11, ECHR

Sidey Ltd v Clackmannanshire Council [2010] CSIH 37; 2010 S.L.T. 607; [2010] Eu. L.R. 649; 2010 G.W.D. 19-383, IH (1 Div) .... *Digested,* 10/**4483**: *Considered* 17/2773

Sidney and North Saanich Memorial Park Society v British Columbia (Attorney General) 2016 BCSC 589; [2017] W.T.L.R. 135; 19 I.T.E.L.R. 182, Sup Ct (BC)

Signature of St Albans (Property) Guernsey Ltd v Wragg [2017] EWHC 2352 (Ch); [2018] 2 W.L.R. 943; [2017] H.L.R. 45; [2018] 1 P. & C.R. 12, Ch D

Silberquelle GmbH v Maselli-Strickmode GmbH (C-495/07) EU:C:2009:10; [2009] E.C.R. I-137; [2009] E.T.M.R. 28; [2009] Bus. L.R. D45, ECJ (1st Chamber) ..... *Digested,* 09/**2447**: *Applied* 17/1393: *Followed* 14/1931, 16/1289

Silver Dry Bulk Co Ltd v Homer Hulbert Maritime Co Ltd [2017] EWHC 44 (Comm); [2017] 1 All E.R. (Comm) 791; [2017] 1 Lloyd's Rep. 154; [2017] 1 C.L.C. 1, QBD (Comm) .... *Digested,* 17/**64**

Silvergate Support Services Ltd v Revenue and Customs Commissioners [2017] UKFTT 388 (TC); [2017] S.T.I. 1180, FTT (Tax)

Silvester v Revenue and Customs Commissioners TC04682, FTT (Tax) *Disapproved* 17/2144

Sim v Rotherham MBC; *joined cases* Townend v Doncaster MBC; Barnfield v Solihull MBC; Rathbone v Croydon LBC [1987] Ch. 216; [1986] 3 W.L.R. 851; [1986] 3 All E.R. 387; [1986] I.C.R. 897; [1986] I.R.L.R. 391; 85 L.G.R. 128; (1986) 83 L.S.G. 3746; (1986) 130 S.J. 839, Ch D .... *Digested,* 86/**1152**:
Approved 17/808: *Considered* 90/1984, 96/2673, 15/863

Simba Toys GmbH & Co KG v EUIPO (C-30/15 P) EU:C:2016:849; [2017] E.T.M.R. 6; [2017] F.S.R. 15, ECJ (1st Chamber)

Simic v Bosnia and Herzegovina (Admissibility) (75255/10) (2017) 64 E.H.R.R. SE14, ECHR

Simmonds v Gammell; *sub nom* Lloyd's Syndicate 994 for 2001 Year of Account, Re; Lloyd's Syndicate 102 for 2001 Year of Account, Re [2016] EWHC 2515 (Comm); [2016] 2 Lloyd's Rep. 631; [2016] 2 C.L.C. 676; [2016] Lloyd's Rep. I.R. 693, QBD (Comm) .... *Digested,* 17/**1355**

Simmonds v Stewart Alexander Group Ltd see Dickinson v Tesco Plc

Simmons v Castle [2012] EWCA Civ 1039; [2013] 1 W.L.R. 1239; [2013] 1 All E.R. 334; [2012] C.P. Rep. 43; [2012] 5 Costs L.R. 931; [2013] E.M.L.R. 3; [2012] P.I.Q.R. P22; [2013] Med. L.R. 1, CA (Civ Div) .... *Digested,* 12/**852**:
Applied 14/2333, 17/782: *Cited* 16/1404, 17/827: *Considered* 14/2311, 14/2326, 15/1904, 15/1915, 16/1636: *Explained* 15/804: *Followed* 15/791, 16/566

Simon v Byford; *sub nom* Simon (Deceased), Re [2014] EWCA Civ 280; [2014] W.T.L.R. 1097; 17 I.T.E.L.R. 536, CA (Civ Div) .... *Digested,* 14/**2838**:
Considered 17/2077

Simon (Deceased), Re see Simon v Byford

Simpkin v Berkeley Group Holdings Plc [2017] EWHC 1472 (QB); [2017] 4 W.L.R. 116, QBD

Simpkin v Berkeley Group Holdings Plc [2016] EWHC 1619 (QB); [2017] 1 Costs L.O. 13, QBD .... *Digested,* 17/**772**

Simplex GE (Holdings) Ltd v Secretary of State for the Environment [2017] P.T.S.R. 1041; (1989) 57 P. & C.R. 306; [1988] 3 P.L.R. 25; Times, June 2, 1988; Independent, May 16, 1988; [1988] J.P.L. 809; Daily Telegraph, May 13, 1988; [1988] E.G. 65 (C.S.), CA (Civ Div) .... *Digested,* 89/**3578**:
Applied 01/4728, 02/3726, 05/3307, 06/3024, 06/37, 13/2501, 15/2016, 16/1696: *Considered* 99/4230: *Followed* 10/2755, 16/1748, 17/1754

Simpson v Downie [2012] CSIH 74; 2013 S.L.T. 178; 2013 S.C.L.R. 377; 2012 Fam. L.R. 121; 2012 G.W.D. 33-673, IH (Ex Div) .... *Digested,* 13/**3719**:
Applied 17/2840

Simpson v Hillcrest Housing Association Ltd 2017 Hous. L.R. 2; 2016 G.W.D. 38-682, Lands Tr (Scot) .... *Digested,* 17/**2707**

Sinclair v 231 Sussex Gardens Right to Manage Ltd see Willow Court Management Co (1985) Ltd v Alexander

Sinclair v Glatt [2015] EWHC 1673 (Admin); [2017] 1 B.C.L.C. 100; [2015] Lloyd's Rep. F.C. 481, Ch D .... *Digested,* 15/**649**

Sinclair Collis Ltd v Lord Advocate [2012] CSIH 80; 2013 S.C. 221; 2013 S.L.T. 100; 2013 S.C.L.R. 49; 2012 G.W.D. 34-685, IH (Ex Div) .... *Digested,* 13/**3826**:
Considered 13/3750, 17/2466

Sinclair Gardens Investments (Kensington) Ltd v Farnborough Road (Calloway House) RTM Co Ltd see Elim Court RTM Co Ltd v Avon Freeholds Ltd

Sinclair Gardens Investments (Kensington) Ltd v Wisbey [2016] UKUT 203 (LC); [2016] L. & T.R. 29, UT (Lands) .... *Digested,* 17/**1439**

Sinclair Roche & Temperley v Heard [2004] I.R.L.R. 763, EAT .... *Digested,* 05/**1274**:
Applied 05/1292, 10/1109, 13/1071, 13/3688, 16/697, 17/788, 17/828: *Considered* 08/1218, 13/974, 15/413

Singer v Beckett; *sub nom* Continental Assurance Co of London Plc (In Liquidation), Re [2007] 2 B.C.L.C. 287; [2001] B.P.I.R. 733, Ch D .... *Digested,* 01/**728**:
Applied 13/479, 16/1212, 17/1298, 17/1318: *Considered* 10/3501

Singh v Minister for Justice and Equality (C-218/14) EU:C:2015:476; [2016] Q.B. 208; [2015] 3 W.L.R. 1311; [2016] 1 C.M.L.R. 12; [2016] C.E.C. 325; [2015] Imm. A.R. 1304; [2016] I.N.L.R. 264, ECJ (Grand Chamber)
Considered 17/1246

Singh v Rajah of Faridkote [1894] A.C. 670, PC (Ind)
Applied 57/522, 71/1548: *Considered* 17/432: *Distinguished* 55/1309

Singh v Secretary of State for the Home Department [2017] EWCA Civ 362; [2017] 1 W.L.R. 4340, CA (Civ Div)

Singh v Secretary of State for the Home Department [2016] EWCA Civ 492; [2016] 4 W.L.R. 183; [2016] I.N.L.R. 679, CA (Civ Div) .... *Digested,* 17/**5**

Singh v Singh [2017] I.C.R. D7, EAT

Singh (Daljit) v Secretary of State for the Home Department 2000 S.C. 219; 2000 S.L.T. 243; 2000 G.W.D. 2-63, IH (1 Div) .... *Digested,* 00/**6491**: *Applied* 05/5439: *Considered* 17/2825: *Distinguished* 03/5730

Singha v Heer; *sub nom* Heer v Singha [2016] EWCA Civ 424; [2017] 1 F.L.R. 1192; [2016] W.T.L.R. 1189; 20 I.T.E.L.R. 345; [2016] Fam. Law 813, CA (Civ Div) .... *Digested,* 16/**2155**

Singularis Holdings Ltd v PricewaterhouseCoopers [2014] UKPC 36; [2015] A.C. 1675; [2015] 2 W.L.R. 971; [2015] B.C.C. 66; [2014] 2 B.C.L.C. 597; (2014) 158(44) S.J.L.B. 37, PC (Ber) *Considered* 17/2447

Singularis Holdings Ltd (In Official Liquidation) v Daiwa Capital Markets Europe Ltd [2017] EWHC 257 (Ch); [2017] 2 All E.R. (Comm) 445; [2017] Bus. L.R. 1386; [2017] 1 Lloyd's Rep. 226; [2017] 1 B.C.L.C. 625; [2017] P.N.L.R. 24, Ch D ...... *Digested,* 17/**174**

Singularis Holdings Ltd (In Official Liquidation) v PricewaterhouseCoopers see PricewaterhouseCoopers v SAAD Investments Co Ltd (In Official Liquidation)

Sinocore International Co Ltd v RBRG Trading (UK) Ltd [2017] EWHC 251 (Comm); [2018] 1 All E.R. (Comm) 576; [2017] 1 Lloyd's Rep. 375, QBD (Comm) .... *Digested,* 17/**81**

Sippchoice Ltd v Revenue and Customs Commissioners; *sub nom* Revenue and Customs Commissioners v Sippchoice Ltd [2017] UKUT 87 (TCC); [2017] S.T.C. 1580; [2017] Pens. L.R. 10; [2017] B.T.C. 510, UT (Tax) .... *Digested,* 17/**2167**

Sippchoice Ltd v Revenue and Customs Commissioners; *sub nom* Revenue and Customs Commissioners v Sippchoice Ltd [2016] UKFTT 464 (TC), FTT (Tax) *Affirmed* 17/2167

Sir Cliff Richard v BBC [2017] EWHC 1291 (Ch); [2017] E.M.L.R. 22, Ch D .... *Digested,* 17/**356**

Sisu Capital Fund Ltd v Tucker (Costs); *joined case* Sisu Capital Fund Ltd v Wallace (Costs) [2005] EWHC 2321 (Ch); [2006] 1 All E.R. 167; [2006] B.C.C. 463; [2006] 2 Costs L.R. 262; [2006] B.P.I.R. 154; [2006] F.S.R. 21; Times, November 4, 2005; (2005) 155 N.L.J. 1686, Ch D (Companies Ct) *Applied* 08/526, 10/1844, 17/1298

Sisu Capital Fund Ltd v Wallace (Costs) see Sisu Capital Fund Ltd v Tucker (Costs)

SISVEL/Postponement of oral proceedings (T1750/14) [2017] E.P.O.R. 24, EPO (Technical Bd App)

Six Continents Ltd v Inland Revenue Commissioners; *sub nom* Six Continents Ltd v Revenue and Customs Commissioners [2016] EWHC 2426 (Ch); [2017] S.T.C. 1228; [2016] B.T.C. 43; [2016] S.T.I. 2749, Ch D .... *Digested,* 17/**2114**

Six Continents Ltd v Revenue and Customs Commissioners see Six Continents Ltd v Inland Revenue Commissioners

SJ&J Monk (A Firm) v Newbigin (Valuation Officer); *sub nom* Newbigin (Valuation Officer) v SJ&J Monk (A Firm) [2017] UKSC 14; [2017] 1 W.L.R. 851; [2017] 2 All E.R. 971; [2017] R.A. 95; Times, March 14, 2017, SC .... *Digested,* 17/**1525**

SJ&J Monk (A Firm) v Newbigin (Valuation Officer); *sub nom* Newbigin (Valuation Officer) v SJ&J Monk (A Firm) [2015] EWCA Civ 78; [2015] 1 W.L.R. 4817; [2015] 4 All E.R. 1014; [2015] R.A. 93, CA (Civ Div) .... *Digested,* 15/**2086**: *Considered* 17/1526: *Followed* 16/1469: *Reversed* 17/1525

Sjelle Autogenbrug I/S v Skatteministeriet (C-471/15) EU:C:2017:20; [2017] B.V.C. 7; [2017] S.T.I. 211, ECJ (3rd Chamber)

Sjumarken v Revenue and Customs Commissioners [2015] UKFTT 375 (TC); [2015] S.T.I. 3242, FTT (Tax) *Affirmed* 17/2143

Sjumarken v Revenue and Customs Commissioners [2016] UKUT 568 (TCC); [2017] S.T.C. 239; [2017] B.T.C. 501, UT (Tax) .... *Digested,* 17/**2143**

Skeen v Sullivan 1980 S.L.T. (Notes) 11, HCJ Appeal .... *Digested,* 80/**3018**: *Considered* 17/2540

Skelton v DBS Homes (Kings Hill) Ltd [2015] UKUT 379 (LC), UT (Lands) *Reversed* 17/1468

Skelton v DBS Homes (Kings Hill) Ltd [2017] EWCA Civ 1139; [2018] 1 W.L.R. 362; [2017] H.L.R. 38; [2018] L. & T.R. 10; [2017] 2 P. & C.R. DG25, CA (Civ Div) ... *Digested,* 17/**1468**

Skelwith (Leisure) Ltd v Armstrong [2015] EWHC 2830 (Ch); [2016] Ch. 345; [2016] 2 W.L.R. 144, Ch D .... *Digested,* 16/**1817**: *Applied* 17/1456

Skerritts of Nottingham Ltd v Secretary of State for the Environment, Transport and the Regions (No.1); *sub nom* Secretary of State for the Environment, Transport and the Regions v Skerritts of Nottingham Ltd [2001] Q.B. 59; [2000] 3 W.L.R. 511; (2000) 80 P. & C.R. 516; [2000] 2 P.L.R. 84; Times, March 8, 2000; Independent, May 8, 2000; [2000] J.P.L. 789; [2000] E.G. 31 (C.S.); (2000) 97(10) L.S.G. 38; [2000] N.P.C. 19, CA (Civ Div) .... *Digested,* 00/**4473**: *Applied* 17/1737: *Considered* 02/3694

Sky Plc v Skykick UK Ltd [2017] EWHC 1769 (Ch); [2017] E.T.M.R. 42; [2018] F.S.R. 2, Ch D

Skyscape Cloud Services Ltd v Sky Plc [2016] EWHC 1340 (IPEC); [2016] E.T.M.R. 40; [2017] F.S.R. 6, IPEC .... *Digested,* 16/**1293**
SL v Croatia (Just Satsifaction) (13712/11) (2017) 64 E.H.R.R. SE1, ECHR
SL v Westminster City Council see R. (on the application of SL) v Westminster City Council
SL (Permission to Vaccinate), Re see Barnet LBC v AL
Slater v Buckinghamshire CC; *joined case* Slater v Stigwood (t/a as Stigwoods) [2004] EWHC 77 (QB); [2004] Lloyd's Rep. I.R. 432, QBD .... *Digested,* 04/**2709**: *Considered* 17/1877
Slater v Stigwood (t/a as Stigwoods) see Slater v Buckinghamshire CC
Slattery v Jagger [2015] EWHC 3976 (Ch); [2017] W.T.L.R. 321, Ch D (Manchester)
Slezak v Secretary of State for Work and Pensions [2017] CSIH 4; 2017 S.C. 262; 2017 S.L.T. 221; 2017 G.W.D. 4-60, IH (Ex Div) .... *Digested,* 17/**2826**
Sloan, Petitioner 1991 S.C. 281; 1991 S.L.T. 527, IH (1 Div) .... *Digested,* 91/**4458**: *Applied* 17/2601
Slough BC v Secretary of State for the Environment see R. v Secretary of State for the Environment Ex p. Slough BC
Slovakia v Cambal see Poland v Celinski
Slovenska Posta AS v European Commission (C-293/15 P) EU:C:2016:511; [2017] 4 C.M.L.R. 6, ECJ (8th Chamber)
SM v CM [2017] CSIH 1; 2017 S.C. 235; 2017 S.L.T. 197; 2017 S.C.L.R. 739; 2017 Fam. L.R. 2; 2017 G.W.D. 3-26, IH (Ex Div) .... *Digested,* 17/**2438**: *Considered* 17/2418
SM v HM see HM (A Child), Re
SM v Secretary of State for the Home Department; *sub nom* Majumder v Secretary of State for the Home Department [2016] EWCA Civ 1167; [2017] 3 All E.R. 756; [2017] Imm. A.R. 582, CA (Civ Div) .... *Digested,* 17/**1228**
SM v Secretary of State for the Home Department; *sub nom* Majumder v Secretary of State for the Home Department [2016] UKUT 229 (IAC), UT (IAC) *Approved* 17/1243: *Reversed* 17/1228
SM v Secretary of State for Work and Pensions [2016] UKUT 245 (AAC); [2016] 3 F.C.R. 566, UT (AAC) .... *Digested,* 17/**954**
SM (Pakistan) v Secretary of State for the Home Department see SM (Withdrawal of Appealed Decision: Effect: Pakistan)
SM (Withdrawal of Appealed Decision: Effect: Pakistan); *sub nom* SM (Pakistan) v Secretary of State for the Home Department [2014] UKUT 64 (IAC); [2014] Imm. A.R. 662; [2014] I.N.L.R. 681, UT (IAC) .... *Digested,* 15/**1386**: *Considered* 17/2280
Small v Shrewsbury and Telford Hospitals NHS Trust UKEAT/0300/14/LA, EAT *Reversed* 17/848
Small v Shrewsbury and Telford Hospitals NHS Trust [2017] EWCA Civ 882; [2017] I.R.L.R. 889, CA (Civ Div) .... *Digested,* 17/**848**
Smallwood v Revenue and Customs Commissioners; *sub nom* Trevor Smallwood Trust, Re; Revenue and Customs Commissioners v Smallwood [2010] EWCA Civ 778; [2010] S.T.C. 2045; 80 T.C. 536; [2010] B.T.C. 637; 12 I.T.L. Rep. 1002; [2010] W.T.L.R. 1771; [2010] S.T.I. 2174; (2010) 154(27) S.J.L.B. 30, CA (Civ Div) .... *Digested,* 10/**3236**: *Considered* 17/2089: *Followed* 17/2130
Smart Card Chips, Re (COMP/AT.39574) [2017] 4 C.M.L.R. 16, CEC
SMAY Investments Ltd v Sachdev [2003] EWHC 474 (Ch); [2003] 1 W.L.R. 1973; Times, April 1, 2003; (2003) 100(19) L.S.G. 30, Ch D .... *Digested,* 03/**599**: *Applied* 17/297
SME (Hammersmith) Ltd v Transport for London [2017] UKUT 91 (LC); [2017] R.V.R. 249, UT (Lands) .... *Digested,* 17/**1699**
Smith v All Other Persons Claiming to be Interested in the Ross Revenge [2017] EWHC 787 (Admlty); [2017] 2 Lloyd's Rep. 288, QBD (Admlty) .... *Digested,* 17/**2019**
Smith v Bar Standards Board [2016] EWHC 3015 (Admin); [2017] A.C.D. 6, QBD (Admin)
Smith v Donnelly 2002 J.C. 65; 2001 S.L.T. 1007; 2001 S.C.C.R. 800; 2001 G.W.D. 26-1011, HCJ Appeal .... *Digested,* 01/**6702**: *Applied* 03/5359, 11/4102, 11/4104, 17/2509: *Cited* 09/4756, 11/4105: *Considered* 04/4632, 05/5098, 06/5164, 08/4637, 10/4061, 10/4062, 15/2968, 15/2991: *Followed* 09/4758
Smith v Gibson see Smith (Richard) v Procurator Fiscal, Hamilton
Smith v Kent CC [2004] EWHC 412 (QB), QBD *Considered* 17/808
Smith v Lancashire Teaching Hospitals NHS Trust [2016] EWHC 2208 (QB); [2017] P.I.Q.R. P4, QBD .... *Digested,* 17/**1645**

Smith v Lawson see Kiss Cards Ltd, Re
Smith v McCarthy [2017] P.N.L.R. 28, CA (Irl)
Smith v Molyneaux [2016] UKPC 35; [2017] 1 P. & C.R. 7, PC (BVI) .... *Digested,* 17/**1824**
Smith v North East Derbyshire Primary Care Trust see Smith v North Eastern Derbyshire Primary Care Trust
Smith v North Eastern Derbyshire Primary Care Trust; *sub nom* Smith v North East Derbyshire Primary Care Trust; R. (on the application of Smith) v North Eastern Derbyshire Primary Care Trust [2006] EWCA Civ 1291; [2006] 1 W.L.R. 3315; (2006) 9 C.C.L. Rep. 663; [2007] LS Law Medical 188; Times, September 11, 2006; (2006) 150 S.J.L.B. 1152, CA (Civ Div) .... *Digested,* 06/**37**:
Applied 08/262, 10/2768, 15/2016: *Considered* 13/2393: *Followed* 10/2590, 17/1464
Smith v Parole Board for England and Wales see R. (on the application of Smith) v Parole Board for England and Wales
Smith v Revenue and Customs Commissioners [2016] UKFTT 783 (TC); [2017] S.T.I. 113, FTT (Tax)
Smith v Stuart [2010] CSIH 29; 2010 S.C. 490; 2010 S.L.T. 1249; 2010 G.W.D. 14-270, IH (2 Div) .... *Digested,* 11/**4546**:
Followed 17/2771
Smith v Taylor see Broadhurst v Tan
Smith v Trafford Housing Trust (Costs) [2012] EWHC 3320 (Ch); (2012) 156(46) S.J.L.B. 31, Ch D
Applied 15/259, 16/225, 17/256
Smith v United Kingdom (Admissibility) (54357/15) [2017] I.R.L.R. 771, ECHR
Smith (Richard) v Procurator Fiscal, Hamilton; *sub nom* Smith v Gibson [2017] SAC (Crim) 10; 2017 S.C.C.R. 373; 2017 G.W.D. 23-401, SAC .... *Digested,* 17/**2815**
Smith (Thomas Bennie) v HM Advocate [2010] HCJAC 118; 2011 S.L.T. 212; 2011 S.C.L. 261; 2011 S.C.C.R. 134; 2010 G.W.D. 38-782, HCJ .... *Digested,* 11/**4586**:
Considered 12/4266, 12/4267, 13/3985, 17/2807
Smith and Nephew Overseas Ltd v Revenue and Customs Commissioners [2017] UKFTT 151 (TC); [2017] S.F.T.D. 678; [2017] S.T.I. 942, FTT (Tax) .... *Digested,* 17/**2108**
Smith New Court Securities Ltd v Citibank NA; *sub nom* Smith New Court Securities Ltd v Scrimgeour Vickers (Asset Management) Ltd [1997] A.C. 254; [1996] 3 W.L.R. 1051; [1996] 4 All E.R. 769; [1997] 1 B.C.L.C. 350; [1996] C.L.C. 1958; Times, November 22, 1996; Independent, November 27, 1996; (1996) 93(46) L.S.G. 28; (1996) 146 N.L.J. 1722; (1997) 141 S.J.L.B. 5, HL .... *Digested,* 96/**996**:
Applied 00/1452, 01/965, 03/535, 04/920, 07/2918, 08/893, 10/828, 11/537: *Considered* 11/857, 14/3215: *Followed* 97/3370, 09/407, 17/636
Smith New Court Securities Ltd v Scrimgeour Vickers (Asset Management) Ltd see Smith New Court Securities Ltd v Citibank NA
SmithKline Beecham Plc's Paroxetine Methanesulfonate Patent (No.2) see Synthon BV v SmithKline Beecham Plc (No.2)
Smithton Ltd (formerly Hobart Capital Markets Ltd) v Naggar [2014] EWCA Civ 939; [2015] 1 W.L.R. 189; [2014] B.C.C. 482; [2015] 2 B.C.L.C. 22; Times, August 19, 2014; (2014) 158(29) S.J.L.B. 37, CA (Civ Div) .... *Digested,* 14/**505**:
Followed 17/1299
SMS Cosmos AS, Re see ITouch Ltd, Re
SMS Group GmbH v Directia Generala Regionala a Finantelor Publice Bucuresti (C-441/16) EU:C:2017:712; [2017] B.V.C. 40, ECJ (10th Chamber)
Smyth v Secretary of State for Communities and Local Government [2015] EWCA Civ 174; [2015] P.T.S.R. 1417; [2016] Env. L.R. 7, CA (Civ Div) .... *Digested,* 16/**1759**:
Applied 16/1750, 17/1775: *Followed* 16/1747
Snamprogetti Ltd v Phillips Petroleum Co (UK) Ltd see Phillips Petroleum Co (UK) Ltd v Snamprogetti Ltd
Snook v London and West Riding Investments Ltd [1967] 2 Q.B. 786; [1967] 2 W.L.R. 1020; [1967] 1 All E.R. 518; (1967) 111 S.J. 71, CA (Civ Div) .... *Digested,* 67/**1836**:
Applied 99/4764, 00/3879, 01/5319, 04/3954, 07/3396, 09/1199, 09/2205, 12/2049, 16/1182, 17/2071: *Considered* 84/1915, 88/2043, 89/2112, 89/2145, 09/1194, 11/1074, 14/2494, 17/2180: *Followed* 99/2485, 02/5841, 05/4313, 13/2420, 13/478
Snowball Assets Ltd v Huntsmore House (Freehold) Ltd [2015] UKUT 338 (LC), UT (Lands)
Applied 17/1830
SO (A Child) (Wardship: Extension of Protective Injunction Orders), Re; *sub nom* O v P [2015] EWHC 935 (Fam); [2016] Fam. 333; [2016] 3 W.L.R. 716; [2016] 1 All E.R. 1021; [2016] 1 F.L.R. 1144; [2016] 1 F.C.R. 447; [2015] Fam. Law 891, Fam Div .... *Digested,* 16/**948**:
Considered 17/1070

Societe Civile des Producteurs de Phonogrammes (SCPP) v Production 31 Distribution (Societe) [2017] E.C.C. 10; [2017] E.C.D.R. 21, Cass (F)
Societe Comateb v Directeur General des Douanes et Droits Indirects (C192/95) EU:C:1997:12; [1997] S.T.C. 1006; [1997] E.C.R. I-165; [1997] 2 C.M.L.R. 649, ECJ .... *Digested,* 97/**1730**: *Applied* 17/2289
Societe des Produits Nestle SA v Cadbury UK Ltd [2017] EWCA Civ 358; [2018] 2 All E.R. 39; [2017] Bus. L.R. 1832; [2017] E.C.C. 28; [2017] E.T.M.R. 31; [2017] F.S.R. 34, CA (Civ Div) .... *Digested,* 17/**1389**
Societe des Produits Nestle SA v Cadbury UK Ltd; *sub nom* Cadbury UK Ltd v Societe des Produits Nestle SA [2013] EWCA Civ 1174; [2014] 1 All E.R. 1079; [2014] Bus. L.R. 134; [2014] E.T.M.R. 3; [2014] R.P.C. 7, CA (Civ Div) .... *Digested,* 14/**1933**: *Considered* 14/1934, 17/1387
Societe des Produits Nestle SA v Cadbury UK Ltd [2016] EWHC 50 (Ch); [2016] 4 All E.R. 1081; [2016] Bus. L.R. 354; [2016] E.T.M.R. 21; [2016] F.S.R. 19, Ch D .... *Digested,* 16/**1332**: *Affirmed* 17/1389: *Applied* 16/1289
Societe des Produits Nestle SA v Mars UK Ltd (C-353/03) EU:C:2005:432; [2005] E.C.R. I-6135; [2005] 3 C.M.L.R. 12; [2006] All E.R. (EC) 348; [2006] C.E.C. 3; [2005] E.T.M.R. 96; [2006] F.S.R. 2; Times, July 20, 2005; (2005) 28(10) I.P.D. 28071, ECJ (2nd Chamber) .... *Digested,* 06/**2587**: *Applied* 09/2424: *Followed* 14/1937, 17/1389
Societe Generale (London Branch) v Geys see Geys v Societe Generale
Societe Generale SA v Saad Trading, Contracting and Financial Services Co [2012] EWCA Civ 695, CA (Civ Div) *Disapproved* 17/203: *Followed* 16/291
Societe pour la Recherche, la Production, le Transport, la Transformation et la Commercialisation des Hydrocarbures SpA v Statoil Natural Gas LLC see Sonatrach v Statoil
Societe Soc(1) v X [2017] E.C.C. 22, Cass (L)
Socrates Training Ltd v Law Society of England and Wales [2016] CAT 19; [2017] Comp. A.R. 45, CAT
Socrates Training Ltd v Law Society of England and Wales [2017] CAT 10; [2017] Comp. A.R. 303; [2017] 5 C.M.L.R. 6, CAT .... *Digested,* 17/**410**
Soering v United Kingdom (A/161) (1989) 11 E.H.R.R. 439; Times, July 8, 1989; Independent, July 11, 1989; Guardian, July 13, 1989; Daily Telegraph, October 2, 1989, ECHR .... *Digested,* 89/**1712**: *Applied* 97/2764, 02/2577, 05/2167, 09/1473, 14/1652: *Considered* 03/2162, 03/2256, 04/2009, 04/839, 05/2058, 05/2076, 08/1940, 09/2033, 10/1265, 10/1266, 10/1736, 12/128, 13/1184, 13/1593, 14/564, 16/41: *Explained* 06/2244, 17/83: *Followed* 02/2514
Sofia v San Marino (Admissibility) (38977/15) (2017) 65 E.H.R.R. SE7, ECHR
Software 2000 Ltd v Andrews [2007] I.C.R. 825; [2007] I.R.L.R. 568, EAT .... *Digested,* 07/**1426**: *Applied* 07/1427, 17/774
Software Box Ltd v Gannon [2016] I.C.R. 148, EAT .... *Digested,* 16/**734**: *Applied* 17/2582
Software Incubator Ltd v Computer Associates Ltd [2016] EWHC 1587 (QB); [2017] Bus. L.R. 245; [2016] 2 C.L.C. 77, QBD (Merc) (London) .... *Digested,* 17/**45**
Sokoya v Revenue and Customs Commissioners [2009] UKFTT 163 (TC); [2009] S.F.T.D. 480; [2009] S.T.I. 2514, FTT (Tax) .... *Digested,* 09/**3878**: *Considered* 17/2111
Solar Century Holdings Ltd v Secretary of State for Energy and Climate Change [2014] EWHC 3677 (Admin); [2015] A.C.D. 24, QBD (Admin) *Affirmed* 16/39: *Applied* 17/1534
Solicitors Regulation Authority v Chan [2015] EWHC 2659 (Admin), DC *Applied* 17/1490
Solicitors Regulation Authority v Clyde & Co LLP [2017] Lloyd's Rep. F.C. 418, Solicitors Disc Tr .... *Digested,* 17/**1489**
Solicitors Regulation Authority v Kadurugamuwa [2017] EWHC 2245 (Admin); [2017] A.C.D. 119, DC
Solicitors Regulation Authority v Libby [2017] EWHC 973 (Admin); [2017] A.C.D. 81, DC
Solicitors Regulation Authority v Solicitors Disciplinary Tribunal [2016] EWHC 2862 (Admin); [2017] A.C.D. 17, DC
Solicitors Regulation Authority v Wingate [2016] EWHC 3455 (Admin); [2017] A.C.D. 31, QBD (Admin)
Solihull MBC v Finn see White v Ealing LBC
Solihull MBC v Gallagher Homes Ltd see Gallagher Homes Ltd v Solihull MBC
Solihull MBC v Special Educational Needs Tribunal see White v Ealing LBC

Solomons v Cheal see Care Matters Partnership Ltd (In Administration), Re
Soltan v Poland see Krolik v Poland
Somerset v Earl Poulett see Somerset, Re
Somerset CC v Barber see Barber v Somerset CC
Somerset, Re; *sub nom* Somerset v Earl Poulett [1894] 1 Ch. 231, CA
Considered 61/8142, 17/2219

Somji v Cadbury Schweppes Plc see Cadbury Schweppes Plc v Somji
Sonatrach v Statoil; *sub nom* Societe pour la Recherche, la Production, le Transport, la Transformation et la Commercialisation des Hydrocarbures SpA v Statoil Natural Gas LLC [2014] EWHC 875 (Comm); [2014] 2 All E.R. (Comm) 857; [2014] 2 Lloyd's Rep. 252; [2014] 1 C.L.C. 473, QBD (Comm) .... *Digested,* 14/**128**: *Applied* 17/67

Soni v General Medical Council [2015] EWHC 364 (Admin); (2015) 143 B.M.L.R. 113, QBD (Admin) .... *Digested,* 15/**1188**: *Considered* 17/1113

Sony Communications International AB v SSH Communications Security Corp; *sub nom* SSH Communications Security Corp v Sony Mobile Communications AB [2016] EWHC 2985 (Pat); [2016] 4 W.L.R. 186; [2016] 6 Costs L.R. 1141, Ch D (Patents Ct) .... *Digested,* 17/**279**

Sony Music Entertainment Ireland Ltd v UPC Communications Ireland Ltd [2017] E.C.D.R. 8, CA (Irl)

Sony/ATV Music Publishing LLC v WPMC Ltd [2017] EWHC 389 (Ch); [2017] 2 Costs L.O. 207, Ch D .... *Digested,* 17/**250**

Sorbie v Dunlevey (Valuation Officer) [2016] UKUT 167 (LC); [2016] R.A. 313, UT (Lands) .... *Digested,* 17/**1521**

Sorpa bs v Icelandic Competition Authority (E-29/15) [2016] 5 C.M.L.R. 23; [2017] 4 C.M.L.R. 21, EFTA

Sorrell v Sorrell [2005] EWHC 1717 (Fam); [2006] 1 F.L.R. 497; [2006] 1 F.C.R. 75; [2006] Fam. Law 12, Fam Div .... *Digested,* 06/**1621**: *Considered* 17/1032

Soulier v Premier ministre (C-301/15) EU:C:2016:878; [2017] 2 C.M.L.R. 9; [2017] C.E.C. 890; [2017] E.C.D.R. 23, ECJ (3rd Chamber)

South Australia Asset Management Corp v York Montague Ltd; *joined cases* Nykredit Mortgage Bank Plc v Edward Erdman Group Ltd; United Bank of Kuwait Plc v Prudential Property Services Ltd [1997] A.C. 191; [1996] 3 W.L.R. 87; [1996] 3 All E.R. 365; [1996] 5 Bank. L.R. 211; [1996] C.L.C. 1179; 80 B.L.R. 1; 50 Con. L.R. 153; [1996] P.N.L.R. 455; [1996] 2 E.G.L.R. 93; [1996] 27 E.G. 125; Times, June 24, 1996; Independent, July 2, 1996; [1996] E.G. 107 (C.S.); (1996) 93(32) L.S.G. 33; (1996) 146 N.L.J. 956; (1996) 140 S.J.L.B. 156; [1996] N.P.C. 100, HL .... *Digested,* 96/**4519**: *Applied* 97/3846, 98/4005, 98/4027, 98/4031, 98/4384, 99/1389, 99/4053, 00/1486, 00/4249, 00/4280, 01/4504, 01/4532, 03/2994, 03/3014, 06/2897, 06/2901, 07/2480, 09/2725, 10/827, 13/487, 16/2136, 16/570, 17/1568: *Considered* 97/3827, 97/3839, 98/3999, 98/4032, 98/5724, 00/4009, 00/4247, 00/4275, 00/4279, 01/2511, 01/4263, 06/2451, 10/626, 11/536, 12/263, 15/683, 17/1357: *Distinguished* 02/3292, 16/1537: *Explained* 08/160, 17/641: *Followed* 98/3959, 98/3987, 99/4018, 99/4057, 99/804, 01/4529, 11/2259, 11/3472, 12/2305, 14/2195, 14/2217, 15/1779, 15/1792, 16/1551, 17/1571: *Referred to* 97/4871

South Buckinghamshire DC v Porter (No.2); *sub nom* South Buckinghamshire DC v Secretary of State for Transport, Local Government and the Regions [2004] UKHL 33; [2004] 1 W.L.R. 1953; [2004] 4 All E.R. 775; [2005] 1 P. & C.R. 6; [2004] 4 P.L.R. 50; Times, July 2, 2004; Independent, July 6, 2004; [2004] 28 E.G. 177 (C.S.); (2004) 101(31) L.S.G. 25; (2004) 148 S.J.L.B. 825; [2004] N.P.C. 108, HL .... *Digested,* 04/**3087**: *Applied* 05/3296, 07/1157, 07/3277, 08/2930, 08/4956, 09/3059, 10/3180, 12/1459, 13/112, 13/2351, 14/70, 15/1987, 15/2164, 16/1078, 16/1678, 16/1703, 16/1737, 17/1765, 17/414: *Considered* 09/4974, 12/51, 16/1757, 17/1727, 17/1785, 17/2635: *Followed* 05/3304, 11/2508, 11/2511, 13/2348, 14/2066, 14/2439, 15/1967, 16/1756, 17/1769

South Buckinghamshire DC v Secretary of State for Transport, Local Government and the Regions see South Buckinghamshire DC v Porter (No.2)
South Coast Construction Ltd v Iverson Road Ltd [2017] EWHC 61 (TCC); [2017] 1 All E.R. (Comm) 653; [2017] B.L.R. 169, QBD (TCC) .... *Digested,* 17/**453**
South Cone Inc v Bessant (t/a REEF) see REEF Trade Mark
South Eastern Power Networks Plc v Revenue and Customs Commissioners see Eastern Power Networks Plc v Revenue and Customs Commissioners

South Lakeland DC v Carlisle Diocesan Parsonages Board see South Lakeland DC v Secretary of State for the Environment

South Lakeland DC v Secretary of State for the Environment; *joined case* South Lakeland DC v Carlisle Diocesan Parsonages Board [1992] 2 A.C. 141; [1992] 2 W.L.R. 204; [1992] 1 All E.R. 573; 90 L.G.R. 201; (1992) 64 P. & C.R. 128; [1992] 1 P.L.R. 143; Times, February 3, 1992; Independent, February 13, 1992; (1992) 156 L.G. Rev. 602; Guardian, February 5, 1992; (1992) 142 N.L.J. 159; (1992) 136 S.J.L.B. 61; [1992] N.P.C. 16, HL .... *Digested,* 92/**4186**: *Applied* 03/3434, 07/3266, 16/1669: *Considered* 10/4470: *Followed* 93/3925, 12/2587, 14/2388, 15/2018, 17/1751, 17/1758

South Manchester Abbeyfield Society Ltd v Hopkins [2011] I.C.R. 254; [2011] I.R.L.R. 300, EAT .... *Digested,* 11/**1100**: *Applied* 17/812: *Considered* 12/1112, 14/1091, 16/696: *Doubted* 14/1092

South Somerset DC v Secretary of State for the Environment [2017] P.T.S.R. 1075; (1993) 66 P. & C.R. 83; [1993] 1 P.L.R. 80; [1993] 26 E.G. 121; [1992] E.G. 134 (C.S.), CA (Civ Div) .... *Digested,* 93/**3927**: *Applied* 16/1684, 16/1703: *Cited* 00/4439: *Considered* 96/4734

Southall v General Medical Council [2010] EWCA Civ 407; [2010] 2 F.L.R. 1550; [2010] 2 F.C.R. 77; [2010] Med. L.R. 235; (2010) 113 B.M.L.R. 178; [2010] Fam. Law 699; (2010) 154(16) S.J.L.B. 28, CA (Civ Div) .... *Digested,* 10/**1547**: *Applied* 13/1442: *Considered* 15/1249: *Followed* 17/1113

Southend BC v CO see Southend BC v O

Southend BC v O; *sub nom* Southend BC v CO [2017] EWHC 1949 (Fam); [2017] 4 W.L.R. 185; [2018] 1 F.L.R. 837, Fam Div

Southern Cross Healthcare Co Ltd v Perkins [2010] EWCA Civ 1442; [2011] I.C.R. 285; [2011] I.R.L.R. 247; Times, February 28, 2011, CA (Civ Div) .... *Digested,* 11/**1081**: *Followed* 11/1077, 17/854

Southern Pacific Mortgages Ltd v Scott see North East Property Buyers Litigation, Re

Southern Rock Insurance Co Ltd v Hafeez [2017] CSOH 127; 2017 S.L.T. 1159; [2018] Lloyd's Rep. I.R. 207; 2017 G.W.D. 32-516, OH .... *Digested,* 17/**2687**

Southwark LBC v Akhtar [2017] UKUT 150 (LC); [2017] L. & T.R. 36, UT (Lands) .... *Digested,* 17/**1469**

Southwark LBC v Dennett [2007] EWCA Civ 1091; [2008] H.L.R. 23; [2008] B.L.G.R. 94; [2008] R.V.R. 115; [2007] N.P.C. 115, CA (Civ Div) .... *Digested,* 08/**1874**: *Applied* 17/325

Southwark LBC v Mills; *sub nom* Southwark LBC v Tanner; *joined case* Baxter v Camden LBC (No.2) [2001] 1 A.C. 1; [1999] 3 W.L.R. 939; [1999] 4 All E.R. 449; [2000] Env. L.R. 112; (2000) 32 H.L.R. 148; [2000] B.L.G.R. 138; [2000] L. & T.R. 159; [1999] 3 E.G.L.R. 35; [1999] 45 E.G. 179; Times, October 22, 1999; [1999] E.G. 122 (C.S.); (1999) 96(42) L.S.G. 41; (1999) 96(42) L.S.G. 45; (1999) 149 N.L.J. 1618; (1999) 143 S.J.L.B. 249; [1999] N.P.C. 123; (2000) 79 P. & C.R. D13, HL .... *Digested,* 99/**3672**: *Applied* 08/2461, 11/2070: *Considered* 06/2918, 11/3220: *Followed* 02/3058, 14/2221, 14/2508, 17/1446

Southwark LBC v Tanner see Southwark LBC v Mills

Southwark LBC v Woelke [2013] UKUT 349 (LC); [2014] L. & T.R. 9, UT (Lands) .... *Digested,* 14/**2007**: *Considered* 17/1469

SOVAG - Schwarzmeer und Ostsee Versicherungs-Aktiengesellschaft v If Vahinkovakuutusyhtio Oy (C-521/14) EU:C:2016:41; [2016] Q.B. 780; [2016] 3 W.L.R. 136; [2016] R.T.R. 11; [2016] C.E.C. 1365; [2016] I.L.Pr. 12, ECJ (4th Chamber) *Followed* 17/338

Sovereign Trustees Ltd v Lewis [2016] EWHC 2593 (Ch); [2016] Pens. L.R. 345, Ch D .... *Digested,* 17/**1627**

Spar Shipping AS v Grand China Logistics Holding (Group) Co Ltd; *sub nom* Grand China Logistics Holding (Group) Co Ltd v Spar Shipping AS [2016] EWCA Civ 982; [2017] 4 All E.R. 124; [2017] 2 All E.R. (Comm) 701; [2017] Bus. L.R. 663; [2016] 2 Lloyd's Rep. 447; [2016] 2 C.L.C. 441, CA (Civ Div) .... *Digested,* 17/**2023**

Spar Shipping AS v Grand China Logistics Holding (Group) Co Ltd; *sub nom* Grand China Logistics Holding (Group) Co Ltd v Spar Shipping AS [2015] EWHC 718 (Comm); [2015] 1 All E.R. (Comm) 879; [2015] 2 Lloyd's Rep. 407; [2015] 1 C.L.C. 356, QBD (Comm) .... *Digested,* 15/**2334**: *Affirmed* 17/2023

Sparekassernes Datacenter (SDC) v Skatteministeriet (C-2/95) EU:C:1997:278; [1997] S.T.C. 932; [1997] E.C.R. I-3017; [1997] 3 C.M.L.R. 999; [1997] All E.R. (EC) 610; [1997] B.T.C. 5395; [1997] B.V.C. 509, ECJ (5th Chamber) .... *Digested,* 97/**4987**: *Applied* 98/4900, 02/4755, 03/4538, 06/4435, 08/3993, 08/4041, 09/4105, 11/3526, 14/3046: *Considered* 00/5294, 07/5568: *Followed* 98/4921, 12/3387, 17/2295

Sparkasse Hilden Ratingen Velbert v Benk [2012] EWHC 2432 (Ch); [2012] B.P.I.R. 1258, Ch D (Birmingham) .... *Digested,* 13/**1688**: *Applied* 14/1786, 15/1412, 17/2325

Spartafield Ltd v Penten Group Ltd [2017] EWHC 1121 (TCC); [2017] 3 Costs L.R. 467, QBD (TCC) .... *Digested,* 17/**267**

Spartafield Ltd v Penten Group Ltd [2016] EWHC 2295 (TCC); 168 Con. L.R. 221, QBD (TCC) .... *Digested,* 17/**473**

Spartan Capital Ltd, Re see Glenn v Watson

Special Opportunity Holdings Ltd, Re see Level One Residential (Jersey) Ltd, Re

Specsavers International Healthcare Ltd v Asda Stores Ltd [2012] EWCA Civ 24; [2012] E.T.M.R. 17; [2012] F.S.R. 19, CA (Civ Div) .... *Digested,* 12/**1915**: *Applied* 13/1761, 14/1930, 15/1539: *Considered* 14/1926, 15/1534: *Followed* 14/1915, 14/1917, 14/1928, 16/1289, 16/1333, 17/1390: *Preliminary ruling given* 14/1912

Spectrum Plus Ltd (In Liquidation), Re; *sub nom* National Westminster Bank Plc v Spectrum Plus Ltd (In Creditors Voluntary Liquidation) [2005] UKHL 41; [2005] 2 A.C. 680; [2005] 3 W.L.R. 58; [2005] 4 All E.R. 209; [2005] 2 Lloyd's Rep. 275; [2005] B.C.C. 694; [2005] 2 B.C.L.C. 269; Times, July 1, 2005; Independent, July 6, 2005; (2005) 155 N.L.J. 1045, HL .... *Digested,* 05/**2320**: *Applied* 06/2325, 08/231: *Considered* 10/1839: *Followed* 17/159

Speight v Diamond Insurance (Unreported, October 18, 2016), CC (Huddersfield) [*IME Law Ltd, Riverside East, 2 Millsands, Sheffield*] .... *Digested,* 17/**1685**

Spencer v Anderson (Paternity Testing: Jurisdiction) see Spencer v Spencer

Spencer v Spencer; *sub nom* Spencer v Anderson (Paternity Testing: Jurisdiction) [2016] EWHC 851 (Fam); [2016] Fam. 391; [2016] 3 W.L.R. 905; [2017] 2 All E.R. 846; [2017] 1 F.L.R. 1204; (2016) 151 B.M.L.R. 92; [2016] Fam. Law 808, Fam Div .... *Digested,* 16/**930**

Spickenreuther's Petition, Re see St Augustine's Churchyard, Droitwich Spa, Re

Spiliada Maritime Corp v Cansulex Ltd (The Spiliada) [1987] A.C. 460; [1986] 3 W.L.R. 972; [1986] 3 All E.R. 843; [1987] 1 Lloyd's Rep. 1; [1987] E.C.C. 168; [1987] 1 F.T.L.R. 103; Financial Times, November 25, 1986; (1987) 84 L.S.G. 113; (1986) 136 N.L.J. 1137; (1986) 130 S.J. 925, HL .... *Digested,* 87/**3135**: *Applied* 89/1722, 89/3095, 90/3768, 91/475, 91/476, 92/475, 93/3571, 93/5876, 94/4040, 94/483, 95/696, 96/846, 97/908, 98/4398, 99/2405, 99/717, 99/719, 99/750, 00/775, 01/815, 03/599, 04/1493, 05/622, 06/634, 07/683, 09/448, 09/449, 09/603, 11/1088, 11/3256, 12/474, 14/2186, 17/940: *Considered* 87/3095, 87/399, 89/2725, 89/3042, 90/3709, 94/3256, 95/3484, 96/1089, 96/1091, 98/764, 02/2756, 02/477, 05/611, 06/24, 09/1497, 10/503, 13/472, 15/434, 17/371, 17/920: *Distinguished* 87/3024, 03/2215, 08/2271: *Explained* 00/769: *Followed* 91/5142, 95/6052, 95/690, 97/2453, 98/748, 98/749, 05/978, 11/325, 11/469, 11/470, 13/1777, 14/477, 14/567, 17/317, 17/982

Spin Master Ltd v PMS International Group [2017] EWHC 1477 (Pat); [2017] Bus. L.R. 1627; [2017] F.S.R. 44, Ch D (Patents Ct) .... *Digested,* 17/**1383**

Spiral Packs (London) Ltd v Revenue and Customs Commissioners [2017] UKFTT 661 (TC); [2017] S.T.I. 1987, FTT (Tax)

Spire Healthcare Ltd v Brooke; *sub nom* Jellett v Brooke [2016] EWHC 2828 (QB); [2017] 1 W.L.R. 1177; [2017] P.I.Q.R. P6, QBD .... *Digested,* 17/**322**

Spire Healthcare Ltd v Royal & Sun Alliance Insurance Plc [2016] EWHC 3278 (Comm); [2016] 2 C.L.C. 1002; [2017] Lloyd's Rep. I.R. 118, QBD (Comm) .... *Digested,* 17/**1345**

Spiro v Glencrown Properties Ltd [1991] Ch. 537; [1991] 2 W.L.R. 931; [1991] 1 All E.R. 600; (1991) 62 P. & C.R. 402; [1991] 02 E.G. 167; Times, December 13, 1990; Independent, December 5, 1990; Financial Times, December 14, 1990; Daily Telegraph, December 17, 1990; [1990] E.G. 148 (C.S.); (1991) 141 N.L.J. 124; (1990) 134 S.J. 1479, Ch D .... *Digested,* 91/**557**: *Applied* 93/2442, 15/2486: *Considered* 93/2491, 93/551, 94/3513, 13/2451, 17/2221

Sportech Plc v Revenue and Customs Commissioners see Revenue and Customs Commissioners v IFX Investment Co Ltd

Sports Management Group Ltd (In Liquidation), Re; *sub nom* Green v Marston [2016] B.P.I.R. 1224, Ch D (Companies Ct) .... *Digested,* 17/**1299**

Spring Capital Ltd v Revenue and Customs Commissioners [2016] UKUT 264 (TCC); [2016] B.T.C. 509, UT (Tax) .... *Digested,* 17/**2115**

Spring Capital Ltd v Revenue and Customs Commissioners [2015] UKFTT 66 (TC); [2015] S.T.I. 1403, FTT (Tax)
Affirmed 17/2115
Spring Capital Ltd v Revenue and Customs Commissioners [2016] UKFTT 232 (TC), FTT (Tax)
Affirmed 17/2171
Spring Capital Ltd v Revenue and Customs Commissioners [2017] UKUT 215 (TCC); [2017] B.T.C. 519, UT (Tax) .... *Digested,* 17/**2171**
Spring Salmon & Seafood Ltd, Re see Advocate General for Scotland, Petitioner
Spring Salmon and Seafood Ltd v Revenue and Customs Commissioners [2017] UKUT 205 (TCC); [2017] B.T.C. 522, UT (Tax)
Springwell Navigation Corp v JP Morgan Chase Bank (formerly Chase Manhattan Bank) [2010] EWCA Civ 1221; [2010] 2 C.L.C. 705, CA (Civ Div) .... *Digested,* 11/**193**:
Applied 11/212, 13/2553: *Considered* 13/595: *Distinguished* 14/1034:
Followed 11/186, 17/1446
Squibb Group Ltd v Pole 2 Pole Scaffolding Ltd; *joined case* Pole 2 Pole Scaffolding Ltd v Sqibb Group Ltd [2017] EWHC 2394 (TCC); [2017] B.L.R. 613, QBD (TCC)
Squier v General Medical Council [2016] EWHC 2739 (Admin); (2017) 155 B.M.L.R. 211; [2016] A.C.D. 139, QBD (Admin) .... *Digested,* 17/**1098**
Squires v HM Advocate 1996 S.C.C.R. 916, HCJ Appeal .... *Digested,* 97/**5803**:
Distinguished 17/2520
Squirrell Ltd v National Westminster Bank Plc [2005] EWHC 664 (Ch); [2006] 1 W.L.R. 637; [2005] 2 All E.R. 784; [2005] 1 All E.R. (Comm) 749; [2005] 2 Lloyd's Rep. 374; Times, May 25, 2005, Ch D .... *Digested,* 05/**459**:
Considered 17/173
Srivatsa v Secretary of State for Health [2016] EWHC 2916 (QB); [2017] I.C.R. D5, QBD
SRN Horizon Ltd v Revenue and Customs Commissioners [2017] UKUT 246 (TCC); [2017] B.T.C. 524, UT (Tax)
SS (Nigeria) v Secretary of State for the Home Department [2013] EWCA Civ 550; [2014] 1 W.L.R. 998; [2013] Imm. A.R. 1106, CA (Civ Div) .... *Digested,* 14/**1668**:
Applied 15/1378, 16/1076, 17/1198: *Followed* 14/1670, 15/1325, 15/1327, 15/1328, 16/1077
SSH Communications Security Corp v Sony Mobile Communications AB see Sony Communications International AB v SSH Communications Security Corp
St Albans City and DC v International Computers Ltd [1996] 4 All E.R. 481; [1997-98] Info. T.L.R. 58; [1997] F.S.R. 251; (1996) 15 Tr. L.R. 444; Times, August 14, 1996; [1998] Masons C.L.R. Rep. 98; (1997) 20(2) I.P.D. 20020, CA (Civ Div) .. *Digested,* 96/**1218**:
Applied 04/682: *Considered* 15/56, 17/508: *Followed* 16/441
St Albans City and District Council v Hunston Properties Ltd see Hunston Properties Ltd v Secretary of State for Communities and Local Government
St Andrew's Churchyard, Fairlight, Re (Unreported, October 16, 2014), Cons Ct (Chichester)
Considered 17/662
St Andrew's Churchyard, Witchford, Re [2017] P.T.S.R. 86, Cons Ct .... *Digested,* 17/**662**
St Andrew's College Bradfield v Revenue and Customs Commissioners [2015] UKFTT 34 (TC); [2015] S.F.T.D. 349; [2015] S.T.I. 331, FTT (Tax) .... *Digested,* 15/**2579**:
Affirmed 17/2266
St Andrew's College Bradfield v Revenue and Customs Commissioners [2016] UKUT 491 (TCC); [2017] S.T.C. 83; [2016] B.V.C. 544; [2016] S.T.I. 2963; [2017] S.T.I. 35, UT (Tax) .... *Digested,* 17/**2266**
St Augustine's Churchyard, Droitwich Spa, Re; *sub nom* Spickenreuther's Petition, Re [2016] 1 W.L.R. 3365, Cons Ct (Worcester) .... *Digested,* 17/**661**
St Chad's Churchyard, Bensham, Re [2017] Fam. 68; [2016] 3 W.L.R. 1707, Cons Ct (Durham) .... *Digested,* 17/**660**
ST Dupont v EI du Pont de Nemours & Co; *sub nom* EI du Pont de Nemours & Co v ST Dupont; DU PONT Trade Mark [2003] EWCA Civ 1368; [2006] 1 W.L.R. 2793; [2006] C.P. Rep. 25; [2004] F.S.R. 15; (2004) 27(2) I.P.D. 27009; (2003) 147 S.J.L.B. 1207, CA (Civ Div) .... *Digested,* 04/**2399**:
Applied 15/1542: *Considered* 05/2563, 10/2580, 17/1356
St Helens MBC v Barnes see Barnes v St Helens MBC
St Martins Property Corp Ltd v Sir Robert McAlpine & Sons see Linden Gardens Trust Ltd v Lenesta Sludge Disposal Ltd
St Mary the Virgin, Eccleston, Re [2017] P.T.S.R. 651, Cons Ct (Blackburn) .... *Digested,* 17/**665**
St Nicholas, Sevenoaks, Re [2005] 1 W.L.R. 1011; Times, October 29, 2004; (2004) 101(44) L.S.G. 31, Arches Ct .... *Digested,* 05/**993**:
Applied 12/885: *Considered* 07/1084, 17/660

St Oswald's Churchyard, Dean, Re [2017] P.T.S.R. 52, Cons Ct .... *Digested,* 17/**669**

St Paul's Church, Woodhouse Eaves, Re [2017] Fam. 1; [2016] 3 W.L.R. 1134, Cons Ct .... *Digested,* 17/**663**

St Philip's, Scholes, Re [2017] Fam. 6; [2016] 3 W.L.R. 932, Cons Ct .... *Digested,* 16/**588**

Staatlich genehmigte Gesellschaft der Autoren, Komponisten und Musikverleger registrierte Genossenschaft mbH (AKM) v Zurs.net Betriebs GmbH (C-138/16) EU:C:2017:218; [2017] E.C.D.R. 15, ECJ (8th Chamber)

Staatssecretaris van Financien v Cooperatieve Vereniging Cooperatieve Aardappelenbewaarplaats GA (154/80) EU:C:1981:38; [1981] E.C.R. 445; [1981] 3 C.M.L.R. 337, ECJ (2nd Chamber)
Applied 11/3568, 13/3226, 17/2262: *Followed* 97/4975, 12/3407

Staatssecretaris van Financien v Nobel Biocare Nederland BV (C□160/13) see VDP Dental Laboratory NV v Staatssecretaris van Financien (C-144/13)

Staatssecretaris van Financien v X BV (C-154/13) see VDP Dental Laboratory NV v Staatssecretaris van Financien (C-144/13)

Stack v Dowden; *sub nom* Dowden v Stack [2007] UKHL 17; [2007] 2 A.C. 432; [2007] 2 W.L.R. 831; [2007] 2 All E.R. 929; [2007] 1 F.L.R. 1858; [2007] 2 F.C.R. 280; [2007] B.P.I.R. 913; [2008] 2 P. & C.R. 4; [2007] W.T.L.R. 1053; (2006-07) 9 I.T.E.L.R. 815; Times, April 26, 2007; [2007] Fam. Law 593; [2007] 18 E.G. 153 (C.S.); (2007) 157 N.L.J. 634; (2007) 151 S.J.L.B. 575; [2007] N.P.C. 47; [2007] 2 P. & C.R. DG11, HL .... *Digested,* 07/**3367**:
Applied 07/3362, 07/3366, 08/2145, 08/3060, 08/3102, 08/3122, 08/3615, 09/3119, 09/3719, 10/2692, 13/2421, 13/693: *Considered* 08/3064, 09/1363, 10/3442, 11/1292, 12/2024, 13/2422, 14/2492, 15/2092, 15/2126, 17/1826: *Distinguished* 08/3104: *Followed* 10/2691, 12/1319, 12/1457, 12/1825, 12/2705, 12/752, 13/2420, 14/3196, 16/1828

Stadt Graz v Strabag AG (C-314/09) EU:C:2010:567; [2011] 1 C.M.L.R. 26, ECJ (3rd Chamber)
Applied 16/1792: *Considered* 17/1813

Stadt Wiener Neustadt v Niederosterreichische Landesregierung (C-348/15) EU:C:2016:882; [2017] 2 C.M.L.R. 11; [2017] Env. L.R. 20, ECJ (1st Chamber)

Staffordshire CC v K; *sub nom* Staffordshire CC v SRK; Secretary of State for Justice v Staffordshire CC [2016] EWCA Civ 1317; [2017] Fam. 278; [2017] 2 W.L.R. 1131; [2017] C.O.P.L.R. 120; Times, February 9, 2017, CA (Civ Div) .... *Digested,* 17/**1546**

Staffordshire CC v K; *sub nom* Staffordshire CC v SRK; Secretary of State for Justice v Staffordshire CC [2016] EWCOP 27; [2016] Fam. 419; [2016] 3 W.L.R. 867; [2016] C.O.P.L.R. 504; [2016] Med. L.R. 398, CP .... *Digested,* 16/**1482**:
Affirmed 17/1546

Staffordshire CC v SRK see Staffordshire CC v K

Stagecoach Group Plc v Revenue and Customs Commissioners [2016] UKFTT 120 (TC); [2016] S.F.T.D. 982; [2016] S.T.I. 1534, FTT (Tax)
Approved 17/2112

Stait v Fenner [1912] 2 Ch. 504, Ch D
Considered 17/1456

Standard Chartered Bank v Mehra see Standard Chartered Bank v Pakistan National Shipping Corp (No.2)

Standard Chartered Bank v Pakistan National Shipping Corp (No.2); *joined case* Standard Chartered Bank v Mehra [2002] UKHL 43; [2003] 1 A.C. 959; [2002] 3 W.L.R. 1547; [2003] 1 All E.R. 173; [2002] 2 All E.R. (Comm) 931; [2003] 1 Lloyd's Rep. 227; [2002] B.C.C. 846; [2003] 1 B.C.L.C. 244; [2002] C.L.C. 1330; Times, November 7, 2002; (2003) 100(1) L.S.G. 26; (2002) 146 S.J.L.B. 258, HL .... *Digested,* 02/**4541**:
Applied 08/3903: *Considered* 11/412: *Followed* 12/3346, 17/169

Standard Chartered Plc v Revenue and Customs Commissioners; *joined case* Lloyds Banking Group Plc v Revenue and Customs Commissioners [2014] UKFTT 316 (TC); [2014] S.F.T.D. 1270, FTT (Tax)
Affirmed 17/2289

Standard Chartered Plc v Revenue and Customs Commissioners see Revenue and Customs Commissioners v MG Rover Group Ltd

Stanford International Bank Ltd v Director of the Serious Fraud Office see Stanford International Bank Ltd (In Receivership), Re

Stanford International Bank Ltd (In Receivership), Re; *sub nom* Serious Fraud Office v Wastell; Janvey v Wastell; Stanford International Bank Ltd v Director of the Serious Fraud Office [2010] EWCA Civ 137; [2011] Ch. 33; [2010] 3 W.L.R. 941; [2010] Bus. L.R. 1270; [2011] B.C.C. 211; [2010] Lloyd's Rep. F.C. 357; [2010] B.P.I.R. 679, CA (Civ Div) .... *Digested,* 10/**1873**:
Applied 11/1873, 13/764, 17/559, 17/597: *Approved* 14/802: *Followed* 14/1817, 14/803

Stanhope Pension Trust Ltd v Registrar of Companies; *sub nom* Forte's (Manufacturing) Ltd, Re [1994] B.C.C. 84; [1994] 1 B.C.L.C. 628; (1995) 69 P. & C.R. 238; [1993] E.G. 206 (C.S.); [1993] N.P.C. 169, CA (Civ Div) .... *Digested,* 94/**425**: *Applied* 13/1705: *Followed* 17/402

Stanley v Wilson [2017] B.P.I.R. 227, Ch D (Leeds)

Stannard v Reay [1967] F.S.R. 140, Ch D .... *Digested,* 67/**3940**: *Applied* 17/1400

Stanton Ltd v Drayton Commercial Investment Co Ltd [1983] 1 A.C. 501; [1982] 3 W.L.R. 214; [1982] 2 All E.R. 942; [1982] S.T.C. 585; [1982] Com. L.R. 198; 55 T.C. 286; (1982) 79 L.S.G. 1176, HL .... *Digested,* 82/**1592**: *Applied* 17/2188

Stapenhill Developments v Customs and Excise Commissioners [1984] V.A.T.T.R. 1, VAT Tr .... *Digested,* 84/**3620**: *Considered* 17/2288

Staples v West Dorset DC 93 L.G.R. 536; [1995] P.I.Q.R. P439; Times, April 28, 1995; (1995) 92(18) L.S.G. 36; (1995) 139 S.J.L.B. 117, CA (Civ Div) .... *Digested,* 95/**4731**: *Applied* 01/4504: *Considered* 98/3918, 01/4496, 04/2723: *Distinguished* 06/5600: *Followed* 17/2200

Star Industrial Co Ltd v Yap Kwee Kor (t/a New Star Industrial Co) [1976] F.S.R. 256, PC (Sing) .... *Digested,* 77/**3040**: *Applied* 17/1394: *Considered* 77/415, 96/3637, 97/4905

Star Polaris LLC v HHIC-Phil Inc [2016] EWHC 2941 (Comm); [2017] 1 Lloyd's Rep. 203; [2016] 2 C.L.C. 832; 169 Con. L.R. 125, QBD (Comm) .... *Digested,* 17/**505**

Starbucks (HK) Ltd v British Sky Broadcasting Group Plc [2015] UKSC 31; [2015] 1 W.L.R. 2628; [2015] 3 All E.R. 469; [2015] E.C.C. 19; [2015] E.T.M.R. 31; [2015] F.S.R. 29; Times, May 28, 2015, SC .... *Digested,* 15/**1495**: *Followed* 17/1394

Stares v Elgin Legal Ltd see Elgin Legal Ltd, Re

Starlight Shipping Co v Allianz Marine & Aviation Versicherungs AG; *joined cases* Brit UW Ltd v Starlight Shipping Co; Brit UW Ltd v Imperial Marine Co [2013] UKSC 70; [2014] 1 All E.R. 590; [2014] 1 All E.R. (Comm) 337; [2014] Bus. L.R. 873; [2014] 1 Lloyd's Rep. 223; [2013] 2 C.L.C. 713; [2014] Lloyd's Rep. I.R. 327, SC .... *Digested,* 14/**565**: *Considered* 14/558, 15/371, 17/428: *Followed* 14/1920, 16/362

Starlight Shipping Co v Allianz Marine & Aviation Versicherungs AG; *sub nom* Brit UW Ltd v Starlight Shipping Co; Brit UW Ltd v Imperial Marine Co; *joined case* Alexandros T, The [2014] EWCA Civ 1010; [2014] 2 Lloyd's Rep. 544; [2014] 2 C.L.C. 492; [2015] Lloyd's Rep. I.R. 49, CA (Civ Div) .... *Digested,* 15/**366**: *Followed* 15/368, 16/362, 17/428

Starr v Ward [2015] EWHC 1987 (QB), QBD *Considered* 17/651

STATE OF ISRAEL/Tomatoes III (T1242/06) [2017] E.P.O.R. 1, EPO (Technical Bd App)

Stati v Kazakhstan [2017] EWHC 1348 (Comm); [2017] 2 Lloyd's Rep. 201, QBD (Comm) .... *Digested,* 17/**80**

Stec v United Kingdom (Admissibility) (65731/01) (2005) 41 E.H.R.R. SE18, ECHR *Applied* 15/2348: *Considered* 07/3867, 07/3875, 10/1694, 10/2197, 16/2417, 16/2599, 17/2386

Steel v Joy see Halsey v Milton Keynes General NHS Trust

Steel Abrasives Cartel, Re (AT.39792) [2017] 4 C.M.L.R. 10, CEC

Steele v Mooney [2005] EWCA Civ 96; [2005] 1 W.L.R. 2819; [2005] 2 All E.R. 256; [2005] C.P. Rep. 26; Times, February 15, 2005, CA (Civ Div) .... *Digested,* 05/**340**: *Applied* 15/362, 16/296: *Considered* 10/274, 17/1475: *Followed* 10/273

Steele v Steele [2001] C.P. Rep. 106; Times, June 5, 2001, Ch D .... *Digested,* 01/**440**: *Applied* 17/772: *Considered* 16/2110

Steele (Inspector of Taxes) v European Vinyls Corp (Holdings) BV see Steele (Inspector of Taxes) v EVC International NV (formerly European Vinyls Corp (Holdings) BV)

Steele (Inspector of Taxes) v EVC International NV (formerly European Vinyls Corp (Holdings) BV); *sub nom* Steele (Inspector of Taxes) v European Vinyls Corp (Holdings) BV; Steeple v European Vinyls Corp (Holdings) BV [1996] S.T.C. 785; 69 T.C. 88; [1996] B.T.C. 425, CA (Civ Div) .... *Digested,* 96/**1291**: *Applied* 13/3094: *Considered* 07/3989, 17/2091

Steele (Kevin Munro) v HM Advocate; *sub nom* R. v Steele; *joined case* Forbes (David Landells) v HM Advocate 1992 J.C. 1; 1992 S.L.T. 847; 1992 S.C.C.R. 30; Times, October 31, 1991, HCJ .... *Digested,* 92/**5502**: *Applied* 08/4625: *Approved* 17/2559: *Considered* 96/1378, 13/3611, 17/2505: *Distinguished* 95/5718, 96/6809: *Referred to* 92/5355

Steeple v European Vinyls Corp (Holdings) BV see Steele (Inspector of Taxes) v EVC International NV (formerly European Vinyls Corp (Holdings) BV)

Steer v Secretary of State for Communities and Local Government [2017] EWHC 1456 (Admin); [2017] J.P.L. 1281, QBD (Admin) .... *Digested*, 17/**1714**

Stefan v General Medical Council (No.1) [1999] 1 W.L.R. 1293; [2000] H.R.L.R. 1; 6 B.H.R.C. 487; [1999] Lloyd's Rep. Med. 90; (1999) 49 B.M.L.R. 161; Times, March 11, 1999; (1999) 143 S.J.L.B. 112, PC (UK) .... *Digested*, 99/**2661**: *Applied* 09/69, 11/3203, 17/1764: *Considered* 03/4713

Steinfeld v Secretary of State for Education; *sub nom* R. (on the application of Steinfeld) v Secretary of State for Education [2017] EWCA Civ 81; [2018] Q.B. 519; [2017] 3 W.L.R. 1237; [2017] 4 All E.R. 47; [2017] 2 F.L.R. 692; [2017] 2 F.C.R. 324; [2017] H.R.L.R. 3, CA (Civ Div) .... *Digested*, 17/**976**

Steinfeld v Secretary of State for Education [2016] EWHC 128 (Admin); [2016] 4 W.L.R. 41; [2016] 4 All E.R. 421; [2016] 1 F.L.R. 1034; [2016] 2 F.C.R. 606; [2016] H.R.L.R. 8; [2016] Fam. Law 296, QBD (Admin) .... *Digested*, 16/**867**: *Affirmed* 17/976

Stellite Construction Ltd v Vascroft Contractors Ltd [2016] EWHC 792 (TCC); [2016] B.L.R. 402; 165 Con. L.R. 108, QBD (TCC) .... *Digested*, 16/**393**: *Applied* 17/450

Stephens v Cannon [2005] EWCA Civ 222; [2005] C.P. Rep. 31; [2006] R.V.R. 126; Times, May 3, 2005, CA (Civ Div) .... *Digested*, 05/**292**: *Applied* 07/2680, 10/2718, 17/1639

Sternbaum v Dhesi [2016] EWCA Civ 155; [2016] H.L.R. 16; [2016] 2 P. & C.R. 4; [2016] 2 P. & C.R. DG12, CA (Civ Div) .... *Digested*, 16/**1366**: *Applied* 17/1563

Stevens v Equity Syndicate Management Ltd [2015] EWCA Civ 93; [2015] 4 All E.R. 458; [2015] R.T.R. 24; [2015] Lloyd's Rep. I.R. 503, CA (Civ Div) .... *Digested*, 15/**681**: *Followed* 17/644

Stevens v University of Birmingham [2015] EWHC 2300 (QB); [2016] 4 All E.R. 258; [2017] I.C.R. 96; [2015] I.R.L.R. 899; [2016] E.L.R. 145; [2015] Med. L.R. 489, QBD .... *Digested*, 15/**811**

Stevensdrake Ltd (t/a Stevensdrake Solicitors) v Hunt [2017] EWCA Civ 1173; [2017] B.C.C. 611; [2017] 4 Costs L.R. 781; [2017] B.P.I.R. 1408, CA (Civ Div) .... *Digested*, 17/**1479**

Stevensdrake Ltd (t/a Stevensdrake Solicitors) v Hunt [2016] EWHC 342 (Ch); [2016] B.C.C. 515; [2017] 1 B.C.L.C. 64; [2016] 2 Costs L.O. 187; [2016] B.P.I.R. 773, Ch D .... *Digested*, 16/**1209**: *Reversed in part* 17/1479

Stevenson v Singh [2012] EWHC 2880 (QB), QBD
Considered 17/44

Stewart v Malik [2009] CSIH 5; 2009 S.C. 265; 2009 S.L.T. 205; 2009 Rep. L.R. 22; 2009 G.W.D. 7-127, IH (1 Div) .... *Digested*, 09/**5076**: *Considered* 17/2464

Stewart v Payne; *joined case* McQuade v Clarke [2016] HCJAC 122; 2017 J.C. 155; 2017 S.L.T. 159; 2017 S.C.L. 263; 2017 S.C.C.R. 56; 2016 G.W.D. 40-707, HCJ .... *Digested*, 17/**2530**

Stewart v Perth and Kinross Council; *sub nom* Stewart v Perth and Kinross DC [2004] UKHL 16; 2004 S.C. (H.L.) 71; 2004 S.L.T. 383; 2004 S.C.L.R. 849; [2004] L.L.R. 598; Times, April 6, 2004; (2004) 148 S.J.L.B. 472; [2004] 28 S.L.L.P. 32; 2004 G.W.D. 12-273, HL .... *Digested*, 04/**5023**: *Applied* 09/5177, 17/2660

Stewart v Perth and Kinross DC see Stewart v Perth and Kinross Council

Stewart v Secretary of State for Work and Pensions (C-503/09) EU:C:2011:500; [2012] P.T.S.R. 1; [2012] 1 C.M.L.R. 13; [2012] C.E.C. 479, ECJ (2nd Chamber) .... *Digested*, 12/**3129**: *Applied* 12/1030: *Considered* 15/2353, 17/2169

Stewart v Watts see Watts v Stewart

Stewart Gill Ltd v Horatio Myer and Co Ltd [1992] Q.B. 600; [1992] 2 W.L.R. 721; [1992] 2 All E.R. 257; 31 Con. L.R. 1; (1991) 11 Tr. L.R. 86; (1992) 142 N.L.J. 241, CA (Civ Div) .... *Digested*, 92/**510**: *Applied* 97/2507, 03/3616: *Considered* 97/906, 02/695, 12/268, 13/597, 17/1566: *Followed* 11/551

Stichting Brein v Wullems (t/a Filmspeler) (C-527/15) EU:C:2017:300; [2017] Bus. L.R. 1816; [2017] 3 C.M.L.R. 30; [2017] E.C.D.R. 14, ECJ (2nd Chamber)

Stichting Brein v Ziggo BV (C-610/15) EU:C:2017:456; [2017] Bus. L.R. 1899; [2018] C.E.C. 191; [2017] E.C.D.R. 19, ECJ (2nd Chamber)

Stichting Brein v Ziggo BV (C-610/15) EU:C:2017:99; [2017] E.C.D.R. 13, AGO

Stichting Goed Wonen v Staatssecretaris van Financien (C-376/02) EU:C:2005:251; [2006] S.T.C. 833; [2005] E.C.R. I-3445; [2005] 2 C.M.L.R. 41; [2007] B.T.C. 5989; [2008] B.V.C. 25; [2005] S.T.I. 890, ECJ (Grand Chamber) .... *Digested,* 06/**4443**: *Applied* 17/2236

Stichting Ostade Blade v Netherlands (8406/06) (2014) 59 E.H.R.R. SE9, ECHR *Considered* 17/290

Stock 94 Szolgaltato Zrt v Nemzeti Ado- es Vamhivatal Del-dunantuli Regionalis Ado Foigazgatosaga (C-208/15) EU:C:2016:936; [2016] B.V.C. 45; [2017] S.T.I. 39, ECJ (5th Chamber)

Stockbrook Investments Ltd v Alexander (Valuation Officer) [2016] R.A. 338, VT .... *Digested,* 17/**1528**

Stocznia Gdynia SA v Gearbulk Holdings Ltd [2009] EWCA Civ 75; [2010] Q.B. 27; [2009] 3 W.L.R. 677; [2009] 2 All E.R. (Comm) 1129; [2009] 1 Lloyd's Rep. 461; [2009] 1 C.L.C. 134; [2009] B.L.R. 196; [2009] C.I.L.L. 2708, CA (Civ Div) *Digested,* 09/**734**: *Applied* 12/1114: *Considered* 17/462

Stodday Land Ltd v Pye; *sub nom* Pye v Stodday Land Ltd [2016] EWHC 2454 (Ch); [2016] 4 W.L.R. 168; [2017] 1 P. & C.R. 5, Ch D (Manchester) .... *Digested,* 17/**1456**

Stoke by Nayland Golf and Leisure Ltd v Revenue and Customs Commissioners [2017] UKFTT 246 (TC); [2017] S.F.T.D. 947; [2017] S.T.I. 1048, FTT (Tax)

Stoker v Lancashire CC [1992] I.R.L.R. 75, CA (Civ Div) .... *Digested,* 92/**1995**: *Considered* 17/852: *Followed* 96/2660

Stokes Pension Fund Trustees v Western Power Distribution (South West) Plc; *sub nom* Trustees of the Stokes Pension Fund v Western Power Distribution (South West) Plc [2005] EWCA Civ 854; [2005] 1 W.L.R. 3595; [2005] 3 All E.R. 775; [2005] C.P. Rep. 40; [2005] B.L.R. 497; [2006] 2 Costs L.R. 226; Times, July 28, 2005; Independent, July 15, 2005; (2005) 102(30) L.S.G. 28, CA (Civ Div) .. *Digested,* 05/**374**: *Applied* 06/358, 06/382, 10/388: *Considered* 12/352, 12/387, 14/369, 15/262, 17/266: *Followed* 12/3050

Stokors SA v IG Markets Ltd [2012] EWCA Civ 1706, CA (Civ Div) *Applied* 17/359: *Considered* 17/360

Stolarczyk v Harrower see Stolarczyk (Grzegorz) v Procurator Fiscal, Stirling

Stolarczyk (Grzegorz) v Procurator Fiscal, Stirling; *sub nom* Stolarczyk v Harrower [2017] HCJAC 23; 2017 S.L.T. 527; 2017 S.C.L. 527; 2017 S.C.C.R. 229; 2017 G.W.D. 13-201, HCJ .... *Digested,* 17/**2482**

Stolkin v Revenue and Customs Commissioners; *sub nom* Revenue and Customs Commissioners v Stolkin [2016] EWCA Civ 447; [2017] 1 W.L.R. 2995; [2017] 2 All E.R. 69; [2016] S.T.C. 1731; [2016] B.T.C. 19; [2016] S.T.I. 1533, CA (Civ Div) .... *Digested,* 16/**2047**

Stolt Loyalty, The [1993] 2 Lloyd's Rep. 281, QBD (Admlty) .... *Digested,* 94/**4047**: *Affirmed* 96/5296: *Considered* 95/689, 17/493

Stone v 54 Hogarth Rd, London SW5 Management Ltd see Willow Court Management Co (1985) Ltd v Alexander

Stone v Bolton see Bolton v Stone

Stone (Inspector of Taxes) v Hitch see Hitch v Stone (Inspector of Taxes)

Stone Rowe Brewer LLP v Just Costs Ltd see Wilsons Solicitors LLP v Bentine

Stoner (Christiane) v HM Advocate [2017] HCJAC 32; 2017 S.C.L. 618; 2017 G.W.D. 18-286, HCJ Appeal .... *Digested,* 17/**2521**

Storck v Germany (61603/00) (2006) 43 E.H.R.R. 6; [2005] M.H.L.R. 211, ECHR *Applied* 07/3913, 16/1482, 16/1517, 17/966: *Considered* 10/3144, 11/3225, 16/1524, 17/1546

Stowarzyszenie Olawska Telewizja Kablowa (OTK) v Stowarzyszenie Filmowcow Polskich (SFP) (C-367/15) EU:C:2017:36; [2017] E.C.D.R. 16, ECJ (5th Chamber)

Stransham-Ford v Minister of Justice and Correctional Services (2017) 156 B.M.L.R. 57, Sup Ct (SA)

Strategic Designs v Thorne (Valuation Officer) [2017] UKUT 201 (LC); [2017] R.V.R. 308, UT (Lands)

Streetmap.EU Ltd v Google Inc [2016] EWHC 253 (Ch), Ch D *Applied* 17/410

Stribog Ltd v FKI Engineering Ltd see FKI Engineering Ltd v Stribog Ltd

Stringfellow v Showmen's Guild of Great Britain [2017] CSOH 62; 2017 S.L.T. 483; 2017 G.W.D. 12-168, OH .... *Digested,* 17/**2393**

Strlekar v Slovenia (40535/14) (2017) 64 E.H.R.R. SE9, ECHR

Stuart v Goldberg; *sub nom* Stuart v Goldberg Linde (A Firm) [2008] EWCA Civ 2; [2008] 1 W.L.R. 823; [2008] C.P. Rep. 18; Times, January 23, 2008; (2008) 152(4) S.J.L.B. 28, CA (Civ Div) .... *Digested,* 08/**271**: *Applied* 10/257, 17/1375: *Considered* 10/425: *Followed* 16/1313

Stuart v Goldberg Linde (A Firm) see Stuart v Goldberg

Stuart v Reid [2015] CSOH 175; 2016 G.W.D. 1-12, OH
Considered 17/2428

Stuart (Michael) v HM Advocate [2017] HCJAC 54; 2017 S.C.L. 798; 2017 G.W.D. 23-389, HCJ Appeal .... *Digested,* 17/**2561**

Studebaker Distributors Ltd v Charlton Steam Shipping Co Ltd [1938] 1 K.B. 459; [1937] 4 All E.R. 304; (1937) 59 Ll. L. Rep. 23, KBD
Applied 58/548, 17/2003: *Considered* 74/3541, 74/3545

Stunt v Associated Newspapers Ltd [2017] EWHC 695 (QB); [2017] 1 W.L.R. 3985; [2017] 3 C.M.L.R. 9; [2017] E.M.L.R. 18, QBD .... *Digested,* 17/**1167**

Sturrock v HM Advocate see S (A) v HM Advocate

Sturrock (Alexander) v HM Advocate [2016] HCJAC 97; 2017 S.C.L. 601; 2017 S.C.C.R. 340; 2017 G.W.D. 17-266, HCJ Appeal .... *Digested,* 17/**2478**

Su v Clarksons Platou Futures Ltd; *sub nom* Su v Clarksons Platou Futures Ltd (also known as Morimoto v Clarksons Platou Futures Ltd); Su v Clarksons Platou Futures Ltd (also known as Chi v Clarksons Platou Futures Ltd) [2017] EWHC 337 (Comm); [2017] 1 Lloyd's Rep. 568, QBD (Comm) .... *Digested,* 17/**326**

Su v Clarksons Platou Futures Ltd (also known as Chi v Clarksons Platou Futures Ltd) see Su v Clarksons Platou Futures Ltd

Su v Clarksons Platou Futures Ltd (also known as Morimoto v Clarksons Platou Futures Ltd) see Su v Clarksons Platou Futures Ltd

SU v SA see SU (Children) (Passports), Re

SU (Children) (Passports), Re; *sub nom* FM v KAH; SU v SA [2017] EWHC 441 (Fam); [2017] 2 F.L.R. 1067; [2017] 2 F.C.R. 375, Fam Div .... *Digested,* 17/**957**

Suffolk Coastal DC v Hopkins Homes Ltd see Secretary of State for Communities and Local Government v Hopkins Homes Ltd

Sufi v United Kingdom (8319/07); *joined case* Elmi v United Kingdom (11449/07) (2012) 54 E.H.R.R. 9; [2011] Crim. L.R. 882; (2011) 108(28) L.S.G. 20, ECHR . *Digested,* 12/**1659**:
Considered 12/1689, 14/1664, 15/1373, 17/1204: *Referred to* 13/1602

Sukul v Bar Standards Board [2014] EWHC 3532 (Admin), QBD (Admin)
Considered 17/1486

Sul America Cia Nacional de Seguros SA v Enesa Engenharia SA see Sulamerica Cia Nacional de Seguros SA v Enesa Engenharia SA

Sulaiman v France; *sub nom* Sulaiman v Tribunal de Grande Instance, Paris [2016] EWHC 2868 (Admin); [2017] Lloyd's Rep. F.C. 111, QBD (Admin) .... *Digested,* 17/**900**

Sulaiman v Tribunal de Grande Instance, Paris see Sulaiman v France

Sulamerica Cia Nacional de Seguros SA v Enesa Engenharia SA; *sub nom* Sul America Cia Nacional de Seguros SA v Enesa Engenharia SA [2012] EWCA Civ 638; [2013] 1 W.L.R. 102; [2012] 2 All E.R. (Comm) 795; [2012] 1 Lloyd's Rep. 671; [2012] 2 C.L.C. 216; [2012] Lloyd's Rep. I.R. 405; Times, August 24, 2012, CA (Civ Div) .... *Digested,* 12/**104**:
Applied 13/801: *Distinguished* 14/629: *Explained* 17/367: *Followed* 13/98

Suleman v Shahsavari [1988] 1 W.L.R. 1181; [1989] 2 All E.R. 460; (1989) 57 P. & C.R. 465; [1989] 09 E.G. 69; Independent, July 12, 1988; (1988) 85(32) L.S.G. 38; (1988) 138 N.L.J. Rep. 241; (1988) 132 S.J. 1243, Ch D .... *Digested,* 89/**1290**:
Applied 12/854: *Explained* 17/497

Sullivan v Bristol Film Studios Ltd; *sub nom* Sullivan (also known as Soloman) v Bristol Film Studios Ltd [2012] EWCA Civ 570; [2012] C.P. Rep. 34; [2012] E.M.L.R. 27, CA (Civ Div) .... *Digested,* 12/**432**:
Considered 17/1574: *Followed* 15/693

Sullivan v Guy's and St Thomas' NHS Foundation Trust [2017] EWHC 602 (QB); [2017] Med. L.R. 260, QBD .... *Digested,* 17/**1562**

Sullivan (also known as Soloman) v Bristol Film Studios Ltd see Sullivan v Bristol Film Studios Ltd

Sully and Lavernock Community Council v Vale of Glamorgan Council [2017] P.A.D. 2, Planning Inspector

Sumal & Sons (Properties) Ltd v Newham LBC; *sub nom* R. v Sumal & Sons (Properties) Ltd [2012] EWCA Crim 1840; [2013] 1 W.L.R. 2078; [2012] Lloyd's Rep. F.C. 692; [2012] H.L.R. 46; [2012] C.T.L.C. 206; [2012] 2 P. & C.R. DG19, CA (Crim Div) .... *Digested,* 13/**688**:
Considered 16/502, 17/577: *Followed* 15/601

Summit Electrical Installations Ltd v Revenue and Customs Commissioners [2017] UKFTT 564 (TC); [2017] S.T.I. 1734, FTT (Tax)

Sun Alliance (Bahamas) Ltd v Scandi Enterprises Ltd [2017] UKPC 10; [2017] 2 All E.R. (Comm) 1019; [2017] B.L.R. 371, PC (Bah)

Sun Life Assurance Co of Canada v Lincoln National Life Insurance Co (Unreported)
Considered 17/191

Sun Microsystems Inc v M-Tech Data Ltd; *sub nom* Oracle America Inc v M-Tech Data Ltd [2012] UKSC 27; [2012] 1 W.L.R. 2026; [2012] 4 All E.R. 338; [2012] Bus. L.R. 1631; [2012] 3 C.M.L.R. 28; [2012] E.C.C. 27; [2012] Eu. L.R. 727; [2012] E.T.M.R. 43; [2012] Info. T.L.R. 173; [2013] F.S.R. 14; Times, July 16, 2012, SC .... *Digested,* 12/**1970**: *Applied* 14/1860: *Followed* 17/1361

Sunca v Iasi Court of Law see Romania v Zagrean

Sunca v Romania see Romania v Zagrean

Surfstone Pty Ltd v Morgan Consulting Engineers Pty Ltd [2016] QCA 213; (2017) 33 Const. L.J. 356, CA (Qld)

Surikov v Ukraine (42788/06) [2017] I.R.L.R. 377, ECHR

Surrey and Sussex Healthcare NHS Trust v Logan Construction (South East) Ltd [2017] EWHC 17 (TCC); [2017] 2 All E.R. (Comm) 586; [2017] B.L.R. 189; 170 Con. L.R. 65; [2017] C.I.L.L. 3954, QBD (TCC) .... *Digested,* 17/**475**

Surrey CC v NR; *sub nom* K (Wardship: Without Notice Return Order), Re [2017] EWHC 153 (Fam); [2017] 2 F.L.R. 901; [2017] 1 F.C.R. 516, Fam Div .... *Digested,* 17/**1066**

Surrey CC v P see Cheshire West and Chester Council v P

Surtees v Middlesbrough BC see Redcar and Cleveland BC v Bainbridge

Surzur Overseas Ltd v Koros [1999] 2 Lloyd's Rep. 611; [1999] C.L.C. 801, CA (Civ Div) .... *Digested,* 99/**528**: *Applied* 17/160: *Considered* 16/2145

Sussex Cars Association v Revenue and Customs Commissioners [2017] UKFTT 691 (TC); [2017] S.T.I. 2070, FTT (Tax)

Sutherland v Harvie see Sutherland (Adam) v HM Advocate

Sutherland v Hatton see Barber v Somerset CC

Sutherland v Lord Advocate [2017] CSOH 32; 2017 S.L.T. 333; 2017 G.W.D. 8-109, OH .... *Digested,* 17/**2389**

Sutherland v V2 Music Ltd [2002] EWHC 14 (Ch); [2002] E.M.L.R. 28, Ch D .... *Digested,* 02/**2780**: *Applied* 17/1400

Sutherland (Adam) v HM Advocate; *sub nom* Sutherland v Harvie [2017] HCJAC 22; 2017 J.C. 268; 2017 S.L.T. 721; 2017 S.C.L. 502; 2017 S.C.C.R. 268; 2017 G.W.D. 14-230, HCJ .... *Digested,* 17/**2798**

Sutherland (Alexander) v HM Advocate [2015] HCJAC 115; 2016 S.L.T. 93; 2016 S.C.L. 233; 2016 S.C.C.R. 41; 2015 G.W.D. 39-621, HCJ .... *Digested,* 16/**2822**: *Not applied* 17/2816

Sutton LBC v Edwards see Edwards v Sutton LBC

Sutton LBC v Gray see C (Care Proceedings: Publication of Judgment), Re

Sutton LBC v H; *sub nom* Sutton LBC v MH [2016] EWHC 1371 (Fam); [2017] 2 F.L.R. 263; [2016] Fam. Law 1076, Fam Div

Sutton LBC v MH see Sutton LBC v H

Svenska Lokmannaforbundet v Sweden (A/20) see Swedish Engine Drivers Union v Sweden (A/20)

Svensson v Retriever Sverige AB (C-466/12) EU:C:2014:76; [2014] Bus. L.R. 259; [2014] 3 C.M.L.R. 4; [2014] All E.R. (EC) 609; [2015] C.E.C. 17; [2014] E.C.D.R. 9; [2015] E.M.L.R. 5, ECJ (4th Chamber) *Applied* 17/1358: *Considered* 15/1476

SW (Human Rights Claim: Procedure) (No.1), Re see W (Children) (Convention Rights Claim: Procedure), Re

Swain v DPP see R. v Jones (Margaret)

Swain v Hillman [2001] 1 All E.R. 91; [2001] C.P. Rep. 16; [1999] C.P.L.R. 779; [2000] P.I.Q.R. P51; Times, November 4, 1999; Independent, November 10, 1999, CA (Civ Div) .... *Digested,* 99/**561**: *Applied* 00/1761, 01/4855, 01/680, 03/3040, 03/387, 06/2389: *Cited* 00/353: *Considered* 01/669, 01/684, 07/538, 16/2687, 17/370: *Followed* 15/356, 17/210

Swainland Builders Ltd v Freehold Properties Ltd [2002] EWCA Civ 560; [2002] 2 E.G.L.R. 71; [2002] 23 E.G. 123; [2002] 17 E.G. 154 (C.S.), CA (Civ Div) .... *Digested,* 02/**3856**: *Applied* 12/2042, 16/438, 17/1817: *Distinguished* 07/2748

Swales v Cox [1981] Q.B. 849; [1981] 2 W.L.R. 814; [1981] 1 All E.R. 1115; (1981) 72 Cr. App. R. 171; [1981] Crim. L.R. 235; (1981) 125 S.J. 133, QBD .... *Digested,* 81/**2102**: *Considered* 94/3491, 17/542

Swanfield Ltd v Revenue and Customs Commissioners; *joined cases* QN Hotels (Wrexham) Ltd v Revenue and Customs Commissioners; QN Hotels (Aylesbury) Ltd v Revenue and Customs Commissioners; QN Hotels Ltd v Revenue and Customs Commissioners [2017] UKUT 88 (TCC); [2017] B.V.C. 507, UT (Tax) .... *Digested,* 17/**2279**

Swanfield Ltd v Revenue and Customs Commissioners; *joined cases* QN Hotels (Wrexham) Ltd v Revenue and Customs Commissioners; QN Hotels (Aylesbury) Ltd v Revenue and Customs Commissioners; QN Hotels Ltd v Revenue and Customs Commissioners [2015] UKFTT 274 (TC), FTT (Tax) *Reversed* 17/2279

Swansea University Pension and Assurance Scheme Trustees v Williams; *sub nom* Williams v Swansea University Pension and Assurance Scheme [2017] EWCA Civ 1008; [2018] I.C.R. 233; [2017] I.R.L.R. 882; [2018] E.L.R. 142; [2017] Pens. L.R. 19, CA (Civ Div) .... *Digested,* 17/**776**

Swansea University Pension and Assurance Scheme Trustees v Williams; *sub nom* Williams v Swansea University Pension and Assurance Scheme [2015] I.C.R. 1197; [2015] I.R.L.R. 885; [2015] Pens. L.R. 489, EAT .... *Digested,* 15/**806**: *Affirmed* 17/776

Swedish Engine Drivers Union v Sweden (A/20); *sub nom* Svenska Lokmannaforbundet v Sweden (A/20) [1978] E.C.C. 1; (1979-80) 1 E.H.R.R. 617, ECHR *Considered* 97/2774, 17/766

Sweetman v An Bord Pleanala (C-258/11) EU:C:2013:220; [2014] P.T.S.R. 1092; [2013] 3 C.M.L.R. 16; [2015] Env. L.R. 18, ECJ (3rd Chamber) *Considered* 15/1970, 15/1987, 15/2027, 16/1701, 17/1775

Swift v Revenue and Customs Commissioners see Anson v Revenue and Customs Commissioners

Swift v Secretary of State for Justice [2013] EWCA Civ 193; [2014] Q.B. 373; [2013] 3 W.L.R. 1151; [2013] 2 F.C.R. 1; [2013] H.R.L.R. 21; [2013] P.I.Q.R. P14; (2013) 163(7555) N.L.J. 17, CA (Civ Div) .... *Digested,* 13/**2196**: *Applied* 14/3226, 17/1466

Swift v Secretary of State for Justice [2012] EWHC 2000 (QB); [2012] P.I.Q.R. P21, QBD .... *Digested,* 12/**1675**: *Affirmed* 13/2196: *Applied* 13/1582, 17/1645

Swiggs v Nagarajan (No.2) see Nagarajan v London Regional Transport

Swindon BC v Webb (t/a Protective Coatings) [2016] EWCA Civ 152; [2016] 1 W.L.R. 3301; [2017] 2 All E.R. 515, CA (Civ Div) .... *Digested,* 16/**6**

Swiss International Air Lines AG v Secretary of State for Energy and Climate Change (C-272/15); *sub nom* R. (on the application of Swiss International Air Lines AG) v Secretary of State for Energy and Climate Change (C-272/15) EU:C:2016:993; [2017] P.T.S.R. 511; [2017] Env. L.R. 23; Times, February 3, 2017, ECJ (4th Chamber)

Swissair Schweizerische Luftverkehr AG, Re see Flightline Ltd v Edwards

Swissport Ltd v Exley [2017] I.C.R. 1288, EAT .... *Digested,* 17/**774**

Sword Services Ltd v Revenue and Customs Commissioners see R. (on the application of Sword Services Ltd) v Revenue and Customs Commissioners

Swynson Ltd v Lowick Rose LLP (In Liquidation) (formerly Hurst Morrison Thomson LLP); *sub nom* Lowick Rose LLP (In Liquidation) v Swynson Ltd [2017] UKSC 32; [2017] 2 W.L.R. 1161; [2017] 3 All E.R. 785; 171 Con. L.R. 75; [2017] P.N.L.R. 18; Times, May 2, 2017, SC .... *Digested,* 17/**637**

Swynson Ltd v Lowick Rose LLP (In Liquidation) (formerly Hurst Morrison Thomson LLP); *sub nom* Lowick Rose LLP (In Liquidation) v Swynson Ltd [2015] EWCA Civ 629; [2016] 1 W.L.R. 1045; [2015] 2 C.L.C. 102; [2015] P.N.L.R. 28, CA (Civ Div) .... *Digested,* 15/**1781**: *Considered* 16/1550: *Reversed* 17/637

SXH v Crown Prosecution Service [2014] EWCA Civ 90; [2014] 1 W.L.R. 3238, CA (Civ Div) .... *Digested,* 14/**1646**: *Affirmed* 17/1240

SXH v Crown Prosecution Service [2017] UKSC 30; [2017] 1 W.L.R. 1401; [2018] 1 All E.R. 267; Times, April 19, 2017; [2017] Crim. L.R. 712, SC .... *Digested,* 17/**1240**

Symbion Power LLC v Venco Imtiaz Construction Co [2017] EWHC 348 (TCC); [2017] B.L.R. 297, QBD (TCC) .... *Digested,* 17/**76**

SYMBOL TECHNOLOGIES/Adapter unit for PDA (T1824/15) [2017] E.P.O.R. 8, EPO (Technical Bd App)

Synectiv Ltd v Revenue and Customs Commissioners [2013] UKFTT 677 (TC), FTT (Tax) *Reversed* 17/2263

Synectiv Ltd v Revenue and Customs Commissioners [2017] UKUT 99 (TCC); [2017] B.V.C. 508, UT (Tax) .... *Digested,* 17/**2263**

Synergi Partners Ltd, Re; *sub nom* Mond v Synergi Partners Ltd [2015] EWHC 964 (Ch); [2015] B.C.C. 333; [2015] 2 B.C.L.C. 229; [2015] B.P.I.R. 1300, Ch D (Manchester) .... *Digested,* 15/**1416**: *Considered* 17/1268

Synthon BV v SmithKline Beecham Plc (No.2); *sub nom* SmithKline Beecham Plc's Paroxetine Methanesulfonate Patent (No.2) [2005] UKHL 59; [2006] 1 All E.R. 685; [2006] R.P.C. 10; (2005) 86 B.M.L.R. 130, HL .... *Digested,* 06/**2525**: *Applied* 07/2614, 09/2362, 09/2394, 09/2406, 09/2407, 10/1960, 10/1966, 10/1981, 10/2014, 16/1298, 16/1322, 17/1378: *Followed* 11/1956, 14/1897, 16/1311

Sysmex (UK) Ltd v Imperial College Healthcare NHS Trust [2017] EWHC 1824 (TCC); [2017] Med. L.R. 569, QBD (TCC)

Systemcare (UK) Ltd v Services Design Technology Ltd [2011] EWCA Civ 546; [2012] 1 B.C.L.C. 14; [2011] 4 Costs L.R. 666, CA (Civ Div) .... *Digested,* 11/**292**: *Followed* 12/376, 16/287, 17/250

Szafranski v Poland (17249/12) (2017) 64 E.H.R.R. 23, ECHR

Szelest v Poland; *sub nom* Szelest v Regional Court in Piotrokow Tribunalski [2016] EWHC 2852 (Admin); [2017] A.C.D. 4, QBD (Admin)

Szelest v Regional Court in Piotrokow Tribunalski see Szelest v Poland

T v Aberash see R. v Secretary of State for the Home Department Ex p. T

T v E (A Child) (Abduction: Refusal to Order Return) [2016] EWHC 3148 (Fam); [2017] 4 W.L.R. 18; [2017] 1 F.C.R. 435, Fam Div

T v K (Egyptian Fostering: UK Adoption) see Z (A Child) (English Adoption: Egyptian Orphan), Re

T v Locality Reporter; *sub nom* MT v Gerry [2014] CSIH 108; 2015 S.C. 359; 2015 Fam. L.R. 2; 2015 G.W.D. 1-23, IH (Ex Div) .... *Digested,* 15/**3072**: *Applied* 17/2604

T v Poland; *sub nom* RT v Circuit Court in Tarnobrzeg, Poland [2017] EWHC 1978 (Admin); [2017] 4 W.L.R. 137; [2017] A.C.D. 114, DC .... *Digested,* 17/**910**

T v R (Maintenance After Remarriage: Agreement) [2016] EWFC 26; [2016] 4 W.L.R. 95; [2017] 2 F.L.R. 18; [2016] Fam. Law 955, Fam Ct .... *Digested,* 16/**921**

T v Scottish Ministers 2017 S.L.T. (Sh Ct) 233; 2017 G.W.D. 29-466, Sh Ct (Tayside) (Falkirk) .... *Digested,* 17/**2748**

T (A Child) (Adoption: Notice of Proceedings), Re [2017] EWFC 19; [2017] 4 W.L.R. 63, Fam Ct .... *Digested,* 17/**916**

T (A Child) (Care Proceedings: Request to Assume Jurisdiction), Re; *sub nom* K (A Child) (Brussels II Revised: Art.15), Re; T (A Child: Article 15 of Brussels II Revised), Re; A Local Authority v A Mother; K (A Child) (Care Proceedings: Jurisdiction), Re [2013] EWHC 521 (Fam); [2013] Fam. 253; [2013] 2 W.L.R. 1263; [2013] 2 F.L.R. 909; [2013] Fam. Law 788, Fam Div .... *Digested,* 13/**1282**: *Affirmed in part* 14/1355: *Considered* 14/1285, 17/980

T (A Child) (Care Proceedings: Request to Assume Jurisdiction), Re; *sub nom* K (A Child) (Brussels II Revised: Art.15), Re; T (A Child: Article 15 of Brussels II Revised), Re; A Local Authority v A Mother; K (A Child) (Care Proceedings: Jurisdiction), Re [2013] EWCA Civ 895; [2014] Fam. 130; [2014] 2 W.L.R. 1204; [2014] 1 F.L.R. 749; [2014] 2 F.C.R. 369; [2014] Fam. Law 281; [2013] Fam. Law 1381, CA (Civ Div) .... *Digested,* 14/**1355**: *Applied* 14/1287: *Followed* 17/926

T (A Child) (Contact: Alienation: Permission to Appeal), Re [2002] EWCA Civ 1736; [2003] 1 F.L.R. 531; [2003] 1 F.C.R. 303; Times, October 30, 2002; [2003] Fam. Law 151, CA (Civ Div) .... *Digested,* 02/**1614**: *Applied* 10/26: *Considered* 12/1357: *Followed* 12/1347, 15/334, 17/1282

T (A Child) (Early Permanence Placement), Re [2015] EWCA Civ 983; [2017] 1 F.L.R. 330; [2016] 1 F.C.R. 521; [2015] Fam. Law 1451, CA (Civ Div) .... *Digested,* 16/**810**

T (A Child) (Suspension of Contact: Section 91(14) CA 1989), Re [2015] EWCA Civ 719; [2016] 1 F.L.R. 916; [2017] 1 F.C.R. 48; [2015] Fam. Law 1180, CA (Civ Div) .... *Digested,* 16/**924**

T (A Child), Re; *sub nom* Medway Council v M ME15C00859, Fam Ct *Applied* 17/995

T (A Child), Re [2016] EWCA Civ 1210; [2017] 1 F.C.R. 428, CA (Civ Div) .... *Digested,* 17/**1056**

T (A Child: Article 15 of Brussels II Revised), Re see T (A Child) (Care Proceedings: Request to Assume Jurisdiction), Re

T (A Minor) (Liver Transplant: Consent), Re see T (A Minor) (Wardship: Medical Treatment), Re

T (A Minor) (Wardship: Medical Treatment), Re; *sub nom* T (A Minor) (Liver Transplant: Consent), Re; C (A Minor) (Medical Treatment: Refusal of Parental Consent), Re [1997] 1 W.L.R. 242; [1997] 1 All E.R. 906; [1997] 1 F.L.R. 502; [1997] 2 F.C.R. 363; [1997] 8 Med. L.R. 166; (1997) 35 B.M.L.R. 63; Times, October 28, 1996; Independent, October 29, 1996; (1996) 93(42) L.S.G. 28; (1996) 146 N.L.J. 1577; (1996) 140 S.J.L.B. 237, CA (Civ Div) .... *Digested,* 96/**546**: *Considered* 03/1777, 17/958: *Followed* 99/2370

Target Holdings Ltd v Redferns [1996] A.C. 421; [1995] 3 W.L.R. 352; [1995] 3 All E.R. 785; [1995] C.L.C. 1052; Times, July 21, 1995; Independent, August 10, 1995; (1995) 139 S.J.L.B. 195; [1995] N.P.C. 136, HL ..... *Digested,* 95/**2195**: *Applied* 00/2332, 03/4472, 13/689: *Considered* 96/3909, 97/3979, 99/1401, 01/729, 03/4475, 11/2707, 12/275, 13/3172: *Followed* 13/227, 14/2055, 15/167, 17/1276

Tartan Army Ltd v SETT GmbH [2017] CSOH 22; 2017 S.L.T. 532; 2017 G.W.D. 8-117, OH ..... *Digested,* 17/**2689**

Taser International Inc v SC Gate 4 Business SRL (C-175/15) EU:C:2016:176; [2016] Q.B. 887; [2016] 3 W.L.R. 683; [2017] 1 All E.R. (Comm) 289; [2017] C.E.C. 147; [2016] E.T.M.R. 28; [2016] I.L.Pr. 28, ECJ (6th Chamber)

Taylor v Betterment Properties (Weymouth) Ltd see Betterment Properties (Weymouth) Ltd v Dorset CC

Taylor v East Midlands Offender Employment; *sub nom* Taylor v Lowe [2000] I.R.L.R. 760, EAT ..... *Digested,* 00/**2177**: *Considered* 17/808

Taylor v General Medical Council [1990] 2 A.C. 539; [1990] 2 W.L.R. 1423; [1990] 2 All E.R. 263; [1990] 2 Med. L.R. 45; (1990) 87(20) L.S.G. 36; (1990) 134 S.J. 757, PC (UK) ..... *Digested,* 90/**88**: *Considered* 08/1804, 17/1807

Taylor v Honiton Town Council [2017] EWHC 101 (Admin); [2017] 1 Costs L.R. 31, QBD (Admin) ..... *Digested,* 17/**228**

Taylor v Honiton Town Council see R. (on the application of Taylor) v Honiton Town Council

Taylor v Ladbrokes Betting and Gaming Ltd [2017] I.R.L.R. 312, EAT ..... *Digested,* 17/**781**

Taylor v Lawrence [2002] EWCA Civ 90; [2003] Q.B. 528; [2002] 3 W.L.R. 640; [2002] 2 All E.R. 353; [2002] C.P. Rep. 29; Times, February 8, 2002; Independent, February 14, 2002; Daily Telegraph, February 14, 2002; (2002) 99(12) L.S.G. 35; (2002) 152 N.L.J. 221; (2002) 146 S.J.L.B. 50, CA (Civ Div) ..... *Digested,* 02/**294**: *Applied* 02/296, 03/443, 04/255, 05/464, 06/30, 11/372, 11/762, 15/616: *Considered* 03/453, 06/518, 07/3387, 07/510, 14/1604, 17/2125: *Distinguished* 08/1937: *Explained* 04/870: *Followed* 03/842, 11/493, 15/339

Taylor v Lowe see Taylor v East Midlands Offender Employment

Taylor v Quigley [2016] CSOH 178; 2017 Rep. L.R. 37; 2017 G.W.D. 1-2, OH ..... *Digested,* 17/**2446**

Taylor v Rover Co Ltd [1966] 1 W.L.R. 1491; [1966] 2 All E.R. 181, Assizes (Birmingham) ..... *Digested,* 66/**8274**: *Applied* 17/2193: *Considered* 93/5668

Taylor v Southern Pacific Mortgages Ltd see North East Property Buyers Litigation, Re

Taylor v Taylor [2017] EWHC 1080 (Ch); [2017] 4 W.L.R. 83; [2017] 2 P. & C.R. DG16, Ch D (Bristol) ..... *Digested,* 17/**1827**

Taylor v Van Dutch Marine Holding Ltd [2017] EWHC 636 (Ch); [2017] 1 W.L.R. 2571; [2017] 4 All E.R. 627; [2018] 1 All E.R. (Comm) 250; [2018] 1 B.C.L.C. 275, Ch D ..... *Digested,* 17/**303**

Taylor Clark Leisure Plc v Revenue and Customs Commissioners [2016] CSIH 54; [2016] S.T.C. 2492; 2016 S.C. 843; 2016 S.L.T. 873; 2017 S.C.L.R. 277; [2016] B.V.C. 27; [2016] L.L.R. 853; 2016 G.W.D. 22-418, IH (Ex Div) ..... *Digested,* 16/**2834**: *Considered* 17/2290: *Followed* 17/2289

Taylor Fashions Ltd v Liverpool Victoria Trustees Co Ltd; *joined case* Old & Campbell Ltd v Liverpool Victoria Friendly Society [1982] Q.B. 133; [1981] 2 W.L.R. 576; [1981] 1 All E.R. 897; [1981] Com. L.R. 34; (1979) 251 E.G. 159, Ch D ..... *Digested,* 79/**1619**: *Applied* 03/2496, 04/2253, 06/3494, 09/1363, 09/3175, 15/2121, 16/1825, 17/406: *Considered* 85/1909, 86/1901, 86/3551, 87/1444, 96/3694, 99/4369, 08/3081, 10/2730, 13/2462: *Followed* 96/988: *Referred to* 82/1145, 92/2054, 95/4938, 97/1056

Taylor Sinclair (Capital) Ltd (In Liquidation), Re see Knights v Seymour Pierce Ellis Ltd (formerly Ellis & Partners Ltd)

Taylor Walton (A Firm) v Laing see Laing v Taylor Walton (A Firm)

Taylor Wimpey Plc v Revenue and Customs Commissioners [2017] UKUT 34 (TCC); [2017] S.T.C. 639; [2017] B.V.C. 505, UT (Tax) ..... *Digested,* 17/**2242**

Tayside Public Transport Co Ltd (t/a Travel Dundee) v Reilly [2012] CSIH 46; 2012 S.L.T. 1191; [2012] I.R.L.R. 755; 2012 G.W.D. 19-386, IH (2 Div) ..... *Digested,* 12/**3988**: *Applied* 17/821

TB (Jamaica) v Secretary of State for the Home Department see R. (on the application of TB (Jamaica)) v Secretary of State for the Home Department

Tchenguiz v Director of the Serious Fraud Office; *sub nom* Rawlinson & Hunter Trustees SA v Director of the Serious Fraud Office [2014] EWCA Civ 1129; [2015] 1 W.L.R. 797; [2014] C.P. Rep. 45, CA (Civ Div) .... *Digested,* 14/**294**: *Applied* 17/183

Tchenguiz v Grant Thornton UK LLP; *sub nom* Tchenguiz v Kaupthing Bank HF [2017] EWCA Civ 83; [2018] 2 W.L.R. 834; [2017] 2 B.C.L.C. 299, CA (Civ Div) *Digested,* 17/**1332**

Tchenguiz v Grant Thornton UK LLP [2017] EWHC 310 (Comm); [2017] 1 W.L.R. 2809; [2017] 4 All E.R. 895; [2018] 1 All E.R. (Comm) 63; [2017] Lloyd's Rep. F.C. 216, QBD (Comm) .... *Digested,* 17/**182**

Tchenguiz v Grant Thornton UK LLP; *sub nom* Tchenguiz v Kaupthing Bank HF [2015] EWHC 1864 (Comm); [2015] 2 B.C.L.C. 307, QBD (Comm) .... *Digested,* 15/**310**: *Affirmed* 17/1332

Tchenguiz v Imerman; *sub nom* Imerman v Tchenguiz; *joined case* Imerman v Imerman [2010] EWCA Civ 908; [2011] Fam. 116; [2011] 2 W.L.R. 592; [2011] 1 All E.R. 555; [2010] 2 F.L.R. 814; [2010] 3 F.C.R. 371; Times, September 2, 2010; [2010] Fam. Law 1177; (2010) 154(30) S.J.L.B. 32, CA (Civ Div) .... *Digested,* 10/**1280**: *Applied* 14/496, 16/893, 17/2195: *Followed* 11/369

Tchenguiz v Kaupthing Bank HF see Tchenguiz v Grant Thornton UK LLP

TCO In-well Technologies UK Ltd v Stuart [2017] I.C.R. 1175, EAT .... *Digested,* 17/**797**

TD (Nigeria) v Secretary of State for the Home Department see HA (Afghanistan) v Secretary of State for the Home Department

Teal Assurance Co Ltd v WR Berkley Insurance (Europe) Ltd; *sub nom* WR Berkley Insurance (Europe) Ltd v Teal Assurance Co Ltd [2017] EWCA Civ 25; [2017] 1 C.L.C. 19; [2017] Lloyd's Rep. I.R. 259, CA (Civ Div) .... *Digested,* 17/**1352**: *Followed* 17/1338

Teal Assurance Co Ltd v WR Berkley Insurance (Europe) Ltd; *sub nom* WR Berkley Insurance (Europe) Ltd v Teal Assurance Co Ltd [2015] EWHC 1000 (Comm); [2015] 1 C.L.C. 925; [2016] Lloyd's Rep. I.R. 134, QBD (Comm) .... *Digested,* 16/**1273**: *Affirmed* 17/1352

Teasdale v HSBC Bank Plc; *joined cases* Atkinson v Bank of Scotland Plc; Cuthbertson v Tesco Personal Finance Plc; Mills v Marks and Spencer Financial Services Plc; Backwell v Royal Bank of Scotland Plc; Jemitus v Bank of Scotland Plc; Brookes v HSBC Bank Plc [2010] EWHC 612 (QB); [2010] 4 All E.R. 630; [2010] 4 Costs L.R. 543; [2010] C.T.L.C. 19, QBD (Merc) (Manchester) .... *Digested,* 10/**299**: *Applied* 13/303, 17/1373

Ted Baker Plc v Axa Insurance UK Plc [2017] EWCA Civ 4097; [2017] Lloyd's Rep. I.R. 682, CA (Civ Div)

Tedcom Finance Ltd v Vetabet Holdings Ltd [2011] EWCA Civ 191; [2012] 1 C.L.C. 950; [2011] Arb. L.R. 8, CA (Civ Div) *Considered* 17/334

Teekay Tankers Ltd v STX Offshore & Shipping Co [2014] EWHC 3612 (Comm); [2015] 2 All E.R. (Comm) 263; [2015] Bus. L.R. 731; [2015] 2 B.C.L.C. 210; [2014] 2 C.L.C. 763, QBD (Comm) .... *Digested,* 15/**361**: *Considered* 17/337

Teekay Tankers Ltd v STX Offshore and Shipbuilding Co Ltd [2017] EWHC 253 (Comm); [2018] 1 All E.R. (Comm) 279; [2017] 1 Lloyd's Rep. 387, QBD (Comm) .... *Digested,* 17/**500**

Tees Esk and Wear Valleys NHS Foundation Trust v Harland [2017] I.C.R. 760; [2017] I.R.L.R. 486, EAT .... *Digested,* 17/**841**

Tekdemir v Kreis Bergstrasse (C-652/15) EU:C:2017:239; [2017] 3 C.M.L.R. 25, ECJ (1st Chamber)

Tele2 Sverige AB v Post- och telestyrelsen (C-203/15); *sub nom* R. (on the application of Watson) v Secretary of State for the Home Department (C-698/15); *joined case* Secretary of State for the Home Department v Watson (C-698/15) EU:C:2016:970; [2017] Q.B. 771; [2017] 2 W.L.R. 1289; [2017] 2 C.M.L.R. 30, ECJ (Grand Chamber) .... *Digested,* 17/**894**

Telegraph Group Plc, Ex p. see R. (on the application of Telegraph Group Plc) v Sherwood

Teletape (A Firm) v Revenue and Customs Commissioners [2016] UKFTT 797 (TC); [2017] S.T.I. 117, FTT (Tax)

Telewest Communications Plc v Customs and Excise Commissioners [2005] EWCA Civ 102; [2005] S.T.C. 481; [2005] B.T.C. 5125; [2005] B.V.C. 156; Times, February 21, 2005; [2005] S.T.I. 220; (2005) 102(17) L.S.G. 33, CA (Civ Div) ... *Digested,* 05/**4419**: *Applied* 17/2248: *Followed* 11/3561

Telfair Shipping Corp v Inersea Carriers SA (The Caroline P) [1985] 1 W.L.R. 553; [1985] 1 All E.R. 243; [1984] 2 Lloyd's Rep. 466; (1985) 82 L.S.G. 1781; (1985) 129 S.J. 283, QBD (Comm) .... *Digested*, 85/**2012**:
Applied 04/2240, 17/1342: *Considered* 00/878

TelNG Ltd v Revenue and Customs Commissioners [2015] UKFTT 327 (TC); [2015] S.T.I. 2416, FTT (Tax)
Affirmed 17/2154

TelNG Ltd v Revenue and Customs Commissioners [2016] UKUT 363 (TCC); [2016] B.V.C. 537; [2016] S.T.I. 2545, UT (Tax) .... *Digested*, 17/**2154**

Temple Finance Ltd v Revenue and Customs Commissioners; *sub nom* Revenue and Customs Commissioners v Temple Finance Ltd [2017] UKUT 315 (TCC); [2017] S.T.C. 1781; [2017] B.V.C. 524; [2017] S.T.I. 1862, UT (Tax) .... *Digested*, 17/**2248**

Temple Finance Ltd v Revenue and Customs Commissioners; *sub nom* Revenue and Customs Commissioners v Temple Finance Ltd [2016] UKFTT 41 (TC); [2016] S.T.I. 369, FTT (Tax)
Affirmed 17/2248

Ten Oever v Stichting Bedrijfspensioenfonds voor het Glazenwassers- en Schoonmaakbedrijf (C-109/91); *joined cases* Coloroll Pension Trustees Ltd v Russell (C-200/91); Neath v Hugh Steeper Ltd (C-152/91); Moroni v Collo GmbH (C-110/91) EU:C:1993:833; [1993] E.C.R. I-4879; [1995] 2 C.M.L.R. 357; [1995] I.C.R. 74; [1993] I.R.L.R. 601; [1993] Pens. L.R. 317; Times, October 12, 1993; Financial Times, October 5, 1993, ECJ .... *Digested*, 94/**4814**:
Applied 08/2732, 14/1120, 15/1858: *Considered* 17/1620: *Followed* 14/1087

TENARIS/Entitlement to priority (T577/11) [2017] E.P.O.R. 19, EPO (Technical Bd App)

Tenax Steamship Co v Owners of the Motor Vessel Brimnes (The Brimnes); *sub nom* Tenax Steamship Co v Reinante Transoceanica Navegacion SA (The Brimnes) [1975] Q.B. 929; [1974] 3 W.L.R. 613; [1974] 3 All E.R. 88; [1974] 2 Lloyd's Rep. 241; (1974) 118 S.J. 808, CA (Civ Div) .... *Digested*, 74/**3560**:
Applied 76/140, 81/2486, 17/344: *Approved* 77/2747: *Considered* 75/3168, 76/2546: *Distinguished* 77/2750

Tenax Steamship Co v Reinante Transoceanica Navegacion SA (The Brimnes) see Tenax Steamship Co v Owners of the Motor Vessel Brimnes (The Brimnes)

Tendler v Sproule [1947] 1 All E.R. 193, CA .... *Digested*, 47-51/**8679**:
Applied 63/1953: *Considered* 17/1443: *Distinguished* 78/1821

Tennant (Thomas) v HM Advocate see Wood (Kenneth) v HM Advocate

Tenzin v Russell 2015 Hous. L.R. 11; 2015 G.W.D. 4-88, IH (Ex Div) .... *Digested*, 15/**3188**:
Applied 17/2840

Terna Bahrain Holding Co WLL v Al Shamsi; *joined case* Al Shamsi v Terna Bahrain Holding Co WLL [2012] EWHC 3283 (Comm); [2013] 1 All E.R. (Comm) 580; [2013] 1 Lloyd's Rep. 86; [2013] 2 C.L.C. 1; 145 Con. L.R. 114, QBD (Comm) .. *Digested*, 13/**113**:
Applied 16/65: *Considered* 14/133, 15/95, 17/66

Tesco Freetime Ltd v Revenue and Customs Commissioners [2017] UKFTT 614 (TC); [2018] S.F.T.D. 274; [2017] S.T.I. 1903, FTT (Tax)

Tesco Stores Ltd v Dundee City Council [2012] UKSC 13; [2012] P.T.S.R. 983; 2012 S.C. (U.K.S.C.) 278; 2012 S.L.T. 739; [2012] 2 P. & C.R. 9; [2012] J.P.L. 1078; [2012] 13 E.G. 91 (C.S.); 2012 G.W.D. 12-235, SC .... *Digested*, 12/**2595**:
Applied 12/2542, 13/2290, 15/2046, 16/1754, 17/1767, 17/22: *Considered* 15/1996, 16/2766, 17/1725: *Explained* 15/1947: *Followed* 14/2384, 14/2395, 14/2397, 16/1722, 17/1097, 17/1724, 17/1769, 17/1785

Tesco Stores Ltd v Fife Council Assessor [2016] CSIH 76; 2016 S.L.T. 1260; [2017] R.A. 83; 2016 G.W.D. 32-581, LVAC .... *Digested*, 17/**2726**

Tesco Stores Ltd v Secretary of State for the Environment; *joined cases* Tesco Stores Ltd v Tarmac Provincial Properties Ltd; Tesco Stores Ltd v West Oxfordshire DC [1995] 1 W.L.R. 759; [1995] 2 All E.R. 636; 93 L.G.R. 403; (1995) 70 P. & C.R. 184; [1995] 2 P.L.R. 72; [1995] 2 E.G.L.R. 147; [1995] 27 E.G. 154; Times, May 13, 1995; [1995] E.G. 82 (C.S.); (1995) 92(24) L.S.G. 39; (1995) 145 N.L.J. 724; (1995) 139 S.J.L.B. 145, HL .... *Digested*, 95/**4784**:
Applied 96/4779, 99/4215, 01/4682, 01/4731, 03/2057, 11/2551, 12/2324, 13/2358, 16/1741, 17/1761: *Considered* 99/3049, 07/2988, 07/3291, 09/1736, 09/2981, 12/2577, 13/2349, 14/2354: *Followed* 03/3438, 13/2348, 14/2399, 14/2422, 16/1714, 16/781

Tesco Stores Ltd v Tarmac Provincial Properties Ltd see Tesco Stores Ltd v Secretary of State for the Environment

Tesco Stores Ltd v West Oxfordshire DC see Tesco Stores Ltd v Secretary of State for the Environment

Tesco Supermarkets Ltd v Nattrass [1972] A.C. 153; [1971] 2 W.L.R. 1166; [1971] 2 All E.R. 127; 69 L.G.R. 403; (1971) 115 S.J. 285, HL .... *Digested,* 71/**10538**: *Applied* 72/3464, 72/594, 82/2783, 85/3116, 87/4197, 93/3642, 96/969, 04/4634: *Considered* 73/3036, 84/958, 88/851, 02/837, 07/2814, 09/3959, 11/696, 17/511: *Distinguished* 88/175, 93/3559, 95/5132, 96/3020: *Followed* 74/**3441**, 12/687

Test Claimants in the FII Group Litigation v Inland Revenue Commissioners (C-35/11); *sub nom* Test Claimants in the FII Group Litigation v Revenue and Customs Commissioners (C-35/11) EU:C:2012:707; [2013] Ch. 431; [2013] 2 W.L.R. 1416; [2013] S.T.C. 612; [2013] 1 C.M.L.R. 50; [2013] B.T.C. 424; [2012] S.T.I. 3271, ECJ (Grand Chamber) *Considered* 16/2054: *Followed* 14/2874, 16/2057, 17/2114

Test Claimants in the FII Group Litigation v Revenue and Customs Commissioners; *sub nom* Test Claimants in the Franked Investment Income Group Litigation v Revenue and Customs Commissioners; Evonik Degussa UK Holdings Ltd v Revenue and Customs Commissioners [2016] EWCA Civ 1180; [2017] S.T.C. 696; [2017] 1 C.M.L.R. 37; [2016] B.T.C. 44, CA (Civ Div) .... *Digested,* 17/**2080**

Test Claimants in the FII Group Litigation v Revenue and Customs Commissioners; *sub nom* Test Claimants in the Franked Investment Income Group Litigation v Revenue and Customs Commissioners; Evonik Degussa UK Holdings Ltd v Revenue and Customs Commissioners [2014] EWHC 4302 (Ch); [2015] S.T.C. 1471; [2015] B.T.C. 3; [2015] S.T.I. 49, Ch D .... *Digested,* 15/**2422**: *Affirmed* 17/2080: *Cited* 16/2054

Test Claimants in the FII Group Litigation v Revenue and Customs Commissioners (C-35/11) see Test Claimants in the FII Group Litigation v Inland Revenue Commissioners (C-35/11)

Test Claimants in the Franked Investment Income Group Litigation v Revenue and Customs Commissioners see Test Claimants in the FII Group Litigation v Revenue and Customs Commissioners

Teva UK Ltd v Boehringer Ingelheim Pharma GmbH & Co KG [2016] EWCA Civ 1296; [2017] 4 All E.R. 976; [2017] F.S.R. 29, CA (Civ Div) .... *Digested,* 17/**1368**

Teva UK Ltd v Merck Sharp & Dohme Corp [2017] EWHC 539 (Pat); (2017) 155 B.M.L.R. 150, Ch D (Patents Ct) .... *Digested,* 17/**1386**

Texan Management Ltd v Pacific Electric Wire and Cable Co Ltd [2009] UKPC 46, PC (BVI) *Applied* 17/297: *Considered* 14/558, 16/269

Texas Keystone Inc v Psari Holdings Ltd see Excalibur Ventures LLC v Texas Keystone Inc

TF v PJ (Reversal of Judgment) see F (A Child) (Return Order: Power to Revoke), Re

TFS Derivatives Ltd v Morgan [2004] EWHC 3181 (QB); [2005] I.R.L.R. 246, QBD ...... *Digested,* 05/**700**: *Applied* 11/1115, 13/1048, 17/824: *Considered* 09/1222

TG (A Child) (Care Proceedings: Biomechanical Engineering Evidence), Re; *sub nom* TG (Children) (Care Proceedings: Case Management: Expert Evidence), Re [2013] EWCA Civ 5; [2013] 1 F.L.R. 1250; [2013] 1 F.C.R. 229; (2013) 130 B.M.L.R. 169; [2013] Fam. Law 264, CA (Civ Div) .... *Digested,* 13/**1224**: *Applied* 14/1322, 15/1004, 16/879: *Followed* 17/998

TG (Children) (Care Proceedings: Case Management: Expert Evidence), Re see TG (A Child) (Care Proceedings: Biomechanical Engineering Evidence), Re

Thaine v London School of Economics [2010] I.C.R. 1422; [2010] Eq. L.R. 268, EAT .. *Digested,* 11/**1046**: *Approved* 17/826: *Cited* 17/2583

Thakkar v Patel [2017] EWCA Civ 117; [2017] 2 Costs L.R. 233, CA (Civ Div) .... *Digested,* 17/**266**

Thakkar v Thakkar [2016] EWHC 2488 (Fam); [2016] 4 W.L.R. 164; [2017] 2 F.L.R. 399, Fam Div .... *Digested,* 16/**869**

Thales UK Ltd v Thales Pension Trustees Ltd [2017] EWHC 666 (Ch); [2017] Pens. L.R. 15, Ch D .... *Digested,* 17/**1617**

Thames Water Utilities Ltd v Marcic see Marcic v Thames Water Utilities Ltd

Thames Water Utilities Ltd v Reynolds [1996] I.R.L.R. 186, EAT .... *Digested,* 96/**2673**: *Considered* 02/1335, 17/808: *Followed* 00/2177

Thatcher v CH Pearce & Sons (Contractors), Ltd [1968] 1 W.L.R. 748; (1968) 19 P. & C.R. 682; (1967) 112 S.J. 379, Assizes (Bristol) .... *Digested,* 68/**2205**: *Applied* 17/1447: *Considered* 84/1916

Thathiah v Revenue and Customs Commissioners [2017] UKFTT 601 (TC); [2017] S.T.I. 1900, FTT (Tax)

The Queensland Mercantile and Agency Company, Limited, and Liquidator v Australasian Investment Company, Limited (1888) 15 R. 935, IH (1 Div) *Considered* 17/2447

Thefaut v Johnston [2017] EWHC 497 (QB); [2017] Med. L.R. 319, QBD .... *Digested,* 17/**1642**

Thera East v Valentine [2017] I.R.L.R. 878, EAT .... *Digested,* 17/**856**

Thermal Energy Construction Ltd v AE&E Lentjes UK Ltd [2009] EWHC 408 (TCC), QBD (TCC)
Considered 10/845, 17/2461

Thermal Systems Cartel, Re (AT.39960) [2017] 5 C.M.L.R. 4, CEC

Thevarajah v Riordan [2015] UKSC 78; [2016] 1 W.L.R. 76; [2017] 1 All E.R. 329; [2015] 6 Costs L.R. 1119; Times, December 23, 2015, SC .... *Digested,* 16/**304**: *Applied* 17/2182

Thomas v Bridgend CBC [2011] EWCA Civ 862; [2012] Q.B. 512; [2012] 2 W.L.R. 624; [2012] P.T.S.R. 441; [2012] H.L.R. 1; [2011] R.V.R. 241; [2012] J.P.L. 25, CA (Civ Div) .... *Digested,* 11/**1686**: *Applied* 13/2506: *Followed* 17/1436

Thomas v Frogmore Real Estate Partners GP1 Ltd; *sub nom* FREP (Belle Vale) Ltd (In Administration), Re; FREP (Ellesmere Port) Ltd (In Administration), Re; FREP (Knowle) Ltd (In Administration), Re; *joined case* Frogmore Real Estate Partners GP1 Ltd v Thomas [2017] EWHC 25 (Ch); [2017] Bus. L.R. 1117; [2018] B.C.C. 67; [2017] 2 B.C.L.C. 101; [2017] B.P.I.R. 771, Ch D (Companies Ct) .... *Digested,* 17/**1257**

Thomas v HM Advocate 2001 G.W.D. 24-913, HCJ Appeal
Followed 17/2799

Thomas v Hugh James Ford Simey Solicitors [2017] EWCA Civ 1303; [2017] 5 Costs L.O. 643; [2018] P.N.L.R. 5, CA (Civ Div) .... *Digested,* 17/**1576**

Thomas v Mariner Properties Ltd see D'Eye, Re

Thomas v Merthyr Tydfil Car Auction Ltd; *joined case* Merthyr Tydfil Car Auction Ltd v Thomas [2013] EWCA Civ 815; 149 Con. L.R. 105; [2014] Env. L.R. 4; [2014] L.L.R. 550, CA (Civ Div) .... *Digested,* 14/**2222**: *Followed* 17/2251

Thomas v Thomas [1947] A.C. 484; [1947] 1 All E.R. 582; 1947 S.C. (H.L.) 45; 1948 S.L.T. 2; 1947 S.L.T. (Notes) 53; 63 T.L.R. 314; [1948] L.J.R. 515; 176 L.T. 498, HL .... *Digested,* 47-51/**7496**: *Applied* 47-51/10957, 47-51/2723, 47-51/9902, 52/987, 55/2078, 59/431, 70/3157, 76/338, 98/5439, 98/6102, 01/6217, 03/3539, 13/3902, 13/3956, 17/2616: *Considered* 74/1069, 91/5082, 94/3280, 94/3439, 03/5285, 05/10, 15/1769, 15/3076, 16/2740: *Distinguished* 90/4099: *Followed* 86/4416, 88/4930, 08/5003, 13/6, 14/1579: *Not applied* 51/3869

Thomas Bates & Son Ltd v Wyndham's (Lingerie) Ltd [1981] 1 W.L.R. 505; [1981] 1 All E.R. 1077; (1981) 41 P. & C.R. 345; (1980) 257 E.G. 381; (1981) 125 S.J. 32, CA (Civ Div) .... *Digested,* 81/**1584**: *Applied* 83/417, 84/1932, 89/2140, 96/3756, 00/4382, 01/5510, 05/3974, 07/806, 17/1817: *Cited* 95/780: *Considered* 83/1215, 84/2943, 96/5784, 06/2689: *Distinguished* 90/2833, 92/5952

Thomas Cook Airlines Ltd v British Airline Pilots Association [2017] EWHC 2253 (QB); [2017] I.R.L.R. 1137, QBD

Thompson v Director of Legal Aid Casework [2017] EWHC 230 (Admin); [2017] 1 Costs L.R. 163, QBD (Admin) .... *Digested,* 17/**1483**

Thompson v News Group Newspapers Ltd see Venables v News Group Newspapers Ltd

Thompson v Renwick Group Plc [2014] EWCA Civ 635; [2015] B.C.C. 855; [2014] 2 B.C.L.C. 97; [2014] P.I.Q.R. P18, CA (Civ Div) .... *Digested,* 14/**2202**: *Applied* 17/2194

Thompson v Sayegh 2015 G.W.D. 7-132, Sh Ct (Lothian) (Edinburgh)
Applied 17/2445

Thomson v Glasgow Corp 1962 S.C. (H.L.) 36; 1962 S.L.T. 105, HL .... *Digested,* 62/**3636**: *Applied* 97/5653: *Considered* 91/5679, 08/4588, 16/2461, 17/2435: *Followed* 11/4278

Thomson v Thomas Muir (Waste Management) Ltd 1995 S.L.T. 403, OH .... *Digested,* 95/**6062**: *Applied* 17/2461

Thomson v Yorkshire Building Society (Bankruptcy: Title to Sue) 1994 S.C.L.R. 1014, Sh Pr .... *Digested,* 95/**5485**: *Distinguished* 17/2677

Thorne v Revenue and Customs Commissioners [2014] UKFTT 730 (TC); [2014] S.T.I. 3025, FTT (Tax)
Reversed 17/2146

Thorne v Revenue and Customs Commissioners [2016] UKUT 349 (TCC); [2016] B.T.C. 516; [2016] S.T.I. 2592, UT (Tax) .... *Digested,* 17/**2146**

Thorner v Curtis see Thorner v Major

Thorner v Major; *sub nom* Thorner v Curtis; Thorner v Majors [2009] UKHL 18; [2009] 1 W.L.R. 776; [2009] 3 All E.R. 945; [2009] 2 F.L.R. 405; [2009] 3 F.C.R. 123; [2009] 2 P. & C.R. 24; [2009] 2 E.G.L.R. 111; [2009] W.T.L.R. 713; (2009-10) 12 I.T.E.L.R. 62; Times, March 26, 2009; [2009] Fam. Law 583; [2009] 13 E.G. 142 (C.S.); (2009) 159 N.L.J. 514; (2009) 153(12) S.J.L.B. 30; [2009] N.P.C. 50; [2009] 2 P. & C.R. DG2, HL .... *Digested,* 09/**3723**:
Applied 10/1240, 15/2411, 16/1825: *Followed* 11/1250, 15/2121, 17/1825

Thorner v Majors see Thorner v Major

Thornton Springer v NEM Insurance Co Ltd [2000] 2 All E.R. 489; [2000] 1 All E.R. (Comm) 486; [2000] C.L.C. 975; [2000] Lloyd's Rep. I.R. 590; (2000) 97(13) L.S.G. 42; (2000) 144 S.J.L.B. 147, QBD (Comm) .... *Digested,* 00/**3555**:
Followed 17/1342

Thorsen v Richmond Society for the Prevention of Cruelty to Animals 19 I.T.E.L.R. 289, US Court

Thrasyvoulou v Secretary of State for the Environment; *joined case* Oliver v Secretary of State for the Environment [1990] 2 A.C. 273; [1990] 2 W.L.R. 1; [1990] 1 All E.R. 65; 88 L.G.R. 217; (1990) 2 Admin. L.R. 289; (1990) 59 P. & C.R. 326; [1990] 1 P.L.R. 69; [1990] 13 E.G. 69; (1990) 154 L.G. Rev. 192; [1989] E.G. 178 (C.S.), HL .... *Digested,* 90/**4426**:
Applied 91/3509, 97/4075, 97/4109, 06/3293, 07/2677: *Considered* 94/4363, 98/1981, 06/1949, 11/1, 13/979, 17/2125: *Distinguished* 92/4216, 07/3225: *Followed* 97/4039

Three Rivers DC v Bank of England (Disclosure) (No.1); *sub nom* Three Rivers DC v HM Treasury; Three Rivers DC v Bank of England (No.5); Three Rivers DC v Bank of England (No.4) [2002] EWCA Civ 1182; [2003] 1 W.L.R. 210; [2002] 4 All E.R. 881; [2003] C.P. Rep. 9; [2003] C.P.L.R. 181; Times, October 4, 2002; Independent, November 11, 2002; (2002) 99(39) L.S.G. 40, CA (Civ Div) .... *Digested,* 02/**426**:
Considered 03/282: *Distinguished* 03/2397: *Followed* 17/187

Three Rivers DC v Bank of England (Disclosure) (No.3) [2003] EWCA Civ 474; [2003] Q.B. 1556; [2003] 3 W.L.R. 667; [2003] C.P.L.R. 349; Times, April 19, 2003; (2003) 100(23) L.S.G. 37, CA (Civ Div) .... *Digested,* 04/**370**:
Considered 11/2116: *Followed* 17/186

Three Rivers DC v Bank of England (Disclosure) (No.4) [2004] UKHL 48; [2005] 1 A.C. 610; [2004] 3 W.L.R. 1274; [2005] 4 All E.R. 948; Times, November 12, 2004; Independent, November 16, 2004; (2004) 101(46) L.S.G. 34; (2004) 154 N.L.J. 1727; (2004) 148 S.J.L.B. 1369, HL .... *Digested,* 05/**299**:
Applied 07/470, 08/3863, 14/2934, 16/155, 16/156: *Considered* 07/999, 09/4206: *Followed* 12/548, 17/530

Three Rivers DC v Bank of England (Indemnity Costs) [2006] EWHC 816 (Comm); [2006] 5 Costs L.R. 714, QBD (Comm) .... *Digested,* 07/**398**:
Applied 16/230, 17/241, 17/263: *Considered* 08/318

Three Rivers DC v Bank of England (No.3) [2003] 2 A.C. 1; [2000] 2 W.L.R. 1220; [2000] 3 All E.R. 1; [2000] Lloyd's Rep. Bank. 235; [2000] 3 C.M.L.R. 205; [2000] Eu. L.R. 583; (2000) 2 L.G.L.R. 769; Times, May 19, 2000; (2000) 97(23) L.S.G. 41, HL .... *Digested,* 00/**270**:
Applied 03/4357, 05/4193, 06/4433, 07/2490, 07/538, 09/979, 15/688, 15/995: *Considered* 02/4546, 04/753, 05/4197, 06/4332: *Followed* 17/1563, 17/379

Three Rivers DC v Bank of England (No.3) (Summary Judgment) [2001] UKHL 16; [2003] 2 A.C. 1; [2001] 2 All E.R. 513; [2001] Lloyd's Rep. Bank. 125; (2001) 3 L.G.L.R. 36; Times, March 23, 2001, HL .... *Digested,* 01/**5355**:
Applied 03/509, 05/578, 07/4193, 08/1874, 08/2208, 08/432, 09/711, 15/276: *Considered* 01/669, 02/505, 03/2462, 04/753, 05/4193, 05/4197, 06/4332, 06/4433, 17/2253: *Distinguished* 05/461: *Followed* 03/478, 13/433

Three Rivers DC v Bank of England (No.4) see Three Rivers DC v Bank of England (Disclosure) (No.1)

Three Rivers DC v Bank of England (No.5) see Three Rivers DC v Bank of England (Disclosure) (No.1)

Three Rivers DC v HM Treasury see Three Rivers DC v Bank of England (Disclosure) (No.1)

Threlfall v ECD Insight Ltd (Costs) [2013] EWCA Civ 1444; [2014] 2 Costs L.O. 129; (2013) 163(7586) N.L.J. 18, CA (Civ Div) .... *Digested,* 14/**337**:
Followed 17/250

Thrumster Estate Ltd v Mindt 2017 S.L.T. (Land Ct) 1; 2016 G.W.D. 21-381, Land Ct . *Digested,* 17/**2694**

Thum v Thum [2016] EWHC 2634 (Fam); [2016] 4 W.L.R. 171; [2017] I.L.Pr. 14; [2017] 1 F.C.R. 69, Fam Div .... *Digested,* 17/**1046**

Thurrock BC v West [2012] EWCA Civ 1435; [2013] H.L.R. 5; [2013] 1 P. & C.R. 12; [2013] L. & T.R. 11; [2013] 1 P. & C.R. DG9, CA (Civ Div) .... *Digested,* 13/**1890**:
Applied 14/2000: *Considered* 17/1163, 17/1168

Thwaite v Thwaite [1982] Fam. 1; [1981] 3 W.L.R. 96; [1981] 2 All E.R. 789; (1981) 125 S.J. 307, CA (Civ Div) .... *Digested,* 81/**701**:
Applied 82/193, 82/199.u, 82/952, 83/143.u: *Considered* 83/1097, 84/1671, 85/1672, 86/1083, 86/1102, 93/168, 17/1016: *Distinguished* 08/1420: *Followed* 82/907

Tibbles v SIG Plc (t/a Asphaltic Roofing Supplies) [2012] EWCA Civ 518; [2012] 1 W.L.R. 2591; [2012] 4 All E.R. 259; [2012] C.P. Rep. 32; [2013] 1 Costs L.O. 41, CA (Civ Div) .... *Digested,* 12/**443**:
Applied 15/1079, 17/1013: *Considered* 17/383: *Followed* 13/451, 14/457, 15/210, 16/683

Tietosuojavaltuutettu v Satakunnan Markkinaporssi Oy (C-73/07) EU:C:2008:727; [2008] E.C.R. I-9831; [2010] All E.R. (EC) 213, ECJ (Grand Chamber)
Followed 17/1167

Tillman v Egon Zehnder Ltd see Egon Zehnder Ltd v Tillman

Timab Industries v European Commission (C-411/15 P) EU:C:2017:11; [2017] 4 C.M.L.R. 12, ECJ (10th Chamber)

Times Newspapers Ltd v Flood; *joined cases* Miller v Associated Newspapers Ltd; Frost v MGN Ltd [2014] EWCA Civ 1574, CA (Civ Div)
Affirmed 17/1478

Times Newspapers Ltd v Flood; *joined cases* Miller v Associated Newspapers Ltd; Frost v MGN Ltd [2017] UKSC 33; [2017] 1 W.L.R. 1415; [2017] 4 All E.R. 733; [2017] 2 Costs L.R. 345; [2017] E.M.L.R. 19, SC .... *Digested,* 17/**1478**

Timmins v Gedling BC; *sub nom* R. (on the application of Timmins) v Gedling BC [2015] EWCA Civ 10; [2016] 1 All E.R. 895; [2015] P.T.S.R. 837; [2015] 2 P. & C.R. 12; [2015] J.P.L. 816, CA (Civ Div) .... *Digested,* 15/**1974**:
Applied 16/1693: *Followed* 17/1724

Timmins v Gormley see Locabail (UK) Ltd v Bayfield Properties Ltd (Leave to Appeal)

Timothy James Consulting Ltd v Wilton; *joined case* Wilton v Timothy James Consulting Ltd [2015] I.C.R. 764; [2015] I.R.L.R. 368, EAT .... *Digested,* 15/**860**:
Considered 17/778: *Not followed* 16/2101

Timperley v Hicks (Unreported, March 28, 2017), CC (Stockport) [*IMe Law Ltd, Riverside West, 1 Millsands. Sheffield*] .... *Digested,* 17/**1661**

Tinsley v Manchester City Council [2016] EWHC 2855 (Admin); (2017) 20 C.C.L. Rep. 50; [2017] Med. L.R. 28; [2017] M.H.L.R. 83, QBD (Admin) .... *Digested,* 17/**1540**

TJ v SB [2017] SAC (Civ) 24; 2017 Fam. L.R. 119; 2017 G.W.D. 25-414, SAC .... *Digested,* 17/**2418**

TJB v RJB (Financial Order: Declaration) [2016] EWHC 1171 (Fam); [2017] 1 F.L.R. 1497; [2016] Fam. Law 956, Fam Div

TL (Human Rights: Relevant Person's Representative), Re; *sub nom* L v L [2017] EWCOP 1; [2017] C.O.P.L.R. 216, CP .... *Digested,* 17/**1535**

TM (EEA nationals: Meaning: NI practitioners: Zimbabwe); *sub nom* TM (Zimbabwe) v Secretary of State for the Home Department [2017] UKUT 165 (IAC); [2017] Imm. A.R. 1058, UT (IAC)

TM (Zimbabwe) v Secretary of State for the Home Department see TM (EEA nationals: Meaning: NI practitioners: Zimbabwe)

TMD Gesellschaft fur transfusionsmedizinische Dienste mbH v Finanzamt Kassel II - Hofgeismar (C-412/15) EU:C:2016:738; [2017] S.T.C. 1807; [2016] B.V.C. 36; [2016] S.T.I. 2827, ECJ (3rd Chamber)

Tobias v Tobias [2017] EWFC 46; [2017] 4 W.L.R. 146; [2018] 1 F.L.R. 616; [2017] 3 F.C.R. 399, Fam Ct .... *Digested,* 17/**988**

Tole (Callum Stephen) v HM Advocate [2013] HCJAC 109; 2013 S.L.T. 1227; 2013 S.C.L. 912; 2014 S.C.C.R. 5; 2013 G.W.D. 30-590, HCJ .... *Digested,* 14/**3373**:
Applied 17/2477: *Considered* 15/2966

Tolley v Secretary of State for Work and Pensions (C-430/15) see Secretary of State for Work and Pensions v Tolley (C-430/15)

Tolsma v Inspecteur der Omzetbelasting, Leeuwarden (C-16/93) EU:C:1994:80; [1994] S.T.C. 509; [1994] E.C.R. I-743; [1994] 2 C.M.L.R. 908; [1994] B.V.C. 117; Times, March 29, 1994; [1994] S.T.I. 424, ECJ (6th Chamber) .... *Digested,* 94/**4962**:
Applied 00/5347, 06/4469, 06/4488, 07/4284, 11/3568, 14/3085, 16/2216, 17/2258, 17/2262: *Considered* 98/4891, 02/4790, 08/4029

Tom Hoskins Plc v EMW Law (A Firm) [2010] EWHC 479 (Ch); [2010] E.C.C. 20; (2010) 160 N.L.J. 584, Ch D .... *Digested,* 10/**2291**:
Considered 17/302

Tomas v Spain (35214/09) (2017) 65 E.H.R.R. 24, ECHR

Tomlin v Standard Telephones & Cables Ltd [1969] 1 W.L.R. 1378; [1969] 3 All E.R. 201; [1969] 1 Lloyd's Rep. 309; (1969) 113 S.J. 641, CA (Civ Div) .... *Digested,* 69/**4990**:
Considered 80/13.u, 93/2451: *Followed* 17/292

Tomlinson v Birmingham City Council see Ali v Birmingham City Council

Tomlinson v Congleton BC [2003] UKHL 47; [2004] 1 A.C. 46; [2003] 3 W.L.R. 705; [2003] 3 All E.R. 1122; [2004] P.I.Q.R. P8; Times, August 1, 2003; Independent, October 7, 2003; [2003] 32 E.G. 68 (C.S.); (2003) 100(34) L.S.G. 33; (2003) 153 N.L.J. 1238; (2003) 147 S.J.L.B. 937; [2003] N.P.C. 102, HL ..... *Digested,* 03/**4360**: *Applied* 03/2980, 05/1955, 06/4334, 06/4338, 08/2761, 13/2084: *Considered* 05/4194, 05/4196, 06/4333: *Followed* 11/3474, 14/2208, 16/2144, 17/1564, 17/2200

Tommy Hilfiger Licensing LLC v Delta Center as (C-494/15) EU:C:2016:528; [2016] Bus. L.R. 1008; [2017] C.E.C. 182; [2017] E.T.M.R. 5, ECJ (2nd Chamber)

Tonbridge and Malling BC v Smith [2015] EWHC 3920 (QB), QBD *Affirmed* 17/1783

Tonkin v UK Insurance Ltd [2006] EWHC 1120 (TCC); [2006] 2 All E.R. (Comm) 550; 107 Con. L.R. 107; [2007] Lloyd's Rep. I.R. 283, QBD (TCC) .... *Digested,* 07/**2486**: *Applied* 15/1472: *Considered* 17/1343

Tooth v Revenue and Customs Commissioners [2016] UKFTT 723 (TC); [2017] S.F.T.D. 338; [2017] S.T.I. 295, FTT (Tax)

Top Brands Ltd v Sharma; *sub nom* Mama Milla Ltd (In Creditors' Voluntary Liquidation), Re; Sharma v Top Brands Ltd [2015] EWCA Civ 1140; [2017] 1 All E.R. 854; [2017] 1 All E.R. (Comm) 158; [2016] B.C.C. 1; [2016] Lloyd's Rep. F.C. 1; [2016] B.P.I.R. 111; [2016] P.N.L.R. 12, CA (Civ Div) .... *Digested,* 16/**1230**

Topping v Ralph Trustees Ltd [2017] EWHC 1954 (QB); [2017] 4 W.L.R. 147, QBD .... *Digested,* 17/**208**

Topps Europe Ltd v European Commission (T-699/14) EU:T:2017:2; [2017] 4 C.M.L.R. 13, GC (3rd Chamber)

Toridas UAB v Valstybine mokesciu inspekcija prie Lietuvos Respublikos finansu ministerijos (C-386/16) EU:C:2017:599; [2017] B.V.C. 34, ECJ (9th Chamber)

Torresi v Consiglio dell'Ordine degli Avvocati di Macerata (C-58/13); *joined case* Torresi v Consiglio dell'Ordine degli Avvocati di Macerata (C-59/13) EU:C:2014:2088; [2015] Q.B. 331; [2015] 2 W.L.R. 29; [2015] All E.R. (EC) 1039, ECJ (Grand Chamber) *Considered* 17/2673

Torresi v Consiglio dell'Ordine degli Avvocati di Macerata (C-59/13) see Torresi v Consiglio dell'Ordine degli Avvocati di Macerata (C-58/13)

Tortladze v Georgia (Admissibility) (28739/06) (2017) 65 E.H.R.R. SE12, ECHR

Toshiba Corp v European Commission (C-180/16 P) EU:C:2017:520; [2017] 5 C.M.L.R. 11, ECJ (7th Chamber)

Toshiba Corp v European Commission (C-623/15 P) EU:C:2017:21; [2017] 4 C.M.L.R. 17, ECJ (8th Chamber)

Toshoku Finance UK Plc (In Liquidation), Re; *sub nom* Khan v Inland Revenue Commissioners; Kahn v Inland Revenue Commissioners; Inland Revenue Commissioners v Kahn [2002] UKHL 6; [2002] 1 W.L.R. 671; [2002] 3 All E.R. 961; [2002] S.T.C. 368; [2002] B.C.C. 110; [2002] 1 B.C.L.C. 598; [2002] B.P.I.R. 790; [2003] R.V.R. 106; [2002] B.T.C. 69; Times, February 25, 2002; [2002] S.T.I. 237; (2002) 99(12) L.S.G. 33; (2002) 146 S.J.L.B. 55, HL .... *Digested,* 02/**2718**: *Applied* 07/2393, 12/1794, 13/287: *Considered* 10/1835, 11/1818, 11/4392, 13/1662, 13/2138: *Distinguished* 05/2260: *Followed* 10/1837, 11/1820, 12/1791, 14/1756, 17/1316

Total Fulfilment Logistics Ltd v May (Valuation Officer); *sub nom* Fulfilment Logistics Ltd v May (Valuation Officer) [2014] UKUT 354 (LC); [2014] R.V.R. 300; [2014] J.P.L. 1395, UT (Lands) .... *Digested,* 15/**25**: *Considered* 17/1515

Total Network SL v Revenue and Customs Commissioners see Customs and Excise Commissioners v Total Network SL

Totel Ltd v Revenue and Customs Commissioners [2016] EWCA Civ 1310; [2017] 1 W.L.R. 2313; [2017] S.T.C. 540; [2017] B.V.C. 3, CA (Civ Div) .... *Digested,* 17/**2228**

Totel Ltd v Revenue and Customs Commissioners [2014] UKUT 485 (TCC); [2015] S.T.C. 610; [2014] B.V.C. 542, UT (Tax) .... *Digested,* 15/**2583**: *Affirmed* 17/2228: *Applied* 17/2281

Tower Hamlets LBC v Begum (Rikha) see Begum (Rikha) v Tower Hamlets LBC

Tower Hamlets LBC v M see C (A Child) (Application for Public Interest Immunity) (No.2), Re

Tower Hamlets LBC v M see C (A Child) (Care Proceedings: Disclosure), Re

Tower MCashback LLP 1 v Revenue and Customs Commissioners; *sub nom* Revenue and Customs Commissioners v Tower MCashback LLP 1 [2011] UKSC 19; [2011] 2 A.C. 457; [2011] 2 W.L.R. 1131; [2011] 3 All E.R. 171; [2011] S.T.C. 1143; 80 T.C. 641; [2011] B.T.C. 294; Times, May 16, 2011; [2011] S.T.I. 1620; (2011) 108(21) L.S.G. 19, SC .... *Digested,* 11/**3277**: *Applied* 12/3255, 13/3086, 14/2905, 14/2926, 17/2180: *Considered* 11/3285, 11/3308, 14/2975, 16/2103: *Followed* 15/2435, 16/2053, 16/2119, 17/2101

Town & County Factors Ltd v Customs and Excise Commissioners (C-498/99) EU:C:2002:494; [2002] S.T.C. 1263; [2002] E.C.R. I-7173; [2002] 3 C.M.L.R. 31; [2003] All E.R. (EC) 33; [2003] C.E.C. 264; [2002] B.T.C. 5558; [2002] B.V.C. 645; Times, October 7, 2002; [2002] S.T.I. 1292, ECJ (6th Chamber) .... *Digested,* 02/**4789**: *Considered* 04/3977: *Followed* 17/2260

Town Investments Ltd v Department of the Environment; *sub nom* HEPC (Mayfair Properties) v Department of the Environment; London County Freehold and Leasehold Properties v Department of the Environment [1978] A.C. 359; [1977] 2 W.L.R. 450; [1977] 1 All E.R. 813; (1977) 34 P. & C.R. 48; (1977) 121 S.J. 203, HL .... *Digested,* 77/**2516**: *Applied* 92/1489, 17/870: *Considered* 83/2150, 86/1837, 87/2569: *Distinguished* 78/494

Townend v Doncaster MBC see Sim v Rotherham MBC

Townsend (Deceased), Re see Crabbe v Townsend

Townsend Carriers Ltd v Pfizer Ltd (1977) 33 P. & C.R. 361; (1977) 242 E.G. 813; (1977) 121 S.J. 375, Ch D .... *Digested,* 78/**1790**: *Applied* 11/2060: *Considered* 89/2104, 89/2160, 89/2162, 93/2455, 16/1464, 17/1514: *Distinguished* 86/358, 98/3608, 07/2755

Townsley (Scott) v HM Advocate [2016] HCJAC 87; 2016 S.C.L. 1006; 2016 G.W.D. 31-559, HCJ .... *Digested,* 17/**2791**

Townson v FCE Bank Plc (t/a Ford Credit) [2016] E.C.C. 30, CC (Birmingham) .... *Digested,* 17/**480**

TOYOBO/Heat shrinkable polyester film roll and process (T971/11) [2017] E.P.O.R. 10, EPO (Technical Bd App)

Tradax Ocean Transportation SA v Pagnan see Pagnan SpA v Tradax Ocean Transportation SA

Tradigrain SA v Intertek Testing Services (ITS) Canada Ltd [2007] EWCA Civ 154; [2007] 1 C.L.C. 188; Times, March 20, 2007; [2007] Bus. L.R. D32, CA (Civ Div) .... *Digested,* 07/**2477**: *Followed* 17/468, 17/502

Tradition Financial Services Ltd v Gamberoni [2017] EWHC 768 (QB); [2017] I.R.L.R. 698, QBD .... *Digested,* 17/**824**

Trafilerie Meridionali SpA v European Commission (C-519/15 P) EU:C:2016:682; [2017] 4 C.M.L.R. 1, ECJ (6th Chamber)

Trainfx Ltd, Re; *sub nom* Hellenic Capital Investments Ltd v Trainfx Ltd [2015] EWHC 3713 (Ch); [2016] B.C.C. 493, Ch D .... *Digested,* 17/**1267**

Training in Compliance Ltd (t/a Matthew Read) v Dewse (t/a Data Research Co) [2001] C.P. Rep. 46, CA (Civ Div) .... *Digested,* 00/**543**: *Applied* 01/673, 17/352: *Followed* 10/336

Transgrain Shipping (Singapore) Pte Ltd v Yangtze Navigation (Hong Kong) Co Ltd [2016] EWHC 3132 (Comm); [2017] Bus. L.R. 814; [2017] 1 Lloyd's Rep. 212; [2016] 2 C.L.C. 848, QBD (Comm) .... *Digested,* 17/**1427**

Transocean Drilling UK Ltd v Providence Resources Plc [2016] EWCA Civ 372; [2016] 2 All E.R. (Comm) 606; [2016] 2 Lloyd's Rep. 51; [2016] 1 C.L.C. 585; [2016] B.L.R. 360; 165 Con. L.R. 1; [2016] C.I.L.L. 3844, CA (Civ Div) .... *Digested,* 16/**428**: *Applied* 17/463

Transocean Drilling UK Ltd v Providence Resources Plc [2016] EWHC 2611 (Comm); 169 Con. L.R. 84; [2016] 6 Costs L.O. 883, QBD (Comm) .... *Digested,* 17/**257**

Trasporti Castelletti Spedizioni Internazionali SpA v Hugo Trumpy SpA (C-159/97) EU:C:1999:142; [1999] E.C.R. I-1597; [1999] I.L.Pr. 492, ECJ .... *Digested,* 99/**736**: *Considered* 09/608, 17/295

Travel Document Service v Revenue and Customs Commissioners [2017] UKUT 45 (TCC); [2017] S.T.C. 973; [2017] B.T.C. 505, UT (Tax) .... *Digested,* 17/**2113**

Travel Document Service v Revenue and Customs Commissioners [2015] UKFTT 582 (TC); [2016] S.F.T.D. 186; [2016] S.T.I. 442, FTT (Tax) .... *Digested,* 16/**2064**: *Affirmed* 17/2113

Travel Vac SL v Sanchis (C423/97) EU:C:1999:197; [1999] E.C.R. I-2195; [1999] 2 C.M.L.R. 1111; [1999] All E.R. (EC) 656; (1999) 96(31) L.S.G. 43, ECJ .... *Digested,* 99/**819**: *Considered* 16/416, 17/479: *Distinguished* 06/697

Travelers Casualty & Surety Co of Canada v Sun Life Assurance Co of Canada (UK) Ltd (Costs) [2006] EWHC 2885 (Comm), QBD (Comm) *Applied* 09/389, 17/241

Treanor v Revenue and Customs Commissioners [2017] UKFTT 73 (TC); [2017] S.T.I. 224, FTT (Tax)

Treebhawon (NIAA 2002 Part 5A: Compelling Circumstances Test), Re; *sub nom* Secretary of State for the Home Department v Treebhawon [2017] UKUT 13 (IAC); [2017] Imm. A.R. 790, UT (IAC)

Trelfa (Rachel) v HM Advocate see Fee (Rachel) v HM Advocate

Trengove v Walsall MBC see Burnip v Birmingham City Council

Trevor Smallwood Trust, Re see Smallwood v Revenue and Customs Commissioners
Triad Timber v Customs and Excise Commissioners (10649) [1993] V.A.T.T.R. 384, VAT Tr (London)
Disapproved 17/2289
Tricor Plc (formerly PNC Telecom Plc) v Revenue and Customs Commissioners [2016] UKUT 362 (TCC); [2016] B.V.C. 534, UT (Tax) .... *Digested,* 17/**2253**
Tricor Plc (Formerly PNC Telecom Plc) v Revenue and Customs Commissioners [2014] UKFTT 241 (TC), FTT (Tax)
Affirmed 17/2253
Trillium Digital Systems Inc's Trade Mark [2000] E.T.M.R. 1054 (Note), OHIM (Cancellation Div)
Applied 01/4009: *Considered* 17/1395
Trilogy Management Ltd v Harcus Sinclair (A Firm) [2016] EWHC 170 (Ch); [2017] W.T.L.R. 707, Ch D
Trilogy Services Scotland Ltd v Windsor Residential [2017] SAC (Civ) 2; 2017 S.C.L.R. 640; 2017 G.W.D. 3-29, SAC .... *Digested,* 17/**2465**
Trimingham v Associated Newspapers Ltd [2012] EWHC 1296 (QB); [2012] 4 All E.R. 717; (2012) 109(25) L.S.G. 21, QBD .... *Digested,* 13/**2042**:
Applied 17/645: *Referred to* 15/2536
Trinity Mirror Plc, Re see R. (on the application of Trinity Mirror Plc) v Croydon Crown Court
Triplerose Ltd v Mill House RTM Co Ltd [2016] UKUT 80 (LC); [2016] L. & T.R. 23, UT (Lands) .... *Digested,* 16/**1386**:
Applied 16/1384: *Approved* 17/1463
Trolex Products Ltd v Merrol Fire Protection Engineers Ltd (Unreported, November 20, 1991), CA (Civ Div)
Followed 17/1566
Trollope & Colls Ltd v North West Metropolitan Regional Hospital Board [1973] 1 W.L.R. 601; [1973] 2 All E.R. 260; 9 B.L.R. 60; (1973) 117 S.J. 355, HL .... *Digested,* 73/**270**:
Applied 82/2940, 92/314, 05/655, 10/1117, 17/2461: *Considered* 80/17, 90/401, 96/1218, 00/4640, 07/816: *Distinguished* 81/828: *Followed* 80/357, 13/592
Trotter v Trotter 2001 S.L.T. (Sh Ct) 42; 2000 Fam. L.R. 94; 2000 G.W.D. 12-425, Sh Pr .... *Digested,* 00/**6274**:
Considered 17/2781
Truex v Toll [2009] EWHC 396 (Ch); [2009] 1 W.L.R. 2121; [2009] 4 All E.R. 419; [2009] 5 Costs L.R. 758; [2009] 2 F.L.R. 250; [2009] B.P.I.R. 692; [2009] P.N.L.R. 21; [2009] Fam. Law 474; (2009) 159 N.L.J. 429, Ch D (Bankruptcy Ct) .... *Digested,* 09/**2221**:
Applied 10/313, 11/1890, 13/1711: *Considered* 13/392: *Followed* 17/1323
Trump International Golf Club Scotland Ltd v Scottish Ministers [2015] UKSC 74; [2016] 1 W.L.R. 85; [2017] 1 All E.R. 307; 2016 S.C. (U.K.S.C.) 25; 2016 S.L.T. 9; 2016 S.C.L.R. 67; [2016] J.P.L. 555; 2016 G.W.D. 1-26, SC .... *Digested,* 16/**1727**:
Applied 16/1754: *Considered* 16/1734: *Distinguished* 17/1735: *Followed* 17/1749
Trust A v X (A Child) see D (A Child) (Deprivation of Liberty: Parental Responsibility), Re
Trust Risk Group SpA v AmTrust Europe Ltd see AmTrust Europe Ltd v Trust Risk Group SpA
Trustee Ex p. v McCarthy see McCarthy (A Bankrupt), Re
Trustee L v Attorney General 19 I.T.E.L.R. 770, Sup Ct (Ber)
Trustees Ex p. v Texaco see Clark (A Bankrupt), Re
Trustees Executors Ltd v Fund Managers Canterbury Ltd [2016] NZHC 2194; [2017] Lloyd's Rep. I.R. 128, HC (NZ)
Trustees of Abdul Gaffoor Trust v Income Tax Commissioner, Colombo see Caffoor (Trustees of the Abdul Gaffoor Trust) v Income Tax Commissioner (Colombo)
Trustees of Celestial Church of Christ, Edward Street Parish (A Charity) v Lawson [2017] EWHC 97 (Ch); [2017] P.T.S.R. 790, Ch D .... *Digested,* 17/**178**
Trustees of FD Fenston Will Trusts v Revenue and Customs Commissioners [2007] S.T.C. (S.C.D.) 316; [2007] S.T.I. 556, Sp Comm .... *Digested,* 07/**3992**:
Applied 17/2097
TRUSTEES OF PRINCETON UNIVERSITY/Complexes of Form L2IrX (T437/14) [2017] E.P.O.R. 7, EPO (Technical Bd App)
Trustees of the BT Pension Scheme v Revenue and Customs Commissioners (C-628/15) EU:C:2017:687; [2017] S.T.C. 2075; [2017] B.T.C. 34; [2017] S.T.I. 2100, ECJ (2nd Chamber)
Trustees of the Morrison 2002 Maintenance Trust v Revenue and Customs Commissioners [2017] UKUT 300 (TCC); [2017] S.T.C. 1741; [2017] B.T.C. 529; [2017] S.T.I. 1865, UT (Tax) .... *Digested,* 17/**2098**

Trustees of the Morrison 2002 Maintenance Trust v Revenue and Customs Commissioners [2016] UKFTT 250 (TC); [2016] S.F.T.D. 894; [2016] S.T.I. 2004, FTT (Tax)
Affirmed 17/2098

Trustees of the P Panayi Accumulation and Maintenance Settlements v Revenue and Customs Commissioners (C-646/15) EU:C:2017:682; [2017] 4 W.L.R. 210; [2017] S.T.C. 2495; [2017] B.T.C. 25; 20 I.T.E.L.R. 624, ECJ (1st Chamber)

Trustees of the Scottish Solicitors Staff Pension Fund v Pattison & Sim see Scottish Solicitors Staff Pension Fund's Trustees v Pattison & Sim

Trustees of the Stokes Pension Fund v Western Power Distribution (South West) Plc see Stokes Pension Fund Trustees v Western Power Distribution (South West) Plc

Trustees of the William Jones's Schools Foundation v Parry see William Jones's Schools Foundation Trustees v Parry

TS v Norway (Admissibility) (15633/15) (2017) 64 E.H.R.R. SE3, ECHR

TSB England and Wales v Department of Trade and Industry see JH Rayner (Mincing Lane) Ltd v Department of Trade and Industry

Tsikata v Newspaper Publishing Plc [1997] 1 All E.R. 655; [1997] E.M.L.R. 117; Independent, October 15, 1996; (1996) 146 N.L.J. 1686, CA (Civ Div) .... *Digested,* 96/**5662**:
Considered 07/1070, 17/653: *Distinguished* 13/799

TT Education Ltd v Pie Corbett Consultancy Ltd; *sub nom* TALK FOR LEARNING Trade Mark Application [2017] E.T.M.R. 26; [2017] R.P.C. 17, App Person .... *Digested,* 17/**1356**

TUI UK Ltd v Tickell [2016] EWHC 2741 (QB); [2016] 6 Costs L.O. 941, QBD .... *Digested,* 17/**229**

Tullett Prebon Plc v BGC Brokers LP; *joined case* BGC Brokers LP v Tullett Prebon Plc [2010] EWHC 484 (QB); [2010] I.R.L.R. 648; (2010) 154(12) S.J.L.B. 37, QBD .... *Digested,* 10/**1034**:
Affirmed 11/1049: *Considered* 11/1068, 14/1022, 17/824

Tum v Secretary of State for the Home Department (C-16/05); *sub nom* R. (on the application of Tum) v Secretary of State for the Home Department (C-16/05); *joined case* R. (on the application of Dari) v Secretary of State for the Home Department (C-16/05) EU:C:2007:530; [2008] 1 W.L.R. 94; [2007] E.C.R. I-7415; [2008] 1 C.M.L.R. 2; [2008] Imm. A.R. 175; [2007] I.N.L.R. 473, ECJ (2nd Chamber) .... *Digested,* 08/**1349**:
Applied 09/1435, 17/1230: *Distinguished* 09/2150

Turgut v Secretary of State for the Home Department see R. v Secretary of State for the Home Department Ex p. Turgut

Turkington v Times Newspapers Ltd see McCartan Turkington Breen v Times Newspapers Ltd

Turner v East Midlands Trains Ltd [2012] EWCA Civ 1470; [2013] 3 All E.R. 375; [2013] I.C.R. 525; [2013] I.R.L.R. 107, CA (Civ Div) .... *Digested,* 13/**1065**:
Considered 16/736, 17/1787

Turner v Plasplugs Ltd [1996] 2 All E.R. 939; Times, February 1, 1996; Independent, February 27, 1996; (1996) 146 N.L.J. 370, CA (Civ Div) .... *Digested,* 96/**3858**:
Followed 99/3760, 17/1477

Turner v Royal Bank of Scotland Plc (Relitigation) [2000] B.P.I.R. 683, CA (Civ Div) .... *Digested,* 00/**3434**:
Applied 01/374, 03/2350, 05/2336, 10/1858, 14/1787, 16/1239, 17/1324:
Considered 05/2279, 06/2333: *Distinguished* 03/2347: *Followed* 10/1857, 14/1788

Turner v Secretary of State for Communities and Local Government [2016] EWCA Civ 466; [2017] 2 P. & C.R. 1; [2016] J.P.L. 1092, CA (Civ Div) .... *Digested,* 16/**1695**:
Followed 17/1724, 17/1757

Turner v South Cambridgeshire DC [2016] EWHC 1017 (Admin); [2016] R.V.R. 355, QBD (Admin) .... *Digested,* 17/**1508**

Turner v United States [2012] EWHC 2426 (Admin), DC
Applied 13/1185: *Followed* 17/901

Turner & Co v O Palomo SA; *sub nom* O Palomo SA v Turner & Co [2000] 1 W.L.R. 37; [1999] 4 All E.R. 353; [1999] 2 Costs L.R. 184; Times, August 30, 1999; [1999] N.P.C. 114, CA (Civ Div) .... *Digested,* 99/**416**:
Applied 06/2388: *Considered* 09/2221, 13/392: *Followed* 17/1323

Turner (t/a Wicked Wang Promotions) v Revenue and Customs Commissioners [2017] UKFTT 100 (TC); [2017] S.T.I. 226, FTT (Tax)

Turvill v Bird [2016] EWCA Civ 703; [2016] B.L.R. 522; [2016] T.C.L.R. 7, CA (Civ Div) .... *Digested,* 16/**287**:
Followed 17/250

TW (Children), Re [2015] EWHC 3054 (Fam); [2016] 2 F.L.R. 1386; [2016] Fam. Law 15, Fam Div .... *Digested,* 17/**1001**

TW Logistics Ltd v Essex CC [2017] EWHC 185 (Ch); [2017] Ch. 310; [2017] 3 W.L.R. 89, Ch D .... *Digested,* 17/**1860**

Tweddle v Southern Pacific Mortgages Ltd see North East Property Buyers Litigation, Re
Twin Benefits Ltd v Barker; *sub nom* Confiance Ltd, Re [2017] EWHC 177 (Ch); [2017] 4 W.L.R. 42; [2017] W.T.L.R. 729, Ch D .... *Digested,* 17/**187**
Twinsectra Ltd v Yardley [2002] UKHL 12; [2002] 2 A.C. 164; [2002] 2 W.L.R. 802; [2002] 2 All E.R. 377; [2002] P.N.L.R. 30; [2002] W.T.L.R. 423; Times, March 25, 2002; [2002] 38 E.G. 204 (C.S.); (2002) 99(19) L.S.G. 32; (2002) 152 N.L.J. 469; (2002) 146 S.J.L.B. 84; [2002] N.P.C. 47, HL .... *Digested,* 02/**249**: *Applied* 04/3940, 05/2731, 05/2732, 06/4381, 07/4251, 08/2169, 08/3944, 09/2586, 10/1876, 10/1930, 13/1952, 15/1184, 15/390: *Considered* 04/2408, 05/2325, 06/4380, 07/4237, 10/3441, 11/3470, 13/1950: *Followed* 11/1896, 11/3495, 14/286, 14/3028, 17/1490, 17/174
Twintec Ltd v Volkerfitzpatrick Ltd [2014] EWHC 10 (TCC); [2014] B.L.R. 150; [2014] C.I.L.L. 3476, QBD (TCC) .... *Digested,* 14/**592**: *Applied* 15/696, 17/656: *Considered* 15/2924
TY (Sri Lanka) v Secretary of State for the Home Department [2015] EWCA Civ 1233; [2016] Imm. A.R. 470; [2016] I.N.L.R. 401, CA (Civ Div) .... *Digested,* 16/**1149**: *Considered* 17/2673: *Followed* 17/1245
Tyrrell v HM Senior Coroner County Durham and Darlington [2016] EWHC 1892 (Admin); (2017) 153 B.M.L.R. 208; [2016] Inquest L.R. 235, DC .... *Digested,* 17/**1593**

U v Glasgow City Council [2017] CSOH 122; 2017 S.L.T. 1109; 2017 G.W.D. 31-491, OH .... *Digested,* 17/**2664**
U v J (Domicile: Habitual Residence) [2017] EWHC 449 (Fam); [2017] 1 F.C.R. 545; [2017] W.T.L.R. 565, Fam Div .... *Digested,* 17/**982**
U v U see U (Children), Re
U (Children), Re; *sub nom* U v U [2016] EWCA Civ 1332; [2017] 4 W.L.R. 67, CA (Civ Div) .... *Digested,* 17/**944**
U-Drive Ltd v Revenue and Customs Commissioners [2017] UKUT 112 (TCC); [2017] S.T.C. 806; [2017] B.V.C. 510; [2017] S.T.I. 1066, UT (Tax) .... *Digested,* 17/**2249**
U-Drive Ltd v Revenue and Customs Commissioners [2015] UKFTT 667 (TC); [2016] S.T.I. 257, FTT (Tax) *Reversed* 17/2249
UAB 'Gelvora' v Valstybine Vartotoju Teisiu Apsaugos Tarnyba (C-357/16) EU:C:2017:573; [2017] Bus. L.R. 1724; [2018] 1 C.M.L.R. 28, ECJ (2nd Chamber)
UB (Sri Lanka) v Secretary of State for the Home Department [2017] EWCA Civ 85; [2017] Imm. A.R. 1182, CA (Civ Div)
UBS AG v HSH Nordbank AG [2009] EWCA Civ 585; [2010] 1 All E.R. (Comm) 727; [2009] 2 Lloyd's Rep. 272; [2009] 1 C.L.C. 934, CA (Civ Div) .... *Digested,* 09/**619**: *Applied* 17/1377: *Considered* 10/353, 10/371, 10/636, 16/369
UBS AG v Revenue and Customs Commissioners; *sub nom* Deutsche Bank Group Services (UK) Ltd v Revenue and Customs Commissioners; *joined case* DB Group Services (UK) Ltd v Revenue and Customs Commissioners [2016] UKSC 13; [2016] 1 W.L.R. 1005; [2016] 3 All E.R. 1; [2016] S.T.C. 934; [2016] B.T.C. 11; Times, March 21, 2016; [2016] S.T.I. 513, SC .... *Digested,* 16/**2098**: *Applied* 16/2097, 16/2120, 17/2156: *Followed* 17/403
UBS AG (London Branch) v Kommunale Wasserwerke Leipzig GmbH; *joined cases* UBS Ltd v DEPFA Bank Plc; UBS AG (London Branch) v Landesbank Baden-Württemberg [2017] EWCA Civ 1567; [2017] 2 Lloyd's Rep. 621, CA (Civ Div)
UBS AG (London Branch) v Kommunale Wasserwerke Leipzig GmbH; *joined cases* UBS Ltd v DEPFA Bank Plc; USB AG (London Branch) v Landesbank Baden-Wurttemberg [2014] EWHC 3615 (Comm), QBD (Comm) [*PR0000203355*] *Considered* 17/2067
UBS AG (London Branch) v Landesbank Baden-Württemberg see UBS AG (London Branch) v Kommunale Wasserwerke Leipzig GmbH
UBS Ltd v DEPFA Bank Plc see UBS AG (London Branch) v Kommunale Wasserwerke Leipzig GmbH
UCB Home Loans Corp Ltd v Moore see Royal Bank of Scotland Plc v Etridge (No.2)
Uddin, Re see L (A Child), Re
UDL Argos Engineering, Re (Unreported, December 1, 2001), CFA (HK) *Applied* 17/404
UE (Nigeria) v Secretary of State for the Home Department [2010] EWCA Civ 975; [2012] 1 W.L.R. 127; [2011] 2 All E.R. 352; [2011] Imm. A.R. 1; [2011] I.N.L.R. 97, CA (Civ Div) .... *Digested,* 11/**1789**: *Applied* 17/1212

Ufficio Distrettuale delle Imposte Dirette di Fiorenzuola d'Arda v Comune di Carpaneto Piacentino (231/87) EU:C:1989:381; [1991] S.T.C. 205; [1989] E.C.R. 3233; Times, November 15, 1989, ECJ .... *Digested,* 91/**3661**: *Applied* 02/4739, 06/4498, 07/4351, 09/4121, 17/2268: *Considered* 01/5579, 01/5609: *Followed* 05/4411

Ugiagbe v Southwark LBC [2009] EWCA Civ 31; [2009] P.T.S.R. 1465; [2009] H.L.R. 35; Times, February 18, 2009; [2009] N.P.C. 25, CA (Civ Div) .... *Digested,* 09/**1904**: *Considered* 15/1268: *Followed* 17/1159

UK Insurance Ltd v Farrow (t/a R Farrow & Sons) [2016] EWHC 190 (QB); [2017] Lloyd's Rep. I.R. 338, QBD (Comm)

UK Insurance Ltd v Holden [2016] EWHC 264 (QB); [2016] 4 W.L.R. 38; [2016] 3 All E.R. 727; [2016] R.T.R. 13; [2016] 2 C.M.L.R. 37; [2016] Lloyd's Rep. I.R. 349, QBD (Merc) .... *Digested,* 16/**1266**: *Reversed* 17/1347

UK Insurance Ltd v Holden see UK Insurance Ltd v R&S Pilling (t/a Phoenix Engineering)

UK Insurance Ltd v R&S Pilling (t/a Phoenix Engineering); *sub nom* UK Insurance Ltd v Holden [2017] EWCA Civ 259; [2017] Q.B. 1357; [2017] 3 W.L.R. 450; [2017] 4 All E.R. 199; [2017] 2 All E.R. (Comm) 905; [2017] R.T.R. 25; [2017] Lloyd's Rep. I.R. 463; Times, May 30, 2017, CA (Civ Div) .... *Digested,* 17/**1347**

UK Power Networks (Transport) Ltd v Revenue and Customs Commissioners see Eastern Power Networks Plc v Revenue and Customs Commissioners

UK Power Reserve Ltd v Read [2014] EWHC 66 (Ch), Ch D *Considered* 17/823

UK Storage Co (SW) Ltd v Revenue and Customs Commissioners; *sub nom* Revenue and Customs Commissioners v UK Storage Co (SW) Ltd [2012] UKUT 359 (TCC); [2013] S.T.C. 361; [2012] B.V.C. 1955; [2012] S.T.I. 3233, UT (Tax) ...... *Digested,* 13/**3194**: *Applied* 14/3052: *Not followed* 17/2238

UK Working Time Guidelines, Re (C-484/04) see Commission of the European Communities v United Kingdom (C-484/04)

UKI (Kingsway) Ltd v Westminster City Council; *sub nom* Westminster City Council v UKI (Kingsway) Ltd [2017] EWCA Civ 430; [2017] P.T.S.R. 1606; [2017] R.A. 179; [2017] 2 P. & C.R. DG23, CA (Civ Div) .... *Digested,* 17/**1514**

UKI (Kingsway) Ltd v Westminster City Council; *sub nom* Westminster City Council v UKI (Kingsway) Ltd [2015] UKUT 301 (LC); [2015] R.A. 433, UT (Lands) .... *Digested,* 16/**1464**: *Reversed* 17/1514

Ukpabi v DPP [2008] EWHC 952 (Admin), DC *Considered* 17/532

UKRS Training Ltd v NSAR Ltd [2017] CAT 14; [2017] Comp. A.R. 368, CAT

UL v BK (Freezing Orders: Safeguards: Standard Examples) [2013] EWHC 1735 (Fam); [2014] Fam. 35; [2014] 2 W.L.R. 914; [2013] Fam. Law 1379, Fam Div .. *Digested,* 14/**496**: *Applied* 17/1051, 17/988

Ullah (Ahsan) v Special Adjudicator see R. (on the application of Ullah) v Special Adjudicator

Ullens de Schooten v Belgium (C-268/15) EU:C:2016:874; [2017] 4 W.L.R. 47, ECJ (Grand Chamber)

Ulster Marine Insurance Co Ltd v Oceanus Mutual Underwriting Association (Bermuda) Ltd see Bragg v Oceanus Mutual Underwriting Association (Bermuda) Ltd

Ulster Metal Refiners Ltd v Revenue and Customs Commissioners [2015] UKFTT 255 (TC), FTT (Tax) *Affirmed* 17/2250

Ulster Metal Refiners Ltd v Revenue and Customs Commissioners [2016] UKUT 342 (TCC); [2016] B.V.C. 529, UT (Tax) .... *Digested,* 17/**2250**

Ultimate Invoice Finance Ltd, Petitioner [2017] CSOH 72; 2017 S.L.T. 791; 2017 G.W.D. 15-243, OH .... *Digested,* 17/**2676**

UMS Holding Ltd v Great Station Properties SA [2017] EWHC 2398 (Comm); [2018] 1 All E.R. (Comm) 856; [2018] Bus. L.R. 650; [2017] 2 Lloyd's Rep. 421, QBD (Comm)

UMS Holdings Ltd v Great Station Properties SA [2017] EWHC 2473 (Comm); [2018] 1 All E.R. (Comm) 892; [2017] 2 Lloyd's Rep. 448, QBD (Comm)

Unal v Sicherheitsdirektion fur das Bundesland Vorarlberg (C136/03) see Dorr v Sicherheitsdirektion fur das Bundesland Karnten (C136/03)

Underwood v Revenue and Customs Commissioners [2008] EWCA Civ 1423; [2009] S.T.C. 239; 79 T.C. 631; [2009] B.T.C. 26; [2009] S.T.I. 256; [2009] 1 E.G. 76 (C.S.); [2008] N.P.C. 139, CA (Civ Div) .... *Digested,* 09/**3749**: *Followed* 17/2094

Undre v Harrow LBC [2016] EWHC 931 (QB); [2017] E.M.L.R. 3, QBD .... *Digested,* 17/**649**: *Considered* 16/578

Undre v Harrow LBC [2016] EWHC 2761 (QB); [2017] E.M.L.R. 8, QBD .... *Digested,* 17/**655**

Unicargo v Flotec Maritime S de RL (The Cienvik) [1996] 2 Lloyd's Rep. 395; [1996] C.L.C. 434; Independent, January 1, 1996, QBD (Admlty) .... *Digested,* 97/**711**: *Applied* 17/334: *Followed* 15/364

Unicom Insurance Services Ltd v Revenue and Customs Commissioners [2016] UKFTT 782 (TC); [2017] S.T.I. 80, FTT (Tax)

Union Castle Mail Steamship Co Ltd v Revenue and Customs Commissioners [2016] UKFTT 526 (TC); [2016] S.F.T.D. 1057; [2016] S.T.I. 2789, FTT (Tax) .... *Digested,* 17/**2106**: *Applied* 17/2108

Union Dampfschiffsrhederei AG v SS Parisian see Albano, The v Allan Line Steamship Co Ltd

Union Marine Classification Services LLC v Comoros [2017] EWHC 2364 (Comm); [2017] 2 Lloyd's Rep. 608, QBD (Comm)

Unionen v Almega Tjansteforbunden (C-336/15) EU:C:2017:276; [2017] I.C.R. 909, ECJ (10th Chamber)

Unison Claimants v Glasgow City Council see HBJ Claimants v Glasgow City Council

Unite the Union v Mills [2017] I.C.R. 693, EAT .... *Digested,* 17/**839**

Unite the Union v Nailard [2017] I.C.R. 121; [2016] I.R.L.R. 906, EAT .... *Digested,* 17/**840**

Unite the Union v United Kingdom (Admissibility) (65397/13) [2017] I.R.L.R. 438; (2016) 63 E.H.R.R. SE7, ECHR
Considered 17/766

United Antwerp Maritime Agencies (Unamar) NV v Navigation Maritime Bulgare (C-184/12) EU:C:2013:663; [2014] 1 All E.R. (Comm) 625; [2014] 1 Lloyd's Rep. 161, ECJ (3rd Chamber)
Applied 17/163

United Bank Ltd v Akhter see United Bank Ltd v Asif

United Bank Ltd v Asif; *joined case* United Bank Ltd v Akhter QBENI 2000/0073/A2, CA (Civ Div)
Considered 17/488: *Not followed* 16/442

United Bank of Kuwait Plc v Prudential Property Services Ltd see South Australia Asset Management Corp v York Montague Ltd

United City Merchants (Investments) Ltd v Royal Bank of Canada (The American Accord) [1983] 1 A.C. 168; [1982] 2 W.L.R. 1039; [1982] 2 All E.R. 720; [1982] 2 Lloyd's Rep. 1; [1982] Com. L.R. 142, HL .... *Digested,* 82/**215**: *Applied* 84/387, 86/394, 87/202, 03/256: *Considered* 83/358, 99/279, 00/5888, 17/166: *Followed* 93/4734, 16/130

United Distillers & Vintners Ltd v Brown EAT/1471/99, EAT
Applied 17/851

United Horse Shoe and Nail Co Ltd v John Stewart & Co (1888) 13 App. Cas. 401; (1888) 15 R. (H.L.) 45, HL
Considered 17/1357

United Lincolnshire Hospitals NHS Foundation Trust v Farren [2017] I.C.R. 513, EAT . *Digested,* 17/**851**

United Lincolnshire Hospitals NHS Trust v N [2014] EWCOP 16; [2014] C.O.P.L.R. 660; (2014) 140 B.M.L.R. 204, CP .... *Digested,* 15/**1227**: *Applied* 17/1124

United Parcel Service Inc v European Commission (T-194/13) EU:T:2017:144; [2017] 4 C.M.L.R. 31, GC (4th Chamber)

United States v Dollfus Mieg et Cie SA see Dollfus Mieg et Compagnie SA v Bank of England (No.1)

United States v Love [2016] Lloyd's Rep. F.C. 597, MC .... *Digested,* 17/**901**

United States v Montgomery (No.1); *sub nom* M (Restraint Order: External Confiscation Order), Re [2001] UKHL 3; [2001] 1 W.L.R. 196; [2001] 1 All E.R. 815; [2002] I.L.Pr. 27; Times, February 6, 2001; Independent, March 12, 2001; Daily Telegraph, February 7, 2001; (2001) 151 N.L.J. 136, HL .... *Digested,* 01/**15**: *Applied* 17/270: *Followed* 15/630

United States v Philip Morris Inc (No.1) [2003] EWHC 3028 (Comm), QBD (Comm)
Affirmed 04/257: *Applied* 17/530

United Trust Bank Ltd v Dohil [2011] EWHC 3302 (QB); [2012] 2 All E.R. (Comm) 765, QBD .... *Digested,* 12/**268**: *Applied* 15/1409, 17/162

United Utilities Group Plc v Hart 35/2015, CC (Liverpool)
Considered 17/366

Universal Music GmbH v X [2017] E.C.C. 27, BGH (Ger)

Universal Music International Holding BV v Schilling (C-12/15) EU:C:2016:449; [2016] Q.B. 967; [2016] 3 W.L.R. 1139; [2017] C.E.C. 272; [2016] I.L.Pr. 30, ECJ (2nd Chamber)

Universal Project Management Services Ltd v Fort Gilkicker Ltd see Fort Gilkicker Ltd, Re

University Hospital Lewisham NHS Trust v Hamuth; *sub nom* Lewisham Hospital NHS Trust v Hamuth [2006] EWHC 1609 (Ch); [2006] Inquest L.R. 141; [2007] W.T.L.R. 309; (2006) 150 S.J.L.B. 168, Ch D .... *Digested,* 07/**1972**: *Applied* 17/961

University Hospital NHS Trust v CA see CA (Natural Delivery or Caesarean Section), Re

University of Brighton v Dovehouse Interiors Ltd see Brighton University v Dovehouse Interiors Ltd

University of Kent v Customs and Excise Commissioners [2004] B.V.C. 2215; [2004] V. & D.R. 372; [2004] S.T.I. 1948, V&DTr (London) .... *Digested,* 05/**4421**: *Applied* 14/3101: *Considered* 17/2238

University of Oxford v Deer see Ittihadieh v 5-11 Cheyne Gardens RTM Co Ltd

University of Sunderland v Drossou [2017] I.R.L.R. 1087; [2017] I.C.R. D23, EAT

Unsped Paket Servisi San Ve Tic AS v Bulgaria (Admissibility) (3503/08) (2017) 64 E.H.R.R. SE10, ECHR

Unwired Planet International Ltd v Huawei Technologies Co Ltd [2017] EWCA Civ 266; [2017] Bus. L.R. 1971, CA (Civ Div)

Unwired Planet International Ltd v Huawei Technologies Co Ltd [2017] EWHC 1304 (Pat); [2017] R.P.C. 20, Ch D (Patents Ct)

Unwired Planet International Ltd v Huawei Technologies Co Ltd [2016] EWHC 958 (Pat); [2016] Bus. L.R. 796; [2017] F.S.R. 4, Ch D (Patents Ct) .... *Digested,* 16/**1308**

Uprichard v Fife Council see Uprichard v Scottish Ministers

Uprichard v Scottish Ministers; *sub nom* Uprichard v Fife Council [2011] CSIH 59; 2012 S.C. 172; 2011 G.W.D. 30-655, IH (2 Div) .... *Digested,* 12/**4225**: *Affirmed* 14/2373: *Considered* 17/2635

Uratemp Ventures Ltd v Carrell see Uratemp Ventures Ltd v Collins

Uratemp Ventures Ltd v Collins; *joined case* Uratemp Ventures Ltd v Carrell [2001] UKHL 43; [2002] 1 A.C. 301; [2001] 3 W.L.R. 806; [2002] 1 All E.R. 46; (2001) 33 H.L.R. 85; [2002] L. & T.R. 15; [2001] 3 E.G.L.R. 93; [2002] R.V.R. 162; 2001 Hous. L.R. 133; Times, October 18, 2001; Independent, December 3, 2001; Daily Telegraph, October 16, 2001; [2001] 43 E.G. 186 (C.S.); (2001) 98(41) L.S.G. 35; [2001] N.P.C. 145; [2002] 1 P. & C.R. DG15, HL .... *Digested,* 01/**4148**: *Applied* 05/2660, 09/2520, 15/1290: *Considered* 06/2046, 07/3250, 10/2090, 13/2336, 15/478, 17/1441

Urso v Department for Work and Pensions [2017] I.R.L.R. 304, EAT .... *Digested,* 17/**778**

USB AG (London Branch) v Landesbank Baden-Wurttemberg see UBS AG (London Branch) v Kommunale Wasserwerke Leipzig GmbH

UsedSoft GmbH v Oracle International Corp (C-128/11) EU:C:2012:407; [2013] Bus. L.R. 911; [2012] 3 C.M.L.R. 44; [2012] All E.R. (EC) 1220; [2013] C.E.C. 323; [2012] E.C.D.R. 19; [2013] R.P.C. 6; Times, September 7, 2012, ECJ (Grand Chamber) *Considered* 15/56, 17/45

Utilise TDS Ltd v Cranstoun Davies see Denton v TH White Ltd

V v Associated Newspapers Ltd see C (Deceased), Re

V v V (Ancillary Relief: Power to Order Child Maintenance) [2001] 2 F.L.R. 799; Times, August 16, 2001; [2001] Fam. Law 649, Fam Div .... *Digested,* 01/**2636**: *Applied* 17/1001

V (A Child) (Recognition of Foreign Adoption), Re; *sub nom* W v Secretary of State for the Home Department [2017] EWHC 1733 (Fam); [2017] 3 F.C.R. 694, Fam Div

V (A Child), Re [2016] EWFC 58; [2017] 1 F.C.R. 292, Fam Ct .... *Digested,* 17/**953**

V (Children) (Long-term Fostering versus Adoption), Re [2013] EWCA Civ 913; [2014] 1 F.L.R. 1009; [2013] 3 F.C.R. 407; [2013] Fam. Law 1362, CA (Civ Div) .... *Digested,* 14/**1249**: *Applied* 17/913

V (European Maintenance Regulation), Re [2016] EWHC 668 (Fam); [2017] 1 F.L.R. 1083; [2016] Fam. Law 682, Fam Div

Vaccine Research LP v Revenue and Customs Commissioners; *sub nom* Revenue and Customs Commissioners v Vaccine Research LP [2014] UKUT 389 (TCC); [2015] S.T.C. 179; [2014] B.T.C. 525, UT (Tax) .... *Digested,* 14/**2905**: *Considered* 17/2180

Vadala v Lawes (1890) 25 Q.B.D. 310, CA *Applied* 47-51/7731, 88/400, 91/471, 92/464: *Considered* 90/610, 17/434

Vairea v Reed Business Information Ltd [2017] I.C.R. D9, EAT
Val Wyatt Marines v Wokingham BC [2017] P.A.D. 27, Planning Inspector
Vald Nielsen Holding A/S v Baldorino [2017] EWHC 1033 (Comm); [2017] 3 Costs L.O. 309, QBD (Comm) .... *Digested,* 17/**359**
Vale do Rio doce Navegacao SA v Shanghai Bao Steel Ocean Shipping Co Ltd (t/a Bao Steel Ocean Shipping Co); *sub nom* Vale do Rio doce Navegacao SA v Shanghai Bao Steel Ocean Shipping Co Ltd (t/a Baosteel Ocean Shipping Co) [2000] 2 All E.R. (Comm) 70; [2000] 2 Lloyd's Rep. 1; [2000] C.L.C. 1200; Times, May 16, 2000, QBD (Comm) .... *Digested,* 00/**240**: *Applied* 17/334: *Considered* 11/130, 11/134, 16/61: *Followed* 15/364
Vale do Rio doce Navegacao SA v Shanghai Bao Steel Ocean Shipping Co Ltd (t/a Baosteel Ocean Shipping Co) see Vale do Rio doce Navegacao SA v Shanghai Bao Steel Ocean Shipping Co Ltd (t/a Bao Steel Ocean Shipping Co)
Valentine v Valentine see Valentine's Settlement, Re
Valentine's Settlement, Re; *sub nom* Valentine v Valentine [1965] Ch. 831; [1965] 2 W.L.R. 1015; [1965] 2 All E.R. 226; (1965) 109 S.J. 237, CA .... *Digested,* 65/**3556**: *Applied* 67/1991, 00/2436, 10/1275: *Distinguished* 17/914: *Followed* 96/467, 13/1194, 14/1242, 17/1034
Vallianatos v Greece (29381/09) (2014) 59 E.H.R.R. 12; 36 B.H.R.C. 149, ECHR (Grand Chamber) *Considered* 16/867, 17/976
Valsts Policijas Rigas Regiona Parvaldes Kartibas Policijas Parvalde v Rigas Pasvaldibas SIA Rigas Satiksme (C-13/16) EU:C:2017:336; [2017] 4 W.L.R. 97; [2017] 3 C.M.L.R. 39; [2018] C.E.C. 255, ECJ (2nd Chamber)
Van Aken v Camden LBC [2002] EWCA Civ 1724; [2003] 1 W.L.R. 684; [2003] 1 All E.R. 552; [2003] H.L.R. 33; Times, October 28, 2002, CA (Civ Div) .... *Digested,* 02/**2344**: *Considered* 17/323: *Followed* 12/1291: *Not applied* 17/12
Van de Water v Staatssecretaris van Financien (C325/99) EU:C:2001:201; [2001] E.C.R. I-2729, ECJ *Followed* 17/632
Van den Boogaard v Laumen (C-220/95) EU:C:1997:91; [1997] Q.B. 759; [1997] 3 W.L.R. 284; [1997] E.C.R. I-1147; [1997] All E.R. (E.C.) 517; [1997] I.L.Pr. 278; [1997] 2 F.L.R. 399; [1997] 3 F.C.R. 493; Times, March 26, 1997; [1997] Fam. Law 599, ECJ (5th Chamber) .... *Digested,* 97/**2454**: *Applied* 07/1697: *Considered* 98/2470, 07/5183, 17/1027: *Followed* 11/1297
Van der Weegen v Belgium (C-580/15) EU:C:2017:429; [2017] S.T.I. 1455, ECJ (5th Chamber)
Van Doren + Q GmbH v Lifestyle Sports + Sportswear Handelsgesellschaft mbH (C-244/00) EU:C:2003:204; [2003] E.C.R. I-3051; [2003] 2 C.M.L.R. 6; [2004] All E.R. (EC) 912; [2003] C.E.C. 348; [2003] E.T.M.R. 75; Times, April 29, 2003, ECJ .... *Digested,* 03/**2621**: *Applied* 11/1996, 12/1970: *Considered* 17/1392: *Followed* 11/1994
Van Gansewinkel Groep BV, Re [2015] EWHC 2151 (Ch); [2015] Bus. L.R. 1046; [2016] B.C.C. 172; [2016] 2 B.C.L.C. 138, Ch D .... *Digested,* 15/**402**: *Considered* 16/349, 16/350, 17/1321
Van Lynden v Gilchrist [2016] CSIH 72; 2017 S.C. 134; 2016 S.L.T. 1187; 2017 S.C.L.R. 351; 2016 G.W.D. 29-525, IH (1 Div) .... *Digested,* 17/**2710**
Van Lynden v Gilchrist [2015] CSOH 147; 2015 S.L.T. 864; 2015 G.W.D. 37-596, OH *Digested,* 16/**2709**: *Reversed* 17/2710
Vanden Recycling Ltd v Bevin Tumulty; *sub nom* Vanden Recycling Ltd v Kras Recycling BV [2015] EWHC 3616 (QB), QBD *Reversed in part* 17/217
Vanden Recycling Ltd v Bevin Tumulty; *sub nom* Vanden Recycling Ltd v Kras Recycling BV [2017] EWCA Civ 354; [2017] C.P. Rep. 33, CA (Civ Div) .... *Digested,* 17/**217**
Vanden Recycling Ltd v Kras Recycling BV see Vanden Recycling Ltd v Bevin Tumulty
Vanderbilt v Wallace see Azumi Ltd v Zuma's Choice Pet Products Ltd
Vanquish Properties (UK) Ltd Partnership v Brook Street (UK) Ltd [2016] EWHC 1508 (Ch); [2016] L. & T.R. 33, Ch D .... *Digested,* 17/**1432**
Vardy Properties v Revenue and Customs Commissioners [2012] UKFTT 564 (TC); [2012] S.F.T.D. 1398; [2013] S.T.I. 67, FTT (Tax) .... *Digested,* 13/**3131**: *Applied* 17/2175
Various Claimants v BACHL see KR v Bryn Alyn Community (Holdings) Ltd (In Liquidation)
Various Claimants v Barclays Bank Plc [2017] EWHC 1929 (QB); [2017] I.R.L.R. 1103, QBD

Various Claimants v Bryn Alyn Community (Holdings) Ltd (In Liquidation) see KR v Bryn Alyn Community (Holdings) Ltd (In Liquidation)

Varney (Scotland) Ltd v Lanark Burgh Council 1974 S.C. 245; 1976 S.L.T. 46, IH (2 Div) .... *Digested,* 76/**2991**: *Considered* 77/3294, 90/4820, 17/2846: *Followed* 01/6753

Vasiliauskas v Lithuania (35343/05) (2016) 62 E.H.R.R. 31; 41 B.H.R.C. 338, ECHR

Vasiliou v Hajigeorgiou; *sub nom* Hajigeorgiou v Vasiliou [2005] EWCA Civ 236; [2005] 1 W.L.R. 2195; [2005] 3 All E.R. 17; [2005] C.P. Rep. 27; Times, March 22, 2005; (2005) 102(18) L.S.G. 22; [2005] N.P.C. 39, CA (Civ Div) .... *Digested,* 05/**296**: *Applied* 14/291: *Considered* 11/327: *Followed* 16/152, 16/154, 17/298

Vaskrsic v Slovenia (31371/12) [2017] H.L.R. 27, ECHR

VAT on Advertising, Re see Commission of the European Communities v France (C-68/92)

Vattenfall Europe Generation AG v Germany (C-457/15) EU:C:2016:613; [2017] Env. L.R. 13, ECJ (6th Chamber)

Vaughan v Lewisham LBC [2013] I.R.L.R. 713, EAT .... *Digested,* 13/**336**: *Applied* 17/795: *Considered* 15/827

VDP Dental Laboratory NV v Staatssecretaris van Financien (C-144/13); *joined cases* Staatssecretaris van Financien v X BV (C-154/13); Staatssecretaris van Financien v Nobel Biocare Nederland BV (C□160/13) EU:C:2015:116; [2015] S.T.C. 1133; [2015] B.V.C. 18, ECJ (1st Chamber) *Applied* 17/2285

Vehicle Control Services Ltd v Mackie 2017 S.L.T. (Sh Ct) 111; 2017 G.W.D. 13-198, Sh Ct (Tayside) (Dundee) .... *Digested,* 17/**2467**

Vehicle Control Services Ltd v Revenue and Customs Commissioners [2016] UKUT 316 (TCC); [2017] S.T.C. 11; [2016] B.V.C. 526; [2016] S.T.I. 2203, UT (Tax) ... *Digested,* 17/**2241**

Vehicle Control Services Ltd v Revenue and Customs Commissioners [2016] UKFTT 443 (TC); [2016] S.T.I. 2171, FTT (Tax) *Affirmed* 17/2241

Veloss International SA v European Parliament (T-667/11) EU:T:2015:5, GC *Considered* 17/1816

Venables v News Group Newspapers Ltd; *joined case* Thompson v News Group Newspapers Ltd [2001] Fam. 430; [2001] 2 W.L.R. 1038; [2001] 1 All E.R. 908; [2001] E.M.L.R. 10; [2001] 1 F.L.R. 791; [2002] 1 F.C.R. 333; [2001] H.R.L.R. 19; [2001] U.K.H.R.R. 628; 9 B.H.R.C. 587; Times, January 16, 2001; Independent, January 17, 2001; [2001] Fam. Law 258; Daily Telegraph, January 16, 2001; (2001) 98(12) L.S.G. 41; (2001) 151 N.L.J. 57; (2001) 145 S.J.L.B. 43, Fam Div .... *Digested,* 01/**3476**: *Applied* 01/3577, 17/3: *Considered* 01/4415: *Distinguished* 03/297

Vento v Chief Constable of West Yorkshire; *sub nom* Chief Constable of West Yorkshire v Vento (No.2) [2002] EWCA Civ 1871; [2003] I.C.R. 318; [2003] I.R.L.R. 102; [2003] Po. L.R. 171; Times, December 27, 2002; (2003) 100(10) L.S.G. 28; (2003) 147 S.J.L.B. 181, CA (Civ Div) .... *Digested,* 03/**1306**: *Applied* 06/1363, 07/1413, 09/3815, 10/1116, 10/1125, 13/1038, 15/791, 15/857, 15/876: *Considered* 04/1276, 04/917, 06/1371, 08/1136, 08/891, 10/1042, 11/1064, 11/1071, 12/1116, 13/794, 14/1099, 14/3476, 16/2101, 16/2141, 17/782: *Followed* 04/1306, 05/1318, 13/786, 15/804, 15/807

Verband Sozialer Wettbewerb eV v DHL Paket GmbH (C-146/16) EU:C:2017:243; [2017] Bus. L.R. 1808; [2017] 3 C.M.L.R. 26, ECJ (10th Chamber)

Vercoe v Rutland Fund Management Ltd [2010] EWHC 424 (Ch); [2010] Bus. L.R. D141, Ch D *Applied* 11/530: *Considered* 17/1357

Verein fur Konsumenteninformation v Amazon EU Sarl (C-191/15) EU:C:2016:612; [2017] Q.B. 252; [2017] 2 W.L.R. 19, ECJ (3rd Chamber)

Verein fur Konsumenteninformation v INKO, Inkasso GmbH (C-127/15) EU:C:2016:934; [2017] Bus. L.R. 846; [2017] 2 C.M.L.R. 19, ECJ (3rd Chamber)

Vereniging Noordelijke Land- en Tuinbouw Organisatie v Staatssecretaris van Financien (C-515/07) EU:C:2009:88; [2009] S.T.C. 935; [2009] E.C.R. I-839; [2009] S.T.I. 511, ECJ (4th Chamber) .... *Digested,* 09/**4052**: *Followed* 17/2241

Vereniging Openbare Bibliotheken v Stichting Leenrecht (C-174/15) EU:C:2016:856; [2018] Bus. L.R. 108; [2017] C.E.C. 811; [2017] E.C.D.R. 3, ECJ (3rd Chamber)

Verlander v Devon Waste Management [2007] EWCA Civ 835, CA (Civ Div) *Applied* 17/1639

Verley v O'Neil see Dickinson v Tesco Plc

Verrechia (t/a Freightmaster Commercials) v Commissioner of Police of the Metropolis see English v Emery Reimbold & Strick Ltd

Verrin v Welcome Financial Services Ltd [2017] E.C.C. 7, CC (Plymouth) .... *Digested,* 17/**481**

Versloot Dredging BV v HDI Gerling Industrie Versicherung AG [2016] UKSC 45; [2017] A.C. 1; [2016] 3 W.L.R. 543; [2016] 4 All E.R. 907; [2016] 2 All E.R. (Comm) 955; [2016] 2 Lloyd's Rep. 198; [2016] 2 C.L.C. 177; [2016] Lloyd's Rep. I.R. 468; Times, August 9, 2016, SC .... *Digested,* 16/**1261**

Verwertungsgesellschaft Rundfunk GmbH v Hettegger Hotel Edelweiss GmbH (C-641/15) EU:C:2017:131; [2017] Bus. L.R. 751; [2017] E.C.D.R. 9, ECJ (2nd Chamber)

Vestergaard Frandsen A/S v BestNet Europe Ltd [2009] EWHC 1456 (Ch); [2010] F.S.R. 2, Ch D .... *Digested,* 10/**1937**: *Applied* 17/2197: *Considered* 11/2200

Vestergaard Frandsen A/S (now called MVF 3 Aps) v Bestnet Europe Ltd; *sub nom* MVF 3 Aps (formerly Vestergaard Frandsen A/S) v Bestnet Europe Ltd [2014] EWHC 3159 (Ch); [2015] Bus. L.R. D1, Ch D .... *Digested,* 15/**1477**: *Affirmed* 17/1357

Vestergaard Frandsen A/S (now called MVF 3 Aps) v Bestnet Europe Ltd; *sub nom* MVF 3 Aps (formerly Vestergaard Frandsen A/S) v Bestnet Europe Ltd [2016] EWCA Civ 541; [2017] F.S.R. 5, CA (Civ Div) .... *Digested,* 17/**1357**

Vestergaard Frandsen S/A (now called MVF3 APS) v Bestnet Europe Ltd [2013] UKSC 31; [2013] 1 W.L.R. 1556; [2013] 4 All E.R. 781; [2013] I.C.R. 981; [2013] I.R.L.R. 654; [2013] E.M.L.R. 24; [2013] R.P.C. 33; Times, June 20, 2013; (2013) 157(21) S.J.L.B. 31, SC .... *Digested,* 13/**1753**: *Applied* 17/1364

VG Cistoca doo v Vladika (C-335/16) EU:C:2017:242; [2017] P.T.S.R. 1224, ECJ (6th Chamber)

Vibert v Zenith Insurance [2016] CSOH 96; 2016 Rep. L.R. 123; 2016 G.W.D. 23-423, OH .... *Digested,* 17/**2442**

Vickers Plc v United Kingdom (9313/81) see Lithgow v United Kingdom (A/102)

Vicky Construction Ltd v Shaw (Inspector of Taxes) see Shaw (Inspector of Taxes) v Vicky Construction Ltd

Victoria Plum Ltd (t/a Victoria Plumb) v Victorian Plumbing Ltd [2016] EWHC 2911 (Ch); [2017] Bus. L.R. 363; [2017] E.C.C. 35; [2017] E.T.M.R. 8; [2017] F.S.R. 17, Ch D .... *Digested,* 17/**1403**

Victoria Recreation Ground, Portslade's Application, Re (1981) 41 P. & C.R. 119, Lands Tr *Considered* 17/1856

Videocon Global Ltd v Goldman Sachs International; *sub nom* Goldman Sachs International v Videocon Global Ltd [2016] EWCA Civ 130; [2017] 2 All E.R. (Comm) 800; [2017] 1 B.C.L.C. 696; [2016] 1 C.L.C. 528, CA (Civ Div)

Vieira v Revenue and Customs Commissioners [2017] EWHC 936 (Ch); [2017] 4 W.L.R. 86; [2017] S.T.C. 1328; [2017] B.P.I.R. 1062; [2017] B.T.C. 11; [2017] B.V.C. 18; [2017] S.T.I. 1118, Ch D .... *Digested,* 17/**1327**

Vieira de Azevedo v CED Portugal Unipessoal Lda (C-558/15) see Azevedo v CED Portugal Unipessoal Lda (C-558/15)

Vigier v Bundesversicherungsanstalt fur Angestellte (C70/80) EU:C:1981:19; [1981] E.C.R. 229; [1982] 2 C.M.L.R. 709, ECJ .... *Digested,* 82/**1317**: *Considered* 17/2169

Vigne (Deceased), Re see Vigne's Representatives v Revenue and Customs Commissioners

Vigne's Representatives v Revenue and Customs Commissioners; *sub nom* Vigne (Deceased), Re [2017] UKFTT 632 (TC); [2017] W.T.L.R. 1193, FTT (Tax)

Vilca v Xstrata Ltd [2017] EWHC 1582 (QB); [2017] B.L.R. 460; [2017] Med. L.R. 457, QBD .... *Digested,* 17/**298**

Villaswan Ltd (In Receivership) v Sheraton Caltrust (Blythswood) Ltd (In Liquidation) 1999 S.C.L.R. 199; [2000] B.C.C. 188; Times, January 27, 1999; 1998 G.W.D. 39-2017, OH .... *Digested,* 99/**6304**

Villeroy & Boch AG v European Commission (C-625/13 P) EU:C:2017:52; [2017] 4 C.M.L.R. 19, ECJ (1st Chamber)

Vince v Wyatt; *sub nom* Wyatt v Vince [2015] UKSC 14; [2015] 1 W.L.R. 1228; [2015] 2 All E.R. 755; [2015] 1 F.L.R. 972; [2015] 1 F.C.R. 566; [2015] Fam. Law 524, SC .... *Digested,* 15/**1093**: *Applied* 15/1090, 17/977: *Considered* 16/892, 16/921: *Followed* 17/1000, 17/1013, 17/1020

Vinci Construction UK Ltd v Beumer Group UK Ltd [2017] EWHC 2196 (TCC); [2017] B.L.R. 547; 174 Con. L.R. 178; [2017] C.I.L.L. 4037, QBD (TCC) .... *Digested,* 17/**461**

Vinnlustodin HF v Sea Tank Shipping AS [2016] EWHC 2514 (Comm); [2017] Bus. L.R. 730; [2016] 2 Lloyd's Rep. 510; [2016] 2 C.L.C. 507; 2016 A.M.C. 2415, QBD (Comm) .... *Digested,* 17/**2003**

Vinos v Marks & Spencer Plc [2001] 3 All E.R. 784; [2001] C.P. Rep. 12; [2000] C.P.L.R. 570; Independent, July 17, 2000, CA (Civ Div)
Applied 00/535, 01/641, 01/645, 04/391, 05/466: *Cited* 03/456: *Considered* 01/643, 01/644, 06/347, 07/522, 11/354, 11/706, 13/2199, 13/3074, 17/1475: *Distinguished* 01/654, 05/340, 07/468: *Followed* 02/479, 16/1953

Vinter v United Kingdom (66069/09); *joined cases* Bamber v United Kingdom (130/10); Moore v United Kingdom (3896/10) (2016) 63 E.H.R.R. 1; 34 B.H.R.C. 605; Times, July 11, 2013; [2014] Crim. L.R. 81, ECHR (Grand Chamber) .... *Digested,* 13/**1550**:
Applied 15/1296, 15/965, 15/971: *Considered* 14/2701, 17/1588

Vinyls Italia SpA v Mediterranea di Navigazione SpA (C-54/16) EU:C:2017:433; [2018] 1 W.L.R. 543; [2017] C.E.C. 1354; [2017] I.L.Pr. 27, ECJ (5th Chamber)

Vion Trading GmbH v Hauptzollamt Hamburg-Jonas (C-202/10) see Ze Fu Fleischhandel GmbH v Hauptzollamt Hamburg-Jonas (C-201/10)

Virgin Atlantic Airways Ltd v Premium Aircraft Interiors UK Ltd; *sub nom* Virgin Atlantic Airways Ltd v Zodiac Seats UK Ltd (formerly Contour Aerospace Ltd) [2013] UKSC 46; [2014] A.C. 160; [2013] 3 W.L.R. 299; [2013] 4 All E.R. 715; [2013] R.P.C. 29, SC .... *Digested,* 13/**1806**:
Applied 17/425: *Considered* 17/1856, 17/190, 17/322: *Distinguished* 17/1013: *Followed* 14/1903, 15/1498, 17/1806, 17/372

Virgin Atlantic Airways Ltd v Zodiac Seats UK Ltd (formerly Contour Aerospace Ltd) see Virgin Atlantic Airways Ltd v Premium Aircraft Interiors UK Ltd

Virgin Enterprises Ltd v One in a Million Ltd see British Telecommunications Plc v One in a Million Ltd

Viridis UK Ltd v Mulalley & Co Ltd [2014] EWHC 268 (TCC), QBD (TCC)
Applied 15/696, 17/465

Vitol SA v Beta Renowable Group SA [2017] EWHC 1734 (Comm); [2018] 1 All E.R. (Comm) 260; [2017] 2 Lloyd's Rep. 338; 173 Con. L.R. 116, QBD (Comm) .... *Digested,* 17/**487**

Vitol SA v Norelf Ltd (The Santa Clara) [1996] A.C. 800; [1996] 3 W.L.R. 105; [1996] 3 All E.R. 193; [1996] 2 Lloyd's Rep. 225; [1996] C.L.C. 1159; (1996) 15 Tr. L.R. 347; Times, July 1, 1996; Independent, June 28, 1996; (1996) 93(26) L.S.G. 19; (1996) 146 N.L.J. 957; (1996) 140 S.J.L.B. 147, HL .... *Digested,* 96/**1242**:
Applied 09/991: *Considered* 08/160: *Followed* 14/624, 17/487

Vivienne Westwood Ltd v Conduit Street Development Ltd [2017] EWHC 350 (Ch); [2017] L. & T.R. 23, Ch D .... *Digested,* 17/**1444**

Vizcaya Partners Ltd v Picard [2016] UKPC 5; [2016] 3 All E.R. 181; [2016] 1 All E.R. (Comm) 891; [2016] Bus. L.R. 413; [2016] 1 B.C.L.C. 683; [2016] 1 C.L.C. 806, PC (Gib) .... *Digested,* 17/**432**

VM v Belgium (60125/11) (2017) 65 E.H.R.R. 14, ECHR

VM v United Kingdom (49734/12) (2017) 64 E.H.R.R. 7, ECHR

VM (Jamaica) v Secretary of State for the Home Department see Secretary of State for the Home Department v VM (Jamaica)

Vnuk v Zavarovalnica Triglav dd (C-162/13) EU:C:2014:2146; [2016] R.T.R. 10; [2015] Lloyd's Rep. I.R. 142, ECJ (3rd Chamber)
Applied 16/1266: *Considered* 17/1877: *Followed* 17/1347

Vodafone 2 v Revenue and Customs Commissioners [2009] EWCA Civ 446; [2010] Ch. 77; [2010] 2 W.L.R. 288; [2010] Bus. L.R. 96; [2009] S.T.C. 1480; [2010] Eu. L.R. 110; [2009] B.T.C. 273; Times, June 26, 2009; [2009] S.T.I. 1795, CA (Civ Div) .... *Digested,* 09/**3765**:
Applied 10/3495, 16/562: *Considered* 14/1063, 16/652, 17/1504: *Followed* 17/2080

Vodafone Group Services Ltd v Infineon Technologies AG [2017] EWHC 1383 (Ch); [2017] 5 C.M.L.R. 15, Ch D

Volcafe Ltd v Compania Sud Americana de Vapores SA (t/a CSAV) [2015] EWHC 516 (Comm); [2016] 1 All E.R. (Comm) 657; [2015] 1 Lloyd's Rep. 639; [2015] 1 C.L.C. 294, QBD (Merc) (London) .... *Digested,* 15/**2308**:
Reversed in part 17/2001

Volcafe Ltd v Compania Sud Americana de Vapores SA (t/a CSAV) [2016] EWCA Civ 1103; [2017] Q.B. 915; [2017] 3 W.L.R. 1; [2017] 1 All E.R. (Comm) 751; [2017] 1 Lloyd's Rep. 32; [2016] 2 C.L.C. 762, CA (Civ Div) .... *Digested,* 17/**2001**

Volk v Goeser 19 I.T.E.L.R. 725, US Court

Volkswagen Financial Services (UK) Ltd v Revenue and Customs Commissioners; *sub nom* Revenue and Customs Commissioners v Volkswagen Financial Services (UK) Ltd [2015] EWCA Civ 832; [2016] S.T.C. 417; [2015] B.V.C. 32; [2015] S.T.I. 2533, CA (Civ Div) .... *Digested,* 15/**2584**: *Affirmed in part* 17/2245: *Applied* 16/2181, 17/2241, 17/2248
Volkswagen Financial Services (UK) Ltd v Revenue and Customs Commissioners; *sub nom* Revenue and Customs Commissioners v Volkswagen Financial Services (UK) Ltd [2017] UKSC 26; [2017] S.T.C. 824; [2017] B.V.C. 15; [2017] S.T.I. 1039, SC .... *Digested,* 17/**2245**
VOM v Secretary of State for the Home Department see VOM (Error of Law: When Appealable)
VOM (Error of Law: When Appealable); *sub nom* VOM v Secretary of State for the Home Department [2016] UKUT 410 (IAC); [2017] Imm. A.R. 117; [2017] I.N.L.R. 464, UT (IAC) .... *Digested,* 17/**384**
Vorarlberger Gebietskrankenkasse v WGV-Schwabische Allgemeine Versicherungs AG (C-347/08) EU:C:2009:561; [2010] 1 All E.R. (Comm) 603; [2009] E.C.R. I-8661; [2010] C.E.C. 377; [2010] I.L.Pr. 2; [2010] Lloyd's Rep. I.R. 77, ECJ (3rd Chamber) *Considered* 17/429
Vosper Plc v United Kingdom (9262/81) see Lithgow v United Kingdom (A/102)
Vrang v Revenue and Customs Commissioners [2017] EWHC 1055 (Admin); [2017] S.T.C. 1192; [2017] B.T.C. 12; [2017] S.T.I. 1197, QBD (Admin) .... *Digested,* 17/**2184**
VS (India) v Secretary of State for the Home Department; *sub nom* S v Secretary of State for the Home Department [2015] CSOH 118; 2015 S.L.T. 651; 2015 G.W.D. 29-493, OH .... *Digested,* 15/**3149**: *Reversed* 17/2665
VS (India) v Secretary of State for the Home Department; *sub nom* S v Secretary of State for the Home Department [2017] CSIH 48; 2017 S.L.T. 977; 2017 G.W.D. 23-397, IH (Ex Div) .... *Digested,* 17/**2665**
VS (Lithuania) v Secretary of State for the Home Department; *sub nom* Sadovska v Secretary of State for the Home Department [2016] CSIH 51; 2016 G.W.D. 24-447, IH *Reversed* 17/1248
VS (Lithuania) v Secretary of State for the Home Department; *sub nom* Sadovska v Secretary of State for the Home Department [2017] UKSC 54; [2017] 1 W.L.R. 2926; [2018] 1 All E.R. 757; 2018 S.C. (U.K.S.C.) 38; 2017 S.L.T. 883; 2018 S.C.L.R. 36; [2018] 1 C.M.L.R. 37; [2017] Imm. A.R. 1473; [2017] I.N.L.R. 944; Times, August 4, 2017; 2017 G.W.D. 23-396, SC .... *Digested,* 17/**1248**
VS (Sri Lanka) v Entry Clearance Officer see Mahad (Ethiopia) v Entry Clearance Officer
VTB Capital Plc v Nutritek International Corp [2013] UKSC 5; [2013] 2 A.C. 337; [2013] 2 W.L.R. 398; [2013] 1 All E.R. 1296; [2013] 1 All E.R. (Comm) 1009; [2013] 1 Lloyd's Rep. 466; [2013] B.C.C. 514; [2013] 1 B.C.L.C. 179; [2013] 1 C.L.C. 153, SC .... *Digested,* 13/**472**: *Applied* 13/362, 13/427: *Considered* 15/2305, 15/430, 17/371: *Followed* 15/431, 17/2194
Vukota-Bojic v Switzerland (61838/10) [2017] I.R.L.R. 94, ECHR
Vyas v Goraya (t/a Taj Construction Roofing) [2016] EWCA Civ 1095; 169 Con. L.R. 21, CA (Civ Div) .... *Digested,* 17/**489**
Vyas v Leyland Cars see Science Research Council v Nasse
Vyse v Foster; *joined case* Vyse v Vyse (1874-75) L.R. 7 H.L. 318, HL *Applied* 47-51/9426, 17/2221
Vyse v Vyse see Vyse v Foster
Vyse v Wyldecrest Parks (Management) Ltd [2017] UKUT 24 (LC); [2017] L.L.R. 390, UT (Lands) .... *Digested,* 17/**1161**

W v G (Financial Provision: Conditional Order for Sale: Equitable Interest); *sub nom* DW v CG [2016] EWHC 2965 (Fam); [2017] 4 W.L.R. 80, Fam Div .... *Digested,* 17/**1846**
W v G see Gray v Work
W v H see Estrada Juffali v Juffali
W v Hertfordshire CC see W (A Minor) (Wardship: Jurisdiction), Re
W v P see C Plc v P
W v Sanofi Pasteur MSD SNC (C-621/15); *sub nom* NW v Sanofi Pasteur MSD SNC (C-621/15) EU:C:2017:484; [2017] 4 W.L.R. 171; [2018] 1 C.M.L.R. 16; [2018] C.E.C. 331; (2017) 158 B.M.L.R. 16; Times, September 4, 2017, ECJ (2nd Chamber)
W v Schaffer 2001 S.L.T. (Sh Ct) 86; 2000 G.W.D. 36-1348, Sh Pr *Applied* 17/2604

W v Secretary of State for the Home Department see R. (on the application of W) v Secretary of State for the Home Department

W v Secretary of State for the Home Department see V (A Child) (Recognition of Foreign Adoption), Re

W v X (Jurisdiction in Matters of Parental Responsibility) (C-499/15) EU:C:2017:118; [2017] Fam. 305; [2017] 2 W.L.R. 1369; [2017] I.L.Pr. 12; [2017] 2 F.L.R. 828; [2017] 2 F.C.R. 389, ECJ (1st Chamber)

W (A Child) (Adoption: Approach to Long Term Welfare), Re see W (A Child) (Adoption: Grandparents' Competing Claim), Re

W (A Child) (Adoption: Delay), Re [2017] EWHC 829 (Fam); [2017] 2 F.L.R. 1628, Fam Div

W (A Child) (Adoption: Grandparents' Competing Claim), Re; *sub nom* W (A Child) (Adoption: Approach to Long Term Welfare), Re [2016] EWCA Civ 793; [2017] 1 W.L.R. 889; [2017] 2 F.L.R. 31; [2016] Fam. Law 1213, CA (Civ Div) .... *Digested,* 17/**912**: *Applied* 17/913: *Considered* 17/911

W (A Child) (Care Proceedings: Child's Representation), Re; *sub nom* W (Representation of Child), Re [2016] EWCA Civ 1051; [2017] 1 W.L.R. 1027; [2017] 2 F.L.R. 199; [2016] 3 F.C.R. 630, CA (Civ Div) .... *Digested,* 17/**929**

W (A Child) (Care Proceedings: Non Party Appeal), Re [2016] EWCA Civ 1140; [2017] 1 W.L.R. 2415; [2017] 1 F.L.R. 1629; [2017] 1 F.C.R. 349, CA (Civ Div) . *Digested,* 17/**999**: *Considered* 17/335

W (A Child) (Designation of Local Authority), Re; *sub nom* Medway Council v Kent CC [2016] EWCA Civ 366; [2017] 1 F.L.R. 1511; [2016] Fam. Law 663, CA (Civ Div) *Followed* 17/925

W (A Child), Re [2017] EWHC 1032 (Fam); [2017] 2 F.L.R. 1714, Fam Div

W (A Minor) (Wardship: Jurisdiction), Re; *sub nom* W v Hertfordshire CC [1985] A.C. 791; [1985] 2 W.L.R. 892; [1985] 2 All E.R. 301; (1985) 149 J.P. 593; 83 L.G.R. 669; [1985] Fam. Law 326; (1985) 82 L.S.G. 2087; (1985) 135 N.L.J. 483; (1985) 129 S.J. 347, HL .... *Digested,* 85/**2255**: *Applied* 86/2181, 86/2214, 86/2218, 87/2460, 88/1215, 90/3122: *Considered* 86/2171, 86/2213, 87/2457, 87/2518, 87/2523, 06/1699: *Distinguished* 86/2212: *Followed* 86/2160, 89/2485, 02/315, 09/1647, 17/1069

W (Adoption Application: Reunification with Family of Origin), Re; *sub nom* H (A Child) (Placement Order: Judge's Understanding of Earlier Proceedings), Re; Prospective Adopters v Brighton and Hove City Council [2015] EWCA Civ 1284; [2016] 2 F.L.R. 1173; [2016] 1 F.C.R. 381; [2016] Fam. Law 274, CA (Civ Div) .... *Digested,* 16/**809**: *Applied* 17/912

W (Children) (Abuse: Oral Evidence), Re see W (Children) (Family Proceedings: Evidence), Re

W (Children) (Convention Rights Claim: Procedure), Re; *sub nom* SW (Human Rights Claim: Procedure) (No.1), Re; Luton BC v PW; *joined case* PW v Luton BC [2017] EWHC 450 (Fam); [2017] 1 W.L.R. 3451; [2017] 2 F.L.R. 1609, Fam Div *Digested,* 17/**975**

W (Children) (Family Proceedings: Evidence), Re; *sub nom* W (Children) (Abuse: Oral Evidence), Re [2010] UKSC 12; [2010] 1 W.L.R. 701; [2010] 2 All E.R. 418; [2010] P.T.S.R. 775; [2010] 1 F.L.R. 1485; [2010] 1 F.C.R. 615; [2010] H.R.L.R. 22; Times, March 8, 2010; [2010] Fam. Law 449; (2010) 107(11) L.S.G. 15; (2010) 160 N.L.J. 389; (2010) 154(9) S.J.L.B. 28, SC .... *Digested,* 10/**1398**: *Applied* 12/1334, 12/1335, 14/1412: *Considered* 12/1336, 14/1309, 17/993: *Followed* 11/1370, 12/1338, 15/1032, 15/1144, 16/856, 16/857

W (Children) (Parental Agreement with Local Authority), Re [2014] EWCA Civ 1065; [2015] 1 F.L.R. 949; [2014] Fam. Law 1394, CA (Civ Div) .... *Digested,* 15/**1136**: *Considered* 17/950: *Followed* 16/821

W (Children), Re [2017] EWFC 61; [2017] 3 F.C.R. 709, Fam Ct

W (Incapacitated Person) (Representatives and Advocates: Duties and Powers), Re see D (Incapacitated Person) (Representatives and Advocates: Duties and Powers), Re

W (R) v HM Advocate; *sub nom* RW v HM Advocate [2017] HCJAC 17; 2017 S.C.L. 459; 2017 S.C.C.R. 203; 2017 G.W.D. 11-152, HCJ .... *Digested,* 17/**2522**

W (Representation of Child), Re see W (A Child) (Care Proceedings: Child's Representation), Re

W Braithwaite & Son Ltd (In Administration), Re [2016] B.P.I.R. 1282, Ch D (Leeds) ... *Digested,* 17/**1273**

W Ltd v M Sdn Bhd [2016] EWHC 422 (Comm); [2017] 1 All E.R. (Comm) 981; [2016] 1 Lloyd's Rep. 552; [2016] 1 C.L.C. 437; 164 Con. L.R. 66; [2016] C.I.L.L. 3828, QBD (Comm) .... *Digested,* 16/**73**

W Nagel (A Firm) v Pluczenik Diamond Co NV [2017] EWHC 1750 (Comm); [2018] 1 All E.R. (Comm) 124; [2017] Bus. L.R. 1691; [2017] 2 Lloyd's Rep. 215; [2018] E.C.C. 2, QBD (Comm) .... *Digested,* 17/**46**

WA Sherratt Ltd v John Bromley (Church Stretton) Ltd [1985] Q.B. 1038; [1985] 2 W.L.R. 742; [1985] 1 All E.R. 216; [1985] F.L.R. 8; (1985) 82 L.S.G. 44; (1985) 129 S.J. 67, CA (Civ Div) .... *Digested,* 85/**2704**: *Applied* 15/358: *Considered* 96/2823, 17/1314

Waaler v Hounslow LBC; *sub nom* Hounslow LBC v Waaler [2015] UKUT 17 (LC); [2015] L. & T.R. 24, UT (Lands) .... *Digested,* 16/**1392**: *Affirmed* 17/1470

Waaler v Hounslow LBC; *sub nom* Hounslow LBC v Waaler [2017] EWCA Civ 45; [2017] 1 W.L.R. 2817; [2017] H.L.R. 16; [2017] 1 P. & C.R. 15; [2017] L. & T.R. 19, CA (Civ Div) .... *Digested,* 17/**1470**

Wade (Philip) v HM Advocate; *joined case* Coats (Colin) v HM Advocate [2014] HCJAC 88; 2014 S.C.L. 680; 2014 G.W.D. 25-481, HCJ .... *Digested,* 14/**3377**: *Considered* 17/2807

Wagner v EUI Ltd (Unreported, February 13, 2017), CC (Slough) [*Louis Zvesper, Barrister, Hardwicke Building, New Square, London*] .... *Digested,* 17/**1673**

Wagner v Luxembourg (76240/01) (Unreported, June 28, 2007), ECHR *Applied* 17/914

Wakelin v Read [2000] O.P.L.R. 277; [2000] Pens. L.R. 319; Times, April 10, 2000, CA (Civ Div) .... *Digested,* 00/**4393**: *Applied* 05/2976, 10/2377, 17/1625: *Followed* 11/2309

Walachowski v Poland see Krolik v Poland

Walapu v Revenue and Customs Commissioners [2016] EWHC 658 (Admin); [2016] 4 All E.R. 955; [2016] S.T.C. 1682; [2016] B.T.C. 14; [2016] S.T.I. 1336, QBD (Admin) .... *Digested,* 16/**2115**: *Considered* 16/2051, 17/2126

Walgate & Son v Scottish Natural Heritage see A I Walgate & Son v Scottish Natural Heritage

Walker v Chief Constable of the West Midlands see Hunter v Chief Constable of the West Midlands

Walker v Emslie. (1899) 3 Adam 102, HCJ *Considered* 17/2540

Walker v Gotgs (Unreported, December 13, 2015), CC (Norwich) [*Irwin Mitchell LLB, Riverside West, 1 Millsands, Sheffield*] .... *Digested,* 17/**1652**

Walker v Innospec Ltd [2017] UKSC 47; [2017] 4 All E.R. 1004; [2018] 1 C.M.L.R. 26; [2017] I.C.R. 1077; [2017] I.R.L.R. 928; [2017] H.R.L.R. 10; [2017] Pens. L.R. 18; Times, July 25, 2017, SC .... *Digested,* 17/**1610**

Walker v Innospec Ltd see O'Brien v Ministry of Justice

Walker v National Westminster Bank Plc [2016] EWHC 315 (Ch); [2016] B.C.C. 355; [2017] 1 B.C.L.C. 124, Ch D (Birmingham)

Walker v Revenue and Customs Commissioners; *sub nom* Revenue and Customs Commissioners v Walker [2016] UKFTT 123 (TC), FTT (Tax) *Reversed* 17/2173

Walker v Revenue and Customs Commissioners; *sub nom* Revenue and Customs Commissioners v Walker [2016] UKUT 32 (TCC); [2017] S.T.C. 1145; [2017] B.T.C. 506, UT (Tax) .... *Digested,* 17/**2173**

Walker (t/a Walkers Financial Planning) v Financial Conduct Authority [2017] B.P.I.R. 1736, UT (Tax)

Wall v Collins [2007] EWCA Civ 444; [2007] Ch. 390; [2007] 3 W.L.R. 459; [2008] 1 All E.R. 122; [2008] 1 P. & C.R. 19; (2007) 104(22) L.S.G. 26; (2007) 151 S.J.L.B. 675; [2007] N.P.C. 64, CA (Civ Div) .... *Digested,* 07/**3426**: *Considered* 17/1840

Wall v Royal Bank of Scotland Plc [2016] EWHC 2460 (Comm); [2017] 4 W.L.R. 2; [2016] 5 Costs L.R. 943, QBD (Comm) .... *Digested,* 16/**280**: *Considered* 17/205

Wall v Standard Telephones & Cables Ltd (No.2) see Alexander v Standard Telephones & Cables Ltd (No.2)

Wallace v Secretary of State for Education [2017] EWHC 109 (Admin); [2017] P.T.S.R. 675; [2017] E.L.R. 237; Times, March 20, 2017; [2017] A.C.D. 37, QBD (Admin) .... *Digested,* 17/**718**

Wallace (James) v HM Advocate [2017] HCJAC 40; 2017 S.C.L. 710; 2017 G.W.D. 20-320, HCJ Appeal .... *Digested,* 17/**2548**

Wallbank v Wallbank Fox Designs Ltd see Weddall v Barchester Healthcare Ltd

Wallenborn Transports SA v Hauptzollamt Giessen (C-571/15) EU:C:2017:417; [2017] B.V.C. 27; [2017] S.T.I. 1236, ECJ (5th Chamber)

Wallersteiner v Moir (No.1); *sub nom* Moir v Wallersteiner (No.1) [1974] 1 W.L.R. 991; [1974] 3 All E.R. 217; (1974) 118 S.J. 464, CA (Civ Div) .... *Digested,* 74/**2143**: *Applied* 78/242, 17/346: *Distinguished* 91/2853
Walters v Babergh DC 82 L.G.R. 235; Times, June 21, 1983; (1983) 127 S.J. 595, QBD .... *Digested,* 84/**2072**: *Applied* 06/1439, 17/872: *Considered* 94/3900: *Followed* 14/3696
Walters (t/a Rosewood) v Barik [2017] I.C.R. D16, EAT
Waltham Forest LBC v Khan [2017] UKUT 153 (LC); [2017] L.L.R. 673, UT (Lands) .... *Digested,* 17/**1162**
Waltham Forest LBC v Mitoo [2016] EWHC 2159 (Admin); [2017] Env. L.R. 9; [2016] A.C.D. 99, DC .... *Digested,* 17/**1580**
Walton v Allman [2015] EWHC 3325 (Ch); [2016] 1 W.L.R. 2053; [2017] 1 F.L.R. 927; [2016] B.P.I.R. 1056; [2016] Fam. Law 168, Ch D .... *Digested,* 16/**171**
Walton v Scottish Ministers [2012] UKSC 44; [2013] P.T.S.R. 51; 2013 S.C. (U.K.S.C.) 67; 2012 S.L.T. 1211; [2013] 1 C.M.L.R. 28; [2013] Env. L.R. 16; [2013] J.P.L. 323; 2012 G.W.D. 34-689, SC .... *Digested,* 13/**3703**: *Applied* 13/2358, 14/3730, 15/2027: *Considered* 13/3409, 14/2419, 17/1814: *Followed* 16/1715
Walton Centre NHS Foundation Group v Briggs see Briggs (Incapacitated Person), Re
Wamala v Tascor Services Ltd (formerly Reliance Secure Task Management Ltd) [2017] EWHC 1461 (QB); [2017] 4 W.L.R. 155, QBD
Wan v Admiral Insurance (Unreported, December 2, 2016), CC (Coventry) [*IMe Law Ltd, Riverside West, 1 Millsands, Sheffield*] .... *Digested,* 17/**1667**
Wandsworth LBC v Griffin [2000] 2 E.G.L.R. 105; [2000] 26 E.G. 147; [2001] R.V.R. 45, Lands Tr .... *Digested,* 00/**3947**: *Considered* 17/1470
Wandsworth LBC v Michalak; *sub nom* Michaelek v Wandsworth LBC; Michalak v Wandsworth LBC [2002] EWCA Civ 271; [2003] 1 W.L.R. 617; [2002] 4 All E.R. 1136; [2003] 1 F.C.R. 713; [2002] H.L.R. 39; [2002] N.P.C. 34, CA (Civ Div) ..... *Digested,* 03/**2789**: *Applied* 03/2079, 03/4265, 04/1889, 04/2782, 04/3731, 04/710, 06/2277, 10/1703, 17/1466: *Considered* 03/2171, 04/2534, 04/2776, 04/4738, 05/3835: *Followed* 02/3079, 04/1898
Wandsworth LBC v Vining [2017] EWCA Civ 1092; [2018] I.C.R. 499; [2017] I.R.L.R. 1140; Times, September 26, 2017, CA (Civ Div)
Wannell v Rothwell (Inspector of Taxes) [1996] S.T.C. 450; 68 T.C. 719; Times, April 11, 1996, Ch D .... *Digested,* 96/**3398**: *Applied* 17/2145: *Considered* 04/3778: *Followed* 16/2096
Ward v Coope; *sub nom* Coope v Ward [2015] EWCA Civ 30; [2015] 1 W.L.R. 4081, CA (Civ Div) .... *Digested,* 15/**1776**: *Followed* 17/2297
Ward of Court (Wardship: Interview), Re; *sub nom* A (A Child) (Ward of Court: Security Service Interview), Re [2017] EWHC 1022 (Fam); [2017] Fam. 369; [2017] 3 W.L.R. 593; [2017] 4 All E.R. 331; [2017] 2 F.L.R. 1515; [2017] 3 F.C.R. 171, Fam Div .... *Digested,* 17/**1069**
Waren Import Gesellschaft Krohn & Co v Internationale Graanhandel Thegra NV [1975] 1 Lloyd's Rep. 146, QBD (Comm) .... *Digested,* 75/**3145**: *Applied* 17/1997: *Considered* 16/1944
Warner v Lewis see Lewis v Warner
Warner v Scapa Flow Charters [2016] CSOH 101; 2016 S.L.T. 918; 2016 G.W.D. 23-436, OH .... *Digested,* 16/**2454**: *Reversed in part* 17/2436
Warner v Scapa Flow Charters [2017] CSIH 13; 2017 S.C. 361; 2017 S.L.T. 239; 2017 G.W.D. 7-106, IH (Ex Div) .... *Digested,* 17/**2436**
Warner-Lambert Co LLC v Actavis Group PTC EHF [2015] EWCA Civ 556; [2015] R.P.C. 25; (2015) 145 B.M.L.R. 216, CA (Civ Div) .... *Digested,* 15/**1515**: *Reversed in part* 17/1366
Warner-Lambert Co LLC v Generics (UK) Ltd (t/a Mylan) see Generics (UK) Ltd (t/a Mylan) v Warner-Lambert Co LLC
Warren v Random House Group Ltd [2008] EWCA Civ 834; [2009] Q.B. 600; [2009] 2 W.L.R. 314; [2009] 2 All E.R. 245; [2009] E.M.L.R. 1, CA (Civ Div) .... *Digested,* 09/**984**: *Applied* 13/797, 17/650: *Considered* 09/983
Warwickshire CC v Matalia; *sub nom* Matalia v Warwickshire CC 3BM30478, Ch D (Birmingham) *Affirmed* 17/2195
Warwickshire CC v Matalia; *sub nom* Matalia v Warwickshire CC [2017] EWCA Civ 991; [2017] E.C.C. 25; [2017] E.L.R. 428, CA (Civ Div) .... *Digested,* 17/**2195**
Wastell v Woodward (Deceased) [2017] Lloyd's Rep. I.R. 474, QBD .... *Digested,* 17/**1877**
Waterfall II, Re see Lehman Brothers International (Europe) (In Administration), Re

Wates Construction Ltd v HGP Greentree Allchurch Evans Ltd [2005] EWHC 2174 (TCC); [2006] B.L.R. 45; 105 Con. L.R. 47, QBD (TCC) .... *Digested,* 06/**383**: *Applied* 06/382, 10/1117, 17/263
Wathelet v Garage Bietheres & Fils SPRL (C-149/15) EU:C:2016:840; [2017] 1 W.L.R. 865; [2017] R.T.R. 10; [2017] 2 C.M.L.R. 6, ECJ (5th Chamber)
Watson v Bogue (No.1) 2000 S.L.T. (Sh Ct) 125; 1998 S.C.L.R. 512; 1998 G.W.D. 18-930, Sh Pr .... *Digested,* 98/**6176**: *Distinguished* 17/2781
Watson v Watchfinder.co.uk Ltd [2017] EWHC 1275 (Comm); [2017] Bus. L.R. 1309, QBD (Comm) .... *Digested,* 17/**399**
Watson v Watson (Wasted Costs Orders) see Ridehalgh v Horsefield
Watt v ABC [2016] EWCOP 2532; [2017] 4 W.L.R. 24; [2016] C.O.P.L.R. 605; [2017] W.T.L.R. 159; [2017] W.T.L.R. 739; [2017] 1 P. & C.R. DG9, CP .... *Digested,* 17/**1549**: *Considered* 17/2217
Watt v Murphy [2016] SAC (Crim) 16; 2016 S.L.T. (Sh Ct) 247; 2016 S.C.L. 798; 2016 S.C.C.R. 314; 2016 G.W.D. 18-333, SAC .... *Digested,* 16/**2793**: *Distinguished* 17/2516
Watts v Driver and Vehicle Standards Agency [2017] EWHC 1019 (Admin); [2017] 1 W.L.R. 3426; [2018] R.T.R. 6; [2018] 1 C.M.L.R. 33, DC .... *Digested,* 17/**1880**
Watts v Secretary of State for Health [2016] EWHC 2835 (QB); [2017] Med. L.R. 14; (2017) 153 B.M.L.R. 179, QBD
Watts v Stewart; *sub nom* Stewart v Watts [2016] EWCA Civ 1247; [2017] 2 W.L.R. 1107; [2017] H.L.R. 8; [2017] L. & T.R. 24; Times, January 10, 2017; [2017] 1 P. & C.R. DG18, CA (Civ Div) .... *Digested,* 17/**1448**
Waydale Ltd v MRM Engineering 1996 S.L.T. (Sh Ct) 6, Sh Pr .... *Digested,* 96/**7112**: *Distinguished* 17/2696
WB v HM Advocate [2014] HCJAC 52; 2014 S.C.C.R. 376; 2014 G.W.D. 17-317, HCJ *Digested,* 14/**3388**: *Considered* 17/2473
WD v HD [2015] EWHC 1547 (Fam); [2017] 1 F.L.R. 160; [2016] Fam. Law 160, Fam Div
Wealden DC v Secretary of State for Communities and Local Government; *sub nom* Secretary of State for Communities and Local Government v Wealden DC [2017] EWCA Civ 39; [2018] Env. L.R. 5; [2017] J.P.L. 625, CA (Civ Div) .... *Digested,* 17/**1775**
Wealden DC v Secretary of State for Communities and Local Government [2017] EWHC 351 (Admin); [2017] Env. L.R. 31, QBD (Admin) .... *Digested,* 17/**1704**
Wealden DC v Secretary of State for Communities and Local Government [2016] EWHC 247 (Admin); [2016] Env. L.R. 19, QBD (Admin) .... *Digested,* 16/**1747**: *Affirmed* 17/1775
Wearside Civil Engineering Ltd v Revenue and Customs Commissioners [2016] UKFTT 780 (TC); [2017] S.T.I. 79, FTT (Tax)
Weatherford Global Products Ltd v Hydropath Holdings Ltd [2014] EWHC 3243 (TCC), QBD (TCC) *Considered* 17/336
Weatherilt v Cathay Pacific Airways Ltd [2017] I.C.R. 985; [2017] I.R.L.R. 609, EAT .... *Digested,* 17/**853**: *Considered* 17/856
Webb v Liverpool Women's NHS Foundation Trust [2016] EWCA Civ 365; [2016] 1 W.L.R. 3899; [2017] 2 All E.R. 313; [2016] C.P. Rep. 30; [2016] 2 Costs L.R. 411; (2016) 150 B.M.L.R. 42, CA (Civ Div) .... *Digested,* 16/**225**
Webb v Webb (C-294/92) EU:C:1994:193; [1994] Q.B. 696; [1994] 3 W.L.R. 801; [1994] 3 All E.R. 911; [1994] E.C.R. I-1717; [1994] I.L.Pr. 389; Times, June 27, 1994; [1994] N.P.C. 97, ECJ .... *Digested,* 94/**4798**: *Applied* 00/3490, 01/3736, 07/1710: *Distinguished* 16/898, 17/1849
Webb-Samann v Seagon (C-454/15) EU:C:2016:891; [2017] 2 C.M.L.R. 18, ECJ (2nd Chamber)
Webber v Department for Education [2016] EWHC 2519 (Ch); [2017] I.C.R. 198; [2017] Pens. L.R. 1, Ch D .... *Digested,* 17/**1625**
Weber's Wine World Handels GmbH v Abgabenberufungskommission Wien (C147/01) EU:C:2003:533; [2003] E.C.R. I-11365; [2004] 1 C.M.L.R. 7; [2005] All E.R. (EC) 224; [2003] C.E.C. 501; [2004] B.T.C. 8019, ECJ (5th Chamber) .. *Digested,* 04/**908**: *Applied* 17/2289: *Considered* 10/3278, 13/3220: *Followed* 14/3074
WebMindLicenses Kft v Nemzeti Ado- es Vamhivatal Kiemelt Ado- es Vam Foigazgatosag (C-419/14) EU:C:2015:832; [2016] 4 W.L.R. 50; [2017] S.T.C. 97; [2016] 2 C.M.L.R. 23; [2016] C.E.C. 1011; [2016] B.V.C. 4; [2016] S.T.I. 203, ECJ (3rd Chamber)
Webster v Brunel University see Wong v Igen Ltd (formerly Leeds Careers Guidance)
Webster v Burton Hospitals NHS Foundation Trust [2017] EWCA Civ 62; [2017] Med. L.R. 113; (2017) 154 B.M.L.R. 129, CA (Civ Div) .... *Digested,* 17/**1556**

Weddall v Barchester Healthcare Ltd; *joined case* Wallbank v Wallbank Fox Designs Ltd [2012] EWCA Civ 25; [2012] I.R.L.R. 307, CA (Civ Div) .... *Digested,* 12/**3344**: *Considered* 14/3000: *Followed* 17/2205

Weeks v Magill see Porter v Magill

Weir v Hilsdon [2017] EWHC 983 (Ch); [2017] B.P.I.R. 1088, Ch D .... *Digested,* 17/**1300**

Welbeck Securities Ltd v Powlson (Inspector of Taxes); *sub nom* Powlson v Welbeck Securities Ltd [1987] S.T.C. 468; [1987] 2 F.T.L.R. 298; 60 T.C. 269; (1987) 84(27) L.S.G. 2120; (1987) 131 S.J. 942, CA (Civ Div) .... *Digested,* 88/**253**: *Applied* 06/4144, 17/2092

Welch v Welch [2017] 3 F.C.R. 405, Fam Ct

Welds v Yorkshire Ambulance Service NHS Trust [2016] EWHC 3325 (QB); (2017) 155 B.M.L.R. 101, QBD .... *Digested,* 17/**1555**

Welford v EDF Energy Networks (LPN) Plc [2007] EWCA Civ 293; [2007] 2 P. & C.R. 15; [2007] 2 E.G.L.R. 1; [2007] 24 E.G. 170; [2007] R.V.R. 172; Times, May 8, 2007; [2007] 15 E.G. 147 (C.S.); [2007] N.P.C. 40; [2007] Bus. L.R. D63, CA (Civ Div) .... *Digested,* 07/**3385**: *Considered* 16/2674, 17/2644

Weller v Associated Newspapers Ltd [2014] EWHC 2127 (QB), QBD *Considered* 17/214

Wellesley v Duke of Beaufort; *sub nom* Long Wellesley's Case 39 E.R. 538; (1831) 2 Russ. & M. 639, Ch D *Applied* 63/2577, 17/8: *Considered* 11/484

Wellesley Partners LLP v Withers LLP [2015] EWCA Civ 1146; [2016] Ch. 529; [2016] 2 W.L.R. 1351; 163 Con. L.R. 53; [2016] P.N.L.R. 19; [2016] C.I.L.L. 3757, CA (Civ Div) .... *Digested,* 16/**1544**: *Followed* 16/1548, 17/1577, 17/2201

Wells v Devani; *sub nom* Devani v Wells [2016] EWCA Civ 1106; [2017] Q.B. 959; [2017] 2 W.L.R. 1391, CA (Civ Div) .... *Digested,* 17/**47**

Wells v United Kingdom (57715/09) see James v United Kingdom (25119/09)

Wells v Vale of White Horse DC [2017] P.A.D. 25, Planning Inspector

Welsh Development Agency v Redpath Dorman Long Ltd [1994] 1 W.L.R. 1409; [1994] 4 All E.R. 10; 67 B.L.R. 1; 38 Con. L.R. 106; Times, April 4, 1994; Independent, May 2, 1994; (1994) 10 Const. L.J. 325; (1994) 91(21) L.S.G. 42; (1994) 138 S.J.L.B. 87, CA (Civ Div) .... *Digested,* 95/**4191**: *Applied* 97/1047, 07/491, 14/426, 14/427: *Considered* 96/859, 97/2719, 99/481, 05/479, 10/394: *Distinguished* 96/820, 99/542: *Followed* 12/308, 17/1342

Welsh Ministers v PJ see PJ (A Patient) v Local Health Board

Wenner v Germany (62303/13) (2017) 64 E.H.R.R. 19; 42 B.H.R.C. 530, ECHR

Wermuth v Wermuth [2003] EWCA Civ 50; [2003] 1 W.L.R. 942; [2003] 4 All E.R. 531; [2003] 1 F.C.R. 289; Times, February 7, 2003; [2003] Fam. Law 308, CA (Civ Div) .... *Digested,* 03/**1585**: *Applied* 07/1772, 14/1326, 17/1042: *Considered* 15/1063

Wes Futures Ltd v Allen Wilson Construction Ltd [2016] EWHC 2863 (TCC); 170 Con. L.R. 121; [2016] 6 Costs L.R. 1083; [2017] C.I.L.L. 3926, QBD (TCC) .... *Digested,* 17/**258**

West v Ian Finlay and Associates [2014] EWCA Civ 316; [2014] B.L.R. 324; 153 Con. L.R. 1; [2014] 2 E.G.L.R. 63; [2014] C.I.L.L. 3507, CA (Civ Div) .... *Digested,* 14/**595**: *Followed* 17/489

West v Revenue and Customs Commissioners [2016] UKFTT 536 (TC); [2017] S.F.T.D. 389; [2016] S.T.I. 168, FTT (Tax)

West v Scottish Prison Service see West v Secretary of State for Scotland

West v Secretary of State for Scotland; *sub nom* West v Scottish Prison Service 1992 S.C. 385; 1992 S.L.T. 636; 1992 S.C.L.R. 504; Times, June 11, 1992; Scotsman, May 5, 1992, IH (1 Div) .... *Digested,* 92/**5191**: *Applied* 95/5443, 97/5714, 97/6043, 97/6359, 03/5265: *Considered* 95/5441, 00/6205, 03/5192, 04/4478, 04/4543, 17/2393: *Explained* 93/4730: *Followed* 00/5832, 10/3995, 11/4329, 12/3822, 14/3301

West Berkshire DC v Department for Communities and Local Government see R. (on the application of West Berkshire DC) v Secretary of State for Communities and Local Government

West Lancashire BC v Secretary of State for Communities and Local Government [2009] EWHC 3631 (Admin), QBD (Admin) *Applied* 17/1758

West Lothian Council v B; *sub nom* EV (A Child), Re; West Lothian Council v MB [2017] UKSC 15; 2017 S.C. (U.K.S.C.) 67; 2017 S.L.T. 319; 2017 Fam. L.R. 34; 2017 G.W.D. 8-114, SC .... *Digested,* 17/**1063**

West Lothian Council v B; *sub nom* EV (A Child), Re; West Lothian Council v MB [2016] CSIH 60; 2017 S.C.L.R. 304; 2016 Fam. L.R. 134; 2016 G.W.D. 25-463, IH (2 Div)
Reversed 17/1063

West Lothian Council v MB see West Lothian Council v B

West Sussex CC v Alma [2016] EWHC 2009 (Fam); [2016] 4 W.L.R. 129; [2017] 1 F.L.R. 1383; [2016] Fam. Law 1217, Fam Div ..... *Digested,* 16/**813**

Westacre Investments Inc v Jugoimport SDPR Holding Co Ltd [2000] Q.B. 288; [1999] 3 W.L.R. 811; [1999] 3 All E.R. 864; [1999] 1 All E.R. (Comm) 865; [1999] 2 Lloyd's Rep. 65; [1999] C.L.C. 1176; [1999] B.L.R. 279; Times, May 25, 1999; Independent, May 25, 1999, CA (Civ Div) ..... *Digested,* 99/**236**:
Applied 99/230, 07/242, 09/182, 17/73: *Followed* 10/174, 16/430

Westermann Lernspielverlage GmbH v EUIPO (C-482/15 P) EU:C:2016:805; [2017] E.T.M.R. 1, ECJ (10th Chamber)

Western Excavating (ECC) Ltd v Sharp [1978] Q.B. 761; [1978] 2 W.L.R. 344; [1978] 1 All E.R. 713; [1978] I.C.R. 221; [1978] I.R.L.R. 27; (1978) 13 I.T.R. 132; Times, November 16, 1977; (1987) 121 S.J. 814, CA (Civ Div) ..... *Digested,* 78/**900**:
Applied 78/891, 78/893, 78/904, 79/838, 80/892, 81/981, 82/1097, 84/1194, 88/1247, 90/1929, 01/2234, 02/1427, 03/1214, 03/1221, 09/1255, 10/1032, 17/770: *Considered* 78/897, 78/905, 80/1008, 80/883, 81/103u, 81/808, 86/1261, 89/1458, 99/2030, 14/3506: *Distinguished* 79/846: *Explained* 80/893

Western Heritable Investment Co Ltd v Hunter 2004 S.C. 635; 2004 S.L.T. 355; 2004 S.C.L.R. 819; 2004 G.W.D. 11-250, IH (1 Div) ..... *Digested,* 04/**4993**:
Considered 17/2699

Western Trading Ltd v Great Lakes Reinsurance (UK) Plc; *sub nom* Great Lakes Reinsurance (UK) SE v Western Trading Ltd [2016] EWCA Civ 1003; [2016] 2 C.L.C. 478; [2016] Lloyd's Rep. I.R. 643, CA (Civ Div) ..... *Digested,* 17/**1343**

Western Trading Ltd v Great Lakes Reinsurance (UK) Plc; *sub nom* Great Lakes Reinsurance (UK) SE v Western Trading Ltd [2015] EWHC 103 (QB); [2015] Lloyd's Rep. I.R. 561, QBD (Merc) (London) ..... *Digested,* 15/**1472**:
Reversed in part 17/1343

Westflische Drahtindustrie GmbH v European Commission (C-523/15 P) EU:C:2016:541; [2017] 4 C.M.L.R. 7, ECJ (6th Chamber)

Westfoot Invesments Ltd v European Property Holdings Inc 2015 S.L.T. (Sh Ct) 201; 2015 Hous. L.R. 57; 2015 G.W.D. 29-492, Sh Ct (Lothian) (Edinburgh) ..... *Digested,* 15/**3286**:
Considered 17/2651

Westland Helicopters Ltd v Arab Organisation for Industrialisation [1995] Q.B. 282; [1995] 2 W.L.R. 126; [1995] 2 All E.R. 387; [1994] 2 Lloyd's Rep. 608, QBD (Comm) ..... *Digested,* 96/**3659**:
Applied 06/2396: *Considered* 17/157

Westminster City Council v National Asylum Support Services see R. (on the application of Westminster City Council) v National Asylum Support Service

Westminster City Council v Owadally [2017] EWHC 1092 (Admin); [2017] 1 W.L.R. 4350; [2017] 2 Cr. App. R. 18; (2017) 181 J.P. 377; Times, June 22, 2017; [2017] Crim. L.R. 806; [2017] A.C.D. 89, DC ..... *Digested,* 17/**573**

Westminster City Council v Secretary of State for Communities and Local Government [2013] EWHC 690 (Admin), QBD (Admin)
Applied 17/1750

Westminster City Council v UKI (Kingsway) Ltd see UKI (Kingsway) Ltd v Westminster City Council

Westminster Trading Ltd v Revenue and Customs Commissioners [2017] UKUT 23 (TCC); [2017] B.V.C. 503, UT (Tax) ..... *Digested,* 17/**2275**

Westwood v Knight [2012] EWPCC 14, PCC
Applied 17/1007

Weszka v Poland; *sub nom* Weszka v Regional Court in Poznan, Poland [2017] EWHC 168 (Admin); [2017] A.C.D. 43, QBD (Admin)

Weszka v Regional Court in Poznan, Poland see Weszka v Poland

Wetheralds Construction Ltd v Revenue and Customs Commissioners [2016] UKFTT 827 (TC); [2017] S.T.I. 170, FTT (Tax)

WF Gozze Frottierweberei GmbH v Baumwollborse (C-689/15) EU:C:2017:434; [2017] Bus. L.R. 1795, ECJ (2nd Chamber)

WH Newson Holding Ltd v IMI Plc; *sub nom* IMI Plc v Delta Ltd [2016] EWCA Civ 773; [2017] Ch. 27; [2016] 3 W.L.R. 1595; [2016] C.P. Rep. 46, CA (Civ Div) ..... *Digested,* 16/**190**

WHA Ltd v Revenue and Customs Commissioners [2013] UKSC 24; [2013] 2 All E.R. 907; [2013] S.T.C. 943; [2013] B.V.C. 155; [2013] S.T.I. 1769, SC ..... *Digested,* 13/**3209**:
Applied 14/3087: *Considered* 17/2249

Wheeldon Bros Waste Ltd v Millennium Insurance Co Ltd [2017] EWHC 218 (TCC); [2017] B.L.R. 234, QBD (TCC) ..... *Digested,* 17/**184**

Wheels Common Investment Fund Trustees Ltd v Revenue and Customs Commissioners [2017] UKFTT 830 (TC); [2017] S.F.T.D. **441**; [2017] S.T.I. 246; [2017] S.T.I. 172, FTT (Tax)

Wheels Private Hire Ltd v Revenue and Customs Commissioners; *sub nom* Revenue and Customs Commissioners v Wheels Private Hire Ltd [2015] UKFTT 363 (TC); [2016] L.L.R. 464; [2015] S.T.I. 2490, FTT (Tax)
Affirmed 17/2265

Wheels Private Hire Ltd v Revenue and Customs Commissioners; *sub nom* Revenue and Customs Commissioners v Wheels Private Hire Ltd [2017] UKUT 51 (TCC); [2017] B.V.C. 506; [2017] L.L.R. 275, UT (Tax) .... *Digested,* 17/**2265**

Whitbread Group Plc v Revenue and Customs Commissioners see Marriott Rewards LLC v Revenue and Customs Commissioners

Whitcombe v Bank of Scotland Plc [2017] CSOH 58; 2017 Hous. L.R. 40; 2017 G.W.D. 14-212, OH .... *Digested,* 17/**2692**

White v Ealing LBC; *joined cases* Richardson v Solihull MBC; Hereford and Worcester CC v Lane; Solihull MBC v Finn; Solihull MBC v Special Educational Needs Tribunal [1999] 1 F.C.R. 356; [1998] Ed. C.R. 308; [1998] E.L.R. 319; (1998) 42 B.M.L.R. 182; Times, April 10, 1998, CA (Civ Div) .... *Digested,* 98/**1977**:
Applied 08/1088, 13/1442: *Considered* 98/1979, 08/922, 17/714:
Distinguished 03/1120

White v Jones [1995] 2 A.C. 207; [1995] 2 W.L.R. 187; [1995] 1 All E.R. 691; [1995] 3 F.C.R. 51; Times, February 17, 1995; Independent, February 17, 1995; (1995) 145 N.L.J. 251; (1995) 139 S.J.L.B. 83; [1995] N.P.C. 31, HL .... *Digested,* 95/**3701**:
Applied 98/4593, 98/4595, 01/4507, 01/4524, 01/4538, 02/3297, 10/2290, 16/1546: *Considered* 97/331, 97/3830, 97/692, 98/3921, 98/3927, 98/3931, 98/3951, 98/4019, 00/4219, 00/4225, 01/4487, 01/4525, 04/2725, 04/2740, 08/2658, 10/2267, 11/4485, 13/2094, 13/4023, 13/4024, 17/1569:
Distinguished 97/3833, 98/4584, 99/3400, 99/4050, 04/2733, 04/3673, 09/5081, 11/4493: *Followed* 97/3834, 98/4021, 00/4253, 00/4259, 01/4534, 01/4537, 02/6000, 14/511, 15/1777: *Referred to* 95/5841

White v Philips [2017] EWHC 386 (Ch); [2017] Med. L.R. 180, Ch D (Leeds) .... *Digested,* 17/**2078**

White v White; *joined cases* Evans v Motor Insurers Bureau; Mighell v Reading [2001] UKHL 9; [2001] 1 W.L.R. 481; [2001] 2 All E.R. 43; [2001] 1 All E.R. (Comm) 1105; [2001] 1 Lloyd's Rep. 679; [2001] R.T.R. 25; [2001] 2 C.M.L.R. 1; [2001] Lloyd's Rep. I.R. 493; [2001] P.I.Q.R. P20; Times, March 6, 2001; Independent, April 30, 2001; (2001) 98(15) L.S.G. 33; (2001) 151 N.L.J. 350; (2001) 145 S.J.L.B. 67, HL .... *Digested,* 01/**3828**:
Applied 05/5054, 09/3954, 17/1350: *Considered* 04/2231, 06/2426, 09/2292, 10/1927, 11/4408: *Followed* 03/2472, 13/1743

White v White [2001] 1 A.C. 596; [2000] 3 W.L.R. 1571; [2001] 1 All E.R. 1; [2000] 2 F.L.R. 981; [2000] 3 F.C.R. 555; Times, October 31, 2000; Independent, November 1, 2000; [2001] Fam. Law 12; Daily Telegraph, November 7, 2000; (2000) 97(43) L.S.G. 38; (2000) 150 N.L.J. 1716; (2000) 144 S.J.L.B. 266; [2000] N.P.C. 111, HL .... *Digested,* 00/**2530**:
Applied 01/5156, 02/1678, 02/1682, 02/1687, 02/1690, 03/1581, 03/1589, 05/1656, 06/1623, 06/1626, 07/1695, 07/1700, 12/1423: *Considered* 01/2632, 01/2635, 01/2639, 03/1579, 04/1515, 04/4216, 05/1688, 06/1633, 06/4090, 07/1691, 07/1706, 08/1422, 09/2739, 10/1288, 10/1292, 11/1311, 12/1427, 12/1440, 14/1361, 15/1102: *Followed* 01/2633, 09/1491, 09/1504, 11/1296, 11/1302, 13/1309, 16/899, 17/983: *Referred to* 12/1421

Whitecap Leisure Ltd v John H Rundle Ltd [2008] EWCA Civ 429; [2008] 2 Lloyd's Rep. 216; [2008] C.P. Rep. 31; (2008) 152(18) S.J.L.B. 31, CA (Civ Div) .... *Digested,* 08/**393**:
Followed 17/461

Whitehead v Searle [2007] EWHC 2046 (QB), QBD
Considered 17/223

Whitehouse (David) v HM Advocate [2017] HCJAC 46; 2017 S.C.L. 742; 2017 G.W.D. 21-342, HCJ Appeal .... *Digested,* 17/**2519**

Whiting, Re [2014] C.O.P.L.R. 107, Fam Div .... *Digested,* 14/**320**:
Applied 17/1065: *Considered* 15/1719

Whittlestone v BJP Home Support Ltd [2014] I.C.R. 275; [2014] I.R.L.R. 176, EAT ...... *Digested,* 14/**1092**:
Applied 17/812: *Considered* 16/696

Whittome v Whittome (No.1) 1994 S.L.T. 114; 1993 S.C.L.R. 137, OH .... *Digested,* 93/**5223**:
Considered 17/2611: *Followed* 99/6074

Why v Cheltenham BC [2017] UKUT 208 (LC); [2017] R.V.R. 284, UT (Lands) .... *Digested,* 17/**1834**

Whyatt v Powell [2017] EWHC 484 (Admin); [2017] Lloyd's Rep. I.R. 478, QBD (Admin) .... *Digested,* 17/**1350**

Whyte v Ticehurst [1986] Fam. 64; [1986] 2 W.L.R. 700; [1986] 2 All E.R. 158; [1986] 2 F.L.R. 83; [1986] Fam. Law 192; (1986) 83 L.S.G. 875; (1985) 130 S.J. 185, Fam Div .... *Digested,* 86/**3548**: *Applied* 89/3812: *Considered* 90/4657, 17/2072

Whyte (Craig) v HM Advocate [2017] HCJAC 14; 2017 J.C. 262; 2017 S.C.L. 751; 2017 S.C.C.R. 354; 2017 G.W.D. 21-341, HCJ Appeal .... *Digested,* 17/**2512**

Wickersham v Revenue and Customs Commissioners [2016] EWHC 2956 (Ch); [2016] B.T.C. 46, Ch D (Leeds) .... *Digested,* 17/**2129**

Wightman (James) v HM Advocate [2017] HCJAC 50; 2017 S.C.L. 804; 2017 S.C.C.R. 437; 2017 G.W.D. 22-364, HCJ Appeal .... *Digested,* 17/**2475**

Wigley-Foster v Wilson [2016] EWCA Civ 454; [2016] 1 W.L.R. 4769; [2017] 1 All E.R. (Comm) 715; [2016] Lloyd's Rep. I.R. 622; [2016] P.I.Q.R. P17; Times, July 5, 2016, CA (Civ Div) .... *Digested,* 16/**1268**

Wildtree Hotels Ltd v Harrow LBC [2001] 2 A.C. 1; [2000] 3 W.L.R. 165; [2000] 3 All E.R. 289; [2000] B.L.G.R. 547; (2001) 81 P. & C.R. 9; [2000] 2 E.G.L.R. 5; [2000] R.V.R. 235; Times, June 27, 2000; Independent, July 31, 2000; [2000] E.G. 80 (C.S.); (2000) 97(28) L.S.G. 31; (2000) 150 N.L.J. 984; [2000] N.P.C. 71; (2001) 81 P. & C.R. DG9, HL .... *Digested,* 00/**4293**: *Applied* 16/1805: *Followed* 17/1832

Wilkes v DePuy International Ltd [2016] EWHC 3096 (QB); [2018] 2 W.L.R. 531; [2017] 3 All E.R. 589; (2017) 153 B.M.L.R. 91, QBD .... *Digested,* 17/**483**

Wilkin v Goldthorpe [1998] E.L.R. 345, QBD .... *Digested,* 98/**1980**: *Considered* 14/906, 17/713: *Followed* 13/900

Wilkinson v City of York Council [2011] EWCA Civ 207; [2011] P.T.S.R. D39, CA (Civ Div) *Applied* 17/1512

Wilkinson v Rossendale BC [2002] EWHC 1204 (Admin); [2003] J.P.L. 82, QBD (Admin) *Not followed* 17/1748

Wilky Group Ltd v Mole Valley DC [2017] P.A.D. 20, Planning Inspector

Will Woodlands (A Charity) v Revenue and Customs Commissioners [2017] UKFTT 578 (TC); [2017] S.T.I. 1833, FTT (Tax)

Willers v Gubay see Willers v Joyce

Willers v Joyce [2016] UKSC 43; [2016] 3 W.L.R. 477; [2017] 2 All E.R. 327; Times, September 2, 2016, SC .... *Digested,* 16/**2140**

Willers v Joyce; *sub nom* Willers v Gubay [2016] UKSC 44; [2016] 3 W.L.R. 534; [2017] 2 All E.R. 383; Times, September 6, 2016; [2016] C.I.L.L. 3876, SC .... *Digested,* 16/**1413**: *Followed* 16/873

William Cory & Son Ltd v CW Harrison see William Cory & Son Ltd v Harrison

William Cory & Son Ltd v Harrison; *sub nom* William Cory & Son Ltd v CW Harrison [1906] A.C. 274, HL *Considered* 17/823

William Jones's Schools Foundation Trustees v Parry; *sub nom* Trustees of the William Jones's Schools Foundation v Parry [2016] I.C.R. 1140, EAT .... *Digested,* 17/**794**

William Sindall Plc v Cambridgeshire CC [1994] 1 W.L.R. 1016; [1994] 3 All E.R. 932; 92 L.G.R. 121; Times, June 8, 1993; [1993] E.G. 105 (C.S.); [1993] N.P.C. 82, CA (Civ Div) .... *Digested,* 94/**572**: *Applied* 17/169: *Distinguished* 00/121: *Followed* 00/818

William Verry (Glazing Systems) Ltd v Furlong Homes Ltd [2005] EWHC 138 (TCC), QBD (TCC) *Applied* 17/658

Williams v British Airways Plc (C-155/10); *sub nom* British Airways Plc v Williams (C-155/10) EU:C:2011:588; [2012] 1 C.M.L.R. 23; [2012] C.E.C. 118; [2012] I.C.R. 847; [2011] I.R.L.R. 948; (2011) 161 N.L.J. 1292, ECJ (1st Chamber) .... *Digested,* 12/**1137**: *Applied* 15/833: *Explained* 17/805

Williams v Bullivant [1983] S.T.C. 107; 56 T.C. 159; [1982] B.T.C. 384, DC .... *Digested,* 83/**1946**: *Applied* 15/2492, 17/2172: *Referred to* 85/237

Williams v Central Bank of Nigeria; *sub nom* Central Bank of Nigeria v Williams [2014] UKSC 10; [2014] A.C. 1189; [2014] 2 W.L.R. 355; [2014] 2 All E.R. 489; [2014] W.T.L.R. 873; 16 I.T.E.L.R. 740; Times, March 5, 2014; (2014) 164(7596) N.L.J. 16, SC .... *Digested,* 14/**3023**: *Applied* 14/2991: *Followed* 17/321

Williams v Dartmoor National Park Authority [2017] P.A.D. 28, Planning Inspector

Williams v Glover see GP Aviation Group International Ltd (In Liquidation), Re

Williams v Hackney LBC; *sub nom* Hackney LBC v Williams [2017] EWCA Civ 26; [2017] 3 W.L.R. 59; [2017] 2 F.L.R. 1216, CA (Civ Div) .... *Digested,* 17/**950**

Williams v Hackney LBC; *sub nom* Hackney LBC v Williams [2015] EWHC 2629 (QB), QBD
Reversed 17/950

Williams v Inspector of Taxes see Locabail (UK) Ltd v Bayfield Properties Ltd (Leave to Appeal)

Williams v Lawrence [2011] EWHC 2001 (Ch); [2011] B.P.I.R. 1761; [2011] W.T.L.R. 1455, Ch D (Birmingham) .... *Digested,* 11/**2660**: *Applied* 17/1277

Williams v NHS Business Services Authority see NHS Business Services Authority v Williams

Williams v Revenue and Customs Commissioners [2016] UKFTT 846 (TC); [2017] S.T.I. 176, FTT (Tax)

Williams v Swansea University Pension and Assurance Scheme see Swansea University Pension and Assurance Scheme Trustees v Williams

Williams v Wednesbury Overseers (Unreported, 1890)
Followed 17/1822

Williams v Williams (1882) 20 Ch. D. 659, Ch D
Applied 07/1972, 09/6: *Considered* 17/661, 17/972

Williams (Valuation Officer) v Scottish & Newcastle Retail Ltd; *sub nom* Scottish & Newcastle Retail Ltd v Williams (Valuation Officer); *joined case* Allied Domecq Retailing Ltd v Williams (Valuation Officer) [2001] EWCA Civ 185; [2001] 1 E.G.L.R. 157; [2001] R.A. 41; [2001] L.L.R. 732; Times, March 6, 2001; Independent, February 21, 2001; [2001] 9 E.G. 227 (C.S.); (2001) 98(19) L.S.G. 37; [2001] N.P.C. 46, CA (Civ Div) .... *Digested,* 01/**4833**: *Applied* 01/4834, 03/3497, 03/3498, 07/3349, 09/3106, 17/1851: *Considered* 03/3528, 08/2546: *Followed* 03/3516, 12/2690

Williamson v Secretary of State for Education and Employment see R. (on the application of Williamson) v Secretary of State for Education and Employment

Williamson v Thompson see Jackson v Hall

Williamson (John) v HM Advocate [2016] HCJAC 115; 2017 S.C.L. 153; 2016 G.W.D. 38-678, HCJ .... *Digested,* 17/**2569**

Willmott v Rotherham NHS Foundation Trust [2017] EWCA Civ 181; (2017) 155 B.M.L.R. 58, CA (Civ Div) .... *Digested,* 17/**1554**

Willmott Dixon Construction Ltd v Robert West Consulting Ltd [2016] EWHC 3291 (TCC); [2017] B.L.R. 67; [2017] T.C.L.R. 1; [2017] P.N.L.R. 17, QBD (TCC) ...... *Digested,* 17/**477**

Willow Court Management Co (1985) Ltd v Alexander; *joined cases* Sinclair v 231 Sussex Gardens Right to Manage Ltd; Stone v 54 Hogarth Rd, London SW5 Management Ltd [2016] UKUT 290 (LC); [2016] L. & T.R. 34, UT (Lands) .... *Digested,* 17/**1460**

Wilsher v Essex AHA [1987] Q.B. 730; [1987] 2 W.L.R. 425; [1986] 3 All E.R. 801; Times, August 6, 1986; (1986) 83 L.S.G. 2661; (1986) 136 N.L.J. 1061; (1986) 130 S.J. 749, CA (Civ Div) .... *Digested,* 87/**2605**: *Considered* 17/1559: *Followed* 06/2866: *Reversed* 88/2415

Wilson v Exel UK Ltd (t/a Exel) [2010] CSIH 35; 2010 S.L.T. 671; 2010 S.C.L.R. 486; 2010 Rep. L.R. 68; 2010 G.W.D. 18-365, IH (1 Div) .... *Digested,* 10/**4499**: *Applied* 17/2205: *Considered* 12/3344, 13/3862, 15/1800: *Distinguished* 12/3901

Wilson v First County Trust Ltd (No.2); *sub nom* Wilson v Secretary of State for Trade and Industry [2003] UKHL 40; [2004] 1 A.C. 816; [2003] 3 W.L.R. 568; [2003] 4 All E.R. 97; [2003] 2 All E.R. (Comm) 491; [2003] H.R.L.R. 33; [2003] U.K.H.R.R. 1085; Times, July 11, 2003; Independent, November 3, 2003; (2003) 100(35) L.S.G. 39; (2003) 147 S.J.L.B. 872, HL .... *Digested,* 04/**628**: *Applied* 04/2222, 05/1410, 05/190, 05/3376, 05/672, 06/2735, 08/3105, 08/860, 10/3523, 12/3366, 13/3058, 13/3182, 13/409, 14/610, 17/719: *Considered* 04/3581, 05/17, 09/2137, 10/3925, 10/4537, 10/594, 12/1205, 12/1654: *Followed* 07/3293, 14/2241, 17/2074

Wilson v North Star Shipping (Aberdeen) Ltd [2014] CSOH 156; 2014 G.W.D. 36-675, OH
Considered 17/2757

Wilson v Secretary of State for Trade and Industry see Wilson v First County Trust Ltd (No.2)

Wilson v United Kingdom (30668/96); *joined cases* Palmer v United Kingdom (30671/96); Doolan v United Kingdom (30678/96) [2002] I.R.L.R. 568; (2002) 35 E.H.R.R. 20; 13 B.H.R.C. 39; Times, July 5, 2002, ECHR .... *Digested,* 02/**2375**: *Applied* 05/1310: *Considered* 06/1375, 17/766

Wilson v Williams [2015] EWHC 1841 (Ch); [2015] B.P.I.R. 1319, Ch D (Leeds)
Applied 17/1300

Wilson (Craig) v HM Advocate [2017] HCJAC 3; 2017 J.C. 135; 2017 S.C.L. 237; 2017 G.W.D. 3-32, HCJ .... *Digested,* 17/**2549**

Wilson (Sean) v HM Advocate [2017] HCJAC 52; 2017 S.C.L. 783; 2017 G.W.D. 23-393, HCJ Appeal .... *Digested,* 17/**2547**

Wilson Leisure Developments Ltd v Revenue and Customs Commissioners [2017] UKFTT 722 (TC); [2017] S.T.I. 2134, FTT (Tax)

Wilson Taylor Asia Pacific Pte Ltd v Dyna-Jet Pte Ltd see Dyna-Jet Pte Ltd v Wilson Taylor Asia Pacific Pte Ltd

Wilsons Solicitors LLP v Bentine; *sub nom* Bentine v Bentine; *joined case* Stone Rowe Brewer LLP v Just Costs Ltd [2015] EWCA Civ 1168; [2016] Ch. 489; [2016] 2 W.L.R. 1035; [2017] 1 All E.R. 345; [2015] 6 Costs L.O. 779, CA (Civ Div) .... *Digested,* 16/**205**: *Considered* 17/288

Wilton v Timothy James Consulting Ltd see Timothy James Consulting Ltd v Wilton

Wilton Park Ltd v Revenue and Customs Commissioners see Wiltonpark Ltd v Revenue and Customs Commissioners

Wiltonpark Ltd v Revenue and Customs Commissioners; *sub nom* Wilton Park Ltd v Revenue and Customs Commissioners [2016] EWCA Civ 1294; [2017] S.T.C. 1131; [2017] B.V.C. 1; [2017] L.L.R. 413; [2017] S.T.I. 32, CA (Civ Div) .... *Digested,* 17/**2283**

Wiltonpark Ltd v Revenue and Customs Commissioners; *sub nom* Wilton Park Ltd v Revenue and Customs Commissioners [2015] UKUT 343 (TCC); [2016] S.T.C. 189; [2015] B.V.C. 522; [2015] L.L.R. 923; [2015] S.T.I. 2398, UT (Tax) .... *Digested,* 15/**2621**: *Affirmed* 17/2283

Wimbledon Construction Co 2000 Ltd v Vago [2005] EWHC 1086 (TCC); [2005] B.L.R. 374; 101 Con. L.R. 99, QBD (TCC) .... *Digested,* 06/**664**: *Applied* 07/526, 08/607, 10/559, 10/560, 11/495, 12/600, 14/579, 14/580, 14/581, 17/471: *Considered* 09/652, 09/656

Winchester City Council v Handcock (Valuation Officer) [2006] R.A. 265, Lands Tr .... *Digested,* 07/**3345**: *Applied* 14/2129: *Followed* 17/1528

Wind Prospect Developments Ltd v Secretary of State for Communities and Local Government [2014] EWHC 4041 (Admin), QBD (Admin) *Applied* 17/1769

Windermere Marina Village Ltd v Wild [2014] UKUT 163 (LC); [2014] L. & T.R. 30; [2014] 3 E.G.L.R. 12, UT (Lands) .... *Digested,* 15/**1603**: *Approved* 17/1472

Windle v Secretary of State for Justice; *sub nom* Secretary of State for Justice v Windle; *joined case* Arada v Windle [2016] EWCA Civ 459; [2017] 3 All E.R. 568; [2016] I.C.R. 721; [2016] I.R.L.R. 628, CA (Civ Div) .... *Digested,* 16/**679**: *Followed* 17/788

Windsurfing Chiemsee Produktions und Vertriebs GmbH v Attenberger (C-109/97) see Windsurfing Chiemsee Produktions- und Vertriebs GmbH v Boots- und Segelzubehor Walter Huber (C-108/97)

Windsurfing Chiemsee Produktions- und Vertriebs GmbH v Boots- und Segelzubehor Walter Huber (C-108/97); *joined case* Windsurfing Chiemsee Produktions und Vertriebs GmbH v Attenberger (C-109/97) EU:C:1999:230; [2000] Ch. 523; [2000] 2 W.L.R. 205; [1999] E.C.R. I-2779; [1999] E.T.M.R. 585; Times, May 18, 1999, ECJ .... *Digested,* 99/**3530**: *Applied* 00/3705, 00/3718, 04/2372, 08/2405: *Considered* 00/3724, 00/3758, 02/2885, 03/2651, 04/2398, 08/2397, 13/1825, 14/1872, 15/1530: *Followed* 05/2557, 14/1917, 17/1389

Windsurfing International Inc v Tabur Marine (Great Britain) Ltd [1985] R.P.C. 59, CA (Civ Div) *Applied* 92/3291, 92/3319, 93/3041, 95/3758, 95/3777, 95/3778, 96/4568, 97/3902, 98/3477, 99/3506, 99/3519, 00/3639, 01/3902, 02/2816, 02/2840, 04/2273, 04/2308, 04/2341, 04/2346, 05/2481, 06/2503, 06/2530, 06/2531, 06/5538, 09/2396, 11/1979: *Considered* 93/3030, 94/2766, 95/3757, 95/3779, 01/3963, 02/2845, 03/5748, 04/2340, 07/2620, 08/4893: *Followed* 96/4543, 97/3901, 00/3678, 01/3967, 10/1980, 12/1940, 16/1311, 17/1376: *Referred to* 94/3438, 99/3480, 99/3514

Wingate v McGlennan 1992 S.L.T. 837; 1991 S.C.C.R. 133, HCJ Appeal .... *Digested,* 91/**4674**: *Considered* 17/2510: *Distinguished* 96/7315

Winterburn v Bennett [2016] EWCA Civ 482; [2017] 1 W.L.R. 646; [2017] R.T.R. 5; [2016] 2 P. & C.R. 11; Times, July 25, 2016; [2016] 2 P. & C.R. DG20, CA (Civ Div) .... *Digested,* 16/**1821**: *Followed* 17/1860

Winters v Secretary of State for Communities and Local Government [2017] EWHC 357 (Admin); [2017] P.T.S.R. 568; [2017] J.P.L. 684, QBD (Admin) .... *Digested,* 17/**1752**

Wintersteiger AG v Products 4U Sondermaschinenbau GmbH (C-523/10) EU:C:2012:220; [2013] Bus. L.R. 150; [2013] C.E.C. 15; [2012] E.T.M.R. 31; [2012] I.L.Pr. 23; Times, July 31, 2012, ECJ (1st Chamber)
Applied 17/1398

Wirral BC v Farthing [2008] EWHC 1919 (Ch); [2008] R.A. 303, Ch D
Applied 17/1504

Wirynska v Poland see Wisniewski v Poland

Wise Finance Ltd v Braymist Ltd see Braymist Ltd v Wise Finance Co Ltd

Wishart v Castlecroft Securities Ltd see Wishart, Petitioner

Wishart, Petitioner; *sub nom* Wishart v Castlecroft Securities Ltd [2009] CSIH 65; 2010 S.C. 16; 2009 S.L.T. 812; 2009 S.C.L.R. 696; [2010] B.C.C. 161; 2009 G.W.D. 28-446, IH (Ex Div) .... *Digested,* 10/**4009**:
Considered 13/354, 17/2422, 17/2423

Wisniewska v Nursing and Midwifery Council [2016] EWHC 2672 (Admin); (2017) 153 B.M.L.R. 127; [2016] A.C.D. 141, QBD (Admin) .... *Digested,* 17/**1116**

Wisniewski v Poland; *sub nom* Wisniewski v Regional Court of Wroclaw; *joined cases* Wirynska v Poland; Sapor v Poland [2016] EWHC 386 (Admin); [2016] 1 W.L.R. 3750; [2016] A.C.D. 66, DC .... *Digested,* 16/**788**:
Applied 17/899

Wisniewski v Regional Court of Wroclaw see Wisniewski v Poland

Witney Town Council v Beam Construction (Cheltenham) Ltd [2011] EWHC 2332 (TCC); [2011] B.L.R. 707; [2011] T.C.L.R. 8; 139 Con. L.R. 1; [2011] C.I.L.L. 3090; (2011) 161 N.L.J. 1369, QBD (TCC) .... *Digested,* 12/**586**:
Applied 13/537, 16/386: *Considered* 16/395, 17/453

Wittenberg v Sunset Personnel Services Ltd [2017] I.C.R. 1012, EAT (SC)

Witter v QHSE Solutions Ltd [2016] SAC (Civ) 8; 2017 S.C. (S.A.C.) 21; 2016 G.W.D. 30-528, SAC .... *Digested,* 17/**2422**

WM v HM (Financial Remedies: Sharing Principle: Special Contribution) see M v M

WM (Afghanistan) v Secretary of State for the Home Department see NA (Pakistan) v Secretary of State for the Home Department

Wm Morrison Supermarkets Plc v Revenue and Customs Commissioners [2013] UKUT 247 (TCC); [2013] S.T.C. 2176; [2013] B.V.C. 1672, UT (Tax) .... *Digested,* 13/**3227**:
Considered 15/2596, 17/2284

WN Hillas & Co Ltd v Arcos Ltd; *joined case* WN Hillas & Co Ltd v Arcos Ltd (Quantum) (1932) 43 Ll. L. Rep. 359; (1932) 147 L.T. 503, HL
Applied 72/508, 86/1827, 96/6703: *Considered* 75/3043, 83/466, 09/719: *Followed* 15/1572, 17/74: *Not followed* 75/409

WN Hillas & Co Ltd v Arcos Ltd (Quantum) see WN Hillas & Co Ltd v Arcos Ltd

Wodzicki v Wodzicki [2017] EWCA Civ 95; [2018] 1 F.L.R. 473; [2017] 2 P. & C.R. DG1, CA (Civ Div)

Woking BC v Johnson [2017] EWHC 2547 (Admin); [2018] H.L.R. 4; [2017] A.C.D. 132, QBD (Admin)

Wolfgang und Dr Wilfried Rey Grundstucksgemeinschaft GbR v Finanzamt Krefeld (C-332/14) EU:C:2016:417; [2017] S.T.C. 1668; [2016] B.V.C. 23; [2016] S.T.I. 1800, ECJ (4th Chamber)

Wolkowicz v Poland; *sub nom* Poland v Wolkowicz; Poland v Biskup; Lithuania v Rizleriene; *joined cases* Biskup v Poland; Rizleriene v Lithuania [2013] EWHC 102 (Admin); [2013] 1 W.L.R. 2402; [2013] A.C.D. 54, QBD (Admin) .... *Digested,* 13/**1185**:
Considered 17/901: *Followed* 16/792

Wong v Igen Ltd (formerly Leeds Careers Guidance); *sub nom* Chambelin Solicitors v Emokpae; Brunel University v Webster; Igen Ltd (formerly Leeds Careers Guidance) v Wong; *joined cases* Webster v Brunel University; Emokpae v Chamberlin Solicitors [2005] EWCA Civ 142; [2005] 3 All E.R. 812; [2005] I.C.R. 931; [2005] I.R.L.R. 258; Times, March 3, 2005; (2005) 102(13) L.S.G. 28; (2005) 149 S.J.L.B. 264, CA (Civ Div) .... *Digested,* 05/**1221**:
Applied 06/1349, 06/1354, 06/1368, 07/1184, 07/1401, 08/4301, 09/4267: *Approved* 12/1072: *Considered* 07/1388, 07/1433, 08/1181, 11/4223, 12/1033, 12/1117, 13/1032, 13/1033, 17/2308, 17/819: *Followed* 10/1123, 11/1103, 14/1010: *Referred to* 13/986

Wood v Capita Insurance Services Ltd [2017] UKSC 24; [2017] A.C. 1173; [2017] 2 W.L.R. 1095; [2017] 4 All E.R. 615; [2018] 1 All E.R. (Comm) 51; 171 Con. L.R. 1; Times, April 7, 2017; [2017] C.I.L.L. 3971, SC .... *Digested,* 17/**498**:
Considered 17/1455: *Followed* 17/1334, 17/474

Wood v Capita Insurance Services Ltd see Wood v Sureterm Direct Ltd

Wood v Chief Constable of the West Midlands [2004] EWCA Civ 1638; [2005] E.M.L.R. 20; [2005] Po. L.R. 277; Times, December 13, 2004; (2005) 149 S.J.L.B. 25, CA (Civ Div) .... *Digested,* 05/**975**:
Followed 11/868, 17/648

Wood v Kingston upon Hull City Council [2017] EWCA Civ 364; [2018] P.T.S.R. 131; [2017] H.L.R. 30, CA (Civ Div) .... *Digested,* 17/**1158**
Wood v Kingston upon Hull City Council [2015] UKUT 165 (LC), UT (Lands)
Affirmed 17/1158
Wood v Musselburgh Joint Racing Committee [2017] L.L.R. 216; 2016 G.W.D. 34-621, Sh Ct (Lothian) (Edinburgh) .... *Digested,* 17/**2716**
Wood v Sureterm Direct Ltd; *sub nom* Wood v Capita Insurance Services Ltd [2015] EWCA Civ 839, CA (Civ Div)
Affirmed 17/498
Wood v TUI Travel Plc (t/a First Choice) [2017] EWCA Civ 11; [2018] 2 W.L.R. 1051; [2017] 2 All E.R. (Comm) 734; [2017] 1 Lloyd's Rep. 322; [2017] P.I.Q.R. P8, CA (Civ Div) .... *Digested,* 17/**1883**
Wood (Kenneth) v HM Advocate; *joined cases* Tennant (Thomas) v HM Advocate; McLean (Darryl) v HM Advocate [2017] HCJAC 2; 2017 J.C. 185; 2017 S.L.T. 190; 2017 S.C.L. 295; 2017 S.C.C.R. 100; 2017 G.W.D. 3-42, HCJ .... *Digested,* 17/**2805**
Wood Floor Solutions Andreas Domberger GmbH v Silva Trade SA (C-19/09) EU:C:2010:137; [2010] 1 W.L.R. 1900; [2010] Bus. L.R. 1050; [2010] 2 Lloyd's Rep. 114; [2010] I.L.Pr. 21, ECJ (3rd Chamber)
Applied 15/446, 17/28: *Considered* 15/433: *Followed* 15/530
Woodar Investment Development Ltd v Wimpey Construction UK Ltd [1980] 1 W.L.R. 277; [1980] 1 All E.R. 571; (1980) 124 S.J. 184, HL .... *Digested,* 80/**2792**:
Applied 81/2855, 83/4027, 94/3698, 95/773, 11/2678: *Considered* 80/883, 81/811, 82/2877, 83/1319, 89/2952, 95/4113, 08/676, 10/576, 11/3117, 17/2008: *Distinguished* 87/1303: *Followed* 97/986: *Referred to* 82/2455
Woodfield v JJ Gallagher Ltd see JJ Gallagher Ltd v Cherwell DC
Woodland v Essex CC see Woodland v Swimming Teachers Association
Woodland v Swimming Teachers Association; *sub nom* Woodland v Essex CC [2013] UKSC 66; [2014] A.C. 537; [2013] 3 W.L.R. 1227; [2014] 1 All E.R. 482; [2014] E.L.R. 67; (2013) 16 C.C.L. Rep. 532; [2014] P.I.Q.R. P6; Times, November 1, 2013; (2013) 163(7582) N.L.J. 15; (2013) 157(41) S.J.L.B. 39, SC .... *Digested,* 14/**2200**:
Applied 17/1033, 17/470: *Considered* 16/2731: *Followed* 15/1113
Woodroffes (Musical Instruments) Ltd, Re [1986] Ch. 366; [1985] 3 W.L.R. 543; [1985] 2 All E.R. 908; [1985] P.C.C. 318; (1985) 82 L.S.G. 3170; (1985) 129 S.J. 589, Ch D .... *Digested,* 85/**281**:
Applied 17/159: *Cited* 00/3471: *Considered* 95/2826: *Distinguished* 93/2390: *Followed* 93/2331
Woolley v Akbar see Woolley v Akram
Woolley v Akram; *sub nom* Woolley v Akbar 2017 S.L.T. (Sh Ct) 175; 2017 S.C.L.R. 647; 2017 G.W.D. 7-92, Sh Ct (Lothian) (Edinburgh) .... *Digested,* 17/**2661**
Woolway (Valuation Officer) v Mazars LLP [2015] UKSC 53; [2015] A.C. 1862; [2015] 3 W.L.R. 386; [2016] 1 All E.R. 299; [2015] R.A. 373; Times, August 12, 2015, SC .... *Digested,* 15/**1702**:
Applied 17/1851: *Followed* 16/1461
Woolwich Plan Managers Ltd, Re see Barclays Bank Plc, Re
Wordie Property Co Ltd v Secretary of State for Scotland 1984 S.L.T. 345, IH (1 Div) .. *Digested,* 84/**4735**:
Applied 89/5083, 92/5890, 93/5939, 96/7151, 97/6113, 04/5080, 06/5520, 11/4207, 11/4452, 11/4609, 12/4103, 15/3197, 17/2719: *Considered* 00/6491, 00/6500, 04/5024, 05/5438, 17/2635: *Followed* 97/6144, 99/6411, 12/4145, 13/4013: *Referred to* 93/5937
Work v Gray see Gray v Work
Working Environments Ltd v Greencoat Construction Ltd [2012] EWHC 1039 (TCC); [2012] B.L.R. 309; 142 Con. L.R. 149; [2012] C.I.L.L. 3188, QBD (TCC) .... *Digested,* 12/**579**:
Applied 17/658: *Considered* 13/520
Workman v Forrester [2017] EWCA Civ 73; [2017] C.P. Rep. 21; [2017] 2 F.C.R. 76, CA (Civ Div) .... *Digested,* 17/**382**
World Online Telecom Ltd (formerly Localtel Ltd) v I-Way Ltd [2002] EWCA Civ 413, CA (Civ Div)
Considered 17/488: *Followed* 16/442
Worrall v Antoniadou [2016] EWCA Civ 1219; (2017) 153 B.M.L.R. 14, CA (Civ Div) ... *Digested,* 17/**1578**
Wotherspoon v Orr see Wotherspoon (David) v Procurator Fiscal, Glasgow
Wotherspoon (David) v Procurator Fiscal, Glasgow; *sub nom* Wotherspoon v Orr [2017] HCJAC 69; 2018 J.C. 79; 2017 S.C.L. 955; 2017 S.C.C.R. 505; 2017 G.W.D. 30-476, HCJ .... *Digested,* 17/**2509**
WR Berkley Insurance (Europe) Ltd v Teal Assurance Co Ltd see Teal Assurance Co Ltd v WR Berkley Insurance (Europe) Ltd
Wray v Wray [1905] 2 Ch. 349, Ch D
Applied 17/1432

Wright v Elderpark Housing Association [2017] CSIH 54; 2017 S.L.T. 995; 2017 Hous. L.R. 71; 2017 G.W.D. 25-424, IH (Ex Div) .... *Digested,* 17/**2699**
Wright v Lewis Silkin LLP [2016] EWCA Civ 1308; [2017] P.N.L.R. 16, CA (Civ Div) .... *Digested,* 17/**1577**
Wright v Lewis Silkin LLP [2015] EWHC 1897 (QB); [2015] P.N.L.R. 32, QBD .... *Digested,* 15/**1793**: *Applied* 16/1545: *Reversed in part* 17/1577
Wright v North Ayrshire Council [2014] I.C.R. 77; [2014] I.R.L.R. 4, EAT (SC) .... *Digested,* 14/**3500**: *Considered* 17/770
Wright v Queen, The [2016] UKPC 18; [2017] Crim. L.R. 137, PC (CI)
Wright v Scottbridge Construction Ltd see Scottbridge Construction Ltd v Wright
Wrotham Park Estate Co Ltd v Parkside Homes Ltd [1974] 1 W.L.R. 798; [1974] 2 All E.R. 321; (1974) 27 P. & C.R. 296; (1973) 118 S.J. 420, Ch D .... *Digested,* 74/**3130**: *Applied* 75/1017, 06/1018, 07/1054, 11/2682, 15/800, 17/2196: *Cited* 11/530: *Considered* 86/2827, 87/1227, 88/2729, 92/1513, 92/1793, 93/427, 95/2968, 95/3766, 98/4341, 03/717, 08/3113, 16/564: *Distinguished* 87/3654, 93/1368: *Explained* 89/3422
Wu (t/a Modern China at the Florence) v Moore (Valuation Officer) [2017] R.V.R. 276, VT
WW Property Investments Ltd v National Westminster Bank Plc [2016] EWCA Civ 1142; [2017] 2 All E.R. (Comm) 624; [2017] 1 Lloyd's Rep. 87, CA (Civ Div) ..... *Digested,* 17/**171**
WW Property Investments Ltd v National Westminster Bank Plc see CGL Group Ltd v Royal Bank of Scotland Plc
WW Realisation 1 Ltd (In Administration), Re [2010] EWHC 3604 (Ch); [2011] B.C.C. 382; [2012] 1 B.C.L.C. 405, Ch D .... *Digested,* 11/**1830**: *Considered* 17/1258
Wyatt v Vince [2016] EWHC 1368 (Fam); [2017] 1 F.L.R. 1766; [2016] Fam. Law 966, Fam Div .... *Digested,* 17/**1029**
Wyatt v Vince see Vince v Wyatt
Wychavon DC v Secretary of State for Communities and Local Government [2016] EWHC 592 (Admin); [2016] P.T.S.R. 675, QBD (Admin) .... *Digested,* 16/**1760**: *Doubted* 17/1779, 17/1780
Wye Valley NHS Trust v B; *sub nom* X NHS Trust v B [2015] EWCOP 60; [2015] C.O.P.L.R. 843; (2015) 18 C.C.L. Rep. 733; [2015] Med. L.R. 552; (2016) 147 B.M.L.R. 187, CP .... *Digested,* 16/**1512**: *Considered* 16/1522, 17/1124, 17/1548
Wyldecrest Parks (Management) Ltd v Kenyon [2017] UKUT 28 (LC), UT (Lands) *Applied* 17/1161
Wylie v Omniasig SA [2012] CSOH 128; 2013 S.L.T. 46; 2012 G.W.D. 28-574, OH ..... *Digested,* 13/**3904**: *Considered* 17/2757

X v A (No.1) 2016 S.L.T. (Sh Ct) 404; 2016 Fam. L.R. 153; 2016 G.W.D. 27-501, Sh Ct (Lothian) (Edinburgh) .... *Digested,* 17/**2840**
X v A (No.2) 2016 S.L.T. (Sh Ct) 411; 2016 Fam. L.R. 159; 2016 G.W.D. 27-488, Sh Ct (Lothian) (Edinburgh) .... *Digested,* 17/**2457**
X v Air France (Societe) [2017] I.L.Pr. 20, Cass (F)
X v Belgium (C-638/16 PPU) EU:C:2017:173; [2017] 4 W.L.R. 89; [2017] 3 C.M.L.R. 15; [2017] C.E.C. 1239, ECJ (Grand Chamber)
X v Sony Europe Ltd [2017] E.C.C. 9, Cass (F)
X v Staatssecretaris van Financien (C-317/15) EU:C:2017:119; [2017] S.T.I. 330, ECJ (9th Chamber)
X v Staatssecretaris van Financien (C-569/15) EU:C:2017:673; [2017] S.T.I. 2005, ECJ (3rd Chamber)
X v Staatssecretaris van Financien (C-570/15) EU:C:2017:674; [2017] S.T.I. 2006, ECJ (3rd Chamber)
X v Wandsworth LBC see A v Hoare
X v X [2016] EWHC 3512 (Fam); [2017] 2 F.C.R. 92, Fam Div .... *Digested,* 17/**1028**
X v X (Financial Remedies: Share Value Discount: Date for Computation of Assets) [2016] EWHC 1995 (Fam); [2017] 2 F.L.R. 840, Fam Div
X v Y see S (Brussels II: Recognition: Best Interests of Child) (No.2), Re
X v Y see Z (Foreign Surrogacy: Allocation of Work: Guidance on Parental Order Reports), Re
X (A Child) v Dartford and Gravesham NHS Trust [2015] EWCA Civ 96; [2015] 1 W.L.R. 3647; [2015] C.P. Rep. 22; [2015] E.M.L.R. 14; [2015] P.I.Q.R. P14; [2015] Med. L.R. 103; (2015) 143 B.M.L.R. 166, CA (Civ Div) .... *Digested,* 15/**4**: *Considered* 17/1015: *Referred to* 16/818
X (A Child) (Application for Reporting Restrictions: Media Notification), Re; *sub nom* X (A Child) (Publicity), Re [2016] EWHC 1668 (Fam); [2016] 4 W.L.R. 116; [2016] E.M.L.R. 24; [2017] 2 F.L.R. 70; [2016] Fam. Law 1224, Fam Div .... *Digested,* 16/**887**

X (A Child) (Care Proceedings: Notice to Father without Parental Responsibility), Re; *sub nom* CD (A Child), Re [2017] EWFC 34; [2017] 4 W.L.R. 110, Fam Ct .... *Digested,* 17/**930**
X (A Child) (Care Proceedings: Rehearing), Re [2016] EWHC 2755 (Fam); [2017] 2 F.L.R. 80, Fam Div .... *Digested,* 17/**935**
X (A Child) (Jurisdiction: Secure Accommodation), Re; *sub nom* X (A Child) (Secure Accommodation: Inherent Jurisdiction), Re; *joined case* Y (A Child) (Jurisdiction: Secure Accommodation), Re [2016] EWHC 2271 (Fam); [2017] Fam. 80; [2016] 3 W.L.R. 1718; [2017] 2 F.L.R. 1717; [2017] 1 F.C.R. 584; [2016] Fam. Law 1327, Fam Div .... *Digested,* 17/**1068**: *Applied* 17/1067: *Considered* 17/2379
X (A Child) (Parental Order: Time Limit), Re; *sub nom* X (A Child) (Surrogacy: Time Limit), Re [2014] EWHC 3135 (Fam); [2015] Fam. 186; [2015] 2 W.L.R. 745; [2015] 1 F.L.R. 349; [2014] Fam. Law 1681, Fam Div (Birmingham) .... *Digested,* 15/**1127**: *Applied* 16/935, 16/936, 16/940, 17/1059: *Considered* 16/939
X (A Child) (Publicity), Re see X (A Child) (Application for Reporting Restrictions: Media Notification), Re
X (A Child) (Review of Fact Finding in Care Proceedings), Re [2016] EWHC 1342 (Fam); [2017] 2 F.L.R. 61; [2016] Fam. Law 960, Fam Div .... *Digested,* 17/**936**: *Considered* 16/931
X (A Child) (Secure Accommodation: Inherent Jurisdiction), Re see X (A Child) (Jurisdiction: Secure Accommodation), Re
X (A Child) (Surrogacy: Time Limit), Re see X (A Child) (Parental Order: Time Limit), Re
X (A Child), Re [2017] EWHC 2084 (Fam); [2018] 1 F.L.R. 1072; [2017] 3 F.C.R. 604; [2017] Med. L.R. 500, Fam Div .... *Digested,* 17/**921**
X (A Child), Re [2017] EWHC 2141 (Fam); [2017] 3 F.C.R. 615, Fam Div
X (A Child), Re; *sub nom* Northumberland CC v Z [2008] EWHC 1324 (Fam), Fam Div *Considered* 17/913
X (A Child), Re [2017] EWHC 2036 (Fam); [2018] 1 F.L.R. 1054; [2017] 3 F.C.R. 584, Fam Div
X (A Child), Re [2017] EWHC 1585 (Fam); [2018] 1 F.L.R. 1041; [2017] 3 F.C.R. 570, Fam Div
X (A Knoll Group Company) v Y (Italian Company) (I ZR 91/11) [2017] E.C.C. 16; [2017] E.C.D.R. 26, BGH (Ger)
X (Children), Re [2017] EWHC 120 (Fam); [2017] 1 F.C.R. 614, Fam Div DR
X (Children), Re [2015] EWHC 3651 (Fam); [2017] 1 F.L.R. 172; [2016] Fam. Law 283, Fam Div
X (Disclosure to the Security Service), Re see Commissioner of Police of the Metropolis v A Local Authority
X (Foreign Surrogacy: Child's Name), Re; *sub nom* CH v SM [2016] EWHC 1068 (Fam); [2017] 4 W.L.R. 211; [2017] 2 F.L.R. 91; [2016] Fam. Law 810, Fam Div
X (formerly known as Bell) v SO [2003] EWHC 1101 (QB); [2003] E.M.L.R. 37; [2003] 2 F.C.R. 686; [2003] A.C.D. 61, QBD .... *Digested,* 03/**297**: *Applied* 17/3
X Council v Mother [2017] 1 F.C.R. 571, Fam Div DR .... *Digested,* 17/**1067**
X Family v Corsair (Societe) [2017] E.C.C. 4, Cass (F)
X NHS Trust v B see Wye Valley NHS Trust v B
X-Fab Semiconductor Foundries AG v Plessey Semiconductors Ltd [2014] EWHC 3190 (QB), QBD *Considered* 17/453
X-Wind Power Ltd v Revenue and Customs Commissioners [2016] UKFTT 317 (TC), FTT (Tax) *Affirmed* 17/2122
X-Wind Power Ltd v Revenue and Customs Commissioners [2017] UKUT 290 (TCC); [2017] B.T.C. 526, UT (Tax) .... *Digested,* 17/**2122**
Xellia Pharmaceuticals APS v Competition and Markets Authority see Generics (UK) Ltd v Competition and Markets Authority
Xellia Pharmaceuticals ApS v European Commission (T-471/13) EU:T:2016:460; [2017] 4 C.M.L.R. 4, GC (9th Chamber)
XH v Secretary of State for the Home Department see R. (on the application of XH) v Secretary of State for the Home Department
XP v Compensa Towarzystwo SA [2016] EWHC 1728 (QB); [2016] Med. L.R. 570, QBD .... *Digested,* 17/**1691**
Xstrata Coal Queensland Pty Ltd v Benxi Iron and Steel (Group) International Economic and Trading Co Ltd [2016] EWHC 2022 (Comm); [2017] 1 All E.R. (Comm) 299; 167 Con. L.R. 1, QBD (Comm) .... *Digested,* 16/**66**
XX v Whittington Hospital NHS Trust [2017] EWHC 2318 (QB); [2018] P.I.Q.R. Q2; [2017] Med. L.R. 545; (2018) 160 B.M.L.R. 205, QBD

XY v Envial SpA [2017] I.L.Pr. 7, Cass (F)
XY v Institution [2017] E.C.D.R. 20, Sad Najwyzszy (PL)
Xydhias v Xydhias [1999] 2 All E.R. 386; [1999] 1 F.L.R. 683; [1999] 1 F.C.R. 289; Times, January 13, 1999; Independent, January 21, 1999; [1999] Fam. Law 301; (1999) 96(6) L.S.G. 34; (1999) 149 N.L.J. 52, CA (Civ Div) .... *Digested,* 99/**2416**:
Applied 07/1709: *Considered* 08/1427, 11/1292, 14/1361: *Followed* 17/1003
XYZ v Various Companies; *sub nom* PIP Breast Implant Litigation, Re [2013] EWHC 3643 (QB); [2014] 2 Costs L.O. 197; [2014] Lloyd's Rep. I.R. 431, QBD .... *Digested,* 14/**465**:
Considered 15/1795, 17/205

Y v I see I (A Child) (Contact Application: Jurisdiction), Re
Y v Secretary of State for Exiting the European Union see R. (on the application of Yalland) v Secretary of State for Exiting the European Union
Y v Secretary of State for the Home Department see EY (Turkey) v Secretary of State for the Home Department
Y v X [2017] I.L.Pr. 28, Cass (F)
Y (A Child) (Jurisdiction: Secure Accommodation), Re see X (A Child) (Jurisdiction: Secure Accommodation), Re
Y (Children), Re [2016] EWHC 503 (Fam); [2017] 1 F.L.R. 1103; [2016] Fam. Law 664, Fam Div
Y (Sri Lanka) v Secretary of State for the Home Department; *joined case* Z (Sri Lanka) v Secretary of State for the Home Department [2009] EWCA Civ 362; [2009] H.R.L.R. 22; [2010] I.N.L.R. 178; Times, May 5, 2009, CA (Civ Div) .... *Digested,* 09/**2082**:
Considered 13/1576, 17/1176: *Followed* 14/1647
Y Trust No.1, Re 19 I.T.E.L.R. 553, Grand Ct (CI)
Yadly Marketing Co Ltd v Secretary of State for the Home Department [2016] EWCA Civ 1143; [2017] 1 W.L.R. 1041; [2017] C.P. Rep. 12; [2017] Imm. A.R. 701, CA (Civ Div) .... *Digested,* 17/**323**
Yalland v Secretary of State for Exiting the European Union see R. (on the application of Yalland) v Secretary of State for Exiting the European Union
Yam Seng Pte Ltd v International Trade Corp Ltd [2013] EWHC 111 (QB); [2013] 1 All E.R. (Comm) 1321; [2013] 1 Lloyd's Rep. 526; [2013] 1 C.L.C. 662; [2013] B.L.R. 147; 146 Con. L.R. 39; [2013] Bus. L.R. D53, QBD .... *Digested,* 13/**587**:
Applied 17/502: *Considered* 16/423
Yang v Official Receiver [2013] EWHC 3577 (Ch); [2014] B.P.I.R. 826; [2015] R.V.R. 274, Ch D (Manchester) .... *Digested,* 14/**1778**:
Applied 16/1197, 17/1292
Yarrow Plc v United Kingdom (9266/81) see Lithgow v United Kingdom (A/102)
Yates v Great Ormond Street Hospital see Great Ormond Street Hospital for Children NHS Foundation Trust v Yates
Yates v Nemo Personal Finance 9HG00904, CC (Manchester)
Applied 17/482: *Distinguished* 11/519
Yates Building Co Ltd v RJ Pulleyn & Sons (York) Ltd (1975) 237 E.G. 183; (1975) 119 S.J. 370, CA (Civ Div) .... *Digested,* 75/**388**:
Applied 98/3440, 17/1583: *Considered* 13/575, 14/1970: *Distinguished* 96/7107, 09/2515: *Followed* 95/6071
Yeboah v Crofton see Crofton v Yeboah
Yegiazaryan v Smagin; *sub nom* A v B [2016] EWCA Civ 1290; [2017] 1 All E.R. (Comm) 1103; [2017] 1 Lloyd's Rep. 102, CA (Civ Div) .... *Digested,* 17/**65**
Yegiazaryan v Smagin; *sub nom* A v B [2015] EWHC 1944 (Comm), QBD (Comm)
Affirmed 17/65
Yegiazaryan v Smagin see K v S
Yen Interest Rate Derivatives, Re (AT.39861) [2017] 5 C.M.L.R. 3, CEC
Yentob v MGN Ltd see Gulati v MGN Ltd
Yeo v Times Newspapers Ltd [2015] EWHC 3375 (QB); [2017] E.M.L.R. 1, QBD
Considered 16/2143
Yeoman's Row Management Ltd v Cobbe see Cobbe v Yeoman's Row Management Ltd
Yerrakalva v Barnsley MBC; *sub nom* Barnsley MBC v Yerrakalva [2011] EWCA Civ 1255; [2012] 2 All E.R. 215; [2012] I.C.R. 420; [2012] I.R.L.R. 78; (2011) 161 N.L.J. 1595, CA (Civ Div) .... *Digested,* 12/**1091**:
Applied 12/1090, 12/1092, 13/969, 14/1073, 15/827, 17/795: *Considered* 13/3518: *Followed* 14/1074
YL v Birmingham City Council see L v Birmingham City Council
Yonge v Toynbee [1910] 1 K.B. 215, CA
Applied 13/308, 17/48: *Considered* 05/489, 15/1662: *Followed* 14/2053
York City Council v Sykes (Valuation Officer); *sub nom* City of York Council v Sykes (Valuation Officer) [2017] UKUT 230 (LC); [2017] R.A. 355, UT (Lands)

Yorkshire Woolcombers Association Ltd, Re see Illingworth v Houldsworth
Younas (Faisal) v HM Advocate [2014] HCJAC 114; 2015 J.C. 180; 2014 S.L.T. 1043; 2015 S.C.L. 30; 2014 S.C.C.R. 628; 2014 G.W.D. 34-646, HCJ .... *Digested,* 15/**3002**: *Considered* 15/2994, 15/3019, 17/2556
Young v Bristol Aeroplane Co Ltd [1944] K.B. 718; [1944] 2 All E.R. 293; (1945) 78 Ll. L. Rep. 6, CA
Applied 47-51/2389, 47-51/3047, 47-51/7882, 55/351, 56/6138, 56/6957, 57/3680, 75/1906, 77/1527, 85/2704, 85/471, 85/568, 90/3733, 08/892, 13/1307, 13/350: *Considered* 47-51/1086, 47-51/7868, 68/3317, 68/496, 68/647, 78/1590, 87/994, 89/631, 90/1522, 02/3096, 07/4518, 08/2306, 17/2202: *Distinguished* 47-51/9934: *Followed* 54/1583, 12/1760, 17/488
Young v Catholic Care (Diocese of Leeds) see A v Hoare
Young v Information Commissioner (2017) 158 B.M.L.R. 220, FTT (GRC)
Young v NHS Business Services Authority; *joined case* NHS Business Services Authority v Young [2015] EWHC 2686 (Ch), Ch D
Affirmed 17/813
Young v NHS Business Services Authority; *joined case* NHS Business Services Authority v Young [2017] EWCA Civ 8; [2018] 1 All E.R. 131; [2017] I.C.R. 599, CA (Civ Div) .... *Digested,* 17/**813**
Young v Official Receiver [2010] EWHC 1591 (Ch); [2010] B.P.I.R. 1477, Ch D .... *Digested,* 11/**1835**: *Applied* 17/1296
Young (A Bankrupt), Re; *sub nom* Allen v Young [2017] B.P.I.R. 1116, Ch D (Bankruptcy Ct) .... *Digested,* 17/**1285**
Your Life Management Services Ltd v Bromley LBC [2017] P.A.D. 16, Planning Inspector
Your Response Ltd v Datateam Business Media Ltd [2014] EWCA Civ 281; [2015] Q.B. 41; [2014] 3 W.L.R. 887; [2014] 4 All E.R. 928; [2014] 2 All E.R. (Comm) 899; [2014] C.P. Rep. 31; [2014] 1 C.L.C. 915; [2014] Info. T.L.R. 1; [2015] F.S.R. 23, CA (Civ Div) .... *Digested,* 14/**2528**: *Applied* 17/768: *Followed* 15/2533
Yrusta v Argentina (1/2013) 42 B.H.R.C. 315, UN CED
Yuanda (UK) Co Ltd v WW Gear Construction Ltd [2010] EWHC 720 (TCC); [2011] 1 All E.R. (Comm) 550; [2011] Bus. L.R. 360; [2010] 1 C.L.C. 491; [2010] B.L.R. 435; [2010] T.C.L.R. 5; 130 Con. L.R. 133; [2010] C.I.L.L. 2849, QBD (TCC) .... *Digested,* 10/**554**: *Applied* 12/2711: *Approved* 17/508: *Considered* 16/398, 16/414
Yukos Capital Sarl v OJSC Rosneft Oil Co [2012] EWCA Civ 855; [2014] Q.B. 458; [2013] 3 W.L.R. 1329; [2013] 1 All E.R. 223; [2013] 1 All E.R. (Comm) 327; [2012] 2 Lloyd's Rep. 208; [2012] 2 C.L.C. 549; 143 Con. L.R. 1, CA (Civ Div) .. *Digested,* 12/**120**: *Applied* 15/1566: *Considered* 14/65, 15/85: *Followed* 17/80
Yukos Oil Co v Dardana Ltd see Dardana Ltd v Yukos Oil Co (No.1)
YZ v NHS Trust 1; *sub nom* YZ v Oxleas NHS Foundation Trust; R. (on the application of YZ) v Oxleas NHS Foundation Trust [2015] EWHC 2296 (Admin); [2015] M.H.L.R. 394, QBD (Admin)
Affirmed 17/1545
YZ v Oxleas NHS Foundation Trust see R. (on the application of YZ) v Oxleas NHS Foundation Trust
YZ v Oxleas NHS Foundation Trust see YZ v NHS Trust 1

Z v Travelers Insurance Co Ltd [2017] EWHC 287 (QB); [2017] Lloyd's Rep. I.R. 269, QBD .... *Digested,* 17/**254**
Z v Y see A (Abduction: Child's Objections to Return), Re
Z v Z; *sub nom* Z (Application for Financial Relief After Foreign Divorce: Stage II: Quantum of Award), Re [2016] EWHC 1720 (Fam); [2017] 2 F.L.R. 456; [2016] Fam. Law 1085, Fam Div
Z v Z (Application for Financial Relief after Foreign Divorce) [2016] EWHC 911 (Fam); [2017] 2 F.L.R. 405; [2016] Fam. Law 807, Fam Div
Z v Z (Legal Professional Privilege: Fraud Exemption); *sub nom* AAZ v BBZ [2016] EWHC 3349 (Fam); [2017] 4 W.L.R. 84; [2017] 2 F.C.R. 450, Fam Div .... *Digested,* 17/**1488**
Z v Z (Recognition of Brazilian Adoption Order) [2013] EWHC 747 (Fam); [2014] 1 F.L.R. 1295; [2013] Fam. Law 937, Fam Div
Considered 17/1034
Z (A Child) (English Adoption: Egyptian Orphan), Re; *sub nom* T v K (Egyptian Fostering: UK Adoption) [2016] EWHC 2963 (Fam); [2017] 4 W.L.R. 20; [2017] 2 F.L.R. 943, Fam Div .... *Digested,* 17/**913**
Z (A Child) (Human Fertilisation and Embryology Act: Parental Order), Re see Z (A Child) (Surrogate Father: Parental Order), Re

Z (A Child) (Public Law: Translation Costs), Re [2017] EWCA Civ 157; [2017] 1 W.L.R. 4255; [2017] 2 Costs L.R. 311; [2018] 1 F.L.R. 956; [2017] 2 F.C.R. 404, CA (Civ Div) .... *Digested,* 17/**998**

Z (A Child) (Recognition of Foreign Order), Re; *sub nom* Health Service Executive of Ireland v Z [2016] EWHC 784 (Fam); [2016] Fam. 375; [2016] 3 W.L.R. 791; [2017] 1 F.L.R. 1236; [2016] Fam. Law 684, Fam Div .... *Digested,* 16/**302**

Z (A Child) (Surrogacy Agreements: Child Arrangements Orders), Re; *sub nom* A v X; M (A Child), Re [2016] EWFC 34; [2017] 1 F.L.R. 946; [2016] Fam. Law 1100, Fam Ct .... *Digested,* 17/**945**

Z (A Child) (Surrogacy: Parental Order), Re see Z (A Child) (Surrogate Father: Parental Order), Re

Z (A Child) (Surrogate Father: Parental Order), Re; *sub nom* Z (A Child) (Human Fertilisation and Embryology Act: Parental Order), Re; Z (A Child) (Surrogacy: Parental Order), Re [2015] EWFC 73; [2015] 1 W.L.R. 4993; [2016] 2 All E.R. 83; [2017] 1 F.L.R. 472; [2015] 3 F.C.R. 586; [2015] Fam. Law 1349, Fam Ct ... *Digested,* 16/**937**

Z (A Child) (Surrogate Father: Parental Order), Re [2016] EWHC 1191 (Fam); [2017] Fam. 25; [2016] 3 W.L.R. 1369; [2016] 2 F.L.R. 327; [2016] H.R.L.R. 15; [2016] Fam. Law 958, Fam Div .... *Digested,* 16/**938**: *Considered* 17/1058

Z (A Minor) (Freedom of Publication), Re; *sub nom* Z (A Minor) (Identification: Restrictions on Publication), Re [1997] Fam. 1; [1996] 2 W.L.R. 88; [1995] 4 All E.R. 961; [1996] 1 F.L.R. 191; [1996] 2 F.C.R. 164; [1996] Fam. Law 90, CA (Civ Div) .... *Digested,* 96/**547**: *Applied* 02/1648, 06/1687, 08/1514: *Considered* 00/2535, 04/1496: *Followed* 00/4162, 09/1647, 10/408, 17/923

Z (A Minor) (Identification: Restrictions on Publication), Re see Z (A Minor) (Freedom of Publication), Re

Z (Application for Financial Relief After Foreign Divorce: Stage II: Quantum of Award), Re see Z v Z

Z (Attorney General for Northern Ireland's Reference), Re see R. v Z

Z (Children) (Care Proceedings: Review of Findings), Re; *sub nom* ZZ (Children) (Care Proceedings: Retraction of Testimony), Re [2014] EWFC 9; [2015] 1 W.L.R. 95; [2014] Fam. Law 1237; (2014) 158(25) S.J.L.B. 45, Fam Ct .... *Digested,* 15/**1005**: *Applied* 15/1004, 17/1047, 17/936

Z (Foreign Surrogacy: Allocation of Work: Guidance on Parental Order Reports), Re; *sub nom* X v Y; L (Children), Re [2015] EWFC 90; [2017] 4 W.L.R. 5; [2016] 2 F.L.R. 803; [2016] Fam. Law 314, Fam Ct .... *Digested,* 16/**935**

Z (Sri Lanka) v Secretary of State for the Home Department see Y (Sri Lanka) v Secretary of State for the Home Department

Z Ltd v A-Z [1982] Q.B. 558; [1982] 2 W.L.R. 288; [1982] 1 All E.R. 556; [1982] 1 Lloyd's Rep. 240; [1982] E.C.C. 362; (1982) 126 S.J. 100, CA (Civ Div) .... *Digested,* 82/**2507**: *Applied* 82/2463, 83/2975: *Considered* 82/2504, 84/2250, 90/3584, 92/208, 95/861, 06/2880, 10/1314, 10/359: *Distinguished* 12/408, 17/303: *Followed* 02/440

Z Trust, Re [2016] JRC 48; 19 I.T.E.L.R. 589, Royal Ct (Jer)

ZA v NA (Abduction: Habitual Residence) see A v A (Children) (Habitual Residence)

Zahid v University of Manchester see R. (on the application of Zahid) v University of Manchester

ZAI Corporate Finance Ltd v AIM Disciplinary Committee of the London Stock Exchange Plc see R. (on the application of ZAI Corporate Finance Ltd) v AIM Disciplinary Committee of the London Stock Exchange Plc

Zakrzewski v Poland [2013] UKSC 2; [2013] 1 W.L.R. 324; [2013] 2 All E.R. 93; [2013] 2 C.M.L.R. 33; Times, January 31, 2013, SC .... *Digested,* 13/**1180**: *Considered* 16/792: *Followed* 16/789, 17/900

Zammit v Malta (1046/12) (2017) 65 E.H.R.R. 17, ECHR

Zas Ventures Ltd v Forkner see Forkner v Zas Ventures Ltd

Zavahir v Shankleman [2016] EWHC 2772 (Ch); [2017] B.C.C. 500, Ch D (Companies Ct)

Zavarco Plc, Re; *sub nom* Blomqvist v Zavarco Plc; *joined case* Blomqvist v Aziz [2015] EWHC 1898 (Ch); [2016] Ch. 128; [2015] 3 W.L.R. 1479; [2017] 1 B.C.L.C. 252, Ch D .... *Digested,* 16/**360**

Zavod Ekran OAO v Magneco Metrel UK Ltd [2017] EWHC 2208 (Comm); [2017] 2 Lloyd's Rep. 566, QBD (Comm)

Ze Fu Fleischhandel GmbH v Hauptzollamt Hamburg-Jonas (C-201/10); *joined case* Vion Trading GmbH v Hauptzollamt Hamburg-Jonas (C-202/10) EU:C:2011:282; [2011] 3 C.M.L.R. 11, ECJ (4th Chamber) *Applied* 17/2230

Zebaida v Secretary of State for Education [2016] EWHC 1181 (Admin); [2016] P.T.S.R. 1490; [2016] E.L.R. 321; [2016] A.C.D. 92, QBD (Admin) .... *Digested,* 16/**630**: *Applied* 17/720

Zelger v Salinitri (129/83) EU:C:1984:215; [1984] E.C.R. 2397; [1985] 3 C.M.L.R. 366, ECJ (4th Chamber) .... *Digested,* 85/**1380**: *Applied* 92/3534, 93/3569, 01/5419, 04/579, 17/1042: *Considered* 91/474, 93/3318, 05/468

Zeligs v Janes 2016 BCCA 280; 19 I.T.E.L.R. 935, CA (BC)

Zelouf v Khanna [2016] EWHC 205 (Ch); [2016] B.P.I.R. 1288, Ch D .... *Digested,* 17/**1308**

Zengota v Poland [2017] EWHC 191 (Admin); [2017] 1 W.L.R. 3103, QBD (Admin) ..... *Digested,* 17/**899**

Zentrale zur Bekampfung unlauteren Wettbewerbs Frankfurt am Main eV v comtech GmbH (C-568/15) EU:C:2017:154; [2017] Bus. L.R. 1232; [2017] 3 C.M.L.R. 14; [2017] C.E.C. 1194, ECJ (7th Chamber)

Zermalt Holdings SA v Nu-Life Upholstery Repairs Ltd [1985] 2 E.G.L.R. 14; (1985) 275 E.G. 1134, QBD (Comm) .... *Digested,* 85/**95**: *Applied* 05/202, 06/196, 06/203, 10/164, 10/178, 13/2834, 15/78, 17/67: *Approved* 89/3857: *Considered* 93/169, 93/182, 94/208, 94/227, 96/3796, 97/3326, 05/2678, 07/250: *Followed* 04/2522

ZH v Switzerland (60119/12) (2017) 65 E.H.R.R. 30; [2016] Imm. A.R. 375, ECHR

ZH (Tanzania) v Secretary of State for the Home Department [2011] UKSC 4; [2011] 2 A.C. 166; [2011] 2 W.L.R. 148; [2011] 2 All E.R. 783; [2011] 1 F.L.R. 2170; [2011] 1 F.C.R. 221; [2011] H.R.L.R. 15; [2011] U.K.H.R.R. 371; [2011] Imm. A.R. 395; [2011] I.N.L.R. 369; Times, February 8, 2011; [2011] Fam. Law 468; (2011) 108(7) L.S.G. 17; (2011) 155(5) S.J.L.B. 30, SC .... *Digested,* 11/**1790**: *Applied* 11/1711, 12/1289, 12/1707, 12/1751, 14/1596, 14/1668, 14/662, 15/1285: *Considered* 12/1293, 12/1663, 12/1738, 12/1750, 12/1775, 12/4099, 13/1605, 13/2366, 13/3776, 13/3778, 14/1650, 14/1704, 15/1337, 15/1353, 17/1952: *Followed* 11/1736, 12/1718, 13/1578, 14/1673, 14/1725, 15/3145

Zielinski v France (24846/94) (2001) 31 E.H.R.R. 19, ECHR .... *Digested,* 01/**3544**: *Applied* 02/2457, 15/2348: *Considered* 17/2033

Zim Properties Ltd v Procter (Inspector of Taxes); *sub nom* Procter (Inspector of Taxes) v Zim Properties [1985] S.T.C. 90; 58 T.C. 371; (1985) 82 L.S.G. 124; (1985) 129 S.J. 68; (1985) 129 S.J. 323, Ch D .... *Digested,* 85/**238**: *Applied* 89/3639, 11/1581: *Considered* 17/2092

Zmyslowski v Governor of Wandsworth Prison see Zmyslowski v Poland

Zmyslowski v Poland; *sub nom* Zmyslowski v Regional Court in Lublin, Poland; *joined case* Zmyslowski v Governor of Wandsworth Prison [2016] EWHC 3271 (Admin); [2017] A.C.D. 9, DC

Zmyslowski v Regional Court in Lublin, Poland see Zmyslowski v Poland

Znamenskaya v Russia (77785/01) [2005] 2 F.C.R. 406; (2007) 44 E.H.R.R. 15, ECHR .... *Digested,* 06/**2199**: *Applied* 17/1645

Zockoll Group Ltd v Mercury Communications Ltd (No.1) [1998] F.S.R. 354, CA (Civ Div) .... *Digested,* 98/**525**: *Cited* 09/509: *Followed* 17/286

Zombory-Moldovan (t/a Craft Carnival) v Revenue and Customs Commissioners; *sub nom* Revenue and Customs Commissioners v Zombory-Moldovan (t/a Craft Carnival) [2016] UKUT 433 (TCC); [2016] S.T.C. 2436; [2016] B.V.C. 541; [2016] S.T.I. 2784, UT (Tax) .... *Digested,* 17/**2237**

Zombory-Moldovan (t/a Craft Carnival) v Revenue and Customs Commissioners; *sub nom* Revenue and Customs Commissioners v Zombory-Moldovan (t/a Craft Carnival) [2015] UKFTT 245 (TC); [2015] S.F.T.D. 784; [2015] S.T.I. 1967, FTT (Tax)
Reversed 17/2237

Zoumbas v Secretary of State for the Home Department see FZ (Democratic Republic of Congo) v Secretary of State for the Home Department

Zoya Ltd v Ahmed (t/a Property Mart) [2016] EWHC 1981 (Ch); [2017] Ch. 127; [2017] 2 W.L.R. 773, Ch D .... *Digested,* 17/**390**

Zoya Ltd v Ahmed (t/a Property Mart) [2016] EWHC 2249 (Ch); [2016] 4 W.L.R. 174; [2017] 2 Costs L.O. 133, Ch D .... *Digested,* 17/**48**

ZT (Kosovo) v Secretary of State for the Home Department [2009] UKHL 6; [2009] 1 W.L.R. 348; [2009] 3 All E.R. 976; [2009] I.N.L.R. 310; Times, February 9, 2009; (2009) 153(5) S.J.L.B. 29, HL .... *Digested,* 09/**2075**: *Applied* 15/3149, 17/1241: *Considered* 09/2105, 10/1758, 11/1716, 17/1210: *Followed* 10/1819, 11/1715

Zucchetti Rubinetteria SpA v European Commission (C-618/13 P) EU:C:2017:48; [2017] 4 C.M.L.R. 25, ECJ (1st Chamber)

Zuk v Poland (48286/11) (2017) 65 E.H.R.R. SE8, ECHR

Zulfikarpasic v Gajer (C-484/15) EU:C:2017:199; [2017] C.E.C. 1065; [2017] I.L.Pr. 16, ECJ (2nd Chamber)
Zumax Nigeria Ltd v First City Monument Bank Plc [2014] EWHC 2075 (Ch), Ch D
Affirmed 17/297
Zumax Nigeria Ltd v First City Monument Bank Plc [2016] EWCA Civ 567; [2016] 1 C.L.C. 953, CA (Civ Div) .... *Digested,* 17/**297**: *Applied* 17/375
Zurich Assurance Ltd v Winchester City Council [2014] EWHC 758 (Admin), QBD (Admin)
Applied 17/1780
Zurich Insurance Co Plc v Hayward [2011] EWCA Civ 641; [2011] C.P. Rep. 39, CA (Civ Div) .... *Digested,* 11/**378**: *Considered* 13/266, 17/322
Zurich Insurance Co Plc v Hayward see Hayward v Zurich Insurance Co Plc
Zurich Insurance Plc v Maccaferri Ltd see Maccaferri Ltd v Zurich Insurance Plc
Zurich Insurance Plc UK v International Energy Group Ltd see International Energy Group Ltd v Zurich Insurance Plc UK
Zwolinski v Poland see Krolik v Poland
ZXC v Bloomberg LP [2017] EWHC 328 (QB); [2017] E.M.L.R. 21; [2017] Lloyd's Rep. F.C. 206, QBD .... *Digested,* 17/**2199**
ZZ (Children) (Care Proceedings: Retraction of Testimony), Re see Z (Children) (Care Proceedings: Review of Findings), Re
ZZ (France) v Secretary of State for the Home Department [2014] EWCA Civ 7; [2014] Q.B. 820; [2014] 2 W.L.R. 791; [2014] 3 All E.R. 587; [2014] 2 C.M.L.R. 49; [2014] I.N.L.R. 858, CA (Civ Div) .... *Digested,* 14/**1708**: *Applied* 15/218, 16/1157: *Followed* 16/1094, 17/442
ZZ (France) v Secretary of State for the Home Department (C-300/11) EU:C:2013:363; [2013] Q.B. 1136; [2013] 3 W.L.R. 813; [2013] 3 C.M.L.R. 46; [2014] All E.R. (EC) 56; [2014] C.E.C. 109; [2014] Imm. A.R. 1; [2014] I.N.L.R. 368, ECJ (Grand Chamber) .... *Digested,* 14/**1223**: *Applied* 15/873: *Considered* 17/43
ZZ (France) v Secretary of State for the Home Department (C-300/11) (Unreported, September 12, 2012), AGO
Followed 17/1250

PART II

SCOTTISH CASE CITATOR 2017

This section contains:
(i) Details of cases decided or judicially considered in the Scottish courts during 2017
(ii) References to English cases judicially considered in Scotland during2017
Scottish cases published in English Law Reports are included in both the English and Scottish sections
Figures appearing in bold type indicate the main substantive paragraph

3D Garages Ltd v Prolatis Co Ltd 2017 S.L.T. (Sh Ct) 9; 2016 G.W.D. 34-617, Sh Ct (Lothian) (Edinburgh) .... *Digested,* 17/**2781**

A v B 2016 S.L.T. (Sh Ct) 389; 2016 G.W.D. 27-492, Sh Ct (Lothian) (Edinburgh) .... *Digested,* 17/**2618**
A v City of Edinburgh Council 2017 Hous. L.R. 4; 2017 G.W.D. 5-67, Sh Ct (Lothian) (Edinburgh) .... *Digested,* 17/**2659**
A v Criminal Injuries Compensation Board [2017] CSIH 46; 2017 S.L.T. 984; 2017 G.W.D. 22-381, IH (2 Div) .... *Digested,* 17/**2386**
A v K 2017 G.W.D. 4-55, Sh Ct (Tayside) (Forfar)
A v Murphy [2014] HCJAC 96; 2014 S.C.L. 784; 2014 G.W.D. 28-565, HCJ .... *Digested,* 14/**3784**: *Applied* 17/2819
A v Secretary of State for the Home Department see AA (Nigeria) v Secretary of State for the Home Department
A v Secretary of State for the Home Department see HMA v Secretary of State for the Home Department
A & B Taxis v Co-operative Insurance 2017 G.W.D. 6-77, Sh Ct (Tayside) (Perth)
A I Walgate & Son v Scottish Natural Heritage; *sub nom* Walgate & Son v Scottish Natural Heritage [2017] CSOH 51; [2017] L.L.R. 651; 2017 G.W.D. 12-167, OH *Digested,* 17/**2407**: *Cited* 17/2408
A Ltd, Petitioner 2016 S.L.T. (Sh Ct) 425; 2016 G.W.D. 35-635, Sh Ct (Lothian) (Edinburgh) .... *Digested,* 17/**2685**
AA v BB 2015 G.W.D. 17-288, Sh Ct (South Strathclyde) (Dumfries) *Reversed* 17/2616
AA (Nigeria) v Secretary of State for the Home Department; *sub nom* A v Secretary of State for the Home Department [2016] CSIH 39; 2016 S.L.T. 1208; 2016 G.W.D. 17-317, IH (2 Div) .... *Digested,* 17/**2672**
AA (Nigeria) v Secretary of State for the Home Department [2017] CSIH 38; 2017 S.L.T. 1088; [2018] Imm. A.R. 1; 2017 G.W.D. 22-377, IH (2 Div) .... *Digested,* 17/**2673**
AB v AT see Contempt of Court Proceedings in Respect of M and L
AB v HM Advocate; *sub nom* B v HM Advocate [2017] UKSC 25; 2017 S.C. (U.K.S.C.) 101; 2017 S.L.T. 401; 2017 S.C.L. 434; 2017 S.C.C.R. 244; 2017 G.W.D. 12-178, SC .... *Digested,* 17/**537**
AB, Petitioner see Contempt of Court Proceedings in Respect of M and L
Abboud (Mohammed) v HM Advocate [2016] HCJAC 124; 2017 S.C.L. 234; 2017 S.C.C.R. 93; 2016 G.W.D. 40-708, HCJ .... *Digested,* 17/**2553**
ABT (Ethiopia) v Secretary of State for the Home Department [2017] CSOH 65; 2017 G.W.D. 14-222, OH
Abu Qatada v United Kingdom (8139/09) see Othman v United Kingdom (8139/09)
Accountant in Bankruptcy v Farrell see Accountant in Bankruptcy v Walker
Accountant in Bankruptcy v Walker; *sub nom* Accountant in Bankruptcy v Farrell [2017] CSOH 78; 2017 S.L.T. 890; [2017] B.P.I.R. 803; 2017 G.W.D. 16-255, OH .... *Digested,* 17/**2684**
Accountant in Bankruptcy, Appellant [2017] SAC (Civ) 5; 2017 S.L.T. (Sh Ct) 77; 2017 G.W.D. 5-71, SAC .... *Digested,* 17/**2682**
Adcock (Edward) v Archibald 1925 J.C. 58; 1925 S.L.T. 258, HCJ *Considered* 17/2512
Advice Centre for Mortgages Ltd v McNicoll 2006 S.L.T. 591; 2006 S.C.L.R. 602; 2006 Hous. L.R. 22; 2006 G.W.D. 19-413, OH .... *Digested,* 06/**5548**: *Applied* 16/2487, 17/2470: *Followed* 14/3631

Advocate General for Scotland v Murray Group Holdings Ltd see RFC 2012 Plc (In Liquidation) (formerly Rangers Football Club Plc) v Advocate General for Scotland
AF v AF 2017 S.L.T. (Sh Ct) 211; 2017 G.W.D. 22-371, Sh Ct (Glasgow)
AF v RF [2017] SAC (Civ) 18; 2017 Fam. L.R. 61; 2017 G.W.D. 16-261, SAC .... *Digested,* 17/**2615**
AH v CH see H v H
AH (Afghanistan) v Secretary of State for the Home Department [2017] CSOH 80; 2017 G.W.D. 19-306, OH
Ahmed v QBE Insurance (Europe) Ltd [2017] SAC (Civ) 22; 2017 G.W.D. 22-368, SAC
Ahmed (Tanveer) v HM Advocate [2016] HCJAC 125; 2017 J.C. 130; 2017 S.C.L. 306; 2016 G.W.D. 40-727, HCJ .... *Digested,* 17/**2806**: *Considered* 17/2807
AJE v HM Advocate see E v HM Advocate
AK (Latvia), Appellant [2017] CSIH 42; 2017 G.W.D. 22-376, IH (Ex Div)
Al v Advocate General for Scotland [2015] CSOH 95; 2015 S.L.T. 507; 2015 G.W.D. 25-439, OH .... *Digested,* 15/**3148**: *Considered* 17/2663
Al-Khawaja v United Kingdom (26766/05); *joined case* Tahery v United Kingdom (22228/06) (2009) 49 E.H.R.R. 1; 26 B.H.R.C. 249; [2009] Crim. L.R. 352, ECHR .... *Digested,* 09/**757**: *Considered* 09/761, 10/658, 17/2603
Al-Khawaja v United Kingdom (26766/05); *joined case* Tahery v United Kingdom (22228/06) [2012] 2 Costs L.O. 139; (2012) 54 E.H.R.R. 23; 32 B.H.R.C. 1; Times, December 22, 2011; [2012] Crim. L.R. 375, ECHR (Grand Chamber) .... *Digested,* 12/**657**: *Applied* 12/653: *Considered* 13/600, 14/287, 17/2474
Alexander Oastler Ltd v Williams 2017 G.W.D. 12-170, Sh Ct (Tayside) (Dundee)
Allan v Plexus Corp (UK) Ltd 2017 S.C.L.R. 214; 2016 Rep. L.R. 119; 2018 Rep. L.R. 32; 2016 G.W.D. 28-502, Sh Ct (Lothian) (Edinburgh) .... *Digested,* 17/**2441**
Allan v Tant (Michael Norman) 1986 J.C. 62; 1986 S.C.C.R. 175, HCJ .... *Digested,* 86/**3893**: *Considered* 17/2478, 17/2479
Alliance Trust Savings Ltd v Currie [2016] CSOH 154; 2017 S.C.L.R. 685; 2016 G.W.D. 35-628, OH
Amlin UK Ltd v Geo-Rope Ltd [2016] CSOH 165; [2017] Lloyd's Rep. I.R. 277; 2017 Rep. L.R. 46; 2016 G.W.D. 39-689, OH .... *Digested,* 17/**2754**
Anchor Line (Henderson Bros) Ltd, Re; *sub nom* Companies Act 1929, Re [1937] Ch. 483; [1937] 2 All E.R. 823, Ch D
Considered 47-51/1270, 17/2447
Anderson v Advocate General for Scotland 2017 G.W.D. 11-163, Sh Ct (Lothian) (Livingston)
Anderson v Imrie [2016] CSOH 171; 2017 Rep. L.R. 21; 2017 G.W.D. 1-11, OH .... *Digested,* 17/**2737**
Anderson (Craig) v HM Advocate [2017] HCJAC 33; 2017 J.C. 287; 2017 S.C.L. 621; 2017 G.W.D. 17-269, HCJ Appeal .... *Digested,* 17/**2499**
Anderson (James McAulay) v HM Advocate 1996 J.C. 29; 1996 S.L.T. 155, HCJ Appeal .... *Digested,* 96/**6764**: *Applied* 04/4679, 06/5173, 08/4663, 15/3114, 17/2532: *Cited* 09/4820: *Considered* 06/5192, 07/5078, 09/4815, 14/3459, 17/2438, 17/2538: *Distinguished* 00/6091, 08/4677: *Followed* 03/5379: *Referred to* 97/5804
Anderson Brown & Co v Morris 1987 S.L.T. (Sh. Ct.) 96; 1987 S.C.L.R. 187, Sh Pr ..... *Digested,* 87/**5078**: *Applied* 17/2413: *Followed* 90/5797, 96/7332
Anderson Strathern LLP v Scottish Legal Complaints Commission [2016] CSIH 71; 2017 S.C. 120; 2016 S.L.T. 967; 2016 G.W.D. 28-511, IH (2 Div) .... *Digested,* 16/**2715**: *Cited* 17/2711
Angus v Nisbet [2010] HCJAC 76; 2011 J.C. 69; 2011 S.L.T. 98; 2011 S.C.L. 33; 2010 S.C.C.R. 873; 2010 G.W.D. 27-532, HCJ .... *Digested,* 11/**4102**: *Considered* 17/2494
Angus Growers Ltd v Scottish Ministers [2016] CSOH 26; 2016 S.L.T. 529; 2016 G.W.D. 6-125, OH .... *Digested,* 16/**2428**: *Considered* 17/2773
Ansari v Aberdeen City Council [2017] CSIH 5; 2017 S.C. 274; 2017 S.L.T. 358; 2017 G.W.D. 4-57, IH (Ex Div) .... *Digested,* 17/**2746**
Ansari v Aberdeen City Council [2015] CSOH 168; 2016 S.L.T. 73; 2016 G.W.D. 1-24, OH .... *Digested,* 16/**2750**: *Affirmed* 17/2746
AP v Duncan [2016] CSOH 111; 2017 S.C.L.R. 341; 2016 G.W.D. 26-480, OH .... *Digested,* 17/**2428**
Apex Property Factor Ltd v C 2017 Hous. L.R. 107; 2017 G.W.D. 31-504, Sh Ct (Glasgow)
AR (Pakistan), Appellant [2017] CSIH 52; 2017 G.W.D. 25-419, IH (Ex Div)

Arbitration Application No.2 of 2016 [2017] CSOH 23; 2017 G.W.D. 6-79, OH
Argyll and Bute Council v Gordon [2017] SAC (Civ) 6; 2017 S.L.T. (Sh Ct) 53; 2017 G.W.D. 6-87, SAC .... *Digested,* 17/**2834**
Argyll and Bute Council v Gordon 2016 S.L.T. (Sh Ct) 196; 2016 S.C.L.R. 192; 2016 G.W.D. 6-135, Sh Ct (Lothian) (Edinburgh) .... *Digested,* 16/**2825**: *Affirmed* 17/2834
Arjo Wiggins Ltd v British Waterways Board [2017] SAC (Civ) 15; 2017 G.W.D. 15-240, SAC
Armia Ltd v Daejan Developments Ltd 1979 S.C. (H.L.) 56; 1979 S.L.T. 147, HL .... *Digested,* 79/**3117**: *Applied* 89/3854, 96/6570, 00/6467, 05/5470: *Followed* 91/5346, 93/5383, 17/2696
Armstrong v Glasgow City Council see HBJ Claimants v Glasgow City Council
Armstrong (Edward) v Procurator Fiscal, Livingston [2017] SAC (Crim) 11; 2017 G.W.D. 24-413, SAC
Arnold v Britton [2015] UKSC 36; [2015] A.C. 1619; [2015] 2 W.L.R. 1593; [2016] 1 All E.R. 1; [2015] H.L.R. 31; [2015] 2 P. & C.R. 14; [2015] L. & T.R. 25; [2015] C.I.L.L. 3689, SC .... *Digested,* 15/**1606**: *Applied* 15/1802, 16/137, 16/1764, 16/426, 17/2468, 17/498: *Cited* 17/2471: *Considered* 16/2704: *Followed* 16/413, 16/440, 17/1334, 17/1443, 17/1455, 17/1474, 17/2463, 17/474, 17/478, 17/493, 17/506
Arthur J Gallagher Insurance Brokers Ltd v Hudson 2017 G.W.D. 3-27, Sh Ct (Grampian) (Banff)
AS v HM Advocate see S (A) v HM Advocate
ASA International Ltd v Kashmiri Properties (Ireland) Ltd [2016] CSIH 70; 2017 S.C. 107; 2016 G.W.D. 27-493, IH (Ex Div) .... *Digested,* 17/**2655**
Ashif (Mohammed) v HM Advocate; *joined case* Ashraf (Aliah) v HM Advocate [2015] HCJAC 100; 2017 J.C. 7; 2016 S.L.T. 1079; 2016 S.C.L. 934; 2016 S.C.C.R. 437; 2016 G.W.D. 33-589, HCJ .... *Digested,* 17/**2496**
Ashraf (Aliah) v HM Advocate see Ashif (Mohammed) v HM Advocate
Asif v Secretary of State for the Home Department 1999 S.L.T. 890; 1999 S.C.L.R. 427; 1999 G.W.D. 6-311, OH .... *Digested,* 99/**6291**: *Affirmed* 02/5878: *Approved* 00/6491: *Considered* 17/2825
Assange v Sweden; *sub nom* Assange v Swedish Prosecution Authority [2011] EWHC 2849 (Admin); (2011) 108(44) L.S.G. 17, DC
Affirmed 12/1284: *Applied* 13/606, 14/1227, 15/963: *Considered* 13/1179, 13/667, 17/2597
Assange v Swedish Prosecution Authority see Assange v Sweden
Assessor for Glasgow v Schuh Ltd [2012] CSIH 40; 2012 S.L.T. 904; [2012] R.A. 245; 2012 G.W.D. 17-355, LVAC .... *Digested,* 12/**4244**: *Applied* 17/2726: *Cited* 14/3676
Attorney General's Reference (No.2 of 2002) [2002] EWCA Crim 2373; [2003] 1 Cr. App. R. 21; Times, October 17, 2002; [2003] Crim. L.R. 192, CA (Crim Div) ...... *Digested,* 02/**748**: *Applied* 17/2559: *Considered* 03/760
Attorney General's Reference (Nos 128 to 141 of 2015 and 8 to 10 of 2016); *sub nom* R. v Stephenson (Nosakhere); R. v Nazran (Sundish Singh); R. v McDermott (Louis Junior); R. v Wiggan (Theodore Junior); R. v Gul (Rowan); R. v Ducram (Fitzroy); R. v Mattu (Joga Singh); R. v Miah (Mohammed Selu); R. v Ghalib (Amar); R. v Abdin (Joynal); R. v Hussain (Ifran); R. v Hussain (Usman); R. v Fedar (Mohammed); R. v Mohammed (Janed); R. v Officer (Clinton); R. v Smith (Jamal Shaka); R. v Mentore (Darren) [2016] EWCA Crim 54; [2016] 4 W.L.R. 83; [2016] 2 Cr. App. R. (S.) 12, CA (Crim Div) .... *Digested,* 16/**1886**: *Considered* 17/2802
AV v AJF [2017] CSOH 103; 2017 Fam. L.R. 110; 2017 G.W.D. 24-408, OH .... *Digested,* 17/**2599**
Aviemore Highland Resort Ltd v Cairngorms National Park Authority 2009 S.L.T. (Sh Ct) 97; 2009 G.W.D. 24-388, Sh Ct (Grampian) (Inverness) .... *Digested,* 09/**4984**: *Distinguished* 17/2643
AWG Business Centres Ltd v Regus Caledonia Ltd [2017] CSIH 22; 2017 G.W.D. 9-131, IH (1 Div)
AWG Group Ltd v HCP II Properties 101 GP Ltd [2017] CSOH 69; 2017 Hous. L.R. 30; 2017 G.W.D. 15-245, OH .... *Digested,* 17/**2696**
Azhar v Dundee City Council [2017] L.L.R. 429; 2017 G.W.D. 19-311, Sh Ct (Tayside) (Dundee) .... *Digested,* 17/**2718**

B v D [2015] CSOH 24; 2015 S.L.T. 217; 2015 G.W.D. 8-148, OH .... *Digested,* 15/**2886**: *Affirmed* 17/2452
B v General Teaching Council for Scotland [2016] CSOH 181; 2017 G.W.D. 2-17, OH
B v HM Advocate [2016] HCJAC 101; 2017 S.C.L. 64; 2016 G.W.D. 37-665, HCJ .... *Digested,* 17/**2550**
B v HM Advocate see AB v HM Advocate

B v Locality Reporter [2017] SAC (Civ) 10; 2017 G.W.D. 13-195, SAC
B v Secretary of State for the Home Department see MIAB v Secretary of State for the Home Department
B v Secretary of State for Work and Pensions [2005] EWCA Civ 929; [2005] 1 W.L.R. 3796; Times, September 16, 2005, CA (Civ Div) .... *Digested,* 06/**3978**: *Considered* 17/2772
B (JP) v HM Advocate [2017] HCJAC 28; 2017 S.C.L. 690; 2017 G.W.D. 18-287, HCJ Appeal .... *Digested,* 17/**2520**
B (R) v HM Advocate; *sub nom* RB v HM Advocate [2017] HCJAC 24; 2017 J.C. 278; 2017 S.L.T. 714; 2017 S.C.L. 545; 2017 S.C.C.R. 278; 2017 G.W.D. 14-216, HCJ .... *Digested,* 17/**2486**
B, Petitioner see Contempt of Court Proceedings in Respect of M and L
BA (Turkey) v Secretary of State for the Home Department [2017] CSOH 27; 2017 S.L.T. 1061; 2017 G.W.D. 8-116, OH .... *Digested,* 17/**2668**
Bain v Brand (1876) 1 App. Cas. 762; (1876) 3 R. (H.L.) 16, HL
Considered 07/5285, 16/2709: *Explained* 86/4106: *Followed* 81/3242, 89/4524, 17/2710
Baisley v South Lanarkshire Council [2017] I.C.R. 365, EAT (SC) .... *Digested,* 17/**2582**
Balfour (Bruce James) v HM Advocate see Ferguson (James Douglas) v HM Advocate
Balgray Ltd v Hodgson [2016] CSIH 55; 2016 S.L.T. 839; 2017 S.C.L.R. 235; 2016 G.W.D. 22-390, IH (Ex Div) .... *Digested,* 16/**2702**
Bamford v Harvey [2012] EWHC 2858 (Ch); [2013] Bus. L.R. 589; [2013] B.C.C. 311; Times, December 7, 2012, Ch D .... *Digested,* 13/**354**: *Considered* 17/2423
Bank Mellat v HM Treasury [2013] UKSC 38; [2014] A.C. 700; [2013] 4 All E.R. 495; [2013] Lloyd's Rep. F.C. 557, SC .... *Digested,* 14/**48**: *Applied* 14/2102, 14/45, 16/1157, 16/2599, 17/2693: *Considered* 15/3243, 17/1231: *Followed* 14/663, 16/1975, 16/632, 17/1155, 17/1513
Banks v Mecca Bookmakers (Scotland) Ltd 1982 S.C. 7; 1982 S.L.T. 150, OH .... *Digested,* 82/**3945**: *Distinguished* 93/5461, 17/2696
Barnes v Chief Constable of the Police Service of Scotland [2017] CSOH 92; 2017 S.L.T. 844; 2017 G.W.D. 21-328, OH .... *Digested,* 17/**2769**
Baronetcy of Pringle of Stichill, Re [2016] UKPC 16; [2016] 1 W.L.R. 2870; [2017] 1 All E.R. 106; 2016 S.C. (P.C.) 1; 2016 S.L.T. 723; [2016] W.T.L.R. 1117; 2016 G.W.D. 20-360, PC (Sc) .... *Digested,* 16/**2744**
Barr v South Lanarkshire Council 2017 G.W.D. 15-247, Lands Tr (Scot)
Barras v Aberdeen Steam Trawling & Fishing Co Ltd [1933] A.C. 402; [1933] All E.R. Rep. 52; (1933) 45 Ll. L. Rep. 199; 1933 S.C. (H.L.) 21; 1933 S.L.T. 338, HL
Applied 14/2936, 16/2102: *Considered* 47-51/9934, 83/538, 16/2697, 17/2679
Barratt Scotland Ltd v Keith 1993 S.C. 142; 1994 S.L.T. 1343; 1993 S.C.L.R. 120, IH (2 Div) .... *Digested,* 93/**5686**: *Cited* 10/4482: *Considered* 04/5093: *Followed* 17/2771
Barrett v Spice Lounge (Scotland) Ltd 2017 G.W.D. 30-485, SPIC
BC (China) v Secretary of State for the Home Department [2017] CSOH 83; 2017 G.W.D. 19-305, OH
Beggs v Scottish Information Commissioner [2016] CSIH 23; 2016 S.C. 615; 2016 G.W.D. 11-225, IH (Ex Div) .... *Digested,* 17/**2395**
Beggs v Scottish Ministers [2017] CSIH 62; 2017 G.W.D. 32-508, IH (Ex Div)
Beggs v Scottish Ministers [2017] CSOH 99; 2017 G.W.D. 22-359, OH
Bell Building Projects Ltd v Arnold Clark Automobiles Ltd [2017] CSOH 55; 2017 G.W.D. 12-174, OH
Bessant v South Cone Inc see REEF Trade Mark
Beyts v Trump International Golf Club Scotland Ltd 2017 S.L.T. (Sh Ct) 93; 2017 G.W.D. 12-187, Sh Ct (Lothian) (Edinburgh) .... *Digested,* 17/**2675**
Bimbo SA v Office for Harmonisation in the Internal Market (Trade Marks and Designs) (OHIM) (T-569/10) EU:T:2012:535; [2013] E.T.M.R. 7, GC (7th Chamber)
Considered 17/2690
Black v Carmichael; *joined case* Carmichael v Black 1992 S.L.T. 897; 1992 S.C.C.R. 709; Times, June 25, 1992; Independent, July 27, 1992; Guardian, July 8, 1992, HCJ Appeal .... *Digested,* 92/**5545**: *Applied* 17/2597: *Distinguished* 96/5698
Bloor Construction (UK) Ltd v Bowmer and Kirkland (London) Ltd [2000] B.L.R. 314; (2000) 2 T.C.L.R. 914, QBD (TCC)
Applied 09/649, 10/566: *Considered* 07/732, 08/607, 17/2461
BM v HM Advocate [2017] HCJAC 55; 2017 S.C.L. 882; 2017 G.W.D. 23-388, HCJ .... *Digested,* 17/**2498**

BM (Albania) v Advocate General for Scotland [2017] CSOH 17; 2017 S.L.T. 247; [2017] Imm. A.R. 1143; 2017 G.W.D. 5-70, OH .... *Digested,* 17/**2671**

Bolitho v City and Hackney Health Authority [1998] A.C. 232; [1997] 3 W.L.R. 1151; [1997] 4 All E.R. 771; [1998] P.I.Q.R. P10; [1998] Lloyd's Rep. Med. 26; (1998) 39 B.M.L.R. 1; [1998] P.N.L.R. 1; Times, November 27, 1997; (1997) 94(47) L.S.G. 30; (1997) 141 S.J.L.B. 238, HL .... *Digested,* 97/**3789**: *Applied* 98/3977, 99/3994, 01/4263, 01/4542, 02/3294, 03/5826, 04/2698, 06/2869, 07/2917, 07/2926, 08/2644, 08/2763, 09/2840, 09/2842, 09/2844, 09/73, 14/2197, 17/1561: *Considered* 98/3986, 03/2989, 07/2923, 07/3068, 16/2731, 17/1568, 17/2736: *Distinguished* 98/3969, 05/2863: *Followed* 98/3963, 99/3989

Bolkiah v KPMG; *sub nom* HRH Prince Jefri Bolkiah v KPMG [1999] 2 A.C. 222; [1999] 2 W.L.R. 215; [1999] 1 All E.R. 517; [1999] 1 B.C.L.C. 1; [1999] C.L.C. 175; [1999] P.N.L.R. 220; Times, April 20, 1999; Independent, January 12, 1999; (1999) 149 N.L.J. 16; (1999) 143 S.J.L.B. 35, HL .... *Digested,* 99/**1**: *Applied* 00/2504, 00/4008, 02/216, 02/3108, 04/2569, 05/2724, 12/2097, 14/2060, 17/184, 17/2712, 17/458: *Considered* 99/2, 99/3796, 00/4007, 03/2821, 06/1042, 11/287, 12/1051, 12/1140, 12/334: *Distinguished* 12/418: *Followed* 00/2469, 10/1379

Bouygues UK Ltd v Dahl-Jensen UK Ltd [2000] B.L.R. 49; (2000) 2 T.C.L.R. 308; 70 Con. L.R. 41; Independent, February 7, 2000, QBD (TCC) *Affirmed* 00/3489: *Applied* 02/654, 10/566, 14/581, 15/459: *Considered* 17/2461: *Followed* 01/6289

Bow v Harvie see Paterson v Harvie

Bowes v Highland Council [2017] CSOH 53; 2017 S.L.T. 749; 2017 Rep. L.R. 52; 2017 G.W.D. 12-193, OH .... *Digested,* 17/**2738**

Bowman v Guthrie 1998 S.L.T. (Land Ct) 2; 1997 S.L.C.R. 40, Land Ct .... *Digested,* 98/**6030**: *Considered* 17/2402

Boyle v CIS Ltd 2017 Rep. L.R. 138; 2017 G.W.D. 20-323, Sh Ct (Lothian) (Edinburgh)

Bradley v Bradley [2017] SAC (Civ) 29; 2017 S.L.T. (Sh Ct) 201; 2017 Fam. L.R. 123; 2017 G.W.D. 31-502, SAC .... *Digested,* 17/**2607**

Bradley v Secretary of State for Business, Innovation and Skills [2016] CSIH 80; 2017 S.C. 153; 2016 S.L.T. 1097; 2016 G.W.D. 33-587, IH (Ex Div) .... *Digested,* 17/**2459**

British Telecommunications Plc v Scottish Water 2017 G.W.D. 14-218, Sh Ct (Lothian) (Edinburgh)

Brits v Kilcoyne & Co [2017] CSIH 47; 2017 G.W.D. 23-386, IH (Ex Div)

Brits v Kilcoyne & Co [2017] CSOH 24; 2017 G.W.D. 7-97, OH

Brown v Aviva Insurance 2017 G.W.D. 1-6, Sh Ct (Lothian) (Livingston)

Brown v McPherson see Brown v Procurator Fiscal, Ayr

Brown v Procurator Fiscal, Ayr; *sub nom* Brown v McPherson [2016] SAC (Crim) 32; 2017 S.L.T. (Sh Ct) 63; 2017 S.C.L. 315; 2016 S.C.C.R. 564; 2016 G.W.D. 36-644, SAC .... *Digested,* 17/**2510**

Brown (Duncan) v HM Advocate [2016] HCJAC 112; 2017 S.C.L. 141; 2016 G.W.D. 38-677, HCJ

Bruce v Tayside Health Board [2017] CSOH 123; 2017 G.W.D. 31-505, OH

Brucefield Estate Trustee Co Ltd v Computacenter (UK) Ltd 2017 Hous. L.R. 66; 2017 G.W.D. 21-350, Sh Ct (Lothian) (Livingston) .... *Digested,* 17/**2697**

Buck v Ainslie [2017] CSOH 73; 2017 G.W.D. 17-279, OH

Buckley v Secretary of State for Business, Energy and Industrial Strategy [2017] CSOH 105; 2017 G.W.D. 24-404, OH

Burke v Laing [2016] SAC (Crim) 31; 2017 S.C.L. 112; 2016 G.W.D. 34-622, SAC .... *Digested,* 17/**2795**

Burnett (Andrew) v Procurator Fiscal, Hamilton [2017] SAC (Crim) 4; 2017 S.C.L. 569; 2017 G.W.D. 11-151, SAC .... *Digested,* 17/**2494**

Burzala (Steven) v HM Advocate [2007] HCJAC 67; 2008 S.L.T. 61; 2008 S.C.L. 305; 2008 S.C.C.R. 199; 2008 G.W.D. 1-10, HCJ .... *Digested,* 08/**4664**: *Applied* 17/2532: *Considered* 10/4116

Butterworth v Supplementary Benefits Commission see Crake v Supplementary Benefits Commission

Byrne (Andrew) v HM Advocate [2016] HCJAC 84; 2016 S.C.L. 998; 2016 G.W.D. 31-562, HCJ Appeal .... *Digested,* 17/**2808**

C v C [2016] SAC (Civ) 6; 2016 S.L.T. (Sh Ct) 433; 2016 Fam. L.R. 141; 2016 G.W.D. 26-472, SAC .... *Digested,* 17/**2458**

C v G [2017] CSOH 5; 2017 S.L.T. 79; 2017 G.W.D. 3-33, OH .... *Digested,* 17/**2779**

C v HM Advocate; *sub nom* RC v HM Advocate [2017] HCJAC 61; 2018 J.C. 1; 2017 S.C.L. 854; 2017 G.W.D. 27-437, HCJ .... *Digested,* 17/**2473**

C v HM Advocate [2016] HCJAC 100; 2017 S.C.L. 53; 2016 G.W.D. 37-658, HCJ .... *Digested,* 17/**2487**

Cafferkey (Daniel) v HM Advocate; *joined case* Frew (Laura) v HM Advocate [2016] HCJAC 114; 2017 S.C.L. 149; 2017 S.C.C.R. 14; 2016 G.W.D. 38-671, HCJ .... *Digested,* 17/**2495**
Cairns v Dundee City Council [2017] CSOH 86; 2017 Rep. L.R. 96; 2017 G.W.D. 21-352, OH
Calderwood v Renfrewshire Council 2004 S.C. 691; 2004 S.L.T. 219; [2004] L.L.R. 171; [2004] 29 S.L.L.P. 22; 2004 G.W.D. 6-100, IH (Ex Div) .... *Digested,* 04/**5024**: *Applied* 17/2719: *Considered* 16/2721
Cameron (David) v HM Advocate [2017] HCJAC 74; 2017 S.C.L. 923; 2017 G.W.D. 31-496, HCJ .... *Digested,* 17/**2567**
Cameron (Stuart) v HM Advocate see Ferguson (James Douglas) v HM Advocate
Campbell v Gordon see Campbell v Peter Gordon Joiners Ltd
Campbell v Peter Gordon Joiners Ltd; *sub nom* Campbell v Gordon [2016] UKSC 38; [2016] A.C. 1513; [2016] 3 W.L.R. 294; [2017] 2 All E.R. 161; 2017 S.C. (U.K.S.C.) 13; 2016 S.L.T. 887; 2016 S.C.L.R. 434; [2016] 2 B.C.L.C. 287; [2016] I.C.R. 862; [2016] Lloyd's Rep. I.R. 591; [2016] P.I.Q.R. P15; Times, July 20, 2016; 2016 G.W.D. 21-380, SC .... *Digested,* 16/**1257**
Campbell v Scottish Ministers [2017] CSOH 35; 2017 G.W.D. 9-124, OH
Campbell (Sharon) v Vannet 1997 S.C.C.R. 787; 1997 G.W.D. 40-2039, HCJ Appeal . *Digested,* 98/**5603**: *Distinguished* 09/5154: *Followed* 17/2472
Carmichael v Black see Black v Carmichael
Carmichael (Alan) v HM Advocate [2016] HCJAC 123; 2017 S.C.L. 230; 2016 G.W.D. 40-709, HCJ .... *Digested,* 17/**2571**
Carse (Liquidator) v Coppen 1951 S.C. 233; 1951 S.L.T. 145, IH (1 Div) .... *Digested,* 47-51/**1270**: *Considered* 17/2447: *Distinguished* 17/2781
Carter v McIntosh (1862) 24 D. 925, IH (2 Div)
Applied 55/3507, 17/2610: *Considered* 97/6106, 07/5335
Cassidy v Trafalgar Housing Association Ltd 2017 G.W.D. 26-433, Lands Tr (Scot)
Cattle v Stockton Waterworks Co (1874-75) L.R. 10 Q.B. 453; [1874-80] All E.R. Rep. 492, QBD
Applied 72/2341, 17/2455: *Considered* 89/3392: *Followed* 65/2671
Cay's Trustee v Cay 1998 S.C. 780; 1999 S.L.T. 321; 1998 S.C.L.R. 456; 1998 G.W.D. 14-722, IH (2 Div) .... *Digested,* 98/**6001**: *Applied* 17/2684: *Followed* 02/5891
CCHG Ltd (t/a Vaporized) v Vapouriz Ltd [2017] CSOH 100; 2017 S.L.T. 907; [2017] E.T.M.R. 35; 2017 G.W.D. 22-378, OH .... *Digested,* 17/**2690**
Centenary 6 Ltd v Joint Liquidators of Centenary Holdings III Ltd [2017] CSOH 95; 2017 G.W.D. 23-384, OH
CF v MF [2017] CSIH 44; 2017 S.L.T. 945; 2017 Fam. L.R. 83; 2017 G.W.D. 23-394, IH (Ex Div) .... *Digested,* 17/**2604**
CF (China) v Secretary of State for the Home Department [2017] CSOH 116; 2017 G.W.D. 29-463, OH
Chalmers v Diageo Scotland Ltd [2017] CSOH 36; [2017] L.L.R. 256; 2017 G.W.D. 9-126, OH .... *Digested,* 17/**2740**
Chalmers (Robert Davidson) v HM Advocate [2014] HCJAC 24; 2014 J.C. 220; 2014 S.L.T. 688; 2014 S.C.L. 442; 2014 S.C.C.R. 291; 2014 G.W.D. 13-249, HCJ .... *Digested,* 14/**3775**: *Considered* 17/2807
Chaudhry v Advocate General for Scotland [2013] CSOH 36; 2013 S.L.T. 548; 2013 S.C.L.R. 635; 2013 G.W.D. 10-211, OH .... *Digested,* 13/**3541**: *Considered* 17/2447
Chaudhry v South Lanarkshire Council 2017 G.W.D. 12-190, Lands Tr (Scot)
Chaudhry (Tariq) v Procurator Fiscal, Hamilton [2017] SAC (Crim) 7; 2017 S.C.L. 646; 2017 G.W.D. 14-231, SAC .... *Digested,* 17/**2818**
Chaudhry (Tariq) v Procurator Fiscal, Hamilton [2017] SAC (Crim) 5; 2017 S.C.L. 573; 2017 G.W.D. 11-153, SAC .... *Digested,* 17/**2543**
Chief Constable of the Police Service of Scotland v A (M) 2017 S.L.T. (Sh Ct) 192; 2017 G.W.D. 21-356, Sh Ct (Lothian) (Edinburgh) .... *Digested,* 17/**2819**
Chiswell v Chiswell [2016] CSOH 45; 2017 S.C.L.R. 49; 2016 G.W.D. 10-186, OH ...... *Digested,* 17/**2677**
Christian Institute v Lord Advocate; *sub nom* Christian Institute, Petitioners; Christian Institute v Scottish Ministers [2016] UKSC 51; 2017 S.C. (U.K.S.C.) 29; 2016 S.L.T. 805; 2016 S.C.L.R. 448; [2016] H.R.L.R. 19; [2016] E.L.R. 474; (2016) 19 C.C.L. Rep. 422; Times, September 26, 2016; 2016 G.W.D. 22-401, SC ...... *Digested,* 16/**848**
Christian Institute v Scottish Ministers see Christian Institute v Lord Advocate
Christian Institute, Petitioners see Christian Institute v Lord Advocate
City of Edinburgh Council v Marcel [2017] CSIH 50; 2017 G.W.D. 23-400, IH (1 Div)
City of Edinburgh Council v Marcel [2017] CSOH 15; 2017 G.W.D. 5-75, OH
City of Edinburgh Council v O; *sub nom* City of Edinburgh Council v RO [2016] SAC (Civ) 15; 2017 Fam. L.R. 27; 2016 G.W.D. 40-716, SAC .... *Digested,* 17/**2602**
City of Edinburgh Council v RO see City of Edinburgh Council v O

Coventry (t/a RDC Promotions) v Lawrence; *sub nom* Coventry v Lawrence; Lawrence v Coventry (t/a RDC Promotions); Lawrence v Fen Tigers Ltd [2014] UKSC 13; [2014] A.C. 822; [2014] 2 W.L.R. 433; [2014] 2 All E.R. 622; [2014] P.T.S.R. 384; [2014] B.L.R. 271; 152 Con. L.R. 1; [2014] Env. L.R. 25; [2014] H.L.R. 21; [2014] 2 P. & C.R. 2; [2014] 1 E.G.L.R. 147; [2014] L.L.R. 423; (2014) 158(9) S.J.L.B. 37, SC .... *Digested,* 14/**2223**:
Applied 14/2526: *Considered* 16/264, 17/2740: *Followed* 16/1554
Cowan (Amanda) v HM Advocate [2017] HCJAC 73; 2017 S.C.L. 1022; 2017 S.C.C.R. 526; 2017 G.W.D. 31-495, HCJ
Coyle (James Thomas) v HM Advocate [2007] HCJAC 52; 2008 J.C. 107; 2008 S.C.L. 131; 2007 S.C.C.R. 479; 2007 G.W.D. 29-508, HCJ .... *Digested,* 08/**5043**:
Applied 08/5055: *Cited* 17/2814
Craig v Mair's Trustees; *sub nom* Healy & Young's Trustee v Mair's Trustees 1914 S.C. 893; 1914 2 S.L.T. 118, IH (1 Div)
Applied 17/2704
Crake v Supplementary Benefits Commission; *joined case* Butterworth v Supplementary Benefits Commission [1982] 1 All E.R. 498; (1981) 2 F.L.R. 264, QBD .... *Digested,* 82/**3035**:
Considered 83/3179, 91/2313, 13/1868, 17/2825: *Followed* 00/2542
Cranwell v Cullen UKEATPAS/0046/14/SM, EAT (SC)
Applied 17/2582
Crofters Commission's Reference, Re 2012 S.L.C.R. 159, Land Ct .... *Digested,* 14/**3627**:
Considered 17/2402
Croly (Theresa) v HM Advocate 2004 S.C.C.R. 389; 2004 G.W.D. 15-334, HCJ
Considered 17/2482
Cruden Buildings and Renewals Ltd v Scottish Water [2017] CSOH 98; [2017] B.L.R. 575; 2017 G.W.D. 22-363, OH .... *Digested,* 17/**2455**
Cullen v Advocate General for Scotland [2016] CSOH 170; 2017 S.L.T. 1; 2016 G.W.D. 40-726, OH .... *Digested,* 17/**2772**
Cumbria CC v X see Cumbria CC, Petitioner
Cumbria CC, Petitioner; *sub nom* Cumbria CC v X [2016] CSIH 92; 2017 S.C. 451; 2017 S.L.T. 34; 2017 Fam. L.R. 15; 2016 G.W.D. 40-703, IH (Ex Div) .... *Digested,* 17/**2379**
Cumming v SSE Plc 2016 Rep. L.R. 75; 2016 G.W.D. 15-286, Sh Ct (Lothian) (Edinburgh) .... *Digested,* 16/**2460**:
Affirmed 17/2429
Cumming v SSE Plc [2017] SAC (Civ) 17; 2017 Rep. L.R. 82; 2017 G.W.D. 15-238, SAC .... *Digested,* 17/**2429**
Cumming v Tayside Health Board [2016] CSOH 58; 2017 S.C.L.R. 176; 2016 Rep. L.R. 85; 2016 G.W.D. 12-233, OH .... *Digested,* 16/**2441**

D v Amec Group Ltd [2016] CSOH 176; 2017 G.W.D. 3-40, OH
D v Lanarkshire Acute Hospitals NHS Trust [2017] CSIH 30; 2017 G.W.D. 15-249, IH (1 Div)
D v Lothian Health Board; *sub nom* JD v Lothian Health Board [2017] CSIH 27; 2018 S.C.L.R. 1; 2017 G.W.D. 15-234, IH (Ex Div)
Considered 17/2697
D Geddes (Contractors) Ltd v Neil Johnson Health & Safety Services Ltd [2017] CSOH 42; [2017] P.N.L.R. 21; 2017 G.W.D. 10-134, OH .... *Digested,* 17/**2735**
David T Morrison & Co Ltd (t/a Gael Home Interiors) v ICL Plastics Ltd [2014] UKSC 48; 2014 S.C. (U.K.S.C.) 222; 2014 S.L.T. 791; 2014 S.C.L.R. 711; [2014] C.I.L.L. 3561; 2014 G.W.D. 25-504, SC .... *Digested,* 14/**2470**:
Considered 17/2449: *Followed* 16/2456
Davidson (William) v HM Advocate [2016] HCJAC 110; 2017 S.C.L. 198; 2016 G.W.D. 38-686, HCJ .... *Digested,* 17/**2813**
Davis v Catto [2011] CSIH 85; 2012 Rep. L.R. 40; 2012 G.W.D. 3-54, IH (Ex Div) .... *Digested,* 12/**4208**:
Considered 17/2442
DAY (Ghana) v Secretary of State for the Home Department [2017] CSIH 7; 2017 G.W.D. 4-52, IH (1 Div)
Dean (Zain Taj) v Lord Advocate; *sub nom* Lord Advocate v Dean [2017] UKSC 44; [2017] 1 W.L.R. 2721; [2018] 1 All E.R. 995; 2018 S.C. (U.K.S.C.) 1; 2017 S.L.T. 773; 2017 S.C.C.R. 388; 2017 G.W.D. 21-345, SC .... *Digested,* 17/**905**
Dem-Master Demolition Ltd v Healthcare Environmental Services Ltd [2017] CSOH 14; 2017 G.W.D. 5-72, OH
Devaseelan v Secretary of State for the Home Department [2002] UKIAT 702; [2003] Imm. A.R. 1, IAT .... *Digested,* 04/**2013**:
Applied 02/2577, 04/2009, 07/926, 08/1940, 08/2025, 13/1187:
Considered 04/2015, 05/2152, 07/2283, 11/1716, 17/2672: *Not applied* 09/358
Dewar v Scottish Borders Council [2017] CSOH 68; 2017 G.W.D. 15-250, OH

Dewar (John) v HM Advocate [2017] HCJAC 31; 2017 G.W.D. 17-274, HCJ Appeal
Dickie v Khandani [2012] CSOH 122; 2012 G.W.D. 26-546, OH
Considered 17/2757
Dickson v Ore Valley Housing Association 2017 G.W.D. 15-246, Lands Tr (Scot)
Dickson v United Dominions Trust Ltd (No.4) 1988 S.L.T. 19, OH .... *Digested,* 87/**4913**:
Applied 95/5485: *Considered* 17/2677: *Referred to* 95/6212
Digipos Store Solutions Group Ltd v Digi International Inc [2008] EWHC 3371 (Ch); [2008] Bus. L.R. 1621; [2008] R.P.C. 24, Ch D .... *Digested,* 08/**2397**:
Considered 17/2690
Dinsmore (Niall Brian) v HM Advocate [2017] HCJAC 11; 2017 S.L.T. 446; 2017 S.C.L. 411; 2017 G.W.D. 8-121, HCJ .... *Digested,* 17/**2810**
Divers (Shaun Patrick) v Procurator Fiscal, Airdrie [2017] SAC (Crim) 12; 2017 S.C.L. 1054; 2017 G.W.D. 28-450, SAC
DK v Secretary of State for Work and Pensions see K v Secretary of State for Work and Pensions
DM v Fife Council see M v Fife Council
DM v HM Advocate see M (D) v HM Advocate
Docherty v Babcock International 2017 Rep. L.R. 132; 2017 G.W.D. 19-295, Sh Ct (Lothian) (Edinburgh)
Docherty v Secretary of State for Business, Innovation and Skills [2017] CSOH 54; 2017 S.L.T. 671; 2017 G.W.D. 13-197, OH .... *Digested,* 17/**2448**
Dogan v Germany (C-138/13) EU:C:2014:2066; [2015] 1 C.M.L.R. 16; [2015] C.E.C. 130, ECJ (2nd Chamber)
Considered 17/2668
Dollar Land (Cumbernauld) Ltd v CIN Properties Ltd 1998 S.C. (H.L.) 90; 1998 S.L.T. 992; 1998 S.C.L.R. 929; [1998] 3 E.G.L.R. 79; [1998] 51 E.G. 83; Times, August 24, 1998; 1998 G.W.D. 25-1268, HL .... *Digested,* 98/**6034**:
Applied 17/2772: *Distinguished* 02/6152: *Followed* 00/6634
Donnelly v Royal Bank of Scotland Plc [2017] SAC (Civ) 1; 2017 S.L.T. (Sh Ct) 41; [2017] B.P.I.R. 400; 2017 G.W.D. 2-22, SAC .... *Digested,* 17/**2678**
Donnelly v Royal Bank of Scotland Plc 2016 S.L.T. (Sh Ct) 307; [2016] B.P.I.R. 606; 2016 G.W.D. 8-159, Sh Ct (Glasgow) .... *Digested,* 16/**2694**:
Reversed in part 17/2678
Donnelly (Brian) v HM Advocate 2000 S.C.C.R. 861, HCJ Appeal .... *Digested,* 01/**6391**:
Considered 17/2505: *Overruled* 17/2559
Dooneen Ltd (t/a McGinnes Associates) v Mond [2016] CSOH 23; 2016 G.W.D. 5-122, OH
Affirmed 17/2845: *Followed* 17/2678
Dooneen Ltd (t/a McGinnes Associates) v Mond [2016] CSIH 59; 2017 S.C.L.R. 199; [2017] B.P.I.R. 380; 2016 G.W.D. 23-441, IH (2 Div) .... *Digested,* 17/**2845**:
Followed 17/2678
Douglas v Perth and Kinross Council [2017] CSIH 28; 2017 S.C. 523; [2018] Env. L.R. 6; 2017 G.W.D. 18-291, IH (Ex Div)
Douglas v Perth and Kinross Council [2016] CSOH 167; 2017 G.W.D. 1-12, OH
DS v HM Advocate see S (D) v HM Advocate
Dulas (Michael) v HM Advocate [2016] HCJAC 91; 2016 S.C.L. 994; 2016 G.W.D. 32-583, HCJ .... *Digested,* 17/**2796**
Duncan's Hotel (Glasgow) Ltd v J&A Ferguson Ltd 1974 S.C. 191, OH
Applied 17/2464: *Considered* 97/6073
Dundee City Council v LT 2017 Fam. L.R. 145; 2017 G.W.D. 32-514, Sh Ct (Tayside) (Dundee)
Dunlea v Cashwell [2017] SAC (Civ) 12; 2017 S.C.L.R. 675; 2017 G.W.D. 13-207, SAC .... *Digested,* 17/**2654**
Dunsire (Lee) v HM Advocate [2017] HCJAC 30; 2017 S.C.L. 611; 2017 S.C.C.R. 348; 2017 G.W.D. 17-267, HCJ Appeal .... *Digested,* 17/**2476**
Durkin v HSBC Bank Plc [2016] CSIH 93; 2017 S.L.T. 125; 2017 S.C.L.R. 731; 2017 G.W.D. 1-3, IH (Ex Div) .... *Digested,* 17/**2412**

E v HM Advocate; *sub nom* AJE v HM Advocate 2002 J.C. 215; 2002 S.L.T. 715; 2002 S.C.C.R. 341; 2002 G.W.D. 13-407, HCJ .... *Digested,* 02/**5526**:
Applied 17/2532: *Considered* 03/5380, 10/4045, 16/2495: *Distinguished* 03/5379, 15/2943
E v Refugee Applications Commissioner (C-493/10) see R. (on the application of NS) v Secretary of State for the Home Department (C-411/10)
Early (Gerald Patrick) v HM Advocate [2006] HCJAC 65; 2007 J.C. 50; 2006 S.L.T. 856; 2006 S.C.C.R. 583; 2006 G.W.D. 28-623, HCJ .... *Digested,* 06/**5205**:
Applied 07/5046, 10/4078, 17/2521: *Cited* 08/4646: *Considered* 07/5068, 09/4798, 16/2535, 17/2520: *Followed* 09/4772

Ferguson (Derek Charles) v HM Advocate [2008] HCJAC 71; 2009 S.L.T. 67; 2009 S.C.L. 250; 2009 S.C.C.R. 78; 2008 G.W.D. 40-595, HCJ .... *Digested,* 09/**4828**: *Applied* 15/2998, 16/2565: *Considered* 09/4805, 10/4113, 13/3602, 15/2987, 15/2999, 17/2558

Ferguson (James Douglas) v HM Advocate; *joined cases* Nolan (Thomas) v HM Advocate; Balfour (Bruce James) v HM Advocate; Cameron (Stuart) v HM Advocate [2014] HCJAC 19; 2014 S.L.T. 431; 2014 S.C.C.R. 244; 2014 G.W.D. 10-194, HCJ .... *Digested,* 14/**3778**: *Applied* 17/2808: *Considered* 17/2809

Fife Council v Royal & Sun Alliance Insurance Plc [2017] CSOH 28; 2017 G.W.D. 8-111, OH

Fife Council v Royal & Sun Alliance Insurance Plc [2017] CSOH 115; 2017 G.W.D. 29-458, OH

Findmypast Ltd (formerly Brightsolid Online Technology Ltd) v Revenue and Customs Commissioners see Findmypast Ltd (formerly DC Thomson Family History Ltd) v Revenue and Customs Commissioners

Findmypast Ltd (formerly DC Thomson Family History Ltd) v Revenue and Customs Commissioners; *sub nom* Findmypast Ltd (formerly Brightsolid Online Technology Ltd) v Revenue and Customs Commissioners [2016] UKUT 17 (TCC); [2016] S.T.C. 1107; [2016] B.V.C. 503; [2016] S.T.I. 241, UT (Tax) .... *Digested,* 16/**2208**: *Affirmed* 17/2848

Finnegan (Harry) v HM Advocate [2016] HCJAC 88; 2016 S.L.T. 1139; 2016 S.C.L. 1003; 2016 G.W.D. 31-557, HCJ .... *Digested,* 17/**2793**

Firm of Malcolm G D Morrison v Scottish Ministers 2017 G.W.D. 24-402, Land Ct

First Time Ltd v Liquidator of Denmore Investments Ltd [2016] SAC (Civ) 9; 2016 S.L.T. (Sh Ct) 430; 2016 G.W.D. 32-568, SAC .... *Digested,* 17/**2451**

First Time Ltd v Liquidator of Denmore Investments Ltd [2017] SAC (Civ) 4; 2017 G.W.D. 5-64, SAC

Forbes (David Landells) v HM Advocate see Steele (Kevin Munro) v HM Advocate

Fortune's Trustee v Cooper Watson Ltd [2017] CSOH 74; 2017 G.W.D. 15-244, OH

Foss v Harbottle 67 E.R. 189; (1843) 2 Hare 461, Ct of Chancery
Applied 56/1149, 64/465, 78/241, 78/366, 82/330, 16/345: *Cited* 01/6300: *Considered* 47-51/10390, 68/445, 82/331, 85/3514, 85/3534, 91/414, 92/3560, 94/421, 96/1213, 96/5732, 02/619, 06/2324, 07/435, 09/510, 13/353, 17/2423, 17/287: *Distinguished* 63/411, 66/1409, 72/3459: *Followed* 10/826

Fox (Victor) v Patterson 1948 J.C. 104; 1948 S.L.T. 547; 1948 S.L.T. (Notes) 48, HCJ Appeal .... *Digested,* 48/**4167**: *Applied* 54/750: *Considered* 52/795, 54/3697, 90/4943, 17/2501

Francis (Angus) v HM Advocate [2017] HCJAC 63; 2017 S.C.L. 909; 2017 G.W.D. 29-459, HCJ .... *Digested,* 17/**2488**

Fraser (Nat Gordon) v HM Advocate [2013] HCJAC 117; 2014 J.C. 115; 2013 S.C.L. 1031; 2013 S.C.C.R. 674; 2013 G.W.D. 33-652, HCJ .... *Digested,* 14/**3448**: *Applied* 17/2529, 17/2567: *Considered* 15/3018

Frew (Laura) v HM Advocate see Cafferkey (Daniel) v HM Advocate

Fyfe v Council of the Law Society of Scotland [2017] CSIH 6; 2017 S.C. 283; 2017 S.L.T. 254; 2017 S.C.L.R. 464; 2017 G.W.D. 5-73, IH (2 Div) .... *Digested,* 17/**2713**

G v G 2017 S.L.T. (Sh Ct) 169; 2017 G.W.D. 20-317, Sh Ct (Grampian) (Aberdeen) ... *Digested,* 17/**2617**

G v Scottish Criminal Cases Review Commission; *sub nom* Gordon v Scottish Criminal Cases Review Commission [2017] UKSC 20; 2017 S.C. (U.K.S.C.) 86; 2017 S.L.T. 365; 2017 S.C.C.R. 214; 2017 G.W.D. 11-144, SC .... *Digested,* 17/**623**

G v Scottish Ministers [2017] CSOH 10; 2017 G.W.D. 4-56, OH

G v Stirling Council [2016] CSOH 121; 2016 Hous. L.R. 64; 2016 G.W.D. 26-483, OH . *Digested,* 17/**2657**

Gajdamowicz v First Glasgow Ltd 2017 G.W.D. 24-411, SPIC

Galbraith v Whitehead, &c (1863) 1 M. 644, IH (2 Div)
Applied 17/2677

Gall (Daniel Campbell) v HM Advocate 1992 J.C. 115; 1993 S.L.T. 290; 1992 S.C.C.R. 447, HCJ .... *Digested,* 92/**5519**: *Considered* 17/2571

Gallemos Ltd (In Receivership) v Barratt Falkirk Ltd 1989 S.C. 239; 1990 S.L.T. 98, IH (Ex Div) .... *Digested,* 89/**4878**: *Applied* 17/2610

Gannon (Anthony) v HM Advocate [2017] HCJAC 58; 2017 S.L.T. 1034; 2017 S.C.L. 892; 2017 G.W.D. 26-432, HCJ .... *Digested,* 17/**2560**

Garnett's Executor, Applicant 2017 S.L.T. (Sh Ct) 50; 2016 G.W.D. 40-729, Sh Ct (Glasgow) .... *Digested,* 17/**2838**

Gay (Grant) v HM Advocate [2017] HCJAC 62; 2017 S.C.L. 913; 2017 G.W.D. 28-448, HCJ .... *Digested,* 17/**2794**

GCMR, Petitioner [2017] CSOH 66; 2017 G.W.D. 17-275, OH
Gemmell (James Kelly) v HM Advocate; *joined cases* Robertson (Paul) v HM Advocate; Gibson (David Alexander) v HM Advocate; McCourt (Peter Stephen) v HM Advocate; Ross v Richardson; Hart v Brown; Nisbet v Ogilvie [2011] HCJAC 129; 2012 J.C. 223; 2012 S.L.T. 484; 2012 S.C.L. 385; 2012 S.C.C.R. 176; 2012 G.W.D. 4-78, HCJ .... *Digested,* 12/**4277**: *Applied* 16/2808, 17/2814: *Cited* 12/3912: *Considered* 13/3972, 13/3990, 14/3771, 16/2779, 16/2821: *Followed* 16/2813
General All Purpose Plastics Ltd v Young [2017] SAC (Civ) 30; 2017 G.W.D. 33-518, SAC
George (Matthew Strannigan Smith) v HM Advocate [2011] HCJAC 88; 2012 S.C.L. 54; 2011 S.C.C.R. 568; 2011 G.W.D. 29-645, HCJ .... *Digested,* 12/**4260**: *Considered* 17/2797
George Leslie Ltd v Halcrow Group Ltd [2017] CSOH 106; 2017 G.W.D. 24-410, OH
Georgieva v Nursing and Midwifery Council 2017 G.W.D. 11-156, Sh Ct (Lothian) (Edinburgh)
GG v WG 2017 G.W.D. 19-294, Sh Ct (Grampian) (Aberdeen)
Gibson (David Alexander) v HM Advocate see Gemmell (James Kelly) v HM Advocate
Gilchrist v McPherson [2016] SAC (Crim) 28; 2016 S.C.L. 1022; 2016 G.W.D. 33-606, SAC .... *Digested,* 17/**2814**
Gillan (Shaun Christopher) v HM Advocate 2002 S.L.T. 551; 2002 S.C.C.R. 502; 2002 G.W.D. 10-305, HCJ Appeal .... *Digested,* 02/**5440**: *Applied* 17/2490
Gilmour (John) v HM Advocate [2014] HCJAC 2; 2014 S.C.L. 162; 2014 G.W.D. 3-61, HCJ .... *Digested,* 14/**3379**: *Distinguished* 17/2477
GL v JL [2017] CSOH 60; 2017 Fam. L.R. 54; 2017 G.W.D. 14-219, OH .... *Digested,* 17/**2619**
Glasgow City Council v M (Transfer of Parental Rights: Jurisdiction) 2001 S.C. 415; 2001 S.L.T. 396; 2001 G.W.D. 3-107, IH (Ex Div) .... *Digested,* 01/**6511**: *Applied* 17/2601
Glasgow City Council v Unison Claimants [2017] CSIH 34; 2017 S.C. 611; 2017 S.L.T. 729; [2017] I.R.L.R. 739; 2017 G.W.D. 19-300, IH (2 Div) .... *Digested,* 17/**2585**
Glenmorie Wind Farm Ltd v Scottish Ministers [2016] CSOH 34; 2016 S.C.L.R. 619; 2016 G.W.D. 8-161, OH .... *Digested,* 17/**2765**
Gordon v National Grid Gas Plc [2017] R.V.R. 138; 2016 G.W.D. 30-535, Lands Tr (Scot) .... *Digested,* 17/**2644**
Gordon v Scottish Criminal Cases Review Commission see G v Scottish Criminal Cases Review Commission
Gough v McFadyen see Robertson (Stewart) v HM Advocate
Gough (Stephen Peter) v HM Advocate see Robertson (Stewart) v HM Advocate
Graham v Mackenzie (1871) 9 M. 798, IH (2 Div) *Applied* 17/2677
Graham (Charles) v HM Advocate [2017] HCJAC 71; 2017 S.C.L. 963; 2017 S.C.C.R. 497; 2017 G.W.D. 30-479, HCJ .... *Digested,* 17/**2546**
Grahame v Secretary of State for Scotland 1951 S.C. 368; 1951 S.L.T. 312; 1951 S.L.C.R. 35, IH (1 Div) .... *Digested,* 51/**4362**: *Applied* 00/5938: *Considered* 17/2412
Grange Trust's Trustees v City of Edinburgh Council [2017] CSOH 102; 2017 G.W.D. 23-387, OH
Gray v Advocate General for Scotland [2016] CSOH 166; 2016 S.L.T. 1287; 2017 Rep. L.R. 14; 2016 G.W.D. 39-688, OH .... *Digested,* 17/**2443**
Gray v Braid Group (Holdings) Ltd; *sub nom* Gray, Petitioners [2016] CSIH 68; 2017 S.C. 409; 2016 S.L.T. 1003; 2017 S.C.L.R. 599; 2016 G.W.D. 29-517, IH (Ex Div) .... *Digested,* 16/**2481**
Gray v Braid Logistics (UK) Ltd [2017] CSOH 44; 2017 G.W.D. 11-146, OH
Gray v MacNeil's Executor 2016 S.L.T. (Sh Ct) 250; 2016 G.W.D. 5-119, Sh Ct (Grampian) (Lochmaddy) .... *Digested,* 16/**2487**: *Reversed* 17/2470
Gray v MacNeil's Executor [2017] SAC (Civ) 9; 2017 S.L.T. (Sh Ct) 83; 2017 S.C.L.R. 666; 2017 Hous. L.R. 47; 2017 G.W.D. 11-149, SAC .... *Digested,* 17/**2470**
Gray (James) v HM Advocate 1999 S.L.T. 528; 1999 S.C.C.R. 24; 1999 G.W.D. 1-17, HCJ Appeal .... *Digested,* 99/**5915**: *Considered* 17/2505: *Overruled* 17/2559
Gray Aitken Partnership Ltd v Link Housing Association Ltd see Link Housing Association Ltd v PBL Construction Ltd
Gray's Executors v Manson's Executor [2017] CSOH 25; 2017 G.W.D. 6-91, OH
Gray, Petitioners see Gray v Braid Group (Holdings) Ltd

Green v Chalmers [2017] SAC (Civ) 8; 2017 S.L.T. (Sh Ct) 69; 2017 G.W.D. 7-94, SAC .... *Digested,* 17/**2432**
Green v Chalmers 2016 S.C.L.R. 413; 2016 G.W.D. 32-565, Sh Ct (Tayside) (Perth) *Reversed in part* 17/2432
Green v Rangers International Football Club Plc [2017] CSIH 37; 2017 S.C. 399; 2017 G.W.D. 21-337, IH (Ex Div)
Green v Rangers International Football Club Plc [2017] CSOH 90; 2017 G.W.D. 21-336, OH
Green (Steven) v HM Advocate [2017] HCJAC 51; 2017 S.C.L. 771; 2017 G.W.D. 21-338, HCJ Appeal .... *Digested,* 17/**2544**
Grubb v Finlay [2017] CSOH 81; 2017 G.W.D. 19-299, OH
Gruszka v Poland; *sub nom* Gruszka v Regional Court in Opole, Poland [2015] EWHC 2564 (Admin), QBD (Admin) *Considered* 17/2597
Gruszka v Regional Court in Opole, Poland see Gruszka v Poland
Gryc (Lech) v Lord Advocate [2017] HCJAC 1; 2017 S.C.L. 260; 2017 G.W.D. 2-18, HCJ .... *Digested,* 17/**2598**
Gubinas (Justinas) v HM Advocate; *joined case* Radavicius (Nerijus) v HM Advocate [2017] HCJAC 59; 2018 J.C. 45; 2017 S.L.T. 1017; 2017 S.C.L. 828; 2017 S.C.C.R. 463; 2017 G.W.D. 26-431, HCJ .... *Digested,* 17/**2559**: *Applied* 17/2560
Gubinas (Justinas) v HM Advocate; *joined case* Radadvicius (Nerijus) v HM Advocate [2017] HCJAC 25; 2017 S.L.T. 663; 2017 S.C.L. 556; 2017 G.W.D. 16-257, HCJ .... *Digested,* 17/**2505**
Gyle Shopping Centre General Partners Ltd v Marks & Spencer Plc [2016] CSIH 19; 2017 S.C.L.R. 221; 2016 G.W.D. 10-205, IH (2 Div)

H v H; *sub nom* AH v CH [2016] CSOH 152; 2016 Fam. L.R. 186; 2016 G.W.D. 34-616, OH .... *Digested,* 17/**2614**
H & H Properties UK Ltd v Douris 2017 G.W.D. 12-188, Sh Ct (Tayside) (Dundee)
HA (Afghanistan) v Secretary of State for the Home Department; *joined case* TD (Nigeria) v Secretary of State for the Home Department [2010] CSIH 28; 2010 S.C. 457; [2010] Imm. A.R. 599; 2010 G.W.D. 14-267, IH (Ex Div) .... *Digested,* 10/**4333**: *Considered* 17/2768
HAA (Iraq) v Secretary of State for the Home Department [2017] CSOH 11; 2017 G.W.D. 4-51, OH
Haggerty v Scottish Ministers [2017] CSOH 61; 2017 G.W.D. 12-165, OH
Haggerty (Barry) v HM Advocate [2009] HCJAC 31; 2009 S.C.L. 810; 2009 G.W.D. 12-187, HCJ .... *Digested,* 10/**4101**: *Considered* 17/2556
Haider (Rehman) v Procurator Fiscal, Glasgow [2017] SAC (Crim) 9; 2017 S.L.T. (Sh Ct) 137; 2017 S.C.L. 822; 2017 G.W.D. 21-354, SAC .... *Digested,* 17/**2816**
Haigh v Charles W Ireland Ltd [1974] 1 W.L.R. 43; [1973] 3 All E.R. 1137; 1974 S.C. (H.L.) 1; 1974 S.L.T. 34; (1973) 15 K.I.R. 283; Times, November 23, 1973; (1973) 117 S.J. 939, HL .... *Digested,* 74/**2612**: *Considered* 17/2679
Hamilton v Scottish Ministers [2017] CSOH 121; 2017 G.W.D. 31-503, OH
Handy (William Thomas) v HM Advocate [2017] HCJAC 20; 2017 S.C.L. 521; 2017 G.W.D. 12-177, HCJ .... *Digested,* 17/**2500**
Harazin (Grzegorz) v Lord Advocate [2010] HCJAC 65; [2011] Eu. L.R. 88; 2010 G.W.D. 26-496, HCJ .... *Digested,* 11/**4262**: *Applied* 17/2597
Harper v Letley [2016] CSOH 39; 2017 S.C.L.R. 1; 2016 Fam. L.R. 50; 2016 G.W.D. 9-165, OH .... *Digested,* 17/**2421**
Harrison v Compass Group, UK and Ireland Ltd 2017 Rep. L.R. 141; 2017 G.W.D. 24-407, SPIC
Hart v Brown see Gemmell (James Kelly) v HM Advocate
Harvie v Robertson (1903) 5 F. 338; (1903) 10 S.L.T. 581, IH (1 Div) *Considered* 17/2740
Hay v Richardson see Hay (Ian Morris) v HM Advocate
Hay (Ian Morris) v HM Advocate; *joined case* Hay v Richardson [2012] HCJAC 28; 2014 J.C. 19; 2012 S.L.T. 569; 2012 S.C.L. 492; 2012 S.C.C.R. 281; 2012 G.W.D. 8-142, HCJ .... *Digested,* 12/**4271**: *Applied* 15/3243, 16/2782, 17/2798
Hayes v Willoughby [2013] UKSC 17; [2013] 1 W.L.R. 935; [2013] 2 All E.R. 405; [2013] 2 Cr. App. R. 11; [2013] E.M.L.R. 19; Times, May 28, 2013; (2013) 163(7554) N.L.J. 25, SC .... *Digested,* 13/**642**: *Considered* 17/2515

HBJ Claimants v Glasgow City Council; *sub nom* Armstrong v Glasgow City Council; McDonald v Glasgow City Council; *joined case* Unison Claimants v Glasgow City Council [2017] CSIH 56; 2017 S.L.T. 1135; [2017] I.R.L.R. 993; 2017 G.W.D. 27-439, IH (2 Div) .... *Digested,* 17/**2584**
Healy & Young's Trustee v Mair's Trustees see Craig v Mair's Trustees
Heather Capital Ltd (in Liquidation) v Burness Paull & Williamsons LLP [2015] CSOH 150; 2015 G.W.D. 38-599, OH
Reversed 17/2449
Heather Capital Ltd (In Liquidation) v Burness Paull LLP see Heather Capital Ltd (In Liquidation) v Levy & McRae
Heather Capital Ltd (In Liquidation) v Levy & McRae; *joined case* Heather Capital Ltd (In Liquidation) v Burness Paull LLP [2017] CSIH 19; 2017 S.L.T. 376; 2017 G.W.D. 9-127, IH (Ex Div) .... *Digested,* 17/**2449**: *Considered* 17/2697
Heather Capital Ltd (In Liquidation) v Levy & McRae [2016] CSOH 107; 2017 S.C.L.R. 317; 2016 G.W.D. 25-457, OH
Reversed 17/2449
Henderson v Foxworth Investments Ltd; *sub nom* Liquidator of Letham Grange Development Co Ltd v Foxworth Investments Ltd [2014] UKSC 41; [2014] 1 W.L.R. 2600; 2014 S.C. (U.K.S.C.) 203; 2014 S.L.T. 775; 2014 S.C.L.R. 692; (2014) 158(27) S.J.L.B. 37; 2014 G.W.D. 23-437, SC .... *Digested,* 14/**1579**: *Applied* 15/2910, 15/3076, 17/2440, 17/2616: *Considered* 15/3133
Henderson (Colin) v HM Advocate [2017] HCJAC 43; 2017 S.C.L. 703; 2017 G.W.D. 20-319, HCJ Appeal .... *Digested,* 17/**2504**
Higham v Stena Sealink Ltd [1996] 1 W.L.R. 1107; [1996] 3 All E.R. 660; [1996] 2 Lloyd's Rep. 26; [1996] C.L.C. 1193; [1996] P.I.Q.R. P351; Times, February 26, 1996, CA (Civ Div) .... *Digested,* 96/**825**: *Considered* 16/2454, 17/2436
Higherdelta Ltd v Covea Insurance Plc [2017] CSOH 84; [2017] Lloyd's Rep. I.R. 650; 2017 G.W.D. 21-349, OH
Hill v Stewart Milne Group Ltd [2016] CSIH 65; 2016 S.C. 892; 2016 G.W.D. 24-444, IH (Ex Div) .... *Digested,* 17/**2426**
Hill v Stewart Milne Group Ltd [2016] CSIH 35; 2017 S.C.L.R. 92; 2016 G.W.D. 16-297, IH (Ex Div) .... *Digested,* 17/**2463**
HM Advocate v Al-Megrahi (Abdelbaset Ali) (No.4); *sub nom* HM Advocate v Megrahi (Abdelbaset Ali) (No.4); Megrahi (Abdelbaset Ali) v HM Advocate (No.4) 2002 J.C. 99; 2002 S.L.T. 1433; 2002 S.C.C.R. 509; 2002 G.W.D. 11-335, HCJ Appeal .... *Digested,* 03/**5384**: *Applied* 08/4627, 08/4632, 09/4732, 09/4740, 09/4768, 14/3389, 17/2473: *Considered* 06/5236
HM Advocate v Alongi (Margo Robertson); *sub nom* HM Advocate v Alongi (Margot Robertson) [2017] HCJAC 18; 2017 S.C.L. 455; 2017 S.C.C.R. 287; 2017 G.W.D. 12-176, HCJ .... *Digested,* 17/**2474**
HM Advocate v Alongi (Margot Robertson) see HM Advocate v Alongi (Margo Robertson)
HM Advocate v Anderson (Neil) see HM Advocate v Clarke (Graham)
HM Advocate v Andrews (Francis) see HM Advocate v Clarke (Graham)
HM Advocate v Ball (Ginette) [2016] HCJAC 109; 2017 S.L.T. 520; 2017 S.C.L. 4; 2017 S.C.C.R. 23; 2016 G.W.D. 40-706, HCJ .... *Digested,* 17/**2540**
HM Advocate v Bell (James Cunningham) 1995 S.L.T. 350; 1995 S.C.C.R. 244, HCJ Appeal .... *Digested,* 95/**5797**: *Applied* 96/6833, 96/6849, 11/4569, 17/2802: *Considered* 96/6862, 08/5054: *Followed* 10/4531
HM Advocate v Chung (Mark) [2017] HCJAC 48; 2017 S.C.L. 758, HCJ .... *Digested,* 17/**2490**
HM Advocate v Clarke (Graham); *joined cases* HM Advocate v Clarke (Lindsay); HM Advocate v Anderson (Neil); HM Advocate v Nixon (Marilyn); HM Advocate v Nixon (Keith); HM Advocate v Davidson (Yvonne); HM Advocate v Andrews (Francis) [2016] HCJAC 2; 2017 S.C.L. 583; 2017 S.C.C.R. 301; 2017 G.W.D. 17-271, HCJ
HM Advocate v Clarke (Lindsay) see HM Advocate v Clarke (Graham)
HM Advocate v Collins (Gordon); *sub nom* Collins (Gordon) v HM Advocate [2016] HCJAC 102; 2017 J.C. 99; 2017 S.L.T. 23; 2017 S.C.L. 202; 2017 S.C.C.R. 31; 2016 G.W.D. 38-685, HCJ .... *Digested,* 17/**2797**
HM Advocate v Cordiner (Jennifer) [2017] HCJAC 53; 2017 S.C.L. 748; 2017 G.W.D. 23-390, HCJ Appeal .... *Digested,* 17/**2528**
HM Advocate v Coulter (Andrew Alexander Marshall) see HM Advocate v Coulter (Ronnie)

HM Advocate v Coulter (Ronnie); *joined cases* HM Advocate v Coulter (Andrew Alexander Marshall); HM Advocate v Montgomery (David Shields) [2016] HCJAC 96; 2017 J.C. 115; 2016 S.L.T. 1276; 2017 S.C.L. 14; 2016 S.C.C.R. 464; 2016 G.W.D. 34-614, HCJ .... *Digested,* 17/**2523**
HM Advocate v Davidson (Yvonne) see HM Advocate v Clarke (Graham)
HM Advocate v Donaldson (Francis Jude) [2017] HCJAC 29; 2017 S.C.L. 672; 2017 G.W.D. 17-272, HCJ Appeal .... *Digested,* 17/**2563**
HM Advocate v ER see HM Advocate v R
HM Advocate v F [2016] HCJAC 106; 2017 S.C.L. 131; 2016 G.W.D. 37-657, HCJ
HM Advocate v Graham (David William) [2010] HCJAC 50; 2011 J.C. 1; 2010 S.L.T. 715; 2010 S.C.L. 789; 2010 S.C.C.R. 641; 2010 G.W.D. 19-384, HCJ .... *Digested,* 10/**4523**: *Applied* 17/2805: *Considered* 16/2587: *Followed* 14/3772
HM Advocate v Grier (David Henry) see HM Advocate v Withey (Gary Martin)
HM Advocate v Hawkins (Jake) [2017] HCJ 79; 2017 S.L.T. 1328; 2018 S.C.C.R. 1; 2017 G.W.D. 39-597, HCJ
HM Advocate v IP see HM Advocate v P
HM Advocate v JM see HM Advocate v V
HM Advocate v KS see HM Advocate v V
HM Advocate v Lisek (Miroslaw Aleksander) [2017] HCJAC 15; 2017 J.C. 223; 2017 S.L.T. 613; 2017 S.C.L. 469; 2017 S.C.C.R. 185; 2017 G.W.D. 11-155, HCJ .... *Digested,* 17/**2597**
HM Advocate v M (C) [2016] HCJAC 79; 2017 S.L.T. 795; 2017 S.C.L. 595; 2017 G.W.D. 18-283, HCJ .... *Digested,* 17/**2481**
HM Advocate v M see HM Advocate v V
HM Advocate v Mac Mowat; *sub nom* HM Advocate v MacMowat 2001 S.L.T. 738; 2001 S.C.C.R. 242; 2001 G.W.D. 12-408, HCJ .... *Digested,* 01/**6302**: *Applied* 17/2476
HM Advocate v MacMowat see HM Advocate v Mac Mowat
HM Advocate v McDonald (Allan McConnell) [2016] HCJAC 121; 2017 S.L.T. 267; 2017 S.C.L. 120; 2016 G.W.D. 39-693, HCJ
HM Advocate v McGuigan (John) 1936 J.C. 16; 1936 S.L.T. 161, HCJ *Cited* 17/2478: *Followed* 17/2472
HM Advocate v Megrahi (Abdelbaset Ali) (No.4) see HM Advocate v Al-Megrahi (Abdelbaset Ali) (No.4)
HM Advocate v Millar (Charles) [2016] HCJAC 104; 2017 J.C. 1; 2016 S.L.T. 1318; 2017 S.C.L. 124; 2017 S.C.C.R. 1; 2016 G.W.D. 37-656, HCJ
HM Advocate v Montgomery (David Shields) see HM Advocate v Coulter (Ronnie)
HM Advocate v Nixon (Keith) see HM Advocate v Clarke (Graham)
HM Advocate v Nixon (Marilyn) see HM Advocate v Clarke (Graham)
HM Advocate v O see HM Advocate v V
HM Advocate v P; *sub nom* HM Advocate v IP [2017] HCJAC 56; 2017 S.C.L. 877; 2017 S.C.C.R. 447; 2017 G.W.D. 23-391, HCJ .... *Digested,* 17/**2534**
HM Advocate v PO see HM Advocate v V
HM Advocate v R; *sub nom* HM Advocate v ER [2016] HCJ 98; 2016 S.L.T. 1267; 2017 S.C.L. 46; 2016 S.C.C.R. 490; 2016 G.W.D. 34-612, HCJ .... *Digested,* 17/**2493**
HM Advocate v RV see HM Advocate v V
HM Advocate v S see HM Advocate v V
HM Advocate v Steven (Andrew) [2017] HCJAC 7; 2017 S.C.L. 395; 2017 G.W.D. 4-59, HCJ Appeal .... *Digested,* 17/**2802**
HM Advocate v Swift (James Aloysius) 1984 J.C. 83; 1985 S.L.T. 26; 1984 S.C.C.R. 216, HCJ .... *Digested,* 84/**3906**: *Applied* 88/3921, 97/5801, 98/5594, 09/4798, 10/4078, 13/3622, 14/3415, 14/3416, 14/3420, 15/2969, 15/2971, 17/2519: *Considered* 97/5861, 97/5862, 06/5205, 07/5068, 08/4646, 13/3621, 14/3417, 17/2522, 17/2564: *Followed* 97/5803, 01/6344, 03/5378: *Referred to* 92/5423, 93/4935
HM Advocate v V; *sub nom* HM Advocate v RV; HM Advocate v PO; HM Advocate v JM; HM Advocate v KS; *joined cases* HM Advocate v O; HM Advocate v M; HM Advocate v S [2016] HCJAC 103; 2017 S.C.L. 29; 2017 S.C.C.R. 7; 2016 G.W.D. 37-663, HCJ .... *Digested,* 17/**2568**
HM Advocate v W [2016] HCJAC 111; 2017 S.C.L. 145; 2016 G.W.D. 38-670, HCJ .... *Digested,* 17/**2480**
HM Advocate v Withey (Gary Martin); *joined case* HM Advocate v Grier (David Henry) [2017] HCJAC 47; 2017 J.C. 249; 2017 S.C.L. 657; 2017 S.C.C.R. 325; 2017 G.W.D. 21-340, HCJ .... *Digested,* 17/**2527**
HM Inspector of Health & Safety v Chevron North Sea Ltd; *sub nom* Conner (HM Inspector of Health and Safety) v Chevron North Sea Ltd [2016] CSIH 29; 2016 S.C. 709; 2016 S.L.T. 561; 2017 S.C.L.R. 247; 2016 G.W.D. 14-273, IH (1 Div) *Digested,* 16/**2671**
HMA v Secretary of State for the Home Department; *sub nom* A v Secretary of State for the Home Department [2016] CSIH 85; 2017 S.C. 186; 2017 S.L.T. 8; 2016 G.W.D. 37-667, IH (Ex Div) .... *Digested,* 17/**2674**

Hoe International Ltd v Andersen [2016] CSOH 33; 2016 G.W.D. 7-142, OH
Reversed 17/2471
Hoe International Ltd v Andersen [2017] CSIH 9; 2017 S.C. 313; 2017 G.W.D. 6-83, IH (2 Div) .... *Digested,* 17/**2471**
Holland (Aaron) v HM Advocate [2016] HCJAC 108; 2017 S.C.L. 35; 2016 G.W.D. 37-661, HCJ
Hollister v MacInnes 2017 G.W.D. 20-315, Land Ct
Holman Fenwick Willan LLP v Orr see Holman Fenwick Willan LLP v Procurator Fiscal, Glasgow
Holman Fenwick Willan LLP v Procurator Fiscal, Glasgow; *sub nom* Holman Fenwick Willan LLP v Orr [2017] HCJAC 38; 2017 J.C. 239; 2017 S.L.T. 899; 2017 S.C.L. 676; 2017 S.C.C.R. 309; 2017 G.W.D. 19-298, HCJ .... *Digested,* 17/**2566**
Holman Fenwick Willan LLP v Procurator Fiscal, Glasgow [2017] HCJAC 39; 2017 S.C.L. 687; 2017 G.W.D. 19-297, HCJ Appeal .... *Digested,* 17/**2535**
Honeyman v Babcock Design and Technology Ltd 2017 G.W.D. 5-76, SPIC
Hood v Council of the Law Society of Scotland [2017] CSIH 21; 2017 S.C. 386; 2017 S.C.L.R. 799; 2017 G.W.D. 9-132, IH (2 Div) .... *Digested,* 17/**2714**
Hooley Ltd v Ganges Jute Private Ltd; *sub nom* Hooley Ltd, Petitioner; Hooley Ltd v Titaghur Plc; Hooley Ltd v Samnuggur Jute Factory Ltd; Hooley Ltd v Victoria Jute Co Ltd [2016] CSOH 141; 2017 S.L.T. 58; [2016] B.C.C. 826; 2016 G.W.D. 33-584, OH .... *Digested,* 17/**2447**
Hooley Ltd v Samnuggur Jute Factory Ltd see Hooley Ltd v Ganges Jute Private Ltd
Hooley Ltd v Titaghur Plc see Hooley Ltd v Ganges Jute Private Ltd
Hooley Ltd v Victoria Jute Co Ltd see Hooley Ltd v Ganges Jute Private Ltd
Hooley Ltd, Petitioner see Hooley Ltd v Ganges Jute Private Ltd
Hopwood v West Lothian Council 2017 G.W.D. 22-380, Lands Tr (Scot)
Horada v Secretary of State for Communities and Local Government [2016] EWCA Civ 169; [2017] 2 All E.R. 86; [2016] P.T.S.R. 1271; Times, May 12, 2016, CA (Civ Div) .... *Digested,* 16/**1678**:
Considered 17/2763
Hosie v West Dunbartonshire Council 2017 G.W.D. 23-399, Lands Tr (Scot)
Howden (John) v HM Advocate 1994 S.C.C.R. 19, HCJ Appeal .... *Digested,* 94/**5531**:
Applied 17/2490: *Cited* 16/2514: *Considered* 96/6722, 02/5440, 10/4103, 15/2993, 16/2518: *Distinguished* 14/3371
Howgate Shopping Centre Ltd v Catercraft Services Ltd 2004 S.L.T. 231; 2004 S.C.L.R. 739; 2004 G.W.D. 4-76, OH .... *Digested,* 04/**4990**:
Applied 17/2704
HRH Prince Jefri Bolkiah v KPMG see Bolkiah v KPMG
Huggins v Trinidad and Tobago; *joined case* Phillip v Trinidad and Tobago [2008] UKPC 32, PC (Trin)
Applied 17/2529
Humphreys v Crabbe [2016] CSIH 82; 2017 S.C.L.R. 699; 2016 G.W.D. 35-634, IH (Ex Div)
Huntaven Properties Ltd v Hunter Construction (Aberdeen) Ltd [2017] CSOH 57; 2017 G.W.D. 14-229, OH
Hunter v Hanley 1955 S.C. 200; 1955 S.L.T. 213; [1955-95] P.N.L.R. 1, IH (1 Div) ...... *Digested,* 55/**3451**:
Applied 83/2548, 83/3962, 84/2322, 90/3264, 97/6302, 00/6588, 03/5826, 04/5055, 13/3857, 14/3688, 15/3230: *Considered* 86/3608, 89/2558, 03/5825, 17/1561: *Distinguished* 00/6585, 17/2389: *Followed* 90/5498: *Not applied* 88/4930, 89/4195: *Referred to* 00/6603
Hussain v Glasgow City Council [2017] CSOH 1; 2017 S.L.T. 231; 2017 Hous. L.R. 8; 2017 G.W.D. 2-19, OH .... *Digested,* 17/**2660**
Hussain (Muzaffar) v Procurator Fiscal, Glasgow [2017] SAC (Crim) 1; 2017 S.C.L. 421; 2017 G.W.D. 1-5, SAC .... *Digested,* 17/**2502**
Hutchison (Alexander Wilson) v HM Advocate 1984 S.L.T. 233; 1983 S.C.C.R. 504, HCJ Appeal .... *Digested,* 84/**3943**:
Considered 17/2571

ICU (Europe) Ltd v Ibrahim [2016] CSIH 62; 2016 S.L.T. 1182; 2016 G.W.D. 23-422, IH (2 Div) .... *Digested,* 17/**2423**
Igoe v Campbell see Courtney's Executors v Campbell
IHA (Somalia) v Secretary of State for the Home Department [2017] CSIH 25; 2017 G.W.D. 11-159, IH (Ex Div)
Inland Revenue Commissioners v Royal Bank of Scotland Ltd see Lord Advocate v Royal Bank of Scotland Ltd
Invest 360 Ltd v Park 2017 G.W.D. 20-316, Sh Ct (Grampian) (Aberdeen)
Iona Hotels Ltd v Craig see Iona Hotels Ltd (In Receivership), Petitioners

Iona Hotels Ltd (In Receivership), Petitioners; *sub nom* Iona Hotels Ltd v Craig 1990 S.C. 330; 1991 S.L.T. 11; 1990 S.C.L.R. 614, IH (1 Div) .... *Digested,* 90/**4772**: *Considered* 16/2697, 17/2679
Iqbal v Parnez [2017] SAC (Civ) 7; 2017 G.W.D. 6-81, SAC
Ironside (Joanne Mary) v HM Advocate see Copolo (John Murray) v HM Advocate
Ironside (Joanne Mary) (also known as Mitchell) v HM Advocate see Copolo (John Murray) v HM Advocate

J v C [2017] CSIH 8; 2017 G.W.D. 5-63, IH (1 Div)
J & S Wight Ltd v McGowan 2017 G.W.D. 17-278, Land Ct
J H & W Lamont of Heathfield Farm v Chattisham Ltd [2017] CSOH 119; 2017 G.W.D. 30-470, OH
J. & P. Coats, Ltd. v Brown. (1909) 6 Adam 19, HCJ
Distinguished 17/2530
JA v WA [2017] CSOH 93; 2017 Fam. L.R. 94; 2017 G.W.D. 22-370, OH .... *Digested,* 17/**2609**
JA (Iran) v Secretary of State for the Home Department [2017] CSOH 39; 2017 G.W.D. 10-138, OH
Jack v Jack [2015] CSOH 91; 2015 Fam. L.R. 95; 2015 G.W.D. 24-425, OH .... *Digested,* 15/**3079**: *Affirmed* 17/2610
Jack v Jack [2016] CSIH 75; 2016 Fam. L.R. 177; 2016 G.W.D. 33-595, IH (Ex Div) ... *Digested,* 17/**2610**
Jackson (Steven) v HM Advocate [2017] HCJAC 72; 2018 J.C. 86; 2017 S.C.L. 1014; 2017 S.C.C.R. 517; 2017 G.W.D. 31-497, HCJ
JAL Fish Ltd Small Self-Administered Pension Scheme Trustees v Robertson Construction Eastern Ltd [2017] CSOH 70; 2017 S.L.T. 577; 2017 G.W.D. 15-251, OH .... *Digested,* 17/**2771**
James v United Kingdom (25119/09); *joined cases* Lee v United Kingdom (57877/09); Wells v United Kingdom (57715/09) (2013) 56 E.H.R.R. 12; 33 B.H.R.C. 617; (2012) 109(37) L.S.G. 20, ECHR .... *Digested,* 13/**1558**: *Approved* 17/1594: *Considered* 13/2112, 13/2113, 13/3878, 14/2234, 15/1813, 15/3242, 17/2745, 17/2746: *Followed* 14/3702: *Not applied* 15/1811
James Richardson & Sons v The Kipp 2017 G.W.D. 20-326, Land Ct
Jamieson (Brian) v HM Advocate (No.2) 1994 J.C. 251; 1995 S.L.T. 666; 1994 S.C.C.R. 610, HCJ .... *Digested,* 94/**5513**: *Considered* 09/4836, 12/3939, 14/3400: *Distinguished* 17/2492
Jarvie v Greater Glasgow Primary Care NHS Trust 2006 G.W.D. 17-347, OH
Considered 17/2428
JD v Lothian Health Board see D v Lothian Health Board
Jeunesse v Netherlands (12738/10) (2015) 60 E.H.R.R. 17, ECHR
Applied 16/1079, 16/1125, 17/1200, 17/1207, 17/1239: *Considered* 17/2670: *Distinguished* 16/1118
JL v HM Advocate see L v HM Advocate
JM v JW see M v W
JMG (Gambia) v Secretary of State for the Home Department [2017] CSOH 128; 2017 G.W.D. 32-515, OH
JO (Nigeria) v Secretary of State for the Home Department [2016] CSOH 179; 2017 G.W.D. 2-20, OH
Jobcenter Berlin Neukolln v Alimanovic (C-67/14) EU:C:2015:597; [2016] Q.B. 308; [2016] 2 W.L.R. 208; [2016] 1 C.M.L.R. 29; [2016] C.E.C. 805, ECJ (Grand Chamber)
Applied 16/1983: *Considered* 17/2658: *Followed* 16/1980
John Douglas v Alexander M'Cutcheon (Carson's Trustee) (1876) 3 R. 565, IH (2 Div)
Considered 17/2781
John Hudson & Co Ltd v Kirkness (Inspector of Taxes) see Kirkness (Inspector of Taxes) v John Hudson & Co Ltd
John Muir Trust v Scottish Ministers [2016] CSIH 33; 2016 S.C. 741; 2017 S.C.L.R. 261; 2016 G.W.D. 16-295, IH (Ex Div) .... *Digested,* 17/**2430**
John Muir Trust v Scottish Ministers [2015] CSOH 163; 2016 G.W.D. 7-148, OH
Reversed 17/2764
John Muir Trust v Scottish Ministers [2016] CSIH 61; 2017 S.C. 207; 2016 G.W.D. 24-453, IH (1 Div) .... *Digested,* 17/**2764**
John Thomas Witherington. (1881) 4 Coup. 475, HCJ
Considered 17/2512
Johnston Press Pension Plan Trustees v Sedgwick Noble Lowndes Ltd [2017] CSOH 21; 2017 G.W.D. 6-88, OH
Johnston's Trustee v Baird [2012] CSOH 117; 2012 G.W.D. 25-514, OH
Applied 17/2684
Joint Administrators of Castlebridge Plant Ltd, Noters; *sub nom* Nimmo & Friar, Noters [2015] CSOH 165; [2017] B.C.C. 87; 2016 G.W.D. 1-17, OH

Jolly (Andrew) v HM Advocate [2013] HCJAC 96; 2014 J.C. 171; 2013 S.L.T. 1100; 2013 S.C.L. 832; 2013 S.C.C.R. 511; 2013 G.W.D. 29-576, HCJ .... *Digested,* 13/**3564**: *Applied* 17/2477: *Considered* 15/2966: *Distinguished* 17/2481: *Overruled* 14/3410
JQ v Mundell see Q (J) v Procurator Fiscal, Paisley
JR v HM Advocate see R (J) v HM Advocate
JS v Children's Reporter see S v Children's Reporter
Julius Samann Ltd v Tetrosyl Ltd [2006] EWHC 529 (Ch); [2006] E.T.M.R. 75; [2006] F.S.R. 42; (2006) 29(6) I.P.D. 29046, Ch D .... *Digested,* 06/**2598**: *Applied* 08/2387, 10/2004: *Considered* 12/1972, 16/1289, 17/2690

K v Marist Bros [2016] CSOH 54; 2016 G.W.D. 13-261, OH *Affirmed* 17/2770
K v Marist Bros [2017] CSIH 2; 2017 S.C. 258; 2017 G.W.D. 2-24, IH (2 Div) .... *Digested,* 17/**2770**
K v Secretary of State for Work and Pensions; *sub nom* DK v Secretary of State for Work and Pensions [2016] CSIH 84; 2017 S.C. 176; 2016 G.W.D. 36-650, IH (Ex Div) .... *Digested,* 17/**2825**
K (B) v HM Advocate [2017] HCJAC 68; 2017 S.C.L. 990; 2017 G.W.D. 30-477, HCJ . *Digested,* 17/**2532**
K (Pakistan) v Secretary of State for the Home Department see MAK (Pakistan) v Secretary of State for the Home Department
Kaizer v Scottish Ministers [2017] CSOH 110; 2017 Rep. L.R. 124; 2017 G.W.D. 27-443, OH
Kapri (Fatjon) v Lord Advocate [2014] HCJAC 63; 2014 G.W.D. 21-395, HCJ *Applied* 17/2440
Karanakaran v Secretary of State for the Home Department [2000] 3 All E.R. 449; [2000] Imm. A.R. 271; [2000] I.N.L.R. 122; Times, February 16, 2000; Independent, February 4, 2000; (2000) 97(5) L.S.G. 34; (2000) 97(10) L.S.G. 36; (2000) 144 S.J.L.B. 81, CA (Civ Div) .... *Digested,* 00/**3307**: *Applied* 03/2218, 03/2275, 03/5733: *Considered* 04/2043, 11/1714, 17/2825: *Followed* 02/5874, 02/5877, 05/2182
KB v MS 2017 S.L.T. (Sh Ct) 160; 2017 Fam. L.R. 66; 2017 G.W.D. 13-204, Sh Ct (Tayside) (Dundee) .... *Digested,* 17/**2612**
Kell (Scotland) Ltd v City of Glasgow Licensing Board 2010 S.L.T. (Sh Ct) 197; [2011] L.L.R. 59; 2010 G.W.D. 23-444, Sh Ct (Glasgow) .... *Digested,* 11/**4445**: *Applied* 17/2719
Kenman Holdings Ltd v Comhairle Nan Eilean Siar [2015] CSOH 170; 2016 G.W.D. 1-28, OH *Reversed in part* 17/2773
Kenman Holdings Ltd v Comhairle Nan Eilean Siar [2017] CSIH 10; 2017 S.C. 339; 2017 S.L.T. 341; 2017 G.W.D. 6-78, IH (Ex Div) .... *Digested,* 17/**2773**
Kennedy v Glenbelle Ltd 1996 S.C. 95; 1996 S.L.T. 1186; 1996 S.C.L.R. 411, IH (1 Div) .... *Digested,* 96/**7230**: *Applied* 13/3870, 17/2740, 17/2741
Kennedy v Mackenzie [2017] CSOH 118; 2017 G.W.D. 30-486, OH
Kennedy v Smith 2017 S.L.T. (Land Ct) 19; 2016 G.W.D. 30-539, Land Ct .... *Digested,* 17/**2402**
Kenyon v Gibson; *sub nom* Kenyon (Ria) v Procurator Fiscal, Hamilton [2016] HCJAC 116; 2017 S.C.L. 162; 2016 G.W.D. 38-673, HCJ .... *Digested,* 17/**2525**
Kenyon (Ria) v Procurator Fiscal, Hamilton see Kenyon v Gibson
Kerseboom (Michel) v HM Advocate [2016] HCJAC 51; 2017 J.C. 47; 2016 S.C.L. 839; 2016 S.C.C.R. 386; 2016 G.W.D. 29-518, HCJ .... *Digested,* 16/**2489**
Kidd v Paull & Williamson LLP [2017] CSOH 124; 2017 G.W.D. 31-499, OH
Kidd v Paull & Williamson LLP [2017] CSOH 16; 2017 G.W.D. 6-80, OH
Kinloch v Coral Racing Ltd [2017] CSOH 43; 2017 S.L.T. 856; [2017] L.L.R. 513; 2017 G.W.D. 10-136, OH .... *Digested,* 17/**2469**
Kirk (Carol) v Procurator Fiscal, Stirling [2017] HCJAC 66; 2017 S.C.L. 982; 2017 G.W.D. 30-475, HCJ .... *Digested,* 17/**2508**
Kirkness (Inspector of Taxes) v John Hudson & Co Ltd; *sub nom* John Hudson & Co Ltd v Kirkness (Inspector of Taxes) [1955] A.C. 696; [1955] 2 W.L.R. 1135; [1955] 2 All E.R. 345; 48 R. & I.T. 352; 36 T.C. 28; (1955) 34 A.T.C. 142; [1955] T.R. 145; (1955) 99 S.J. 368, HL .... *Digested,* 55/**1257**: *Considered* 57/280, 59/1549, 62/2916, 95/525, 99/4669, 15/2482, 17/2673
KL (Algeria) v Secretary of State for the Home Department; *sub nom* L (Algeria) v Secretary of State for the Home Department [2016] CSIH 14; 2016 S.C. 543; 2016 G.W.D. 9-176, IH (1 Div) .... *Digested,* 17/**2669**
Kleinwort Benson Ltd v Glasgow City Council (No.3) 2002 S.L.T. 1190; 2002 S.C.L.R. 714; 2002 G.W.D. 16-544, OH .... *Digested,* 02/**5344**: *Applied* 17/2448
KMI v SMO 2017 Fam. L.R. 73; 2017 G.W.D. 13-196, Sh Ct (South Strathclyde) (Hamilton) .... *Digested,* 17/**2608**

Knight v Chief Constable of the Police Service of Scotland 2017 G.W.D. 28-452, Sh Ct (Lothian) (Edinburgh)
Kookmin Bank v Rainy Sky SA see Rainy Sky SA v Kookmin Bank
KP v HM Advocate see P v HM Advocate
KS v MG [2017] CSOH 26; 2017 G.W.D. 7-102, OH
Kukanauza (Ruslanas) v HM Advocate [2017] HCJAC 26; 2017 S.C.L. 629; 2017 S.C.C.R. 290; 2017 G.W.D. 16-258, HCJ Appeal .... *Digested,* 17/**2558**

L v HM Advocate; *sub nom* JL v HM Advocate [2016] HCJAC 61; 2016 S.C.L. 715; 2016 S.C.C.R. 365; 2016 G.W.D. 22-393, HCJ .... *Digested,* 16/**2498**: *Applied* 17/2552: *Cited* 16/2496
L v HM Advocate [2016] HCJAC 120; 2017 S.C.L. 166; 2016 G.W.D. 38-676, HCJ ...... *Digested,* 17/**2485**
L (Algeria) v Secretary of State for the Home Department see KL (Algeria) v Secretary of State for the Home Department
L, Petitioners (No.3) 1996 S.L.T. 928, IH (1 Div) .... *Digested,* 96/**7129**: *Considered* 02/5935, 17/2426: *Followed* 01/6758
Laidlaw v Richardson see Laidlaw (Robert) v Procurator Fiscal, Livingston
Laidlaw (Robert) v Procurator Fiscal, Livingston; *sub nom* Laidlaw v Richardson [2017] SAC (Crim) 8; 2017 S.C.L. 719; 2017 S.C.C.R. 359; 2017 G.W.D. 21-355, SAC .... *Digested,* 17/**2799**
Lamont v Kennedy 2010 S.L.C.R. 76, Land Ct
Considered 17/2402
Laughlan v Harrower [2016] SAC (Crim) 30; 2017 S.C. (S.A.C.) 17; 2016 S.L.T. (Sh Ct) 427; 2017 S.C.L. 108; 2016 S.C.C.R. 544; 2016 G.W.D. 32-570, SAC .... *Digested,* 17/**2526**
Laverie v Scottish Ministers [2017] CSOH 45; 2017 S.L.T. 640; 2017 G.W.D. 11-145, OH .... *Digested,* 17/**2575**
Lawrence v Coventry (t/a RDC Promotions) see Coventry (t/a RDC Promotions) v Lawrence
Lawrence v Fen Tigers Ltd see Coventry (t/a RDC Promotions) v Lawrence
Lawrie (Jeanie) v Muir 1950 J.C. 19; 1950 S.L.T. 37; 1949 S.L.T. (Notes) 58, HCJ Appeal .... *Digested,* 47-51/**2075**: *Applied* 47-51/2076, 01/6303, 05/5088, 17/2495: *Considered* 94/5508, 15/2952: *Referred to* 01/6385
Lawrie (Joshua) v HM Advocate see McDowall (Luke) v HM Advocate
Leach v Linderman see Leach (Deceased), Re
Leach (Deceased), Re; *sub nom* Leach v Linderman [1986] Ch. 226; [1985] 3 W.L.R. 413; [1985] 2 All E.R. 754; [1985] Fam. Law 319; (1985) 82 L.S.G. 2081; (1985) 135 N.L.J. 392; (1985) 129 S.J. 318, CA (Civ Div) .... *Digested,* 85/**3644**: *Considered* 17/2443
Leathem (John) v HM Advocate [2017] HCJAC 10; 2017 J.C. 214; 2017 S.L.T. 215; 2017 S.C.L. 401; 2017 S.C.C.R. 157; 2017 G.W.D. 6-89, HCJ .... *Digested,* 17/**2807**
Lebara Ltd v Revenue and Customs Commissioners (C-520/10) EU:C:2012:264; [2012] S.T.C. 1536; [2012] B.V.C. 219, ECJ (3rd Chamber)
Applied 16/2208: *Considered* 17/2848: *Followed* 16/2187
Lee v United Kingdom (57877/09) see James v United Kingdom (25119/09)
Lewis v Hunter 2017 G.W.D. 19-308, Land Ct
Lindsays v Campbell [2017] SAC (Civ) 23; 2017 G.W.D. 25-416, SAC
Link Housing Association Ltd v Gray Aitken Partnership Ltd see Link Housing Association Ltd v PBL Construction Ltd
Link Housing Association Ltd v PBL Construction Ltd; *sub nom* Gray Aitken Partnership Ltd v Link Housing Association Ltd; Link Housing Association Ltd v Gray Aitken Partnership Ltd [2007] CSIH 4; 2007 S.C. 294; 2007 S.C.L.R. 343; 2007 G.W.D. 17-305, IH (1 Div) .... *Digested,* 08/**4591**: *Distinguished* 08/4593, 16/2475, 17/2454
Liquidator of Letham Grange Development Co Ltd v Foxworth Investments Ltd see Henderson v Foxworth Investments Ltd
Liquidators of Grampian Maclennan's Distribution Services Ltd v Carnbroe Estates Ltd [2017] CSOH 8; 2017 G.W.D. 3-37, OH
Liu v Anderson's Solicitors LLP [2017] CSIH 45; 2017 G.W.D. 22-358, IH (1 Div)
Lizanec v Procurator Fiscal, Edinburgh see Lizanec v Richardson
Lizanec v Richardson; *sub nom* Lizanec v Procurator Fiscal, Edinburgh [2016] SAC (Crim) 33; 2017 S.C.L. 417; 2016 G.W.D. 37-660, SAC .... *Digested,* 17/**2517**
LM v Criminal Injuries Compensation Authority; *sub nom* M v Criminal Injuries Compensation Authority [2016] CSOH 156; 2017 S.C.L.R. 716; 2016 G.W.D. 35-624, OH
LO v N [2017] CSIH 14; 2017 Fam. L.R. 44; 2017 G.W.D. 7-101, IH (Ex Div) .... *Digested,* 17/**2600**

Loch Hill Windfarm (Scotland) Ltd v Scottish Ministers [2015] CSIH 37; 2015 G.W.D. 17-294, IH (Ex Div)
Considered 17/2765
Loch Lomond and Trossachs National Park Authority v Anstalt [2017] SAC (Civ) 11; 2017 S.L.T. (Sh Ct) 138; 2017 G.W.D. 13-206, SAC .... *Digested,* 17/**2643**
Lord Advocate v Dean (Zain Taj) [2016] HCJAC 117; 2017 S.L.T. 121; 2017 S.C.L. 170; 2017 S.C.C.R. 17; 2016 G.W.D. 38-672, HCJ .... *Digested,* 17/**2440**
Lord Advocate v Dean see Dean (Zain Taj) v Lord Advocate
Lord Advocate v Royal Bank of Scotland Ltd; *sub nom* Inland Revenue Commissioners v Royal Bank of Scotland Ltd 1977 S.C. 155; 1978 S.L.T. 38, IH (1 Div) .... *Digested,* 78/**3157**:
Distinguished 90/4772: *Followed* 83/4001, 16/2697: *Not followed* 17/2679
Love v Dunn see Paterson v Harvie
Luckhurst v Harrower see Luckhurst v Procurator Fiscal, Forfar
Luckhurst v Procurator Fiscal, Forfar; *sub nom* Luckhurst v Harrower [2016] SAC (Crim) 29; 2017 S.L.T. (Sh Ct) 7; 2017 S.C.L. 104; 2016 G.W.D. 31-543, SAC .. *Digested,* 17/**2511**
Lumsden (Paul William) v HM Advocate [2011] HCJAC 89; 2012 J.C. 133; 2012 S.C.L. 175; 2011 S.C.C.R. 648; 2011 G.W.D. 33-693, HCJ .... *Digested,* 12/**3936**:
Considered 17/2556
Lusona Consultancy (Accountancy & Finance) Ltd v McEwan [2017] CSOH 52; 2017 G.W.D. 12-175, OH
Lyons v Fraser [2016] HCJAC 92; 2017 S.C.L. 44; 2016 G.W.D. 32-571, HCJ .... *Digested,* 17/**2536**

M v Aviva Insurance UK Ltd; *sub nom* CM v Aviva Insurance UK Ltd 2017 Rep. L.R. 32; 2016 G.W.D. 40-704, Sh Ct (Lothian) (Edinburgh) .... *Digested,* 17/**2445**
M v Criminal Injuries Compensation Authority see LM v Criminal Injuries Compensation Authority
M v Fife Council; *sub nom* DM v Fife Council [2016] CSIH 17; 2016 S.C. 556; 2016 S.L.T. 489; 2017 S.C.L.R. 8; [2016] E.L.R. 237; 2016 G.W.D. 11-215, IH (Ex Div) .... *Digested,* 16/**2590**
M v HM Advocate (No.2); *sub nom* CJM v HM Advocate [2013] HCJAC 22; 2013 S.L.T. 380; 2013 S.C.L. 361; 2013 S.C.C.R. 215; 2013 G.W.D. 8-170, HCJ ...... *Digested,* 13/**3558**:
Applied 16/2489: *Considered* 13/3561, 14/3371, 17/2480: *Followed* 15/2953
M v Locality Reporter [2016] SAC (Civ) 16; 2017 G.W.D. 1-7, SAC
M v M; *sub nom* EM v AM [2016] CSIH 2; 2016 S.C.L.R. 571; 2016 Fam. L.R. 2; 2016 G.W.D. 3-75, IH (Ex Div) .... *Digested,* 17/**2616**
M v Nursing and Midwifery Council [2016] CSIH 95; 2017 G.W.D. 1-8, IH (Ex Div)
M v Nursing and Midwifery Council [2016] CSIH 86; 2017 S.C. 224; 2017 S.L.T. 53; 2016 G.W.D. 39-696, IH (Ex Div) .... *Digested,* 17/**2640**
M v State Hospitals Board for Scotland see McCann v State Hospitals Board for Scotland
M v W; *sub nom* JM v JW [2017] SAC (Civ) 3; 2017 Fam. L.R. 50; 2017 G.W.D. 4-43, SAC .... *Digested,* 17/**2413**
M (D) v HM Advocate; *sub nom* DM v HM Advocate [2017] HCJAC 19; 2017 S.C.L. 535; 2017 S.C.C.R. 235; 2017 G.W.D. 12-180, HCJ .... *Digested,* 17/**2552**
M, Petitioner [2016] CSOH 115; 2016 S.L.T. 911; 2016 G.W.D. 23-435, OH .... *Digested,* 16/**2417**:
Affirmed 17/2386
MA (Pakistan) v Secretary of State for the Home Department [2017] CSOH 109; 2017 G.W.D. 27-441, OH
MA (Pakistan) v Secretary of State for the Home Department [2017] CSOH 13; 2017 G.W.D. 6-86, OH
MA (Pakistan) v Secretary of State for the Home Department [2017] CSOH 12; 2017 G.W.D. 5-69, OH
Macallans v W Burrell Homes Ltd 2017 S.L.T. (Sh Ct) 1; 2016 G.W.D. 37-652, Sh Ct (Glasgow) .... *Digested,* 17/**2437**
Macaulay v Morrison 2017 G.W.D. 19-307, Land Ct
MacDonald v Aberdeenshire Council [2013] CSIH 83; 2014 S.C. 114; 2014 S.L.T. 2; 2014 S.C.L.R. 111; 2014 Rep. L.R. 2; 2013 G.W.D. 36-709, IH (Ex Div) .... *Digested,* 14/**3690**:
Applied 17/2738: *Considered* 17/2739
Macguire v Grant & Wilson Property Management Ltd [2017] SAC (Civ) 20; 2017 S.L.T. (Sh Ct) 107; 2017 G.W.D. 16-254, SAC .... *Digested,* 17/**2439**
Machin's Trustee v Machin 2017 G.W.D. 15-253, Sh Ct (Glasgow)
MacKay (Scott Henry) v HM Advocate [2017] HCJAC 44; 2017 J.C. 311; 2017 S.L.T. 1127; 2017 S.C.L. 761; 2017 S.C.C.R. 364; 2017 G.W.D. 21-344, HCJ Appeal *Digested,* 17/**2551**
Mackie v Maxi Construction Ltd 2017 S.L.T. (Sh Ct) 97; 2017 G.W.D. 9-130, Sh Ct (Lothian) (Livingston) .... *Digested,* 17/**2688**
Maclachlan v Strathclyde Partnership for Transport 2017 G.W.D. 14-227, SPIC

MacLeod's Legal Representatives v Highland Health Board [2016] CSIH 25; 2016 S.C. 647; 2017 S.C.L.R. 115; 2016 G.W.D. 12-241, IH (Ex Div) .... *Digested,* 17/**2736**

MacMillan v MacKenzie 1995 S.L.T. (Land Ct) 7, Land Ct (Full Ct) .... *Digested,* 95/**6416**: *Considered* 17/2402

MacMillan v T Leith Developments Ltd (In Receivership and Liquidation) [2016] CSOH 19; 2016 S.L.T. 477; 2016 G.W.D. 7-146, OH .... *Digested,* 16/**2697**: *Reversed in part* 17/2679

MacMillan v T Leith Developments Ltd (In Receivership and Liquidation) [2017] CSIH 23; 2017 S.C. 642; 2017 S.L.T. 415; 2017 S.C.L.R. 477; 2017 G.W.D. 10-141, IH (1 Div) .... *Digested,* 17/**2679**

MacRoberts LLP v McCrindle Group Ltd [2016] CSIH 27; 2017 S.C. 1; [2016] P.N.L.R. 28; 2016 G.W.D. 13-258, IH (Ex Div) .... *Digested,* 16/**2718**

MAK (Pakistan) v Secretary of State for the Home Department; *sub nom* K (Pakistan) v Secretary of State for the Home Department [2016] CSIH 13; 2016 S.C. 536; 2016 G.W.D. 9-175, IH (1 Div) .... *Digested,* 17/**2670**: *Applied* 17/2669: *Considered* 17/2665

Malcolm v Dundee City Council [2017] CSIH 32; 2017 S.L.T. 1008; 2017 G.W.D. 18-288, IH (2 Div) .... *Digested,* 17/**2583**

Malloch v Aberdeen Corp (No.1) [1971] 1 W.L.R. 1578; [1971] 2 All E.R. 1278; 1971 S.C. (H.L.) 85; 1971 S.L.T. 245; (1971) 115 S.J. 756, HL .... *Digested,* 71/**3866**: *Applied* 83/15: *Considered* 75/3760, 76/3084, 77/3072, 80/99, 87/3162, 92/5290, 95/5443, 04/466, 17/2768: *Distinguished* 84/14, 93/5405, 98/2242, 03/3475: *Followed* 83/24, 96/3961

Malone v Greater Glasgow and Clyde Health Board [2017] CSOH 31; 2017 G.W.D. 8-118, OH

Maloney v City of Edinburgh Council 2017 G.W.D. 22-379, Lands Tr (Scot)

Malpas v Fife Council 1999 S.L.T. 499; 1999 S.C.L.R. 550; 1999 G.W.D. 6-308, OH ... *Digested,* 99/**5688**: *Considered* 17/2428

Mannai Investment Co Ltd v Eagle Star Life Assurance Co Ltd [1997] A.C. 749; [1997] 2 W.L.R. 945; [1997] 3 All E.R. 352; [1997] C.L.C. 1124; [1997] 1 E.G.L.R. 57; [1997] 25 E.G. 138; [1997] 24 E.G. 122; (1997) 16 Tr. L.R. 432; Times, May 26, 1997; [1997] E.G. 82 (C.S.); (1997) 94(30) L.S.G. 30; (1997) 147 N.L.J. 846; (1997) 141 S.J.L.B. 130; [1997] N.P.C. 81, HL .... *Digested,* 97/**3256**: *Applied* 98/3598, 00/5612, 01/4156, 01/4182, 02/3008, 03/2723, 04/2243, 04/2497, 04/670, 05/2646, 05/523, 06/284, 07/2728, 07/807, 08/2438, 11/2060, 12/3364, 14/1996, 14/2970, 16/2060, 17/2111: *Considered* 03/2758, 05/475, 07/2754, 09/5040, 10/4356, 12/4124, 16/2707, 17/1432: *Distinguished* 98/3033, 98/3608, 00/3910, 04/2488, 08/2437, 12/2022: *Explained* 06/2703: *Followed* 00/3885, 00/4421, 10/2049, 14/1970, 14/2226, 15/2847, 17/2471: *Overruled* 99/3660

Manson v Henry Robb Ltd [2017] CSOH 126; 2017 S.L.T. 1173; 2017 Rep. L.R. 118; 2017 G.W.D. 31-498, OH .... *Digested,* 17/**2572**

Marin Subsea Ltd v EDS [2017] CSOH 120; 2017 G.W.D. 30-472, OH

Marine and Offshore (Scotland) Ltd v Jack [2017] CSOH 89; 2017 G.W.D. 22-360, OH

Marshall v Marshall 2007 Fam. L.R. 48; 2007 G.W.D. 10-188, OH .... *Digested,* 07/**5188**: *Applied* 17/2610

Martin (Matthew) v HM Advocate [2016] HCJAC 42; 2016 S.C.L. 524; 2016 S.C.C.R. 276; 2016 G.W.D. 15-282, HCJ .... *Digested,* 16/**2514**: *Applied* 17/2490

Martin (Ronald O'Neill) v HM Advocate [2006] HCJAC 86; 2007 J.C. 70; 2006 S.C.C.R. 683; 2006 G.W.D. 37-740, HCJ .... *Digested,* 07/**5518**: *Applied* 16/2802: *Considered* 17/2812

Martin McColl Ltd v West Dunbartonshire Licensing Board [2017] L.L.R. 551; 2017 G.W.D. 14-226, Sh Ct (North Strathclyde) (Dumbarton) .... *Digested,* 17/**2719**

Masocha (Walter) v HM Advocate [2016] HCJAC 15; 2016 S.C.L. 369; 2016 G.W.D. 7-144, HCJ Appeal .... *Digested,* 16/**2563**: *Considered* 17/2555

Mauger v Chief Constable of the Police Service of Scotland [2016] CSIH 44; 2017 S.C. 20; 2016 G.W.D. 20-355, IH (1 Div) .... *Digested,* 17/**2768**

Mauger v Chief Constable of the Police Service of Scotland [2016] CSOH 22; 2016 G.W.D. 9-164, OH
Affirmed 17/2768

Maxwell (Ivan Keith David) v HM Advocate [2017] HCJAC 64; 2017 S.C.L. 947; 2017 G.W.D. 29-462, HCJ .... *Digested,* 17/**2542**

Maynard v Oliver [2003] 3 Q.R. 6; [2002] 5 Q.R. 5, CC (Lincoln) [*Irwin Mitchell Solicitors, St. Peter's House, Hartshead, Sheffield*] .... *Digested,* 03/**3183**: *Considered* 17/2757

McAllister (Lesley) v Procurator Fiscal, Aberdeen [2017] SAC (Crim) 15; 2017 S.L.T. (Sh Ct) 243; 2017 S.C.L. 1058; 2017 G.W.D. 31-494, SAC .... *Digested,* 17/**2516**
McAteer (Connor) v HM Advocate [2016] HCJAC 95; 2017 S.C.L. 41; 2016 G.W.D. 33-590, HCJ
McAteer (Conor) v HM Advocate [2016] HCJAC 90; 2016 S.C.L. 1009; 2016 G.W.D. 31-558, HCJ .... *Digested,* 17/**2800**
McBrearty (Samuel) v HM Advocate 2004 J.C. 122; 2004 S.L.T. 917; 2004 S.C.C.R. 337; 2004 G.W.D. 15-329, HCJ .... *Digested,* 04/**4679**:
McBride v Scottish Police Authority see Scottish Police Services Authority v McBride
McBride v Scottish Police Services Authority see Scottish Police Services Authority v McBride
McBride v Strathclyde Police Joint Board see Scottish Police Services Authority v McBride
McCallum v City of Edinburgh Council [2017] CSIH 24; 2017 S.L.T. 466; 2017 Hous. L.R. 42; 2017 G.W.D. 11-162, IH (Ex Div) .... *Digested,* 17/**2705**
McCallum v City of Edinburgh Council 2017 S.L.T. (Lands Tr) 9; 2016 G.W.D. 24-450, Lands Tr (Scot)
Affirmed 17/2705
McCann v State Hospitals Board for Scotland; *sub nom* CM, Petitioner; CM v State Hospitals Board for Scotland; M v State Hospitals Board for Scotland [2017] UKSC 31; [2017] 1 W.L.R. 1455; [2017] 4 All E.R. 449; 2017 S.C. (U.K.S.C.) 121; 2017 S.L.T. 451; 43 B.H.R.C. 1; (2017) 156 B.M.L.R. 35; [2017] M.H.L.R. 306; Times, April 25, 2017; 2017 G.W.D. 12-169, SC .... *Digested,* 17/**1118**
McClure Naismith v Harley Haddow Partnership [2017] CSOH 125; 2017 G.W.D. 32-509, OH
McCormick (Adam) v HM Advocate [2016] HCJAC 50; 2016 S.L.T. 793; 2016 S.C.L. 651; 2016 S.C.C.R. 308; 2016 G.W.D. 18-334, HCJ .... *Digested,* 16/**2795**:
Considered 17/2817
McCourt (Peter Stephen) v HM Advocate see Gemmell (James Kelly) v HM Advocate
McCrae (Kyle) v HM Advocate [2017] HCJAC 27; 2017 S.C.L. 637; 2017 G.W.D. 16-256, HCJ Appeal .... *Digested,* 17/**2491**
McCue v Scottish Daily Record & Sunday Mail Ltd (No.1) 1998 S.C. 811; 1998 S.L.T. 983; 1998 S.C.L.R. 742; 1998 G.W.D. 23-1153, IH (Ct of 5 judges) .... *Digested,* 98/**5493**:
Considered 99/5680, 17/2435: *Distinguished* 00/5940: *Followed* 12/3831
McDonald v Glasgow City Council see HBJ Claimants v Glasgow City Council
McDonald v McDonald; *sub nom* McDonald v Newton [2017] UKSC 52; 2017 S.C. (U.K.S.C.) 142; 2017 S.L.T. 837; 2018 S.C.L.R. 26; 2017 Fam. L.R. 78; 2017 G.W.D. 23-395, SC .... *Digested,* 17/**1014**
McDonald v Newton see McDonald v McDonald
McDonald's Trustee v Aberdeen City Council 2000 S.C. 185; 2000 S.L.T. 985; 2000 Hous. L.R. 30; 2000 G.W.D. 1-24, IH (Ex Div) .... *Digested,* 00/**6465**:
Distinguished 17/2694
McDowall v G4S Care and Justice Services (UK) Ltd 2016 S.L.T. (Sh Ct) 371; 2017 Rep. L.R. 2; 2016 G.W.D. 32-580, Sh Ct (Lothian) (Edinburgh) .... *Digested,* 16/**2748**
McDowall (Luke) v HM Advocate; *joined cases* Lawrie (Joshua) v HM Advocate; Scott (Jordan) v HM Advocate [2016] HCJAC 105; 2017 S.C.L. 158; 2016 G.W.D. 37-659, HCJ .... *Digested,* 17/**2501**
McGeoch v Lord President of the Council [2011] CSOH 65; 2011 S.L.T. 633; 2011 G.W.D. 14-320, OH
Affirmed 12/3970: *Considered* 17/2773
McGraddie v McGraddie [2013] UKSC 58; [2013] 1 W.L.R. 2477; 2014 S.C. (U.K.S.C.) 12; 2013 S.L.T. 1212; 2015 S.C.L.R. 109; 2013 G.W.D. 25-471, SC *Digested,* 13/**6**:
Applied 17/2440: *Considered* 15/300, 15/3133: *Followed* 14/1579
McGuire (William Bennett) v HM Advocate [2016] HCJAC 113; 2017 S.C.L. 137; 2016 G.W.D. 38-675, HCJ
McHale (Joseph Francis) v HM Advocate; *joined case* Schruyers (Kevin Charles) v HM Advocate [2017] HCJAC 35; 2018 J.C. 11; 2017 S.C.L. 866; 2017 S.C.C.R. 427; 2017 G.W.D. 27-438, HCJ .... *Digested,* 17/**2503**
McHugh v Harvie [2015] HCJAC 86; 2015 S.C.L. 987; 2015 S.C.C.R. 430; 2015 G.W.D. 34-556, HCJ .... *Digested,* 16/**2818**:
Distinguished 17/2798
McInally (John Francis) v HM Advocate [2006] HCJAC 48; 2006 J.C. 224; 2006 S.C.C.R. 391; 2006 G.W.D. 23-503, HCJ
Applied 17/2482
McKechnie v Murray [2016] CSIH 4; 2016 S.C. 339; 2016 G.W.D. 9-167, IH (Ex Div) .. *Digested,* 17/**2452**
McKenna v O'Hare [2017] SAC (Civ) 16; 2017 S.C. (S.A.C.) 33; 2017 S.L.T. (Sh Ct) 117; 2017 G.W.D. 14-228, SAC .... *Digested,* 17/**2741**

McKie v Scottish Ministers [2006] CSOH 54; 2006 S.C. 528; 2006 S.L.T. 668; 2006 G.W.D. 20-437, OH .... *Digested,* 06/**5105**: *Applied* 17/2427
McLean (Darryl) v HM Advocate see Wood (Kenneth) v HM Advocate
McLeish v Lothian NHS Board [2017] CSOH 71; 2017 Rep. L.R. 90; 2017 G.W.D. 15-248, OH .... *Digested,* 17/**2642**
McLeod v Cedar Holdings Ltd 1989 S.L.T. 620, IH (2 Div) .... *Digested,* 89/**4794**: *Applied* 17/2677: *Distinguished* 93/5393: *Referred to* 94/5914
McManus v City Link Development Co Ltd [2017] CSIH 12; 2017 Hous. L.R. 84; 2017 G.W.D. 6-82, IH (Ex Div)
McMaster v Scottish Ministers [2017] CSOH 46; 2017 S.L.T. 586; 2017 G.W.D. 11-143, OH .... *Digested,* 17/**2693**
McMillan v Mundell see McMillan (Graham) v Procurator Fiscal, Paisley
McMillan (Graham) v Procurator Fiscal, Paisley; *sub nom* McMillan v Mundell [2017] SAC (Crim) 2; 2017 S.L.T. (Sh Ct) 80; 2017 S.C.L. 489; 2017 S.C.C.R. 96; 2017 G.W.D. 4-44, SAC .... *Digested,* 17/**2570**
McMultan (Christopher) v HM Advocate [2016] HCJAC 89; 2016 S.C.L. 973; 2016 S.C.C.R. 496; 2016 G.W.D. 31-544, HCJ .... *Digested,* 17/**2541**
McNair (Ryan) v HM Advocate [2017] HCJAC 6; 2017 S.L.T. 229; 2017 S.C.L. 312; 2017 G.W.D. 4-58, HCJ .... *Digested,* 17/**2804**
McNulty v McNulty 2016 Fam. L.R. 145; 2016 G.W.D. 36-646, Sh Ct (Tayside) (Dunfermline) .... *Digested,* 17/**2611**
McPhail v Lanarkshire CC (No.2) 1951 S.C. 301; 1951 S.L.T. 167, IH (1 Div) .... *Digested,* 51/**3988**: *Considered* 17/2448
McQuade v Clarke see Stewart v Payne
McWilliam v Gibson see McWilliam v Harvie
McWilliam v Harvie; *sub nom* McWilliam v Gibson [2016] HCJAC 29; 2017 J.C. 31; 2016 S.L.T. 648; 2016 S.C.L. 434; 2016 G.W.D. 13-254, HCJ .... *Digested,* 16/**2588**: *Applied* 17/2570
McWilliams v Russell 2017 G.W.D. 32-510, Sh Ct (Glasgow)
ME v Refugee Applications Commissioner (C-493/10) see R. (on the application of NS) v Secretary of State for the Home Department (C-411/10)
Megrahi (Abdelbaset Ali) v HM Advocate (No.4) see HM Advocate v Al-Megrahi (Abdelbaset Ali) (No.4)
MH (Bangladesh) v Secretary of State for the Home Department [2014] CSOH 143; 2014 G.W.D. 30-597, OH *Considered* 17/2663
MIAB v Secretary of State for the Home Department; *sub nom* B v Secretary of State for the Home Department [2016] CSIH 64; 2016 S.C. 871; 2016 S.L.T. 1220; 2017 S.C.L.R. 557; 2016 G.W.D. 28-509, IH (1 Div) .... *Digested,* 17/**2663**: *Applied* 17/2671
Midlothian Council v Bracewell Stirling Architects [2017] CSOH 87; [2017] P.N.L.R. 33; 2017 G.W.D. 21-330, OH .... *Digested,* 17/**2468**
Midlothian Council v Greens 2017 Hous. L.R. 111; 2017 G.W.D. 30-484, Sh Ct (Lothian) (Edinburgh)
Miller v Chivas Brothers Ltd [2014] CSIH 65; 2015 S.C. 85; 2014 G.W.D. 24-452, IH (Ex Div) .... *Digested,* 15/**2895**: *Applied* 17/2426: *Considered* 16/2445
Miller v Smith [2017] SAC (Civ) 26; 2017 G.W.D. 28-444, SAC
Miller's Executor v Miller 2016 S.L.T. (Sh Ct) 399; 2016 G.W.D. 23-431, Sh Ct (Lothian) (Livingston) .... *Digested,* 17/**2683**
Mills (Kenneth Anthony) v HM Advocate (No.1) 1999 J.C. 216; 1999 S.L.T. 680; 1999 S.C.C.R. 202; 1999 G.W.D. 11-495, HCJ .... *Digested,* 99/**5857**: *Applied* 17/2532
Milne v Harrower [2016] SAC (Crim) 26; 2017 S.C. (S.A.C.) 1; 2016 S.C.L. 1011; 2016 S.C.C.R. 392; 2016 G.W.D. 29-519, SAC .... *Digested,* 17/**2515**
Minister voor Immigratie, Integratie en Asiel v B (C-456/12) see O v Minister voor Immigratie, Integratie en Asiel (C-456/12)
Mirga v Secretary of State for Work and Pensions; *joined case* Samin v Westminster City Council [2016] UKSC 1; [2016] 1 W.L.R. 481; [2016] 2 All E.R. 447; [2016] 2 C.M.L.R. 31; [2016] H.L.R. 7; Times, February 8, 2016, SC .... *Digested,* 16/**1983**: *Considered* 17/2658
Mitchell v Harrower see Mitchell (Fraser) v Procurator Fiscal, Kirkcaldy
Mitchell v Somerville [2017] CSIH 60; 2017 G.W.D. 31-493, IH (Ex Div)
Mitchell (Darrell) v HM Advocate [2017] HCJAC 60; 2018 J.C. 67; 2017 S.C.L. 896; 2017 S.C.C.R. 485; 2017 G.W.D. 26-430, HCJ .... *Digested,* 17/**2554**

Mitchell (Fraser) v Procurator Fiscal, Kirkcaldy; *sub nom* Mitchell v Harrower [2017] SAC (Crim) 14; 2017 S.L.T. (Sh Ct) 207; 2017 S.C.L. 1066; 2017 S.C.C.R. 512; 2017 G.W.D. 29-460, SAC .... *Digested,* 17/**2477**
ML v ANS see S v L
MM (Iran) v Secretary of State for the Home Department [2017] CSOH 82; 2017 G.W.D. 20-325, OH
Mohammed v Advocate General for Scotland [2017] L.L.R. 570; 2017 G.W.D. 14-217, Sh Ct (Lothian) (Livingston) .... *Digested,* 17/**2666**
Moir v Memsie 2017 Rep. L.R. 78; 2017 G.W.D. 12-173, Sh Ct (Lothian) (Edinburgh) . *Digested,* 17/**2444**
Moneybarn No.1 Ltd v Bell 2016 S.L.T. (Sh Ct) 419; 2016 G.W.D. 32-569, Sh Ct (South Strathclyde) (Dumfries) .... *Digested,* 17/**2456**
Moor Row Ltd v DWF LLP [2017] CSOH 63; 2017 G.W.D. 14-213, OH
Moran v Freyssinet Ltd [2014] CSOH 173; 2015 Rep. L.R. 15; 2015 G.W.D. 1-7, OH .. *Digested,* 15/**2912**: *Affirmed* 16/2461: *Applied* 17/2445
Moray Council v Scottish Ministers [2006] CSIH 41; 2006 S.C. 691; 2007 S.C.L.R. 55; 2006 G.W.D. 25-578, IH (2 Div) .... *Digested,* 07/**5464**: *Considered* 17/2765
Morton (Henry) v HM Advocate [2017] HCJAC 21; 2017 S.C.L. 513; 2017 G.W.D. 13-211, HCJ .... *Digested,* 17/**2811**
Mowlem Plc (t/a Mowlem Marine) v Scrabster Harbour Trust see Scrabster Harbour Trust v Mowlem Plc (t/a Mowlem Marine)
Moynihan (Sean Barry) v HM Advocate [2016] HCJAC 85; 2017 J.C. 71; 2016 S.C.L. 977; 2016 S.C.C.R. 548; 2016 G.W.D. 31-546, HCJ .... *Digested,* 17/**2556**: *Considered* 17/2555
MP Burke Transport Ltd v Charles Scott & Partners LLP [2017] CSOH 67; 2017 G.W.D. 14-214, OH
MR (Syria) v Secretary of State for the Home Department [2017] CSOH 97; 2017 G.W.D. 22-373, OH
Mrs Maggie Brack Ferguson and Others v Andrew Paul (1885) 12 R. 1222, IH (2 Div) *Considered* 17/2710: *Followed* 16/2709
MS (India) v Secretary of State for the Home Department [2013] CSIH 52; 2013 G.W.D. 23-441, IH (Ex Div) *Applied* 15/3149, 15/3157: *Considered* 17/2665
MS (Pakistan), Applicants [2017] CSIH 55; 2017 G.W.D. 25-415, IH (Ex Div)
MT v Gerry see T v Locality Reporter
MTM Construction Ltd v William Reid Engineering Ltd 1998 S.L.T. 211; 1997 S.C.L.R. 778; 1997 Rep. L.R. 27; Times, April 22, 1997; 1997 G.W.D. 7-260, OH .... *Digested,* 97/**6073**: *Applied* 17/2464
Muldoon (John Scott) v Herron 1970 J.C. 30; 1970 S.L.T. 228, HCJ .... *Digested,* 70/**3070**: *Applied* 90/4852, 91/4586, 94/5513, 17/2492
Mull Shellfish Ltd v Golden Sea Produce Ltd 1992 S.L.T. 703; Times, October 17, 1991; Scotsman, August 28, 1991, IH (2 Div) .... *Digested,* 91/**5457**: *Considered* 17/2455
Mullan v Anderson 1993 S.L.T. 835; 1993 S.C.L.R. 506, IH (Ct of 5 judges) .... *Digested,* 93/**5815**: *Applied* 04/4564: *Considered* 03/5293, 13/3728, 17/2779: *Followed* 96/6627, 09/5044: *Referred to* 08/5003
Munnoch v Tay-Forth Foundries Ltd 2008 S.C.L.R. 232; 2007 G.W.D. 31-530, OH *Considered* 17/2757
Munro v Keeper of the Registers of Scotland 2017 G.W.D. 22-366, Lands Tr (Scot)
Munro v Keeper of the Registers of Scotland 2017 G.W.D. 17-277, Lands Tr (Scot)
Murphy (Charles) v HM Advocate [2016] HCJAC 118; 2017 S.L.T. 143; 2017 S.C.L. 176; 2016 G.W.D. 39-691, HCJ .... *Digested,* 17/**2538**
Murray Group Holdings Ltd v Revenue and Customs Commissioners see RFC 2012 Plc (In Liquidation) (formerly Rangers Football Club Plc) v Advocate General for Scotland
Murray, Petitioner 2012 S.L.T. (Sh Ct) 57; 2012 G.W.D. 14-300, Sh Ct (Tayside) (Kirkcaldy) .... *Digested,* 12/**4294**: *Considered* 17/2839
MZ (Iran) v Secretary of State for the Home Department [2017] CSOH 104; 2017 G.W.D. 23-398, OH
MZ (Pakistan) v Secretary of State for the Home Department 2017 G.W.D. 16-264, OH

Nacap Ltd v Moffat Plant Ltd 1987 S.L.T. 221, IH (1 Div) .... *Digested,* 87/**4767**: *Considered* 17/2455: *Followed* 03/5772: *Referred to* 91/5457
Nadaf (Allabaksh) v HM Advocate [2017] HCJAC 37; 2017 S.C.L. 699; 2017 G.W.D. 19-296, HCJ Appeal .... *Digested,* 17/**2497**

Othman v United Kingdom (8139/09); *sub nom* Abu Qatada v United Kingdom (8139/09) (2012) 55 E.H.R.R. 1; 32 B.H.R.C. 62; Times, January 25, 2012, ECHR .... *Digested,* 12/**1664**:
Applied 14/3521: *Considered* 13/1187, 16/2634, 16/794, 16/796, 17/2440, 17/903

Outlook Finance Ltd v Lindsay's Executor Nominate 2016 Hous. L.R. 75; 2016 G.W.D. 28-508, Sh Ct (South Strathclyde) (Lanark) .... *Digested,* 17/**2780**

Owens (Hugh) v HM Advocate 1946 J.C. 119; 1946 S.L.T. 227, HCJ Appeal
Considered 17/2482: *Disapproved* 73/3603: *Followed* 63/785, 82/683, 90/4891: *Referred to* 93/5031

P v HM Advocate; *sub nom* KP v HM Advocate [2017] HCJAC 57; 2018 J.C. 33; 2017 S.C.L. 729; 2017 S.C.C.R. 451; 2017 G.W.D. 24-406, HCJ Appeal .... *Digested,* 17/**2529**

P v Scottish Ministers [2017] CSOH 33; 2017 S.L.T. 271; 2017 G.W.D. 8-110, OH .... *Digested,* 17/**2749**

P, Applicant [2017] CSIH 3; 2017 G.W.D. 5-62, IH (Ex Div)

Pacitti v Manganiello 1995 S.C.L.R. 557, Sh Pr .... *Digested,* 95/**6058**:
Applied 17/2704

ParkingEye Ltd v Beavis [2015] EWCA Civ 402; [2015] R.T.R. 27; [2015] C.T.L.C. 82, CA (Civ Div) .... *Digested,* 15/**2153**:
Affirmed 16/437: *Considered* 17/2467

Paterson v Harvie; *joined cases* Bow v Harvie; Love v Dunn [2014] HCJAC 87; 2015 J.C. 118; 2014 S.L.T. 857; 2014 S.C.L. 606; 2014 S.C.C.R. 521; 2014 G.W.D. 26-517, HCJ .... *Digested,* 14/**3410**:
Applied 16/2508, 17/2494

Paterson v Macleod [2017] CSOH 20; 2017 G.W.D. 7-107, OH

Patrick v Patrick 2017 Fam. L.R. 128; 2017 G.W.D. 27-440, Sh Ct (Glasgow) .... *Digested,* 17/**2613**

Pattullo's Application, Re 2017 G.W.D. 25-422, Sh Ct (Glasgow)

Paxton v North Ayrshire Council [2017] SAC (Civ) 14; 2017 Rep. L.R. 87; 2017 G.W.D. 13-202, SAC .... *Digested,* 17/**2756**

Peebles v Rembrand Builders Merchants Ltd 2017 G.W.D. 15-236, Sh Ct (Tayside) (Dundee)

Pensionsversicherungsanstalt v Brey (C-140/12) EU:C:2013:565; [2014] 1 W.L.R. 1080; [2014] 1 C.M.L.R. 37; [2014] All E.R. (EC) 534, ECJ (3rd Chamber)
Applied 14/1739: *Considered* 17/2658

Perth and Kinross Council v Scottish Water Ltd [2015] CSOH 138; 2015 S.L.T. 788; 2015 G.W.D. 34-547, OH .... *Digested,* 16/**2475**:
Affirmed 17/2454

Perth and Kinross Council v Scottish Water Ltd [2016] CSIH 83; 2017 S.C. 164; 2016 S.L.T. 1251; 2016 G.W.D. 35-627, IH (Ex Div) .... *Digested,* 17/**2454**:
Considered 17/2448

Perth and Kinross Council, Petitioner [2017] CSOH 101; 2017 G.W.D. 24-409, OH

Petroineos Manufacturing Scotland Ltd v Clydeport Operations Ltd [2017] CSOH 49; 2017 G.W.D. 14-215, OH

Pettigrew v River Clyde Homes 2017 Hous. L.R. 15; 2017 G.W.D. 12-189, Lands Tr (Scot) .... *Digested,* 17/**2708**

Phensrisai v Yutikan [2017] CSOH 48; 2017 S.L.T. 631; 2017 G.W.D. 12-181, OH .... *Digested,* 17/**2757**

Phillip v Trinidad and Tobago see Huggins v Trinidad and Tobago

Phosphate Sewage Co Ltd v Molleson (Res Judicata); *joined case* Official Liquidator v Molleson (1879) 4 App. Cas. 801; (1879) 6 R. (H.L.) 113, HL
Applied 80/2609, 82/2382, 90/3542, 08/1432, 08/272, 14/2209: *Considered* 17/2412: *Followed* 17/372

Plewa v Chief Adjudication Officer [1995] 1 A.C. 249; [1994] 3 W.L.R. 317; [1994] 3 All E.R. 323; Times, July 9, 1994; Independent, July 29, 1994; (1994) 91(30) L.S.G. 32; (1994) 138 S.J.L.B. 152, HL .... *Digested,* 94/**4179**:
Applied 97/2241, 17/2772

Pocock v Highland Council [2017] CSOH 40; 2017 Rep. L.R. 69; 2017 G.W.D. 10-142, OH .... *Digested,* 17/**2739**

Politakis v Spencely [2017] SAC (Civ) 19; 2017 G.W.D. 18-281, SAC

Pollock v Drogo Developments Ltd [2017] CSOH 64; 2017 G.W.D. 14-221, OH

Pompa's Trustees v Edinburgh Burgh Council 1942 S.C. 119; 1942 S.L.T. 118, IH (2 Div)
Applied 63/4108, 83/4964, 90/5395, 08/4591: *Considered* 91/5470, 08/4593, 17/2454: *Distinguished* 61/10496

Potts v Gibson [2016] SAC (Crim) 25; 2016 S.C.L. 819; 2016 S.C.C.R. 412; 2016 G.W.D. 29-520, SAC .... *Digested,* 16/**2583**:
Affirmed 17/2564

Potts v Gibson see Potts (Donnie Daniel) v Procurator Fiscal, Hamilton

Potts (Donnie Daniel) v Procurator Fiscal, Hamilton; *sub nom* Potts v Gibson [2017] HCJAC 8; 2017 J.C. 194; 2017 S.L.T. 313; 2017 S.C.L. 222; 2017 S.C.C.R. 109; 2017 G.W.D. 7-98, HCJ .... *Digested,* 17/**2564**

Prescott v University of St Andrews [2016] CSOH 3; 2016 G.W.D. 4-99, OH
Considered 17/2429

Presslie v Cochrane McGregor Group Ltd (No.1) 1996 S.C. 289; 1996 S.L.T. 988, IH (2 Div) .... *Digested,* 96/**6570**: *Considered* 17/2696

Principal Reporter v LZ [2017] CSIH 51; 2017 S.L.T. 961; 2017 G.W.D. 24-403, IH (Ex Div) .... *Digested,* 17/**2601**

Principal Reporter, Applicant 2017 S.L.T. (Sh Ct) 21; 2017 G.W.D. 3-35, Sh Ct (Glasgow)
Reversed 17/2601

Priya Properties Ltd v Inverclyde Council 2017 Hous. L.R. 19; 2016 G.W.D. 40-718, Sh Ct (North Strathclyde) (Greenock) .... *Digested,* 17/**2656**

Procurator Fiscal, Forfar v B (D) 2017 S.L.T. (Sh Ct) 44; 2017 G.W.D. 4-54, Sh Ct (Tayside) (Forfar) .... *Digested,* 17/**2533**

Procurator Fiscal, Peterhead v Elrick (Lyn) 2017 S.L.T. (Sh Ct) 157; 2017 S.C.L. 1072; 2017 G.W.D. 18-285, Sh Ct (Grampian) (Peterhead) .... *Digested,* 17/**2518**

Procurator Fiscal, Peterhead v Elrick (Lyn) 2017 S.L.T. (Sh Ct) 67; 2017 G.W.D. 12-179, Sh Ct (Grampian) (Peterhead) .... *Digested,* 17/**2514**

Professional Standards Authority for Health and Social Care v General Dental Council [2016] CSIH 58; 2017 S.C.L.R. 185; 2016 G.W.D. 24-445, IH (Ex Div) .... *Digested,* 17/**2635**

Professional Standards Authority for Health and Social Care v General Medical Council [2015] EWHC 1304 (Admin); [2015] Med. L.R. 327, QBD (Admin) .... *Digested,* 15/**1203**: *Considered* 17/2638

Professional Standards Authority for Health and Social Care v Nursing and Midwifery Council [2017] CSIH 29; 2017 S.C. 542; 2017 S.L.T. 625; 2017 G.W.D. 16-262, IH (Ex Div) .... *Digested,* 17/**2638**

Promontoria (Ram) Ltd v Moore [2017] CSOH 88; 2017 G.W.D. 21-331, OH

Prospect Healthcare (Hairmyres) Ltd v Keir Build Ltd [2017] CSOH 112; 2017 G.W.D. 28-446, OH

PS (Georgia) v Advocate General for Scotland [2017] CSOH 34; 2017 G.W.D. 10-140, OH

Purewall, Appellant [2017] SAC (Civ) 28; 2017 S.L.T. (Sh Ct) 251; 2017 G.W.D. 30-483, SAC

PW (Poland) v Secretary of State for the Home Department [2017] CSOH 47; 2017 G.W.D. 11-161, OH

Q (J) v Procurator Fiscal, Paisley; *sub nom* JQ v Mundell [2017] HCJAC 9; 2017 J.C. 201; 2017 S.L.T. 398; 2017 S.C.L. 332; 2017 S.C.C.R. 116; 2017 G.W.D. 5-65, HCJ .... *Digested,* 17/**2537**

Quinn v Scottish Ministers [2017] CSIH 53; 2017 S.L.T. 1036; 2017 Rep. L.R. 98; 2017 G.W.D. 25-427, IH (Ex Div) .... *Digested,* 17/**2745**

Quinn v Scottish Ministers [2016] CSOH 67; 2017 Rep. L.R. 104; 2016 G.W.D. 17-303, OH
Reversed 17/2745

R v A University [2017] CSIH 11; 2017 S.L.T. 284; 2017 S.C.L.R. 762; 2017 G.W.D. 7-100, IH (2 Div) .... *Digested,* 17/**2580**

R v HM Advocate [2016] HCJAC 94; 2017 S.L.T. 177; 2017 S.C.L. 77; 2016 G.W.D. 32-582, HCJ .... *Digested,* 17/**2792**

R (J) v HM Advocate; *sub nom* JR v HM Advocate [2017] HCJAC 49; 2017 S.C.L. 814; 2017 S.C.C.R. 402; 2017 G.W.D. 22-383, HCJ Appeal .... *Digested,* 17/**2809**

R. v Abdin (Joynal) see Attorney General's Reference (Nos 128 to 141 of 2015 and 8 to 10 of 2016)

R. v Ducram (Fitzroy) see Attorney General's Reference (Nos 128 to 141 of 2015 and 8 to 10 of 2016)

R. v Fedar (Mohammed) see Attorney General's Reference (Nos 128 to 141 of 2015 and 8 to 10 of 2016)

R. v Ghalib (Amar) see Attorney General's Reference (Nos 128 to 141 of 2015 and 8 to 10 of 2016)

R. v Gul (Rowan) see Attorney General's Reference (Nos 128 to 141 of 2015 and 8 to 10 of 2016)

R. v Hertfordshire CC Ex p. Cheung; *joined case* R. v Sefton MBC Ex p. Pau Times, April 4, 1986, CA (Civ Div) .... *Digested,* 86/**1135**: *Applied* 14/787: *Considered* 10/1432, 17/2711

R. v Hussain (Ifran) see Attorney General's Reference (Nos 128 to 141 of 2015 and 8 to 10 of 2016)
R. v Hussain (Usman) see Attorney General's Reference (Nos 128 to 141 of 2015 and 8 to 10 of 2016)
R. v Immigration Appeal Tribunal Ex p. Antonissen (C-292/89) EU:C:1991:80; [1991] E.C.R. I-745; [1991] 2 C.M.L.R. 373; Times, February 27, 1991; Guardian, March 7, 1991; (1991) 135 S.J. 6, ECJ .... *Digested,* 91/**4007**:
Applied 96/3164, 06/2041: *Considered* 95/52, 98/4539, 06/1589, 08/2094, 17/2658: *Followed* 11/1794
R. v Immigration Appeal Tribunal Ex p. Secretary of State for the Home Department (C370/90) EU:C:1992:296; [1992] 3 All E.R. 798; [1992] E.C.R. I-4265; [1992] 3 C.M.L.R. 358; [1993] 1 F.L.R. 798; [1992] Imm. A.R. 565; Times, August 31, 1992; Independent, July 17, 1992; [1993] Fam. Law 294; Guardian, July 15, 1992, ECJ .... *Digested,* 92/**4802**:
Applied 95/2715: *Cited* 17/2673: *Considered* 97/2919, 98/3250, 06/1573: *Followed* 04/2071
R. v Lundt-Smith [1964] 2 Q.B. 167; [1964] 2 W.L.R. 1063; [1964] 3 All E.R. 225 (Note); (1964) 128 J.P. 534; 62 L.G.R. 376; (1964) 108 S.J. 425, Assizes .... *Digested,* 64/**3194**:
Approved 71/10171: *Considered* 69/3177, 98/1365, 16/2793: *Distinguished* 17/2516
R. v Mattu (Joga Singh) see Attorney General's Reference (Nos 128 to 141 of 2015 and 8 to 10 of 2016)
R. v McDermott (Louis Junior) see Attorney General's Reference (Nos 128 to 141 of 2015 and 8 to 10 of 2016)
R. v Mentore (Darren) see Attorney General's Reference (Nos 128 to 141 of 2015 and 8 to 10 of 2016)
R. v Miah (Mohammed Selu) see Attorney General's Reference (Nos 128 to 141 of 2015 and 8 to 10 of 2016)
R. v Mohammed (Janed) see Attorney General's Reference (Nos 128 to 141 of 2015 and 8 to 10 of 2016)
R. v Nazran (Sundish Singh) see Attorney General's Reference (Nos 128 to 141 of 2015 and 8 to 10 of 2016)
R. v Officer (Clinton) see Attorney General's Reference (Nos 128 to 141 of 2015 and 8 to 10 of 2016)
R. v Reynolds (Jacqueline) [2017] EWCA Crim 57; 2017 S.C.L. 324, CA (Crim Div) .... *Digested,* 17/**581**
R. v Sefton MBC Ex p. Pau see R. v Hertfordshire CC Ex p. Cheung
R. v Smith (Jamal Shaka) see Attorney General's Reference (Nos 128 to 141 of 2015 and 8 to 10 of 2016)
R. v Steele see Steele (Kevin Munro) v HM Advocate
R. v Stephenson (Nosakhere) see Attorney General's Reference (Nos 128 to 141 of 2015 and 8 to 10 of 2016)
R. v Wiggan (Theodore Junior) see Attorney General's Reference (Nos 128 to 141 of 2015 and 8 to 10 of 2016)
R. (on the application of A) v Secretary of State for Work and Pensions see R. (on the application of Carmichael) v Secretary of State for Work and Pensions
R. (on the application of Agyarko) v Secretary of State for the Home Department; *joined cases* R. (on the application of Evans) v Secretary of State for the Home Department; R. (on the application of Ikuga) v Secretary of State for the Home Department [2017] UKSC 11; [2017] 1 W.L.R. 823; [2017] 4 All E.R. 575; [2017] 3 C.M.L.R. 3; [2017] Imm. A.R. 764; [2017] I.N.L.R. 548; Times, March 1, 2017, SC .... *Digested,* 17/**1239**:
Considered 17/2665
R. (on the application of Agyarko) v Secretary of State for the Home Department; *joined cases* R. (on the application of Evans) v Secretary of State for the Home Department; R. (on the application of Ikuga) v Secretary of State for the Home Department [2015] EWCA Civ 440; [2016] 1 W.L.R. 390; [2015] Imm. A.R. 1201; [2016] I.N.L.R. 198, CA (Civ Div) .... *Digested,* 16/**1141**:
Affirmed 17/1239: *Considered* 17/1200, 17/2670
R. (on the application of Alvi) v Secretary of State for the Home Department [2012] UKSC 33; [2012] 1 W.L.R. 2208; [2012] 4 All E.R. 1041; [2012] Imm. A.R. 998; [2012] I.N.L.R. 504, SC .... *Digested,* 12/**1755**:
Applied 13/1648, 14/1688, 14/1716, 15/1347, 16/1145, 17/1230: *Considered* 14/1653, 16/1129, 16/2683, 17/2668: *Followed* 17/1209
R. (on the application of AW) v Secretary of State for the Home Department see R. (on the application of T) v Chief Constable of Greater Manchester
R. (on the application of B) v Secretary of State for the Home Department see R. (on the application of T) v Chief Constable of Greater Manchester

R. (on the application of Buer) v Secretary of State for the Home Department; *joined cases* Eroglu v Secretary of State for the Home Department; R. (on the application of KP (Turkey) v Secretary of State for the Home Department [2014] EWCA Civ 1109; [2015] 1 C.M.L.R. 3; [2015] Imm. A.R. 82, CA (Civ Div) .... *Digested,* 15/**959**: *Considered* 17/2668

R. (on the application of Carmichael) v Secretary of State for Work and Pensions; *sub nom* R. (on the application of MA) v Secretary of State for Work and Pensions; *joined cases* R. (on the application of Rutherford) v Secretary of State for Work and Pensions; R. (on the application of A) v Secretary of State for Work and Pensions; R. (on the application of Daly) v Secretary of State for Work and Pensions [2016] UKSC 58; [2016] 1 W.L.R. 4550; [2017] 1 All E.R. 869; [2016] P.T.S.R. 1422; [2016] H.R.L.R. 24; [2016] H.L.R. 46; (2017) 20 C.C.L. Rep. 103; Times, November 22, 2016, SC .... *Digested,* 17/**2030**: *Considered* 17/2824: *Followed* 17/2026

R. (on the application of Child Poverty Action Group) v Secretary of State for Work and Pensions [2010] UKSC 54; [2011] 2 A.C. 15; [2011] 2 W.L.R. 1; [2011] 1 All E.R. 729; [2011] P.T.S.R. 185; Times, December 13, 2010; (2010) 108(2) L.S.G. 19; (2010) 154(47) S.J.L.B. 30, SC .... *Digested,* 11/**3157**: *Applied* 13/397, 14/1542: *Considered* 16/1835, 17/2772

R. (on the application of CN) v Lewisham LBC see R. (on the application of N) v Lewisham LBC

R. (on the application of Daly) v Secretary of State for Work and Pensions see R. (on the application of Carmichael) v Secretary of State for Work and Pensions

R. (on the application of Edwards) v Environment Agency (C-260/11); *sub nom* Edwards v Environment Agency (C-260/11) EU:C:2013:221; [2013] 1 W.L.R. 2914; [2013] 3 C.M.L.R. 18; [2014] All E.R. (EC) 207, ECJ (4th Chamber) .... *Digested,* 14/**1183**: *Applied* 14/333, 14/339, 17/280: *Considered* 14/3338, 17/2430: *Followed* 14/442

R. (on the application of Evans) v Secretary of State for the Home Department see R. (on the application of Agyarko) v Secretary of State for the Home Department

R. (on the application of H (A Child)) v Newham LBC see R. (on the application of N) v Lewisham LBC

R. (on the application of Haney) v Secretary of State for Justice see R. (on the application of Kaiyam) v Secretary of State for Justice

R. (on the application of Ikuga) v Secretary of State for the Home Department see R. (on the application of Agyarko) v Secretary of State for the Home Department

R. (on the application of JB) v Secretary of State for the Home Department see R. (on the application of T) v Chief Constable of Greater Manchester

R. (on the application of Kaiyam) v Secretary of State for Justice; *sub nom* R. (on the application of Haney) v Secretary of State for Justice; R. (on the application of Massey) v Secretary of State for Justice; *joined case* R. (on the application of Robinson) v Governor of Whatton Prison [2014] UKSC 66; [2015] A.C. 1344; [2015] 2 W.L.R. 76; [2015] 2 All E.R. 822; 38 B.H.R.C. 313; Times, December 15, 2014, SC .... *Digested,* 15/**1811**: *Applied* 17/2745: *Considered* 15/3242, 16/2750, 16/2751, 17/1588, 17/2746, 17/2747: *Followed* 17/1591: *Superseded* 17/1594

R. (on the application of KP (Turkey) v Secretary of State for the Home Department see R. (on the application of Buer) v Secretary of State for the Home Department

R. (on the application of MA) v Secretary of State for Work and Pensions see R. (on the application of Carmichael) v Secretary of State for Work and Pensions

R. (on the application of Massey) v Secretary of State for Justice see R. (on the application of Kaiyam) v Secretary of State for Justice

R. (on the application of N) v Lewisham LBC; *sub nom* R. (on the application of CN) v Lewisham LBC; R. (on the application of ZH) v Newham LBC; *joined case* R. (on the application of H (A Child)) v Newham LBC [2014] UKSC 62; [2015] A.C. 1259; [2014] 3 W.L.R. 1548; [2015] 1 All E.R. 783; [2015] H.L.R. 6; [2014] B.L.G.R. 842; [2015] 1 P. & C.R. 13; Times, December 1, 2014; (2014) 158(45) S.J.L.B. 37, SC .... *Digested,* 15/**1290**: *Considered* 17/2679: *Followed* 17/562

R. (on the application of NS) v Secretary of State for the Home Department (C-411/10); *sub nom* ME v Refugee Applications Commissioner (C-493/10); NS v Secretary of State for the Home Department (C-411/10); *joined case* E v Refugee Applications Commissioner (C-493/10) EU:C:2011:865; [2013] Q.B. 102; [2012] 3 W.L.R. 1374; [2012] 2 C.M.L.R. 9; [2012] All E.R. (EC) 1011; (2012) 109(29) L.S.G. 26, ECJ (Grand Chamber) .... *Digested,* 12/**1698**: *Applied* 14/1672, 16/1066: *Considered* 13/1577, 17/2663: *Explained* 14/1652: *Followed* 13/1578

R. (on the application of Robinson) v Governor of Whatton Prison see R. (on the application of Kaiyam) v Secretary of State for Justice

R. (on the application of Rutherford) v Secretary of State for Work and Pensions see R. (on the application of Carmichael) v Secretary of State for Work and Pensions

R. (on the application of T) v Chief Constable of Greater Manchester; *sub nom* R. (on the application of B) v Secretary of State for the Home Department; *joined cases* R. (on the application of JB) v Secretary of State for the Home Department; R. (on the application of AW) v Secretary of State for the Home Department; R. (on the application of T) v Secretary of State for the Home Department [2014] UKSC 35; [2015] A.C. 49; [2014] 3 W.L.R. 96; [2014] 4 All E.R. 159; [2014] 2 Cr. App. R. 24; 38 B.H.R.C. 505; Times, June 23, 2014, SC *Digested,* 14/**1637**: *Applied* 16/1769: *Followed* 17/2749

R. (on the application of T) v Secretary of State for the Home Department see R. (on the application of T) v Chief Constable of Greater Manchester

R. (on the application of ZH) v Newham LBC see R. (on the application of N) v Lewisham LBC

RA (Iraq) v Secretary of State for the Home Department [2016] CSOH 182; 2017 G.W.D. 1-9, OH

Radadvicius (Nerijus) v HM Advocate see Gubinas (Justinas) v HM Advocate

Raeshaw Farms Ltd v Scottish Natural Heritage [2017] CSOH 50; 2017 S.L.T. 683; [2017] L.L.R. 632; 2017 G.W.D. 12-166, OH .... *Digested,* 17/**2408**: *Cited* 17/2407

Rainy Sky SA v Kookmin Bank; *sub nom* Kookmin Bank v Rainy Sky SA [2011] UKSC 50; [2011] 1 W.L.R. 2900; [2012] 1 All E.R. 1137; [2012] 1 All E.R. (Comm) 1; [2012] Bus. L.R. 313; [2012] 1 Lloyd's Rep. 34; [2011] 2 C.L.C. 923; [2012] B.L.R. 132; 138 Con. L.R. 1; Times, November 18, 2011; [2011] C.I.L.L. 3105, SC .... *Digested,* 12/**637**: *Applied* 12/2057, 12/2372, 12/2389, 13/2154, 14/2714, 14/2739, 14/474, 15/1861, 15/368, 15/475, 16/142, 17/2468, 17/498: *Considered* 12/1053, 13/1893, 15/383: *Followed* 13/2840, 14/117, 14/1775, 15/1606, 15/2113, 15/517, 16/1947, 16/424, 17/474

Ralston v HM Advocate 1987 S.C.C.R. 467, HCJ Appeal .... *Digested,* 88/**3890**: *Applied* 89/3997: *Considered* 94/5656, 97/5765: *Distinguished* 97/5766: *Followed* 11/4093, 17/2492: *Referred to* 95/5625

Randall (Barry Victor) v Queen, The [2002] UKPC 19; [2002] 1 W.L.R. 2237; [2002] 2 Cr. App. R. 17; Times, April 24, 2002; [2002] Crim. L.R. 928, PC (CI) .... *Digested,* 02/**905**: *Applied* 07/1027: *Considered* 06/958, 10/4093, 10/770: *Distinguished* 17/2529

Rangers FC Group Ltd v Joint Liquidators of RFC 2012 Plc [2017] CSOH 85; 2017 G.W.D. 21-329, OH

Rankin v Meek 1995 S.L.T. 526, OH .... *Digested,* 95/**5554**: *Considered* 17/2781

Ray v Ray 2017 G.W.D. 31-501, Sh Ct (Grampian) (Banff)

Raza v Orr see Raza (Ali) v Procurator Fiscal, Glasgow

Raza (Ali) v Procurator Fiscal, Glasgow; *sub nom* Raza v Orr [2017] SAC (Crim) 6; 2017 S.C.L. 649; 2017 S.C.C.R. 263; 2017 G.W.D. 13-199, SAC .... *Digested,* 17/**2483**

Razzaq (Mohammed) v HM Advocate [2017] HCJAC 45; 2018 J.C. 21; 2017 S.C.L. 786; 2017 S.C.C.R. 376; 2017 G.W.D. 21-339, HCJ Appeal .... *Digested,* 17/**2489**

RB v HM Advocate see B (R) v HM Advocate

RC v HM Advocate see C v HM Advocate

Redcar and Cleveland BC v Bainbridge; *joined case* Surtees v Middlesbrough BC [2008] EWCA Civ 885; [2009] I.C.R. 133; [2008] I.R.L.R. 776, CA (Civ Div) .... *Digested,* 08/**1156**: *Applied* 10/1020, 10/1082, 11/1116, 12/1097, 17/2585: *Considered* 09/1207, 10/1026

REEF Trade Mark; *sub nom* Bessant v South Cone Inc; South Cone Inc v Bessant (t/a REEF) [2002] EWCA Civ 763; [2003] R.P.C. 5; Times, May 31, 2002, CA (Civ Div) .... *Digested,* 02/**2897**: *Applied* 05/2568, 07/2684, 12/1981: *Considered* 14/1938, 17/1356, 17/2690: *Followed* 08/2395

Reeve v Thomas Dykfs (1829) 7 S. 632, IH (1 Div) *Considered* 17/2431

Reid v Harrower see Reid v Murphy

Reid v Murphy; *sub nom* Reid v Harrower [2016] SAC (Crim) 27; 2016 S.C.L. 1019; 2016 G.W.D. 33-607, SAC .... *Digested,* 17/**2821**

Reid v Scottish Ministers [2017] CSIH 20; 2017 S.C. 372; 2017 G.W.D. 9-123, IH (Ex Div) .... *Digested,* 17/**2747**

Reid v Scottish Ministers [2015] CSOH 84; 2015 G.W.D. 21-357, OH *Affirmed* 17/2747

Reid (Colin) v HM Advocate [2016] HCJAC 41; 2017 J.C. 37; 2016 S.L.T. 797; 2016 S.C.L. 448; 2016 S.C.C.R. 233; 2016 G.W.D. 14-270, HCJ .... *Digested,* 16/**2506**

Reilly (Andrew) v HM Advocate [2017] HCJAC 5; 2017 S.C.L. 347; 2017 S.C.C.R. 142; 2017 G.W.D. 6-84, HCJ .... *Digested,* 17/**2484**

Renfrew Golf Club v Motocaddy Ltd [2016] CSIH 57; 2016 S.C. 860; 2016 S.L.T. 781; 2017 S.C.L.R. 294; 2016 G.W.D. 22-415, IH (1 Div) .... *Digested,* 16/**2735**

Revenue and Customs Commissioners v Findmypast Ltd; *sub nom* Revenue and Customs Commissioners, Appellants [2017] CSIH 59; [2017] S.T.C. 2335; 2018 S.C. 24; 2017 S.L.T. 1071; [2017] B.V.C. 38; 2017 G.W.D. 30-488, IH (1 Div) .... *Digested,* 17/**2848**

Revenue and Customs Commissioners v Murray Group Holdings Ltd see RFC 2012 Plc (In Liquidation) (formerly Rangers Football Club Plc) v Advocate General for Scotland

Revenue and Customs Commissioners, Appellants see Revenue and Customs Commissioners v Findmypast Ltd

RFC 2012 Plc (In Liquidation) (formerly Rangers Football Club Plc) v Advocate General for Scotland; *sub nom* Revenue and Customs Commissioners v Murray Group Holdings Ltd; Advocate General for Scotland v Murray Group Holdings Ltd; Murray Group Holdings Ltd v Revenue and Customs Commissioners [2017] UKSC 45; [2017] 1 W.L.R. 2767; [2017] 4 All E.R. 654; [2017] S.T.C. 1556; 2018 S.C. (U.K.S.C.) 15; 2017 S.L.T. 799; 2017 S.C.L.R. 517; [2017] B.T.C. 22; [2017] W.T.L.R. 1093; Times, July 17, 2017; [2017] S.T.I. 1610; 2017 G.W.D. 21-357, SC .... *Digested,* 17/**2131**

RHM Bakeries (Scotland) Ltd v Strathclyde RC 1985 S.C. (H.L.) 17; 1985 S.L.T. 214; Times, January 29, 1985, HL .... *Digested,* 85/**4458**:
Applied 13/3870, 17/2741: *Considered* 88/4575, 95/6164, 96/7230, 00/6600:
Followed 95/6162, 12/4231

Riaviz (Loreno Carlo) v HM Advocate [2017] HCJAC 36; 2017 S.C.L. 695; 2017 G.W.D. 18-284, HCJ Appeal

Richards v Pharmacia Ltd c/o Pfizer Ltd [2017] CSOH 77; 2017 G.W.D. 18-282, OH

Robertson v Dunn [2015] SAC (Crim) 1; 2016 S.L.T. (Sh Ct) 51; 2015 G.W.D. 40-641, SAC .... *Digested,* 16/**2802**:
Considered 17/2812

Robertson v Edinburgh City Council 2017 G.W.D. 22-367, SPIC

Robertson v Muir [2016] SAC (Civ) 10; 2017 S.C. (S.A.C.) 9; 2016 Fam. L.R. 194; 2016 G.W.D. 34-615, SAC .... *Digested,* 17/**2425**

Robertson (Paul) v HM Advocate see Gemmell (James Kelly) v HM Advocate

Robertson (Stewart) v HM Advocate; *sub nom* Robertson, Petitioner; Gough v McFadyen; *joined case* Gough (Stephen Peter) v HM Advocate [2007] HCJAC 63; 2008 J.C. 146; 2007 S.L.T. 1153; 2008 S.C.L. 80; 2008 S.C.C.R. 20; 2007 G.W.D. 37-643, HCJ .... *Digested,* 08/**4650**:
Applied 15/2978, 16/19: *Considered* 17/2571: *Followed* 14/3427

Robertson, Petitioner see Robertson (Stewart) v HM Advocate

Rodger (Stephen) v HM Advocate [2017] HCJAC 65; 2017 S.C.L. 971; 2017 G.W.D. 29-461, HCJ .... *Digested,* 17/**2531**

Rodgers (Christopher) v HM Advocate [2017] HCJAC 34; 2017 S.C.L. 591; 2017 G.W.D. 17-270, HCJ Appeal

Romein v Advocate General for Scotland [2016] CSIH 24; 2016 S.C. 629; 2016 S.L.T. 459; 2016 S.C.L.R. 789; [2016] Imm. A.R. 909; [2017] I.N.L.R. 76; 2016 G.W.D. 11-224, IH (Ex Div) .... *Digested,* 16/**2688**

Ross v Richardson see Gemmell (James Kelly) v HM Advocate

Royal Bank of Scotland Plc v Mirza [2017] SAC (Civ) 13; 2017 S.L.T. (Sh Ct) 105; 2017 Hous. L.R. 45; 2017 G.W.D. 13-208, SAC .... *Digested,* 17/**2651**

Royal Bank of Scotland Plc v Wilson [2010] UKSC 50; 2011 S.C. (U.K.S.C.) 66; 2010 S.L.T. 1227; 2010 Hous. L.R. 88; 2010 G.W.D. 39-792, SC .... *Digested,* 11/**2717**:
Cited 12/4069: *Considered* 17/2781: *Followed* 13/3951

Royal Dornoch Golf Club v Crofters having Rights in Hilton of Embo Common Grazings 2017 S.L.T. (Land Ct) 14; 2016 G.W.D. 25-462, Land Ct .... *Digested,* 17/**2427**

Royal Insurance (UK) Ltd v Amec Construction Scotland Ltd [2007] CSOH 179; 2008 S.C. 201; 2008 S.L.T. 427; [2008] B.L.R. 53; 2008 G.W.D. 4-63, OH .... *Digested,* 08/**4587**:
Applied 17/2840

Royal Society for the Protection of Birds v Scottish Ministers [2017] CSIH 31; 2017 S.C. 552; [2018] Env. L.R. 1; 2017 G.W.D. 18-290, IH (1 Div)

Ruddy v Chief Constable of Strathclyde [2012] UKSC 57; 2013 S.C. (U.K.S.C.) 126; 2013 S.L.T. 119; 2013 S.C.L.R. 110; [2013] H.R.L.R. 10; 2013 Rep. L.R. 67; 2012 G.W.D. 40-779, SC .... *Digested,* 13/**3527**:
Applied 13/3779: *Considered* 17/2773

Rule v Hazelhaw Properties Ltd 2017 G.W.D. 2-16, Sh Ct (Glasgow)

Ruscillo v Council for the Regulation of Health Care Professionals see Council for the Regulation of Health Care Professionals v General Medical Council
Russell v McNair's Executrix 2017 S.L.T. (Sh Ct) 247; 2017 G.W.D. 26-436, Sh Ct (Glasgow) .... *Digested,* 17/**2839**
RW v HM Advocate see W (R) v HM Advocate

S v Children's Reporter; *sub nom* JS v Children's Reporter [2016] CSIH 74; 2017 S.C. 31; 2016 S.L.T. 1235; 2017 S.C.L.R. 539; 2016 Fam. L.R. 166; 2016 G.W.D. 31-547, IH (Ex Div) .... *Digested,* 17/**2603**
S v L; *sub nom* ML v ANS [2012] UKSC 30; 2013 S.C. (U.K.S.C.) 20; 2012 S.L.T. 961; [2012] H.R.L.R. 27; 2012 Fam. L.R. 108; Times, October 8, 2012; (2012) 156(28) S.J.L.B. 31; 2012 G.W.D. 24-488, SC .... *Digested,* 12/**1297**: *Considered* 17/2600: *Followed* 16/2653
S v Secretary of State for the Home Department see VS (India) v Secretary of State for the Home Department
S (A) v HM Advocate; *sub nom* AS v HM Advocate; Sturrock v HM Advocate [2016] HCJAC 126; 2017 J.C. 180; 2017 S.L.T. 264; 2017 S.C.L. 290; 2017 S.C.C.R. 80; 2017 G.W.D. 1-4, HCJ .... *Digested,* 17/**2479**
S (A) v Procurator Fiscal, Kilmarnock [2017] SAC (Crim) 3; 2017 S.L.T. (Sh Ct) 89; 2017 S.C.L. 493; 2017 G.W.D. 9-128, SAC .... *Digested,* 17/**2790**
S (D) v HM Advocate; *sub nom* DS v HM Advocate [2017] HCJAC 12; 2017 S.C.L. 363; 2017 S.C.C.R. 129; 2017 G.W.D. 8-112, HCJ .... *Digested,* 17/**2801**
SA (Bangladesh) v Secretary of State for the Home Department [2017] CSOH 117; 2017 S.L.T. 1245; 2017 G.W.D. 30-482, OH
SAA (Iraq) v Secretary of State for the Home Department [2017] CSOH 59; 2017 G.W.D. 13-209, OH
Sadiq (Alam) v HM Advocate; *joined case* Sadiq (Omar) v HM Advocate [2017] HCJAC 67; 2017 S.C.L. 940; 2017 S.C.C.R. 421; 2017 G.W.D. 30-473, HCJ .... *Digested,* 17/**2472**
Sadiq (Omar) v HM Advocate see Sadiq (Alam) v HM Advocate
Sadovska v Secretary of State for the Home Department see VS (Lithuania) v Secretary of State for the Home Department
Salvesen v Riddell [2013] UKSC 22; 2013 S.C. (U.K.S.C.) 236; 2013 S.L.T. 863; 2014 S.C.L.R. 44; [2013] H.R.L.R. 23; 2013 G.W.D. 14-304, SC .... *Digested,* 13/**1865**: *Cited* 17/2693
Samin v Westminster City Council see Mirga v Secretary of State for Work and Pensions
Sangster (Stephen) v HM Advocate [2017] HCJAC 4; 2017 J.C. 204; 2017 S.C.L. 336; 2017 S.C.C.R. 119; 2017 G.W.D. 6-85, HCJ .... *Digested,* 17/**2492**
Sargent v Dewar see Sargent v Secretary of State for Scotland
Sargent v Secretary of State for Scotland; *sub nom* Sargent v Dewar 2001 S.C.L.R. 190; 2000 Rep. L.R. 118; 2000 G.W.D. 28-1089, OH .... *Digested,* 01/**6817**: *Considered* 17/2738
Scanmudring AS v James Fisher MFE Ltd [2017] CSOH 91; 2017 G.W.D. 21-334, OH
Schatschaschwili v Germany (9154/10) (2016) 63 E.H.R.R. 14; 41 B.H.R.C. 474; [2017] Crim. L.R. 140, ECHR
Considered 17/2603
Schruyers (Kevin Charles) v HM Advocate see McHale (Joseph Francis) v HM Advocate
Schuh Ltd v Assessor for Glasgow [2013] CSIH 93; 2014 S.L.T. 184; [2014] R.V.R. 62; 2013 G.W.D. 39-754, LVAC .... *Digested,* 14/**3678**: *Applied* 17/2726: *Cited* 14/3676
Scotch Whisky Association v Lord Advocate [2013] CSOH 70; 2013 S.L.T. 776; [2013] 3 C.M.L.R. 34; [2013] L.L.R. 811; Times, June 13, 2013; 2013 G.W.D. 16-328, OH .... *Digested,* 13/**3750**: *Affirmed* 17/2466
Scotch Whisky Association v Lord Advocate [2016] CSIH 77; 2017 S.C. 465; 2016 S.L.T. 1141; 2017 S.C.L.R. 410; [2017] 1 C.M.L.R. 41; 2016 G.W.D. 33-588, IH (1 Div) .... *Digested,* 17/**2466**
Scott (Jordan) v HM Advocate see McDowall (Luke) v HM Advocate
Scottish Hydro Electric Transmission Plc v Auquhirie Land Co Ltd 2016 G.W.D. 32-575, Lands Tr (Scot)
Affirmed 17/2647
Scottish Hydro Electric Transmission Plc v Auquhirie Land Co Ltd [2017] CSIH 39; [2017] R.V.R. 315; 2017 G.W.D. 21-346, IH (Ex Div) .... *Digested,* 17/**2647**
Scottish Ministers v Stirton [2014] CSIH 92; 2015 S.C.L.R. 350; 2014 G.W.D. 37-683, IH (2 Div) .... *Digested,* 15/**3011**: *Considered* 17/2736

Scottish Parliamentary Corporate Body v Sovereign Indigenous Peoples of Scotland [2016] CSIH 81; 2016 S.L.T. 1307; 2016 Hous. L.R. 109; 2016 G.W.D. 34-610, IH (2 Div) .... *Digested,* 17/**2662**

Scottish Parliamentary Corporate Body v Sovereign Indigenous Peoples of Scotland [2016] CSOH 113; 2016 S.L.T. 862; 2016 Hous. L.R. 87; 2016 G.W.D. 24-446, OH .... *Digested,* 16/**2682**: *Affirmed* 17/2662

Scottish Police Services Authority v McBride; *sub nom* McBride v Scottish Police Authority; McBride v Scottish Police Services Authority; McBride v Strathclyde Police Joint Board [2016] UKSC 27; [2017] 2 All E.R. 875; 2017 S.C. (U.K.S.C.) 1; [2016] I.C.R. 788; [2016] I.R.L.R. 633; Times, June 22, 2016; 2016 G.W.D. 19-339, SC .... *Digested,* 16/**738**: *Followed* 17/851

Scottish Power Generation Ltd v HM Advocate [2016] HCJAC 99; 2017 J.C. 85; 2016 S.L.T. 1296; 2017 S.C.L. 88; 2016 S.C.C.R. 569; 2016 G.W.D. 35-640, HCJ .... *Digested,* 17/**2641**

Scottish Solicitors Staff Pension Fund's Trustees v Pattison & Sim; *sub nom* Trustees of the Scottish Solicitors Staff Pension Fund v Pattison & Sim [2014] CSOH 119; 2014 G.W.D. 26-533, OH *Affirmed* 17/2844

Scottish Solicitors Staff Pension Fund's Trustees v Pattison & Sim; *sub nom* Trustees of the Scottish Solicitors Staff Pension Fund v Pattison & Sim [2015] CSIH 96; 2016 S.C. 284; 2016 G.W.D. 2-60, IH (Ex Div) .... *Digested,* 17/**2844**

Scottish Water Business Stream Ltd v Ford 2017 G.W.D. 30-489, Sh Ct (Lothian) (Edinburgh)

Scottish Water Business Stream Ltd v GSL Property Management Ltd 2017 G.W.D. 30-471, Sh Ct (Glasgow)

Scottish Water Business Stream Ltd v Phillips 2017 G.W.D. 28-455, Sh Ct (Glasgow)

Scottish Water Business Stream Ltd v Sharma 2017 G.W.D. 28-454, Sh Ct (Lothian) (Edinburgh)

Scrabster Harbour Trust v Mowlem Plc (t/a Mowlem Marine); *joined case* Mowlem Plc (t/a Mowlem Marine) v Scrabster Harbour Trust [2006] CSIH 12; 2006 S.C. 469; 2006 S.L.T. 250; [2006] B.L.R. 207; 2006 G.W.D. 7-122, IH (1 Div) .... *Digested,* 06/**5154**: *Cited* 17/2471

Secretary of State for Work and Pensions v City of Glasgow Council [2017] CSIH 35; 2017 S.C. 707; 2017 S.L.T. 783; 2017 Hous. L.R. 94; 2017 G.W.D. 19-314, IH (Ex Div) .... *Digested,* 17/**2824**

Secretary of State for Work and Pensions v M; *sub nom* Secretary of State for Work and Pensions v MMcK [2017] CSIH 57; 2018 S.C. 1; 2017 S.L.T. 1045; 2017 G.W.D. 29-468, IH (Ex Div) .... *Digested,* 17/**2827**

Secretary of State for Work and Pensions v MMcK see Secretary of State for Work and Pensions v M

Sellar v Greater Glasgow Health Board [2017] CSOH 56; 2017 G.W.D. 12-172, OH

Sellars v IMI Yorkshire Imperial Ltd 1986 S.C. 235; 1986 S.L.T. 629, IH (2 Div) .... *Digested,* 86/**4228**: *Considered* 17/2454

Sheridan v News Group Newspapers Ltd [2016] CSIH 67; 2017 S.C. 63; 2016 S.L.T. 941; 2017 S.C.L.R. 576; 2016 G.W.D. 26-473, IH (Ex Div) .... *Digested,* 16/**2432**

Shetland Islands Council, Applicant 2017 S.L.T. (Sh Ct) 59; 2017 G.W.D. 5-66, Sh Ct (Grampian) (Lerwick) .... *Digested,* 17/**2605**

Shilliday v Smith 1998 S.C. 725; 1998 S.L.T. 976; 1998 S.C.L.R. 502; 1998 G.W.D. 16-821, IH (1 Div) .... *Digested,* 98/**6215**: *Considered* 17/2846

Short's Trustee v Chung (No.1) 1991 S.L.T. 472; 1991 S.C.L.R. 629, IH (2 Div) .... *Digested,* 91/**4415**: *Applied* 17/2684: *Considered* 96/7035: *Followed* 93/4825, 98/6001, 02/5891

Short's Trustee v Chung (No.2) 1999 S.C. 471; 1999 S.L.T. 751; 1999 S.C.L.R. 815; 1999 G.W.D. 12-537, IH (Ex Div) .... *Digested,* 99/**5709**: *Applied* 00/5938: *Considered* 17/2412

Sidey Ltd v Clackmannanshire Council [2010] CSIH 37; 2010 S.L.T. 607; [2010] Eu. L.R. 649; 2010 G.W.D. 19-383, IH (1 Div) .... *Digested,* 10/**4483**: *Considered* 17/2773

Simpson v Downie [2012] CSIH 74; 2013 S.L.T. 178; 2013 S.C.L.R. 377; 2012 Fam. L.R. 121; 2012 G.W.D. 33-673, IH (Ex Div) .... *Digested,* 13/**3719**: *Applied* 17/2840

Simpson v Hillcrest Housing Association Ltd 2017 Hous. L.R. 2; 2016 G.W.D. 38-682, Lands Tr (Scot) .... *Digested,* 17/**2707**

Sinclair Collis Ltd v Lord Advocate [2012] CSIH 80; 2013 S.C. 221; 2013 S.L.T. 100; 2013 S.C.L.R. 49; 2012 G.W.D. 34-685, IH (Ex Div) .... *Digested,* 13/**3826**: *Considered* 13/3750, 17/2466

Singh (Daljit) v Secretary of State for the Home Department 2000 S.C. 219; 2000 S.L.T. 243; 2000 G.W.D. 2-63, IH (1 Div) .... *Digested,* 00/**6491**: *Applied* 05/5439: *Considered* 17/2825: *Distinguished* 03/5730

Singularis Holdings Ltd v PricewaterhouseCoopers [2014] UKPC 36; [2015] A.C. 1675; [2015] 2 W.L.R. 971; [2015] B.C.C. 66; [2014] 2 B.C.L.C. 597; (2014) 158(44) S.J.L.B. 37, PC (Ber) *Considered* 17/2447

SK (Iraq) v Secretary of State for the Home Department [2017] CSOH 3; 2017 G.W.D. 3-36, OH

Skeen v Sullivan 1980 S.L.T. (Notes) 11, HCJ Appeal .... *Digested,* 80/**3018**: *Considered* 17/2540

Slezak v Secretary of State for Work and Pensions [2017] CSIH 4; 2017 S.C. 262; 2017 S.L.T. 221; 2017 G.W.D. 4-60, IH (Ex Div) .... *Digested,* 17/**2826**

Sloan, Petitioner 1991 S.C. 281; 1991 S.L.T. 527, IH (1 Div) .... *Digested,* 91/**4458**: *Applied* 17/2601

SM v CM [2017] CSIH 1; 2017 S.C. 235; 2017 S.L.T. 197; 2017 S.C.L.R. 739; 2017 Fam. L.R. 2; 2017 G.W.D. 3-26, IH (Ex Div) .... *Digested,* 17/**2438**: *Considered* 17/2418

Smith v Donnelly 2002 J.C. 65; 2001 S.L.T. 1007; 2001 S.C.C.R. 800; 2001 G.W.D. 26-1011, HCJ Appeal .... *Digested,* 01/**6702**: *Applied* 03/5359, 11/4102, 11/4104, 17/2509: *Cited* 09/4756, 11/4105: *Considered* 04/4632, 05/5098, 06/5164, 08/4637, 10/4061, 10/4062, 15/2968, 15/2991: *Followed* 09/4758

Smith v Gibson see Smith (Richard) v Procurator Fiscal, Hamilton

Smith v Stuart [2010] CSIH 29; 2010 S.C. 490; 2010 S.L.T. 1249; 2010 G.W.D. 14-270, IH (2 Div) .... *Digested,* 11/**4546**: *Followed* 17/2771

Smith (George Donald) v HM Advocate [2016] HCJAC 67; 2017 J.C. 54; 2016 S.C.L. 773; 2016 G.W.D. 26-476, HCJ .... *Digested,* 16/**2520**

Smith (Richard) v Procurator Fiscal, Hamilton; *sub nom* Smith v Gibson [2017] SAC (Crim) 10; 2017 S.C.C.R. 373; 2017 G.W.D. 23-401, SAC .... *Digested,* 17/**2815**

Smith (Thomas Bennie) v HM Advocate [2010] HCJAC 118; 2011 S.L.T. 212; 2011 S.C.L. 261; 2011 S.C.C.R. 134; 2010 G.W.D. 38-782, HCJ .... *Digested,* 11/**4586**: *Considered* 12/4266, 12/4267, 13/3985, 17/2807

Software Box Ltd v Gannon [2016] I.C.R. 148, EAT .... *Digested,* 16/**734**: *Applied* 17/2582

Soofi v Dykes [2017] CSOH 2; 2017 G.W.D. 2-14, OH

Soofi v Dykes [2017] CSIH 40; 2017 G.W.D. 21-332, IH (1 Div)

South Buckinghamshire DC v Porter (No.2); *sub nom* South Buckinghamshire DC v Secretary of State for Transport, Local Government and the Regions [2004] UKHL 33; [2004] 1 W.L.R. 1953; [2004] 4 All E.R. 775; [2005] 1 P. & C.R. 6; [2004] 4 P.L.R. 50; Times, July 2, 2004; Independent, July 6, 2004; [2004] 28 E.G. 177 (C.S.); (2004) 101(31) L.S.G. 25; (2004) 148 S.J.L.B. 825; [2004] N.P.C. 108, HL .... *Digested,* 04/**3087**: *Applied* 05/3296, 07/1157, 07/3277, 08/2930, 08/4956, 09/3059, 10/3180, 12/1459, 13/112, 13/2351, 14/70, 15/1987, 15/2164, 16/1078, 16/1678, 16/1703, 16/1737, 17/1765, 17/414: *Considered* 09/4974, 12/51, 16/1757, 17/1727, 17/1785, 17/2635: *Followed* 05/3304, 11/2508, 11/2511, 13/2348, 14/2066, 14/2439, 15/1967, 16/1756, 17/1769

South Buckinghamshire DC v Secretary of State for Transport, Local Government and the Regions see South Buckinghamshire DC v Porter (No.2)

South Cone Inc v Bessant (t/a REEF) see REEF Trade Mark

Southern Rock Insurance Co Ltd v Hafeez [2017] CSOH 127; 2017 S.L.T. 1159; [2018] Lloyd's Rep. I.R. 207; 2017 G.W.D. 32-516, OH .... *Digested,* 17/**2687**

Squires v HM Advocate 1996 S.C.C.R. 916, HCJ Appeal .... *Digested,* 97/**5803**: *Distinguished* 17/2520

SS (India) v Secretary of State for the Home Department [2017] CSIH 43; 2017 G.W.D. 22-374, IH (Ex Div)

SSE Generation Ltd v Hochtief Solutions AG [2016] CSOH 177; 2017 G.W.D. 3-39, OH

St Andrew's Environmental Protection Association Ltd v Fife Council see St Andrews Environmental Protection Association Ltd, Petitioner

St Andrews Environmental Protection Association Ltd, Petitioner; *sub nom* St Andrew's Environmental Protection Association Ltd v Fife Council [2016] CSIH 22; 2016 S.L.T. 979; 2017 S.C.L.R. 35; 2016 G.W.D. 10-208, IH (Ex Div) .... *Digested,* 16/**2766**

St Andrews Forest Lodges Ltd v Grieve 2017 G.W.D. 14-224, Sh Ct (Tayside) (Dundee)

Taylor Clark Leisure Plc v Revenue and Customs Commissioners [2016] CSIH 54; [2016] S.T.C. 2492; 2016 S.C. 843; 2016 S.L.T. 873; 2017 S.C.L.R. 277; [2016] B.V.C. 27; [2016] L.L.R. 853; 2016 G.W.D. 22-418, IH (Ex Div) .... *Digested,* 16/**2834**: *Considered* 17/2290: *Followed* 17/2289
Taylor Wimpey UK Ltd v Scottish Ministers [2016] CSIH 94; 2017 G.W.D. 1-13, IH (Ex Div)
Tayside Contracts v D Geddes (Contractors) Ltd [2017] CSOH 108; 2017 G.W.D. 26-429, OH
TD (Nigeria) v Secretary of State for the Home Department see HA (Afghanistan) v Secretary of State for the Home Department
Tennant (Thomas) v HM Advocate see Wood (Kenneth) v HM Advocate
Tenzin v Russell 2015 Hous. L.R. 11; 2015 G.W.D. 4-88, IH (Ex Div) .... *Digested,* 15/**3188**: *Applied* 17/2840
Tesco Stores Ltd v Fife Council Assessor [2016] CSIH 76; 2016 S.L.T. 1260; [2017] R.A. 83; 2016 G.W.D. 32-581, LVAC .... *Digested,* 17/**2726**
Thaine v London School of Economics [2010] I.C.R. 1422; [2010] Eq. L.R. 268, EAT .. *Digested,* 11/**1046**: *Approved* 17/826: *Cited* 17/2583
The Queensland Mercantile and Agency Company, Limited, and Liquidator v Australasian Investment Company, Limited (1888) 15 R. 935, IH (1 Div) *Considered* 17/2447
Thermal Energy Construction Ltd v AE&E Lentjes UK Ltd [2009] EWHC 408 (TCC), QBD (TCC) *Considered* 10/845, 17/2461
Thomas v HM Advocate 2001 G.W.D. 24-913, HCJ Appeal *Followed* 17/2799
Thomas v Thomas [1947] A.C. 484; [1947] 1 All E.R. 582; 1947 S.C. (H.L.) 45; 1948 S.L.T. 2; 1947 S.L.T. (Notes) 53; 63 T.L.R. 314; [1948] L.J.R. 515; 176 L.T. 498, HL .... *Digested,* 47-51/**7496**: *Applied* 47-51/10957, 47-51/2723, 47-51/9902, 52/987, 55/2078, 59/431, 70/3157, 76/338, 98/5439, 98/6102, 01/6217, 03/3539, 13/3902, 13/3956, 17/2616: *Considered* 74/1069, 91/5082, 94/3280, 94/3439, 03/5285, 05/10, 15/1769, 15/3076, 16/2740: *Distinguished* 90/4099: *Followed* 86/4416, 88/4930, 08/5003, 13/6, 14/1579: *Not applied* 51/3869
Thompson v Sayegh 2015 G.W.D. 7-132, Sh Ct (Lothian) (Edinburgh) *Applied* 17/2445
Thomson v Glasgow Corp 1962 S.C. (H.L.) 36; 1962 S.L.T. 105, HL .... *Digested,* 62/**3636**: *Applied* 97/5653: *Considered* 91/5679, 08/4588, 16/2461, 17/2435: *Followed* 11/4278
Thomson v Scottish Ministers [2017] CSIH 16; 2017 G.W.D. 8-119, IH (Ex Div)
Thomson v Thomas Muir (Waste Management) Ltd 1995 S.L.T. 403, OH .... *Digested,* 95/**6062**: *Applied* 17/2461
Thomson v Yorkshire Building Society (Bankruptcy: Title to Sue) 1994 S.C.L.R. 1014, Sh Pr .... *Digested,* 95/**5485**: *Distinguished* 17/2677
Thrumster Estate Ltd v Mindt 2017 S.L.T. (Land Ct) 1; 2016 G.W.D. 21-381, Land Ct . *Digested,* 17/**2694**
Till v Tayside Public Transport Co Ltd [2017] CSOH 6; 2017 G.W.D. 3-41, OH
TJ v SB [2017] SAC (Civ) 24; 2017 Fam. L.R. 119; 2017 G.W.D. 25-414, SAC .... *Digested,* 17/**2418**
TM (Democratic Republic of Congo) v Secretary of State for the Home Department [2017] CSOH 19; 2017 G.W.D. 5-68, OH
Tock v Keeper of the Registers of Scotland 2017 G.W.D. 12-182, Lands Tr (Scot)
Tock v Keeper of the Registers of Scotland 2017 G.W.D. 12-183, Lands Tr (Scot)
Tole (Callum Stephen) v HM Advocate [2013] HCJAC 109; 2013 S.L.T. 1227; 2013 S.C.L. 912; 2014 S.C.C.R. 5; 2013 G.W.D. 30-590, HCJ .... *Digested,* 14/**3373**: *Applied* 17/2477: *Considered* 15/2966
Tomczak v Reid 2017 G.W.D. 32-512, SPIC
Torresi v Consiglio dell'Ordine degli Avvocati di Macerata (C-58/13); *joined case* Torresi v Consiglio dell'Ordine degli Avvocati di Macerata (C-59/13) EU:C:2014:2088; [2015] Q.B. 331; [2015] 2 W.L.R. 29; [2015] All E.R. (EC) 1039, ECJ (Grand Chamber) *Considered* 17/2673
Torresi v Consiglio dell'Ordine degli Avvocati di Macerata (C-59/13) see Torresi v Consiglio dell'Ordine degli Avvocati di Macerata (C-58/13)
Townsley (Scott) v HM Advocate [2016] HCJAC 87; 2016 S.C.L. 1006; 2016 G.W.D. 31-559, HCJ .... *Digested,* 17/**2791**
Trelfa (Rachel) v HM Advocate see Fee (Rachel) v HM Advocate
Trilogy Services Scotland Ltd v Windsor Residential [2017] SAC (Civ) 2; 2017 S.C.L.R. 640; 2017 G.W.D. 3-29, SAC .... *Digested,* 17/**2465**

Trollope & Colls Ltd v North West Metropolitan Regional Hospital Board [1973] 1 W.L.R. 601; [1973] 2 All E.R. 260; 9 B.L.R. 60; (1973) 117 S.J. 355, HL .... *Digested,* 73/**270**: *Applied* 82/2940, 92/314, 05/655, 10/1117, 17/2461: *Considered* 80/17, 90/401, 96/1218, 00/4640, 07/816: *Distinguished* 81/828: *Followed* 80/357, 13/592

Trotter v Trotter 2001 S.L.T. (Sh Ct) 42; 2000 Fam. L.R. 94; 2000 G.W.D. 12-425, Sh Pr .... *Digested,* 00/**6274**: *Considered* 17/2781

Trustees of the Scottish Solicitors Staff Pension Fund v Pattison & Sim see Scottish Solicitors Staff Pension Fund's Trustees v Pattison & Sim

TY (Sri Lanka) v Secretary of State for the Home Department [2015] EWCA Civ 1233; [2016] Imm. A.R. 470; [2016] I.N.L.R. 401, CA (Civ Div) .... *Digested,* 16/**1149**: *Considered* 17/2673: *Followed* 17/1245

U v Glasgow City Council [2017] CSOH 122; 2017 S.L.T. 1109; 2017 G.W.D. 31-491, OH .... *Digested,* 17/**2664**

Ultimate Invoice Finance Ltd, Petitioner [2017] CSOH 72; 2017 S.L.T. 791; 2017 G.W.D. 15-243, OH .... *Digested,* 17/**2676**

Unison Claimants v Glasgow City Council see HBJ Claimants v Glasgow City Council

University Court of the University of St Andrews v Headon Holdings Ltd [2017] CSIH 61; 2017 G.W.D. 32-507, IH (Ex Div)

Uprichard v Fife Council see Uprichard v Scottish Ministers

Uprichard v Scottish Ministers; *sub nom* Uprichard v Fife Council [2011] CSIH 59; 2012 S.C. 172; 2011 G.W.D. 30-655, IH (2 Div) .... *Digested,* 12/**4225**: *Affirmed* 14/2373: *Considered* 17/2635

Van Lynden v Gilchrist [2016] CSIH 72; 2017 S.C. 134; 2016 S.L.T. 1187; 2017 S.C.L.R. 351; 2016 G.W.D. 29-525, IH (1 Div) .... *Digested,* 17/**2710**

Van Lynden v Gilchrist [2015] CSOH 147; 2015 S.L.T. 864; 2015 G.W.D. 37-596, OH *Digested,* 16/**2709**: *Reversed* 17/2710

Varney (Scotland) Ltd v Lanark Burgh Council 1974 S.C. 245; 1976 S.L.T. 46, IH (2 Div) .... *Digested,* 76/**2991**: *Considered* 77/3294, 90/4820, 17/2846: *Followed* 01/6753

Veen v Keeper of the Registers of Scotland 2017 G.W.D. 17-276, Lands Tr (Scot)

Vehicle Control Services Ltd v Mackie 2017 S.L.T. (Sh Ct) 111; 2017 G.W.D. 13-198, Sh Ct (Tayside) (Dundee) .... *Digested,* 17/**2467**

Vibert v Zenith Insurance [2016] CSOH 96; 2016 Rep. L.R. 123; 2016 G.W.D. 23-423, OH .... *Digested,* 17/**2442**

Villaswan Ltd (In Receivership) v Sheraton Caltrust (Blythswood) Ltd (In Liquidation) 1999 S.C.L.R. 199; [2000] B.C.C. 188; Times, January 27, 1999; 1998 G.W.D. 39-2017, OH .... *Digested,* 99/**6304**

VS (India) v Secretary of State for the Home Department; *sub nom* S v Secretary of State for the Home Department [2015] CSOH 118; 2015 S.L.T. 651; 2015 G.W.D. 29-493, OH .... *Digested,* 15/**3149**: *Reversed* 17/2665

VS (India) v Secretary of State for the Home Department; *sub nom* S v Secretary of State for the Home Department [2017] CSIH 48; 2017 S.L.T. 977; 2017 G.W.D. 23-397, IH (Ex Div) .... *Digested,* 17/**2665**

VS (Lithuania) v Secretary of State for the Home Department; *sub nom* Sadovska v Secretary of State for the Home Department [2017] UKSC 54; [2017] 1 W.L.R. 2926; [2018] 1 All E.R. 757; 2018 S.C. (U.K.S.C.) 38; 2017 S.L.T. 883; 2018 S.C.L.R. 36; [2018] 1 C.M.L.R. 37; [2017] Imm. A.R. 1473; [2017] I.N.L.R. 944; Times, August 4, 2017; 2017 G.W.D. 23-396, SC .... *Digested,* 17/**1248**

W v Greater Glasgow Health Board [2017] CSIH 58; 2017 G.W.D. 29-465, IH (2 Div)

W v Schaffer 2001 S.L.T. (Sh Ct) 86; 2000 G.W.D. 36-1348, Sh Pr *Applied* 17/2604

W (R) v HM Advocate; *sub nom* RW v HM Advocate [2017] HCJAC 17; 2017 S.C.L. 459; 2017 S.C.C.R. 203; 2017 G.W.D. 11-152, HCJ .... *Digested,* 17/**2522**

WA v Secretary of State for the Home Department [2017] CSOH 30; 2017 G.W.D. 7-104, OH

Wade (Philip) v HM Advocate; *joined case* Coats (Colin) v HM Advocate [2014] HCJAC 88; 2014 S.C.L. 680; 2014 G.W.D. 25-481, HCJ .... *Digested,* 14/**3377**: *Considered* 17/2807

Wagner v Grant [2016] CSIH 34; 2016 S.L.T. 699; 2017 S.C.L.R. 79; 2016 G.W.D. 15-287, IH (Ex Div) .... *Digested,* 16/**2740**

Walgate & Son v Scottish Natural Heritage see A I Walgate & Son v Scottish Natural Heritage

Walker v Emslie. (1899) 3 Adam 102, HCJ
Considered 17/2540
Wallace (James) v HM Advocate [2017] HCJAC 40; 2017 S.C.L. 710; 2017 G.W.D. 20-320, HCJ Appeal .... *Digested,* 17/**2548**
Warner v Scapa Flow Charters [2016] CSOH 101; 2016 S.L.T. 918; 2016 G.W.D. 23-436, OH .... *Digested,* 16/**2454**:
Reversed in part 17/2436
Warner v Scapa Flow Charters [2017] CSIH 13; 2017 S.C. 361; 2017 S.L.T. 239; 2017 G.W.D. 7-106, IH (Ex Div) .... *Digested,* 17/**2436**
Watson v Bogue (No.1) 2000 S.L.T. (Sh Ct) 125; 1998 S.C.L.R. 512; 1998 G.W.D. 18-930, Sh Pr .... *Digested,* 98/**6176**:
Distinguished 17/2781
Watt v Murphy [2016] SAC (Crim) 16; 2016 S.L.T. (Sh Ct) 247; 2016 S.C.L. 798; 2016 S.C.C.R. 314; 2016 G.W.D. 18-333, SAC .... *Digested,* 16/**2793**:
Distinguished 17/2516
Waydale Ltd v MRM Engineering 1996 S.L.T. (Sh Ct) 6, Sh Pr .... *Digested,* 96/**7112**:
Distinguished 17/2696
WB v HM Advocate [2014] HCJAC 52; 2014 S.C.C.R. 376; 2014 G.W.D. 17-317, HCJ *Digested,* 14/**3388**:
Considered 17/2473
Welford v EDF Energy Networks (LPN) Plc [2007] EWCA Civ 293; [2007] 2 P. & C.R. 15; [2007] 2 E.G.L.R. 1; [2007] 24 E.G. 170; [2007] R.V.R. 172; Times, May 8, 2007; [2007] 15 E.G. 147 (C.S.); [2007] N.P.C. 40; [2007] Bus. L.R. D63, CA (Civ Div) .... *Digested,* 07/**3385**:
Considered 16/2674, 17/2644
Wells v United Kingdom (57715/09) see James v United Kingdom (25119/09)
West v Scottish Prison Service see West v Secretary of State for Scotland
West v Secretary of State for Scotland; *sub nom* West v Scottish Prison Service 1992 S.C. 385; 1992 S.L.T. 636; 1992 S.C.L.R. 504; Times, June 11, 1992; Scotsman, May 5, 1992, IH (1 Div) .... *Digested,* 92/**5191**:
Applied 95/5443, 97/5714, 97/6043, 97/6359, 03/5265: *Considered* 95/5441, 00/6205, 03/5192, 04/4478, 04/4543, 17/2393: *Explained* 93/4730: *Followed* 00/5832, 10/3995, 11/4329, 12/3822, 14/3301
West Lothian Council v B; *sub nom* EV (A Child), Re; West Lothian Council v MB [2017] UKSC 15; 2017 S.C. (U.K.S.C.) 67; 2017 S.L.T. 319; 2017 Fam. L.R. 34; 2017 G.W.D. 8-114, SC .... *Digested,* 17/**1063**
West Lothian Council v B; *sub nom* EV (A Child), Re; West Lothian Council v MB [2016] CSOH 48; 2017 S.C.L.R. 65; 2016 G.W.D. 11-218, OH
West Lothian Council v B; *sub nom* EV (A Child), Re; West Lothian Council v MB [2016] CSIH 60; 2017 S.C.L.R. 304; 2016 Fam. L.R. 134; 2016 G.W.D. 25-463, IH (2 Div)
Reversed 17/1063
West Lothian Council v MB see West Lothian Council v B
Western Heritable Investment Co Ltd v Hunter 2004 S.C. 635; 2004 S.L.T. 355; 2004 S.C.L.R. 819; 2004 G.W.D. 11-250, IH (1 Div) .... *Digested,* 04/**4993**:
Considered 17/2699
Westfoot Invesments Ltd v European Property Holdings Inc 2015 S.L.T. (Sh Ct) 201; 2015 Hous. L.R. 57; 2015 G.W.D. 29-492, Sh Ct (Lothian) (Edinburgh) .... *Digested,* 15/**3286**:
Considered 17/2651
Whitcombe v Bank of Scotland Plc [2017] CSOH 58; 2017 Hous. L.R. 40; 2017 G.W.D. 14-212, OH .... *Digested,* 17/**2692**
Whitehouse (David) v HM Advocate [2017] HCJAC 46; 2017 S.C.L. 742; 2017 G.W.D. 21-342, HCJ Appeal .... *Digested,* 17/**2519**
Whittome v Whittome (No.1) 1994 S.L.T. 114; 1993 S.C.L.R. 137, OH .... *Digested,* 93/**5223**:
Considered 17/2611: *Followed* 99/6074
Whyte (Craig) v HM Advocate [2017] HCJAC 14; 2017 J.C. 262; 2017 S.C.L. 751; 2017 S.C.C.R. 354; 2017 G.W.D. 21-341, HCJ Appeal .... *Digested,* 17/**2512**
Wightman (James) v HM Advocate [2017] HCJAC 50; 2017 S.C.L. 804; 2017 S.C.C.R. 437; 2017 G.W.D. 22-364, HCJ Appeal .... *Digested,* 17/**2475**
Wildland Ltd v Scottish Ministers [2017] CSOH 113; 2017 G.W.D. 30-487, OH
William Tracey Ltd v Scottish Ministers [2016] CSOH 131; 2016 S.L.T. 1049; 2017 S.C.L.R. 368; 2016 G.W.D. 30-536, OH .... *Digested,* 16/**2674**
Williamson (John) v HM Advocate [2016] HCJAC 115; 2017 S.C.L. 153; 2016 G.W.D. 38-678, HCJ .... *Digested,* 17/**2569**
Wilson v North Star Shipping (Aberdeen) Ltd [2014] CSOH 156; 2014 G.W.D. 36-675, OH
Considered 17/2757
Wilson (Craig) v HM Advocate [2017] HCJAC 3; 2017 J.C. 135; 2017 S.C.L. 237; 2017 G.W.D. 3-32, HCJ .... *Digested,* 17/**2549**

Wilson (James) v HM Advocate [2016] HCJAC 70; 2017 J.C. 64; 2016 S.C.L. 785; 2016 S.C.C.R. 425; 2016 G.W.D. 28-505, HCJ ... *Digested,* 16/**2518**
Wilson (Sean) v HM Advocate [2017] HCJAC 52; 2017 S.C.L. 783; 2017 G.W.D. 23-393, HCJ Appeal ... *Digested,* 17/**2547**
Wingate v McGlennan 1992 S.L.T. 837; 1991 S.C.C.R. 133, HCJ Appeal ... *Digested,* 91/**4674**: *Considered* 17/2510: *Distinguished* 96/7315
Winton (Stewart) v HM Advocate [2016] HCJAC 19; 2016 S.L.T. 393; 2016 S.C.L. 406; 2017 S.C.C.R. 320; 2016 G.W.D. 8-154, HCJ Appeal ... *Digested,* 16/**2566**
Wishart v Castlecroft Securities Ltd see Wishart, Petitioner
Wishart, Petitioner; *sub nom* Wishart v Castlecroft Securities Ltd [2009] CSIH 65; 2010 S.C. 16; 2009 S.L.T. 812; 2009 S.C.L.R. 696; [2010] B.C.C. 161; 2009 G.W.D. 28-446, IH (Ex Div) ... *Digested,* 10/**4009**: *Considered* 13/354, 17/2422, 17/2423
Wittenberg v Sunset Personnel Services Ltd [2017] I.C.R. 1012, EAT (SC)
Witter v QHSE Solutions Ltd [2016] SAC (Civ) 8; 2017 S.C. (S.A.C.) 21; 2016 G.W.D. 30-528, SAC ... *Digested,* 17/**2422**
Wood v Musselburgh Joint Racing Committee [2017] L.L.R. 216; 2016 G.W.D. 34-621, Sh Ct (Lothian) (Edinburgh) ... *Digested,* 17/**2716**
Wood (Kenneth) v HM Advocate; *joined cases* Tennant (Thomas) v HM Advocate; McLean (Darryl) v HM Advocate [2017] HCJAC 2; 2017 J.C. 185; 2017 S.L.T. 190; 2017 S.C.L. 295; 2017 S.C.C.R. 100; 2017 G.W.D. 3-42, HCJ ... *Digested,* 17/**2805**
Woolley v Akbar see Woolley v Akram
Woolley v Akram; *sub nom* Woolley v Akbar 2017 S.L.T. (Sh Ct) 175; 2017 S.C.L.R. 647; 2017 G.W.D. 7-92, Sh Ct (Lothian) (Edinburgh) ... *Digested,* 17/**2661**
Worbey v Campbell [2017] CSIH 49; 2017 G.W.D. 24-412, IH (Ex Div)
Wordie Property Co Ltd v Secretary of State for Scotland 1984 S.L.T. 345, IH (1 Div) .. *Digested,* 84/**4735**: *Applied* 89/5083, 92/5890, 93/5939, 96/7151, 97/6113, 04/5080, 06/5520, 11/4207, 11/4452, 11/4609, 12/4103, 15/3197, 17/2719: *Considered* 00/6491, 00/6500, 04/5024, 05/5438, 17/2635: *Followed* 97/6144, 99/6411, 12/4145, 13/4013: *Referred to* 93/5937
Wotherspoon v Orr see Wotherspoon (David) v Procurator Fiscal, Glasgow
Wotherspoon (David) v Procurator Fiscal, Glasgow; *sub nom* Wotherspoon v Orr [2017] HCJAC 69; 2018 J.C. 79; 2017 S.C.L. 955; 2017 S.C.C.R. 505; 2017 G.W.D. 30-476, HCJ ... *Digested,* 17/**2509**
Wright v Elderpark Housing Association [2017] CSIH 54; 2017 S.L.T. 995; 2017 Hous. L.R. 71; 2017 G.W.D. 25-424, IH (Ex Div) ... *Digested,* 17/**2699**
Wylie v Omniasig SA [2012] CSOH 128; 2013 S.L.T. 46; 2012 G.W.D. 28-574, OH ..... *Digested,* 13/**3904**: *Considered* 17/2757

X v A (No.1) 2016 S.L.T. (Sh Ct) 404; 2016 Fam. L.R. 153; 2016 G.W.D. 27-501, Sh Ct (Lothian) (Edinburgh) ... *Digested,* 17/**2840**
X v A (No.2) 2016 S.L.T. (Sh Ct) 411; 2016 Fam. L.R. 159; 2016 G.W.D. 27-488, Sh Ct (Lothian) (Edinburgh) ... *Digested,* 17/**2457**
X (A Child) (Jurisdiction: Secure Accommodation), Re; *sub nom* X (A Child) (Secure Accommodation: Inherent Jurisdiction), Re; *joined case* Y (A Child) (Jurisdiction: Secure Accommodation), Re [2016] EWHC 2271 (Fam); [2017] Fam. 80; [2016] 3 W.L.R. 1718; [2017] 2 F.L.R. 1717; [2017] 1 F.C.R. 584; [2016] Fam. Law 1327, Fam Div ... *Digested,* 17/**1068**: *Applied* 17/1067: *Considered* 17/2379
X (A Child) (Secure Accommodation: Inherent Jurisdiction), Re see X (A Child) (Jurisdiction: Secure Accommodation), Re
X, Petitioners 2017 G.W.D. 28-453, Sh Ct (Lothian) (Edinburgh)
XL (China) v Secretary of State for the Home Department [2017] CSOH 41; 2017 G.W.D. 10-139, OH

Y v Secretary of State for the Home Department see EY (Turkey) v Secretary of State for the Home Department
Y (A Child) (Jurisdiction: Secure Accommodation), Re see X (A Child) (Jurisdiction: Secure Accommodation), Re
YG v EP [2017] CSOH 75; 2017 G.W.D. 16-260, OH
Younas (Faisal) v HM Advocate [2014] HCJAC 114; 2015 J.C. 180; 2014 S.L.T. 1043; 2015 S.C.L. 30; 2014 S.C.C.R. 628; 2014 G.W.D. 34-646, HCJ ... *Digested,* 15/**3002**: *Considered* 15/2994, 15/3019, 17/2556
YZ (China) v Secretary of State for the Home Department [2017] CSIH 41; 2017 G.W.D. 22-375, IH (Ex Div)

PART III

SHIPS' NAME INDEX 2017